MICROSOFT
OFFICE
Introductory Concepts and Techniques

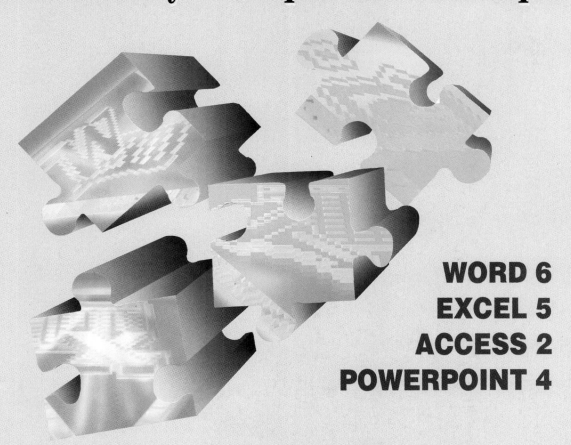

WORD 6
EXCEL 5
ACCESS 2
POWERPOINT 4

Course One

MICROSOFT
OFFICE
Introductory Concepts and Techniques

Course One

**WORD 6
EXCEL 5
ACCESS 2
POWERPOINT 4**

**Gary B. Shelly
Thomas J. Cashman
Misty E. Vermaat**

Contributing Authors

Marvin M. Boetcher
Steven G. Forsythe
Sherry L. Green
Philip J. Pratt
James E. Quasney

**boyd & fraser
publishing company**

An International Thomson Publishing Company

Danvers • Albany • Bonn • Boston • Cincinnati • Detroit • London • Madrid • Melbourne
Mexico City • New York • Paris • San Francisco • Singapore • Tokyo • Toronto • Washington

Special thanks go to the following reviewers of the Shelly Cashman Series Windows Applications textbooks:

Susan Conners, Purdue University Calumet; **William Dorin**, Indiana University Northwest; **Robert Erickson**, University of Vermont; **Deborah Fansler**, Purdue University Calumet; **Roger Franklin**, The College of William and Mary; **Roy O. Foreman**, Purdue University Calumet; **Patricia Harris**, Mesa Community College; **Cynthia Kachik**, Santa Fe Community College; **Suzanne Lambert**, Broward Community College; **Anne McCoy**, Miami-Dade Community College/Kendall Campus; **Karen Meyer**, Wright State University; **Mike Michaelson**, Palomar College; **Michael Mick**, Purdue University Calumet; **Cathy Paprocki**, Harper College; **Jeffrey Quasney**, Educational Consultant; **Denise Rall**, Purdue University; **Sorel Reisman**, California State University, Fullerton; **John Ross**, Fox Valley Technical College; **Lorie Szalapski**, St. Paul Technical College; **Susan Sebok**, South Suburban College; **Betty Svendsen**, Oakton Community College; **Jeanie Thibault**, Educational Dynamics Institute; **Margaret Thomas**, Ohio University; **Carole Turner**, University of Wisconsin; **Diane Vaught**, National Business College; **Dwight Watt**, Swainsboro Technical Institute; **Melinda White**, Santa Fe Community College; **Eileen Zisk**, Community College of Rhode Island; and **Sue Zulauf**, Sinclair Community College.

© 1995 boyd & fraser publishing company
One Corporate Place • Ferncroft Village
Danvers, Massachusetts 01923

International Thomson Publishing
boyd & fraser publishing company is an ITP company.
The ITP trademark is used under license.

Printed in the United States of America

For more information, contact boyd & fraser publishing company:

boyd & fraser publishing company
One Corporate Place • Ferncroft Village
Danvers, Massachusetts 01923, USA

International Thomson Publishing Europe
Berkshire House 168-173
High Holborn
London, WC1V 7AA, England

Thomas Nelson Australia
102 Dodds Street
South Melbourne 3205
Victoria, Australia

Nelson Canada
1120 Birchmont Road
Scarborough, Ontario
Canada M1K 5G4

International Thomson Editores
Campose Eliseos 385, Piso 7
Col. Polanco
11560 Mexico D.F. Mexico

International Thomson Publishing GmbH
Konigswinterer Strasse 418
53227 Bonn, Germany

International Thomson Publishing Asia
221 Henderson Road
#05-10 Henderson Building
Singapore 0315

International Thomson Publishing Japan
Hirakawacho Kyowa Building, 3F
2-2-1 Hirakawacho
Chiyoda-ku, Tokyo 102, Japan

ISBN 0-87709-861-1 (Perfect bound)

ISBN 0-87709-885-9 (Spiral bound)

1 2 3 4 5 6 7 8 9 10   BC   9 8 7 6 5

This book was designed using Windows 3.11, QuarkXpress 3.31 for Windows, and CorelDraw 3.0 & 5.0 for Windows.

$\mathcal{C}$ ONTENTS

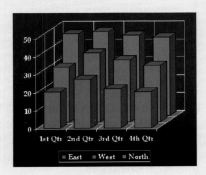

MICROSOFT OFFICE MO1

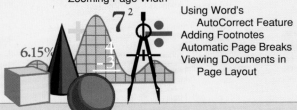

SPREADSHEETS USING MICROSOFT EXCEL 5 FOR WINDOWS   E1

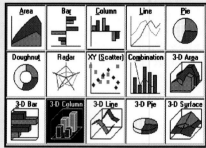

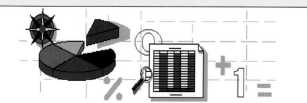

OBJECT LINKING AND EMBEDDING (OLE)   OLE1

▶ PROJECT ONE
Sharing Data and Graphics Between
Applications   OLE2

DATABASE USING MICROSOFT ACCESS 2 FOR WINDOWS   A1

▶ PROJECT ONE
Creating a Database   A2

▶ PROJECT TWO
Querying a Database   A63

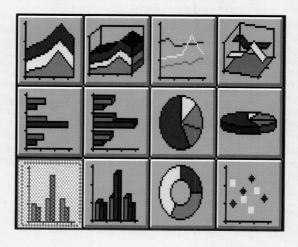

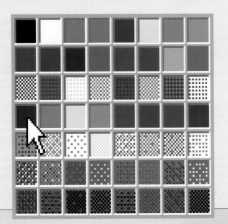

PRESENTATION GRAPHICS USING MICROSOFT POWERPOINT 4 FOR WINDOWS   PP1

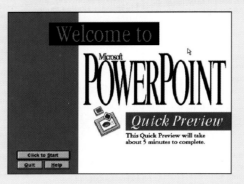

P R E F A C E

▶ THE WINDOWS ENVIRONMENT

S ince the introduction of Microsoft Windows version 3.1, the personal computing industry has moved rapidly toward establishing Windows as the de facto user interface. The majority of software development funds in software vendor companies are devoted to Windows applications. Virtually all PCs purchased today, at any price, come preloaded with Windows and, often, with one or more Windows applications packages. With an enormous installed base, it is clear that Windows is the operating environment for both now and the future.

The Windows environment places the novice as well as the experienced user in the world of the mouse and a common graphical user interface between all applications. An up-to-date educational institution that teaches applications software to students for their immediate use and as a skill to be used within industry must teach Windows-based applications software.

▶ OBJECTIVES OF THIS TEXTBOOK

M *icrosoft Office: Introductory Concepts and Techniques* was specifically developed for an introductory personal computer applications course. No previous experience with a computer is assumed, and no mathematics beyond the high school freshman level is required. The objectives of this book are as follows:

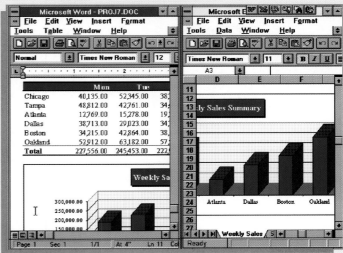

FIGURE P-1

- ▶ To teach the fundamentals of Microsoft Windows 3.1, Microsoft Office Manager, Microsoft Word 6, Microsoft Excel 5, Microsoft Access 2, Microsoft PowerPoint 4, and object linking and embedding (OLE)
- ▶ To acquaint the student with the proper way to solve personal computer application-type problems
- ▶ To use practical problems to illustrate personal computer applications
- ▶ To take advantage of the many new capabilities of word processing, spreadsheet creation, database development, and presentation graphics in a Windows environment
- ▶ To develop integrated solutions to problems through the use OLE (see Figure P-1)

This textbook covers all essential aspects of Microsoft Windows, Microsoft Office Manager, the four application tools, and OLE. When students complete a course using this textbook, they will have a firm knowledge of Windows and will be able to solve a variety of personal computer-related problems. In addition, because they will be learning Windows, students will find the migration to other Windows applications software to be relatively simple and straightforward. For those desiring additional coverage of Microsoft Office, a follow-up textbook is available titled *Microsoft Office: Advanced Concepts and Techniques*.

▶ THE SHELLY CASHMAN APPROACH

T he Shelly Cashman Series Windows Applications books present word processing, spreadsheet, database, programming, presentation graphics, and Windows itself by showing the actual screens displayed by Windows and the applications software. Because the student interacts with pictorial displays when using Windows, written words in a textbook does not suffice. For this reason, the Shelly Cashman Series emphasizes screen displays as the primary means of teaching Windows applications software. Every screen shown in the Shelly Cashman Series Windows Applications books appears in color, because the student views color on the screen. In addition, the screens display exactly as the student will see them. The screens in this book were captured while using the software. Nothing has been altered or changed except to highlight portions of the screen when appropriate (see the screens in Figure P-2).

The Shelly Cashman Series Windows Applications books present the material using a unique pedagogy designed specifically for the graphical environment of Windows. The textbooks are primarily designed for a lecture/lab method of presentation, although they are equally suited for a tutorial/hands-on approach wherein the student learns by actually completing each project following the step-by-step instructions. Features of this pedagogy include the following:

▶ **Project Orientation:** Each project in the book solves a complete problem, meaning that the student is introduced to a problem to be solved and is then given the step-by-step process to solve the problem.

▶ **Step-by-Step Instructions:** Each of the tasks required to complete a project is identified throughout the development of the project. For example, a task might be to copy one cell to adjacent cells in a row using Excel. Then, each step to accomplish the task is specified. The steps are accompanied by screens (see Figure P-2). The student is not told to perform a step without seeing the result of the step on a color screen. Hence, students learn from this book the same as if they were using the computer. This attention to detail in accomplishing a task and showing the resulting screen makes the Shelly Cashman Series Windows Applications textbooks unique.

▶ **Multiple Ways to Use the Book:** Because each step to accomplish a task is illustrated with a screen, the book can be used in a number of ways, including: (a) Lecture and textbook approach — The instructor lectures on the material in the book. The student reads and studies the material and then applies the knowledge to an application on a computer; (b) Tutorial approach — The student performs each specified step on a computer. At the end of the project, the student has solved the problem and is ready to solve comparable student assignments; (c) Reference — Each task in a project is clearly identified. Therefore, the material serves as a complete reference because the student can refer to any task to determine how to accomplish it.

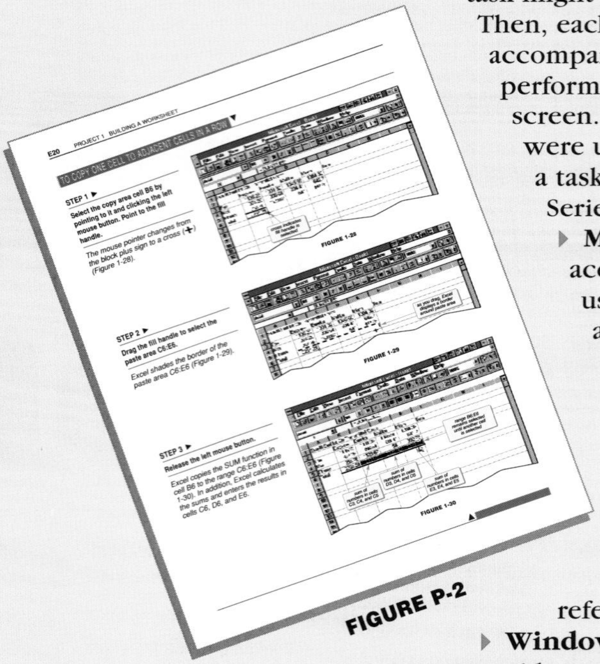

▶ **Windows/Graphical User Interface Approach:** Windows provides a graphical user interface. All of the examples in the book use this interface. Thus, the mouse is used for the majority of control functions and is the preferred user communication tool. When specifying a command to be executed, the sequence is as follows: (a) If a button invokes the command, use the button; (b) If a button is not available, use the command from a menu; (c) If a button or a menu cannot be used, only then is the keyboard used to implement a Windows command.

FIGURE P-2

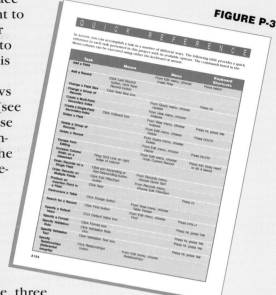

▸ **Emphasis on Windows Techniques:** The most general techniques to implement commands, enter information, and generally interface with Windows are presented. This approach allows the student to move from one application software package to another under Windows with a minimum amount of relearning with respect to interfacing with the software. An application-specific method is taught only when no other option is available.

▸ **Reference for All Techniques:** Even though general Windows techniques are used in all examples, a Quick Reference chart (see Figure P-3) at the end of each project details not only the mouse and menu methods for implementing a command, but also contains the keyboard shortcuts for the commands presented in the project. Therefore, students are exposed to all means for implementing a command.

FIGURE P-3

▶ ORGANIZATION OF THIS TEXTBOOK

M *icrosoft Office: Introductory Concepts and Techniques* consists of an introduction to computers, two projects on Microsoft Windows 3.1, an introducution to Microsoft Office, three projects each on the four Microsoft applications for Windows: Word 6, Excel 5, Access 2, and PowerPoint 4, and a project on object linking and embedding (OLE).

An Introduction to Computers

Many students taking a course in the use of Microsoft Office will have little previous experience using computers. For this reason, the textbook begins with a section titled *Introduction to Computers* that covers computer hardware and software concepts important to first-time computer users.

Using Microsoft Windows 3.1

To effectively use the Microsoft Office family of application software products, students need a practical knowledge of Microsoft Windows. Thus, two Microsoft Windows projects are included as an introduction to the graphical user interface.

Project 1 – An Introduction to Windows The first project introduces the students to Windows concepts, Windows terminology, and how to communicate with Windows using the mouse and keyboard. Topics include starting and exiting Windows; opening group windows; maximizing windows; scrolling; selecting menus; choosing a command from a menu; starting and exiting Windows applications; obtaining online Help; and responding to dialog boxes.

Project 2 – Disk and File Management The second project introduces the students to File Manager. Topics include formatting a diskette; copying a group of files; renaming and deleting files; searching for help topics; activating, resizing, and closing a group window; switching between applications; and minimizing an application window to an application icon.

Microsoft Office Manager

The Microsoft Office family includes Microsoft Word 6, Microsoft Excel 5, Microsoft Access 2, Microsoft PowerPoint 4, and a license to use Microsoft Mail. The Microsoft Office Manager allows students to manage the use of these software products as if they were all a single program via the Microsoft Office Manager toolbar. Therefore, a project introducing the Microsoft Office family and how to use and manipulate the Microsoft Office Manager toolbar immediately follows the two projects on Microsoft Windows.

Project 1 – An Introduction to Microsoft Office   This project introduces the student to the Microsoft Office product line and to Microsoft Office Manager. Topics include using the Microsoft Office Manager toolbar to start an application, switch to another application, and quit an application; adding a button and removing a button from the Microsoft Office Manager toolbar; changing the size of the Microsoft Office Manager toolbar; and locating files on disk using Find File.

Word Processing Using Microsoft Word 6 for Windows

After presenting the basic computer, Microsoft Windows, and Microsoft Office Manager concepts, this txtbook provides detailed instruction on how to use Microsoft Word 6. The material is divided into three projects as follows:

Project 1 – Creating and Editing a Document   In Project 1, students are introduced to Word terminology and the Word window by preparing an announcement (Figure P-4). Topics include starting and quitting Word; entering text; saving a document; selecting characters, lines, and paragraphs; centering, bolding, italicizing, and changing the font and font size of selected text; adding bullets to paragraphs; importing and scaling a clip art file; checking spelling; printing a document; opening a document; correcting errors; and using Word's online Help.

FIGURE P-4

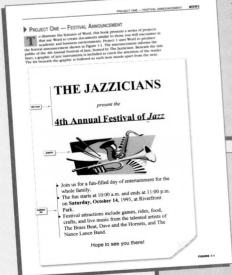

Project 2 – Using Wizards to Create a Document   In Project 2, students learn the basic components of a business letter. Students use the Letter Wizard to create a resume cover letter and the Resume Wizard to create a resume; replace selected text with new text; right-align text; add a border beneath a paragraph; create and insert an AutoText entry; drag and drop a paragraph; vertically align text with the TAB key; view and print in print preview; switch from one open document to another; and arrange multiple open documents on the same Word screen.

Project 3 – Creating the Research Paper   In Project 3, students use the MLA style of documentation to create a research paper. Topics include changing margins; adjusting line spacing; using a header to number pages; centering text before typing; first-line indenting paragraphs; zooming page width; using Word's Auto-Correct feature; adding footnotes; viewing documents in page layout view; inserting a hard page break; creating a hanging indent; sorting paragraphs; going to a specific location in a document; finding and replacing text; editing a document in print preview; using the Thesaurus; and counting words in a document.

Spreadsheets Using Microsoft Excel 5 for Windows

Following the three projects on Microcosft Word 6 for Windows, this textbook presents three projects on Microsoft Excel 5. The topics presented are as follows:

Project 1 – Building a Worksheet In Project 1, students are introduced to Excel terminology, the Excel window, and the basic characteristics of a worksheet and workbook. Topics include starting and exiting Excel; entering text and numbers; selecting a range; using the AutoSum button; copying using the fill handle; changing font size; bolding; centering across columns; using the AutoFormat command; charting using the ChartWizard button; saving and opening a worksheet; editing a worksheet; and obtaining online Help.

Project 2 – Formulas, Formatting, and Creating Charts In Project 2, students use formulas and functions to build a worksheet and learn more about formatting and printing a worksheet. Topics include entering formulas; using the AVERAGE, MAX, and MIN functions; formatting text; formatting numbers; drawing borders and adding colors; changing the widths of columns and heights of rows; spell checking; creating a 3-D column chart on a separate sheet; previewing a worksheet; printing a section of the worksheet; and displaying and printing the formulas in a worksheet.

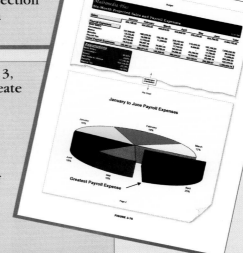

FIGURE P-5

Project 3 – Enhancing a Worksheet and Chart In Project 3, students learn how to work with larger worksheets, how to create a worksheet based on assumptions, how to use the IF function and absolute references, how to create and format a 3-D pie chart (Figure P-5), and how to perform what-if analysis. Topics include using the fill handle to create a series; deleting, inserting, copying, and moving data on a worksheet; displaying and docking toolbars; freezing titles; changing the magnification of worksheets; displaying different parts of the worksheet using panes; changing the type, size, and color of fonts; in-depth charting of data; previewing a printout; printing in landscape; printing to fit; and simple what-if analysis and goal seeking.

Object Linking and Embedding (OLE)

After the projects on Microsoft Word 6 and Microsoft Excel 5, the student is introduced to object linking and embedding as described below:

Project 1 – Sharing Data and Graphics Between Applications In this project, the student is acquainted with the three methods for copying objects between a source document and a destination document: (1) copy and paste; (2) copy and embed; and (3) copy and link. The project also shows how to tile active applications and then copy and embed by using the drag and drop procedure.

Databases Using Microsoft Access 2 for Windows

Following the project on object linking and embedding, this textbook provides detailed instrucion on Microsoft Access 2. The topics are divided into three projects as follows:

Project 1 – Creating a Database   In Project 1, students are introduced to Access terminology, the Access window, and the basic characteristics of databases. Topics include starting and exiting Access; creating a database; creating a table; defining fields; opening a table; adding records to an empty table; closing a table; opening and closing a database; adding records to a non-empty table; and printing the contents of a table. Other topics in this project include using a form to view data; creating a graph using the GraphWizard; and using online Help. Students also learn how to design a database to eliminate redundancy.

Project 2 – Querying a Database   In Project 2, students learn how to ask questions concerning the data in their databases by using queries. Topics include creating and running queries and printing the results; displaying only selected fields; using character data in criteria; using wildcards; using numeric data in criteria; using various comparison operators; and creating compound criteria. Other topics include sorting; joining multiple tables; and restricting records in a join. Students use computed fields, statistics, and grouping, and also graph the results of a query.

FIGURE P-6

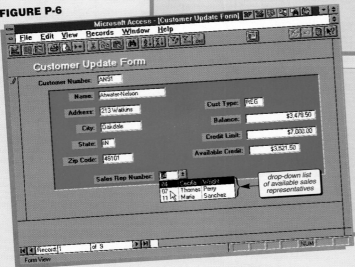

Project 3 – Maintaining a Database   In Project 3, students learn how to maintain a database. Topics include using Datasheet view and Form view to add new records, to change existing records, and to delete records; changing the structure of a table; creating validation rules; and specifying referential integrity. Students perform mass changes and deletes using queries and create and use single-field and multiple-field indexes.

Presentation Graphics Using Microsoft PowerPoint 4 for Windows

The final Windows application software package covered in this textbook is Microsoft PowerPoint 4. The material is presented in three projects as follows:

Project 1 – Building a Slide Presentation   In Project 1, students are introduced to PowerPoint terminology; the PowerPoint window; and the basics of creating a bulleted list presentation. Topics include starting PowerPoint; establishing the foundation of a presentation using the Pick a Look Wizard; selecting a template; displaying information on every slide; changing text style; decreasing font size; saving a presentation; changing line spacing; checking spelling; printing a presentation; exiting PowerPoint and opening an existing presentation; correcting errors; and obtaining online Help.

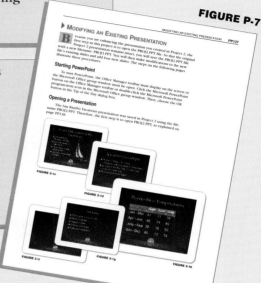
Project 2 – Creating a Presentation in Outline View   In Project 2, students create a presentation in Outline view and learn how to insert clip art. Topics include arranging text using the Promote and Demote butons; changing slide layouts; adding clip art; drawing an object and adding text to the object; changing text color and fill color; rearranging slide order; copying and pasting; reversing the last edit using the Undo button; and printing an outline.

Project 3 – Enhancing a Presentation and Adding Graphs and Tables   In Project 3, students enhance the presentation created in Project 2 by adding a graph, a table, and transition and build effects, and running an automatic slide show (see Figure P-7). Topics include saving the presentation with a new name; changing templates; deleting objects; adding a graph using Microsoft Graph 5; adding a table using Microsoft Word 6; adding slide transition effects; adding build effects; establishing slide show timings; and running an automatic slide show.

FIGURE P-7

▶ END-OF-PROJECT STUDENT ACTIVITIES

ach project ends with a wealth of student activities including most or all of the following features:

▸ A list of key terms for review
▸ A Quick Reference that lists the ways to carry out a task using the mouse, menu, or keyboard shortcuts
▸ Student Assignments for homework and classroom discussion
▸ Computer Laboratory Exercises that usually require the student to load and manipulate a file, a document, a spreadsheet, a database, or a slide from the Student Diskette that accompanies this book
▸ Computer Laboratory Assignments that require the student to develop a complete project assignment (see Figure P-8); the assignments increase in difficulty from a relatively easy assignment to a case study

FIGURE P-8

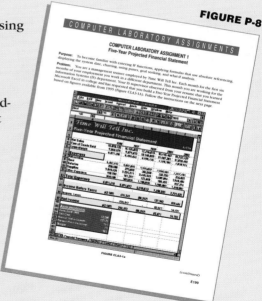

▶ ANCILLARY MATERIALS FOR TEACHING FROM THE SHELLY CASHMAN SERIES WINDOWS APPLICATIONS TEXTBOOKS

A comprehensive instructor's support package accompanies all textbooks in the Shelly Cashman Series.

Annotated Instructor's Edition (AIE)   The AIE is designed to assist you with your lectures by suggesting illustrations to use, summarizing key points, proposing pertinent questions, offering important tips, alerting you to pitfalls, and by incorporating the answers to the Student Assignments. There are several hundred annotations throughout the textbook (see Figure P-9).

FIGURE P-9

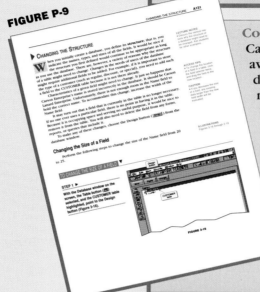

Computer-Based LCD Lecture Success System   The Shelly Cashman Series proudly presents the finest LCD learning material available in textbook publishing. The Lecture Success System diskette, together with a personal computer and LCD technology, are used in lieu of transparencies. The system enables you to explain and illustrate the step-by-step, screen-by-screen development of a project in the textbook without entering large amounts of data, thereby improving your students' grasp of the material. The Lecture Success System leads to a smooth, easy, error-free lecture.

The Lecture Success System diskette comes with files that correspond to key figures in the book. You load the files that pertain to a project and display them as needed. If the students want to see a series of steps a second time, simply reopen the file you want to start with and redo the steps. This presentation system is available to adopters without charge.

Instructor's Materials   The instructor's ancillary contains the following:

▶ Detailed lesson plans including project objectives, project overview, and a three-column outline of each project that includes page references and illustration references
▶ Answers to all student assignments at the end of the projects
▶ A test bank of more than 600 True/False, Multiple Choice, and Fill-In questions
▶ Illustrations for every screen, diagram, and table in the textbook on CD-ROM — for selection and display in a lecture or to print and make transparencies
▶ An Instructor's Diskette that includes the projects and solutions to the Computer Laboratory Assignments at the end of each project
▶ A Lesson Plans and Test Bank Diskette that includes the detailed lesson plans and test bank for customizing to individual instructor's needs

MicroExam IV   MicroExam IV, a computerized test-generating system, is available free to adopters of any Shelly Cashman Series textbooks. It includes all of the questions from the test bank just described. MicroExam IV is an easy-to-use, menu-driven software package that provides instructors with testing flexibility and allows customizing of testing documents.

NetTest IV   NetTest IV allows instructors to take a MicroExam IV file made up of True/False and Multiple Choice questions and proctor a paperless examination in a network environment. The same questions display in a different order on each PC. Students have the option of instantaneous feedback. Tests are electronically graded, and an item analysis is produced.

▶ ACKNOWLEDGMENTS

T he Shelly Cashman Series would not be the success it is without the contributions of outstanding publishing professionals. First, and foremost, among them is Becky Herrington, director of production and designer. She is the heart and soul of the Shelly Cashman Series, and it is only through her leadership, dedication, and untiring efforts that superior products are produced.

Under Becky's direction, the following individuals made significant contributions to these books: Ginny Harvey, series administrator and manuscript editor; Peter Schiller, production manager, Ken Russo, senior illustrator and cover art; Mike Bodnar, Greg Herrington, Dave Bonnewitz, and Dave Wyer, illustrators; Jeanne Black, Betty Hopkins, and Rebecca Evans, typographers; Tracy Murphy, series coordinator; Sue Sebok and Melissa Dowling LaRoe, copy editors; Marilyn Martin and Nancy Lamm, proofreaders; Henry Blackham, cover and opener photography; and Dennis Woelky, glass etchings.

Special recognition for a job well done must go to James Quasney, who, together with writing, assumed the responsibilities as series editor. Particular thanks go to Thomas Walker, president and CEO of boyd & fraser publishing company, who recognized the need, and provided the support, to produce the full-color Shelly Cashman Series Windows Applications textbooks.

We hope you will find using the book an enriching and rewarding experience.

Gary B. Shelly
Thomas J. Cashman

▶ SHELLY CASHMAN SERIES – TRADITIONALLY BOUND TEXTBOOKS

 he Shelly Cashman Series presents both Windows- and DOS-based personal computer applications in a variety of traditionally bound textbooks, as shown in the table below. For more information, see your ITP representative or call 1-800-423-0563.

COMPUTERS	
Computers	Using Computers: A Gateway to Information
	Using Computers: A Gateway to Information Brief Edition
Computers and Windows Applications	Using Computers and Microsoft Office: Introductory Concepts and Techniques (also available in spiral bound)
	Using Computers and Microsoft Office: Advanced Concepts and Techniques (also available in spiral bound)
	Using Computers and Works 3.0 (also available in spiral bound)
	Complete Computer Concepts and Microsoft Works 2.0 (also available in spiral bound)
Computers and DOS Applications	Complete Computer Concepts and WordPerfect 5.1, Lotus 1-2-3 Release 2.2, and dBASE IV Version 1.1 (also available in spiral bound)
	Complete Computer Concepts and WordPerfect 5.1, Lotus 1-2-3 Release 2.2, and dBASE III PLUS (also available in spiral bound)
Computers and Programming	Using Computers and Programming in QuickBASIC
	Using Computers and Programming in Microsoft BASIC

WINDOWS APPLICATIONS	
Integrated Packages	Microsoft Office: Introductory Concepts and Techniques (also available in spiral bound)
	Microsoft Office: Advanced Concepts and Techniques (also available in spiral bound)
	Microsoft Works 3.0 (also available in spiral bound)
	Microsoft Works 2.0 (also available in spiral bound)
Graphical User Interface	Microsoft Windows 3.1 Introductory Concepts and Techniques
	Microsoft Windows 3.1 Complete Concepts and Techniques
Windows Applications	Microsoft Word 2.0, Microsoft Excel 4, and Paradox 1.0 (also available in spiral bound)
Word Processing	Microsoft Word 6* • Microsoft Word 2.0
	WordPerfect 6* • WordPerfect 5.2
Spreadsheets	Microsoft Excel 5* • Microsoft Excel 4
	Lotus 1-2-3 Release 5* • Lotus 1-2-3 Release 4*
	Quattro Pro 5*
Database Management	Paradox 5* • Paradox 4.5 • Paradox 1.0
	Microsoft Access 2*
Presentation Graphics	Microsoft PowerPoint 4*

DOS APPLICATIONS	
Operating Systems	DOS 6 Introductory Concepts and Techniques
	DOS 6 and Microsoft Windows 3.1 Introductory Concepts and Techniques
Integrated Package	Microsoft Works 3.0 (also available in spiral bound)
DOS Applications	WordPerfect 5.1, Lotus 1-2-3 Release 2.2, and dBASE IV Version 1.1 (also available in spiral bound)
	WordPerfect 5.1, Lotus 1-2-3 Release 2.2, and dBASE III PLUS (also available in spiral bound)
Word Processing	WordPerfect 6.0
	WordPerfect 5.1 Step-by-Step Function Key Edition
	WordPerfect 5.1
	WordPerfect 5.1 Function Key Edition
	WordPerfect 4.2 (with Educational Software)
	WordStar 6.0 (with Educational Software)
Spreadsheets	Lotus 1-2-3 Release 4 • Lotus 1-2-3 Release 2.4 • Lotus 1-2-3 Release 2.3
	Lotus 1-2-3 Release 2.2 • Lotus 1-2-3 Release 2.01
	Quattro Pro 3.0
	Quattro with 1-2-3 Menus (with Educational Software)
Database Management	dBASE 5
	dBASE IV Version 1.1
	dBASE III PLUS (with Educational Software)
	Paradox 4.5
	Paradox 3.5 (with Educational Software)

PROGRAMMING AND NETWORKING	
Programming	Microsoft BASIC
	QuickBASIC
	Microsoft Visual Basic 3.0 for Windows*
Networking	Novell Netware for Users
Internet	The Internet: Introductory Concepts and Techniques

*Also available as a mini book in the Double Diamond Edition

▶ SHELLY CASHMAN SERIES – Custom Edition PROGRAM

If you do not find a Shelly Cashman Series traditionally bound textbook to fit your needs, boyd & fraser's unique **Custom Edition** program allows you to choose from a number of options and create a textbook perfectly suited to your course. The customized materials are available in a variety of binding styles, including boyd & fraser's patented **Custom Edition** kit, spiral bound, and notebook bound. Features of the **Custom Edition** program are:

▶ Textbooks that match the content of your course

▶ Windows- and DOS-based materials for the latest versions of personal computer applications software

▶ Shelly Cashman Series quality, with the same full-color materials and Shelly Cashman Series pedagogy found in the traditionally bound books

▶ Affordable pricing so your students receive the **Custom Edition** at a cost similar to that of traditionally bound books

The table on the right summarizes the available materials. For more information, see your ITP representative or call 1-800-423-0563.

COMPUTERS	
Computers	Using Computers: A Gateway to Information
	Using Computers: A Gateway to Information Brief Edition
	Introduction to Computers (32-page)
OPERATING SYSTEMS	
Graphical User Interface	Microsoft Windows 3.1 Introductory Concepts and Techniques
	Microsoft Windows 3.1 Complete Concepts and Techniques
Operating Systems	Introduction to DOS 6 (using DOS prompt)
	Introduction to DOS 5.0 (using DOS shell)
	Introduction to DOS 5.0 or earlier (using DOS prompt)
WINDOWS APPLICATIONS	
Integrated Packages	Microsoft Works 3.0
	Microsoft Works 2.0
Microsoft Office	Microsoft Office (16-page)
	Object Linking and Embedding (OLE) (32-page)
Word Processing	Microsoft Word 6*
	Microsoft Word 2.0
	WordPerfect 6*
	WordPerfect 5.2
Spreadsheets	Microsoft Excel 5*
	Microsoft Excel 4
	Lotus 1-2-3 Release 5*
	Lotus 1-2-3 Release 4*
	Quattro Pro 5*
Database Management	Paradox 5*
	Paradox 4.5
	Paradox 1.0
	Microsoft Access 2*
Presentation Graphics	Microsoft PowerPoint 4*
DOS APPLICATIONS	
Integrated Package	Microsoft Works 3.0
Word Processing	WordPerfect 6.0
	WordPerfect 5.1 Step-by-Step Function Key Edition
	WordPerfect 5.1
	WordPerfect 5.1 Function Key Edition
	Microsoft Word 5.0
	WordPerfect 4.2
	WordStar 6.0
Spreadsheets	Lotus 1-2-3 Release 4
	Lotus 1-2-3 Release 2.4
	Lotus 1-2-3 Release 2.3
	Lotus 1-2-3 Release 2.2
	Lotus 1-2-3 Release 2.01
	Quattro Pro 3.0
	Quattro with 1-2-3 Menus
Database Management	dBASE 5
	dBASE IV Version 1.1
	dBASE III PLUS
	Paradox 4.5
	Paradox 3.5
PROGRAMMING AND NETWORKING	
Programming	Microsoft BASIC
	QuickBASIC
	Microsoft Visual Basic 3.0 for Windows*
Networking	Novell Netware for Users
Internet	The Internet: Introductory Concepts and Techniques

* Also available as a mini-module

Introduction to Computers

Objectives

After completing this chapter, you will be able to:

▶ Define the term computer and discuss the four basic computer operations: input, processing, output, and storage

▶ Define data and information

▶ Explain the principal components of the computer and their use

▶ Describe the use and handling of diskettes and hard disks

▶ Discuss computer software and explain the difference between system software and application software

▶ Describe several types of personal computer applications software

▶ Discuss computer communications channels and equipment and LAN and WAN computer networks

▶ Explain how to purchase, install, and maintain a personal computer system

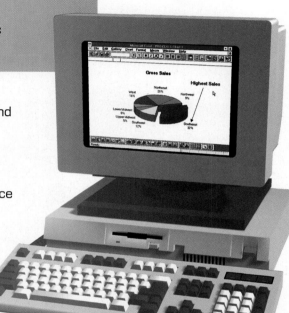

Every day, computers impact how individuals work and how they live. The use of small computers, called personal computers or microcomputers , continues to increase and has made computing available to almost anyone. In addition, advances in communication technology allow people to use personal computer systems to easily and quickly access and send information to other computers and computer users. At home, at work, and in the field, computers are helping people to do their work faster, more accurately, and in some cases, in ways that previously would not have been possible.

Why Study Computers and Application Software?

T oday, many people believe that knowing how to use a computer, especially a personal computer, is a basic skill necessary to succeed in business or to function effectively in society. As you can see in Figure 1, the use of computer technology is widespread in the world. It is important to understand that while computers are used in many different ways, there are certain types of common applications computer users need to know. It is this type of software that you will learn as you use this book. Given the widespread use and availability of computer systems, knowing how to use common application software on a computer system is an essential skill for practically everyone.

FIGURE 1
Computers in use in a wide variety of applications and professions. New applications are being developed every day.

Before you learn about application software, however, it will help if you understand what a computer is, the components of a computer, and the types of software used on computers. These topics are explained in this introduction. Also included is information that describes computer networks and a list of guidelines for purchasing, installing, and maintaining a personal computer.

What Is a Computer?

T he most obvious question related to understanding computers is, "What is a computer?" A computer is an electronic device, operating under the control of instructions stored in its own memory unit, that can accept data (input), process data arithmetically and logically, produce output from the processing, and store the results for future use. Generally the term is used to describe a collection of devices that function together as a system. An example of the devices that make up a personal computer, or microcomputer, is shown in Figure 2.

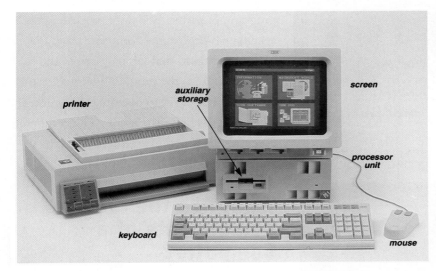

FIGURE 2
Devices that comprise a personal computer.

What Does a Computer Do?

W hether small or large, computers can perform four general operations. These operations comprise the information processing cycle and are: input, process, output, and storage. Collectively, these operations describe the procedures a computer performs to process data into information and store it for future use.

All computer processing requires data. Data refers to the raw facts, including numbers, words, images, and sounds, given to a computer during the input operation. In the processing phase, the computer manipulates the data to create information. Information refers to data processed into a form that has meaning and is useful. During the output operation, the information that has been created is put into some form, such as a printed report, that people can use. The information can also be placed in computer storage for future use.

These operations occur through the use of electronic circuits contained on small silicon chips inside the computer (Figure 3). Because these electronic circuits rarely fail and the data flows along these circuits at close to the speed of light, processing can be accomplished in billionths of a second. Thus, the computer is a powerful tool because it can perform these four operations reliably and quickly.

The people who either use the computer directly or use the information it provides are called computer users, end users, or sometimes, just users.

FIGURE 3
Inside a computer are chips and other electronic components that process data in billionths of a second.

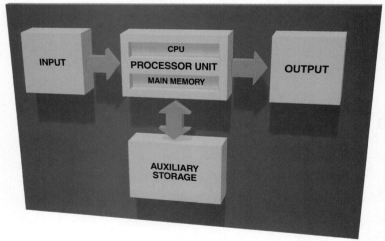

FIGURE 4
A computer is composed of input devices through which data is entered into the computer; the processor that processes data stored in main memory; output devices on which the results of the processing are made available; and auxiliary storage units that store data for future processing.

How Does a Computer Know What to Do?

For a computer to perform the operations in the information processing cycle, it must be given a detailed set of instructions that tell it exactly what to do. These instructions are called a computer program, or software. Before processing for a specific job begins, the computer program corresponding to that job is stored in the computer. Once the program is stored, the computer can begin to operate by executing the program's first instruction. The computer executes one program instruction after another until the job is complete.

What Are the Components of a Computer?

To understand how computers process data into information, you need to examine the primary components of the computer. The four primary components of a computer are: input devices, the processor unit, output devices, and auxiliary storage units (Figure 4).

Input Devices

Input devices enter data into main memory. Many input devices exist. The two most commonly used are the keyboard and the mouse.

The Keyboard   The most commonly used input device is the keyboard, on which data is entered by manually keying in or typing. The keyboard on most computers is laid out in much the same manner as the one shown in Figure 5. The alphabetic keys are arranged like those on a typewriter.

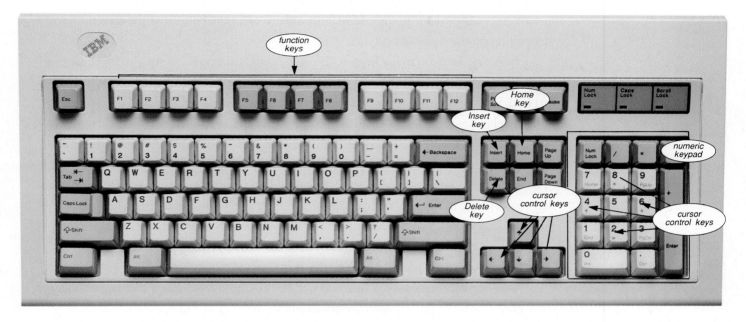

A **numeric keypad** is located on the right side of most keyboards. This arrangement of keys allows you to enter numeric data rapidly. To activate the numeric keypad you press and engage the NUMLOCK key located above the numeric keypad. The NUMLOCK key activates the numeric keypad so when the keys are pressed, numeric characters are entered into the computer memory and appear on the screen. A light turns on at the top right of the keyboard to indicate that the numeric keys are in use.

The **cursor** is a symbol, such as an underline character, which indicates where you are working on the screen. The **cursor control keys**, or **arrow keys**, allow you to move the cursor around the screen. Pressing the UP ARROW (↑) key causes the cursor to move upward on the screen. The DOWN ARROW (↓) key causes the cursor to move down; the LEFT ARROW (←) and RIGHT ARROW (→) keys cause the cursor to move left and right on the screen. On the keyboard in Figure 5, there are two sets of cursor control keys. One set is included as part of the numeric keypad. The second set of cursor control keys is located between the typewriter keys and the numeric keypad. To use the numeric keypad for cursor control, the NUMLOCK key must be disengaged. If the NUMLOCK key is engaged (indicated by the fact that as you press any numeric keypad key, a number appears on the screen), you can return to the cursor mode by pressing the NUMLOCK key. On most keyboards, a NUMLOCK light will indicate when the numeric keypad is in the numeric mode or the cursor mode.

FIGURE 5
This keyboard represents most desktop personal computer keyboards.

The other keys on the keypad—PAGE UP, PAGE DOWN, HOME, and END—have various functions depending on the software you use. Some programs make no use of these keys; others use the PAGE UP and PAGE DOWN keys, for example, to display previous or following pages of data on the screen. Some software uses the HOME key to move the cursor to the upper left corner of the screen. Likewise, the END key may be used to move the cursor to the end of a line of text or to the bottom of the screen, depending on the software.

Function keys on many keyboards can be programmed to accomplish specific tasks. For example, a function key might be used as a help key. Whenever that key is pressed, messages display that give instructions to help the user. The keyboard in Figure 5 has twelve function keys located across the top of the keyboard.

Other keys have special uses in some applications. The SHIFT keys have several functions. They work as they do on a typewriter, allowing you to type capital letters. The SHIFT key is always used to type the symbol on the upper portion of any key on the keyboard. Also, to temporarily use the cursor control keys on the numeric keypad as numeric entry keys, you can press the SHIFT key to switch into numeric mode. If you have instead pressed the NUMLOCK key to use the numeric keys, you can press the SHIFT key to shift temporarily back to the cursor mode.

The keyboard has a BACKSPACE key, a TAB key, an INSERT key and a DELETE key that perform the functions their names indicate.

The ESCAPE (ESC) key is generally used by computer software to cancel an instruction or exit from a situation. The use of the ESC key varies between software packages.

As with the ESC key, many keys are assigned special meaning by the computer software. Certain keys may be used more frequently than others by one piece of software but rarely used by another. It is this flexibility that allows you to use the computer in so many different applications.

The Mouse   A mouse (Figure 6) is a pointing device you can use instead of the cursor control keys. You lay the palm of your hand over the mouse and move it across the surface of a pad that provides traction for a rolling ball on the bottom of the mouse. The mouse detects the direction of the ball movement and sends this information to the screen to move the cursor. You push buttons on top of the mouse to indicate your choices of actions from lists or icons displayed on the screen.

FIGURE 6
The mouse input device is used to move the cursor and choose selections on the computer screen.

The Processor Unit

The **processor unit** is composed of the central processing unit and main memory. The **central processing unit (CPU)** contains the electronic circuits that cause processing to occur. The CPU interprets instructions to the computer, performs the logical and arithmetic processing operations, and causes the input and output operations to occur. On personal computers, the CPU is designed into a chip called a **microprocessor** (Figure 7).

  Main memory, also called **random access memory**, or **RAM**, consists of electronic components that store data including numbers, letters of the alphabet, graphics, and sound. Any data to be processed must be stored in main memory. The amount of main memory in computers is typically measured in kilobytes or megabytes. One **kilobyte (K or KB)** equals 1,024 memory locations and one **megabyte (M or MB)** equals approximately 1 million memory locations. A memory location, or **byte**, usually stores one character. Therefore, a computer with 4MB can store approximately 4 million characters. One megabyte of memory can hold approximately 500 pages of text information.

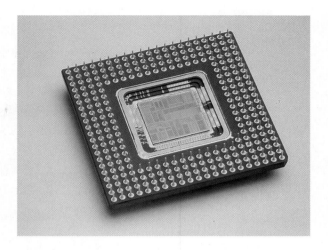

FIGURE 7
A Pentium microprocessor from Intel Corporation. The microprocessor circuits are located in the center. Small gold wires lead from the circuits to the pins that fit in the microprocessor socket on the main circuit board of the computer. The pins provide an electronic connection to different parts of the computer.

Output Devices

Output devices make the information resulting from processing available for use. The output from computers can be presented in many forms, such as a printed report or color graphics. When a computer is used for processing tasks, such as word processing, spreadsheets, or database management, the two output devices most commonly used are the printer and the television-like display device called a screen, monitor, or CRT (cathode ray tube).

Printers Printers used with computers can be either impact printers or nonimpact printers. An **impact printer** prints by striking an inked ribbon against the paper. One type of impact printer often used with personal computers is the dot matrix printer (Figure 8).

FIGURE 8
Dot matrix are the least expensive of the personal computer printers. Some can be purchased for less than $200. Advantages of dot matrix printers include the capability to handle wide paper and to print multipart forms.

FIGURE 9
On a dot matrix printer with a nine-pin print head, the letter E is formed with seven vertical and five horizontal dots. As the nine-pin print head moves from left to right, it fires one or more pins into the ribbon, making a dot on the paper. At the first print position, it fires pins 1 through 7. At print positions 2 through 4, it fires pins 1,4, and 7. At print position 5, it fires pins 1 and 7. Pins 8 and 9 are used for lowercase characters such as g, j, p, q, and y that extend below the line.

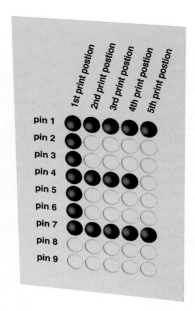

To print a character, a **dot matrix printer** generates a dot pattern representing a particular character. The printer then activates wires in a print head contained on the printer, so selected wires press against the ribbon and paper, creating a character. As you see in Figure 9, the character consists of a series of dots produced by the print head wires. In the actual size created by the printer, the characters are clear and easy to read.

Dot matrix printers vary in the speed with which they can print characters. These speeds range from 50 to more than 300 characters per second. Generally, the higher the speed, the higher the cost of the printer. Compared to other printers, dot matrix offer the lowest initial cost and the lowest per-page operating costs. Other advantages of dot matrix printers are that they can print on multipart forms and they can be purchased with wide carriages that can handle paper larger than 8 1/2 by 11 inches.

Nonimpact printers, such as ink jet printers and laser printers, form characters by means other than striking a ribbon against paper (Figure 10). Advantages of using a nonimpact printer are that it can print graphics and it can print in varying type sizes and styles called **fonts** (Figure 11). An **ink jet printer** forms a character by using a nozzle that sprays drops of ink onto the page. Ink jet printers produce relatively high-quality images and print between 30 and 150 characters per second in text mode and one to two pages per minute in graphics mode.

FIGURE 10 ▲
Two types of nonimpact printers are the laser printer (top) and the ink jet printer. Nonimpact printers are excellent for printing work that includes graphics.

FIGURE 11 ▶
Nonimpact printers do an excellent job of printing text in different typefaces, usually referred to as fonts. Technically, a font is a typeface in a particular size. It is common, however, to refer to the different typefaces as fonts. Dot matrix printers can print some fonts but usually at a slower rate and quality than nonimpact printers. The names of four different typefaces (fonts) are shown.

Laser printers work similar to a copying machine by converting data from the computer into a beam of light that is focused on a photoconductor drum, forming the images to be printed. The photoconductor attracts particles of toner that are fused by heat and pressure onto paper to produce an image. Laser printers produce high-quality output and are used for applications that combine text and graphics such as **desktop publishing** (Figure 12). Laser printers for personal computers can cost from $500 to more than $10,000. They can print four to sixteen pages of text and graphics per minute.

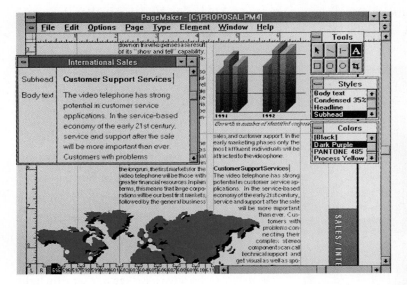

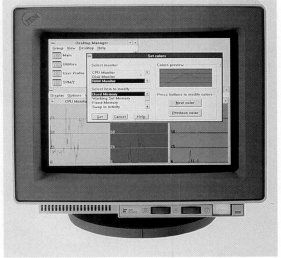

FIGURE 12
High-quality printed documents can be produced with laser printers and desktop publishing software.

Computer Screens Most full-size personal computers use a TV-like display device called a **screen**, **monitor**, or **CRT** (cathode ray tube) (Figure 13). Portable computers use a flat panel display that uses **liquid crystal display (LCD)** technology similar to a digital watch. The surface of the screen is made up of individual picture elements called **pixels**. Each pixel can be illuminated to form characters and graphic shapes (Figure 14). Color screens have three colored dots (red, green, and blue) for each pixel. These dots can be turned on to display different colors. Most color monitors today use super VGA (video graphics array) technology that can display 800 × 600 (width × height) pixels.

FIGURE 13
Many personal computer systems now come with color screens. Color can be used to enhance the information displayed so the user can understand it more quickly.

FIGURE 14
Pixel is an abreviation of the words picture element, one of thousands of spots on a computer screen that can be turned on and off to form text and graphics.

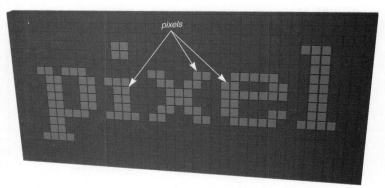

Auxiliary Storage

Auxiliary storage devices are used to store instructions and data when they are not being used in main memory. Two types of auxiliary storage most often used on personal computers are diskettes and hard disks. CD-ROM disk drives are also becoming common.

Diskettes   A **diskette** is a circular piece of oxide-coated plastic that stores data as magnetic spots. Diskettes are available in various sizes and storage capacities. Personal computers most commonly use diskettes that are 5 1/4 inches or 3 1/2 inches in diameter (Figure 15).

FIGURE 15
The most commonly used diskettes for personal computers are the 5 1/4-inch size on the left and the 3 1/2-inch size on the right. Although they are smaller in size, the 3 1/2-inch diskettes can store more data.

To read data stored on a diskette or to store data on a diskette, you insert the diskette in a disk drive (Figure 16). You can tell that the computer is reading data on the diskette or writing data on it because a light on the disk drive will come on while read/write operations are taking place. Do not try to insert or remove a diskette when the light is on as you could cause permanent damage to the data stored on it.

The storage capacities of disk drives and the related diskettes can vary widely (Figure 17). The number of characters that can be stored on a diskette by a disk drive depends on two factors: (1) the recording density of the bits on a track; and (2) the number of tracks on the diskette.

FIGURE 16
A user inserts a 3 1/2-inch diskette into the disk drive of a personal computer.

DIAMETER (INCHES)	DESCRIPTION	CAPACITY (BYTES)
5.25	Double-sided, double-density	360KB
5.25	Double-sided high-density	1.25MB
3.5	Double-sided double-density	720KB
3.5	Double-sided high-density	1.44MB

FIGURE 17
Storage capacities of different size and type diskettes.

Disk drives found on many personal computers are 5 1/4-inch, double-sided disk drives that can store from 360,000 bytes to 1.25 million bytes on the diskette. Another popular type is the 3 1/2-inch diskette, which, although physically smaller, stores from 720,000 bytes to 1.44 million bytes. An added benefit of the 3 1/2-inch diskette is its rigid plastic housing that protects the magnetic surface of the diskette.

The recording density is stated in bits per inch (bpi)—the number of magnetic spots that can be recorded on a diskette in a one-inch circumference of the innermost track on the diskette. Diskettes and disk drives used today are identified as being double-density or high-density. You need to be aware of the density of diskettes used by your system because data stored on high-density diskettes, for example, cannot be processed by a computer that has only double-density disk drives.

The second factor that influences the number of characters that can be stored on a diskette is the number of tracks on the diskette. A **track** is a very narrow recording band forming a full circle around the diskette (Figure 18).

FIGURE 18
Each track on a diskette is a narrow, circular band. On a diskette containing 80 tracks, the outside track is called track 0 and the inside track is called track 79. The disk surface is divided into sectors.

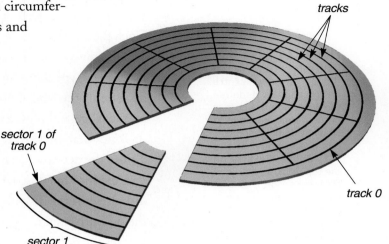

tracks

sector 1 of track 0

track 0

sector 1

The tracks are separated from each other by a very narrow blank gap. Each track on a diskette is divided into sectors. The term sector is used to refer to a pie-shaped section of the disk. It is also used to refer to a section of track. Sectors are the basic units for diskette storage. When data is read from a diskette, it reads a minimum of one full sector from a track. When data is stored on a diskette, it writes one full sector on a track at a time. The tracks and sectors on the diskette and the number of characters that can be stored in each sector are defined by a special formatting program that is used with the computer.

Data stored in sectors on a diskette must be retrieved and placed into main memory to be processed. The time required to access and retrieve data, called the **access time,** can be important in some applications. The access time for diskettes varies from about 175 milliseconds (one millisecond equals 1/1000 of a second) to approximately 300 milliseconds. On average, data stored in a single sector on a diskette can be retrieved in approximately 1/15 to 1/3 of a second.

Diskette care is important to preserve stored data. Properly handled, diskettes can store data indefinitely. However, the surface of the diskette can be damaged and the data stored can be lost if the diskette is handled improperly.

A diskette will give you very good service if you follow a few simple procedures:

1. Keep diskettes in their original box or in a special diskette storage box to protect them from dirt and dust and prevent them from being accidentally bent. Store 5 1/4-inch diskettes in their protective envelopes. Store the container away from heat and direct sunlight. Magnetic and electrical equipment, including telephones, radios, and televisions, can erase the data on a diskette, so do not place diskettes near such devices. Do not place heavy objects on a diskette, because the weight can pinch the covering, causing damage when the disk drive attempts to rotate.

2. To affix one of the self-adhesive labels supplied with most diskettes, it is best to write or type the information on the label before you place the label on the diskette. If the label is already on the diskette, use only a felt-tip pen to write on the label, and press lightly. Do not use ball point pens, pencils, or erasers on lables that are already on diskettes.

3. To use the diskette, grasp the diskette on the side away from the side to be inserted into the disk drive. Slide the diskette carefully into the slot on the disk drive. If the disk drive has a latch or door, close it. If it is difficult to close the disk drive door, do not force it—the diskette may not be inserted fully, and forcing the door closed may damage the diskette. Reinsert the diskette if necessary, and try again to close the door.

The diskette write-protect feature (Figure 19) prevents the accidental erasure of the data stored on a diskette by preventing the disk drive from writing new data or erasing existing data. On a 5 1/4-inch diskette, a write-protect notch is located on the side of the diskette. A special write-protect label is placed over this notch whenever you want to protect the data. On the 3 1/2-inch diskette, a small switch can slide to cover and uncover the write-protection window. On a 3 1/2-inch diskette, when the window is uncovered the data is protected.

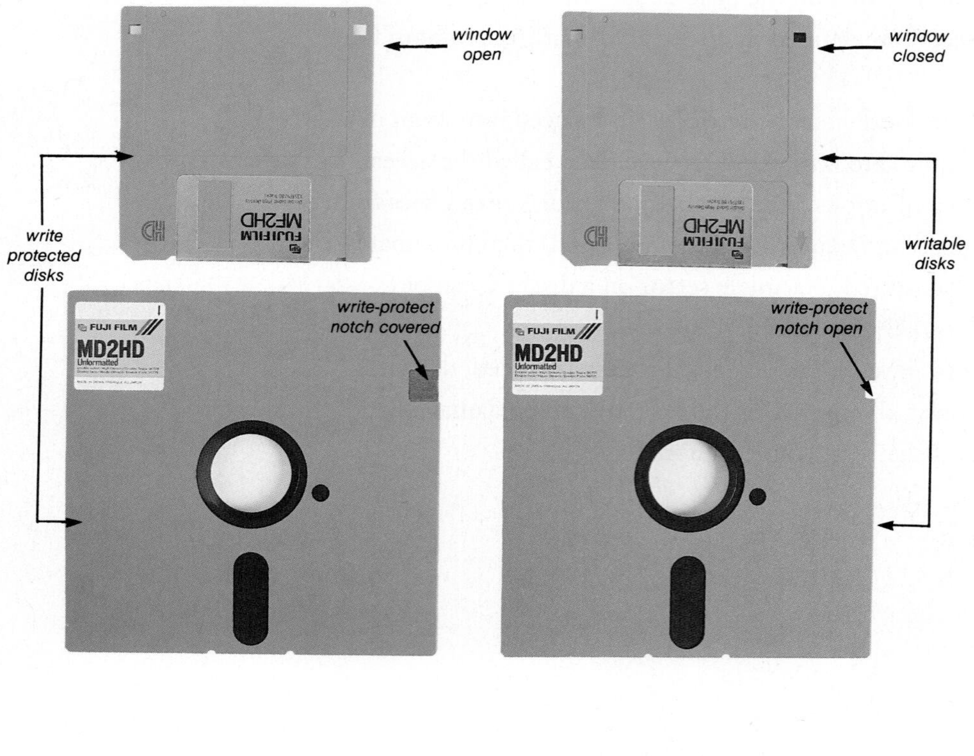

FIGURE 19
Data cannot be written on the 3 1/2-inch diskette on the top left because the window in the corner of the diskette is open. A small piece of plastic covers the window of the 3 1/2-inch diskette on the top right, so data can be written on this diskette. The reverse situation is true for the 5 1/4-inch diskettes. The write-protect notch of the 5 1/4-inch diskette on the bottom left is covered and, therefore, data cannot be written to the diskette. The notch of the 5 1/4-inch diskette on the bottom right, however, is open. Data can be written to this diskette.

Hard Disk   Another form of auxiliary storage is a hard disk. A hard disk consists of one or more rigid metal platters coated with a metal oxide material that allows data to be magnetically recorded on the surface of the platters (Figure 20). Although hard disks are available in removable cartridge form, most disks cannot be removed from the computer. As with diskettes, the data is recorded on hard disks on a series of tracks. The tracks are divided into sectors when the disk is formatted

spindle   disk surface

read/write head

access arm

The hard disk platters spin at a high rate of speed, typically 3,600 revolutions per minute. When reading data from the disk, the read head senses the magnetic spots that are recorded on the disk along the various tracks and transfers that data to main memory. When writing, the data is transferred from main memory and is stored as magnetic spots on the tracks on the recording surface of one or more of the disk platters. Unlike diskette drives, the read/write heads on a hard disk drive do not actually touch the surface of the disk.

FIGURE 20
The protective cover of this hard disk drive has been removed. A read/write head is at the end of the access arm that extends over the recording surface, called a platter.

The number of platters permanently mounted on the spindle of a hard disk varies. On most drives, each surface of the platter can be used to store data. Thus, if a hard disk drive uses one platter, two surfaces are available for data. If the drive uses two platters, four sets of read/write heads read and record data from the four surfaces. Storage capacities of internally mounted fixed disks for personal computers range from 80 million characters to more than 500 million characters. Larger capacity, stand-alone hard disk units are also available that can store more than one billion bytes of information. One billion bytes is called a gigabyte.

FIGURE 21
CD-ROM disk drives allow the user to access tremendous amounts of prerecorded information — more than 600MB of data can be stored on one CD-ROM disk.

The amount of effective storage on both hard disks and diskettes can be increased by the use of compression programs. Compression programs use sophisticated formulas to replace spaces and repeated text and graphics patterns with codes that can later be used to recreate the compressed data. Text files can be compressed the most; as much as an eighth of their original volume. Graphics files can be compressed the least. Overall, a 2-to-1 compression ratio is average.

CD-ROM   Compact disk read-only memory (CD-ROM) disks are increasingly used to store large amounts of prerecorded information (Figure 21). Each CD-ROM disk can store more than 600 million bytes of data—the equivalent of 300,000 pages of text. Because of their large storage capacity, CD-ROM is often used for multimedia material. Multimedia combines text, graphics, video (pictures), and audio (sound) (Figure 22 on the next page).

Computer Software

Computer software is the key to productive use of computers. With the correct software, a computer can become a valuable tool. Software can be categorized into two types: system software and application software.

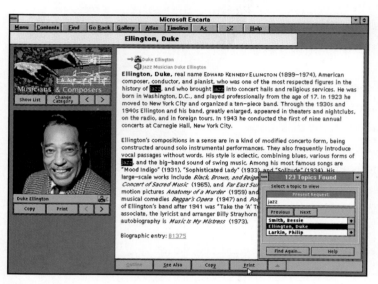

FIGURE 22
Microsoft Encarta is a multimedia encyclopedia available on a CD-ROM disk. Text, graphics, sound, and animation are all available. The camera-shaped icon at the top of the text indicates that a photograph is available for viewing. The speaker-shaped icon just below the camera indicates that a sound item is available. In this topic, if the user chooses the speaker icon with the mouse, a portion of Duke Ellington's music is played.

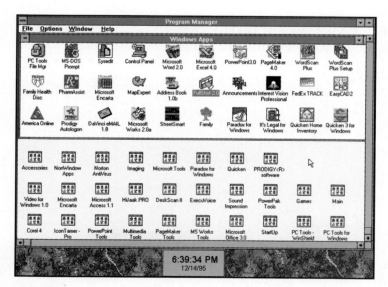

FIGURE 23
Microsoft Windows is a graphical user interface that works with the DOS operating system to make the computer easier to use. The small pictures or symbols on the main part of the screen are called icons. The icons represent different processing options, such as word processing or electronic spreadsheet applications, the user can choose.

System Software

System software consists of programs to control the operations of computer equipment. An important part of system software is a set of programs called the **operating system**. Instructions in the operating system tell the computer how to perform the functions of loading, storing, and executing an application and how to transfer data. For a computer to operate, an operating system must be stored in the computer's main memory. When a computer is started, the operating system is loaded into the computer and stored in main memory. This process is called **booting**. The most commonly used operating system on personal computers is **DOS (Disk Operating System)**.

Many computers use an **operating environment** that works with the operating system to make the computer system easier to use. Operating environments have a **graphical user interface (GUI)** displaying visual clues such as icon symbols to help the user. Each **icon** represents an application software package, such as word processing or a file or document where data is stored. **Microsoft Windows** (Figure 23) is a graphical user interface that works with DOS. Apple Macintosh computers also have a built in graphical user interface in the operating system.

Application Software

Application software consists of programs that tell a computer how to produce information. The different ways people use computers in their careers or in their personal lives, are examples of types of application software. Business, scientific, and educational programs are all examples of application software.

Personal Computer Application Software Packages

Personal computer users often use application software packages. Some of the most commonly used packages are: word processing, electronic spreadsheet, presentation graphics, database, communications, and electronic mail software.

Word processing software (Figure 24) is used to create and print documents. A key advantage of word processing software is its capability to make changes easily in documents, such as correcting spelling, changing margins, and adding, deleting, or relocating entire paragraphs. These changes would be difficult and time consuming to make using manual methods such as a typewriter. With a word processor, documents can be printed quickly and accurately and easily stored on a disk for future use. Word processing software is oriented toward working with text, but most word processing packages can also include numeric and graphic information.

Electronic spreadsheet software (Figure 25) allows the user to add, subtract, and perform user-defined calculations on rows and columns of numbers. These numbers can be changed and the spreadsheet quickly recalculates the new results. Electronic spreadsheet software eliminates the tedious recalculations required with manual methods. Spreadsheet information is frequently converted into a graphic form. Graphics capabilities are now included in most spreadsheet packages.

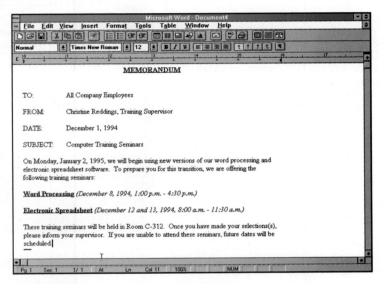

FIGURE 24
Word processing software is used to write letters, memos, and other documents. As the user types words and letters, they display on the screen. The user can easily add, delete, and change any text entered until the document looks exactly as desired. The user can then save the document on auxiliary storage and can also print it on a printer.

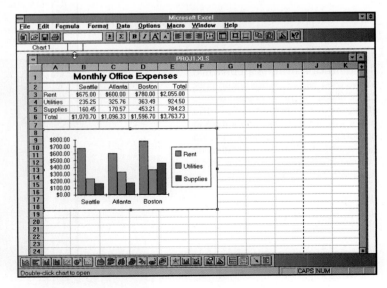

FIGURE 25
Electronic spreadsheet software is frequently used by people who work with numbers. The user enters the data and the formulas to be used on the data and calculates the results. Most spreadsheet programs have the capability to use numeric data to generate charts, such as the bar chart.

Database software (Figure 26) allows the user to enter, retrieve, and update data in an organized and efficient manner. These software packages have flexible inquiry and reporting capabilities that allow users to access the data in different ways and create custom reports that include some or all of the information in the database.

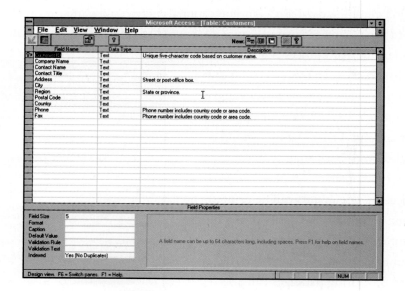

FIGURE 26
Database software allows the user to enter, retrieve, and update data in an organized and efficient manner. This database table illustrates how a business organized customer information. Once the table is defined, the user can add, delete, change, display, print, or reorganize the database records.

Presentation graphics software (Figure 27) allows the user to create documents called slides to be used in making presentations. Using special projection devices, the slides are projected directly from the computer. In addition, the slides can be printed and used as handouts, or converted into transparencies and displayed on overhead projectors. Presentation graphics software includes many special effects, color, and art that enhance information presented on a slide. Because slides frequently include numeric data, presentation graphics software includes the capability to convert the numeric data into many forms of charts.

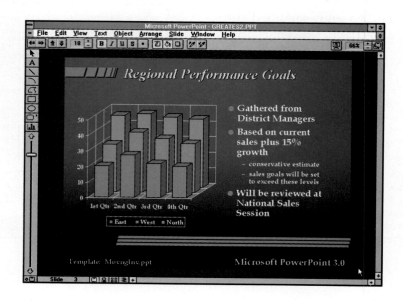

FIGURE 27
Presentation graphics software allows the user to create documents called slides for use in presentations. Using special projection devices, the slides display as they appear on the computer screen. The slides can also be printed and used as handouts or converted into transparencies to be used with overhead projectors.

Communications software (Figure 28) is used to transmit data and information from one computer to another. For the transfer to take place, each computer must have communications software. Organizations use communications software to transfer information from one location to another. Many individuals use communications software to access on-line databases that provide information on current events, airline schedules, finances, weather, and hundreds of other subjects.

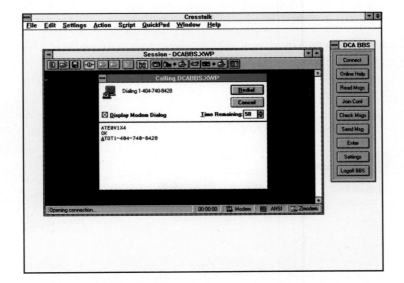

FIGURE 28
Communications software allows users to transmit data from one computer to another. This software enables the user to choose a previously entered phone number of another computer. Once the number is chosen, the communications software dials the number and establishes a communication link. The user can then transfer data or run programs on the remote computer.

Electronic mail software, also called **e-mail** (Figure 29), allows users to send messages to and receive messages from other computer users. The other users may be on the same computer network or on a separate computer system reached through the use of communications equipment and software.

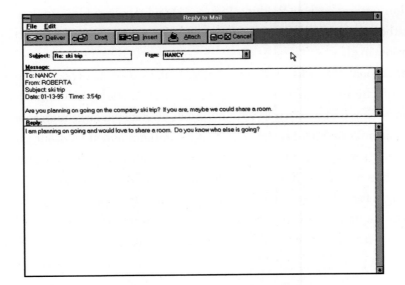

FIGURE 29
Electronic mail software allows users to send and receive messages with other computer users. Each user has an electronic mail box to which messages are sent. This software enables a user to add a reply to a received message and then send the reply back to the person who sent the original message.

What Is Communications?

Communications refers to the transmission of data and information over a communications channel, such as a standard telephone line, between one computer and another computer. Figure 30 shows the basic model for a communications system. This model consists of the following equipment:

1. A computer.
2. Communications equipment that sends (and can usually receive) data.
3. The communications channel over which the data is sent.
4. Communications equipment that receives (and can usually send) data.
5. Another computer.

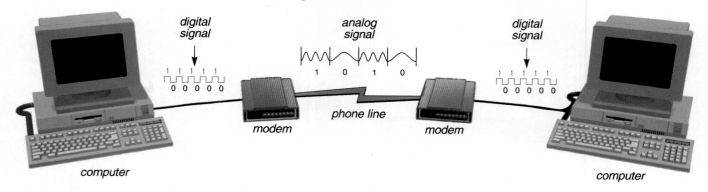

FIGURE 30
The basic model of a communications system. Individual electrical pulses of the digital signal from the computer are converted into analog (electrical wave) signals for transmission over voice telephone lines. At the main computer receiving end, another modem converts the analog signals back into digital signals that can be processed by the computer.

The basic model also includes communications software. When two computers are communicating with each other, compatible communications software is required on each system.

Communications is important to understand because of on-line services and the trend to network computers. With communications equipment and software, access is available to an increasing amount and variety of information and services. **On-line information services** such as Prodigy (Figure 31) and America On-Line offer the latest news, weather, sports, and financial information along with shopping, entertainment, and electronic mail.

International networks such as the Internet allow users to access information at thousands of Internet member organizations around the world. Electronic bulletin boards can be found in most cities with hundreds available in large metropolitan areas. An electronic **bulletin board system (BBS)** is a computer and at least one phone line that allows users to *chat* with the computer operator, called the **system operator (sys op)** or, if more than one phone line is available, with other BBS users. BBS users can also leave messages for other users. BBSs are often devoted to a specific subject area such as games, hobbies, or a specific type of computer or software. Many computer hardware and software companies operate BBSs so users of their products can share information.

Communications Channels

A **communications channel** is the path the data follows as it is transmitted from the sending equipment to the receiving equipment in a communications system. These channels are made up of one or more **transmission media,** including twisted pair wire, coaxial cable, fiber optics, microwave transmission, satellite transmission, and wireless transmission.

Communications Equipment

If a personal computer is within approximately 1,000 feet of another computer, the two devices can usually be directly connected by a cable. If the devices are more than 1,000 feet, however, the electrical signal weakens to the point that some type of special communications equipment is required to increase or change the signal to transmit it farther. A variety of communications equipment exists to perform this task, but the equipment most often used is a modem.

FIGURE 31
Prodigy is one of several on-line service providers offering information on a number of general-interest subjects. The topic areas display on the right. Users access Prodigy and other on-line services by using a modem and special communications software.

Computer equipment is designed to process data as **digital signals,** individual electrical pulses grouped together to represent characters. Telephone equipment was originally designed to carry only voice transmission, which is comprised of a continuous electrical wave called an **analog signal** (see Figure 30). Thus, a special piece of equipment called a modem converts between the digital signals and analog signals so telephone lines can carry data. A **modem** converts the digital signals of a computer to analog signals that are transmitted over a communications channel. A modem also converts analog signals it receives into digital signals used by a computer. The word modem comes from a combination of the words *mo*dulate, which means to change into a sound or analog signal,and *dem*odulate, which means to convert an analog signal into a digital signal. A modem is needed at both the sending and receiving ends of a communications channel. A modem may be an external stand-alone device that is connected to the computer and phone line or an internal circuit board that is installed inside the computer.

Modems can transmit data at rates from 300 to 38,400 bits per second (bps). Most personal computers use a 2,400 bps or higher modem. Business or heavier volume users would use faster and more expensive modems.

Communication Networks

A communication **network** is a collection of computers and other equipment using communications channels to share hardware, software, data, and information. Networks are classified as either local area networks or wide area networks.

Local Area Networks (LANs)

A **local area network**, or LAN, is a privately owned communications network and covers a limited geographic area, such as a school computer laboratory, an office, a building, or a group of buildings.

The LAN consists of a communications channel connecting a group of personal computers to one another. Very sophisticated LANs are capable of connecting a variety of office devices, such as word processing equipment, computer terminals, video equipment, and personal computers.

Three common applications of local area networks are hardware, software, and information resource sharing. **Hardware resource sharing** allows each personal computer in the network to access and use devices that would be too expensive to provide for each user or would not be justified for each user because of only occasional use. For example, when a number of personal computers are used on the network, each may need to use a laser printer. Using a LAN, the purchase of one laser printer serves the entire network. Whenever a personal computer user on the network needs the laser printer, it is accessed over the network. Figure 32 depicts a simple local area network consisting of four personal computers linked together by a cable. Three of the personal computers (computer 1 in the sales and marketing department, computer 2 in the accounting department, and computer 3 in the personnel department) are available for use at all times. Computer 4 is used as a **server**, which is dedicated to handling the communications needs of the other computers in the network. The users of this LAN have connected the laser printer to the server. Using the LAN, all computers and the server can use the printer.

FIGURE 32
A local area network (LAN) consists of multiple personal computers connected to one another. The LAN allows users to share softwre, hardware, and information.

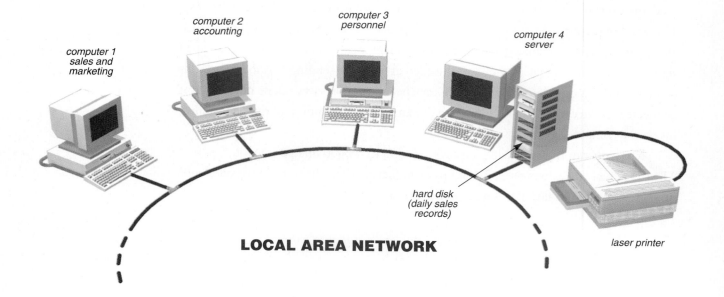

computer 1
sales and
marketing

computer 2
accounting

computer 3
personnel

computer 4
server

hard disk
(daily sales
records)

laser printer

LOCAL AREA NETWORK

Frequently used software is another type of resource sharing that often occurs on a local area network. For example, if all users need access to word processing software, the software can be stored on the hard disk of the server and accessed by all users as needed. This is more convenient and faster than having the software stored on a diskette and available at each computer.

Information resource sharing allows anyone using a personal computer on the local area network to access data stored on any other computer in the network. In actual practice, hardware resource sharing and information resource sharing are often combined. The capability to access and store data on common auxiliary storage is an important feature of many local area networks.

Information resource sharing is usually provided by using either the file-server or client-server method. Using the **file-server** method, the server sends an entire file at a time. The requesting computer then performs the processing. With the **client-server** method, processing tasks are divided between the server computer

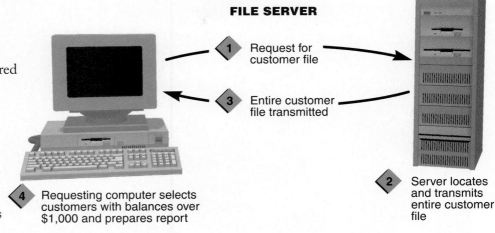

FILE SERVER

1 Request for customer file

3 Entire customer file transmitted

2 Server locates and transmits entire customer file

4 Requesting computer selects customers with balances over $1,000 and prepares report

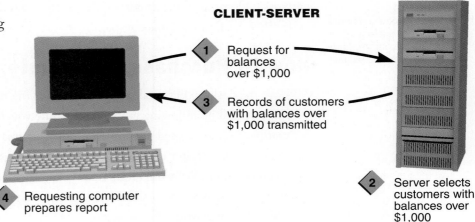

CLIENT-SERVER

1 Request for balances over $1,000

3 Records of customers with balances over $1,000 transmitted

2 Server selects customers with balances over $1,000

4 Requesting computer prepares report

and the *client* computer requesting the information. Figure 33 illustrates how the two methods would process a request for information stored on the server system for customers with balances over $1,000. With the file-server method, all customer records would be transferred to the requesting computer. The requesting computer would then process the records to identify the customers with balances over $1,000. With the client-server method, the server system would review the customers' records and only transfer records of customers meeting the criteria. The client-server method greatly reduces the amount of data sent over a network but requires a more powerful server system.

FIGURE 33
A request for information about customers with balances over $1,000 would be processed differently by the file-server and client-server networks.

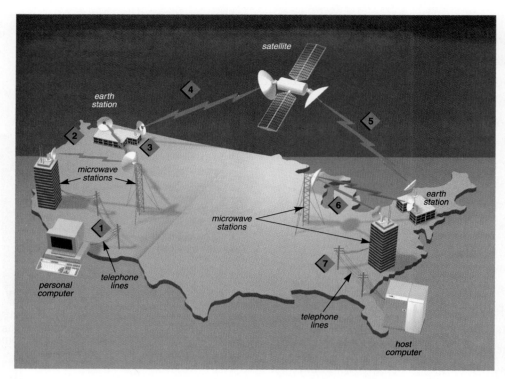

Wide Area Networks (WANs)

A wide area network, or WAN, is geographic in scope (as opposed to local) and uses telephone lines, microwaves, satellites, or a combination of communications channels (Figure 34). Public wide area network companies include common carriers such as the telephone companies. Telephone company deregulation has encouraged a number of companies to build their own wide area

FIGURE 34
A wide area network (WAN) may use a number of different communications channels such as telephone lines, microwaves, and satellites.

networks. Communications companies, such as MCI, have built WANs to compete with other communications companies.

How to Purchase a Computer System

T he desktop personal computer (PC) is the most widely purchased type of system. The following guidelines assume you are purchasing a desktop IBM-compatible PC, to be used for home or light business use. That is not meant to imply that Macintosh or other non DOS or Windows operating system computers are not worth considering. Software requirements and the need to be compatible with other systems you may work with should determine the type of system you purchase. A portable computer would be an appropriate choice if your situation requires that you have a computer with you when you travel.

1. Determine what applications you will use on your computer. This decision will guide you as to the type and size of computer.

2. Choose your software first. Some packages only run on Macintosh computers, others only on a PC. Some packages only run under the Windows operating system. In addition, some software requires more memory and disk space than other packages.

3. Be aware of hidden costs. Realize that there will be some additional costs associated with buying a computer. Such costs might include; an additional phone line or outlet to use the modem, computer furniture, consumable supplies such as diskettes and paper, diskette holders, reference manuals on specific software

packages, and special training classes you may want to take. Depending on where you buy your computer, the seller may be willing to include some or all of these in the system purchase price.

4. **Buy equipment that meets the *Energy Star* power consumption guidelines.** These guidelines require that computer systems, monitors, and printers, reduce electrical consumption if they have not been used for some period of time, usually several minutes. Equipment meeting the guidelines can display the *Energy Star* logo.

5. **Use a spreadsheet like the one shown in Figure 35 to compare purchase alternatives.** Use a separate sheet of paper to take notes on each vendor's system and then summarize the information on the spreadsheet.

6. **Consider buying from local computer dealers and direct mail companies.** Each has certain advantages. The local dealer can more easily provide hands-on support, if necessary. With a mail order company, you are usually limited to speaking to someone over the phone. Mail order companies usually, but not always, offer the lowest prices. The important thing to do when shopping for a system is to make sure you are comparing identical or similar configurations.

System Cost Comparison Worksheet			Desired	#1	#2	#3	#4
Base System	Mfr		—	Delway			
	Model			4500X			
	Processor		486DX	486DX			
	Speed		50MHz	50			
	Pwr Supply		200watts	220			
	Exp Slots		5	5			
	Price			$995			
Memory	8MB Ram			incl			
Disk	Mfr			Conner			
	Size		>300MB	340			
	Price			incl			
Diskette	3 1/2						
	5 1/4						
	Combination			$50			
Monitor	Mfr			NEC			
	Model			5FG			
	Size		15in	15			
	Price			$300			
Sound	Mfr			Media Labs			
	Model			Pro			
	Price			$75			
CDROM	Mfr			NEC			
	Speed			450/200			
	Price			$100			
Mouse	Mfr			Logitech			
	Price			incl			
Modem	Mfr			Boca			
	Mod/fax Speeds		14.4/14.4	14.4/14.4			
	Price			$125			
Printer	Mfr			HP			
	Model			4Z			
	Type			laser			
	Speed		6ppm	8ppm			
	Price			$675			
Surge Protector	Mfr			Brooks			
	Price			$35			
Options	Tape Backup						
	UPS						
Other	Sales Tax			0			
	Shipping			$30			
	1 YR Warranty			incl			
	1 YR On-Site Svc			incl			
	3 YR On-Site Svc			$150			
Software	List free software			Windows			
				MS Works			
				diagnostics			
	TOTAL			**$2,535**			

FIGURE 35
A spreadsheet is an effective way to summarize and compare the prices and equipment offered by different system vendors.

7. **Consider more than just price.** Don't necessarily buy the lowest cost system. Consider intangibles such as how long the vendor has been in business, its reputation for quality, and reputation for support.

8. **Look for free software.** Many system vendors now include free software with their systems. Some even let you choose which software you want. Such software only has value, however, if you would have purchased it if it had not come with the computer.

9. **Buy a system compatible with the one you use elsewhere.** If you use a personal computer at work or at some other organization, make sure the computer you buy is compatible. That way, if you need or want to, you can work on projects at home.

10. **Consider purchasing an on-site service agreement.** If you use your system for business or otherwise can't afford to be without your computer, consider purchasing an on-site service agreement. Many of the mail order vendors offer such support through third-party companies. Such agreements usually state that a technician will be on-site within 24 hours. Some systems include on-site service for only the first year. It is usually less expensive to extend the service for two or three years when you buy the computer rather than waiting to buy the service agreement later.

11. **Use a credit card to purchase your system.** Many credit cards now have purchase protection benefits that cover you in case of loss or damage to purchased goods. Some also extend the warranty of any products purchased with the card. Paying by credit card also gives you time to install and use the system before you have to pay for it. Finally, if you're dissatisfied with the system and can't reach an agreement with the seller, paying by credit card gives you certain rights regarding withholding payment until the dispute is resolved. Check your credit card agreement for specific details.

12. **Buy a system that will last you for at least three years.** Studies show that many users become dissatisfied because they didn't buy a powerful enough system. Consider the following system configuration guidelines. Each of the components will be discussed separately:

Base System Components:	Optional Equipment:
486SX or 486DX processor, 33 megahertz	5 1/4" diskette drive
150 watt power supply	14.4K fax modem
160 to 300MB hard disk	laser printer
4 to 8MB RAM	sound card and speakers
3 to 5 expansion slots	CD-ROM drive
3 1/2" diskette drive	tape backup
14" or 15" color monitor	uninterruptable power supply (UPS)
mouse or other pointing device	
enhanced keyboard	
ink jet or bubble jet printer	
surge protector	

Processor: A 486SX or 486DX processor with a speed rating of at least 33 mega-hertz is needed for today's more sophisticated software, even word processing soft-ware. Buy a system that can be upgraded to the Pentium processor.

Power Supply: 150 watts. If the power supply is too small, it won't be able to support additional expansion cards that you might want to add in the future.

Hard Disk: 160 to 300 megabytes (MB). Each new release of software requires more hard disk space. Even with disk compression programs, disk space is used up fast. Start with more disk than you ever think you'll need.

Memory (RAM): 4 to 8 megabytes (MB). Like disk space, the new applications are demanding more memory. It's easier and less expensive to obtain the memory when you buy the system than if you wait until later.

Expansion Slots: 3 to 5 open slots on the base system. Expansion slots are needed for scanners, tape drives, video boards, and other equipment you may want to add in the future as your needs change and the price of this equipment becomes lower.

Diskette Drives: Most software is now distributed on 3 1/2-inch disks. Consider adding a 5 1/4-inch diskette to read data and programs that may have been stored on that format. The best way to achieve this is to buy a combination diskette drive which is only slightly more expensive than a single 3 1/2-inch diskette drive. The combination device has both 3 1/2- and 5 1/4-inch diskette drives in a single unit.

Color Monitor: 14 to 15 inch. This is one device where it pays to spend a little more money. A 15-inch super VGA monitor will display graphics better than a 14-inch model. For health reasons, make sure you pick a low radiation model.

Pointing Device: Most systems include a mouse as part of the base package.

Enhanced Keyboard: The keyboard is usually included with the system. Check to make sure the keyboard is the *enhanced* and not the older *standard* model. The enhanced keyboard is sometimes called the *101* keyboard because it has 101 keys.

Printer: The price of nonimpact printers has come within several hundred dollars of the lowest cost dot matrix printers. Unless you need the wide carriage or multi-part form capabilities of a dot matrix, purchase a nonimpact printer.

Surge Protector: A voltage spike can literally destroy your system. It is low-cost insurance to protect yourself with a surge protector. Don't merely buy a fused multi-plug outlet from the local hardware store. Buy a surge protector designed for com-puters with a separate protected jack for your phone (modem) line.

Fax Modem: Volumes of information are available via on-line databases. In addition, many software vendors provide assistance and free software upgrades via bulletin boards. For the speed they provide, 14.4K modems are worth the extra money. Facsimile (fax) capability only costs a few dollars more and gives you more communication options.

Sound Card and Speakers: More and more software and support materials are incorporating sound.

CD-ROM Drive: Multimedia is the wave of the future and it requires a CD-ROM drive. Get a double- or triple-speed model.

Tape Backup: Larger hard disks make backing up data on diskettes impractical. Internal or external tape backup systems are the most common solution. Some portable units, great if you have more than one system, are designed to connect to your printer port. The small cassette tapes can store the equivalent of hundreds of diskettes.

Uninterruptable Power Supply (UPS): A UPS uses batteries to start or keep your system running if the main electrical power is turned off. The length of time they provide depends on the size of the batteries and the electrical requirements of your system but is usually at least 10 minutes. The idea of a UPS is to give you enough time to save your work. Get a UPS that is rated for your size system.

Remember that the types of applications you want to use on your system will guide you as to the type and size of computer that is right for you. The ideal computer system you choose may differ from the general recommendation that is presented here. Determine your needs and buy the best system your budget will allow.

How to Install a Computer System

1. **Allow for adequate workspace around the computer.** A workspace of at least two feet by four feet is recommended.

2. **Install bookshelves.** Bookshelves above and/or to the side of the computer area are useful for keeping manuals and other reference materials handy.

3. **Install your computer in a well-designed work area.** The height of your chair, keyboard, monitor, and work surface is important and can affect your health. See Figure 36 for specific guidelines.

4. **Use a document holder.** To minimize neck and eye strain, obtain a document holder that holds documents at the same height and distance as your computer screen.

5. **Provide adequate lighting.**

6. **While working at your computer, be aware of health issues.** See Figure 37 for a list of computer user health guidelines.

7. **Install or move a phone near the computer.** Having a phone near the computer really helps if you need to call a vendor about a hardware or software problem. Oftentimes the vendor support person can talk you through the correction while you're on the phone. To avoid data loss, however, don't place diskettes on the phone or any other electrical or electronic equipment.

8. **Obtain a computer tool set.** Computer tool sets are available from computer dealers, office supply stores, and mail order companies. These sets will have the right-sized screwdrivers and other tools to work on your system. Get one that comes in a zippered carrying case to keep all the tools together.

9. **Save all the paperwork that comes with your system.** Keep it in an accessible place with the paperwork from your other computer-related purchases. To keep different-sized documents together, consider putting them in a plastic zip-lock bag.

10. **Record the serial numbers of all your equipment and software.** Write the serial numbers on the outside of the manuals that came with the equipment as well as in a single list that contains the serial numbers of all your equipment and software.

11. **Keep the shipping containers and packing materials for all your equipment.** This material will come in handy if you have to return your equipment for servicing or have to move it to another location.

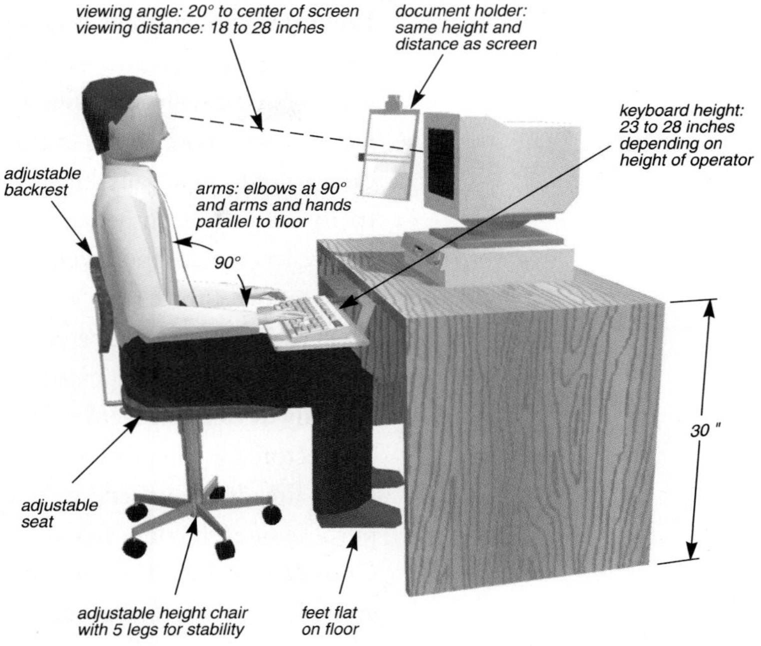

viewing angle: 20° to center of screen
viewing distance: 18 to 28 inches

document holder: same height and distance as screen

keyboard height: 23 to 28 inches depending on height of operator

adjustable backrest

arms: elbows at 90° and arms and hands parallel to floor

90°

30 "

adjustable seat

adjustable height chair with 5 legs for stability

feet flat on floor

FIGURE 36
More than anything else, a well-designed work area should be flexible to allow adjustment to the height and build of different individuals. Good lighting and air quality should also be considered.

COMPUTER USER HEALTH GUIDELINES
1. Work in a well-designed work area. Figure 36 illustrates the guidelines.
2. Alternate work activities to prevent physical and mental fatigue. If possible, change the order of your work to provide some variety.
3. Take frequent breaks. At least once per hour, get out of your chair and move around. Every two hours, take at least a 15 minute break.
4. Incorporate hand, arm, and body stretching exercises into your breaks. At lunch, try to get outside and walk.
5. Make sure your computer monitor is designed to minimize electromagnetic radiation
6. Try to eliminate or minimize surrounding noise. Noisy environments contribute to stress and tension.
7. If you frequently have to use the phone and the computer at the same time, consider using a telephone headset. Cradling the phone between your head and shoulder can cause muscle strain.
8. Be aware of symptoms of repetitive strain injuries; soreness, pain, numbness, or weakness in neck, shoulders, arms, wrists, and hands. Don't ignore early signs; seek medical advice.

FIGURE 37
All computer users should follow the Computer User Health Guidelines to maintain their health.

12. **Look at the inside of your computer.** Before you connect power to your system, remove the computer case cover and visually inspect the internal components. The user manual usually identifies what each component does. Look for any disconnected wires, loose screws or washers, or any other obvious signs of trouble. Be careful not to touch anything inside the case unless you are grounded. Static electricity can permanently damage the microprocessor chips on the circuit boards. Before you replace the cover, take several photographs of the computer showing the location of the circuit boards. These photos may save you from taking the cover off in the future if you or a vendor has a question about what equipment controller card is installed in what expansion slot.

13. **Identify device connectors.** At the back of your system there are a number of connectors for the printer, the monitor, the mouse, a phone line, etc. If they aren't already identified by the manufacturer, use a marking pen to write the purpose of each connector on the back of the computer case.

14. **Complete and send in your equipment and software registration cards right away.** If you're already entered in the vendors user database, it can save you time when you call in with a support question. Being a registered user also makes you eligible for special pricing on software upgrades.

15. **Install your system in an area where the temperature and humidity can be maintained.** Try to maintain a constant temperature between 60 and 80 degrees farenheight when the computer is operating. High temperatures and humidity can damage electronic components. Be careful when using space heaters; their hot, dry air has been known to cause disk problems.

16. **Keep your computer area clean.** Avoid eating and drinking around the computer. Smoking should be avoided also. Cigarette smoke can quickly cause damage to the diskette drives and diskette surfaces.

17. **Check your insurance.** Some policies have limits on the amount of computer equipment they cover. Other policies don't cover computer equipment at all if it is used for a business (a separate policy is required).

How to Maintain Your Computer System

1. **Learn to use system diagnostic programs.** If a set didn't come with your system, obtain one. These programs help you identify and possibly solve problems before you call for technical assistance. Some system manufacturers now include diagnostic programs with their systems and ask that you run the programs before you call for help.

2. **Start a notebook that includes information on your system.** This notebook should be a single source of information about your entire system, both hardware and software. Each time you make a change to your system, adding or removing hardware or software, or when you change system parameters, you should record the change in the notebook. Items to include in the notebook are the following:

✓ Serial numbers of all equipment and software.

✓ Vendor support phone numbers. These numbers are often buried in user manuals. Look up these numbers once and record all of them on a single sheet of paper at the front of your notebook.

✓ Date and vendor for each equipment and software purchase.

✓ File listings for key system files (e.g., autoexec.bat and config.sys).

✓ Notes on discussions with vendor support personnel.

✓ A chronological history of any equipment or software problems. This history can be helpful if the problem persists and you have to call several times.

3. **Periodically review disk directories and delete unneeded files.** Files have a way of building up and can quickly use up your disk space. If you think you may need a file in the future, back it up to a diskette.

4. **Any time you work inside your computer turn the power off and disconnect the equipment from the power source.** In addition, before you touch anything inside the computer, touch an unpainted metal surface such as the power supply. This will discharge any static electricity that could damage internal components.

5. **Reduce the need to clean the inside of your system by keeping the surrounding area dirt and dust free.** Diskette cleaners are available but should be used sparingly (some owners never use them unless they experience diskette problems). If dust builds up inside the computer it should be carefully removed with compressed air and a small vacuum. Don't touch the components with the vacuum.

6. **Back up key files and data.** At a minimum, you should have a diskette with your **command.com, autoexec.bat,** and **config.sys** files. If your system crashes, these files will help you get going again. In addition, backup any files with a file extension of **.sys.** For Windows systems, all files with a file extension of **.ini** and **.grp** should be backed up.

7. **Protect your system from computer viruses.** Computer viruses are programs designed to *infect* computer systems by copying themselves into other computer files (Figure 38). The virus program spreads when the infected files are used by or copied to another system.

FIGURE 38
How a virus program can be transmitted from one computer to another.

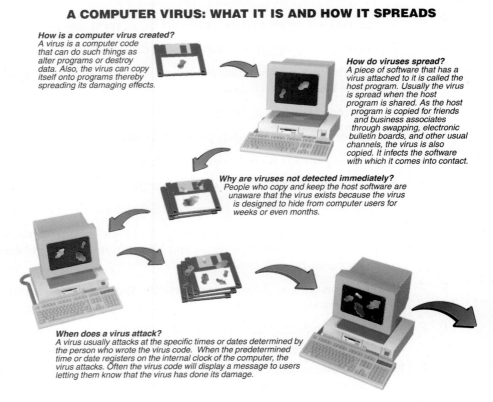

A COMPUTER VIRUS: WHAT IT IS AND HOW IT SPREADS

How is a computer virus created?
A virus is a computer code that can do such things as alter programs or destroy data. Also, the virus can copy itself onto programs thereby spreading its damaging effects.

How do viruses spread?
A piece of software that has a virus attached to it is called the host program. Usually the virus is spread when the host program is shared. As the host program is copied for friends and business associates through swapping, electronic bulletin boards, and other usual channels, the virus is also copied. It infects the software with which it comes into contact.

Why are viruses not detected immediately?
People who copy and keep the host software are unaware that the virus exists because the virus is designed to hide from computer users for weeks or even months.

When does a virus attack?
A virus usually attacks at the specific times or dates determined by the person who wrote the virus code. When the predetermined time or date registers on the internal clock of the computer, the virus attacks. Often the virus code will display a message to users letting them know that the virus has done its damage.

Virus programs are dangerous because they are often designed to damage the files of the infected system. Protect yourself from viruses by installing an anti-virus program on your computer.

Summary of Introduction to Computers

A s you learn to use the software taught in this book, you will also become familiar with the components and operation of your computer system. When you need help understanding how the components of your system function, refer to this introduction. You can also refer to this section for information on computer communications and for guidelines when you decide to purchase a computer system of your own.

Student Assignments

Student Assignment 1: True/False

Instructions: Circle T if the statement is true or F if the statement is false.

T F   1. A computer is an electronic device, operating under the control of instructions stored in its own memory unit, that can accept data (input), process data arithmetically and logically, produce output from the processing, and store the results for future use.

T F   2. Information refers to data processed into a form that has meaning and is useful.

T F   3. A computer program is a detailed set of instructions that tells a computer exactly what to do.

T F   4. A mouse is a communications device used to convert between digital and analog signals so telephone lines can carry data.

T F   5. The central processing unit contains the processor unit and main memory.

T F   6. A laser printer is an impact printer that provides high-quality output.

T F   7. Auxiliary storage is used to store instructions and data when they are not being used in main memory.

T F   8. A diskette is considered to be a form of main memory.

T F   9. CD-ROM is often used for multimedia material that combines text, graphics, video, and sound.

T F   10. The operating system tells the computer how to perform functions such as how to load, store, and execute an application program and how to transfer data between the input/output devices and main memory.

T F   11. Programs such as database management, spreadsheet, and word processing software are called system software.

T F   12. For data to be transferred from one computer to another over communications lines, communications software is required only on the sending computer.

T F   13. A communications network is a collection of computers and other equipment that use communications channels to share hardware, software, data, and information.

T F 14. Determining what applications you will use on your computer will help you to purchase a computer that is the type and size that meets your needs.

T F 15. The path the data follows as it is transmitted from the sending equipment to the receiving equipment in a communications system is called a modem.

T F 16. Computer equipment that meets the power consumption guidelines can display the *Energy Star* logo.

T F 17. An on-site maintenance agreement is important if you cannot be without the use of your computer.

T F 18. An anit-virus program is used to protect your computer equipment and software.

T F 19. When purchasing a computer, consider only the price because one computer is no different from another.

T F 20. A LAN allows you to share software but not hardware.

Student Assignment 2: Multiple Choice

Instructions: Circle the correct response.

1. The four operations performed by a computer include _____ .
   a. input, control, output, and storage
   b. interface, processing, output, and memory
   c. input, output, processing, and storage
   d. input, logical/rational, arithmetic, and output

2. A hand-held input device that controls the cursor location is _____ .
   a. the cursor control keyboard
   b. a mouse
   c. a modem
   d. the CRT

3. A printer that forms images without striking the paper is _____ .
   a. an impact printer   b. a nonimpact printer   c. an ink jet printer   d. both b and c

4. The amount of storage provided by a diskette is a function of _____ .
   a. the thickness of the disk
   b. the recording density of bits on the track
   c. the number of recording tracks on the diskette
   d. both b and c

5. Portable computers use a flat panel screen called a _____ .
   a. a multichrome monitor
   b. a cathode ray tube
   c. a liquid crystal display
   d. a monochrome monitor

6. When not in use, diskettes should be _____ .
   a. stored away from magnetic fields
   b. stored away from heat and direct sunlight
   c. stored in a diskette box or cabinet
   d. all of the above

7. CD-ROM is a type of _____ .
   a. main memory
   b. auxiliary storage
   c. communications equipment
   d. system software

8. An operating system is considered part of _____ .
   a. word processing software
   b. database software
   c. system software
   d. spreadsheet software

9. The type of application software most commonly used to create and print documents is _____ .
   a. word processing   b. electronic spreadsheet   c. database   d. none of the above

10. The type of application software most commonly used to send messages to and receive messages from other computer users is _____ .
    a. electronic mail   b. database   c. presentation graphics   d. none of the above

Student Assignment 3: Comparing Personal Computer Advertisements

Instructions: Obtain a copy of a recent computer magazine and review the advertisements for desktop personal computer systems. Compare ads for the least and most expensive desktop systems you can find. Discuss the differences.

Student Assignment 4: Evaluating On-Line Information Services

Instructions: Prodigy and America On-Line both offer consumer oriented on-line information services. Contact each company and request each to send you information on the specific services it offers. Try to talk to someone who actually uses one or both of the services. Discuss how each service is priced and the differences between the two on-line services.

Student Assignment 5: Visiting Local Computer Retail Stores

Instructions: Visit local computer retail stores and compare the various types of computers and support equipment available. Ask about warranties, repair services, hardware setup, training, and related issues. Report on the knowledge of the sales staff assisting you and their willingness to answer your questions. Does the store have standard hardware packages, or are they willing to configure a system to your specific needs? Would you feel confident buying a computer from this store?

Index

Photo Credits

Figure 1, (1) Compaq Computer Corp. All rights reserved.; (2) International Business Machines Corp.; (3) UNISYS Corp.; (4) Compaq Computer Corp. All rights reserved.; (5) International Business Machines Corp.; (6) Zenith Data Systems; (7) International Business Machines Corp.; (8) International Business Machines Corp.; (9) Hewlett-Packard Co.; Figure 2, International Business Machines Corp.; Figure 3, Compaq Computer Corp. All rights reserved.; Figure 5, International Business Machines Corp.; Figure 6, Logitech, Inc.; Figure 7, Intel Corp.; Figure 8, Epson America, Inc.; Figure 10 (top), Hewlett-Packard Co.; Figure 10 (bottom), Epson America, Inc.; Figure 12, Aldus Corp.; Figure 13, International Business Machines Corp.; Figure 15, Jerry Spagnoli; Figure 16, Greg Hadel; Figure 19, Jerry Spagnoli; Figure 20, Microscience International Corp.; Figure 21, 3M Corp.; Illustrations, Dave Wyer.

W I N D O W S

USING *M*ICROSOFT *W*INDOWS 3.1

MICROSOFT WINDOWS 3.1

PROJECT ONE

▼

AN INTRODUCTION TO WINDOWS

OBJECTIVES You will have mastered the material in this project when you can:

▶ Describe a user interface
▶ Describe Microsoft Windows
▶ Identify the elements of a window
▶ Perform the four basic mouse operations of pointing, clicking, double-clicking, and dragging
▶ Correct errors made while performing mouse operations
▶ Understand the keyboard shortcut notation
▶ Select a menu
▶ Choose a command from a menu

▶ Respond to dialog boxes
▶ Start and exit an application
▶ Name a file
▶ Understand directories and subdirectories
▶ Understand directory structures and directory paths
▶ Create, save, open, and print a document
▶ Open, maximize, and scroll a window
▶ Obtain online Help while using an application

▶ INTRODUCTION

T he most popular and widely used graphical user interface available today is **Microsoft Windows**, or **Windows**. Microsoft Windows allows you to easily communicate with and control your computer. In addition, Microsoft Windows makes it easy to learn the application software installed on your computer, transfer data between the applications, and manage the data created while using an application.

In Project 1, you learn about user interfaces, the computer hardware and computer software that comprise a user interface, and Microsoft Windows. Using Microsoft Windows, you perform the operations of opening a group window, starting and exiting an application, maximizing an application window, entering and editing data within an application, printing a document on the printer, saving a document on disk, opening a document, and obtaining online Help while using an application.

What Is a User Interface?

A **user interface** is the combination of hardware and software that allows the computer user to communicate with and control the computer. Through the user interface, you are able to control the computer, request information from the computer, and respond to messages displayed by the computer. Thus, a user interface provides the means for dialogue between you and the computer.

Hardware and software together form the user interface. Among the hardware associated with a user interface is the monitor, keyboard, and mouse (Figure 1–1). The monitor displays messages and provides information. You respond by entering data in the form of a command or other response using the keyboard or mouse. Among the responses

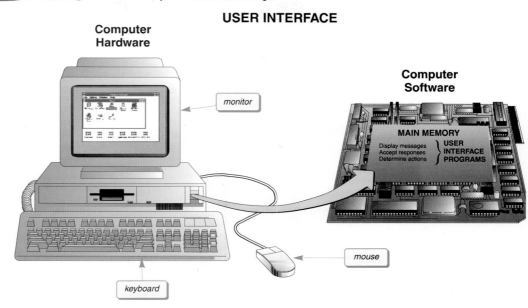

USER INTERFACE

Computer Hardware

monitor

Computer Software

MAIN MEMORY
Display messages
Accept responses
Determine actions
} **USER INTERFACE PROGRAMS**

mouse

keyboard

FIGURE 1-1

available to you are responses that specify what application software to run, when to print, and where to store data for future use.

The computer software associated with the user interface are the programs that engage you in dialogue (Figure 1-1). The computer software determines the messages you receive, the manner in which you should respond, and the actions that occur based on your responses. The goal of an effective user interface is to be **user friendly**, meaning that the software can be easily used by individuals with limited training. Research studies have indicated that the use of graphics can play an important role in aiding users to effectively interact with a computer. A **graphical user interface**, or **GUI** is a user interface that displays graphics in addition to text when it communicates with the user.

▶ MICROSOFT WINDOWS

Microsoft Windows, or Windows, the most popular graphical user interface, makes it easy to learn and work with **application software**, which is software that performs an application-related function, such as word processing. Numerous application software packages are available for purchase from retail computer stores, and several applications are included with the Windows interface software. In Windows terminology, these application software packages are referred to as **applications**.

Starting Microsoft Windows

When you turn on the computer, an introductory screen consisting of the Windows logos, Windows name, version number (3.1), and copyright notices displays momentarily (Figure 1-2 on the next page). Next, a blank screen containing an hourglass icon (⧗) displays (Figure 1-3 on the next page). The **hourglass icon** indicates that Windows requires a brief interval of time to change the display on the screen, and you should wait until the hourglass icon disappears. Next, a rectangular area, called a **window**, and the introductory Microsoft Office screen display momentarily (Figure 1-4). The Microsoft Office screen displays on top of and partially hides the window. The horizontal area at the top of the window, called the **title bar**, contains the **window title** (Program Manager).

Finally, the introductory Microsoft Office screen disappears and the window that was partially visible in Figure 1-4 and another window become visible (Figure 1-5). The double-line, or **window border**, surrounding each window determines its shape and size. The title bar at the top of each window contains a window title that identifies each window. In Figure 1-5, the Program Manager and Main titles identify each window.

FIGURE 1-2

FIGURE 1-3

The screen background on which the windows are displayed is called the **desktop.** The **Microsoft Office Manager toolbar** displays in the upper right corner of the desktop when **Microsoft Office** starts. The **toolbar** contains six buttons that allow you to start and switch between Microsoft Office applications, search for files on disk, and customize the toolbar. If your desktop does not look similar to the desktop in Figure 1-5, your instructor will inform you of the modifications necessary to change your desktop.

The Program Manager window represents the **Program Manager** application. The Program Manager application starts when you start Windows and is central to the operation of Windows. Program Manager organizes related applications into groups and displays the groups in the Program Manager window. A window that represents an

FIGURE 1-4

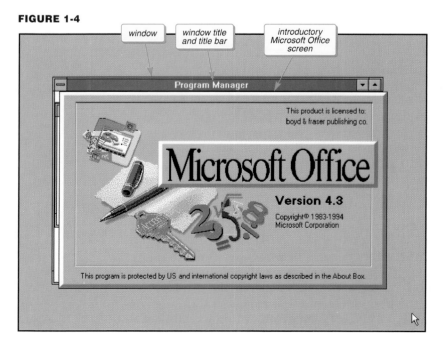

application, such as the Program Manager window, is called an **application window**.

Small pictures, or **icons**, represent an individual application or groups of applications. In Figure 1-5, the Main window contains eight icons (File Manager, Control Panel, Print Manager, Clipboard Viewer, MS-DOS Prompt, Windows Setup, PIF Editor, and Read Me). A window that contains a group of icons, such as the Main window, is called a **group window**. The icons in a group window, called **program-item icons**, each represent an individual application. A name below each program-item icon identifies the application. The program-item icons are unique and, therefore, easily distinguished from one another.

The six icons at the bottom of the Program Manager window in Figure 1-5 (Accessories, Games, StartUp, Applications, Microsoft Tools, and Microsoft Office), called **group icons**, each represent a group of applications. Groups icons are similar in appearance and only the name below the icon distinguishes one icon from another icon. Although the program-item icons of the individual applications in these groups are not visible in Figure 1-5, a method to view these icons will be demonstrated later in this project.

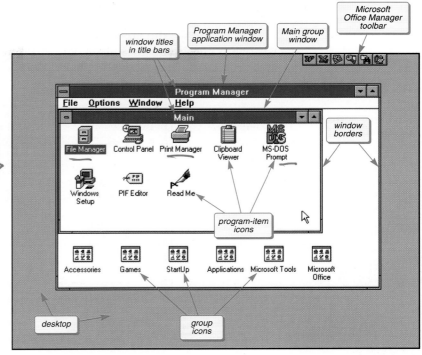

FIGURE 1-5

▶ COMMUNICATING WITH MICROSOFT WINDOWS

The Windows interface software provides the means for dialogue between you and the computer. Part of this dialogue involves requesting information from the computer and responding to messages displayed by the computer. You can request information and respond to messages using either the mouse or keyboard.

The Mouse and Mouse Pointer

A **mouse** is a pointing device commonly used with Windows that is attached to the computer by a cable and contains one or more buttons. The mouse in Figure 1-6 contains two buttons, the left mouse button and the right mouse button. On the bottom of this mouse is a ball (Figure 1-7).

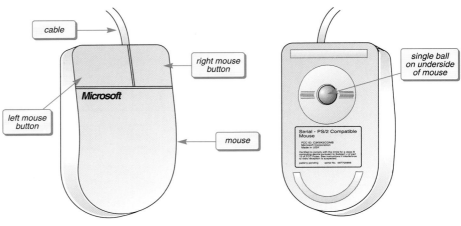

FIGURE 1-6   **FIGURE 1-7**

As you move the mouse across a flat surface (Figure 1-8), the movement of the ball is electronically sensed, and a **mouse pointer** in the shape of a block arrow ( ) moves across the desktop in the same direction.

Mouse moves diagonally across flat surface

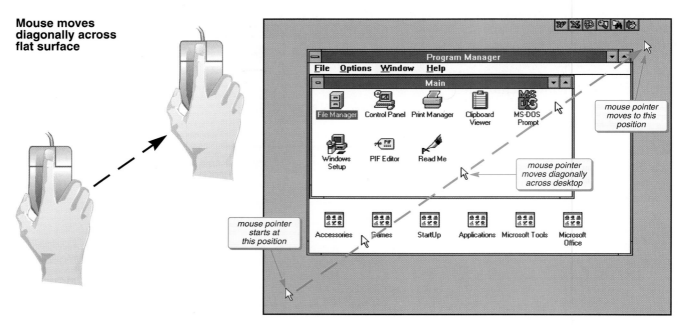

FIGURE 1-8

Mouse Operations

You use the mouse to perform four basic operations: (1) pointing; (2) clicking; (3) double-clicking; and (4) dragging. **Pointing** means moving the mouse across a flat surface until the mouse pointer rests on the item of choice on the desktop. In Figure 1-9, you move the mouse diagonally across a flat surface until the tip of the mouse pointer rests on the Print Manager program-item icon.

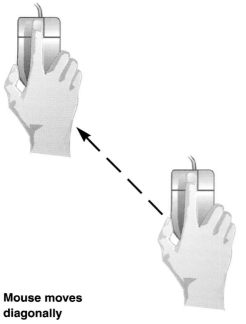

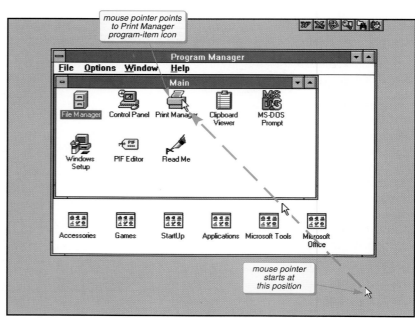

Mouse moves diagonally

FIGURE 1-9

Clicking means pressing and releasing a mouse button. In most cases, you must point to an item before pressing and releasing a mouse button. In Figure 1-10, you highlight the Print Manager program-item icon by pointing to the Print Manager icon (Step 1) and pressing and releasing the left mouse button (Step 2). These steps are commonly referred to as clicking the Print Manager icon. When you click the Print Manager icon, Windows highlights, or places color behind, the name below the Print Manager icon (Step 3).

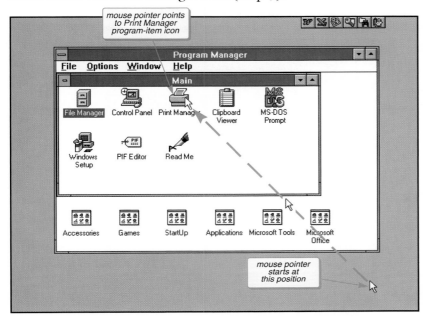

Step 1: Point to the Print Manager icon.

Step 2: Press and release the left mouse button.

Step 3: Windows highlights the Print Manager name.

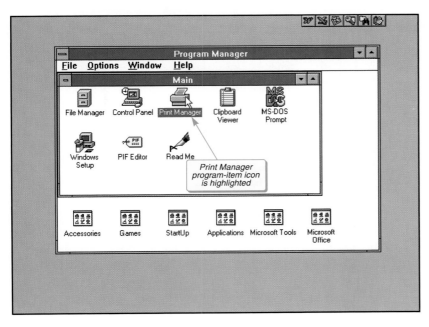

FIGURE 1-10

Double-clicking means quickly pressing and releasing a mouse button twice without moving the mouse. In most cases, you must point to an item before quickly pressing and releasing a mouse button twice. In Figure 1-11, to open the Accessories group window, point to the Accessories group icon (Step 1), and quickly press and release the left mouse button twice (Step 2). These steps are commonly referred to as double-clicking the Accessories icon. When you double-click the Accessories icon, Windows opens a group window with the same name (Step 3).

Step 1: Point to the Accessories icon.

Step 2: Quickly press and release the left mouse button twice.

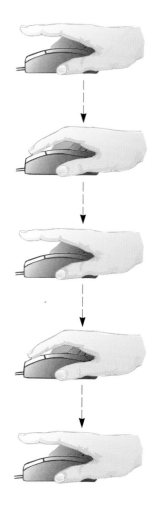

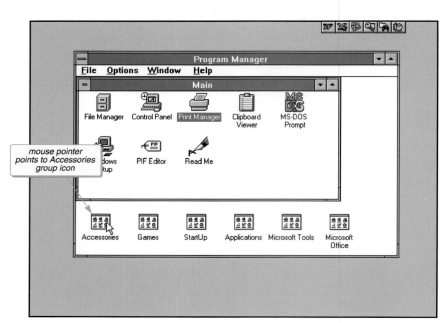

Step 3: Windows opens the Accessories group window.

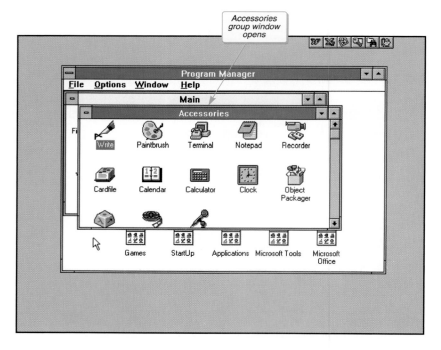

FIGURE 1-11

Dragging means holding down the left mouse button, moving an item to the desired location, and then releasing the left mouse button. In most cases, you must point to an item before dragging. In Figure 1-12, you move the Control Panel program-item icon by pointing to the Control Panel icon (Step 1), holding down the left mouse button while moving the icon to its new location (Step 2), and releasing the left mouse button (Step 3). These steps are commonly referred to as dragging the Control Panel icon.

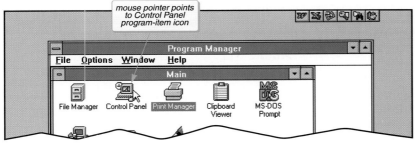

Step 1: Point to the Control Panel icon.

Step 2: Hold down the left mouse button and move the icon to its new location.

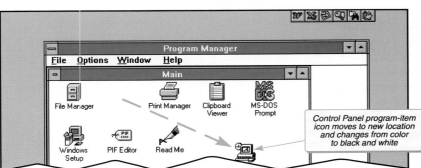

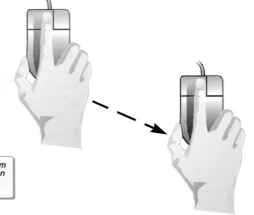

Step 3: Release the left mouse button.

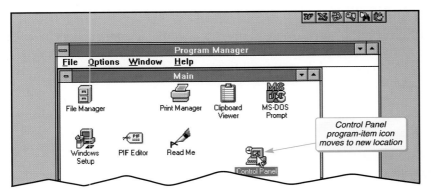

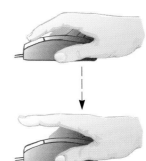

FIGURE 1-12

The Keyboard and Keyboard Shortcuts

The **keyboard** is an input device on which you manually key, or type, data. Figure 1-13 on the next page shows the enhanced IBM PS/2 keyboard. Any task you accomplish with a mouse you can also accomplish with the keyboard. Although the choice of whether to use the mouse or keyboard is a matter of personal preference, the mouse is strongly recommended.

FIGURE 1-13

The Quick Reference at the end of each project provides a list of the tasks presented in the project and the manner in which to complete the tasks using a mouse, menu, or keyboard.

To perform tasks using the keyboard, you must understand the notation used to identify which keys to press. This notation is used throughout Windows to identify **keyboard shortcuts** and in the Quick Reference at the end of each project. Keyboard shortcuts can consist of pressing a single key (RIGHT ARROW), pressing two keys simultaneously as shown by two key names separated by a plus sign (CTRL+F6), or pressing three keys simultaneously as shown by three key names separated by plus signs (CTRL+SHIFT+LEFT ARROW).

For example, to move the highlight from one program-item icon to the next program-item icon, you can press the RIGHT ARROW key (RIGHT ARROW). To move the highlight from the Main window to a group icon, hold down the CTRL key and press the F6 key (CTRL+F6). To move to the previous word in certain Windows applications, hold down the CTRL and SHIFT keys and press the LEFT ARROW key (CTRL+SHIFT+LEFT ARROW).

Menus and Commands

A **command** directs the software to perform a specific action, such as printing on the printer or saving data for use at a future time. One method of carrying out a command is by choosing the command from a list of available commands, called a menu.

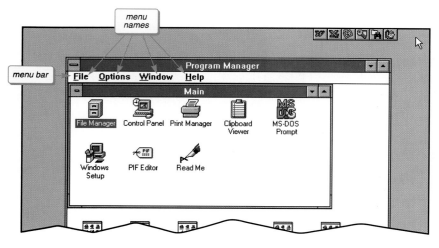

FIGURE 1-14

Windows organizes related groups of commands into **menus** and assigns a menu name to each menu. The **menu bar**, a horizontal bar below the title bar of an application window, contains a list of the available menu names for that application. The menu bar for the Program Manager window in Figure 1-14 contains the following menu names: File, Options, Window, and Help. One letter in each menu name is underlined.

Selecting a Menu

To open a menu, you select the menu name. **Selecting** means marking an item. In some cases, when you select an item, Windows marks the item with a highlight by placing color behind the item. You select a menu name by pointing to the menu name in the menu bar and pressing the left mouse button (called clicking) or by using the keyboard to press the ALT key and then the keyboard key of the underlined letter in the menu name. Clicking the menu name File in the menu bar or pressing the ALT key and then the F key opens the File menu (Figure 1-15).

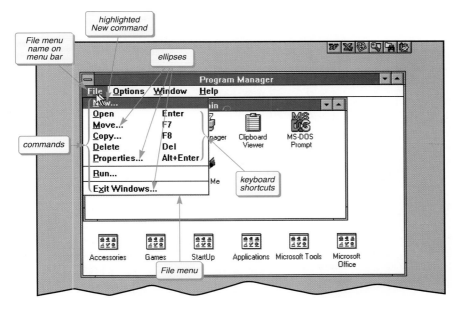

FIGURE 1-15

The File menu in Figure 1-15 contains the following commands: New, Open, Move, Copy, Delete, Properties, Run, and Exit Windows. The first command in the menu (New) is highlighted and a single character in each command is underlined. Some commands (New, Move, Copy, Properties, Run, and Exit Windows) are followed by an ellipsis (...). An **ellipsis** indicates Windows requires more information before executing the command. Commands without an ellipsis, such as the Open command, execute immediately.

Choosing a Command

You **choose** an item to carry out an action. You can choose using a mouse or the keyboard. For example, to choose a command using a mouse, either click the command name in the menu or drag the highlight to the command name. To choose a command using the keyboard, either press the keyboard key of the underlined character in the command name or use the arrow keys to move the highlight to the command name and then press the ENTER key.

Some command names are followed by a keyboard shortcut. In Figure 1-15, the Open, Move, Copy, Delete, and Properties command names have keyboard shortcuts. The keyboard shortcut for the Properties command is ALT+ENTER. Holding down the ALT key and then pressing the ENTER key chooses the Properties command without selecting the File menu.

Dialog Boxes

When you choose a command whose command name is followed by an ellipsis (…), Windows opens a dialog box. A **dialog box** is a window that displays when Windows needs to supply information to you or wants you to enter information or select among several options.

For example, Windows may inform you that a document is printing on the printer through the use of a dialog box; or Windows may ask you whether you want to print all pages in a printed report or just certain pages in the report.

A dialog box contains a title bar that identifies the name of the dialog box. In Figure 1-16, the name of the dialog box is Print.

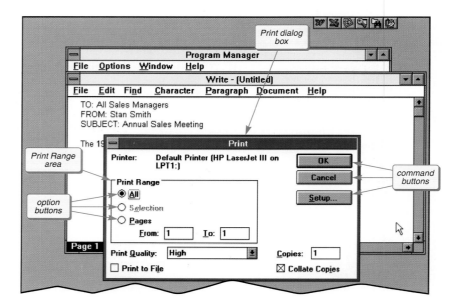

FIGURE 1-16

The types of responses Windows will ask for when working with dialog boxes fall into five categories: (1) Selecting mutually exclusive options; (2) Selecting one or more multiple options; (3) Entering specific information from the keyboard; (4) Selecting one item from a list of items; and (5) Choosing a command to be implemented from the dialog box.

Each of these types of responses is discussed in the following paragraphs, together with the method of specifying them.

The Print dialog box in Figure 1-16 opens when you choose the Print command from the File menu of some windows. The Print Range area, defined by the name Print Range and a rectangular box, contains three option buttons.

The **option buttons** give you the choice of printing all pages of a report (All), selected parts of a report (Selection), or certain pages of a report (Pages). The option button containing the black dot (All) is the **selected button**. You can select only one option button at a time. A dimmed option button, such as the Selection button, cannot be selected. To select an option button, use the mouse to click the option button or press the TAB key until the area containing the option button is selected and press the arrow keys to highlight the option button.

The Print dialog box in Figure 1-16 on the previous page contains the OK, Cancel, and Setup command buttons. **Command buttons** execute an action. The OK button executes the Print command, and the Cancel button cancels the Print command. The Setup button changes the setup of the printer by allowing you to select a printer from a list of printers, select the paper size, and so on.

Figure 1-17 illustrates text boxes and check boxes. A **text box** is a rectangular area in which Windows displays text or you enter text. In the Print dialog box in Figure 1-17, the Pages option button is selected, which means only certain pages of a report are to print. You select which pages by entering the first page in the From text box (1) and the last page in the To text box (4). To enter text into a text box, select the text box by clicking it or pressing the TAB key until the text in the text box is highlighted, and then type the text using the keyboard. The Copies text box in Figure 1-17 contains the number of copies to be printed (3).

FIGURE 1-17

Check boxes represent options that you can turn on or off. An X in a check box indicates the option is turned on. To place an X in the box, click the box, or press the TAB key until the check box is highlighted, and then press the SPACEBAR. In Figure 1-17, the Print to File check box, which does not contain an X, indicates the Print to File option is turned off and the pages will print on the printer. The Collate Copies check box, which contains an X, indicates the Collate Copies feature is turned on and the pages will print in collated order.

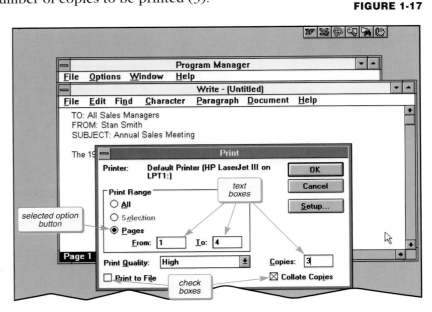

The Print dialog boxes in Figure 1-18 and Figure 1-19 on the next page, illustrate the Print Quality drop-down list box. When first selected, a **drop-down list box** is a rectangular box containing highlighted text and a down arrow box on the right. In Figure 1-18, the highlighted text, or **current selection**, is High.

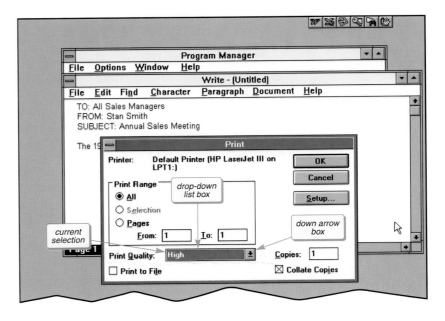

FIGURE 1-18

When you click the down arrow, the drop-down list box in Figure 1-19 displays. The list contains three choices (High, Medium, and Low). The current selection, High, is highlighted. To select from the list, use the mouse to click the selection or press the DOWN ARROW key to highlight the selection, and then press ALT+UP ARROW or ALT+DOWN ARROW to make the selection.

Windows uses drop-down list boxes when a list of options must be presented but the dialog box is not big enough to contain the entire list. After you make your selection, the list disappears and only the current selection displays.

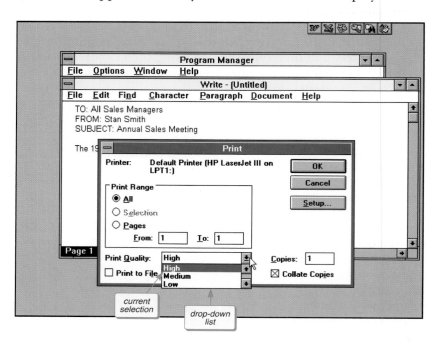

FIGURE 1-19

▶ USING MICROSOFT WINDOWS

T he remainder of this project illustrates how to use Windows to perform the common operations of starting and quitting an application, creating a document, saving a document on disk, opening a document, editing a document, printing a document and using Windows online Help. Understanding how to perform these operations will make completing the remainder of the projects in this book easier. These operations are illustrated by the use of the Notepad and Paintbrush applications.

One of the many applications included with Windows is the Notepad application. **Notepad** allows you to enter, edit, save, and print notes. Items that you create while using an application, such as a note, are called **documents**. In the following section, you will use the Notepad application to learn to (1) open a group window, (2) start an application from a group window, (3) maximize an application window, (4) create a document, (5) select a menu, (6) choose a command from a menu, (7) print a document, (8) save a document, and (9) quit an application. In the process, you will enter and print a note.

Opening a Group Window

Each group icon at the bottom of the Program Manager window represents a group window that contains program-item icons. To open the group window and view the program-item icons in that window, use the mouse to point to the group icon and then double-click the left mouse button, as shown in the steps on the next page.

TO OPEN A GROUP WINDOW ▼

STEP 1 ►

Point to the Accessories group icon at the bottom of the Program Manager window.

The mouse pointer points to the Accessories group icon (▦) (Figure 1-20).

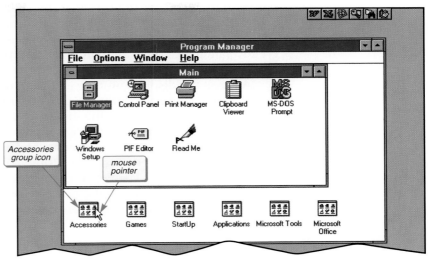

FIGURE 1-20

STEP 2 ►

Double-click the left mouse button.

Windows removes the Accessories icon from the Program Manager window and opens the Accessories window on top of the Program Manager and Main windows (Figure 1-21). The Accessories window contains the Notepad program-item icon (▤).

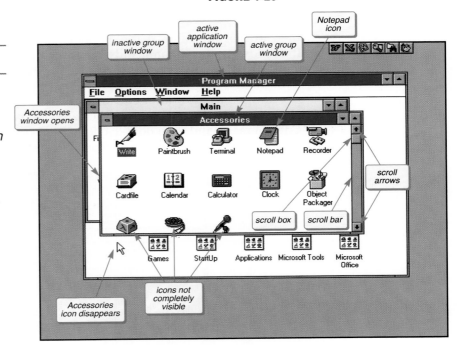

FIGURE 1-21

Opening a group window when one or more group windows are already open in the Program Manager window causes the new group window to open on top of the other group windows. The title bar of the newly opened group window is a different color or intensity than the title bars of the other group windows. This indicates the new group window is the active window. The **active window** is the window currently being used. Only one application window and one group window can be active at the same time. In Figure 1-21 on the previous page, the colors of the title bars indicate that the Program Manager window is the active application window (green title bar) and the Accessories group window is the active group window (green title bar). The color of the Main window title bar (yellow) indicates the Main window is inactive. The colors may not be the same on the computer you use.

A scroll bar displays on the right edge of the Accessories window. A **scroll bar** is a bar that displays at the right and/or bottom edge of a window whose contents are not completely visible. In Figure 1-21 on the previous page, the third row of program-item icons in the Accessories window are not completely visible. A scroll bar contains two **scroll arrows** and a **scroll box** which enable you to view areas of the window not currently visible. To view areas of the Accessories window not currently visible, you can click the down scroll arrow repeatedly, click the scroll bar between the down scroll arrow and the scroll box, or drag the scroll box towards the down scroll arrow until the area you want to view is visible in the window.

Correcting an Error While Double-Clicking a Group Icon

While double-clicking, it is easy to mistakenly click once instead of double-clicking. When you click a group icon such as the Accessories group icon once, the **Control menu** for that icon opens (Figure 1-22). The Control menu contains the following seven commands: Restore, Move, Size, Minimize, Maximize, Close, and Next. You choose one of these commands to carry out an action associated with the Accessories group icon. To remove the Control menu and open the Accessories window after clicking the Accessories group icon once, you can choose the Restore command; click any open area outside the menu to remove the Control menu and then double-click the Accessories group icon; or simply double-click the Accessories group icon as if you had not clicked the icon at all.

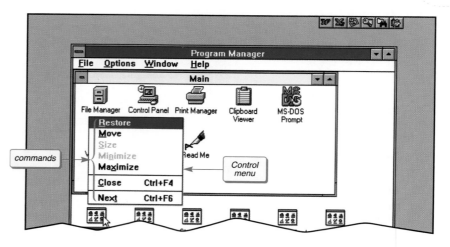

FIGURE 1-22

Starting an Application

Each program-item icon in a group window represents an application. To start an application, double-click the program-item icon. In this project, you want to start the Notepad application. To start the Notepad application, perform the steps on the opposite page.

TO START AN APPLICATION ▼

STEP 1 ►

Point to the Notepad program-item icon.

The mouse pointer points to the Notepad icon in the Accessories window (Figure 1-23).

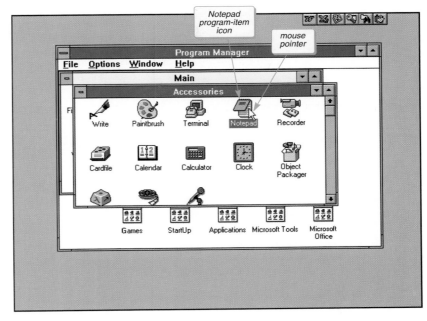

FIGURE 1-23

STEP 2 ►

Double-click the left mouse button.

*Windows opens the Notepad window on the desktop (Figure 1-24). Program Manager becomes the inactive application (yellow title bar) and Notepad is the active application (green title bar). The word Untitled in the window title (Notepad - [Untitled]) indicates a document has not been created and saved on disk. The menu bar contains the following menus: File, Edit, Search, and Help. The area below the menu bar contains an insertion point, mouse pointer, and two scroll bars. The **insertion point** is a flashing vertical line that indicates the point at which text from the keyboard will be displayed. When you point to the interior of the Notepad window, the mouse pointer changes from a block arrow to an I-beam icon ($\mathcal{I}$).*

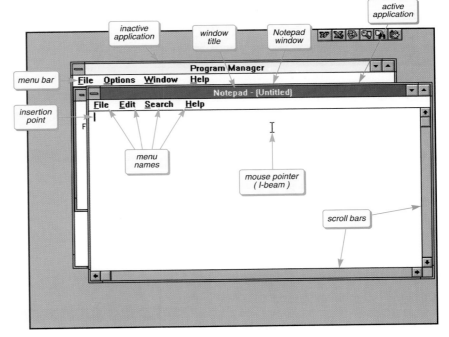

FIGURE 1-24

Correcting an Error While Double-Clicking a Program-Item Icon

While double-clicking a program-item icon you can easily click once instead. When you click a program-item icon such as the Notepad icon once, the icon becomes the **active icon** and Windows highlights the icon name (Figure 1-25). To start the Notepad application after clicking the Notepad icon once, double-click the Notepad icon as if you had not clicked the icon at all.

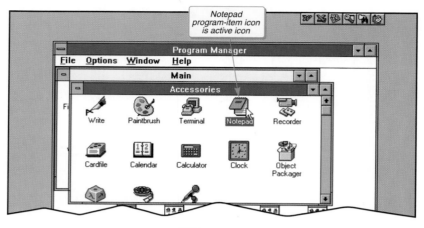

FIGURE 1-25

Maximizing an Application Window

Before you work with an application, maximizing the application window makes it easier to see the contents of the window. You can maximize an application window so the window fills the entire desktop. To maximize an application window to its maximum size, choose the **Maximize button** (▲) by pointing to the Maximize button and then clicking the left mouse button. When you maximize an application window, the Microsoft Office Manager toolbar displays on the title bar of the application window (see Figure 1-27). Complete the following steps to maximize the Notepad window.

TO MAXIMIZE AN APPLICATION WINDOW ▼

STEP 1 ▶

Point to the Maximize button in the upper right corner of the Notepad window.

The mouse pointer becomes a block arrow and points to the Maximize button (Figure 1-26).

FIGURE 1-26

STEP 2 ▶

Click the left mouse button.

*The Notepad window fills the desktop (Figure 1-27). The **Restore button** (▲▼) replaces the Maximize button at the right side of the title bar. Clicking the Restore button will return the window to its size before maximizing. The Microsoft Office Manager toolbar displays to the left of the Restore button on the title bar.*

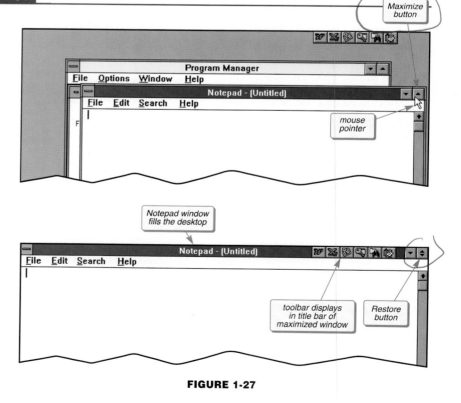

FIGURE 1-27

Creating a Document

To create a document in Notepad, type the text you want to display in the document. After typing a line of text, press the ENTER key to terminate the entry of the line. To create a document, enter the note shown in Figure 1-28 by performing the steps below.

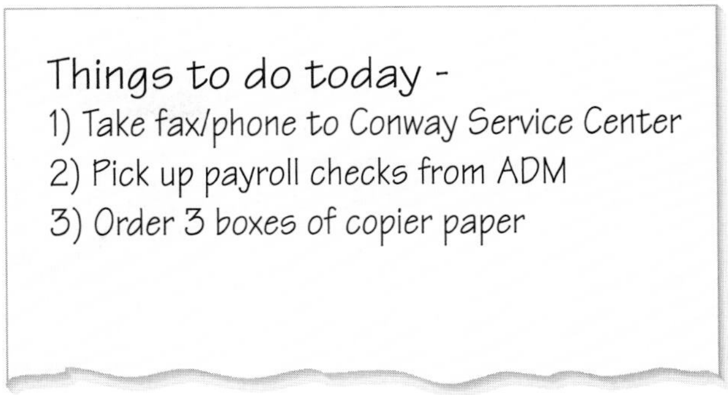

Things to do today -
1) Take fax/phone to Conway Service Center
2) Pick up payroll checks from ADM
3) Order 3 boxes of copier paper

FIGURE 1-28

TO CREATE A NOTEPAD DOCUMENT ▼

STEP 1 ▶

Type Things to do today — **and press the ENTER key.**

The first line of the note is entered and the insertion point displays at the beginning of the next line (Figure 1-29).

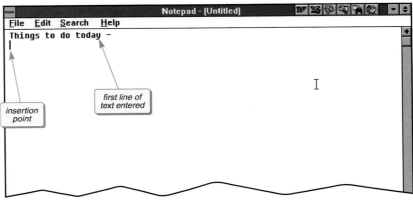

FIGURE 1-29

STEP 2 ▶

Type the remaining lines of the note. Press the ENTER key after typing each line.

The remaining lines in the note are entered and the insertion point is located at the beginning of the line following the note (Figure 1-30).

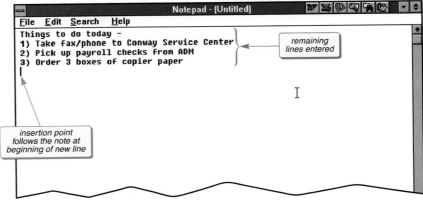

FIGURE 1-30

Printing a Document by Choosing a Command from a Menu

After creating a document, you often print the document on the printer. To print the note, complete the following steps.

TO PRINT A DOCUMENT ▼

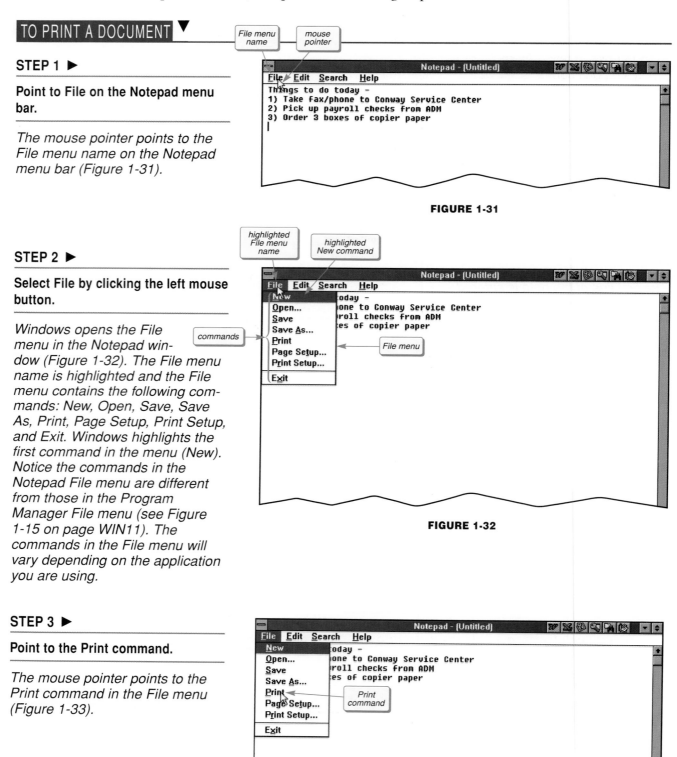

STEP 1 ▶

Point to File on the Notepad menu bar.

The mouse pointer points to the File menu name on the Notepad menu bar (Figure 1-31).

FIGURE 1-31

STEP 2 ▶

Select File by clicking the left mouse button.

Windows opens the File menu in the Notepad window (Figure 1-32). The File menu name is highlighted and the File menu contains the following commands: New, Open, Save, Save As, Print, Page Setup, Print Setup, and Exit. Windows highlights the first command in the menu (New). Notice the commands in the Notepad File menu are different from those in the Program Manager File menu (see Figure 1-15 on page WIN11). The commands in the File menu will vary depending on the application you are using.

FIGURE 1-32

STEP 3 ▶

Point to the Print command.

The mouse pointer points to the Print command in the File menu (Figure 1-33).

FIGURE 1-33

STEP 4 ►

Choose the Print command from the File menu by clicking the left mouse button.

Windows momentarily opens the Notepad dialog box (Figure 1-34). The dialog box contains the Now Printing text message and the Cancel command button (Cancel). When the Notepad dialog box closes, Windows prints the document on the printer (Figure 1-35).

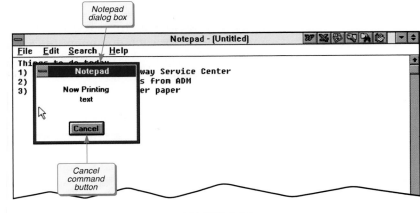

FIGURE 1-34

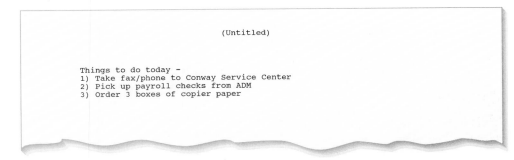

(Untitled)

Things to do today -
1) Take fax/phone to Conway Service Center
2) Pick up payroll checks from ADM
3) Order 3 boxes of copier paper

FIGURE 1-35

► FILE AND DISK CONCEPTS

To protect against the accidental loss of a document and to save a document for use in the future, you should save a document on disk. Before saving a document on disk, however, you must understand the concepts of naming a file, directories, subdirectories, directory structures, and directory paths. The following section explains these concepts.

Naming a File

When you create a document using an application, the document is stored in main memory. If you quit the application without saving the document on disk, the document is lost. To save the document for future use, you must store the document in a **document file** on the hard disk or on a diskette before quitting the application. Before saving a document, you must assign a name to the document file.

All files are identified on disk by a **filename** and an **extension**. For example, the name SALES.TXT consists of a filename (SALES) and an extension (.TXT). A filename can contain from one to eight characters and the extension begins with a period and can contain from one to three characters. Filenames must start with a letter or number. Any uppercase character or lowercase character is valid except a period (.), quotation mark ("), slash (/), backslash (\), brackets ([]), colon (:), semicolon (;), vertical bar (|), equal sign (=), comma (,), or blank space. Filenames cannot be CON, AUX, COM1, COM2, COM3, COM4, LPT1, LPT2, LPT3, PRN, and NUL.

To more easily identify document files on disk, it is convenient to assign the same extension for each document file saved on disk. Typical filenames and extensions of document files saved using Notepad are: SHOPPING.TXT, 1994.TXT, and MECHANIC.TXT.

You can use the asterisk character (*) in place of a filename or extension to refer to a group of files. For instance, the asterisk in the expression *.TXT tells Windows to reference any file that contains the .TXT extension, regardless of the filename. This group of files might consist of the HOME.TXT, AUTOPART.TXT, MARKET.TXT, JONES.TXT, and FRANK.TXT files.

The asterisk in MONTHLY.* tells Windows to reference any file that contains the filename MONTHLY, regardless of the extension. Files in this group might consist of the MONTHLY.TXT, MONTHLY.CAL, and MONTHLY.CRD files.

Directory Structures and Directory Paths

HARD DISK

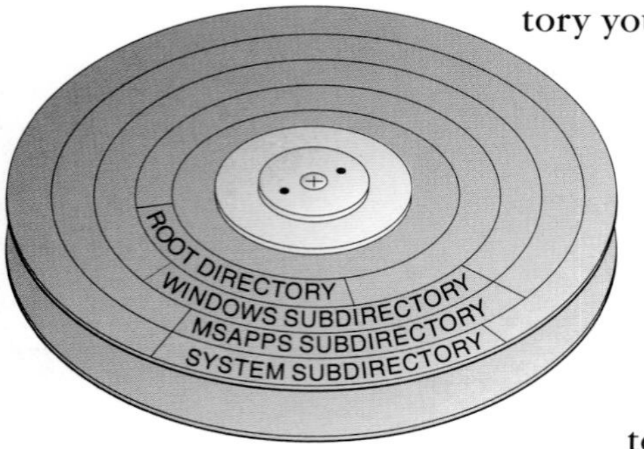

FIGURE 1-36

After selecting a name and extension for a file, you must decide which auxiliary storage device (hard drive or diskette) to use and in which directory you want to save the file. A **directory** is an area of a disk created to store related groups of files. When you first prepare a disk for use on a computer, a single directory, called the **root directory**, is created on the disk. You can create **subdirectories** in the root directory to store additional groups of related files. The hard disk in Figure 1-36 contains the root directory and the WINDOWS, MSAPPS, and SYSTEM subdirectories. The WINDOWS, MSAPPS, and SYSTEM subdirectories are created when Windows is installed and contain files related to Windows.

The relationship between the root directory and any subdirectories is called the **directory structure**. Each directory or subdirectory in the directory structure has an associated directory path. The **directory path** is the path Windows follows to find a file in a directory. Table 1-1 contains a graphic representation of the directory structure and the associated directory paths of drive C.

Each directory and subdirectory on drive C is represented by a file folder icon in the directory structure. The first file folder icon, an unshaded open file folder (📂), represents the root directory of the current drive (drive C). The c:\ entry to the right of the icon symbolizes the root directory (identified by the \ character) of drive C (c:). The path is C:\. Thus, to find a file in this directory, Windows locates drive C (C:) and the root directory (\) on drive C.

▶ **TABLE 1-1**

Directory Structure	Directory Path
📂 c:\	C:\
📂 windows	C:\WINDOWS
📁 msapps	C:\WINDOWS\MSAPPS
📁 system	C:\WINDOWS\SYSTEM

The second icon, a shaded open file folder (📂), represents the current subdirectory. This icon is indented and below the first file folder icon because it is a subdirectory. The name of the subdirectory (windows) displays to the right of the shaded file folder icon. Because the WINDOWS subdirectory was created in the root directory, the path for the WINDOWS subdirectory is C:\WINDOWS. To find a file in this subdirectory, Windows locates drive C, locates the root directory on drive C, and then locates the WINDOWS subdirectory in the root directory.

Because the current path is C:\WINDOWS, the file folder icons for both the root directory and WINDOWS subdirectory are open file folders. An open file folder indicates the directory or subdirectory is in the current path. Unopened file folders represent subdirectories not in the current path.

The third and fourth icons in Table 1-1, unopened file folders (▢), represent the MSAPPS and SYSTEM subdirectories. The unopened file folders indicate that these subdirectories are not part of the path of the current path. These file folder icons are indented below the file folder for the WINDOWS subdirectory which means they were created in the WINDOWS subdirectory. The subdirectory names (msapps and system) display to the right of the file folder icons.

Because the MSAPPS and SYSTEM subdirectories were created in the WINDOWS subdirectory, the paths for these subdirectories are C:\WINDOWS\MSAPPS and C:\WINDOWS\SYSTEM. The second backslash (\) in these paths separates the two subdirectory names. To find a file in these subdirectories, Windows locates drive C, locates the root directory on drive C, then locates the WINDOWS subdirectory in the root directory, and finally locates the MSAPPS or SYSTEM subdirectory in the WINDOWS subdirectory.

Saving a Document on Disk

After entering data into a document, you will often save it on the hard disk or a diskette to protect against accidental loss and to make the document available for use later. The screen before you begin to save the document is shown in Figure 1-37. To save the document on a diskette in drive A using the filename, agenda, perform the following steps.

FIGURE 1-37

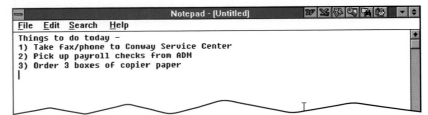

TO SAVE A FILE ▼

STEP 1 ▶

Insert a formatted diskette into drive A (Figure 1-38).

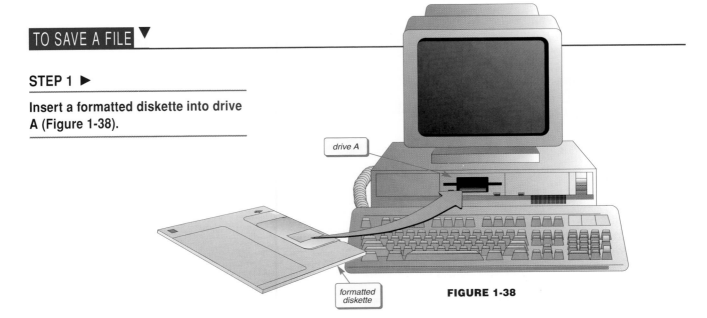

FIGURE 1-38

STEP 2 ▶

Select File on the Notepad menu bar, and then point to the Save As command.

Windows opens the File menu in the Notepad window and the mouse pointer points to the Save As command (Figure 1-39). The ellipsis (...) following the Save As command indicates Windows will open a dialog box when you choose this command.

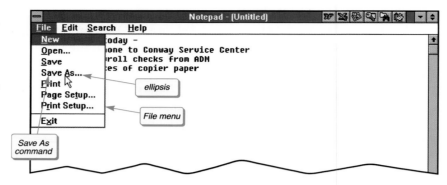

FIGURE 1-39

STEP 3 ▶

Choose the Save As command from the File menu by clicking the left mouse button.

The Save As dialog box opens (Figure 1-40). The File Name text box contains the highlighted *.txt entry. Typing a filename from the keyboard will replace the entire *.txt entry with the filename entered from the keyboard. The current path is c:\windows and the Directories list box contains the directory structure of the current subdirectory (windows). The drive selection in the Drives drop-down list box is c:. The dialog box contains the OK (OK) and Cancel (Cancel) command buttons.

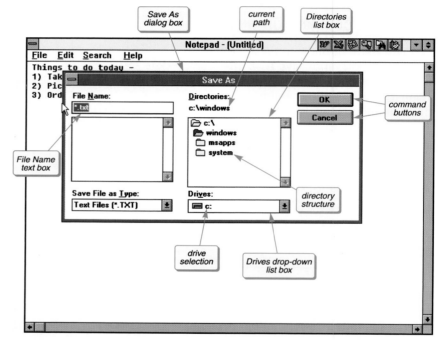

FIGURE 1-40

STEP 4 ▶

Type agenda **in the File Name text box, and then point to the Drives drop-down list box arrow.**

The filename, agenda, and an insertion point display in the File Name text box (Figure 1-41). When you save this document, Notepad will automatically add the .TXT extension to the agenda filename and save the file on disk using the name AGENDA.TXT. The mouse pointer points to the Drives drop-down list box arrow.

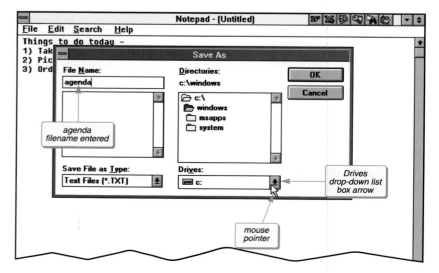

FIGURE 1-41

STEP 5 ▶

Choose the Drives drop-down list box arrow by clicking the left mouse button, and then point to the drive a: icon ( ) in the Drives drop-down list.

Windows displays the Drives drop-down list (Figure 1-42). The drive a: icon, drive c: icon, and drive h: icon display in the drop-down list. The drive h: icon represents a special area of the hard drive used by the DOS operating system and may not display in the drop-down list on your computer. The mouse pointer points to the drive a: icon.

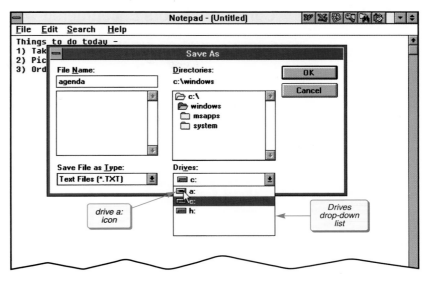

FIGURE 1-42

STEP 6 ▶

Choose the drive a: icon by clicking the left mouse button, and then point to the OK button.

The selection is highlighted and the light on drive A turns on while Windows checks for a diskette in drive A (Figure 1-43). The current path changes to a:\ and the Directories list box contains the directory structure of drive A.

FIGURE 1-43

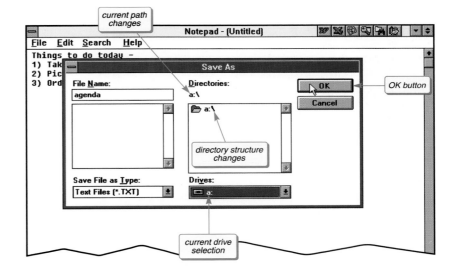

STEP 7 ▶

Choose the OK button in the Save As dialog box by clicking the left mouse button.

Windows closes the Save As dialog box and displays an hourglass icon while saving the AGENDA.TXT document file on the diskette in drive A. After the file is saved, Windows changes the window title of the Notepad window to reflect the name of the AGENDA.TXT file (Figure 1-44).

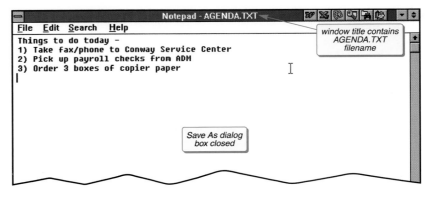

FIGURE 1-44

Correcting Errors Encountered While Saving a Document File

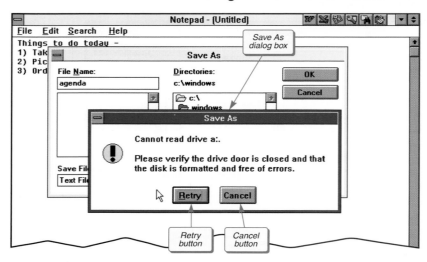

FIGURE 1-45

Before you save a document file to a diskette, you must insert a formatted diskette into the diskette drive. **Formatting** is the process of preparing a diskette for use on a computer by establishing the sectors and cylinders on a disk, analyzing the diskette for defective cylinders, and establishing the root directory. The technique for formatting a diskette is shown in Project 2. If you try to save a file on a diskette and forget to insert a diskette, forget to close the diskette drive door after inserting a diskette, insert an unformatted diskette, or insert a damaged diskette, Windows opens the Save As dialog box in Figure 1-45.

The dialog box contains the messages telling you the condition found and the Retry (Retry) and Cancel buttons. To save a file on the diskette in drive A after receiving this message, insert a formatted diskette into the diskette drive, point to the Retry button, and click the left mouse button.

In addition, you cannot save a document file to a write-protected diskette. A **write-protected diskette** prevents accidental erasure of data stored on the diskette by not letting the disk drive write new data or erase existing data on the diskette. If you try to save a file on a write-protected diskette, Windows opens the Save As dialog box shown in Figure 1-46.

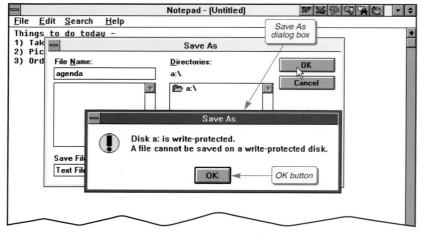

FIGURE 1-46

The Save As dialog box in Figure 1-46 contains the messages, Disk a: is write-protected., and, A file cannot be saved on a write-protected disk., and the OK button. To save a file on diskette after inserting a write-protected diskette into drive A, remove the diskette, remove the write-protection from the diskette, insert the diskette into the diskette drive, point to the OK button, and click the left mouse button.

Quitting an Application

When you have finished the document, quit the application by completing the steps on the next page.

TO QUIT AN APPLICATION ▼

STEP 1 ▶

Point to File on the Notepad menu
bar (Figure 1-47).

FIGURE 1-47

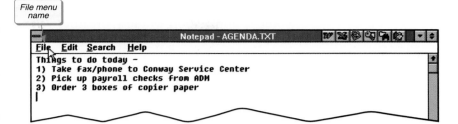

File menu
name

STEP 2 ▶

Select File by clicking the left mouse
button, and then point to the Exit
command.

*Windows opens the File menu and
the mouse pointer points to the
Exit command (Figure 1-48).*

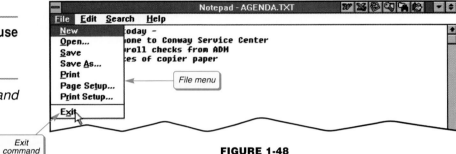

File menu

Exit
command

FIGURE 1-48

STEP 3 ▶

Choose the Exit command from the
File menu by clicking the left mouse
button.

*Windows closes the Notepad
window and exits the Notepad
application (Figure 1-49). The
Microsoft Office Manager toolbar
displays in the upper right corner
of the desktop.*

FIGURE 1-49

Microsoft
Office Manager
toolbar

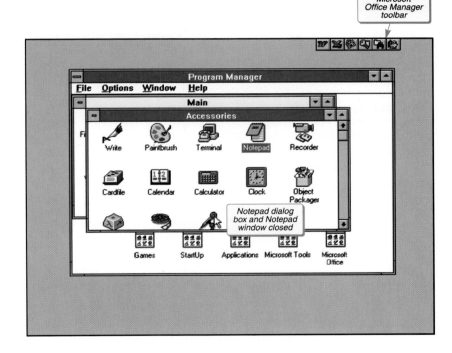

Notepad dialog
box and Notepad
window closed

In the preceding example, you used the Microsoft Windows graphical user interface to accomplish the tasks of opening the Accessories group window, starting the Notepad application from the Accessories group window, maximizing the Notepad application window, creating a document in the Notepad application window, printing the document on the printer, saving the document on disk, and quitting the Notepad application.

▶ MODIFYING A DOCUMENT FILE

Changes are frequently made to a document saved on disk. To make these changes, you must first open the document file by retrieving the file from disk using the Open command. After modifying the document, you save the modified document file on disk using the Save command. Using the Notepad application, you will learn to (1) open a document file and (2) save an edited document file on diskette. In the process, you will add the following line to the AGENDA.TXT file: 4) Buy copier toner.

Starting the Notepad Application and Maximizing the Notepad Window

To start the Notepad application and maximize the Notepad window, perform the following step.

TO START AN APPLICATION AND MAXIMIZE ITS WINDOW ▼

STEP 1 ▶

Double-click the Notepad icon in the Accessories group window. When the Notepad window opens, click the Maximize button.

Double-clicking the Notepad icon opens the Notepad window. Clicking the Maximize button maximizes the Notepad window (Figure 1-50).

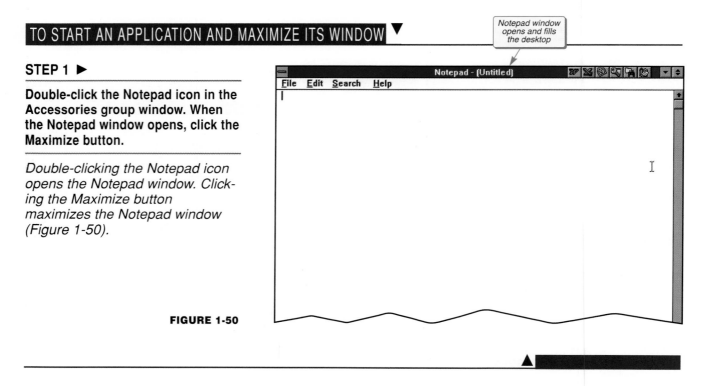

Notepad window opens and fills the desktop

FIGURE 1-50

Opening a Document File

Before you can modify the AGENDA.TXT file, you must open the file from the diskette on which it was stored. To do this, ensure the diskette containing the file is inserted into drive A, and then perform the following steps.

TO OPEN A DOCUMENT FILE ▼

STEP 1 ▶

Select File on the menu bar, and then point to the Open command.

Windows opens the File menu and the mouse pointer points to the Open command (Figure 1-51).

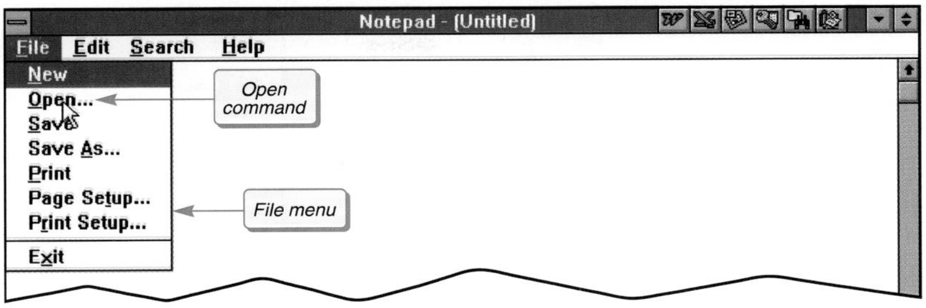

FIGURE 1-51

STEP 2 ▶

Choose the Open command from the File menu by clicking the left mouse button, and then point to the Drives drop-down list box arrow.

Windows opens the Open dialog box (Figure 1-52). The File Name text box contains the *.txt entry, and the File Name list box is empty because no files with the .TXT extension appear in the current directory. The current path is c:\windows. The Directories list box contains the directory structure of the current subdirectory (WINDOWS). The selected drive in the Drives drop-down list box is c:. The mouse pointer points to the Drives drop-down list box arrow.

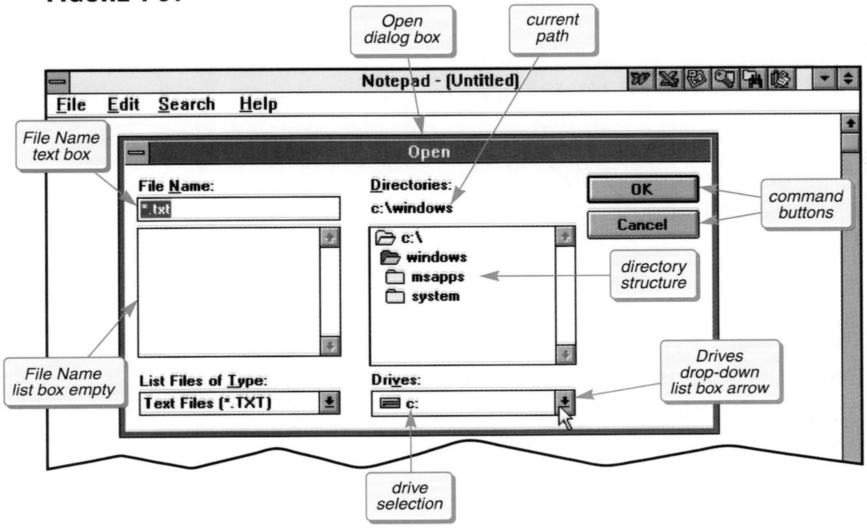

FIGURE 1-52

STEP 3 ▶

Choose the Drives drop-down list box arrow by clicking the left mouse button, and then point to the drive a: icon.

Windows displays the Drives drop-down list (Figure 1-53). The drive a: icon, drive c: icon, and drive h: icon display in the drop-down list. The current selection is c:. The mouse pointer points to the drive a: icon.

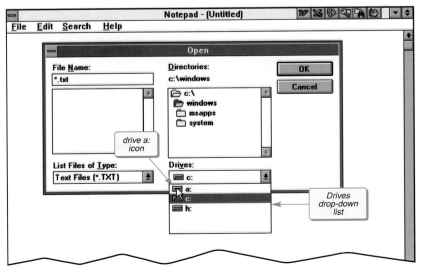

FIGURE 1-53

STEP 4 ▶

Select the drive a: icon by clicking the left mouse button, and then point to the agenda.txt entry in the File Name list box.

The light on drive A turns on, and Windows checks for a diskette in drive A. If there is no diskette in drive A, a dialog box opens to indicate this fact. The current selection in the Drives drop-down list box is highlighted (Figure 1-54). The File Name list box contains the filename agenda.txt, the current path is a:\, and the Directories list box contains the directory structure of drive A. The mouse pointer points to the agenda.txt entry.

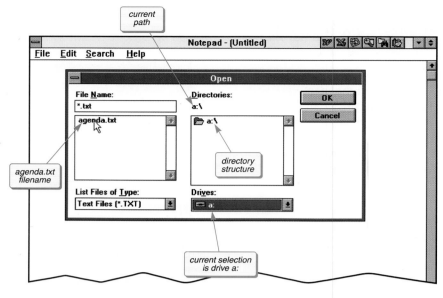

FIGURE 1-54

STEP 5 ▶

Select the agenda.txt file by clicking the left mouse button, and then point to the OK button.

Notepad highlights the agenda.txt entry in the File Name text box, and the agenda.txt filename displays in the File Name text box (Figure 1-55). The mouse pointer points to the OK button.

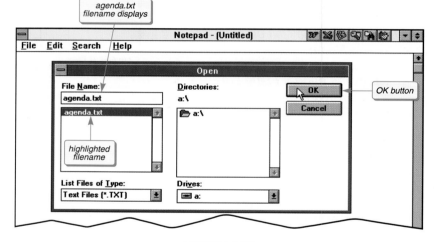

FIGURE 1-55

STEP 6 ▶

Choose the OK button from the Open dialog box by clicking the left mouse button.

Windows retrieves the agenda.txt file from the diskette in drive A and opens the AGENDA.TXT document in the Notepad window (Figure 1-56).

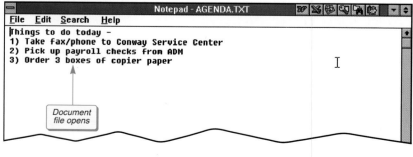

FIGURE 1-56

Editing the Document File

Edit the AGENDA.TXT document file by entering the fifth line of text.

TO EDIT THE DOCUMENT ▼

STEP 1 ►

Press the DOWN ARROW key four times to position the insertion point, and then type 4) Buy copier toner

The new line displays in the Notepad document (Figure 1-57).

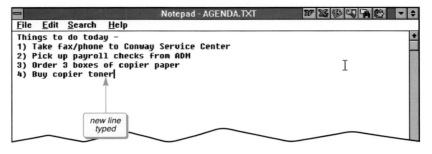

FIGURE 1-57

Saving the Modified Document File

After modifying the AGENDA.TXT file, you should save the modified document file on disk using the same AGENDA.TXT filename. To save a modified file on disk, choose the Save command. The Save command differs from the Save As command in that you choose the Save command to save changes to an existing file, whereas you choose the Save As command to name and save a new file or to save an existing file under a new name.

TO SAVE A MODIFIED DOCUMENT FILE ▼

STEP 1 ►

Select File on the Notepad menu bar, and then point to the Save command.

Windows opens the File menu and the mouse pointer points to the Save command (Figure 1-58).

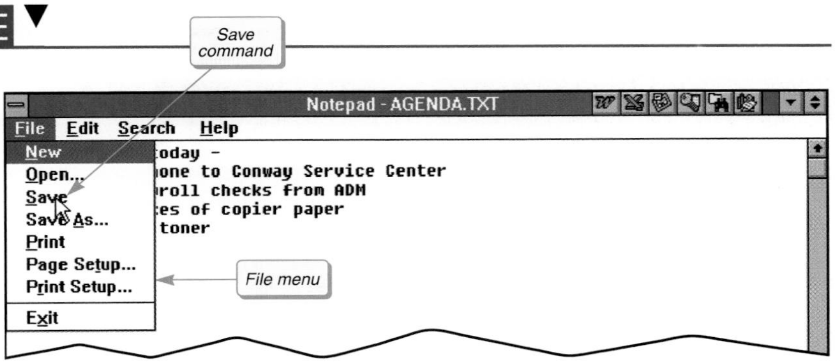

FIGURE 1-58

STEP 2 ►

Choose the Save command from the File menu by clicking the left mouse button.

Windows closes the File menu, displays the hourglass icon momentarily, and saves the AGENDA.TXT document on the diskette in drive A (Figure 1-59).

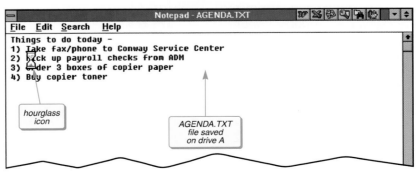

FIGURE 1-59

STEP 3 ▶

**Remove the diskette from drive A
(Figure 1-60).**

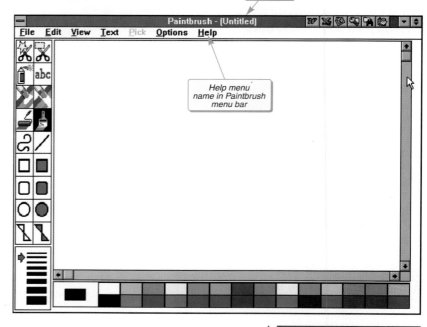

FIGURE 1-60

When you have finished saving the modified AGENDA.TXT file, quit the
Notepad application by performing the following steps.

TO QUIT NOTEPAD

Step 1: Select File on the Notepad menu bar.
Step 2: Choose the Exit command from the File menu.

▶ USING WINDOWS HELP

I f you require help while using an application, you can use Windows
online Help. **Online Help** is available for all applications except Clock.
To illustrate Windows online Help, you will start the Paintbrush application and obtain help about the commands on the Edit menu. **Paintbrush** is a
drawing program that allows you to create, edit, and print full-color illustrations.

TO START AN APPLICATION AND MAXIMIZE ITS WINDOW ▼

STEP 1 ▶

**Double-click the Paintbrush icon
(🎨) in the Accessories group
window in Program Manager, and
then click the Maximize button on
the Paintbrush - [Untitled] window.**

*Windows opens and maximizes
the Paintbrush window (Figure
1-61).*

Paintbrush
window

Help menu
name in Paintbrush
menu bar

FIGURE 1-61

TO OBTAIN HELP ▼

STEP 1 ▶

Select Help on the Paintbrush menu bar, and then point to the Contents command.

Windows opens the Help menu (Figure 1-62). The Help menu contains four commands. The mouse pointer points to the Contents command.

STEP 2 ▶

Choose the Contents command from the Help menu by clicking the left mouse button. Then click the Maximize button on the Paintbrush Help window.

Windows opens the Paintbrush Help window (Figure 1-63), and when you click the Maximize button, it maximizes the window.

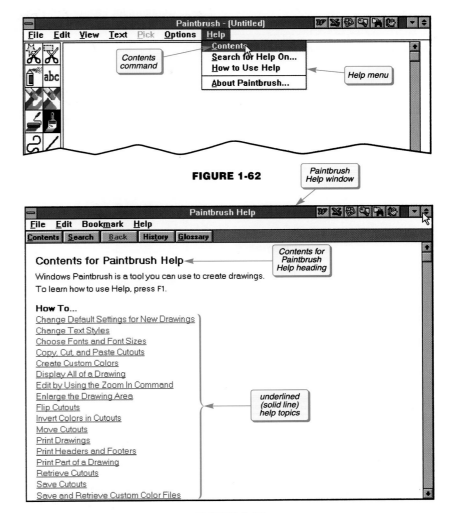

FIGURE 1-62

FIGURE 1-63

The Contents for Paintbrush Help heading displays in the window followed by information about the Paintbrush application, how to learn to use Help (press F1), and an alphabetical list of all help topics for the Paintbrush application. Each **help topic** is underlined with a solid line. The solid line indicates additional information relating to the topic is available. Underlined help topics are called jumps. A **jump** provides a link to viewing information about another help topic or more information about the current topic. A jump may be either text or graphics.

Choosing a Help Topic

To choose an underlined help topic, scroll the help topics to make the help topic you want visible, then point to the help topic and click the left mouse button. When you place the mouse pointer on a help topic, the mouse pointer changes to a hand ( ). To obtain help about the Edit menu, perform the steps on the next page.

TO CHOOSE A HELP TOPIC ▼

STEP 1 ►

Point to the down scroll arrow.

The mouse pointer points to the down scroll arrow in the Paintbrush Help window (Figure 1-64).

FIGURE 1-64

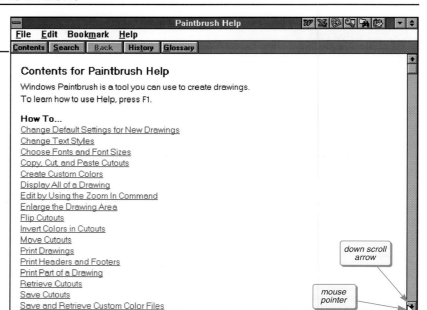

STEP 2 ►

Hold down the left mouse button (scroll) until the Commands heading and the Edit Menu Commands topic are visible, and then point to the Edit Menu Commands topic.

The Commands heading and the Edit Menu Commands topic are visible (Figure 1-65). The mouse pointer changes to a hand and points to the Edit Menu Commands topic.

FIGURE 1-65

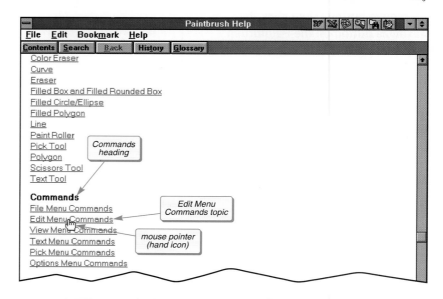

STEP 3 ►

Choose the Edit Menu Commands topic by clicking the left mouse button.

The Edit Menu Commands heading and information about each of the commands in the Edit menu display (Figure 1-66). Two terms (scroll bar and cutout) are underlined with a dotted line. Terms underlined with a dotted line have an associated glossary definition. To display a term's glossary definition, point to the term and click the left mouse button.

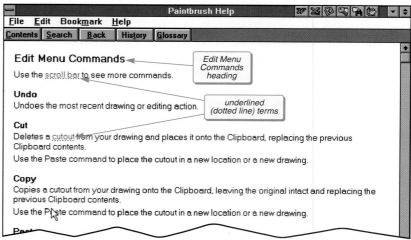

FIGURE 1-66

TO DISPLAY A DEFINITION ▼

STEP 1 ►

Point to the term, scroll bar.

The mouse pointer changes to a hand and points to the term, scroll bar (Figure 1-67).

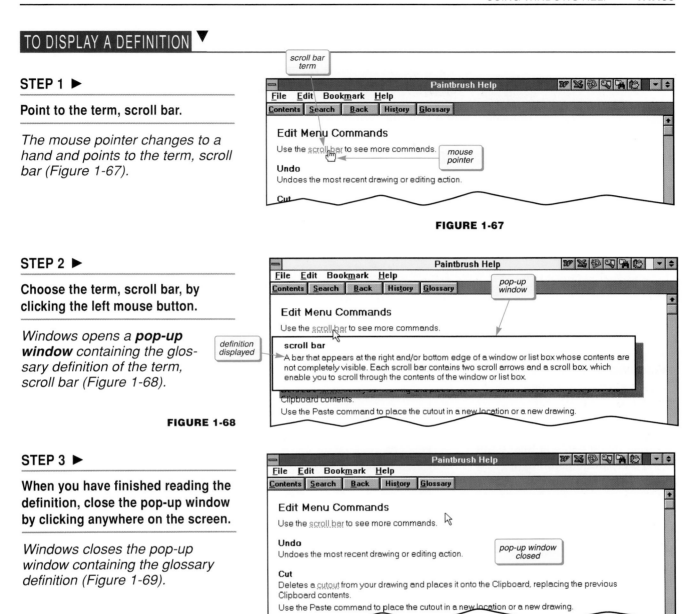

FIGURE 1-67

STEP 2 ►

Choose the term, scroll bar, by clicking the left mouse button.

*Windows opens a **pop-up window** containing the glossary definition of the term, scroll bar (Figure 1-68).*

FIGURE 1-68

STEP 3 ►

When you have finished reading the definition, close the pop-up window by clicking anywhere on the screen.

Windows closes the pop-up window containing the glossary definition (Figure 1-69).

FIGURE 1-69

Exiting the Online Help and Paintbrush Applications

After obtaining help about the Edit menu commands, quit Help by choosing the Exit command from the Help File menu. Then, quit Paintbrush by choosing the Exit command from the Paintbrush File menu. The steps are summarized as follows.

TO QUIT PAINTBRUSH HELP

Step 1: Select File on the Paintbrush Help menu bar.
Step 2: Choose the Exit command from the File menu.

TO QUIT PAINTBRUSH

Step 1: Select File on the Paintbrush menu bar.
Step 2: Choose the Exit command from the File menu.

▶ QUITTING WINDOWS

Y ou always want to return the desktop to its original state before beginning your next session with Windows. Therefore, before exiting Windows, you must verify that any changes made to the desktop are not saved when you quit Windows.

Verify Changes to the Desktop Will Not Be Saved

Because you want to return the desktop to its state before you started Windows, no changes should be saved. The Save Settings on Exit command on the Program Manager Options menu controls whether changes to the desktop are saved or are not saved when you quit Windows. A check mark (✔) preceding the Save Settings on Exit command indicates the command is active and all changes to the layout of the desktop will be saved when you quit Windows. If the command is preceded by a check mark, choose the Save Settings on Exit command by pointing to the command name and clicking the left mouse button to remove the check mark, so the changes will not be saved. Perform the following steps to verify that changes are not saved to the desktop.

TO VERIFY CHANGES ARE NOT SAVED TO THE DESKTOP ▼

STEP 1 ▶

Select Options on the Program Manager menu bar, and then point to the Save Settings on Exit command.

The Options menu opens (Figure 1-70). A check mark (✔) precedes the Save Settings on Exit command.

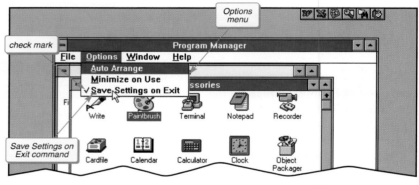

FIGURE 1-70

STEP 2 ▶

To remove the check mark, choose the Save Settings on Exit command from the Options menu by clicking the left mouse button.

Windows closes the Options menu (Figure 1-71). Although not visible in Figure 1-71, the check mark preceding the Save Settings on Exit command has been removed. This means any changes made to the desktop will not be saved when you exit Windows.

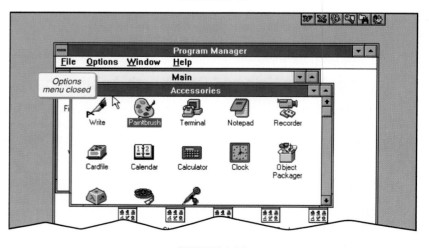

FIGURE 1-71

Quitting Windows Without Saving Changes

After verifying the Save Settings on Exit command is not active, quit Windows by choosing the Exit command from the File menu, as shown below.

 TO QUIT WINDOWS ▼

STEP 1 ►

Select File on the Program Manager menu bar, and then point to the Exit Windows command.

Windows opens the File menu and the mouse pointer points to the Exit Windows command (Figure 1-72).

FIGURE 1-72

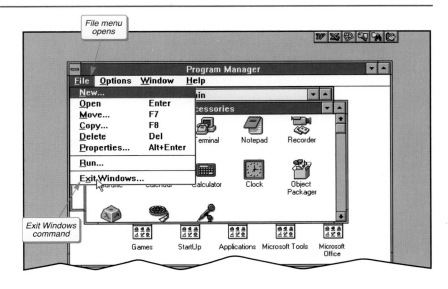

STEP 2 ►

Choose the Exit Windows command from the File menu by clicking the left mouse button, and then point to the OK button.

The Exit Windows dialog box opens and contains the message, This will end your Windows session., and the OK and Cancel buttons (Figure 1-73). Choosing the OK button exits Windows. Choosing the Cancel button cancels the exit from Windows and returns you to the Program Manager window. The mouse pointer points to the OK button.

STEP 3 ►

Choose the OK button by clicking the left mouse button.

When you quit Windows, all windows are removed from the desktop and control is returned to the DOS operating system.

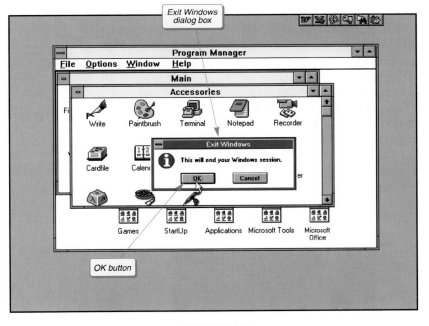

FIGURE 1-73

▶ PROJECT SUMMARY

Project 1 illustrated user interfaces and the Microsoft Windows graphical user interface. You started and exited Windows and learned the parts of a window. You started Notepad, entered and printed a note, edited the note, opened and saved files, and exited the application. You opened group windows, maximized application windows, and scrolled the windows. You used the mouse to select a menu, chose a command from a menu, and respond to dialog boxes. You used Windows online Help to obtain help about the Paintbrush application.

▶ KEY TERMS AND INDEX

active icon *(WIN18)*
active window *(WIN15)*
applications *(WIN3)*
application software *(WIN3)*
application window *(WIN5)*
check boxes *(WIN13)*
choose *(WIN11)*
choosing a command *(WIN11)*
choosing a help topic *(WIN33)*
clicking *(WIN7)*
command *(WIN10)*
command buttons *(WIN13)*
Control menu *(WIN16)*
creating a document *(WIN19)*
current selection *(WIN13)*
desktop *(WIN4)*
dialog box *(WIN12)*
directory *(WIN22)*
directory path *(WIN22)*
directory structure *(WIN22)*
displaying a definition *(WIN35)*
documents *(WIN14)*
document file *(WIN21)*
double-clicking *(WIN8)*
dragging *(WIN9)*
drop-down list box *(WIN13)*
ellipsis *(WIN11)*
editing the document *(WIN31)*
error correction *(WIN16, WIN18, WIN26)*
extension *(WIN21)*
file and disk concepts *(WIN21–WIN27)*
filename *(WIN21)*
formatting *(WIN26)*

graphical user interface (GUI) *(WIN3)*
group icons *(WIN5)*
group window *(WIN5)*
GUI *(WIN3)*
help topic *(WIN33)*
hourglass icon *(WIN3)*
icons *(WIN5)*
insertion point *(WIN17)*
jump *(WIN33)*
keyboard *(WIN9)*
keyboard shortcuts *(WIN10)*
Maximize button *(WIN18)*
maximizing an application window *(WIN18)*
menus *(WIN10)*
menu bar *(WIN10)*
Microsoft Office *(WIN 4)*
Microsoft Office Manager toolbar *(WIN4)*
Microsoft Windows *(WIN2)*
mouse *(WIN5)*
mouse operations *(WIN6–WIN9)*
mouse pointer *(WIN6)*
naming a file *(WIN21)*
Notepad *(WIN14)*
online Help *(WIN32)*
opening a document file *(WIN28)*
opening a group window *(WIN14)*
option buttons *(WIN12)*
Paintbrush *(WIN32)*
pointing *(WIN6)*
pop-up window *(WIN35)*

printing a document *(WIN20)*
Program Manager *(WIN4)*
program-item icons *(WIN5)*
quitting an application *(WIN26, WIN32)*
quitting Windows *(WIN35)*
Restore button *(WIN18)*
root directory *(WIN22)*
saving a document *(WIN23)*
saving a modified document file *(WIN31)*
scroll arrows *(WIN16)*
scroll bar *(WIN16)*
scroll box *(WIN16)*
selected button *(WIN12)*
selecting *(WIN11)*
selecting a menu *(WIN11)*
starting an application *(WIN16)*
starting Microsoft Windows *(WIN3)*
subdirectories *(WIN22)*
text box *(WIN13)*
title bar *(WIN4)*
toolbar *(WIN4)*
user friendly *(WIN3)*
user interface *(WIN2)*
using Windows Help *(WIN32)*
windows *(WIN4)*
window border *(WIN4)*
window title *(WIN4)*
Windows *(WIN2)*
write-protected diskette *(WIN26)*

In Microsoft Windows, you can accomplish a task in a number of ways. The following table provides a quick reference to each task presented in this project with its available options. The commands listed in the Menu column can be executed using either the keyboard or mouse.

Task	Mouse	Menu	Keyboard Shortcuts
Choose a Command from a Menu	Click command name, drag highlight to command name and release mouse button		Press underlined character; or press arrow keys to select command and press ENTER
Choose a Help Topic	Click help topic		Press TAB, ENTER
Display a Definition	Click definition		Press TAB, ENTER
Maximize an Application Window	Click Maximize button	From Control menu, choose Maximize	
Obtain Online Help		From Help menu, choose Contents	Press F1
Open a Document		From File menu, choose Open	
Open a Group Window	Double-click group icon	From Window menu, choose group window name	Press CTRL+F6 (or CTRL+TAB) to select group icon; press ENTER
Print a File		From File menu, choose Print	
Quit an Application	Double-click Control-menu box	From File menu, choose Exit	
Quit Windows	Double-click Control-menu box; click OK button	From File menu, choose Exit Windows, choose OK button	
Remove a Definition	Click open space on desktop		Press ENTER
Save a Document on Disk		From File menu, choose Save As	
Save an Edited Document on Disk		From File menu, choose Save	
Save Changes when Quitting Windows		From Options menu, choose Save Settings on Exit if no check mark precedes command	
Save No Changes when Quitting Windows		From Options menu, choose Save Settings on Exit if check mark precedes command	
Scroll a Window	Click up or down scroll arrow, drag scroll arrow box, click scroll bar		Press UP ARROW or DOWN ARROW
Select a Menu	Click menu name on menu bar		Press ALT + underlined character (or F10 + underlined character)
Start an Application	Double-click program-item icon	From File menu, choose Open	Press arrow keys to select program-item icon; press ENTER

STUDENT ASSIGNMENT 1
True/False

Instructions: Circle T if the statement is true or F if the statement is false.

T F 1. A user interface is a combination of computer hardware and computer software.
T F 2. Microsoft Windows is a graphical user interface.
T F 3. The Program Manager window is a group window.
T F 4. The toolbar displays in the upper right corner of the desktop when Microsoft Office starts.
T F 5. A menu is a small picture that can represent an application or a group of applications.
T F 6. Clicking means quickly pressing and releasing a mouse button twice without moving the mouse.
T F 7. CTRL+SHIFT+LEFT ARROW is an example of a keyboard shortcut.
T F 8. You carry out an action in an application by choosing a command from a menu.
T F 9. Selecting means marking an item.
T F 10. Windows opens a dialog box to supply information, allow you to enter information, or choose among several options.
T F 11. A program-item icon represents a group of applications.
T F 12. You open a group window by pointing to its icon and double-clicking the left mouse button.
T F 13. A scroll bar allows you to view areas of a window that are not currently visible.
T F 14. Notepad and Paintbrush are applications.
T F 15. Choosing the Restore button maximizes a window to its maximum size.
T F 16. APPLICATION.TXT is a valid name for a document file.
T F 17. The directory structure is the relationship between the root directory and any subdirectories.
T F 18. You save a new document on disk by choosing the Save As command from the File menu.
T F 19. You open a document by choosing the Retrieve command from the File menu.
T F 20. Help is available while using Windows only in the *User's Guide* that accompanies the Windows software.

STUDENT ASSIGNMENT 2
Multiple Choice

Instructions: Circle the correct response.

1. Through a user interface, the user is able to _____.
   a. control the computer
   b. request information from the computer
   c. respond to messages displayed by the computer
   d. all of the above
2. _____ is quickly pressing and releasing a mouse button twice without moving the mouse.
   a. Double-clicking
   b. Clicking
   c. Dragging
   d. Pointing
3. To view the commands in a menu, you _____ the menu name.
   a. choose
   b. maximize
   c. close
   d. select

4. A(n) _____ is a window that displays to supply information, allows you to enter information, or choose among several options.
   a. group window
   b. dialog box
   c. application window
   d. drop-down list box

5. A _____ is a rectangular area in which Windows displays text or you enter text.
   a. dialog box
   b. text box
   c. drop-down list box
   d. list box

6. The title bar of one group window that is a different color or intensity than the title bars of the other group windows indicates a(n) _____ window.
   a. inactive
   b. application
   c. group
   d. active

7. To view an area of a window that is not currently visible in a window, use the _____.
   a. title bar
   b. scroll bar
   c. menu bar
   d. Restore button

8. The _____ menu in the Notepad application contains the Save, Open, and Print commands.
   a. Window
   b. Options
   c. Help
   d. File

9. Before exiting Windows, you should check the _____ command to verify that no changes to the desktop will be saved.
   a. Open
   b. Exit Windows
   c. Save Settings on Exit
   d. Save Changes

10. Online Help is available for all applications except _____.
    a. Program Manager
    b. Calendar
    c. Clock
    d. File Manager

STUDENT ASSIGNMENT 3
Identifying Items in the Program Manager Window

Instructions: On the desktop in Figure SA1-3, arrows point to several items in the Program Manager window. Identify the items in the spaces provided.

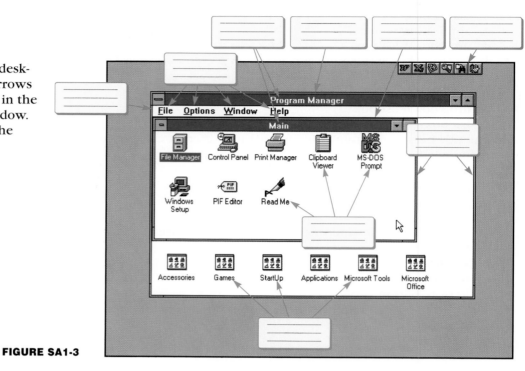

FIGURE SA1-3

STUDENT ASSIGNMENT 4
Starting an Application

Instructions: Using the desktop in Figure SA1-4, list the steps in the spaces provided to open the Accessories window and start the Notepad application.

Step 1: _____

_____

Step 2: _____

_____

Step 3: _____

_____

Step 4: _____

_____

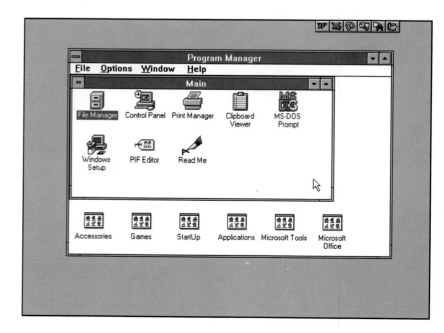

FIGURE SA1-4

STUDENT ASSIGNMENT 5
Saving a File to Disk

Instructions: Using the desktop in Figure SA1-5, list the steps in the spaces provided to save the notepad document on drive A using the AGENDA.TXT filename.

Step 1: _____

_____

Step 2: _____

_____

Step 3: _____

_____

Step 4: _____

_____

Step 5: _____

_____

Step 6: _____

_____

Step 7: _____

_____

```
┌─────────────────────────────────────────────────────────────┐
│ —            Notepad - (Untitled)         w ✕ 🖴 🖴 🖴 🖴  ▼ ◆ │
├─────────────────────────────────────────────────────────────┤
│ File  Edit  Search  Help                                   ▲  │
│ Things to do today -                                          │
│ 1) Take fax/phone to Conway Service Center                    │
│ 2) Pick up payroll checks from ADM                            │
│ 3) Order 3 boxes of copier paper                              │
│ |                                                             │
│                                                               │
│                              I                                │
│                                                               │
```

FIGURE SA1-5

STUDENT ASSIGNMENT 6
Using Online Help

Instructions: Using the desktop in Figure SA1-6, list the steps in the spaces provided to obtain online Help about the Paint Roller tool.

Step 1: _____

_____

Step 2: _____

_____

Step 3: _____

_____

Step 4: _____

_____

Step 5: _____

_____

FIGURE SA1-6

COMPUTER LABORATORY EXERCISE 1
Improving Your Mouse Skills

Instructions: Use a computer to perform the following tasks:

1. Start Microsoft Windows.
2. If necessary, double-click the Games group icon ( ) to open the Games window.
3. Double-click the Solitaire program-item icon ( ) in the Games window.
4. Choose the Maximize button in the Solitaire window (Figure CLE1-1).
5. Select Help from the menu bar of the Solitaire window.
6. Choose the Contents command from the Help menu.

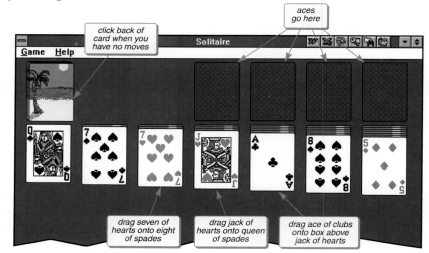

FIGURE CLE1-1

7. Review each help topic below the Contents for Solitaire Help heading. After reviewing each topic, choose the Contents button below the menu bar to return to the Contents for Solitaire Help screen.
8. Select File from the menu bar of the Solitaire Help window.
9. Choose the Exit command from the File menu to quit the Solitaire Help application.
10. Play the game of Solitaire.
11. Select Game from the menu bar of the Solitaire window.
12. Choose the Exit command from the Game menu to quit Solitaire.

COMPUTER LABORATORY EXERCISE 2
Running the Windows Tutorial

Instructions: Use a computer to perform the following tasks:

1. Start Microsoft Windows.
2. Select Help from the menu bar of the Program Manager window.
3. Choose the Windows Tutorial command from the Help menu (Figure CLE1-2). The Windows Tutorial has two lessons (Mouse lesson and Windows Basics lesson).
4. Press the M key to begin the Mouse lesson.
5. Follow the instructions on the screen to step through the Mouse lesson.
6. When you have completed the Mouse lesson, choose the Go on to the Windows Basics lesson button.

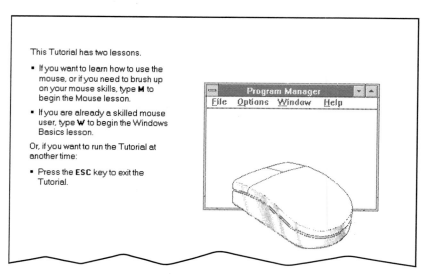

FIGURE CLE1-2

7. Click the Instructions button (Instructions) and read the information in the Instructions box.
8. When finished, choose the Return to the Tutorial button (Return to the Tutorial).
9. Choose the Continue button to begin the Windows Basics lesson. Respond as needed to the questions and instructions on the screen.
10. When you have completed the Windows Basics lesson, press the ESC key and then press the Y key to exit the tutorial.

COMPUTER LABORATORY EXERCISE 3
Creating, Saving, and Printing Documents

Instructions: Use a computer to perform the following tasks:

1. Start Microsoft Windows if necessary.
2. Double-click the Accessories icon to open the Accessories window.
3. Double-click the Notepad icon to start the Notepad application.
4. Choose the Maximize button to maximize the Notepad window.
5. Enter the note shown at the right at the insertion point on the screen.
6. Insert the Student Diskette that accompanies this book into drive A.
7. Select File on the Notepad menu bar.
8. Choose the Save As command.
9. Type grocery in the File Name text box.
10. Change the current selection in the Drives drop-down list box to a:.
11. Click the OK button to save the document on drive A.
12. Select File on the Notepad menu bar.
13. Choose the Print command to print the document on the printer (Figure CLE1-3).
14. Remove the Student Diskette from drive A.
15. Select File on the Notepad menu bar.
16. Choose the Exit command from the File menu to quit Notepad.

Grocery List -
1/2 Gallon of Low Fat Milk
1 Dozen Medium Size Eggs
1 Loaf of Wheat Bread

```
                              (Untitled)




        Grocery List -
        1/2 Gallon of Low Fat Milk
        1 Dozen Medium Size Eggs
        1 Loaf of Wheat Bread
```

FIGURE CLE1-3

COMPUTER LABORATORY EXERCISE 4
Opening, Editing, and Saving Documents

Instructions: Use a computer to perform the following tasks:

1. Start Microsoft Windows.
2. Double-click the Accessories icon to open the Accessories window.
3. Double-click the Calendar icon (📖) to start the Calendar application.

(continued)

COMPUTER LABORATORY EXERCISE 4 (continued)

4. Choose the Maximize button to maximize the Calendar window.
5. Insert the Student Diskette that accompanies this book into drive A.
6. Select File on the Calendar menu bar.
7. Choose the Open command from the File menu.
8. Change the current selection in the Drives drop-down list box to a:.
9. Select the thompson.cal filename in the File Name list box. The THOMPSON.CAL file contains the daily appointments for Mr. Thompson.
10. Choose the OK button in the Open dialog box to open the THOMPSON.CAL document.
11. Select Show on the Calendar menu bar.
12. Choose the Date command from the Show menu.
13. Type 9/29/95 in the Show Date text box.
14. Choose the OK button. The document on your screen is shown in Figure CLE1-4a.
15. Make the changes shown at the right to the document.
16. Select File on the Calendar menu bar.
17. Choose the Save As command from the File menu to save the THOMPSON.CAL document on drive A. Use the filename PETER.CAL.

TIME	CHANGE
11:00 AM	Stay at Auto Show one more hour
2:00 PM	Change the Designer's Meeting from 2:00 PM to 3:00 PM
4:00 PM	Remove the Quality Control Meeting

18. Select File on the Calendar menu bar.
19. Choose the Print command from the File menu.
20. Choose the OK button in the Print dialog box to print the document on the printer (Figure CLE1-4b).
21. Remove the Student Diskette from drive A.
22. Select File on the Calendar menu bar.
23. Choose the Exit command from the File menu to quit Calendar.

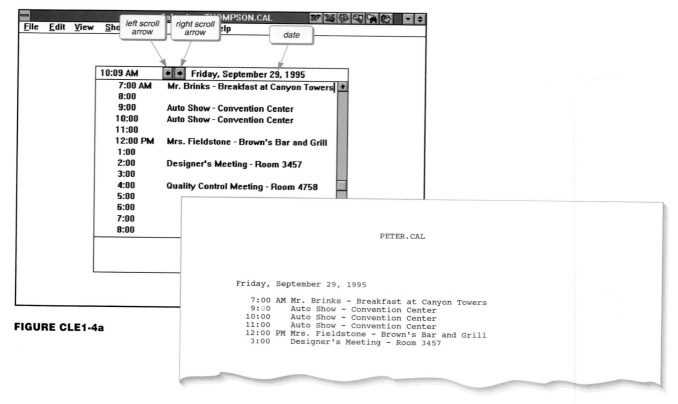

FIGURE CLE1-4a

FIGURE CLE1-4b

COMPUTER LABORATORY EXERCISE 5
Using Online Help

Instructions: Use a computer to perform the following tasks:

1. Start Microsoft Windows.
2. Double-click the Accessories icon to open the Accessories window.
3. Double-click the Cardfile icon (🗄) to start the Cardfile application.
4. Click the Maximize button in the Cardfile window to maximize the Cardfile window.
5. Select Help on the Cardfile menu bar.
6. Choose the Contents command from the Help menu.
7. Choose the Maximize button in the Cardfile Help window to maximize the Cardfile Help window.
8. Choose the Add More Cards help topic.
9. Select File on the Cardfile Help menu bar.
10. Choose the Print Topic command from the File menu to print the Adding More Cards help topic on the printer (Figure CLE1-5a).
11. Display the definition of the term, index line.
12. Remove the index line definition from the desktop.
13. Choose the Contents button below the menu bar to return to the Contents for Cardfile Help screen.
14. Choose the Delete Cards help topic.
15. Choose the Selecting Cards help topic at the bottom of the Deleting Cards screen.
16. Select File on the Cardfile Help menu bar.
17. Choose the Print Topic command to print the Selecting Cards help topic (Figure CLE1-5b).
18. Select File on the Cardfile Help menu bar.
19. Choose the Exit command from the File menu to quit Cardfile Help.
20. Select File on the Cardfile menu bar.
21. Choose the Exit command from the File menu to quit Cardfile.

Adding More Cards

Cardfile adds new cards in the correct alphabetic order and scrolls to display the new card at the front.

To add a new card to a file
1 From the Card menu, choose Add.
2 Type the text you want to appear on the index line.
3 Choose the OK button.
4 In the information area, type text.

FIGURE CLE1-5a

Selecting Cards

To select a card in Card view
▸ Click the card's index line if it is visible.
   Or click the arrows in the status bar until the index line is visible, and then click it.
   If you are using the keyboard, press and hold down CTRL+SHIFT and type the first letter of the index line.

To select a card by using the Go To command
1 From the Search menu, choose Go To.
2 Type text from the card's index line.
3 Choose the OK button.

To select a card in List view
▸ Click the card's index line.
   Or use the arrow keys to move to the card's index line.

See Also
Moving Through a Card File

FIGURE CLE1-5b

$\mathcal{M}$ICROSOFT $\mathcal{W}$INDOWS 3.1

P R O J E C T   T W O

▼

DISK AND FILE MANAGEMENT

OBJECTIVES You will have mastered the material in this project when you can:

- ▶ Identify the elements of the directory tree window
- ▶ Understand the concepts of diskette size and capacity
- ▶ Format and copy a diskette
- ▶ Select and copy one file or a group of files
- ▶ Change the current drive
- ▶ Rename or delete a file

- ▶ Create a backup diskette
- ▶ Search for help topics using Windows online Help
- ▶ Switch between applications
- ▶ Activate, resize, and close a group window
- ▶ Arrange the icons in a group window
- ▶ Minimize an application window to an icon

▶ INTRODUCTION

File Manager is an application included with Windows that allows you to organize and work with your hard disk and diskettes and the files on those disks. In this project, you will use File Manager to (1) format a diskette; (2) copy files between the hard disk and a diskette; (3) copy a diskette; (4) rename a file on diskette; and (5) delete a file from diskette.

Formatting a diskette and copying files to a diskette are common operations illustrated in this project that you should understand how to perform. While performing the Computer Laboratory Exercises at the end of each application project, you will save documents on a diskette that accompanies this textbook. To prevent the accidental loss of stored documents on a diskette, it is important to periodically make a copy of the entire diskette. A copy of a diskette is called a **backup diskette**. In this project, you will learn how to create a backup diskette to protect against the accidental loss of documents on a diskette.

You will also use Windows online Help in this project. In Project 1, you obtained help by choosing a topic from a list of help topics. In this project, you will use the Search feature to search for help topics.

▶ STARTING WINDOWS

A s explained in Project 1, when you turn on the computer, an introductory screen consisting of the Windows logo, Windows name, version number, and copyright notices displays momentarily. Next, a blank screen containing an hourglass icon displays followed by the Program Manager and introductory Microsoft Office screen consisting of the Microsoft Office name, version (Version 4.3), and copyright notices.

Finally, the Program Manager and Main windows display on the desktop (Figure 2-1). The Microsoft Office Manager toolbar displays in the upper right corner of the desktop. The File Manager program-item icon displays in the Main window. If your desktop does not look similar to the desktop in Figure 2-1, your instructor will inform you of the modifications necessary to change your desktop.

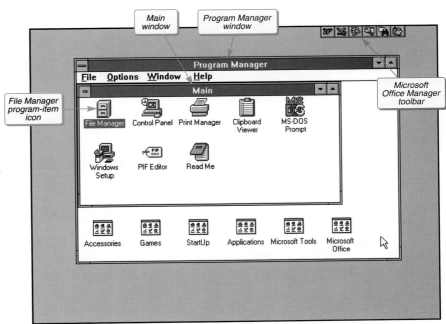

FIGURE 2-1

Starting File Manager and Maximizing the File Manager Window

To start File Manager, double-click the File Manager icon (🗎) in the Main window. To maximize the File Manager window, choose the Maximize button on the File Manager window by pointing to the Maximize button and clicking the left mouse button.

TO START AN APPLICATION AND MAXIMIZE ITS WINDOW ▼

STEP 1 ▶

Double-click the File Manager icon in the Main window (see Figure 2-1), then click the Maximize button on the File Manager title bar.

Windows opens and maximizes the File Manager window (Figure 2-2).

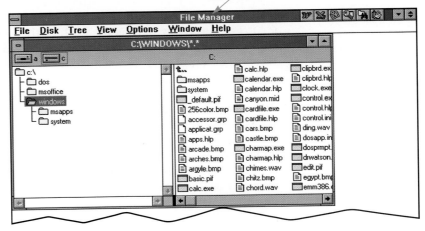

FIGURE 2-2

▶ FILE MANAGER

When you start File Manager, Windows opens the File Manager window (Figure 2-3). The menu bar contains the File, Disk, Tree, View, Options, Window, and Help menus. These menus contain the commands to organize and work with the disks and the files on those disks.

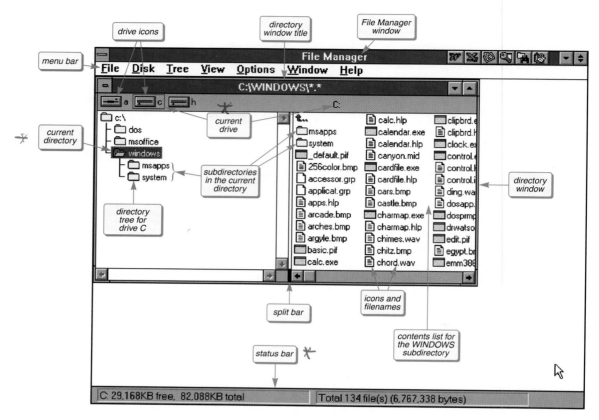

FIGURE 2-3

Below the menu bar is a **directory window** titled C:\WINDOWS*.*. The window title consists of a directory path (C:\WINDOWS), backslash (\), and filename (*.*). The directory path is the path of the current directory on drive C (WINDOWS subdirectory). The backslash separates the path and filename. The filename (*.*) references a group of files whose filename and extension can be any valid filename and extension.

Below the title bar is a horizontal bar that contains two **drive icons**. The drive icons represent the disk drives attached to the computer. The first drive icon (⬜ a) represents drive A (diskette drive) and the second drive icon (⬜ c) represents drive C (hard drive). Depending upon the number of disk drives attached to your computer, there may be more than two drive icons in the horizontal bar. A rectangular box surrounding the drive C icon indicates drive C is the **current drive**. The entry to the right of the icons (C:) also indicates drive C is the current drive.

The directory window is divided into two equal-sized areas. Each area is separated by a split bar. The **directory tree** in the area on the left contains the directory structure. The **directory tree** in the **directory structure** shows the relationship between the root directory and any subdirectories on the current drive (drive C). You can drag the **split bar** to the left or right to change the size of the two areas.

In the left area, a file folder icon represents each directory or subdirectory in the directory structure (see Figure 2-3). The shaded open file folder (📂) and subdirectory name for the current directory (WINDOWS subdirectory) are high-lighted. The unopened file folder icons (📁) for the two subdirectories in the WINDOWS subdirectory (MSAPPS and SYSTEM) are indented below the icon for the WINDOWS subdirectory.

The area on the right contains the contents list. The **contents list** is a list of the files in the current directory (WINDOWS subdirectory). Each entry in the contents list consists of an icon and name. The shaded file folder icons for the two subdirectories in the current directory (MSAPPS and SYSTEM) display at the top of the first column in the list.

The status bar at the bottom of the File Manager window indicates the amount of unused disk space on the current drive (29,168KB free), amount of total disk space on the current drive (82,088KB total), number of files in the current directory (134 files), and the amount of disk space the files occupy (6,767,338 bytes).

▶ FORMATTING A DISKETTE

Before saving a document file on a diskette or copying a file onto a diskette, you must format the diskette. **Formatting** prepares a diskette for use on a computer by establishing the sectors and cylinders on the diskette, analyzing the diskette for defective cylinders, and establishing the root directory. To avoid errors while formatting a diskette, you should understand the concepts of diskette size and capacity that are explained in the following section.

Diskette Size and Capacity

How a diskette is formatted is determined by the size of the diskette, capacity of the diskette as established by the diskette manufacturer, and capabilities of the disk drive you use to format the diskette. **Diskette size** is the physical size of the diskette. Common diskette sizes are 5 1/4-inch and 3 1/2-inch.

Diskette capacity is the amount of space on the disk, measured in kilobytes (K) or megabytes (MB), available to store data. A diskette's capacity is established by the diskette manufacturer. Common diskette capacities are 360K and 1.2MB for a 5 1/4-inch diskette and 720K and 1.44MB for a 3 1/2-inch diskette.

A diskette drive's capability is established by the diskette drive manufacturer. There are 3 1/2-inch diskette drives that are capable of formatting a diskette with a capacity of 720K or 1.44MB and there are 5 1/4-inch diskette drives capable of formatting a diskette with a capacity of 360K or 1.2MB.

Before formatting a diskette, you must consider two things. First, the diskette drive you use to format a diskette must be capable of formatting the size of diskette you want to format. You can use a 3 1/2-inch diskette drive to format a 3 1/2-inch diskette, but you cannot use a 3 1/2-inch diskette drive to format a 5 1/4-inch diskette. Similarly, you can use a 5 1/4-inch diskette drive to format a 5 1/4-inch diskette, but you cannot use a 5 1/4-inch diskette drive to format a 3 1/2-inch diskette.

Second, the diskette drive you use to format a diskette must be capable of formatting the capacity of the diskette you want to format. A 5 1/4-inch diskette drive capable of formatting 1.2MB diskettes can be used to either format a 360K or 1.2MB diskette. However, because of the differences in the diskette manufacturing process, you cannot use a diskette drive capable of formatting 360K diskettes to format a 1.2MB diskette. A 3 1/2-inch diskette drive capable of formatting 1.44MB diskettes can be used to format either a 720K or 1.44MB diskette. Since the 1.44 MB diskette is manufactured with two square holes in the plastic cover and the 720K diskette is manufactured with only one square hole, you cannot use a diskette drive capable of formatting 720K diskette to format a 1.44MB diskette.

The computer you use to complete this project should have a 3 1/2-inch diskette drive capable of formatting a diskette with 1.44MB of disk storage. Trying to format a 3 1/2-inch diskette with any other diskette drive may result in an error. Typical errors encountered because of incorrect diskette capacity and diskette drive capabilities are explained later in this project. For more information about the diskette drive you will use to complete the projects in this textbook, contact your instructor.

Formatting a Diskette

To store a file on a diskette, the diskette must already be formatted. If the diskette is not formatted, you must format the diskette using File Manager. When formatting a diskette, use either an unformatted diskette or a diskette containing files you no longer need. Do not format the Student Diskette that accompanies this book.

To format a diskette using File Manager, you insert the diskette into the diskette drive, and then choose the **Format Disk command** from the Disk menu. Perform the following steps to format a diskette.

TO FORMAT A DISKETTE ▼

STEP 1 ►

Insert an unformatted diskette or a formatted diskette containing files you no longer need into drive A.

STEP 2 ►

Select the Disk menu, and then point to the Format Disk command.

*Windows opens the **Disk menu** (Figure 2-4). The mouse pointer points to the Format Disk command.*

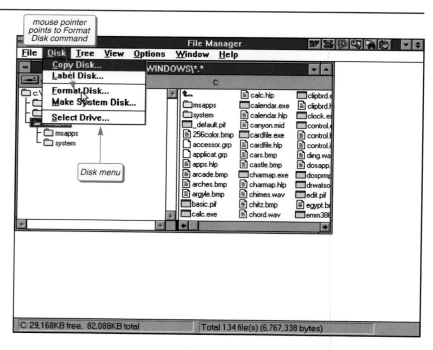

FIGURE 2-4

STEP 3 ▶

Choose the Format Disk command from the Disk menu, and then point to the OK button.

Windows opens the Format Disk dialog box (Figure 2-5). The current selections in the Disk In and Capacity boxes are Drive A: and 1.44 MB, respectively. With these selections, the diskette in drive A will be formatted with a capacity of 1.44MB. The Options list box is not required to format a diskette in this project. The mouse pointer points to the OK button.

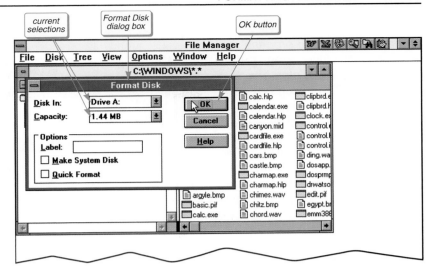

FIGURE 2-5

STEP 4 ▶

Choose the OK button by clicking the left mouse button, and then point to the Yes button.

Windows opens the Confirm Format Disk dialog box (Figure 2-6). This dialog box reminds you that if you continue, Windows will erase all data on the diskette in drive A. The mouse pointer points to the Yes button.

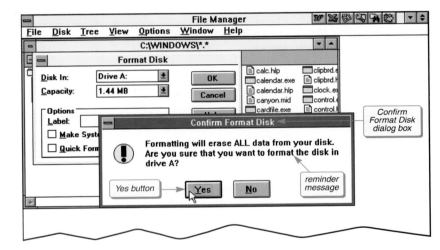

FIGURE 2-6

STEP 5 ▶

Choose the Yes button by clicking the left mouse button.

Windows opens the Formatting Disk dialog box (Figure 2-7). As the formatting process progresses, a value from 1 to 100 indicates what percent of the formatting process is complete. Toward the end of the formatting process, the creating root directory message replaces the 1% completed message to indicate Windows is creating the root directory on the diskette. The formatting process takes approximately two minutes.

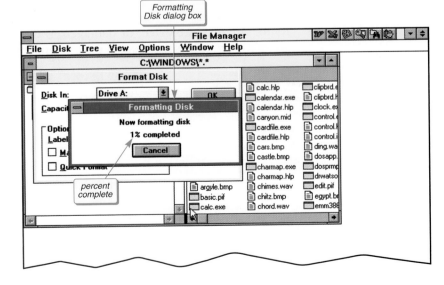

FIGURE 2-7

When the formatting process is complete, Windows opens the Format Complete dialog box (Figure 2-8). The dialog box contains the total disk space (1,457,664 bytes) and available disk space (1,457,664 bytes) of the newly formatted diskette. The values for the total disk space and available disk space in the Format Complete dialog box may be different for your computer.

STEP 6 ▶

Choose the No button by pointing to the No button, and then clicking the left mouse button.

Windows closes the Format Disk and Format Complete dialog boxes.

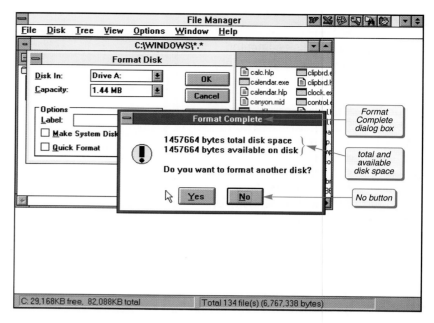

FIGURE 2-8

Correcting Errors Encountered While Formatting a Diskette

When you try to format a diskette but forget to insert a diskette into the diskette drive or the diskette you inserted is write-protected, damaged, or does not have the correct capacity for the diskette drive, Windows opens the Format Disk Error dialog box shown in Figure 2-9. The dialog box contains an error message (Cannot format disk.), a suggested action (Make sure the disk is in the drive and not write-protected, damaged, or of wrong density rating.), and the OK button. To format a diskette after forgetting to insert the diskette into the diskette drive, insert the diskette into the diskette drive, choose the OK button, and format the diskette.

If the same dialog box opens after inserting a diskette into drive A, remove the diskette and determine if the diskette is write-protected, not the correct capacity for the diskette drive, or damaged. If the diskette is write-protected, remove the write-protection from the diskette, choose the OK button and format the diskette.

FIGURE 2-9

If the diskette is not write-protected, check the diskette to determine if the diskette is the same capacity as the diskette drive. If it is not, insert a diskette with the correct capacity into the diskette drive, choose the OK button and format the diskette. If the diskette is not write-protected and the correct capacity, throw the damaged diskette away and insert another diskette into drive A, choose the OK button, and format the new diskette.

▶ COPYING FILES TO A DISKETTE

After formatting a diskette, you can save files on the diskette or copy files to the diskette from the hard drive or another diskette. You can easily copy a single file or group of files from one directory to another directory using File Manager. When copying files, the drive and directory containing the files to be copied are called the **source drive** and **source directory**, respectively. The drive and directory to which the files are copied are called the **destination drive** and **destination directory**, respectively.

To copy a file, select the filename in the contents list and drag the highlighted filename to the destination drive icon or destination directory icon. Groups of files are copied in a similar fashion. You select the filenames in the contents list and drag the highlighted group of filenames to the destination drive or destination directory icon. In this project, you will copy a group of files consisting of the ARCADE.BMP, CARS.BMP, and EGYPT.BMP files from the WINDOWS subdirectory of drive C to the root directory of the diskette that you formatted earlier in this project. Before copying the files, maximize the directory window to make it easier to view the contents of the window.

Maximizing the Directory Window

To enlarge the C:\WINDOWS*. * window, click the Maximize button on the right side of the directory window title bar. When you maximize a directory window, the window fills the File Manager window.

TO MAXIMIZE A DIRECTORY WINDOW ▼

STEP 1 ▶

Click the Maximize button on the right side of the C:\WINDOWS*.* window title bar.

The directory window fills the File Manager window (Figure 2-10). Windows changes the File Manager window title to contain the directory window title (File Manager - [C:\WINDOWS. *]) and removes the title bar of the directory tree window. A Restore button displays at the right side of the File Manager menu bar. Clicking the Restore button returns the directory window to its previous size.*

FIGURE 2-10

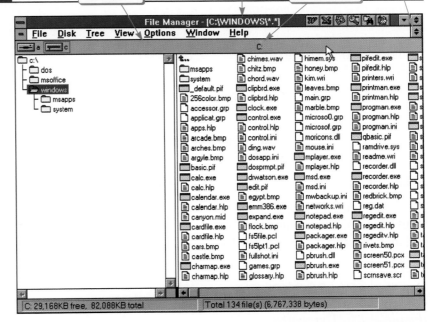

Selecting a Group of Files

Before copying a group of files, you must select (highlight) each file in the contents list. You select the first file in a group of files by pointing to its icon or filename and clicking the left mouse button. You select the remaining files in the group by pointing to each file icon or filename, holding down the CTRL key, clicking the left mouse button, and releasing the CTRL key. The steps on the following pages show how to select the group of files consisting of the ARCADE.BMP, CARS.BMP, and EGYPT.BMP files.

TO SELECT A GROUP OF FILES ▼

STEP 1 ►

Point to the ARCADE.BMP filename in the contents list (Figure 2-11).

FIGURE 2-11

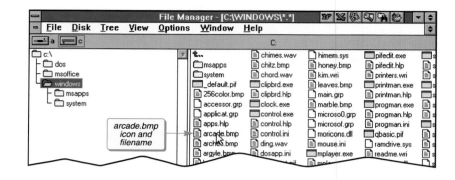

STEP 2 ►

Select the ARCADE.BMP file by clicking the left mouse button, and then point to the CARS.BMP filename.

When you select the first file, the highlight on the current directory (WINDOWS) in the directory tree changes to a rectangular box (Figure 2-12). The ARCADE.BMP entry is highlighted, and the mouse pointer points to the CARS.BMP filename.

FIGURE 2-12

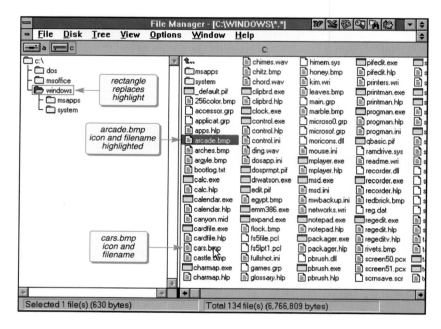

STEP 3 ►

Hold down the CTRL key, click the left mouse button, release the CTRL key, and then point to the EGYPT.BMP filename.

Two files, ARCADE.BMP and CARS.BMP, are highlighted (Figure 2-13). The mouse pointer points to the EGYPT.BMP filename.

FIGURE 2-13

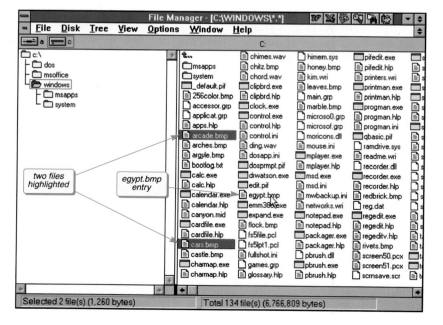

STEP 4 ▶

Hold down the CTRL key, click the left mouse button, and then release the CTRL key.

The group of files consisting of the ARCADE.BMP, CARS.BMP, and EGYPT.BMP files is highlighted (Figure 2-14).

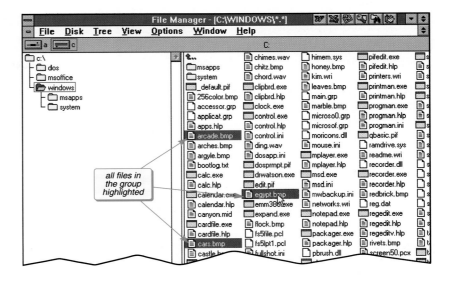

FIGURE 2-14

The ARCADE.BMP, CARS.BMP, and EGYPT.BMP files in Figure 2-14 are not located next to each other (sequentially) in the contents list. To select this group of files you selected the first file by pointing to its filename and clicking the left mouse button. Then, you selected each of the other files by pointing to their file-names, holding down the CTRL key, and clicking the left mouse button. If a group of files is located sequentially in the contents list, you select the group by pointing to the first filename in the list and clicking the left mouse button, and then hold down the SHIFT key, point to the last filename in the group and click the left mouse button.

Copying a Group of Files

After selecting each file in the group, insert the formatted diskette into drive A, and then copy the files to drive A by pointing to any highlighted filename and dragging the filename to the drive A icon.

TO COPY A GROUP OF FILES ▼

STEP 1 ▶

Verify that the formatted diskette is in drive A.

STEP 2 ▶

Point to the highlighted ARCADE.BMP entry (Figure 2-15).

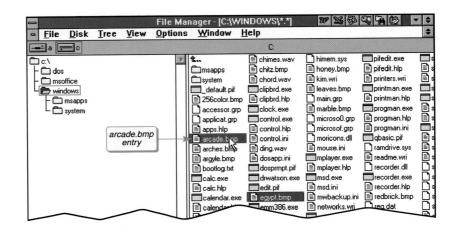

FIGURE 2-15

STEP 3 ▶

Drag the ARCADE.BMP filename over to the drive A icon.

As you drag the entry, the mouse pointer changes to an outline of a group of documents (🗐) (Figure 2-16). The outline contains a plus sign to indicate the group of files is being copied, not moved.

FIGURE 2-16

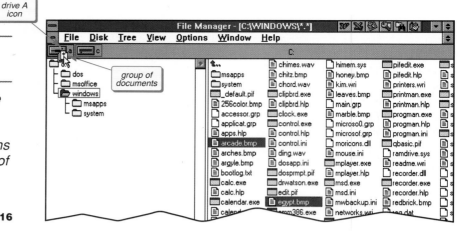

STEP 4 ▶

Release the mouse button, and then point to the Yes button.

Windows opens the Confirm Mouse Operation dialog box (Figure 2-17). The dialog box opens to confirm that you want to copy the files to the root directory of drive A (A:\). The highlight over the CARS.BMP entry is replaced with a dashed rectangular box. The mouse pointer points to the Yes button.

FIGURE 2-17

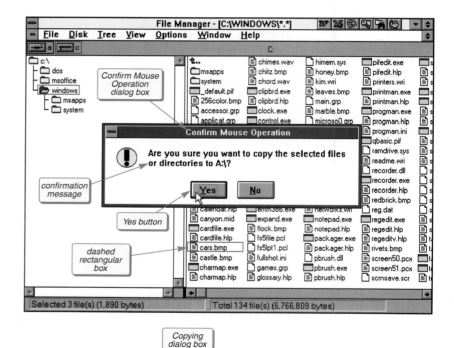

STEP 5 ▶

Choose the Yes button by clicking the left mouse button.

Windows opens the Copying dialog box, and the dialog box remains on the screen while Windows copies each file to the diskette in drive A (Figure 2-18). The dialog box in Figure 2-18 indicates the EGYPT.BMP file is currently being copied.

FIGURE 2-18

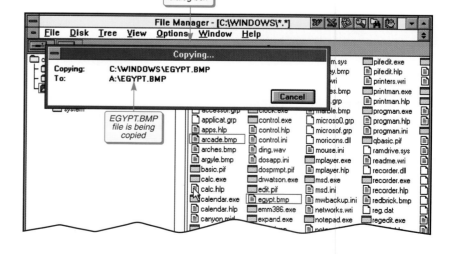

Correcting Errors Encountered While Copying Files

When you try to copy a file to an unformatted diskette, Windows opens the Error Copying File dialog box illustrated in Figure 2-19. The dialog box contains an error message (The disk in drive A is not formatted.), a question (Do you want to format it now?), and the Yes and No buttons. To continue the copy operation, format the diskette by choosing the Yes button. To cancel the copy operation, choose the No button.

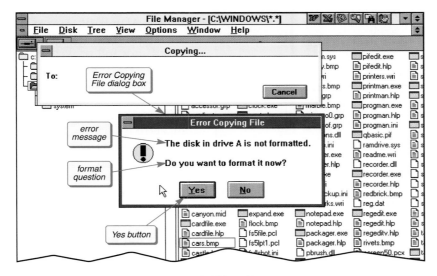

FIGURE 2-19

When you try to copy a file to a diskette but forget to insert a diskette into the diskette drive, Windows opens the Error Copying File dialog box shown in Figure 2-20. The dialog box contains an error message (There is no disk in drive A.), a suggested action (Insert a disk, and then try again.), and the Retry and Cancel buttons. To continue the copy operation, insert a diskette into drive A, and then choose the Retry button.

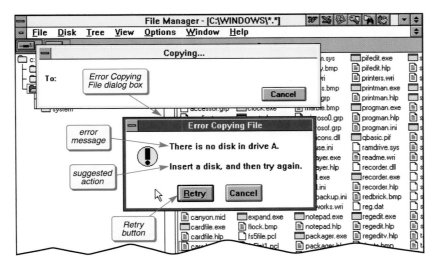

FIGURE 2-20

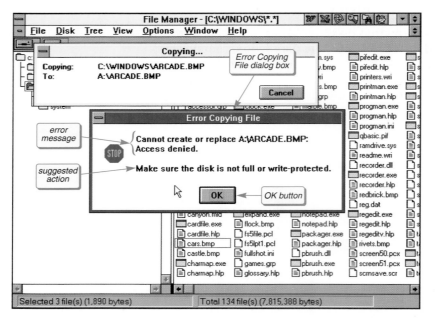

FIGURE 2-21

If you try to copy a file to a diskette that does not have enough room for the file, or you have inserted a write-protected diskette into the diskette drive, Windows opens the Error Copying File dialog box in Figure 2-21. The dialog box contains an error message (Cannot create or replace A:\ARCADE.BMP: Access denied.), a suggested action (Make sure the disk is not full or write-protected.), and the OK button. To continue with the copy operation, first remove the diskette from the diskette drive. Next, determine if the diskette is write-protected. If it is, remove the write-protection from the diskette, insert the diskette into the diskette drive, and then choose the OK button. If you determine the diskette is not write-protected, insert a diskette that is not full into the diskette drive, and then choose the OK button.

Replacing a File on Disk

If you try to copy a file to a diskette that already contains a file with the same filename and extension, Windows opens the Confirm File Replace dialog box (Figure 2-22). The Confirm File Replace dialog box contains information about the file being replaced (A:\ARCADE.BMP), the file being copied (C:\WINDOWS\ARCADE.BMP), and the Yes, Yes to All, No, and Cancel buttons. If you want to replace the file, on the diskette with the file being copied, choose the Yes button. If you do not want to replace the file choose the No button. If you want to cancel the copy operation, choose the Cancel button.

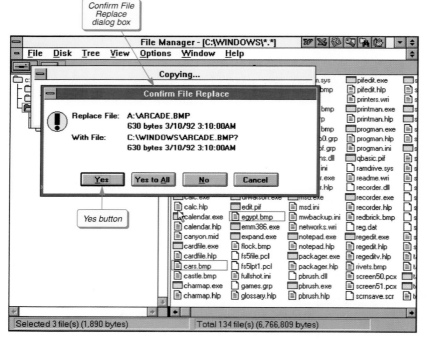

FIGURE 2-22

Changing the Current Drive

After copying a group of files, you should verify the files were copied onto the correct drive and into the correct directory. To view the files on drive A, change the current drive to drive A by pointing to the drive A icon and clicking the left mouse button.

TO CHANGE THE CURRENT DRIVE ▼

STEP 1 ▶

Point to the drive A icon.

The mouse pointer points to the drive A icon and the current drive is drive C (Figure 2-23).

FIGURE 2-23

STEP 2 ▶

Choose the drive A icon by clicking the left mouse button.

A rectangular box surrounds the drive A icon and the current drive entry changes to drive A (Figure 2-24). The directory tree of drive A and the contents list consisting of the files in the root directory of drive A display in the directory window. Another rectangular box surrounds the a:\ entry in the directory tree to indicate the current drive is drive A and the current directory is the root directory (\).

FIGURE 2-24

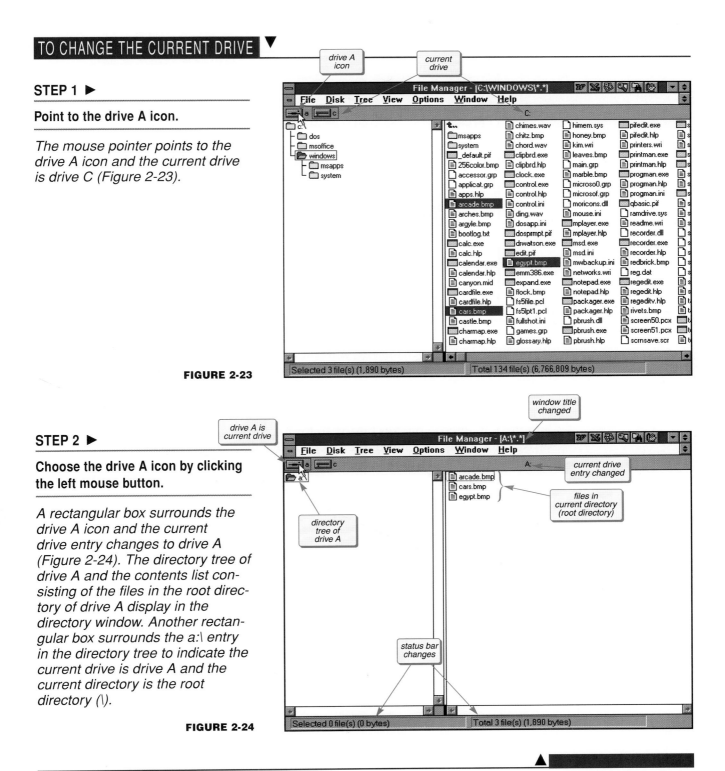

Correcting Errors Encountered While Changing the Current Drive

When you try to change the current drive before inserting a diskette into the diskette drive, Windows opens the Error Selecting Drive dialog box illustrated in Figure 2-25. The dialog box contains an error message (There is no disk in drive A.), a suggested action (Insert a disk, and then try again.), and the Retry and Cancel buttons. To change the current drive after forgetting to insert a diskette into drive A, insert a diskette into drive A, and choose the Retry button.

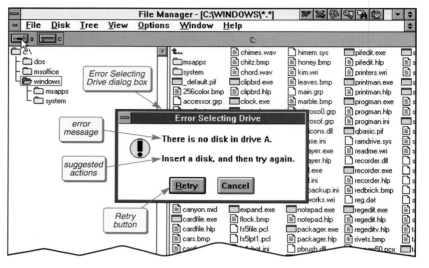

FIGURE 2-25

When you try to change the current drive and there is an unformatted diskette in the diskette drive, Windows opens the Error Selecting Drive dialog box shown in Figure 2-26. The dialog box contains an error message (The disk in drive A is not formatted.), a suggested action (Do you want to format it now?), and the Yes and No buttons. To change the current drive after inserting an unformatted diskette into drive A, choose the Yes button to format the diskette and change the current drive. Choose the No button to cancel the change.

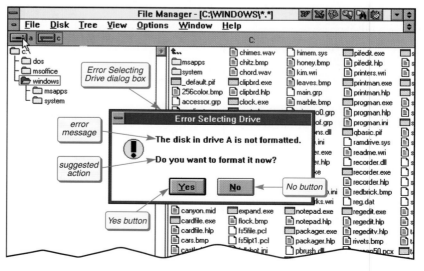

FIGURE 2-26

▶ RENAMING A FILE

 ometimes you may want to rename a file by changing its name or file-name extension. You change the name or extension of a file by selecting the filename in the contents list, choosing the **Rename command** from the File menu, entering the new filename, and choosing the OK button. In this project, you will change the name of the CARS.BMP file on the diskette in drive A to AUTOS.BMP.

TO RENAME A FILE ▼

STEP 1 ▶

Select the CARS.BMP entry by clicking the CARS.BMP filename in the contents list.

The CARS.BMP entry is high-lighted (Figure 2-27).

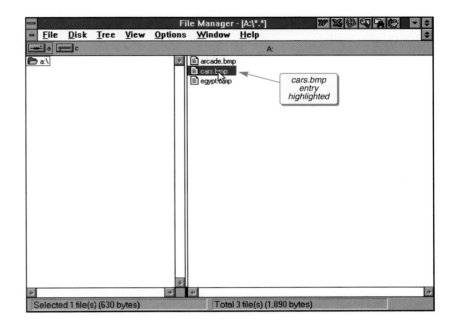

FIGURE 2-27

STEP 2 ▶

Select the File menu, and then point to the Rename command.

Windows opens the File menu (Figure 2-28). The mouse pointer points to the Rename command.

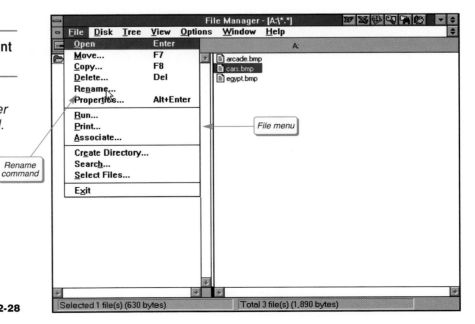

FIGURE 2-28

STEP 3 ►

Choose the Rename command from the File menu by clicking the left mouse button.

Windows opens the Rename dialog box (Figure 2-29). The dialog box contains the Current Directory : A:\ message, the From and To text boxes, and the OK, Cancel, and Help buttons. The From text box contains the CARS.BMP filename and the To text box contains an insertion point.

FIGURE 2-29

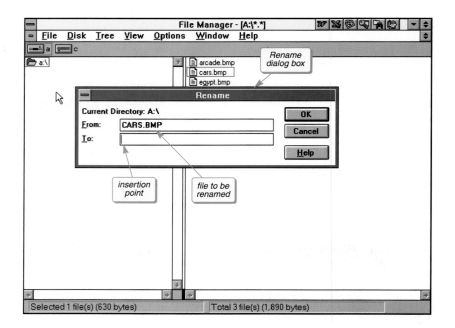

STEP 4 ►

Type `autos.bmp` **in the To text box, and then point to the OK button.**

The To text box contains the AUTOS.BMP filename and the mouse pointer points to the OK button (Figure 2-30).

FIGURE 2-30

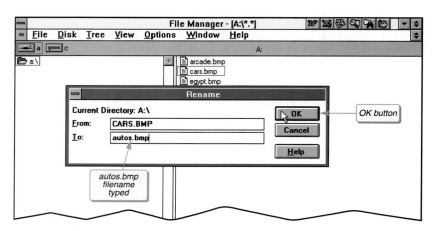

STEP 5 ►

Choose the OK button by clicking the left mouse button.

The filename in the cars.bmp entry changes to autos.bmp (Figure 2-31).

FIGURE 2-31

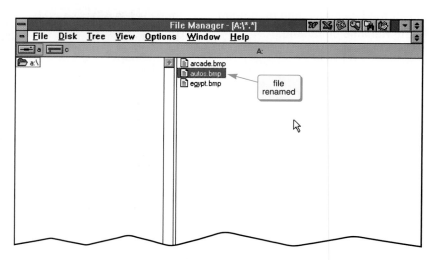

▶ DELETING A FILE

 hen you no longer need a file, you can delete it by selecting the filename in the contents list, choosing the **Delete command** from the File menu, choosing the OK button, and then choosing the Yes button. In this project, you will delete the EGYPT.BMP file from the diskette in drive A.

TO DELETE A FILE ▼

STEP 1 ▶

Select the EGYPT.BMP entry.

The EGYPT.BMP entry is high-lighted (Figure 2-32).

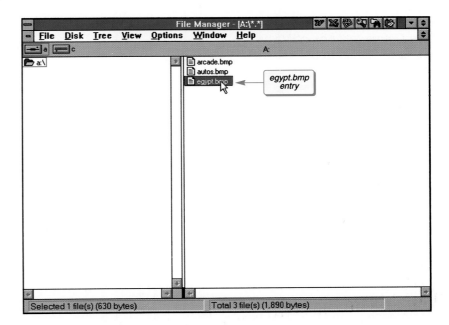

FIGURE 2-32

STEP 2 ▶

Select the File menu from the menu bar, and then point to the Delete command.

Windows opens the File menu (Figure 2-33). The mouse pointer points to the Delete command.

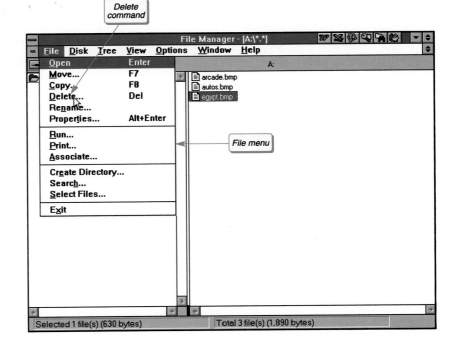

FIGURE 2-33

STEP 3 ▶

Choose the Delete command from the File menu by clicking the left mouse button, and then point to the OK button.

Windows opens the Delete dialog box (Figure 2-34). The dialog box contains the Current Directory: A:\ message, Delete text box, and the OK, Cancel, and Help buttons. The Delete text box contains the name of the file to be deleted (EGYPT.BMP), and the mouse pointer points to the OK button.

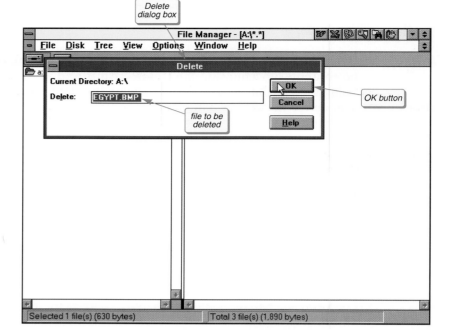

FIGURE 2-34

STEP 4 ▶

Choose the OK button by clicking the left mouse button, and then point to the Yes button.

Windows opens the Confirm File Delete dialog box (Figure 2-35). The dialog box contains the Delete File message and the path and filename of the file to delete (A:\EGYPT.BMP). The mouse pointer points to the Yes button.

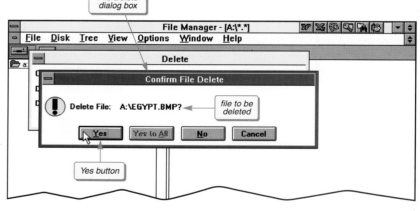

FIGURE 2-35

STEP 5 ▶

Choose the Yes button by clicking the left mouse button.

Windows deletes the EGYPT.BMP file from the diskette on drive A, removes the EGYPT.BMP entry from the contents list, and highlights the AUTOS.BMP file (Figure 2-36).

STEP 6

Remove the diskette from drive A.

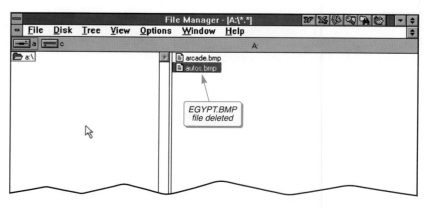

FIGURE 2-36

▶ CREATING A BACKUP DISKETTE

T o prevent accidental loss of a file on a diskette, you should make a backup copy of the diskette. A copy of a diskette made to prevent accidental loss of data is called a **backup diskette**. Always be sure to make backup diskettes before installing software stored on diskettes onto the hard drive.

The first step in creating a backup diskette is to protect the diskette to be copied, or **source diskette**, from accidental erasure by write-protecting the diskette. After write-protecting the source diskette, choose the **Copy Disk command** from the Disk menu to copy the contents of the source diskette to another diskette, called the **destination diskette**. After copying the source diskette to the destination diskette, remove the write-protection from the source diskette and identify the destination diskette by writing a name on the paper label supplied with the diskette and affixing the label to the diskette.

In this project, you will use File Manager to create a backup diskette for the Student Diskette included with this book. The Student Diskette contains valuable documents that should be backed up to prevent accidental loss. The source diskette will be the Student Diskette and the destination diskette will be a formatted diskette that will later be labeled Student Diskette Backup. To create a backup diskette, both the Student Diskette and the formatted diskette must be the same size and capacity.

File Manager copies a diskette by asking you to insert the source diskette into drive A, reading data from the source diskette into main memory, asking you to insert the destination disk, and then copying the data from main memory to the destination disk. Depending on the size of main memory on your computer, you may have to insert and remove the source and destination diskettes several times before the copy process is complete. The copy process takes about three minutes to complete.

TO COPY A DISKETTE ▼

STEP 1 ▶

Write-protect the Student Diskette by opening the write-protect window (Figure 2-37).

write-protect window
open means diskette
is write-protected

Student
Diskette

FIGURE 2-37

STEP 2 ▶

Select the Disk menu from the menu bar, and then point to the Copy Disk command.

Windows opens the Disk menu (Figure 2-38). The mouse pointer points to the Copy Disk command.

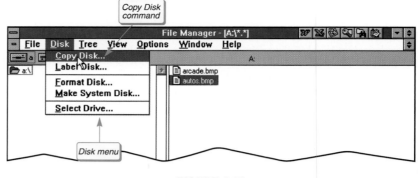

FIGURE 2-38

STEP 3 ▶

Choose the Copy Disk command from the Disk menu by clicking the left mouse button, and then point to the Yes button.

Windows opens the Confirm Copy Disk dialog box (Figure 2-39). The dialog box reminds you that the copy process will erase all data on the destination disk. The mouse pointer points to the Yes button.

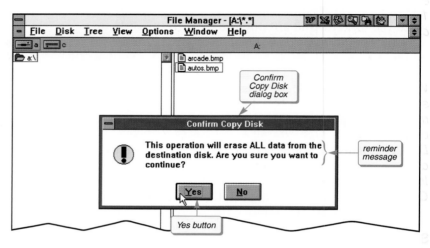

FIGURE 2-39

STEP 4 ▶

Choose the Yes button by clicking the left mouse button, and then point to the OK button.

Windows opens the Copy Disk dialog box (Figure 2-40). The dialog box contains the Insert source disk. message and the mouse pointer points to the OK button.

STEP 5

Insert the source diskette, the Student Diskette, into drive A.

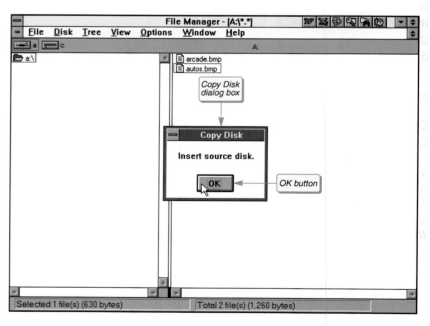

FIGURE 2-40

STEP 6 ▶

Choose the OK button in the Copy Disk dialog box by clicking the left mouse button.

Windows opens the Copying Disk dialog box (Figure 2-41). The dialog box contains the messages, Now Copying disk in Drive A:. and 1% completed. As the copy process progresses, a value from 1 to 100 indicates what percent of the copy process is complete.

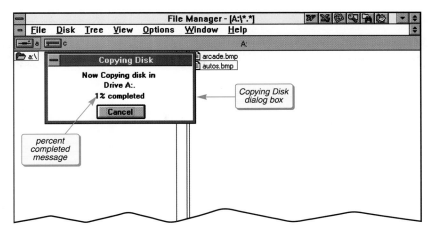

FIGURE 2-41

When as much data from the source diskette as will fit in main memory is copied to main memory, Windows opens the Copy Disk dialog box (Figure 2-42). The dialog box contains the message, Insert destination disk., and the OK button.

STEP 7 ▶

Remove the source diskette (Student Diskette) from drive A and insert the destination diskette (Student Diskette Backup diskette) into drive A.

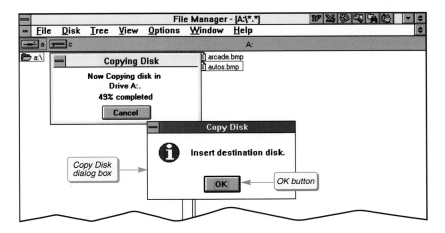

FIGURE 2-42

STEP 8 ▶

Choose the OK button from the Copy Disk dialog box.

Windows opens the Copying Disk dialog box (Figure 2-43). A value from 50 to 100 displays as the data in main memory is copied to the destination disk.

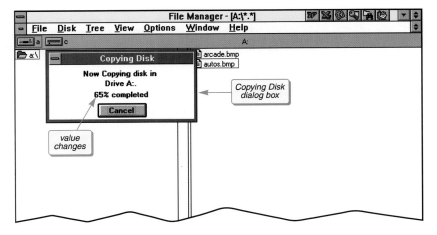

FIGURE 2-43

STEP 9 ▶

Remove the Student Diskette Backup diskette from drive A and remove the write-protection from the Student Diskette by closing the write-protect window.

The write-protection is removed from the 3 1/2-inch Student Diskette (Figure 2-44).

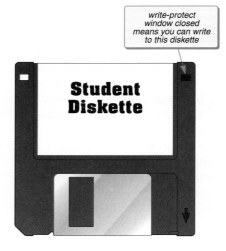

write-protect window closed means you can write to this diskette

FIGURE 2-44

STEP 10 ▶

Identify the Student Diskette Backup diskette by writing the words Student Diskette Backup on the paper label supplied with the diskette and then affix the label to the diskette (Figure 2-45).

FIGURE 2-45

Depending on the size of main memory on your computer, you may have to insert and remove the source and destination diskettes several times before the copy process is complete. If prompted by Windows to insert the source diskette, remove the destination diskette (Student Diskette Backup diskette) from drive A, insert the source diskette (Student Diskette) into drive A, and then choose the OK button. If prompted to insert the destination diskette, remove the source diskette (Student Diskette) from drive A, insert the destination diskette (Student Diskette Backup diskette) into drive A, and then choose the OK button.

In the future if you change the contents of the Student Diskette, choose the Copy Disk command to copy the contents of the Student Diskette to the Student Diskette Backup diskette. If the Student Diskette becomes unusable, you can format a diskette, choose the Copy Disk command to copy the contents of the Student Diskette Backup diskette (source diskette) to the formatted diskette (destination diskette), label the formatted diskette, Student Diskette, and use the new Student Diskette in place of the unusable Student Diskette.

Correcting Errors Encountered While Copying a Diskette

When you try to copy a disk and forget to insert the source diskette when prompted, insert an unformatted source diskette, forget to insert the destination diskette when prompted, or insert a write-protected destination diskette, Windows opens the Copy Disk Error dialog box illustrated in Figure 2-46. The dialog box contains the Unable to copy disk. error message, and OK button. To complete the copy process after forgetting to insert a source diskette or inserting an unformatted source diskette, choose the OK button, insert the formatted source diskette into the diskette drive, and choose the **Disk Copy command** to start over the disk copy process. To complete the copy process after forgetting to insert a destination diskette or inserting a write-protected destination diskette, choose the OK button, insert a nonwrite-protected diskette in the diskette drive, and choose the Disk Copy command to restart the disk copy process.

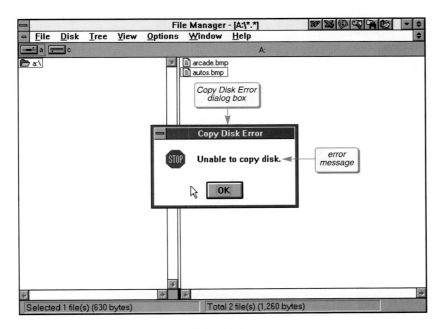

FIGURE 2-46

▶ SEARCHING FOR HELP USING ONLINE HELP

I n Project 1, you obtained help about the Paintbrush application by choosing the Contents command from the Help menu of the Paintbrush window (see pages WIN33 through WIN35). You then chose a topic from a list of help topics on the screen. In addition to choosing a topic from a list of available help topics, you can use the Search feature to search for help topics. In this project, you will use the Search feature to obtain help about copying files and selecting groups of files using the keyboard.

Searching for a Help Topic

In this project, you used a mouse to select and copy a group of files. If you want to obtain information about how to select a group of files using the keyboard instead of the mouse, you can use the Search feature. A search can be performed in one of two ways. The first method allows you to select a search topic from a list of search topics. A list of help topics associated with the search topic displays. You then select a help topic from this list. To begin the search, choose the **Search for Help on command** from the Help menu.

TO SEARCH FOR A HELP TOPIC ▼

STEP 1 ►

Select the Help menu from the File Manager window menu bar, and then point to the Search for Help on command.

*Windows opens the **Help menu** (Figure 2-47). The mouse pointer points to the Search for Help on command.*

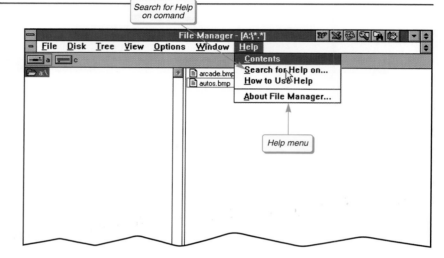

FIGURE 2-47

STEP 2 ►

Choose the Search for Help on command from the Help menu by clicking the left mouse button.

Windows opens the Search dialog box (Figure 2-48). The dialog box consists of two areas separated by a horizontal line. The top area contains the Search For text box, Search For list box, and Cancel and Show Topics buttons. The Search For list box contains an alphabetical list of search topics. A vertical scroll bar indicates there are more search topics than appear in the list box. The Cancel button cancels the Search operation. The Show Topics button is dimmed and cannot be chosen. The bottom area of the dialog box contains the empty Help Topics list box and the dimmed Go To button.

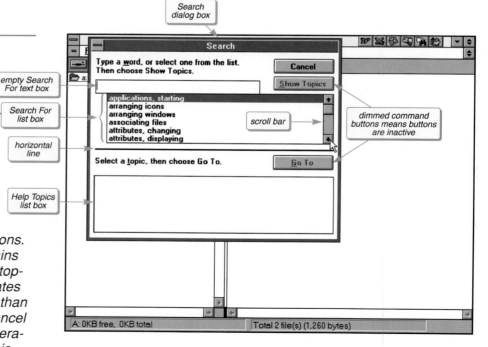

FIGURE 2-48

STEP 3 ▶

Point to the down scroll arrow in the Search For list box (Figure 2-49).

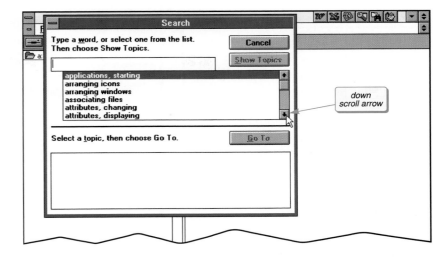

FIGURE 2-49

STEP 4 ▶

Hold down the left mouse button until the selecting files search topic is visible, and then point to the selecting files search topic (Figure 2-50).

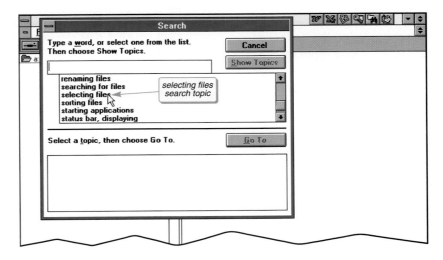

FIGURE 2-50

STEP 5 ▶

Select the selecting files search topic by clicking the left mouse button, and then point to the Show Topics button (Show Topics).

The selecting files search topic is highlighted in the Search For list box and displays in the Search For text box (Figure 2-51). The Show Topics button is no longer dimmed and the mouse pointer points to the Show Topics button.

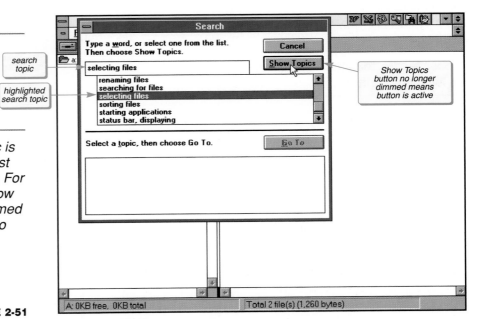

FIGURE 2-51

STEP 6 ▶

Choose the Show Topics button by clicking the left mouse button, and then point to the Using the Keyboard to Select Files help topic.

*The Help Topics list box contains four help topics (Figure 2-52). The Go To button (*Go To*) is no longer dimmed, and the mouse pointer points to the Using the Keyboard to Select Files help topic.*

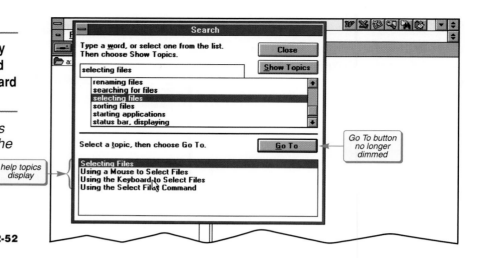

FIGURE 2-52

STEP 7 ▶

Select the Using the Keyboard to Select Files help topic by clicking the left mouse button, and then point to the Go To button.

The Using the Keyboard to Select Files help topic is highlighted in the Help Topics list box and the mouse pointer points to the Go To button (Figure 2-53).

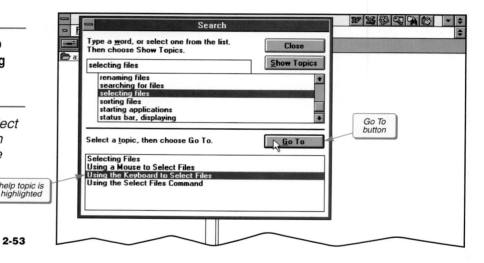

FIGURE 2-53

STEP 8 ▶

Choose the Go To button by clicking the left mouse button.

Windows closes the Search dialog box and opens the File Manager Help window (Figure 2-54). The Using the Keyboard to Select Files screen displays in the window.

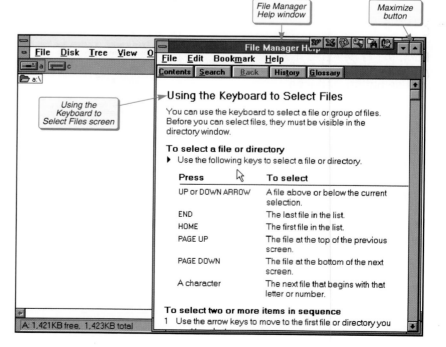

FIGURE 2-54

STEP 9 ▶

Click the Maximize button (▲) to maximize the File Manager Help window (Figure 2-55).

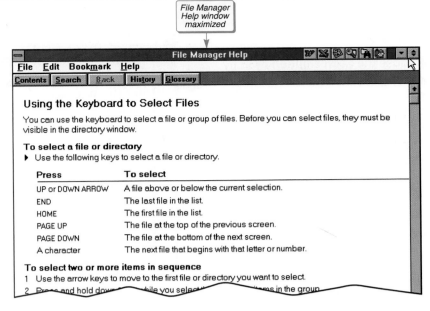

FIGURE 2-55

Searching for Help Using a Word or Phrase

The second method you can use to search for help involves entering a word or phrase to assist the Search feature in finding help related to the word or phrase. In this project, you copied a group of files from the hard disk to a diskette. To obtain additional information about copying files, choose the Search button and type copy from the keyboard.

TO SEARCH FOR A HELP TOPIC ▼

STEP 1 ▶

Point to the Search button (Search) (Figure 2-56).

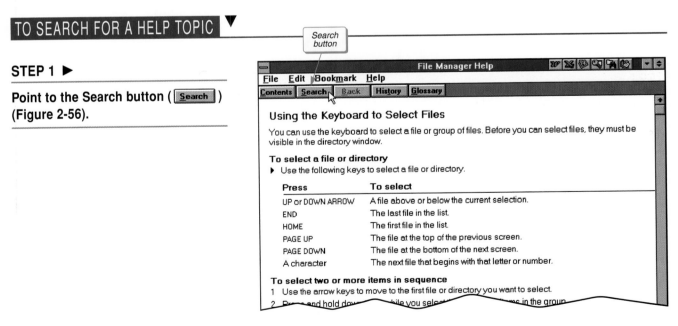

FIGURE 2-56

STEP 2 ▶

Choose the Search button by clicking the left mouse button, and then type `copy`

Windows opens the Search dialog box (Figure 2-57). As you type the word copy, each letter of the word displays in the Search For text box and the Search For Topics in the Search For Topics list box change. When the entry of the word is complete, the word copy displays in the Search For text box and the Search For topics beginning with the four letters c-o-p-y display first in the Search For list box.

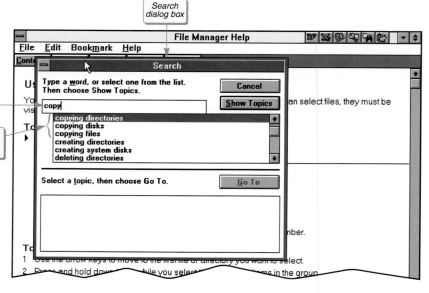

FIGURE 2-57

STEP 3 ▶

Select the copying files search topic by pointing to the topic and clicking the left mouse button, and then point to the Show Topics button.

The copying files search topic is highlighted in the Search For list box and displays in the Search For text box (Figure 2-58).

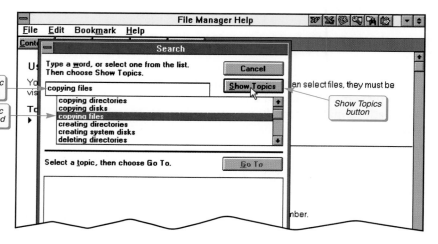

FIGURE 2-58

STEP 4 ▶

Choose the Show Topics button by clicking the left mouse button, and then point to the Go To button.

Only the Copying Files and Directories help topic displays in the Help Topic list box (Figure 2-59).

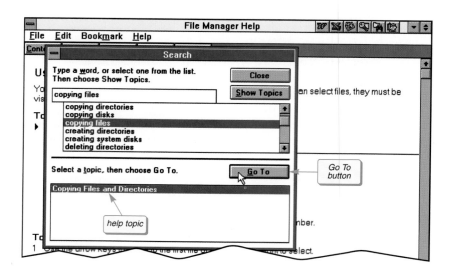

FIGURE 2-59

STEP 5 ▶

Choose the Go To button by clicking the left mouse button.

Windows closes the Search dialog box and displays the Copying Files and Directories help screen (Figure 2-60).

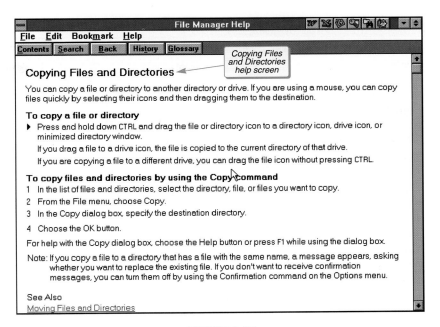

FIGURE 2-60

Quitting File Manager and Online Help

When you finish using File Manager and Windows online Help, you should quit the File Manager Help and File Manager applications. One method of quitting these applications is to first quit the File Manager Help application, and then quit the File Manager application. However, because quitting an application automatically quits the help application associated with that application, you can simply quit the File Manager application to quit both applications. Because the Program Manager and File Manager windows are hidden behind the File Manager Help window (see Figure 2-60), you must move the File Manager window on top of the other windows before quitting File Manager. To do this, you must switch to the File Manager application.

▶ SWITCHING BETWEEN APPLICATIONS

Each time you start an application and maximize its window, its application window displays on top of the other windows on the desktop. To display a hidden application window, you must switch between applications on the desktop using the ALT and TAB keys. To switch to another application, hold down the ALT key, press the TAB key one or more times, and then release the ALT key. Each time you press the TAB key, a box containing an application icon and application window title opens on the desktop. To display the File Manager window, you will have to press the TAB key only once.

TO SWITCH BETWEEN APPLICATIONS ▼

STEP 1 ▶

Hold down the ALT key, and then press the TAB key.

A box containing the File Manager application icon and window title (File Manager) displays (Figure 2-61).

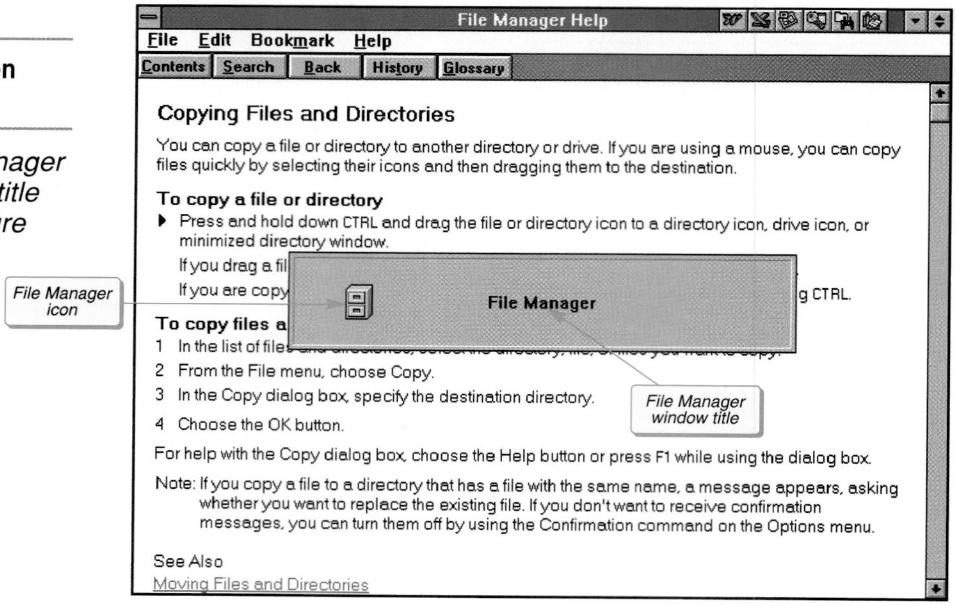

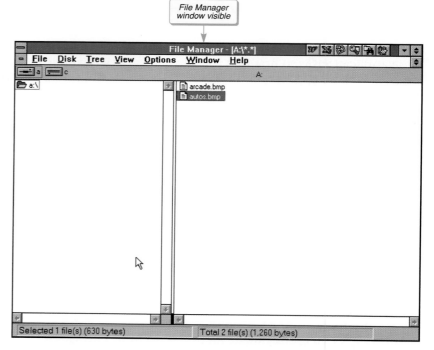

FIGURE 2-61

STEP 2 ▶

Release the ALT key.

The File Manager window moves on top of the other windows on the desktop (Figure 2-62).

FIGURE 2-62

Verify Changes to the File Manager Window Will Not Be Saved

Because you want to return the File Manager window to its state before you started the application, no changes should be saved. The **Save Settings on Exit command** on the Options menu controls whether changes to the File Manager window are saved or not saved when you quit File Manager. A check mark ($\sqrt{}$) preceding the Save Settings on Exit command indicates the command is active and all changes to the layout of the File Manager window will be saved when you quit File Manager. If the command is preceded by a check mark, choose the Save Settings on Exit command by clicking the left mouse button to remove the check mark, so the changes will not be saved. Perform the following steps to verify that changes are not saved to the File Manager window.

TO VERIFY CHANGES WILL NOT BE SAVED ▼

STEP 1 ▶

Select the Options menu from the File Manager menu bar.

*The **Options menu** opens (Figure 2-63). A check mark ($\sqrt{}$) precedes the Save Settings on Exit command.*

STEP 2

To remove the check mark, choose the Save Settings on Exit command from the Options menu by pointing to the Save Settings on Exit command and clicking the left mouse button.

Windows closes the Options menu. Although not visible, the check mark preceding the Save Settings on Exit command has been removed. This means any changes made to the desktop will not be saved when you exit File Manager.

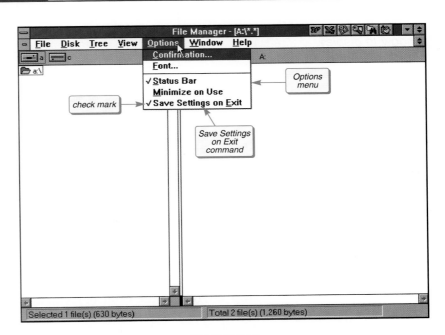

FIGURE 2-63

Quitting File Manager

After verifying no changes to the File Manager window will be saved, the Save Settings on Exit command is not active, so you can quit the File Manager application. In Project 1 you chose the Exit command from the File menu to quit an application. In addition to choosing a command from a menu, you can also quit an application by pointing to the **Control-menu box** in the upper left corner of the application window and double-clicking the left mouse button, as shown in the steps on the next page.

TO QUIT AN APPLICATION ▼

STEP 1 ▶

Point to the Control-menu box in the upper left corner of the File Manager window (Figure 2-64).

STEP 2 ▶

Double-click the left mouse button to exit the File Manager application.

Windows closes the File Manager and File Manager Help windows, causing the Program Manager window to display.

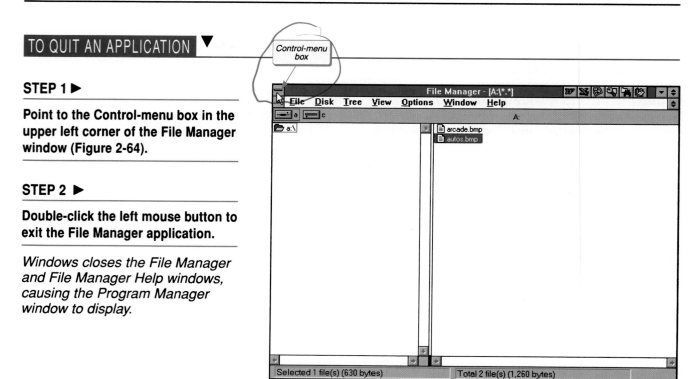

FIGURE 2-64

TO QUIT WINDOWS

Step 1: Select the Options menu from the Program Manager menu bar.
Step 2: If a check mark precedes the Save Settings on Exit command, choose the Save Settings on Exit command.
Step 3: Point to the Control-menu box in the upper left corner of the Program Manager window.
Step 4: Double-click the left mouse button.
Step 5: Choose the OK button to exit Windows.

▶ ADDITIONAL COMMANDS AND CONCEPTS

I n addition to the commands and concepts presented in Project 1 and this project, you should understand how to activate a group window, arrange the program-item icons in a group window, and close a group window. These topics are discussed on the following pages. In addition, methods to resize a window and minimize an application window to an application icon are explained.

Activating a Group Window

Frequently, several group windows are open in the Program Manager window at the same time. In Figure 2-65, two group windows (Main and Accessories) are open. The Accessories window is the active group window, and the inactive Main window is partially hidden behind the Accessories window. To view a group window that is partially hidden, activate the hidden window by selecting the Window menu and then choosing the name of the group window you wish to view.

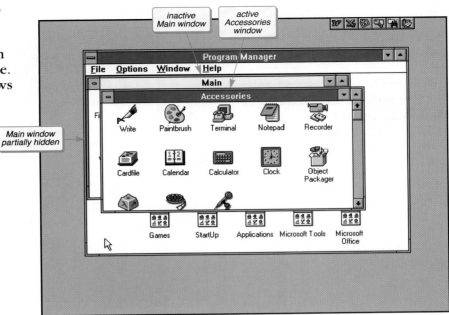

FIGURE 2-65

TO ACTIVATE A GROUP WINDOW ▼

STEP 1 ►

Select the Window menu from the Program Manager menu bar, and then point to the Main group window name.

*The **Window menu** consists of two areas separated by a horizontal line (Figure 2-66). Below the line is a list of the group windows and group icons in the Program Manager window. Each entry in the list is preceded by a value from one to seven. The number of the active window (Accessories) is preceded by a check mark and the mouse pointer points to the Main group window name.*

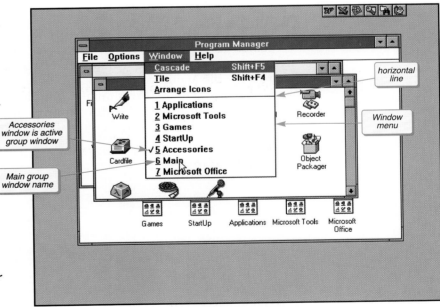

FIGURE 2-66

STEP 2 ▶

Choose the Main group window name by clicking the left mouse button.

The Main window moves on top of the Accessories window (Figure 2-67). The Main window is now the active window.

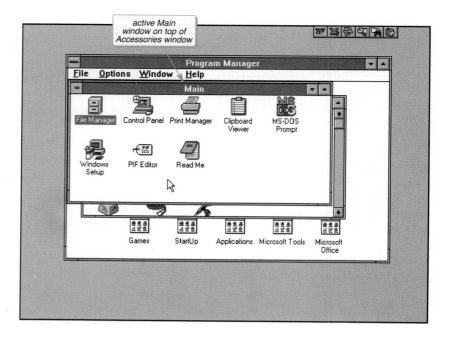

FIGURE 2-67

An alternative method of activating an inactive window is to point to any open area of the window and click the left mouse button. This method cannot be used if the inactive window is completely hidden behind another window.

Closing a Group Window

When several group windows are open in the Program Manager window, you may want to close a group window to reduce the number of open windows. In Figure 2-68, the Main, Accessories, and Games windows are open. To close the Games window, choose the Minimize button on the right side of the Games title bar. Choosing the Minimize button removes the group window from the desktop and displays the Games group icon at the bottom of the Program Manager window.

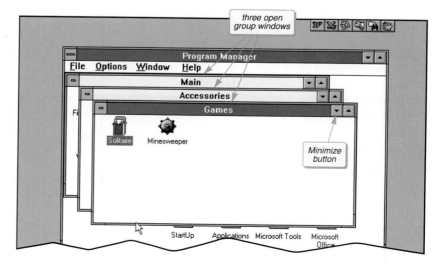

FIGURE 2-68

TO CLOSE A GROUP WINDOW ▼

STEP 1 ►

Choose the Minimize button (▾) on the Games title bar.

The Games window closes and the Games icon displays at the bottom edge of the Program Manager window (Figure 2-69).

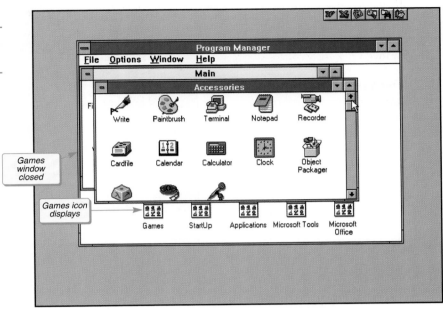

FIGURE 2-69

Resizing a Group Window

When more than six group icons display at the bottom of the Program Manager window, some group icons may not be completely visible. In Figure 2-70, the name of the CompuServe icon is partially visible. To make the icon visible, resize the Main window by dragging the bottom window border toward the window title.

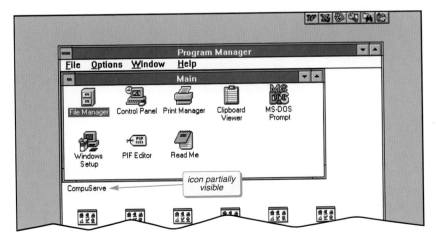

FIGURE 2-70

TO RESIZE A WINDOW ▼

STEP 1 ▶

Point to the bottom border of the Main window.

As the mouse pointer approaches the window border, the mouse pointer changes to a double-headed arrow icon (⬍) (Figure 2-71).

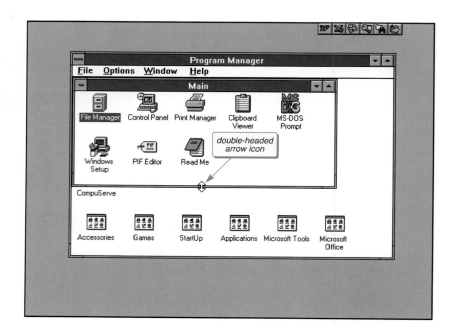

FIGURE 2-71

STEP 2 ▶

Drag the bottom border toward the window title until the CompuServe icon is visible.

The Main window changes shape, and the CompuServe icon is visible (Figure 2-72).

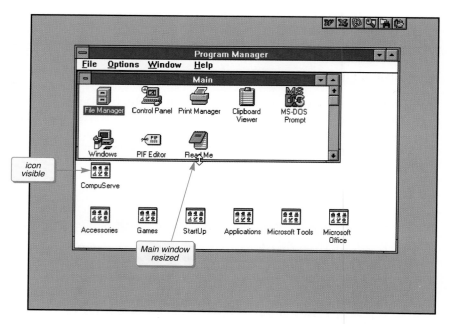

FIGURE 2-72

In addition to dragging a window border to resize a window, you can also drag a window corner to resize the window. By dragging a corner, you can change both the width and length of a window.

Arranging Icons

Occasionally, a program-item icon is either accidentally or intentionally moved within a group window. The result is that the program-item icons are not arranged in an organized fashion in the window. Figure 2-73 shows the eight program-item icons in the Main window. One icon, the File Manager icon, is not aligned with the other icons. As a result, the icons in the Main window appear unorganized. To arrange the icons in the Main window, choose the **Arrange Icons command** from the Window menu.

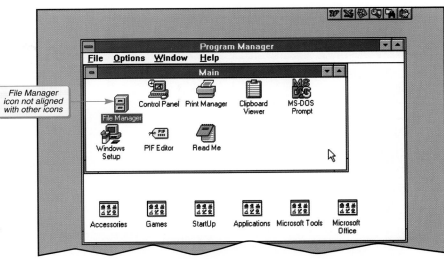

FIGURE 2-73

TO ARRANGE PROGRAM-ITEM ICONS ▼

STEP 1 ▶

Select the Window menu from the Program Manager menu bar, and then point to the Arrange Icons command.

Windows opens the Window menu (Figure 2-74). The mouse pointer points to the Arrange Icons command.

FIGURE 2-74

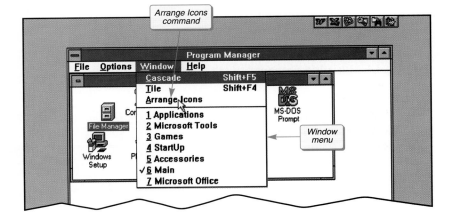

STEP 2 ▶

Choose the Arrange Icons command by clicking the left mouse button.

The icons in the Main window are arranged (Figure 2-75).

FIGURE 2-75

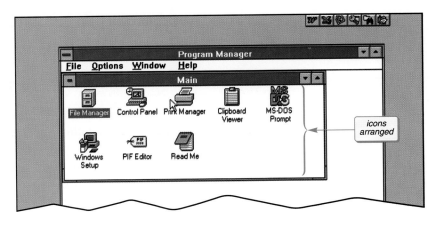

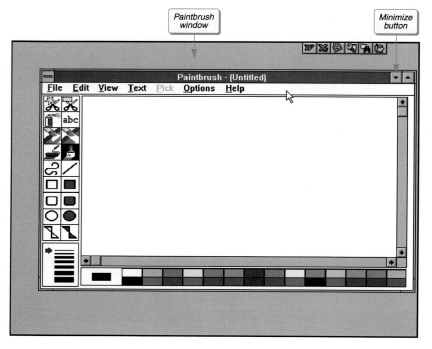

FIGURE 2-76

Minimizing an Application Window to an Icon

When you finish work in an application and there is a possibility of using the application again before quitting Windows, you should minimize the application window to an application icon instead of quitting the application. An **application icon** represents an application that was started and then minimized. Minimizing a window to an application icon saves you the time of starting the application and maximizing its window if you decide to use the application again. In addition, you free space on the desktop without quitting the application. The desktop in Figure 2-76 contains the Paintbrush window. To minimize the Paintbrush window to an application icon, click the Minimize button on the right side of the Paintbrush title bar.

TO MINIMIZE AN APPLICATION WINDOW TO AN ICON ▼

STEP 1 ▶

Click the Minimize button on the right side of the Paintbrush title bar.

Windows closes the Paintbrush window and displays the Paintbrush application icon at the bottom of the desktop (Figure 2-77).

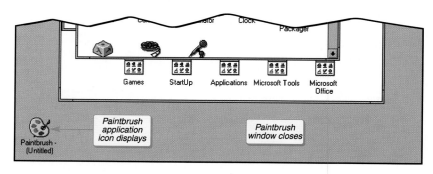

FIGURE 2-77

After minimizing an application window to an application icon, you can start the application again by double-clicking the application icon.

▶ PROJECT SUMMARY

In this project, you used File Manager to format and copy a diskette, copy a group of files, and rename and delete a file. You searched for help about File Manager using the Search feature of online Help, and you switched between applications on the desktop. In addition, you activated, resized, and closed a group window, arranged the icons in a group window, and minimized an application window to an application icon.

▶ KEY TERMS AND INDEX

application icon *(WIN86)*
Arrange Icons command
  (WIN85)
backup diskette *(WIN48,*
  WIN67)
Cascade command *(WIN94)*
contents list *(WIN51)*
Control-menu box *(WIN79)*
Copy Disk command *(WIN67)*
current drive *(WIN50)*
Delete command *(WIN65)*
destination directory *(WIN55)*
destination diskette *(WIN67)*

destination drive *(WIN55)*
directory structure *(WIN50)*
directory tree *(WIN50)*
directory window *(WIN50)*
Disk Copy command *(WIN71)*
Disk menu *(WIN52)*
diskette capacity *(WIN51)*
diskette size *(WIN51)*
drive icons *(WIN50)*
File Manager *(WIN48)*
Format Disk command *(WIN52)*
formatting *(WIN51)*
Help menu *(WIN72)*

Options menu *(WIN79)*
Rename command *(WIN63)*
Save Settings on Exit command
  (WIN79)
Search for Help on command
  (WIN72)
source directory *(WIN55)*
source diskette *(WIN67)*
source drive *(WIN55)*
split bar *(WIN50)*
Tile command *(WIN94)*
Window menu *(WIN81)*

Q U I C K   R E F E R E N C E

In Windows you can accomplish a task in a number of ways. The following table provides a quick reference to each task presented in the project with its available options. The commands listed in the Menu column can be executed using either the keyboard or mouse.

Task	Mouse	Menu	Keyboard Shortcuts
Activate a Group Window	Click group window	From Window menu, choose window title	
Arrange Program-Item Icons in a Group Window		From Window menu, choose Arrange Icons	
Change the Current Drive	Click drive icon		Press TAB to move highlight to drive icon area, press arrow keys to outline drive icon, and press ENTER
Close a Group Window	Click Minimize button or double-click Control-menu box	From Control menu, choose Close	Press CTRL+F4
Copy a Diskette		From Disk menu, choose Copy Disk	
Copy a File or Group of Files	Drag highlighted file-name(s) to destination drive or directory icon	From File menu, choose Copy	
Delete a File		From File menu, choose Delete	Press DEL
Format a Diskette		From Disk menu, choose Format Disk	

(continued)

QUICK REFERENCE (continued)

Task	Mouse	Menu	Keyboard Shortcuts
Maximize a Directory Window	Click Maximize button	From Control menu, choose Maximize	
Minimize an Application Window	Click Minimize button	From Control menu, choose Minimize	Press ALT, SPACEBAR, N
Rename a File		From File menu, choose Rename	
Resize a Window	Drag window border or corner	From Control menu, choose Size	
Save Changes when Quitting File Manager		From Options menu, choose Save Settings on Exit if no check mark precedes command	
Save No Changes when Quitting Windows		From Options menu, choose Save Settings on Exit if check mark precedes command	
Search for a Help Topic		From Help menu, choose Search for Help on	
Select a File in the Contents List	Click the filename		Press arrow keys to outline filename, press SHIFT+F8
Select a Group of Files in the Contents list	Select first file, hold down CTRL key and select other files		Press arrow keys to outline first file, press SHIFT+F8, press arrow keys to outline each additional filename, and press SPACEBAR
Switch between Applications	Click application window		Hold down ALT, press TAB (or ESC), release ALT

S T U D E N T   A S S I G N M E N T S

STUDENT ASSIGNMENT 1
True/False

Instructions: Circle T if the statement is true or F if the statement if false.

T   F   1. Formatting prepares a diskette for use on a computer.

T   F   2. It is not important to create a backup diskette of the Student Diskette.

T   F   3. Program Manager is an application you can use to organize and work with your hard disk and diskettes and the files on those disks.

T   F   4. A directory window title bar usually contains the current directory path.

T   F   5. A directory window consists of a directory tree and contents list.

T   F   6. The directory tree contains a list of the files in the current directory.

T   F   7. The disk capacity of a 3 1/2-inch diskette is typically 360K or 1.2MB.

T   F   8. The source drive is the drive from which files are copied.

T F 9. You select a single file in the contents list by pointing to the filename and clicking the left mouse button.

T F 10. You select a group of files in the contents list by pointing to each filename and clicking the left mouse button.

T F 11. Windows opens the Error Copying File dialog box if you try to copy a file to an unformatted diskette.

T F 12. You change the filename or extension of a file using the Change command.

T F 13. Windows opens the Confirm File Delete dialog box when you try to delete a file.

T F 14. When creating a backup diskette, the disk to receive the copy is the source disk.

T F 15. The first step in creating a backup diskette is to choose the Copy Disk command from the Disk menu.

T F 16. On some computers, you may have to insert and remove the source and destination diskettes several times to copy a diskette.

T F 17. Both the Search for Help on command and the Search button initiate a search for help.

T F 18. An application icon represents an application that was started and then minimized.

T F 19. You hold down the TAB key, press the ALT key, and then release the TAB key to switch between applications on the desktop.

T F 20. An application icon displays on the desktop when you minimize an application window.

STUDENT ASSIGNMENT 2
Multiple Choice

Instructions: Circle the correct response.

1. The _____ application allows you to format a diskette.
   a. Program Manager
   b. File Manager
   c. online Help
   d. Paintbrush
2. The _____ contains the directory structure of the current drive.
   a. contents list
   b. status bar
   c. split bar
   d. directory tree
3. The _____ key is used when selecting a group of files.
   a. CTRL
   b. ALT
   c. TAB
   d. ESC
4. After selecting a group of files, you _____ the group of files to copy the files to a new drive or directory.
   a. click
   b. double-click
   c. drag
   d. none of the above
5. The commands to rename and delete a file are located on the _____ menu.
   a. Window
   b. Options
   c. Disk
   d. File
6. The first step in creating a backup diskette is to _____.
   a. write-protect the destination diskette
   b. choose the Copy command from the Disk menu
   c. write-protect the source diskette
   d. label the destination diskette

(continued)

STUDENT ASSIGNMENT 2 (continued)

7. When searching for help, the _____ button displays a list of Help topics.
   a. Go To
   b. Topics
   c. Show Topics
   d. Search

8. You use the _____ and _____ keys to switch between applications on the desktop.
   a. ALT, TAB
   b. SHIFT, ALT
   c. ALT, CTRL
   d. ESC, CTRL

9. When you choose a window title from the Window menu, Windows _____ the associated group window.
   a. opens
   b. closes
   c. enlarges
   d. activates

10. To resize a group window, you can use the _____.
    a. title bar
    b. window border
    c. Resize command on the Window menu
    d. Arrange Icons command on the Options menu

STUDENT ASSIGNMENT 3
Identifying the Parts of a Directory Window

Instructions: On the desktop in Figure SA2-3, arrows point to several items in the C:\WINDOWS*.* directory window. Identify the items in the spaces provided.

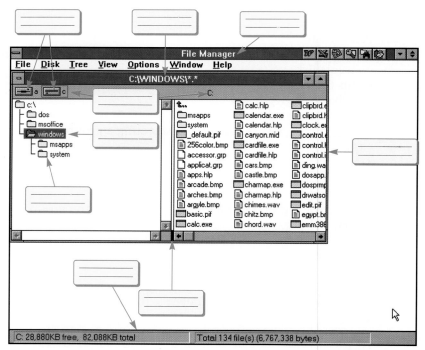

FIGURE SA2-3

STUDENT ASSIGNMENT 4
Selecting a Group of Files

Instructions: Using the desktop in Figure SA2-4, list the steps to select the group of files consisting of the ARCADE.BMP, CARS.BMP, and EGYPT.BMP files in the spaces provided.

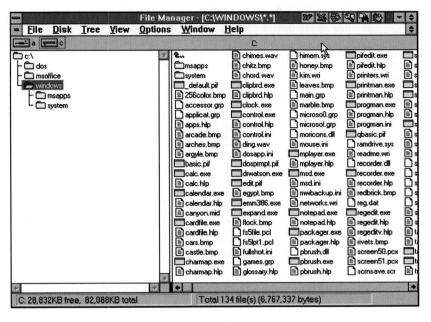

FIGURE SA2-4

Step 1: _____

Step 2: _____

Step 3: _____

Step 4: _____

STUDENT ASSIGNMENT 5
Copying a Group of Files

Instructions: Using the desktop in Figure SA2-5, list the steps to copy the group of files selected in Student Assignment 4 to the root directory of drive A. Write the steps in the spaces provided.

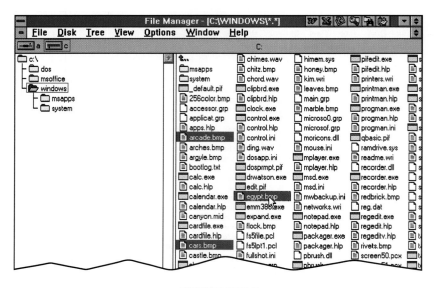

FIGURE SA2-5

Step 1: _____

Step 2: _____

Step 3: _____

Step 4: _____

STUDENT ASSIGNMENT 6
Searching for Help

Instructions: Using the desktop in Figure SA2-6, list the steps to complete the search for the Using the Keyboard to Select Files help topic. The mouse pointer points to the down scroll arrow. Write the steps in the spaces provided.

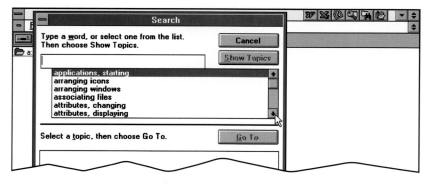

FIGURE SA2-6

Step 1: _____

Step 2: _____

Step 3: _____

Step 4: _____

Step 5: _____

Step 6: _____

C O M P U T E R   L A B O R A T O R Y   E X E R C I S E S

COMPUTER LABORATORY EXERCISE 1
Selecting and Copying Files

Instructions: Perform the following tasks using a computer:

Part 1:

1. Start Windows.
2. Double-click the File Manager icon to start File Manager.
3. Click the Maximize button on the File Manager window to enlarge the File Manager window.
4. Click the Maximize button on the C:\WINDOWS*.* window to enlarge the C:\WINDOWS*.* window.
5. Select the CHITZ.BMP file.
6. Hold down the CTRL key and click the LEAVES.BMP filename to select the LEAVES.BMP file. The CHITZ.BMP and LEAVES.BMP files should both be highlighted.
7. Insert the Student Diskette into drive A.
8. Drag the group of files to the drive A icon.
9. Choose the Yes button in the Confirm Mouse Operation dialog box.
10. Choose the drive A icon to change the current drive to drive A.
11. Select the CHITZ.BMP file.
12. Choose the Delete command from the File menu.
13. Choose the OK button in the Delete dialog box.
14. Choose the Yes button in the Confirm File Delete dialog box.
15. If the LEAVES.BMP file is not highlighted, select the LEAVES.BMP file.
16. Choose the Rename command from the File menu.
17. Type AUTUMN.BMP in the To text box.
18. Choose the OK button in the Rename dialog box to rename the LEAVES.BMP file.

Part 2:

1. Hold down the ALT key, press the TAB key, and release the ALT key to switch to the Program Manager application.
2. Double-click the Accessories icon to open the Accessories window.
3. Double-click the Paintbrush icon to start Paintbrush.
4. Click the Maximize button on the Paintbrush window to enlarge the Paintbrush window.
5. Choose the Open command from the File menu.
6. Click the Down Arrow button in the Drives drop-down list box to display the Drives drop-down list.
7. Select the drive A icon.
8. Select the AUTUMN.BMP file in the File Name list box.
9. Choose the OK button to retrieve the AUTUMN.BMP file into Paintbrush.
10. Choose the Print command from the File menu.

(continued)

COMPUTER LABORATORY EXERCISE 1 (continued)

11. Click the Draft option button in the Print dialog box.
12. Choose the OK button in the Print dialog box to print the contents of the AUTUMN.BMP file.
13. Remove the Student Diskette from drive A.
14. Choose the Exit command from the File menu to quit Paintbrush.
15. Hold down the ALT key, press the TAB key, and release the ALT key to switch to the File Manager application.
16. Select the Options menu.
17. If a check mark precedes the Save Settings on Exit command, choose the Save Settings on Exit command.
18. Choose the Exit command from the File menu of the File Manager window to quit File Manager.
19. Choose the Exit Windows command from the File menu of the Program Manager window.
20. Click the OK button to quit Windows.

COMPUTER LABORATORY EXERCISE 2
Searching with Online Help

Instructions: Perform the following tasks using a computer:

1. Start Microsoft Windows.
2. Double-click the Accessories icon to open the Accessories window.
3. Double-click the Write icon to start the Write application.
4. Click the Maximize button on the Write window to enlarge the Write window.
5. Choose the Search for Help on command from the Help menu.
6. Scroll the Search For list box to make the cutting text topic visible.
7. Select the cutting text topic.
8. Choose the Show Topics button.
9. Choose the Go To button to display the Copying, Cutting, and Pasting Text topic.
10. Click the Maximize button on the Write Help window to enlarge the window.
11. Choose the Print Topic command from the File menu to print the Copying, Cutting, and Pasting Text topic on the printer.
12. Choose the Search button.
13. Enter the word paste in the Search For list box.
14. Select the Pasting Pictures search topic.
15. Choose the Show Topics button.
16. Choose the Go To button to display the Copying, Cutting, and Pasting Pictures topic.
17. Choose the Print Topic command from the File menu to print the Copying, Cutting, and Pasting Pictures topic on the printer.
18. Choose the Exit command from the File menu to quit Write Help.
19. Choose the Exit command from the File menu to quit Write.
20. Select the Options menu.
21. If a check mark precedes the Save Settings on Exit command, choose the Save Settings on Exit command.
22. Choose the Exit Windows command from the File menu.
23. Click the OK button to quit Windows.

COMPUTER LABORATORY EXERCISE 3
Working with Group Windows

Instructions: Perform the following tasks using a computer:

1. Start Windows. The Main window should be open in the Program Manager window.
2. Double-click the Accessories icon to open the Accessories window.
3. Double-click the Games icon to open the Games window.
4. Choose the Accessories window title from the Window menu to activate the Accessories window.
5. Click the Minimize button on the Accessories window to close the Accessories window.
6. Choose the **Tile command** from the Window menu. The Tile command arranges a group of windows so no windows overlap, all windows are visible, and each window occupies an equal portion of the screen.
7. Move and resize the Main and Games windows to resemble the desktop in Figure CLE2-3. To resize a window, drag the window border or corner. To move a group window, drag the window title bar. Choose the Arrange Icons command from the Window menu to arrange the icons in each window.

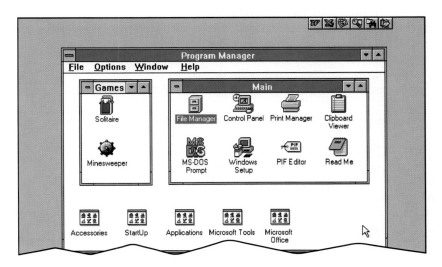

FIGURE CLE2-3

8. Press the PRINT SCREEN key to capture the desktop.
9. Open the Accessories window.
10. Choose the **Cascade command** from the Window menu. The Cascade command arranges a group of windows so the windows overlap and the title bar of each window is visible.
11. Double-click the Paintbrush icon to start Paintbrush.
12. Click the Maximize button on the Paintbrush window to enlarge the Paintbrush window.
13. Choose the Paste command from the Edit menu to place the picture of the desktop in the window.
14. Choose the Print command from the File menu.
15. Click the Draft option button.
16. Choose the OK button in the Print dialog box to print the desktop.
17. Choose the Exit command from the File menu of the Paintbrush window.
18. Choose the No button to not save current changes and quit Paintbrush.
19. Select the Options menu.
20. If a check mark precedes the Save Settings on Exit command, choose the Save Settings on Exit command.
21. Choose the Exit Windows command from the File menu.
22. Click the OK button.

COMPUTER LABORATORY EXERCISE 4
Backing Up Your Student Diskette

Instructions: Perform the following tasks using a computer to back up your Student Diskette:

Part 1:

1. Start Windows.
2. Double-click the File Manager icon to start the File Manager application.
3. Click the Maximize button on the File Manager window to enlarge the File Manager window.
4. Write-protect the Student Diskette.
5. Choose the Copy Disk command from the Disk menu.
6. Choose the Yes button in the Confirm Copy Disk dialog box.
7. Insert the source diskette (Student Diskette) into drive A.
8. Choose the OK button in the Copy Disk dialog box.
9. When prompted, insert the destination diskette (the formatted diskette created in this project) into drive A.
10. Choose the OK button in the Copy Disk dialog box.
11. Insert and remove the source and destination diskette until the copy process is complete.
12. Click the drive A icon to change the current drive to drive A.
13. Press the PRINT SCREEN key to capture the desktop.
14. Select the Options menu on the File Manager menu bar.
15. If a check mark precedes the Save Settings on Exit command, choose the Save Settings on Exit command.
16. Choose the Exit command from the File menu on the File Manager menu bar to quit File Manager.

Part 2:

1. Double-click the Accessories icon to open the Accessories window.
2. Double-click the Paintbrush icon to start Paintbrush.
3. Click the Maximize button to enlarge the Paintbrush window.
4. Choose the Paste command from the Edit menu to place the picture of the desktop in the window.
5. Choose the Print command from the File menu.
6. Click the Draft option button.
7. Choose the OK button in the Print dialog box to print the picture of the desktop on the printer.
8. Choose the Exit command from the File menu.
9. Choose the No button to not save current changes and quit Paintbrush.
10. Select the Options menu.
11. If a check mark precedes the Save Settings on Exit command, choose the Save Settings on Exit command.
12. Choose the Exit Windows command from the File menu of the Program Manager menu bar.
13. Click the OK button to quit Windows.
14. Remove the diskette from drive A.
15. Remove the write-protection from the Student Diskette.

USING *M*ICROSOFT *O*FFICE

Microsoft Office

AN INTRODUCTION TO MICROSOFT OFFICE

OBJECTIVES You will have mastered the material in this project when you can:

- ▸ Identify the applications in the Microsoft Office family
- ▸ Distinguish between the different versions of Microsoft Office
- ▸ Recognize the Microsoft Office Manager toolbar
- ▸ Start and quit an application using the Microsoft Office Manager toolbar
- ▸ Switch between applications using the Microsoft Office Manager toolbar

- ▸ Identify the commands on the Office menu
- ▸ Add a button to and remove a button from the Microsoft Office Manager toolbar
- ▸ Identify the commands on the shortcut menu
- ▸ Change the size of the Microsoft Office Manager toolbar
- ▸ Locate a file on disk using Find File

▶ THE MICROSOFT OFFICE FAMILY

T he **Microsoft Office family** is a collection of the most popular Microsoft application software products that work alike and work together as if they were a single program. Microsoft Office includes Microsoft Word, Microsoft Excel, Microsoft Access, and Microsoft PowerPoint. Microsoft Office also includes a license to use Microsoft Mail on your personal computer. An explanation of each of these application software packages is given on the following pages.

Microsoft Word

Microsoft Word is a powerful application software program that allows you to create documents by word processing. You use Microsoft Word to prepare all types of personal and business communications, including announcements, letters, memos, resumes, business and academic reports, as well as other forms of written documents. Microsoft Word can check a written document for incorrectly spelled words and grammar and automatically correct typing errors and expand abbreviations as you type. You can also use Microsoft Word's desktop publishing features to create professional looking brochures, advertisements, and newsletters.

Figure 1-1 illustrates the announcement created in Project 1 of the Microsoft Word section of this book. Also shown is the top portion of the announcement as it displays in the Microsoft Word window that opens when you start Microsoft Word from within Microsoft Office. The steps to create this announcement are shown in Project 1 of Microsoft Word.

THE JAZZICIANS

present the

4th Annual Festival of *Jazz*

- Join us for a fun-filled day of entertainment for the whole family.
- The fun starts at 10:00 a.m. and ends at 11:00 p.m. on **Saturday, October 14**, 1995, at Riverfront Park.
- Festival attractions include games, rides, food, crafts, and live music from the talented artists of The Brass Beat, Dave and the Hornets, and The Nance Lance Band.

Hope to see you there!

printed announcement

announcement displayed in Microsoft Word window

FIGURE 1-1

Microsoft Excel

Microsoft Excel is a spreadsheet program that allows you to organize data, perform calculations on the data, make decisions, create graphs and charts based upon the data, and develop professional looking reports.

Figure 1-2 illustrates the worksheet and column chart created in Project 1 of the Microsoft Excel section of this book. Also shown is the worksheet and column chart as it displays in the Microsoft Excel window that opens when you start Microsoft Excel from within Microsoft Office. The steps to create this worksheet and column chart are shown in Project 1 of Microsoft Excel.

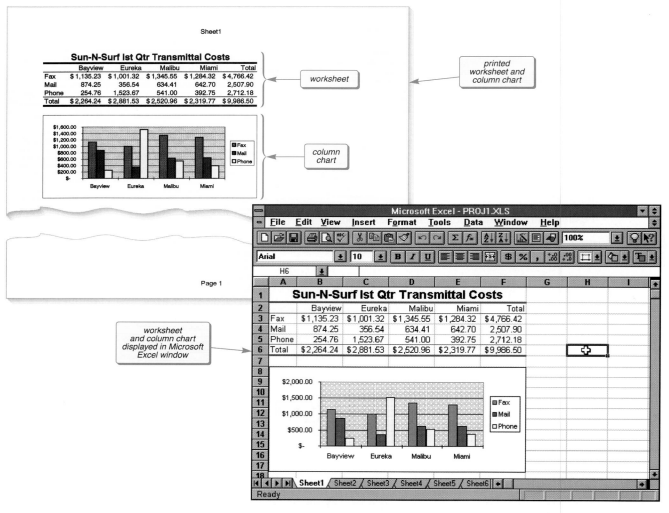

FIGURE 1-2

Microsoft Access

A **database** is a collection of data organized in a manner that allows access, retrieval, and use of that data. **Microsoft Access** is a **database management system**. Microsoft Access allows you to create a database; add, change, and delete data in the database; sort data in the database; retrieve data from the database; and create forms and reports using the data in the database.

Figure 1-3 illustrates the database created in Project 1 of the Microsoft Access section of this book. Also shown is the database as it displays in the Microsoft Access window that opens when you start Microsoft Access from within Microsoft Office. The steps to create this database are shown in Project 1 of Microsoft Access.

printed database

Customer Number	Name	Address	City	State	Zip Code	Balance	Credit Limit	Sales Rep Number
AN91	Atwater-Nelson	215 Watkins	Oakdale	IN	48101	$3,478.50	$7,000.00	04
AW52	Alliance West	266 Ralston	Allanson	IN	48102	$492.20	$4,000.00	07
BD22	Betodial	542 Prairie	Oakdale	IN	48101	$57.00	$4,000.00	07
CE76	Carson Enterprise	96 Prospect	Bishop	IL	61354	$4,125.00	$9,000.00	11
FC63	Forrest Co.	85 Stocking	Fergus	MI	48902	$7,822.00	$7,000.00	04
FY16	Fedder-Yansen	198 Pearl	Oakdale	IN	48101	$3,912.00	$7,000.00	07
LR72	Lanross, Inc.	195 Grayton	Bishop	IL	61354	$0.00	$7,000.00	07
MT19	Morton Trent	867 Bedford	Acme	IL	62127	$1,867.50	$7,000.00	04
RO22	Robertson, Inc.	682 Maumee	Allanson	IN	48102	$2,336.25	$9,000.00	11
RO92	Ronald A. Orten	872 Devonshire	Benson	MI	49246	$6,420.00	$9,000.00	07

database displayed in Microsoft Access window

Microsoft PowerPoint

Microsoft PowerPoint is a complete **presentation graphics program** that allows you to produce professional looking presentations. Microsoft PowerPoint gives you the flexibility to make an informal presentation in a small conference room using overhead transparencies, to make an electronic presentation using a projection device attached to a personal computer, or to make a formal presentation to a large audience using 35mm slides.

Figure 1-4 illustrates the first slide in a presentation created in Project 1 of the Microsoft PowerPoint section of this book. Also shown is the beginning screen of the presentation as it displays in the Microsoft PowerPoint window that opens when you start Microsoft PowerPoint from within Microsoft Office. The steps to create the presentation are shown in Project 1 of Microsoft PowerPoint.

FIGURE 1-3

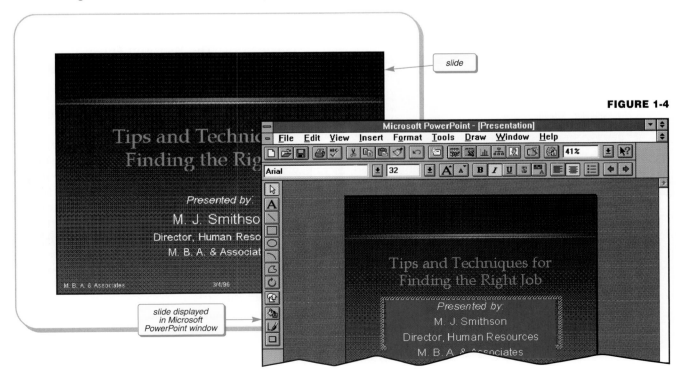

slide

FIGURE 1-4

slide displayed in Microsoft PowerPoint window

Microsoft Mail

Microsoft Mail is an **electronic mail system**. Microsoft Mail allows you to send electronic messages to and receive electronic messages from the other computers connected to a computer network. In addition, Microsoft Mail allows you to add charts, graphs, and sounds to your electronic messages. Microsoft Office includes a license to use Microsoft Mail. This license entitles you to install and use Microsoft Mail on one personal computer. To use Microsoft Mail, you must acquire the Server version of Microsoft Mail for PC Networks. Because the Microsoft Mail software is not included with Microsoft Office, this application is not covered in this book.

Versions of Microsoft Office

Two versions of Microsoft Office are currently available: Standard and Professional. **Microsoft Office 4.3 Standard** contains Microsoft Excel Version 5.0, Microsoft Word Version 6.0, and Microsoft PowerPoint Version 4.0. **Microsoft Office 4.3 Professional** contains Microsoft Access Version 2.0 in addition to Microsoft Excel Version 5.0, Microsoft Word Version 6.0, and Microsoft Power-Point Version 4.0.

As updates to the current versions of Microsoft Word 6.0, Microsoft Excel 5.0, Microsoft PowerPoint 4.0, and Microsoft Access 2.0 are released, the older versions will be replaced with the newer versions, resulting in a change in Microsoft Office and a new version number for Microsoft Office. This book is written using the Microsoft Office 4.3 Professional version.

▶ THE MICROSOFT OFFICE MANAGER TOOLBAR

When Microsoft Windows is installed, a StartUp group window is created in the Program Manager window. When Microsoft Office is installed, the Microsoft Office icon ( ) is added to the StartUp group window (Figure 1-5). With the Microsoft Office icon in the StartUp group window, Microsoft Office automatically starts when you start Microsoft Windows. When Microsoft Office starts, the Microsoft Office Manager (MOM) toolbar displays in the upper right corner of the desktop (Figure 1-6). The **Microsoft Office Manager (MOM) toolbar** allows you to start applications and switch between applications with a single click of the left mouse button.

FIGURE 1-5

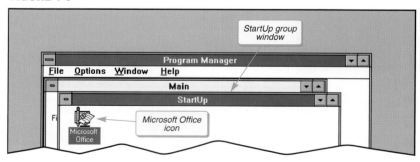

The Microsoft Office Manager toolbar in Figure 1-6 contains six buttons. The first five buttons, called **application buttons**, allow you to start an application from the toolbar. The first four buttons ( ) start Microsoft Word, Microsoft Excel, Microsoft Power-Point, and Microsoft Access, respectively. You start an application by pointing to its application button and clicking the left mouse button. The fifth application button ( ) starts Find File. **Find File** allows you to search for a file or files on disk. The sixth button ( ), called the Microsoft Office button, opens the Office menu used to customize the buttons on the toolbar and the appearance of the toolbar.

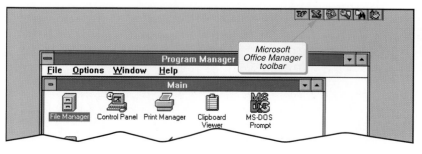

FIGURE 1-6

Starting an Application

In Project 1 of *Microsoft Windows 3.1*, one method of starting an application was explained. You started the Notepad application by pointing to the Notepad icon in the Accessories group window (see page WIN17) and double-clicking the left mouse button. An easier way to start an application that has a corresponding application button on the Microsoft Office Manager toolbar is to point to the application button and click the left mouse button.

TO START AN APPLICATION USING THE TOOLBAR ▼

STEP 1 ►

Point to the Microsoft Word button on the Microsoft Office Manager toolbar.

The mouse pointer points to the Microsoft Word button (Figure 1-7). The help prompt, Microsoft Word, displays below the mouse pointer.

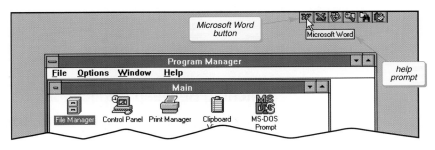

FIGURE 1-7

STEP 2 ►

Click the left mouse button to start Microsoft Word.

Windows displays the Microsoft Word Version 6.0 title screen momentarily and then opens the maximized Microsoft Word application window and maximized Document1 document window (Figure 1-8). The title bar contains the application window name and document window name.

STEP 3

If the Tip of the Day dialog box opens, point to the OK button in the dialog box and click the left mouse button to close the dialog box.

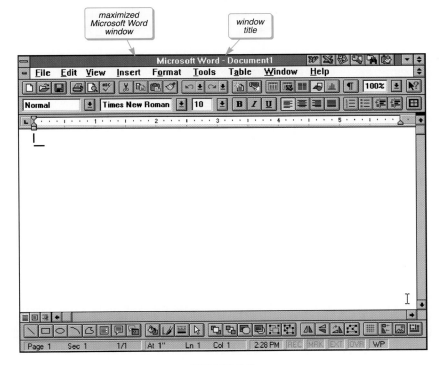

FIGURE 1-8

Starting a Second Application

A benefit of Microsoft Windows and Microsoft Office is the capability of running several applications at the same time. To illustrate how to start a second application, start Microsoft Excel by pointing to the Microsoft Excel application button on the Microsoft Office Manager toolbar and clicking the left mouse button. The steps to start Microsoft Excel are summarized on the next page.

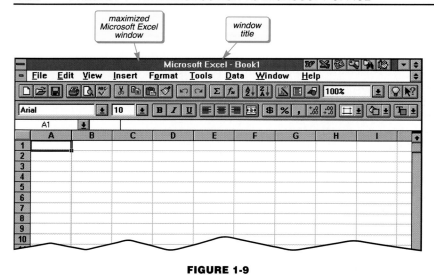

FIGURE 1-9

TO START MICROSOFT EXCEL

Step 1: Point to the Microsoft Excel button on the Microsoft Office Manager toolbar.
Step 2: Click the left mouse button.

Windows displays the Microsoft Excel Version 5.0 title screen momentarily and then opens the maximized Microsoft Excel application window and maximized Book1 document window (Figure 1-9). The title bar contains the application window name and the document window name.

Switching Between Applications on the Desktop

One feature of the Microsoft Office Manager toolbar is its capability to switch between applications on the desktop. After starting two or more applications, you can easily switch between the applications using the application buttons on the toolbar. To demonstrate the capability to switch between applications, switch to Microsoft Word by pointing to the Microsoft Word button on the toolbar and clicking the left mouse button. Perform the following steps to switch to Microsoft Word.

TO SWITCH TO ANOTHER APPLICATION ▼

STEP 1 ▶

Point to the Microsoft Word button on the Microsoft Office Manager toolbar (Figure 1-10).

FIGURE 1-10

STEP 2 ▶

Click the left mouse button to switch to Microsoft Word.

The maximized Microsoft Word window displays on the desktop (Figure 1-11).

FIGURE 1-11

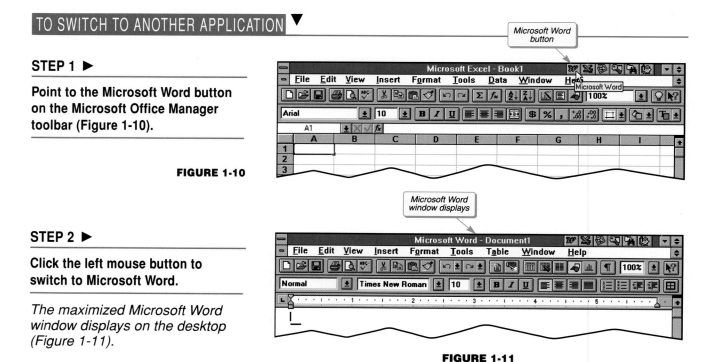

Tiling Applications

In the previous example, the maximized Microsoft Word application window was open on the desktop when you switched to the other open application window (Microsoft Excel window). When multiple application windows are open on the desktop, you often tile the windows to make transferring information between windows easier. To tile two application windows when one application window is opened on the desktop, you hold down the SHIFT key, point to the application button of the other application and click the left mouse button. An in-depth explanation of tiling application windows using the Microsoft Office Manager toolbar and transferring information between two application windows is given in Project 1 of the Object Linking and Embedding section of this book.

Quitting an Application

As explained in Project 1 of *Microsoft Windows 3.1*, you can quit an application by choosing the Exit command from the File menu (see Page WIN27). You can quit an application using the toolbar by holding down the ALT key and clicking the application's button on the toolbar. Follow the steps below to quit Microsoft Word.

TO QUIT AN APPLICATION ▼

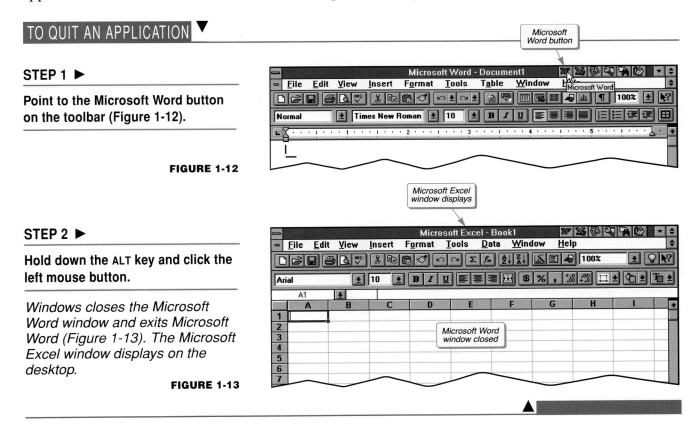

STEP 1 ▶

Point to the Microsoft Word button on the toolbar (Figure 1-12).

FIGURE 1-12

STEP 2 ▶

Hold down the ALT key and click the left mouse button.

Windows closes the Microsoft Word window and exits Microsoft Word (Figure 1-13). The Microsoft Excel window displays on the desktop.

FIGURE 1-13

▶ CUSTOMIZING THE MICROSOFT OFFICE MANAGER TOOLBAR

When Microsoft Office starts, the Microsoft Office Manager toolbar displays in the upper right corner of the desktop (see Figure 1-6 on page MO6). The toolbar contains six buttons. You can customize the toolbar by adding an application button, deleting an application button, rearranging the order of the application buttons on the toolbar, and changing the size and position of the toolbar. You use the Customize command on the Office menu to customize the Microsoft Office Manager toolbar.

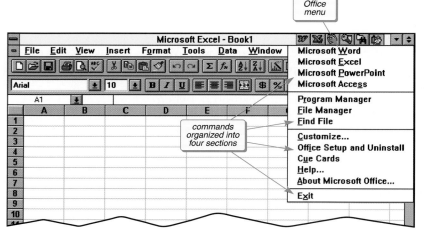

FIGURE 1-14

The Office Menu

When you point to the Microsoft Office button on the toolbar and click the left mouse button, the **Office menu** opens (Figure 1-14). The commands on the Office menu are organized into four sections. The first section contains the four commands to start Microsoft Word, Microsoft Excel, Microsoft PowerPoint, and Microsoft Access. The second section contains the commands to switch to Program Manager, start File Manager, and start Find File.

The third section contains commands to customize the toolbar (Customize), change the setup of Microsoft Office and uninstall Microsoft Office (Office Setup and Uninstall), use Cue Cards (Cue Cards), obtain help about Microsoft Office (Help), and display general information about the current version of Microsoft Office (About Microsoft Office). **Cue Cards** is an online tool to help you learn a Microsoft Office application. Cue Cards display step-by-step instructions that remain visible on the screen while you use an application. The Exit command in the fourth section of the Office menu allows you to exit Microsoft Office.

Adding an Application Button to the Microsoft Office Manager Toolbar

To add an application button to the toolbar, you use the Customize command on the Office menu. Perform the following steps to add an application button to the toolbar for the Windows Calculator application.

TO ADD AN APPLICATION BUTTON TO THE TOOLBAR ▼

STEP 1 ►

Point to the Microsoft Office button on the Microsoft Office Manager toolbar.

The mouse pointer points to the Microsoft Office button on the toolbar (Figure 1-15). The help prompt, Microsoft Office, displays below the mouse pointer.

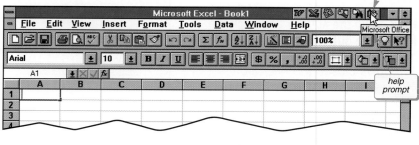

FIGURE 1-15

STEP 2 ►

Click the left mouse button to open the Office menu, and then point to the Customize command.

The Office menu opens (Figure 1-16). The mouse pointer points to the Customize command.

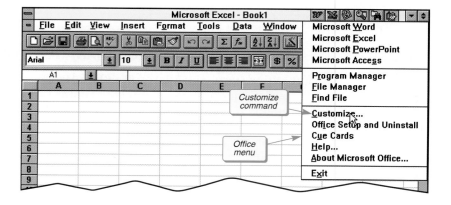

FIGURE 1-16

STEP 3 ►

Choose the Customize command by clicking the left mouse button. If the Toolbar folder does not display on top of the Menu and View folders, point to the Toolbar tab and click the left mouse button.

Windows opens the Customize dialog box (Figure 1-17). The dialog box contains three folders (Toolbar, Menu, and View). The **Toolbar folder** *displays on top of the other two folders and contains the Toolbar list box, up and down*

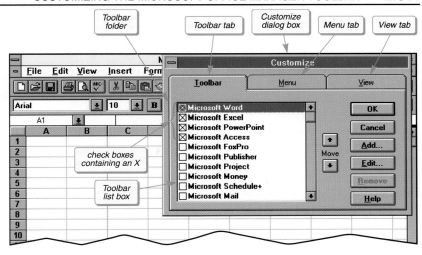

FIGURE 1-17

arrows, and several command buttons. The Toolbar list box contains a list of the Microsoft Office applications for which buttons can be added to the toolbar. A check box displays to the left of each application name in the Toolbar list box. An X displays in each of the first four check boxes (Microsoft Word, Microsoft Excel, Microsoft PowerPoint, and Microsoft Access) to indicate buttons for those applications currently display on the toolbar. Although not visible, the check box to the left of the Find File entry also contains an X.

STEP 4 ►

Scroll the Toolbar list box until the Calculator entry is visible, and then point to the check box to the left of the Calculator entry.

The Calculator entry displays in the Toolbar list box (Figure 1-18). The mouse pointer points to the check box to the left of the Calcu- lator application name. The Find File entry is also visible in the Toolbar list box.

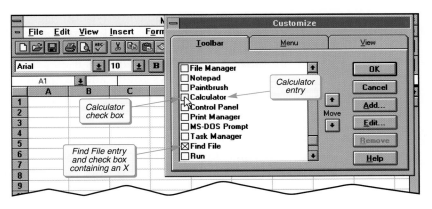

FIGURE 1-18

STEP 5 ►

Click the left mouse button to place an X in the check box to the left of the Calculator application name, and then point to the OK button.

The Calculator entry is highlighted and an X displays in the check box to the left of the entry (Figure 1-19). The mouse pointer points to the OK button.

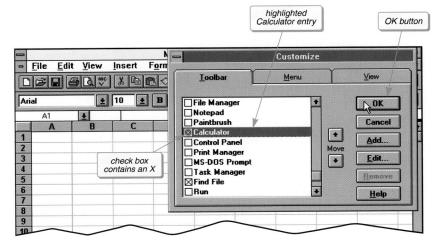

FIGURE 1-19

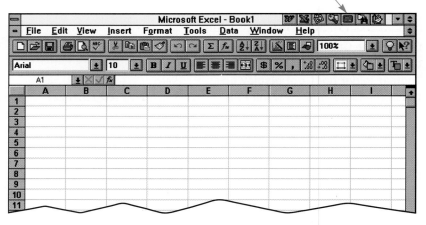

FIGURE 1-20

STEP 6 ▶

Choose the OK button by clicking the left mouse button.

The Calculator button is inserted between the Microsoft Access and Find File buttons on the toolbar (Figure 1-20). The Calculator button occupies this position because the Calculator entry is between the Microsoft Access and Find File entries in the Toolbar list box in the Customize dialog box.

In addition to adding an application button, you can also choose the position a button occupies among the other buttons on the Microsoft Office Manager toolbar by choosing the Customize command and selecting the corresponding entry in the Toolbar list box. Then, press the up or down arrow to move the application name upward or downward in the list of applications in the Toolbar list box.

As illustrated in Figure 1-17 on page MO11, three folders display in the Customize dialog box. The Toolbar folder allows you to add a button to the toolbar, remove a button from the toolbar, and change the position of a button on the toolbar. The Toolbar folder was used previously to add a button to the toolbar. The **Menu folder** allows you to add an application name to the Office menu, remove an application name from the Office menu, change the position of an application name on the Office menu, and control which commands display in the four sections of the Office menu. The **View folder** allows you to change the size of the toolbar and determines whether the toolbar displays, if ToolTips is used, and whether the title screen displays when you start an application. **ToolTips** displays the help prompts whenever the mouse pointer points to the button on the toolbar.

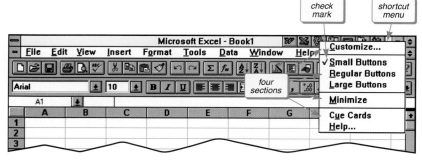

FIGURE 1-21

Opening the Shortcut Menu

In addition to using the Customize command on the Office menu to open the Customize dialog box, you can also use the Customize command on the shortcut menu. A **shortcut menu** contains commands related to an object on the desktop, such as the Microsoft Office Manager toolbar or an area of the desktop. When you point to any button on the toolbar and click the right mouse button, a shortcut menu opens (Figure 1-21). The commands on the shortcut menu are organized into four sections.

The first section contains the Customize command. The second section contains the three commands to change the size of the Microsoft Office Manager toolbar (Small Buttons, Regular Buttons, and Large Buttons). The Small Buttons command is preceded by a check mark to indicate the smallest version of the toolbar displays. The third section contains the Minimize command to remove the toolbar from the desktop and display the Microsoft Office icon in the lower left corner of the desktop. The fourth section contains the Cue Cards and Help commands.

Changing the Size of the Microsoft Office Manager Toolbar

Perform the following steps to change the size of the Microsoft Office Manager toolbar from its current size (Small Buttons) to the Regular Buttons size.

TO CHANGE THE SIZE OF THE TOOLBAR ▼

STEP 1 ▶

Point to any button on the Microsoft Office Manager toolbar.

The mouse pointer points to the Microsoft PowerPoint button on the Microsoft Office Manager toolbar (Figure 1-22). The Microsoft PowerPoint help prompt displays below the mouse pointer.

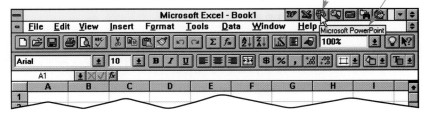

FIGURE 1-22

STEP 2 ▶

Click the right mouse button to open a shortcut menu, and then, point to the Regular Buttons command.

Windows opens a shortcut menu (Figure 1-23). The mouse pointer points to the Regular Buttons command.

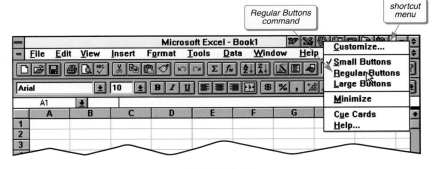

FIGURE 1-23

STEP 3 ▶

Choose the Regular Buttons command by clicking the left mouse button.

The Microsoft Office Manager toolbar displays in a window titled Microsoft Office Manager (Figure 1-24). The toolbar may display in a different area on your computer.

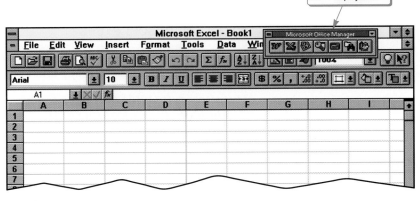

FIGURE 1-24

▶ Locating a File on Disk Using the Toolbar

U sing the Find File button on the toolbar, you can locate and retrieve a file from disk. You can search for a file based on its filename, its location on disk, the summary information entered for the file, or a specific string of text in the file. You can also copy, delete, or print a file without having to switch to File Manager or the application.

For detailed instructions on how to find a file on disk, click the Microsoft Office button on the Microsoft Office Manager toolbar, choose the Help command, click the Search button in the Microsoft Office Help window, scroll the Search list box to make the Find File command (Office menu) topic visible, select the topic, click the Show Topics button, and then click the Go To button. For practice in finding a file on disk, complete Computer Laboratory Exercise 2 at the end of this project.

▶ Restoring the Toolbar and Quitting Excel

N ext, return the size of the Microsoft Office Manager toolbar to its original size when Microsoft Office was first started (Small Buttons). Return the toolbar to its original appearance by removing the Calculator button from the toolbar and quit Microsoft Excel. The steps to accomplish these tasks are summarized below.

TO CHANGE THE TOOLBAR SIZE TO SMALL BUTTONS

Step 1: Point to any button on the toolbar and click the right mouse button to open the shortcut menu.
Step 2: Point to the Small Buttons command and click the left mouse button.

TO REMOVE THE CALCULATOR BUTTON

Step 1: Point to the Microsoft Office button on the toolbar and click the left mouse button to open the Office menu.
Step 2: Choose the Customize command from the Office menu.
Step 3: Scroll the entries in the Toolbar list box to make the Calculator entry visible.
Step 4: Point to the check box to the left of the Calculator entry and click the left mouse button to remove the X from the check box.
Step 5: Choose the OK button in the Customize dialog box.

TO QUIT MICROSOFT EXCEL

Step 1: Point to the Microsoft Excel button on the toolbar.
Step 2: Hold down the ALT key and click the left mouse button.

The Microsoft Office Manager toolbar displays in the upper right corner of the desktop, the Calculator button is removed from the toolbar, and Windows exits Microsoft Excel.

▶ Project Summary

The purpose of this project is to introduce you to Microsoft Office. Important topics include using the Microsoft Office Manager toolbar to start an application, switch to another application, and quit an application; adding a button to and removing a button from the toolbar; and changing the size of the toolbar. With this introduction you are ready to begin the study of each of the Microsoft Office applications explained later in this book.

▶ KEY TERMS AND INDEX

application buttons (MO6)
Cue Cards (MO10)
database (MO4)
database management system
   (MO4)
electronic mail system (MO6)
Find File (MO6, MO13)
Menu folder (MO12)
Microsoft Access (MO4)

Microsoft Excel (MO4)
Microsoft Mail (MO6)
Microsoft Office family (MO2)
Microsoft Office Manager (MOM)
   toolbar (MO6)
Microsoft Office 4.3 Professional
   (MO6)
Microsoft Office 4.3 Standard
   (MO6)

Microsoft PowerPoint (MO5)
Microsoft Word (MO2)
Office menu (MO10)
presentation graphics program
   (MO5)
shortcut menu (MO12)
Toolbar folder (MO11)
ToolTips (MO12)
View folder (MO12)

Q U I C K   R E F E R E N C E

In Microsoft Office, you can accomplish a task in a number of ways. The following table provides a quick reference to each task presented in this project with its available options. The commands listed in the Menu column can be executed using either the keyboard or mouse.

Task	Mouse	Menu	Shortcut Keys
Add a Button to the Toolbar		From Office or shortcut menu, choose Customize, then select Toolbar tab and click a check box	
Change the Size of the Toolbar		From shortcut menu, choose button size; from Office menu, choose Customize, select View tab, and select a toolbar size	
Open the Shortcut Menu	Point to toolbar and click right mouse button		
Quit an Application	Hold down ALT key and click application button		
Remove a Button from the Toolbar		From Office or shortcut menu, choose Customize, then select Toolbar tab and click a check box	
Search for a File on Disk	Click Find File button	From Office menu, choose Find File	
Start an Application	Click application button	From Office menu, choose application name	
Switch to Another Application	Click application button	From Office menu, choose application name	

COMPUTER LABORATORY EXERCISE 1
Using Cue Cards to Add a Button to the Toolbar

Instructions: Use your computer to perform the following tasks to obtain experience in adding a button to the Microsoft Office Manager toolbar using Cue Cards.

1. Click the Microsoft Office button on the Microsoft Office Manager toolbar.
2. Choose the Cue Cards command.
3. When the Microsoft Office Cue Cards dialog box opens, select the View Cue Cards on using and customizing Office Manager topic by clicking the button to the left of the topic.
4. When the Office Cue Cards dialog box opens, select the Customize the Office Manager toolbar topic by clicking the button to the left of the topic.
5. When the Customize the Office Manager Toolbar topic displays in the Office Cue Cards dialog box, read the help information and choose the Add a button to the toolbar topic by clicking the button to the left of the topic.
6. When the Add a Button to the Toolbar topic displays in the Office Cue Cards dialog box, follow the instructions to add a button for the Notepad application.
7. When you are finished, exit Cue Cards by double-clicking the Control-menu box in the upper left corner of the Office Cue Cards dialog box.
8. Without using Cue Cards, remove the Notepad button from the toolbar.

COMPUTER LABORATORY EXERCISE 2
Searching for a File Using Find File

Instructions: Use your computer to perform the following tasks to obtain experience in finding a file on disk using Find File.

1. Insert the Student Diskette that accompanies this book in Drive A.
2. Click the Find File button on the toolbar to start Find File.
3. When the Find File dialog box opens, choose the Search button. The File Name drop-down list box contains the highlighted *.doc;*.xl*;*.ppt entry to indicate a search will be performed for Microsoft Word, Microsoft Excel, and Microsoft Power Point documents. The Location drop-down list box contains the c:\ entry to indicate a search will be performed on drive C.
4. Point to the down arrow to the right of the Location drop-down list box and click the left mouse button to open the Location drop-down list.
5. Select the drive A icon from the Location drop-down list. Selecting the drive A icon will cause files on the diskette in drive A to be searched.
6. Point to the Include Subdirectories check box and click the left mouse button to place an X in the check box. The X will cause all subdirectories on the diskette in drive A to be searched.
7. Choose the OK button. Find File searches the files on drive A. The Listed Files list box in the Find File dialog box contains a drive icon for drive A, a subdirectory icon for the excel5 subdirectory on drive A, and a partial list of Microsoft Word, Microsoft Excel, and Microsoft PowerPoint files on drive A. The cla4-2.xlt filename is highlighted in the Listed Files list box and the Preview of area contains a portion of this file.
8. Select the cle2-2.xls entry in the Listed Files list box.
9. Choose the Open button to start Microsoft Excel and open the cle2-2.xls file.
10. When you are finished, quit Excel by double-clicking the Control-menu box in the Microsoft Excel window.
11. Remove the Student Diskette from drive A.

WORD PROCESSING

USING MICROSOFT WORD 6 FOR WINDOWS

MICROSOFT WORD 6 FOR WINDOWS

▼

CREATING AND EDITING A DOCUMENT

OBJECTIVES You will have mastered the material in this project when you can:

▶ Start Word
▶ Describe the Word screen
▶ Change the default font size of all text
▶ Enter text into a document
▶ Import a graphic
▶ Scale an imported graphic
▶ Save a document
▶ Select text
▶ Center a paragraph
▶ Underline selected text

▶ Bold selected text
▶ Italicize selected text
▶ Change the font size of selected text
▶ Change the font of selected text
▶ Check a document for spelling errors
▶ Print a document
▶ Correct errors in a document
▶ Use Word's Help facility
▶ Quit Word

▶ WHAT IS MICROSOFT WORD?

Microsoft Word is a full-featured **word processing program** that allows you to efficiently and economically create professional-looking documents, such as announcements, letters, resumes, and reports, and revise them easily. Word has many features designed to simplify the production of documents. For example, you can instruct Word to create a prewritten document for you, and then you can modify the document to meet your needs. Using its new **Auto features**, Word can perform tasks like automatically correcting typing errors, expanding codes to phrases, and analyzing and formatting a document. To improve the accuracy of your writing, Word can check your spelling and grammar. You can use Word's thesaurus to add variety and precision to your writing. With Word, you can easily include tables and graphics in your documents. You can also use Word's desktop publishing features to create professional-looking brochures, advertisements, and newsletters.

▶ PROJECT ONE — FESTIVAL ANNOUNCEMENT

T o illustrate the features of Word, this book presents a series of projects that use Word to create documents similar to those you will encounter in academic and business environments. Project 1 uses Word to produce the festival announcement shown in Figure 1-1. The announcement informs the public of the 4th Annual Festival of Jazz, hosted by The Jazzicians. Beneath the title lines, a graphic of jazz instruments is included to catch the attention of the reader. The list beneath the graphic is bulleted so each item stands apart from the next.

FIGURE 1-1

Document Preparation Steps

The following document preparation steps give you an overview of how the document shown in Figure 1-1 on the previous page will be developed in this project. If you are preparing the document in this project on a personal computer, read these steps without doing them.

1. Start Word.
2. Change the size of the displayed and printed characters.
3. Enter the document text.
4. Save the document on disk.
5. Format the document title lines (center, bold, underline, italicize, and enlarge).
6. Add bullets to the list.
7. Bold the festival date.
8. Change the font of the last line of the announcement.
9. Import the graphic.
10. Resize the graphic.
11. Check the spelling of the document.
12. Save the document again.
13. Print the document.
14. Quit Word.

The following pages contain a detailed explanation of each of these steps.

▶ STARTING WORD

To start Word, the Office Manager toolbar must display on the screen or the Microsoft Office group window must be open. Follow these steps to start Word, or ask your instructor how to start Word on your computer.

TO START WORD ▼

STEP 1 ▶

If the Office Manager toolbar displays, use the mouse to point to the Microsoft Word button ( ) (Figure 1-2). If the Office Manager toolbar does not display at the top right of your screen, then point to the Microsoft Word program-item icon (🖋) in the Microsoft Office group window.

Your Office Manager toolbar may contain more or fewer buttons than shown in Figure 1-2.

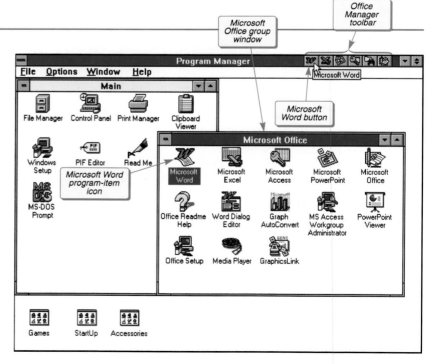

FIGURE 1-2

STEP 2 ►

Double-click the left mouse button.

Word displays the Tip of the Day dialog box (Figure 1-3). Each time you start Word, a different tip displays. These tips are designed to help you be more productive. Depending on how Word was installed on your system, the Tip of the Day dialog box may or may not display.

STEP 3

In the Tip of the Day dialog box, point to the OK button (OK).

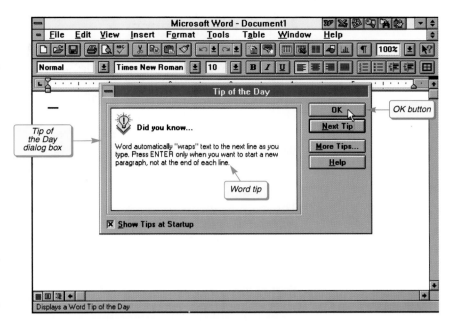

FIGURE 1-3

STEP 4 ►

Click the left mouse button.

Word removes the Tip of the Day dialog box and displays an empty document titled Document1 (Figure 1-4).

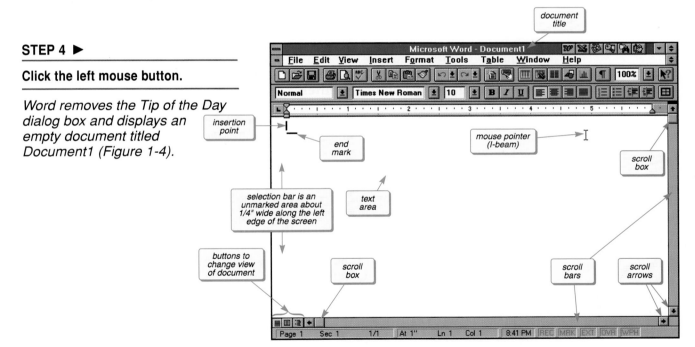

FIGURE 1-4

▶ THE WORD SCREEN

he **Word screen** (Figure 1-4 on the previous page), also called the **Word workplace**, consists of a variety of features to make your work more efficient and results more professional. If you are following along on a personal computer and your screen differs from Figure 1-4, select the View menu and choose the Normal command.

Word Document Window

The Word document window contains several elements similar to the document windows in other applications, as well as some elements unique to Word. The main elements of the Word document window are the text area, insertion point, end mark, mouse pointer, scroll bars, and selection bar (Figure 1-4 on the previous page).

TEXT AREA   As you type or insert graphics, your text and graphics display in the **text area.**

INSERTION POINT   The **insertion point** is a blinking vertical bar indicating where the text will be inserted as you type. As you type, the insertion point moves to the right, and when you reach the end of a line, it moves downward to the next line. You also insert graphics at the location of the insertion point.

END MARK   The **end mark** indicates the end of your document. Each time you begin a new line as you type, the end mark moves downward.

MOUSE POINTER   The **mouse pointer** can become one of eight different shapes, depending on the task you are performing in Word and the pointer's location on the screen. The mouse pointer in Figure 1-4 on the previous page has the shape of an I-beam ($\mathbb{I}$). The mouse pointer displays as an I-beam when it is in the text area. Other mouse pointer shapes are described as they appear on the screen during this and subsequent projects.

SCROLL BARS   **Scroll bars** are used to display different portions of your document in the document window. At the right edge of the document window is a vertical scroll bar, and at the bottom of the document window is a horizontal scroll bar. On both scroll bars, the **scroll box** indicates your current location in the document. At the left edge of the horizontal scroll bar, Word provides three buttons to change the view of a document. These buttons are discussed as they are used in a later project.

SELECTION BAR   The **selection bar** is an unmarked area about 1/4" wide along the left edge of the text area that is used to select text with the mouse.

Word is preset to use standard 8 1/2 by 11-inch paper, with 1.25-inch left and right margins and 1-inch top and bottom margins. Only a portion of your document, however, displays on the screen at one time. The portion of the document displayed on the screen is viewed through the **document window** (Figure 1-5).

FIGURE 1-5

Menu Bar, Toolbars, Rulers, and Status Bar

The menu bar, toolbars, and horizontal ruler appear at the top of the screen just below the title bar (Figure 1-6 on the next page). The status bar appears at the bottom of the screen.

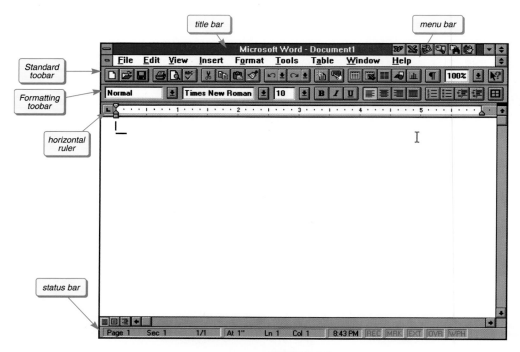

FIGURE 1-6

MENU BAR   The **menu bar** displays the Word menu names. Each menu name represents a menu of commands that can be used to retrieve, store, print, and format data in your document. To display a menu, such as the File menu, select the menu name by pointing to it and clicking the left mouse button.

TOOLBARS   Just below the menu bar is the **Standard toolbar**. Immediately below the Standard toolbar is the **Formatting toolbar**.

    Toolbars contain buttons and boxes that allow you to perform tasks more quickly than using the menu bar. For example, to print, point to the Print button (🖨) on the Standard toolbar and press the left mouse button (called clicking the Print button on the Standard toolbar). Each button has a picture on the face to help you remember its function. Figure 1-7 illustrates the Standard toolbar and identifies its buttons and boxes. Figure 1-8 illustrates the Formatting toolbar. Each button and box is explained in detail as it is used in the projects.

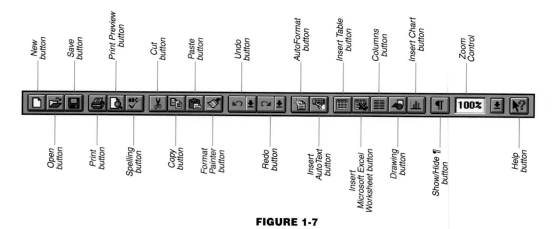

FIGURE 1-7

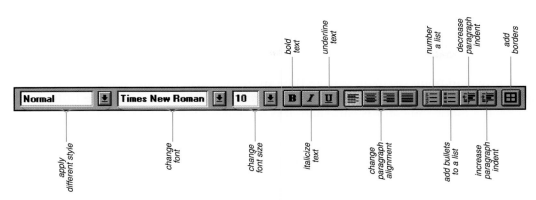

FIGURE 1-8

The Standard and Formatting toolbars initially display **anchored**, or locked, below the menu bar. Additional toolbars may automatically display on the Word screen, depending on the task you are performing. These additional toolbars either display stacked beneath the Formatting toolbar or floating on the Word screen. You can rearrange the order of **stacked toolbars** and can move **floating toolbars** anywhere on the Word screen. Later, you'll learn how to float an anchored toolbar and anchor a floating toolbar.

RULERS   Below the Formatting toolbar is the **horizontal ruler** (Figure 1-9). It is used to set tab stops, indent paragraphs, adjust column widths, and change page margins. The horizontal ruler, sometimes just called the **ruler**, always displays beneath the Formatting toolbar. An additional ruler, called the **vertical ruler** displays when you are performing certain tasks. The vertical ruler is discussed as it displays on the screen in a later project.

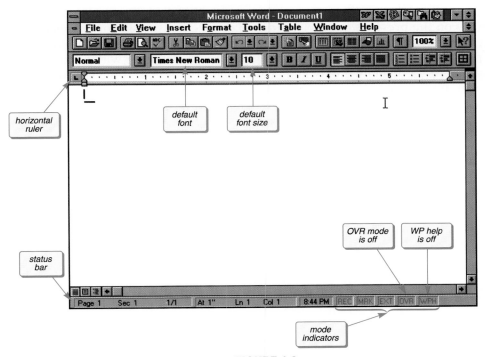

FIGURE 1-9

STATUS BAR   The **status bar** is located at the bottom of the screen. The following information about the page shown in Figure 1-9 on the previous page displays left to right: the page number; the section number; the page visible in the document window, followed by the total number of pages in the document; the position of the insertion point (in inches) from the top of the page; the line number and column number of the insertion point; the current time; and several **mode indicators**. If a mode indicator is darkened, it is on. For example, the dimmed OVR indicates overtype mode is off. To turn most modes on or off, double-click the mode indicator. Mode indicators are discussed as they are used in the projects.

Depending on how Word was installed and the status of certain keys on the keyboard, your status bar may have different mode indicators on or off. For example, the dimmed WPH at the right edge of the status bar indicates WordPerfect help is off. If your status bar displays a darkened WP or a dimmed WPN, WordPerfect help is active and you need to deactivate it. When WordPerfect help is on, the keys you press on the keyboard work according to WordPerfect rather than Word. To deactive the WordPerfect help, ask for assistance from your instructor or choose the Options command from the Tools menu; click the General tab; click the Help for WordPerfect Users and the Navigation Keys for WordPerfect Users check boxes; then choose the OK button in the Options dialog box.

When you have selected a command from a menu, the status bar displays a brief description of the currently selected command. If a task you select requires several seconds, the status bar displays a message informing you of the progress of the task.

▶ CHANGING THE DEFAULT FONT SIZE

Characters that display on the screen are a specific shape and size. The **font**, or typeface, defines the appearance and shape of letters, numbers, and special characters. The preset, or default, font is Times New Roman (Figure 1-9 on the previous page). The **font size** specifies the size of the characters on the screen. Font size is gauged by a measurement system called points. A single point is about 1/72 of an inch in height. Thus, a character with a font size of ten is about 10/72 of an inch in height. The default font size in some versions of Word is 10. If most of the characters in your document require a larger font size, you can easily change the default font size before you type. In Project 1, many of the characters in the announcement are a font size of 20. Follow these steps to change the font size before you begin entering text.

TO CHANGE THE DEFAULT FONT SIZE BEFORE TYPING ▼

STEP 1 ►

Point to the Font Size box arrow.

*The mouse pointer changes to a left-pointing block arrow ( ) in a toolbar (Figure 1-10). When you point to a toolbar button, Word displays a **ToolTip**, which is Font Size in this case, immediately beneath the button and also displays a brief description of the button at the left edge of the status bar.*

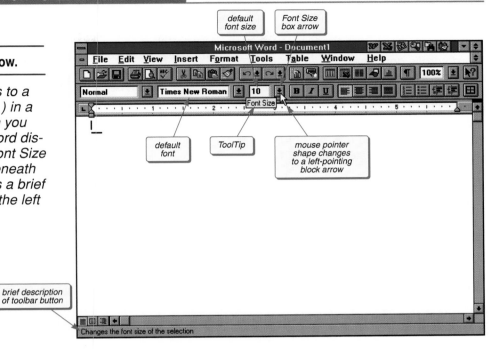

FIGURE 1-10

STEP 2 ►

Click the Font Size box arrow.

A list of available font sizes displays in the Font Size drop-down list box (Figure 1-11).

STEP 3

Point to the down scroll arrow on the Font Size scroll bar.

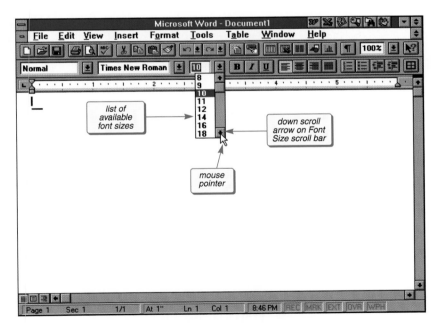

FIGURE 1-11

STEP 4 ▶

Click the down scroll arrow once. Point to the font size 20.

Word scrolls down one line in the available font sizes (Figure 1-12). The font size 20 now displays in the list. To make room for the display of font size 20, the font size 8 no longer displays at the top of the list. Thus, the font size 8 **scrolled** *off the top of the list.*

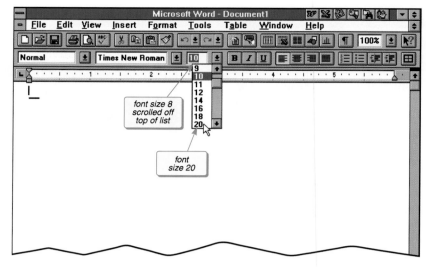

FIGURE 1-12

STEP 5 ▶

Select font size 20 by clicking the left mouse button.

The font size for this document changes to 20 (Figure 1-13).

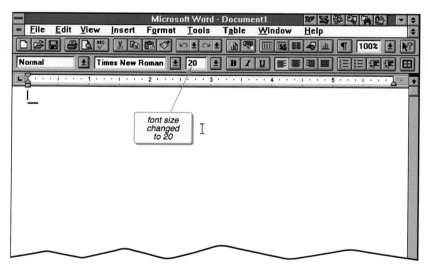

FIGURE 1-13

The new default font size takes effect immediately in your document. Word uses this font size for the remainder of this announcement.

▶ ENTERING TEXT

To prepare a document in Word, you enter text by typing on the keyboard. In Project 1, the first title line (THE JAZZICIANS) appears capitalized. The following example explains the steps to enter the first title line in all capital letters at the left margin. Later in the project, this title line will be centered across the top of the document, formatted in bold, and enlarged.

TO ENTER CAPITALIZED WORDS INTO A DOCUMENT ▼

STEP 1 ►

If the CAPS LOCK indicator is off on your keyboard, press the CAPS LOCK key. Type THE JAZZICIANS

Word places the letter T in THE at the location of the insertion point. As you continue typing this title line, the insertion point moves to the right (Figure 1-14). If at any time during typing you make an error, press the BACKSPACE *key until you have deleted the text in error and then retype the text correctly.*

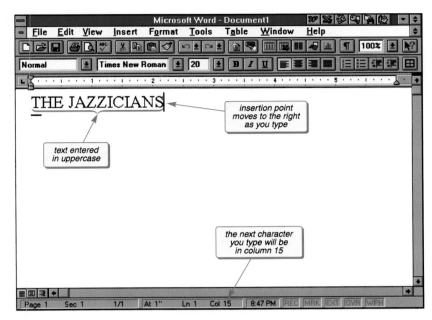

FIGURE 1-14

STEP 2 ►

Press the CAPS LOCK key. Press the ENTER key.

Word creates a new paragraph by moving the insertion point to the beginning of the next line (Figure 1-15). Whenever you press the ENTER *key, Word considers the previous line and the next line to be different paragraphs. Notice the status bar indicates the current position of the insertion point.*

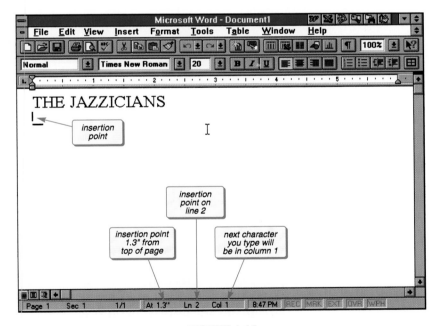

FIGURE 1-15

Entering Blank Lines into a Document

To enter a blank line into a document, press the ENTER key without typing anything on the line. The following example explains how to enter one blank line after the first title line THE JAZZICIANS.

TO ENTER A BLANK LINE INTO A DOCUMENT ▼

STEP 1 ▶

Press the ENTER key once.

Word inserts one blank line into your document beneath the first title line (Figure 1-16).

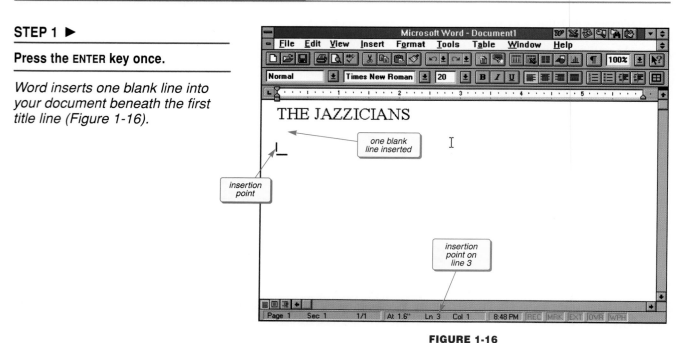

FIGURE 1-16

Displaying Nonprinting Characters

You will find it helpful to display **nonprinting characters** indicating where in the document you pressed the ENTER key or the SPACEBAR. The paragraph mark (¶) is a nonprinting character that indicates where you pressed the ENTER key. A raised dot (·) shows where you pressed the SPACEBAR. Nonprinting characters display only on the screen. They do not appear in printed documents. Other non-printing characters are discussed as they display on the screen in subsequent projects. The following steps illustrate how to display nonprinting characters, if they are not already displaying on your screen.

TO DISPLAY NONPRINTING CHARACTERS ▼

STEP 1 ►

Point to the Show/Hide ¶ button (¶) on the Standard toolbar.

Word displays the ToolTip for the button (Figure 1-17).

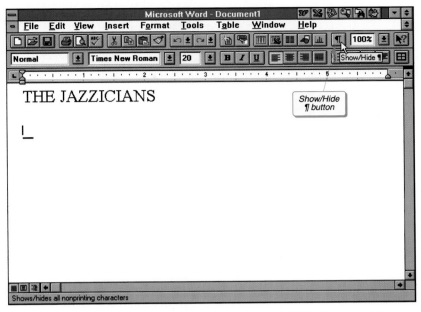

FIGURE 1-17

STEP 2 ►

Click the Show/Hide ¶ button.

Word displays nonprinting characters on the screen and the Show/Hide ¶ button on the Standard toolbar is recessed (Figure 1-18).

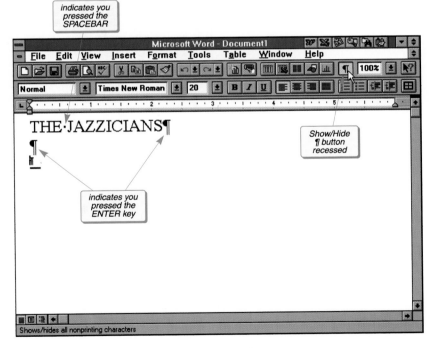

FIGURE 1-18

Notice several changes to your screen display (Figure 1-18 on the previous page). A paragraph mark appears at the end of each line to indicate you pressed the ENTER key. Recall that each time you press the ENTER key, Word creates a new paragraph. Because you changed the font size, the first two paragraph marks are 20 point and the one above the end mark is 10 point, the default. Between each word, a raised dot appears, indicating you pressed the SPACEBAR. Finally, the Show/Hide ¶ button is recessed, or ghosted, to indicate it is selected. If you feel the nonprinting characters clutter your screen, you can hide them by clicking the Show/Hide ¶ button again.

Entering the Remaining Title Lines

The next step is to enter the second and third title lines into the document window as shown in the steps below.

TO ENTER THE REMAINING TITLE LINES

Step 1: Type present the and press the ENTER key twice.
Step 2: Type 4th Annual Festival of Jazz and press the ENTER key four times.

The title lines display as shown in Figure 1-19.

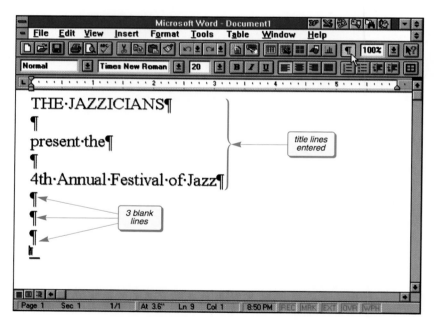

FIGURE 1-19

Using the Wordwrap Feature

Wordwrap allows you to type words in a paragraph continually without pressing the ENTER key at the end of each line. When the insertion point moves beyond the right margin, Word automatically positions it at the beginning of the next line. As you type, if a word extends beyond the right margin, Word also automatically positions the word on the next line with the insertion point. Thus, as you enter text, do not press the ENTER key when the insertion point reaches the right margin. Because Word creates a new paragraph each time you press the ENTER key, press the ENTER key only in these circumstances:

1. to insert blank lines into a document
2. to begin a new paragraph
3. to terminate a short line of text and advance to the next line
4. in response to certain Word commands

TO USE WORDWRAP ▼

STEP 1 ►

Type the first paragraph in the body of the announcement: Join us for a fun-filled day of entertainment for the whole family.

Word automatically wraps the word "whole" to the beginning of line 10 because it is too long to fit on line 9 (Figure 1-20). Your document may wordwrap on a different word, depending on the type of printer you are using.

word "whole" could not fit on line 9, so Word wrapped it around to beginning of line 10

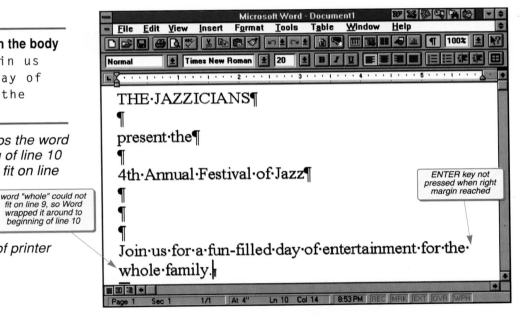

ENTER key not pressed when right margin reached

FIGURE 1-20

Entering Documents that Scroll through the Document Window

As you type more lines of text than Word can display in the text area, Word scrolls the top portion of the document upward off of the screen. Although you cannot see the text once it scrolls off the screen, it still remains in the document. Recall that the document window allows you to view only a portion of your document at one time (Figure 1-5 on page MSW7).

TO ENTER A DOCUMENT THAT SCROLLS THROUGH THE DOCUMENT WINDOW ▼

STEP 1 ▶

Press the ENTER key. Type the next paragraph in the body of the announcement: The fun starts at 10:00 a.m. and ends at 11:00 p.m. on Saturday, October 14, 1995, at Riverfront Park.

Word scrolls the first title, THE JAZZICIANS, off the top of the screen (Figure 1-21). The paragraph mark at the end of the first sentence indicates the next sentence will be a separate paragraph. Recall that each time you press the ENTER key, Word considers the text before and after the paragraph mark separate paragraphs. Your screen may scroll differently, depending on the type of monitor or printer you are using.

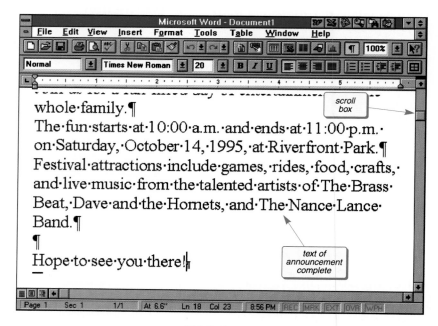

FIGURE 1-21

STEP 2 ▶

Press the ENTER key. Type the last paragraph in the body of the announcement: Festival attractions include games, rides, food, crafts, and live music from the talented artists of The Brass Beat, Dave and the Hornets, and The Nance Lance Band. **Press the ENTER key twice. Type the last line of the announcement:** Hope to see you there!

Word scrolls much of the announcement off of the screen (Figure 1-22). All the text in the announcement has been entered.

FIGURE 1-22

When Word scrolls text off the top of the screen, the scroll box on the scroll bar at the right edge of the document window moves downward (Figure 1-22). The scroll box indicates the current relative location of the insertion point in the document. You may use either the mouse or the keyboard to move the insertion point to a different location in a document. With the mouse, you use the scroll bars to bring a different portion of the document into the document window, then click the mouse to move the insertion point to that location. When you use the keyboard, the insertion point automatically moves when you press the appropriate keys.

To move the insertion point to a portion of the document that has scrolled off the screen, drag the scroll box upward or downward. To move the document up or down one entire screen at a time, click anywhere above or below the scroll box on the scroll bar or press the PAGE UP or PAGE DOWN key on the keyboard. To move the document up or down one line at a time in the window, click the scroll arrow at the top or bottom of the scroll bar. To move the insertion point to the top of the document using the keyboard, press CTRL+HOME; to move to the end of the document, press CTRL+END.

▶ SAVING A DOCUMENT

When you are creating a document in Word, the computer stores it in main memory. If the computer is turned off, or if you lose electrical power, the document is lost. Hence, it is mandatory to save on disk any document you will use later. The following steps illustrate how to save a document on a diskette inserted in drive A using the Save button on the Standard toolbar.

TO SAVE A NEW DOCUMENT ▼

STEP 1 ▶

Insert a formatted diskette into drive A. Point to the Save button (▣) on the Standard toolbar and click.

Word responds by displaying the Save As dialog box with the insertion point blinking after the default filename doc1.doc in the File Name box (Figure 1-23). Because doc1.doc is initially selected when the Save As dialog box displays, you can change the filename by typing the new name. If you do not enter a new filename, the document will be saved with the default filename doc1.doc.

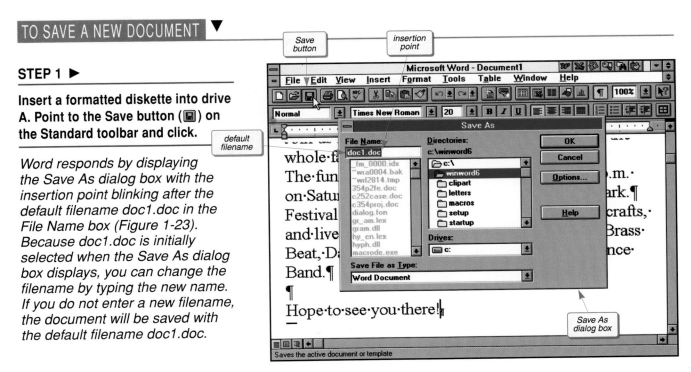

FIGURE 1-23

STEP 2 ▶

Type the filename `proj1` in the File
Name box. Do not press the ENTER
key after typing the filename.
Point to the Drives drop-down
list box arrow.

*The filename proj1 displays in the
File Name box (Figure 1-24).*

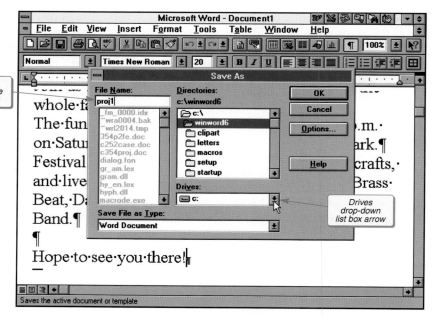

FIGURE 1-24

STEP 3 ▶

Click the Drives drop-down list box
arrow and point to ▭ a:

*A list of the available drives dis-
plays (Figure 1-25). Your list may
differ, depending on your system
configuration.*

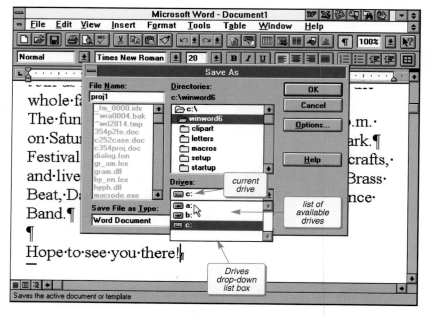

FIGURE 1-25

STEP 4 ▶

Select drive a: by clicking it. Point to the OK button.

Drive A becomes the selected drive (Figure 1-26). The names of existing files stored on the diskette in drive A display in the File Name list box. In Figure 1-26, no files are currently stored on the diskette in drive A.

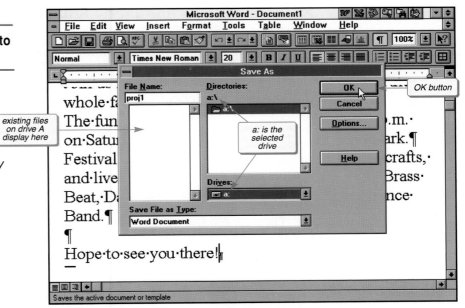

FIGURE 1-26

STEP 5 ▶

Choose the OK button in the Save As dialog box.

Word saves the document on the diskette in drive A with the filename PROJ1.DOC (Figure 1-27). Word automatically appends the extension .DOC which stands for Word document, to the filename PROJ1. Although the announcement is saved on diskette, it also remains in main memory and displays on the screen.

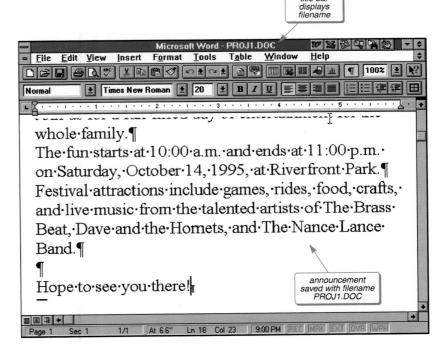

FIGURE 1-27

▶ FORMATTING PARAGAPHS AND CHARACTERS IN A DOCUMENT

T he text for Project 1 is now complete. The next step is to format the characters and paragraphs within the announcement. Paragraphs encompass the text up to and including the paragraph mark (¶). **Paragraph formatting** is the process of changing the appearance of a paragraph. For example, you can center or indent a paragraph.

Characters include letters, numbers, punctuation marks, and symbols. **Character formatting** is the process of changing the way characters appear on the screen and in print. You use character formatting to emphasize certain words and to improve the readability of a document. With Word, you can format before you type or apply new formats after you type. Earlier, you changed the font size before you typed any text, then, you entered the text. In this section, you will format existing text.

Figure 1-28a shows the announcement before formatting the paragraphs and characters in it. Figure 1-28b shows the announcement after formatting it. As you can see from the two figures, a document that is formatted is not only easier to read, but it looks more professional as well.

In the pages that follow, you will change the unformatted announcement in Figure 1-28a to the formatted announcement in Figure 1-28b using these steps:

1. Center the three title lines across the page.
2. Bold and enlarge the first title line.
3. Italicize the second title line.
4. Bold, enlarge, and underline the third title line.
5. Italicize the word Jazz in the third title line.
6. Add bullets to the body paragraphs.
7. Bold the festival date.
8. Center and change the font of the last line of the announcement.

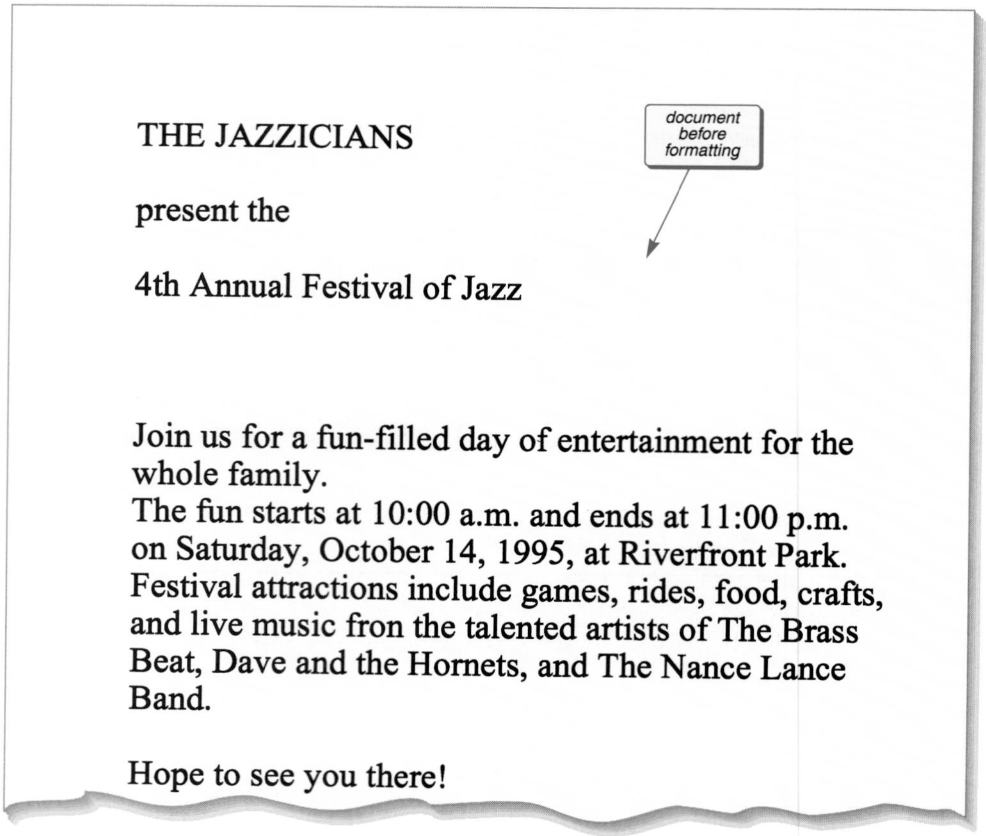

THE JAZZICIANS

document
before
formatting

present the

4th Annual Festival of Jazz

Join us for a fun-filled day of entertainment for the whole family.
The fun starts at 10:00 a.m. and ends at 11:00 p.m. on Saturday, October 14, 1995, at Riverfront Park. Festival attractions include games, rides, food, crafts, and live music fron the talented artists of The Brass Beat, Dave and the Hornets, and The Nance Lance Band.

Hope to see you there!

FIGURE 1-28a

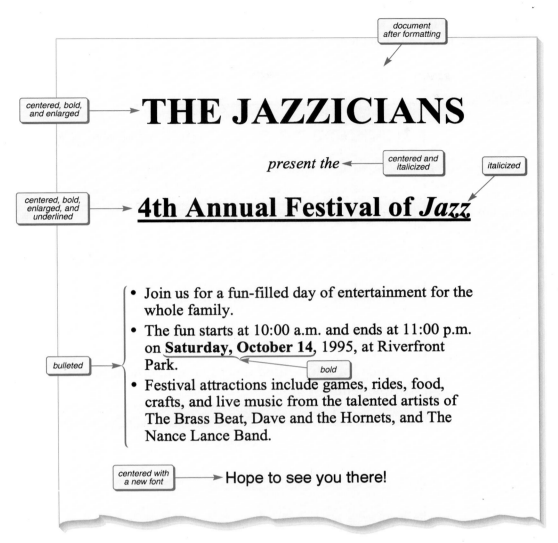

document after formatting

centered, bold, and enlarged → **THE JAZZICIANS**

present the ← *centered and italicized*

italicized

centered, bold, enlarged, and underlined → **<u>4th Annual Festival of *Jazz*</u>**

bulleted →
- Join us for a fun-filled day of entertainment for the whole family.
- The fun starts at 10:00 a.m. and ends at 11:00 p.m. on **Saturday, October 14**, 1995, at Riverfront Park.

  bold
- Festival attractions include games, rides, food, crafts, and live music from the talented artists of The Brass Beat, Dave and the Hornets, and The Nance Lance Band.

centered with a new font → Hope to see you there!

FIGURE 1-28b

The process required to format the announcement is explained on the following pages. The first formatting step is to center the three title lines between the margins. Recall that each title line is considered a separate paragraph because each line ends with a paragraph mark.

Selecting and Formatting Paragraphs and Characters

To format a single paragraph, move the insertion point into the paragraph and then format it. However, to format multiple paragraphs in a document, the paragraphs you want to format must first be selected and then they can be formatted. Likewise, to format characters, you must first select the characters to be formatted and then format your selection. Selected text is highlighted. For example, if your screen normally displays dark letters on a light background, then selected text appears as light letters on a dark background.

To center the first three title lines in Project 1, you must first select them. Then, center the selected paragraphs as shown in the following steps.

TO SELECT MULTIPLE PARAGRAPHS ▼

STEP 1 ►

Press CTRL+HOME to position the insertion point at the top of the document. Position the mouse pointer in the selection bar to the left of the first paragraph to be centered.

The mouse pointer changes to a right-pointing block arrow (⇗) in the selection bar (Figure 1-29). The selection bar is an unmarked area about 1/4-inch wide along the left edge of the screen.

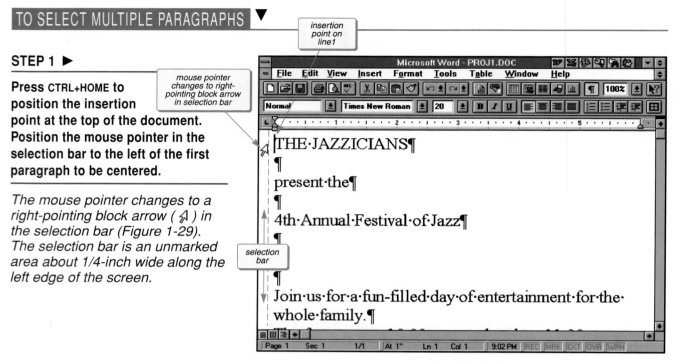

FIGURE 1-29

STEP 2 ►

Press and hold down the left mouse button. Drag the mouse pointer to the last line of the last paragraph to be centered. Release the mouse button.

All of the paragraphs to be centered are selected (Figure 1-30).

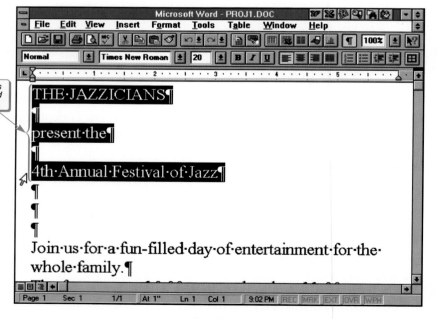

FIGURE 1-30

TO CENTER SELECTED PARAGRAPHS ▼

STEP 1 ▶

Point to the Center button (▦) on the Formatting toolbar.

The ToolTip, Center, displays beneath the mouse pointer (Figure 1-31).

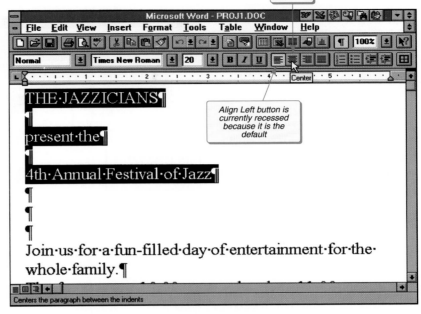

FIGURE 1-31

STEP 2 ▶

Click the Center button on the Formatting toolbar.

Word centers the three title lines between the left and right margins (Figure 1-32). The Center button on the Formatting toolbar is recessed, indicating the paragraphs are centered. When the paragraph containing the insertion point is centered, the Center button on the Formatting toolbar is recessed. If, for some reason, you wanted to return the paragraph to left-justified, you would click the Align Left button on the Formatting toolbar.

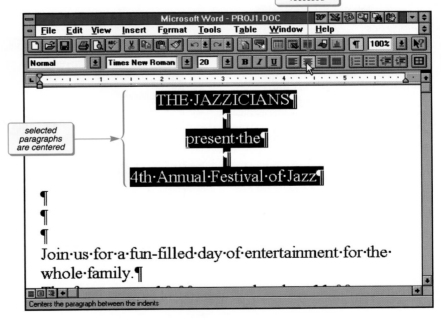

FIGURE 1-32

The next step is to select the first title line and format the characters in the selected line. Follow the steps on the next page to select the first title line, to bold the selected characters, and then to increase the font size of the selected characters to 48.

TO SELECT A SINGLE LINE ▼

STEP 1 ►

Position the mouse pointer in the selection bar to the left of the line of characters to be formatted. Click the left mouse button.

The mouse pointer changes to a right-pointing block arrow, and the entire line to the right of the mouse pointer is selected (Figure 1-33).

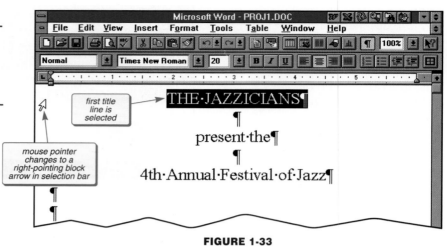

FIGURE 1-33

TO BOLD SELECTED TEXT ▼

STEP 1 ►

While the text is selected, point to the Bold button (B) on the Formatting toolbar and click.

Word formats the first title line in bold (Figure 1-34).

FIGURE 1-34

When the selected text is bold, the Bold button on the Formatting toolbar is recessed. If, for some reason, you wanted to remove the bold format while the text is selected, you would click the Bold button a second time.

The final step in formatting the first title line is to increase its font size. Recall that the font size specifies the size of the characters on the screen. Earlier in this project, you changed the font size for the entire announcement from 10 to 20. The first title line, however, requires a larger font size than the rest of the document.

Follow the steps on the next page to format the first title line to 48 point.

TO CHANGE THE FONT SIZE OF SELECTED TEXT ▼

STEP 1 ▶

While the text is selected, point to the Font Size box arrow on the Formatting toolbar and click. Point to the down arrow on the scroll bar and hold down the left mouse button until the font size 48 displays in the list. Then, point to 48.

A list of the available font sizes appears (Figure 1-35).

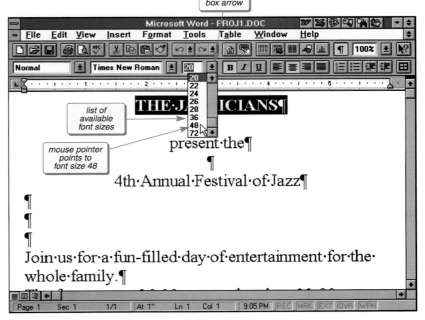

FIGURE 1-35

STEP 2 ▶

Select font size 48 by clicking the left mouse button.

Word increases the font size of the first title line from 20 to 48 (Figure 1-36). The Font Size box on the Formatting toolbar displays 48, indicating the selected text has a font size of 48.

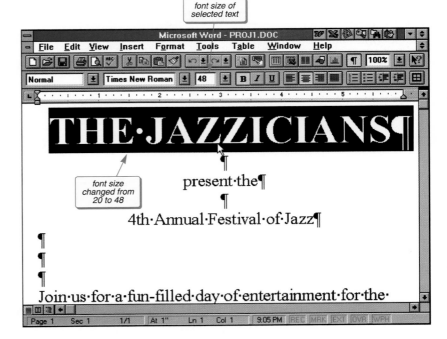

FIGURE 1-36

The next step is to select the second title line and italicize the characters in it, as shown in the steps on the next page.

TO ITALICIZE TEXT ▼

STEP 1 ►

Position the mouse pointer in the selection bar to the left of the line to be formatted and click.

The second title line is selected (Figure 1-37).

FIGURE 1-37

STEP 2 ►

With the text selected, point to the Italic button (*I*) on the Formatting toolbar and click.

The second title line is italicized (Figure 1-38).

FIGURE 1-38

When the selected text is italicized, the Italic button on the Formatting toolbar is recessed. If, for some reason, you want to remove the italic format from selected text, you would click the Italic button a second time.

The next step is to format the third title line. First, you select it. Then, you increase its font size to 36, bold it, and underline it.

FIGURE 1-39

STEP 1 ▶

Click in the selection bar to the left of the line to be formatted. Click the Font Size box arrow and scroll to font size 36. Select font size 36 by clicking it. Click the Bold button on the Formatting toolbar. Click the Underline button (☐) on the Formatting toolbar.

The third title line is enlarged, bold, and underlined (Figure 1-39).

When the selected text is underlined, the Underline button on the Formatting toolbar is recessed. If, for some reason, you want to remove the underline format from selected text, you would click the Underline button a second time.

The final step in formatting the third title line is to select the word Jazz and italicize it, as shown in the following steps.

TO SELECT A SINGLE WORD AND FORMAT IT ▼

STEP 1 ▶

Position the mouse pointer somewhere in the word to be formatted (Figure 1-40).

FIGURE 1-40

STEP 2 ▶

Double-click the left mouse button.

The word "Jazz" is selected (Figure 1-41).

FIGURE 1-41

STEP 3 ▶

Click the Italic button on the Formatting toolbar.

The word "Jazz" is italicized (Figure 1-42). It also remains bold, underlined, and enlarged from your previous character formatting.

FIGURE 1-42

The next formatting step is to add **bullets** to the paragraphs in the body of the announcement. Bullets are small, raised dots. Bullets differ from the nonprinting character for the SPACEBAR because bullets print.

Because the paragraphs to be bulleted do not display in the document window, you must first use the scroll bar to bring the paragraphs into view. Then, you must select the paragraphs and add bullets to them, as shown in the following steps.

TO ADD BULLETS TO PARAGRAPHS ▼

STEP 1 ►

Position the mouse pointer on the vertical scroll bar beneath the scroll box (Figure 1-43).

FIGURE 1-43

STEP 2 ►

Click the left mouse button. Position the mouse pointer in the selection bar to the left of the first paragraph to be bulleted.

Word scrolls down one screenful in the document (Figure 1-44).

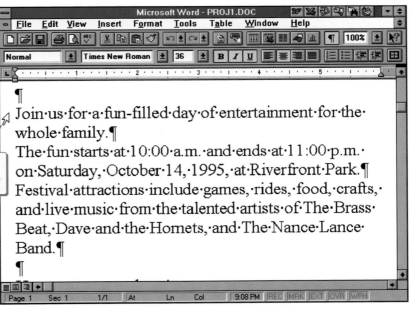

FIGURE 1-44

STEP 3 ►

Drag the mouse pointer to the last line of the last paragraph to be bulleted. Point to the Bullets button (▤).

Word selects the paragraphs to be bulleted and displays the ToolTip, Bullets, beneath the button (Figure 1-45).

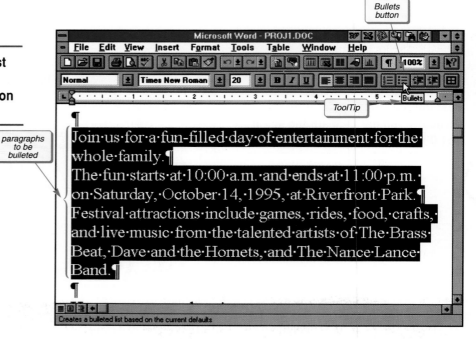

FIGURE 1-45

STEP 4 ►

Click the Bullets button. Click inside the selected paragraphs to remove the highlight.

Word adds bullets to the paragraphs (Figure 1-46).

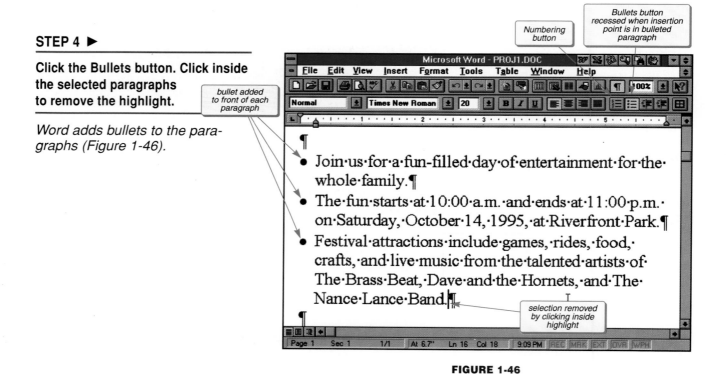

FIGURE 1-46

To remove a highlight, click the mouse. If you click inside the highlight, the Formatting toolbar displays the characteristics of characters and paragraphs containing the insertion point.

To add numbers to the front of a list instead of bullets, click the Numbering button () instead of the Bullets button. To remove bullets or numbers from a list, select the list and choose the Bullets and Numbering command from the Format menu. Then, choose the Remove button in the Bullets and Numbering dialog box.

The next step is to bold the day of the festival. The day consists of the group of words, "Saturday, October 14". Follow these steps to select the day, a group of words, and bold them.

TO SELECT A GROUP OF WORDS AND BOLD THEM ▼

STEP 1 ▶

Position the mouse pointer on the first character of the first word to be selected.

The mouse pointer is at the beginning of the word "Saturday" (Figure 1-47).

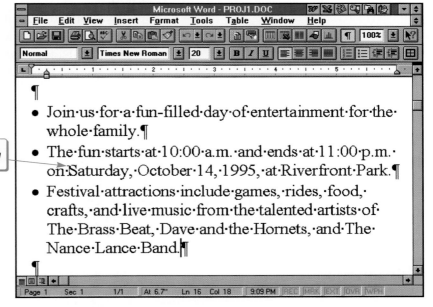

FIGURE 1-47

STEP 2 ▶

Drag the mouse pointer through the last character of the last word to be selected.

The words "Saturday, October 14" are selected (Figure 1-48). When the mouse pointer is in selected text, its shape is a left-pointing block arrow.

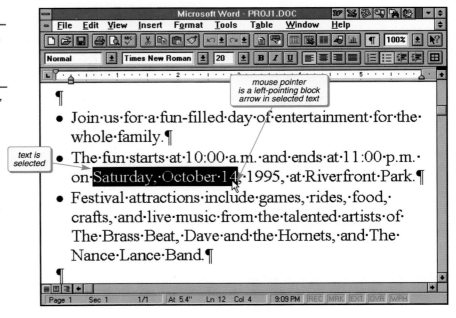

FIGURE 1-48

STEP 3 ►

Click the Bold button on the Formatting toolbar. Click inside the selected text to remove the highlight.

Word bolds the text and positions the insertion point inside the bold text (Figure 1-49). When the insertion point is inside the bold text, the Bold button on the Formatting toolbar is recessed.

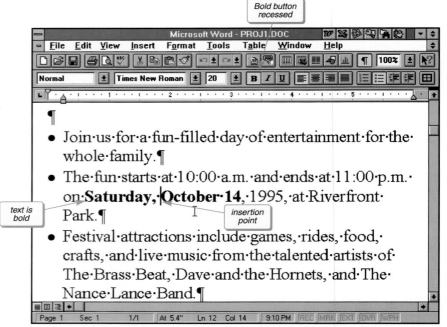

FIGURE 1-49

The final step in formatting the announcement is to select the last line and change its font and then center the entire line, as shown in the following steps.

TO CHANGE A FONT ▼

STEP 1 ►

Click beneath the scroll box on the vertical scroll bar to bring the last line of the announcement into the document window. Click in the selection bar to the left of the last line of the announcement to select it. Click the Font box arrow. Point to the up arrow on the Font scroll bar and hold down the mouse button until the Arial font displays in the list. Point to the Arial font (or a similar Font).

Word displays a list of available fonts (Figure 1-50). The font you select will be applied to the highlighted text. Your list of available fonts may differ, depending on the type of printer you are using.

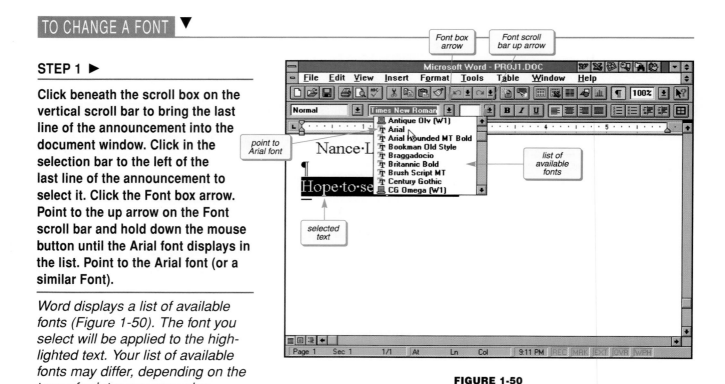

FIGURE 1-50

STEP 2 ▶

Click the Arial font. Click inside the selected text to remove the highlight. Click the Center button on the Formatting toolbar.

Word changes the font of the text to Arial (Figure 1-51). The last line of the document is centered. Recall when you are centering just one paragraph, the paragraph does not have to be selected – just place the insertion point somewhere inside the paragraph to be centered.

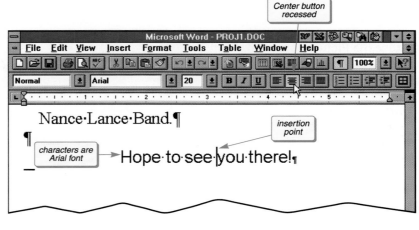

FIGURE 1-51

The formatting for the announcement is now complete. The next step is to import a graphic and resize it.

▶ ADDING A CLIP ART FILE TO A DOCUMENT

Word for Windows software includes a series of predefined graphics called **clip art files** or **Windows metafiles**. You insert, or **import**, these graphics into a Word document by choosing the Picture command from the Insert menu. Follow these steps to import the Windows metafile called jazz.wmf into your document (see Figure 1-56 on page MSW37). Windows metafiles have a file extension of **.wmf**.

TO IMPORT A GRAPHIC ▼

STEP 1 ▶

Press CTRL+HOME and position the insertion point where you want the graphic to be inserted. Select the Insert menu and point to the Picture command.

The insertion point is positioned on the second paragraph mark beneath the third title line of the announcement (Figure 1-52).

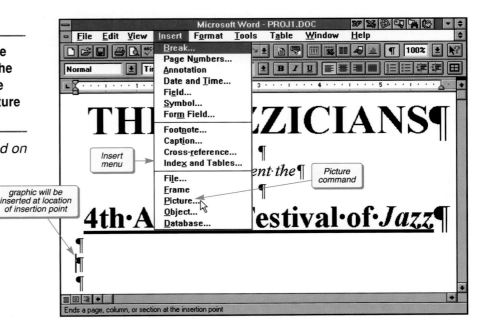

FIGURE 1-52

STEP 2 ►

Choose the Picture command. Point to the down scroll arrow on the File Name scroll bar.

Word displays the Insert Picture dialog box (Figure 1-53). The current subdirectory is clipart on drive C. The Windows metafiles are located in the clipart subdirectory. Word displays the Windows metafiles in the File Name list box. The filename to be imported, jazz.wmf, is not in view in the File Name list box.

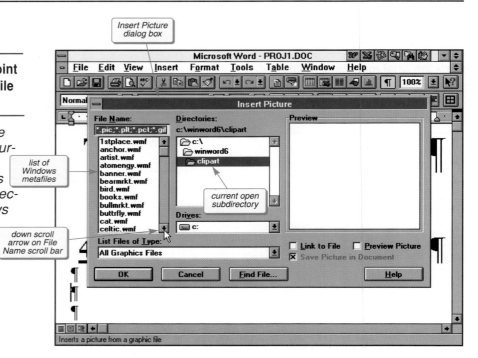

FIGURE 1-53

STEP 3 ►

Hold down the left mouse button until the filename jazz.wmf appears in the File Name list box. Point to the file jazz.wmf (Figure 1-54).

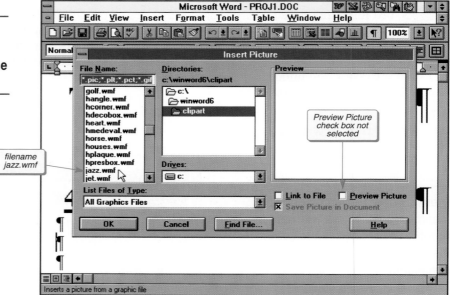

FIGURE 1-54

STEP 4 ▶

Select the filename jazz.wmf by clicking it. If it is not already selected, click the Preview Picture check box. Point to the OK button.

Word highlights the file-name and places it in the File Name box (Figure 1-55). Because the Preview Picture check box is selected, Word displays a preview of jazz.wmf, the selected Windows metafile, in the Preview area.

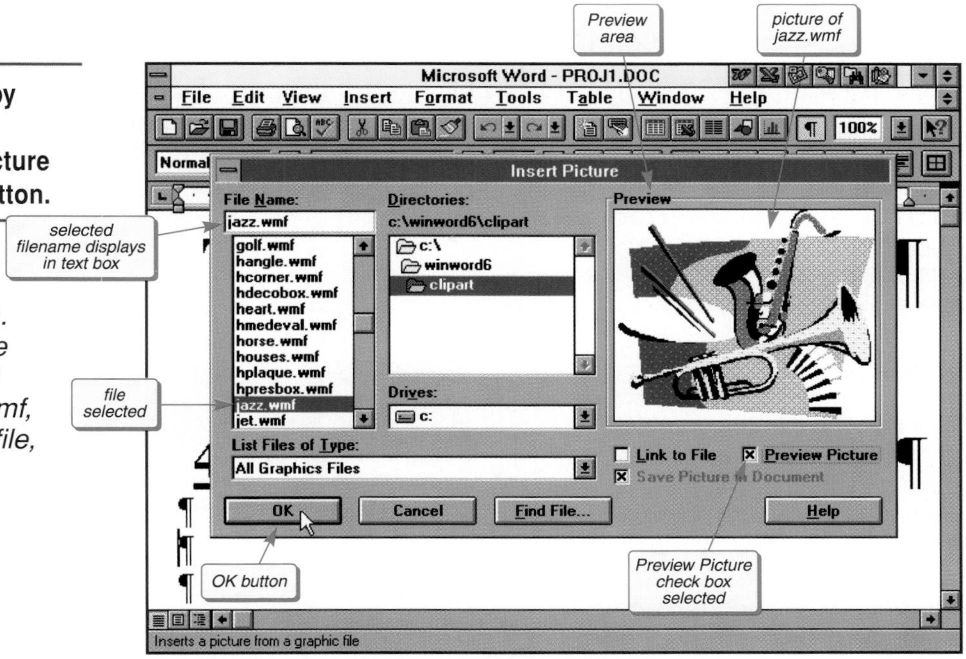

FIGURE 1-55

STEP 5 ▶

Choose the OK button in the Insert Picture dialog box.

Word inserts the graphic into your document at the location of the insertion point (Figure 1-56).

FIGURE 1-56

The graphic in the document is part of a paragraph. Therefore, you can use any of the paragraph alignment buttons on the Formatting toolbar to reposition the graphic.

Compare the graphic in Figure 1-56 to the one in Figure 1-1 on page MSW3. The graphic in Figure 1-1 is much larger and centered. Thus, the next step is to resize and center the imported graphic.

Scaling an Imported Graphic

Once a graphic has been imported into a document, you can easily change its size, or **scale** it. Scaling includes both enlarging and reducing the size of a graphic. To scale a graphic, you must first select it. The following steps show how to select and scale the graphic you just imported.

TO SCALE A GRAPHIC ▼

STEP 1 ▶

Click anywhere in the graphic.

*Word selects the graphic (Figure 1-57). Selected graphics display surrounded by a box with small black squares, called **sizing handles,** at each corner and middle location. The mouse is used to drag the sizing handles until the graphic is the desired size.*

STEP 2

Position the mouse pointer on the right, middle sizing handle.

The mouse pointer changes to a two-headed arrow (↔) when it is on a sizing handle.

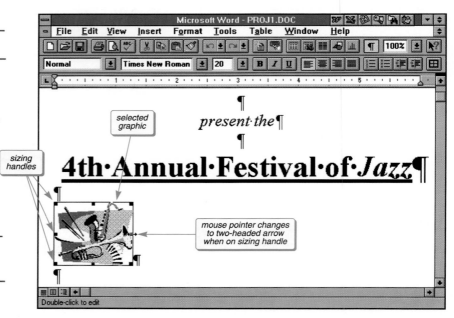

FIGURE 1-57

STEP 3 ▶

Drag the sizing handle to the right until the scaling percentage displayed on the status bar is 384% Wide.

As you drag the sizing handle to the right, Word displays the percentage of the imported graphic's original width on the status bar (Figure 1-58).

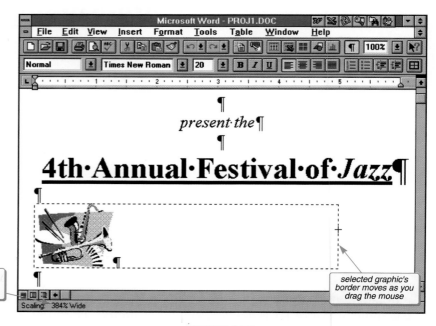

FIGURE 1-58

STEP 4 ▶

Release the mouse button.

Word resizes the graphic based on the new width (Figure 1-59).

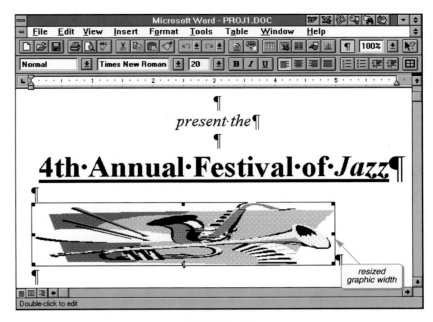

FIGURE 1-59

STEP 5 ▶

Click the down arrow on the vertical scroll bar three times. Drag the bottom, middle sizing handle downward until the scaling percentage displayed on the status bar reads 205% High. Then, click the Center button on the Formatting toolbar to center the graphic.

Word resizes the imported graphic in the document (Figure 1-60).

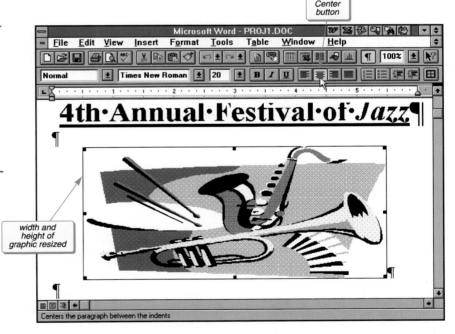

FIGURE 1-60

When you drag a middle sizing handle, as demonstrated in the above steps, the proportions of the original graphic are not maintained. To resize a graphic and maintain its original proportions, drag a corner sizing handle.

Rather than scaling a selected graphic with the mouse, you can also use the Picture command on the Format menu to resize a graphic. With the Picture command, you enter exact width and height measurements. If you have a precise measurement for the graphic, use the Picture command; otherwise, drag the sizing handles to resize the graphic.

Restoring a Scaled Graphic to its Original Size

Sometimes you might scale a graphic and realize it is the wrong size. In these cases, you might want to return the graphic to its original size and start over. To return a scaled graphic to its original size, select the graphic and choose the Picture command from the Format menu. Then, choose the Reset button in the Picture dialog box. Finally, choose the OK button in the Picture dialog box.

After you have entered and formatted a document, you should ensure that no typographical errors have occurred by checking the spelling of the words in your document.

▶ CHECKING SPELLING

Word checks your document for spelling errors using a main dictionary contained in the Word program. If a word is not found in the dictionary, the word is displayed in the Spelling dialog box with a message indicating the word is not in the main dictionary. In the Spelling dialog box, you may correct the word. Sometimes, however, the word is spelled correctly. For example, many names, abbreviations, and specialized terms are not in the main dictionary. In these cases, you ignore the message and continue the spelling check.

When you invoke Word's **spell checker**, it checks all of your document. The following steps illustrate how to spell check PROJ1.DOC. (In the following example, the word "whole" has intentionally been misspelled as "whol" to illustrate the use of Word's spell checker. If you are doing this project on a personal computer, your announcement may have different misspelled words, depending on the accuracy of your typing.)

TO CHECK THE SPELLING OF A DOCUMENT ▼

STEP 1 ▶

Press CTRL+HOME to position the insertion point at the top of the document. Point to the Spelling button ( ) on the Standard toolbar as shown in Figure 1-61.

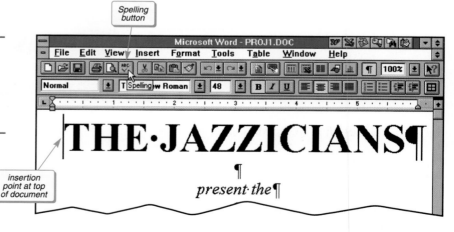

FIGURE 1-61

STEP 2 ▶

Click the Spelling button on the Standard toolbar.

Word begins the spelling check at the top of your document. When a word is not found in the main dictionary, it displays the Spelling: English (US) dialog box (Figure 1-62). Word did not find JAZZICIANS in its main dictionary because JAZZICIANS is a proper name and is spelled correctly.

STEP 3

Point to the Ignore All button (Ignore All) in the Spelling: English (US) dialog box.

FIGURE 1-62

STEP 4 ▶

Choose the Ignore All button.

The spelling check ignores all future occurrences of the word JAZZICIANS. Word continues the spelling check until it finds the next error or reaches the end of the document. The spelling check did not find the word "whol" in its main dictionary. The spelling check lists suggested corrections in the Suggestions list box and places its choice (whole) in the Change To box (Figure 1-63).

STEP 5

Choose the Change button (Change) in the Spelling: English (US) dialog box.

The spelling check changes the misspelled word (whol) to its suggestion (whole). Word continues to check spelling until it finds the next error or reaches the end of the document.

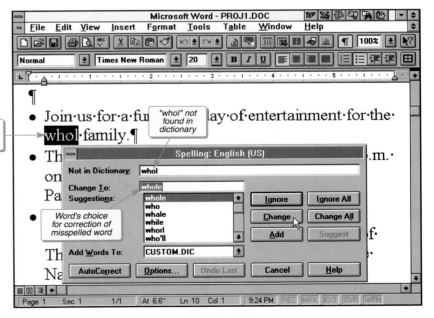

FIGURE 1-63

STEP 6 ▶

When Word stops on Riverfront, choose the Ignore All button because Riverfront is a proper name. When Word stops on Nance, choose the Ignore All button because Nanceis a proper name.

Word displays a message that it has checked the entire document (Figure 1-64).

STEP 7

Choose the OK button.

Word returns to your document.

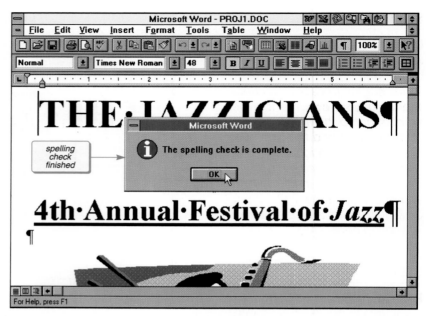

FIGURE 1-64

If the suggested change made by the spelling check is not your choice, you can select any of the other words in the list of suggested words by clicking the desired word. The word you click appears in the Change To box. If your choice is not in the list of suggested words, you may type your desired word directly into the Change To box. When you choose the Change button, the word in the Change To box replaces the misspelled word.

▶ SAVING AN EXISTING DOCUMENT WITH THE SAME FILENAME

The announcement for Project 1 is now complete. To transfer the formatting changes, imported graphic, and spelling corrections to your diskette in drive A, you must save the document again. When you saved the document the first time, you assigned a filename to it (PROJ1). Word automatically assigns this filename to the document each time you save it when you use the following procedure.

TO SAVE AN EXISTING DOCUMENT WITH THE SAME FILENAME ▼

STEP 1 ►

Point to the Save button on the Standard toolbar and click.

Word saves the document on a diskette inserted in drive A using the currently assigned filename, PROJ1. When the save is finished, the document remains in main memory and displays on the screen (Figure 1-65).

FIGURE 1-65

If you want to save an existing document with a different filename, choose the Save As command from the File menu to display the Save As dialog box. Then, follow the procedures as discussed in Steps 2 through 5 on pages MSW20-21.

▶ PRINTING A DOCUMENT

he next step is to print the document you created. A printed version of the document is called a **hardcopy** or **printout**. Perform the following steps to print the announcement created in Project 1.

TO PRINT A DOCUMENT ▼

STEP 1 ►

Ready the printer according to the printer instructions. Point to the Print button (⬛) on the Standard toolbar (Figure 1-66).

STEP 2 ►

Click the Print button.

The mouse pointer briefly changes to an hourglass shape (⧗), and then Word quickly displays a message on the status bar, indicating it is preparing to print the document. A few moments later, the document begins printing on the printer.

FIGURE 1-66

STEP 3 ▶

When the printer stops, retrieve the
printout (Figure 1-67).

FIGURE 1-67

THE JAZZICIANS

present the

4th Annual Festival of *Jazz*

- Join us for a fun-filled day of entertainment for the whole family.
- The fun starts at 10:00 a.m. and ends at 11:00 p.m. on **Saturday, October 14**, 1995, at Riverfront Park.
- Festival attractions include games, rides, food, crafts, and live music from the talented artists of The Brass Beat, Dave and the Hornets, and The Nance Lance Band.

Hope to see you there!

When you use the Print button to print a document, Word automatically prints the entire document. You may then distribute the hardcopy or keep it as a permanent record of the document.

▶ QUITTING WORD

fter you create, save, and print the announcement, Project 1 is complete. To quit Word and return control to Program Manager, perform the following steps.

TO QUIT WORD ▼

STEP 1 ▶

Select the File menu and point to the Exit command (Figure 1-68).

FIGURE 1-68

STEP 2 ▶

Choose the Exit command.

If you made changes to the document since the last save, Word displays a message asking if you want to save the changes (Figure 1-69). Choose the Yes button (Yes) to save changes; choose the No button (No) to ignore the changes; or choose the Cancel button (Cancel) to return to the document. If you made no changes since saving the document, this dialog box does not display.

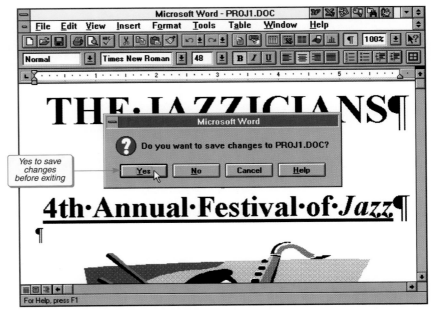

FIGURE 1-69

You can also quit Word by double-clicking the Control-menu box on the left edge of the title bar.

Project 1 is now complete. You created, formatted, added a graphic, checked spelling, and printed it. You might, however, decide to change the announcement at a later date. To do this, you must start Word and then retrieve your document from the diskette in drive A, as shown in the following steps.

▶ OPENING A DOCUMENT

Earlier, you saved on disk the document built in Project 1 using the file-name PROJ1.DOC. Once you have created and saved a document, you will often have reason to retrieve it from diskette. For example, you might want to revise the document or print another copy of it. To do this, you must first start Word and then open the document. The following steps illustrate how to open the file PROJ1.DOC using the Open button (⬚) on the Standard toolbar.

TO OPEN A DOCUMENT ▼

STEP 1 ▶

Point to the Open button on the Standard toolbar and click.

Word displays the Open dialog box (Figure 1-70).

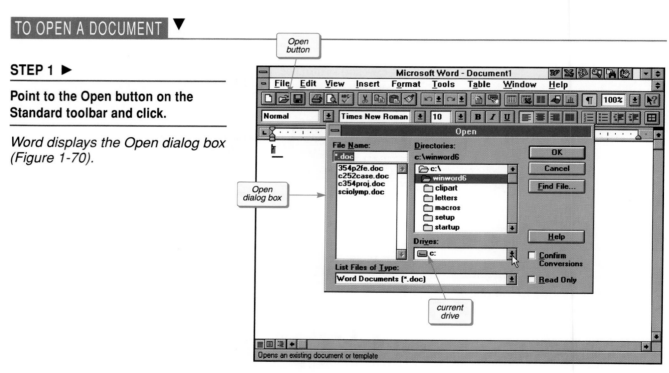

FIGURE 1-70

STEP 2 ▶

If drive A is not the selected drive, select a: in the Drives drop-down list box (refer to Figures 1-24 through 1-26 on pages MSW20-21 to review this technique). Then, select the filename proj1.doc by clicking the filename in the File Name list box. Point to the OK button (Figure 1-71).

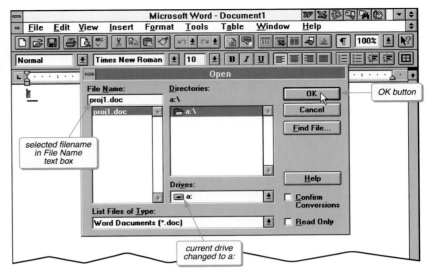

FIGURE 1-71

STEP 3 ▶

Choose the OK button in the Open dialog box.

Word opens the document PROJ1.DOC from the diskette in drive A and displays it on the screen (Figure 1-72).

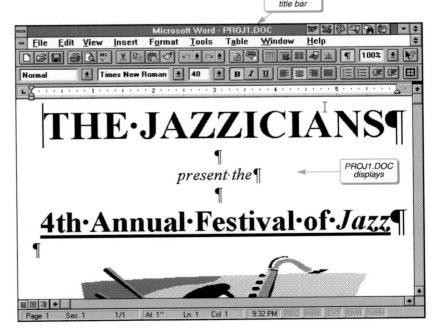

FIGURE 1-72

▶ CORRECTING ERRORS

fter creating a document, you will often find you must make changes to the document. Changes can be required because the document contains an error or because of new circumstances.

Types of Changes Made to Documents

The types of changes made to documents normally fall into one of the three following categories: additions, deletions, or modifications.

ADDITIONS   You might have to place additional words, sentences, or paragraphs in the document. Additions occur when you omit text from a document and are required to add it later. For example, you might accidentally forget to put the word Annual in the third title line in Project 1.

DELETIONS   Sometimes text in a document is incorrect or is no longer needed. For example, Dave and the Hornets might cancel their appearance at the jazz festival. In this case, you would delete them from the announcement.

MODIFICATIONS   If an error is made in a document, you might have to revise the word(s) in the text. For example, the date of the festival in Project 1 might change to October 21.

Word provides several methods for correcting errors in a document. For each of the error correction techniques, you must first move the insertion point to the error.

Inserting Text into an Existing Document

If you leave a word or phrase out of a sentence, you can insert it into the sentence by positioning the insertion point where you would like the text inserted. Word always inserts the text to the left of the insertion point. The text to the right of the insertion point moves to the right and downward to accommodate the added text. The following steps illustrate adding the word *live* before the word *entertainment* in the first bulleted paragraph beneath the graphic in Project 1.

TO INSERT TEXT INTO AN EXISTING DOCUMENT ▼

STEP 1 ▶

Scroll through the document and position the mouse pointer immediately to the left of the letter e in entertainment and click.

The insertion point displays immediately to the left of the letter e in entertainment (Figure 1-73).

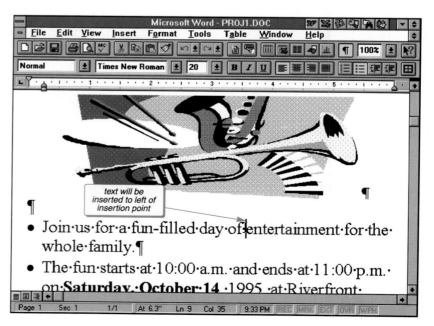

FIGURE 1-73

STEP 2 ▶

Type the word live **followed by a space.**

The word "live" is now inserted between the words "of" and "enter-tainment" in the announcement for Project 1 (Figure 1-74).

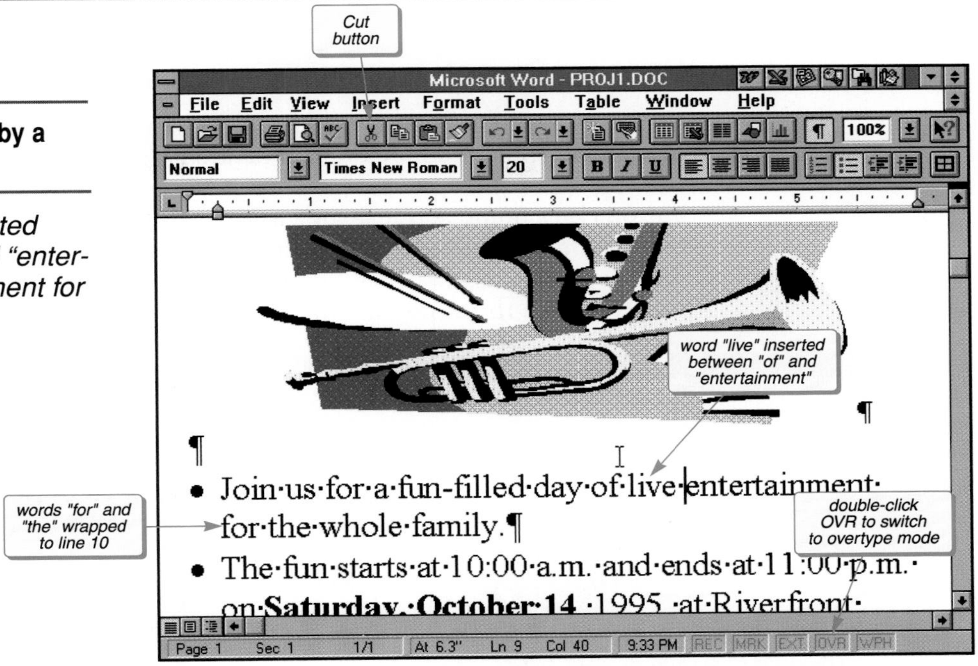

Cut button

word "live" inserted between "of" and "entertainment"

words "for" and "the" wrapped to line 10

double-click OVR to switch to overtype mode

FIGURE 1-74

In Figure 1-74, the text to the right of the word *entertainment* moved to the right and downward to accommodate the insertion of the word *live*. That is, the words *for* and *the* moved down to line 10.

In Word, the default typing mode is **insert mode**. In insert mode, as you type a character, Word inserts the character and moves all the characters to the right of the typed character one position to the right. You can change to **overtype mode** by double-clicking the **OVR mode indicator** on the status bar (Figure 1-74). In overtype mode, Word overtypes characters to the right of the insertion point. Clicking the OVR mode indicator a second time returns you to insert mode.

Deleting Text from an Existing Document

It is not unusual to type incorrect characters or words in a document. In such a case, to correct the error, you might want to delete certain letters or words. Perform the following steps to delete an incorrect character or word.

TO DELETE AN INCORRECT CHARACTER IN A DOCUMENT

Step 1: Position the insertion point next to the incorrect character.
Step 2: Press the BACKSPACE key to erase to the left of the insertion point; or press the DELETE key to erase to the right of the insertion point.

TO DELETE AN INCORRECT WORD OR PHRASE IN A DOCUMENT

Step 1: Select the word or phrase you want to erase.
Step 2: Click the Cut button (✄) on the Standard toolbar.

Undoing Recent Actions

Word provides an Undo button (▢) on the Standard toolbar you can use to cancel your recent command(s) or action(s). If you accidentally delete some text, you can make it reappear. If you want to cancel your undo, you can use the Redo button (▢). Some actions, such as saving or printing a document, cannot be undone or redone.

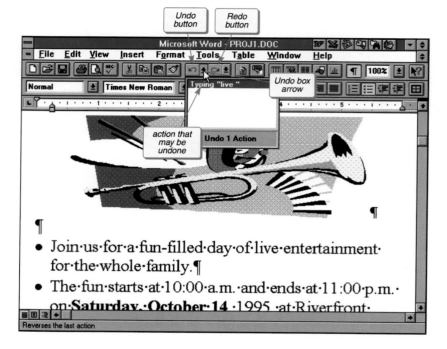

**TO CANCEL YOUR
MOST RECENT ACTION**

Step 1: Click the Undo button on
the Standard toolbar.

**TO CANCEL YOUR
MOST RECENT UNDO**

Step 1: Click the Redo button on
the Standard toolbar.

TO CANCEL A PRIOR ACTION

Step 1: Click the Undo box arrow
to display the Undo Actions
list (Figure 1-75).
Step 2: Select the action to be
undone by clicking it.

FIGURE 1-75

You may also select multiple actions by dragging the mouse through them in the undo list to undo a group of sequential actions.

Closing the Entire Document

Sometimes, everything goes wrong. If this happens, you may want to close the document entirely and start over. You may also want to close a document when you are finished with it so you can begin your next document. To close the document, follow these steps.

TO CLOSE THE ENTIRE DOCUMENT AND START OVER

Step 1: Select the File menu.
Step 2: Choose the Close command.
Step 3: When Word displays the dialog box, choose the No button to ignore the
changes since the last time you saved the document.
Step 4: Click the New button (▢) on the Standard toolbar.

You can also close the document by double-clicking on the Control-menu box on the left edge of the menu bar.

▶ WORD'S HELP FACILITY

 t any time while you are using Word, you can select the Help menu to gain access to **online Help** (Figure 1-76). The Word Help menu provides a table of contents and an index for navigating around the Help facility. Also, every Word dialog box has a Help button you can click to obtain help about the current activity on which you are working.

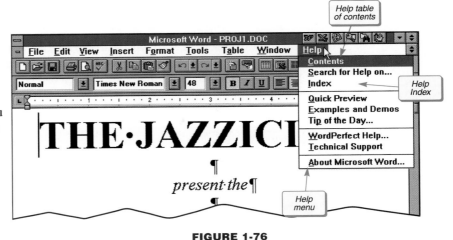

FIGURE 1-76

The Help Button

To obtain help on an item on the Word screen, you can click the Help button (▨) on the Standard toolbar. When you click the Help button, the mouse pointer changes to an arrow with a question mark (▨?) as shown in Figure 1-77. You move the mouse pointer to any item on the Word screen and click to obtain **context-sensitive** help. The term context-sensitive help means that Word will display immediate information for the topic on which you click. For example, clicking the Undo button displays the Help window shown in Figure 1-78.

You can print the Help information in the Help window by choosing the Print Topic command from the File menu in the Help window. You close a Help window by choosing Exit from the File menu in the Help window or by double-clicking the Control-menu box in the title bar on the Help window.

Word's online Help has features that make it powerful and easy to use. The best way to familiarize yourself with online Help is to use it.

FIGURE 1-77

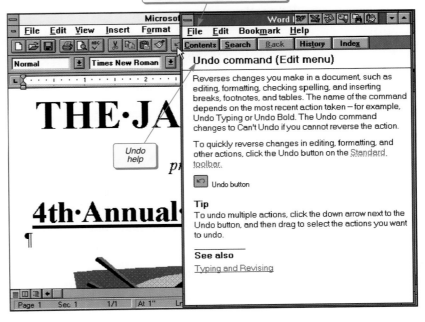

FIGURE 1-78

Tip of the Day

Each time you start Word, a **Tip of the Day** dialog box displays on the Word screen (Figure 1-3 on page MSW5). These tips are designed to help you be a more productive Word user. You can view Word tips at any time by choosing the Tip of the Day command from the Help menu (Figure 1-76 on the previous page).

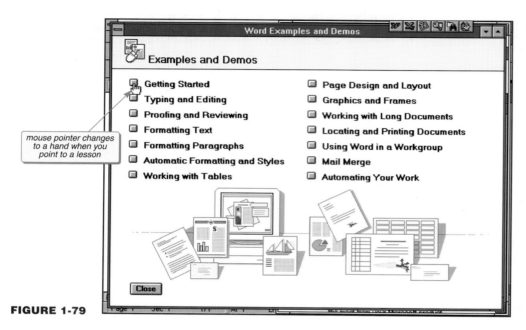

FIGURE 1-79

Word's Online Examples and Demonstrations

You can improve your Word skills by stepping through the online **examples and demonstrations** supplied with Word. If you have an open document on your screen, before you begin the examples and demonstrations, click the Save button on the Standard toolbar to save the document with your latest changes.

Next, choose Examples and Demos from the Help menu (Figure 1-76 on the previous page). Word responds by displaying a Word Examples and Demos window (Figure 1-79). The mouse pointer changes to a small hand when you point to a lesson. Select any of the fourteen lessons. When you select a lesson, Word displays another menu so you can customize your lessons.

Wizards

Word supplies **wizards** to assist you in creating common types of documents, such as letters, memos, resumes, and newsletters. To use a wizard, choose the New command from the File menu, and then select the wizard you desire. The wizard asks you a few basic questions, then displays a basic formatted document on the screen for you to customize or fill in blanks. In Project 2, you will use wizards to create a cover letter and a resume.

▶ PROJECT SUMMARY

Project 1 introduced you to starting Word and creating a document. You learned how to change the font size before entering any text in the document. You also learned how to save and print a document. Once you saved the document, you learned how to format paragraphs and characters in the document. Then, you imported and scaled a graphic file. You used the spelling checker to check the document for typographical errors. You learned to move the insertion point so you could insert, delete, and modify text. Finally, you learned to use Word's online Help.

▶ KEY TERMS AND INDEX

Q U I C K   R E F E R E N C E

In Microsoft Word 6, you can accomplish a task in a number of ways. The following table provides a quick reference to each task presented in this project with its available options. The commands listed in the Menu column can be executed using either the keyboard or mouse. If you have WordPerfect help activated, the key combinations listed in the Keyboard Shortcuts column will not work as shown.

Task	Mouse	Menu	Keyboard Shortcuts
Bold Selected Text	Click Bold button on Formatting toolbar	From Format menu, choose Font	Press CTRL+B
Cancel a Selection	Click anywhere in text area of document window		Press arrow key
Center a Paragraph	Click Center button on Formatting toolbar	From Format menu, choose Paragraph	Press CTRL+E
Change a Font Size	Click Font Size box on Formatting toolbar	From Format menu, choose Font	Press CTRL+SHIFT+P
Check Spelling	Click Spelling button on Standard toolbar	From Tools menu, choose Spelling	Press F7
Close a Document	Double-click Control-menu box on menu bar	From File menu, choose Close	Press CTRL+W

(continued)

QUICK REFERENCE (continued)

Task	Mouse	Menu	Keyboard Shortcuts
Decrease to Next Available Font Size			Press CTRL+<
Display Nonprinting Characters	Click Show/Hide ¶ button on Standard toolbar	From Tools menu, choose Options	Press CTRL+SHIFT+*
Increase to Next Available Font Size			Press CTRL+>
Italicize Selected Text	Click Italic button on Formatting toolbar	From Format menu, choose Font	Press CTRL+I
Move the Insertion Point	Point mouse pointer to desired location and click		Press RIGHT, LEFT, DOWN, or UP ARROW
Move the Insertion Point to the Beginning/End of a Document	Drag scroll box to top/bottom of vertical scroll bar and click		Press CTRL+HOME or CTRL+END
Obtain Context-Sensitive Help	Click Help button on Standard toolbar		Press SHIFT+F1
Obtain Online Help		Select Help menu	Press F1
Open a Document	Click Open button on Standard toolbar	From File menu, choose Open	Press CTRL+O
Print a Document	Click Print button on Standard toolbar	From File menu, choose Exit	Press CTRL+P
Quit Word	Double-click Control-menu box on title bar	From File menu, choose Exit	Press ALT+F4
Redo the Last Undo	Click Redo button on Standard toolbar	From Edit menu, choose Redo	Press CTRL+Y
Save a Document	Click Save button on Standard toolbar	From File menu, choose Save	Press CTRL+S
Scroll Up/Down One Line	Click up/down scroll arrow on vertical scroll bar		Press UP or DOWN ARROW
Scroll Up/Down One Screen	Click scroll bar above/below scroll box		Press PAGE UP or PAGE DOWN
Select a Graphic	Click in graphic		
Select a Line	Click in selection bar to left of line		Press SHIFT+DOWN ARROW
Select a Group of Words	Move insertion point to first word and drag to end of last word		Press F8, then arrow key until desired words are selected
Select One Word	Double-click in word		Press CTRL+SHIFT+RIGHT ARROW
Underline Selected Text	Click Underline button on Formatting toolbar	From Format menu, choose Font	Press CTRL+U
Undo the Last Change	Click Undo button on Standard toolbar	From Edit menu, choose Undo	Press CTRL+Z

STUDENT ASSIGNMENT 1
True/False

Instructions: Circle T if the statement is true or F if the statement is false.

T F 1. Microsoft Word 6.0 is a word processing program that allows you to create and revise documents.
T F 2. The status bar is used to retrieve a document and display it in the document window.
T F 3. To create a new paragraph, press the ENTER key.
T F 4. To enter a blank line into a document, click the Blank Line button on the Standard toolbar.
T F 5. Toolbars contain buttons and boxes that allow you to perform tasks more quickly than using the menu bar.
T F 6. You should always hide nonprinting characters before printing a document because nonprinting characters can make your printed document difficult to read.
T F 7. Wordwrap allows you to type continually without pressing the ENTER key at the end of each line.
T F 8. To save a document with the same filename, click the Save button on the Standard toolbar.
T F 9. When you select a word, it appears on the status bar.
T F 10. The Underline button is located on the Formatting toolbar.
T F 11. When you check spelling of a document, Word displays a list of suggestions for the misspelled word(s).
T F 12. When you save a document, it disappears from the screen.
T F 13. A printed version of a document is called a hardcopy, or printout.
T F 14. Click the Exit button on the Standard toolbar to quit Word.
T F 15. In insert mode, Word always inserts text to the left of the insertion point.
T F 16. To open a document, click the New button on the Standard toolbar.
T F 17. If you don't assign a filename when you save a document, Word automatically assigns one for you.
T F 18. When selected text has been centered, the Center button appears recessed.
T F 19. If you accidentally delete a word, you can make it reappear by clicking the Undo button.
T F 20. To select a graphic, click anywhere inside the graphic.

STUDENT ASSIGNMENT 2
Multiple Choice

Instructions: Circle the correct response.

1. Word is preset to use standard 8 1/2 by 11-inch paper, with _____ inch left and right margins and _____ inch top and bottom margins.
   a. 1 1/4, 1
   b. 1 1/2, 1 1/4
   c. 1, 1 1/2
   d. 1, 1 1/4
2. As you type or insert graphs, your text and graphics display in the _____.
   a. scroll bars
   b. text area
   c. insertion area
   d. selection bar

(continued)

STUDENT ASSIGNMENT 2 (continued)

3. When the mouse pointer is in an open menu, it has the shape of a(n) _____.
   a. I-beam
   b. hourglass
   c. left-pointing block arrow
   d. vertical bar

4. To move the document up one entire screen at a time, _____.
   a. click the scroll box
   b. click anywhere on the scroll bar above the scroll box
   c. click the up scroll button at the top of the scroll bar
   d. both b and c

5. Word automatically adds the extension of _____ to a filename when you save a document.
   a. .doc
   b. .txt
   c. .wrd
   d. .mwd

6. To erase the character to the left of the insertion point, press the _____ key.
   a. DELETE
   b. INSERT
   c. BACKSPACE
   d. both a and c

7. Selected graphics display _____ handles at the corner and middle points.
   a. selection
   b. sizing
   c. scaling
   d. resizing

8. When nonprinting characters display in the document window, spaces are indicated by _____.
   a. raised dots
   b. right-pointing arrows
   c. a superscripted letter S
   d. question marks

9. _____ the OVR mode indicator to toggle between overtype and insert mode.
   a. Click
   b. Double-click
   c. Drag
   d. Point to

10. When you close a document, _____.
   a. it is erased from disk
   b. it is removed from the screen
   c. control is returned to Program Manager
   d. both a and c

STUDENT ASSIGNMENT 3
Understanding the Word Screen

Instructions: In Figure SA1-3, arrows point to major components of the Word screen. Identify the various parts of the screen in the spaces provided.

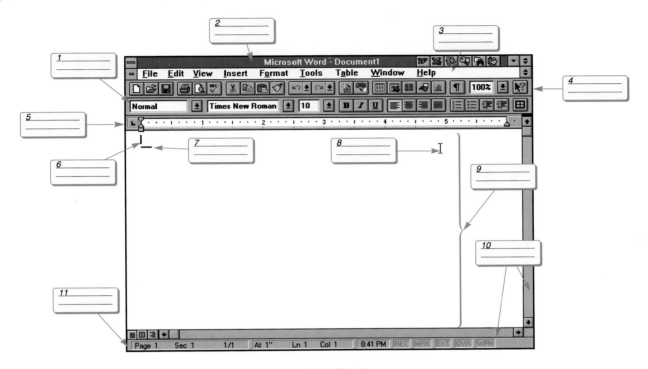

FIGURE SA1-3

STUDENT ASSIGNMENT 4
Understanding the Standard Toolbar

Instructions: In Figure SA1-4, arrows point to several of the buttons on the Standard toolbar. In the spaces provided, briefly explain the purpose of each button.

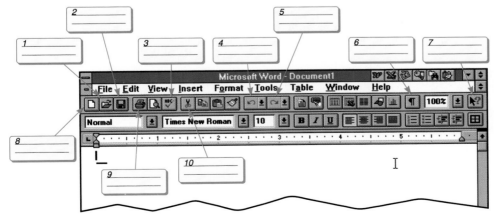

FIGURE SA1-4

STUDENT ASSIGNMENT 5
Understanding the Formatting Toolbar

Instructions: Answer the following questions concerning the Formatting toolbar in Figure SA1-5.

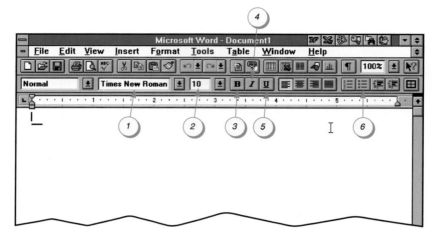

FIGURE SA1-5

1. What do the words Times New Roman indicate? _____

2. What does the 10 indicate? _____

3. What is the purpose of the button that contains the dark capital B? _____

4. What is the purpose of the button that contains the slanted capital I? _____

5. What is the purpose of the button that contains the capital U with the line under it?

   _____

6. What is the purpose of the button with the three large dots to the left of three horizontal lines?

   _____

STUDENT ASSIGNMENT 6
Understanding Methods of Deleting Text

Instructions: Describe the result of various methods of deleting text in the space provided.

METHOD	RESULT
Position the insertion point and press the DELETE key.	_____
Position the insertion point and press the BACKSPACE key.	_____
Select a word or phrase and click the Cut button.	_____

COMPUTER LABORATORY EXERCISE 1
Using the Help Menu, Help Button, and Examples and Demonstrations

Instructions: Perform the following tasks using a computer:

1. Start Word.
2. Select Help from the menu bar by pointing to Help and clicking the left mouse button.
3. Choose the Contents command by pointing to it and clicking the left mouse button. A screen with the title Word Help displays.
4. Press F1 to display the How to Use Help window. Read the contents of the window.
5. Select File from the Help window by pointing to File and clicking the left mouse button.
6. Ready the printer and choose the Print Topic command by pointing to it and clicking the left mouse button. Word produces a hardcopy of the How to Use Help window.
7. To return to Word Help, choose the Contents button by pointing to it and clicking the left mouse button.
8. To close the Help window, choose the Exit command from the File menu in the Help window.
9. Click the Help button on the Standard toolbar.
10. Point to the Spelling button on the Formatting toolbar and click.
11. Print the contents of the Spelling command Help window as described in Steps 5 and 6 above. Then, close the Help window as described in Step 8 above.
12. From the Help menu, choose Quick Preview.
13. Read the Getting Started lesson.
14. From the Help menu, choose Examples and Demos.
15. Select and read these three lessons: Typing and Editing, Proofing and Reviewing, and Formatting Text.
16. When you have completed reading the three lessons, return to the Word text screen by choosing the Close button from the Word Examples and Demos window. Then, close the Word Help window.

COMPUTER LABORATORY EXERCISE 2
Importing and Scaling a Graphic File

Instructions: Import a lightbulb graphic file. First, resize it without retaining its original proportions, as shown in Figure CLE1-2. Then, reset it to its original dimensions and resize it again, retaining its original proportions.

Perform the following tasks:

1. Start Word.
2. From the Insert menu, choose the Picture command.
3. Point to the down arrow at the bottom of the scroll bar in the File Name box and hold down the left mouse button until the filename lightblb.wmf displays. Select this file by clicking it. If it is not selected, click the Preview Picture check box to display the file in the Preview area.

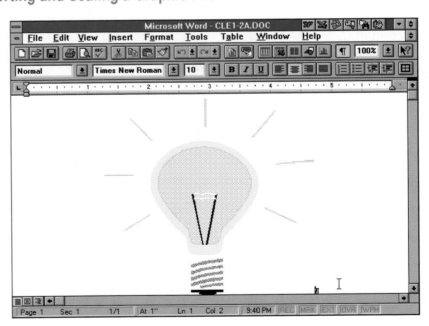

FIGURE CLE1-2

(continued)

COMPUTER LABORATORY ASSIGNMENT 2 (continued)

4. Choose the OK button in the Insert Picture dialog box.
5. Select the lightbulb graphic by clicking it.
6. Center the graphic by clicking the Center button on the Formatting toolbar.
7. Resize the graphic as follows: drag the right, middle sizing handle until the status bar reads 250% Wide; drag the bottom, middle sizing handle until the status bar reads 220% High.
8. Save the scaled graphic with the filename CLE1-2A.
9. Print the graphic by clicking the Print button on the Standard toolbar.
10. Restore the graphic to its original dimensions by choosing the Picture command from the Format menu. In the Picture dialog box, choose the Reset button. Then, choose the OK button.
11. Resize the graphic again, this time retaining its original proportions by dragging the bottom, right corner sizing handle until the status bar reads 225% Wide and 225% High.
12. Use the Save As command on the File menu to save the scaled graphic with the filename CLE1-2B.
13. Print the graphic.

COMPUTER LABORATORY EXERCISE 3
Checking Spelling of a Document

Instructions: Start Word. Open the document CLE1-3.DOC from the Word subdirectory on the Student Diskette that accompanies this book. As shown in Figure CLE1-3, the document is an employee announcement containing many typographical errors. You are to use Word's spelling checker to correct the errors.

Perform the following tasks:

1. Position the insertion point at the beginning of the document and start the spelling checker by clicking the Spelling button on the Standard toolbar.
2. Change the incorrect word NOTACE to NOTICE by clicking the Change button.
3. Change the incorrect word EMPLOYES to EMPLOYEES by clicking the Change button.
4. Click the Delete button to remove the duplicate occurrence of the word has.
5. Change the incorrect word insurence to insurance by clicking the Change button.
6. Change the incorrect word cns to cons by pointing to cons in the suggested list of words and clicking. Then, click the Change button.
7. Change the incorrect word crrent to current by clicking the Change button.
8. Change the incorrect word p;sn to plan by typing plan in the Change To box. Then, click the Change button.
9. Change the incorrect word Alternitive to Alternative by clicking the Change button.
10. Use the Save As command on the File menu to save the document on your data disk with the filename CLE1-3A.
11. Print the new document.

NOTACE

incorrect entries are circled to help you identify them

ALL EMPLOYES

- A meeting has has been scheduled on August 18 in Lunchroom A from 9:00 a.m. to 11:00 a.m. covering our insurence plan.

- Be prepared to discuss the pros and cns of our crrent insurance p;sn.

- Alternitive plans for 1996 will be distributed following our meeting.

PLEASE PLAN TO ATTEND

FIGURE CLE1-3

COMPUTER LABORATORY ASSIGNMENT 1
Creating an Announcement with an Imported Graphic

Purpose: To become familiar with creating a document, formatting and spell checking a document, importing a graphic, and saving and printing a document.

Problem: As a student in the Athletic Department at Jefferson High School (JHS), your coach has asked you to create an announcement for two current events: the sale of SuperSaver Coupon Books and the Big Brother/Sister search. You prepare the document shown in Figure CLA1-1.

SHOW YOUR SUPPORT

for the

JHS Athletic Department

- SuperSaver Coupon Books are now on sale for $25.00 each. Use these books for savings at restaurants and hotels.

- We are looking for individuals to serve as big brothers and big sisters for our students. Monthly events are planned for each student and his or her big brother/sister.

CALL **555-2323** FOR INFORMATION

FIGURE CLA1-1

Instructions: Perform the following tasks:

1. Change the font size from 10 to 20 by clicking the Font Size box arrow and selecting 20.
2. If it is not already selected, click the Show/Hide ¶ button on the Formatting toolbar to display paragraph marks and spaces.
3. Create the announcement shown in Figure CLA1-1. Enter the document without the graphic file and unformatted, that is, without any bolding, underlining, italicizing, or centering.
4. Save the document on a diskette with the filename CLA1-1.
5. Select the first three title lines. Center them.
6. Select the first title line. Bold it. Change its font size from 20 to 36.
7. Select the second title line. Italicize it.
8. Select the third title line. Bold and underline it. Change its font size from 20 to 36.
9. Import the graphic filename called sports.wmf on the second paragraph mark beneath the third title line. Select it and center it.
10. Select the two paragraphs beneath the graphic. Add bullets to them.
11. Select the last line of the announcement. Change its font to Arial. Select the telephone number and bold it.
12. Check the spelling of the announcement.
13. Save the announcement again with the same filename.
14. Print the announcement.

COMPUTER LABORATORY ASSIGNMENT 2
Creating an Announcement with a Scaled Graphic

Purpose: To become familiar with creating a document, formatting and spell checking a document, importing and scaling a graphic, and saving and printing a document.

Problem: You are the secretary of The Math Club for your college. One of your responsibilities is to announce monthly meetings. For the May meeting, you prepare the document shown in Figure CLA1-2 on the next page.

Instructions: Perform the following tasks:

1. Change the font size from 10 to 20 by clicking the Font Size box arrow and selecting 20.
2. If it is not already selected, click the Show/Hide ¶ button on the Formatting toolbar to display paragraph marks and spaces.
3. Create the announcement shown in Figure CLA1-2 on the next page. Enter the document without the graphic file and unformatted, that is, without any bolding, underlining, italicizing, or centering.
4. Save the document on a diskette with the filename CLA1-2.
5. Select the first three title lines. Center them.
6. Select the first title line. Bold it. Change its font size from 20 to 48.
7. Select the second title line. Italicize it.
8. Select the third title line. Bold and underline it. Change its font size from 20 to 36.
9. Import the graphic filename called math.wmf. Select it and center it. Change its width to 320%. Change its height to 270%.
10. Select the three paragraphs beneath the graphic. Add bullets to them.
11. In the first bulleted paragraph, select the date, May 1, 1995, and bold it.
12. Select the last line of the announcement. Change its font to Arial.
13. Check the spelling of the announcement.
14. Save the announcement again with the same filename.
15. Print the announcement.

(continued)

COMPUTER LABORATORY ASSIGNMENT 2 (continued)

THE MATH CLUB

announces its

MONTHLY MEETING

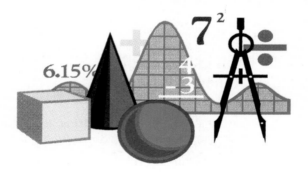

- This month's meeting is scheduled for Monday, **May 1, 1995**, from 6:00 p.m. to 9:00 p.m. in Alumni Hall. Bring one dish to pass.

- Guest speaker will address the math requirements on the GMAT exam.

- Food will be served at 6:00 p.m. Guest speaker will begin at 7:00 p.m.

QUESTIONS? CALL 555-9898

FIGURE CLA1-2

COMPUTER LABORATORY ASSIGNMENT 3
Composing an Announcement

Purpose: To become familiar with designing and creating a document from notes, formatting and spell checking a document, importing and scaling a graphic, and saving and printing a document.

Problem: You are the director of theater events for the town of New Cambridge, Florida. An upcoming planned play is *To Kill a Mockingbird*. You want to announce when and where auditions will be held for anyone interested in a role in this play.

Instructions: Create an announcement for auditions for the upcoming play, *To Kill a Mockingbird*, using the guidelines below. You are to format the announcement so it looks professional. Save the announcement with the filename CLA1-3.

Perform the following tasks:

1. First title line: CALLING ALL ACTORS
2. Second title line: for a role in
3. Third title line: TO KILL A MOCKINGBIRD
4. Beneath the title lines: Use the graphic filename called theatre.wmf. You will need to scale it.
5. First bulleted paragraph: Auditions will take place on Saturday, June 17, 1995, at the Town Square in New Cambridge, Florida.
6. Second bulleted paragraph: Only amateur actors are permitted to audition for a role. Each actor may audition for only one role.
7. Third bulleted paragraph: Interested parties should call 555-1234 to sign up for an audition.
8. Last line of announcement: RESERVE YOUR SPOT TODAY!

COMPUTER LABORATORY ASSIGNMENT 4
Designing and Creating an Announcement

Purpose: To provide practice in planning and building a document.

Problem: You are to scan through the list of available Windows metafiles in the clipart subdirectory and select one that pertains to an area of interest to you. Assume you are the secretary of an upcoming event that relates to the graphic file you have chosen.

Instructions: Create an announcement that uses the Windows metafile you selected. In your announcement, use a variety of font sizes, fonts, bold, italics, and underlining. Be creative. Scale the graphic. Be sure to check the spelling of your announcement before printing it. Save the announcement with the filename CLA1-4.

▼

USING WIZARDS TO CREATE A DOCUMENT

OBJECTIVES   You will have mastered the material in this project when you can:

▸ Explain the components of a business letter
▸ Create a letter using the Letter Wizard
▸ Understand styles in a document
▸ Replace selected text with new text
▸ Right-align text
▸ Add a border beneath a paragraph
▸ Remove a paragraph mark
▸ Select characters with click and SHIFT+click
▸ Create an AutoText entry
▸ Insert an AutoText entry
▸ Select and replace sentences
▸ Drag and drop a paragraph

▸ Cut and paste a paragraph
▸ Create a resume using the Resume Wizard
▸ Understand the Word screen in page layout view
▸ Use the TAB key to vertically-align text
▸ Insert a line break
▸ Use print preview to view and print a document
▸ Switch from one open document to another
▸ Display multiple open documents on the Word screen
▸ Use shortcut menus

▶ INTRODUCTION

t one time in your professional life, you will prepare a resume along with a personalized cover letter to send to a prospective employer(s). In addition to some personal information, a **resume** usually contains the applicant's educational background and job experience. Because employers review many resumes for each vacant position, you should carefully design your resume so it presents you as the best candidate for the job. You should attach a personalized cover letter to each resume you send. A **cover letter** enables you to elaborate on positive points in your resume; it also provides you with the opportunity to show the potential employer your written communication skills. Thus, it is important your cover letter be well written and follow proper business letter rules.

Because composing letters and resumes from scratch is a difficult process for many people, Word provides **wizards** to assist you in these document preparations. By asking you several basic questions, Word's wizards create a document for you based on your responses. You then either fill in the blanks or replace prewritten words in the documents prepared by the wizards.

▶ Project Two — Cover Letter and Resume

Project 2 uses Word to produce the cover letter and resume shown in Figure 2-1. Mary Jo Williams, an upcoming college graduate, is seeking a full-time position as a software specialist in a growing firm in the Chicagoland area. In addition to her resume, she would like to send a personalized cover letter to Mr. James Parker at Chambers Electric Company detailing her work experience.

cover letter

Mary Jo Williams
667 North Street, Chicago, IL 60605

March 7, 1995

Mr. James Parker
Chambers Electric Company
515 Lake Avenue
Chicago, IL 60604

Dear Mr. Parker:

I am interested in working as a software specialist for your organization. I am currently a help desk consultant with over two years of experience to offer you. I enclose my resume as a first step in exploring the possibilities of employment with Chambers Electric Company.

As a software specialist with your organization, I would bring quality, timely, and friendly user support. Furthermore, I work well with others, and I am experienced in many software packages, including word processing, spreadsheet, database, communications, and presentation graphics.

My responsibilities include assisting faculty and staff at Hillside University with software problems. I also answer and log calls and forward hardware problems to the correct department. In addition, I have developed a call tracking system for the university.

As I will be graduating in May, my current position must be relinquished to a registered student. Thus, I am seeking full-time employment outside the university. I will call you in a few days to arrange an interview at a convenient time for you. Thank you for your consideration.

Sincerely,

Mary Jo Williams

resume

Mary Jo Williams
667 North Street
Chicago, IL 60605
312-555-2345 (W) 312-555-6868 (H)

Objective

To obtain a software specialist position with a growing firm in the Chicagoland area.

Education

1991 - 1995

Hillside University
Chicago, IL
B.S. in Office Automation	May 1995	GPA	3.8/4.0
A.S. in PC Applications	May 1993	GPA	3.7/4.0

Awards received
1994 Student of the Year

Software experience
Windows Products: Word, Excel, Access, Quattro Pro, WordPerfect, FoxPro, PowerPoint
DOS Products: Word, Lotus, dBASE IV, Quattro Pro, WordPerfect, FoxPro, Harvard Graphics

Work experience

1992 - 1995

Hillside University
Chicago, IL
Assist faculty and staff with software problems. Responsibilities include answering and logging calls, solving software problems, and forwarding hardware problems to correct department. Also developed a call tracking system for the university.

Volunteer experience
Train employees at the local United Way each Saturday on a variety of software packages.

Interests and activities
Chicagoland Windows User Group Member
Subscribe to several PC and software magazines

Hobbies
SCUBA Diving, Photography, and Snow Skiing

References
Available upon request

FIGURE 2-1

Document Preparation Steps

The following document preparation steps give you an overview of how the cover letter and resume in Figure 2-1 on the previous page will be developed in this project. If you are preparing the documents in this project on a personal computer, read these steps without doing them.

1. Start Word.
2. Use the Letter Wizard to create a prewritten cover letter.
3. Enhance the letterhead on the cover letter.
4. Change the font size of the characters in the cover letter.
5. Create an AutoText entry.
6. Personalize the cover letter.
7. Save the cover letter.
8. Move a paragraph in the cover letter.
9. Save the cover letter again, spell check it, and print it.
10. Use the Resume Wizard to create a resume.
11. Personalize the resume.
12. Spell check and save the resume.
13. View and print the resume in print preview.

The following pages contain a detailed explanation of each of these steps.

▶ STARTING WORD

T o start Word, the Office Manager toolbar must display on the screen or the Microsoft Office group window must be open. Click the Microsoft Word button on the Office Manager toolbar or double-click the Microsoft Word program-item icon in the Microsoft Office group window. If your computer displays the Tip of the Day dialog box, choose the OK button to display the Word screen. These steps are illustrated in Project 1 on pages MSW4 and MSW5.

Displaying Nonprinting Characters

As discussed in Project 1, it is helpful to display nonprinting characters that indicate where in the document you pressed the ENTER key and SPACEBAR. If nonprinting characters are not displaying, you should display them by clicking the Show/Hide ¶ button on the Standard toolbar as illustrated in Project 1 on page MSW15.

▶ CREATING A COVER LETTER

Y ou can follow many different styles when you create business letters. The cover letter in Figure 2-1 on the previous page is a **block letter**. In a block letter, all of the text begins at the left margin. Whether you create a block letter or a different style of letter, all business letters have the same basic components.

Components of a Business Letter

You should take care when preparing business letters to include all essential elements. Essential business letter elements include the date line, inside address, message, and signature block (Figure 2-2). The **date line**, which consists of the month, day, and year, is positioned two to six lines below the letterhead. The **inside address**, placed two to eight lines below the date line, usually contains the addressee's courtesy title (e.g., Mr.) plus full name; business affiliation; and full geographical address. The **salutation**, if present, begins two lines beneath the last line of the inside address. The body of the letter, or the **message**, begins two lines beneath the salutation. Within the message, paragraphs are single-spaced internally; double-spaced between paragraphs. Two lines below the last line of the message, the **complimentary close** displays, if one is present. The **signature block** is typed at least four lines below the complimentary close, allowing room for the author to sign his or her name.

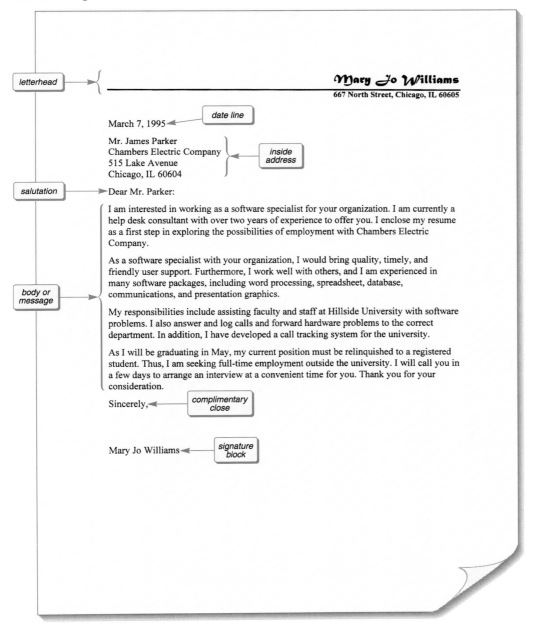

FIGURE 2-2

Using the Letter Wizard to Create a Resume Cover Letter

You can type a letter from scratch into a blank document window by following the rules listed in the preceding paragraph on the previous page, or you can use a wizard and let Word format the letter with appropriate spacing and layout. With a wizard, you can also instruct Word to prewrite the letter for you. Then, you customize the letter by selecting and replacing text. Follow the steps on the next several pages to create the cover letter for the resume using the **Letter Wizard**.

TO CREATE A LETTER USING A WIZARD ▼

STEP 1 ▶

Select the File menu and point to the New command (Figure 2-3).

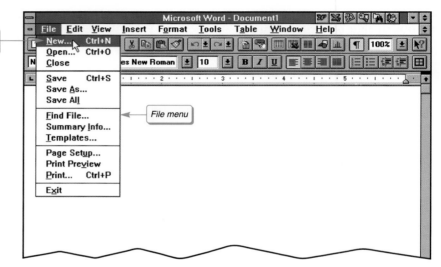

FIGURE 2-3

STEP 2 ▶

Choose the New command.

*Word displays the New dialog box (Figure 2-4). The default template, Normal, is listed in the Template box. A list of available templates and wizards display in the Template list box. A **template** is a pattern or blueprint for a document. When you create a new document using the New button on the Standard toolbar, you use the **Normal Document Template**. If you want to use a different template or a wizard, you must use the New command in the File menu.*

STEP 3

Point to Letter Wizard in the Template list box.

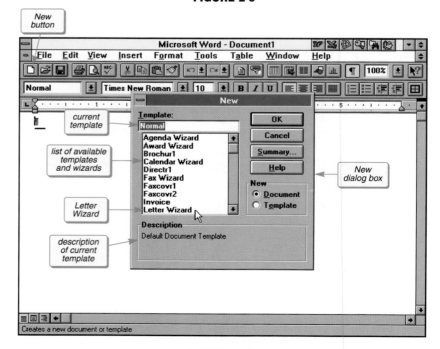

FIGURE 2-4

STEP 4 ▶

Select Letter Wizard by clicking the left mouse button. If the Document option button is not already selected, click it. Point to the OK button in the New dialog box.

Word places Letter Wizard in the Template box (Figure 2-5). The Letter Wizard is currently selected. Because you are creating a document, the Document option button is selected.

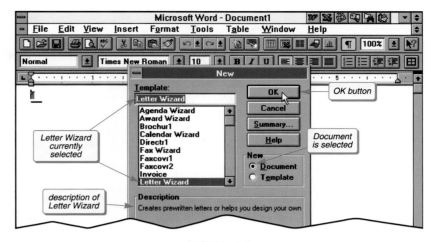

FIGURE 2-5

STEP 5 ▶

Choose the OK button.

After a few seconds, Word displays the first in a series of Letter Wizard dialog boxes (Figure 2-6). Each Letter Wizard dialog box presents you with questions. You respond to the questions by selecting appropriate options.

STEP 6

Read the TIP in the Letter Wizard dialog box. Click the Select a prewritten business letter option button. Then, point to the Next button (Next>).

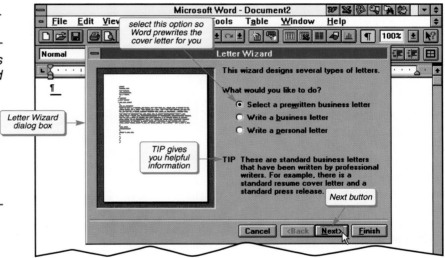

FIGURE 2-6

STEP 7 ▶

Choose the Next button. Select Resume cover letter in the list of prewritten letter types. Point to the Next button.

Word displays the second of the series of Letter Wizard dialog boxes (Figure 2-7). Word provides fifteen different types of prewritten letters.

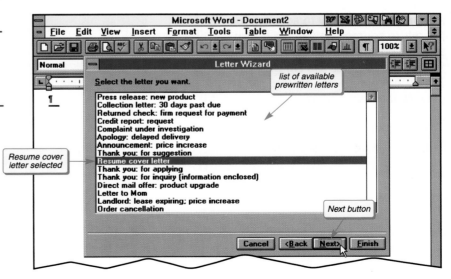

FIGURE 2-7

STEP 8 ▶

Choose the Next button. Click the Plain paper option button. Point to the Next button.

Word displays the third Letter Wizard dialog box (Figure 2-8). If you select the Letterhead stationery option, Word allows space at the top of your letter for the letterhead. The Plain paper option begins the letter at the top of the paper.

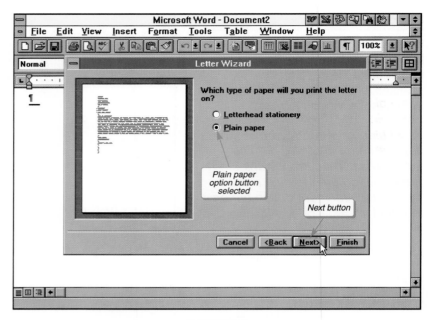

FIGURE 2-8

STEP 9 ▶

Choose the Next button. If the Letter Wizard dialog box already has the recipient information in the recipient's name and address box, select the information by dragging the mouse through it. In the recipient's name and address box, type Mr. James Parker **and press the ENTER key. Type** Chambers Electric Company **and press the ENTER key. Type** 515 Lake Avenue **and press the ENTER key. Type** Chicago, IL 60604 **and press the TAB key to advance to the return address box. In the return address box, type** 667 North Street **and press the ENTER key. Type** Chicago, IL 60605 **and point to the Next button.**

Word displays the fourth Letter Wizard dialog box (Figure 2-9).

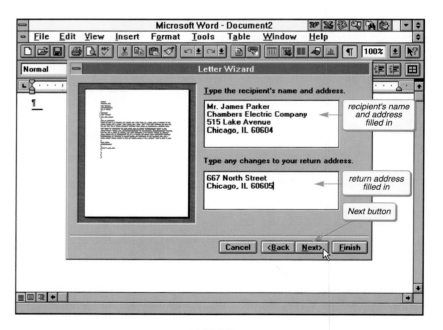

FIGURE 2-9

STEP 10 ►

Choose the Next button. Click the Classic option button. Point to the Next button.

Word displays the fifth Letter Wizard dialog box (Figure 2-10). You may select one of three styles of cover letters: Classic, Contemporary, or Typewriter. The sample area displays the layout of the selected style for you.

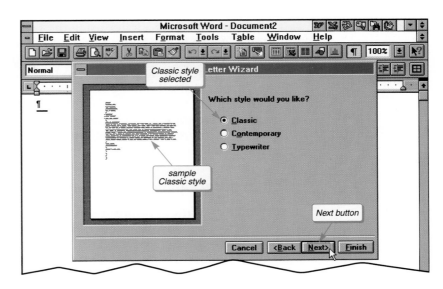

FIGURE 2-10

STEP 11 ►

Choose the Next button. Click the Just display the letter option button. Point to the Finish button (Finish).

Word displays the final Letter Wizard dialog box (Figure 2-11). The Just display the letter option button instructs Word to place the letter in the document window when you exit the Letter Wizard. The Next button is dimmed because there are no more Letter Wizard dialog boxes.

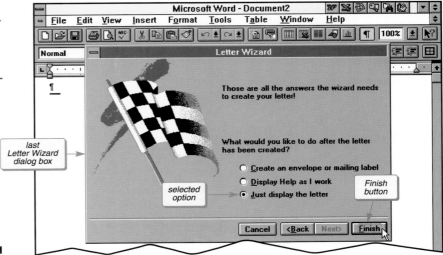

FIGURE 2-11

STEP 12 ►

Choose the Finish button.

After a few seconds, Word displays the prewritten cover letter in the document window (Figure 2-12). Because Word displays the current date in the letter, your date line may display a different date.

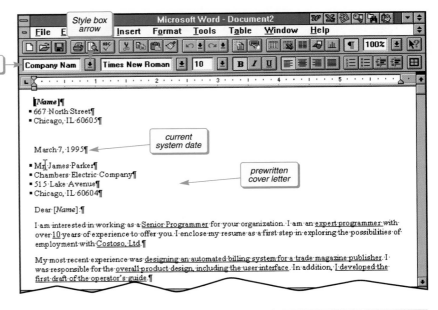

FIGURE 2-12

When you create a letter using the Letter Wizard, you can choose the Back button (Back) in any Letter Wizard dialog box to change any of the previous option(s) you selected. To exit from the Letter Wizard and return to the document window without creating the letter, choose the Cancel button (Cancel) from any Letter Wizard dialog box.

In addition to the Letter Wizard, Word provides eight other wizards to assist you in creating these documents: agenda, award, calendar, fax cover sheet, legal pleading, memo, newsletter, and resume. Later in this project, you will use the Resume Wizard.

Printing the Cover Letter Generated by the Letter Wizard

You may want to print the cover letter generated by the Letter Wizard so you can review it and identify words, phrases, and sentences you need to revise. To print the cover letter generated by the Letter Wizard, click the Print button on the Standard toolbar. The resulting printout is shown in Figure 2-13.

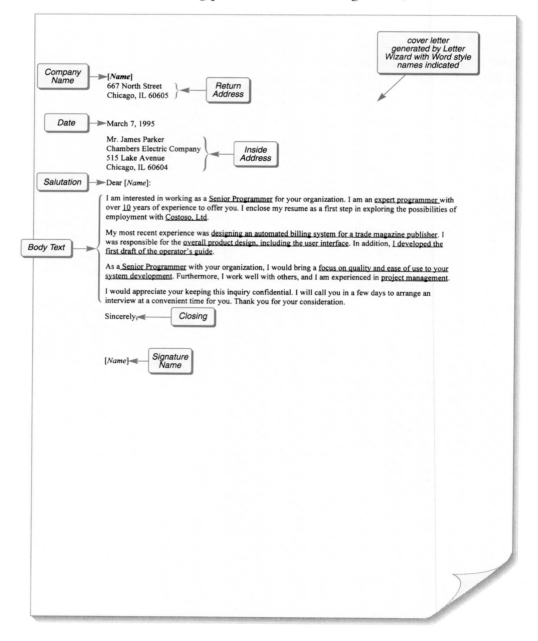

FIGURE 2-13

Styles

When you use a wizard to create a document, Word formats the document using styles. A **style** is a customized format applied to characters or paragraphs. The Style box displays the name of the style associated to the location of the insertion point. In Figure 2-12 on page MSW73, the insertion point is in the Company Name style. If you click the Style box arrow, the list of styles in a document displays. The bold style names are **paragraph styles**, and the dimmed style names are **character styles**. If you add text to a document that contains styles, you may select the appropriate style from the Style list before entering the text so the text you type will be formatted according to the selected style.

The styles created by the Letter Wizard are indicated in the printout of the cover letter in Figure 2-13. When you modify the cover letter, the style associated at the location of the insertion point will be applied to the text you type.

▶ MODIFYING THE PREWRITTEN COVER LETTER

If you compare the printout in Figure 2-13 to the cover letter in Figure 2-1 on page MSW67, you will notice several modifications need to be made. First, the letterhead (consisting of the Company Name and Return Address styles) needs to be modified to make the letter look more professional. Next, the font size of the text beneath the letterhead needs to be increased. All of the underlined words in the prewritten letter must be changed to address the applicant's requirements. Finally, the middle two paragraphs should be reversed so the letter flows better. The steps on the following pages illustrate these modifications.

Enhancing the Letterhead on the Cover Letter

The letterhead created by the Letter Wizard is dull and plain. Because you want to convey creativity and professionalism to your prospective employer, you should enhance the letterhead presented by the Letter Wizard. The first step in enhancing the letterhead is to select the company name line and change its font to Matura MT Script Capital and its font size to 16, as shown in the following steps.

TO CHANGE THE FORMATTING OF THE COMPANY NAME LINE

Step 1: Click the mouse in the selection bar to the left of the company name line, which is indicated by the notation **[Name]** at the top of the document. Word selects **[Name]**.

Step 2: Click the Font box arrow on the Formatting toolbar to display the list of available fonts. Select the font Matura MT Script Capital (or a similar font) by clicking it.

Step 3: Click the Font Size box arrow on the Formatting toolbar to display the list of available font sizes. Select font size 16 by clicking it.

Word changes the font and font size of the company name line (Figure 2-14).

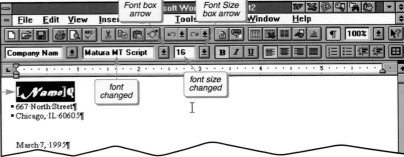

FIGURE 2-14

The next step is to type a name in place of the notation [*Name*]. Because the notation [*Name*] is still selected from the previous steps, the next character(s) you type will replace the selected text. Thus, to replace selected text with new text, type the new text, as shown in the following step.

TO REPLACE SELECTED TEXT WITH NEW TEXT ▼

STEP 1 ▶

Type Mary Jo Williams

Word replaces the selection of [Name] with the name Mary Jo Williams (Figure 2-15). Because the insertion point is inside the name, the Formatting toolbar displays the characteristics of the text.

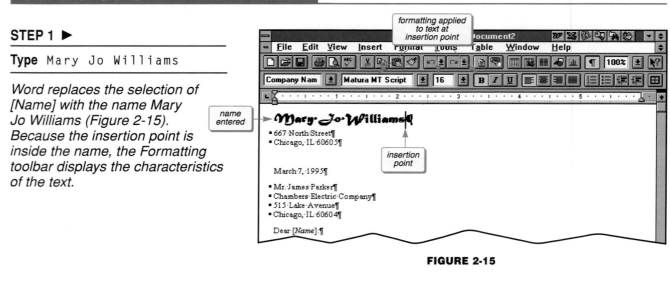

FIGURE 2-15

The next step is to **right-align** the name line. That is, the name should be placed at the right margin of the page as shown below.

TO RIGHT-ALIGN TEXT ▼

STEP 1 ▶

Click the Align Right button (▤) on the Formatting toolbar.

Word right aligns the Company Name line (Figure 2-16). The Align Right button is recessed on the Formatting toolbar. Recall that to adjust paragraph formatting, the insertion point must be positioned somewhere inside the paragraph.

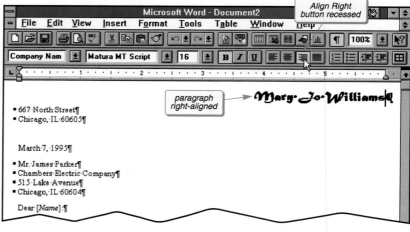

FIGURE 2-16

To add professionalism to your letterhead, you should draw a solid line, called a **border** in Word, beneath the name. You can add a border, also called a **rule** or **ruling line**, to any edge of a paragraph. That is, borders may be added above or below a paragraph, to the left or right of a paragraph, or any combination of these sides. You add borders by clicking the Borders button ( ) on the Formatting toolbar. When you click the Borders button, a **Borders toolbar** displays beneath the Formatting toolbar and the Borders button is recessed. Follow these steps to add a ruling line beneath the name.

TO ADD A BORDER BENEATH A PARAGRAPH ▼

STEP 1 ▶

If the Borders button on your Formatting toolbar is not recessed, click it to display the Borders toolbar.

Word displays a Borders toolbar beneath the Formatting toolbar (Figure 2-17). The Borders button on the Formatting toolbar is recessed.

STEP 2

Point to the Line Style box arrow on the Borders toolbar.

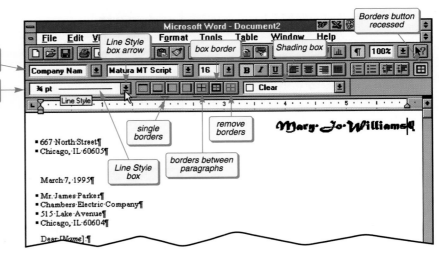

FIGURE 2-17

STEP 3 ▶

Click the Line Style box arrow and point to the 1 1/2 pt line style.

Word displays a list of available point sizes for the border (Figure 2-18). You may choose from a variety of solid single lines, solid double lines, or dotted lines.

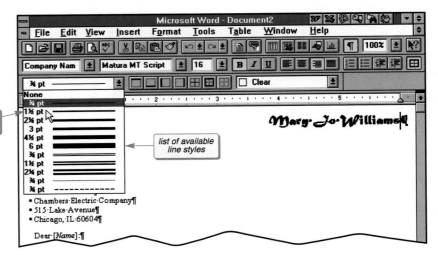

FIGURE 2-18

STEP 4 ▶

Select the 1 1/2 pt line style by clicking the left mouse button. Point to the Bottom Border button (▦) on the Borders toolbar.

Word places 1 1/2 pt and a sample line style in the Line Style box (Figure 2-19).

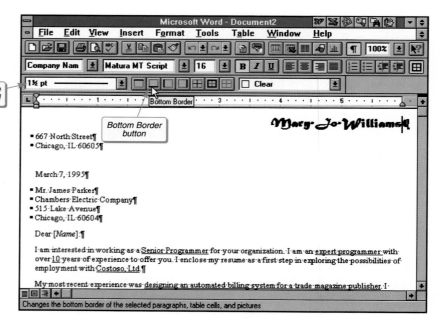

FIGURE 2-19

STEP 5 ▶

Click the Bottom Border button. Point to the Borders button on the Formatting toolbar.

Word draws a ruling line beneath the paragraph containing the company name in your cover letter (Figure 2-20).

STEP 6

Click the Borders button.

Word removes the Borders toolbar from the Word screen.

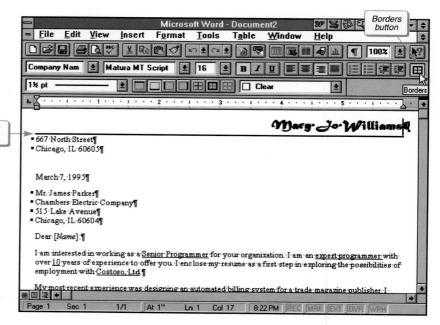

FIGURE 2-20

You can add a border to any edge of a paragraph by placing the insertion point in the paragraph to be bordered and clicking the appropriate button on the Borders toolbar. To add a box border around an entire paragraph, click the Outside Border button (▦). To remove a border from a paragraph, click the No Border button (▦) on the Borders toolbar.

The Borders toolbar is initially stacked (or anchored) beneath the Formatting toolbar; that is, it is placed below the Formatting toolbar. You can, however, float (or move) this toolbar by holding down the SHIFT key while double-clicking in a blank area on the toolbar. Then, to re-anchor the floating toolbar (or put it back below the Formatting toolbar), double-click in a blank area of it.

The return address information is currently split into two lines: one line containing the street address and the other line containing the city, state, and zip code. The next step in enhancing the letterhead is to modify these address lines so the entire address displays on a single line beneath the ruling line. To do this, you must delete the paragraph mark following the word "Street," as shown in these steps.

TO REMOVE A PARAGRAPH MARK ▼

STEP 1 ▶

Click to the right of the paragraph mark to be deleted.

Word positions the insertion point between the letter "t" in "Street" and the paragraph mark on line 2 (Figure 2-21).

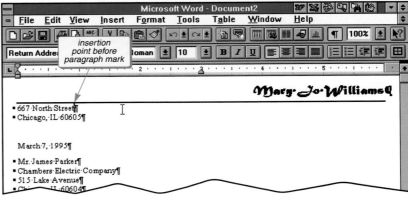

FIGURE 2-21

STEP 2 ▶

Press the DELETE key. Type a comma followed by a space. Press the END key to move the insertion point to the end of the line.

Word removes the paragraph mark on line 2 and brings the city, state, and zip code line up and to the right of the comma on line 2 (Figure 2-22). Recall that to delete to the right of the insertion point, press the DELETE key; to delete to the left of the insertion point, press the BACKSPACE key.

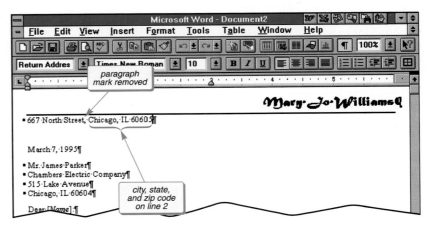

FIGURE 2-22

The next step in enhancing the letterhead is to bold the address line and align it with the right margin. Because the Letter Wizard moved the right indent marker for line 2 to the 3-inch mark on the horizontal ruler (Figure 2-23 on the next page), you must first move the right indent marker back to the right margin. Then, you can click the Align Right button, as shown in the steps on the next page.

TO FORMAT THE RETURN ADDRESS LINE ▼

STEP 1 ►

Click in the selection bar to the left of the return address line to select the address line. Click the Bold button on the Formatting toolbar. Click to the right of the paragraph mark on the return address line. Point to the right indent marker on the horizontal ruler.

Word bolds the return address line (Figure 2-23). The Bold button is recessed, indicating the text at the location of the insertion point is bold. The insertion point is before the paragraph mark on line 2, the return address line.

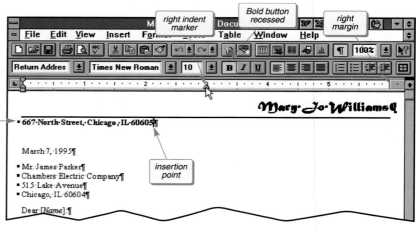

FIGURE 2-23

STEP 2 ►

Drag the right indent marker to the right margin.

As the mouse pointer moves, a vertical dotted line displays beneath the mouse pointer (Figure 2-24). The vertical dotted line indicates the position of the right indent marker if you release the mouse at that location.

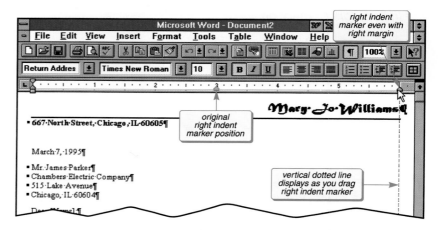

FIGURE 2-24

STEP 3 ►

Release the left mouse button. Click the Align Right button on the Formatting toolbar.

Word right-aligns the return address line at the right margin (Figure 2-25). The Align Right button is recessed, indicating the text at the insertion point is right-aligned.

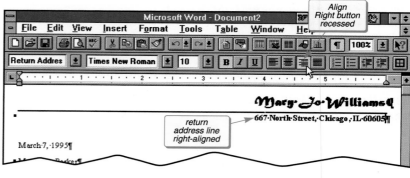

FIGURE 2-25

The letterhead is now complete.

Changing the Font Size of the Characters Below the Letterhead in the Cover Letter

The next process in modifying the resume cover letter is to change the font size of all of the characters in the letter below the letterhead. To do this, you must first select the text below the letterhead and then change its font size. To select text that is not a word or sentence, you can drag over the text as you learned in Project 1, or you can position the insertion point at the beginning of the text to select and then use the SHIFT+click technique at the end of the text to select it, as shown in these steps.

TO CHANGE FONT SIZE OF THE COVER LETTER CHARACTERS ▼

STEP 1 ▶

Position the insertion point to the left of the first character to be changed. Point to the scroll box on the vertical scroll bar.

The insertion point is to the left of the letter M in March (Figure 2-26). Depending on your system date, your month may be different.

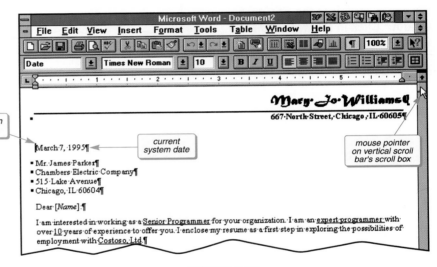

FIGURE 2-26

STEP 2 ▶

Drag the scroll box to the bottom of the vertical scroll bar. Press and hold down the SHIFT key. Then, position the mouse pointer to the right of the last paragraph mark in the document and click the left mouse button. Release the SHIFT key.

*Word selects all text between the insertion point to the left of the date line and the bottom of the document (Figure 2-27). The process of holding down the SHIFT key and clicking the left mouse button is called a **SHIFT+click**. You may SHIFT+click instead of dragging the mouse to select text.*

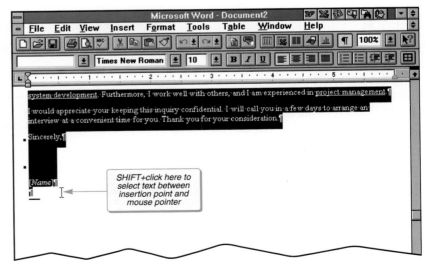

FIGURE 2-27

STEP 3 ▶

Click the Font Size box arrow on the Formatting toolbar and select font size 12 by clicking it. Point to the scroll box on the vertical scroll bar.

Word changes the font size of the selected text from 10 to 12 (Figure 2-28).

STEP 4

Drag the scroll box to the top of the vertical scroll bar to bring the top of the cover letter into the document window. Click in the document window to remove the highlight.

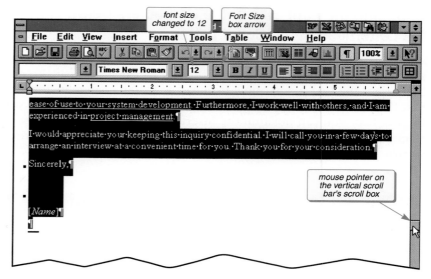

FIGURE 2-28

Creating an AutoText Entry

If you use text frequently, you can store the text in an **AutoText entry** and then use the entry throughout your document. That is, you only need to type the entry once, and for all future occurrences of the text, you select the appropriate text from the AutoText dialog box. In this way, you avoid entering the text inconsistently and incorrectly in different places in the same document. Follow these steps to create an AutoText entry for the prospective employer's company name.

TO CREATE AN AUTOTEXT ENTRY ▼

STEP 1 ▶

Select the text to be stored by dragging the mouse through it or using the SHIFT+click technique. (Be sure to not select the paragraph mark at the end of the text.) Then, point to the Edit AutoText button (■) on the Standard toolbar.

Word highlights the name, Chambers Electric Company, in the inside address (Figure 2-29).

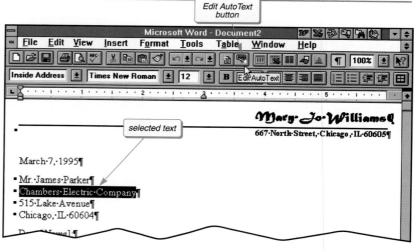

FIGURE 2-29

STEP 2 ▶

Click the Edit AutoText button. When the AutoText dialog box displays, point to the Add button (Add).

Word displays the AutoText dialog box (Figure 2-30). The selected text displays in the Selection area of the AutoText dialog box. A name for the selected text, the first few characters of the selection, displays in the Name box. You can change the name or keep the one proposed by Word.

STEP 3

Click the Add button.

Word stores the entry, removes the AutoText dialog box, and returns to the document window.

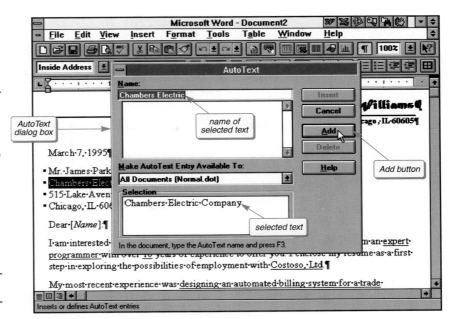

FIGURE 2-30

The name has been stored as an AutoText entry. Later in the project, you will use the AutoText entry instead of typing the name again.

Customizing the Cover Letter

The next step in modifying the cover letter generated by the Letter Wizard is to customize it. Notice in the printout of the cover letter in Figure 2-13 on page MSW74 that several words and phrases are underlined and italicized. You are to replace these words and phrases with text that meets your needs. That is, the Letter Wizard has supplied default text that you must change. You should, however, read through the entire letter because you may need to change other words and phrases that are not underlined or italicized. To make these changes, you must first select the text to be changed. Then, type the new text. To select the text, you can either drag the mouse through the text or click at the beginning of the text and SHIFT+click at the end of the text. Follow the steps on the next page to begin customizing the cover letter.

TO BEGIN CUSTOMIZING THE COVER LETTER

Step 1: Select the notation [*Name*]: in the salutation of the cover letter. Type
`Mr. Parker:`

Step 2: Select the underlined words, Senior Programmer, in the first paragraph of the cover letter. Click the Underline button on the Formatting toolbar and type `software specialist`

Step 3: Select the words, an expert programmer, in the first paragraph of the cover letter. Type `currently a help desk consultant` (If an underline remains in the space after the word "consultant," select the space by dragging the mouse pointer through it and then click the Underline button on the Formatting toolbar.)

Step 4: Select the underlined number 10 in the first paragraph of the cover letter. Click the Underline button on the Formatting toolbar and type `two`

The salutation and first paragraph of the cover letter now display, as shown in Figure 2-31.

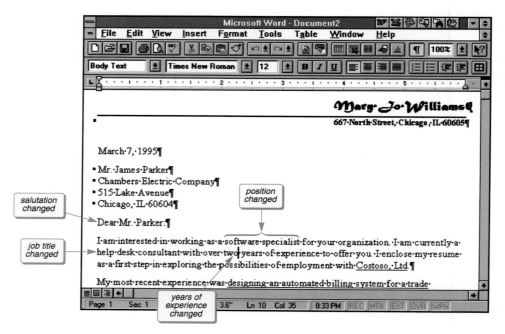

FIGURE 2-31

The next step is to replace the company name, Costoso, Ltd, with the company name Chambers Electric Company. Recall that you stored an AutoText entry for Chambers Electric Company. Thus, once you select Costoso, Ltd, you instruct Word to replace the selection with a stored AutoText entry, as shown in these steps.

TO INSERT AN AUTOTEXT ENTRY ▼

STEP 1 ▶

Select the underlined company name, Costoso, Ltd, in the first paragraph of the cover letter. (Be sure not to select the period following the company name.) Click the Underline button on the Formatting toolbar. Select the Edit menu and point to the AutoText command.

The company name is high-lighted in the cover letter (Figure 2-32). You will replace the selection with a stored AutoText entry.

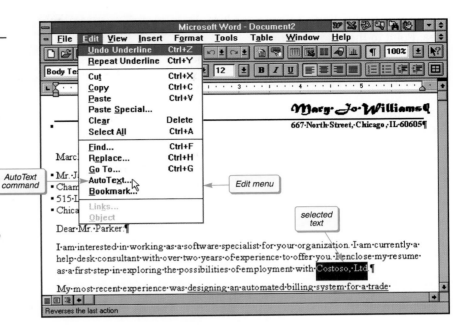

FIGURE 2-32

STEP 2 ▶

Choose the AutoText command.

Word displays the AutoText dialog box (Figure 2-33). The Selection area, as well as the Name box, display the selected text. The stored AutoText entry name displays in the Name list box. The Insert button (Insert) is dimmed because you have not selected a stored AutoText entry yet.

STEP 3

Point to Chambers Electric in the Name list box.

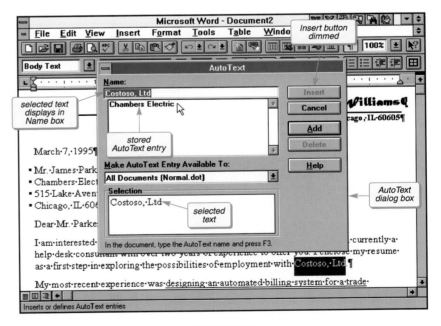

FIGURE 2-33

STEP 4 ▶

Click the stored AutoText entry, Chambers Electric. Click the Plain Text option button in the Insert As area. Point to the Insert button.

Word places the name of the selected AutoText entry in the Name box (Figure 2-34). The Insert button is active because you have selected a stored AutoText entry from the list. The bottom of the AutoText dialog box now displays an Insert As area and a Preview area. You can insert the selected AutoText entry with or without its formatting. The Preview area displays the text as it will be inserted over the selection.

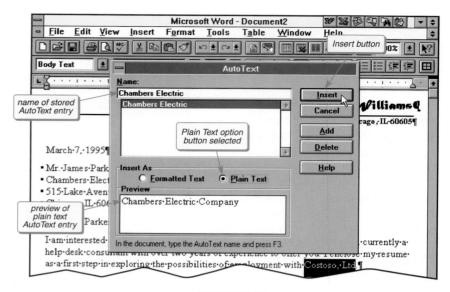

FIGURE 2-34

STEP 5 ▶

Choose the Insert button.

Word replaces the selected text in the cover letter with the selected AutoText entry (Figure 2-35).

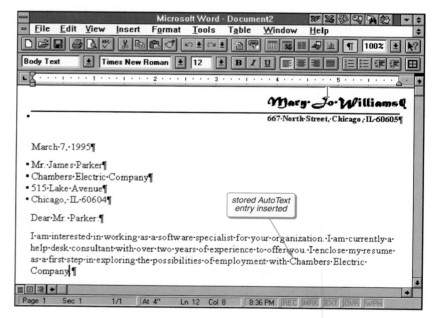

FIGURE 2-35

If you store the AutoText entries with short names, instead of accepting the default name supplied by Word, you can type the AutoText entry name directly in the document and then click the AutoText button to insert the stored AutoText entry at the location of the insertion point. When you use this technique, Word inserts the AutoText entry with the same formatting it originally contained. That is, it is not inserted as plain text.

The next step is to customize the remaining text of the cover letter. In the second paragraph, the entire first two sentences need to be revised. To select a sentence, position the mouse pointer in the sentence and **CTRL+click**. That is, press and hold the CTRL key while clicking the left mouse button. Follow these steps to select and replace sentences in the second paragraph of the cover letter.

TO SELECT AND REPLACE SENTENCES

STEP 1 ▶

Press the PAGE DOWN key to scroll down one screenful. Position the mouse pointer in the sentence you want to select. Then, CTRL+click.

The first sentence in the second paragraph of the cover letter is selected (Figure 2-36). The mouse pointer is a left-pointing block arrow when in selected text.

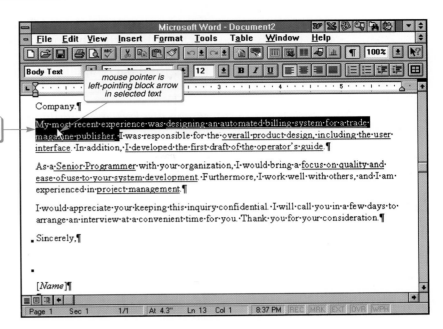

FIGURE 2-36

STEP 2 ▶

Type My responsibilities include assisting faculty and staff at Hillside University with software problems. **Press the SPACEBAR. Select the next sentence in the same paragraph by positioning the mouse pointer in it and then CTRL+click. Press the SPACEBAR and type** I also answer and log calls and forward hardware problems to the correct department. **Press the SPACEBAR.**

Word changes the text in the first two sentences (Figure 2-37).

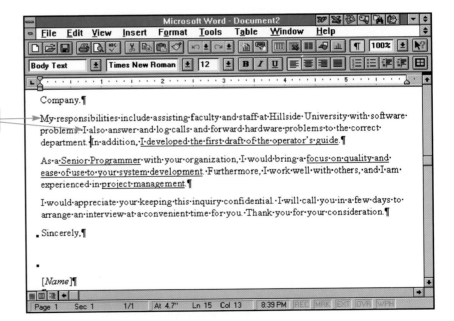

FIGURE 2-37

The final step in customizing the cover letter is to replace the remaining words and phrases in the letter, as shown in the steps on the next page.

TO FINISH CUSTOMIZING THE COVER LETTER

Step 1: In the last sentence in the second paragraph of the cover letter, select the underlined text, I developed the first draft of the operator's guide, click the Underline button on the Formatting toolbar and type `I have developed a call tracking system for the university`

Step 2: In the third paragraph of the cover letter, select the underlined words, Senior Programmer. Click the Underline button on the Formatting toolbar, press the SPACEBAR, and type `software specialist` (If your screen displays an underline in the space before the words, Senior Programmer, select the space by dragging the mouse pointer through it and click the Underline button to remove the underline.)

Step 3: In the third paragraph of the cover letter, select the words, a focus on quality and ease of use to your system development, and type `quality, timely, and friendly user support`

Step 4: In the third paragraph of the cover letter, select the underlined words, project management. Click the Underline button on the Formatting toolbar and type `many software packages, including word processing, spreadsheet, database, communications, and presentation graphics`

Step 5: In the fourth paragraph of the cover letter, select the entire first sentence and type `As I will be graduating in May, my current position must be relinquished to a registered student. Thus, I am seeking full-time employment outside the university.` Press the SPACEBAR.

Step 6: Click the down arrow on the vertical scroll bar until the signature block displays in the document window. Select the notation [*Name*] in the signature block at the bottom of the cover letter and type `Mary Jo Williams`

The customized cover letter displays as shown in Figure 2-38.

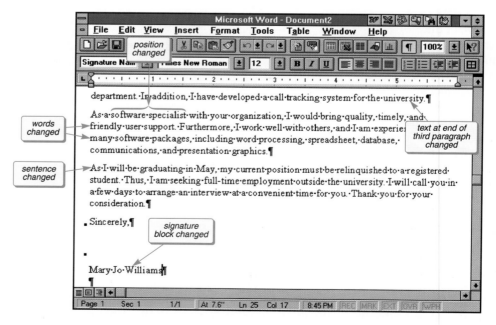

FIGURE 2-38

Saving the Cover Letter

Recall from Project 1 that it is prudent to save your work on disk at regular intervals. Because you have performed several tasks thus far, you should save your cover letter. For a detailed example of the procedure summarized below, refer to pages MSW19 through MSW21 in Project 1.

TO SAVE A DOCUMENT

Step 1: Insert your data disk into drive A.

Step 2: Click the Save button on the Standard toolbar.

Step 3: Type the filename `proj2ltr` in the File Name box. Do not press the ENTER key.

Step 4: Click the Drives drop-down box arrow and select drive A.

Step 5: Choose the OK button in the Save As dialog box.

Switching Two Paragraphs in the Cover Letter

When you proofread the customized cover letter, you realize the second and third paragraphs would flow better if they were reversed. That is, you want to move the second paragraph so it is positioned above the fourth paragraph.

To move paragraphs, you can either **drag and drop** one of the paragraphs or **cut and paste** one of the paragraphs. Both techniques require you to first select the paragraph to be moved. With dragging and dropping, you drag the selected paragraph to its new location and insert, or drop, it there. Cutting involves removing the selected text from the document and placing it on the **Clipboard**, a temporary storage area. Pasting is the process of copying an item from the Clipboard into the document at the location of the insertion point.

You should use the drag and drop technique to move paragraphs a short distance. When you are moving between several pages, however, the cut and paste technique is more efficient. Thus, use the drag and drop technique to move the second paragraph, as shown in the following steps (see Figure 2-42 on page MSW91).

TO DRAG AND DROP A PARAGRAPH ▼

STEP 1 ▶

Scroll up through the document and position the mouse pointer in the selection bar to the left of the paragraph to be moved. Double-click the mouse.

Word selects the entire paragraph (Figure 2-39). To select an entire paragraph, you can either double-click in the selection bar to the left of the paragraph or triple-click somewhere inside the paragraph.

paragraph to be moved is selected

mouse pointer in selection bar

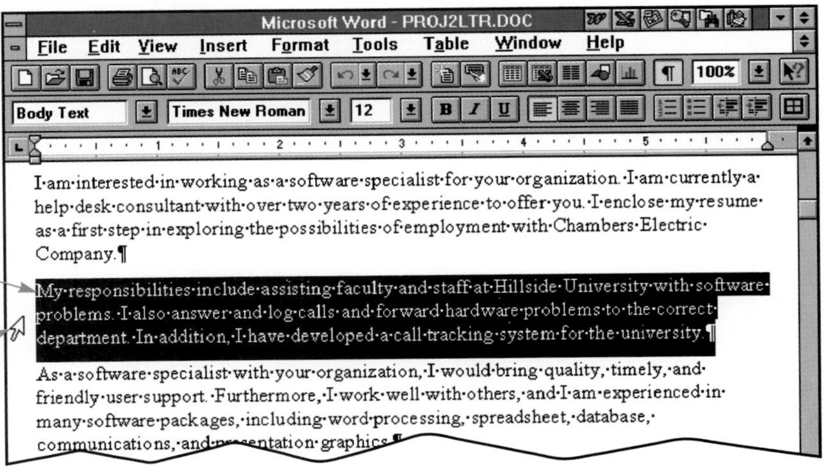

Microsoft Word - PROJ2LTR.DOC

File Edit View Insert Format Tools Table Window Help

Body Text   Times New Roman   12   **B** *I* U

I·am·interested·in·working·as·a·software·specialist·for·your·organization.·I·am·currently·a· help·desk·consultant·with·over·two·years·of·experience·to·offer·you.·I·enclose·my·resume· as·a·first·step·in·exploring·the·possibilities·of·employment·with·Chambers·Electric· Company.¶

My·responsibilities·include·assisting·faculty·and·staff·at·Hillside·University·with·software· problems.·I·also·answer·and·log·calls·and·forward·hardware·problems·to·the·correct· department.·In·addition,·I·have·developed·a·call·tracking·system·for·the·university.¶

As·a·software·specialist·with·your·organization,·I·would·bring·quality,·timely,·and· friendly·user·support.·Furthermore,·I·work·well·with·others,·and·I·am·experienced·in· many·software·packages,·including·word·processing,·spreadsheet,·database,· communications,·and·presentation·graphics.¶

FIGURE 2-39

STEP 2 ▶

Move the mouse pointer into the selection. Press and hold the left mouse button.

The insertion point changes to a dotted insertion point and the mouse pointer has a small dotted box beneath it when you begin to drag the selected text (Figure 2-40).

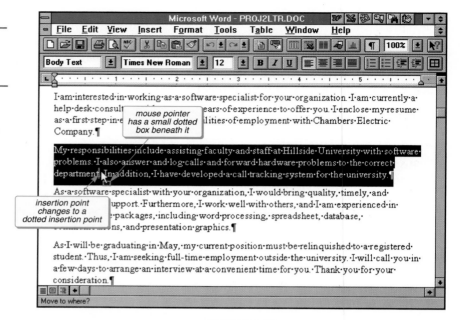

FIGURE 2-40

STEP 3 ▶

Drag the dotted insertion point to the location where the paragraph is to be moved.

The dotted insertion point is positioned to the left of the fourth paragraph in the cover letter (Figure 2-41).

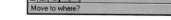

FIGURE 2-41

STEP 4 ▶

Release the left mouse button. Click outside the selection to remove the highlight.

The selected paragraph is moved to the location of the dotted insertion point in the document (Figure 2-42). The second paragraph is moved.

STEP 5

Press CTRL+HOME to move the insertion point to the top of the document.

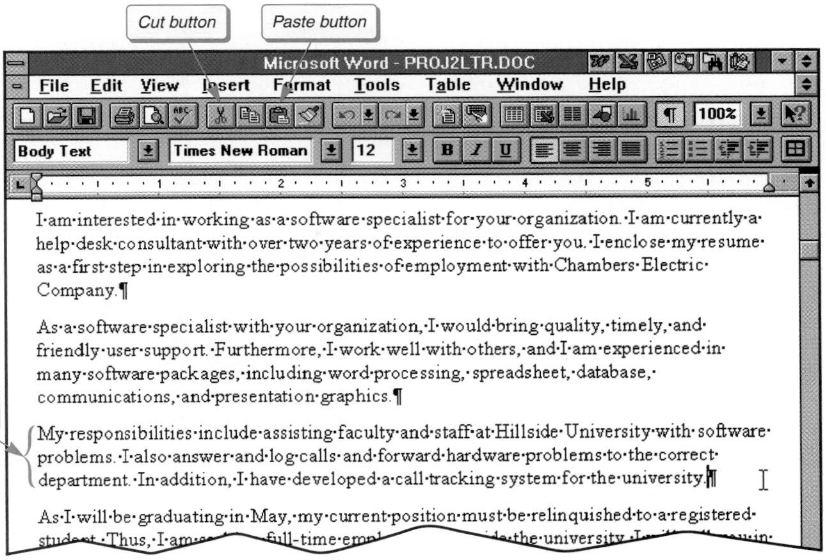

FIGURE 2-42

As mentioned earlier, you may choose to use the cut and paste method, instead of the drag and drop technique, to move a paragraph.

TO CUT AND PASTE A PARAGRAPH

Step 1: Position the mouse pointer in the selection bar to the left of the paragraph to be moved.
Step 2: Double-click the mouse.
Step 3: Click the **Cut button** (✂)on the Standard toolbar. Word removes the selected paragraph from the screen and places it on the Clipboard.
Step 4: Move the insertion point to the location where the paragraph on the Clipboard is to be pasted.
Step 5: Click the **Paste button** (📋) on the Standard toolbar.

Recall that you can use the Undo button on the Standard toolbar if you accidentally drag and drop incorrectly or cut the wrong text.

You can use the drag and drop and cut and paste techniques to move any selection. That is, you can move words, sentences, and phrases by selecting them and then dragging and dropping them or cutting and pasting them.

Saving Again, Spell Checking, and Printing the Cover Letter

The cover letter for the resume is now complete. After completing the cover letter, you should check the spelling of the document by clicking the Spelling button on the Standard toolbar. For a detailed example of spell checking, refer to pages MSW40 through MSW42 in Project 1. Because you have performed several tasks since the last save, you should save the cover letter again by clicking the Save button on the Standard toolbar. Finally, you should print the cover letter by clicking the Print button on the Standard toolbar. When you remove the document from the printer, the printout displays the finished cover letter (Figure 2-43 on the next page).

Mary Jo Williams
667 North Street, Chicago, IL 60605

March 7, 1995

Mr. James Parker
Chambers Electric Company
515 Lake Avenue
Chicago, IL 60604

Dear Mr. Parker:

I am interested in working as a software specialist for your organization. I am currently a help desk consultant with over two years of experience to offer you. I enclose my resume as a first step in exploring the possibilities of employment with Chambers Electric Company.

As a software specialist with your organization, I would bring quality, timely, and friendly user support. Furthermore, I work well with others, and I am experienced in many software packages, including word processing, spreadsheet, database, communications, and presentation graphics.

My responsibilities include assisting faculty and staff at Hillside University with software problems. I also answer and log calls and forward hardware problems to the correct department. In addition, I have developed a call tracking system for the university.

As I will be graduating in May, my current position must be relinquished to a registered student. Thus, I am seeking full-time employment outside the university. I will call you in a few days to arrange an interview at a convenient time for you. Thank you for your consideration.

Sincerely,

Mary Jo Williams

finished
cover letter

FIGURE 2-43

▶ Creating a Resume

Now that the cover letter is complete, you need to create a resume to send with the cover letter to your potential employer. Word supplies a **Resume Wizard** to assist you in building your resume. Once the Resume Wizard creates the resume, you will need to customize it like you did the cover letter generated by the Letter Wizard. Then, you will save and print the resume. Because you will later display multiple open documents on the screen, do not close the cover letter before beginning the resume.

Using the Resume Wizard to Create a Resume

Just as the Letter Wizard asked you several questions necessary to build your cover letter, the Resume Wizard will ask you questions necessary to build a resume, as shown in the following steps.

TO CREATE A RESUME USING THE RESUME WIZARD ▼

STEP 1 ▶

From the File menu, choose the New command. When the New dialog box displays, click the down arrow on the vertical scroll bar until Resume Wizard displays in the Template list box. Then, click Resume Wizard and point to the OK button.

Resume Wizard is selected in the New dialog box (Figure 2-44).

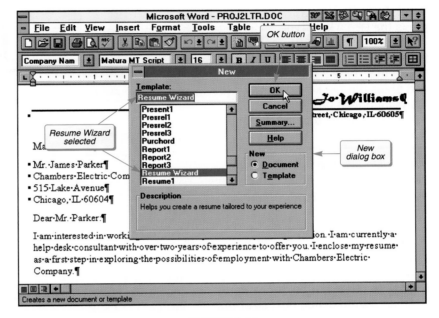

FIGURE 2-44

STEP 2 ▶

Choose the OK button.

After few seconds, Word displays the first of a series of Resume Wizard dialog boxes, asking for the type of resume you want to create (Figure 2-45). Be sure to read the TIP in the Resume Wizard dialog boxes for helpful information.

STEP 3

Select the Entry-level resume option button and point to the Next button.

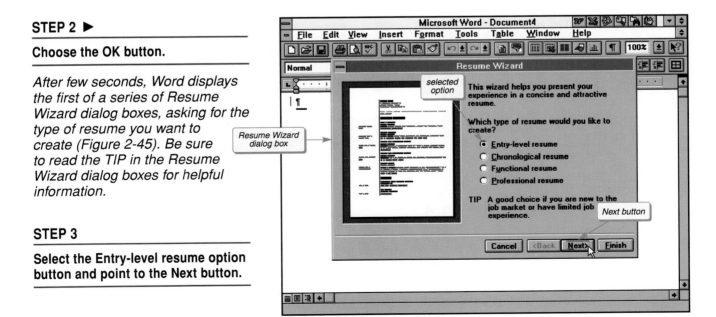

FIGURE 2-45

STEP 4 ▶

Choose the Next button. If the second Resume Wizard dialog box already has a name in the Name box, select the name by dragging the mouse pointer through it; otherwise, click in the Name box. Type Mary Jo Williams and press the TAB key to advance to the Address box. Type 667 North Street and press the ENTER key. Type Chicago, IL 60605 and press the TAB key to advance to the Home phone box. Type 312-555-6868 and press the TAB key to advance to the Work phone box. Type 312-555-2345 and point to the Next button.

Word displays the next Resume Wizard dialog box, in which you enter your personal information (Figure 2-46).

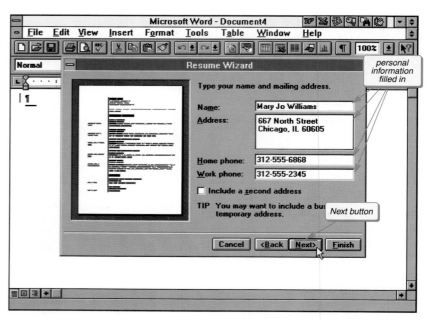

FIGURE 2-46

STEP 5 ▶

Choose the Next button. In the third Resume Wizard dialog box, clear the Languages check box by clicking it. Point to the Next button.

Word displays the third Resume Wizard dialog box, requesting the headings you want on your resume (Figure 2-47). You want all headings, except the Languages heading, on your resume.

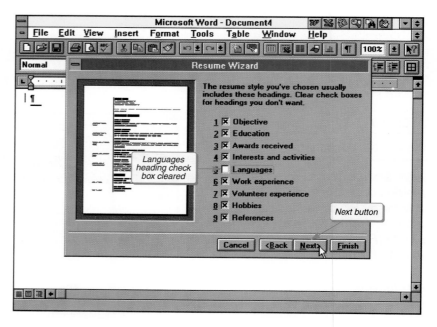

FIGURE 2-47

STEP 6 ►

Choose the Next button. Point to the Next button in the fourth Resume Wizard dialog box.

Word displays the next Resume Wizard dialog box, which allows you to choose additional headings for your resume (Figure 2-48). All of these check boxes should be cleared because you do not want these headings on your resume.

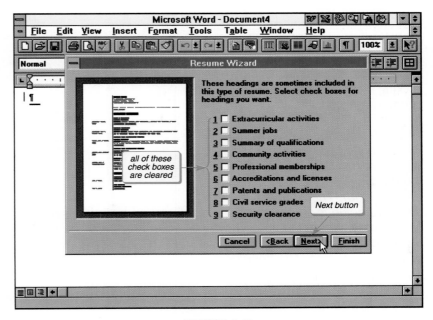

FIGURE 2-48

STEP 7 ►

Choose the Next button. In the fifth Resume Wizard dialog box, type Software experience **in the additional headings box. Point to the Add button.**

Word displays the fifth Resume Wizard dialog box, which allows you to enter any additional headings you want on your resume (Figure 2-49).

STEP 8

Choose the Add button.

Word adds the heading you entered into the list of resume headings.

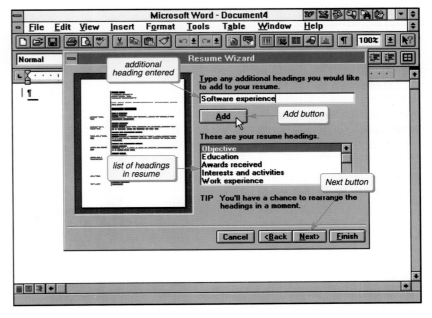

FIGURE 2-49

STEP 9 ▶

Choose the Next button. In the sixth Resume Wizard dialog box, select the Software experience heading by clicking it and point to the Move Up button (Move Up).

Word displays the sixth Resume Wizard dialog box, which enables you to rearrange the order of the headings on your resume (Figure 2-50). The Software experience heading is selected. You can move any heading up or down by selecting it and clicking the appropriate button. The headings will display on the resume in the order the names are displayed in this dialog box.

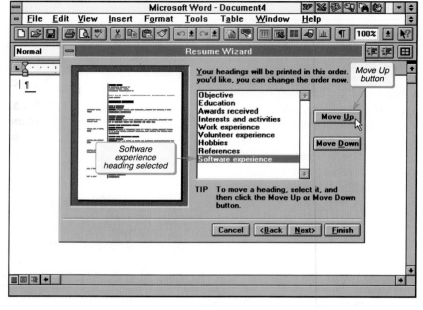

FIGURE 2-50

STEP 10 ▶

Click the Move Up button five times. Select the Interests and activities heading by clicking it and point to the Move Down button (Move Down).

Word moves the heading Software experience up above the Interests and activities heading (Figure 2-51). The Interests and activities heading is selected, ready to be moved down.

STEP 11

Click the Move Down button two times.

Word moves the Interests and activities heading below the Volunteer experience heading.

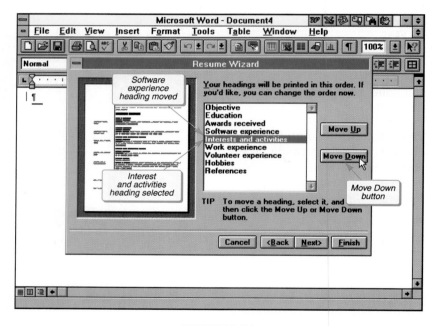

FIGURE 2-51

STEP 12 ▶

Choose the Next button. In the seventh Resume Wizard dialog box, select the Classic style by clicking it and point to the Next button.

Word displays the seventh Resume Wizard dialog box, requesting the style of your resume (Figure 2-52).

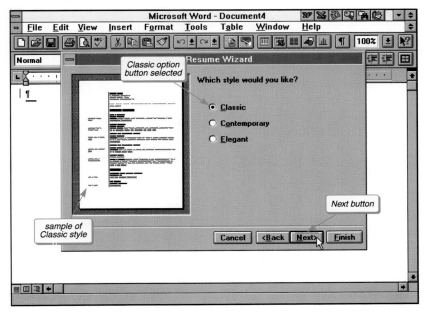

FIGURE 2-52

STEP 13 ▶

Choose the Next button. In the final Resume Wizard dialog box, select the Just display the resume option button by clicking it and point to the Finish button.

Word displays the final Resume Wizard dialog box (Figure 2-53).

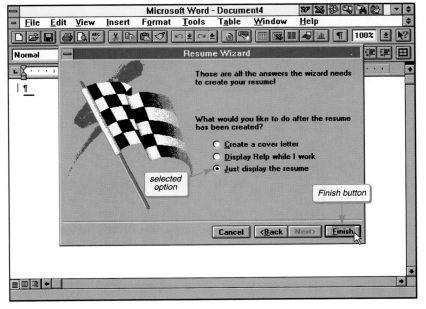

FIGURE 2-53

STEP 14 ▶

Choose the Finish button.

Word creates an entry-level classic style resume layout for you (Figure 2-54). You are to fill in the blanks accordingly. If your screen looks different than Figure 2-54, click the Zoom Control box arrow and select 100% from the list by clicking it.

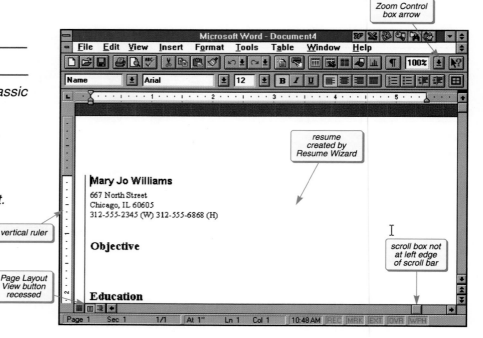

FIGURE 2-54

When Word displays the resume in the document window, it switches from **normal view** to **page layout view**. All of the documents you have created thus far have been in normal view. That is, the announcement in Project 1 and the cover letter in this project were created in normal view. In both normal and page layout views, you can type and edit text. The difference is that page layout view shows you exactly what the printed page will look like.

To see the entire resume created by the Resume Wizard, you should print the resume.

TO PRINT THE RESUME CREATED BY THE RESUME WIZARD

Step 1: Ready the printer.
Step 2: Click the Print button on the Standard toolbar.
Step 3: When the printer stops, retrieve the hardcopy resume from the printer.

The printed resume is shown in Figure 2-55.

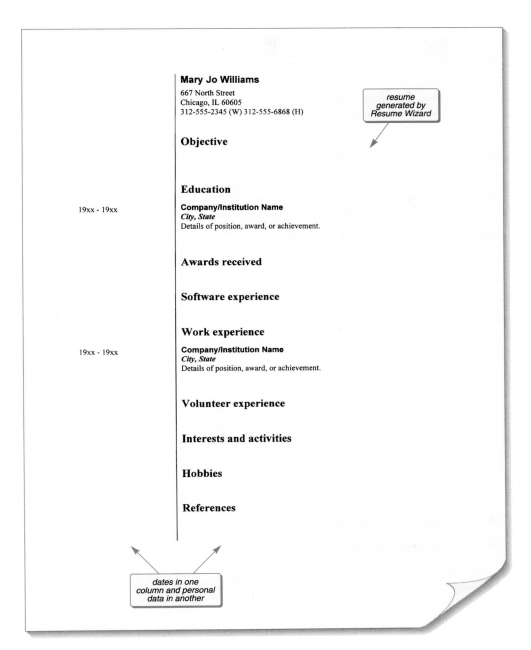

Mary Jo Williams
667 North Street
Chicago, IL 60605
312-555-2345 (W) 312-555-6868 (H)

Objective

Education

19xx - 19xx | **Company/Institution Name**
City, State
Details of position, award, or achievement.

Awards received

Software experience

Work experience

19xx - 19xx | **Company/Institution Name**
City, State
Details of position, award, or achievement.

Volunteer experience

Interests and activities

Hobbies

References

resume
generated by
Resume Wizard

dates in one
column and personal
data in another

FIGURE 2-55

Notice in Figure 2-55 that the Resume Wizard placed the Education and Work experience dates in one column and the rest of the resume in a second column. Because the resume is divided into columns, Word displays the document in page layout view. In normal view, columns are intermixed within one another.

Notice in Figure 2-54 that the scroll box on the horizontal scroll bar is positioned near the right edge of the scroll bar, indicating text is to the left of the insertion point. From the printout of the resume, you can see that the Education and Work experience dates are to the left of the insertion point in the document window. In page layout view, you also have a vertical ruler at the left edge of the document window. Page layout view is discussed in more depth in Projects 3 and 6.

▶ PERSONALIZING THE RESUME

T he next step is to personalize the resume. That is, you fill in blanks beneath the Objective, Awards received, Software experience, Volunteer experience, Interests and activities, Hobbies, and References headings, and select and replace text beneath the Education and Work experience headings, as shown in the following pages.

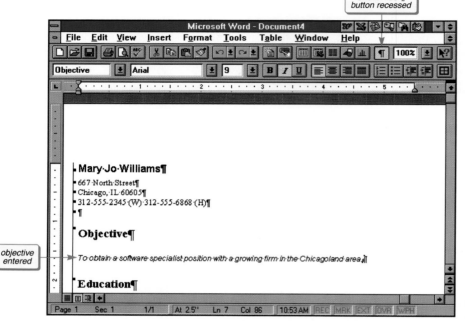

FIGURE 2-56

TO ENTER THE OBJECTIVE

Step 1: If it is not recessed, click the Show/Hide ¶ button on the Standard toolbar to display nonprinting characters.

Step 2: Position the insertion point on the paragraph mark below the Objective heading. Type `To obtain a software specialist position with a growing firm in the Chicagoland area.`

The objective, automatically formatted in italics by the Resume Wizard, displays (Figure 2-56).

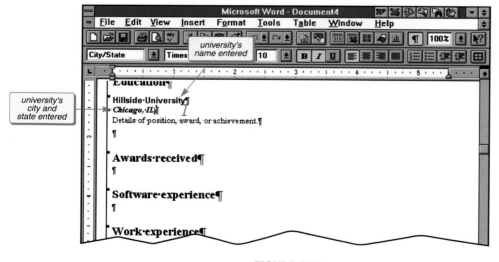

FIGURE 2-57

TO ENTER THE UNIVERSITY'S NAME, CITY, AND STATE

Step 1: Click beneath the scroll box on the vertical scroll bar to bring the Education heading and text into the document window.

Step 2: Select the words, Company/Institution Name, and type `Hillside University`

Step 3: Select the words, *City, State,* and type `Chicago, IL`

The university's name, city, and state display (Figure 2-57).

Using the TAB Key

The next step is to enter the degrees you obtained beneath the university's city and state. Notice in Figure 2-58 that the degree award dates and grade point averages are vertically-aligned. That is, the letter M in May 1995 is directly above the letter M in May 1993; the two letter Gs in GPA are directly above each other; and the number 3 in 3.8 is directly above the number 3 in 3.7. Press the TAB key to vertically-align text in a document.

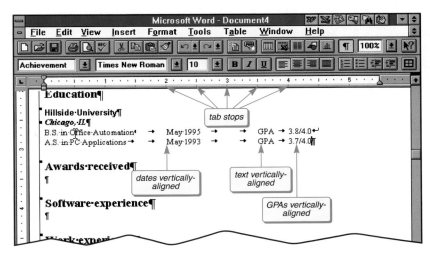

FIGURE 2-58

Word presets tab stops at every one-half inch. These preset, or default, tabs are indicated on the horizontal ruler by small tick marks (Figure 2-58). In a later project, you will learn how to change the preset tab stops.

TO VERTICALLY-ALIGN THE DEGREE INFORMATION WITH THE TAB KEY ▼

STEP 1 ▶

Select the sentence, Details of position, award, or achievement., beneath the university's city and state. Type B.S. in Office Automation

Word replaces the text beneath Chicago, IL (Figure 2-59).

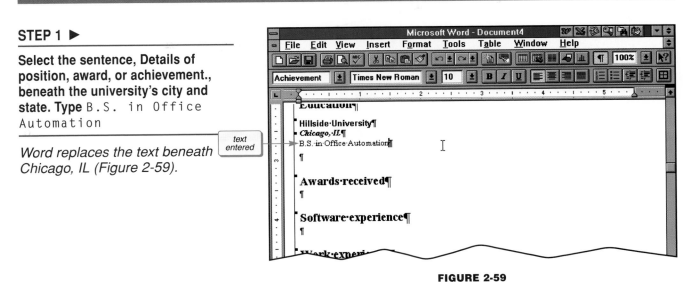

FIGURE 2-59

STEP 2 ▶

Press the TAB key twice and type
May 1995

*The insertion point moves two tab stops to the right, which is two inches from the left margin. Thus, the degree date is entered at the fourth tab stop (Figure 2-60). Notice the **right-pointing arrows** (→) between the degree name and date. A nonprinting character, a right-pointing arrow, displays each time you press the TAB key. Recall that nonprinting characters do not print; they only display in the document window. Notice that only a portion of the first right-pointing arrow displays because it is positioned so close to the tab stop.*

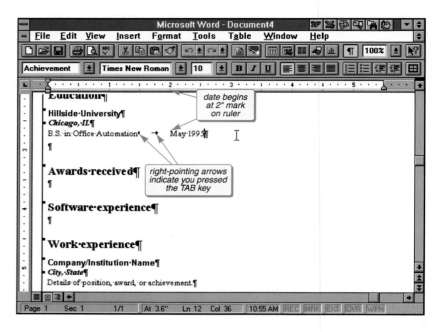

FIGURE 2-60

STEP 3 ▶

Press the TAB key twice. Type GPA **and press the TAB key once. Type** 3.8/4.0

The first degree information is entered (Figure 2-61). GPA is aligned at the 3.5-inch mark and the 3.8 is aligned at the 4-inch mark.

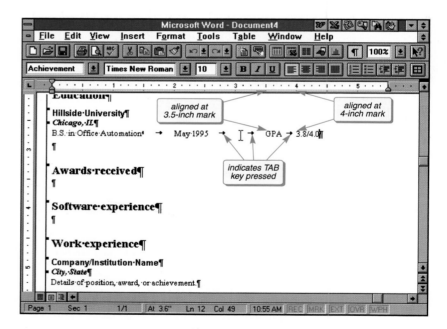

FIGURE 2-61

STEP 4 ▶

Press SHIFT+ENTER.

*Word inserts a **line break** after the grade point average and moves the insertion point to the beginning of the next line (Figure 2-62). The ENTER key would create a new paragraph and advance the insertion point down two lines due to the paragraph formatting created by the Resume Wizard. You do not want to create a new paragraph; instead, you want to keep the same formatting for both degree lines. Thus, a line break is entered to start a new line. The **line break character** (↵) is a nonprinting character that displays on the screen each time you enter a line break.*

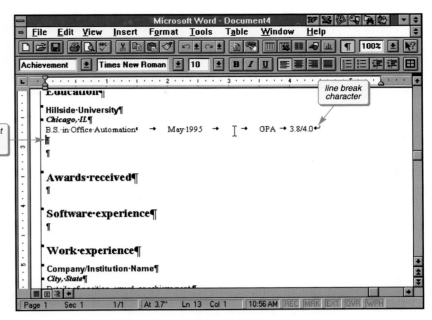

FIGURE 2-62

STEP 5 ▶

Type A.S. in PC Applications **and press the** TAB **key twice. Type** May 1993 **and press the** TAB **key twice. Type** GPA **and press the** TAB **key once. Type** 3.7/4.0 **and press the** DELETE **key to remove the extra paragraph mark.**

The Education section of the resume is complete (Figure 2-63).

FIGURE 2-63

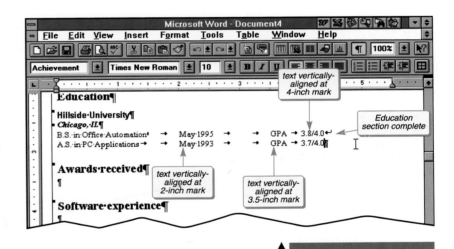

The next step is to enter the details beneath the remaining headings on the resume.

TO ENTER THE AWARDS RECEIVED AND SOFTWARE EXPERIENCE SECTIONS

Step 1: Position the insertion point on the paragraph mark beneath the Awards received heading. Type 1994 Student of the Year

Step 2: Position the insertion point on the paragraph mark beneath the Software experience heading. Type Windows Products: Word, Excel, Access, Quattro Pro, WordPerfect, FoxPro, PowerPoint and press SHIFT+ENTER to create a line break and advance the insertion point to the next line. Type DOS Products: Word, Lotus, dBASE IV, Quattro Pro, WordPerfect, FoxPro, Harvard Graphics

The Awards received and Software experience sections are complete (Figure 2-64 on the next page).

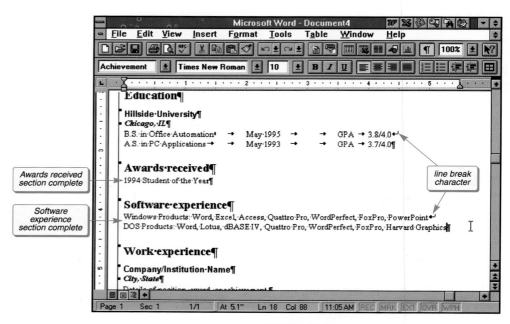

FIGURE 2-64

TO ENTER THE WORK EXPERIENCE SECTION

Step 1: Select the words, Company/Institution Name, beneath the Work experience heading. Type
```
Hillside University
```
Step 2: Select the words, *City, State,* beneath the company's name. Type
```
Chicago, IL
```

Step 3: Select the sentence, Details of position, award, or achievement., beneath the city and state. Type Assist faculty and staff with software problems. Responsibilities include answering and logging calls, solving software problems, and forwarding hardware problems to correct department. Also developed a call tracking system for the university. Press the DELETE key to remove the extra paragraph mark.

The Work experience section is complete (Figure 2-65).

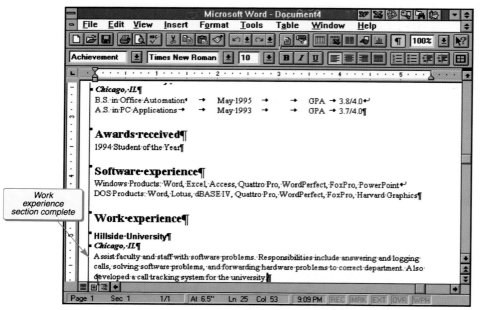

FIGURE 2-65

TO ENTER THE REMAINING SECTIONS OF THE RESUME

Step 1: Scroll through the resume to bring the Volunteer experience section into the document window. Position the insertion point on the paragraph mark beneath the Volunteer experience heading. Type `Train employees at the local United Way each Saturday on a variety of software packages.`

Step 2: Position the insertion point on the paragraph mark beneath the Interests and activities heading. Type `Chicagoland Windows User Group Member` and press SHIFT+ENTER to create a line break. Type `Subscribe to several PC and software magazines`

Step 3: Position the insertion point on the paragraph mark beneath the Hobbies heading. Type `SCUBA Diving, Photography, and Snow Skiing`

Step 4: Position the insertion point on the paragraph mark beneath the References heading. Type `Available upon request`

The Volunteer experience, Interests and activities, Hobbies, and References sections of the resume are complete (Figure 2-66).

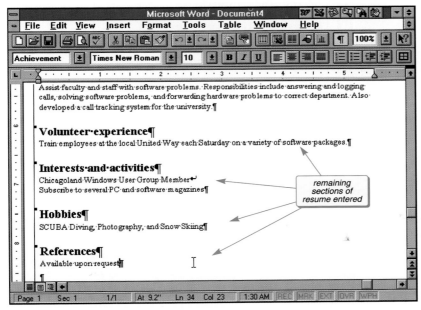

FIGURE 2-66

Saving the Resume

Because you have performed several tasks thus far, you should save your resume. For a detailed example of the procedure summarized below, refer to pages MSW19 through MSW21 in Project 1.

TO SAVE A DOCUMENT

Step 1: Insert your data disk into drive A.

Step 2: Click the Save button on the Standard toolbar.

Step 3: Type the filenam**e** `proj2res` in the File Name box. Do not press the ENTER key.

Step 4: If necessary, click the Drives drop-down box arrow and select drive A.

Step 5: Choose the OK button in the Save As dialog box.

Scrolling Through a Document

The final step in personalizing the resume is to enter the education and work experience dates into column one of the resume. To do this, you must first scroll left to bring the dates into the document window, as shown in these steps.

TO ENTER DATES INTO COLUMN ONE OF THE RESUME ▼

STEP 1 ►

Point to the left of the scroll box on the horizontal scroll bar (Figure 2-67).

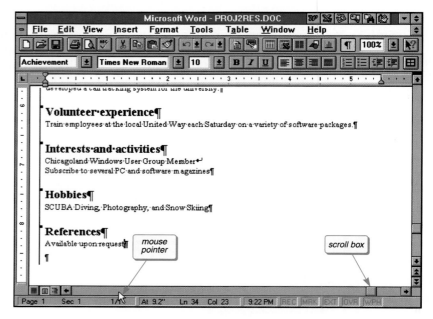

FIGURE 2-67

STEP 2 ►

Click the mouse. Point to the up arrow on the vertical scroll bar.

Word scrolls one screen to the left (Figure 2-68). Column one is now in view, but the dates are not.

STEP 3

Hold down the left mouse button until both dates display in the document window.

Word scrolls up one screen to bring the Education and Work experience dates into the document window. You need to replace the xx's in the dates with actual numbers.

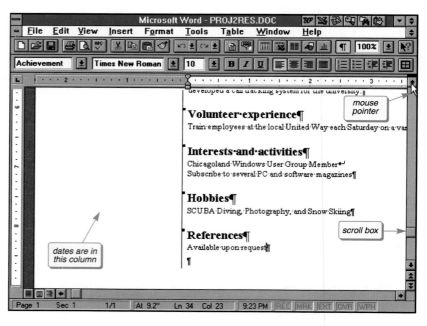

FIGURE 2-68

STEP 4 ▶

In the Education section, select xx in the first 19xx.

Word places a slashed rectangle around the Education section dates, called a frame, and selects the xx (Figure 2-69). Frames are discussed in Project 6.

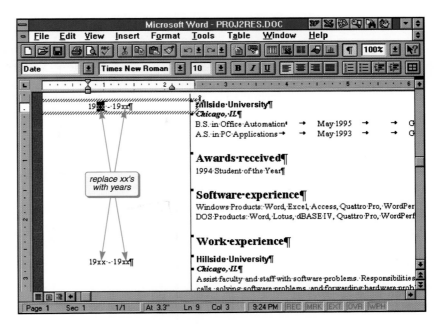

FIGURE 2-69

STEP 5 ▶

Type 91 **and select xx in the second 19xx in the Education section. Type** 95 **and select xx in the first 19xx in the Work experience section. Type** 92 **and select xx in the second 19xx in the Work experience section. Type** 95

The dates are entered and the resume is complete (Figure 2-70).

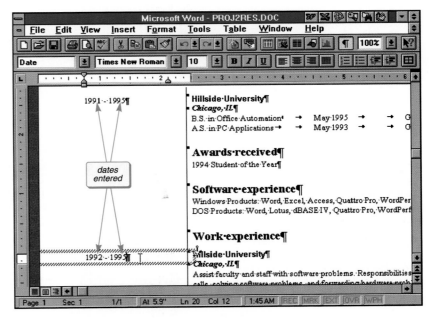

FIGURE 2-70

Saving Again and Spell Checking

The resume is now complete (see Figure 2-1 on page MSW67). After completing the resume, you should check the spelling of the document by clicking the Spelling button on the Standard toolbar. Because you have performed tasks since the last save, you should save the resume again by clicking the Save button on the Standard toolbar.

You have now completed Project 2. The final step is to print the document.

▶ VIEWING AND PRINTING THE RESUME IN PRINT PREVIEW

T o see exactly how a document will look when you print it, you should display it in **print preview**. Print preview displays the entire document in reduced size on the Word screen. In print preview, you can edit and format text, adjust margins, and view multiple pages. Once you preview the document, you can print it directly from within print preview.

TO USE PRINT PREVIEW ▼

STEP 1 ▶

Press CTRL+HOME to move the insertion point to the top of the resume. Point to the Print Preview button (▧) on the Standard toolbar (Figure 2-71).

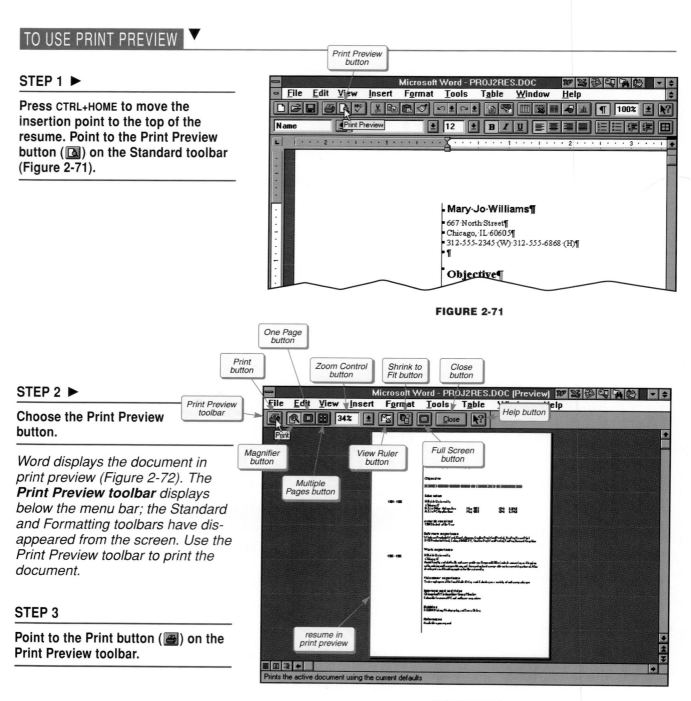

FIGURE 2-71

STEP 2 ▶

Choose the Print Preview button.

*Word displays the document in print preview (Figure 2-72). The **Print Preview toolbar** displays below the menu bar; the Standard and Formatting toolbars have disappeared from the screen. Use the Print Preview toolbar to print the document.*

STEP 3

Point to the Print button (▧) on the Print Preview toolbar.

FIGURE 2-72

STEP 4 ▼

Ready the printer. Choose the Print button. When the printer stops, retrieve the printout.

Word prints the document on the printer (Figure 2-73).

STEP 5

Choose the Close button (Close) on the Print Preview toolbar.

Word returns you to the document window.

Mary Jo Williams
667 North Street
Chicago, IL 60605
312-555-2345 (W) 312-555-6868 (H)

Objective

To obtain a software specialist position with a growing firm in the Chicagoland area.

Education

	Hillside University			
1991 - 1995	*Chicago, IL*			
	B.S. in Office Automation	May 1995	GPA	3.8/4.0
	A.S. in PC Applications	May 1993	GPA	3.7/4.0

Awards received
1994 Student of the Year

Software experience
Windows Products: Word, Excel, Access, Quattro Pro, WordPerfect, FoxPro, PowerPoint
DOS Products: Word, Lotus, dBASE IV, Quattro Pro, WordPerfect, FoxPro, Harvard Graphics

Work experience

1992 - 1995   **Hillside University**
Chicago, IL
Assist faculty and staff with software problems. Responsibilities include answering and logging calls, solving software problems, and forwarding hardware problems to correct department. Also developed a call tracking system for the university.

Volunteer experience
Train employees at the local United Way each Saturday on a variety of software packages.

Interests and activities
Chicagoland Windows User Group Member
Subscribe to several PC and software magazines

Hobbies
SCUBA Diving, Photography, and Snow Skiing

References
Available upon request

FIGURE 2-73

▶ WORKING WITH MULTIPLE OPEN DOCUMENTS

You currently have two documents open: PROJ2LTR.DOC and PROJ2RES.DOC. Each document is in a different document window. You can easily switch back and forth between the two documents, or you can split the document window into two even sections, each containing a different document.

TO SWITCH FROM ONE DOCUMENT TO ANOTHER ▼

STEP 1 ▶

Select the Window menu and point to the 1 PROJ2LTR.DOC document name (Figure 2-74).

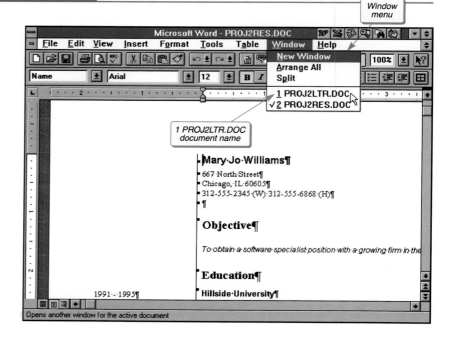

FIGURE 2-74

STEP 2 ▶

Choose the 1 PROJ2LTR.DOC document name.

Word switches from the resume to the cover letter (Figure 2-75). The document window now displays the cover letter you created earlier in this project.

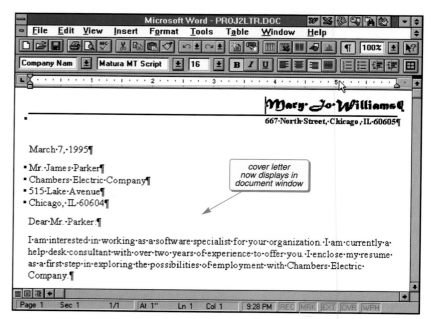

FIGURE 2-75

TO ARRANGE BOTH DOCUMENTS ON THE SAME WORD SCREEN ▼

STEP 1 ▶

Select the Window menu and point to the Arrange All command (Figure 2-76).

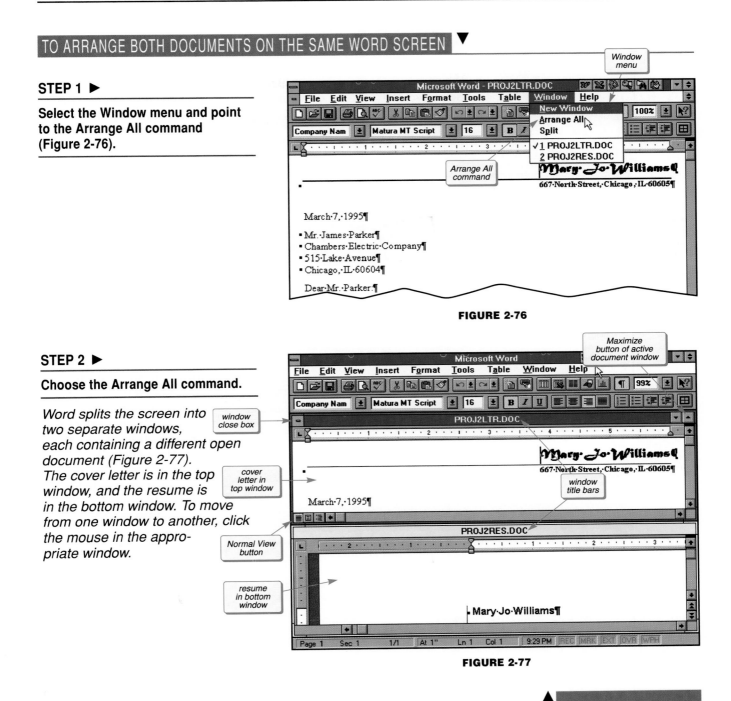

FIGURE 2-76

STEP 2 ▶

Choose the Arrange All command.

Word splits the screen into two separate windows, each containing a different open document (Figure 2-77). The cover letter is in the top window, and the resume is in the bottom window. To move from one window to another, click the mouse in the appropriate window.

FIGURE 2-77

To return to one document window on the screen, maximize the active document by clicking its Maximize button at the right edge of the window title bar (Figure 2-77). If you are in page layout view, and want to return to normal view, click the Normal View button on the horizontal scroll bar.

▶ SHORTCUT MENUS

 hen you select or point to certain text or graphics in Word, you can use **shortcut menus** to accomplish some tasks. Shortcut menus are context sensitive; that is, they contain commands related to the item with which you are working. Use shortcut menus instead of toolbar buttons or commands from menus to perform tasks. For example, you can cut and paste text with a shortcut menu instead of using the Cut and Paste buttons on the Standard toolbar. To display a shortcut menu, click the right mouse button while the insertion point is at the correct location in the document window. Then, select the appropriate command from the shortcut menu.

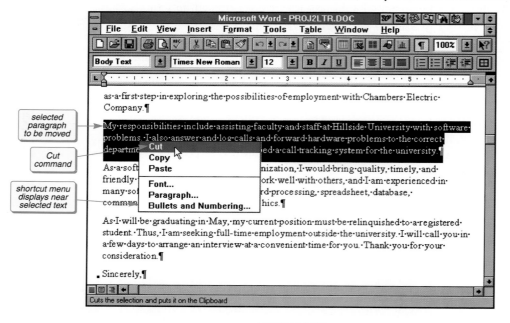

FIGURE 2-78

For example to use a shortcut menu to move a paragraph, first select the paragraph to be moved and then click the right mouse button. Word displays a shortcut menu applicable to selected paragraphs (Figure 2-78). Choose the Cut command from the shortcut menu. Move the insertion point to the location where the paragraph should be moved. Click the right mouse button again to display the shortcut menu applicable to nonselected text (Figure 2-79). Notice in this shortcut menu that the Cut and Copy commands are dimmed because you can only cut or copy selected text. Next, choose the Paste command to copy the cut paragraph from the Clipboard and place it at the location of the insertion point in the document.

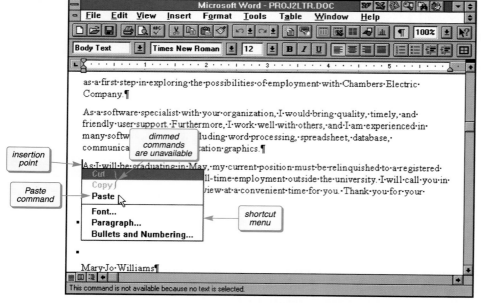

FIGURE 2-79

▶ PROJECT SUMMARY

Project 2 introduced you to creating a cover letter and a resume using Word wizards. You used the Letter Wizard to create a prewritten cover letter. Then, you enhanced the letterhead on the cover letter. You created an AutoText entry, which you used when you personalized the cover letter. Next, you moved a paragraph in the cover letter. Then, you used the Resume Wizard to create an accompanying resume. You viewed and printed the resume in print preview. Then, you learned how to switch between both open documents and how to display them both on the Word screen at the same time. Finally, you learned how to use shortcut menus.

▶ KEY TERMS AND INDEX

AutoText entry *(MSW82)*
block letter *(MSW68)*
border *(MSW77)*
Borders toolbar *(MSW77)*
character styles *(MSW75)*
Clipboard *(MSW89)*
complimentary close *(MSW69)*
cover letter *(MSW66)*
CTRL+click *(MSW86)*
cut and paste *(MSW89)*
Cut button *(MSW91)*
date line *(MSW69)*
drag and drop *(MSW89)*
Edit AutoText button *(MSW82)*

inside address *(MSW69)*
Letter Wizard *(MSW70)*
line break *(MSW103)*
line break character *(MSW103)*
message *(MSW69)*
Normal Document Template *(MSW70)*
normal view *(MSW98)*
Normal View button *(MSW111)*
page layout view *(MSW98)*
paragraph styles *(MSW75)*
Paste button *(MSW91)*
print preview *(MSW108)*
Print Preview toolbar *(MSW108)*

resume *(MSW66)*
Resume Wizard *(MSW92)*
right-align *(MSW76)*
right-pointing arrows *(MSW102)*
rule *(MSW77)*
ruling line *(MSW77)*
salutation *(MSW69)*
SHIFT+click *(MSW81)*
SHIFT+ENTER *(MSW103)*
shortcut menus *(MSW112)*
signature block *(MSW69)*
style *(MSW75)*
template *(MSW70)*
wizards *(MSW66)*

In Microsoft Word 6, you can accomplish a task in a number of ways. The following table provides a quick reference to each task presented in this project with its available options. The commands listed in the Menu column can be executed using either the keyboard or mouse. Some of the commands in the Menu column are also available in shortcut menus. If you have WordPerfect help activated, the key combinations listed in the Keyboard Shortcuts column will not work as shown.

Task	Mouse	Menu	Keyboard Shortcuts
Add a Border	Click Borders button on Formatting toolbar	From Format menu, choose Borders and Shading	
Arrange Open Documents		From Window menu, choose Arrange All	
Create an AutoText Entry	Click Edit AutoText button on Standard toolbar	From Edit menu, choose AutoText	
Create a Letter Using the Letter Wizard		From File menu, choose New	Press CTRL+N
Create a Resume Using the Resume Wizard		From File menu, choose New	Press CTRL+N
Insert an AutoText Entry	Click Insert AutoText button on Standard toolbar	From Edit menu, choose AutoText	
Insert a Line Break			Press SHIFT+ENTER
Move a Paragraph	Drag and drop text	From Edit menu, choose Cut; then Paste	Press CTRL+X; then CTRL+V
Print Preview a Document	Click Print Preview button on Standard toolbar	From File menu, choose Print Preview	Press CTRL+F2
Right-Align Text	Click Align Right button on Formatting toolbar	From Format menu, choose Paragraph	
Select a Sentence	CTRL+click in sentence		
Switch from One Document to Another		From Window menu, choose document name	
Use the Shortcut Menu	Click the right mouse button		Press SHIFT+F10

STUDENT ASSIGNMENT 1
True/False

Instructions: Circle T if the statement is true or F if the statement is false.

T F 1. A resume usually contains the applicant's educational background and job experience.
T F 2. Word provides wizards to assist you in document preparation.
T F 3. In a block letter, the date is printed at the right margin.
T F 4. All business letters should contain a date line, inside address, message, and signature block.
T F 5. When using a wizard to create a document, you must first specify your desired document spacing for the wizard.
T F 6. To create a document using a wizard, click the New button on the Standard toolbar.
T F 7. A style is a customized format applied to characters or paragraphs.
T F 8. A border is a line added to the edge of a paragraph.
T F 9. When you click the Borders button, the Borders dialog box displays on the screen.
T F 10. You can store text in an AutoText entry and then use the AutoText entry throughout your document.
T F 11. One way to move paragraphs is to drag and drop them.
T F 12. When you paste text, the Clipboard contents are erased.
T F 13. You should use cut and paste to move paragraphs a short distance.
T F 14. The TAB key is used to horizontally align text in a document.
T F 15. Print preview displays the entire document in reduced size on the Word screen.
T F 16. You can print a document from the print preview window.
T F 17. To switch from one open document to another, choose the Switch button on the Standard toolbar.
T F 18. To display all open documents on the Word screen, choose the Arrange All command from the Window menu.
T F 19. In print preview, the Print Preview toolbar displays stacked beneath the Formatting toolbar.
T F 20. Shortcut menus are help menus that display shortcut keys.

STUDENT ASSIGNMENT 2
Multiple Choice

Instructions: Circle the correct response.

1. Which of the following is optional in a business letter?
   a. date line
   b. inside address
   c. message
   d. complimentary close
2. In the Style list box, bold style names are _____.
   a. active styles
   b. inactive styles
   c. paragraph styles
   d. character styles
3. To align a paragraph at the right margin, click the _____ button on the Formatting toolbar.
   a. Align Left
   b. Align Right
   c. Center
   d. Justify

STUDENT ASSIGNMENT 2 (continued)

4. You can add a border _____.
   a. above a paragraph
   b. below a paragraph
   c. between paragraphs
   d. all of the above

5. Instead of dragging the mouse to select text, you can position the insertion point at the beginning of the text to select and then _____ at the end of the text to select.
   a. click
   b. CTRL+click
   c. SHIFT+click
   d. ALT+click

6. To select a sentence, _____ in the sentence.
   a. SHIFT+click
   b. CTRL+click
   c. double-click
   d. triple-click

7. The nonprinting character for the TAB key is a _____.
   a. raised dot
   b. paragraph mark
   c. right-pointing arrow
   d. letter T

8. Press _____ to insert a line break.
   a. ENTER
   b. CTRL+ENTER
   c. SHIFT+ENTER
   d. ALT+ENTER

9. To display a shortcut menu, you _____.
   a. click the left mouse button
   b. click the right mouse button
   c. CTRL+click
   d. SHIFT+click

10. In print preview, the Standard toolbar _____.
    a. displays above the Print Preview toolbar
    b. displays below the Print Preview toolbar
    c. displays above the Formatting toolbar
    d. does not display

STUDENT ASSIGNMENT 3
Understanding the Components of a Business Letter

Instructions: In Figure SA2-3, arrows point to the components of a business letter. Identify the various elements of the letter in the spaces provided.

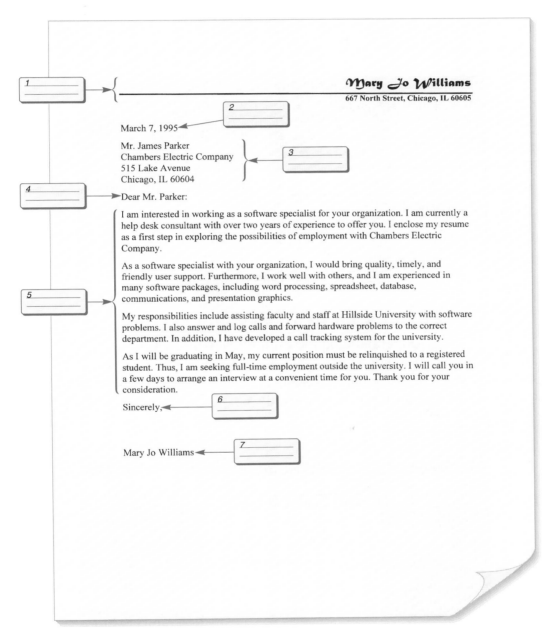

FIGURE SA2-3

STUDENT ASSIGNMENT 4
Understanding the Borders Toolbar

Instructions: In Figure SA2-4, arrows point to several of the boxes and buttons on the Borders toolbar. In the spaces provided, briefly explain the purpose of each button or box.

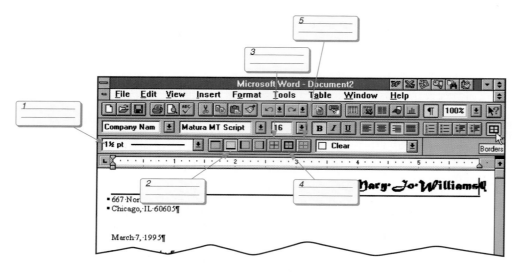

FIGURE SA2-4

STUDENT ASSIGNMENT 5
Understanding the Print Preview Toolbar

Instructions: In Figure SA2-5, arrows point to several of the buttons on the Print Preview toolbar. In the spaces provided, briefly explain the purpose of each button.

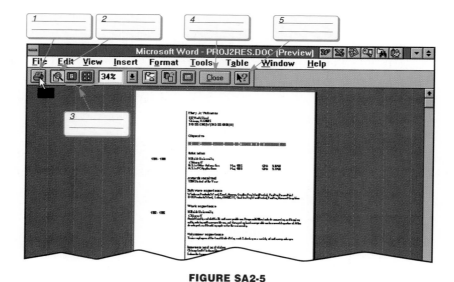

FIGURE SA2-5

STUDENT ASSIGNMENT 6
Understanding the Drag and Drop Procedure

Instructions: Fill in the step numbers below to correctly order the process of moving a paragraph.

Step _____: Drag the dotted insertion point to the location where the paragraph is to be moved.

Step _____: Double-click the left mouse button. Move the mouse pointer into the selected text.

Step _____: Press and hold down the left mouse button.

Step _____: Position the mouse pointer in the selection bar to the left of the paragraph to be moved.

Step _____: Release the left mouse button.

C O M P U T E R   L A B O R A T O R Y   E X E R C I S E S

COMPUTER LABORATORY EXERCISE 1
Using the Help Menu to Learn About Wizards

Instructions: Perform the following tasks using a computer:

1. Start Word.
2. From the Help menu, choose the Search for Help on command. Type `wizards` and press the ENTER key. Select Starting a new document from a template or by using a wizard. Choose the Go To button. Read and print the information.
3. Choose the Close button. Choose the Search button. Choose the Show Topics button. Select Starting a wizard. Choose the Go To button. Read and print the information.
4. Choose the Close button. Choose the Index button. Click the letter S. Scroll through the topics until you find switching to a different open document. Select switching to a different open document. Read and print the information.
5. Choose the Close button. From the Word Help File menu, choose the Exit command.

COMPUTER LABORATORY EXERCISE 2
Adding a Border Beneath a Paragraph

Instructions: Start Word. Open the document CLE2-2.DOC from the Word subdirectory on the Student Diskette that accompanies this book. Given the letterhead shown in Figure CLE2-2, add a border beneath the name.

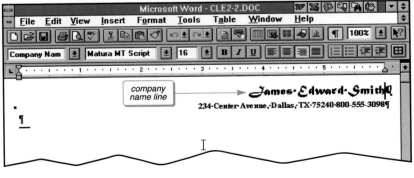

FIGURE CLE2-2

(continued)

COMPUTER LABORATORY EXERCISE 2 (continued)

Perform the following tasks:

1. Position the insertion point in the Company Name line of the letter, which in this letter is a person's name.
2. If the Borders button on the Formatting toolbar is not already recessed, click the Borders button to display the Borders toolbar.
3. Click the Line Style box arrow to display the list of available line styles. Select 1 1/2 pt line style by clicking it.
4. Click the Bottom Border button on the Borders toolbar.
5. Practice floating the anchored Borders toolbar by holding down the SHIFT key and double-clicking in a blank area on the toolbar. Then, re-anchor the Borders toolbar by double-clicking in a blank area of the Borders toolbar or in the title bar of the floating Borders toolbar.
6. Click the Borders button to remove the Borders toolbar.
7. Use the Save As command on the File menu to save the revised letterhead with the filename CLE2-2A.
8. Print the letterhead.

COMPUTER LABORATORY EXERCISE 3
Moving a Paragraph

FIGURE CLE2-3

Instructions: Start Word. Open the document CLE2-3.DOC from the Word subdirectory on the Student Diskette that accompanies this book. As shown in Figure CLE2-3, the document is a letter to mom. You are to move the fourth paragraph.

Karen Lyn Anderson
667 North Street, Chicago, IL 60605

June 7, 1995

Ms. Jean Shephard
78 Baker Court
Chicago, IL 60601

Dear Mom,

How are you doing? Everything is fine with me!

I'm sorry that I haven't written for a while, but I've been really busy! As you know, I really like computers, and I'm spending long hours in front of a screen both at work and at home.

In fact, I just bought a great program. It's really neat — a collection of business letters that I can customize any way I want. For example, there's a letter to people who are late paying their bills and another one that complains about a defective product.

move this paragraph → Too bad they don't have one for writing to you! Ha ha ha. They should also have one for thanking Aunt Patty for the cookies! Nah — form letters could never replace the personal touch!

I'm sure it'll save me a lot of time and energy — you know how hard it is for me to write letters! Now I'll be able to think about business instead of worrying about what to say in letters.

Gotta run now, Mom! All my love!

Perform the following tasks:

1. Position the mouse pointer in the selection bar to the left of the fourth paragraph, which begins, Too bad they don't have one for ... .
2. Double-click the mouse to select the paragraph. Position the mouse pointer in the selected paragraph.
3. Press and hold down the left mouse button. Drag the insertion point to the left of the letter G in the paragraph beginning, Gotta run now, ...
4. Use the Save As command on the File menu to save the document on your data disk with the filename CLE2-3A.
5. Print the revised document.

COMPUTER LABORATORY ASSIGNMENT 1
Using the Letter Wizard to Create a Cover Letter

Purpose: To become familiar with using the Letter Wizard to create a cover letter, personalizing the cover letter, and saving and printing the cover letter.

Problem: As a current employee of Carter Manufacturing, you are seeking employment at Williamsburg Metal Makers as a sales representative. You prepare the cover letter shown in Figure CLA2-1.

Theresa Dawn Carrington

23 Palm Court, Williamsburg, FL 30984

September 10, 1995

Mr. Jerry Dougan
Williamsburg Metal Makers
89 Third Avenue
Williamsburg, FL 30984

Dear Mr. Dougan:

I am interested in working as a sales representative for your organization. I am a highly motivated sales representative with over 3 years of experience to offer you. I enclose my resume as a first step in exploring the possibilities of employment with Williamsburg Metal Makers.

My most recent experience was selling for a major manufacturing firm in the Williamsburg area. I was responsible for the south surburban territory. In addition, I exceeded my sales quota each month.

As a sales representative with your organization, I would bring a base of happy, satisfied customers. Furthermore, I work well with others, and I am experienced in cold calls.

I would appreciate your keeping this inquiry confidential. I will call you in a few days to arrange an interview at a convenient time for you. Thank you for your consideration.

Sincerely,

Theresa Dawn Carrington

FIGURE CLA2-1

Instructions: Perform the tasks below and on the next page.

1. If it is not already selected, click the Show/Hide ¶ button on the Formatting toolbar to display paragraph marks and spaces.
2. Create a prewritten cover letter using the Letter Wizard. Refer to Figure CLA2-2 for the address information requested by the Letter Wizard.

(continued)

COMPUTER LABORATORY ASSIGNMENT 1 (continued)

Theresa Dawn Carrington

23 Palm Court
Williamsburg, FL 30984
506-555-2818 (W) 506-555-0923 (H)

Objective

To obtain a sales representative position with a large metropolitan firm.

Education

1988 - 1992

Florida State University
Tampa, FL

M.S.	Business Administration	May 1992	GPA 3.8/4.0
B.S.	Marketing Management	May 1990	GPA 3.9/4.0
A.S.	Information Technology	May 1988	GPA 3.7/4.0

Foreign languages

Spanish	4 semesters
French	2 semesters
German	2 semesters

Work experience

1992 - 1995

Carter Manufacturing
Tampa, FL
I have maintained top sales representative status for 34 of the past 36 months. My territory includes the suburban Tampa area. Each month I have worked at Carter Manufacturing, I have acquired 10 new customers. Because of my ability to speak multiple foreign languages, I am able to call on many culturally diverse clients in the Tampa suburbs. I have been promoted three times since my employment began with Carter Manufacturing.

Professional memberships

American Institute of Sales Representatives

Awards received

1994 and 1995 Sales Representative of the Year at Carter Manufacturing

Hobbies

Sailing, Traveling, and Tennis

References

Available upon request

FIGURE CLA2-2

3. Save the letterhead with the filename CLA2-1.
4. Modify the letterhead so it looks like Figure CLA2-1 on the previous page.
5. Change the font size of all characters beneath the letterhead to 12 point.
6. Create an AutoText entry for Williamsburg Metal Makers that displays in the inside address.
7. Select and replace the underlined words in the prewritten letter so the revised letter matches the words in Figure CLA2-1 on the previous page. Use the AutoText entry you created in Step 6 when you replace the company name.
8. Check the spelling of the cover letter.
9. Save the cover letter again with the same filename.
10. Print the cover letter.

COMPUTER LABORATORY ASSIGNMENT 2
Using the Resume Wizard to Create a Resume

Purpose: To become familiar with using the Resume Wizard to create a resume, personalizing the resume, using the TAB key, inserting line breaks, and saving and printing a document.

Problem: You have prepared the cover letter displayed in Figure CLA2-1 on page MSW121 and would like to prepare an accompanying resume. You prepare the document shown in Figure CLA2-2.

Instructions: Perform the following tasks:

1. Use the Resume Wizard to create a resume. Use the name and address information in Figure CLA2-2 when the Resume Wizard requests it.
2. Save the resume with the filename CLA2-2.
3. Click the Show/Hide ¶ button on the Formatting toolbar to display paragraph marks and spaces.
4. Personalize the resume, as shown in Figure CLA2-2. When entering multiple paragraphs beneath a heading, be sure to enter a line break instead of a paragraph break. Use the TAB key to align Education and Foreign language data. Do not forget to enter the date information in column one.
5. Check the spelling of the resume.
6. Save the resume again with the same filename.
7. Print the resume from within print preview.

COMPUTER LABORATORY ASSIGNMENT 3
Using Wizards to Compose a Cover Letter and Resume

Purpose: To become familiar with creating a prewritten cover letter and resume from a recent want ad, personalizing the cover letter and resume, and saving and printing the cover letter and want ad.

Problem: You are currently in the market for a new job. You want to use Word's wizards to prepare a cover letter and resume from a recent want ad.

Instructions: Obtain a copy of last Sunday's newspaper. Look through the classified section and cut out a want ad in an area of interest to you. Create a cover letter and resume for the want ad following the guidelines listed below. Save the cover letter with the filename CLA2-3A and the resume with the filename CLA2-3B. Perform the following tasks:

1. Enhance the letterhead in the prewritten cover letter.
2. Change the font size of all characters beneath the letterhead to 12 point.
3. Replace all underlined words and phrases in the cover letter to meet your background and the advertisement.
4. In the resume, use dates in the future for when you will receive your degree.
5. Try to be as accurate as possible when composing the cover letter and resume.
6. Turn in the want ad with printouts of the files CLA2-3A and CLA2-3B.

COMPUTER LABORATORY ASSIGNMENT 4
Designing and Creating a Cover Letter and Resume

Purpose: To provide practice in creating a cover letter and resume without using a Word wizard.

Problem: You are to obtain a job advertisement in your field from a recent classified section of a local newspaper. Assume you are in the market for the position being sought.

Instructions: You are not to use Word's wizards in this assignment. Create a cover letter and accompanying resume for the job advertisement. Use proper spacing for a business letter. Use a variety of formatting in the cover letter and resume to make them look professional. Be sure to check the spelling of your cover letter and resume before printing them. Save the cover letter with the filename CLA2-4A and the resume with the filename CLA2-4B.

Microsoft Word 6 for Windows

PROJECT THREE

CREATING A RESEARCH PAPER

OBJECTIVES You will have mastered the material in this project when you can:

- Describe the MLA documentation style
- Change the margin settings in a document
- Adjust line spacing in a document
- Use a header to number pages
- Indent paragraphs
- Use Word's AutoCorrect feature
- Add footnotes to a research paper
- Switch from normal to page layout view

- Insert hard page breaks
- Sort selected paragraphs
- Go to specified footnotes or pages
- Find and replace specified text
- View multiple pages in print preview
- Edit a document in print preview
- Use Word's thesaurus
- Display the number of words in a document

▶ INTRODUCTION

In both the academic and business environments, you will be asked to write reports. Business reports range from proposals to cost justifications to five-year plans to research findings. Academic reports focus mostly on research findings. Whether you are writing a business report or an academic report, you should follow a standard style when preparing it.

Many different styles of documentation exist for report preparation, depending on the nature of the report. Each style requires the same basic information; the differences among styles appear in the manner of presenting the information. For example, one documentation style may use the term *bibliography*; whereas, another uses *references*, and yet a third prefers *works cited*. A popular documentation style used today for research papers is presented by the **Modern Language Association (MLA)**. Thus, this project uses the **MLA style of documentation**.

▶ PROJECT THREE — RESEARCH PAPER

Project 3 illustrates the creation of a short research paper describing power disturbances that can damage a computer and its peripherals. As shown in Figure 3-1, the paper follows the MLA documentation style. The first two pages present the research paper, and the third page lists the works cited.

MSW124

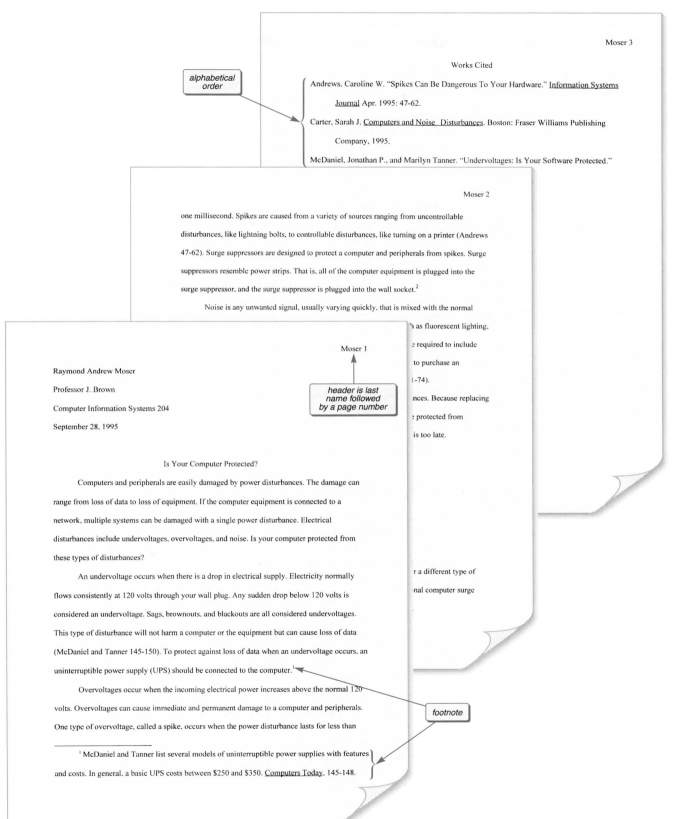

Moser 3

Works Cited

alphabetical order

Andrews, Caroline W. "Spikes Can Be Dangerous To Your Hardware." <u>Information Systems</u>
<u>Journal</u> Apr. 1995: 47-62.

Carter, Sarah J. <u>Computers and Noise Disturbances</u>. Boston: Fraser Williams Publishing
Company, 1995.

McDaniel, Jonathan P., and Marilyn Tanner. "Undervoltages: Is Your Software Protected."

Moser 2

one millisecond. Spikes are caused from a variety of sources ranging from uncontrollable

disturbances, like lightning bolts, to controllable disturbances, like turning on a printer (Andrews

47-62). Surge suppressors are designed to protect a computer and peripherals from spikes. Surge

suppressors resemble power strips. That is, all of the computer equipment is plugged into the

surge suppressor, and the surge suppressor is plugged into the wall socket.[2]

Noise is any unwanted signal, usually varying quickly, that is mixed with the normal

... h as fluorescent lighting.

... e required to include

... to purchase an

...1-74).

... nces. Because replacing

... e protected from

... is too late.

Moser 1

Raymond Andrew Moser

Professor J. Brown

Computer Information Systems 204

September 28, 1995

header is last name followed by a page number

Is Your Computer Protected?

Computers and peripherals are easily damaged by power disturbances. The damage can

range from loss of data to loss of equipment. If the computer equipment is connected to a

network, multiple systems can be damaged with a single power disturbance. Electrical

disturbances include undervoltages, overvoltages, and noise. Is your computer protected from

these types of disturbances?

An undervoltage occurs when there is a drop in electrical supply. Electricity normally

flows consistently at 120 volts through your wall plug. Any sudden drop below 120 volts is

considered an undervoltage. Sags, brownouts, and blackouts are all considered undervoltages.

This type of disturbance will not harm a computer or the equipment but can cause loss of data

(McDaniel and Tanner 145-150). To protect against loss of data when an undervoltage occurs, an

uninterruptible power supply (UPS) should be connected to the computer.[1]

Overvoltages occur when the incoming electrical power increases above the normal 120

volts. Overvoltages can cause immediate and permanent damage to a computer and peripherals.

One type of overvoltage, called a spike, occurs when the power disturbance lasts for less than

... r a different type of

... nal computer surge

footnote

[1] McDaniel and Tanner list several models of uninterruptible power supplies with features
and costs. In general, a basic UPS costs between $250 and $350. <u>Computers Today</u>, 145-148.

FIGURE 3-1

MLA Documentation Style

When writing papers, you must be sure to adhere to some form of documentation style. The research paper in this project follows the guidelines presented by the MLA. To follow the MLA style, double-space all pages of the paper with one-inch top, bottom, left, and right margins. Indent the first word of each paragraph one-half inch from the left margin. At the right margin of each page, place a page number one-half inch from the top margin. On each page, precede the page number with your last name.

The MLA style does not require a title page; instead, place your name and course information in a block at the left margin beginning one inch from the top of the page. Center the title two double-spaces below your name and course information. In the body of the paper, place author references in parentheses with the page number(s) where the referenced information is located. These in-text **parenthetical citations** are used instead of footnoting each source at the bottom of the page or at the end of the paper. In the MLA style, footnotes are used only for explanatory notes. In the body of the paper, use **superscripts** (raised numbers) to signal that an explanatory note exists.

According to the MLA style, explanatory notes are optional. **Explanatory notes** are used to elaborate on points discussed in the body of the paper. Explanatory notes may be placed either at the bottom of the page as footnotes or at the end of the paper as endnotes. Double-space the explanatory notes. Superscript each note's reference number, and indent it one-half inch from the left margin. Place one space following the note number before beginning the note text. At the end of the note text, you may list bibliographic information for further reference.

The MLA style uses the term **works cited** for the bibliographic references. The works cited page lists works alphabetically by each author's last name that is directly referenced in the paper. Place the works cited on a separate numbered page. Center the title, Works Cited, one inch from the top margin. Double-space all lines. Begin the first line of each work cited at the left margin; indent subsequent lines of the same work one-half inch from the left margin.

Document Preparation Steps

The following document preparation steps give you an overview of how the document shown in Figure 3-1 on the previous page will be developed in this project. If you are preparing the document in this project on a personal computer, read these steps without doing them.

1. Start Word.
2. Change the margin settings for the document.
3. Adjust the line spacing for the document.
4. Create a header to number pages.
5. Change the font size to 12.
6. Enter your name and course information.
7. Center the paper title.
8. Save the research paper.
9. First-line indent paragraphs in the paper.
10. Enter the research paper with footnotes, using the AutoCorrect feature.
11. Insert a hard page break.
12. Enter the works cited page.
13. Sort the paragraphs on the works cited page.
14. Save the document again.
15. Print the research paper.
16. Modify the research paper.
17. Save and print the revised research paper.
18. Quit Word.

Displaying Nonprinting Characters

As discussed in the previous projects, it is helpful to display nonprinting characters that indicate where in the document you pressed the ENTER key, SPACEBAR, or TAB key. Thus, if the Show/Hide¶ button on the Formatting toolbar is not already recessed, you should display the nonprinting characters by clicking it.

▶ CHANGING THE MARGINS

Word is preset to use standard 8.5 by 11-inch paper, with 1.25-inch left and right margins and 1-inch top and bottom margins. These margin settings affect every paragraph in the document. Often, you may want to change these default margin settings. For example, the MLA documentation style requires one-inch top, bottom, left, and right margins throughout the paper.

To change the margins, use the rulers. Use the horizontal ruler to change the left and right margins and use the vertical ruler to change the top and bottom margins. Currently, only the horizontal ruler displays in the document window because you are in normal view. To display both the horizontal and vertical rulers, you must switch to **page layout view** or print preview. Recall from Project 2 that Word automatically switched from normal to page layout view when you used the Resume Wizard to create a resume.

Normal view is the default view. That is, when you first install and invoke Word, the document window is in normal view. Thus, the first step in changing the default margin settings for a document is to switch from normal to page layout view, as shown in the following steps.

TO CHANGE THE DEFAULT MARGIN SETTINGS ▼

STEP 1 ▶

Point to the Page Layout View button (📄) on the horizontal scroll bar at the bottom of the Word screen (Figure 3-2).

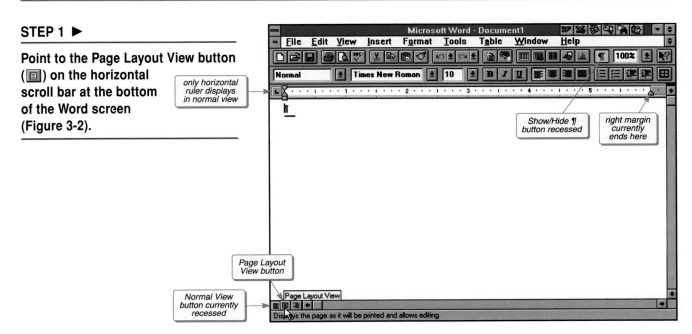

FIGURE 3-2

STEP 2 ▶

If it is not already recessed, click the Page Layout View button. Point to the left of the scroll box on the horizontal scroll bar.

Word switches the document window to page layout view (Figure 3-3). In page layout view, both a horizontal and vertical ruler display. On the rulers, the tick marks are set every 1/8 or .125 inches; that is, eight ticks equal 1 inch. The shaded gray area at the top of the vertical ruler indicates the top margin setting; thus, the top margin is currently 1 inch. You cannot see the left margin setting on the horizontal ruler when you initially switch to page layout view.

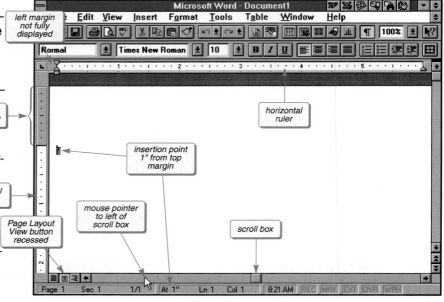

FIGURE 3-3

STEP 3 ▶

Click the left mouse button. When the document window scrolls to the left, point to the left margin boundary.

Word brings the left margin completely into view in the document window. The current left margin setting is 1 1/4 inches (10 ticks on the horizontal ruler). To change the left margin, drag its boundary. The mouse pointer changes to a double-headed arrow (↔) when you position it on a margin boundary (Figure 3-4).

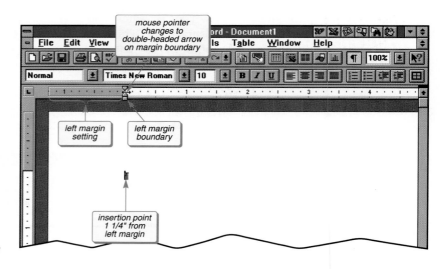

FIGURE 3-4

STEP 4 ▶

Press and hold the ALT key. While holding down the ALT key, press and hold the left mouse button and drag the left margin boundary until the gray shaded margin area reads 1".

Word displays a dotted vertical line in the document window indicating the left margin boundary position as you drag the mouse (Figure 3-5).

FIGURE 3-5

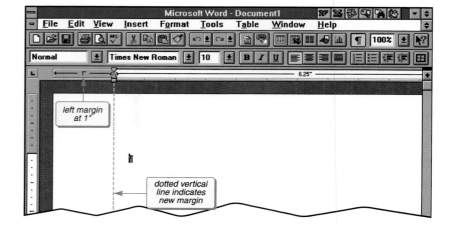

STEP 5 ▶

Release the left mouse button and the ALT key. Point to the right of the scroll box on the horizontal scroll bar.

Word changes the left margin setting to 1 inch (Figure 3-6). To change the right margin, bring the right margin on the ruler into the document window.

FIGURE 3-6

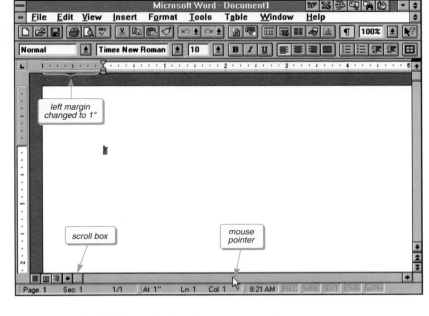

STEP 6 ▶

Click the left mouse button. Position the mouse pointer on the right margin boundary.

Word brings the right margin completely into view in the document window (Figure 3-7). Currently, the right margin is set at 1 1/4 inches.

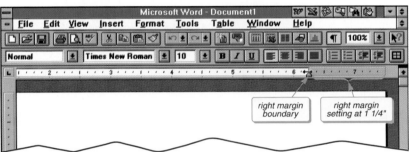

FIGURE 3-7

STEP 7 ▶

With the mouse pointer on the right margin boundary, press and hold the ALT key and press and hold the left mouse button and drag the margin boundary until the gray shaded margin area reads 1". Release the left mouse button and the ALT key. Then, point to the Normal View button (▦) on the horizontal scroll bar.

Word changes the right margin setting to 1 inch (Figure 3-8).

FIGURE 3-8

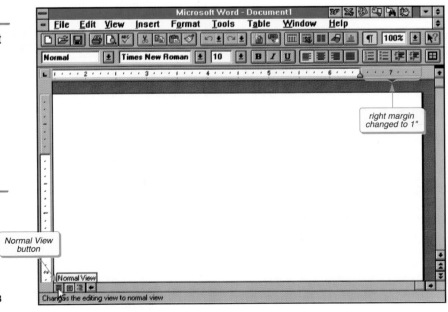

STEP 8 ▶

Click the Normal View button.

Word switches from page layout back to normal view (Figure 3-9).

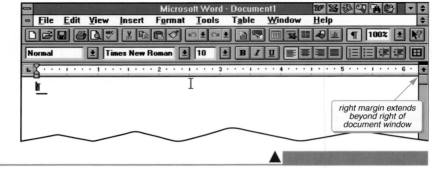

right margin extends beyond right of document window

FIGURE 3-9

Compare Figure 3-2 on page MSW127 to Figure 3-9 above. Notice that the right margin does not display in the document window in Figure 3-9 (as it did in Figure 3-2) because you increased the width of your typing area when you changed the margins. The new margin settings take effect immediately in the document. Word uses these margins for the entire document.

▶ ADJUSTING LINE SPACING

 ord, by default, single-spaces between lines of text and automatically adjusts line height to accommodate various font sizes and graphics. The MLA documentation style requires that you double-space the entire paper. Thus, you must adjust the line spacing as described in the following steps.

TO ADJUST LINE SPACING ▼

STEP 1 ▶

Position the mouse pointer in the document window and click the right mouse button. When the shortcut menu displays, point to the Paragraph command.

Word displays a shortcut menu (Figure 3-10).

FIGURE 3-10

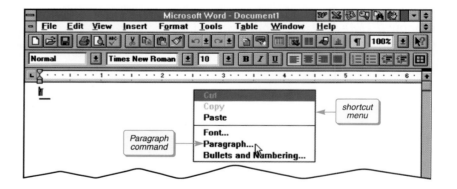

shortcut menu

Paragraph command

STEP 2 ▶

Choose the Paragraph command. In the Paragraph dialog box, point to the Line Spacing box arrow.

Word displays the Paragraph dialog box, listing the current settings in the text boxes and displaying them graphically in the Preview area (Figure 3-11). If your Paragraph dialog box displays a different set of options than Figure 3-11, click the Indents and Spacing tab.

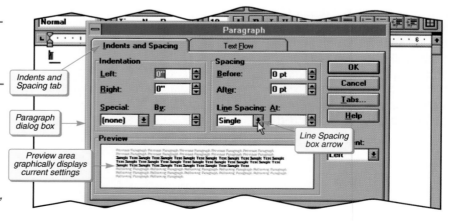

Indents and Spacing tab

Paragraph dialog box

Preview area graphically displays current settings

Line Spacing box arrow

FIGURE 3-11

STEP 3 ▶

Click the Line Spacing box arrow and point to Double.

A list of available line spacing options displays (Figure 3-12).

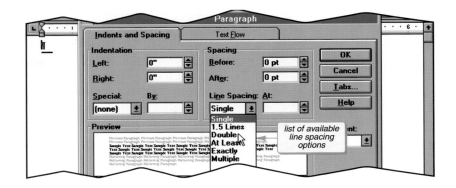

FIGURE 3-12

STEP 4 ▶

Select Double by clicking it. Point to the OK button.

Word displays Double in the Line Spacing box and graphically portrays the new line spacing in the Preview area (Figure 3-13).

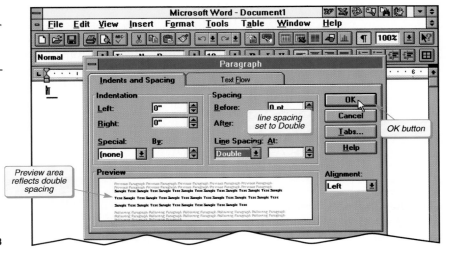

FIGURE 3-13

STEP 5 ▶

Choose the OK button.

Word changes the line spacing to Double (Figure 3-14). Notice that when line spacing is Double, the end mark is positioned one blank line beneath the insertion point.

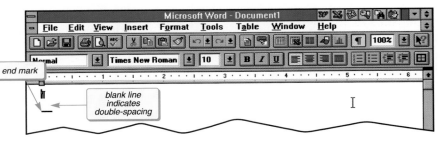

FIGURE 3-14

In the Line Spacing drop-down list box, you have a variety of options for the line spacing settings (Figure 3-12). The default, Single, and the options, 1.5 lines and Double, allow Word to adjust line spacing automatically to accommodate the largest font or graphic on a line. The next two options, At Least and Exactly, enable you to specify a line spacing not provided in the first three options. The difference is that the At Least option allows Word to increase the designation if necessary; whereas, the Exactly option does not allow Word to increase the specification. With the last option, Multiple, you enter a multiple. For example, a multiple of 2 is the same as double-spacing.

▶ USING A HEADER TO NUMBER PAGES

I n Word, you can easily number pages by choosing the Page Numbers command from the Insert menu. Once chosen, this command places page numbers on every page after the first. You cannot, however, place your name as required by the MLA style in front of the page number with the Page Numbers command. To place your name in front of the page number, you must create a header that contains the page number.

Headers and Footers

A **header** is text you want printed at the top of each page in the document. A **footer** is text you want printed at the bottom of every page. In Word, headers are printed in the top margin one-half inch from the top of every page, and footers are printed in the bottom margin one-half inch from the bottom of each page, which meets the MLA style. Headers and footers can include both text and graphics, as well as the page number, current date, and current time.

In this project, you are to precede the page number with your last name placed one-half inch from the top of each page. Your name and the page number should print right-aligned; that is, at the right margin. Use the procedures in these steps to create the header with page numbers according to the MLA style.

TO CREATE A HEADER ▼

STEP 1 ▶

Select the View menu and point to the Header and Footer command (Figure 3-15).

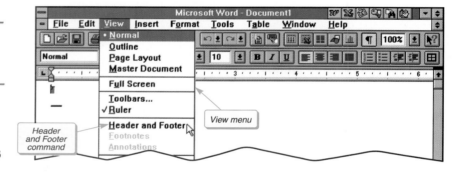

FIGURE 3-15

STEP 2 ▶

Choose the Header and Footer command.

Word switches from normal to page layout view and displays the **Header and Footer toolbar** *(Figure 3-16). The Header and Footer toolbar initially floats in the middle of the document window. Recall that you can anchor it beneath the Formatting toolbar by double-clicking the toolbar title bar or double-clicking in a blank area of the toolbar. The header text is typed in the* **header area***, which initially displays enclosed by a nonprinting dashed rectangle above the Header and Footer toolbar.*

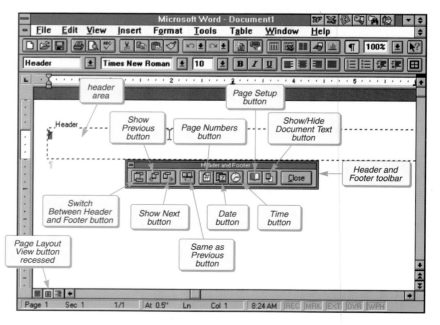

FIGURE 3-16

STEP 3 ▶

Click the Align Right button on the Formatting toolbar. Type Moser **and press the** SPACEBAR. **Point to the Page Numbers button ( ) on the Header and Footer toolbar.**

Word displays Moser right-aligned in the header area (Figure 3-17). The Align Right button is recessed because the paragraph containing the insertion point is right-aligned. The document window and the header area have scrolled right so the right margin is visible.

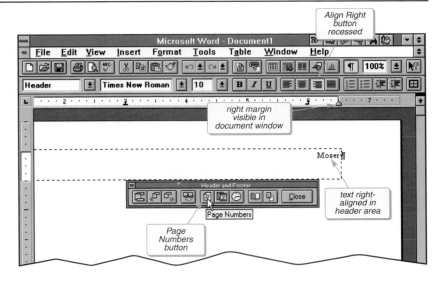

FIGURE 3-17

STEP 4 ▶

Click the Page Numbers button.

Word displays the page number 1 in the header area (Figure 3-18). Notice the header text font size is 10 point. You want all text in your research paper to be in 12 point.

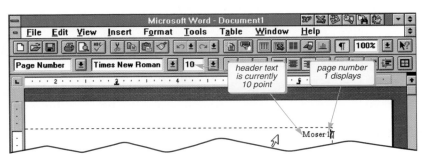

FIGURE 3-18

STEP 5 ▶

Select the text Moser 1 by clicking in the selection bar to its left. Click the Font Size box arrow and point to 12.

Word highlights the text, Moser 1, in the header area (Figure 3-19).

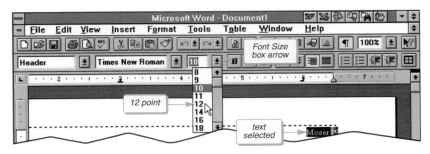

FIGURE 3-19

STEP 6 ▶

Click font size 12.

Word changes the font size of the header to 12 (Figure 3-20).

STEP 7

Choose the Close button ( ) on the Header and Footer toolbar.

Word closes the Header and Footer toolbar and returns to normal view (see Figure 3-14 on page MSW131).

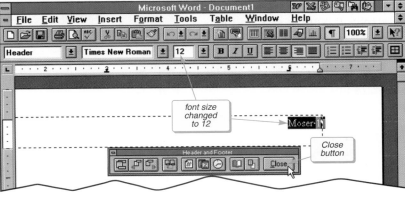

FIGURE 3-20

The header does not display on the screen when the document window is in normal view because it tends to clutter the screen. You will, however, want to verify that the header will print correctly. To see the header in the document window, you must switch to page layout view or display the document in print preview. These views display the header on the screen with the rest of the text.

Just as the Page Numbers button on the Header and Footer toolbar inserts the page number into the document, you can use two other buttons on the Header and Footer toolbar (Figure 3-16 on page MSW132) to insert items into the document. The Date button (▢) inserts the current date into the document and the Time button (◷) inserts the current time.

To edit an existing header, follow the same procedure as to create a new header. That is, choose the Header and Footer command from the View menu. Then, if necessary, click the Show Next button (▣) on the Header and Footer toolbar, edit the header, and choose the Close button on the Header and Footer toolbar.

To create a footer, choose the Header and Footer command from the View menu, click the Switch Between Header and Footer button (▣) on the Header and Footer toolbar and follow the same procedures as to create a header.

▶ TYPING THE BODY OF THE RESEARCH PAPER

The body of the research paper encompasses the first two pages in Figure 3-1 on page MSW125. The steps on the following pages illustrate how to enter the body of the research paper.

Changing the Font Size for All Characters in a Paragraph

In the prior two projects, you learned how to change the font size of characters in a document by clicking the Font Size box arrow and selecting the desired font size. This affected the character at the location of the insertion point or the selected text. In this project, all characters in all paragraphs should be a font size of 12. Thus, you should select the paragraph mark before changing the font size. This way, if you move the insertion point out of the current paragraph, the font size will remain at 12 when you return to the paragraph to continue typing.

TO CHANGE THE FONT SIZE OF ALL CHARACTERS IN A PARAGRAPH ▼

STEP 1 ▶

Select the paragraph mark in the upper left corner of the document window by clicking in the selection bar to its left. Click the Font Size box arrow and point to 12.

Word highlights the paragraph mark (Figure 3-21).

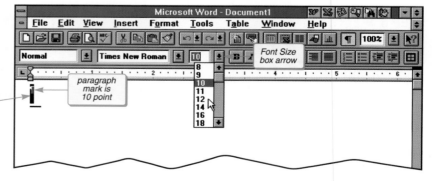

FIGURE 3-21

STEP 2 ►

Select font size 12 by clicking it. Click in the document window to remove the selection.

Word changes the paragraph mark to 12 point and removes the selection (Figure 3-22).

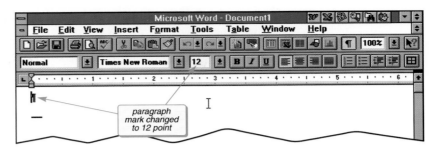

FIGURE 3-22

Compare the size of the paragraph marks in Figures 3-21 and 3-22. Notice that the paragraph mark in Figure 3-22 is larger, indicating it is now 12 point.

Entering Name and Course Information

Recall that the MLA style does not require a separate title page for research papers. Instead, you place your name and course information at the top of the page at the left margin. Follow the step below to begin the body of the research paper.

TO ENTER NAME AND COURSE INFORMATION ▼

STEP 1 ►

Type Raymond Andrew Moser **and press ENTER. Type** Professor J. Brown **and press ENTER. Type** Computer Information Systems 204 **and press ENTER. Type** September 28, 1995 **and press ENTER twice.**

The student name appears on line 1, the professor name on line 2, the course name on line 3, and the date on line 4 (Figure 3-23). Each time you press ENTER, Word advances two lines but increments the line counter on the status bar by only one because earlier you set line spacing to double.

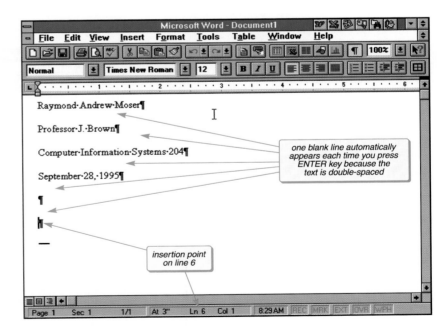

FIGURE 3-23

Centering a Paragraph Before Typing

In Project 1, you learned how to center a paragraph after you typed it. You can also center a paragraph before you type it by performing the following steps.

TO CENTER A PARAGRAPH BEFORE TYPING

STEP 1 ▶

Click the Center button on the Formatting toolbar.

Word centers the paragraph mark and the insertion point between the left and right margins (Figure 3-24). The Center button on the Formatting toolbar is recessed, indicating the text you type will be centered.

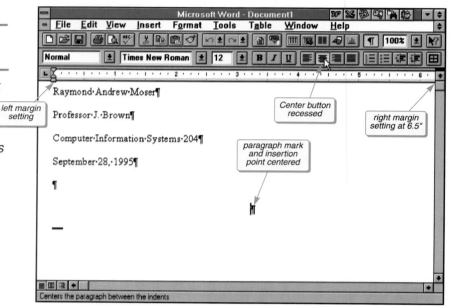

FIGURE 3-24

STEP 2 ▶

Type Is Your Computer Protected? **and press the ENTER key.**

The title is centered on line 6 and the insertion point advances to line 7 (Figure 3-25). Notice that the paragraph mark and insertion point on line 7 are centered because the formatting specified in the prior paragraph (line 6) is carried forward to the next paragraph (line 7).

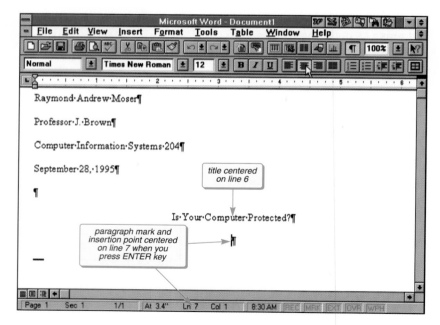

FIGURE 3-25

STEP 3 ▶

Click the Align Left button (▤) on the Formatting toolbar.

Word positions the paragraph mark and the insertion point at the left margin (Figure 3-26). The next text you type will be left-aligned.

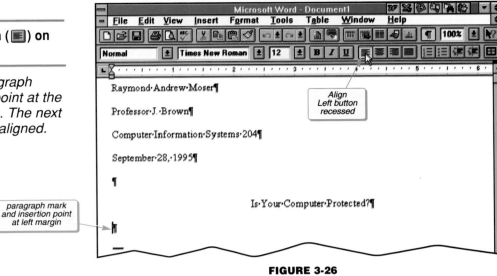

FIGURE 3-26

Saving the Research Paper

Recall that it is prudent to save your work on disk at regular intervals. Because you have performed several tasks thus far, you should save your research paper.

TO SAVE A DOCUMENT

Step 1: Insert your data disk into drive A.
Step 2: Click the Save button on the Standard toolbar.
Step 3: Type the filename `proj3` in the File Name box. Do not press ENTER.
Step 4: Click the Drives box arrow and select drive A.
Step 5: Choose the OK button in the Save As dialog box.

Indenting Paragraphs

According to the MLA style, the first line of each paragraph in the research paper is to be indented one-half inch from the left margin. This procedure, called **first-line indent,** can be accomplished using the ruler, as shown below.

TO FIRST-LINE INDENT PARAGRAPHS ▼

STEP 1 ▶

Point to the first-line indent marker (▽) on the ruler (Figure 3-27).

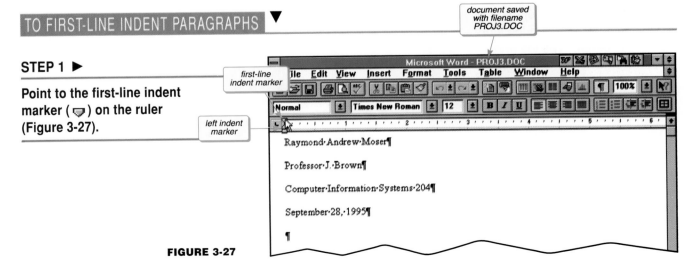

FIGURE 3-27

STEP 2 ▶

Drag the first-line indent marker to the 1/2" mark on the ruler.

As you drag the mouse, a vertical dotted line displays in the document window, indicating the location of the first-line indent marker (Figure 3-28).

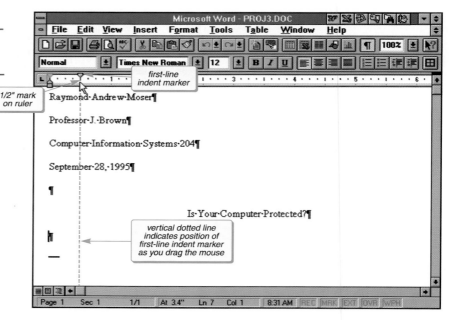

FIGURE 3-28

STEP 3 ▶

Release the left mouse button.

The first-line indent marker displays at the location of the first tab stop, one-half inch from the left margin (Figure 3-29). The paragraph mark containing the insertion point in the document window also moves one-half inch to the right.

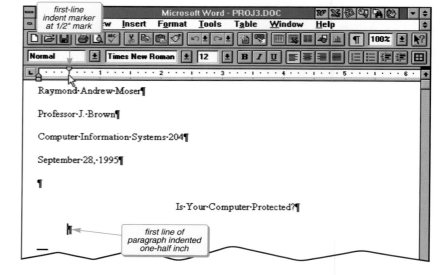

FIGURE 3-29

STEP 4 ▶

Type the first paragraph of the research paper, as shown in Figure 3-31. Press ENTER. Type the first sentence of the second paragraph: Overvoltages occur when the incoming electrical power increases above the normal 120 volts.

When you press ENTER at the end of the first paragraph, the insertion point automatically indents the first line of the second paragraph by one-half inch (Figure 3-30).

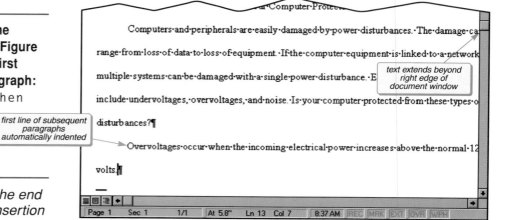

FIGURE 3-30

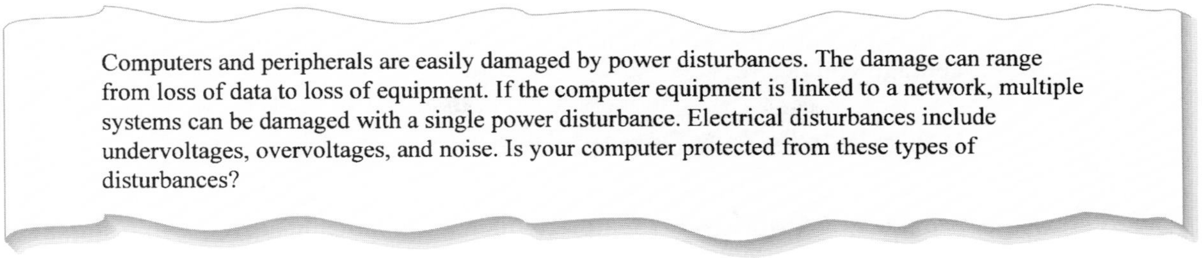

Computers and peripherals are easily damaged by power disturbances. The damage can range from loss of data to loss of equipment. If the computer equipment is linked to a network, multiple systems can be damaged with a single power disturbance. Electrical disturbances include undervoltages, overvoltages, and noise. Is your computer protected from these types of disturbances?

FIGURE 3-31

You may be tempted to use the TAB key to indent the first line of each paragraph in your research paper. Using the TAB key for this task is inefficient because you must press it each time you begin a new paragraph. However, the first-line indent format is automatically carried to each subsequent paragraph you type.

Zooming Page Width

When you changed the margins earlier in this project, the right margin moved beyond the right edge of the document window. (Depending on your Word settings, your right margin may already appear in the document window.) Thus, some of the text at the right edge of the document does not display in the document window (see Figure 3-30). For this reason, Word enables you to **zoom** a document, meaning you can control how much of it displays in the document window. That is, you can magnify or *zoom in on* a document, or you can reduce or *zoom out on* a document.

Because you often want to see both margins in the document window at the same time, Word provides **page width zoom** as shown in the following steps.

TO ZOOM PAGE WIDTH ▼

STEP 1 ►

Click the Zoom Control box arrow on the Standard toolbar. Point to the Page Width option in the list box.

Word displays a list of available zoom percentages and the Page Width option (Figure 3-32).

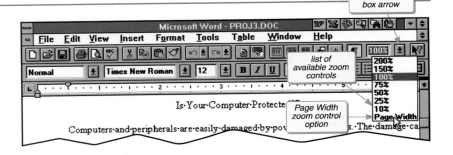

FIGURE 3-32

STEP 2 ►

Select Page Width by clicking the left mouse button.

Word brings both the left and right margins into view in the document window (Figure 3-33). The Zoom Control box now displays 92%, or a different percentage, which Word computes based on your margin settings.

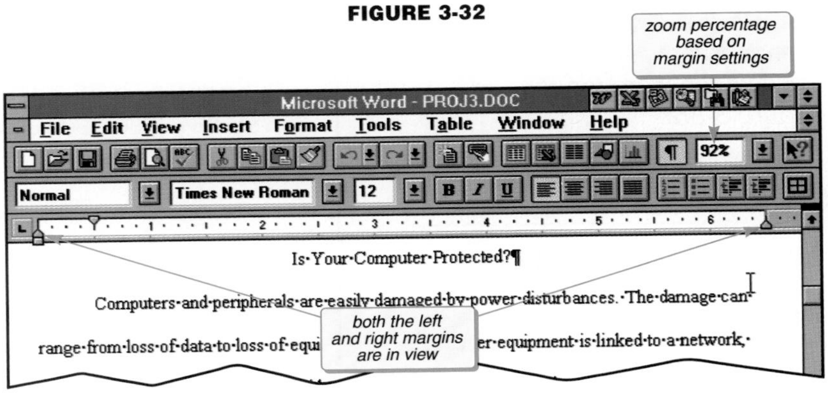

FIGURE 3-33

If you want to zoom a percentage not displayed in the Zoom Control list box, you can choose the Zoom command from the View menu and enter any zoom percentage you desire.

Using Word's AutoCorrect Feature

Because you often misspell the same words or phrases when you type, Word provides an **AutoCorrect** feature, which automatically corrects your misspelled words as you type them into the document. For example, if you type *teh*, Word will automatically change it to *the* for you. Word has predefined the following commonly misspelled words: adn, don;t, i, occurence, recieve, seperate, and teh. That is, if you enter any of these words exactly as shown here, Word will automatically correct them for you, as shown below.

TO ILLUSTRATE WORD'S AUTOCORRECT FEATURE ▼

STEP 1 ►

Press the SPACEBAR. Type the beginning of the second sentence in the second paragraph, misspelling the word "and": `Overvoltages can cause immediate adn` (Figure 3-34).

FIGURE 3-34

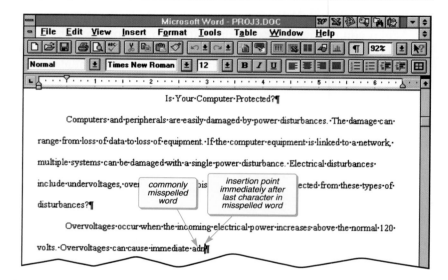

STEP 2 ►

Press the SPACEBAR.

As soon as you press the SPACEBAR, Word's AutoCorrect feature detects the misspelling and corrects the word for you (Figure 3-35).

STEP 3

Type `permanent damage to a computer and peripherals.` followed by a space.

The second sentence of the second paragraph is complete.

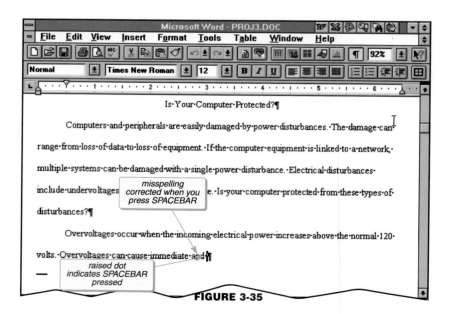

FIGURE 3-35

In addition to the commonly misspelled words predefined by the AutoCorrect feature, you can create your own AutoCorrect entries. For example, if you often misspell the word *computer* as *comptuer*, you should make an AutoCorrect entry for it, as shown in these steps.

TO CREATE AN AUTOCORRECT ENTRY ▼

STEP 1 ►

Select the Tools menu and point to the AutoCorrect command (Figure 3-36).

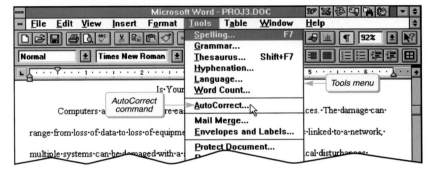

FIGURE 3-36

STEP 2 ►

Choose the AutoCorrect command.

Word displays the AutoCorrect dialog box (Figure 3-37). The insertion point is blinking in the Replace box, waiting for you to create an AutoCorrect entry.

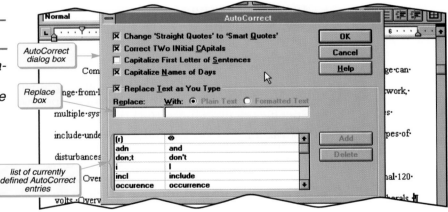

FIGURE 3-37

STEP 3 ►

Type comptuer **in the Replace box. Press the TAB key to advance to the With box. Type** computer **in the With box. Point to the Add button.**

The Replace box contains the misspelled word, and the With box contains its correct spelling (Figure 3-38).

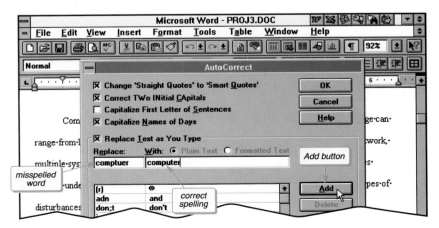

FIGURE 3-38

STEP 4 ▶

Choose the Add button.

Word alphabetically adds the entry to the list of words to automatically correct as you type (Figure 3-39).

STEP 5

Choose the OK button.

Word returns to the document window.

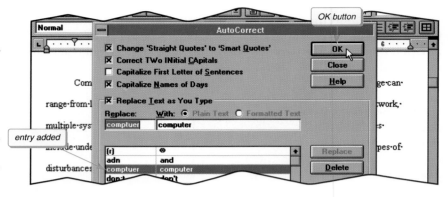

FIGURE 3-39

In addition to creating AutoCorrect entries for words you commonly misspell, you can create entries for abbreviations, codes, etc. For example, you could create an AutoCorrect entry for *asap*, indicating that Word should replace this text with the phrase *as soon as possible*.

In Project 2, you learned how to use the AutoText feature, which enables you to create entries (just as you did for the AutoCorrect feature) and insert them into the document. The difference is that the AutoCorrect feature automatically makes the corrections for you; whereas, you must choose the AutoText command or button before Word will make an AutoText correction.

Adding Footnotes

Recall that explanatory notes are optional in the MLA documentation style. They are used primarily to elaborate on points discussed in the paper. The style specifies to use superscripts (raised numbers) to signal that an explanatory note exists either at the bottom of the page as a **footnote** or at the end of the paper as an **endnote**.

Word, by default, places notes at the bottom of each page. In Word, **note text** can be of any length and format. Word automatically numbers notes sequentially by placing a **note reference mark** in the body of the document and in front of the note text. If, however, you rearrange, insert, or remove notes, the remaining note text and reference marks are renumbered according to their new sequence in the document. Follow these steps to add a footnote to the research paper.

One type of overvoltage, called a spike, occurs when the power disturbance lasts for less than one millisecond. Spikes are caused from a variety of sources ranging from uncontrollable disturbances, like lightning bolts, to controllable disturbances, like turning on a printer (Andrews 47-62). Surge suppressors are designed to protect a computer and peripherals from spikes. Surge suppressors resemble power strips. That is, all of the computer equipment is plugged into the surge suppressor, and the surge suppressor is plugged into the wall socket.

FIGURE 3-40

TO ADD A FOOTNOTE ▼

STEP 1 ►

Type the remainder of the second paragraph, as shown in Figure 3-40. Position the insertion point in the document where you want the note reference mark to appear (immediately after the period at the end of paragraph 2). Select the Insert menu and point to the Footnote command.

The insertion point is positioned immediately after the period following the word "socket" in the research paper (Figure 3-41).

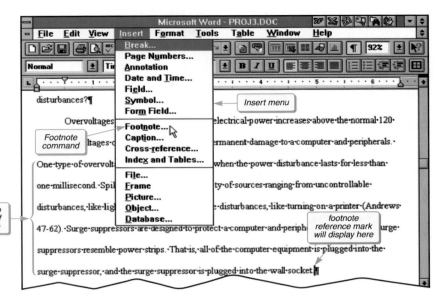

FIGURE 3-41

STEP 2 ►

Choose the Footnote command. Point to the OK button in the Footnote and Endnote dialog box.

Word displays the Footnote and Endnote dialog box (Figure 3-42). The bullet next to the Footnote option indicates that footnotes are the default placement for notes.

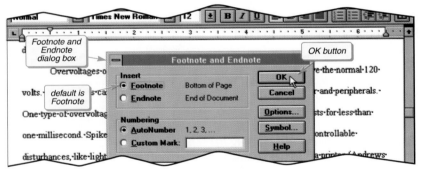

FIGURE 3-42

STEP 3 ►

Choose the OK button.

*Word opens a **note pane** in the lower portion of the window with the note reference mark (a super-scripted 1) positioned at the left margin of the pane (Figure 3-43). A pane is an area at the bottom of the screen, containing an option bar, a text area, and a scroll bar. The note reference mark also displays in the document window at the location of the insertion point. Note reference marks are, by default, super-scripted; that is, they are raised above other letters.*

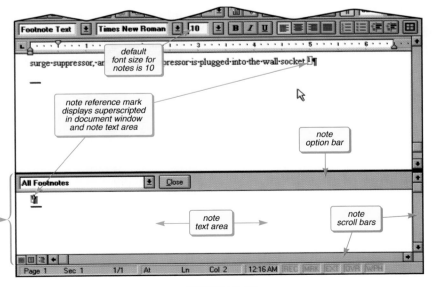

FIGURE 3-43

STEP 4 ▶

Change the font size to 12 by clicking the Font Size box arrow and selecting 12. Position the mouse pointer to the right of the paragraph mark in the note pane, and click the right mouse button. In the shortcut menu, point to the Paragraph command.

Word displays a shortcut menu (Figure 3-44). Because you want to change both first-line indent and line spacing for the notes, you will use the Paragraph dialog box to perform both changes.

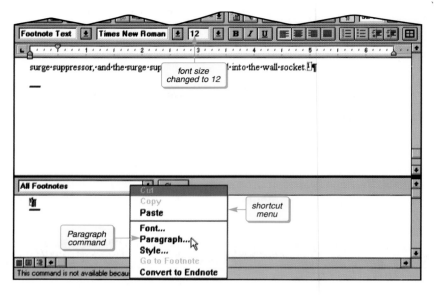

FIGURE 3-44

STEP 5 ▶

Choose the Paragraph command. In the Paragraph dialog box, click the Special box arrow. Point to First Line.

Word displays the Paragraph dialog box (Figure 3-45). You can change the first-line indent in the dialog box. If the Indents and Spacing options do not display in your Paragraph dialog box, click the Indents and Spacing tab.

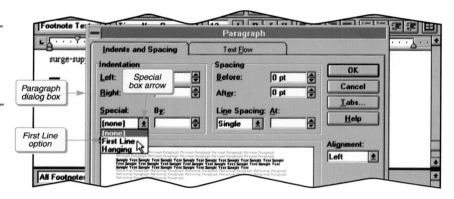

FIGURE 3-45

STEP 6 ▶

Select First Line by clicking the left mouse button. Click the Line Spacing box arrow and select Double by clicking it. Point to the OK button.

Word displays First Line in the Special box and Double in the Line Spacing box (Figure 3-46).

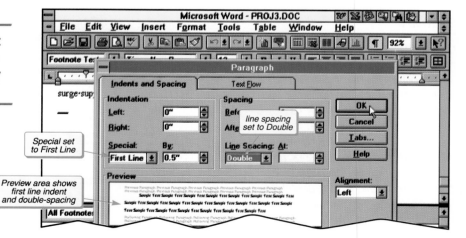

FIGURE 3-46

STEP 7 ▶

Choose the OK button.

Word indents the first line of the note by one-half inch and sets the line spacing for the note to Double (Figure 3-47).

FIGURE 3-47

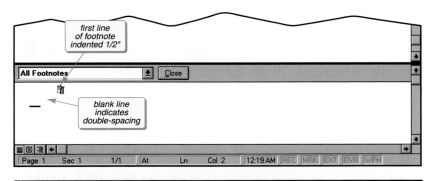

STEP 8 ▶

Press the SPACEBAR and type : Andrews rates the top ten surge suppressors. Each is designed for a different type of computer system, from personal computers to supercomputers. The personal computer surge suppressors cost approximately $75. **Press the SPACEBAR once. Press CTRL+U.**

The text displays (Figure 3-48). The book title should be underlined. Because you pressed CTRL+U, the Underline button on the Formatting toolbar is recessed. When your fingers are on the keyboard, it is more efficient to use a keyboard shortcut, instead of using the mouse to click a button.

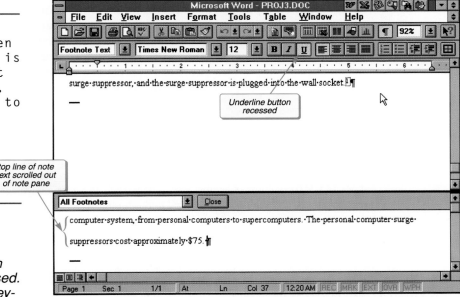

FIGURE 3-48

STEP 9 ▶

Type Information Systems Journal **and press CTRL+U. Type** , 55-59.

*The first note is entered in the note pane with the book name underlined (Figure 3-49). The Underline button is no longer recessed. CTRL+U is a **toggle**. That is, the keyboard shortcut is entered once to activate the button and entered again to deactivate the button.*

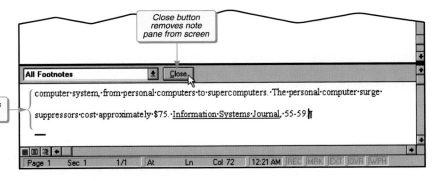

FIGURE 3-49

STEP 10

Choose the Close button.

Word closes the note pane.

When Word closes the note pane and returns to the document, the note text disappears from the screen. The note text still exists; however, it is not visible in normal view. Later in this project when you change the document window from normal view to page layout view, you will be able to see the note text on the screen.

Automatic Page Breaks

As you type documents that exceed one page, Word automatically inserts page breaks when it determines the text has filled one page according to paper size, margin settings, line spacing, and other settings. These **automatic page breaks** are often referred to as **soft page breaks**. If you add text, delete text, or modify text on a page, Word recomputes the position of soft page breaks and adjusts them accordingly. Word performs page recomputation between the keystrokes; that is, it recomputes in between the pauses in your typing. Thus, Word refers to the automatic page break task as **background repagination**. In normal view, soft page breaks appear on the Word screen as a single horizontal thinly dotted line. Word's automatic page break feature is illustrated below.

An undervoltage occurs when there is a drop in electrical supply. Electricity normally flows consistently at 120 volts through your wall plug. Any sudden drop below 120 volts is considered an undervoltage. Sags, brownouts, and blackouts are all considered undervoltages. This type of disturbance will not harm a computer or the equipment but can cause loss of data (McDaniel and Tanner 145-150). To protect against loss of data when an undervoltage occurs, an uninterruptible power supply (UPS) should be connected to the computer.

FIGURE 3-50

TO USE AUTOMATIC PAGE BREAK ▼

STEP 1 ▶

Press the ENTER key and type the next paragraph of the research paper, as shown in Figure 3-50 above.

Word automatically inserts a soft page break above the line beginning "An undervoltage occurs when..." (Figure 3-51). The status bar now displays Page 2 as the current page.

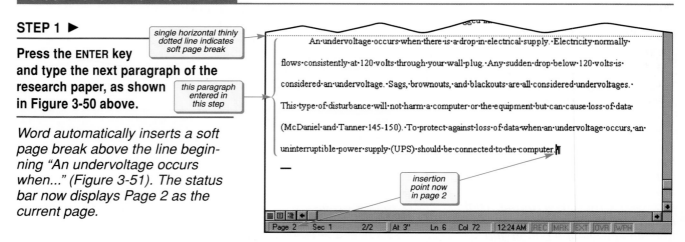

FIGURE 3-51

The next step in Project 3 is to add a second footnote at the end of the paragraph entered in Figure 3-51 and to type the last two paragraphs of the research paper.

TO ADD ANOTHER FOOTNOTE AND FINISH THE PAPER ▼

STEP 1 ►

Be sure the insertion point is positioned at the end of the last sentence in the third paragraph. Select the Insert menu and point to the Footnote command. Follow Steps 2 through 7 in Figures 3-42 through 3-47 to format the footnote. Change the point size to 12. Press the SPACEBAR and type: McDaniel and Tanner list several models of uninterruptible power supplies with features and costs. In general, a basic UPS costs between $250 and $350. **Press the SPACEBAR. Press CTRL+U. Type** Computers Today **and press CTRL+U. Type** , 145-148.

The second note is entered (Figure 3-52).

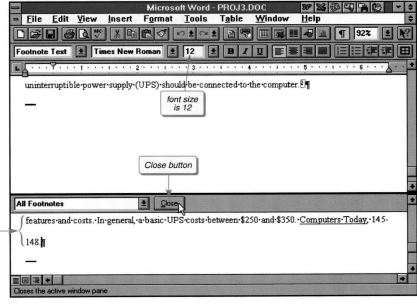

FIGURE 3-52

STEP 2 ►

Choose the Close button on the note pane option bar. Press the ENTER key and type the last two paragraphs of the research paper, as shown in Figure 3-54.

Word closes the note pane and returns to the document. The body of the research paper is complete (Figure 3-53).

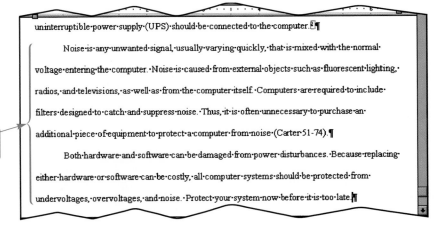

FIGURE 3-53

Noise is any unwanted signal, usually varying quickly, that is mixed with the normal voltage entering the computer. Noise is caused from external objects such as fluorescent lighting, radios, and televisions, as well as from the computer itself. Computers are required to include filters designed to catch and suppress noise. Thus, it is often unnecessary to purchase an additional piece of equipment to protect a computer from noise (Carter 51-74).

Both hardware and software can be damaged from power disturbances. Because replacing either hardware or software can be costly, all computer systems should be protected from undervoltages, overvoltages, and noise. Protect your system now before it is too late.

FIGURE 3-54

Viewing Documents in Page Layout

The notes you entered do not appear at the bottom of the page in the document window when you are in normal view. In normal view, Word does not display headers, footers, or notes. Often, you like to verify the contents of note or header text. In order to illustrate how to display headers, footers, and footnotes on the screen, switch to page layout view as shown below.

TO SWITCH TO PAGE LAYOUT VIEW ▼

STEP 1 ►

Click above the scroll box on the vertical scroll bar to scroll up one screen and to display the soft page break in the document window.

The soft page break is in the document window (Figure 3-55). Notice that the footnote does not display on the screen in normal view.

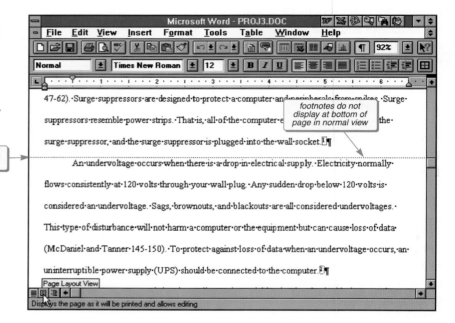

FIGURE 3-55

STEP 2 ►

Click the Page Layout View button. Point beneath the scroll box on the vertical scroll bar.

*Word switches from normal to page layout view (Figure 3-56). The notes display positioned on the screen at the bottom of each page when you are in page layout view. The footnotes are separated from the text by a **note separator**, which is a solid line two inches long beginning at the left margin.*

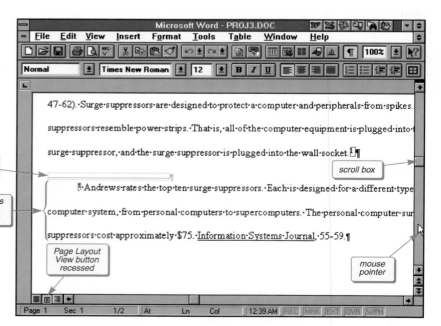

FIGURE 3-56

STEP 3 ▶

Click beneath the scroll box on the vertical scroll bar. Point to the right of the scroll box on the horizontal scroll bar.

The right margin is not in the document window in page layout view (Figure 3-57).

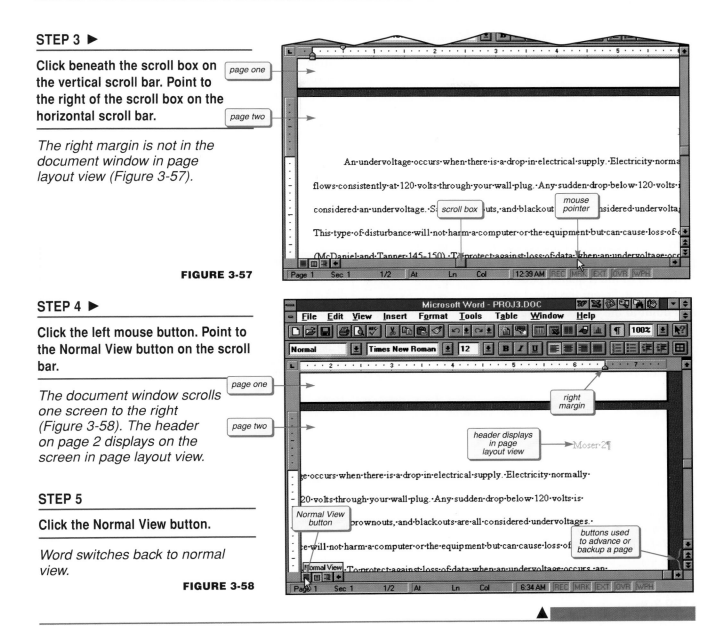

FIGURE 3-57

STEP 4 ▶

Click the left mouse button. Point to the Normal View button on the scroll bar.

The document window scrolls one screen to the right (Figure 3-58). The header on page 2 displays on the screen in page layout view.

STEP 5

Click the Normal View button.

Word switches back to normal view.

FIGURE 3-58

In page layout view, you can type and edit text in the same manner as in normal view. The only difference is that the headers, footers, and notes display properly positioned in the document in page layout view.

In page layout view, click the double arrows (⬍) at the bottom of the vertical scroll bar to advance or backup a page in the document window.

▶ CREATING AN ALPHABETICAL WORKS CITED PAGE

According to the MLA style, the works cited page is a bibliographic list of works you directly reference in your paper. The list is placed on a separate page with the title, Works Cited, centered one inch from the top margin. The works are to be alphabetized by author's last name. The first line of each work begins at the left margin; subsequent lines of the same work are indented one-half inch from the left margin.

Hard Page Breaks

Because the works cited are to display on a separate numbered page, you need to insert a hard page break following the body of the research paper. A **hard page break** is one that is forced into the document at a specific location. Word never moves or adjusts hard page breaks. When you insert hard page breaks, however, Word adjusts any soft page breaks that follow in the document. Word inserts a hard page break just before the insertion point, as shown below.

TO INSERT A HARD PAGE BREAK ▼

STEP 1 ▶

Scroll to the bottom of the research paper. Be sure the insertion point is at the end of the research paper. Press ENTER. Select the Insert menu and point to the Break command.

The insertion point is positioned one line below the body of the research paper (Figure 3-59).

FIGURE 3-59

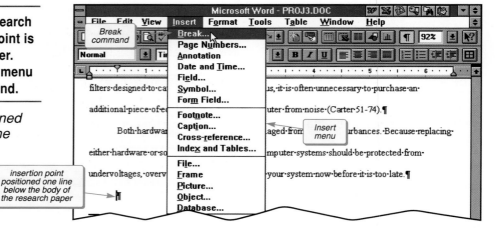

STEP 2 ▶

Choose the Break command.

Word displays the Break dialog box (Figure 3-60). The default option button is Page Break in the Break dialog box.

FIGURE 3-60

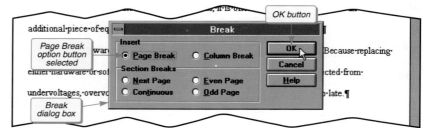

STEP 3 ▶

Choose the OK button in the Break dialog box.

Word inserts a hard page break above the insertion point (Figure 3-61). The hard page break displays as a thinly dotted horizontal line separated by the words Page Break. The status bar indicates the insertion point is on page 3.

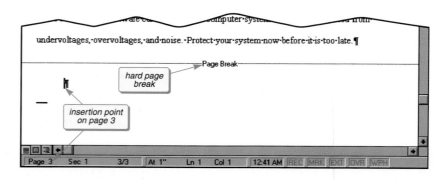

FIGURE 3-61 ▲

To remove a hard page break, you must select it first by pointing to it and double-clicking. Then, choose the Cut button on the Standard toolbar.

Centering the Title of the Works Cited Page

The works cited title is to be centered. If you simply click the Center button, however, the title will not be properly centered; instead, it will be one-half inch to the right of the center point because earlier you set a first-line indent at the first tab stop. Thus, the first line of every paragraph is indented one-half inch. You must move the first-line indent marker back to the left margin prior to clicking the Center button as described below.

TO CENTER THE TITLE OF THE WORKS CITED PAGE

Step 1: Drag the first-line indent marker to the 0" mark on the ruler.

Step 2: Click the Center button on the Formatting toolbar.

Step 3: Type `Works Cited` and press ENTER.

Step 4: Click the Align Left button on the Formatting toolbar.

The title displays properly centered (Figure 3-62). If your screen scrolls left after Step 1, click to the right of the scroll box on the horizontal scroll bar; then click to its left.

FIGURE 3-62

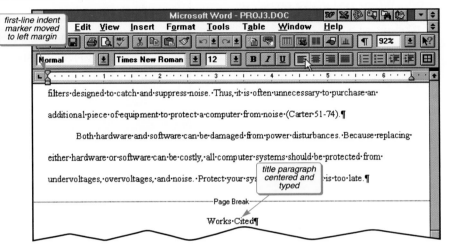

Creating a Hanging Indent

On the works cited page, the paragraphs begin at the left margin. Subsequent lines in the same paragraph are indented one-half inch. In essence, the first line *hangs* to the left of the rest of the paragraph; thus, this type of formatting is called a **hanging indent**. Follow these steps to create a hanging indent.

FIGURE 3-63

Carter, Sarah J. <u>Computers and Noise Disturbances</u>. Boston: Fraser Williams Publishing Company, 1995.
McDaniel, Jonathan P., and Marilyn Tanner. "Undervoltages: Is Your Software Protected."
<u>Computers Today</u> 10 Jul. 1995: 145-150.
Andrews, Caroline W. "Spikes Can Be Dangerous To Your Hardware." <u>Information Systems</u>
<u>Journal</u> Apr. 1995: 47-62.

TO CREATE A HANGING INDENT ▼

STEP 1 ▶

Drag the left indent marker (🔒) to the one-half inch mark on the ruler.

The left indent marker appears at the location of the first tab stop, one-half inch from the left margin (Figure 3-64).

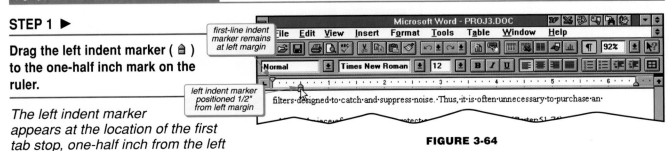

FIGURE 3-64

STEP 2 ▶

Type the works cited paragraphs, as shown in Figure 3-63 on the previous page.

When Word wraps the text in each works cited paragraph, it automatically indents the second line of the paragraph by one-half inch (Figure 3-65). When you press ENTER at the end of the first paragraph, the insertion point automatically returns to the left margin for the next paragraph. Recall that each time you press ENTER, the paragraph formatting in the prior paragraph is carried forward to the next.

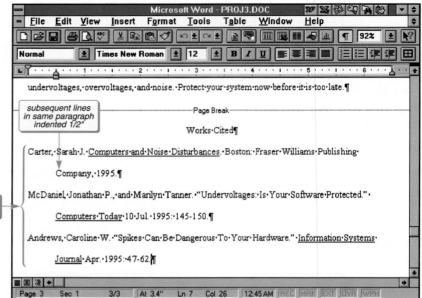

FIGURE 3-65

To drag both the first-line indent and left indent markers at the same time, you drag the small box beneath the left indent marker. When you do this, the left margin is the same for all lines in a paragraph.

Sorting Paragraphs

The MLA style requires that the works cited be listed in alphabetical order by author's last name. With Word, you can arrange paragraphs in alphabetic, numeric, or date order, based on the first character in each paragraph. Ordering characters in this manner is called **sorting**. Arrange the works cited paragraphs in alphabetic order as illustrated in the following steps.

TO SORT PARAGRAPHS ▼

STEP 1 ▶

Select all of the works cited paragraphs by dragging the mouse through the selection bar to the left of the paragraphs. Select the Table menu and point to the Sort Text command.

All of the paragraphs to be sorted are selected (Figure 3-66).

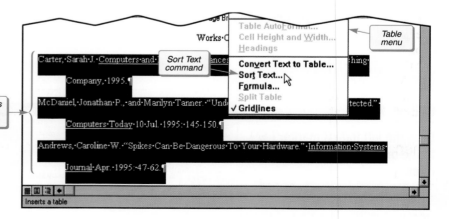

FIGURE 3-66

STEP 2 ►

Choose the Sort Text command.

Word displays a Sort Text dialog box (Figure 3-67). In the Sort By area, the Ascending option is selected. Ascending sorts in alphabetic or numeric order.

FIGURE 3-67

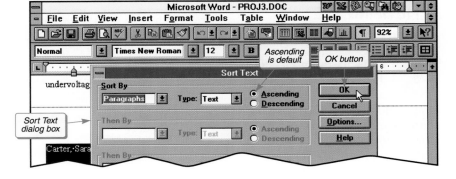

STEP 3 ►

Choose the OK button in the Sort Text dialog box. Click outside of the selection to remove the highlight.

Word alphabetically sorts the works cited paragraphs (Figure 3-68).

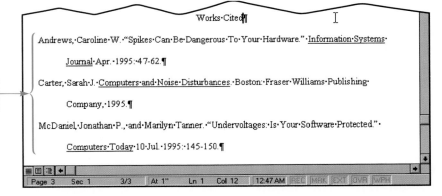

FIGURE 3-68

If you accidentally sort the wrong paragraphs, you can undo a sort by clicking the Undo button on the Standard toolbar.

In the Sort Text dialog box (Figure 3-67), the default sort order is Ascending. If the first character of each paragraph to be sorted is a letter, Word sorts alphabetically on the first letter of the paragraphs. If the first character of each paragraph to be sorted is a number, Word sorts numerically on the first number of the paragraphs. Word by default, orders in **ascending sort order**, meaning from the beginning of the alphabet, lowest number, or earliest date. If the first character of the paragraphs to be sorted contains a mixture of letters, numbers, and dates, then the numbers and dates appear first and the letters appear last once the paragraphs are sorted. Uppercase letters appear before lowercase letters. In case of ties, Word looks to the first position with a non-identical character and sorts on that character for the paragraphs where the tie occurs.

You can also sort in descending order by choosing the Descending option button in the Sort Text dialog box. **Descending sort order** begins sorting from the end of the alphabet, the highest number, or the most recent date.

Checking Spelling, Saving Again, and Printing the Document

The research paper is now complete and ready for proofing. After completing the document, you should check the spelling of the document. You should save the research paper again. Finally, you should print the research paper. When you remove the document from the printer, proofread it carefully and mark anything that needs to be changed (Figure 3-69 on the next page).

▶ REVISING THE
RESEARCH PAPER

A s discussed in Project 1, once you complete a document, you might find it necessary to make changes to it. For example, when reviewing the printout of the research paper (Figure 3-69), you notice that you would rather use the word *microcomputer(s)* instead of the words *personal computer(s)*. You also notice that the paper would read better if the second paragraph were moved to above the fourth paragraph. With Word, you can easily accomplish these editing tasks.

Going to a Specific Location in a Document

Often, you would like to bring a certain page or footnote into view in the document window. To bring a page into view, you could scroll through the document to find it. To bring a footnote into view, you must first switch to page layout view, then scroll through the document to find the footnote. Instead of scrolling through the document, Word provides an easier method of going to a specific location in a document via the Go To dialog box.

Because you want to change the occurrences of the words *personal computer(s)* to *microcomputer(s)* and the only occurrences of the words *personal computer* are in the first footnote of the research paper, you would like to display this footnote in the document window, as shown in the following steps.

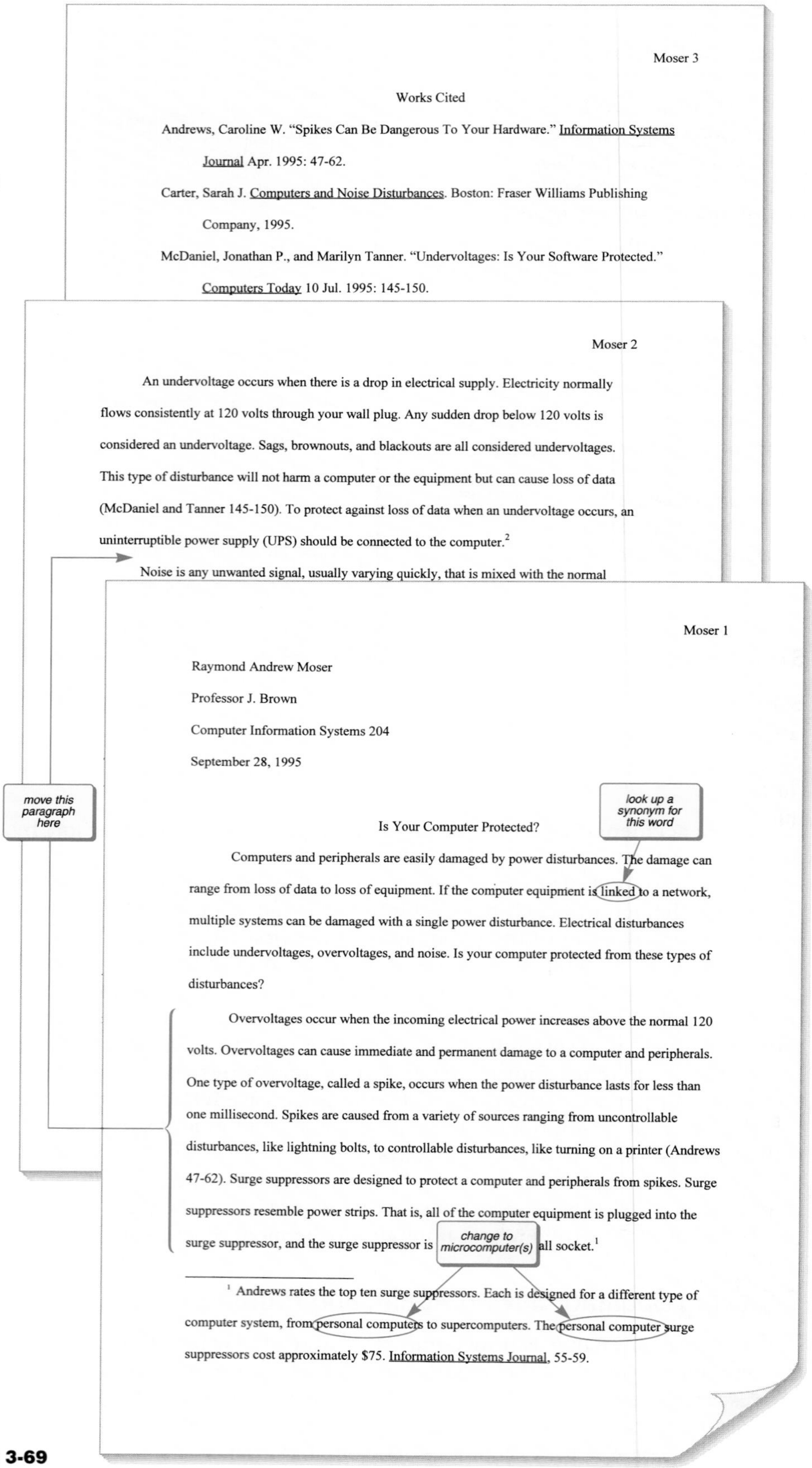

FIGURE 3-69

Moser 3

Works Cited

Andrews, Caroline W. "Spikes Can Be Dangerous To Your Hardware." Information Systems Journal Apr. 1995: 47-62.

Carter, Sarah J. Computers and Noise Disturbances. Boston: Fraser Williams Publishing Company, 1995.

McDaniel, Jonathan P., and Marilyn Tanner. "Undervoltages: Is Your Software Protected." Computers Today 10 Jul. 1995: 145-150.

Moser 2

An undervoltage occurs when there is a drop in electrical supply. Electricity normally flows consistently at 120 volts through your wall plug. Any sudden drop below 120 volts is considered an undervoltage. Sags, brownouts, and blackouts are all considered undervoltages. This type of disturbance will not harm a computer or the equipment but can cause loss of data (McDaniel and Tanner 145-150). To protect against loss of data when an undervoltage occurs, an uninterruptible power supply (UPS) should be connected to the computer.[2]

Noise is any unwanted signal, usually varying quickly, that is mixed with the normal

---

move this paragraph here

Moser 1

Raymond Andrew Moser

Professor J. Brown

Computer Information Systems 204

September 28, 1995

look up a synonym for this word

Is Your Computer Protected?

Computers and peripherals are easily damaged by power disturbances. The damage can range from loss of data to loss of equipment. If the computer equipment is linked to a network, multiple systems can be damaged with a single power disturbance. Electrical disturbances include undervoltages, overvoltages, and noise. Is your computer protected from these types of disturbances?

Overvoltages occur when the incoming electrical power increases above the normal 120 volts. Overvoltages can cause immediate and permanent damage to a computer and peripherals. One type of overvoltage, called a spike, occurs when the power disturbance lasts for less than one millisecond. Spikes are caused from a variety of sources ranging from uncontrollable disturbances, like lightning bolts, to controllable disturbances, like turning on a printer (Andrews 47-62). Surge suppressors are designed to protect a computer and peripherals from spikes. Surge suppressors resemble power strips. That is, all of the computer equipment is plugged into the surge suppressor, and the surge suppressor is *change to microcomputer(s)* all socket.[1]

---

[1] Andrews rates the top ten surge suppressors. Each is designed for a different type of computer system, from personal computers to supercomputers. The personal computer surge suppressors cost approximately $75. Information Systems Journal, 55-59.

TO LOCATE A PAGE OR FOOTNOTE ▼

STEP 1 ►

Press CTRL+HOME. Double-click the page area of the status bar.

Word displays the Go To dialog box (Figure 3-70). In the Go To dialog box, among other areas, you can go directly to a specified page or footnote.

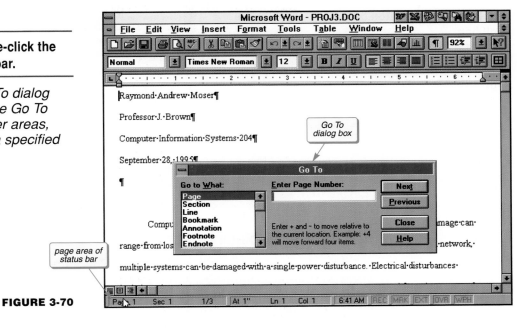

FIGURE 3-70

STEP 2 ►

Select Footnote by clicking it in the Go to What area of the Go To dialog box. Click in the Enter Footnote Number box, type 1 and then point to the Go To button (Figure 3-71).

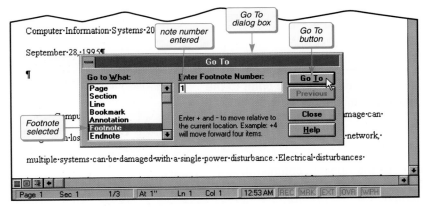

FIGURE 3-71

STEP 3 ►

Choose the Go To button. Point to the Close button in the Go To dialog box.

Word locates the first footnote reference number and places that portion of the document in the document window (Figure 3-72). The footnote text does not display in the document window because you are in normal view.

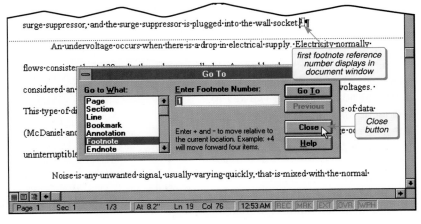

FIGURE 3-72

STEP 4 ▶

Choose the Close button. Click the
Page Layout View button on the
scroll bar.

*Word closes the Go To dialog box
and switches from normal view to
page layout view (Figure 3-73).
The footnote text displays
in page layout view.*

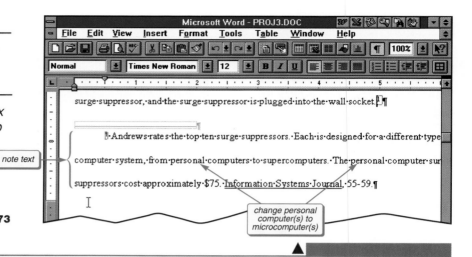

FIGURE 3-73

Finding and Replacing Text

Because you want to change all occurrences of the words *personal com-
puter(s)* to *microcomputer(s)*, you can use Word's find and replace feature, which
automatically locates each occurrence of a specified word or phrase and replaces
it with specified text as shown in these steps.

TO FIND AND REPLACE TEXT ▼

STEP 1 ▶

Select the Edit menu and point to the
Replace command (Figure 3-74).

STEP 2

Choose the Replace command.

*Word displays the Replace dialog
box.*

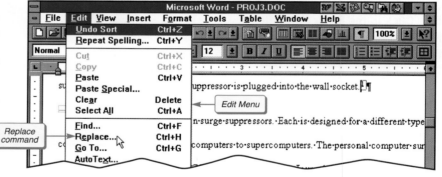

FIGURE 3-74

STEP 3 ▶

Type personal computer **in the
Find What box. Press the TAB key to
advance to the Replace With box.
Type** microcomputer **and point to
the Replace All button (** Replace All **).**

*The Find What box displays
personal computer and the
Replace With box displays microcomputer (Figure 3-75).*

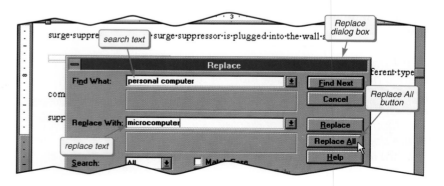

FIGURE 3-75

STEP 4 ▶

Choose the Replace All button.

Word replaces all occurrences of the search text with the replace text and displays a Microsoft Word dialog box indicating the number of replacements that were made (Figure 3-76).

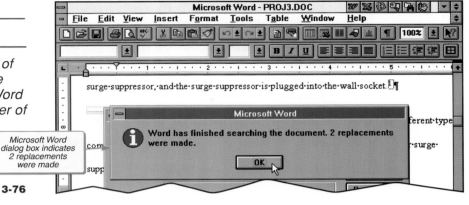

FIGURE 3-76

STEP 5 ▶

Choose the OK button in the Microsoft Word dialog box. Choose the Close button in the Replace dialog box.

Word replaces the occurrences of the words personal computer(s) in the footnote with microcomputer(s) (Figure 3-77).

STEP 6

Choose the Normal View button.

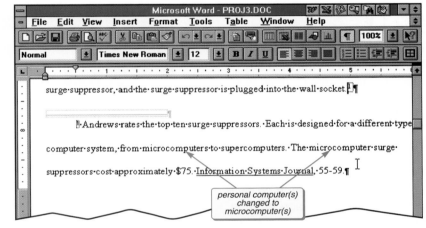

FIGURE 3-77

In some cases, you may only want to replace certain occurrences of the text, not all of them. To instruct Word to confirm each change, choose the Find Next button in the Replace dialog box (Figure 3-75), instead of the Replace All button. When Word finds an occurrence of the text in the Find What box, it pauses and waits for you to choose either the Replace button (Replace) or the Find Next button. The Replace button changes the text; the Find Next button instructs Word to disregard the replacement and to look for the next occurrence of the search text.

If you accidentally replace the wrong text, you can undo a replacement by clicking the Undo button on the Standard toolbar. If you used the Replace All button, Word undoes all replacements. If you used the Replace button, Word only undoes the most recent replacement.

Finding Text

Sometimes, you may only want to find text, instead of find and replace text. To search just for an occurrence of text, you would follow these steps.

TO FIND TEXT

Step 1: Position the insertion point where you want to begin the search.
Step 2: From the Edit menu, choose the Find command.
Step 3: Type the text you want to locate in the Find What box.
Step 4: Choose the Find Next button.
Step 5: To edit the text, choose the Close button; to search for the next occurrence of the text, choose the Find Next button.

Editing a Document in Print Preview

In Project 2, you learned how to move a paragraph using the drag and drop technique. You also learned the cut and paste technique, which was recommended when moving paragraphs over more than one page. When you are moving paragraphs across pages, an alternative to the cut and paste technique is to edit the document in print preview. In print preview, you can display multiple pages in the document window at the same time and edit them.

In this project, you want the paragraph at the bottom of page 1 to be moved after the paragraph at the top of page 2 as shown in these steps.

TO EDIT A DOCUMENT IN PRINT PREVIEW ▼

STEP 1 ▶

Press CTRL+HOME. Click the Print Preview button on the Standard toolbar. Point to the Multiple Pages button ( ) on the Print Preview toolbar.

Word displays the document in print preview (Figure 3-78). Word, by default, displays only one page in print preview. Depending on previous settings, your screen may display more than one page. You can display up to 6 pages in the document window.

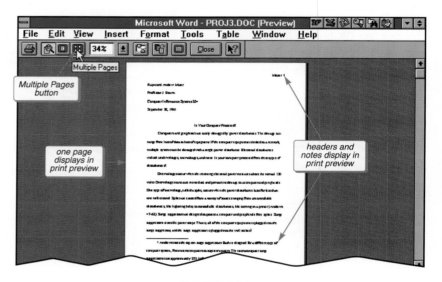

FIGURE 3-78

STEP 2 ▶

Click the Multiple Pages button. Drag the mouse pointer through the grid to select one row of two pages.

Word displays a grid containing a maximum of six pages (Figure 3-79). The grid displays two rows of three pages. Once you select pages in the grid, Word displays the document pages according to the layout you select. In this project, you select 1 x 2 pages; that is, one row of two pages.

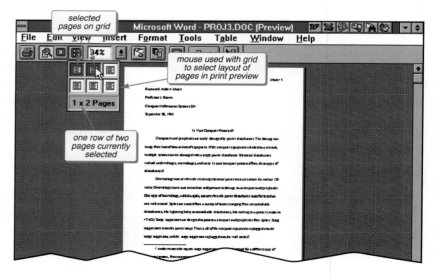

FIGURE 3-79

STEP 3 ▶

Release the left mouse button. Move the mouse pointer into a page.

Word displays two pages in print preview (Figure 3-80). The mouse pointer shape is a magnifier (⊕) when inside a page in print preview. The Magnifier button (⊕) on the Print Preview toolbar is recessed. To enlarge a section of a page, click in the page when the mouse pointer is a magnifier. To edit a page, you must first change the mouse pointer to an I-beam.

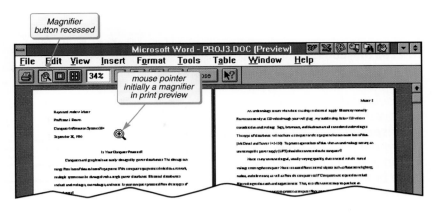

FIGURE 3-80

STEP 4 ▶

Click the Magnifier button. Double-click the mouse in the selection bar to the left of the paragraph to be moved.

The mouse pointer initially changes to an I-beam and then changes to a right-pointing arrow when positioned in the selection bar (Figure 3-81). The last paragraph on page 1 is highlighted. The Magnifier button is not recessed, meaning you can edit the pages displayed in print preview.

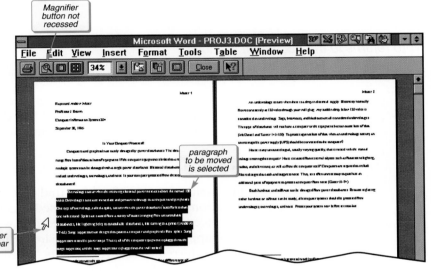

FIGURE 3-81

STEP 5 ▶

Position the mouse pointer inside the selected paragraph and drag the dotted insertion point to the left of the letter N in Noise at the beginning of the second paragraph on page 2.

The insertion point changes to a dotted insertion point, and the mouse pointer has a small dotted box beneath it (Figure 3-82).

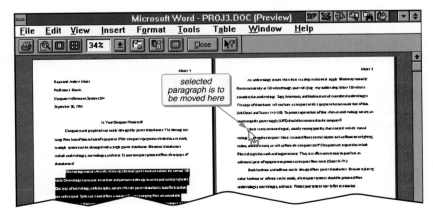

FIGURE 3-82

STEP 6 ▶

Release the mouse button. Click in the page to remove the highlight.

The selected paragraph on page 1 is moved to the location of the dotted insertion point on page 2 in the document (Figure 3-83). Depending on your printer driver, your page break may occur in a different place.

STEP 7

Choose the Close button on the Print Preview toolbar.

Word returns to the document window.

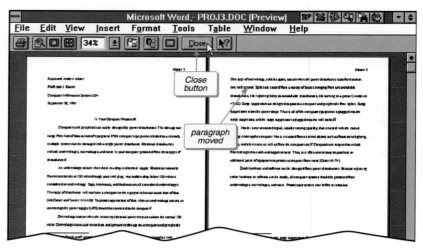

FIGURE 3-83

In print preview, click the up or down arrows on the scroll bar, click above or below the scroll box on the vertical scroll bar, drag the scroll box, or press the PAGE UP key or PAGE DOWN key to bring different pages into the window area.

▶ USING THE THESAURUS

When writing papers, you may find that you used the same word in multiple locations or that a word you used was not quite appropriate. In these instances, you will want to look up a word similar in meaning to the duplicate or inappropriate word. These similar words are called **synonyms**. A book of synonyms is referred to as a **thesaurus**. Word provides an online thesaurus for your convenience. The following steps illustrate how to use Word's thesaurus to locate a synonym for the word *linked* in the first paragraph of Project 3.

TO USE WORD'S THESAURUS ▼

STEP 1 ▶

Select the word for which you want to look up a synonym by double-clicking it. Select the Tools menu and point to the Thesaurus command.

The word "linked" is highlighted in the document (Figure 3-84).

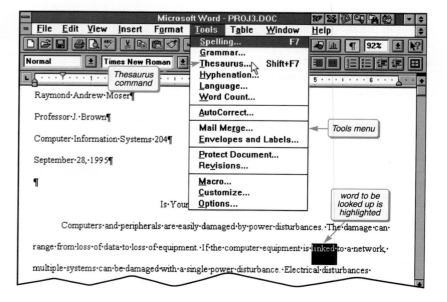

FIGURE 3-84

STEP 2 ▶

Choose the Thesaurus command. Select the synonym connected by clicking it.

Word displays the Thesaurus: English (US) dialog box. The Meanings area displays the definition of the selected word, and the Replace with Synonym area displays a variety of words with similar meanings. The word "connected" is highlighted (Figure 3-85).

STEP 3

Choose the Replace button. Press CTRL+HOME.

Word replaces the word "linked" with "connected" (see Figure 3-86).

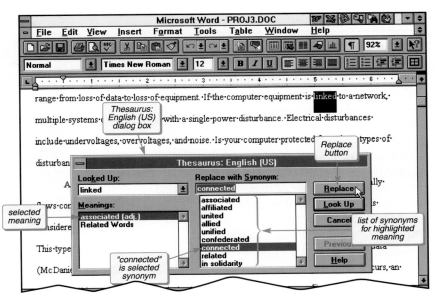

FIGURE 3-85

If multiple meanings are listed in the Meanings area, select the appropriate meaning by clicking it. The Replace with Synonym area will change, based on the meaning you select.

▶ USING WORD COUNT

O ften, when you write papers, you are required to compose a paper with a specified number of words. For this reason, Word provides a command that displays the number of words, as well as pages, characters, paragraphs, and lines, in your document.

TO USE WORD COUNT ▼

STEP 1 ▶

Select the Tools menu and point to the Word Count command (Figure 3-86).

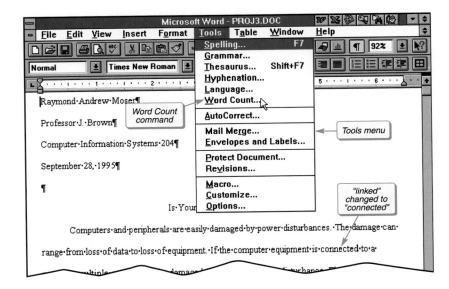

FIGURE 3-86

STEP 2 ►

Choose the Word Count command. In the Word Count dialog box, select the Include Footnotes and Endnotes check box by clicking it.

Word displays the Word Count dialog box (Figure 3-87). Word presents you with a variety of statistics on the current document, including the number of pages, words, characters, paragraphs, and lines. You can choose to have note text included or not included in these statistics.

STEP 3

Click the Include Footnotes and Endnotes check box to deselect it. Choose the Close button in the Word Count dialog box.

Word returns you to the document.

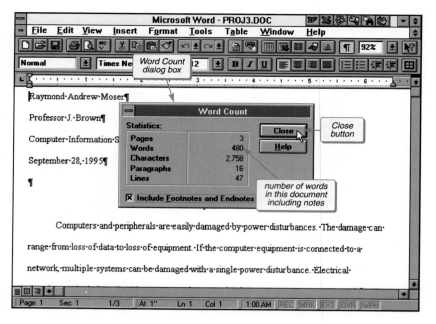

FIGURE 3-87

If you want statistics on only a section of your document, select the section before invoking the Word Count command.

You should change the zoom control back to 100% so the next person who uses Word will not have a reduced display.

TO RETURN ZOOM CONTROL TO 100%

Step 1: Click the Zoom Control box arrow.
Step 2: Click 100% in the list of zoom percentages.

The research paper is now complete. Be sure to spell check and save your research paper one final time before printing it. The final step is to print the revised document by clicking the Print button on the Standard toolbar. The revised document which is shown in Figure 3-1 on page MSW125.

▶ PROJECT SUMMARY

Project 3 introduced you to creating and revising a research paper in Word, using the MLA documentation style. You learned how to change margin settings, adjust line spacing, create headers with page numbers, and indent paragraphs. You learned how to use Word's AutoCorrect feature. Then, you added footnotes to the research paper. You sorted the paragraphs on the works cited page. Next, you revised the research paper by finding and replacing text and moving a paragraph in print preview. Finally, you used Word's thesaurus to look up synonyms and saw how to display statistics about your document.

▶ KEY TERMS AND INDEX

adjusting line spacing (*MSW130*)
ascending sort order (*MSW153*)
AutoCorrect (*MSW140*)
automatic page breaks (*MSW146*)
background repagination
   (*MSW146*)
changing margins (*MSW127*)
descending sort order (*MSW153*)
endnote (*MSW142*)
explanatory notes (*MSW126*)
first-line indent (*MSW137*)
footer (*MSW132*)
footnote (*MSW142*)
hanging indent (*MSW151*)

hard page break (*MSW150*)
header (*MSW132*)
Header and Footer toolbar
   (*MSW132*)
header area (*MSW132*)
MLA style of documentation
   (*MSW124*)
Modern Language Association
   (MLA) (*MSW124*)
normal view (*MSW127*)
note pane (*MSW143*)
note reference mark (*MSW142*)
note separator (*MSW148*)
note text (*MSW142*)

page layout view (*MSW127*)
page width zoom (*MSW139*)
parenthetical citations (*MSW126*)
print preview (*MSW158*)
soft page breaks (*MSW146*)
sorting (*MSW152*)
superscripts (*MSW126*)
synonyms (*MSW160*)
thesaurus (*MSW160*)
toggle (*MSW145*)
works cited (*MSW126*)
zoom (*MSW139*)

Q U I C K   R E F E R E N C E

In Microsoft Word 6 you can accomplish a task in a number of ways. The following table provides a quick reference to each task presented in this project with its available options. The commands listed in the Menu column can be executed using either the keyboard or mouse. Some of the commands in the Menu column are also available in shortcut menus. If you have WordPerfect help activated, the key combinations listed in the Keyboard Shortcuts column will not work as shown.

Task	Mouse	Menu	Keyboard Shortcuts
Add Footnotes		From Insert menu, choose Footnote	Press ALT+CTRL+F
Change Margins	In page layout view, drag margin boundaries	From File menu, choose Page Setup	
Creating an AutoCorrect entry		From Tools menu, choose AutoCorrect	
Create a Hanging Indent	Drag left indent marker on ruler	From Format menu, choose Paragraph	Press CTRL+T
Create a Header		From View menu, choose Header and Footer	
Double-Space Lines		From Format menu, choose Paragraph	Press CTRL+2
First-Line Indent Paragraphs	Drag first-line indent marker on ruler	From Format menu, choose Paragraph	
Go To a Page or Footnote	Double-click page area of status bar	From Edit menu, choose Go To	Press CTRL+G or F5
Insert a Hard Page Break		From Insert menu, choose Break	Press CTRL+ENTER
Insert a Page Number	Click Page Numbers button on Header and Footer toolbar	From Insert menu, choose Page Numbers	Press ALT+SHIFT+P
Left-Align a Paragraph	Click Align Left button on Formatting toolbar	From Format menu, choose Paragraph	Press CTRL+L
Remove a Selected Hard Page Break	Click Cut button on Standard toolbar	From Edit menu, choose Cut	Press DELETE

QUICK REFERENCE (continued)

Task	Mouse	Menu	Keyboard Shortcuts
Replace Text		From Edit menu, choose Replace	Press CTRL+H
Single-Space Lines		From Format menu, choose Paragraph	Press CTRL+1
Sort Paragraphs		From Table menu, choose Sort Text	
Switch to Normal View	Click Normal View button on scroll bar	From View menu, choose Normal	Press ALT+CTRL+N
Switch to Page Layout View	Click Page Layout View button on scroll bar	From View menu, choose Page Layout	Press ALT+CTRL+P
Use the Thesaurus		From Tools menu, choose Thesaurus	Press SHIFT+F7
Use Word Count		From Tools menu, choose Word Count	
Zoom Page Width	Click Zoom box arrow on Standard toolbar	From View menu, choose Zoom	

S T U D E N T   A S S I G N M E N T S

STUDENT ASSIGNMENT 1
True/False

Instructions: Circle T if the statement is true or F if the statement is false.

T F 1. A popular documentation style used today for research papers is presented by the Modern Language Association (MLA).

T F 2. The MLA style uses the term references instead of bibliography.

T F 3. To change margin settings, choose the Margins command from the Format menu.

T F 4. Word, by default, single-spaces between lines of text and automatically adjusts line height to accommodate various font sizes and graphics.

T F 5. A header is text you want to print at the top of each page in a document.

T F 6. A header displays on the screen in normal view.

T F 7. Type the words PAGE NUMBER wherever the page number should appear in the document.

T F 8. Superscripted numbers are those that appear raised above other text in a document.

T F 9. You cannot create your own AutoCorrect entries in Word.

T F 10. Word, by default, prints footnotes on the page that contains the footnote reference mark.

T F 11. In page layout view, Word displays headers, footers, and notes in the document.

T F 12. Hard page breaks display on the screen as a single horizontal thinly dotted line, separated by the words Page Break.

T F 13. Word's default note separator is a two-inch solid line placed at the left margin of the document.

T F 14. A hanging indent indents the first line of each paragraph one-half inch from the left margin.

T F 15. To sort selected paragraphs, click the Sort button on the Standard toolbar.

T F 16. To find and replace text in a document, choose the Find command from the Edit menu.

T F 17. You can drag and drop paragraphs while in print preview.

T F 18. Before you can edit text in print preview, you must be sure the Magnifier button is recessed.

T F 19. Word's thesaurus enables you to look up homonyms for a selected word.

T F 20. To obtain statistics about a document, click the Word Count button on the Standard toolbar.

STUDENT ASSIGNMENT 2
Multiple Choice

Instructions: Circle the correct response.

1. The MLA documentation style suggests all pages of a research paper should be _____-spaced with _____ inch top, bottom, left, and right margins.
   - a. single, 1
   - b. double, 1
   - c. single, 1 1/4
   - d. double, 1 1/4

2. Which command can you use to insert page numbers into a document?
   - a. Page Numbers command from the Insert menu
   - b. Header and Footer command from the View menu
   - c. either a or b
   - d. none of the above

3. The AutoCorrect feature automatically fixes misspelled words when you _____ after entering the misspelled word.
   - a. press the SPACEBAR
   - b. choose the AutoCorrect button
   - c. type a period
   - d. press the ESC key

4. To efficiently indent the first line of each paragraph in a document, _____.
   - a. press the TAB key at the beginning of each paragraph
   - b. drag the first-line indent marker on the ruler
   - c. click the First-Line button on the Standard toolbar
   - d. choose the Indent Paragraph command from the Format menu

5. When Word automatically inserts page breaks, these page breaks are called _____.
   - a. automatic page breaks
   - b. soft page breaks
   - c. hard page breaks
   - d. both a and b

6. If the screen displays a horizontal thinly dotted line completely across the screen with the words Page Break in the middle, you have a(n) _____ in the document.
   - a. soft page break
   - b. hard page break
   - c. footnote separator
   - d. automatic page break

7. To sort selected paragraphs in alphabetic order, choose the _____ option button in the Sort Text dialog box.
   - a. Alphabetical
   - b. Ascending
   - c. Descending
   - d. either a or b

8. By choosing the Word Count command, you can display the number of _____ in a document.
   - a. words
   - b. paragraphs
   - c. lines
   - d. all of the above

9. To view different pages in print preview, _____.
   - a. press the PAGE UP or PAGE DOWN key
   - b. click the up or down arrow on the scroll bar
   - c. drag the scroll box on the scroll bar
   - d. all of the above

10. Headers, footers, and footnotes appear when Word is in _____.
    - a. normal view
    - b. page layout view
    - c. print preview
    - d. both b and c

STUDENT ASSIGNMENT 3
Understanding the Ruler

Instructions: Answer the following questions concerning the ruler in Figure SA3-3. The numbers in the figure in most cases correspond to the numbers of the questions below.

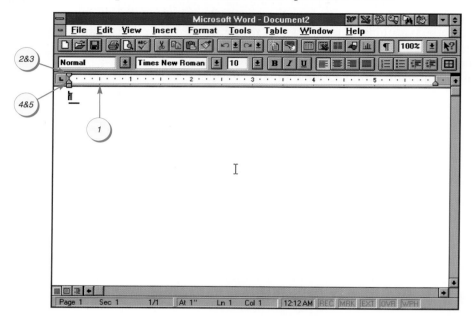

FIGURE SA3-3

1. How many inches from the left margin is the first tab stop?
    _____

2. What is the name of the top triangle at the left margin?
    _____

3. What is the purpose of dragging the top triangle to the first tab stop?
    _____

4. What is the name of the bottom triangle at the left margin?
    _____

5. What is the purpose of dragging the bottom triangle to the first tab stop?
    _____

6. How do you move both triangles at the same time?
    _____

STUDENT ASSIGNMENT 4
Understanding Page Layout View

Instructions: Answer the following questions concerning the page layout view in Figure SA3-4.

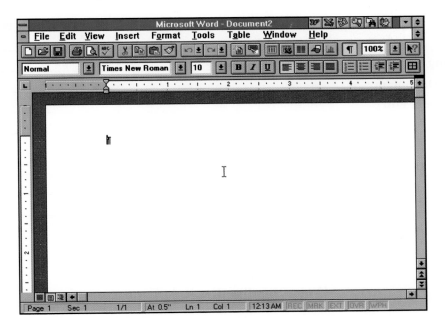

FIGURE SA3-4

1. Identify a feature that indicates you are in page layout view.

   _____

2. What is the top margin setting in the document (in inches)?

   _____

3. What is the left margin setting in the document (in inches)?

   _____

4. How far apart is each tick mark on the ruler (in inches)?

   _____

5. How do you switch from page layout view back to normal view?

   _____

STUDENT ASSIGNMENT 5
Understanding Commands in Menus

Instructions: Write the appropriate command name to accomplish each task and the menu in which each command is located.

TASK	COMMAND NAME	MENU NAME
Add Footnotes		
Adjust Line Spacing		
Count Words in a Document		
Create an AutoCorrect Entry		
Create a Header		
Insert Hard Page Break		
Search and Replace Text		
Sort Paragraphs		
Use Thesaurus		

STUDENT ASSIGNMENT 6
Understanding the Note Pane

Instructions: In Figure SA3-6, arrows point to major components of the note pane. Identify the various parts of the note pane in the spaces provided.

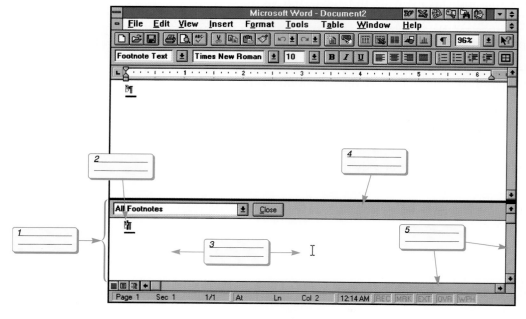

FIGURE SA3-6

COMPUTER LABORATORY EXERCISE 1
Using the Help Menu to Learn About AutoCorrect, Print Preview, Margins, and Headers

Instructions: Perform the following tasks:

1. From the Help menu, choose the Search for Help on command. Type `AutoCorrect` and press the ENTER key. Select AutoCorrect and AutoText: Reusing Text and Graphics. Choose the Go To button. Select Creating an AutoCorrect entry. Read and print the information.

2. Choose the Close button. Select Deleting an AutoCorrect entry. Read and print the information.

3. Choose the Close button. Choose the Search button. Choose the Show Topics button. Select AutoCorrect tips. Choose the Go To button. Read and print the information.

4. Choose the Search button. Type `print preview` and press the ENTER key. Select Editing text in print preview. Choose the Go To button. Read and print the information.

5. Choose the Close button. Choose the Search button. Type `margins` and press the ENTER key. Select Setting margins with the ruler. Choose the Go To button. Read and print the information.

6. Choose the Close button. Choose the Search button. Type `header` and press the ENTER key. Choose the Go To button. Read and print the information.

7. Close the Help window.

COMPUTER LABORATORY EXERCISE 2
Using the Thesaurus

Instructions: Start Word. Open the document CLE3-2 from the Word subdirectory on the Student Diskette that accompanies this book. A portion of the document is shown in Figure CLE3-2.

Perform the following tasks:

1. Select the word *imperative* in the first paragraph of the research paper.
2. From the Tools menu, choose the Thesaurus command.
3. Select the synonym *crucial* by clicking it.
4. Choose the Replace button to replace the word *imperative* with the word *crucial*.
5. Select the word *keep* in the first paragraph.
6. From the Tools menu, choose the Thesaurus command.
7. In the Thesaurus dialog box, select the meaning *hold* in the Meanings area. Then, select the synonym *retain* in the Replace with Synonym area. Choose the Replace button.
8. Save the revised document with the filename CLE3-2A.
9. Print the revised document.

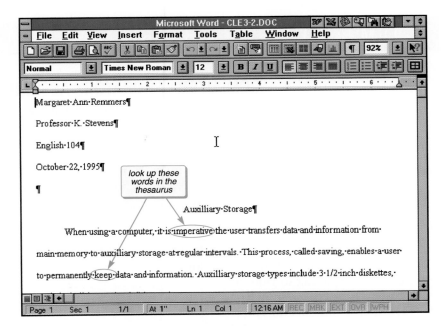

FIGURE CLE3-2

COMPUTER LABORATORY EXERCISE 3
Sorting Paragraphs

Instructions: Start Word. Open the document CLE3-3 from the Word subdirectory on the Student Diskette that accompanies this book. The document is shown in Figure CLE3-3.

Perform the following tasks:

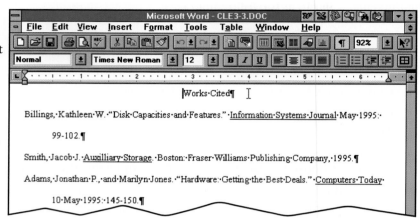

1. Position the mouse pointer in the selection bar to the left of the first works cited paragraph.
2. Drag the mouse pointer through the last works cited paragraph.
3. From the Table menu, choose the Sort Text command.
4. Select the Descending option button in the Sort Text dialog box.
5. Choose the OK button in the Sort Text dialog box.
6. Select the title Works Cited by clicking in the selection bar to its left.

FIGURE CLE3-3

7. Type the new title `Works Cited in Descending Order`
8. Save the revised document with the filename CLE3-3A.
9. Print the works cited page.
10. Repeat Steps 1, 2, and 3.
11. Select the Ascending option button in the Sort Text dialog box and then choose the OK button.
12. Select the title and type a new title `Works Cited in Ascending Order`
13. Save the revised document with the filename CLE3-3B.
14. Print the revised works cited page by clicking the Print button on the Standard toolbar.

COMPUTER LABORATORY ASSIGNMENTS

COMPUTER LABORATORY ASSIGNMENT 1
Preparing a Research Paper and Works Cited Page

Purpose: To become familiar with creating a research paper according to the MLA documentation style.

Problem: You are a college student currently enrolled in a computer class. Your assignment is to prepare a short research paper about application software. The requirements are that the paper be presented according to the MLA documentation style and that it has three references (Figure CLA3-1).

Instructions: Perform the following tasks:

1. If it is not already recessed, click the Show/Hide¶ button on the Formatting toolbar.
2. Change all margin settings to one inch.
3. Adjust line spacing to Double.
4. Create a header to number pages.
5. Change the font size to 12.
6. Type the name and course information at the left margin.
7. Center and type the title.
8. First-line indent all paragraphs in the paper.

9. Type the body of the paper, as shown in Figures CLA3-1a and CLA3-1b. At the end of the body of the research paper, press the ENTER key once and insert a hard page break.
10. Create the works cited page. Be sure to alphabetize the works.
11. Check the spelling of the document.
12. Save the document on a disk with the filename CLA3-1.
13. View the document in print preview.
14. Print the document from within print preview.

Parker 1

Gerald Charles Parker

Professor C. Mason

Computer Information Systems 204

September 13, 1995

Application Software

Computer systems contain both hardware and software. Hardware is any tangible item in a computer system, like the system unit, keyboard, or printer. Software, or a computer program, is the set of instructions that direct the computer to perform a task. Software falls into one of two categories: system software and application software. System software controls the operation of the computer hardware; whereas, application software enables a user to perform tasks. Three major types of application software on the market today for personal computers are word processors, electronic spreadsheets, and database management systems (Little and Benson 10-42).

A word processing program allows a user to efficiently and economically create professional looking documents such as memoranda, letters, reports, and resumes. With a word processor, one can easily revise a document. To improve the accuracy of one's writing, word processors can check the spelling and grammar in a document. They also provide a thesaurus to enable a user to add variety and precision to his or her writing. Many word processing programs also provide desktop publishing features to create brochures, advertisements, and newsletters.

An electronic spreadsheet program enables a user to organize data in a fashion similar to a paper spreadsheet. The difference is the user does not need to perform calculations manually; electronic spreadsheets can be instructed to perform any computation desired. The contents of an electronic spreadsheet can be easily modified by a user. Once the data is modified, all calculations in the spreadsheet are recomputed automatically. Many electronic spreadsheet packages also enable a user to graph the data in his or her spreadsheet (Wakefield 98-110).

(continued)

FIGURE CLA3-1a

COMPUTER LABORATORY ASSIGNMENT 1 (continued)

Parker 2

A database management system (DBMS) is a software program that allows a user to efficiently store a large amount of data in a centralized location. Data is one of the most valuable resources to any organization. For this reason, users desire data be organized and readily accessible in a variety of formats. With a DBMS, a user can then easily store data, retrieve data, modify data, analyze data, and create a variety of reports from the data (Aldrin 25-37).

Many organizations today have all three of these types of application software packages installed on their personal computers. Word processors, electronic spreadsheets, and database management systems make users' tasks more efficient. When users are more efficient, the company as a whole operates more economically and efficiently.

Parker 3

Works Cited

Aldrin, James F. "A Discussion of Database Management Systems." <u>Database Monthly</u> May 1995: 25-37.

Little, Karen A. and Jeffrey W. Benson. <u>Word Processors</u>. Boston: Boyd Publishing Company, 1995.

Wakefield, Sheila A. "What Can An Electronic Spreadsheet Do For You," <u>PC Analyzer</u> Apr. 1995: 98-110.

FIGURE CLA3-1b

COMPUTER LABORATORY ASSIGNMENT 2
Preparing a Research Paper with Footnotes

Purpose: To become familiar with creating a research paper according to the MLA documentation style.

Problem: You are a college student currently enrolled in an English class. Your assignment is to prepare a short research paper in any area of interest to you. The only requirements are that the paper be presented according to the MLA documentation style and that it has three references. You decide to prepare a paper discussing upper and lower respiratory infections (Figure CLA3-2).

Kramer 1

Mary Ann Kramer

Professor S. Barrington

English 104

October 17, 1995

Commonly Confused Infections

Throughout the course of your life, you will experience many upper and lower respiratory infections. Common names used to refer to these infections include influenza, pneumonia, and the common cold. Some of these infections have similar symptoms, like coughing. Each, however, has unique symptoms to differentiate it from the others. Successful treatment of these types of infections depends on correct identification of the virus.

Viruses that affect the lungs are called lower respiratory tract infections. Pneumonia is an infection that attacks the lungs. Pneumonia can be caused by either a virus or bacteria. Influenza is one type of viral pneumonia, commonly called the flu[1]. Patients with a flu virus often experience sudden weakness and severe fatigue, as well as upper respiratory symptoms like sore throat, watery eyes, muscle aches, headache, and nasal stuffiness. Following these ailments, the patient suffers from fever, a dry cough, and chest pain. Treatment of the flu virus includes bed rest, plenty of fluids, and aspirin (Jones 68-75).

Bacterial pneumonia, on the other hand, is more severe than viral pneumonia. Bacteria enters the lungs from many sources, ranging from normal breathing to infection in another part of the body. Bacterial pneumonia inflames the lungs, and the air space begins to fill with fluid. Symptoms the patient experiences are deep cough, fever, chest pain, and chills. Treatment includes ridding the lungs of these fluids and reducing the inflammation with antibiotics. Depending on the severity of the pneumonia, some patients require physical therapy (Spencer and Williams 15-30).

---

[1] Jones states other types of lower respiratory tract diseases include epiglottitis, laryngitis, and tracheobronchitis. Medical Journal, 70.

FIGURE CLA3-2a

(continued)

COMPUTER LABORATORY ASSIGNMENT 2 (continued)

Kramer 2

Viruses that affect the nose and sinuses are called upper respiratory tract infections. Rhinitis, or the common cold, affects the nose. Symptoms include watery eyes, cough, running nose, and may be accompanied by a fever. A common cold that also attacks the sinus openings is called sinusitis. Patients with sinusitis also experience pain in the sinus area over the face. Both rhinitis and sinusitis can be treated with antibiotics[2] and decongestants (McMillan 40-50).

Although the symptoms may be similar, each infection is different from the others. Pneumonia affects the lower respiratory tract and is caused by either a virus or bacteria. Influenza is a type of viral pneumonia; bacterial pneumonia is much more serious and requires a doctor's care. Rhinitis, the common cold, and sinusitis are infections of the upper respiratory tract that can be treated with decongestants and antibiotics. Proper treatment of these infections requires proper diagnosis.

[2] McMillan notes that if a sinus infection is not treated, the patient could suffer from recurrent sinusitis. Once the infection becomes chronic, the only treatment is surgery. Medicine Today, 45-46.

FIGURE CLA3-2b

Part 1 Instructions: Perform the following tasks:

1. If it is not already recessed, click the Show/Hide¶ button on the Formatting toolbar.
2. Change all margin settings to one inch.
3. Adjust line spacing to Double.
4. Create a header to number pages.
5. Change the font size to 12.
6. Type the name and course information at the left margin.
7. Center and type the title.
8. First-line indent all paragraphs in the paper.
9. Type the body of the paper as shown in Figures CLA3-2a and CLA3-2b with appropriate footnotes. At the end of the body of the research paper, press the ENTER key once and insert a hard page break.
10. Create the works cited page. Enter the works cited as shown here. Then, alphabetize them.
    McMillan, Fredrick L. "Rhinitis and Sinusitis: Diagnosis and Treatment." *Medicine Today* Apr. 1995: 30-50.
    Jones, Andrea C. "Pneumonia." *Medicine Journal* May 1995: 63-79.
    Spencer, Jason R., and Karen M. Williams. *Common Bacterial Infections*. Boston: Fraser Publishing Company, 1995.
11. Check the spelling of the document.
12. Save the document on a disk with the filename CLA3-2A.
13. View the document in print preview.
14. Print the document from within print preview.

Part 2 Instructions: Perform the following tasks to modify the research paper:

1. Switch from normal to print preview.
2. Move the fourth paragraph so it is the second paragraph. That is, the paragraph discussing the common cold should appear immediately beneath the introductory paragraph.
3. Switch back to normal view.
4. Use Word's thesaurus to change the word *differentiate* in the first paragraph to a word of your choice. Be sure you have the proper meaning highlighted when looking for a synonym.
5. Use Word's thesaurus to change the word similar in the last paragraph to a word of your choice.
6. Change all occurrences of the word *patient*(s) to *victim*(s).
7. Save the document on a disk with the filename CLA3-2B.
8. Print the document.

COMPUTER LABORATORY ASSIGNMENT 3
Composing a Research Paper with Footnotes

Purpose: To become familiar with composing a research paper from your notes according to the MLA style of documentation.

Problem: You have drafted the notes shown in Figure CLA3-3 on the next page. Your assignment is to prepare a short research paper based on these notes. You are to review the notes and then rearrange and reword. Embellish the paper as you deem necessary. Add two footnotes, elaborating on personal experiences you have had. The requirements are that the paper be presented according to the MLA documentation style.

Instructions: Perform the following tasks:

1. If it is not already recessed, click the Show/Hide¶ button on the Formatting toolbar.
2. Change all margin settings to one inch.
3. Adjust line spacing to Double.
4. Create a header to number pages.
5. Change the font size to 12.
6. Type the name and course information at the left margin.
7. Center and type the title.
8. First-line indent all paragraphs in the paper.
9. Compose the body of the paper from the notes in Figure CLA3-3 with footnotes as specified in the problem definition. At the end of the body of the research paper, press the ENTER key once and insert a hard page break.
10. Create the works cited page from the listed sources. Be sure to alphabetize the works.
11. Check the spelling of the document.
12. Save the document on a disk with the filename CLA3-3.
13. Print the document from within print preview.

(continued)

COMPUTER LABORATORY ASSIGNMENT 3 (continued)

Computers perform three basic activities: input, processing, and output.

The processor transforms input into output.
The processor contains one or more small semiconductor circuits on a piece of silicon, called an integrated circuit or computer chip.
Types of processing include adding, subtracting, multiplying, dividing, organizing, and sorting.
Source: Computers Today, a book published by Fraser Publishing Company in Boston, 1995, pages 45-55, author Kathy L. Stinson.

Input devices send data into the computer.
Examples of input devices are a keyboard, mouse, joystick, and light pen.
Data is input into a computer.
Examples of data include employee timecards, debits and credits, and student grades.
Input and output devices are often referred to as peripheral devices because they are attached to the main unit of the computer.
Source: "Input Data", an article in Peripherals Today, April 1995 issue, pages 109-118, author Nancy C. Walters.

Output devices receive information from the computer.
Information is processed data. Information is output from a computer.
Output can be hardcopy or softcopy.
Printers and plotters are examples of hardcopy output devices.
A monitor is an example of a softcopy output device.
Examples of information include employee paychecks, balance sheets, and report cards.
Source: "Information is Output", an article in Information Magazine, June 1995 issue, pages 80-97, author William E. Trainor.

FIGURE CLA3-3

COMPUTER LABORATORY ASSIGNMENT 4
Creating a Research Paper

Purpose: To become familiar with researching a topic of interest and preparing a research paper that conforms to the MLA style of documentation.

Problem: You are to visit a library and research a topic of interest to you that relates to a current event in the computer industry. You are to obtain a minimum of two references dated sometime within the past two years. Prepare a research paper based on your findings.

Instructions: Create your research paper according to the MLA documentation style. Your paper should be at least one and one-fourth pages in length and should contain a minimum of five paragraphs: introduction, three supporting, and conclusion. Use complete sentences, proper punctuation, and good grammar. Place at least one explanatory note in your paper and include both of your references in the works cited. Check the spelling of your document before printing it. Save your document with the filename CLA3-4.

SPREADSHEETS

USING MICROSOFT EXCEL 5 FOR WINDOWS

MICROSOFT EXCEL 5 FOR WINDOWS

PROJECT ONE

▼

BUILDING A WORKSHEET

OBJECTIVES You will have mastered the material in this project when you can:

▸ Start Excel
▸ Describe the Excel worksheet and workbook
▸ Select a cell or range of cells
▸ Enter text and numbers
▸ Use the AutoSum button to sum a range of cells
▸ Copy a cell to a range of cells using the fill handle
▸ Change the size of the font in a cell
▸ Bold entries on a worksheet
▸ Center cell contents over a series of columns
▸ Apply the AutoFormat command to format a range

▸ Use the reference area to select a cell
▸ Create a column chart using the ChartWizard
▸ Save a workbook
▸ Print a worksheet
▸ Open a workbook
▸ Quit Excel
▸ Correct errors on a worksheet
▸ Use Excel online Help
▸ Use Excel online tutorials
▸ Use the TipWizard
▸ Plan a worksheet

▶ WHAT IS EXCEL?

xcel is a spreadsheet program that allows you to organize data, complete calculations, make decisions, graph data, and develop professional looking reports. The three major parts of Excel are:

▸ **Worksheets** Worksheets allow you to enter, calculate, manipulate, and analyze data such as numbers and text.
▸ **Charts** Charts pictorially represent data. Excel can draw two-dimensional and three-dimensional column charts, pie charts, and other types of charts.
▸ **Databases** Databases manage data. For example, once you enter data onto a worksheet, Excel can sort the data, search for specific data, and select data that meets certain criteria.

▶ PROJECT ONE — SUN-N-SURF 1ST QUARTER TRANSMITTAL COSTS

To illustrate the features of Microsoft Excel, this book presents a series of projects that use Excel to solve typical business problems. Project 1 uses Excel to produce the worksheet and column chart shown in Figure 1-1.

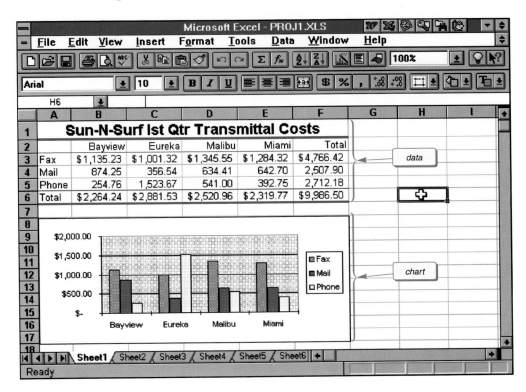

FIGURE 1-1

The worksheet contains the Sun-N-Surf 1st Quarterly Transmittal Costs (Fax, Mail, and Phone) for four locations — Bayview, Eureka, Malibu, and Miami. The worksheet also includes total transmittal costs for each city, each type of transmittal device, and the total transmittal cost for the quarter. Excel calculates the totals by summing the appropriate numbers.

Beneath the worksheet, Excel displays a column chart that it easily creates from the data contained in the worksheet. The column chart compares the three transmittal costs for each of the four cities. For example, you can see from the column chart that for the Eureka office during the first quarter, the greatest transmittal expense was the phone and the smallest transmittal expense was the mail.

Worksheet and Column Chart Preparation Steps

The steps on the next page provide you with an overview of how the worksheet and chart in Figure 1-1 will be built in this project. If you are building the worksheet and chart in this project on a personal computer, read these ten steps without doing them.

1. Start the Excel program.
2. Enter the worksheet title (Sun-N-Surf 1st Qtr Transmittal Costs), the column titles (Bayview, Eureka, Malibu, Miami, and Total), and the row titles (Fax, Mail, Phone, and Total).
3. Enter the first quarter costs (fax, mail, phone) for Bayview, Eureka, Malibu, and Miami.
4. Use the AutoSum button to calculate the first quarter totals for each city, for each type of transmittal, and for the total quarterly transmittal cost for Sun-N-Surf.
5. Format the worksheet title (center it across the five columns, enlarge it, and make it bold).
6. Format the body of the worksheet (add underlines, display the numbers in dollars and cents, and add dollar signs).
7. Direct Excel to create the chart.
8. Save the workbook on disk.
9. Print the worksheet.
10. Quit Excel.

The following pages contain a detailed explanation of each of these steps.

▶ STARTING EXCEL

o start Excel, the Office Manager toolbar must display on the screen or the Microsoft Office group window must be open. Follow these steps to start Excel, or ask your instructor how to start Excel on your computer.

TO START EXCEL ▼

STEP 1 ▶

If the Office Manager toolbar displays, use the mouse to point to the Microsoft Excel button (⬛) (Figure 1-2). If the Office Manager toolbar does not display at the top right of your screen, then point to the Microsoft Excel program-item icon (⬛) in the Microsoft Office group window.

Your Office Manager toolbar may contain more of fewer buttons than shown in Figure 1-2.

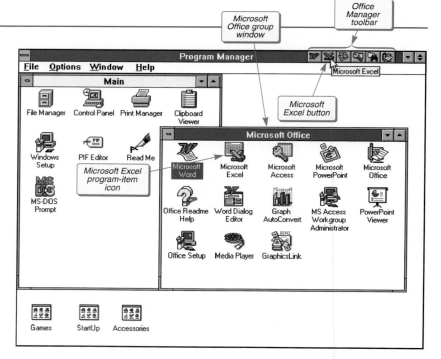

FIGURE 1-2

STEP 2 ►

If the Office Manager toolbar displays, then with the mouse pointer pointing to the Microsoft Excel button, click the left mouse button. If the Office Manager toolbar does not display at the top right of your screen, then double-click the Microsoft Excel program-item icon in the Microsoft Office group window.

Excel displays an empty workbook titled Book1 (Figure 1-3).

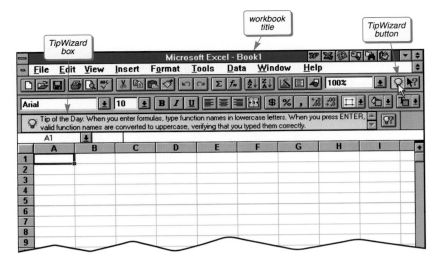

FIGURE 1-3

STEP 3 ►

If the TipWizard box displays (Figure 1-3), point to the TipWizard button on the Standard toolbar (📭) and click the left mouse button.

Excel removes the TipWizard box from the window and increases the display of the worksheet (Figure 1-4). The purpose of the TipWizard box will be discussed later in this project.

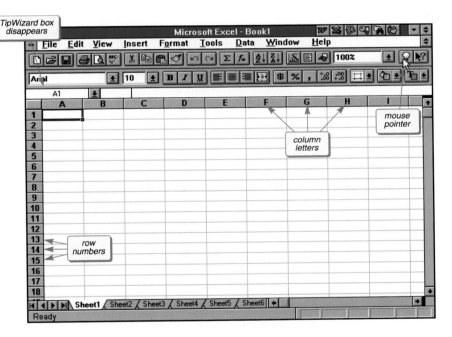

FIGURE 1-4

► THE EXCEL WINDOW

The Excel window consists of a variety of features to make your work more efficient. It contains a title bar, menu bar, toolbars, formula bar, the worksheet window, sheet tabs, scroll bars, and the status bar. Each of these Excel window features and its components is described in this section.

The Workbook

When Excel starts, it creates a new empty workbook, called Book1. The **workbook** (Figure 1-5), is like a notebook. Inside the workbook are sheets, called **worksheets**. On each worksheet you can enter any number of sets of data and charts. Usually, however, you enter one set of data and possibly one or more charts per worksheet. Each sheet name appears on a **sheet tab** at the bottom of the workbook. For example, Sheet1 is the name of the active worksheet displayed in the workbook called Book1. If you click the tab labeled Sheet2, Excel displays the Sheet2 worksheet. To the left of the sheet tabs are the tab scrolling buttons. The **tab scrolling buttons** can be used to scroll through the sheet tabs.

A new workbook opens with 16 worksheets. If necessary, you can add additional worksheets up to a maximum of 255. This project will only use the Sheet1 worksheet. Later projects will use multiple worksheets.

The Worksheet

The worksheet is organized into a rectangular grid containing columns (vertical) and rows (horizontal). A column letter above the grid, also called the column heading, identifies each **column**. A row number on the left side of the grid, also called the row heading, identifies each **row**. Nine complete columns (A through I) and eighteen complete rows (1 through 18) of the worksheet display on the screen when the worksheet is maximized and the TipWizard box is closed (Figure 1-5).

Cell, Gridlines, Active Cell, and Mouse Pointer

The intersection of each column and row is a **cell**. A cell is the basic unit of a worksheet into which you enter data. A cell is referred to by its unique address, or **cell reference**, which is composed of the coordinates of the intersection of a column and a row. To identify a cell, specify the column letter first, followed by the row number. For example, cell reference D3 refers to the cell located at the intersection of column D and row 3 (Figure 1-5).

The horizontal and vertical lines on the worksheet itself are called **gridlines**. Gridlines make it easier to see and identify each cell on the worksheet. If desired, you can remove the gridlines from the worksheet, but it is recommended that you leave the gridlines on.

One cell on the worksheet, designated the **active cell**, is the one in which you can enter data. The active cell in Figure 1-5 is A1. Cell A1 is identified in two ways. First, a heavy border surrounds the cell. Second, the **active cell reference** displays immediately above column A in the **reference area** in the formula bar.

The mouse pointer can become one of fourteen different shapes, depending on the task you are performing in Excel and the pointer's location on the screen. The mouse pointer in Figure 1-5 has the shape of a block plus sign (✚). The mouse pointer displays as a block plus sign whenever it is located in a cell on the worksheet.

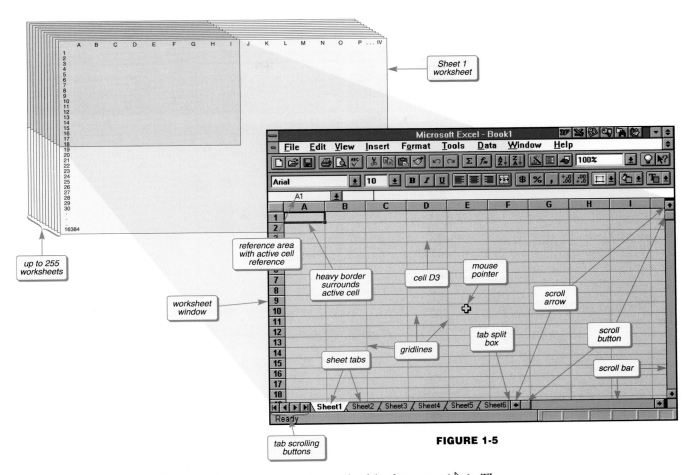

FIGURE 1-5

Another common shape of the mouse pointer is the block arrow ( ). The mouse pointer turns into the block arrow whenever you move it outside the window or when you drag cell contents between rows or columns.

The other mouse pointer shapes are described when they appear on the screen during this and subsequent projects.

Worksheet Window

Each worksheet in a workbook has 256 columns and 16,384 rows for a total of 4,194,304 cells. The column headings begin with A and end with IV. The row headings begin with 1 and end with 16,384. Only a small fraction of the active worksheet displays on the screen at one time. You view the portion of the worksheet displayed on the screen through a **worksheet window** (Figure 1-5). Below and to the right of the worksheet window are the **scroll bars**, **scroll arrows**, and **scroll boxes,** which you can use to move the window around the active worksheet. To the right of the sheet tabs is the tab split box. You can drag the **tab split box** to increase or decrease the length of the horizontal scroll bar.

Menu Bar, Standard Toolbar, Formatting Toolbar, Formula Bar, and Status Bar

The menu bar, Standard toolbar, Formatting toolbar, and formula bar appear at the top of the screen just below the title bar (Figure 1-6 on the next page). The status bar appears at the bottom of the screen.

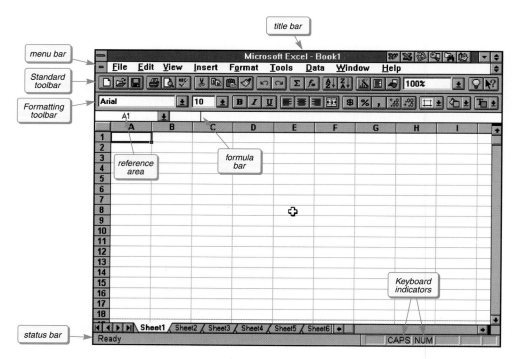

FIGURE 1-6

MENU BAR   The **menu bar** displays the Excel menu names (Figure 1-6). Each menu name represents a pull-down menu of commands that you can use to retrieve, store, print, and manipulate data on the worksheet. To pull down a menu, such as the **File menu**, select the menu name by clicking it.

The menu bar can change to include other menu names, depending on the type of work you are doing in Excel. For example, if you are working with a chart sheet rather than a worksheet, the menu bar will consist of menu names for use specifically with charts.

STANDARD TOOLBAR AND FORMATTING TOOLBAR   The **Standard toolbar** and **Formatting toolbar** (Figure 1-6) contain buttons and drop-down list boxes that allow you to perform frequent tasks quicker than when using the menu bar. For example, to print, you point to the Print button and press the left mouse button. Each button has a picture on the button face that helps you remember the button's function. In addition, when you move the mouse pointer over a button or box, the name of the button or box appears below it.

Figures 1-7a and 1-7b illustrate the Standard and Formatting toolbars and describe the functions of the buttons. Each of the buttons and drop-down list boxes will be explained in detail when they are used in the projects.

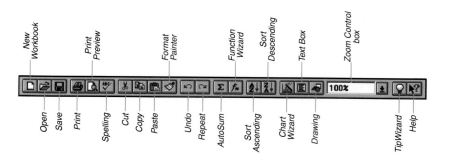

FIGURE 1-7a

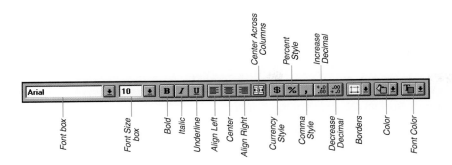

FIGURE 1-7b

Excel has several additional toolbars you can activate through the View menu on the menu bar.

FORMULA BAR   Below the Formatting toolbar is the **formula bar** (Figure 1-6). As you type, the data appears in the formula bar. Excel also displays the active cell reference on the left side of the formula bar in the reference area.

STATUS BAR   The left side of the **status bar** at the bottom of the screen displays a brief description of the command selected (highlighted) in a menu, the function of the button the mouse pointer is on, or the current activity (mode) in progress (Figure 1-6). **Mode indicators**, such as Enter and Ready, specify the current mode of Excel. When the mode is Ready, as shown in Figure 1-6, Excel is ready to accept the next command or data entry. When the mode indicator is Enter, Excel is in the process of accepting data for the active cell.

Keyboard indicators, such as CAPS (Caps Lock), OVR (overtype), and NUM (Num Lock), indicate which keys are engaged and display on the right side of the status bar within the small rectangular boxes (Figure 1-6).

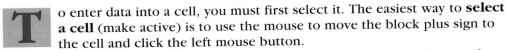

▶ SELECTING A CELL

To enter data into a cell, you must first select it. The easiest way to **select a cell** (make active) is to use the mouse to move the block plus sign to the cell and click the left mouse button.

An alternative method is to use the **arrow keys** that are located just to the right of the typewriter keys on the keyboard. An arrow key selects the cell adjacent to the active cell in the direction of the arrow on the key.

You know a cell is selected (active) when a heavy border surrounds the cell and the active cell reference displays in the reference area in the formula bar.

▶ ENTERING TEXT

In Excel, any set of characters containing a letter is considered **text**. Text is used to place titles on the worksheet, such as the spreadsheet titles, column titles, and row titles. In Project 1 (Figure 1-8 on the next page), the centered worksheet title Sun-N-Surf 1st Qtr Transmittal Costs identifies the worksheet. The column titles are the names of cities (Bayview, Eureka, Malibu, and Miami) and Total. The row titles (Fax, Mail, Phone, and Total) identify the data in each row.

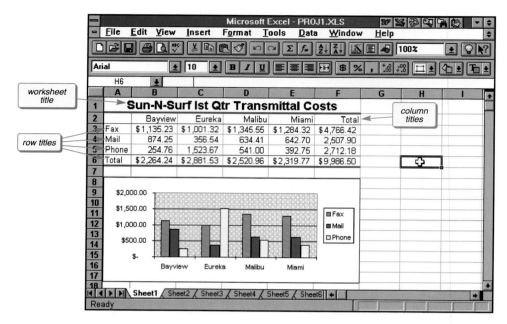

FIGURE 1-8

Entering the Worksheet Title

The following example explains the steps to enter the worksheet title into cell A1. Later in this project, the worksheet title will be centered over the column titles.

TO ENTER THE WORKSHEET TITLE ▼

STEP 1 ▶

Select cell A1 by pointing to it and clicking the left mouse button.

Cell A1 becomes the active cell and a heavy border surrounds it (Figure 1-9).

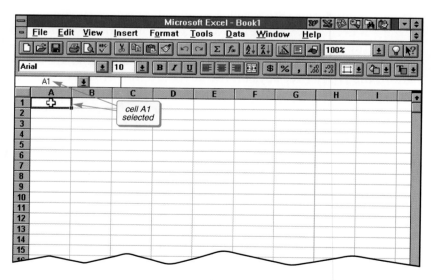

FIGURE 1-9

STEP 2 ►

Type Sun-N-Surf 1st Qtr
Transmittal Costs

*When you type the first character, the mode indicator in the status bar changes from Ready to Enter and Excel displays two boxes: one called the **cancel box** (█) and the other called the **enter box** (█) in the formula bar (Figure 1-10). The entire title displays in the formula bar. The text also appears in cell A1 followed immediately by the insertion point. The **insertion point** is a blinking vertical line that indicates where the next character typed will appear.*

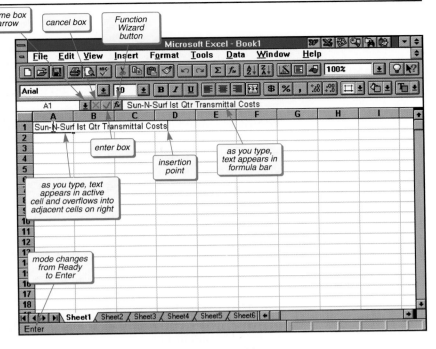

FIGURE 1-10

STEP 3 ►

After you type the text, point to the enter box (Figure 1-11).

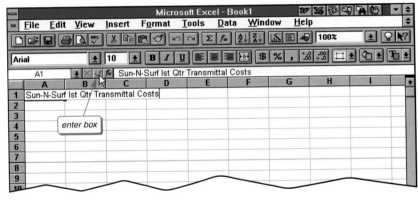

FIGURE 1-11

STEP 4 ►

Click the left mouse button to complete the entry.

Excel enters the worksheet title in cell A1 (Figure 1-12).

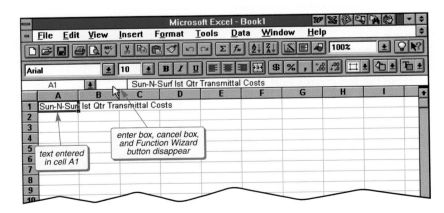

FIGURE 1-12

In the previous example, instead of using the mouse to complete an entry, you can press the ENTER key after typing the text. Pressing the ENTER key replaces Step 3 and Step 4.

When you complete a text entry into a cell, a series of events occurs. First, Excel positions the text **left-justified** in the active cell. Therefore, the S in the company name Sun-N-Surf begins in the leftmost position of cell A1.

Second, when the text is longer than the width of a column, Excel displays the overflow characters in adjacent cells to the right as long as these adjacent columns contain no data. In Figure 1-12, the width of cell A1 is approximately nine characters. The text entered consists of 35 characters. Therefore, Excel displays the overflow characters in cells B1, C1, and D1 because all three cells are empty.

If cell B1 contained data, only the first nine characters of cell A1 would display on the worksheet. Excel would hide the overflow characters, but they would still remain stored in cell A1 and display in the formula bar whenever cell A1 was the active cell.

Third, when you complete an entry into a cell by clicking the enter box or pressing the ENTER key, the cell in which the text is entered remains the active cell. If pressing the ENTER key changes the active cell, then select the Move Selection after Enter check box on the Edit tab that displays when you choose the Options command from the Tools menu.

Correcting a Mistake While Typing

If you type the wrong letter and notice the error before clicking the enter box or pressing the ENTER key, use the **BACKSPACE key** to erase all the characters back to and including the one that is wrong. To cancel the entire entry before entering it into the cell, click the cancel box in the formula bar or press the ESC **key**. If you see an error in a cell, select the cell and retype the entry. Later in this project, additional error-correction techniques are covered.

Entering Column Titles

To enter the column titles, select the appropriate cell and then enter the text, as described in the following steps.

TO ENTER THE COLUMN TITLES ▼

STEP 1 ▶

Select cell B2 by pointing to it and clicking the left mouse button.

Cell B2 becomes the active cell. The active cell reference in the reference area changes from A1 to B2 (Figure 1-13).

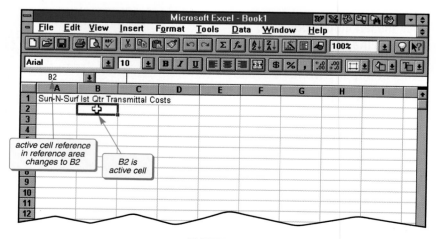

FIGURE 1-13

STEP 2 ▶

Type the column title Bayview

Excel displays Bayview in the formula bar and in cell B2 (Figure 1-14).

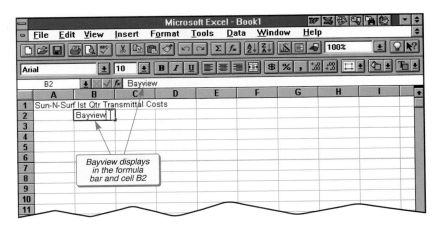

FIGURE 1-14

STEP 3 ▶

Press the RIGHT ARROW **key.**

Excel enters the column title, Bayview, in cell B2 and makes cell C2 the active cell (Figure 1-15). When you press an arrow key to complete an entry, the adjacent cell in the direction of the arrow (up, down, left, or right) becomes the active cell.

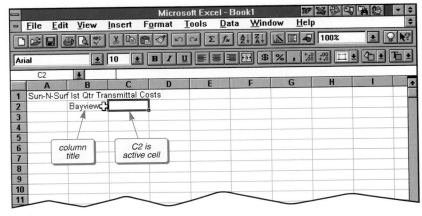

FIGURE 1-15

STEP 4 ▶

Repeat Step 2 and Step 3 for the remaining column titles in row 2. That is, enter Eureka **in cell C2,** Malibu **in cell D2,** Miami **in cell E2, and** Total **in cell F2. Complete the last column title entry in cell F2 by clicking the enter box or by pressing the** ENTER **key.**

The column titles display left-justified as shown in Figure 1-16.

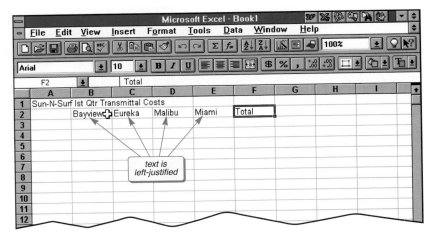

FIGURE 1-16

To complete an entry in a cell, use the arrow keys if the next entry is in an adjacent cell. If the next entry is not in an adjacent cell, click the next cell in which you plan to enter data or click the enter box in the formula bar or press the ENTER key and then use the mouse to select the appropriate cell for the next entry.

Entering Row Titles

The next step in developing the worksheet in Project 1 is to enter the row titles in column A. This process is similar to entering the column titles and is described in the following steps.

TO ENTER ROW TITLES ▼

STEP 1 ▶

Select cell A3 by pointing to it and clicking the left mouse button.

Cell A3 becomes the active cell (Figure 1-17). The cell reference in the reference area changes from F2 to A3.

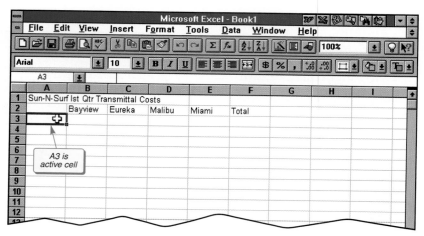

FIGURE 1-17

STEP 2 ▶

Type Fax **and press the** DOWN ARROW **key.**

Excel enters the row title Fax in cell A3 and cell A4 becomes the active cell (Figure 1-18).

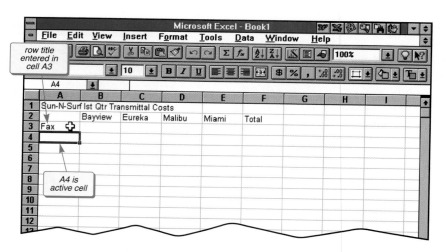

FIGURE 1-18

STEP 3 ►

Repeat the procedure used in Step 2 for the remaining row titles in column A. Enter `Mail` in cell A4, `Phone` in cell A5, and `Total` in cell A6. Complete the last row title in cell A6 by clicking the enter box or by pressing the ENTER key.

The row titles display as shown in Figure 1-19.

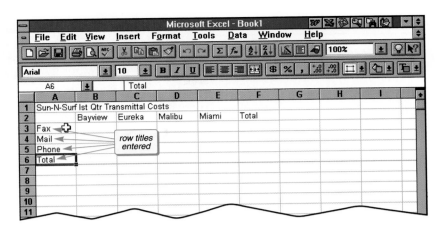

FIGURE 1-19

► ENTERING NUMBERS

In Excel, you can enter numbers into cells to represent amounts. **Numbers** can include the digits zero through nine and any one of the following special characters:

+ - ( ) , / . $ % E e

If a cell entry contains any other character (including spaces) from the keyboard, Excel interprets the entry as text and treats it accordingly. Use of the special characters is explained when they are required in a project.

In Project 1, the costs for Fax, Mail, and Phone for each of the four cities (Bayview, Eureka, Malibu, and Miami) are to be entered in rows three, four, and five. The following steps illustrate how to enter these values one row at a time.

TO ENTER NUMERIC DATA ▼

STEP 1 ►

Select cell B3 by pointing to it and clicking the left mouse button.

Cell B3 becomes the active cell (Figure 1-20).

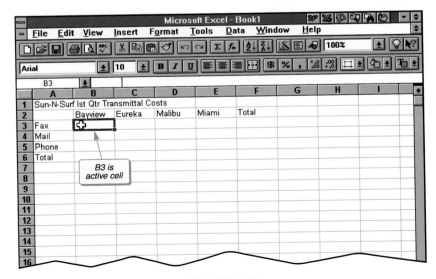

FIGURE 1-20

STEP 2 ►

Type 1135.23 **and press the** RIGHT
ARROW **key.**

Excel enters the number 1135.23
right-justified *in cell B3 and*
changes the active cell to cell C3
(Figure 1-21). The numbers on the
worksheet are formatted with dol-
lar signs and cents later in this
project.

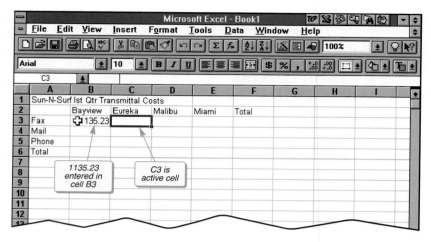

FIGURE 1-21

STEP 3 ►

Enter 1001.32 **in cell C3,** 1345.55
in cell D3, and 1284.32 **in cell E3.**

Row 3 now contains the first
quarter fax costs all right-justified
(Figure 1-22).

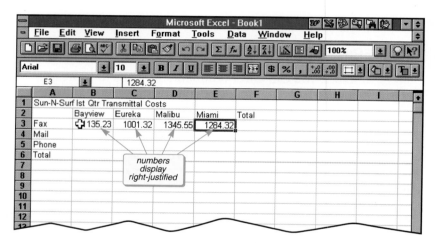

FIGURE 1-22

STEP 4 ►

Select cell B4 (Figure 1-23).

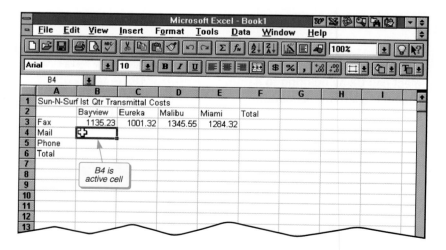

FIGURE 1-23

STEP 5 ►

Enter the 1st Quarter mail costs for the four cities (874.25 for Bayview, 356.54 for Eureka, 634.41 for Malibu, and 642.7 for Miami) and the first quarter phone costs for the four cities (254.76 for Bayview, 1523.67 for Eureka, 541 for Malibu, and 392.75 for Miami).

The first quarter mail and phone costs for the four cities display in row 4 and row 5 (Figure 1-24).

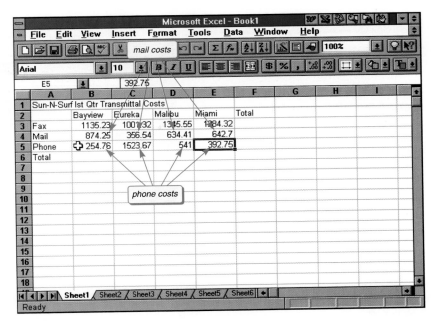

FIGURE 1-24

Step 1 through Step 5 complete the numeric entries. Notice several important points. First, you are not required to type dollar signs and trailing zeros. Later, dollar signs will be added as previously shown in Figure 1-1 on page E3. However, when you enter a number that has cents, you must add the decimal point and the numbers representing the cents when you enter the number.

Second, Excel stores numbers **right-justified** in the cells which means they occupy the rightmost positions in the cells.

Third, Excel will calculate the totals in row 6 and in column F. Indeed, the capability of Excel to perform calculations is one of its major features.

► CALCULATING A SUM

The next step in creating the Sun-N-Surf 1st Qtr Transmittal Costs worksheet is to determine the total costs for the Bayview office. To calculate this value in cell B6, Excel must add the numbers in cells B3, B4, and B5. Excel's **SUM function** provides a convenient means to accomplish this task.

To use the SUM function, you must first identify the cell in which the sum will be stored after it is calculated. Then, you can use the **AutoSum button** (Σ) on the Standard toolbar to enter the SUM function.

Although you can enter the SUM function in cell B6 through the keyboard as =SUM(B3:B5), the following steps illustrate how to use the AutoSum button to accomplish the same task.

TO SUM A COLUMN OF NUMBERS ▼

STEP 1 ►

Select cell B6 by pointing to it and clicking the left mouse button.

Cell B6 becomes the active cell (Figure 1-25).

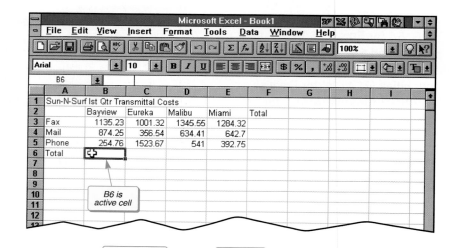

FIGURE 1-25

STEP 2 ►

Point to the AutoSum button on the Standard toolbar and click the left mouse button.

*Excel responds by displaying =SUM(B3:B5) in the form- ula bar and in the active cell B6 (Figure 1-26). The =SUM entry identifies the SUM function. The B3:B5 within paren- theses following the function name SUM is Excel's way of identifying the cells B3, B4, and B5. Excel also surrounds the proposed cells to sum with a moving border, also called the **marquis**.*

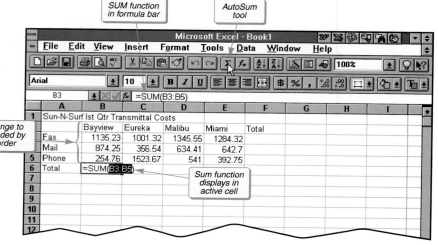

FIGURE 1-26

STEP 3 ►

Click the AutoSum button a second time.

Excel enters the sum of the costs for Bayview (2264.24 = 1135.23 + 874.25 + 254.76) in cell B6 (Figure 1-27). The function assigned to cell B6 displays in the formula bar when cell B6 is the active cell.

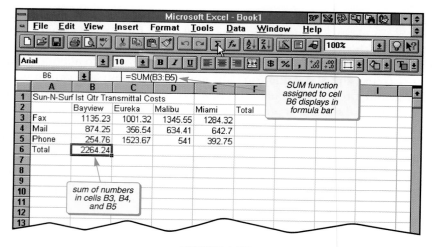

FIGURE 1-27

When you enter the SUM function using the AutoSum button, Excel automatically selects what it considers to be your choice of the group of cells to sum. The group of cells B3, B4, and B5 is called a range. A **range** is a series of two or more adjacent cells in a column or row, or a rectangular group of cells. Many Excel operations, such as summing numbers, take place on cells within a range.

In proposing the range to sum, Excel first looks for a range of cells with numbers above the active cell and then to the left. If Excel proposes the wrong range, you can drag the mouse pointer to select the correct range anytime prior to clicking the AutoSum button a second time. You can also enter the correct range in the formula bar by typing the beginning cell reference, a colon (:), and the ending cell reference.

When using the AutoSum button, you can click it once and then click the enter box or press the ENTER key to complete the entry. However, double-clicking the AutoSum button is the quickest way to enter the SUM function.

▶ USING THE FILL HANDLE TO COPY A CELL TO ADJACENT CELLS

On the Sun-N-Surf 1st Qtr Transmittal Costs worksheet, Excel must also calculate the totals for Eureka in cell C6, for Malibu in cell D6, and for Miami in cell E6. Table 1-1 illustrates the similarity between the entry in cell B6 and the entries required for the totals in cells C6, D6, and E6.

▶ **TABLE 1-1**

CELL	SUM FUNCTION ENTRIES	REMARK
B6	=SUM(B3:B5)	Sums cells B3, B4, and B5
C6	=SUM(C3:C5)	Sums cells C3, C4, and C5
D6	=SUM(D3:D5)	Sums cells D3, D4, and D5
E6	=SUM(E3:E5)	Sums cells E3, E4, and E5

To place the SUM functions in cells C6, D6, and E6, you can follow the same steps that were shown in Figures 1-25 through 1-27. A second, more efficient method is to copy the SUM function from cell B6 to the range C6:E6. The cell being copied is called the **copy area**. The range of cells receiving the copy is called the **paste area**.

Notice from Table 1-1 that although the SUM function entries are similar, they are not exact copies. Each cell to the right of cell B6 has a range that is one column to the right of the previous column. When you copy cell addresses, Excel adjusts them for each new position, resulting in the SUM entries illustrated in Table 1-1. Each adjusted cell reference is called a **relative reference**.

The easiest way to copy the SUM formula from cell B6 to cells C6 and D6 is to use the fill handle. The **fill handle** is the small rectangular dot located in the lower right corner of the heavy border around the active cell (Figure 1-27). The following steps show how to use the fill handle to copy one cell to adjacent cells.

TO COPY ONE CELL TO ADJACENT CELLS IN A ROW ▼

STEP 1 ►

Select the copy area cell B6 by pointing to it and clicking the left mouse button. Point to the fill handle.

The mouse pointer changes from the block plus sign to a cross (✛) (Figure 1-28).

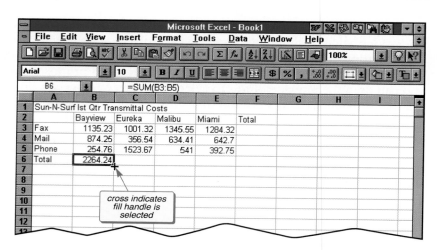

FIGURE 1-28

STEP 2 ►

Drag the fill handle to select the paste area C6:E6.

Excel shades the border of the paste area C6:E6 (Figure 1-29).

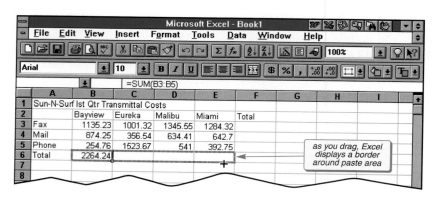

FIGURE 1-29

STEP 3 ►

Release the left mouse button.

Excel copies the SUM function in cell B6 to the range C6:E6 (Figure 1-30). In addition, Excel calculates the sums and enters the results in cells C6, D6, and E6.

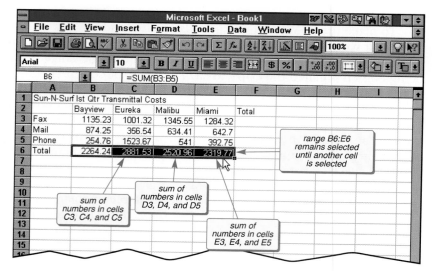

FIGURE 1-30

After the copy is complete, the range remains selected. To remove the range selection, select any cell.

Summing the Row Totals

The next step in building the Sun-N-Surf 1st Qtr Transmittal Costs worksheet is to total the fax, mail, phone, and company total costs and place the sums in column F. The SUM function is used in the same manner as it was when the costs by city were totaled in row 6. However, in this example, all the rows will be totaled at the same time. The following steps illustrate this process.

TO SUM THE ROWS ▼

STEP 1 ▶

Select cell F3 by pointing to it and clicking the left mouse button.

Cell F3 becomes the active cell (Figure 1-31).

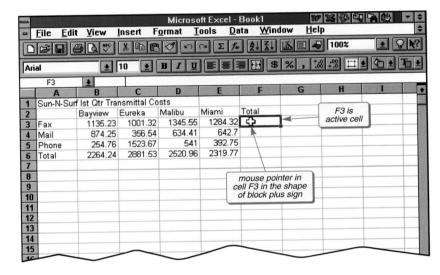

FIGURE 1-31

STEP 2 ▶

With the mouse pointer in cell F3 and in the shape of a block plus sign (), drag the mouse pointer down to cell F6.

Excel highlights the range F3:F6 (Figure 1-32).

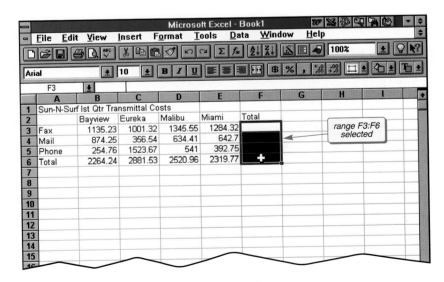

FIGURE 1-32

STEP 3 ▶

Point to the AutoSum button on the Standard toolbar and click.

Excel assigns the functions =SUM(B3:E3) to cell F3, =SUM(B4:E4) to cell F4, =SUM(B5:E5) to cell F5, and =SUM(B6:E6) to cell F6, and then computes and displays the sums in the respective cells (Figure 1-33).

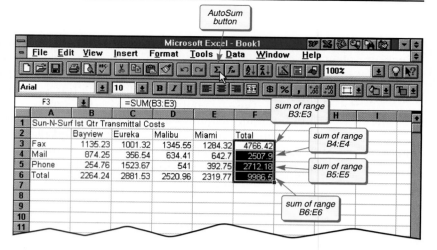

FIGURE 1-33

Because a range was selected next to rows of numbers, Excel assigned the SUM function to each cell in the selected range. Thus, four SUM functions with different ranges were assigned to the selected range, one for each row. This same procedure could have been used earlier to sum the columns. That is, rather than selecting cell B6 and double-clicking the AutoSum button and then copying the SUM function to the range C6:E6, you could have selected the range B6:E6 and clicked the AutoSum button once.

An alternative to finding the totals in row 6 and column F is to select the range B3:F6. This range includes the numbers to sum plus an additional row (row 6) and an additional column (column F). Next, click the AutoSum button. Excel immediately assigns the appropriate SUM functions to the empty cells in the range and displays the desired totals all at once.

▶ FORMATTING THE WORKSHEET

T he text, numeric entries, and functions for the worksheet are now complete. The next step is to format the worksheet. You **format** a worksheet to emphasize certain entries and make the worksheet easier to read and understand.

Figure 1-34a shows the worksheet before formatting it. Figure 1-34b shows the worksheet after formatting it. As you can see from the two figures, a worksheet that is formatted is not only easier to read, but it looks more professional.

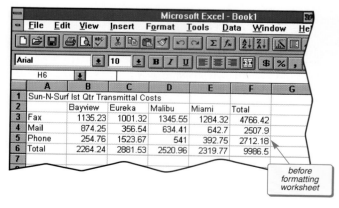

FIGURE 1-34a

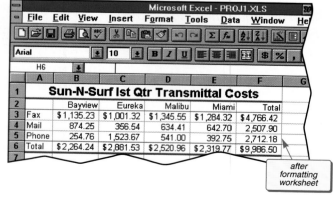

FIGURE 1-34b

To change the unformatted worksheet in Figure 1-34a to the formatted worksheet in Figure 1-34b, begin by bolding the worksheet title, Sun-N-Surf 1st Qtr Transmittal Costs, in cell A1. Next, enlarge the title and center it across columns A through F. Finally, format the body of the worksheet using the AutoFormat command. The body of the worksheet, range A2:F6, includes the column titles, row titles, and numbers. The result is numbers represented in a dollars-and-cents format, dollar signs in the first row of numbers and the total row, and underlines that emphasize portions of the worksheet.

The process required to format the Sun-N-Surf 1st Qtr Transmittal Costs worksheet is explained on the following pages.

Font, Font Size, and Font Style

Characters that appear on the screen are a specific shape and size. The **font type** defines the appearance and shape of the letters, numbers, and special characters. The **font size** specifies the size of the characters on the screen. Character size is gauged by a measurement system called points. A single **point** is about 1/72 of one inch in height. Thus, a character with a **point size** of 10 is about 10/72 of one inch in height.

Font style indicates how the characters appear. They may be normal, bold, underlined, or italicized.

When Excel begins, the default font type for the entire worksheet is Arial with a font size of 10 points, no bold, no underline, and no italic. With Excel you have the capability to change the font characteristics in a single cell, a range of cells, or for the entire worksheet.

To change the worksheet title (Sun-N-Surf 1st Qtr Transmittal Costs) from the Excel default presentation (Figure 1-34a) to the desired formatting (Figure 1-34b), these procedures must be completed: (a) the characters must be changed from normal to bold; (b) the size of the characters must be increased from 10 point to 14 point; and (c) the worksheet title must be centered across columns A through F of the worksheet.

Although the three procedures will be carried out in the order presented, you should be aware that you can make these changes in any order.

TO APPLY THE BOLD FORMAT TO A CELL ▼

STEP 1 ▶

Select cell A1 (Figure 1-35).

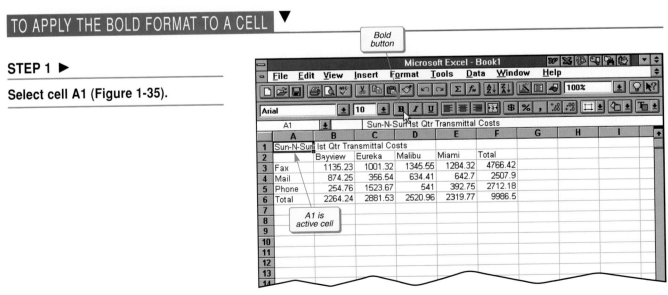

FIGURE 1-35

STEP 2 ▶

Click the Bold button (B) on the Formatting toolbar.

Excel applies a bold format to the worksheet title, Sun-N-Surf 1st Qtr Transmittal Costs (Figure 1-36).

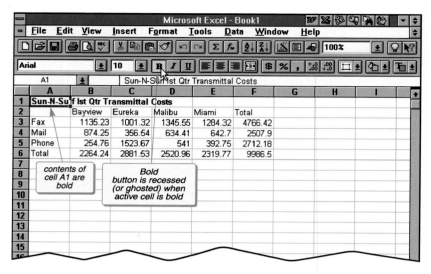

FIGURE 1-36

When the active cell is bold, the Bold button is recessed (or **ghosted**) as shown in Figure 1-36. Clicking the Bold button a second time removes the bold format and the Bold button is no longer be recessed.

Increasing the font size is the next step in formatting the worksheet title.

TO INCREASE THE FONT SIZE ▼

STEP 1 ▶

With cell A1 selected, click the Font Size box arrow on the Formatting toolbar and point to 14 in the drop-down list box (Figure 1-37).

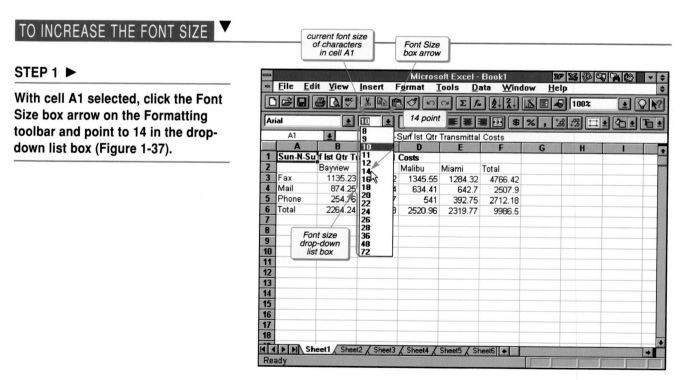

FIGURE 1-37

STEP 2 ▶

Click the left mouse button to choose 14 point.

The characters in the worksheet title in cell A1 increase from 10 point to 14 point (Figure 1-38).

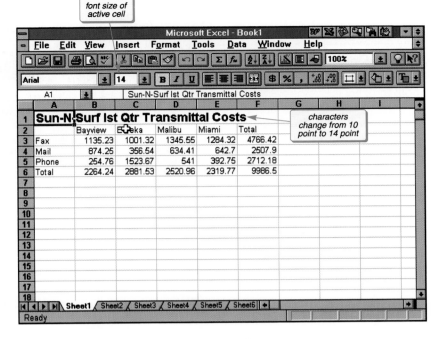

FIGURE 1-38

The final step in formatting the worksheet title is to center it over columns A through F.

TO CENTER A CELL'S CONTENTS ACROSS COLUMNS ▼

STEP 1 ▶

With cell A1 selected, drag the block plus sign to the rightmost cell (F1) in the range over which to center.

When you drag the mouse pointer over the range A1:F1, Excel highlights the cells (Figure 1-39).

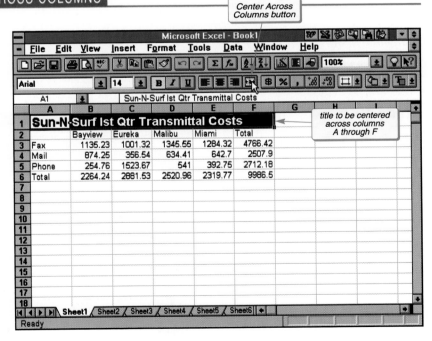

FIGURE 1-39

STEP 2 ▶

Click the Center Across Columns button (▦) on the Formatting toolbar.

Excel centers the contents of cell A1 across columns A through F (Figure 1-40). For the Center Across Columns button to work properly, all the cells except the leftmost cell in the range of cells must be empty.

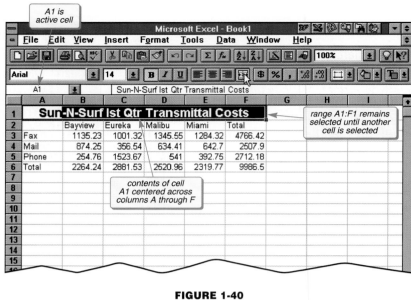

FIGURE 1-40

To remove the selection from range A1:E1, select any cell on the worksheet.

▶ USING AUTOFORMAT TO FORMAT THE WORKSHEET

Excel has several customized format styles called **table formats** that allow you to format the body of the worksheet. The table formats can be used to give a worksheet a professional appearance. Follow these steps to automatically format the range A2:F6 in the Sun-N-Surf 1st Qtr Transmittal Costs worksheet.

TO USE THE AUTOFORMAT COMMAND ▼

STEP 1 ▶

Select cell A2, the upper left corner cell of the rectangular range to format (Figure 1-41).

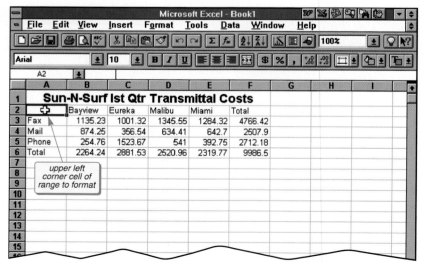

FIGURE 1-41

STEP 2 ▶

Drag the mouse pointer to cell F6, the lower right corner cell of the range to format, and release the left mouse button.

Excel highlights the range to format (Figure 1-42).

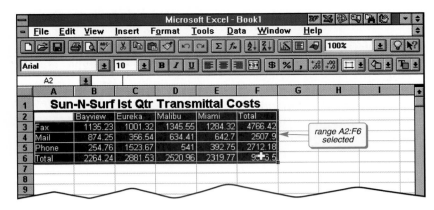

FIGURE 1-42

STEP 3 ▶

Select the Format menu.

The Format menu displays (Figure 1-43).

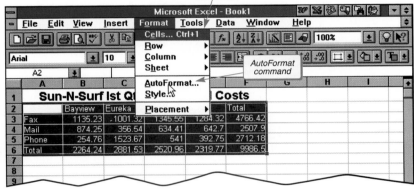

FIGURE 1-43

STEP 4 ▶

Choose the AutoFormat command.

*Excel displays the **AutoFormat dialog box** (Figure 1-44). On the left side of the dialog box is the Table Format list box with the Table Format name Simple highlighted. In the Sample area of the dialog box is a sample of the format that corresponds to the highlighted Table Format name, Simple.*

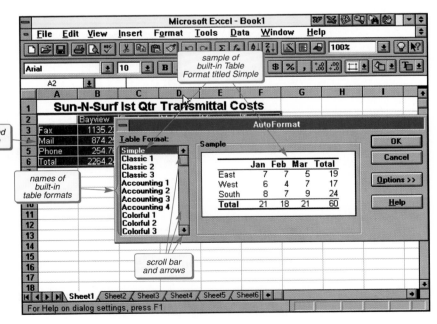

FIGURE 1-44

STEP 5 ►

Point to Accounting 2 in the Table Format list box and click.

The Sample area in the dialog box now shows the Accounting 2 format selected (Figure 1-45).

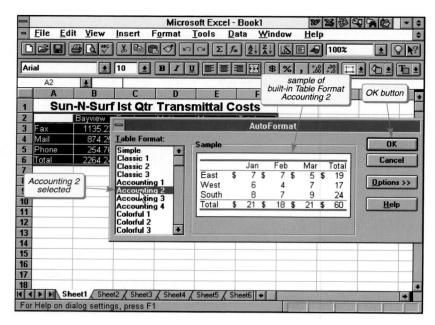

FIGURE 1-45

STEP 6 ►

Choose the OK button (OK) in the AutoFormat dialog box. Select cell H6 to deselect the range A2:F6.

Excel displays the worksheet with the range A2:F6 using the customized format, Accounting 2 (Figure 1-46).

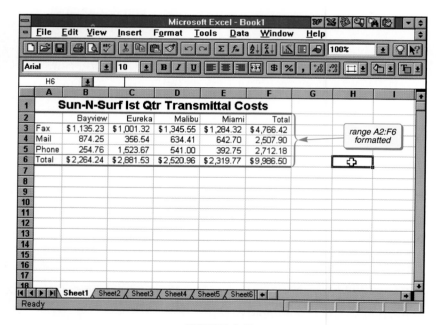

FIGURE 1-46

Excel provides fifteen customized format styles from which to choose. Each format style has different characteristics. The format characteristics associated with the customized format, Accounting 2 (Figure 1-46), include right-justification of column titles, numeric values displayed as dollars and cents, comma placement, numbers aligned on the decimal point, dollar signs in the first row of numbers and in the total row, and top and bottom borders emphasized. The width of column A has also been reduced so the longest row title fits in the column.

The worksheet is now complete. The next step is to chart the Sun-N-Surf 1st Qtr Transmittal Costs for the four offices. To create the chart, the active cell must be cell A2, the cell in the upper left corner of the range to chart. To select cell A2, you can move the mouse pointer to it and click. This is the procedure used in previous examples. You can also use the reference area in the formula bar to select a cell.

Using the Reference Area to Select a Cell

The reference area is located in the left side of the formula bar. To select any cell, click in the reference area and enter the cell reference of the cell you want to select. The following steps show how to select cell A2.

TO USE THE REFERENCE AREA TO SELECT A CELL ▼

STEP 1 ▶

Point to the reference area in the formula bar and click the left mouse button. Type a 2

Even though cell H6 is the active cell, the reference area displays the cell reference a2 (Figure 1-47).

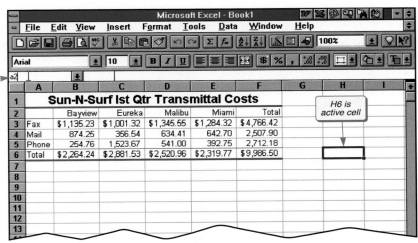

FIGURE 1-47

STEP 2 ▶

Press the ENTER key.

Excel changes the active cell from cell H6 to cell A2 (Figure 1-48).

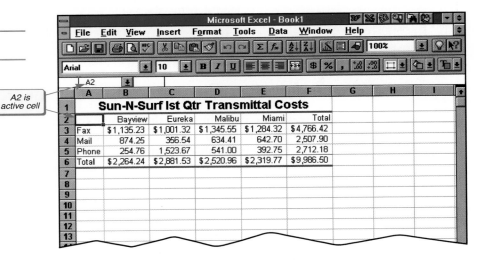

FIGURE 1-48

As you will see in later projects, besides using the reference area to select any cell, you can also click the Name box arrow to the right of the reference area to assign names to a cell or range of cells.

Excel supports several additional ways to select a cell. They are summarized in Table 1-2.

▸ **TABLE 1-2**

KEY, BOX, OR COMMAND	FUNCTION
ARROW	Selects the adjacent cell in the direction of the arrow on the key.
HOME	Selects the cell at the beginning of the row that contains the active cell and moves the window accordingly.
CTRL+HOME	Selects cell A1 or the cell below and to the right of frozen titles and moves the window to the upper left corner of the worksheet.
CTRL+ARROW	Selects the border cell of the worksheet in combination with the arrow keys and moves the window accordingly. For example, to select the rightmost cell in the row that contains the active cell, press CTRL+RIGHT ARROW. You can also press the END key, release it, and then press the arrow key to accomplish the same task.
Go To command on Edit menu	Selects the cell in the worksheet that corresponds to the cell reference you enter in the Go To dialog box and moves the window accordingly. You can press F5 as a shortcut to display the Go To dialog box.
Find command on Edit menu	Finds and selects a cell in the worksheet with specific contents that you enter in the Find dialog box. If necessary, Excel moves the window to display the cell. You can press SHIFT+F5 to display the Find Dialog box.
Reference Area	Selects the cell in the workbook that corresponds to the cell reference you enter in the reference area.
PAGE UP	Selects the cell one window up from the active cell and moves the window accordingly.
ALT+PAGE UP	Selects the cell one window to the left and moves the window accordingly.
PAGE DOWN	Selects the cell one window down from the active cell and moves the window accordingly.
ALT+PAGE DOWN	Selects the cell one window to the right and moves the window accordingly.

▶ ADDING A CHART TO THE WORKSHEET

The column chart drawn by Excel in this project is based on the data in the Sun-N-Surf 1st Qtr Transmittal Costs worksheet (Figure 1-49). It is called an **embedded chart** because it is part of the worksheet.

For Bayview, the light blue column represents the quarterly cost of faxing ($1,135.23), the purple column represents the quarterly cost of mailing ($874.25), and the light yellow column represents the quarterly cost of using the phone ($254.76). For Eureka, Malibu, and Miami, the same color columns represent the comparable costs. Notice in this chart that the totals from the worksheet are not represented because the totals were not in the range specified for charting.

Excel derived the dollar values along the y-axis (or vertical axis) of the chart on the basis of the values in the worksheet. It also automatically determines the $500.00 increments. The value $2,000.00 is greater than any value in the worksheet, so it is the maximum value Excel included on the chart.

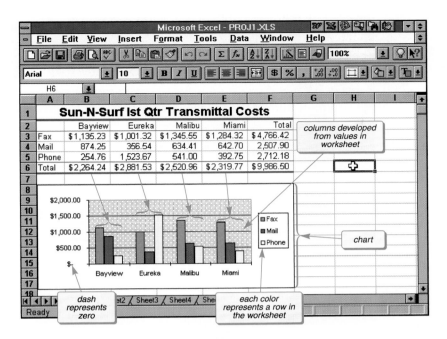

FIGURE 1-49

To draw a chart like the one in Figure 1-49, select the range to chart, click the **ChartWizard button** (![icon]) on the Standard toolbar, and select the area on the worksheet where you want the chart drawn. In Figure 1-49, the chart is located immediately below the worksheet. When you determine the location of the chart on the worksheet, you also determine its size by dragging the mouse pointer from the upper left corner of the chart location to the lower right corner of the chart location.

Follow these detailed steps to draw a **column chart** that compares the Sun-N-Surf 1st Qtr Transmittal Costs for the four cities.

TO DRAW AN EMBEDDED COLUMN CHART ▼

STEP 1 ▶

With cell A2 selected, position the block plus sign within the cell's border (Figure 1-50).

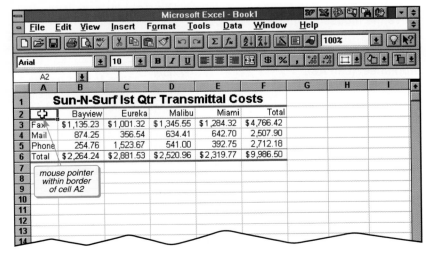

FIGURE 1-50

STEP 2 ▶

Drag the mouse pointer to the lower right corner cell (cell E5) of the range to chart (A2:E5).

Excel highlights the range to chart (Figure 1-51).

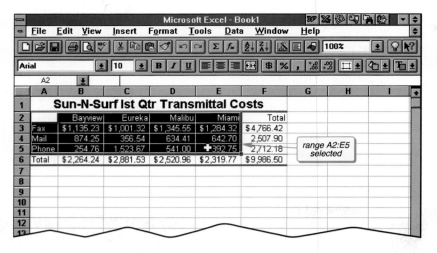

FIGURE 1-51

STEP 3 ▶

Click the ChartWizard button on the Standard toolbar and move the mouse pointer into the window (Figure 1-52).

The mouse pointer changes to a cross hair with a chart symbol ($+$) (Figure 1-52).

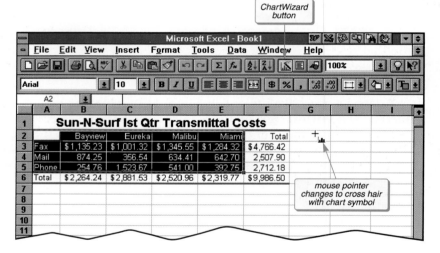

FIGURE 1-52

STEP 4 ▶

Move the mouse pointer to the upper left corner of the desired chart location, immediately below the worksheet (cell A8).

A moving border surrounds the range to chart A2:E5. (Figure 1-53).

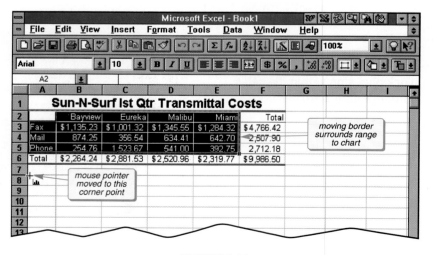

FIGURE 1-53

STEP 5 ▶

Drag the mouse pointer to the lower right corner of the chart location (cell F17).

The mouse pointer is positioned at the lower right corner of cell F17, and the chart location is surrounded by a solid line rectangle (Figure 1-54).

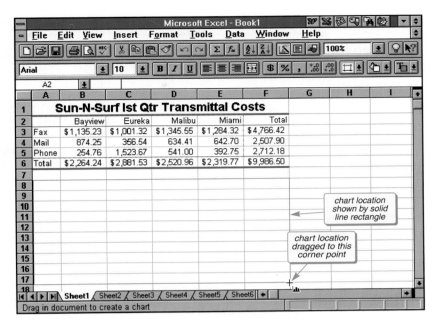

FIGURE 1-54

STEP 6 ▶

Release the left mouse button.

Excel responds by displaying the ChartWizard dialog box (Figure 1-55).

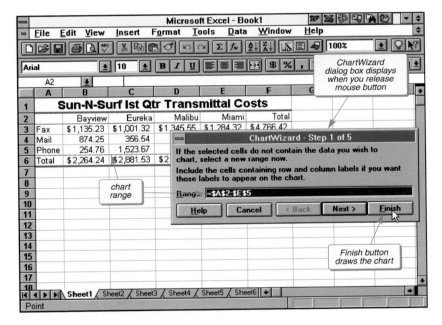

FIGURE 1-55

STEP 7 ▶

In the ChartWizard dialog box, choose the Finish button (Finish).

Excel draws a column chart over the chart location comparing the Sun-N-Surf first quarter transmittal costs for the four cities (Figure 1-56). The small selection squares, or handles, on the border of the chart area indicate the chart is selected. While the chart is selected, you can click on and drag the chart to any location on the worksheet. You can also resize the chart by dragging on the handles.

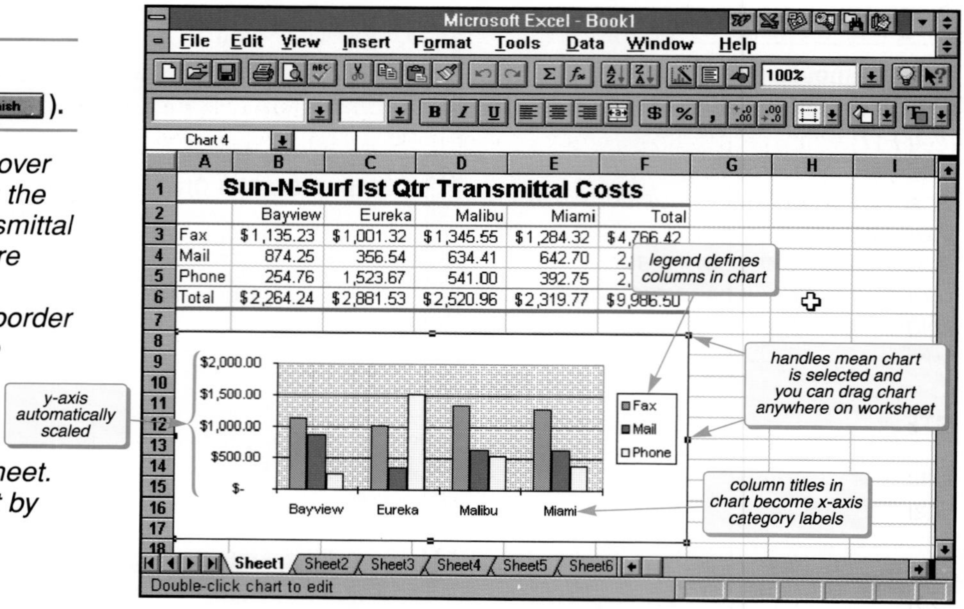

STEP 8 ▶

Select a cell outside the chart location to remove the chart selection.

FIGURE 1-56

The embedded column chart in Figure 1-56 compares the first quarter transmittal costs for each city. It also allows you to compare the costs between the cities. Notice that Excel automatically selects the entries in the row at the top of the range (row 2) as the titles for the x-axis (or horizontal axis) and draws a column for each of the twelve cells containing numbers in the range. The small box to the right of the column chart in Figure 1-56 contains the legend. The **legend** identifies each column in the chart. Excel automatically selects the leftmost column of the range (column A) as titles within the legend. Excel also automatically scales the y-axis on the basis of the magnitude of the numbers in the graph range.

Excel offers 15 different chart types from which you can choose. The **default chart type** is the chart Excel draws when you initially create the chart. When you first load Excel on a computer, the default chart type is the two-dimensional column chart. You can change the chart type by double-clicking the chart and choosing the Chart Type command on the Format menu. The Chart Type command only appears on the Format menu when the chart is active. Subsequent projects will discuss changing charts, sizing charts, and adding text to charts.

▶ SAVING THE WORKBOOK

While you are building a worksheet, the computer stores it in main memory. If the computer is turned off, or if you lose electrical power, the workbook is lost. Hence, it is mandatory to save on disk any workbook that you will use later. The steps below and on the next two pages illustrate how to save a workbook to drive A using the Save button on the Standard toolbar. Be sure you have a formatted disk in drive A.

TO SAVE THE WORKBOOK ▼

STEP 1 ▶

Click the Save button (▣) on the Standard toolbar.

Excel responds by displaying the Save As dialog box (Figure 1-57).

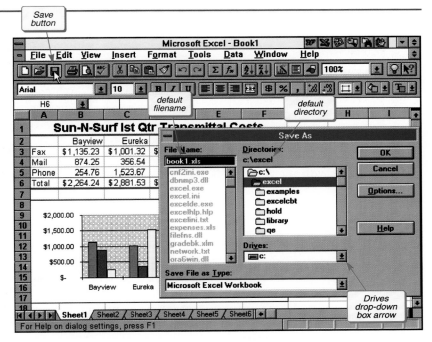

FIGURE 1-57

STEP 2 ▶

Type `proj1` **in the File Name text box.**

The filename proj1 replaces book1.xls in the File Name text box (Figure 1-58).

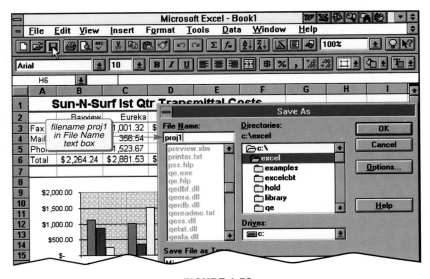

FIGURE 1-58

STEP 3 ▶

Click the Drives drop-down box arrow.

A list of available drives displays (Figure 1-59). If the drive A symbol does not appear in the Drives drop-down list, use the UP ARROW key on the scroll bar.

FIGURE 1-59

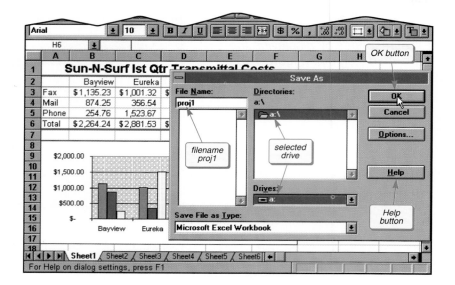

STEP 4 ▶

Select drive A (▭a:) and point to the OK button.

Drive A becomes the selected drive (Figure 1-60).

FIGURE 1-60

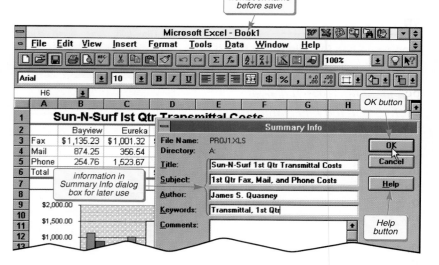

STEP 5 ▶

Choose the OK button in the Save As dialog box.

Excel displays the Summary Info dialog box with the Title, Subject, Author, Keywords, and Comments boxes empty. If you wish, you may enter information such as a title, subject area, author name and keywords in the Summary Info dialog box as shown in Figure 1-61. If you enter information into the text boxes, be sure to press the TAB key to advance from one text box to the next.

FIGURE 1-61

STEP 6 ▶

Choose the OK button in the Summary Info dialog box.

Excel saves the workbook to drive A using the filename PROJ1. XLS. Excel automatically appends to the filename proj1 the extension .XLS, which stands for Excel work-sheet. Although the Sun-N-Surf 1st Qtr Transmittal Costs work-sheet is saved on disk, it also remains in main memory and dis-plays on the screen (Figure 1-62).

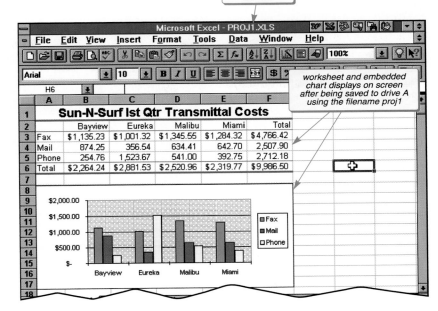

title bar displays new workbook filename

worksheet and embedded chart displays on screen after being saved to drive A using the filename proj1

FIGURE 1-62

While Excel is saving the workbook, it momentarily changes the word Ready in the status bar to Saving PROJ1.XLS. It also displays a horizontal bar next to the words Saving PROJ1.XLS indicating the amount of the workbook saved. After the save operation is complete, Excel changes the name of the workbook in the title bar from Book1 to PROJ1.XLS (Figure 1-62).

▶ PRINTING THE WORKSHEET

nce you have created the worksheet and saved the workbook on disk, you may want to print the worksheet. A printed version of the worksheet is called a **hard copy** or **printout**.

There are several reasons why you may want a printout. First, to present the worksheet to someone who does not have access to your computer, it must be in printed form. In addition, worksheets and charts are often kept for reference by persons other than those who prepare them. In many cases, the worksheets are printed and kept in binders for use by others. This section describes how to print a worksheet.

By default, Excel prints the gridlines that display on the screen along with the worksheet. To print without gridlines, you must turn them off by removing the X in the Gridlines check box on the **Sheet tab** in the Page Setup dialog box. In this section, you will see that some dialog boxes are made up of tabs, each with its own name. A **tab** in a dialog box contains selections that are grouped under the **tab name**.

A number of ways to remove gridlines from the printout are available using the Page Setup command. One way is to choose the Page Setup command from the File menu. Another way is to use the shortcut menu. Excel provides a **short-cut menu** that contains the commands most often used for the current activity. To activate the shortcut menu that pertains to the entire workbook, point to the menu bar and click the right mouse button as described in the following steps.

TO PRINT A WORKSHEET ▼

STEP 1 ►

Ready the printer according to the printer instructions.

STEP 2 ►

Point to the menu bar and click the right mouse button.

Excel displays the shortcut menu (Figure 1-63).

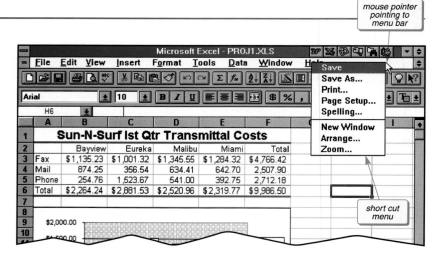

FIGURE 1-63

STEP 3 ►

Choose the Page Setup command from the shortcut menu.

Excel displays the Page Setup dialog box (Figure 1-64). The Page tab displays.

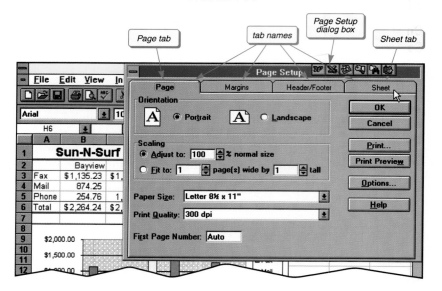

FIGURE 1-64

STEP 4 ►

Click the Sheet tab in the Page Setup dialog box.

Excel displays the Sheet tab in place of the Page tab (Figure 1-65).

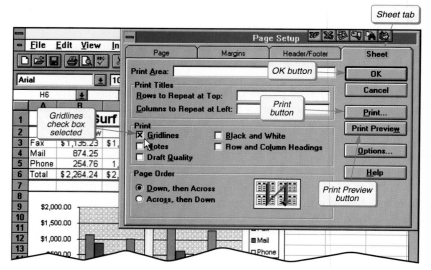

FIGURE 1-65

STEP 5 ▶

If an X appears in the Gridlines check box in the Print area of the Sheet tab, select the check box by clicking it so the X disappears.

The Gridlines check box is empty (Figure 1-66). The gridlines on the screen will not print.

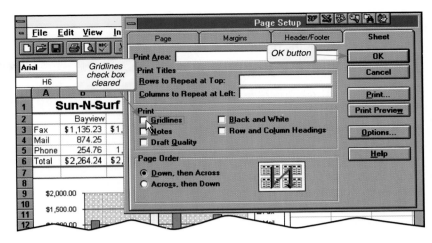

FIGURE 1-66

STEP 6 ▶

Choose the OK button in the Page Setup dialog box.

The Page Setup dialog box disappears and the worksheet and embedded chart display with a dashed line showing the right boundary of the page that Excel will print (Figure 1-67).

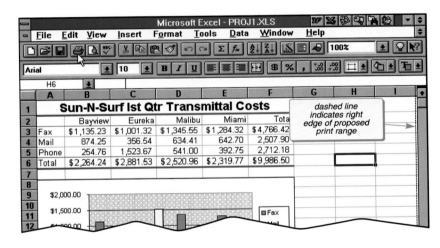

FIGURE 1-67

STEP 7 ▶

Click the Print button (🖨) on the Standard toolbar.

Excel displays the Printing dialog box (Figure 1-68) that allows you to cancel the print job at any time while the system is internally creating the worksheet to send to the printer. When the Printing dialog box disappears, the printing begins.

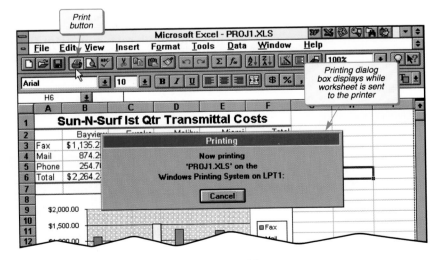

FIGURE 1-68

STEP 8 ▶

When the printer stops, retrieve the printout (Figure 1-69).

STEP 9 ▶

Point to the Save button on the Standard toolbar and click.

Excel saves the workbook with the page setup characteristics shown in Figure 1-66. Saving the workbook after changing the page setup means that you do not have to perform Step 2 through Step 6 the next time you print the worksheet and chart unless you want to make other page setup changes.

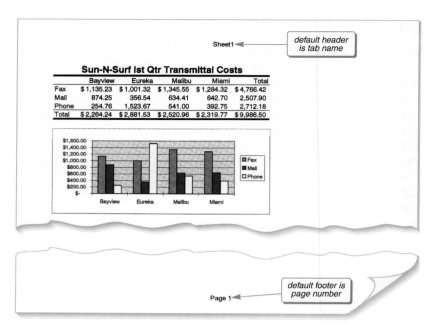

FIGURE 1-69

Notice in Figure 1-69 that Excel adds a header and footer. A **header** is a line of text that prints at the top of each page. A **footer** is a line of text that prints at the bottom of each page. By default, Excel prints the name on the worksheet tab at the bottom of the screen as the header and the page number as the footer.

If you already know the Gridlines check box is clear, then you can skip Step 2 through Step 6 in the previous list. In other words, if the printer is ready, click the Print button on the Standard toolbar to print the worksheet and chart.

▶ EXITING EXCEL

A fter you build, save, and print the worksheet and chart, Project 1 is complete. To quit Excel and return control to Program Manager, perform the following steps.

TO EXIT EXCEL ▼

STEP 1 ▶

Point to the Control-menu box in the title bar (Figure 1-70).

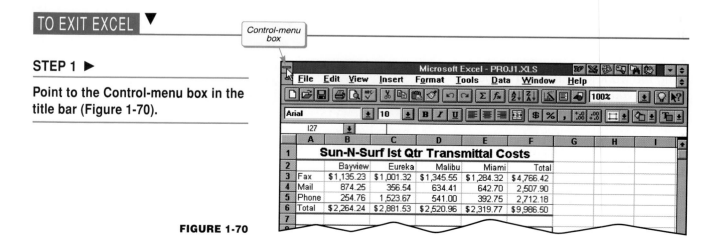

FIGURE 1-70

STEP 2 ▶

Double-click the left mouse button.

If you made changes to the work-book, Excel displays the question, Save changes in 'PROJ1. XLS'? in the Microsoft Excel dialog box (Figure 1-71). Choose the Yes button to save the changes to PROJ1. XLS before quiting Excel. Choose the No button to quit Excel without saving the changes to PROJ1. XLS. Choose the Can-cel button to terminate the Exit command and return to the workbook.

FIGURE 1-71

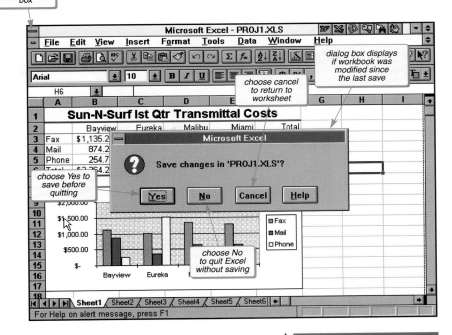

Rather than double-clicking the Control-menu box in the title bar you can also quit Excel by choosing the Exit command on the File menu.

▶ OPENING A WORKBOOK

Earlier, you saved the workbook built in Project 1 on disk using the file-name PROJ1.XLS. Once you have created and saved a workbook, you will often have reason to retrieve it from disk. For example, you may want to enter revised data, review the calculations on the worksheet, or add more data to the worksheet. After starting Excel (see page E4), you can use the following steps to open PROJ1.XLS using the Open button (📂).

TO OPEN A WORKBOOK ▼

STEP 1 ▶

Point to the Open button on the Standard toolbar and click.

Excel displays the Open dialog box.

STEP 2 ▶

If drive A is not the selected drive, select drive A in the Drives drop-down list box (refer to Figures 1-59 and 1-60 on page E36 to review this technique). Select the filename proj1.xls by clicking the filename in the File Name list box (Figure 1-72).

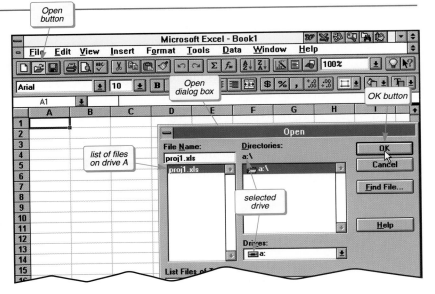

FIGURE 1-72

STEP 3 ▶

Choose the OK button in the Open dialog box.

Excel loads the workbook PROJ1. XLS from drive A into main memory, and displays it on the screen (Figure 1-73).

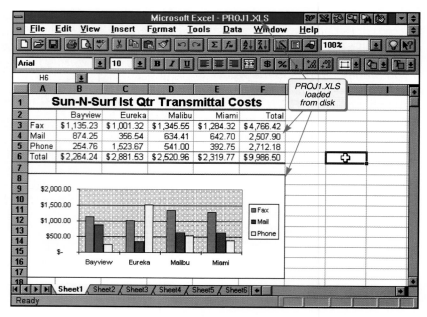

FIGURE 1-73

▶ CORRECTING ERRORS

Several methods are available for correcting errors on a worksheet. The one you choose will depend on the severity of the error and whether you notice it while typing the data in the formula bar or after you have entered the incorrect data into the cell.

Correcting Errors Prior to Entering Data into a Cell

If you notice an error prior to entering data into a cell, use one of the following techniques:

1. Use the BACKSPACE key to erase the portion in error and then type the correct characters; or
2. If the error is too severe, click the cancel box or press the ESC key to erase the entire entry in the formula bar and reenter the data from the beginning.

In-Cell Editing

If you find an error in the worksheet after entering the data, you can correct the error in one of two ways:

1. If the entry is short, select the cell, retype the entry correctly, and click the enter box or press the ENTER key. The new entry will replace the old entry.
2. If the entry in the cell is long and the errors are minor, the **Edit mode** may be a better choice. Use the Edit mode as described at the top of the next page.

a. Double-click the cell containing the error. Excel switches to Edit mode, the cell contents appear in the formula bar, and a flashing insertion point appears in the cell (Figure 1-74). This editing procedure is called **in-cell editing** because you can edit the contents directly in the cell. The cell contents also appear in the formula bar. An alternative to double-clicking the cell is to select the cell and press the function key F2.

b. Make your changes, as specified below:

  (1) To insert between two characters, place the insertion point between the two characters and begin typing. Excel inserts the new characters at the location of the insertion point.

  (2) To delete a character in the cell, move the insertion point to the left of the character you want to delete and press the DELETE **key**, or place the insertion point to the right of the character you want to delete and press the BACKSPACE key. You can also use the mouse to drag over the character or adjacent characters to delete and press the DELETE key or click the Cut button ([✂]) on the Standard toolbar.

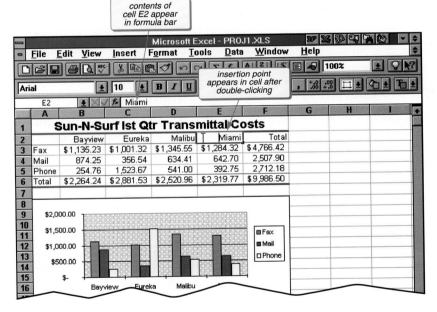

FIGURE 1-74

When you have finished editing an entry, click the enter box or press the ENTER key.

When Excel enters the Edit mode, the keyboard is usually in **Insert mode** (OVR does not display in the status bar). In Insert mode, as you type a character, Excel inserts the character and moves all characters to the right of the typed character one position to the right. You can change to **Overtype mode** (OVR displays in the status bar) by pressing the INSERT **key**. In Overtype mode, Excel overtypes the character to the right of the insertion point. The INSERT key toggles the keyboard between Insert mode and Overtype mode.

While in Edit mode, you may have occasion to move the insertion point to various points in the cell, select portions of the data in the cell, or switch from inserting characters to overtyping characters. Table 1-3 summarizes the most common tasks used during in-cell editing.

▶ **TABLE 1-3**

TASK	MOUSE	KEYBOARD
Move the insertion point to the beginning of data in a cell	Point to the left of the first character and click	Press HOME
Move the insertion point to the end of data in a cell	Point to the right of the last character and click	Press END
Move the insertion point anywhere in a cell	Click the character at the appropriate position	Press RIGHT ARROW or LEFT ARROW
Highlight one or more adjacent characters	Drag the mouse pointer over adjacent characters	Press SHIFT+RIGHT or LEFT ARROW
Select all data in a cell	Double-click the cell with the insertion point in the cell	
Delete selected characters	Click the Cut button on the Standard toolbar	Press DELETE
Toggle between Insert and Overtype modes		Press INSERT

Undoing the Last Entry — The Undo Command

Excel provides an Undo button (⟲) on the Standard toolbar (Figure 1-75) that you can use to erase the most recent cell entry. Thus, if you enter incorrect data in a cell, click the Undo button and Excel changes the cell contents to what they were prior to entering the incorrect data.

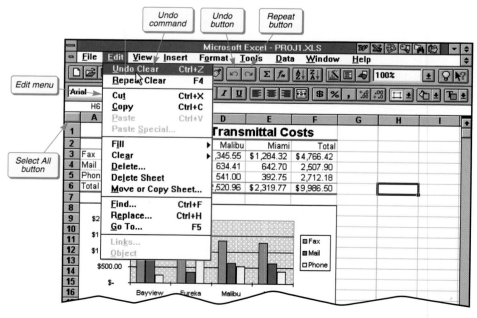

FIGURE 1-75

Using the Undo button you can undo more complicated worksheet activities than a single cell entry. For example, most commands you issue can be undone if you choose the Undo command before making another entry. The general rule is that the Undo command can restore the worksheet data and settings to what they were the last time Excel was in Ready mode. If Excel cannot undo an operation, then the button is inoperative. Next to the Undo button on the Standard toolbar is the Repeat button (⟳). The Repeat button allows you to repeat the last activity.

Finally, you can choose the Undo command from the Edit menu rather than using the Undo button. If Excel cannot undo an operation, then the words, Can't Undo, appear on the Edit menu in place of Undo.

Clearing a Cell or Range of Cells

It is not unusual to enter data into the wrong cell or range of cells. In such a case, to correct the error, you might want to erase or clear the data. **Never press the SPACEBAR to enter a blank character to clear a cell.** A blank character is text and is different than an empty cell, even though the cell may appear empty.

Excel provides three methods to clear the contents of a cell or a range of cells.

TO CLEAR CELL CONTENTS USING THE FILL HANDLE

Step 1: Select the cell or range of cells and point to the fill handle so the mouse pointer changes to a cross.
Step 2: Drag the fill handle back into the selected cell or range until a shadow covers the cell or cells you want to erase.
Step 3: Release the left mouse button.

TO CLEAR CELL CONTENTS USING THE DELETE KEY

Step 1: Select the cell or range of cells to be cleared.
Step 2: Press the DELETE key.

TO CLEAR CELL CONTENTS USING THE CLEAR COMMAND

Step 1: Select the cell or range of cells to be cleared.
Step 2: Choose Clear from the Edit menu.
Step 3: Choose All.

You can also select a range of cells and click the Cut button on the Standard toolbar, or choose the Cut command on the Edit menu. However, in addition to deleting the contents from the range, they also copy the contents of the range to the Clipboard.

Clearing the Entire Worksheet

Sometimes, everything goes wrong. If this happens, you may want to clear the worksheet entirely and start over. To clear the worksheet, follow these steps.

TO CLEAR THE ENTIRE WORKSHEET

Step 1: Select the entire worksheet by clicking the Select All button (▨)which is just above row heading 1 and immediately to the left of column heading A (Figure 1-75).
Step 2: Press the DELETE key or choose the Clear command from the Edit menu and choose All.

TO DELETE AN EMBEDDED CHART

Step 1: Click the chart.
Step 2: Press the DELETE key or choose the Clear command from the Edit menu and choose All.

An alternative to using the Select All button and the DELETE key or Clear command from the Edit menu to clear an entire worksheet is to delete the sheet from the workbook by using the Delete Sheet command on the Edit menu or choose the Close command on the File menu to close the workbook. If you choose the Close command to close a workbook, click the New Workbook button on the Standard toolbar or choose the **New command** on the File menu to begin working on an empty workbook.

▶ EXCEL ONLINE HELP

At any time while you are using Excel, you can select the **Help menu** to gain access to the **online Help** (Figure 1-76). The Excel Help menu provides a table of contents, a search command for navigating around the online Help, and an index of Help topics you may use to request help. Pressing function key F1 also allows you to obtain help on various topics.

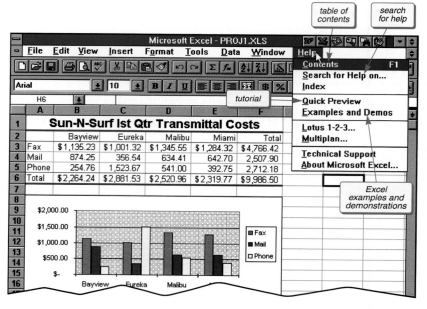

FIGURE 1-76

The **Quick Preview command** on the Help menu steps you through four short **tutorials** (Figure 1-77) that introduce you to the basics of Excel. Below each topic, Excel tells you approximately how long it will take to step through the tutorial (usually 4 to 7 minutes). The lesson titled Getting Started is highly recommended to help you become familiar with Excel. Before you begin the quick preview of Excel, click the Save button to save the workbook with your latest changes.

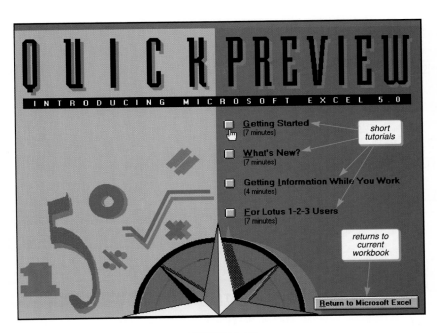

FIGURE 1-77

In many Excel dialog boxes you can click a Help button to obtain help about the current activity on which you are working. If there is no Help button in a dialog box, press function key F1 while the dialog box is on the screen.

Help Button on the Standard Toolbar

To use Excel online Help, you can click the **Help button** (⬚) on the Standard toolbar (top screen of Figure 1-78 on the next page). Move the arrow and question mark pointer (⬚) to any menu name, button, or cell, and click to get context-sensitive help. The term **context-sensitive help** means that Excel will display immediate information on the topic to which the arrow and question mark pointer is pointing. For example, clicking the Bold button displays the **Help window** shown in the bottom screen of Figure 1-78.

To print the Help information in the Help window, choose the **Print Topic command** from the File menu in the Help window. You close a Help window by choosing Exit from the File menu in the Help window.

Excel online Help has features that make it powerful and easy to use. The best way to familiarize yourself with the online Help is to use it.

Excel Online Examples and Demonstrations

To improve your Excel skills, you can step through the examples and demonstrations that come with Excel. Choose the **Examples and Demos command** on the Help menu (Figure 1-76). Excel responds by displaying the screen shown in Figure 1-79 on the next page. Click any of the twenty buttons to select a category of examples and demonstrations. Excel then displays a list of subtopics from which to choose. The Examples and Demos command provides interactive practice sessions on the features of Excel.

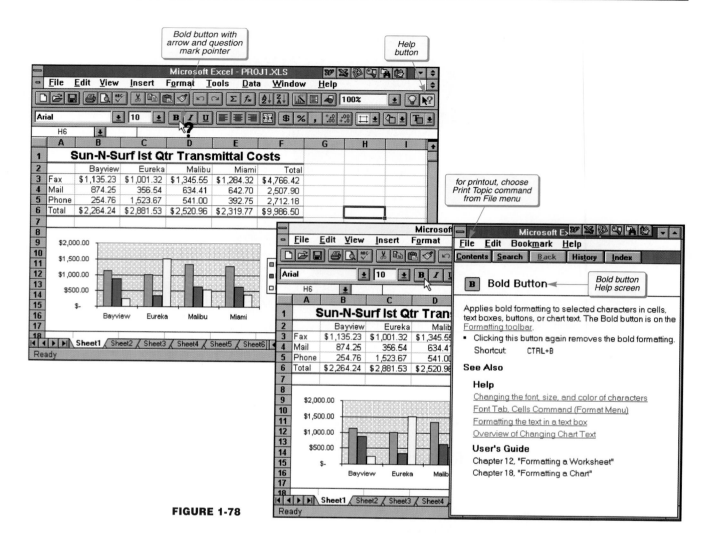

FIGURE 1-78

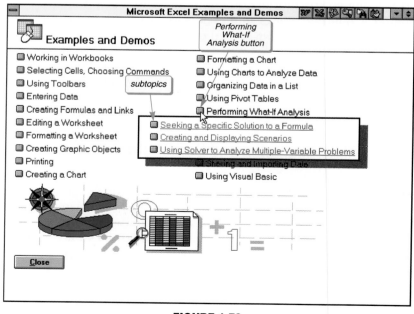

FIGURE 1-79

Information at Your Fingertips — TipWizard

Excel displays tips on how to work more efficiently in the **TipWizard Box**. When toggled on, the TipWizard Box displays at the top of the screen between the Formatting toolbar and formula bar (Figure 1-80). You toggle the TipWizard Box on or off by clicking the **TipWizard button** on the Standard toolbar. If toggled on when you start Excel, the TipWizard Box begins with a tip of the day. As you work through creating and editing a workbook, Excel adds tips to the TipWizard Box. The tips explain how to complete the activities you just performed more efficiently. You can scroll through these tips using the arrows to the right of the Tip-Wizard Box.

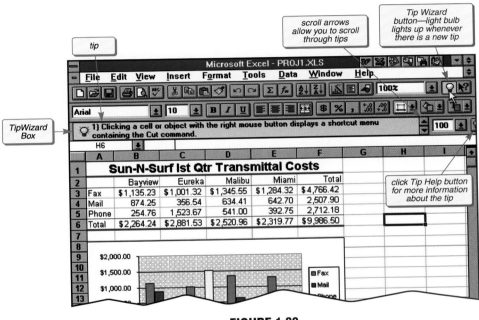

FIGURE 1-80

If the TipWizard Box is toggled off and Excel has a tip to offer you, the bulb on the TipWizard button lights up. To view the tip, click the TipWizard button.

▶ PLANNING A WORKSHEET

At the beginning of this project, the completed Sun-N-Surf 1st Qtr Transmittal Costs worksheet was presented in Figure 1-1 on page E3 and then built step by step. In the business world, you are seldom given the worksheet specifications in this form. Usually, the specifications for a worksheet are given to you verbally or in paragraph form on paper, and it is your responsibility to plan the worksheet from start to finish. Careful planning can significantly reduce your effort and result in a worksheet that is accurate, easy to read, flexible, and useful.

In planning a worksheet, you should follow these steps: (1) define the problem; (2) design the worksheet; (3) enter the worksheet; and, (4) test the worksheet. The following paragraphs describe these four steps in detail and outline how the Sun-N-Surf 1st Qtr Transmittal Costs worksheet in Figure 1-1 was planned.

Define the Problem

In this first step, write down on paper the following information:

1. The purpose of the worksheet.
2. The results or output you want, including such items as totals and charts.
3. Identify the data needed to determine the results.
4. List the required calculations to transform the data to the desired results.

Figure 1-81 shows one way to define the Sun-N-Surf 1st Qtr Transmittal Costs problem.

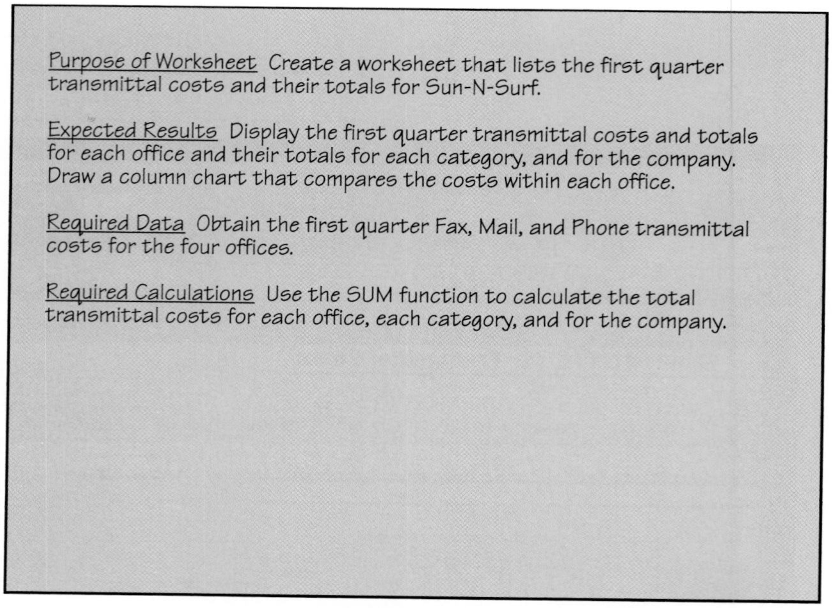

<u>Purpose of Worksheet</u> Create a worksheet that lists the first quarter transmittal costs and their totals for Sun-N-Surf.

<u>Expected Results</u> Display the first quarter transmittal costs and totals for each office and their totals for each category, and for the company. Draw a column chart that compares the costs within each office.

<u>Required Data</u> Obtain the first quarter Fax, Mail, and Phone transmittal costs for the four offices.

<u>Required Calculations</u> Use the SUM function to calculate the total transmittal costs for each office, each category, and for the company.

FIGURE 1-81

Design the Worksheet

In this second step, outline the worksheet on paper. Include the worksheet title, column titles, row titles, totals, and chart location if required.

Don't worry about the specific formats that will eventually be assigned to the worksheet. Figure 1-82 illustrates the outline for the Sun-N-Surf 1st Qtr Transmittal Costs worksheet. The series of 9s in Figure 1-82 indicates numeric entries.

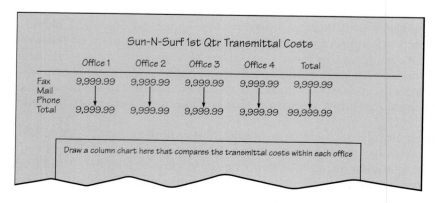

FIGURE 1-82

Enter the Worksheet

After defining the problem and outlining the worksheet, start Excel and enter the worksheet. One technique used by worksheet professionals is to type, in order: (1) the worksheet title; (2) column titles; (3) row titles; (4) numeric data; (5) functions or formulas; (6) after the worksheet is entered, format it to make it easier to read; and, (7) finally, add any required charts.

Test the Worksheet

Test the worksheet until it is error free. You want to be sure that the worksheet generates accurate results. Develop test data that evaluates the functions and formulas in the worksheet. Verify the results using paper, pencil, and a calculator. Begin by entering numbers that are easy to compute by hand and move to more complex entries that test the limits of the worksheet.

▶ PROJECT SUMMARY

Project 1 introduced you to starting Excel and entering text and numbers into a worksheet. You learned how to select a range and how to use the AutoSum button to sum numbers in a column or row. Using the fill handle, you learned how to copy a cell to adjacent cells.

Once the worksheet was built, you learned how to change the font size of the title, bold the title, and center the title over a range using buttons on the Formatting toolbar. Using the steps and techniques presented in the project, you formatted the body of the worksheet with the AutoFormat command, and you used the ChartWizard button to add a column chart. After completing the worksheet, you saved it on disk and printed it. You learned how to edit data in cells and previewed the use of Excel online Help. Finally, you learned how to plan a worksheet.

▶ KEY TERMS AND INDEX

active cell *(E6)*
active cell reference *(E6)*
arrow keys *(E9)*
AutoFormat command *(E27)*
AutoFormat dialog box *(E27)*
AutoSum button *(E17)*
BACKSPACE key *(E12)*
Bold button *(E23)*
cancel box *(E11)*
cell *(E6)*
cell gridlines *(E6)*
cell reference *(E6)*
Center Across Columns button *(E25)*
chart *(E30)*
chart sheet *(E37)*
ChartWizard button *(E31)*
clear cells *(E45)*
clear chart *(E46)*
clear worksheet *(E45)*
Close command *(E36)*
column *(E6)*
column chart *(E31)*

context-sensitive help *(E47)*
copy *(E19)*
copy area *(E19)*
database *(E2)*
decimal numbers *(E17)*
default chart type *(E34)*
DELETE key *(E43)*
Drives box *(E36)*
Edit menu *(E44)*
Edit mode *(E43)*
editing cells *(E43)*
embedded chart *(E30)*
empty cells *(E45)*
enter box *(E11)*
ENTER key *(E12)*
Enter mode *(E9)*
ESC key *(E12)*
Examples and Demos command *(E47)*
Excel *(E2)*
File menu *(E8)*
fill handle *(E19)*
font size *(E23)*

font style *(E23)*
font type *(E23)*
footer *(E40)*
format *(E22)*
Format menu *(E27)*
Formatting toolbar *(E8)*
formula bar *(E9)*
ghosted *(E24)*
gridlines *(E6)*
handle for charts *(E34)*
hard copy *(E37)*
header *(E40)*
Help button *(E47)*
Help menu *(E46)*
Help window *(E47)*
in-cell editing *(E43)*
Insert mode *(E43)*
insertion point *(E11)*
keyboard indicators *(E9)*
left-justified *(E12)*
legend *(E34)*
marquis *(E18)*
menu bar *(E8)*

KEY TERMS (continued)

mode indicators *(E9)*
mouse pointer shapes *(E6)*
name box *(E35)*
New command *(E46)*
numbers *(E15)*
online help *(E46)*
Open a worksheet *(E42)*
Open dialog box *(E41)*
Open File button *(E41)*
Overtype mode *(E43)*
paste area *(E19)*
point *(E23)*
point size *(E23)*
Print button *(E39)*
printing a worksheet *(E37)*
Print topic command *(E47)*
printout *(E37)*
Quick Preview command *(E46)*

quitting Excel *(E40)*
range *(E19)*
Ready mode *(E9)*
reference area *(E6)*
relative reference *(E19)*
right-justified *(E16)*
row *(E6)*
Save button *(E35)*
saving a worksheet *(E35)*
scroll arrow *(E7)*
scroll bar *(E7)*
scroll box *(E7)*
Select All button *(E44)*
select a cell *(E9)*
sheet tab *(E37)*
Shortcut menu *(E37)*
Standard toolbar *(E8)*
starting Excel *(E4)*

status bar *(E9)*
SUM function *(E17)*
tab *(E37)*
tab name *(E37)*
tab scrolling buttons *(E6)*
tab split box *(E7)*
table formats *(E26)*
text *(E9)*
TipWizard Box *(E5, E49)*
TipWizard button *(E5, E49)*
tutorial *(E46)*
Undo command *(E44)*
window *(E5)*
workbook *(E6)*
worksheet *(E6)*
worksheet window *(E7)*
. XLS *(E37)*

Q U I C K   R E F E R E N C E

In Microsoft Excel, you can accomplish a task in a number of ways. The following table provides a quick reference to each task presented in this project with its available options. The commands listed in the Menu column can be executed using either the keyboard or mouse. Many of the commands in the Menu column are also available on the shortcut menu.

Task	Mouse	Menu	Keyboard Shortcuts
AutoFormat	Click AutoFormat button on Standard toolbar	From Format menu, choose AutoFormat	
Bold	Click Bold button Standard toolbar	From Format menu, choose Cells; then select Font tab	Press CTRL+B
Cancel an Entry in the Formula Bar	Click cancel box in formula bar		Press ESC
Center Across Columns	Click Center Across Columns button on Formatting toolbar	From Format menu, choose Cells; then select Alignment tab	Press CTRL+1
Chart	Click ChartWizard button on Standard toolbar	From Insert menu, choose Chart	
Clear Cell Gridlines from Printout		From File menu, choose Page Setup; then select Sheet tab	
Clear Selected Cell or Range	Drag fill handle into cell or range	From Edit menu, choose Clear	Press DELETE

Task	Mouse	Menu	Keyboard Shortcuts
Clear Selected Worksheet		From Edit menu, choose Clear	Press DELETE
Complete an Entry in the Formula Bar	Click enter box in formula bar or click any cell		Press ENTER
Context-Sensitive Help	Click Help button on Standard toolbar		Press SHIFT+F1
Copy a Cell to Adjacent Cells	Drag fill handle across adjacent cells or click Copy button to copy and Paste button on Standard toolbar to paste	From Edit menu, choose Copy, select paste area, and from Edit menu, choose Paste	Press CTRL+C to copy; CTRL+V to paste
Delete a Selected Chart		From Edit menu, choose Clear	Press DELETE
Edit Cell Contents	Double-click cell to edit		Select cell; press F2
Font Size	Click Font Size box arrow on Formatting toolbar	From Format menu, choose Cells; then select Font tab	Press CTRL+1
Help		Select Help menu	Press F1
New Workbook	Click New Workbook button on Standard toolbar	From File menu, choose New	Press CTRL+N
Open a Workbook	Click Open button on Standard toolbar	From File menu, choose Open	Press CTRL+O
Print a Worksheet	Click Print button on Standard toolbar	From File menu, choose Print	Press CTRL+P
Quit Excel	Double-click Control-menu box	From File menu, choose Exit	Press ALT+F4
Save a Workbook	Click Save button on Standard toolbar	From File menu, choose Save As	Press CTRL+S or press F12
Select a Cell	Click cell or reference area and enter cell reference	From Edit menu, choose Goto	Press arrow or press F5
Select a Range	Drag mouse		Press SHIFT+arrow
Select the Entire Worksheet	Click Select All button		Press CTRL+A
Shortcut Menu	Click right mouse button		
Start Excel	Click Microsoft Excel button on Office Manager toolbar or double-click Microsoft Excel program-item icon	From File menu in Program Manager, choose Run; enter EXCEL.EXE	
Sum a Column or Row	Double-click AutoSum button on Standard toolbar	From Insert menu, choose Function	Press ALT+=
TipWizard	Click TipWizard on Standard toolbar		
Undo the Last Operation	Click Undo button on Standard toolbar	From Edit menu, choose Undo	Press CTRL+Z

STUDENT ASSIGNMENT 1
True/False

Instructions: Circle T if the statement is true or F if the statement is false.

T F 1. An Excel worksheet can contain up to 256 columns and 16,384 rows.
T F 2. One or more letters of the alphabet identify a worksheet column.
T F 3. Only rows numbered 0 through 18 are available when Excel begins.
T F 4. When Excel begins, it displays an empty workbook titled Sheet1.
T F 5. The TipWizard allows you to step through the list of tips provided in the current session.
T F 6. The active cell has a heavy border around it.
T F 7. The active cell reference displays at the bottom of the screen in the status bar.
T F 8. The Font Size box can be used to increase or decrease the font size of the entry in the selected cell.
T F 9. To clear the entry in the active cell, press the DELETE key.
T F 10. If you have not yet clicked the enter box or pressed the ENTER key or an arrow key to complete an entry in the formula bar, use the ESC key to erase the entry from the formula bar.
T F 11. The Select All button that selects the entire worksheet is located on the Standard toolbar.
T F 12. To copy a cell to adjacent cells, drag the fill handle on the lower right corner of the heavy border surrounding the active cell to adjacent cells.
T F 13. Numbers entered into a worksheet cannot contain decimal points.
T F 14. Text that is longer than the width of the column will always occupy two or more cells.
T F 15. When a number is entered in an active cell, it is normally aligned to the right in the cell.
T F 16. If you make a mistake while typing a number in the formula bar, you can use the BACKSPACE key to delete unwanted characters.
T F 17. A number entered into an active cell cannot contain a dollar sign, comma, or percent sign.
T F 18. When you click the AutoSum button, Excel proposes a range of cells to sum.
T F 19. Clicking the cancel box in the formula bar clears the entire worksheet.
T F 20. To open a workbook, click the Save button.

STUDENT ASSIGNMENT 2
Multiple Choice

Instructions: Circle the correct response.

1. A _____ is at the intersection of a column and a row.
   a. window
   b. cell
   c. button
   d. range
2. To enter a number into a cell, the cell must be _____.
   a. blank
   b. defined as a numeric cell
   c. the active cell
   d. both a and c

3. Which of the following is a valid number you can enter on a worksheet?
   a. 3.25
   b. 3.25%
   c. $3.25
   d. all of the above

4. When you enter text into the active cell, the text is _____ in the cell.
   a. aligned to the right
   b. aligned to the left
   c. centered
   d. decimal-aligned

5. Keyboard indicators display in the _____ bar.
   a. status
   b. menu
   c. title
   d. button

6. Excel uses the _____ between cell references to indicate a range.
   a. period (.)
   b. colon (:)
   c. semicolon (;)
   d. tilde (~)

7. To display a shortcut menu, _____.
   a. click the right mouse button
   b. click the left mouse button
   c. choose the Shortcut command from the File menu
   d. click the Select All button

8. The fill handle is located _____.
   a. on the menu bar
   b. on the toolbar
   c. on the heavy border that surrounds the active cell
   d. in the status bar

9. Which one of the following will quit Excel and return control to Windows?
   a. double-click the Control-menu box
   b. choose the Close command from the File menu
   c. click the New Workbook button on the Standard toolbar
   d. choose the Clear command from the Edit menu

10. To select the entire worksheet, click the _____.
    a. Select All button
    b. ChartWizard button
    c. Open button
    d. Save button

STUDENT ASSIGNMENT 3
Understanding the Excel Worksheet

Instructions: In Figure SA1-3, arrows point to the major components of the Excel window and bars. Identify the various parts of the windows and bars in the space provided.

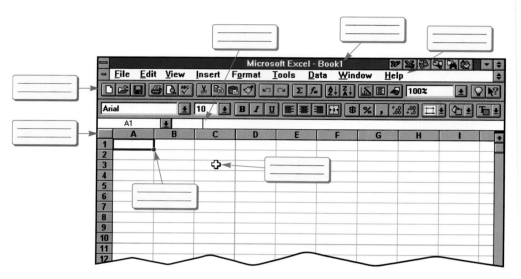

FIGURE SA1-3

STUDENT ASSIGNMENT 4
Understanding Toolbars

Instructions: In the worksheet in Figure SA1-4, arrows point to several of the buttons on the Standard and Formatting toolbars. In the space provided, briefly explain the purpose of each button.

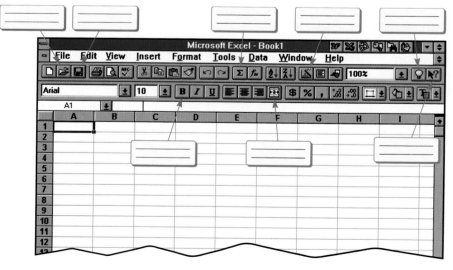

FIGURE SA1-4

STUDENT ASSIGNMENT 5
Understanding the Formula Bar on the Worksheet

Instructions: Answer the following questions concerning the contents of the formula bar area in Figure SA1-5.

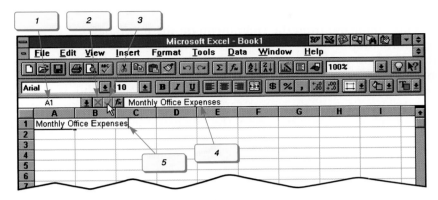

FIGURE SA1-5

1. What does the A1 signify in the reference area on the left side of the formula bar? _____

2. What is the purpose of the box in the formula bar that contains the letter X? _____

3. What is the purpose of the box in the formula bar that contains the check mark? _____

4. How would you complete the entry of the text in the formula bar, Monthly Office Expenses, into cell A1 without using the mouse and maintain cell A1 as the active cell? _____

5. What do you call the vertical line that follows the text in cell A1? _____

STUDENT ASSIGNMENT 6
Understanding the AutoSum Button on the Standard Toolbar

Instructions: Answer the following questions after reviewing the entries on the worksheet in Figure SA1-6.

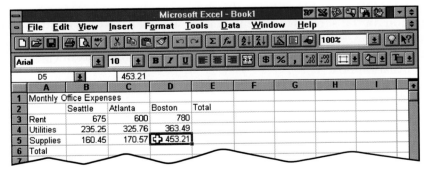

FIGURE SA1-6

1. List the steps to use the AutoSum button to sum the range B3:B5 and assign it to cell B6. Then, copy the SUM function to cells C6 and D6.

_____

2. List the steps to use the AutoSum button on the Standard toolbar to sum the range B3:D5 and produce both the row totals and column totals in the most efficient manner.

_____

COMPUTER LABORATORY EXERCISE 1
Using the Help Menu, Help Button, and Excel Tutorial

Part 1 Instructions: Start Excel and perform the following tasks using a computer.

1. Choose the Contents command from the Help menu on the menu bar.
2. Click Reference Information.
3. Click Parts of the Microsoft Excel Screen.
4. Click Sheet Tab.
5. Read the paragraph. Use the scroll arrow in the lower right corner of the Help window to scroll through and read the rest of the topic.
6. Ready the printer and choose Print Topic from the File menu in the Help window to print a hard copy of the Sheet Tab help topic.
7. To return to the original Help screen, click the Contents button in the upper left corner of the Help window.
8. Use the technique described in Steps 3 and 4 to display help on any other topic listed.
9. To close the Help window, double-click the Control-menu box in the Help window title bar.
10. Click the Help button on the Standard toolbar.
11. Point at the AutoSum button and click.
12. Ready the printer and choose Print Topic from the File menu in the Help window.
13. Close the Help window as described in Step 9.

Part 2 Instructions: Start Excel and perform the following tasks using a computer.

1. Choose Quick Preview from the Help menu and select, one at a time, these previews: Getting Started and Getting Information While You Work.
2. Close the Quick Preview by clicking on the Close button (Close) in the lower left corner of the screen and then click the Return to Microsoft Excel button (Return to Microsoft Excel) in the lower right corner of the screen.

Part 3 Instructions: Start Excel and perform the following tasks using a computer.

1. Choose Examples and Demos from the Help menu.
2. Click the Using Toolbars button.
3. Click the Displaying, Hiding, and Moving Toolbars button.
4. Read the information on the screen and then click the Practice (Practice) button in the lower right corner of the screen.
5. Read the information about displaying a toolbar and click the Hint button (Hint) in the lower right corner of the information box.
6. Read the hint and click the Show me button (Show Me) in the lower right corner of the hint box.
7. Read the information in the show me box and observe the floating toolbar that appears on the sample worksheet on the screen.
8. Close the Examples and Demos by clicking the Close button in the lower left corner of the show me box. Next, click the Close button in the lower left corner of the Examples and Demos screen.

COMPUTER LABORATORY EXERCISE 2
Formatting a Worksheet

Instructions: Start Excel. Open the workbook CLE1-2 from the subdirectory Excel5 on the Student Diskette that accompanies this book. The worksheet is shown at the top of Figure CLE1-2. Perform the tasks at the top of the next page to change it so it resembles the worksheet in the lower portion of Figure CLE1-2.

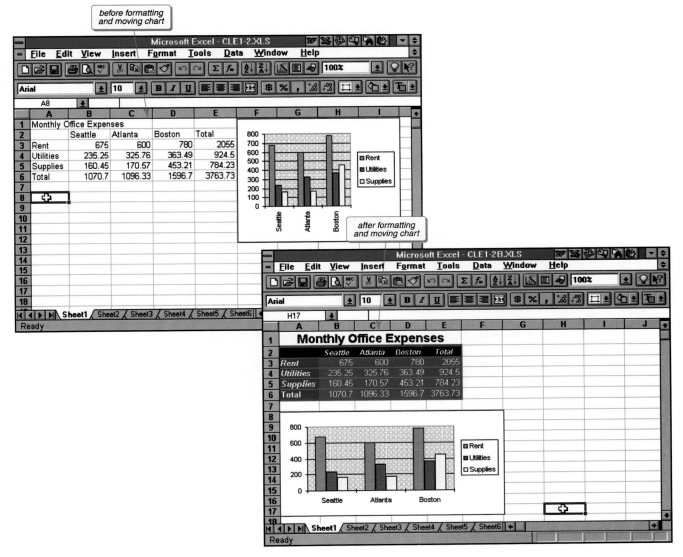

FIGURE CLE1-2

(continued)

COMPUTER LABORATORY EXERCISE 2 (continued)

1. Increase the font size of the worksheet title in cell A1 to 14 point by clicking the Font Size box arrow on the Formatting toolbar and selecting 14 in the Font Size drop-down list box.
2. Bold the worksheet title in cell A1.
3. Center the worksheet title in cell A1 across columns A through E.
4. Select the range A2:E6.
5. Choose the AutoFormat command from the Format menu and review the seventeen formats in the Sample box by selecting each one using the mouse.
6. Select the Colorful 1 format and choose OK from the AutoFormat dialog box.
7. Move the chart from its current location to the range A8:F17 as shown in the lower portion of Figure CLE1-2.
8. Choose the Page Setup command from the shortcut menu or File menu. Select the Sheet tab. Turn Gridlines off. Choose OK from the Page Setup dialog box.
9. Click the Print button on the Standard toolbar to print the worksheet with the new format.
10. Save the workbook using the filename CLE1-2B.
11. Select the column chart and delete it using the DELETE key.
12. Click the Print button to print the worksheet.
13. Choose the Close command from the File menu to close the workbook.

COMPUTER LABORATORY EXERCISE 3
Changing Data in a Worksheet

Instructions: Start Excel. Open the workbook CLE1-3 from the subdirectory Excel5 on the Student Diskette that accompanies this book. As shown in Figure CLE1-3, the worksheet is a semiannual income and expense worksheet. Perform the tasks at the top of the next page.

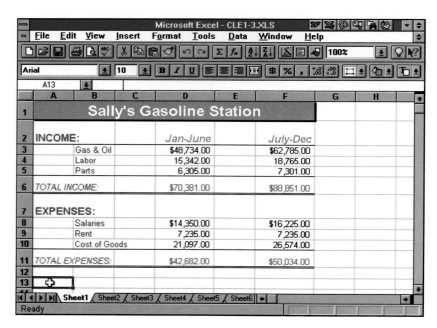

FIGURE CLE1-3

1. Make the changes to the worksheet described in the table below. As you edit the values in the cells containing numeric data, watch the total income (cells D6 and F6) and total expenses (cells D11 and F11). Each of the values in these four cells is based on the SUM function. When you enter a new value, Excel automatically recalculates the SUM functions. After you have successfully made the changes listed in the table, the total incomes in cells D6 and F6 should equal $126,882.00 and $127,811.00, respectively. The total expenses in cells D11 and F11 should equal $50,689.00 and $53,685.00, respectively.
2. Save the workbook using the filename CLE1-3B.
3. Print the revised worksheet without gridlines.

CELL	CURRENT CELL CONTENTS	CHANGE CELL CONTENTS TO
A1	Sally's Gasoline Station	Sal's Gas Station
D3	48734	48535
F3	62785	61523
D5	6305	63005
F5	7301	47523
D8	14350	22357
F8	16225	19876

COMPUTER LABORATORY ASSIGNMENTS

COMPUTER LABORATORY ASSIGNMENT 1
Building and Modifying a College Cost Analysis Worksheet

Purpose: To become familiar with building a worksheet, formatting a worksheet, embedding a column chart, printing a worksheet, and saving a workbook.

Problem: As a student assistant working in the Financial Aid office, you have been asked by the director to project the expenses for attending college for two semesters and a summer session. The estimated costs are shown in the table on the next page.

Instructions: Perform the tasks below and on the next page:

1. Create the worksheet shown in Figure CLA1-1 on the next page using the numbers in the table. Enter the text and numbers into the cells described in the worksheet.
2. Direct Excel to determine the totals for Semester 1, Semester 2, Summer, Tuition, Books, Lab Fees, and a total for the three semesters.

(continued)

COMPUTER LABORATORY ASSIGNMENT 1 (continued)

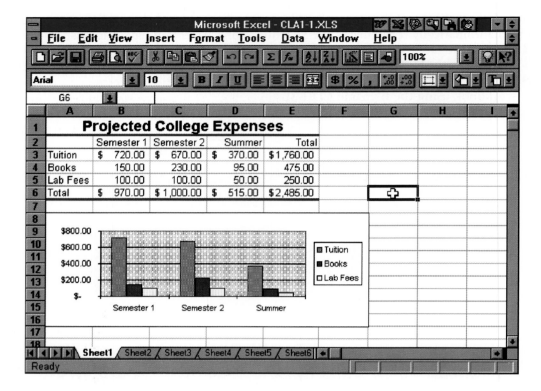

FIGURE CLA1-1

	SEMESTER 1	SEMESTER 2	SUMMER
TUITION	720.00	670.00	370.00
BOOKS	150.00	230.00	95.00
LAB FEES	100.00	100.00	50.00

3. Format the worksheet title, Projected College Expenses, as 14 point, bold, and centered over columns A through E.
4. Format the range A2:E6 using the table format Accounting 2 as shown in the worksheet in Figure CLA1-1.
5. Use the ChartWizard button to draw the column chart shown on the worksheet in Figure CLA1-1. Chart the range A2:D5.
6. Enter your name in cell A19. Enter your course, computer laboratory assignment number (CLA1-1), date, and instructor name below in cells A20 through A23.
7. Save the workbook using the filename CLA1-1.
8. Print the worksheet with cell gridlines off.
9. Increase the tuition by $200.00 for Semester 1 and Semester 2. Increase the cost of books by $25.00 for all three semesters. Increase the Lab fees by $25.00 for Semester 2. The three semester totals should be $1,195.00, $1,250.00, and $540.00, respectively. Print the worksheet containing the new values with cell gridlines off.

COMPUTER LABORATORY ASSIGNMENT 2
Creating a Daily Sales Report Worksheet

Purpose: To become familiar with building a worksheet, formatting a worksheet, embedding a column chart, printing a worksheet, and saving a workbook.

Problem: The Music City company has hired you to work in its Information Systems Department as a part-time consultant. The president of the company has requested that a worksheet be created showing a daily sales summary report for the company's three stores. The request has been turned over to you to handle. The report is to list the daily sales in each store for compact discs (CDs), cassettes, and videos. The daily sales are shown in the table below.

Instructions: Perform the tasks below and on the next page:

1. Create the worksheet shown in Figure CLA1-2 using the numbers in the table below.

	STORE 1	STORE 2	STORE 3
CDs	775.29	600.51	995.17
CASSETTES	550.38	425.43	605.24
VIDEOS	350.65	250.33	400.17

2. Direct Excel to determine the totals for Store 1, Store 2, Store 3, CDs, Cassettes, Videos, and all the stores.

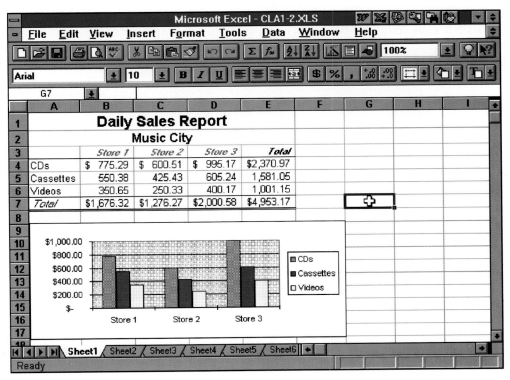

FIGURE CLA1-2

(continued)

COMPUTER LABORATORY ASSIGNMENT 2 (continued)

3. Format the worksheet title, Daily Sales Report, as 14 point, bold, and centered over columns A through E.
4. Format the worksheet subtitle, Music City, as 12 point, bold, and centered over columns A through E.
5. Format the range A3:E7 using the table format Accounting 1 as shown on Figure CLA1-2.
6. Use the ChartWizard button to draw the column chart shown on the worksheet in Figure CLA1-2. Chart the range A3:D6.
7. Enter your name in cell A19. Enter your course, computer laboratory assignment number (CLA1-2), date, and instructor name below the chart in cells A20 through A23.
8. Save the workbook using the filename CLA1-2.
9. Print the worksheet with cell gridlines on.
10. Print the worksheet with cell gridlines off. Save the workbook using the filename CLA1-2.
11. Make the following changes to the daily sales: Store 1, CDs — $546.34, Store 2, Videos — $395.45, and Store 3, Cassettes — $943.67. The new three-store totals should be $1,447.37, $1,421.39, and $2,339.01.
12. Select the chart and increase its width by one column.
13. Print the modified worksheet with cell gridlines off.

COMPUTER LABORATORY ASSIGNMENT 3
Creating a Personal Financial Statement

Purpose: To become familiar with building a worksheet, formatting a worksheet, embedding a column chart, printing a worksheet, and saving a workbook.

Problem: To obtain a bank loan, the bank has requested you to supply a personal financial statement. The statement is to include your average monthly income for the last three years and all major expenses. The data required to prepare your financial statement is shown in the table below.

	1993	1994	1995
INCOME:			
Wages	1200.00	1450.00	1550.00
Tips	300.00	425.00	550.00
EXPENSES:			
Rent	650.00	700.00	850.00
Utilities	125.00	150.00	160.00
Insurance	125.00	140.00	200.00

Instructions: Using the numbers in the table, create the worksheet shown in Figure CLA1-3 including the chart of expenses. Use the AutoSum button to calculate the total income and total expenses for each of the three years. Enter your name in cell A19 and your course, computer laboratory assignment number (CLA1-3), date, and instructor name in cells A20 through A23.

To format the worksheet, use the table format Accounting 1 for the Income table and then again for the Expenses table.

Save the workbook using the filename CLA1-3. Print the worksheet without cell gridlines.

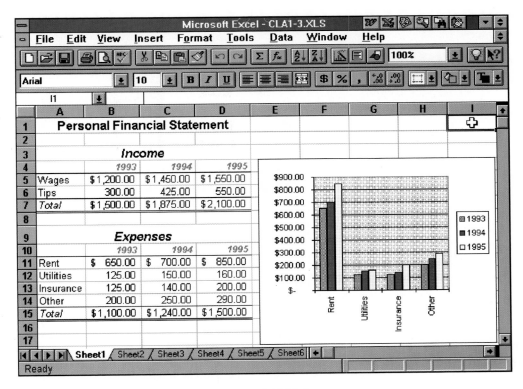

FIGURE CLA1-3

COMPUTER LABORATORY ASSIGNMENT 4
Planning a Weekly Expense Account Report

Purpose: To provide practice in planning and building a worksheet.

Problem: While in college, you are serving an internship in the Office Automation department of the Academic Textbook Company (ATC). ATC is a publishing company that sells textbooks to high schools and colleges throughout the United States. The company has sales representatives that are reimbursed for the following expenses: lodging, meals, and travel.

You have been asked to create for distribution a worksheet that the sales representatives can use as a weekly expense report. Beginning next month, the weekly expense report must be submitted by each sales representative to the regional sales manager of the company by Wednesday of the following week. The sheet should summarize the daily expenses and the total weekly expense. Expenses are only paid for Monday, Tuesday, Wednesday, Thursday, and Friday, the days on which the sales representatives can call upon teachers at the schools.

Instructions: Design and create the Weekly Expense Report. Develop your own test data. Submit the following:

1. A description of the problem. Include the purpose of the worksheet, a statement outlining the results, the required data, and calculations.
2. A handwritten design of the worksheet. This document should be approved by your manager (your instructor) before you build the worksheet.
3. A printed copy of the worksheet without cell gridlines.
4. A one-page, double-spaced typewritten description of the worksheet explaining to the sales representatives its purpose, how to retrieve it, how to enter data into it, save it, and print it.
5. Use the techniques you learned in this project to format the worksheet. Include a column chart that compares the daily costs.
6. Enter your name, course, computer laboratory assignment number (CLA1-4), date, and instructor name below the chart in column A. Save the workbook using the filename CLA1-4.

MICROSOFT EXCEL 5 FOR WINDOWS

PROJECT TWO

FORMULAS, FORMATTING, AND CREATING CHARTS

OBJECTIVES You will have mastered the material in this project when you can:

- ▸ Enter a formula
- ▸ Use the Point mode to enter formulas
- ▸ Identify the arithmetic operators +, −, *, /, %, and ^
- ▸ Determine a percentage
- ▸ Apply the AVERAGE, MAX, and MIN functions
- ▸ Change a cell's font
- ▸ Change the font of individual characters in a cell
- ▸ Color the characters and background of a cell
- ▸ Align text in cells
- ▸ Add borders to a range of cells
- ▸ Change a column width or row height to best fit

- ▸ Change the width of a series of adjacent columns
- ▸ Change the height of a row
- ▸ Check the spelling of a worksheet
- ▸ Create a chart on a separate sheet
- ▸ Format chart items
- ▸ Rename sheet tabs
- ▸ Preview how a printed copy of the worksheet and chart sheet will look
- ▸ Print an entire workbook
- ▸ Print a partial or complete worksheet
- ▸ Display and print the formulas version of a worksheet
- ▸ Print to fit
- ▸ Distinguish between portrait and landscape orientation

▶ INTRODUCTION

In Project 1, you learned about entering data, summing values, making the worksheet easier to read, and drawing a chart. You also learned about online Help and saving, printing, and loading a workbook from disk into main memory. This project continues to emphasize these topics and presents some new ones.

The new topics include entering formulas, changing fonts, coloring characters in a cell and the background of a cell, adding borders, changing the widths of columns and heights of rows, spell checking, using additional charting techniques, and producing alternative types of printouts. One alternative display and printout shows the formulas rather than the values in the worksheet. When you display the formulas in the worksheet, you see exactly what text, data, formulas, and functions you have entered into it.

E66

▶ PROJECT TWO — AWESOME SOUND INTERNATIONAL SALES ANALYSIS

T he worksheet in Project 2 (Figure 2-1) contains a sales report for the month of May that shows the gross sales, returns, net sales, and percent returns by division for Awesome Sound International. In addition, for the gross sales, returns, net sales, and percent returns, the worksheet includes totals in row 9, averages in row 10, and highest and lowest values in rows 11 and 12. On a separate sheet, a 3-D column chart compares the sales by division.

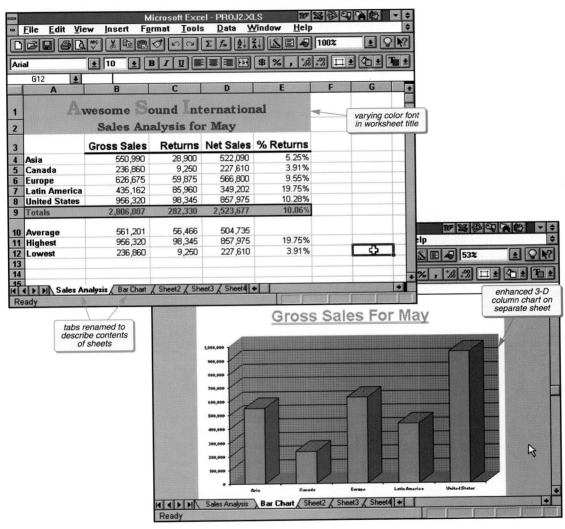

FIGURE 2-1

To improve the appearance of the worksheet and to make it easier to read, the numbers in the worksheet are formatted. The widths of columns A through E and the heights of rows 3 and 10 are increased to add more space between the titles and numbers.

In Figure 2-1, the gross sales in column B and the returns in column C make up the data sent to the accounting department from the division offices throughout the world. You enter the numbers into the worksheet in the same fashion as described in Project 1.

Each division's net sales figure in column D is equal to the gross sales in column B minus the returns in column C and is calculated from a formula. Each division's percent return in column E is the quotient of the returns in column C divided by the gross sales in column B. Row 9 contains the total gross sales, total returns, total net sales, and percent returns for all sales. Finally, rows 10 through 12 contain the average, maximum and minimum gross sales, returns, and net sales.

▶ ENTERING THE TITLES AND NUMBERS INTO THE WORKSHEET

T he worksheet title and subtitle in Figure 2-1 on the previous page are centered over columns A through E in rows 1 and 2. Because the centered text must first be entered into the leftmost column of the area over which it is to be centered, it will be entered into cells A1 and A2. The column headings in row 3 begin in cell B3 and extend through cell E3. The row titles in column A begin in cell A4 and continue down to cell A12. The numbers are entered into the range B4:C8. The total gross sales in cell B9 and the total returns in cell C9 are determined using the SUM function. The steps required to enter the worksheet title, column titles, row titles, numbers, and determine the totals in cells B9 and C9 are outlined in the remainder of this section and are shown in Figure 2-2.

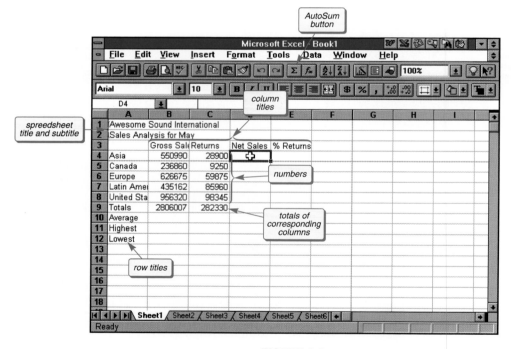

FIGURE 2-2

TO ENTER THE WORKSHEET TITLES

Step 1: Select cell A1. Type Awesome Sound International and click the enter box or press the ENTER key

Step 2: Select cell A2. Type Sales Analysis for May and click the enter box or press the ENTER key.

The worksheet titles display as shown in cells A1 and A2 of Figure 2-2.

TO ENTER THE COLUMN TITLES

Step 1: Select cell B3. Type `Gross Sales` and press the RIGHT ARROW key.
Step 2: Enter the column titles `Returns`, `Net Sales`, and `% Returns` in cells C3, D3, and E3 in the same fashion as described in Step 1.

The column titles display as shown in row 3 of Figure 2-2. Don't be concerned that a portion of the column title Gross Sales is hidden. Later, the column widths will be increased so it will display in its entirety.

TO ENTER THE ROW TITLES

Step 1: Select cell A4. Type `Asia` and press the DOWN ARROW key.
Step 2: Enter the row titles `Canada`, `Europe`, `Latin America`, `United States`, `Totals`, `Average`, `Highest`, and `Lowest` in cells A5 through A12.

The row titles display as shown in column A of Figure 2-2.

TO ENTER THE NUMBERS

Step 1: Enter `550990` in cell B4 and `28900` in cell C4.
Step 2: Enter `236860` in cell B5 and `9250` in cell C5.
Step 3: Enter `626675` in cell B6 and `59875` in cell C6.
Step 4: Enter `435162` in cell B7 and `85960` in cell C7.
Step 5: Enter `956320` in cell B8 and `98345` in cell C8.

The numeric entries display as shown in the range B4:C8 of Figure 2-2.

TO ENTER THE TOTALS

Step 1: Select the range B9:C9.
Step 2: Click the AutoSum button on the Standard toolbar.
Step 3: Select cell D4.

The totals for the gross sales and returns display in cells B9 and C9, respectively (Figure 2-2).

▶ ENTERING FORMULAS

The net sales for each division, which displays in column D, is equal to the corresponding gross sales in column B minus the corresponding returns in column C. Thus, the net sales for the Asia division in row 4 is obtained by subtracting 28900 (cell C4) from 550990 (cell B4).

One of the reasons Excel is such a valuable tool is because you can assign a **formula** to a cell and Excel will calculate the result. In this example, the formula in cell D4 subtracts the value in cell C4 from the value in cell B4 and displays the result in cell D4. The steps to enter the formula using the keyboard are described on the next page.

TO ENTER A FORMULA THROUGH THE KEYBOARD ▼

STEP 1 ►

Select cell D4. Type =b4-c4

The formula displays in the formula bar and in cell D4 (Figure 2-3).

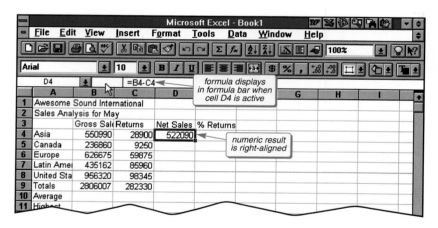

FIGURE 2-3

STEP 2 ►

Click the enter box or press the ENTER key.

Instead of displaying the formula in cell D4, Excel completes the arithmetic indicated by the formula and displays the result, 522090 in cell D4 (Figure 2-4).

FIGURE 2-4

The equal sign (=) preceding b4-c4 is an important part of the formula. It alerts Excel that you are entering a formula or function and not text, such as words. The minus sign (–) following b4 is the arithmetic operator, which directs Excel to perform the subtraction operation. Other valid Excel arithmetic operators include + (**addition**), * (**multiplication**), / (**division**), % (**percentage**), and ^ (**exponentiation**).

You can enter formulas in uppercase or lowercase, and you can add spaces between the arithmetic operators to make the formulas easier to read. That is, =b4-c4 is the same as =B4-C4, =b4 - c4 or =B4 - C4. Notice in Figure 2-4 that Excel displays the formula in the formula bar in uppercase when cell D4 is the active cell even though it was entered earlier in lowercase.

Except for row references, the formulas required to compute the net sales for the other regions in column D are the same as the formula in cell D4. Hence, you can use the fill handle in the lower right corner of the heavy border that surrounds the active cell (Figure 2-4) to copy cell D4 down through the range D5:D9.

TO COPY A FORMULA IN ONE CELL TO ADJACENT CELLS ▼

STEP 1 ▶

Select cell D4, the cell to copy. Point to the fill handle.

The mouse pointer changes to a cross (Figure 2-5).

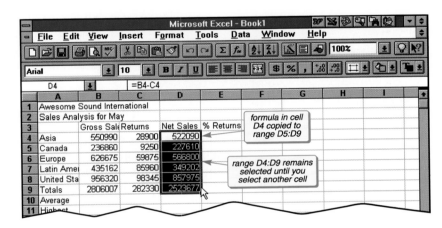

FIGURE 2-5

STEP 2 ▶

Drag the fill handle down to select the range D5:D9 and then release the left mouse button.

Excel copies the formula in cell D4 (=B4-C4) to the range D5:D9 and displays the net sales for the remaining divisions (Figure 2-6).

FIGURE 2-6

Select any cell to remove the selection from the range D4:D9.

When Excel copies the formula =B4-C4 in cell D4 to the range D5:D9, the row references in the formula are adjusted as the formula is copied downward. For example, the formula assigned to cell D5 is =B5-C5. Similarly, Excel assigns cell D6 the formula =B6-C6, cell D7 the formula =B7-C7, cell D8 the formula =B8-C8, and cell D9 the formula =B9-C9. When you copy downward, the row reference changes in the formula.

Order of Operations

In the formulas in column D, only one arithmetic operation is involved, subtraction. When more than one operator is involved in a formula, Excel uses the same order of operations that algebra follows. Moving from left to right in a formula, the **order of operations** is as follows: first negation (-), then all percents (%), then all exponentiations (^), then all multiplications (*) and divisions (/), and finally all additions (+) and subtractions (-). You can use **parentheses** to override the order of operations. All operations within parentheses ae performed before the operations outside the parentheses.

For example, following the order of operations, 8 * 5 - 2 is equal to 38. However, 8 * (5 - 2) is equal to 24 because the parentheses instruct Excel to subtract 2 from 5 before multiplying by 8. Table 2-1 illustrates several examples of valid formulas.

▸ **TABLE 2-1**

FORMULA	REMARK
=E3	Assigns the value in cell E3 to the active cell.
=5 + -10^2	Assigns 105 to the active cell.
=7 * F5 or =F5 * 7 or =(7 * F5)	Assigns seven times the contents of cell F5 to the active cell.
=525 * 15%	Assigns the product of 525 times 0.15 to the active cell.
=-G44 * G45	Assigns the negative value of the product of the values contained in cells G44 and G45 to the active cell.
=2 * (J12 - F2)	Assigns the product of two times the difference between the values contained in cells J12 and F2 to the active cell.
=A1 / C6 - A3 * A4 + A5 ^ A6	From left to right: first exponentiation (A5 ^ A6), then division (A1 / C6), then multiplication (A3 * A4), then subtraction (A1 / C6 - A3 * A4), and finally addition (A1 / C6 - A3 * A4 + A5 ^ A6). If cells A1 = 10, A3 = 6, A4 = 2, A5 = 5, A6 = 2, and C6 = 2, then Excel assigns the active cell the value 18 (10 / 2 - 6 * 2 + 5 ^ 2 = 18).

▸ ENTERING FORMULAS USING THE POINT MODE

In the worksheet shown in Figure 2-1 on page E67, the percent returns for each division display in column E. The percent returns for the Asia division in cell E4 is equal to the returns (cell C4) divided by the gross sales (cell B4). Recall that the slash (/) represents the operation of division.

Rather than entering the formula =c4/b4 in cell E4 completely through the keyboard as was done with net sales in cell D4, the following steps show how to use the mouse and the Point mode to enter a formula. **Point mode** allows you to select cells to be used in a formula by using the mouse.

TO ENTER A FORMULA USING POINT MODE ▾

STEP 1 ▶

Select cell E4. Type the equal sign (=) in the formula bar to begin the formula and click cell C4.

Excel responds by highlighting cell C4 with a moving border and by appending cell C4 to the equal sign in the formula bar and in cell E4 (Figure 2-7).

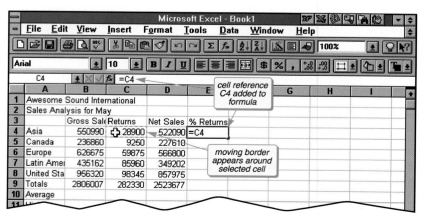

FIGURE 2-7

STEP 2 ▶

Type the slash (/) in the formula bar and click cell B4.

Excel highlights cell B4 with a moving border and appends cell B4 to the slash (/) in the formula bar and in cell E4 (Figure 2-8).

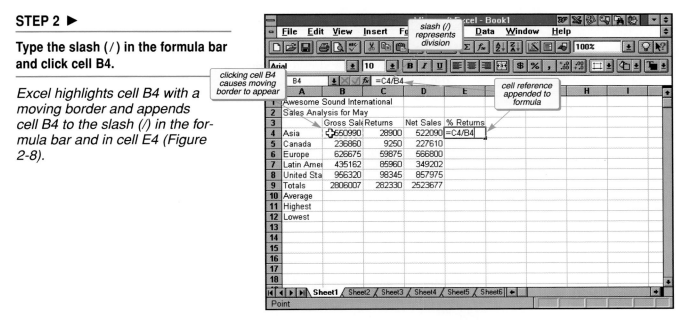

FIGURE 2-8

STEP 3 ▶

Click the enter box or press the ENTER key.

Excel determines the quotient of =C4/B4 and stores the result, 0.052451, in cell E4 (Figure 2-9).

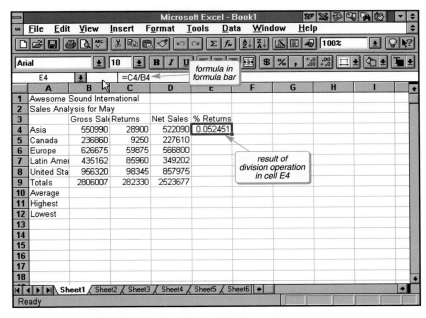

FIGURE 2-9

Later in this project the percent returns, 0.052451, will be formatted to 5.25%.

To complete the percent returns for the remaining divisions and the total line in row 9, use the fill handle to copy cell E4 to the range E5:E9. Perform the following steps to complete the copy.

TO COPY A FORMULA IN ONE CELL TO ADJACENT CELLS

Step 1: Select E4, the cell to copy. Point to the fill handle.
Step 2: Drag the fill handle down to select the range E5:E9 and then release the left mouse button.

Excel copies the formula in cell E4 to the range E5:E9 and displays the percent returns in decimal form for those cells (Figure 2-10).

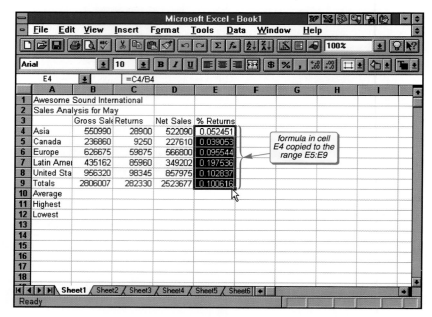

FIGURE 2-10

▶ USING THE AVERAGE, MAX, AND MIN FUNCTIONS

The next step in creating the Sales Analysis report is to compute the average gross sales, place it in cell B10, and then copy it to the range C10:D10 to calculate the average returns and average net sales. The average gross sales can be computed by assigning to cell B10 the formula =(B4 + B5 + B6 + B7 + B8) / 5, but Excel includes an **AVERAGE function** that is much easier to use.

A **function** is a prewritten formula that takes a value or values, performs an operation, and returns a value or values. The values that you give to a function to perform operations on are called the **arguments**. All functions begin with an equal sign and include the arguments in parentheses after the function name. For example, in the function =AVERAGE(B4:B8), the function name is AVERAGE and the argument is the range B4:B8. Perform the following steps to assign the AVERAGE function to cell B10.

TO FIND THE AVERAGE OF A GROUP OF NUMBERS ▼

STEP 1 ▶

Select cell B10. Type =average(

Excel displays the beginning of the AVERAGE function in the formula bar and in cell B10 (Figure 2-11).

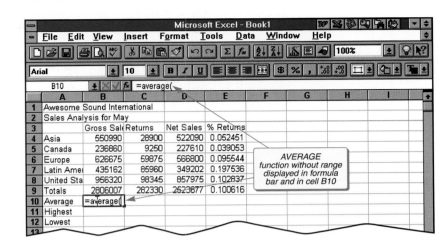

FIGURE 2-11

STEP 2 ▶

Select cell B4, the first end point of the range to average. Drag the mouse pointer down to cell B8, the second end point of the range to average.

A marquis surrounds the range B4:B8. When you select cell B4, Excel appends cell B4 to the left parenthesis in the formula bar and highlights cell B4 with a moving border. When you begin dragging, Excel appends a colon (:) to the function and also the cell reference of the cell where the mouse pointer is located (Figure 2-12).

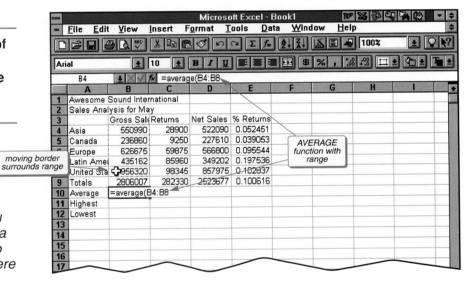

FIGURE 2-12

STEP 4 ▶

Release the left mouse button, and then click the enter box or press the ENTER key.

Excel computes the average, 561201.4, of the five numbers in the range B4:B8 and assigns it to cell B10 (Figure 2-13).

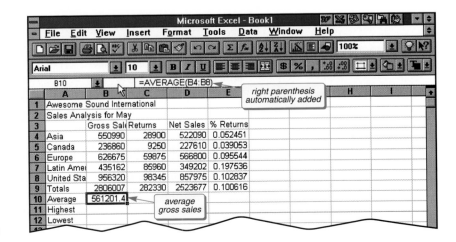

FIGURE 2-13

Notice that Excel automatically appends the right parenthesis to complete the AVERAGE function when you click the enter box or press the ENTER key. The AVERAGE function requires that the range (the argument) be included within parentheses following the function name.

The example just illustrated used the Point mode to select the range following the left parenthesis. Instead of using Point mode, you can type the range. If you decide to type a range, remember that the colon (:) separating the endpoints of the range is required punctuation.

The next two required entries are the average returns in cell C10 and the average net sales in cell D10. Except for the ranges, these two entries are identical to the AVERAGE function in cell B9. Thus, you can use the fill handle to copy cell B10 to the range C10:D10.

Notice this project does not average in cell E10 the percent returns in column E because these values use different denominators. Thus, the average percent returns would make no sense.

TO COPY A FUNCTION IN ONE CELL TO ADJACENT CELLS

Step 1: Select cell B10, the cell to copy. Point to the fill handle.
Step 2: Drag the fill handle across the range C10:D10 and then release the left mouse button.

Excel copies the AVERAGE function in cell B10 to the range C10:D10 and displays 56466 in cell C10 and 504735.4 in cell D10 (Figure 2-14).

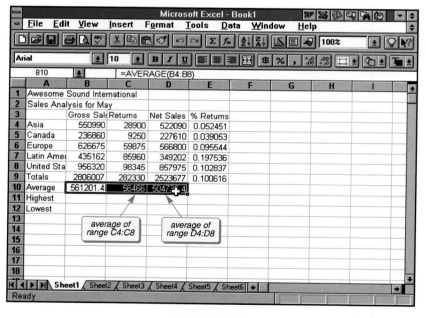

FIGURE 2-14

Calculating the Highest Value in a Range Using the MAX Function

The next step is to select cell B11 and determine the highest value in the range B4:B8. Excel has a function for displaying the highest value in a range called the **MAX function**. Enter the function name and use the Point mode as described in the steps on the opposite page.

TO FIND THE HIGHEST NUMBER IN A RANGE.

Step 1: Select cell B11. Type =max(

Step 2: Select cell B4, the first end point of the desired range. Drag the mouse pointer down to cell B8, the second end point of the desired range.

Step 3: Release the left mouse button and then click the enter box or press the ENTER key.

Excel determines the highest value in the range B4:B8 as 956320 (cell B8) and displays it in cell B11 (Figure 2-15).

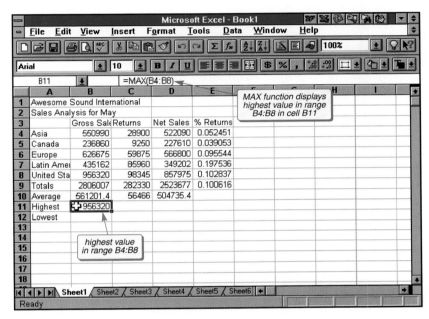

FIGURE 2-15

Certainly it would be as easy as entering the MAX function to scan the range B4:B8 to determine the highest value in the range B4:B8 and enter the number 956320 as a constant in cell B11. The display would be the same as shown in Figure 2-15. However, if the values in the range B4:B8 change, cell B11 would continue to display 956320. By using the MAX function, you are guaranteed that Excel will recalculate the highest value in the range B4:B8 each time a new value is entered into the worksheet.

Calculating the Lowest Value in a Range Using the MIN Function

The next step is to enter the **MIN function** in cell B12 to determine the lowest value in the range B4:B8. Although you could enter the MIN function in the same fashion as the MAX function, the following steps show an alternative using Excel's **Function Wizard button** on the Standard toolbar.

TO ENTER A FUNCTION USING THE FUNCTION WIZARD BUTTON ▼

STEP 1 ►

Select cell B12 and point to the Function Wizard button (f_x) on the Standard toolbar (Figure 2-16).

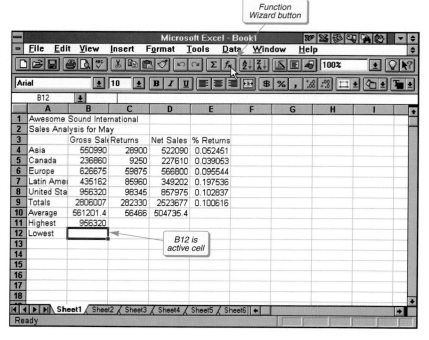

FIGURE 2-16

STEP 2 ►

Click the Function Wizard button. Select MIN in the Function Name list box and point to the Next button (Next).

Excel displays the Function Wizard – Step 1 of 2 dialog box with Most Recently Used selected in the Function Category list box, MIN selected in the Function Name list box, and the mouse pointer pointing to the Next button (Figure 2-17).

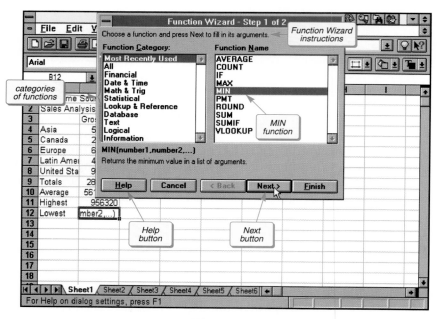

FIGURE 2-17

STEP 3 ▶

Choose the Next button.

Excel displays the Function Wizard – Step 2 of 2 dialog box.

STEP 4 ▶

Use the mouse and Point mode to select the range B4:B8 on the worksheet and then point to the Finish button (Finish).

Excel enters the range in the number 1 box and displays the result of =MIN(B4:B8) in the Value box (236860) of the dialog box (Figure 2-18).

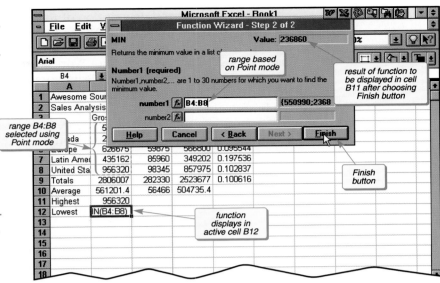

FIGURE 2-18

STEP 5 ▶

Choose the Finish button.

Excel determines the lowest value in the range B4:B8 and displays it in cell B12 (Figure 2-19).

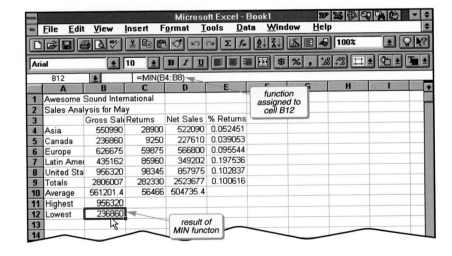

FIGURE 2-19

You can see from the previous example that using the Function Wizard button on the Standard toolbar allows you to easily enter a function into a cell without requiring you to memorize its format. Any time you are to enter a function, simply click the Function Wizard button on the Standard toolbar, select the desired function, and enter the arguments.

An alternative to using the Function Wizard button on the Standard toolbar, is to use the Function Wizard button, which is next to the enter box on the formula bar. This button only displays when the formula bar is active (see Figure 2-12 on page E75) and is primarily used to enter a function in the middle of a formula you are entering into a cell. A third alternative for entering a function into a cell is to choose the Function command on the Insert menu.

Thus far, you have learned to use the SUM, AVERAGE, MAX, and MIN functions. Besides these four functions, Excel has more than 400 additional functions that handle just about every type of calculation you can imagine. These functions are categorized as shown in the Function Category box in Figure 2-17.

To obtain a list and description of the available functions, choose the Contents command from the Help menu. When Excel displays the Microsoft Excel Help screen, choose Reference Information. Then choose Worksheet Functions, and finally choose Alphabetical List of Worksheet Functions or choose Worksheet Functions listed by Category. Use the Print command on the File menu of the Microsoft Help Screen to obtain a hardcopy of any desired topics.

In the Function Wizard dialog box in Figure 2-18 on the previous page, there are five buttons from which to choose. If a button is dimmed (or ghosted), that means you cannot choose it. The functions of the five Function Wizard buttons are described in Table 2-2.

▶ **TABLE 2-2**

BUTTON	FUNCTION
Help	Displays help on the Function Wizard
Cancel	Cancels the Function Wizard and returns you to the worksheet
Back	Displays the previous dialog box
Next	Displays the next dialog box
Finish	Assigns the cell the selections made thus far

Copying the MAX and MIN Functions

The final step before formatting the worksheet is to copy the MAX and MIN functions in the range B11:B12 to the range C11:E12. Using the fill handle you can complete the copy. This example illustrates that the fill handle can be used to copy a range of cells to an adjacent range.

TO COPY A RANGE OF CELLS TO ANOTHER RANGE USING THE FILL HANDLE

Step 1: Select the range B11:B12. Point to the fill handle.
Step 2: Drag the fill handle to the right to select the range C11:E12 and then release the left mouse button.

Excel copies the MAX function across the range C11:E11 and the MIN function across the range C12:E12 (Figure 2-20).

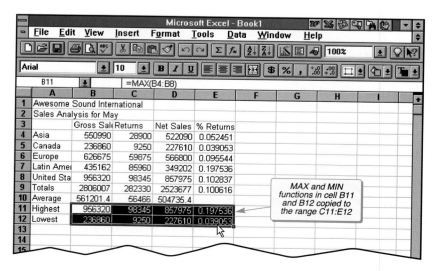

FIGURE 2-20

Here again, you must remember that Excel adjusts the ranges in the copied function so each function refers to the column of numbers above it. Review the numbers in rows 11 and 12 in Figure 2-20. You should see that each MAX function is determining the highest value in the column above it for rows 4 through 8 and each MIN function is determining the lowest value in the column above it for rows 4 through 8.

Select any cell in the worksheet to remove the selection from the range B11:E12. This concludes entering the data and formulas into the worksheet. The next step is to apply formatting to the worksheet so it is easier to read. However, before moving on, it is best to save the workbook.

▶ SAVING AN INTERMEDIATE COPY OF THE WORKBOOK

A good practice is to save intermediate copies of your work. That way, if your computer loses power or you make a serious mistake, you can always retrieve the latest copy from disk. It is recommended that you save an intermediate copy of the worksheet every 50 to 75 keystrokes. Use the Save button on the Standard toolbar often, because you can save keying time later if the unexpected happens. For the following steps, it is assumed you have a formatted disk in drive A.

TO SAVE AN INTERMEDIATE COPY OF THE WORKBOOK ▼

STEP 1 ▶

Click the Save button on the Standard toolbar. When the Save As dialog box displays, type proj2 in the File Name box. If necessary, use the Drives box to change to drive A.

The Save As dialog box displays as shown in Figure 2-21.

STEP 2 ▶

Choose the OK button from the Save As dialog box, and then choose the OK button in the Summary Info dialog box.

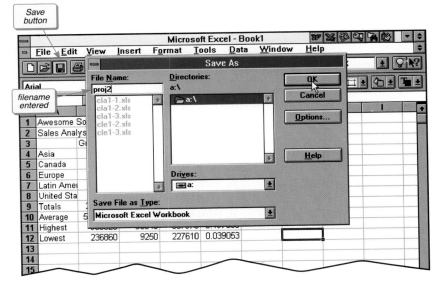

FIGURE 2-21

After Excel completes the save, the worksheet remains on the screen with PROJ2.XLS in the title bar. You can immediately continue with the next activity.

▶ APPLYING FORMATS TO THE WORKSHEET

 lthough the worksheet contains the data, formulas, and functions that make up the Sales Analysis Report, the text and numbers need to be formatted to improve their appearance and readability.

In Project 1, you used the AutoFormat command to apply formatting to the majority of the worksheet. However, you may not always find an acceptable Format Table layout to use. This section describes how to change the unformatted worksheet in Figure 2-22a to the formatted worksheet in Figure 2-22b without using the AutoFormat command.

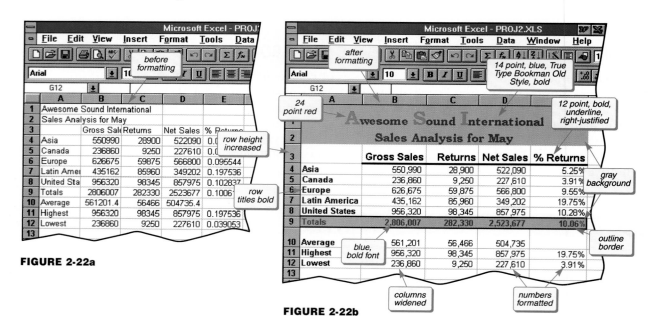

FIGURE 2-22a

FIGURE 2-22b

The type of formatting required in the Project 2 worksheet is outlined as follows:

1. Worksheet titles
   a. font type — TrueType (TT) Bookman Old Style (or TT Courier New if your system does not have TT Bookman Old Style)
   b. font size — 14
   c. font style — bold
   d. font color — blue
   e. font size and font color of first character in each word in main title — 24 red.
   f. alignment — center across columns A through E
   g. background color (range A1:E2) — gray
2. Column titles
   a. font size — 12
   b. font style — bold
   c. alignment — right-justified
   d. border — underline
3. Row titles
   a. font style — bold
4. Total line
   a. font style — bold
   b. font color — blue
   c. background color — gray
   d. border — outline

5. Numbers in range B4:D12
    a. Comma style with no decimal places
6. Numbers in range E4:E12
    a. Percent style with two decimal places
7. Increase the column widths as follows: A to best fit; B to 13.71 characters; C and D to 11.00 characters; and E to 12.14 characters.
8. Increase the heights of rows 3 and 10 to 24.00 points

All of the above formatting can be applied by using the mouse and Formatting toolbar.

Applying Formats to the Worksheet Titles

To emphasize the worksheet title in cells A1 and A2, the font type, size, style, and color are changed as described in the following steps.

TO APPLY FORMATS TO THE CHARACTERS IN THE WORKSHEET TITLE ▼

STEP 1 ▶

Select the range A1:A2.

STEP 2 ▶

Click the Font box arrow on the Formatting toolbar and point to TT Bookman Old Style (or TT Courier New if your system does not have TT Bookman Old Style).

The Font drop-down list box displays (Figure 2-23).

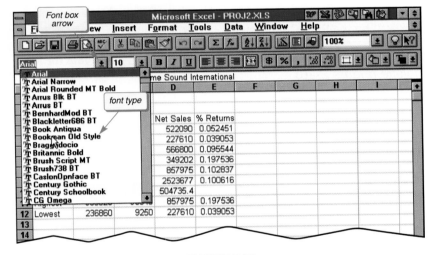

FIGURE 2-23

STEP 3 ▶

Click the left mouse button to choose TT Bookman Old Style (or TT Courier New). Click the Font Size box arrow on the Formatting toolbar and point to 14.

The characters in cells A1 and A2 display using TT Bookman Old Style (or TT Courier New). The mouse pointer points to 14 in the Font Size drop-down list box (Figure 2-24).

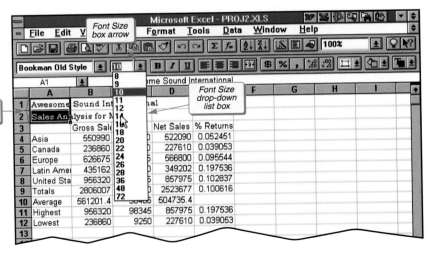

FIGURE 2-24

STEP 4 ▶

Click the left mouse button to change the font size to 14 point and click the Bold button on the Formatting toolbar.

The font in cells A1 and A2 displays in 14 point bold (Figure 2-25). Excel automatically increases the row heights of rows 1 and 2 so the larger characters fit in the cells.

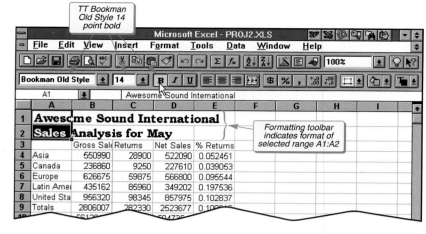

FIGURE 2-25

STEP 5 ▶

Click the Font Color button arrow (■) on the Formatting toolbar and point to the dark blue color (column 1, row 4) on the Font Color palette.

Excel displays the Font Color palette (Figure 2-26).

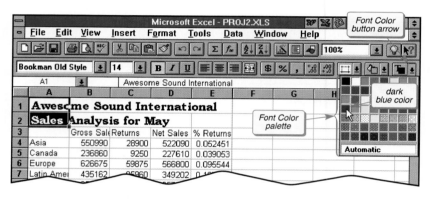

FIGURE 2-26

STEP 6 ▶

Click the left mouse button to choose the dark blue font color.

Excel changes the font color of the characters in cells A1 and A2 from black to dark blue.

STEP 7 ▶

Double-click cell A1 to edit the contents of the cell. Drag across the letter A in Awesome. Click the Font Size box arrow and point to 24.

Excel enters the Edit mode and the letter A in Awesome is selected (Figure 2-27). The Font Size drop-down list box displays.

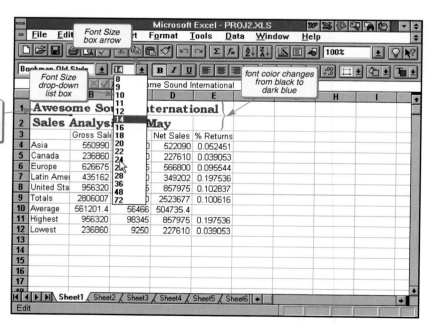

FIGURE 2-27

STEP 8 ▶

Click the left mouse button to choose 24. Click the Font Color button arrow, and then point to the color red (column 3, row 1) on the Font Color palette.

The letter A in Awesome increases to 24 points and the mouse pointer points to the red color on the palette (Figure 2-28).

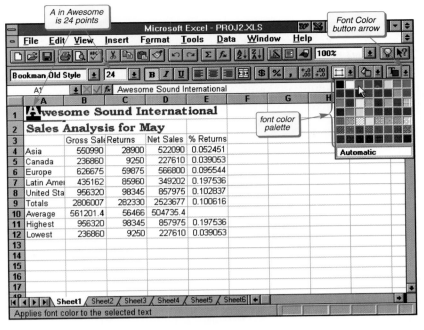

FIGURE 2-28

STEP 9 ▶

Click the left mouse button to choose the red font color for the selected letter A in Awesome.

STEP 10 ▶

Repeat Step 7 through Step 9 for the letter S in Sound and the letter I in International. To choose red using the Font Color button, click the Font Color button, which displays the last color applied.

STEP 11 ▶

Click the check box on the formula bar or press the ENTER key to complete editing the contents of cell A1.

The text making up the worksheet titles displays in the desired format (Figure 2-29).

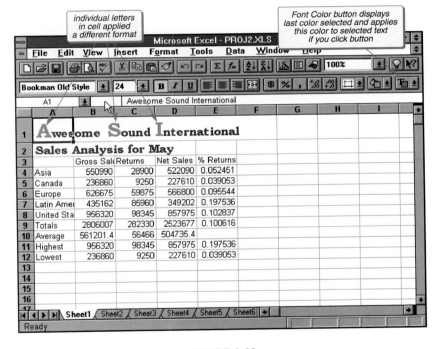

FIGURE 2-29

Excel allows you to change the font of individual characters in a cell or all of the characters in a cell, in a range of cells, or in the entire worksheet. You can also change the font any time while the worksheet is active. For example, some Excel users prefer to change the font before they enter any data. Others change the font while they are building the worksheet or after they have entered all the data. When developing presentation-quality worksheets, several different fonts are often used in the same worksheet.

Recall that the Bold button is like a toggle switch. Click it once and Excel bolds the selected range. Click it again with the same range selected and Excel removes the bold style.

The next step is to center the worksheet titles across columns A through E.

TO CENTER THE WORKSHEET TITLE

Step 1: Select the range A1:E2.
Step 2: Click the Center Across Columns button on the Formatting toolbar.
Step 3: Select cell B3.

Excel centers the worksheet titles in cells A1 and A2 across columns A through E (Figure 2-30).

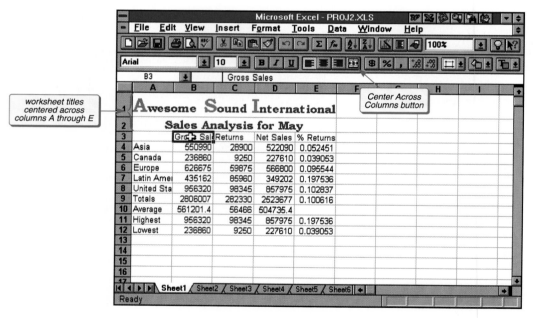

worksheet titles centered across columns A through E

Center Across Columns button

FIGURE 2-30

The final format to be applied to the worksheet title is the gray background color (Figure 2-22b on page E82). This format will be completed later when the background color of the totals in row 9 is applied.

Applying Formats to the Column Titles

According to Figure 2-22b, the text making up the column titles in row 3 are a font size of 12, a font style of bold, aligned right-justified, and underlined. The following steps apply these formats to the column titles.

TO APPLY FORMATS TO THE COLUMN TITLES ▼

STEP 1 ►

Select the range B3:E3. Click the Font Size box arrow on the Formatting toolbar and point to 12.

The Font Size drop-down list box displays (Figure 2-31).

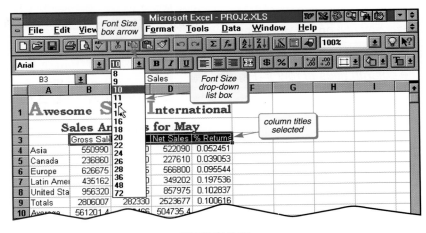

FIGURE 2-31

STEP 2 ►

Click the left mouse button to choose 12 point. Click the Bold button and then the Align Right button (▤) on the Formatting toolbar, and point to the Borders button arrow (▦▾) on the Formatting toolbar.

Excel applies 12 point bold and right-aligns the text in the column titles (Figure 2-32).

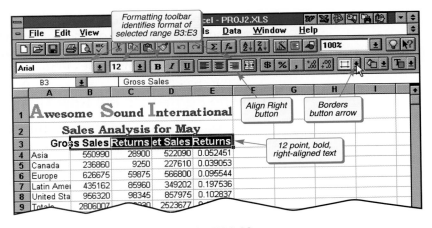

FIGURE 2-32

STEP 3 ►

Click the Borders button arrow and point to the second border in the second row on the Borders palette.

The Borders palette displays (Figure 2-33). Any border selected will be applied to the selected range.

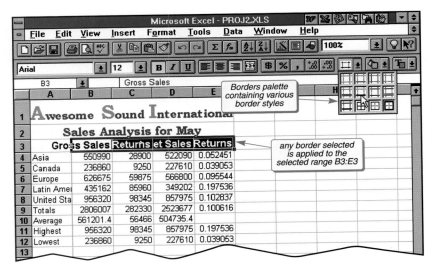

FIGURE 2-33

STEP 4 ▶

Click the left mouse button to choose the underline style, and select any cell on the worksheet.

Excel draws an underline below the column titles in row 3 (Figure 2-34).

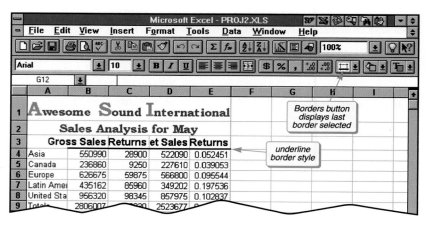

FIGURE 2-34

Notice, thus far, how all the formats have been applied using the mouse and Formatting toolbar. An alternative method to formatting the selected cells is to choose the Cells command on the **Format menu** or the **Format Cells command** on the shortcut menu. In either case, the Format Cells dialog box displays which allows you to apply format styles to the selected cells.

Applying Formats to the Row Titles

The next step is to bold the row titles in column A. Perform the following steps to complete this task.

TO APPLY FORMATS TO THE ROW TITLES

Step 1: Select the range A4:A12.
Step 2: Click the Bold button on the Formatting toolbar.

Excel bolds the text in the range A4:A12 (Figure 2-35).

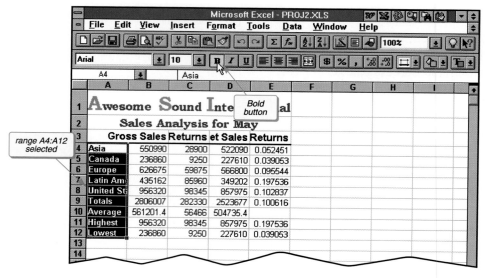

FIGURE 2-35

Applying Formats to the Totals Row and Changing the Background Color of the Worksheet Titles

According to Figure 2-22b on page E82 the totals in row 9 are formatted in a bold style and colored blue. To make the totals stand out, an outline surrounds the totals and the background is colored gray. The **background color** of a cell is the color of the area behind the characters in a cell. The background color of the worksheet titles (A1:E2) is also gray. To illustrate how you can select a **nonadjacent range** using the CTRL key, the background color of the worksheet titles will be changed at the same time the background color of the totals row is changed. Follow these steps to apply the desired format styles.

TO APPLY FORMATS TO THE TOTALS ROW AND CHANGE THE BACKGROUND COLOR ▼

STEP 1 ►

Select the range A9:E9. Click the Bold button twice. Click the Borders button arrow, and point to the bold outline border on the Borders palette.

The Borders palette displays (Figure 2-36). The Bold button is clicked twice because cell A9 in the range A9:E9 is already bold.

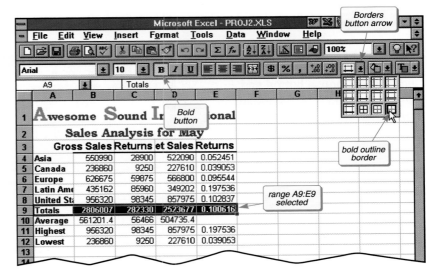

FIGURE 2-36

STEP 2 ►

Click the left mouse button to choose the bold outline border and then click the Font Color arrow and point to the dark blue color (column 1, row 4) on the Font Color palette.

Excel draws an outline around the totals and the Font Color palette displays (Figure 2-37).

STEP 3 ►

Click the left mouse button to choose the dark blue color on the Font Color palette.

Excel colors the font blue in the range A9:E9.

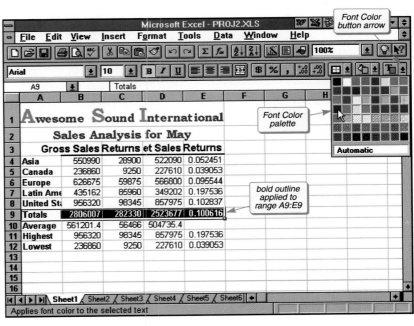

FIGURE 2-37

STEP 4 ▶

With the range A9:E9 selected, hold down the CTRL key and drag across the range A1:E2. Point to the Color button arrow ( ) on the Formatting toolbar.

The nonadjacent ranges A1:E2 and A9:E9 are selected (Figure 2-38).

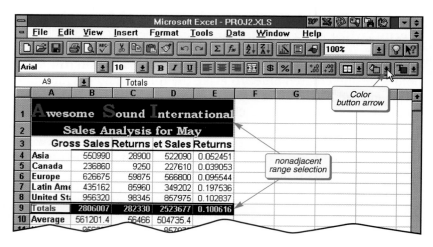

FIGURE 2-38

STEP 5 ▶

Click the left mouse button and point to the light gray color (column 7, row 2) on the Color palette (Figure 2-39).

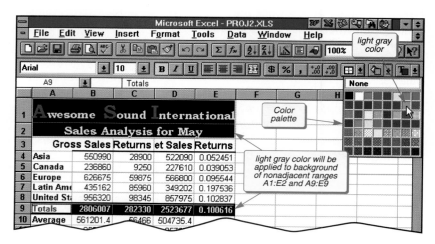

FIGURE 2-39

STEP 6 ▶

Click the left mouse button to choose the light gray color.

Excel colors the background of the nonadjacent ranges A1:E2 and A9:E9 light gray (Figure 2-40).

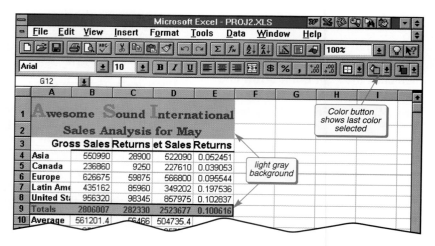

FIGURE 2-40

In the previous steps, you learned how to outline a range of cells, how to select nonadjacent ranges, and how to color the background of a range of cells. These format styles along with the ones previously discussed will allow you to develop professional looking worksheets that will be easy to read and understand.

▶ APPLYING NUMBER FORMATS

hen using Excel, you can apply formats to represent dollar amounts, whole numbers with comma placement, percentages, and decimal numbers through the use of buttons on the Formatting toolbar.

According to Figure 2-22b on page E82, the numbers in columns B through D are formatted to the Comma style with no decimal places. The **Comma style** inserts a comma every three positions to the left of the decimal point. The numbers in the % Returns column are formatted to the Percent style with two decimal places. The **Percent style** inserts a percent sign (%) to the right of the number.

The remainder of this section describes how to use the Comma style, Percent style, Increase Decimal, and Decrease Decimal buttons on the Formatting toolbar to format the numbers in the worksheet. Besides inserting a comma in a number, the **Comma Style button** adds two decimal places to the right of the decimal point. Because this project requires no decimal places in the dollar amounts, the **Decrease Decimal button** on the Formatting toolbar is used to eliminate the decimal places.

The **Percent style button** displays a number in Percent style with no decimal places. Because this project requires two decimal places in the % Returns column, the **Increase Decimal button** is used to add two decimal places. Follow these steps to apply number formatting.

TO APPLY NUMBER FORMATS TO THE WORKSHEET ▼

STEP 1 ▶

Select the range B4:D12. Point to the Comma Style button ( ) on the Formatting toolbar (Figure 2-41).

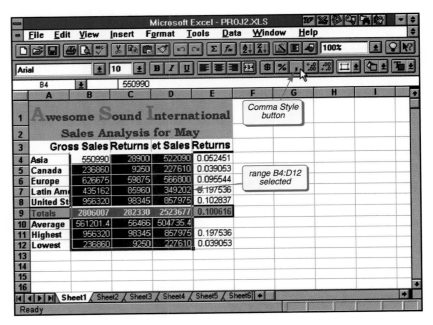

FIGURE 2-41

STEP 2 ▶

Click the left mouse button to apply the Comma style and point to the Decrease Decimal button ( ) on the Formatting toolbar.

*The majority of numbers in the range B4:D12 display as a sequence of **number signs** (#) indicating they are too large to fit in the width of the cells (Figure 2-42).*

FIGURE 2-42

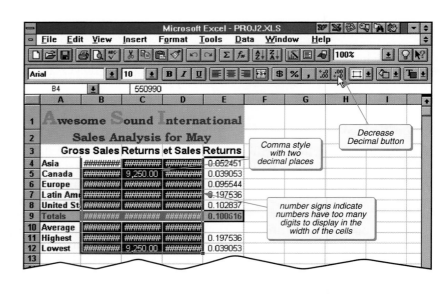

STEP 3 ▶

Click the Decrease Decimal button twice to eliminate the two decimal places in the numbers in the range B4:D12.

The majority of numbers in the range B4:D12 display as whole numbers with comma placement (Figure 2-43). Later the column widths will be increased so the remaining numbers will display properly.

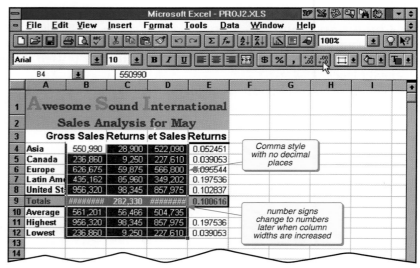

FIGURE 2-43

STEP 4 ▶

Select the range E4:E12 and point to the Percent style button ( ) on the Formatting toolbar (Figure 2-44).

FIGURE 2-44

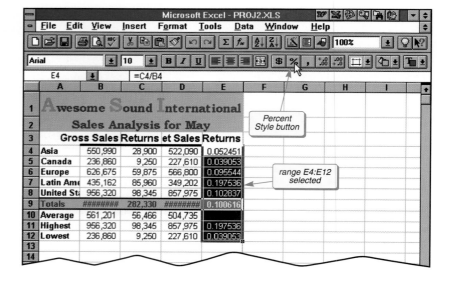

STEP 5 ▶

Click the left mouse button to apply the Percent style. Then, point to and click the Increase Decimal button (⊞) twice.

The decimal numbers in column E display using the Percent style with two decimal places (Figure 2-45).

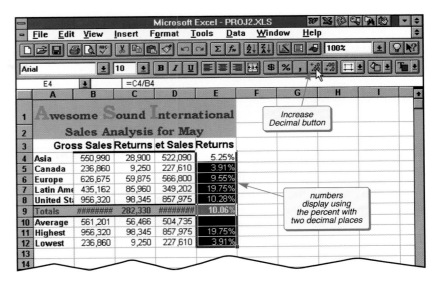

FIGURE 2-45

Excel rounds a number to fit the format selected. For example, in cell E4, Excel rounds the actual value 0.052451 up to 5.25%. In cell E8, Excel rounds the actual value 0.102837 down to 10.28%.

Applying Number Formats Using the Cells Command on the Format Menu or Format Cells Command on the Shortcut Menu

Thus far, you have been introduced to two ways to apply number formats in a worksheet. In Project 1, you formatted the numbers using the AutoFormat command on the Format menu. In the previous section, you were introduced to using the Formatting toolbar as a means of selecting a format style. A third way to format numbers is to use the Cells command on the Format menu or the Format Cells command on the shortcut menu. Using the Cells command allows you to display numbers in any desired format you can imagine.

▶ CHANGING THE WIDTHS OF COLUMNS AND HEIGHTS OF ROWS

When Excel begins and the blank worksheet displays on the screen, all the columns have a default width of 8.43 characters and a height of 12.75 points. At any time, you can change the width of the columns or height of the rows to make the worksheet easier to read or to ensure that entries will display properly in the cells to which they are assigned. The width of columns is measured in characters. A **character** is defined as TT Arial, 10 point, the default font used by Excel.

Changing the Widths of Columns

Excel provides two ways to increase or decrease the width of the columns in a worksheet. First, you can change the width of one column at a time. Second, you can change the width of a series of adjacent columns. This project demonstrates both methods.

When changing the column width, you can manually set the width or you can instruct Excel to size the column to best fit. **Best fit** means that the width of the column will be increased or decreased so the widest entry will fit in the column.

TO CHANGE THE WIDTH OF A COLUMN TO BEST FIT ▼

STEP 1 ▶

Position the mouse pointer on the border line between the column A and column B headings above row 1.

The mouse pointer becomes a split double arrow (↔) (Figure 2-46).

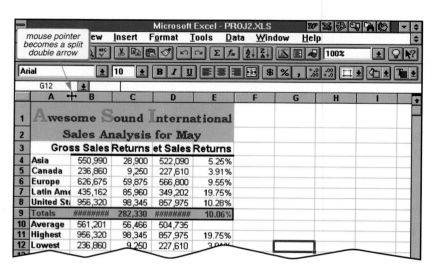

FIGURE 2-46

STEP 2 ▶

Double-click the left mouse button.

The width of column A increases just enough so the widest entry in column A, Latin America, fits in cell A7 (Figure 2-47).

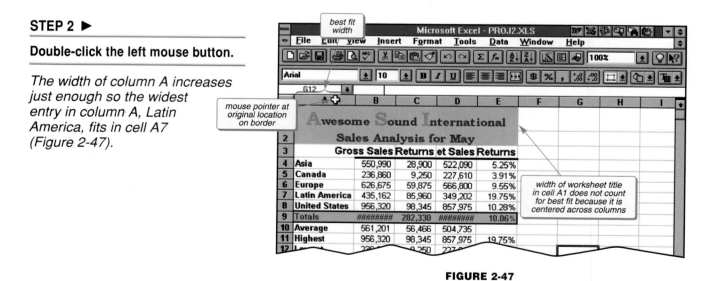

FIGURE 2-47

Compare the entries in column A of Figure 2-47 to Figure 2-46. Notice how Excel has increased the width of column A just enough so all the characters in column A display. To determine the exact character width of column A, you can move the mouse pointer to the border line between the column A and column B headings. When the mouse pointer changes to a split double arrow, hold down the left mouse button. Excel displays the new column width (13 for column A) in place of the cell reference in the reference area in the formula bar.

Recall that the worksheet title, Awesome Sound International, is assigned to cell A1. Because it was centered earlier across columns A through E, Excel does not take the width of the title into consideration when determining the best fit for column A.

If you decide to undo a new column width prior to entering the next command or data item, you can choose the Undo Column Width command from the Edit menu.

The next step is to change the column widths of column B to 13.71, columns C and D to 11.00, and column E to 12.14. In these cases, best fit will not be used because more space is preferred between the columns to improve the appearance of the report.

TO CHANGE THE WIDTH OF COLUMNS ▼

STEP 1 ▶

Position the mouse pointer on the border line between the column B and column C headings above row 1 and drag to the right until the number 13.71 displays in the reference area in the formula bar.

A dotted line shows the new right border of column B and the number 13.71 displays in the reference area in the formula bar (Figure 2-48).

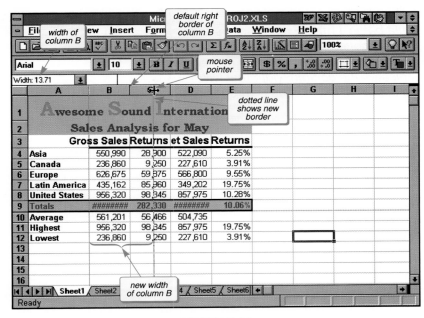

FIGURE 2-48

STEP 2 ▶

Release the left mouse button.

Excel sets the width of column B to 13.71 (Figure 2-49).

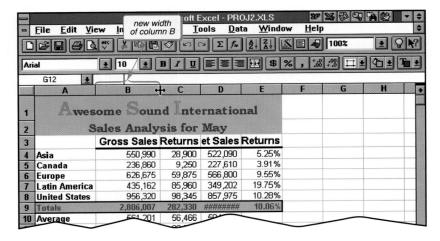

FIGURE 2-49

STEP 3 ▶

Drag the mouse pointer from column heading C through column heading D and then release the left mouse button to select both columns. Move the mouse pointer to the right border of column heading D. When the mouse pointer changes to a split double arrow, drag to the right until a width of 11.00 displays in the reference area in the formula bar.

Columns C and D are selected and the right border of column D is dragged to the right until the width in the Reference area in the for-mula bar is 11.00. Excel displays a vertical dotted line, that when added to the width of column D, indicates the column width that will be assigned to columns C through D (Figure 2-50).

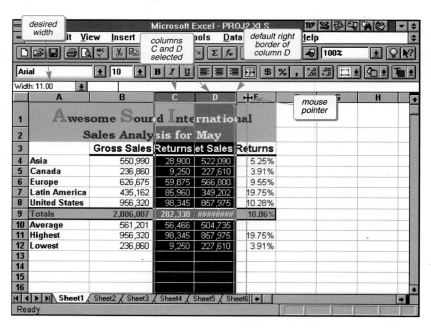

FIGURE 2-50

STEP 4 ▶

Release the left mouse button.

Excel assigns a new width of 11.00 characters to columns C and D (Figure 2-51).

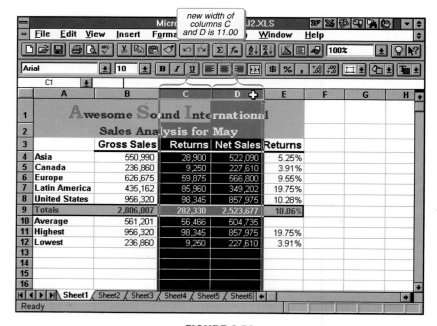

FIGURE 2-51

STEP 5 ▶

Click column heading E to select the column. Click the right mouse button to display the shortcut menu. Point to the Column Width command (Figure 2-52).

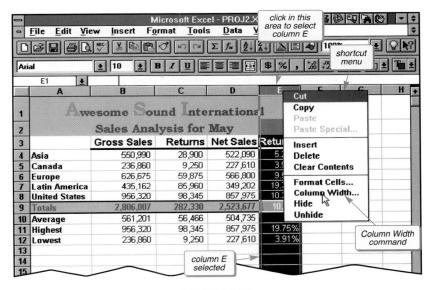

FIGURE 2-52

STEP 6 ▶

Choose the Column Width command. When the Column Width dialog box displays, type the number 12.14 in the Column Width box and point to the OK button.

The Column Width dialog box displays, which allows you to enter a column width between 0 and 255 (Figure 2-53).

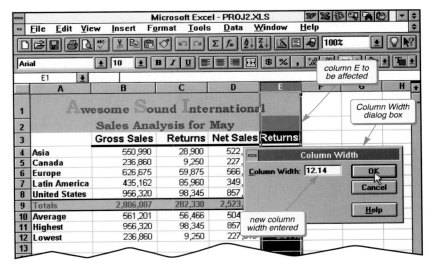

FIGURE 2-53

STEP 7 ▶

Choose the OK button.

The width of column E increases from the default 8.43 to 12.14 characters (Figure 2-54).

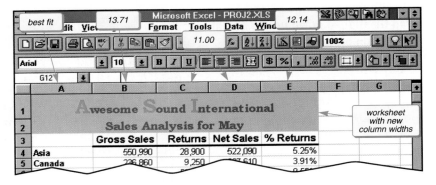

FIGURE 2-54

Step 6 and Step 7 show that you can use the Column Width command instead of dragging the mouse to change the column width. Select any cell in the column or range of columns to be affected, choose the **Column command** from the Format menu or the Column Width command from the shortcut menu, and type in the desired width. The Column Width command only appears on the shortcut menu when one or more entire columns are selected. You select entire columns by dragging through the column headings. Use the Column Width command instead of the mouse when you want to increase or decrease the column width significantly.

The column width can vary between zero and 255 characters. When you decrease the column width to zero, the column is hidden. **Hiding columns** is a technique you can use to hide sensitive data on the screen that you don't want other people to see. When you print a worksheet, hidden columns do not print. To unhide a hidden column, position the mouse pointer to the left of the heading border where the the hidden column is located and drag to the right.

Changing the Heights of Rows

When you change the font size of a cell entry, such as Awesome Sound International in cell A1, Excel automatically adjusts the row height to the best fit. You can also manually adjust the height of a row to add space that improves the appearance of the worksheet. The row height is measured in point size. The default row height is 12.75 points. Recall from Project 1 that a point is equal to 1/72 of an inch. Thus, 12.75 points is equal to about one-sixth of an inch.

The following steps show how to use the mouse to increase the height of rows 3 and 10 from their default height to 24.00 points so there is extra space between the worksheet subtitle in row 2 and the column titles in row 3 and the totals in row 9 and the averages in row 10. In the following example, the CTRL key is used to select the nonadjacent rows 3 and 10 and the bottom border of row 10 is dragged down until the row height in the reference area in the formula bar is 24.00 points.

TO INCREASE THE HEIGHT OF A ROW BY DRAGGING THE MOUSE ▼

STEP 1 ▶

Click row heading 3. Hold down the CTRL key and click row heading 10. Release the CTRL key. Move the mouse pointer to the border line between row headings 10 and 11. Drag the mouse down until a height of 24.00 displays in the reference area in the formula bar.

Excel displays a horizontal dotted line (Figure 2-55). The distance between the dotted line and the top of row 10 indicates the new row height for rows 3 and 10.

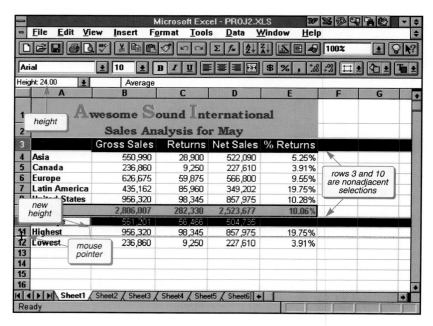

FIGURE 2-55

STEP 2 ►

Release the left mouse button.

Rows 3 and 10 have a new height of 24.00 points (Figure 2-56).

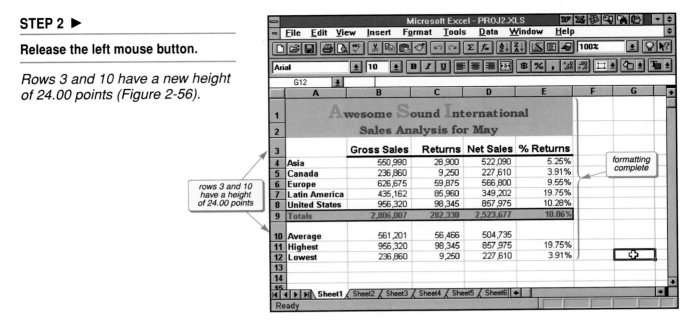

FIGURE 2-56

The row height can vary between zero and 409 points. When you decrease the row height to zero, the row is hidden. To show a hidden row, point just below the row heading border where the row is hidden and drag down.

To use a dialog box to change the row height, select any cell in the row or a series of cells down a column, choose the **Row command** from the Format menu or the **Row Height command** from the shortcut menu, and type the desired height in the Row Height dialog box. As with the Column Width command, the Row Height command only shows on the shortcut menu when one or more rows are selected.

If for some reason you want to switch back to the default row height, simply move the mouse pointer to the row border and double-click.

The task of formatting the worksheet is complete. The next step is to check the spelling of the worksheet.

► CHECKING SPELLING

Excel has a spell checker you can use to check the worksheet for spelling errors. The spell checker checks for spelling errors against its standard dictionary. If you have any specialized terms that are not in the standard dictionary, you can add them to a **custom dictionary** through the **Spelling dialog box**.

When the spell checker finds a word that is not in the dictionaries, it displays the word in the Spelling dialog box so you can correct it if it is misspelled.

You invoke the spell checker by clicking the **Spelling button** on the Standard toolbar or by choosing the Spelling command from the Tools menu. To illustrate Excel's reaction to a misspelled word, the word Lowest in cell A12 is purposely misspelled as Liwest, as shown in Figure 2-57 on the next page.

TO CHECK SPELLING IN THE WORKSHEET ▼

STEP 1 ▶

Select cell A1. Click the Spelling button (🖫) on the Standard toolbar.

The spell checker begins checking the spelling of the text in the worksheet with the active cell (cell A1) and continues checking to the right and down row by row. If the spell checker comes across a word that is not in the standard or custom dictionaries, it displays the Spelling dialog box (Figure 2-57).

STEP 2 ▶

When the spell checker displays a word in the Change To box, select one of the six buttons to the right in the Spelling dialog box.

In Figure 2-57, the word Lowest in cell A12 is misspelled as Liwest. The spell checker displays its best guess of the word you wanted (Lowest) in the Change To box. Because Lowest is in fact the correct spelling, choose the Change button (Change).

STEP 3 ▶

Choose the OK button when Excel displays the Microsoft Excel dialog box to indicate the spell check is complete (Figure 2-58).

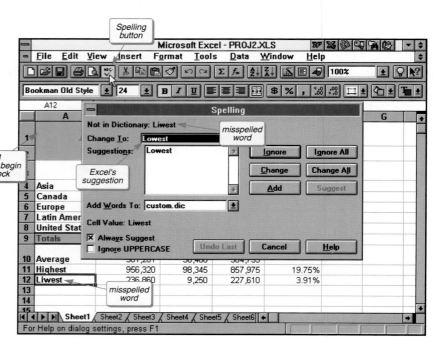

FIGURE 2-57

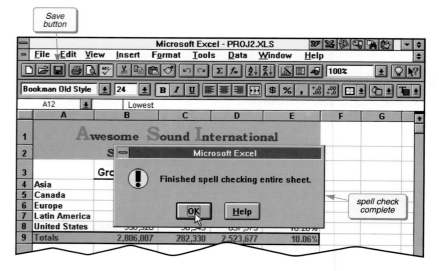

FIGURE 2-58

When the spell checker identifies a word not in the dictionaries, it changes the active cell to the cell containing the word not in the dictionaries. The Spelling dialog box (Figure 2-57) lists the word not in the dictionaries, a suggested correction, and a list of alternative spellings. If you agree with the suggested correction in the Change To box, choose the Change button. To change the word throughout the worksheet, choose the Change All button (Change All).

If one of the words in the Suggestions list box is correct, select the word and choose the Change button or double-click the word. If none of the listed words is correct, type the correct word and choose the Change button. To skip correcting the word, choose the Ignore button (Ignore). To have Excel ignore the word for the remainder of the worksheet, choose the Ignore All button (Ignore All).

Consider these additional points regarding the spell checker:

1. To check the spelling of the text in a single cell, double-click the cell and click the Spelling button on the Standard toolbar.
2. When you select a single cell and the formula bar is not active before invoking the spell checker, Excel checks the entire worksheet, which includes the worksheet, notes, and embedded charts.
3. If you select a range of cells before invoking the spell checker, Excel only checks the spelling of the words in the selected range.
4. To check the spelling of a chart, select the chart before invoking the spell checker.
5. To check the spelling of all the sheets in a workbook, choose the Select All Sheets command from the sheet tab shortcut menu, and then invoke the spell checker. You display the sheet tab shortcut menu by pointing to it and clicking the right mouse button.
6. If you select a cell other than cell A1 before you start the spell checker, a dialog box displays after Excel checks to the end of the worksheet asking if you want to continue checking at the beginning.
7. To add words that are not in the standard dictionary to the custom dictionary, choose the Add button (Add) in the Spelling dialog box (Figure 2-57) when Excel identifies the word.

▶ SAVING THE WORKBOOK A SECOND TIME USING THE SAME FILENAME

Earlier, you saved an intermediate version of the workbook using the filename PROJ2.XLS. To save the workbook a second time using the same filename, click the Save button on the Standard toolbar (Figure 2-58). Excel automatically stores the latest version of the worksheet under the same filename PROJ2.XLS without displaying the Save As dialog box as it did when you saved the workbook the first time.

If you want to save the workbook under a new name, choose the Save As command from the File menu or shortcut menu. For example, some Excel users use the Save button to save the latest version of the workbook to the default drive. They then use the Save As command to save a second copy to another drive.

You can also instruct Excel to automatically create a backup of a workbook on the default drive every time you save it by choosing the Options button (Options...) in the Save As dialog box and selecting the Always Create Backup check box. A **backup** copy is the previous version of the worksheet, renamed with a .BAK extension. Saving a backup copy of the workbook is another form of protection against losing all your work.

▶ CREATING A 3-D COLUMN CHART ON A CHART SHEET

T he next step in this project is to draw the 3-D column chart shown in Figure 2-59. A **column chart** is used to show trends and comparisons. Each column emphasizes the magnitude of the value it represents. The column chart in Figure 2-59 compares the gross sales for the month of May for the international divisions. It is easy to see from the column chart that the United States had the greatest gross sales and Canada had the smallest gross sales.

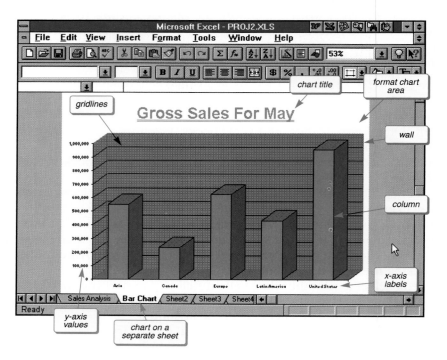

FIGURE 2-59

The column chart in Figure 2-59 differs from the one in Project 1 in that it is not embedded in the worksheet. Instead, it is created on a separate sheet, called a **chart sheet**.

The range of the worksheet to graph is A4:B8 (see Figure 2-60). The division names in the range A4:A8 identify the columns and show at the bottom of the column chart. The entries in column A are called the **category names.** The range B4:B8 contains the data that determines the magnitude of the columns. The entries in column B are called the **data series**. Because there are five category names and five numbers in the data series, the column chart contains five columns.

Drawing the 3-D Column Chart

In Project 1, you used the ChartWizard button on the Standard toolbar to draw an embedded 2-D column chart. Embedded means the chart is on the same sheet with the worksheet. Anytime you want to create an embedded chart, the ChartWizard button is the best choice. However, you will often want to create a chart on a sheet separate from the worksheet, but in the same workbook. To create a chart on a separate sheet, use the **Chart command** on the **Insert menu**. This command takes you into the ChartWizard, but first asks you if you want to create the chart on the same sheet or a separate sheet.

The following steps illustrate how to create a 3-D column chart on a separate sheet.

TO DRAW A 3-D COLUMN CHART ON A CHART SHEET ▼

STEP 1 ▶

Select the range A4:B8. Choose the Chart command on the Insert menu. Point to the As New Sheet command on the cascading menu.

*Excel displays a cascading menu that allows you to choose where the chart will be created (Figure 2-60). A **cascading menu** is one that displays to the right of the current menu with a list of commands.*

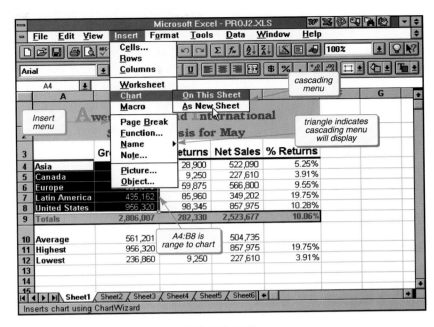

FIGURE 2-60

STEP 2 ▶

Choose the As New Sheet command from the cascading menu.

Excel displays the ChartWizard – Step 1 of 5 dialog box which displays the selected range in the worksheet (Figure 2-61). You can type in a new range or use the mouse to change the range in the worksheet if you decide you want to change your original selection.

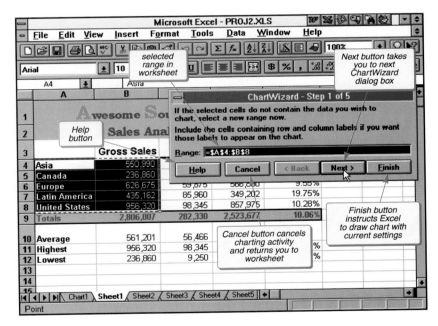

FIGURE 2-61

STEP 3 ▶

Choose the Next button. Select the 3-D Column chart in the ChartWizard – Step 2 of 5 dialog box (Figure 2-62).

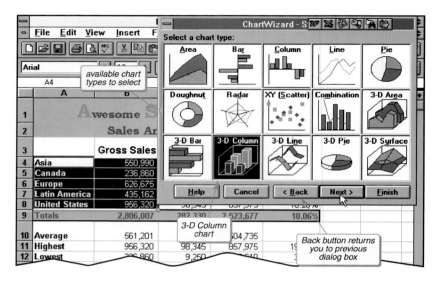

FIGURE 2-62

STEP 4 ▶

Choose the Next button. Select format number 4 for the chart (Figure 2-63).

The ChartWizard – Step 3 of 5 dialog box displays with eight different 3-D formats from which to select.

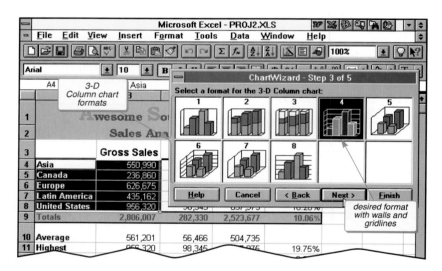

FIGURE 2-63

STEP 5 ▶

Choose the Next button.

The ChartWizard – Step 4 of 5 dialog box displays with a sample of the 3-D column chart. (Figure 2-64).

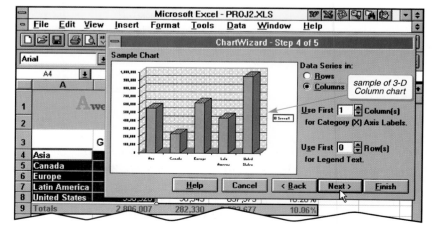

FIGURE 2-64

STEP 6 ▶

Choose the Next button. Select the No option button in the Add a Legend? area. Select the Chart Title box. Type Gross Sales For May **in the Chart Title box (Figure 2-65).**

The ChartWizard – Step 5 of 5 dialog box displays. You have the opportunity in this dialog box to add a chart title, y-axis title, x-axis title, and select whether or not you want legends to display alongside the chart. Excel dynamically changes the sample chart in the dialog box as you enter titles.

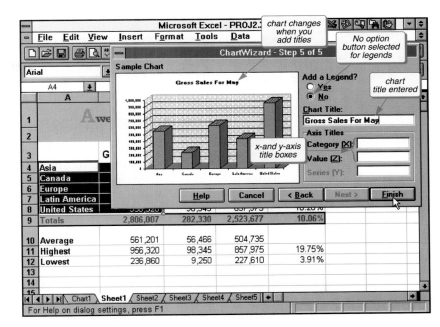

FIGURE 2-65

STEP 7 ▶

Choose the Finish button.

Excel displays the 3-D column chart on a separate sheet (Figure 2-66).

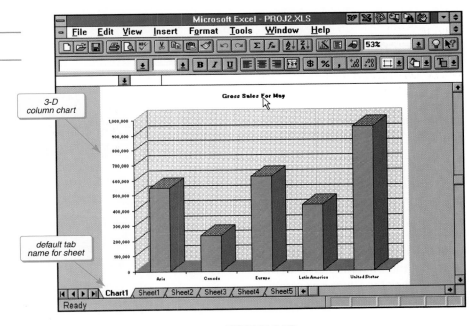

FIGURE 2-66

Each column in the chart in Figure 2-66 represents a division of the company. The names of the divisions display below the corresponding columns on the **x-axis**. The values along the **y-axis** (the vertical line to the left of the columns) are automatically determined by Excel from the highest and lowest gross sales amounts in the range B4:B8 of the worksheet.

Notice in the five ChartWizard dialog boxes (Figures 2-61 through 2-65 on pages E103 through E105) that you can return to the previous ChartWizard dialog box by choosing the Back button. The functions of the buttons for the ChartWizard dialog box are the same as those described for the Chart Wizard dialog box in Table 2-2 on page E80.

Enhancing the 3-D Column Chart

Excel allows you to change the appearance of any chart item labeled in Figure 2-59 on page E102. All you have to do is double-click the chart item you want to change and Excel displays a dialog box containing the changeable characteristics. To change the 3-D column chart in Figure 2-66 so it looks like the one in Figure 2-59, the following changes must be made:

1. Chart title — increase the font size, add a double-underline, and change the font color to red.
2. Walls — change the color to a light blue.
3. Columns — change the color to red.

Applying Formats to the Chart Title

Perform the following steps to increase the chart title font size, double-underline the chart title, and change the color of the chart title to red.

TO APPLY FORMATS TO THE CHART TITLE ▼

STEP 1 ▶

Double-click the chart title. Click the Font tab.

The Font tab displays in the Format Chart Title dialog box.

STEP 2 ▶

Select 36 in the Size list box and Double in the Underline drop-down list box. Click the Color box arrow and select the color red (column 3, row 1) on the palette.

The Format Chart Title dialog box should display as shown in Figure 2-67.

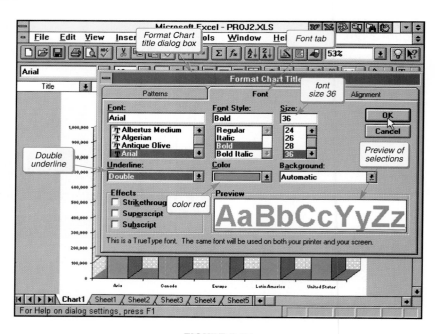

FIGURE 2-67

STEP 3 ▶

Choose the OK button.

Excel displays the column chart with the chart title formatted as required (Figure 2-68).

FIGURE 2-68

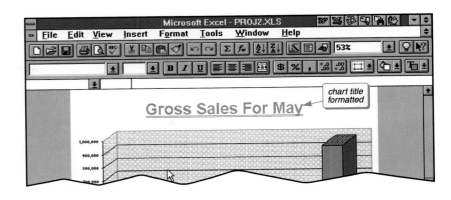

Compare the chart title in Figure 2-68 to the one in Figure 2-66 on page E105. You can see that the chart title stands out after formatting is applied. One of the drawbacks to increasing the font size of the chart title is that Excel decreases the size of the chart itself to make room for the larger font. However, you can select the chart and increase its size if you so desire.

Notice that when you double-click the chart title, Excel immediately opens the Format Chart Title dialog box which includes three tabs — Patterns, Font, and Alignment. Click any tab to display it.

An alternative to formatting the chart title by double-clicking it is to click it to select it and use the buttons on the Formatting toolbar.

Applying Formats to the Walls and the Columns

The next step is to format the walls and the columns. The **walls** are behind and to the left of the columns in the chart. The following steps show how to select a chart item and use the Formatting toolbar to format it.

TO APPLY FORMATS TO THE WALLS AND COLUMNS ▼

STEP 1 ▶

Click any part of the walls except on a gridline.

Black handles surround the walls.

STEP 2 ▶

Click the Color button arrow on the Formatting toolbar and point to the light blue color (column 1, row 5) on the color palette.

The Color palette displays (Figure 2-69).

FIGURE 2-69

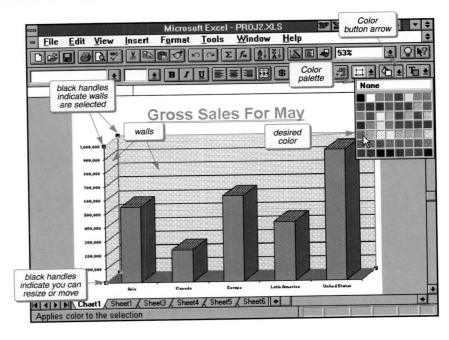

STEP 3 ▶

Click the left mouse button.

Excel changes the color of the walls to a light blue (Figure 2-70).

STEP 4 ▶

Click any one of the five columns.

White handles surround the columns in the chart.

STEP 5 ▶

Click the Color button arrow on the Formatting toolbar and point to red (column 3, row 1) on the color palette.

The Color palette displays (Figure 2-70).

STEP 6 ▶

Click the left mouse button.

The formatted 3-D column chart displays as shown in Figure 2-71.

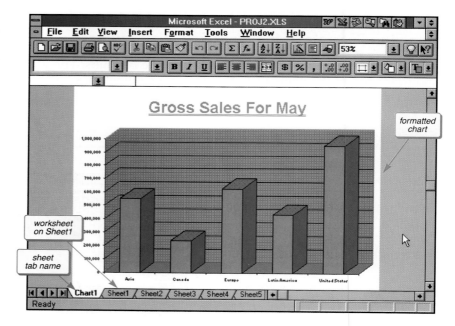

FIGURE 2-70

FIGURE 2-71

You can easily format the chart to a variety of styles. The four ways to apply formats to chart items are:

1. Double-click a chart item and select format styles from a dialog box; the technique applied on the chart title.

2. Click a chart item and use the buttons on the Formatting toolbar; the technique applied on the chart walls and columns in the previous steps.
3. Click a chart item, click the right mouse button to display the shortcut menu, and choose the command that describes the selection, such as Format Walls.
4. Click a chart item, select the Format menu, and choose the command that describes the selection, such as Selected Walls.

One of the commands available on the shortcut menu or the Format menu is the AutoFormat command. The **AutoFormat command** allows you to change the 3-D column chart to any of the other fourteen chart types displayed in Figure 2-62 on page E104.

When you select a chart item, Excel surrounds it with white selection squares or black selection squares, also called **handles**. Chart items marked with **white handles** (such as the columns in Figure 2-70) can be formatted, but cannot be moved or resized. Chart items marked with **black handles** can be formatted, moved, and resized. For example, in Figure 2-69, you can drag the handles on the corners of the wall to resize the chart and change it's perspective.

Changing the Names on the Sheet Tabs and Rearranging the Order of the Sheets

At the bottom of the screen (Figure 2-71) are the tabs that allow you to display any sheet in the workbook. By default, the tab names are Sheet1, Sheet2, and so on. When you draw a chart on a separate sheet, Excel assigns the name Chart1 to the sheet tab. The following steps show you how to rename the sheet tabs and reorder the sheets so the worksheet comes before the chart sheet.

TO RENAME THE SHEET TABS AND REARRANGE THE ORDER OF THE SHEETS ▼

STEP 1 ▶

Double-click the sheet tab named Chart1 at the bottom of the screen.

Excel displays the Rename Sheet dialog box.

STEP 2 ▶

Type Bar Chart **in the Name box.**

The Rename Sheet dialog box displays as shown in Figure 2-72.

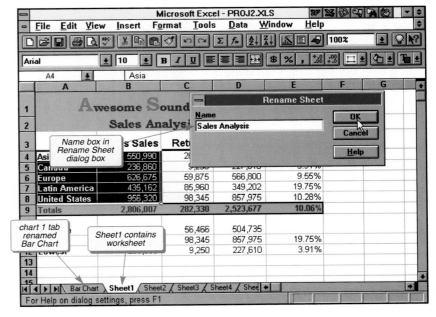

FIGURE 2-72

STEP 3 ▶

Choose the OK button.

Excel renames the Chart1 tab Bar Chart (Figure 2-73).

STEP 4 ▶

Double-click the Sheet1 tab.

Excel displays the Rename Sheet dialog box.

STEP 5 ▶

Type Sales Analysis **in the Name box.**

The Rename Sheet dialog box displays as shown in Figure 2-73.

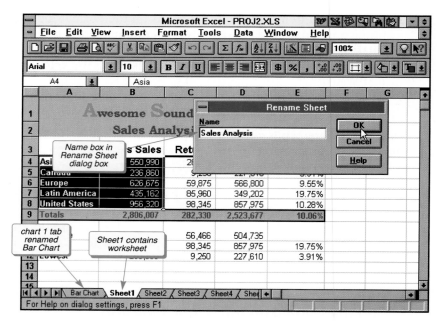

FIGURE 2-73

STEP 6 ▶

Choose the OK button.

Excel renames the Sheet1 tab Sales Analysis (Figure 2-74).

STEP 7 ▶

Point to the Sales Analysis tab and drag it over the Bar Chart tab (Figure 2-74).

The mouse pointer changes to a pointer and a document. A small dark triangle indicates where the Sales Analysis sheet will be moved.

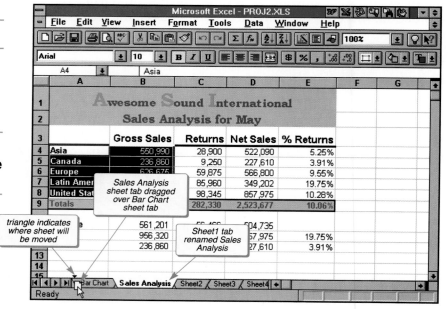

FIGURE 2-74

STEP 8 ►

Release the left mouse button.

*Excel moves the sheet named Sales Analysis in front of the sheet named Bar Chart. The workbook for Project 2 is complete (Figure 2-75). You can also move a sheet by choosing the **Move or Copy Sheet** command on the Edit menu.*

STEP 9 ►

Click the Save button on the Standard toolbar to save the workbook to disk using the filename PROJ2.

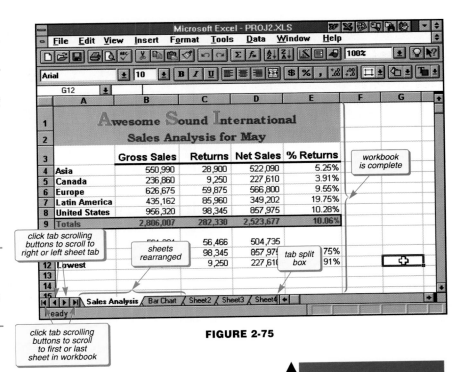

FIGURE 2-75

The previous steps showed you how to rename the sheet tabs at the bottom of the screen and how to resequence them. Sheet names can be up to 31 characters in length. The longer the tab names, the fewer tabs will show. However, you can increase the number of tabs that show by dragging the **tab split box** next to the scroll arrow (Figure 2-75) to the right. This will reduce the size of the scroll bar at the bottom of the screen. Double-click the tab split box to reset it to its normal position.

You can also use the **tab scrolling buttons** to the left of the sheet tabs (Figure 2-75) to scroll between sheet tabs. The leftmost and rightmost tab scrolling buttons scroll to the first or last sheet tab in the workbook. The two middle tab scrolling buttons scroll one sheet tab to the left or right. Tab scrolling buttons do not select sheet tabs. Click a sheet tab to select it.

▶ PREVIEWING AND PRINTING THE WORKBOOK

I n Project 1, you printed the workbook (the worksheet with the embedded chart) without previewing it on the screen. By previewing the workbook, you see exactly how it will look without generating a hard copy. Previewing a workbook can save time, paper, and the frustration of waiting for a printout only to find out it is not what you want.

The **Print Preview command**, as well as the Print command, will only preview selected sheets. You know a sheet is selected when the sheet tab at the bottom of the screen is white. Thus, in Figure 2-75 the Sales Analysis sheet is selected, but the Bar Chart tab is not. To select additional sheets, hold down the SHIFT key and click any sheet tabs you want included in the preview or printout.

TO PREVIEW THE WORKBOOK AND PREPARE IT FOR PRINTING ▼

STEP 1 ▶

Hold down the SHIFT key and click the Bar Chart tab. Point to the Print Preview button ( ) on the Standard toolbar.

Both sheets are selected (Figure 2-76).

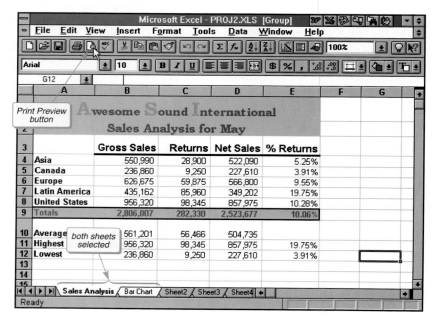

FIGURE 2-76

STEP 2 ▶

Click the Print Preview button.

*Excel displays a preview of the worksheet (possibly with cell gridlines) in the **preview window** and the mouse pointer changes to a magnifying glass ( ) (Figure 2-77).*

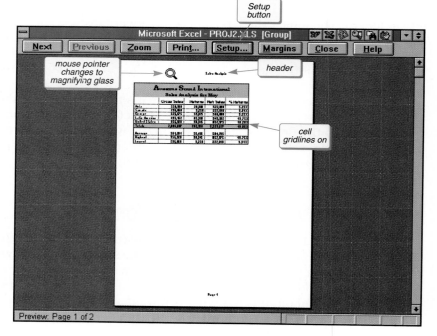

FIGURE 2-77

STEP 3 ►

If the cell gridlines display in the preview as in Figure 2-77, click the Setup button (Setup...) at the top of the preview window. Click the Sheet tab and clear the Gridlines check box in the Print area so the cell gridlines in the preview do not print.

Excel displays the Page Setup dialog box with the Gridlines check box cleared (Figure 2-78).

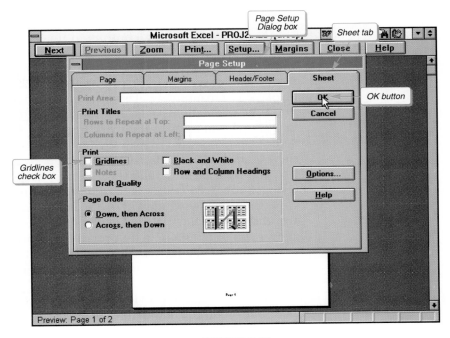

FIGURE 2-78

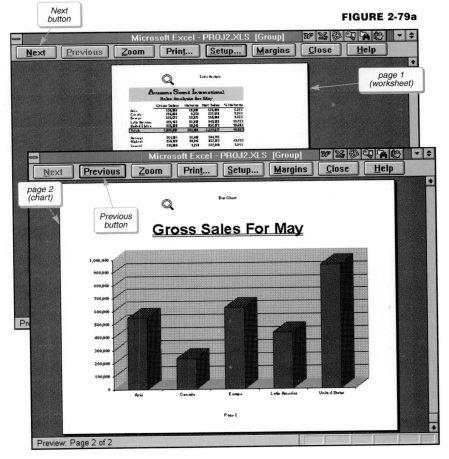

STEP 4 ►

Choose the OK button in the Page Setup dialog box.

Excel displays the preview of the worksheet without cell gridlines (Figure 2-79a).

STEP 5 ►

Click the Next button (Next) to display a preview of the chart.

A preview of the column chart displays (Figure 2-79b).

STEP 6 ►

Click the Close button (Close) in the preview window to return to the workbook.

FIGURE 2-79a

FIGURE 2-79b

Excel displays several buttons at the top of the preview window (Figure 2-79 on the previous page). The first two buttons on the left allow you to page back and forth in a multiple-page worksheet. You use the Zoom button (Zoom) for magnifying or reducing the print preview. Clicking the mouse when the pointer displays as a magnifying glass on the worksheet carries out the same function.

When you click the Print button (Print...), Excel displays a Print dialog box that allows you to print the worksheet. The Setup button displays the same Print Setup dialog box that displays when you choose the Print Setup command from the File menu. The Margins button (Margins) allows you to adjust the top, bottom, left, and right margins, and the column widths. Whatever margin or column width changes you make with the Margins button remain with the worksheet when you close the preview window. The Close button closes the preview window and the workbook redisplays in the Excel workbook window. The Help button (Help) allows you to obtain help on previewing a printout.

Because a change was made in the Print Setup dialog box, Excel draws a dashed line on the worksheet to show the right edge of the page. This is illustrated in Figure 2-80.

After closing the preview window, you can print the worksheet using the Print button on the Standard toolbar.

TO PRINT THE WORKBOOK ▼

STEP 1 ►

Ready the printer.

STEP 2 ►

With both sheets selected, point to the Print button on the Standard toolbar (Figure 2-80).

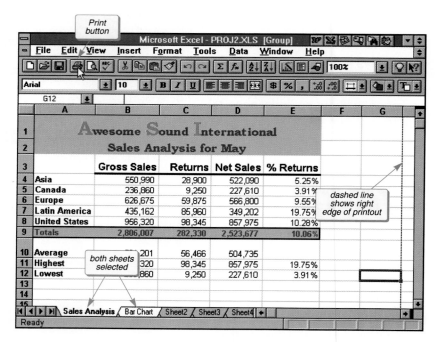

FIGURE 2-80

STEP 3 ▶

Click the left mouse button.

Excel prints the worksheet and column chart on the printer (Figure 2-81).

STEP 4 ▶

Hold down the SHIFT key and click the Sales Analysis tab at the bottom of the window to deselect the Bar Chart tab.

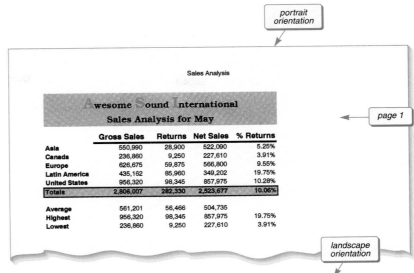

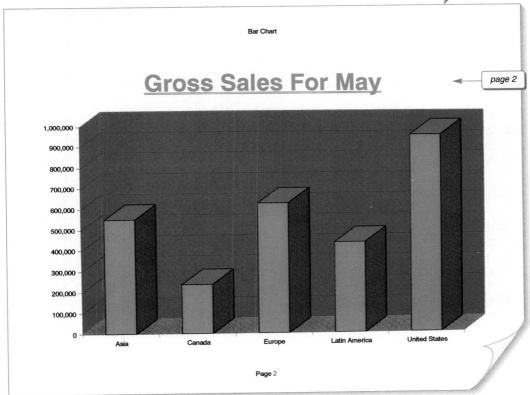

FIGURE 2-81

Notice that the worksheet prints in portrait orientation and the chart prints landscape orientation. **Portrait orientation** means the printout is across the page width of 8.5 inches. **Landscape orientation** means the printout is across the page length of 11 inches. Excel automatically selects landscape orientation for the chart.

▶ PRINTING A SECTION OF THE WORKSHEET

Y ou may not always want to print the entire worksheet. You can print portions of the worksheet by selecting the range of cells to print and then selecting the Selection option button in the Print dialog box. Perform the following steps to print the range A3:C8.

TO PRINT A SECTION OF THE WORKSHEET ▼

STEP 1 ▶

Ready the printer.

STEP 2 ▶

Select the range A3:C8. Point to the menu bar and click the right mouse button. Choose the Print command from the shortcut menu. Click the Selection option button in the Print dialog box.

Excel displays the Print dialog box (Figure 2-82).

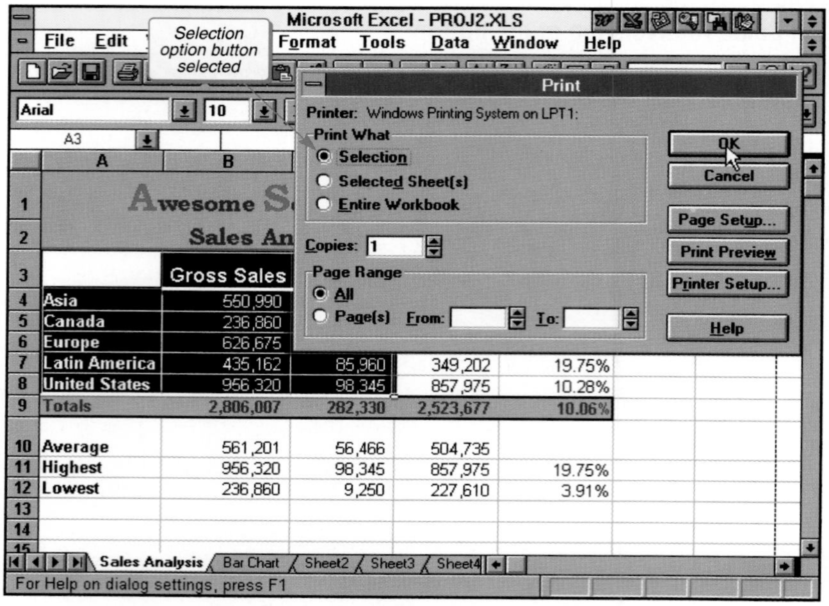

FIGURE 2-82

STEP 3 ▶

Choose the OK button in the Print dialog box.

Excel prints the selected range of the worksheet on the printer (Figure 2-83).

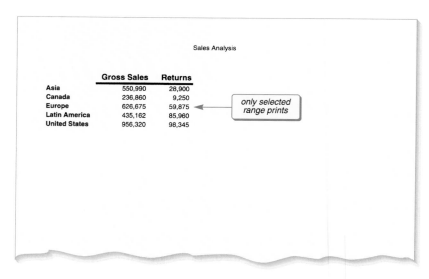

FIGURE 2-83

In the Print What area in the Print dialog box, there are three option buttons (Figure 2-82). The Selection option button instructs Excel to print the selected range. The Selected Sheet(s) option button instructs Excel to print the active sheet (the one displaying on the screen) or the selected sheets. Finally, the Entire Workbook option button instructs Excel to print all the sheets in the workbook. Selecting Entire Workbook is an alternative to selecting tabs by holding down the SHIFT key and clicking tabs to select their sheets. To deselect sheets, click the tab of the one you want to keep active. Next, hold down the SHIFT key and click the active sheet tab again.

▶ DISPLAYING AND PRINTING THE FORMULAS IN THE WORKSHEET

Thus far, the worksheet has been printed exactly as it appears on the screen. This is called the **values version** of the worksheet. Another variation that you can display and print is called the formulas version. The **formulas version** displays and prints what was originally entered into the cells instead of the values in the cells. You can toggle between the values version and formulas version by pressing CTRL+` (single quotation mark next to the 1 key).

The formulas version is useful for debugging a worksheet because the formulas and functions display and print out, instead of the numeric results. **Debugging** is the process of finding and correcting errors in the worksheet.

When you change from values to formulas, Excel increases the width of the columns so the formulas and text do not overflow into adjacent cells on the right. Thus, the worksheet usually becomes significantly wider when the formulas display. To fit the wide printout on one page you can use the **Fit to option** in the Page Setup dialog box and landscape orientation. To change from values to formulas and print the formulas on one page, perform the following steps.

TO DISPLAY THE FORMULAS IN THE WORKSHEET AND FIT THE PRINTOUT ON ONE PAGE ▼

STEP 1 ▶

Press CTRL+` (single quotation mark next to 1 key).

Excel changes the display of the worksheet from values to formulas (Figure 2-84). The formulas in the worksheet display showing unformatted numbers, formulas, and functions that were assigned to the cells. Excel automatically increases the width of the columns.

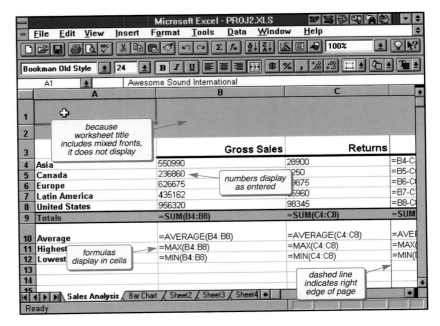

FIGURE2-84

STEP 2 ▶

Choose the Page Setup command from the shortcut menu or File menu. From the Page Setup dialog box, click the Page tab, select the Landscape option, and Fit to option to fit the wide printout on one page in landscape orientation.

Excel displays the Page Setup dialog box with the Landscape and Fit to options selected (Figure 2-85).

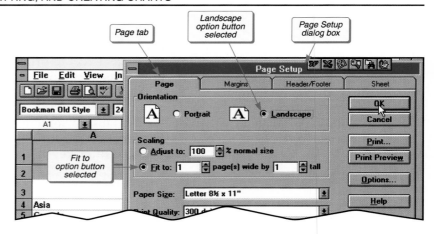

FIGURE 2-85

STEP 3 ▶

Choose the OK button from the Page Setup dialog box. Ready the printer and click the Print tool on the Standard toolbar.

Excel prints the formulas in the worksheet on one page in landscape orientation (Figure 2-86).

STEP 4 ▶

When you're finished with the formulas version, press CTRL+` (single quotation mark next to 1 key) to display the values version.

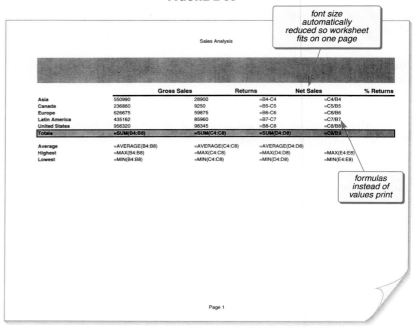

FIGURE 2-86

Although the formulas in the worksheet were printed in the previous example, you can see from Figure 2-84 on page E117 that the display on the screen can also be used for debugging errors in the worksheet.

The formulas in the worksheet were printed using the fit to option so they would fit on one page. Anytime characters extend past the dashed line that represents the rightmost edge of the printed worksheet, the printout will be made up of multiple pages. If you prefer to print the worksheet on one page, select the Fit to option button in the Page Setup dialog box (Figure 2-85) before you print.

An alternative to using CTRL+` to toggle between formulas and values is to select the Formulas check box on the View tab. You display the View tab by choosing the Options command on the Tools menu.

Changing the Print Scaling Option Back to 100%

Depending on your printer driver, you may have to change the Print Scaling option back to 100% after using the Fit to option. Follow the steps below to reset the Scaling option so future worksheets print at 100%, instead of being squeezed on one page.

TO CHANGE THE PRINT SCALING OPTION BACK TO 100%

Step 1: Choose the Page Setup command from the shortcut menu or File menu.
Step 2: Select the Adjust to option button in the Scaling area.
Step 3: If necessary, type 100 in the Adjust to box.
Step 4: Choose the OK button in the Page Setup dialog box.

Through the Adjust to box you can specify the percentage of reduction or enlargement in the printout of a worksheet. The default percentage is 100%. The 100% automatically changes to the appropriate percent whenever you select the Fit to option.

▶ PROJECT SUMMARY

In Project 2, you learned how to enter formulas, calculate an average, find the highest and lowest numbers in a range, change fonts, draw borders, apply number formats, and change column widths and row heights. The techniques and steps presented showed you how to chart on a separate sheet, rename sheet tabs, preview a worksheet, print a workbook, print a section of a worksheet, and display and print the formulas in the worksheet using the Fit to option.

▶ KEY TERMS AND INDEX

addition operator *(E70)*
arguments *(E74)*
Align Left button *(E121)*
Align Right button *(E87)*
As New Sheet command *(E102)*
AutoFormat command *(E109)*
AVERAGE function *(E74)*
background color *(E89)*
backup *(E101)*
best fit *(E94)*
cascading menu *(E102)*
category names *(E102)*
character *(E93)*
Cells command *(E93)*
Chart command *(E102)*
chart sheet *(E102)*
Chart title box *(E105)*
Color button *(E107)*
Color palette *(E107)*
column chart *(E102)*
Column command *(E98)*
column width *(E93)*
Column Width command *(E97)*
Column Width dialog box *(E97)*
Comma style *(E91)*
Comma Style button *(E91)*
custom dictionary *(E99)*
data series *(E102)*
debugging *(E117)*

Decrease Decimal button *(E91)*
division operator *(E70)*
exponentiation operator *(E70)*
Fit to option *(E117)*
Font box *(E83)*
Font Color button *(E84)*
Font Color palette *(E89)*
font color *(E84)*
font size *(E84)*
Font Size box *(E83)*
font styles *(E83)*
Format Cells command *(E88)*
Format menu *(E88)*
formatting numbers *(E91)*
formula *(E69)*
formulas version *(E117)*
function *(E74)*
Function Wizard button *(E77)*
handles *(E109)*
hiding columns *(E98)*
Increase Decimal button *(E91)*
Insert menu *(E102)*
landscape orientation *(E115)*
MAX function *(E76)*
MIN function *(E77)*
Move or Copy sheet command *(E111)*
multiplication operator *(E70)*
negation operator *(E71)*

nonadjacent range *(E89)*
number sign *(E92)*
order of operations *(E71)*
parentheses in formulas *(E71)*
Percent style *(E91)*
Percent Style button *(E91)*
percentage operator *(E70)*
Point mode *(E72)*
portrait orientation *(E115)*
preview window *(E112)*
previewing a worksheet *(E112)*
Print Preview button *(E112)*
Print Preview command *(E111)*
Rename Sheet dialog box *(E109)*
Row command *(E99)*
row height *(E98)*
Row Height command *(E99)*
select sheets *(E117)*
shortcut menu *(E116)*
Spelling button *(E99)*
Spelling dialog box *(E99)*
subtraction operator *(E70)*
tab scrolling buttons *(E111)*
tab split box *(E111)*
values version *(E117)*
walls of chart *(E107)*
white handles *(E109)*
x axis of chart *(E105)*
y axis of chart *(E105)*

In Microsoft Excel, you can accomplish a task in a number of ways. The following table provides a quick reference to each task presented in this project with its available options. The commands listed in the Menu column can be executed using either the keyboard or mouse. Many of the commands in the Menu column are also available on the shortcut menu.

Task	Mouse	Menu	Keyboard Shortcuts
Add a Border	Click Borders button arrow on Formatting toolbar	From Format menu, choose Cells, then select Border tab	Press CTRL+1 Press CTRL+SHIFT+<- (remove border)
Apply Comma Style	Click Comma Style button on Formatting toolbar	From Format menu, choose Cells, then select Number tab	Press CTRL+SHIFT+I
Apply Percent Style	Click Percent Style button on Formatting toolbar	From Format menu, choose Cells, then select Number tab	Press CTRL+SHIFT+%
Change a Column Width	Drag column heading border; double-click column heading right border for best fit	From Format menu, choose Column	Press CTRL+0 (Hide) Press CTRL+SHIFT+) (Unhide)
Change Font Color	Click Font Color arrow on Formatting toolbar	From Format menu choose Cells, then select Font tab	Press CTRL+1
Change Font Size	Click Font Size arrow on Formatting toolbar	From Format menu choose Cells, then select Font tab	Press CTRL+1
Change Font Type	Click Font Type arrow on Formatting toolbar	From Format menu choose Cells, then select Font tab	Press CTRL+1
Change a Row Height	Drag row heading border, double-click row heading bottom border for best fit	From Format menu, choose Row	Press CTRL+9 (Hide) Press CTRL+SHIFT+((Unhide)
Check Spelling	Click Spelling button on Standard toolbar	From Tools menu, choose Spelling	Press F7
Decrease Decimal Places	Click Decrease Decimal button on Formatting toolbar	From Format menu, choose Cells, then select Number tab	Press CTRL+1
Display a Shortcut Menu	Click right mouse button		
Fit to Print Across Page		From File menu, choose Page Setup, then select Page tab	Press CTRL+P and choose Page Setup button
Increase Decimal Places	Click Increase Decimal button on Formatting toolbar	From Format menu, choose Cells, then select Number tab	Press CTRL+1
Left Align Text	Click Align Left button on Formatting toolbar	From Format menu, choose Cells, then select Alignment tab	Press CTRL+1
Move a Sheet	Drag sheet tab to new location	From Edit menu, choose Move or Copy Sheet	

Task	Mouse	Menu	Keyboard Shortcuts
Print Preview	Click Print Preview button on Standard toolbar	From File menu, choose Print Preview	Press CTRL+P and choose Print Preview button
Print an Entire Workbook		From File menu, choose Print	Press CTRL+P
Print a Selected Range		From File menu, choose Print	Press CTRL+P
Rename a Sheet Tab	Double-click tab	From shortcut menu, choose Rename	
Right-Align Text	Click Align Right button on Formatting toolbar	From Format menu choose Cells, then select Alignment tab	Press CTRL+1
Select Sheets	Hold down SHIFT key and click desired sheet tab		
Shade Cells or a Range of Cells	Click Color button on Formatting toolbar	From Format menu, choose Cells, then select Patterns tab	Press CTRL+1
View the Formulas Version or the Values Version		From Tools menu, choose Options, then select View tab	Press CTRL+'

S T U D E N T   A S S I G N M E N T S

STUDENT ASSIGNMENT 1
True/False

Instructions: Circle T if the statement is true or F if the statement is false.

T   F   1. Click the right mouse button to display the shortcut menu.

T   F   2. Use the Currency Style button on the Formatting toolbar to change the entry in a cell to different international monetary value.

T   F   3. The minimum column width is zero.

T   F   4. If you assign a cell the formula =8 / 4, the number 2 displays in the cell.

T   F   5. To remove decimal places in an entry, click the Increase Decimal button.

T   F   6. In the formula =8 + 6 / 2, the addition operation (+) is completed before the division operation (/).

T   F   7. The formulas =a2 - a3, =A2 - A3, and =A2-A3 result in the same value being assigned to the active cell.

T   F   8. The Function Wizard button on the Standard toolbar must be used to enter functions.

T   F   9. If you use the Point mode to enter a formula or select a range, you must click the enter box to complete the entry.

T   F   10. Use the AVERAGE function to assign a cell the average of the entries in a range of cells.

T   F   11. To save an intermediate copy of the workbook to disk, you must choose the Save As command from the File menu.

T   F   12. If you save a workbook a second time using the Save button, Excel will save it under the same filename that was used the first time it was saved.

STUDENT ASSIGNMENT 1 (continued)

T F 13. If the function =SUM(B4:B8) assigns a value of 10 to cell B9, and B9 is copied to C9, cell C9 may or may not equal 10.
T F 14. To select a second sheet, hold down the SHIFT key and click its tab.
T F 15. When a number is too large to fit in a cell, Excel displays asterisks (*) in place of the number in the cell.
T F 16. It is not possible to apply different format styles to individual characters in a cell.
T F 17. Use the Font box to change the font in a cell or range of cells.
T F 18. To increase or decrease the width of a column, use the mouse to point to the column heading name and drag it to the left or right.
T F 19. To select an entire row, click the row heading.
T F 20. When the formulas in the worksheet display, Excel displays numeric and text entries without the format applied to them.

STUDENT ASSIGNMENT 2
Multiple Choice

Instructions: Circle the correct response.

1. Which one of the following arithmetic operations is completed first if they are all found in a formula with no parentheses?
   a. + b. − c. ^ d. *
2. The Comma Style button on the Formatting toolbar causes 5000 to display as:
   a. $5,000 b. 5000 c. 5,000 d. 5,000. 00
3. Which one of the following formulas is valid?
   a. =C3 + b3 b. =c3 + b3 c. =C3 + B3 d. all of these
4. When you use the Print Preview button on the Standard toolbar, the mouse pointer becomes a _____ when it is pointed at the worksheet.
   a. cross b. magnifying glass c. split double arrow d. block plus sign
5. The maximum height of a row is approximately _____ points.
   a. 100 b. 200 c. 300 d. 400
6. A listing on the printer of the worksheet in which formulas display instead of numbers is called the _____ version of the worksheet.
   a. formulas b. displayed c. formatted d. content
7. If 0. 052451 is assigned to a cell that is formatted by clicking the Percent Style button and clicking the Increase Decimal button twice on the Formatting toolbar, then the cell contents display as _____.
   a. 5. 25% b. 5. 24% c. 0. 05% d. 5. 00%
8. Which one of the following describes a column width where the user has requested that Excel determine the width to use?
   a. custom fit b. usual fit c. close fit d. best fit
9. The function =AVERAGE(B3:B7) is equal to _____.
   a. =b3 + b4 + b5 + b6 + b7 / 5 c. both a and b
   b. =(b3 + b4 + b5 + b6 + b7) / 5 d. none of these
10. To print two sheets in the workbook at one time, first select the two sheets by holding down the _____ key and clicking the sheet that is not selected, and then clicking the Print button on the Standard toolbar.
    a. SHIFT b. CTRL c. ALT d. ESC

STUDENT ASSIGNMENT 3
Entering Formulas

Instructions: Using the values in the worksheet in Figure SA2-3, write the formula that accomplishes the task for each of the following items and manually compute the value assigned to the specified cell.

	A	B	C	D	E	F	G	H	I
1	1	3	7	5					
2	8	5	12	3					
3	12	9	15	49					
4	5	12	13	4					
5	8	6	2	1					
6									
7									
8									
9									

FIGURE SA2-3

1. Assign cell A7 the product of cells A2 and D2.

   Formula: _____   Result: _____

2. Assign cell F4 the product of cells B1, C1, and D5.

   Formula: _____   Result: _____

3. Assign cell D6 the sum of the range B1:C2, less cell A5.

   Formula: _____   Result: _____

4. Assign cell G2 five times the quotient of cell B2 divided by cell B1.

   Formula: _____   Result: _____

5. Assign cell E1 the sum of the range of cells D2:D5 minus the product of cells C1 and C3.

   Formula: _____   Result: _____

6. Assign cell G6 the result of cell A5 less cell A4 raised to cell B1.

   Formula: _____   Result: _____

7. Assign cell A6 the expression $(X \wedge 2 - 4 * Y * Z) / (2 * Y)$ where the value of X is in cell C2, the value of Y is in cell D2, and the value of Z is in cell D4.

   Formula: _____   Result: _____

STUDENT ASSIGNMENT 4
Understanding Formulas

Instructions: Figure SA2-4 displays the formula version of a worksheet. In the space provided, indicate in the fill-ins, the numeric value assigned to the cells if the numbers display instead of the formulas.

	A	B	C	D	E
1	3	2	5	=A1 + B1 + C1	
2	7	7	6	=A3 * B2 - C3	
3	5	3	9	=2 * (B3 + C1)	
4	=A2 ^ B1	=20 / (A3 + C1)	=A1	=A2 ^ B3 - C3 * B2	
5					
6					
7					
8					
9					

FIGURE SA2-4

1. D1 _____
2. D2 _____
3. D3 _____
4. A4 _____
5. B4 _____
6. C4 _____
7. D4 _____

STUDENT ASSIGNMENT 5
Understanding Functions

Instructions: Figure SA2-5 displays the formula version of a worksheet. In the space provided, indicate the numeric value assigned to the cells if the numbers display instead of the functions.

1. D1 _____

2. D2 _____

3. D3 _____

4. A4 _____

5. B4 _____

6. C4 _____

7. D4 _____

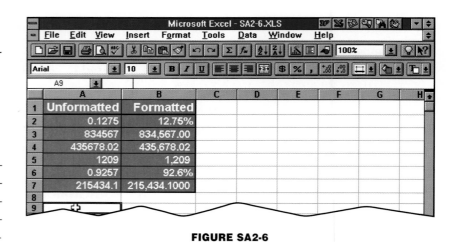

FIGURE SA2-5

STUDENT ASSIGNMENT 6
Applying Number Formats

Instructions: Indicate the buttons you would use on the Formatting toolbar to apply formats to the numbers in column A of Figure SA2-6 so they appear the same as the corresponding number in column B of Figure SA2-6.

Cell	Button(s)
B2	_____
B3	_____
B4	_____
B5	_____
B6	_____
B7	_____

FIGURE SA2-6

COMPUTER LABORATORY EXERCISES

COMPUTER LABORATORY EXERCISE 1
Using the Search for Help on Command on the Help Menu

Instructions: Start Excel and perform the following tasks using a computer.

1. Choose the Search for Help on command from the Help menu.
2. Type column width in the Search dialog box and choose the Show Topics button. With the topic, Adjusting column width, highlighted in the lower list, choose the Go To button. Read the information

displayed on the topic. Ready the printer. Click the Print button in the How To window. Click the Close button in the How To window. Double-click the Control-menu box in the Help window to close.

3. Choose the Search for Help on command from the Help menu. Type borders and click the Show Topics button. Select the topic Tips for Formatting Data in the lower list and choose the Go To button. Read the information and print the information by choosing Print Topic from the File menu in the Help window. Close the Help window.

4. Choose the Search for Help on command from the Help menu. Type function wizard and choose the Show Topics button. Select New Function Wizard and Help for Worksheet Functions from the lower list. Read and print the information in the Help window. Close the Help window.

COMPUTER LABORATORY EXERCISE 2
Applying Formats and Copying Formulas and Functions

Instructions: Start Excel. Open the workbook CLE2-2 from the subdirectory Excel5 on the Student Diskette that accompanies this book. The worksheet resembles the Awesome Sound International Sales Analysis worksheet created in Project 2. Perform the tasks below and on the next page so the worksheet CLE2-2 appears the same as the one shown in Figure CLE2-2.

FIGURE CLE2-2

1. Copy the formula in cell E3 to the range E4:E8.
2. Use the appropriate function in cell B10 to calculate the maximum value in the range B3:B7. Copy cell B10 to the range C10:E10.
3. Use the appropriate function in cell B11 to calculate the minimum value in the range B3:B7. Copy cell B11 to the range C11:E11.
4. Enter your name, course, computer laboratory exercise number (CLE2-2), date, and instructor name in cells A13 through A17.
5. Save an intermediate copy of the workbook. Use the filename CLE2-2A.
6. Apply the following formats to the worksheet title in cell A1: (a) bold; (b) font size 24; (c) text color white (column 2, row 1 on the Color palette); (d) center across columns A through E; (e) background color of range A1:E1 green (column 2, row 2 on the Color palette); and (f) bold outline around the range A1:E1.
7. Change the column width as follows: (a) column A to best fit; (b) columns B through D to 13.00; and (c) column E to 11.00.
8. Bold, italicize, and right-align the column titles in the range B2 through E2. Draw a bold bottom border below row 2 in the range B2:E2 and below row 7 in the range A7:E7.
9. Bold the row titles in the range A3:A11, italicize the row title in cell A8, and bold the totals in the range B8:E8.
10. Draw a double underline border below row 8 in the range A8:E8.
11. Apply the Comma style with no decimal places to the range B3:D11.
12. Apply the Percent style with two decimal places to the range E3:E11.
13. Change the row height for row 1 to 45 points and the row height for rows 2 and 9 to 24 points.

(continued)

COMPUTER LABORATORY EXERCISE 2 (continued)

14. Save the workbook a second time using the same filename.
15. Preview the worksheet. Print the worksheet without gridlines.
16. Save the workbook again.
17. Print the range A2:C9.
18. Press CTRL+` (next to 1 key) to change the display from values to formulas. Print the formulas in the worksheet. After printing the formulas, change the display back to values by pressing CTRL+`.
19. Hide columns B and C by changing their column widths to zero. Print the worksheet.

COMPUTER LABORATORY EXERCISE 3
Changing Values in a Worksheet and Changing Appearance of a Chart

Instructions Part 1: Start Excel and perform the following tasks to change values in a worksheet. Open the worksheet CLE2-3 from the subdirectory Excel5 on the Student Diskette that accompanies this book. The worksheet CLE2-3 is shown in Figure CLE2-3a.

FIGURE CLE2-3a

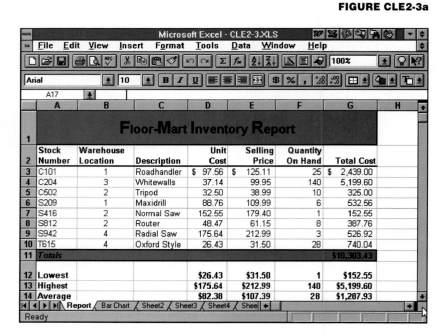

1. Increase the Quantity On Hand amounts in column F as listed in the table to the right. Notice as you change the values in column F that the values in column G change accordingly. You should end up with the following totals: cell G11 is $20,189.18; cell G12 is $812.50; cell G13 is $5,756.70; and cell G14 is $2,523.65.
2. With gridlines off, print a copy of the worksheet with the new values.
3. Close the workbook without saving the changes.

Instructions Part 2: Perform the following tasks to change the appearance of the bar chart that accompanies worksheet CLE2-3 to make it look like Figure CLE2-3b.

1. Open the worksheet CLE2-3.
2. Click the Bar Chart tab at the bottom of the screen to display the worksheet's accompanying bar chart. Steps 3, 4, and 5 will change the chart you see on your screen to look like the one in Figure CLE2-3b.

	OLD QUANTITY ON HAND	NEW QUANTITY ON HAND
Roadhandler	25	40
Whitewalls	140	155
Tripod	10	25
Maxidrill	6	21
Normal Saw	1	16
Router	8	23
Radial Saw	3	18
Oxford Style	28	43

3. Move the columns in the chart so they are in the sequence shown in Figure CLE2-3b by (a) selecting any column on the chart; (b) clicking the right mouse button; (c) selecting Format 3-D Column Group; (d) displaying the Series Order tab; (e) one by one selecting the name in the Series Order box that corresponds to each column; (f) clicking the Move Up button or the Move Down button until the columns are in the same sequence as shown in Figure CLE2-3b; and (g) choosing the OK button.

4. Change the color of the chart walls to blue (column 8, row 1 on the Color palette). You must first click the chart wall (not a gridline) to change the color.

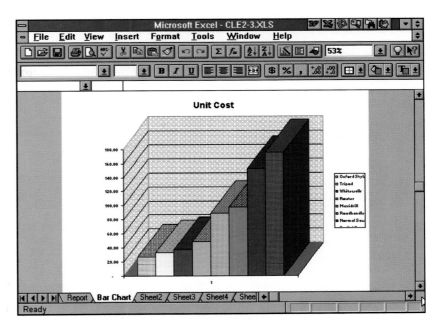

FIGURE CLE2-3b

5. Change the perspective of the chart to agree with the perspective shown in Figure CLE2-3b by (a) clicking on the chart; (b) moving the mouse pointer to the black handle located at the upper left corner of the chart; (c) clicking the handle (the mouse pointer will change to a cross shape); dragging the chart to a new location; and (d) releasing the left mouse button.

6. Click the Report tab at the bottom of the screen to return to the worksheet and enter your name, course, computer laboratory exercise number (CLE2-3B), date, and instructor name in cells A16 through A20.

7. Save the modified workbook. Use the filename CLE2-3B.

8. Print both the worksheet and the column chart.

C O M P U T E R   L A B O R A T O R Y   A S S I G N M E N T S

COMPUTER LABORATORY ASSIGNMENT 1
Building a Monthly Sales Analysis Worksheet and 3-D Column Chart

Purpose: To become familiar with building a worksheet that includes formulas, formatting a worksheet, using the recalculation features of Excel, printing different versions of the worksheet and building a 3-D column chart based on values in the worksheet.

Problem: The computer consulting firm you and a friend started recently on a part-time basis has received its first contract. The client has specified in the contract that you are to build a monthly sales analysis worksheet that determines the sales quota and percentage of quota met for the following salespeople:

NAME	SALES AMOUNT	SALES RETURNS	SALES QUOTA
Sandy Lane	$15,789.00	$245.00	$12,000.00
George Ade	8,500.00	500.00	10,000.00
Mary Markam	17,895.00	1,376.00	12,000.00
Tom Rich	12,843.00	843.00	11,000.00

(continued)

COMPUTER LABORATORY ASSIGNMENT 1 (continued)

Part 1 Instructions: Perform the following tasks to build the worksheet shown in Figure CLA2-1a.

FIGURE CLA2-1a

1. Use the Select All button and the Bold button to bold the entire worksheet.
2. Increase the widths of columns A through F to 13.00 characters.
3. Enter the worksheet title, Monthly Sales Report, in cell A1, column titles in row 2, and the row titles in column A as shown in Figure CLA2-1a.
4. Enter the sales data described in the previous table in columns A, B, C, and E as shown in Figure CLA2-1a. Do not enter the numbers with dollar signs or commas.
5. Obtain the net sales in column D of the worksheet by subtracting the sales returns in column C from the sales amount in column B. Enter the formula in cell D3 and copy it to the range D4:D6.
6. Obtain the above quota amounts in column F by subtracting the sales quota in column E from the net sales in column D. Enter the formula in cell F3 and copy it to the range F4:F6.
7. Obtain the totals in row 7 by adding the column values for each salesperson. The averages in row 8 contain the column averages.
8. In cell A9, enter the % of Quota Sold title with equal signs and the greater than sign to create the arrow shown in Figure CLA2-1a. Obtain the percent of quota sold in cell C9 by dividing the total net sales amount in cell D7 by the total sales quota amount in cell E7.
9. Change the worksheet title font in cell A1 to CG Times and increase its size to 22 point. Center the title across columns A through F.
10. Italicize the column titles in row 2. Right-align the titles in columns B through F. Draw a bold bottom border in the range A2:F2.
11. Select the ranges A1:F1 and A7:F7. Change the background color to purple (column 1, row 2 of the Color palette). Change the text color of the worksheet title to white (column 2, row 1 of the Color palette). Outline both of these ranges with a bold border as shown in Figure CLA2-1.
12. Increase the height of row 1 to 42.00 points and increase the heights of rows 2, 8, and 9 to 24.00 points.
13. Use the buttons on the Formatting toolbar to apply number formats in the range B3:F8 to the Comma style with two decimal places. Format cell C9 to the Percent style with two decimal places.
14 Change the color of cell C9 to yellow (column 4, row 5 of the Color palette) and place an outline around it.

15. Enter your name, course, computer laboratory assignment number (CLA2-1), date, and instructor name below the entries in column A in separate cells.
16. Save the workbook using the filename CLA2-1A.
17. Print the worksheet without gridlines.
18. Save the workbook again.
19. Display the formulas by pressing CTRL+`. Print the formulas in the worksheet using the Fit to option button in the Scaling area on the Page tab in the Page Setup dialog box. After printing the worksheet, reset Scaling by selecting the Adjust to option button on the Page tab in the Page Setup dialog box and changing the percent value to 100%. Change the display from formulas back to values by pressing CTRL+`.
20. Print only the range A2:B8.

Part 2 Instructions: Increment each of the four values in the sales quota column by $1,000.00 until the percent of quota sold in cell C9 is below, yet as close as possible to, 100%. All four values in column E must be incremented the same number of times. The percent of quota sold in cell C9 should equal 98.23%. Save the workbook as CLA2-1B. Print the worksheet without cell gridlines.

Part 3 Instructions: With the percent of quota sold in cell C9 equal to 98.23% from Part 2, decrement each of the four values in the sales return column by $100.00 until the percent of quota sold in cell C9 is below, yet as close as possible to, 100%. Decrement all four values in column C the same number of times. Your worksheet is correct when the percent of quota sold in cell C9 is equal to 99.74%. Save the workbook as CLA2-1C. Print the worksheet without cell gridlines.

Part 4 Instructions: Select the range A3:B6. Use the Chart command on the Insert menu to create a chart on a new sheet. Draw a 3-D Column Chart with a number 4 format like the one shown in Figure CLA2-1b. Notice the following about the chart: (a) the data series for this chart is in columns; (b) there is no legend on the chart; and (c) the chart does have a title of Monthly Sales by Salesperson. Next, change the color of the chart background to yellow (column 4, row 5 on the Color palette) and change the color of the columns to purple (column 1, row 2 on the Color palette). Change the font size of the chart title to 24 point and the color of the text to the same color as the columns. Rename the Sheet tabs at the bottom of the screen to read Sales for the sheet tab corresponding to the worksheet and Bar Chart for the sheet tab corresponding to the chart. Rearrange the order of the sheet tabs so the worksheet appears first with the chart following it. Save the workbook as CLA2-1D. Print the entire workbook without cell gridlines.

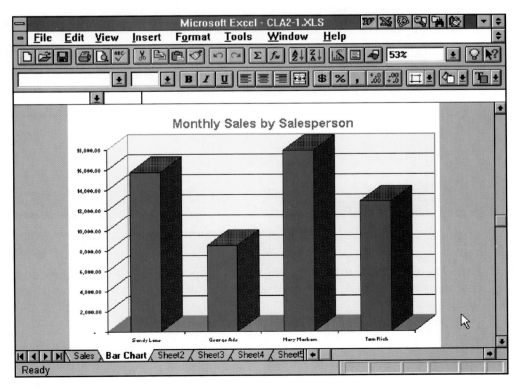

FIGURE CLA2-1b

COMPUTER LABORATORY ASSIGNMENT 2
Building a Biweekly Payroll Worksheet

Purpose: To become familiar with entering complex formulas.

Problem: You are employed by the Payroll department of a construction firm. You have been asked to prepare a biweekly payroll report for the following six employees:

EMPLOYEE	RATE PER HOUR	HOURS	DEPENDENTS
Col, Lisa	12.50	81.00	2
Fel, Jeff	18.00	64.00	4
Di, Marci	13.00	96.25	0
Sno, Niki	4.50	122.50	1
Hi, Mandi	3.35	16.50	1
Bri, Jodi	10.40	80.00	3

Instructions: Perform the following tasks to create a worksheet similar to the one in Figure CLA2-2.

FIGURE CLA2-2

1. Enter the worksheet title, Biweekly Payroll Report, in cell A1. Enter the column titles in row 2, the row titles in column A, and the data in columns B through D from the above table as shown in Figure CLA2-2.

2. Use the following formulas to determine the gross pay, federal tax, state tax, and net pay:
   a. Gross Pay = Rate * Hours (Hint: Assign the first employee in cell E3 the formula =B3 * C3, and copy the formula in E3 to the range E4:E8 for the remaining employees.)
   b. Federal Tax = 20% * (Gross Pay - Dependents * 38. 46)
   c. State Tax = 3. 2% * Gross Pay
   d. Net Pay = Gross Pay - (Federal Tax + State Tax)
3. Show totals for the hours, gross pay, federal tax, state tax, and net pay in row 9.
4. Determine the average, highest, and lowest values of each column in rows 10 through 12 by using the appropriate functions.
5. Do the following to apply formatting to the worksheet title in cell A1: (a) bold; (b) change the font style to TrueType Times New Roman; (c) increase the font size to 18 point; (d) individually change the first character in each word to 28 point; (e) center the title across columns A through H; (f) change the background color of the range to red (column 3, row 1 on the Color palette); and (g) draw a bold outline around the range A1 through H1.
6. Use the buttons on the Formatting toolbar. Apply the Comma style with two decimal places to the range B3:H12. Notice that Excel displays a dash in any cell that has a value of zero and has been formatted to the Comma style.
7. Bold, italicize, and right-align the column titles and draw a bold border under them in the range B2:H2. Change the background color for the range A2:H2 to gray (column 8, row 2 on the Color palette) and change the column title text to white (column 2, row 1 on the Color palette).
8. Select the range H3:H8 and change the background color to black (column 1, row 1 on the Color palette) and change the text color to white (column 2, row 1 on the Color palette). Draw an outline around this range.
9. Bold the names and row titles in column A. Italicize the row titles and change the Font style to MS Sans Serif in the range A9:A12.
10. Change the heights of rows 2 and 10 to 24.00 points and the width of columns A through H to 9.00 points. Draw the borders above and below the totals in row 9 as shown in Figure CLA2-2.
11. Enter your name, course, computer laboratory assignment number (CLA2-2), date, and instructor name below the entries in column A in separate but adjacent cells.
12. Save the workbook using the filename CLA2-2.
13. Preview the worksheet. Print the worksheet with gridlines off.
14. Save the workbook a second time.
15. Press CTRL+` to change the display from values to formulas. Print the formulas to fit on one page in the worksheet. After the printer is finished, reset the worksheet to display the numbers by pressing CTRL+`. Reset Scaling to 100% by selecting the Adjust to option button on the Page tab in the Page Setup dialog box and setting the percent value to 100%.
16. Increase the number of hours worked for each employee by 7. 5. Total net pay (cell H9) should be 4,168.38. Print the worksheet with the new values. Do not save the worksheet with the new values.

COMPUTER LABORATORY ASSIGNMENT 3
Determining the Monthly Accounts Receivable Balance

Purpose: To become familiar with entering and copying formulas, applying formatting to a worksheet, creating a bar chart, and printing different versions of the worksheet.

Problem: You are enrolled in a sophomore Office Information Systems course in which the students are given projects in the local business community. You have been assigned to LakeView Hardware. LakeView Hardware wants you to generate a much-needed report that summarizes their monthly accounts receivable balance. The monthly information contained in the table on the next page is available for test purposes.

(continued)

COMPUTER LABORATORY ASSIGNMENT 3 (continued)

ACCOUNT NUMBER	CUSTOMER NAME	BEGINNING BALANCE	PURCHASES	PAYMENTS	RETURNS
A203	Kelly	1,782.32	324.12	400.00	6.25
C609	Bates	235.68	23.00	25.00	23.15
F812	Webb	435.92	10.00	50.00	212.25
F933	Silver	1,678.54	212.78	25.00	15.00
H234	Abram	3,098.75	89.43	10.00	45.00

Part 1 Instructions: Construct a worksheet similar to the one shown in Figure CLA2-3a. Include all six fields in the report plus the service charge and new balance. (Assume no negative unpaid monthly balances.) Use the following formulas to determine the service charge and the new balance at the end of month for each account:

a. Service Charge = 2.25% * (Beginning Balance - Payments - Returns)
b. New Balance = Beginning Balance + Purchases - Payments - Returns + Service Charge

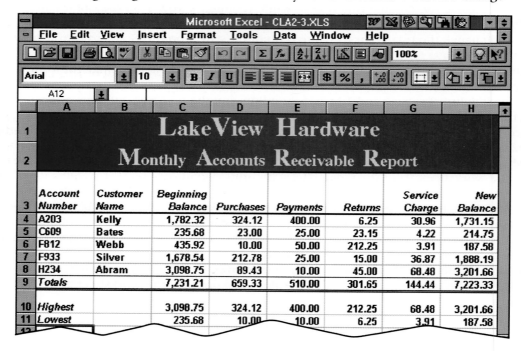

FIGURE CLA2-3a

Perform the following tasks:

1. Use the Select All button and Bold button on the Formatting toolbar to bold the entire worksheet.
2. Assign the worksheet title, LakeView Hardware, to cell A1. Assign the worksheet subtitle, Monthly Accounts Receivable Report, to cell A2.
3. Enter the column titles in the range A3:H3 as shown in Figure CLA2-3a. In the column titles that contain two words (such as Account Number in cell A3), press ALT+ENTER after the first word and ENTER after the second word.
4. Enter the account numbers and row titles in column A
5. Cell C10 should contain the appropriate function to calculate the maximum value in the range C4:C8. Copy cell C10 to the range D10:H10.
6. Cell C11 should contain the appropriate function to calculate the minimum value in the range C4:C8. Copy cell C11 to the range D11:H11.

7. Change the worksheet title font in cell A1, to CG Times 22 point. Change the font size of the first letter of each word in the worksheet title to 28 point. Format the worksheet subtitle font in cell A2 to CG Times 16 point and the first letter of each word in the subtitle to 24 point.

8. Select the range A1:H2 and change the background color to blue (column 5, row 1 of the Color palette). Change the text color in the range A1:H2 to yellow (column 3, row 4 of the Color palette). Center both the worksheet title and subtitle across the range A1:H2. Change the heights of rows 1 and 2 to 30.00 points.

9. Change the widths of columns A through H to 10.00 points. Italicize the column titles and place a bold border below them. Right-align the column titles in the range C3:H3. Change the row height of row 3 to 42.00 points.

10. Italicize the titles in rows 9, 10, and 11. Change the height of row 10 to 24.00 points. Select row 9 and place a single upper border and double underline border in the range A9:H9.

11. Using the buttons on the Formatting toolbar, apply the Comma style with two decimal places to the ranges C4:H11.

12. Enter your name, course, computer laboratory assignment number (CLA2-3), date, and instructor name below the entries in column A in separate but adjacent cells.

13. Save the workbook using the filename CLA2-3.

14. Print the worksheet in landscape orientation without gridlines.

15. Save the workbook again.

16. Print the range A3:C9 in portrait orientation.

17. Press CTRL+` to change the display from values to formulas. Print to fit on one page in landscape orientation, the formulas in the worksheet. After the printer is finished, reset the worksheet to display values by pressing CTRL+`. Reset Scaling to 100% by selecting the Adjust to option button on the Page tab in the Page Setup dialog box and setting the percent value to 100%.

Part 2 Instructions: Select the range B4:C8. Use the Chart command on the Insert menu, to create a chart as a new sheet. Draw a 3-D Bar Chart with a number 1 format like the one shown in Figure CLA2-3b. Notice the following about the chart: (a) the data series for this chart is in columns; (b) there is no legend on the chart; and (c) the chart does have a title of Monthly Accounts Receivable. Once the chart is drawn, change the color of the chart walls to medium blue (column 1, row 3 on the Color palette) and change the color of the bars to yellow (column 3, row 4 on the Color palette). Change the font size and color of the title to 18 point with a color of dark blue (column 1, row 4 on the Color palette). Rename the sheet tabs at the bottom of the screen to read Report for the sheet tab corresponding to the worksheet and Bar Chart for the sheet tab corresponding to the chart. Rearrange the order of the sheet tabs so the worksheet appears first with the chart following it. Save the workbook using the filename CLA2-3A. Print the chart.

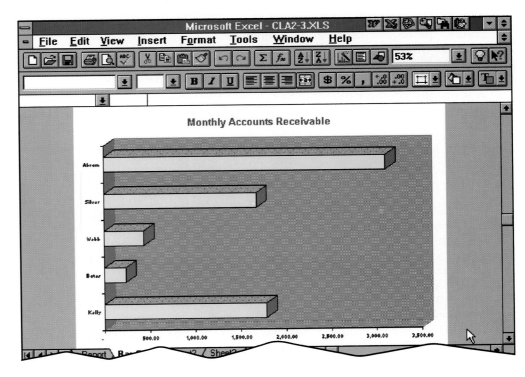

FIGURE CLA2-3b

COMPUTER LABORATORY ASSIGNMENT 4
Inflation Gauge

Purpose: To become familiar with planning a worksheet.

Problem: You are employed as a summer intern by the State Budget department. One of the department's responsibilities is to report to the state legislature the expected inflation rate of food for the next year. They obtain their data by selecting a few often-used grocery items and keeping track of the prices over a period of time. They then determine and report the individual inflation rates and the expected prices in one year. As a summer intern with a knowledge of Excel, they have asked you to create an Inflation Gauge worksheet.

Instructions: Perform the following tasks to determine the price change, inflation rate, and expected price using the pricing information data below.

ITEM	CURRENT PRICE	BEGINNING PRICE	NUMBER OF WEEKS
1 doz. eggs	$0.93	$0.92	13
1 lb. butter	2.59	2.50	15
1 gal. milk	1.92	1.85	18
1 loaf bread	1.10	1.07	6

Assign these three formulas to the first item — 1 doz. eggs in row 4 — and copy them to the rest of the items.
   a. Price Change = 52 * (Current Price - Beginning Price) / Weeks
   b. Inflation Rate = Price Change / Beginning Price
   c. Price in One Year = Current Price + Inflation Rate * Current Price

Use the techniques you learned in this project to apply formatting to the worksheet and to illustrate totals. Enter your name, course, computer laboratory assignment number (CLA2-4), date, and instructor name below the entries in column A in separate but adjacent cells. Save the worksheet using the filename CLA2-4. Submit the following:

1. A description of the problem. Include the purpose of the worksheet, a statement outlining the results, the required data, and calculations.
2. A handwritten design of the worksheet.
3. A printed copy of the worksheet without cell gridlines.
4. A printed copy of the formulas in the worksheet.
5. A short description explaining how to use the worksheet.
6. Draw a chart that compares the inflation rate of the four items in the worksheet. Apply appropriate formatting to the chart.

MICROSOFT EXCEL 5 FOR WINDOWS

PROJECT THREE

ENHANCING A WORKSHEET AND CHART

OBJECTIVES You will have mastered the material in this project when you can:

- ▶ Use the fill handle to create a series of month names
- ▶ Copy a cell's format to another cell using the Format Painter button
- ▶ Copy a range of cells to a nonadjacent paste area
- ▶ Freeze the column and row titles
- ▶ Insert and delete cells
- ▶ Format numbers by entering them with a format symbol
- ▶ Display the system date using the NOW function and format it
- ▶ Use the IF function to enter one value or another in a cell on the basis of a logical test
- ▶ Copy absolute cell references

- ▶ Italicize text
- ▶ Add a drop shadow to a range of cells
- ▶ Display and dock toolbars
- ▶ Create a 3-D pie chart
- ▶ Explode a 3-D pie chart
- ▶ Rotate a chart
- ▶ Add an arrow and text to a chart
- ▶ Use the Zoom Control box to change the appearance of the worksheet
- ▶ View different parts of the worksheet through window panes
- ▶ Use Excel to answer what-if questions
- ▶ Analyze worksheet data by using the Goal Seek command

▶ INTRODUCTION

This project introduces you to techniques to enhance your ability to create worksheets and draw charts. You will learn about alternative methods for entering values in cells and formatting them. You will also learn how to use absolute cell references and how to use the IF function to assign one value or another to a cell based on a logical test.

In the previous projects, you learned how to use the Standard toolbar and Formatting toolbar. Excel has several other toolbars that can make your work easier. One such toolbar is the **Drawing toolbar**, which allows you to draw shapes, arrows, and drop shadows around cells you want to emphasize in the worksheet.

Worksheets are normally much larger than those presented in the previous projects. Worksheets that extend beyond the size of the window present a viewing problem because you cannot see the entire worksheet at one time. For this reason, Excel provides several commands that allow you to rearrange the view on the screen to display critical parts of a large worksheet. These commands allow you to maintain the row and column titles on the screen at all times by freezing the titles and to view different parts of a worksheet through window panes.

From your work in Projects 1 and 2, you are aware of the ease in creating charts. This project goes a step further and introduces you to methods for improving a chart's appearance. With only a little effort, you can use Excel to create, display, and print professional looking charts and convey your message in a dramatic pictorial fashion.

When you set up a worksheet, you should use as many cell references in formulas as possible, rather than constant values. The cell references in a formula are often called assumptions. **Assumptions** are cells whose values you can change to determine new values for formulas. This project emphasizes the use of assumptions and introduces you to answering what-if questions such as: What if you decrease the base salary assumption (cell B15 in Figure 3-1a) by 1% — how would the decrease affect the total projected payroll expenses (cell H12 in Figure 3-1a)? This capability of quickly analyzing the effect of changing values in a worksheet is important in making business decisions.

FIGURE 3-1a

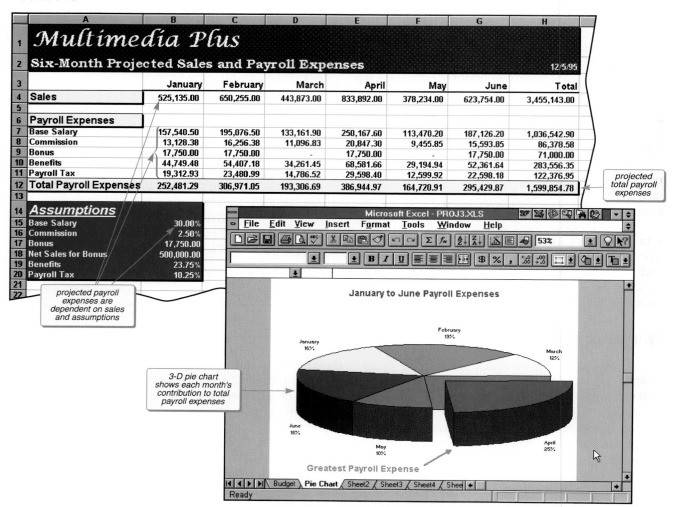

FIGURE 3-1b

▶ PROJECT THREE — MULTIMEDIA PLUS SIX-MONTH PROJECTED SALES AND PAYROLL EXPENSES

T he worksheet in Figure 3-1a contains a company's projected sales and pay-roll expenses for a six-month period. The date in cell H2 (12/5/95) indi-cates that the January to June projections are being made a month before the six-month period begins. The sales in row 4 are estimates based on previous years' sales. In addition, the worksheet includes the projected six-month total sales in cell H4.

Each of the monthly projected payroll expenses in the range B7:G11 — base salary, commission, bonus, benefits, and payroll tax — is determined by taking a percentage of the corresponding monthly sales in row 4. The percent values (assumptions) located in the range B15:B20 are as follows:

1. The monthly base salary is 30% of the projected sales.
2. The monthly commission is 2.5% of the projected sales.
3. The monthly bonus is $17,750 if the monthly projected sales exceed the net sales for bonus in cell B18 ($500,000).
4. The monthly benefits is 23.75% of the projected sales.
5. The monthly payroll tax is 10.25% of the projected sales.

The total projected payroll expenses for each month in row 12 of Figure 3-1a are the sum of the corresponding monthly projected expenses in rows 7 through 11. Finally, the six-month totals in column H are determined by summing the monthly values in each row.

Because the monthly expenses in rows 7 through 11 are dependent on the percent expenses and bonus (assumptions), you can use Excel's what-if capability to determine the impact of changing these percent expenses on the total payroll expenses in row 12.

The 3-D pie chart (Figure 3-1b) shows the contribution of each month to the total projected payroll expenses for the six-month period. The slice representing April has been slightly removed from the main portion of the pie to emphasize the fact that it is expected to contribute more to payroll expenses than any other. The text, Greatest Payroll Expense, at the bottom of the chart sheet and an arrow pointing to the April slice are also used to highlight the April slice.

Worksheet and Chart Preparation Steps

The following list is an overview of how the worksheet in Figure 3-1a and chart in Figure 3-1b will be built in this project. If you are building the worksheet and chart in this project on a personal computer, read these 15 steps without doing them.

1. Start the Excel program.
2. Assign the bold style to all the cells in the worksheet.
3. Enter the worksheet titles, column titles, and row titles. Increase the column widths.
4. Save the workbook.
5. Enter the assumptions in the range B15:B20.
6. Enter the projected sales in row 4.
7. Display the system date in cell H2.
8. Enter the formulas that determine the payroll expenses (B7:G12) and the totals in column H.
9. Format the worksheet so it appears as shown in Figure 3-1a.
10. Create the 3-D pie chart using the nonadjacent range selections B3:G3 and B12:G12.
11. Format the pie chart.

12. Check spelling, preview, print the worksheet and chart, and save the workbook.
13. Use the Zoom Control box on the Standard toolbar to change the appearance of the worksheet.
14. Divide the window into panes.
15. Analyze the data in the worksheet by changing the assumptions (B15:B20) and by goal seeking.

The following sections contain a detailed explanation of each of these steps.

Starting Excel

To start Excel, follow the steps you used at the beginning of Project 1. These steps are summarized below.

TO START EXCEL

Step 1: Click the Microsoft Excel button on the Office Manager toolbar or double-click the Microsoft Excel program-item icon in the Microsoft Office group window.
Step 2: If necessary, enlarge the window by clicking the Maximize button in the upper right corner of the screen.

Changing the Font of the Entire Worksheet to Bold

The first step in this project is to change the font of the entire worksheet to bold, so all entries are emphasized.

TO CHANGE THE FONT OF THE ENTIRE WORKSHEET TO BOLD

Step 1: Click the Select All button immediately above row heading 1.
Step 2: Click the Bold button on the Standard toolbar.

There is no immediate change on the screen. However, as you enter text and numbers into the worksheet, Excel will display them in bold.

Entering the Worksheet Titles

There are two worksheet titles, one in cell A1 and one in cell A2. In the previous projects, the titles were centered over the worksheet. With large worksheets that extend beyond the width of a window, it is best to display them in the upper left corner as shown in Figure 3-1a on page E136.

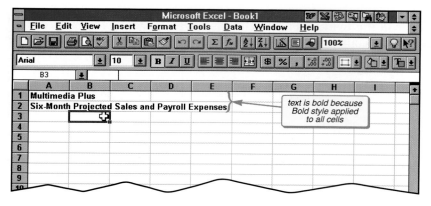

FIGURE 3-2

TO ENTER THE WORKSHEET TITLES

Step 1: Select cell A1 and type
Multimedia Plus
Step 2: Select cell A2 and type
Six-Month Projected
Sales and Payroll
Expenses
Step 3: Select cell B3.

The worksheet titles in cells A1 and A2 display in bold (Figure 3-2).

▶ USING THE FILL HANDLE TO CREATE A SERIES

I n Projects 1 and 2, you used the fill handle to copy a cell or a range of cells to adjacent cells. You can also use the fill handle to automatically create a series of numbers, dates, or month names. Perform the following steps to enter the month name January in cell B3, format cell B3, and then create the remaining five month names, February, March, April, May, and June, in the range C3:G3 (see Figure 3-5).

TO USE THE FILL HANDLE TO CREATE A SERIES OF MONTH NAMES ▼

STEP 1 ▶

With cell B3 selected, enter January. On the Formatting toolbar, choose 11 point in the Font Size box, click the Align Right button, and choose a heavy bottom border from the Borders palette. Point to the fill handle.

The text, January, in cell B3 displays using the applied formats (Figure 3-3). The mouse pointer changes to a cross.

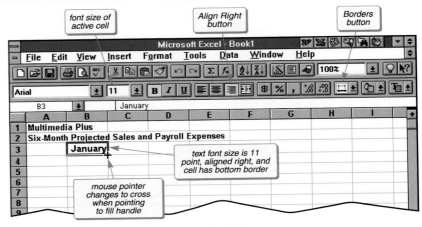

FIGURE 3-3

STEP 2 ▶

Drag the fill handle to the right to select the range C3:G3.

Excel displays a light border that surrounds the range selected (Figure 3-4).

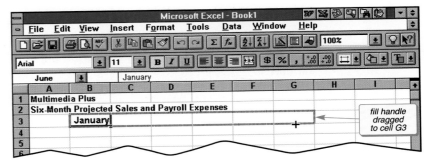

FIGURE 3-4

STEP 3 ▶

Release the left mouse button.

Using January in cell B3 as the basis, Excel creates the month name series, February through June, in the range C3:G3 (Figure 3-5). The formats applied to cell B3 are copied (propagated) to the range C3:G3.

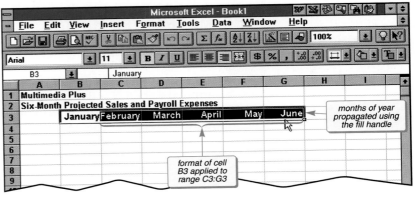

FIGURE 3-5

Besides creating a series of values, the fill handle also copies the format of cell B3 (11 point, right-aligned, and heavy bottom border) to the range C3:G3. If you drag the fill handle past cell G3 (after June) in Step 2, Excel continues to increment the months and will logically repeat January, February, and so on.

You can create different types of series using the fill handle. Table 3-1 illustrates several examples. Notice in Examples 4 through 7 in Table 3-1 that if you use the fill handle to create a series of numbers or nonsequential months, you are required to enter the first number in the series in one cell and the second number in the series in an adjacent cell. You then select both cells and drag the fill handle across the paste area.

If you want to use the fill handle to copy the same text, such as January, to each cell in the paste area without creating a series, hold down the CTRL key while you drag.

▸ **TABLE 3-1**

EXAMPLE	CONTENTS OF CELL(S) COPIED USING FILL HANDLE	NEXT THREE VALUES OF EXTENDED SERIES
1	6:00	7:00, 8:00, 9:00
2	Qtr3	Qtr4, Qtr1, Qtr2
3	Quarter 1	Quarter 2, Quarter 3, Quarter 4
4	Jul-93, Oct-93	Jan-94, Apr-94, Jul-94
5	1999, 2000	2001, 2002, 2003
6	1, 2	3, 4, 5
7	200, 195	190, 185, 180
8	Sun	Mon, Tue, Wed
9	Tuesday	Wednesday, Thursday, Friday
10	1st Part	2nd Part, 3rd Part, 4th Part
11	-1, -3	-5, -7, -9

Customizing the Series

You can instruct Excel on what type of series you want to create by using the **AutoFill shortcut menu** or **Fill command** on the Edit menu. To display the AutoFill shortcut menu, point to the fill handle. When it changes to a cross, hold down the right mouse button. The mouse pointer changes from the cross to a block arrow ( ). Drag the fill handle over the desired range. Then, release the right mouse button and the AutoFill shortcut menu displays. You can then select the type of series you want to create.

▸ COPYING A CELL'S FORMAT USING THE FORMAT PAINTER BUTTON

Because it is not part of the series, the last column title, Total, in cell H3 must be entered separately. Furthermore, to ensure that it appears the same as the other column titles, the same formats applied to the months must be applied to cell H3. Excel has a button on the Standard toolbar, called the **Format Painter** ( ), which allows you to copy a cell's format to another cell. The following steps enter the column title, Total, in cell H3 and format the cell using the Format Painter button.

TO COPY A CELL'S FORMAT ▼

STEP 1 ▶

Select cell H3 and enter `Total`

STEP 2 ▶

Select cell G3 and click the Format Painter button on the Standard toolbar. Move the mouse pointer over cell H3.

The mouse pointer changes to a block plus sign and paint brush (⊕🖌) (Figure 3-6).

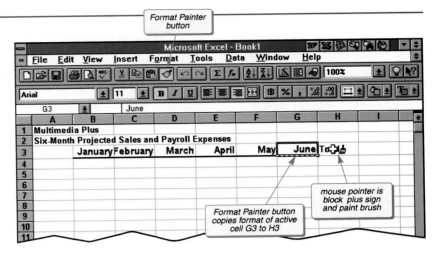

FIGURE 3-6

STEP 3 ▶

Click the left mouse button to assign the format of cell G3 to H3. Select cell A4.

The format of cell G3 (11 point, right-aligned, and a heavy bottom border) is applied to cell H3 (Figure 3-7).

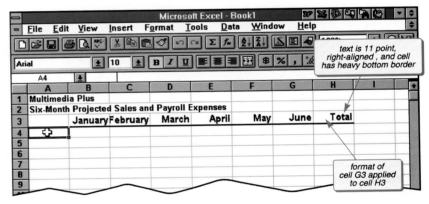

FIGURE 3-7

The Format Painter button can be used to copy the formats of a cell to a range or to copy a range to another range. To copy formats to a range of cells, select the cell or range to copy from, click the Format Painter button, and then drag through the range you want to paste the formats to.

If you want to copy formats to more than one range (nonadjacent ranges), double-click the Format Painter button and then, one by one, drag through the ranges. Finally, click the Format Painter button to deactivate it.

▶ INCREASING THE COLUMN WIDTHS AND ENTERING ROW TITLES

I n Project 2, you increased the column widths after entering the values into the worksheet. Sometimes, you may want to increase the column widths before you enter the values and then, if necessary, adjust them later. The following steps increase the column widths and add the row titles in column A down to Assumptions in cell A14. The last step saves the workbook using the filename PROJ3.XLS.

TO INCREASE COLUMN WIDTHS AND ENTER ROW TITLES ▼

STEP 1 ►

Move the mouse pointer to the border between column heading A and column heading B so the pointer changes to a split double arrow. Drag the mouse pointer to the right until the width displayed in the reference area in the formula bar is equal to 25.00.

The distance between the left edge of column A and the vertical dotted line below the mouse pointer shows the proposed column width and 25.00 displays in the reference area (Figure 3-8).

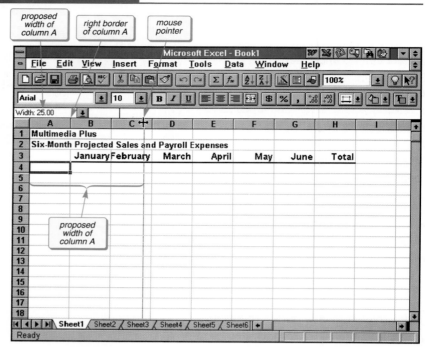

FIGURE 3-8

STEP 2 ►

Release the left mouse button. Select columns B through G by pointing to column heading B and dragging though column heading G. Move the mouse pointer to the borderline between column headings G and H and drag the mouse to the right until the width displayed in the reference area is 13.00.

The distance between the left edge of column G and the vertical line below the mouse pointer shows the proposed column width and 13.00 displays in the reference area (Figure 3-9).

STEP 3 ►

Release the left mouse button. Use the technique in Step 1 to increase the width of column H to 15.00.

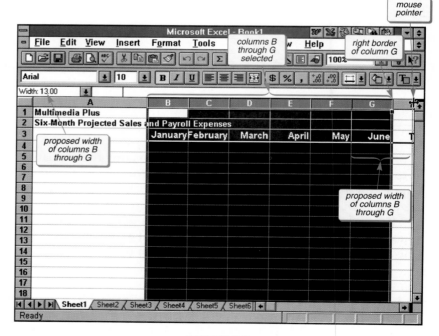

FIGURE 3-9

STEP 4 ▶

Enter Sales in cell A4, Payroll Expenses in cell A6, Base Salary in cell A7, and Commission in cell A8. Enter Bonus in cell A9, Benefits in cell A10, Payroll Tax in cell A11, Total Payroll Expenses in cell A12, and Assumptions in cell A14 as shown in Figure 3-10. Click the Save button on the Standard toolbar. Type the filename PROJ3 in the File Name box. If necessary, select drive A in the Directories box. Choose the OK button. If a Summary Info dialog box displays, choose the OK button.

The workbook name in the title bar changes from Book1 to PROJ3.XLS (Figure 3-10). Only columns A through E display in the window.

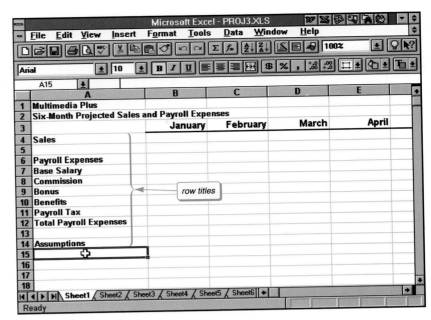

FIGURE 3-10

▶ COPYING A RANGE OF CELLS TO A NONADJACENT PASTE AREA

A ccording to Figure 3-1a on page E136, the row titles in the Assumptions table in the range A15:B20 are the same as the row titles in the range A7:A11, except for the additional entry in cell A18. Hence, the range A7:A11 can be copied to the range A15:A19 and the additional entry in cell A18 can be inserted. Notice that the range to copy (A7:A11) is not adjacent to the paste area (A15:A19). In the first two projects, the fill handle worked well for copying a range of cells to an adjacent paste area, but you cannot use the fill handle to copy a range of cells to a nonadjacent paste area.

A more versatile method of copying a cell or range of cells is to use the Copy button and Paste button on the Standard toolbar. You can use these two buttons to copy a range of cells to an adjacent or nonadjacent paste area.

When you click the **Copy button** (🖺), it copies the contents and format of the selected range and places the entries on the Clipboard, replacing the Clipboard's contents. The **Copy command** on the Edit menu or shortcut menu works the same as the Copy button.

The **Paste button** (🖺) copies the contents of the Clipboard to the paste area. The **Paste command** on the Edit menu or shortcut menu works in the same way as the Paste button. You can also complete the paste operation by pressing the ENTER key.

TO COPY A RANGE OF CELLS TO A NONADJACENT PASTE AREA ▼

STEP 1 ►

Select the range A7:A11 and click the Copy button on the Standard toolbar. Scroll down until row 20 is visible and then select cell A15, the top cell of the paste area.

Excel surrounds the range A7:A11 with a marquis when the Copy button is clicked (Figure 3-11). Excel also copies the values and formats of the range A7:A11 onto the Clipboard.

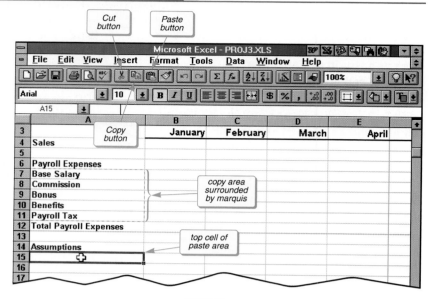

FIGURE 3-11

STEP 2 ►

Press the ENTER key to complete the copy.

Excel copies the contents of the Clipboard (range A7:A11) to the paste area A15:A19 (Figure 3-12).

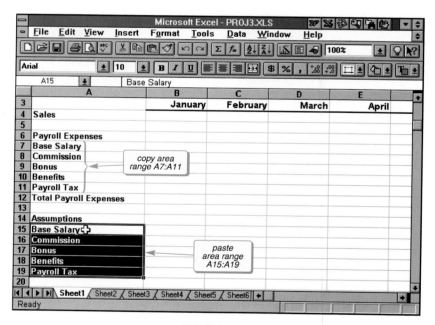

FIGURE 3-12

Notice in Figure 3-11 that you are not required to highlight the entire paste area (A15:A19) before pressing the ENTER key to complete the copy. Because the paste area is exactly the same size as the range you are copying, you need to select only the top left cell of the paste area. In the case of a single column range such as A15:A19, the top cell of the paste area (cell A15) is the upper left cell of the paste area.

When you complete a copy, the values and formats in the paste area are replaced with the values and formats on the Clipboard. Any data contained in the paste area prior to the copy and paste is lost. If you accidentally delete valuable data, immediately click the Undo button on the Standard toolbar or use the **Undo Paste command** from the Edit menu to undo the paste.

Whenever you want to copy a range only once, it is more efficient to use the ENTER key to complete the copy than it is to use the Paste button.

When you use the ENTER key to paste, the contents on the Clipboard are erased after the copy is complete. When you paste using the Paste button or Paste command on the Edit menu or shortcut menu, the contents of the Clipboard remain available for additional copying. Thus, if you plan to copy the cells to more than one paste area, click the Paste button or choose the Paste command from the Edit menu or shortcut menu instead of pressing the ENTER key. Then, select the next paste area and invoke the Paste command again. If you paste using the Paste button or the Paste command from the Edit menu or shortcut menu, the marquis around the range to copy remains to remind you that the copied range is still on the Clipboard. To erase the marquis, press the ESC key.

Using Drag and Drop to Move or Copy Cells

You can use the mouse to move or copy cells. Select the copy area and point to the border of the range. You know you are pointing to the border of a range when the mouse pointer changes to a block arrow. To move the selected cells, drag the selection to its new location. To copy a range, hold down the CTRL key while dragging. Then release the left mouse button before you release the CTRL key. Using the mouse to move or copy cells is called **drag and drop**.

Another way to move cells is to select them, click the Cut button on the Standard toolbar, select the new area, and then click the Paste button on the Standard toolbar or press the ENTER key. You can also use the **Cut command** on the Edit menu or shortcut menu to copy the selected cells to the Clipboard and delete them from their current location.

Moving Cells Versus Copying Cells

In Excel, moving cells is not the same as copying cells. When you copy cells, the copy area remains intact. When you move cells, the original location is blanked and the format is reset to the default. Copy cells to duplicate them on the worksheet. Move cells to rearrange a worksheet.

▶ INSERTING AND DELETING CELLS IN A WORKSHEET

t any time while the worksheet is on the screen, you can add cells to insert new data or delete cells to remove unwanted data. You can insert or delete individual cells, a range of cells, entire rows, or entire columns.

Inserting Rows

The **Rows command** on the Insert menu or the **Insert command** on the shortcut menu allows you to insert rows between rows that already contain values. In the Assumptions table at the bottom of the worksheet, room must be made between rows 17 and 18 to add a row for the Net Sales for Bonus (see Figure 3-1a on page E136). The following steps show how to accomplish the task of inserting a new row into the worksheet.

TO INSERT ROWS

STEP 1 ▶

Click row heading 18 to select the entire row.

STEP 2 ▶

Position the mouse pointer within the selected row and click the right mouse button.

The shortcut menu displays as shown in Figure 3-13.

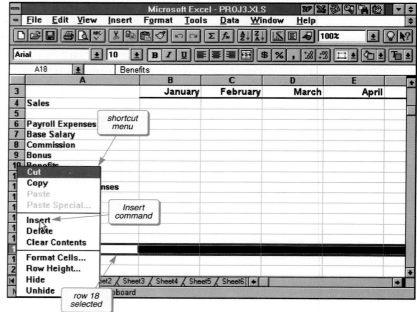

FIGURE 3-13

STEP 3 ▶

Choose the Insert command.

Excel inserts a new row by pushing down all rows below and including row 18, the one originally selected (Figure 3-14).

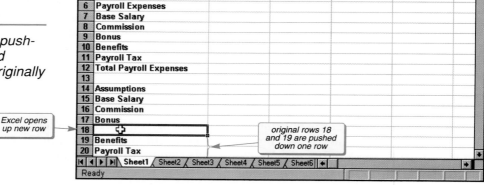

FIGURE 3-14

If the rows pushed down include any formulas, Excel adjusts the cell references to the new locations. Thus, if a formula in the worksheet references a cell in row 18 before the insert, then after the insert, the cell reference in the formula is adjusted to row 19.

The primary difference between the Insert command on the shortcut menu and the Rows command on the Insert menu is that you must select entire rows to insert rows when you use the Insert command on the shortcut menu. The Rows command on the Insert menu only requires that you select a cell in the row to push down or a range of cells to indicate the number of rows to insert. Inserted rows duplicate the format (including colors) of the row above them.

Inserting Columns

Inserting columns into a worksheet is achieved in the same way as inserting rows. To insert columns, begin your column selection immediately to the right of where you want Excel to insert the new blank columns. Select the number of columns you want to insert. Next, choose the Columns command from the Insert menu or the Insert command from the shortcut menu. Here again, if you use the **Columns command**, you need to select only the cells in the columns to push to the right; whereas, you must select entire columns to use the Insert command on the shortcut menu. Inserted columns duplicate the format of the column to their left.

Inserting Individual Cells or a Range of Cells

The Insert command on the shortcut menu or the Cells command on the Insert menu allows you to insert a single cell or a range of cells. However, be aware that if you shift a single cell or a range of cells, they may no longer be lined up with their associated cells. To ensure that the values in the worksheet do not get out of order, it is recommended that you insert only entire rows or entire columns.

Deleting Columns and Rows

The **Delete command** on the Edit menu or shortcut menu removes cells (including the data and format) from the worksheet. Deleting cells is not the same as clearing cells. The Clear command described earlier in Project 1, clears the data out of the cells, but the cells remain in the worksheet. The Delete command removes the cells from the worksheet and moves rows up when you delete rows or moves columns to the left when you delete columns.

Excel does not adjust cell references to the deleted row or column in formulas in the worksheet. Excel displays the error message **#REF!** (meaning cell reference error) in those cells containing formulas that reference cells in the deleted area. For example, if cell A7 contains the formula =A4 + A5 and you delete row 5, then Excel assigns the formula =A4 + #REF! to cell A6 (originally cell A7) and displays the error message #REF! in cell A6, which was originally cell A7.

Deleting Individual Cells or a Range of Cells

Although Excel allows you to delete an individual cell or range of cells, be aware if you shift a cell or range of cells on the worksheet, they may no longer be lined up with their associated cells. For this reason, it is recommended that you delete only entire rows or entire columns.

▶ ENTERING NUMBERS WITH A FORMAT SYMBOL

The next step is to enter the row title, Net Sales for Bonus, in cell A18 and enter the assumption values in the range B15:B20. These numbers can be entered as decimal numbers as was done in Projects 1 and 2 and formatted later, or you can enter them with format symbols. When you enter a number with a **format symbol**, Excel immediately applies number formatting to the cell. Valid format symbols include the percent sign (%), comma (,), and dollar sign ($). If the number entered is a whole number, then it displays without any decimal places.

▶ **TABLE 3-2**

FORMAT SYMBOL	ENTERED IN FORMULA BAR	DISPLAYS IN CELL	COMPARABLE FORMAT
$	$112	$112	Currency (0)
	$3798.12	$3,798.12	Currency (2)
	$44,123.3	$44,123.30	Currency (2)
,	7,876	7,876	Comma (0)
	4,913.6	4,913.60	Comma (2)
%	4%	4%	Percent (0)
	6.1%	6.10%	Percent (2)
	7.25%	7.25%	Percent (2)

If the number has one or more decimal places, then Excel displays the number with two decimal places. Table 3-2 illustrates several examples of numbers entered with format symbols. The number in parentheses in column 4 indicates the number of decimal places.

The following steps describe how to complete the entries in the Assumptions table.

TO ENTER A NUMBER WITH A FORMAT SYMBOL ▼

STEP 1 ▶

Select cell A18 and enter the text
Net Sales for Bonus

STEP 2 ▶

Enter 30.00% in cell B15, 2.50% in cell B16, 17,750.00 in cell B17, 500,000.00 in cell B18, 23.75% in cell B19, and 10.25% in cell B20.

The entries display in a format based on the format symbols entered with the numbers (Figure 3-15).

FIGURE 3-15

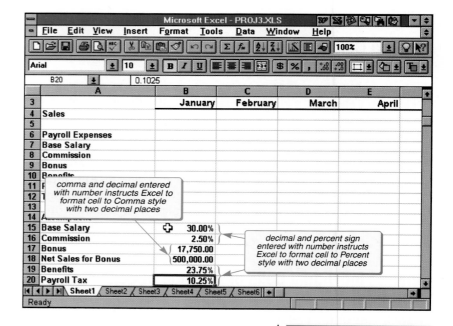

▶ FREEZING WORKSHEET TITLES

Freezing worksheet titles is a useful technique for viewing large work sheets that extend beyond the window. For example, when you scroll down or to the right, the column titles in row 3 and the row titles in column A that define the numbers disappear off the screen. This makes it difficult to remember what the numbers represent. To alleviate this problem, Excel allows you to freeze the titles so they remain on the screen no matter how far down, or to the right, you scroll.

Follow these steps to freeze the worksheet titles and column titles in rows 1 through 3, and the row titles in column A using the **Freeze Panes command** on the Window menu.

TO FREEZE COLUMN AND ROW TITLES ▼

STEP 1 ▶

Select cell B4, the cell below the column headings you want to freeze and to the right of the row titles you want to freeze. Select the Window menu (Figure 3-16).

FIGURE 3-16

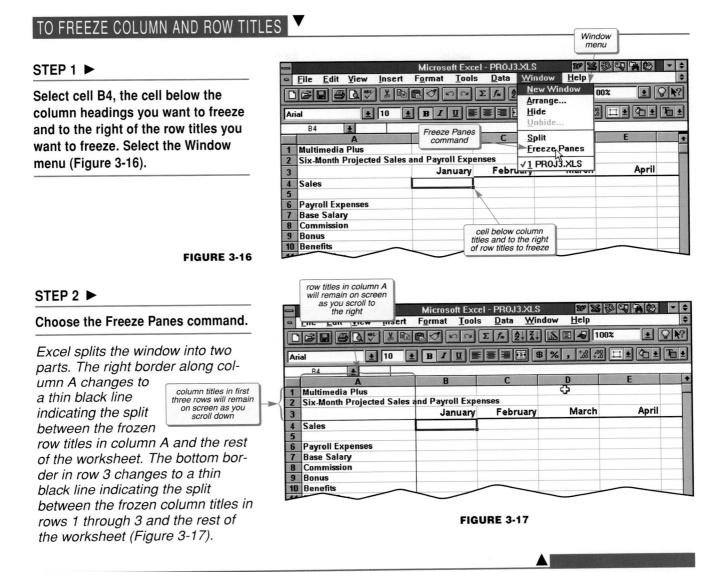

FIGURE 3-17

STEP 2 ▶

Choose the Freeze Panes command.

Excel splits the window into two parts. The right border along column A changes to a thin black line indicating the split between the frozen row titles in column A and the rest of the worksheet. The bottom border in row 3 changes to a thin black line indicating the split between the frozen column titles in rows 1 through 3 and the rest of the worksheet (Figure 3-17).

The row titles in column A remain on the screen even when you use the right scroll arrow to move the window to the right to display column G.

The titles are frozen until you unfreeze them. Later steps in this project show you how to use the Unfreeze Panes command.

Entering the Projected Sales

The next step is to enter the projected sales and their total in row 4.

TO ENTER THE PROJECTED SALES

Step 1: Select cell B4. Enter 525135 in cell B4, 650255 in cell C4, 443873 in cell D4, 833892 in cell E4, 378234 in cell F4, 623754 in cell G4.

Step 2: Select cell H4, click the AutoSum button twice.

The projected sales for the last three months and the total projected sales display as shown on the next page in Figure 3-18. Notice that columns B, C, and D have scrolled off the screen, but column A remains because it was frozen earlier.

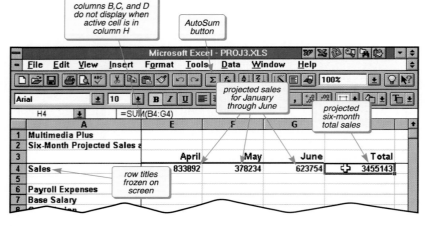

FIGURE 3-18

▶ DISPLAYING THE SYSTEM DATE

he worksheet in Project 3 (Figure 3-1a on page E136) includes a date stamp in cell H2. A **date stamp** is the system date of which your computer keeps track. If the computer's system date is set to the current date, which it normally is, then the date stamp is equivalent to the current date. In information processing, a report such as a printout of the worksheet is often meaningless without a date stamp. For example, the date stamp in Project 3 is useful for showing when the six-month projections were made.

To enter the system date in a cell in the worksheet use the **NOW function**. The NOW function is one of fourteen date and time functions available in Excel. When assigned to a cell, the NOW function returns a decimal number in the range 1 to 65,380, corresponding to the dates January 1, 1900 through December 31, 2078 and the time of day. Excel automatically formats the number representing the system's date and time to the date and time format m/d/yy h:mm where the first m is the month, d is the day of the month, yy is the last two digits of the year, h is the hour of the day, and mm is the minutes past the hour.

The following steps show how to enter the NOW function and change the format from m/d/yy h:mm to m/d/yy where m is the month number, d is day of the month, and yy is the last two digits of the year.

TO ENTER AND FORMAT THE SYSTEM DATE ▼

STEP 1 ▶

Select cell H2 and click the Function Wizard button on the Standard toolbar.

The Function Wizard – Step 1 of 2 dialog box displays.

STEP 2 ▶

Select Date & Time in the Function Category box and select NOW in the Function Name box.

The Function Wizard – Step 1 of 2 dialog box displays as shown in Figure 3-19.

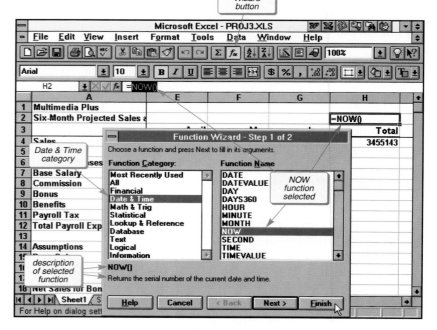

FIGURE 3-19

STEP 3 ▶

Choose the Finish button.

Excel displays the system date and system time in cell H2 using the default date and time format m/d/yy h:mm (Figure 3-20).

FIGURE 3-20

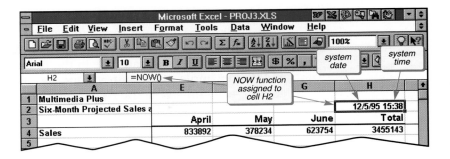

STEP 4 ▶

With cell H2 selected and the mouse pointer within the cell, click the right mouse button.

Excel displays the shortcut menu (Figure 3-21).

FIGURE 3-21

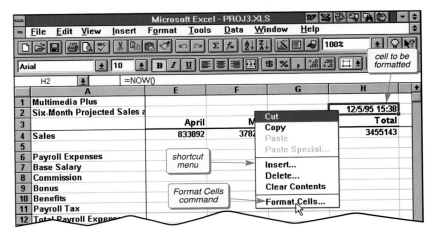

STEP 5 ▶

Choose the Format Cells command. If necessary, click the Number tab, select Date in the Category box, and select m/d/yy in the Format Codes box.

Excel displays the Format Cells dialog box with Date and m/d/yy selected (Figure 3-22).

FIGURE 3-22

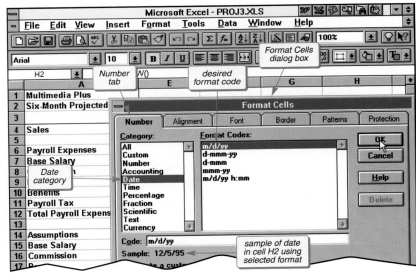

STEP 6 ▶

Choose the OK button in the Format Cells dialog box.

Excel displays the date in the form m/d/yy (Figure 3-23).

FIGURE 3-23

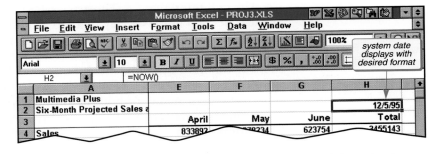

Notice in Figure 3-23 the date displays in the cell right-aligned because Excel treats a date as a number. If you format the date by applying the **General format** (Excel's default for numbers), the date displays as a number. To format a cell to General, select the All category in the Format Cells dialog box and then select General. For example, if the system time and date is 12:00 noon on December 5, 1995 and the cell containing the NOW function is assigned the General format, then Excel displays the following number in the cell:

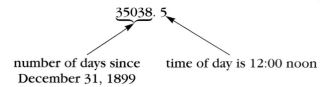

The whole number portion of the number (35038) represents the number of days since December 31, 1899. The decimal portion (.5) represents the time of day (12:00 noon).

▶ ABSOLUTE VERSUS RELATIVE ADDRESSING

The next step is to enter the formulas that determine the projected payroll expenses in the range B7:G11 (Figure 3-1a on page E136). The projected payroll expenses are based on the projected sales in row 4 and the assumptions in the range B15:B20. The formulas for each column are the same, except for the sales in row 4. Thus, the formulas can be entered for January in column B and copied to columns C through G. The formulas for determining the January projected payroll expenses are shown in Table 3-3.

▶ **TABLE 3-3**

CELL	PAYROLL EXPENSE	FORMULA	COMMENT
B7	Base Salary	=B15 * B4	Base Salary % times January Sales
B8	Commission	=B16 * B4	Commission % times January Sales
B9	Bonus	=IF(B4 >= B18, B17, 0)	Bonus equals value in cell B17 or zero
B10	Benefits	=B19 * (B7 + B8 + B9)	Benefits % times sum of Base Salary, Commission, and Bonus
B11	Payroll Tax	=B20 * (B7 + B8 + B9)	Payroll Tax % times sum of Base Salary, Commission, and Bonus

The problem is, if you enter these formulas in column B and then copy them to columns C through G, Excel automatically adjusts the cell references for each column. Thus, after the copy, the February base salary in cell C7 would be =C15 * C4. The cell reference C4 (February sales) is correct. However, cell C15 is empty. What is needed here is a way to keep a cell reference in a formula the same when it is copied. The formula for cell C7 should read =B15 * C4 instead of =C15 * C4.

Excel has the ability to keep a cell reference constant when it copies a formula or function by using a technique called **absolute referencing**. To specify an absolute reference in a formula, add a dollar sign ($) to the beginning of the column name, row name, or both in formulas you plan to copy. For example, $B$15 is an absolute reference and B15 is a relative reference. Both reference the same cell. The difference shows when they are copied. A formula using $B$15 instructs Excel to use the same cell (B15) as it copies the formula to a new location. A formula using B15 instructs Excel to adjust the cell reference as it copies. Table 3-4 gives some additional examples of absolute references. A cell reference with one dollar sign before either the column or the row is called a **mixed cell reference**.

Entering the January Base Salary and Commission Formulas

The following steps show how to enter the base salary formula (=$B$15 * B4) in cell B7 and the commission formula (=$B$16 * B4) in cell B8 for the month of January using the Point mode. When you enter an absolute reference, you can type the $ or you can press F4 with the insertion point in, or to the right of, the cell reference you want to change to absolute.

▶ **TABLE 3-4**

CELL REFERENCE	MEANING
$B$15	Both column and row references remain the same when you copy this cell reference because they are absolute.
B$15	The column reference changes when you copy this cell reference to another column because it is relative. The row reference does not change because it is absolute.
$B15	The row reference changes when you copy this cell reference to another row because it is relative. The column reference does not change because it is absolute.
B15	Both column and row references are relative. When copied to another row and column, both the row and column in the cell reference are adjusted to reflect the new location.

TO ENTER THE JANUARY BASE SALARY AND COMMISSION FORMULAS ▼

STEP 1 ▶

Select cell B7. Type the equal sign (=) and click cell B15. Press F4 to change B15 to an absolute reference in the formula. Type the asterisk (*) and click cell B4.

The formula displays in cell B7 and in the formula bar (Figure 3-24).

STEP 2 ▶

Click the enter box in the formula bar or press the ENTER key.

Excel displays the result (157540.5) in cell B7 (Figure 3-25).

STEP 3 ▶

Select cell B8. Type the equal sign (=) and click cell B16. Press F4 to change cell B16 to an absolute reference in the formula. Type the asterisk (*) and click cell B4. Click the enter box or press the ENTER key.

Excel displays the result of the formula (13128.375) in cell B8 (Figure 3-25).

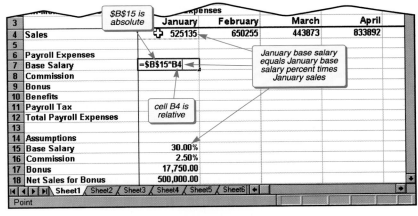

FIGURE 3-24

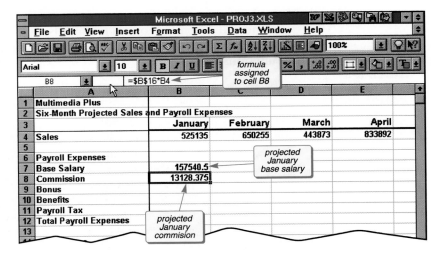

FIGURE 3-25

When you enter a formula that contains an absolute reference, you can use the F4 key to cycle the cell reference on which the insertion point is positioned, or immediately to the right of, from relative to absolute to mixed.

▶ MAKING DECISIONS — THE IF FUNCTION

I f the January sales in cell B4 are greater than or equal to the net sales for bonus in cell B18, then the January bonus in cell B9 is equal to the amount in cell B17 (17,550.00); otherwise, cell B9 is equal to zero. One way to assign the bonus in row 9 is to manually compare the sales for each month in row 4 to the net sales for bonus in cell B17 and enter 17750 when the corresponding month sales equals or exceeds the amount in cell B17. However, because the data in the worksheet changes each time you prepare the report, you will find it preferable to automatically assign the monthly bonus to the entries in the appropriate cells. What you need in cell B8 is an entry that displays 17750 or zero, depending on whether the projected January sales in cell B4 is greater than or equal to or less than the number in cell B18.

Excel has the **IF function** that is useful when the value you want to assign to a cell is dependent on a logical test. A **logical test** is made up of two expressions and a comparison operator. Each expression can be a cell reference, a number, text, a function, or a formula. A **comparison operator** is one of the following: > (greater than), < (less than), = (equal to), >= (greater than or equal to), <= (less than or equal to), <> (not equal to). For example, assume you assign cell B9 the IF function:

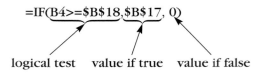

$$=IF(B4>=\$B\$18,\$B\$17, 0)$$

logical test   value if true   value if false

If the January projected sales in cell B4 are greater than or equal to the value in cell B18, then 17,750 displays in cell B9. If the January projected sales in cell B4 are less than the value in cell B18, then cell B9 displays a zero.

The general form of the IF function is:

=IF(logical-test, value-if-true, value-if-false)

The argument, value-if-true, is the value you want displayed in the cell when the logical-test is true. The argument, value-if-false, is the value you want displayed in the cell when the logical-test is false.

Table 3-5 lists the valid comparison operators and examples of their use in IF functions.

▶ **TABLE 3-5**

COMPARISON OPERATOR	MEANING	EXAMPLE
=	Equal to	=IF(A5 = B7, A22 - A3, G5 + E3)
<	Less than	=IF(E12 / D5 < 6, A15, B13 - 5)
>	Greater than	=IF(=SUM(A1:A5) > 100, 1, 0)
>=	Greater than or equal to	=IF(A12 >= $E$2, A4 * D5, 1)
<=	Less than or equal to	=IF(A1 + D5 <= 10, H15, 7 * A3)
<>	Not equal to	=IF(C5 <> B5, "Valid", "Invalid")

The following steps assign the IF function =IF(B4>= $B$18,$B$17,0) to cell B9. This function will determine whether the worksheet projects a bonus or not for January.

TO ENTER AN IF FUNCTION ▼

STEP 1 ►

Select cell B9 and type
=if(b4>=b18,b17,0

The IF function displays in cell B9 and in the formula bar (Figure 3-26).

FIGURE 3-26

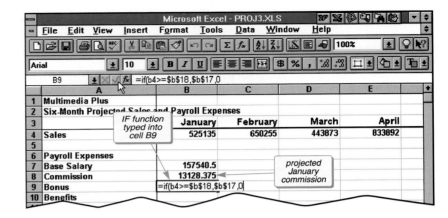

STEP 2 ►

Click the enter box in the formula bar or press the ENTER key.

Excel displays 17750 in cell B9 because the value in cell B4 is greater than or equal to the value in cell B18 (Figure 3-27). Recall that it is not necessary to type the closing parenthesis when you enter a function.

FIGURE 3-27

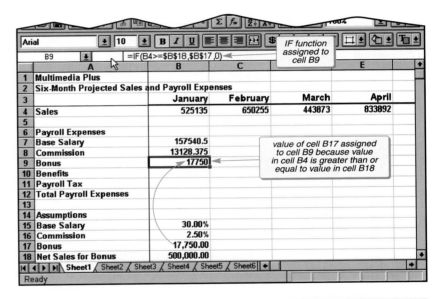

The value that Excel displays in cell B9 depends on the values assigned to cells B4, B17, and B18. For example, if the projected sales in cell B4 are reduced below 500,000, then the IF function in cell B9 will change the display from 17750 to zero. Changing the net sales for bonus in cell B18 to a greater amount has the same effect.

Entering the January Benefits, Payroll Tax Formulas, and Total Payroll Expenses

The January projected benefits in cell B10 are equal to the benefits percent in cell B19 times the sum of the January projected base salary, commission, and bonus in cells B7, B8, and B9. In the same manner, the January projected payroll tax in cell B11 is equal to the payroll tax percent in cell B20 times the sum of the January projected base salary, commission, and bonus in cells B7, B8, and B9. The total January projected payroll expenses in cell B12 are equal to the sum of the January projected payroll expenses in the range B7:B11. The steps on the next page enter the three formulas into the worksheet.

TO ENTER THE JANUARY BENEFITS AND PAYROLL TAX FORMULAS AND TOTAL PAYROLL EXPENSES

Step 1: Select cell B10. Enter =b19*(b7+b8+b9)
Step 2: Select cell B11. Enter =b20*(b7+b8+b9)
Step 3: Select cell B12. Click the AutoSum button on the Standard toolbar twice.

The January projected benefits, payroll tax, and total payroll expenses display in cells B10, B11, and B12 (the left screen in Figure 3-28).

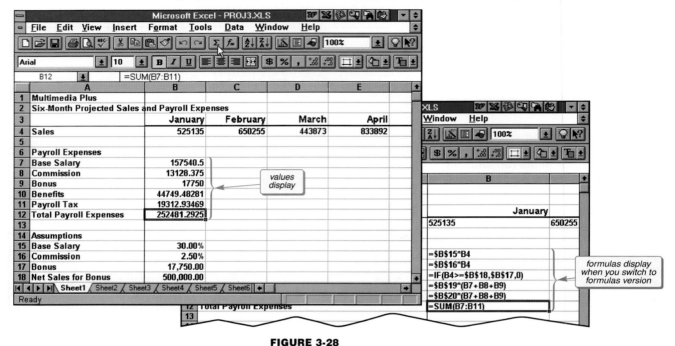

FIGURE 3-28

You can view the formulas in the worksheet by pressing CTRL+` (left apostrophe key — next to the number 1 key on the keyboard). The display changes from the left screen in Figure 3-28 to the right screen in Figure 3-28. Press CTRL+` to display the values again.

TO COPY THE JANUARY PROJECTED PAYROLL EXPENSES AND TOTALS USING THE FILL HANDLE ▼

STEP 1 ▶

Select the range B7:B12. Point to the fill handle near the lower right corner of cell B12.

The range B7:B12 is selected, and the mouse pointer changes to a cross (Figure 3-29).

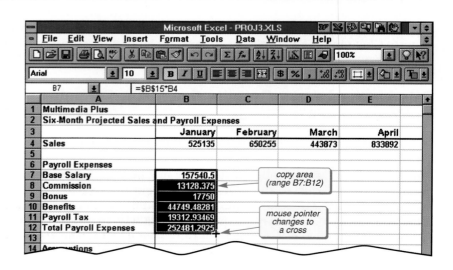

FIGURE 3-29

STEP 2 ▶

Drag the fill handle to select the paste area, range C7:G12, and then release the left mouse button.

Excel copies the formulas in the range B7:B12 to the paste area C7:G12. The last three columns of the paste area display as shown in Figure 3-30.

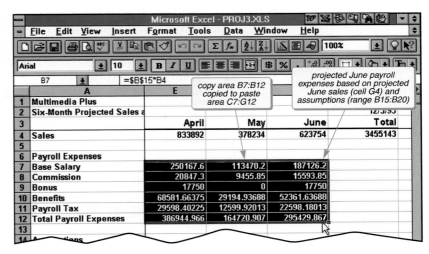

FIGURE 3-30

Determining the Projected Total Payroll Expenses

Follow these steps to determine the total projected payroll expenses in the range H7:H12.

TO DETERMINE THE PROJECTED TOTAL PAYROLL EXPENSES

Step 1: Select the range H7:H12.
Step 2: Click the AutoSum button on the Standard toolbar.

The projected total payroll expenses display in the range H7:H12 (Figure 3-31).

Unfreezing Worksheet Titles and Saving the Workbook

FIGURE 3-31

All the text, data, and formulas have been entered into the worksheet. The next step is to improve the appearance of the worksheet. Before modifying the appearance, the following steps unfreeze the titles and save the workbook under its current filename PROJ3.XLS.

TO UNFREEZE THE WORKSHEET TITLES AND SAVE THE WORKBOOK

Step 1: Select cell B4 to clear the range selection from the previous steps.
Step 2: Select the Window menu and point to the **Unfreeze Panes command** (Figure 3-32 on the next page).
Step 3: Choose the Unfreeze Panes command.
Step 4: Click the Save button on the Standard toolbar.

Excel unfreezes the titles so column A scrolls off the screen when you scroll to the right and the first three rows scroll off the screen when you scroll down. The workbook is saved using the filename PROJ3.XLS.

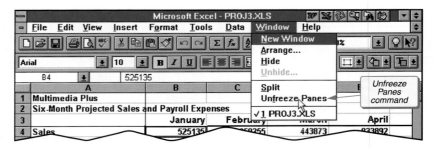

FIGURE 3-32

▶ FORMATTING THE WORKSHEET

he worksheet in Figure 3-32 determines the projected payroll expenses. However, its appearance is uninteresting, even though some minimal formatting was done earlier. This section will complete the formatting of the worksheet so the numbers are easier to read and to emphasize the titles, assumptions, categories, and totals (Figure 3-33).

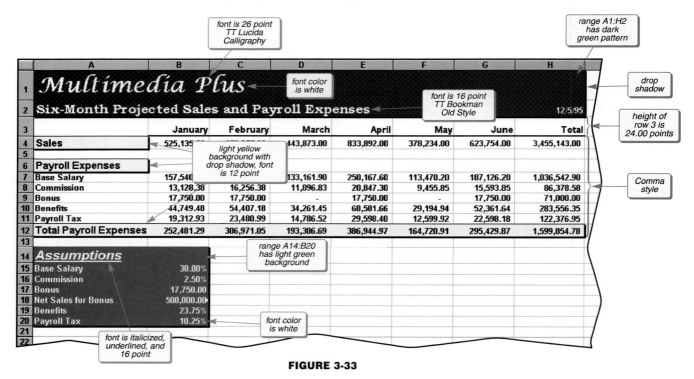

FIGURE 3-33

Formatting the Projected Sales and Payroll Expenses

Apply the Comma style to the projected sales and payroll expenses as described in the following steps.

TO FORMAT THE PROJECTED SALES AND PAYROLL EXPENSES

Step 1: Select the range B4:G12.
Step 2: Click the Comma Style button on the Formatting toolbar.

Excel formats the range B4:H12 to the Comma style (Figure 3-34).

Not all the cells in the range formatted have numbers. Some of the cells are empty (range B5:H6). Applying the Comma style to the empty cells has no impact on the worksheet because the format remains hidden unless numbers are entered into these cells.

An alternative way to apply the Comma style to the range B4:G12 is to use the Format Painter button on the Standard toolbar. For example, you could select cell B17, which was formatted earlier to the Comma style, click the Format Painter button, and drag over the range B4:G12.

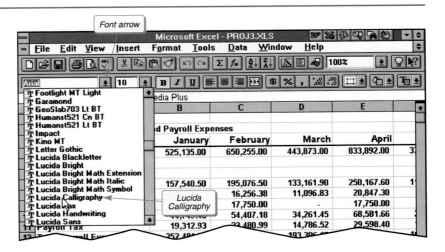

FIGURE 3-34

Compare cell D9 in Figure 3-34 to Figure 3-31. Notice that Excel changes a zero value to a dash (-) when the cell is assigned the Comma style. The dash (-) means the cell contains a numeric value of zero.

Formatting the Titles

To emphasize the worksheet titles in cells A1 and A2, the font type, size, and color are changed as described in the following steps.

TO FORMAT THE TITLES ▼

STEP 1 ▶

Select cell A1. Click the Font arrow on the Formatting toolbar. Scroll down until TT Lucida Calligraphy displays. If your system does not have TT Lucida Calligraphy, select another font.

The Font drop-down list box displays (Figure 3-35).

FIGURE 3-35

STEP 2 ▶

Choose TT Lucida Calligraphy. Click the Font Size arrow and choose 26.

The title in A1 displays as shown in Figure 3-36.

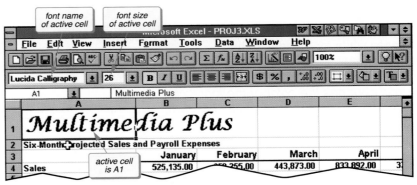

FIGURE 3-36

STEP 3 ▶

Select cell A2. Click the Font arrow on the Formatting toolbar. Choose TT Bookman Old Style. If your system does not have TT Bookman Old Style, select another font. Click the Font Size arrow and choose 16.

The subtitle in cell A2 displays as shown in Figure 3-37.

FIGURE 3-37

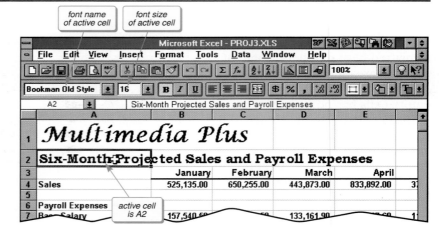

STEP 4 ▶

Select the range A1:H2. Click the Color button arrow on the Formatting toolbar and point to the dark green pattern (column 3, row 7) on the Color palette.

The Color palette displays as shown in Figure 3-38.

FIGURE 3-38

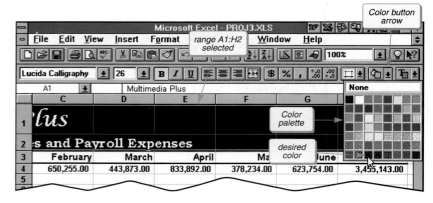

STEP 5 ▶

Choose the dark green pattern. Click the Font Color button arrow on the Formatting toolbar and point to white (column 2, row 1) on the Font Color palette.

The background color of the range A1:H2 changes to the dark green pattern (Figure 3-39). The Font Color palette displays. Because the range remains selected, the true background color does not show.

STEP 6 ▶

Choose white for the font in the titles.

Excel changes the color of the font in the titles from black to white (see Figure 3-33 on page E158).

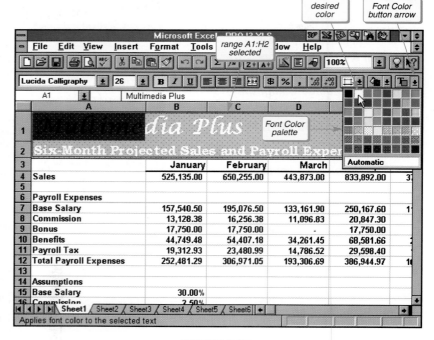

FIGURE 3-39

With the range A1:H2 selected, the next step is to add a drop shadow. To add a drop shadow, the Drawing toolbar must display on the screen. The following section describes how to display and dock an inactive (hidden) toolbar.

Displaying the Drawing Toolbar

Excel toolbars can display more than 200 buttons. Most of the buttons display on thirteen built-in toolbars. You can also create customized toolbars containing the buttons that you often use. Two of the thirteen built-in toolbars are the Standard toolbar and Formatting toolbar that usually display at the top of the screen. Another built-in toolbar is the Drawing toolbar. The **Drawing toolbar** provides tools that can simplify adding lines, boxes, and other figures to a worksheet. You can display the Drawing toolbar using one of the following techniques:

1. Point to a toolbar and click the right mouse button to display a shortcut menu of toolbars. Choose the Drawing toolbar from the list of toolbars.
2. Choose the Toolbars command from the View menu. Select the Drawing toolbar from the list in the Toolbars dialog box.
3. Click the Drawing button on the Standard toolbar.

Perform the following steps to display and then dock the Drawing toolbar at the bottom of the screen.

TO DISPLAY THE DRAWING TOOLBAR ▼

STEP 1 ▶

Point to the Drawing button (🖭) on the Standard toolbar.

STEP 2 ▶

Click the left mouse button.

The Drawing toolbar displays (Figure 3-40). Excel locates the Drawing toolbar on the screen wherever it displayed and in whatever shape it displayed the last time it was used.

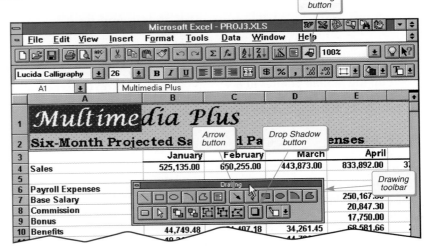

FIGURE 3-40

This project uses the Drop Shadow and Arrow buttons (Figure 3-40). To obtain information on any button, perform the following steps.

TO LIST THE FUNCTIONS OF BUTTONS ON A TOOLBAR

Step 1: From the Help menu, choose the Search for Help on command.
Step 2: When the Search dialog box displays, type `buttons` in the top box and choose the Show Topics button (Show Topics).
Step 3: Select Using Toolbar Buttons in the lower box and choose the Go To button (Go To) scroll down and choose the topic Button Category Summary .
Step 4: Choose the Drawing Buttons Category (or any other category of buttons). When you're finished with one category, click the Back button (Back) to select another category of buttons.
Step 5: When you are finished, double-click the Control-menu box in the Help window.

Moving and Shaping a Toolbar

The Drawing toolbar in Figure 3-40 is called a **floating toolbar** because you can move it anywhere in the window. You move the toolbar by positioning the mouse pointer in a blank area within the toolbar (not on a button) and dragging it to its new location. A floating toolbar always displays in its own window with a title bar and Control-menu box. As with any window, you can drag the toolbar window borders to resize it and you can click the Control-menu box in the title bar to hide a floating toolbar.

Sometimes, a floating toolbar gets in the way no matter where you move it. Hiding the toolbar is one solution. However, there are times when you want to keep it active because you plan to use it. For this reason, Excel allows you to locate toolbars on the edge of its window. If you drag the toolbar close to the edge of the window, Excel positions the toolbar in a **toolbar dock**.

Excel provides four toolbar docks, one on each of the four sides of the window. You can add as many toolbars to a dock as you want. However, each time you dock a toolbar, the window decreases slightly in size to compensate for the room taken up by the toolbar. The following steps show how to dock the Drawing toolbar at the bottom of the screen below the scroll bar.

TO DOCK A TOOLBAR AT THE BOTTOM OF THE SCREEN ▼

STEP 1 ▶

Position the mouse pointer in a blank area in the Drawing toolbar.

STEP 2 ▶

Drag the Drawing toolbar below the scroll bar at the bottom of the screen and release the left mouse button.

Excel docks the Drawing toolbar at the bottom of the screen (Figure 3-41).

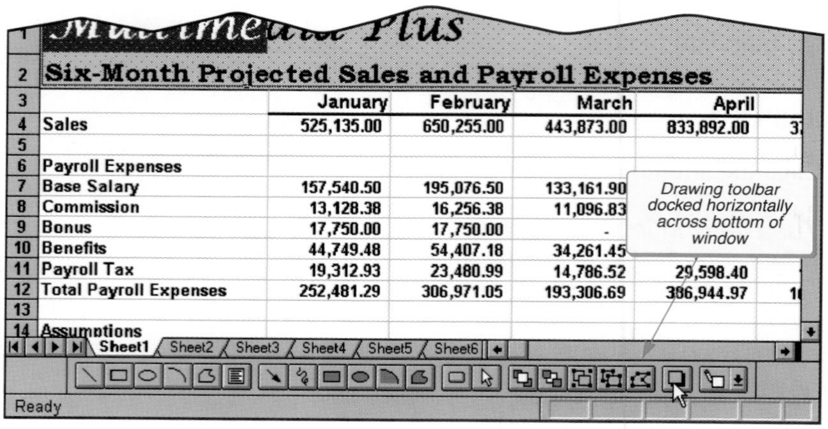

FIGURE 3-41

Compare Figure 3-41 to Figure 3-40 on the previous page. Notice how Excel automatically resizes the Drawing toolbar to fit across the window and between the scroll bar and status bar. Also, the heavy window border that surrounded the floating toolbar has changed to a thin border. To move a toolbar to any of the other three docks, drag the toolbar to the desired edge before releasing the left mouse button. A toolbar that has a drop-down list box, such as the Pattern button ( ) on the right side of the Drawing toolbar cannot be docked on the left or right edge of the window. To change a docked toolbar to a floating toolbar, double-click a blank area in the toolbar.

Adding a Drop Shadow to the Title Area

With the Drawing toolbar at the bottom of the screen, the next step is to add the drop shadow to the selected title area in the range A1:H2.

TO ADD A DROP SHADOW ▼

STEP 1 ▶

With the range A1:H2 selected, point to the Drop Shadow button (🔲) on the Drawing toolbar.

STEP 2 ▶

Click the left mouse button. Select any cell in the worksheet to deselect the drop shadow assigned to the the range A1:H2.

Excel adds a drop shadow to the title area in the range A1:H2 (Figure 3-42).

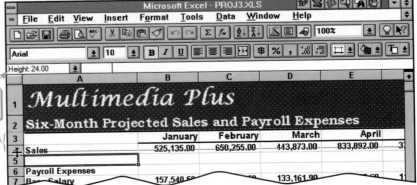

FIGURE 3-42

When you add a drop shadow to a range, Excel selects the drop shadow and surrounds it with black handles. To deselect the drop shadow, select any cell.

To remove an unwanted drop shadow, point to it and click the left mouse button. Next, press the DELETE key. You should also notice that the handles surrounding the drop shadow are black, meaning you can move and resize it.

Increasing the Height of the Row Containing the Column Headings

Row 3 contains the column headings. The next step is to increase the white space between the worksheet title and the column titles by increasing the height of row 3 to 24.00 points.

TO INCREASE THE HEIGHT OF A ROW ▼

STEP 1 ▶

Point to the border line between row headings 3 and 4. Drag the mouse down until a height of 24.00 displays in the reference area in the formula bar (Figure 3-43).

STEP 2 ▶

Release the left mouse button.

Excel increases the height of row 3 to 24.00 points (Figure 3-44 on the next page).

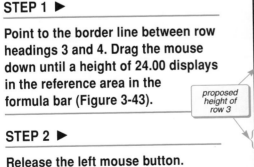

FIGURE 3-43

Changing Font Size, Adding Color, and Adding Drop Shadows to the Category Row Titles and Total Payroll Expenses Row

This project requires a font size of 12 point in cells A4, A6, and A12. Also, cells A4, A6, and the range A12:H12 all require the same background color and drop shadows (see Figure 3-33 on page E158). The following steps change the font size in cells A4, A6, and A12 and then add the background color and drop shadows.

TO CHANGE FONT SIZE , ADD COLOR, AND A DROP SHADOW TO NONADJACENT SELECTIONS ▼

STEP 1 ▶

Select cell A4. Hold down the CTRL key and select cells A6 and A12. Click the Font Size arrow on the Formatting toolbar and choose 12 from the drop-down list.

The font size in cells A4, A6, and A12 changes to 12 point.

STEP 2 ▶

Select cell A4. Hold down the CTRL key and select cell A6. Hold down the CTRL key and select the range A12:H12. Click the Color button arrow on the Formatting toolbar.

The nonadjacent ranges are selected and the Color palette displays (Figure 3-44).

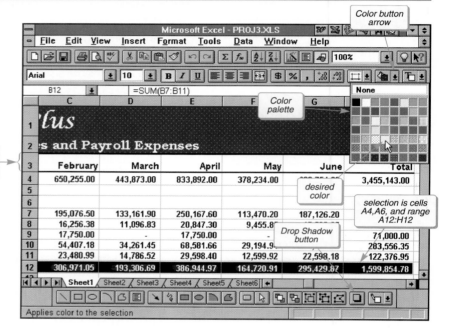

FIGURE 3-44

STEP 3 ▶

Choose light yellow (column 4, row 5) on the Color palette. Click the Drop Shadow button on the Drawing toolbar.

Excel colors the nonadjacent selection and adds a drop shadow to cells A4, A6, and the range A12:H12. The drop shadow on the range A12:H12 remains selected (Figure 3-45).

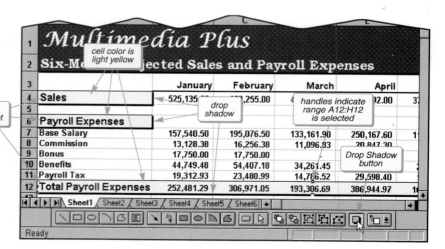

FIGURE 3-45

An alternative to formatting all three areas at once is to select each one separately and apply the formats. Although formatting cell A4 first, and then using the Format Painter button on the Standard toolbar may sound like a good idea, the drop shadow is considered a shape and not a format. Thus, Excel would not paint the drop shadow on cell A6 and the range A12:H12. However, it would paint the background color and change the font size.

Formatting the Assumptions Table

The last step to improving the appearance of the worksheet is to format the Assumptions table in the range A14:B20. Project 3 in Figure 3-33 on page E158 requires a 16 point underlined italics font for the title in cell A14. The background of the range A14:B20 is colored light green, and a drop shadow surrounds it.

TO FORMAT THE ASSUMPTIONS TABLE ▼

STEP 1 ►

Select cell A14. Click the Font Size arrow on the Formatting toolbar and choose 16 point. Click the Italic button (*I*) and Underline button (U) on the Formatting toolbar.

The table heading, Assumptions, displays as shown in Figure 3-46.

FIGURE 3-46

STEP 2 ►

Select the range A14:B20. Click the Color button arrow on the Formatting toolbar. Point to the color green (column 2, row 2) of the Color palette.

The Color palette displays as shown in Figure 3-47.

STEP 3 ►

Click the left mouse button to choose the color green. Click the Font Color button on the Formatting toolbar.

The background of the Assumptions table is colored green and the font is colored white.

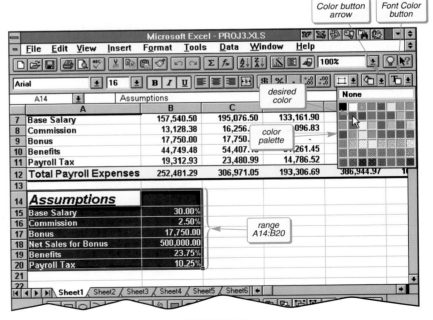

FIGURE 3-47

STEP 4 ▶

Click the Drop Shadow button on the Drawing toolbar. Select cell D20.

The Assumption table displays as shown in Figure 3-48.

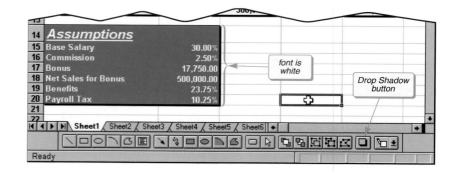

FIGURE 3-48

Because the last font color applied to the worksheet titles was white and Excel applies the last color used, you can click the Font Color button instead of the arrow to choose the color white.

Notice when you apply the **italic** font style to a cell, Excel slants the characters slightly to the right as shown in cell A14 in Figure 3-48. Applying underlining to a font is different from assigning a bottom border to a cell. When you **underline**, only the characters in the cell are underlined. When you assign a bottom border to a cell, the border displays whether or not characters are in the cell.

▶ HIDING A TOOLBAR

ith the formatting of the worksheet complete, the next step is to hide the Drawing toolbar docked at the bottom of the screen. As shown in the following steps, you can hide the Drawing toolbar by clicking on the Drawing button on the Standard toolbar.

TO HIDE THE DRAWING TOOLBAR ▼

STEP 1 ▶

Point to the Drawing button on the Standard toolbar.

STEP 2 ▶

Click the left mouse button.

The Drawing toolbar is removed from the screen (Figure 3-49).

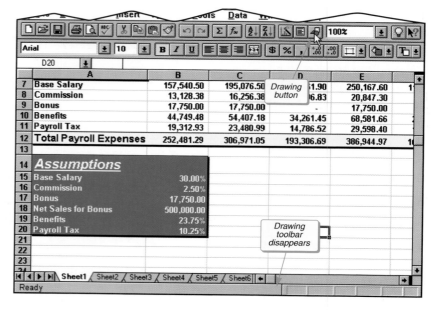

FIGURE 3-49

If you want to hide other toolbars displaying on the screen, use one of the following techniques:

1. Drag the toolbar onto the screen and double-click its Control-menu box.
2. Choose the Toolbars command from the View menu and remove the X from the selected toolbar to hide and then choose the OK button.
3. Point to the toolbar you want to hide, click the right mouse button to display the shortcut menu, and click its name in the shortcut menu to hide it.

The worksheet is complete. Before moving on to create the pie chart, save the workbook by clicking the Save button on the Standard toolbar.

ADDING A PIE CHART TO THE WORKBOOK

FIGURE 3-50

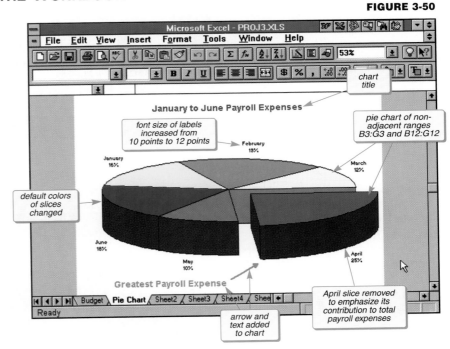

The next step in this project is to draw the 3-D pie chart on a separate sheet as shown in Figure 3-50. A **pie chart** is used to show how 100% of an amount is divided. Each slice (or wedge) of the pie represents a contribution to the whole. The pie chart in Figure 3-50 shows the contribution of each month to the total projected payroll expenses.

The cells in the worksheet to graph are the nonadjacent ranges B3:G3 and B12:G12 (see Figure 3-51). The month names in the range B3:G3 will identify the slices. The cells in row 3 are the category names. The range B12:G12 contains the data that determines the size of the slices. The cells in row 12 make up the data series. Because there are six months, the pie chart has six slices.

This project also calls for emphasizing the month with the greatest projected payroll expenses (April) by offsetting its slice from the main portion and adding an arrow and the text, Greatest Payroll Expense. A pie chart with one or more slices offset is called an **exploded pie chart**.

Drawing the Pie Chart

To draw the pie chart on a separate sheet, select the nonadjacent ranges B3:G3 and B12:G12 and choose the Chart command from the Insert menu. Once the chart is created, it will be formatted as shown in Figure 3-50 in the following fashion:

1. Increase the font size and color the font in the chart title.
2. Increase the font size of the labels that identify the slices.
3. Explode the April slice.
4. Rotate the pie chart so the April slice will display more prominently.
5. Change the color of the slices of the pie chart.
6. Add the words, Greatest Payroll Expense, below the pie chart.
7. Add and format an arrow pointing from the text box to the April slice.

TO DRAW A PIE CHART ▼

STEP 1 ▶

Select the range B3:G3. Hold down the CTRL key and select the range B12:G12. Choose the Chart command from the Insert menu

The Chart cascading menu displays (Figure 3-51).

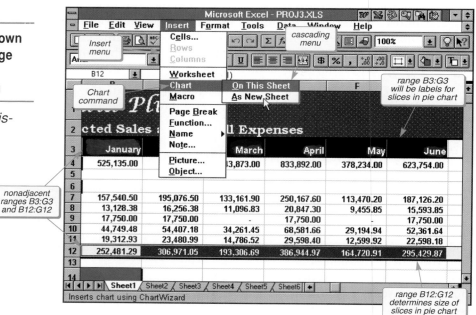

FIGURE 3-51

STEP 2 ▶

Choose the As New Sheet command from the Chart cascading menu.

Excel displays the ChartWizard Step – 1 of 5 dialog box, which shows the selected range to chart (Figure 3-52).

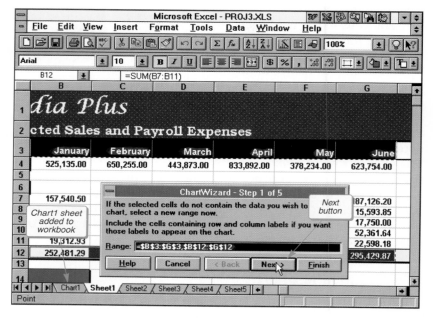

FIGURE 3-52

STEP 3 ▶

Choose the Next button in the
ChartWizard – Step 1 of 5 dialog
box.

*The ChartWizard – Step 2 of 5
dialog box displays with fifteen
charts from which to choose
(Figure 3-53). The first nine charts
in the dialog box are two-
dimensional. The last six charts
are three-dimensional.*

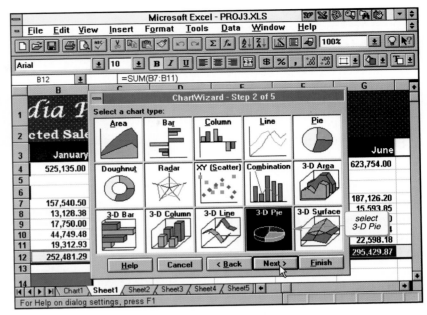

FIGURE 3-53

STEP 4 ▶

Select 3-D Pie (column 4, row 3).

Excel highlights the 3-D pie chart.

STEP 5 ▶

Choose the Next button in the
ChartWizard – Step 2 of 5 dialog
box.

*The ChartWizard – Step 3 of 5
dialog box displays with seven different built-in pie chart formats
from which to choose (Figure
3-54).*

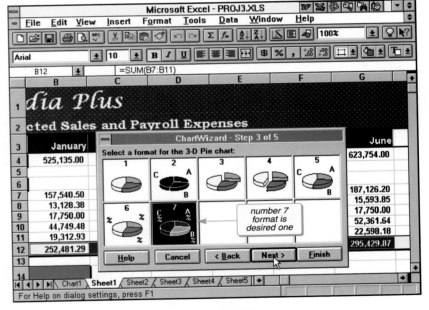

FIGURE 3-54

STEP 6 ▶

Select box 7, the one with the letters C, A, and B and the percent signs.

Excel highlights the selected pie chart format.

STEP 7 ▶

Choose the Next button on the ChartWizard – Step 3 of 5 dialog box. If a Microsoft Excel dialog box displays, choose the OK button. If necessary, change the settings in the ChartWizard – Step 4 of 5 dialog box to agree with those shown in Figure 3-55.

The ChartWizard – Step 4 of 5 dialog box displays showing a sample 3-D pie chart (Figure 3-55).

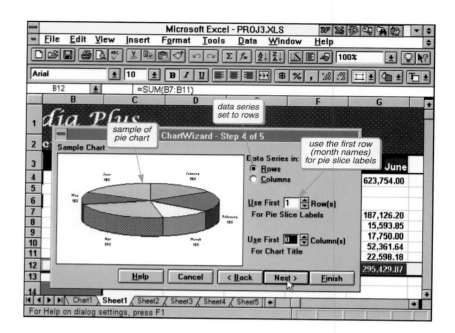

FIGURE 3-55

STEP 8 ▶

Choose the Next button in the ChartWizard – Step 4 of 5 dialog box.

The ChartWizard – Step 5 of 5 dialog box displays on the screen (Figure 3-56). The dialog box gives you the opportunity to add a legend and a chart title.

STEP 9 ▶

Type January to June Payroll Expenses **in the Chart Title box as shown in Figure 3-56.**

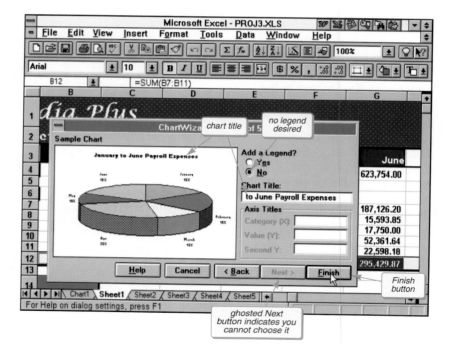

FIGURE 3-56

STEP 10 ▶

Choose the Finish button in the ChartWizard – Step 5 of 5 dialog box.

Excel draws the 3-D pie chart and displays it on a sheet titled Chart1 (Figure 3-57).

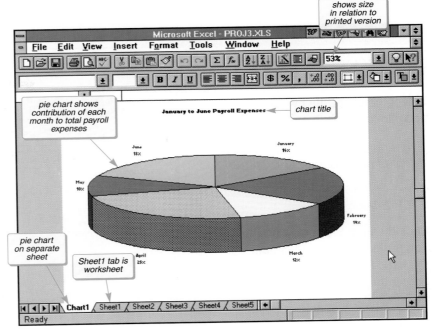

FIGURE 3-57

Each slice of the pie chart represents one of the six months, January through June. The names of the months and the percent contribution to the total projected payroll expense display outside the slices. The chart title, January to June Payroll Expenses, displays immediately above the pie chart.

Excel determines the direction of the data series range (down a column or across a row) on the basis of the selected range. Because the selection for the pie chart is across the worksheet (ranges B3:G3 and B12:G12), Excel automatically sets the data series to rows as shown in Figure 3-55.

Notice in the five ChartWizard dialog boxes (Figure 3-52 through Figure 3-56) that you can return to the previous ChartWizard dialog box, return to the beginning of the ChartWizard, or create the chart with the options selected thus far while any one of the five ChartWizard dialog boxes is on the screen.

Formatting the Chart Title and Chart Labels

In Project 2, the chart title was formatted by double-clicking it and entering the format changes in the Format Chart Title dialog box. This project formats the chart title and labels that identify the slices of the pie by selecting them and using the Formatting toolbar.

TO FORMAT THE CHART TITLE AND LABELS ▼

STEP 1 ▶

Select the chart title by pointing to it and clicking the left mouse button.

Excel displays a box with black handles around the chart title.

STEP 2 ▶

Click the Font Size arrow on the Formatting toolbar and choose 20. Click the Font Color arrow on the Formatting toolbar

The Chart1 sheet displays as shown in Figure 3-58.

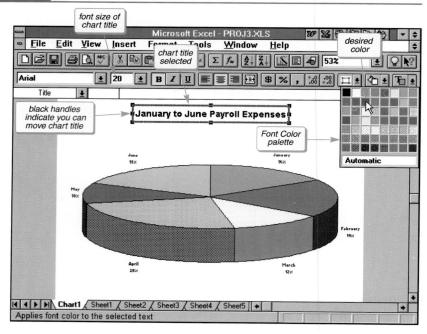

FIGURE 3-58

STEP 3 ▶

Choose blue (column 3, row 2) on the Font Color palette. Point to any one of the labels identifying the slices of the pie and click the left mouse button. Click the Font Size arrow on the Formatting toolbar and choose 12.

The chart title displays in blue, and all the labels increase slightly in size (Figure 3-59).

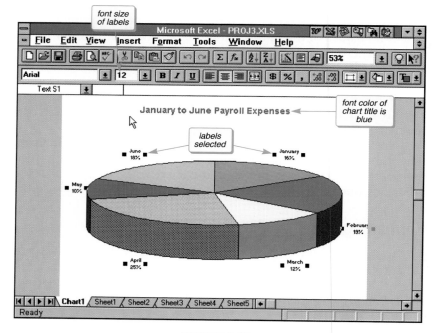

FIGURE 3-59

Notice the labels in Figure 3-59 have black handles. This means you can move and resize them. You can also select and format individual labels by pointing to a label after all the labels have been selected and clicking the left mouse button again.

Exploding the Pie Chart

The next step is to emphasize the slice representing the April payroll expenses by offsetting, or exploding, it from the rest of the pie. Perform the following steps to offset a slice of the pie chart.

TO EXPLODE THE PIE CHART ▼

STEP 1 ▶

Click the slice labeled April twice. Do not double-click.

Excel surrounds the April slice with black handles.

STEP 2 ▶

Drag the slice to the desired position, and release the left mouse button.

Excel redraws the pie chart with the April slice offset from the rest of the pie chart (Figure 3-60).

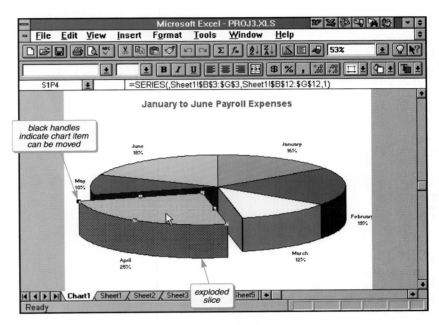

FIGURE 3-60

Although you can offset as many slices as you want, as you drag more slices away from the main portion of the pie chart, the slices become smaller. If you continue to offset slices, the pie chart becomes too small to have an impact on the reader.

Rotating the Pie Chart

In a 3-D chart, you can change the view to better display the section of the chart you are trying to emphasize. Excel allows you to control the rotation angle, elevation, perspective, height, and angle of the axes by using the **3-D View command** on the Format menu or shortcut menu.

To obtain a better view of the offset of the April slice, you can rotate the pie chart 80 degrees to the left. The **rotation angle** of a pie chart is defined by the line that divides the June and January slices (Figure 3-60). Excel initially draws a pie chart with one of the dividing lines pointing to 12:00 (or zero degrees). Complete the steps on the next page to rotate the angle of the pie chart.

TO ROTATE THE PIE CHART ▼

STEP 1 ▶

With the April slice selected, click the right mouse button.

The shortcut menu displays (Figure 3-61).

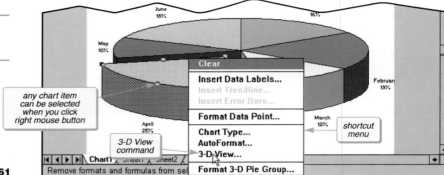

FIGURE 3-61

STEP 2 ▶

Choose the 3-D View command.

The Format 3-D View dialog box displays.

STEP 3 ▶

Click the Rotate Left button (🔄) until the Rotation box displays 280.

Excel displays a sample of the rotated pie chart in the dialog box (Figure 3-62). Between clicks of the Rotate Left button, you can choose the Apply button to apply the current rotation to the pie chart.

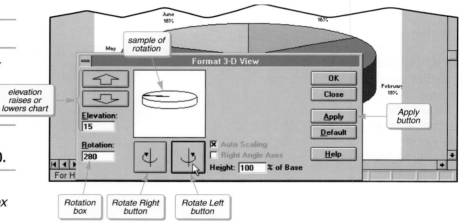

FIGURE 3-62

STEP 4 ▶

Choose the OK button on the Format 3-D View dialog box. Click outside the chart area.

Excel displays the pie chart rotated to the left so the gap between the April slice and the main portion of the pie is more prominent (Figure 3-63).

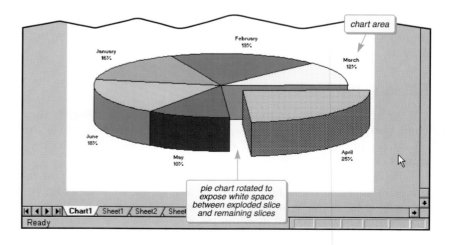

FIGURE 3-63

Compare Figure 3-63 to Figure 3-60 on page E173. The offset of the April slice is more noticeable in Figure 3-63 because the pie chart has been rotated to the left to expose the white space between the main portion of the pie and the April slice.

Besides controlling the rotation angle, additional buttons and boxes in the Format 3-D View dialog box (Figure 3-62 on the previous page) allow you to control the elevation and height of the pie chart. When you change characteristics, Excel always redraws the pie chart in the small window in the Format 3-D View dialog box.

Changing the Colors of the Slices

The next step is to change the colors of the slices of the pie. The colors you see in Figure 3-63 are the default colors Excel uses when you first create a pie chart. The Project 3 chart requires the colors shown in Figure 3-65 on the next page. To change the colors of the slices, select them one at a time and use the Color button on the Formatting toolbar as shown in the following steps.

TO CHANGE THE COLORS OF THE SLICES ▼

STEP 1 ▶

Click the slice labeled April twice. Do not double-click.

Excel displays black handles around the April slice.

STEP 2 ▶

Click the Color button arrow on the Formatting toolbar.

The Color palette displays (Figure 3-64).

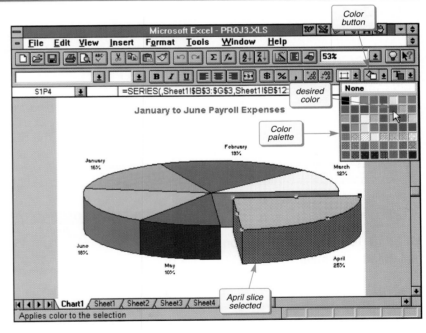

FIGURE 3-64

STEP 3 ▶

Choose teal (column 6, row 2) on the Color palette.

Excel changes the April slice to the color teal.

STEP 4 ▶

Repeat Step 1 through Step 3 and use the following colors on the Color palette for the months specified: January – yellow (column 6, row 1); February – red (column 3, row 1); March – tan (column 3, row 3); May – brown (column 4, row 2); and June – blue (column 3, row 2).

The pie chart displays as shown in Figure 3-65.

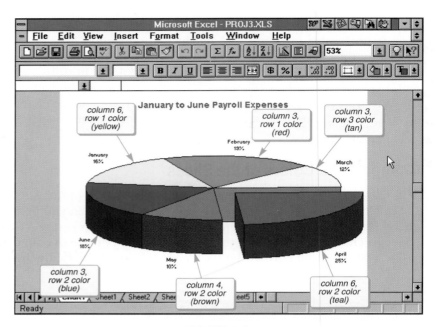

FIGURE 3-65

Adding a Text Box

Excel automatically adds some text to a chart, such as the labels that identify the slices. You can add even more text to clarify or emphasize a chart item. The next step is to add a **text box** with the text, Greatest Payroll Expenses.

TO ADD A TEXT BOX AND FORMAT ITS CONTENTS ▼

STEP 1 ▶

Click the Text Box button (▤) on the Standard toolbar.

The mouse pointer shape changes to a cross.

STEP 2 ▶

Move the mouse pointer approximately three-eighths of an inch above the S in the Sheet1 tab. Drag the mouse to the location shown in Figure 3-66.

A rectangle identifies the text box location on the chart sheet. When you release the left mouse button, the text box will disappear and an insertion point will appear.

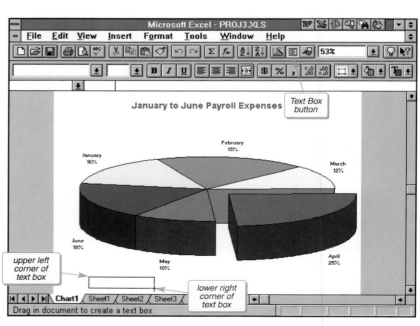

FIGURE 3-66

STEP 3 ▶

Release the left mouse button and type Greatest Payroll Expense

The text displays below and to the left of the pie chart (Figure 3-67).

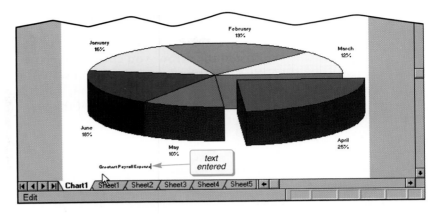

FIGURE 3-67

STEP 4 ▶

Click the text, Greatest Payroll Expense and drag the text box to increase its width as shown in Figure 3-68. Make sure the text box is wide enough or the next step will not work properly.

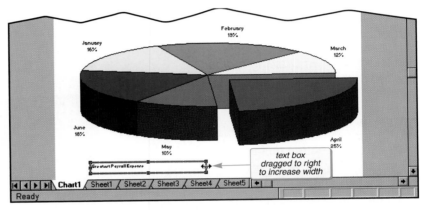

FIGURE 3-68

STEP 5 ▶

With the text box selected, click the Font Size arrow on the Formatting toolbar and choose 20. Click the Bold button on the Formatting toolbar. Click the Font Color button arrow and choose the color red (column 3, row 1) on the Font Color palette.

The text in the text box displays as shown in Figure 3-69.

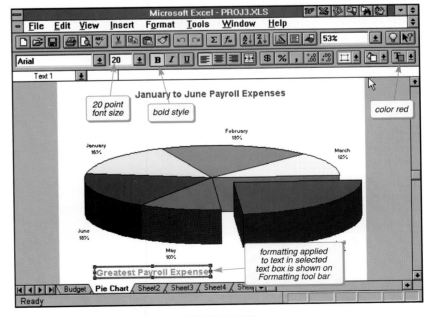

FIGURE 3-69

Adding and Formatting a Chart Arrow

You can add an arrow to the chart and point it at any chart item to emphasize it. To add the arrow, you click the **Arrow button** () on the Drawing toolbar. Next, click the screen where you want the arrow to start. Then drag the arrow in the direction you want it to point. The following steps add and then format an arrow that begins on the right of the text added to the text box and extends toward the April slice.

TO ADD AND FORMAT A CHART ARROW ▼

STEP 1 ▶

Click the Drawing button on the Standard toolbar. If necessary, scroll down until the text box is on the screen.

Excel displays the Drawing toolbar docked at the bottom of the screen.

STEP 2 ▶

Click the Arrow button on the Drawing toolbar. Move the mouse pointer above and to the right of the last letter e in Expense. Drag the mouse pointer to a point immediately below the left edge of the April slice. Release the left mouse button.

An arrow displays between the text box and the April slice (Figure 3-70). The black handles indicate the arrow is selected.

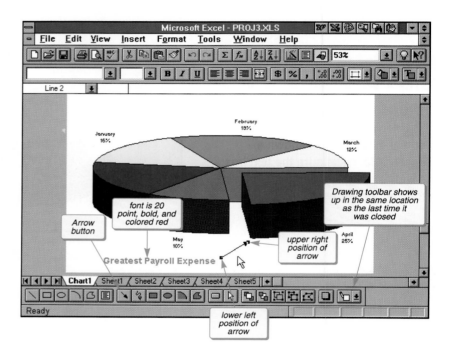

FIGURE 3-70

STEP 3 ▶

With the arrow selected and the mouse pointer pointing to it, click the right mouse button.

The shortcut menu displays (Figure 3-71).

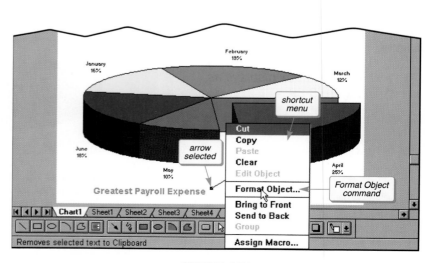

FIGURE 3-71

STEP 4 ▶

Choose the Format Object command. When the Format Object dialog box displays, click the Patterns tab, click the Color arrow, and select the color red (column 3, row 1 on the palette). Click the Weight arrow and select the heaviest weight line.

The Format Object dialog box displays with the selected settings (Figure 3-72).

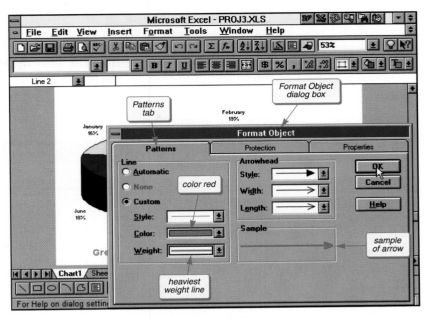

FIGURE 3-72

STEP 5 ▶

Choose the OK button in the Format Object dialog box. Click the Drawing button on the Standard toolbar to hide the Drawing toolbar. Press the ESC key to remove the selection from the arrow.

The formatted arrow displays as shown in Figure 3-73.

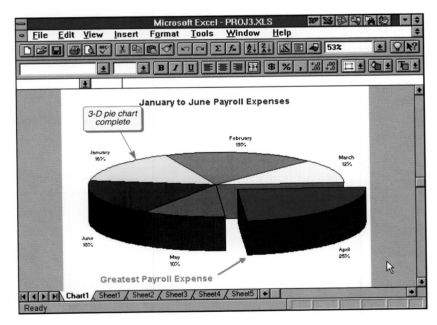

FIGURE 3-73

You can add as many arrows as you want to a chart. However, more than two arrows tend to clutter the chart. As you can see from the Format Object dialog box (Figure 3-72), you can modify the arrow to take on a variety of appearances.

The offset of the slice, the text, and the arrow pointing to the April slice clearly emphasize the month with the greatest projected payroll expenses in the pie chart.

Changing the Name of the Sheet Tabs and Rearranging the Order of the Sheets

The final step in creating the worksheet and pie chart in Project 3 is to change the names of the tabs at the bottom of the screen. The following steps show you how to rename the sheet tabs and reorder the sheets so the worksheet comes before the chart sheet.

TO RENAME THE SHEET TABS AND REARRANGE THE ORDER OF THE SHEETS ▼

STEP 1 ▶

Double-click the tab named Chart1 at the bottom of the screen. When the Rename Sheet dialog box displays, type `Pie Chart` (Figure 3-74).

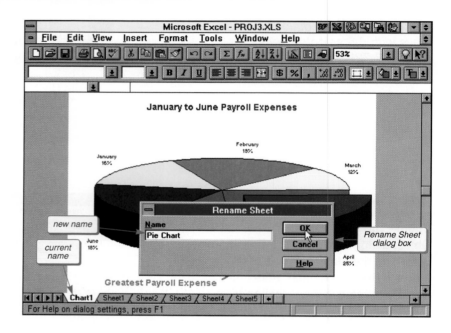

FIGURE 3-74

STEP 2 ▶

Choose the OK button in the Rename Sheet dialog box.

STEP 3 ▶

Repeat Step 1 and Step 2 for the Sheet1 tab. Type `Budget` for the tab name.

STEP 4 ▶

Drag the Budget tab to the left over the Pie Chart tab.

Excel rearranges the sequence of the sheets and displays the worksheet (Figure 3-75).

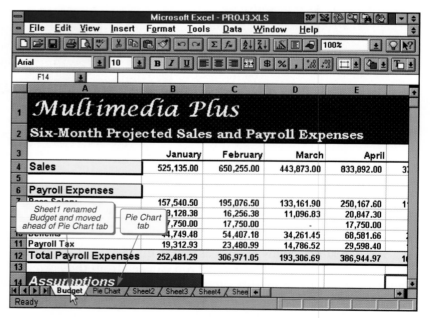

FIGURE 3-75

▶ CHECKING SPELLING, SAVING, PREVIEWING, AND PRINTING THE WORKBOOK

With the workbook complete, the next series of steps is to check spelling, save, preview, and print the workbook. The spell checker only checks the spelling of the selected sheets. Thus, before checking the spelling, hold down the SHIFT key and click the Pie Chart tab. Next, click the Spelling button on the Standard toolbar. After correcting any errors, save the workbook to disk by clicking the Save button on the Standard toolbar before attempting to print it.

Previewing and Printing the Workbook

With the worksheet and pie chart complete, the next step is to print the workbook. You may want to preview it first by clicking the Print Preview button on the Standard toolbar. Recall that Excel only previews selected sheets. Thus, if you want to preview both the worksheet and pie chart, hold down the SHIFT key and click the Pie Chart tab while the Budget sheet displays. Next, click the Print Preview button. After you are finished previewing, follow these steps to print the workbook and save it with the print settings.

TO PRINT THE WORKBOOK

Step 1: Ready the printer.

Step 2: Make sure the worksheet is on the screen. If both sheets are not selected, hold down the SHIFT key and click the Pie Chart tab.

Step 3: Point to the menu bar and click the right mouse button. Excel displays a shortcut menu.

Step 4: Choose the Page Setup command. When the Page Setup dialog box displays, select the Sheet tab and remove the X from the Gridlines check box by clicking it. Next, select the Page tab and select Landscape in the Orientation area. Choose the OK button in the Page Setup dialog box.

Step 5: Click the Print button on the Standard toolbar.

Step 6: Hold down the SHIFT key and click the Budget tab to deselect the Pie Chart tab.

Step 7: Click the Save button on the Standard toolbar to save the workbook with the print settings.

The worksheet and pie chart print as shown in Figure 3-76 on the next page.

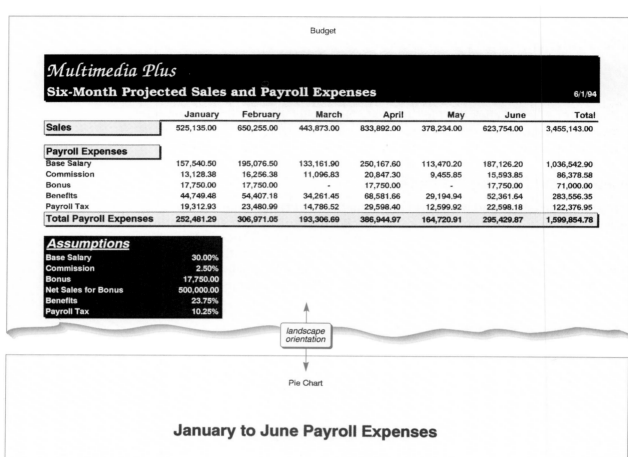

Budget

Multimedia Plus
Six-Month Projected Sales and Payroll Expenses   6/1/94

	January	February	March	April	May	June	Total
Sales	525,135.00	650,255.00	443,873.00	833,892.00	378,234.00	623,754.00	3,455,143.00
Payroll Expenses							
Base Salary	157,540.50	195,076.50	133,161.90	250,167.60	113,470.20	187,126.20	1,036,542.90
Commission	13,128.38	16,256.38	11,096.83	20,847.30	9,455.85	15,593.85	86,378.58
Bonus	17,750.00	17,750.00	-	17,750.00	-	17,750.00	71,000.00
Benefits	44,749.48	54,407.18	34,261.45	68,581.66	29,194.94	52,361.64	283,556.35
Payroll Tax	19,312.93	23,480.99	14,786.52	29,598.40	12,599.92	22,598.18	122,376.95
Total Payroll Expenses	252,481.29	306,971.05	193,306.69	386,944.97	164,720.91	295,429.87	1,599,854.78

Assumptions
Base Salary	30.00%
Commission	2.50%
Bonus	17,750.00
Net Sales for Bonus	500,000.00
Benefits	23.75%
Payroll Tax	10.25%

landscape orientation

Pie Chart

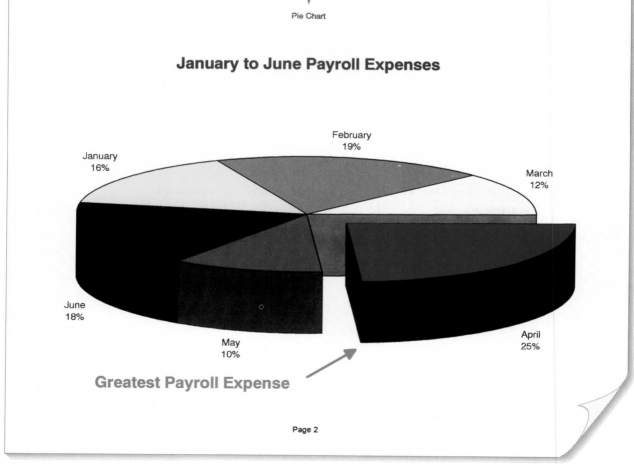

January to June Payroll Expenses

February
19%

January
16%

March
12%

June
18%

April
25%

May
10%

Greatest Payroll Expense

FIGURE 3-76

▶ CHANGING THE VIEW OF THE WORKSHEET

 ith Excel, you can easily change the view of the worksheet. For example, you can magnify or shrink the worksheet on the screen. You can also view different parts of the worksheet through **window panes**.

Shrinking and Magnifying the View of a Worksheet or Chart

To change the view of the worksheet, you can magnify (zoom in) or shrink (zoom out) the display of a worksheet or chart. When you magnify a worksheet, the characters on the screen become large and fewer columns and rows display. Alternatively, when you shrink a worksheet, more columns and rows display. Magnifying or shrinking a worksheet affects only the view; it does not change the window size or printout of the worksheet or chart. Perform the following steps to change the view.

TO SHRINK AND MAGNIFY THE DISPLAY OF A WORKSHEET OR CHART ▼

STEP 1 ▶

Click the Zoom Control box arrow on the Standard toolbar.

A drop-down list of percentages display (Figure 3-77).

FIGURE 3-77

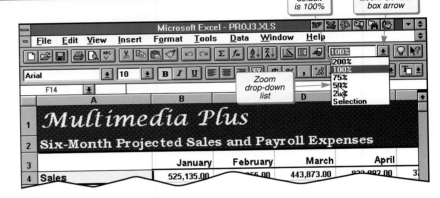

STEP 2 ▶

Choose 50% in the drop-down list.

Excel shrinks the display of the worksheet to a magnification of 50% of its normal display (Figure 3-78). With the worksheet zoomed to 50%, you can see more rows and columns than you did at 100% magnification.

STEP 3 ▶

Click the Zoom Control box arrow on the Standard toolbar and choose 100%.

Excel returns to a normal display.

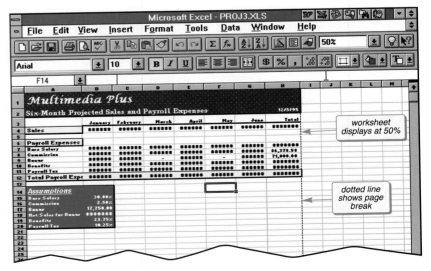

FIGURE 3-78

Notice in Figure 3-78 how you get a better view of the page breaks when you shrink the display of the worksheet. Depending on your printer driver, you may end up with different page breaks.

Splitting the Window into Panes

In Excel, you can split the window into two or four window panes so that you can view different parts of a large worksheet at the same time. To split the window into four panes, select the cell where you want the four panes to intersect. Next, choose the **Split command** from the Window menu. Use the following steps to split the window into four panes.

TO SPLIT A WINDOW INTO FOUR PANES ▼

STEP 1 ▶

Select cell D5, the intersection of the proposed four panes. Select the Window menu.

The Window menu displays as shown in Figure 3-79.

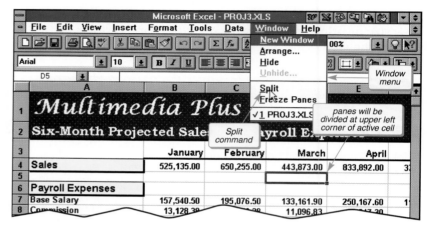

FIGURE 3-79

STEP 2 ▶

Choose the Split command. Use the scroll arrows to display the four corners of the worksheet.

Excel divides the window into four panes and the four corners of the work-sheet display (Figure 3-80).

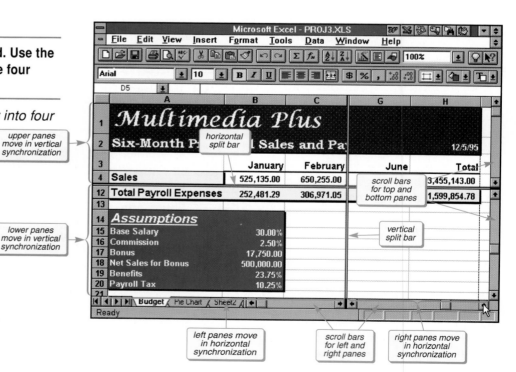

FIGURE 3-80

The four panes in Figure 3-80 are used to display the following: (1) the upper left pane displays the range A1:C4; (2) the upper right pane displays the range G1:H4; (3) the lower left pane displays the range A12:C20; and (4) the lower right pane displays the range G12:H20.

The vertical bar going up and down the middle of the window is called the **vertical split bar**. The horizontal bar going across the middle of the window is called the **horizontal split bar**. If you look closely at the scroll bars below the window and to the right of the window, you will see that the panes split by the horizontal split bar scroll together vertically. The panes split by the vertical split bar scroll together horizontally. To resize the panes, drag either split bar to the desired location in the window.

You can change the values of cells in any of the four panes. Any change you make in one pane also takes effect in the other panes.

If you want to split the window into only two panes instead of four, replace the previous two steps with the following: (1) position the mouse pointer on the **vertical split box** or the **horizontal split box** (Figure 3-81 on the next page); and (2) drag either split box to where you want to split the window.

You can also use the split bars when four panes are on the window to resize the panes. To remove one of the split bars from the window, drag the split box back to its original location or double-click the split bar. Follow these steps to remove both split bars.

TO REMOVE THE FOUR PANES FROM THE WINDOWS

Step 1: Position the mouse pointer at the intersection of the horizontal and vertical split bars.

Step 2: When the mouse pointer shape changes to a cross with four arrow-heads (✛), double-click the left mouse button.

Excel removes the four panes from the window.

▶ CHANGING VALUES IN CELLS THAT ARE REFERENCED IN A FORMULA

Excel's automatic recalculation feature is a powerful tool that can be used to analyze worksheet data. Using Excel to scrutinize the impact of changing values in cells that are referenced by a formula in another cell is called **what-if analysis** or **sensitivity analysis**. Not only does Excel recalculate all formulas in a worksheet when new data is entered, it also redraws any associated charts.

In Project 3, the projected payroll expenses in the range A7:G11 are dependent on the **assumptions** in the range A15:B20. Thus, if you change any of the assumptions, Excel immediately recalculates the projected payroll expenses in rows 7 through 11 and the monthly total projected payroll expenses in row 12. The new values cause Excel to recalculate a new total projected payroll expense for the six-month period in cell H12. Because the monthly totals in row 12 change, Excel redraws the pie chart which is based on these numbers.

A what-if question for the worksheet in Project 3 might be, What if the first four assumptions in the range A15:B20 are changed as follows: Base Salary 30.00% to 27.00%; Commission 2.50% to 1.50%; Bonus $17,750.00 to $15,000.00; Net Sales for Bonus $500,000.00 to $600,000.00 — how would these changes affect the total projected payroll expenses in cell H12? To answer questions like this, you need to change only the first four values in the assumptions table. Excel immediately answers the question regarding the total projected payroll expenses in cell H12 by instantaneously recalculating these figures.

The following steps change the first four assumptions as indicated in the previous paragraph and determine the new total projected payroll expenses in cell H12. To ensure that the Assumptions table (range A14:B20) and the total projected payroll expenses in cell H12 show on the screen at the same time, the following steps also divide the window into two vertical panes.

TO ANALYZE DATA IN A WORKSHEET BY CHANGING VALUES ▼

STEP 1 ►

Use the vertical scroll bar to move the window so cell A4 is in the upper left corner of the screen.

STEP 2 ►

Drag the vertical split box (**|**) from the lower right corner of the screen so the vertical split bar is positioned immediately to the right of column D and then release the left mouse button. Use the right scroll arrow in the right pane to display the totals in column H.

Excel divides the window into two vertical panes and shows the totals in column H in the pane on the right side of the window (Figure 3-81).

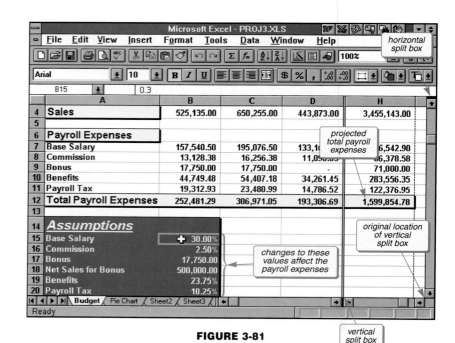

FIGURE 3-81

STEP 3 ►

Enter 27% in cell B15, 1.50% in cell B16, 15,000 in cell B17, 600,000 in cell B18.

Excel immediately recalculates all the formulas in the worksheet, including the total projected payroll expenses in cell H12 (Figure 3-82).

FIGURE 3-82

Each time you enter one of the new percent expenses, Excel recalculates the worksheet. This process usually takes less than one second, depending on how many calculations must be performed and the speed of your computer. Compare the total projected payroll expenses in Figures 3-82 and 3-81. By changing the values of the four assumptions (Figure 3-82), the total projected payroll expenses in cell H12, changes from $1,599,854.78 to $1,379,819.11. The change in the assumptions translates into a savings of $220,045.67 for the six-month period.

▶ GOAL SEEKING

I f you know the result you want a formula to produce, you can use **goal seeking** to determine the value of a cell on which the formula depends. The following example re-opens PROJ3.XLS and uses the **Goal Seek command** on the Tools menu to determine the base salary percentage in cell B15 that yields a total projected payroll expense in cell H12 of $1,300,000.

TO GOAL SEEK ▼

STEP 1 ▶

Close PROJ3.XLS without saving changes by choosing the Close command on the File menu. Click the Open button on the Standard toolbar and reopen PROJ3.XLS. Drag the vertical split box to the right of column D. Select cell H12, the cell that contains the total projected payroll expense. Select the Tools menu.

The Tools menu displays (Figure 3-83).

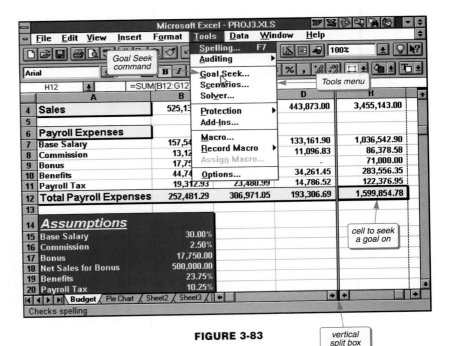

FIGURE 3-83

STEP 2 ▶

Choose the Goal Seek command on the Tools menu.

The Goal Seek dialog box displays. The Set cell box is automatically assigned the cell reference of the active cell in the worksheet (cell H12).

STEP 3 ▶

Type 1,300,000 **in the To value box. Type** B15 **in the By changing cell box.**

The Goal Seek dialog box displays as shown in Figure 3-84.

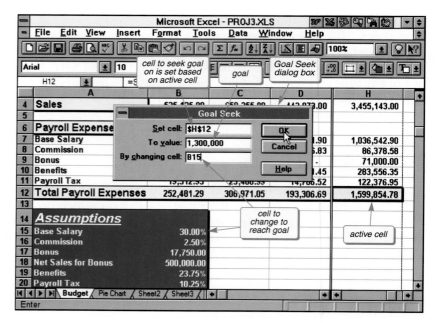

FIGURE 3-84

STEP 4 ▶

Choose the OK button on the Goal Seek dialog box.

Excel immediately changes cell H12 from 1,599,854.78 to the desired value 1,300,000.00. More importantly, Excel changes the base salary percentage in cell B15 to 23.52% (Figure 3-85).

STEP 5 ▶

When the Goal Seeking Status dialog box displays, choose the OK button.

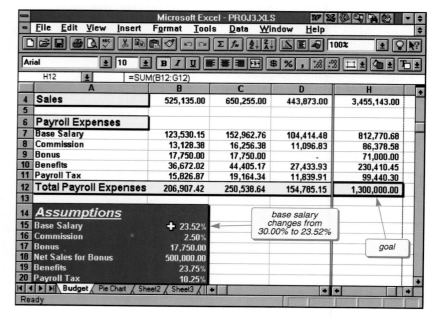

FIGURE 3-85

▲

Goal seeking allows you to change the value of only one cell referenced directly or indirectly in a formula in another cell. In this example, to change the total projected payroll expense in cell H12 to $1,300,000, the base salary percentage in cell B15 must decrease by 6.48% to 23.52%.

Notice that this goal seeking example does not require the cell to vary (cell B15) to be directly referenced in the formula or function. For example, the total projected payroll expense function in cell H12 is =SUM(B12:G12). There is no mention of the base salary percentage (cell B15) in the function. However, because the base salary percentage, on which the monthly sums in row 12 are based, is referenced in the formulas in rows 7 through 11, Excel is able to goal seek on the total projected payroll expense by varying the base salary percentage.

▶ PROJECT SUMMARY

Project 3 introduced you to working with worksheets that extend beyond the window. Using the fill handle, you learned how to create a series. The project presented steps and techniques showing you how to display hidden toolbars, how to freeze titles, and how to change the magnification of the worksheet. You displayed different parts of the worksheet through panes and improved the appearance of a chart. Finally, you used Excel to perform what-if analysis by means of goal seeking and by changing values in cells on which formulas depend.

▶ KEY TERMS AND INDEX

3-D View command *(E173)*
#REF! *(E147)*
absolute referencing *(E152)*
Arrow button *(E178)*
assumptions *(E136)*
AutoFill shortcut menu *(E140)*
Columns command *(E147)*
comparison operator *(E154)*
Copy button *(E143)*
Copy command *(E143)*
Cut command *(E145)*
date stamp *(E150)*
delete columns *(E147)*
Delete command *(E147)*
delete rows *(E147)*
docking a toolbar *(E162)*
drag and drop *(E145)*
drop shadow *(E162)*
Drawing button *(E178)*
Drawing toolbar *(E135, E161)*
exploded pie chart *(E167)*
Fill command *(E140)*

floating toolbar *(E162)*
Format Cells command *(E151)*
Format Object command *(E179)*
Format Painter button *(E140)*
format symbols *(E147)*
Freeze Panes command *(E148)*
freezing worksheet titles *(E148)*
General format *(E152)*
Goal Seek command *(E187)*
goal seeking *(E187)*
hiding a toolbar *(E166)*
horizontal split bar *(E185)*
horizontal split box *(E185)*
IF function *(E154)*
insert columns *(E147)*
Insert command *(E145)*
insert rows *(E145)*
Italic button *(E165)*
line weight *(E179)*
logical test *(E154)*
mixed cell reference *(E152)*
NOW function *(E150)*

Paste button *(E143)*
Paste command *(E143)*
pie chart *(E167)*
rotation angle *(E173)*
Rows command *(E145)*
sensitivity analysis *(E185)*
Split command *(E184)*
text box *(E176)*
Text Box button *(E176)*
toolbar dock *(E162)*
underline *(E166)*
Underline button *(E165)*
Undo Paste command *(E145)*
Unfreeze Panes command *(E157)*
vertical split bar *(E185)*
vertical split box *(E185)*
what-if analysis *(E185)*
window pane *(E183)*
Zoom Control box arrow *(E183)*

In Microsoft Excel, you can accomplish a task in a number of ways. The following table provides a quick reference to each task presented in this project with its available options. The commands listed in the Menu column can be executed using either the keyboard or mouse. Many of the commands in the Menu column are also available on the shortcut menu.

Task	Mouse	Menu	Keyboard Shortcuts
Add a Drop Shadow	Click Drop Shadow button on Drawing toolbar		
Copy a Selection onto the Clipboard	Click Copy button on Standard toolbar	From Edit menu, choose Copy	Press CTRL+C
Copy Cells	Drag selection to paste area while holding down CTRL key or use Copy and Paste buttons on Standard toolbar	From Edit menu, choose Copy; from Edit menu, choose Paste	Press CTRL+C and CTRL+V
Create a Series	Drag fill handle	From Edit menu, choose Fill	
Cut a Selection and Place It on the Clipboard	Click Cut button on Standard toolbar	From Edit menu, choose Cut	Press CTRL+X
Freeze Worksheet Titles		From Window menu, choose Freeze Panes	
Goal Seek		From Tools menu, choose Goal Seek	
Italicize	Click Italic button on Formatting toolbar	From Format menu, choose Cells	Press CTRL+I
Move Cells	Drag selection to its new location or use Cut and Paste buttons on Standard toolbar	From Edit menu, choose Cut; from Edit menu choose Paste	Press CTRL+X and CTRL+V
Paste a Selection from the Clipboard	Click Paste button on Standard toolbar	From Edit menu, choose Paste	Press CTRL+V
Remove Splits	Drag split bars or double-click split bars	From Window menu, choose Remove Split	
Show or Hide a Toolbar	Position mouse pointer in toolbar and click right mouse button	From View menu, choose Toolbars	
Split Window into Panes	Drag vertical split box or horizontal split box	From Window menu, choose Split	
Underline	Click Underline button on Formatting toolbar	From Format menu, choose Cells	Press CTRL+U
Unfreeze Worksheet Titles		From Window menu, choose Unfreeze Panes	
Zoom In or Zoom Out	Click Zoom Control arrow on Standard toolbar	From View menu, choose Zoom	

STUDENT ASSIGNMENT 1
True/False

Instructions: Circle T if the statement is true or F if the statement is false.

T F 1. If you enter 1899 in cell B3, 1900 in cell B4, select the range B3:B4, and then drag the fill handle down to cell B10, Excel assigns cell B10 the value 1900.

T F 2. To copy the text January in cell B3 to all the cells in the range B4:B10, hold down the ALT key while you drag the fill handle from cell B3 to cell B10.

T F 3. The Copy button on the Standard toolbar copies the selection onto the Clipboard.

T F 4. You can invoke the Paste command on the Edit menu by pressing the ENTER key.

T F 5. You can move a floating toolbar anywhere in the window.

T F 6. Excel has toolbar docks on each of the four sides of the window.

T F 7. You can dock more than one toolbar on a toolbar dock.

T F 8. You can dock any toolbar on any toolbar dock.

T F 9. You can freeze vertical titles (columns) but you cannot freeze horizontal titles (rows).

T F 10. The $ in a cell reference affects only the Move command on the Edit menu.

T F 11. If you save a workbook after changing the page setup characteristics, the next time you open the workbook the page characteristics will be the same as when you saved it.

T F 12. You can split a window into eight panes.

T F 13. You must enter a percentage value such as 5.3% as a decimal number (.053) in the formula bar.

T F 14. D23 is an absolute reference, and $D$23 is a relative reference.

T F 15. Although you can insert an entire row or entire column, you cannot insert a cell or range of cells within a row or column.

T F 16. Excel does not allow you to delete a row with a cell that is referenced elsewhere in the worksheet.

T F 17. When you copy cells, Excel adjusts the relative cell references in formulas copied to the paste area.

T F 18. Press the ESC key to remove the selection from a chart item.

T F 19. If you assign cell A4 the IF function =IF(A5 > A7, 1, 0) and cells A5 and A7 are equal to 7, then Excel displays the value 1 in cell A4.

T F 20. If you select a chart item and Excel surrounds it with black handles, then you can drag the chart item to any location in the window.

STUDENT ASSIGNMENT 2
Multiple Choice

Instructions: Circle the correct response.

1. Use function key _____ to change a relative reference in the formula bar to an absolute reference.
   a. F1
   b. F2
   c. F3
   d. F4

2. To use the drag and drop method for copying a range of cells, the mouse pointer must point to the border of the range and change to the _____ shape.
   a. cross
   b. block arrow
   c. block plus sign
   d. split double arrow

STUDENT ASSIGNMENT 2 (continued)

3. If you assign cell A5 the value 10, cell B6 the value 3, and cell B7 the function
   =IF(A5 > 4 * B6, ''Valid'', ''Invalid'')
   then _____ displays in cell B7.
   a. Valid
   b. Invalid
   c. #REF!
   d. none of the above

4. Which one of the following buttons in the ChartWizard dialog boxes instructs Excel to draw the chart using the options selected thus far?
   a. Next>
   b. Cancel
   c. <Back
   d. Finish

5. If you drag the fill handle to the right on cell A4, which contains Monday, then cell B4 will contain
   _____.
   a. Sunday
   b. Monday
   c. Tuesday
   d. #REF!

6. You can split the window into _____.
   a. two horizontal panes
   b. two vertical panes
   c. four panes
   d. none of the above

7. The horizontal and vertical split boxes are located _____.
   a. on the Standard toolbar
   b. on the Formatting toolbar
   c. next to the scroll arrows
   d. immediately to the left of the Select All button

8. To select nonadjacent cells, hold down the _____ key to make additional selections after you make the first selection.
   a. ALT
   b. SHIFT
   c. CTRL
   d. CAPS LOCK

9. You cannot dock a toolbar that contains a drop-down list box on the _____ of the window.
   a. bottom
   b. side
   c. top
   d. all of the above

10. When you insert rows in a worksheet, Excel _____ below the point of insertion to open up the worksheet.
    a. writes over the existing rows
    b. pushes up the rows
    c. reduces the height of the cells
    d. pushes down the rows

STUDENT ASSIGNMENT 3
Using the Standard and Formatting Toolbars

Instructions: The Standard and Formatting toolbars display above the formula bar in Figure SA3-3. Use Figure SA3-3 to answer the questions in this assignment.

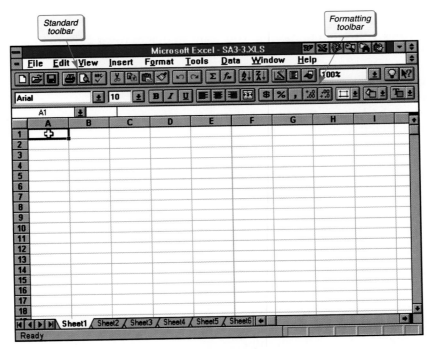

FIGURE SA3-3

1. Describe the function of the following buttons on the Standard toolbar.

   a. Undo button (⟲) _____

   b. Format Painter button (⬧) _____

   c. AutoSum button (Σ) _____

   d. ChartWizard button (⬚) _____

   e. Text Box button (▤) _____

   f. Copy button (▣) _____

2. Describe the function of the following buttons on the Formatting toolbar.

   a. Color button (⬛) _____

   b. Center Across Columns button (▦) _____

   c. Borders button (▦) _____

   d. Bold button (**B**) _____

   e. Comma Style button (▣) _____

   f. Increase Decimal button (▣) _____

STUDENT ASSIGNMENT 4
Understanding the Insert and Delete Commands

Instructions: Fill in the correct answers

1. Assume you want to insert four rows between rows 5 and 6.
   a. Select rows _____ through _____
   b. From the shortcut menu, choose the _____ command.
2. You have data in rows 1 through 6. Assume you want to delete rows 2 thorugh 4 and move rows up to replace them.
   a. Select rows _____ through _____
   b. From the shortcut menu, choose the _____ command.
   c. In which row would the data from row 6 be located? _____
3. Which command on the Edit menu results in formulas receiving the error message #REF! from cells referenced in the affected range? _____

STUDENT ASSIGNMENT 5
Understanding the IF Function

Instructions: Enter the correct answers.

1. Determine the truth value of the logical tests, given the following cell values: E1 = 500; F1 = 500; G1 = 2; H1 = 50; and I1 = 40. Enter true or false.

   a. E1 < 400   Truth value: _____

   b. F1 = E1   Truth value: _____

   c. 10 * H1 + I1 <> E1   Truth value: _____

   d. E1 + F1 >= 1000   Truth value: _____

   e. E1/H1 > G1 * 6   Truth value: _____

   f. 5 * G1 + I1 = H1   Truth value: _____

   g. 10 * I1 + 2 <= F1 + 2   Truth value: _____

   h. H1 -10 < I1   Truth value: _____

2. The active cell is cell F15. Write a function that assigns the value zero (0) or 1 to cell F15. Assign zero to cell F15 if the value in cell B3 is greater than the value in cell C12; otherwise assign 1 to cell F15.

   Function: _____

3. The active cell is cell F15. Write a function that assigns the value Credit OK or Credit Not OK to cell F15. Assign the label Credit OK if the value in cell A1 is not equal to the vlaue in cell B1; otherwise assign the label Credit Not OK.

   Function: _____

STUDENT ASSIGNMENT 6
Understanding Absolute, Mixed, and Relative Referencing

Instructions: Fill in the correct answers. Use Figure SA3-6 for problems 2 through 5.

FIGURE SA3-6

1. Write cell D15 as a relative reference, absolute reference, mixed reference with the row varying, and mixed reference with the column varying.

   Relative reference: _____   Mixed, row varying: _____

   Absolute reference: _____   Mixed, column varying: _____

2. Write the formula for cell B8 that multiplies cell B1 times the sum of cells B4, B5, and B6. Write the formula so that when it is copied to cells C8 and D8, cell B1 remains absolute. Verify your formula by checking it with the values found in cells B8, C8, and D8.

   Formula for cell B8: _____

3. Write the formula for cell E4 that multiplies cell A4 times the sum of cells B4, C4, and D4. Write the formula so that when it is copied to cells E5 and E6, cell A4 remains absolute. Verify your formula by checking it with the values found in cells E4, E5, and E6.

   Formula for cell E4: _____

4. Write the formula for cell B10 that multiplies cell B1 times the sum of cells B4, B5, and B6. Write the formula so that when it is copied to cells C10 and D10, Excel adjusts all the cell references according to the new location. Verify your formula by checking it with the values found in cells B10, C10, and D10.

   Formula for cell B10: _____

5. Write the formula for cell F4 that multiplies cell A4 times the sum of cells B4, C4, and D4. Write the formula so that when it is copied to cells F5 and F6, Excel adjusts all the cell addresses according to the new location. Verify your formula by checking it with the values found in cells F4, F5, and F6.

   Formula for cell F4: _____

COMPUTER LABORATORY EXERCISE 1
Using the Help Menu to Understand
IF Functions, Formulas, and What-if Analysis

Part 1 Instructions: Start Excel and perform the following tasks using a computer.

1. Choose the Search for Help on command from the Help menu.
2. Type `if functions` in the Search dialog box and choose the Show Topics button.
3. With the topic IF highlighted in the lower list, choose the Go To button.
4. Read the information displayed. Choose Print Topic from the Help window File menu to print the information.
5. To exit Help, double-click the Control-menu box in the Help window.

Part 2 Instructions: Start Excel and perform the following tasks using a computer.

1. Choose the Search for Help on command from the Help menu.
2. Type `formulas` in the Search dialog box.
3. In the upper list, select formulas, cell references in and then choose the Show Topics button.
4. In the lower list, choose the Go To button to display the Overview of Using References topic.
5. Read the information and then, under the See Also Help that appears at the bottom of the screen, click Changing a cell's reference type.
6. Read the information that appears in the How To window. Click the Print button in the How To window to print the information.
7. Click the Close button to close the How To window.
8. To exit Help, double-click the Control-menu box in the Help window.

Part 3 Instructions: Start Excel and perform the following tasks using a computer.

1. Choose the Search for Help on command from the Help menu.
2. Type `what-if` in the Search dialog box and then choose the Show Topics button.
3. In the lower list, choose the Go To button to display the Solving What-if Problems topic.
4. Click Seeking a specific solution to a formula using the Goal Seek command.
5. Read the information that appears in the How To window. Click the Print button in the How To window. Click the Close button in the How To window.
6. To exit Help, double-click the Control-menu box in the Help window.

COMPUTER LABORATORY EXERCISE 2
Using the Fill Handle and Mixed Cell Referencing

Instructions: Start Excel. Perform the tasks below Figure CLE3-2 to create the multiplication table shown.

FIGURE CLE3-2

1. Change the width of all the columns in the worksheet to 4.57 characters.
2. Use the fill handle to create the series of numbers between column B and column P in row 1 (2, 4, 6, . . . , 30) and the series of numbers between rows 2 and 17 in column A (1, 2, 3,. . . ,17). Recall that the fill handle requires the first two entries to determine a numeric series.
3. Color the background of column A and row 1 purple (column 5, row 2 on the Color palette).
4. Add a bold outline around column A and then add a bold outline around row 1.
5. Enter the formula =$A2 * B$1 in cell B2. Copy the formula in cell B2 to the range B2:P18. Bold the range A1:P17.
6. Enter your name, course, computer laboratory exercise number (CLE3-2), date, and instructor name in column A in separate but adjacent cells beginning in cell A19. Save the workbook using the filename CLE3-2.
7. Print the worksheet without gridlines.
8. Save the workbook again using the same filename
9. Press CTRL+` (single left quotation mark) to change the display to formulas. Print the formulas version in landscape orientation using the Fit To option on the Page tab in the Page Setup dialog box. Press CTRL+` (single left quotation mark) to change the display to values.

COMPUTER LABORATORY EXERCISE 3
Creating a Series

Instructions: Start Excel. Open CLE3-3 from the subdirectory Excel5 on the Student Diskette that accompanies this book. The worksheet shown in (Figure CLE3-3a) contains the initial values for eight different series.

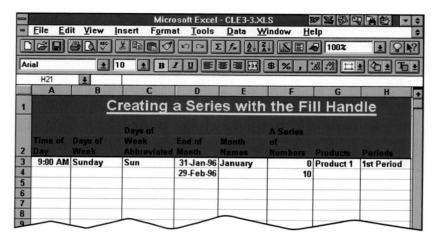

FIGURE CLE3-3a

Use the fill handle on one column at a time to propagate the eight different series through row 17 as shown in Figure CLE3-3b. For example, in column A, select cell A3 and drag the fill handle down to cell A17. Your final result should be 11:00 PM in cell A17. In column D, select the range D3:D4 and drag the fill handle down to cell D17. Save the workbook using the filename CLE3-3A. Print the worksheet on one page without cell gridlines.

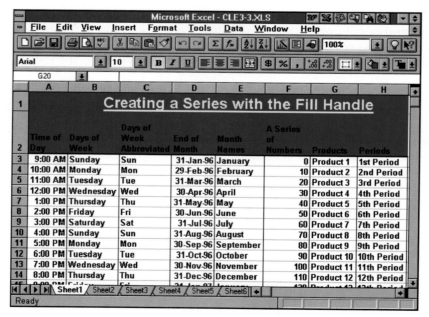

FIGURE CLE3-3b

COMPUTER LABORATORY ASSIGNMENT 1
Five-Year Projected Financial Statement

Purpose: To become familiar with entering IF functions, applying formulas that use absolute referencing, displaying the system date, charting, using panes, goal seeking, and what-if analysis.

Problem: You are a management trainee employed by Time Will Tell Inc. Each month for the first six months of your employment you work in a different department. This month you are working for the Information Systems (IS) department. Your IS supervisor observed from your resume that you learned Microsoft Excel in college and has requested that you build a Five-Year Projected Financial Statement based on figures available from 1995 (Figure CLA3-1A). Follow the instructions on the next page.

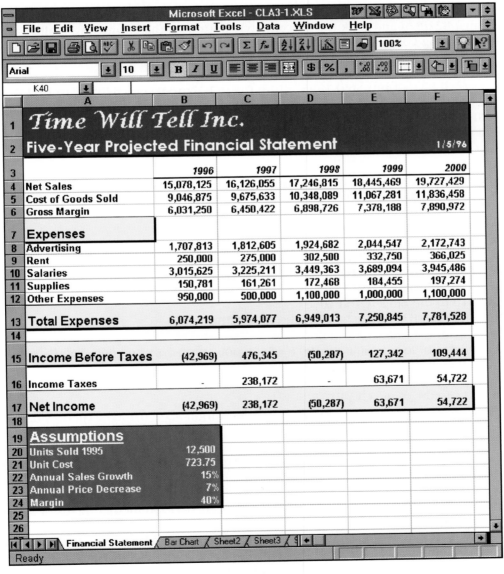

FIGURE CLA3-1a

(continued)

COMPUTER LABORATORY ASSIGNMENT 1(continued)

Part 1 Instructions: Perform the following tasks to create the worksheet shown in Figure CLA3-1a on the previous page.

1. Format the entire worksheet to bold, comma style with no decimal places by clicking the Select All button, the Bold button, the Comma Style button, and finally click the Decrease Decimal button on the Formatting toolbar twice. Enter the worksheet titles in cells A1 and A2. Enter the system date using the NOW function in cell F2. Format the date to the m/d/yy style.
2. Enter 1996 in cell B3, 1997 in cell C3, and generate the series 1996 through 2000 in the range B3:F3 using fill handle. Use the Cells command on the Format menu to assign the range B3:F3 the General format (Number tab, All category, General format code).
3. Enter the row titles in the range A4:A24. Change the font size in cells A7, A13, A15, and A17 to 12 point. Change the font size in cell A19 to 14 point and underline the characters in the cell.
4. Enter the following assumptions in the range B20:B24: Units Sold 1995: 12,500; Unit Cost: 723.75; Annual Sales Growth: 15%; Annual Price Decrease: 7%; Margin: 40%.
   Select the range B22:B24 and click the Percent Style button on the Formatting toolbar.
5. Change the following column widths: A = 23.43 and B through F = 11.00. Change the heights of rows 3, 7, 13, 15, 16, and 17 to 24.00 and row 19 to 18.00.
6. Complete the following entries:
   a. 1996 Sales (cell B4) = Units Sold 1995 * (Unit Cost/(1-Margin)) or =B20*(B21/(1-B24))
   b. 1997 Sales (cell C4) = 1996 Sales * (1+Annual Sales Growth)*(1-Annual Price Decrease) or =B4*(1+$B$22)*(1-$B$23)
   c. Copy cell C4 to the range D4:F4
   d. 1996 Cost of Goods Sold (cell B5) = 1996 Sales - (1996 Sales * Margin) or =B4*(1-$B$24)
   e. Copy cell B5 to the range C5:F5
   f. 1996 Gross Margin (cell B6) = 1995 Sales – 1995 Cost of Goods Sold or =B4-B5
   g. Copy cell B6 to the range C6:F6
   h. 1996 Advertising (cell B8) = $200,000+10%*1996 Sales or =200000+10%*B4
   i. Copy cell B8 to the range C8:F8
   j. 1996 Rent (cell B9) = $250,000
   k. 1997 Rent (cell C9) = 1996 Rent + 10%*1996 Rent or =B9*(1+10%)
   l. Copy cell C9 to the range D9:F9
   m. 1996 Salaries (cell B10) = 20% * 1996 Sales or =20%*B4
   n. Copy cell B10 to the range C10:F10
   o. 1996 Supplies (cell B11) = 1% * 1996 Sales or =1%*B4
   p. Copy cell B11 to the range C11:F11
   q. Other Expenses: 1996 = $950,000; 1997 = $500,000; 1998 = $1,100,000; 1999 = $1,000,000; and 2000 = $1,100,000
   r. 1996 Total Expenses (cell B13) = SUM(B8:B12)
   s. Copy cell B13 to the range C13:F13
   t. 1996 Income Before Taxes (cell B15 = 1996 Gross Margin – 1996 Total Expenses or =B6-B13
   u. Copy cell B15 to the range C15:F15
   v. 1996 Income Taxes (cell B16): If 1996 Income Before Taxes is less than zero, then 1996 Income Taxes equal zero; otherwise, 1996 Income Taxes equal 50% * 1996 Income Before Taxes or =IF(B15<0,0,50%*B15)
   w. Copy cell B16 to the range C16:F16
   x. 1996 Net Income (cell B17) = 1996 Income Before Taxes – 1996 Income Taxes or =B15-B16
   y. Copy cell B17 to the range C17:F17
7. Change the font in cell A1 to 20 point Lucida Calligraphy (or a similar font). Change the font in cell A2 to 16 point Century Gothic (or a similar font). Change the font in cell F2 to 10 point Century Gothic (or a similar font). Change the background and font colors and add drop shadows as shown in Figure CLA3-1a on the previous page.
8. Enter your name, course, computer laboratory assignment (CLA3-1), date, and instructor name in the range A27:A31. Save the workbook using the filename CLA3-1A.

9. Preview and print the worksheet without cell gridlines. Preview and print the formulas (CTRL+') in landscape orientation using the Fit to option button in the Page Setup dialog box. Press CTRL+` to display the values version of the worksheet.
10. Save the workbook again.

Part 2 Instructions: If you did not do Part 1, ask your instructor for a copy of CLA3-1. Draw a 3-D Column chart (Figure CLA3-1B) that compares the projected net incomes for years 1996 through 2000. Use the nonadjacent ranges B3:F3 and B17:F17. Add the chart title and format it as shown in Figure CLA3-1b. Rename and rearrange the tabs as shown in Figure CLA3-1b. Save the workbook using the filename CLA3-1B. Print both sheets.

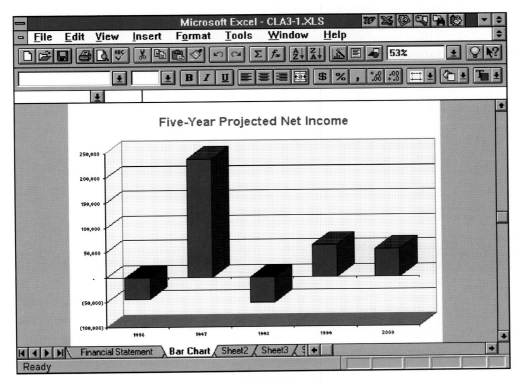

FIGURE CLA3-1b

Part 3 Instructions: If you did not do Parts 1 or 2, ask your instructor for a copy of CLA3-1. If the 3-D column chart is on the screen, click the Financial Statement tab to display the worksheet. Divide the window into two panes by dragging the horizontal split bar between rows 6 and 7. Use the scroll bars to display both the top and bottom of the worksheet. Using the numbers in the following table, analyze the effect of changing the annual sales growth (cell B22) and annual price decrease (cell B23) on the annual net incomes in row 17. Print both the worksheet and chart for each case.

CASE	ANNUAL SALES GROWTH	ANNUAL PRICE DECREASE	1997 RESULTING NET INCOME
1	5%	1%	$217,817
2	10%	-2%	$273,795
3	25%	10%	$275,830

Close CLA3-1B without saving it, and then re-open it. Use the Goal Seek command to determine a margin (cell B24) that would result in a net income of $500,000 for 1996 in cell B17. You should end up with a margin of 45%. Print only the worksheet after the goal seeking is complete. Do not save the workbook.

COMPUTER LABORATORY ASSIGNMENT 2
Modifying a Biweekly Payroll Worksheet

Purpose: To become familiar with entering IF functions with absolute referencing, freezing titles, zooming in and zooming out, and adding, changing, and deleting values and formats in a worksheet.

Note: Before you can begin this assignment, you must first complete Computer Laboratory Assignment 2 in Project 2 on page E134 or obtain the workbook CLA2-2 from your instructor.

Problem: Your supervisor in the Payroll department has asked you to modify the payroll workbook developed in Computer Laboratory Assignment 2 in Project 2 so that it appears as shown in Figure CLA3-2a. The major modifications include reformatting the worksheet, time-and-one-half for hours worked greater than 80, no federal tax if the federal tax is greater than the gross pay, and computation of the social security deduction. The worksheet (CLA2-2) created earlier in Project 2 is shown in Figure CLA2-2 on page E134.

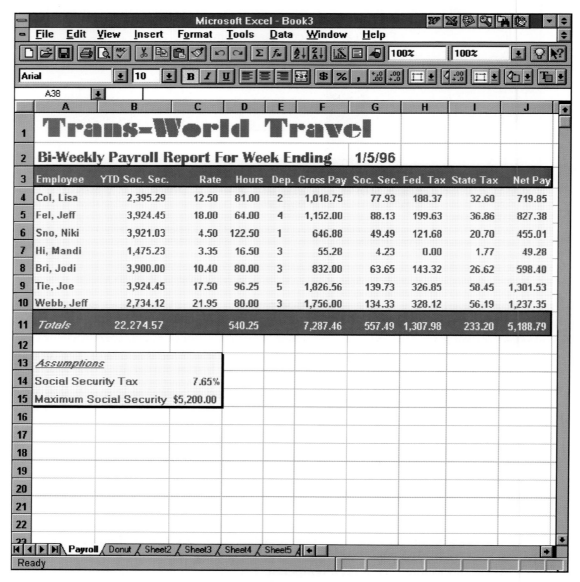

FIGURE CLA3-2a

Part 1 Instructions: Open the workbook CLA2-2 created in Project 2. Perform the following tasks:

1. Bold the entire worksheet. Delete rows 10 through 12. Insert a row above row 1. Enter the worksheet title, Trans-World Travel, in cell A1. Change the worksheet subtitle in row 2 to Bi-weekly Payroll Report for Week Ending. Assign the NOW function to cell G2 and format it to m/d/yy. Change the font in cell A1 to 24 point Braggadocio (or a similar font). Change the font in the range A2:G2 to 16 point Britannic Bold (or a similar font). Change the colors of the worksheet titles area so it appears as shown in Figure CLA3-2a.

2. Insert a new column between columns A and B. Title the new column YTD Soc. Sec.. Insert a new column between columns F and G. Title the new column Soc. Sec.. Format the column titles as shown in Figure CLA3-2a. Freeze the titles in column A and rows 1 through 3.

3. Increase the column widths and row heights as follows: A = 11.00; B = 13.00; C, F, G, I and J = 9.00; D = 7.00; E = 5.00; H = 8.00; row 2 = 24.00; row 3 = 21.00; rows 4 through 10 = 18.00; row 11 = 24.00; and rows 12 through 15 = 18.00.

4. Delete row 6 (Marci Di). Change Mandi Hi's number of dependents from 1 to 3.

5. Enter the following YTD social security values in row B.

NAME	YTD SOC. SEC.
Col, Lisa	$2,395.29
Fel, Jeff	3,924.45
Sno, Niki	3,921.03
Hi, Mandi	1,475.23
Bri, Jodi	3,900.00

6. Insert two new rows immediately above the Totals row. Add the following new employees:

EMPLOYEE	YTD SOC. SEC.	RATE	HOURS	DEPENDENTS
Tie, Joe	$3,924.45	$17.50	96.25	5
Webb, Jeff	2,734.12	21.95	80	3

7. Enter the Assumptions table in the range A13:C15 and format it as shown in Figure CLA3-2a. Place the titles in column A and the numbers in column C.

8. Change the background colors and font colors and add borders in the range A3:J11 as shown in Figure CLA3-2a.

9. Change the formulas to determine the gross pay in column F and the federal tax in column H.
   a. In cell F4, enter an IF function that applies the following logic:
      If Hours <= 80, then Gross Pay = Rate * Hours, otherwise Gross Pay = Rate * Hours + 0. 5 * Rate * (Hours - 80)
   b. Copy the IF function in cell F4 to the range F5:F10.
   c. In cell H4, enter the IF function that applies the following logic:
      If (Gross Pay - Dependents * 38. 46) > 0, then Federal Tax = 20% * (Gross Pay - Dependents * 38. 46), otherwise Federal Tax = 0
   d. Copy the IF function in cell H4 to the range H5:H10.

10. Copy the state tax and net pay formulas in the range I4:J4 to the range I10:H10.

11. An employee pays social security tax only if his or her YTD social security is less than the maximum social security in cell C15.
   a. Use the following logic to determine the social security tax for Lisa Col in cell G4:
      If Soc. Sec. Tax * Gross Pay + YTD Soc. Sec.> Maximum Soc. Sec., then Maximum Soc. Sec. - YTD Soc. Sec., else Soc. Sec. Tax * Gross Pay
   b. Copy the IF function to the range G5:G10.

(continued)

COMPUTER LABORATORY ASSIGNMENT 2 (continued)

    c. Make sure references to the values in the Assumptions table are absolute.

    d. Treat the social security tax as a deduction in determining the net pay.

    e. Determine any new totals as shown in row 11 of Figure CLA3-2a.

    f. Scroll over so the Net Pay column is adjacent to the row titles in column A.

12. Enter your name, course, computer laboratory assignment (CLA3-2), date, and instructor name in the range A18:A22. Save the workbook using the filename CLA3-2A.

13. Use the Zoom Control box on the Standard toolbar to change the view of the worksheet. One by one, select all the percents in the Zoom Control box. Change back to 100%.

14. Preview the worksheet in landscape orientation. Adjust column widths if number signs display in place of numbers. Print the worksheet without cell gridlines. Save the worksheet again.

15. Preview and print the formulas (CTRL+') in landscape orientation using the Fit to option button in the Page Setup dialog box. Close the worksheet without saving the latest changes.

Part 2 Instructions: If you did not do Part 1, ask your instructor for a copy of CLA3-2. Open the workbook CLA3-2A. Using the range A4:A10 (category names) and the range J4:J10 (data series), draw a donut chart (column 1, row 2 in the ChartWizard – Step 2 of 5 dialog box) with the labels inside each piece (Figure CLA3-2b). Add a chart title and format it appropriately. Add the text box with a drop shadow and the arrows as shown in Figure CLA3-2b. Format the text box and arrows appropriately. Rename and rearrange the tabs as shown in Figure CLA3-2b. Save the workbook using the filename CLA3-2B. Print both sheets.

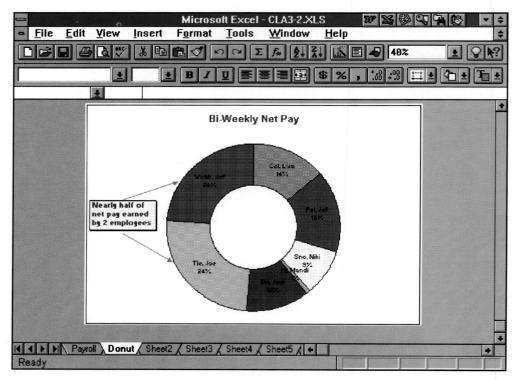

FIGURE CLA3-2b

Part 3 Instructions: If you did not do Parts 1 or 2, ask your instructor for a copy of CLA3-2. If the donut chart is on the screen, click the Payroll tab to display the worksheet. Using the numbers in the following table, analyze the effect of changing the Social Security Tax in cell C14 and the Maximum Social Security in cell C15. Print both the worksheet and chart for each case.

CASE	TAX	MAXIMUM SOCIAL SECURITY TAX	TOTAL SOCIAL SECURITY
1	8%	$5,000	$583.00
2	7.65%	5,200	557.49

COMPUTER LABORATORY ASSIGNMENT 3
Projected Quarterly Report

Purpose: To become familiar with creating a data series, using the Format Painter button, copying a range to a nonadjacent range, applying formulas that use absolute referencing, charting, goal seeking, and what-if analysis.

Problem: You are employed as a worksheet specialist by Plant A Tree Inc. The company utilizes assumptions, based on past business practice, to plan for the next quarter. You have been asked to create a worksheet similar to the one shown in Figure CLA3-3a. Follow the instructions on the next page.

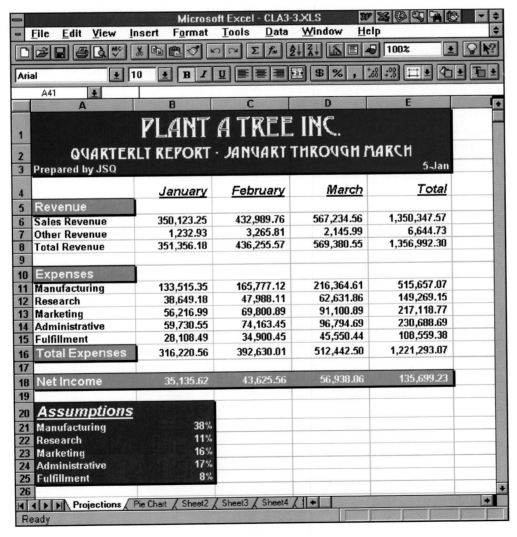

FIGURE CLA3-3a

(continued)

COMPUTER LABORATORY ASSIGNMENT 3 (continued)

Part 1 Instructions: Do the following to create the worksheet shown in Figure CLA3-3a.

1. Bold the entire worksheet. Enter the worksheet titles in cells A1, A2, and A3. Enter the NOW function in cell E3 and format it to d-mmm. Enter January in cell B4 and underline, italicize, and right align it. Use the fill handle to create the month series in row 4. Enter Total in cell E4 and use the Format Painter button on the Standard toolbar to format it the same as cell D4. Enter the row titles down through Assumptions in cell A20. Copy the row titles in the range A11:A15 to the range A21:A25.

2. Change the column widths as follows: A = 18.29; B through D = 13.71; and E = 14.86. Change the height of row 4 to 24.00.

3. Enter the sales revenue and other revenue from the table to the right in the range B6:D7.

	JANUARY	FEBRUARY	MARCH
Sales Revenue	$350,123.25	$432,989.76	$567,234.56
Other Revenue	1,232.93	3,265.81	2,145.99

4. Each of the expense categories in the range B11:D15 are determined by multiplying the total revenue for the month times the corresponding assumption in the Assumption table (range A20:B25). For example, the Manufacturing expense in cell B11 is equal to cell B21 times cell B8 or =B21*B8. Once the formulas are assigned to the range B11:B15, they can be copied to the range C11:D15. However, for the copy to work properly, you must make the first cell reference absolute. Thus, enter the following formulas in the designated cells:
   B11 = $B$21*B8; B12 = $B$22*B8; B13 = $B$23*B8; B14 = $B$24*B8; and B15 = $B$25*B8.

5. Use the SUM function to determine all the totals. The net income is equal to the total revenue for each month minus the total expenses for each month.

6. Enter your name, course, computer laboratory assignment (CLA3-3), date, and instructor name in the range A28:A32.

7. Save the workbook using the filename CLA3-3A.

8. Print the worksheet without cell gridlines. Preview and print the formulas (CTRL+') in landscape orientation using the Fit to option button in the Page Setup dialog box. Press CTRL+' to display the values version of the worksheet.

9. Save the workbook again.

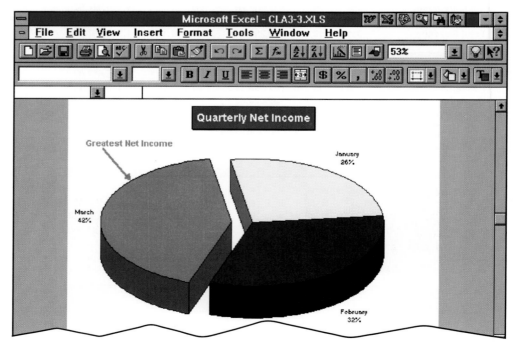

FIGURE CLA3-3b

Part 2 Instructions: If you did not do Part 1, ask your instructor for a copy of CLA3-3. Draw a 3-D pie chart (Figure CLA3-3b) that shows the monthly contribution to the quarterly net income. That is, chart the nonadjacent ranges B4:D4 (category names) and B18:D18 (data series).

Make the following changes to the pie chart:

1. Add the chart title and format it as shown in Figure CLA3-3b.
2. Explode the March slice.
3. Select a slice and use the 3-D View command on the shortcut menu to change the elevation to 30° and the rotation to 350°.
4. Change the color of the slices as shown in Figure CLA3-3b.
5. Add a text box with the phrase, Greatest Net Income, and an arrow pointing to the March slice. Format the text box and arrow as shown in Figure CLA3-3b.
6. Rename the tabs as follows: Chart1 to Pie Chart and Sheet1 to Projections. Rearrange the tabs so the Projections tab is to the left of the Pie Chart tab.
7. Save the workbook using the filename CLA3-3B.
8. Print both sheets.

Part 3 Instructions: If you did not do Parts 1 or 2, ask your instructor for a copy of CLA3-3. If the 3-D pie chart is on the screen, click the Projections tab to display the worksheet shown in Figure CLA3-3a. Using the numbers in the following table, analyze the effect of changing the assumptions in rows 21 through 25 on the quarterly net income in cell E18. Print both the worksheet and chart for each case.

	CASE 1	CASE 2	CASE 3
Manufacturing	35%	37%	40%
Research	10%	10%	15%
Marketing	14%	15%	17%
Administrative	16%	16%	20%
Fulfillment	5%	7%	5%

You should end up with the following quarterly net incomes in cell E18: Case 1 = $271,398.46; Case 2 = $203,548.85; and Case 3 = $40,709.77.

Close CLA3-3B without saving it and then re-open it. Use the Goal Seek command to determine the marketing percentage (cell B23) that would result in a quarterly net income of $200,000 in cell E18. (You should end up with a marketing percentage of 11%.) Print only the worksheet.

COMPUTER LABORATORY ASSIGNMENT 4
Stock Analysis Worksheet

Purpose: To become familiar with planning a worksheet.

Problem: You are rich and famous and own stock in many different companies. Your computer stock portfolio includes the companies listed in the following table on the next page. The number of shares you own in each company are in parentheses. Your investment analysts tell you that on average the computer industry will return 5% per year for the next ten years. Create a worksheet that organizes your computer stock portfolio and projects its annual worth for each of the next ten years. Make sure the 5% return is assigned to a cell so that you can modify this value as circumstances change.

(continued)

COMPUTER LABORATORY ASSIGNMENT 4 (continued)

HARDWARE	SOFTWARE	NETWORKING
Apple (5,000)	Autodesk (3,000)	3Com (2,500)
Compaq (11,500)	Borland (4,500)	Compaq (11,250)
DEC (6,550)	Lotus (11,250)	Novell (16,750)
IBM (22,500)	Microsoft (58,000)	
Intel (7,000)	Symantec (6,500)	

Instructions: Obtain the latest stock prices from the newspaper for your computer stocks. Using the figures in the table, compute the amount of your investment in each stock and list it under the current year. Next, use the 5% return per year to project the annual worth of these stocks for each of the next ten years. Group the companies in the worksheet by major segments (Hardware, Software, Networking). Show totals for each segment. Use goal seeking to modify the grand total by changing the appropriate cells. Use the techniques developed in this project to manipulate the large worksheet. Submit the following:

1. A description of the problem. Include the purpose of the worksheet, a statement outlining the results, the required data, and calculations.
2. A handwritten design of the worksheet.
3. A printed copy of the worksheet without cell gridlines.
4. A printed copy of the formulas in the worksheet.

USING *O*BJECT *L*INKING AND *E*MBEDDING (OLE)

$\mathcal{O}$BJECT $\mathcal{L}$INKING AND $\mathcal{E}$MBEDDING (OLE)

PROJECT ONE

▼

SHARING DATA AND GRAPHICS BETWEEN APPLICATIONS

OBJECTIVES You will have mastered the material in this project when you can:

- ▸ Start two applications
- ▸ Explain source document, destination document, and object
- ▸ Select a range to copy in the source document
- ▸ Copy the selected range in the source document to the Clipboard
- ▸ Switch from the source document application to the destination document application
- ▸ Paste the object on the Clipboard in the destination document

- ▸ Embed the object on the Clipboard in the destination document
- ▸ Link the object on the Clipboard to the destination document
- ▸ Tile two application windows on the screen to view both at the same time
- ▸ Drag and drop an object between tiled applications
- ▸ Embed an existing file or create and embed an object without leaving an application

▶ INTRODUCTION

ne of the powerful features of Windows applications is that you can incorporate parts of documents or entire documents called **objects** from one application in another application. For example, you can copy a worksheet in Excel to a document in Word. In this case, the worksheet in Excel is called the **source document** (copied from) and the document in Word is called the **destination document** (pasted to or linked to). Copying objects between applications can be accomplished in three ways:

1. Copy and paste
2. Copy and embed
3. Copy and link

All of the Microsoft Office applications (Word 6, Excel 5, Access 2, and PowerPoint 4) allow you to use these three methods to copy objects between the applications.

OLE2

The method you select depends on what you plan to do after the task is complete. The first method, *copy and paste*, involves using the Copy and Paste buttons. The latter two methods, *copy and embed* and *copy and link*, are referred to as Object Linking and Embedding, or **OLE**. Each of these three methods is presented in this project. The following paragraphs describe the differences among the three methods.

Method 1 – Copy and Paste   When an object is copied from the source document and pasted in the destination document (standard **copy and paste**), it becomes part of the destination document. The object may be edited, but the editing features are, for the most part, limited to those available in the destination document. Thus, if you copy and paste an Excel worksheet into a Word document, the worksheet displays as a Word table and you use Word to edit the table. If you change values that are totaled, the totals will not be adjusted. This method is further weakened because you cannot directly copy and paste an embedded chart into a Word document. In addition, if you change the table contents in the Word document, the changes are *not* reflected in the worksheet when you display it later in Excel, because no link back to the worksheet is established. Of the three methods described, the *copy and paste* is by far the weakest. On the positive side, the *copy and paste* method is quick and easy.

Method 2 – Copy and Embed   When the same object is copied and embedded in a destination document, it becomes part of the document itself as with the *copy and paste* method. However, more importantly, the editing features made available are those of the source document's application. Thus, if you **copy and embed** an Excel worksheet in a Word document, it displays much like a worksheet in the Word document. When you double-click the worksheet to edit it, the menu bar and toolbars at the top of the Word screen change to the Excel menu bar and toolbars. Hence, when you copy and embed, you edit the worksheet in Word, but with Excel editing capabilities. Here again, if you change the worksheet in the Word document using Excel editing capabilities, the changes are **not** reflected in the worksheet when you display it later in Excel. You can also embed a worksheet with an embedded chart. In addition, the chart in the Word document will change when you change the data on which it depends.

You would choose *copy and embed* over *copy and paste* when you want to use the source application's editing capabilities or, as in this project, you want to copy an embedded chart. You would choose *copy and embed* over *copy and link* (method 3) when the object is fairly stable, or you don't need to have the most current version of the object in your document, or the object is small. Another reason to choose the *copy and embed* method would be when you plan to use the destination document and you do not have a copy of the source document.

Remember, when you copy and embed, the object is saved along with the destination document, thus taking up additional disk storage.

Method 3 – Copy and Link   When the same object is copied and linked to a destination document, the system returns to the source application when you edit the object because only a **link**, or reference, is established. Thus, if you **copy and link** an Excel worksheet to a Word document, it displays similarly to a worksheet in the Word document, but it does not take up space in the document (i.e., the worksheet is not saved with the Word document).

When you click the worksheet to edit, the system switches you to the source application (Excel). Hence, when you copy and link, you edit the object in the source application. For example, if you link an Excel worksheet to a Word document and you double-click the object while Word is active, Windows will start Excel and open the linked worksheet. Any changes you make to the worksheet will show up in the Word document.

Use *copy and link* over the first two methods when an object is likely to change and you want to make sure the object always reflects the changes in the source document or if the object is large, such as a video clip or sound clip. Thus, if you link a worksheet to a memorandum, and update the worksheet weekly, any time you open the memorandum the latest update of the worksheet will display.

Another useful feature is tiling. With the use of tiling, it is possible to start two or more applications, open documents in each of the applications, and place all of the open application's windows on the screen. When some Windows applications are tiled, such as the latest versions of Word, Excel, Access, and PowerPoint, you can copy and embed by using drag and drop between tiled applications.

▶ PROJECT ONE — KING'S COMPUTER OUTLET WEEKLY SALES MEMORANDUM

Each week, the vice president of sales for King's Computer Outlet sends out a memorandum to the regional sales managers showing the previous week's daily sales for all regions. She currently uses only Word to produce the memorandum that includes a table of the daily sales. The wording in the memorandum remains constant week to week. The table of daily sales changes each week.

She recently heard of the OLE capabilities of Microsoft's applications packages and would like to use them so she can create the basic memorandum (upper left screen in Figure 1-1) using Word and maintain the daily sales in a worksheet (upper right screen in Figure 1-1) using Excel. She would like to insert the worksheet from Excel into the Word document (bottom screen Figure 1-1). She plans to experiment with OLE and has decided to test each of the three methods described in the previous section: *copy and paste*; *copy and embed*; and *copy and link*.

▶ COPYING AND PASTING AN OBJECT BETWEEN APPLICATIONS

The first method being used to incorporate the worksheet in the document is a familiar one. It involves a copy and paste. You start Word and open the memorandum shown in the upper left screen in Figure 1-1. Next, you switch to Program Manager, start Excel, and open the worksheet shown in the upper right screen of Figure 1-1. While in Excel, you copy to the Clipboard the portion of the worksheet (called the object) you want to paste in the Word document. In this first example, the range A3:G10 is copied. Finally, you switch to Word and paste the object on the Clipboard into the memorandum. The chart below the data in the upper right screen in Figure 1-1 (range A12:G25) is not included because the *copy and paste* method cannot be used to copy an embedded chart.

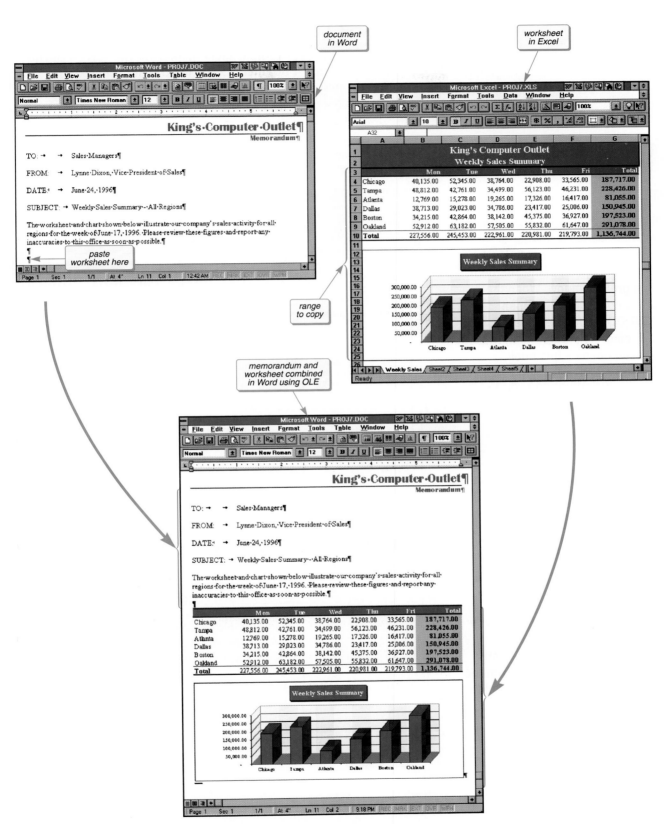

FIGURE 1-1

Starting Word and Excel

To start Word, the Office Manager toolbar must display on the screen or the Microsoft Office group window must be open. Once Word is started and the appropriate document is opened, start Excel, and open the appropriate worksheet as shown in the following steps.

TO START WORD AND EXCEL ▼

STEP 1 ▶

Click the Microsoft Word button on the Office Manager toolbar or double-click the Microsoft Word program-item icon in the Microsoft Office group window. When the Word window displays, open PROJ7.DOC from the Excel5 subdirectory on the Student Diskette that accompanies this book.

The memorandum shown in Figure 1-2 displays.

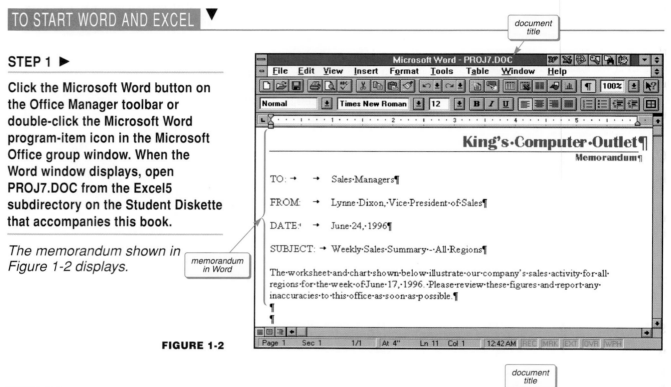

FIGURE 1-2

STEP 2 ▶

Click the Microsoft Excel button on the Office Manager toolbar or press ALT+TAB to return to Program Manager and double-click the Microsoft Excel program-item icon in the Microsoft Office group window. When the Excel window displays, open PROJ7.XLS from the Excel5 subdirectory on the Student Diskette.

The worksheet shown in Figure 1-3 displays. There are two applications open at this time, Word and Excel. Excel is the active application.

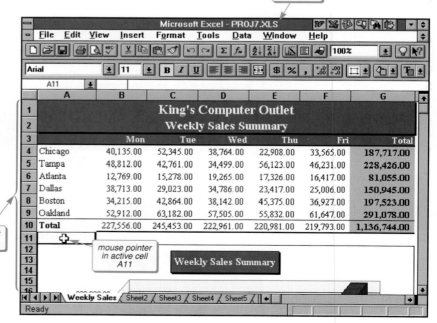

FIGURE 1-3

When you click a button on the Office Manager toolbar to start an application, Microsoft Windows first checks to see if it was started earlier in the session. If the application was started earlier, then Microsoft Windows switches to it and displays it on the screen. If the application was not started earlier, then Microsoft Windows starts it and displays it on the screen.

If the Office Manager toolbar does not display at the top-right of your screen, then to start a second application you activate Program Manager by holding down the ALT key and pressing the TAB key until the box titled Program Manager appears in the middle of the screen. Release the TAB key and then the ALT key. With the Program Manager on the screen, start the second application by double-clicking the program-item icon. You can also switch to Program Manager by pressing CTRL+ESC or by clicking the Control-menu box and choosing the Switch To command.

With the memorandum opened in Word and the worksheet opened in Excel, the next step is to complete the *copy and paste* operation.

Copying the Object in the Source Document and Pasting It in the Destination Document

The steps below and on the next page show how to copy the range A3:G10 to the Clipboard, switch to Word, and paste the object on the Clipboard below the last paragraph in the memorandum.

TO COPY AN OBJECT IN EXCEL AND PASTE IT IN WORD ▼

STEP 1 ▶

With Excel active and PROJ7.XLS on the screen, select the range A3:G10 (Figure 1-4).

STEP 2 ▶

Click the Copy button on the Standard toolbar.

A marquis surrounds the range A3:G10 indicating it has been copied to the Clipboard.

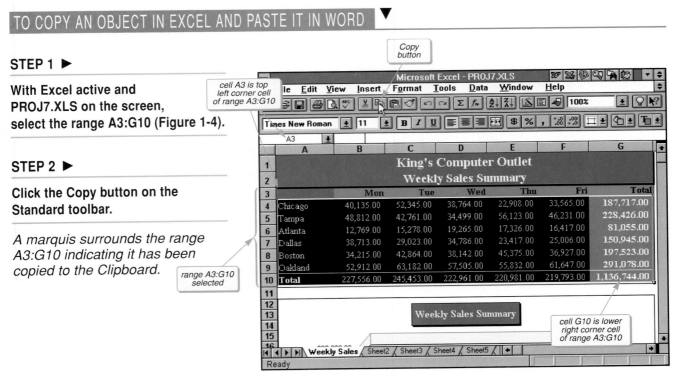

FIGURE 1-4

STEP 3 ▶

Click the Microsoft Word button on the Office Manager toolbar or hold down the ALT key and press the TAB key until the box shown in the middle of the screen contains the title Microsoft Word – PROJ7.DOC. Release the TAB key and then the ALT key. Press CTRL+END.

The document PROJ7.DOC displays with the insertion point at the bottom of the document as shown in Figure 1-5.

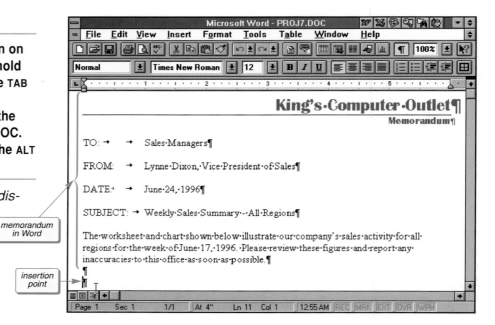

memorandum in Word

insertion point

FIGURE 1-5

STEP 4 ▶

Click the Paste button on the Standard toolbar.

The object on the Clipboard (range A3:G10 from PROJ7.XLS) is copied into the Word document as a table beginning at the insertion point (Figure 1-6).

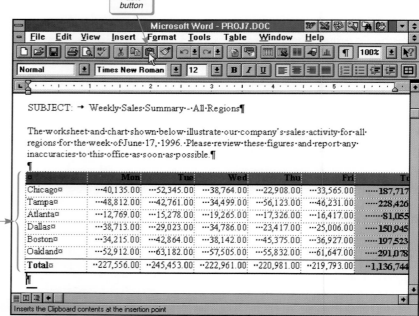

copy of worksheet pasted in memorandum displays as a Word table

FIGURE 1-6

The copy and paste operation is complete. The memorandum contains an object that was originally created in Excel. Although this method of inserting a portion of an Excel worksheet into a Word document is relatively simple, it lacks the required editing capabilities. For example, if any of the numbers change, you would probably make the adjustments to the worksheet in Excel and complete the copy and paste again. You could change the numbers in the table in Word, but then there would be inconsistency between the table in the Word document and the Excel worksheet.

Saving, Printing, and Closing the Memorandum

The following steps save, print, and close the memorandum.

TO SAVE, PRINT, AND CLOSE THE MEMORANDUM

Step 1: With Word active, use the Save As command on the File menu to save the memorandum to drive A using the filename PROJ7A.DOC.

Step 2: Click the Print button on the Standard toolbar. The memorandum prints as shown in Figure 1-7.

Step 3: Choose the Close command from the File menu.

Copying and pasting an object between applications using the Copy and Paste buttons is a quick and easy way for the vice president of sales for King's Computer Outlet to add the worksheet information to the memorandum. However, with this method, it was not possible to copy the chart in the worksheet to the memorandum. Also, if the table in the memorandum is modified, the table will no longer agree with the worksheet unless it too is modified.

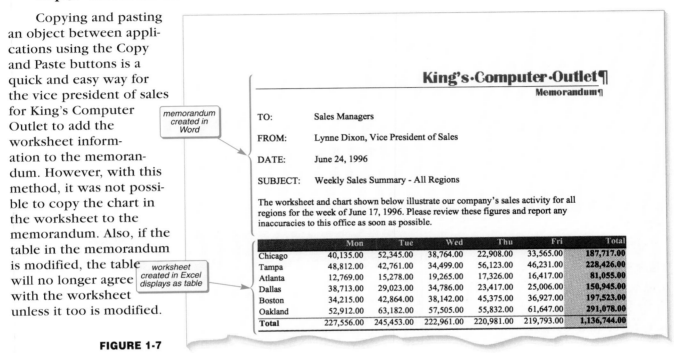

FIGURE 1-7

▶ COPYING AND EMBEDDING AN OBJECT BETWEEN APPLICATIONS

The *copy and embed* method involves using the Copy button and the Paste Special command on the Edit menu. As with the *copy and paste* method, you start both applications and open the document and worksheet. With Excel active, you copy the portion of the worksheet (range A3:G25) you want to the Clipboard. Once the object is on the Clipboard, you return to Word and use the **Paste Special command** to paste the object on the Clipboard into the memorandum.

Using the Paste Special Command to Embed an Object

Follow the steps on the next two pages to open the Word document, copy the worksheet to the Clipboard, and embed the worksheet in the Word document.

TO COPY AND EMBED AN OBJECT BETWEEN APPLICATIONS ▼

STEP 1 ►

With Word active, open PROJ7.DOC from the Excel5 subdirectory on the Student Diskette.

The memorandum shown in Figure 1-8 displays.

STEP 2 ►

Click the Microsoft Excel button on the Office Manager toolbar or press ALT+TAB to switch to Excel. If Excel was not active, start Excel and open PROJ7.XLS from the Excel5 subdirectory on the Student Diskette.

Excel is active and the worksheet PROJ7.XLS displays.

STEP 3 ►

Select the range A3:G25 and click the Copy button on the Standard toolbar.

A marquis surrounds the range A3:G25 (Figure 1-9) indicating that a copy of it is on the Clipboard.

FIGURE 1-8

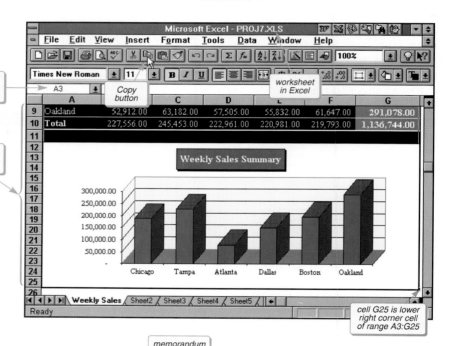

FIGURE 1-9

STEP 4 ►

Click the Microsoft Word button on the Office Manager toolbar or hold down the ALT key and press the TAB key until the box shown in the middle of the screen contains the title Microsoft Word – PROJ7.DOC. Release the TAB key and then the ALT key. Press CTRL+END. Select the Edit menu.

Word is active and the Edit menu displays as shown in Figure 1-10.

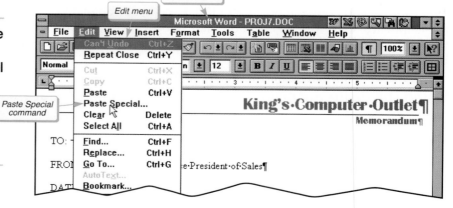

FIGURE 1-10

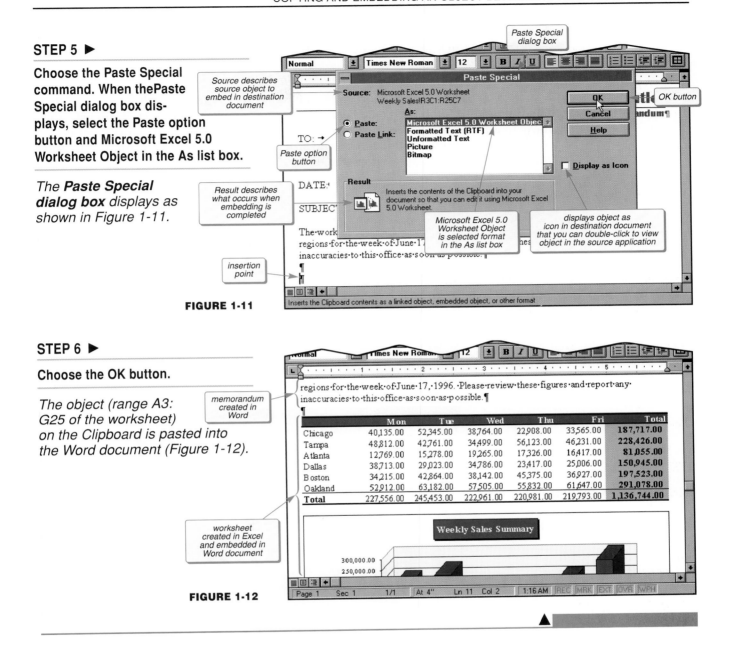

STEP 5 ▶

Choose the Paste Special command. When the Paste Special dialog box displays, select the Paste option button and Microsoft Excel 5.0 Worksheet Object in the As list box.

*The **Paste Special** dialog box* displays as shown in Figure 1-11.

FIGURE 1-11

STEP 6 ▶

Choose the OK button.

The object (range A3: G25 of the worksheet) on the Clipboard is pasted into the Word document (Figure 1-12).

FIGURE 1-12

If you paste the object and the results are not what you expect, click the Undo button on the Standard toolbar or choose the Undo command from the Edit menu. If you have entered other commands between the time you embed the document and your decision to remove the object, click the embedded object to select it and press the DELETE key.

Saving and Printing the Memorandum

The step below and on the next page save and print the memorandum with the embedded worksheet.

TO SAVE AND PRINT THE MEMORANDUM

Step 1: With Word active, use the Save As command on the File menu to save the memorandum with the embedded worksheet to drive A using the filename PROJ7B.DOC.

Step 2: Click the Print button on the Standard toolbar.

The memorandum prints as shown in Figure 1-13.

As you can see from Figure 1-13, the worksheet is added to the bottom of the memorandum as required (see Figure 1-1 on page OLE5). The next section shows how to edit the worksheet portion of the document. Because the worksheet is embedded in the Word document, the size of the file PROJ7B.DOC on disk is larger than the original memorandum (PROJ7.DOC).

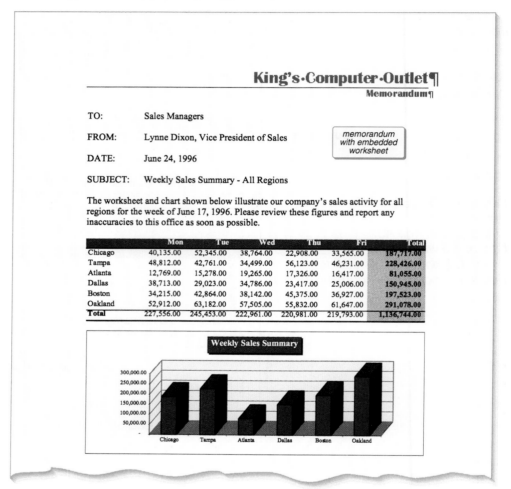

FIGURE 1-13

Editing the Embedded Object

To change information in the worksheet portion of the memorandum, you do not have to make the changes in Excel, delete the worksheet from the memorandum, and then copy and embed again. All you have to do is double-click the worksheet while in Word.

When you double-click the embedded worksheet, the Word toolbars immediately change to Excel toolbars. The status bar changes. Except for the File and Window menus, the menu bar also changes. Thus, you use the editing capabilities of Excel while Word is the active application. This is called **in-place activation**. The following steps show how to change the contents of cell B8 from $34,215.00 to $14,217.00 and the contents of cell C9 from $63,182.00 to $3,182.00 while Word is the active application. As the changes are made, the chart is redrawn to represent the new sales amounts.

TO EDIT THE EMBEDDED WORKSHEET ▼

STEP 1 ►

With Word active, point to the embedded worksheet and double-click.

Excel surrounds the worksheet in the memorandum with a heavy blue border as shown in Figure 1-14. The Excel menu bar, toolbars, formula bar, and status bar display on the screen, even though the title bar shows that Word is active. An Excel window has been opened within Word and the Excel source document displays in the Excel window. Notice the column and row headings and the vertical scroll bar within the Excel window. The mouse pointer changes from an I-beam to a block plus sign.

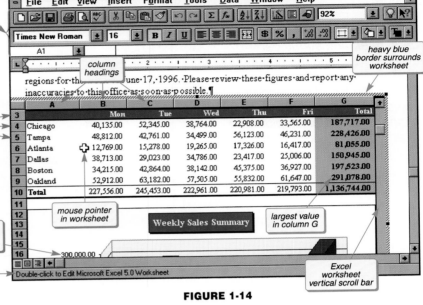

FIGURE 1-14

STEP 2 ►

Use the Excel scroll bar to scroll down so row 8 displays at the top of the window. Select cell B8. Enter 14217 and select cell C9. Enter 3182

The new numbers display in cells B8 and C9 and the chart is redrawn to represent the new amounts (Figure 1-15). The new total amounts cause the y-axis in the chart to be rescaled. The largest amount at the top of the y-axis on the chart was 300,000.00. It is now 250,000.00.

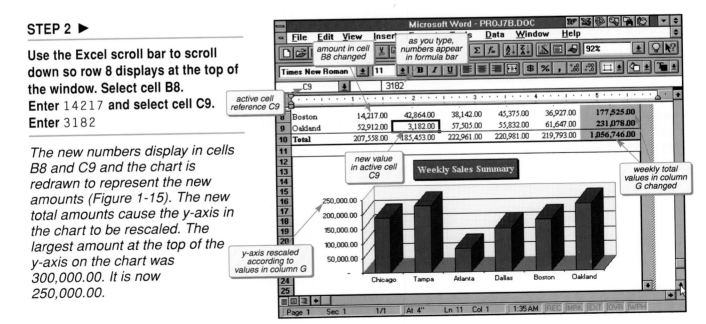

FIGURE 1-15

STEP 3 ▶

Double-click outside the heavy blue border that represents the Excel window.

The Word menu bar, tool-bars, ruler, and status bar are restored, and the heavy blue border no longer sur-rounds the Excel embedded object. The mouse pointer changes from a block plus sign to an I-beam (Figure 1-16).

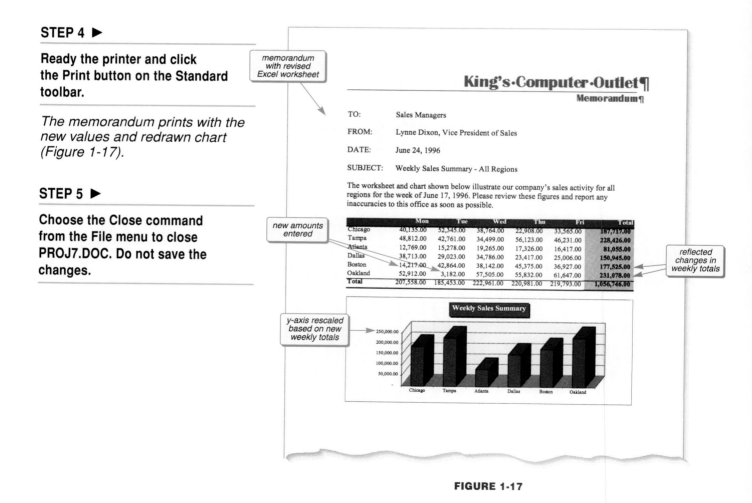

FIGURE 1-16

STEP 4 ▶

Ready the printer and click the Print button on the Standard toolbar.

The memorandum prints with the new values and redrawn chart (Figure 1-17).

STEP 5 ▶

Choose the Close command from the File menu to close PROJ7.DOC. Do not save the changes.

FIGURE 1-17

As shown in Figure 1-14 on page OLE13, when an object is embedded in a document, you can open one application from within another by double-clicking the object. You can then use the editing capabilities of the source application. However, the embedded worksheet has no connection to the original worksheet from which it was copied. Thus, the changes made to the worksheet while Word was active will not show up in the worksheet PROJ7.XLS, if you open it later in Excel.

▶ COPYING AND LINKING AN OBJECT BETWEEN APPLICATIONS

U nlike the previous two methods, when you link an object, you are not making a copy of it in the destination document. You create a link to the source document that contains the object. Thus, when you initiate an edit of a linked object by double-clicking on it in the destination document, the system activates the **source application**. In the case of the memorandum and worksheet in this project, when you link the worksheet to the memorandum and double-click the worksheet, the system activates Excel and opens the appropriate worksheet. The following steps show how to copy and link the worksheet to the memorandum.

TO COPY AND LINK AN OBJECT BETWEEN APPLICATIONS ▼

STEP 1 ▶

With Word active, open PROJ7.DOC from the Excel5 subdirectory on the Student Diskette. Switch to Excel by clicking the Microsoft Excel button on the Office Manager toolbar or press ALT+TAB until the box titled Microsoft Excel – PROJ7.XLS appears in the middle of the screen. Open PROJ7.XLS from the Excel5 subdirectory on the Student Diskette.

Excel is active and the work-sheet PROJ7.XLS displays. You can link objects only from saved documents. Thus, it is important that PROJ7.XLS exists on disk.

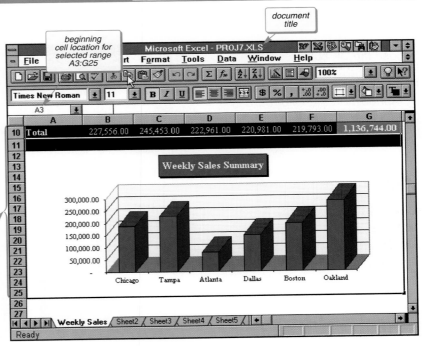

FIGURE 1-18

STEP 2 ▶

Select the range A3:G25 and click the Copy button on the Standard toolbar.

The range A3:G25 (Figure 1-18) is copied onto the Clipboard.

STEP 3 ►

Switch to Word by clicking the Microsoft Word button on the Office Manager toolbar or hold down the ALT key and press the TAB key until the box shown in the middle of the screen contains the title Microsoft Word – PROJ7.DOC. Press CTRL+END. Choose the Paste Special command from the Edit menu. Select the Paste Link option button. Select Microsoft Excel 5.0 Worksheet Object in the As list box.

The Paste Special dialog box displays as shown in Figure 1-19.

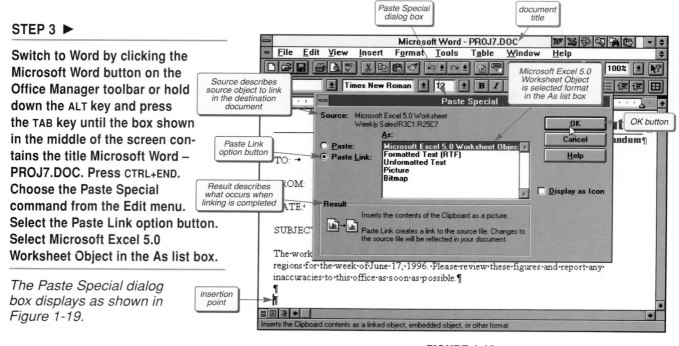

FIGURE 1-19

STEP 4 ►

Choose the OK button.

The object (range A3:G25 of the worksheet) on the Clipboard is paste linked to the Word document (Figure 1-20).

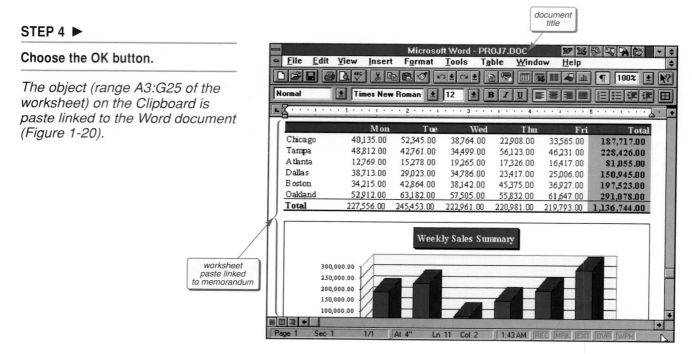

FIGURE 1-20

It appears the result in Figure 1-20 is the same as the result achieved by copying and embedding shown earlier in Figure 1-12 on page OLE11. However, there is a big difference. In Figure 1-12, the object is embedded, or made part of the Word document. In Figure 1-19, the object is linked and, therefore, is not part of the Word document. The difference becomes apparent when you edit the two documents. Before editing the linked worksheet, the following section saves and prints the Word document and then exits both Word and Excel.

Saving and Printing the Memorandum and Exiting Word and Excel

Use the following steps to save and print the memorandum and exit both Word and Excel so you can see how Windows treats a linked object when the source application is closed.

TO SAVE, PRINT, AND EXIT WORD AND EXCEL

Step 1: With Word active, use the Save As command on the File menu to save the memorandum to drive A using the filename PROJ7C.

Step 2: Click the Print button on the Standard toolbar.

Step 3: Double-click the Control-menu box to exit Word.

Step 4: Switch to Excel by clicking the Microsoft Excel button on the Office Manager toolbar or press ALT+TAB to activate Excel, if it does not display on the screen when you exit Word. Double-click the Control-menu box to close Excel. Do not save changes.

The memorandum prints as shown in Figure 1-13 on page OLE12. When the memorandum is saved to disk, the link (reference) to the worksheet is saved with it. Because it is only a link, the size of the memorandum file is not as large as when the worksheet was embedded in the document earlier.

Starting Word and Opening a Document with a Linked Object

The following steps open the memorandum with the linked worksheet.

TO START WORD AND OPEN A DOCUMENT WITH A LINKED OBJECT

Step 1: Click the Microsoft Word button on the Office Manager toolbar or with Program Manager active and the Microsoft Office group window open, double-click the Microsoft Word program-item icon.

Step 2: Click the Open button on the Standard toolbar and open PROJ7C.DOC from drive A.

The memorandum with the linked worksheet displays as shown earlier in Figure 1-20. Word takes considerably longer to open the document because of the link to the worksheet. Once the memorandum is open, Word is active but Excel remains closed.

Editing the Linked Worksheet

When you double-click the worksheet in the Word document, Windows automatically starts Excel, makes it the active application, and opens the original worksheet PROJ7.XLS. The following steps on the next page change the contents of cell B8 from $34,215.00 to $14,217.00 and the contents of cell C9 from $63,182.00 to $3,182.00. As the changes are made, the chart is redrawn to represent the new sales amounts. When you switch to Word, the worksheet represents the most recent changes.

TO EDIT THE LINKED WORKSHEET ▼

STEP 1 ►

With Word active, point to the linked worksheet and double-click.

Windows starts Excel and displays the worksheet PROJ7.XLS in a minimized window.

STEP 2 ►

Click the Maximize button in the PROJ7.XLS window and then scroll down so the worksheet appears as shown in Figure 1-21.

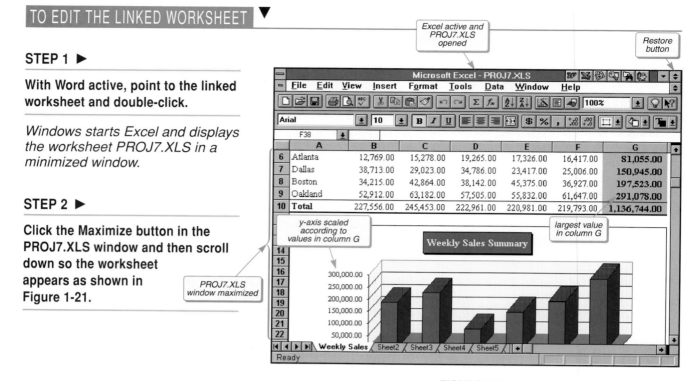

FIGURE 1-21

STEP 3 ►

Select cell B8. Enter `14217` and select cell C9. Enter `3182`

The new numbers display in cells B8 and C9 and the chart is redrawn to represent the new amounts in column G (Figure 1-22). The new total amounts cause the y-axis in the chart to be rescaled. The largest amount at the top of the y-axis on the chart was 300,000.00 (Figure 1-21). It is now 250,000.00.

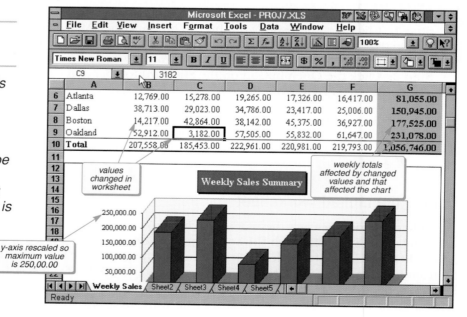

FIGURE 1-22

STEP 4 ▶

Switch to Word by clicking the Microsoft Word button on the Office Manager toolbar or hold down the ALT key and press the TAB key until the box shown in the middle of the screen contains the title Microsoft Word – PROJ7C.DOC.

Windows switches to Word. The memorandum displays with the worksheet updated (Figure 1-23).

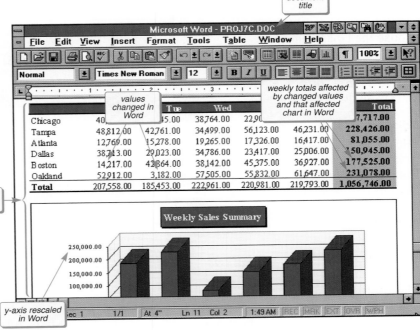

FIGURE 1-23

Displaying and Modifying the Links

To check the links to a document you can choose the **Links command** on the Edit menu. If the command is ghosted, no links exist. You can link as many objects as you want to a document provided you have enough main memory. The following steps show how to check the links.

TO DISPLAY AND EDIT THE LINKS ▼

STEP 1 ▶

Press CTRL+HOME to move the insertion point to the top of the document. Select the Edit menu (Figure 1-24).

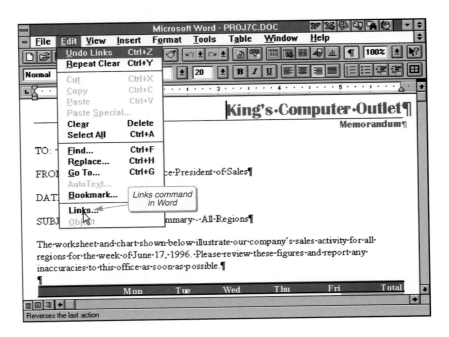

FIGURE 1-24

STEP 2 ►

Choose the Links command.

*The **Links dialog box** displays (Figure 1-25). The Source File list box displays the links. In this case, there is a link to PROJ7.XLS on drive A to PROJ7.DOC. The sheet name and range display in row-column form. That is, R3 stands for row 3. The three dots following R3 mean to the end of the worksheet (R25).*

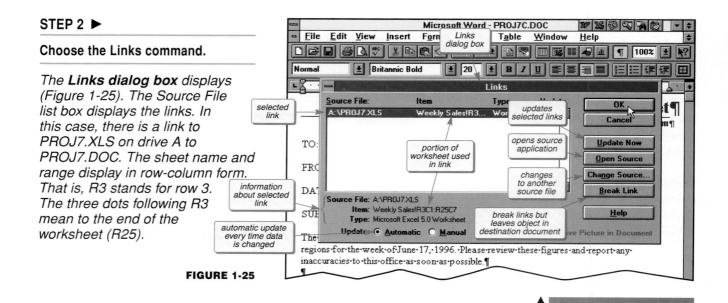

FIGURE 1-25

Both internal links and external links display in the Links dialog box. **Internal links** refer to links within Word itself. **External links** refer to other applications such as Excel. While the Links dialog box is on the screen, you can change links to other files or remove links. For more information, choose the Help button in the Links dialog box.

Saving and Printing the Memorandum and Exiting Word and Excel

The following steps save and print the memorandum. Then, both Word and Excel are closed. Excel is closed *without* saving changes. Thus, when the memorandum is opened later, the updates to the linked object will not appear.

TO SAVE AND PRINT THE MEMORANDUM AND EXIT WORD AND EXCEL

Step 1: With Word active, use the Save As command on the File menu to save the memorandum to drive A using the filename PROJ7D.DOC.

Step 2: Click the Print button on the Standard toolbar.

The memorandum prints as shown in Figure 1-17 on page OLE14.

Step 3: Double-click Word's Control-menu box to exit Word.

Excel becomes the active document and PROJ7.XLS displays.

Step 4: Double-click Excel's Control-menu box to exit Excel.

The Microsoft Excel dialog box displays which allows you to save the changes to the workbook.

Step 5: Choose the No button.

The worksheet PROJ7.XLS is closed and the changes made earlier in Step 3 on page OLE18 (Figure 1-22) are lost.

Step 6: Start Word. Open PROJ7C.DOC from drive A.

The memorandum with the linked worksheet displays (Figure 1-26). The changes made earlier do not show up because the Excel worksheet was not saved in Step 5.

Step 7: Double-click the Word Control-menu box to exit Word.

Consider this important point in the last set of steps. Even though the memorandum was saved after the worksheet was updated, the updates did not show up in Figure 1-26 because the worksheet was not saved when Excel was closed in Step 5. This example further solidifies the fact that the linked worksheet is independent of the memorandum. Thus, the worksheet must be saved for the updates to show when the memorandum is opened later. This was not true when the *copy and embed* method was used earlier.

You can see that if the vice president of sales plans to maintain the worksheet in Excel and send out the memorandum once a week, then the *copy and link* is the better choice over the *copy and paste* and *copy and embed*.

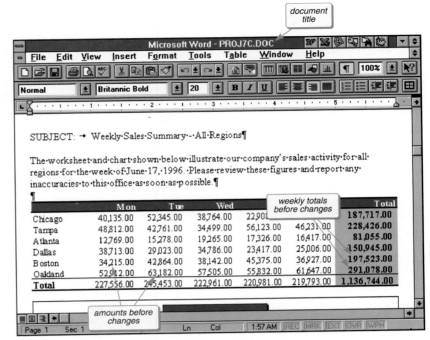

FIGURE 1-26

TILING APPLICATIONS AND USING DRAG AND DROP TO COPY AND EMBED

Earlier in this project, the *copy and embed* method was presented using the Copy button and Paste Special command. An alternative procedure to copy and embed is to tile the applications and then drag and drop the object from the source document to the destination document. To use this procedure with the memorandum and worksheet, you first start Excel, open PROJ7.XLS, then start Word, and open PROJ7.DOC. With Word on the screen, you switch to Excel and tile. **Tiling** is the process of arranging the open windows in smaller sizes to fit next to each other on the desktop. Each application will display in its own window in the same fashion group windows display in Program Manager. You can then use the drag and drop procedure to copy and embed.

The following steps start the applications and open the memorandum and worksheet.

TO START EXCEL AND WORD AND MINIMIZE PROGRAM MANAGER

Step 1: Click the Microsoft Excel button on the Office Manager toolbar or with Program Manager on the screen, double-click the Excel program-item icon in the Microsoft Office group window. If necessary, click the Maximize button in the Excel title bar. Open PROJ7.XLS.

Step 2: Click the Microsoft Word button on the Office Manager toolbar or hold down the ALT key and press the TAB key until the box shown in the middle of the screen contains the title Program Manager and double-click the Word program-item icon to start Word.

Step 3: If necessary, click the Maximize button in the Word window. Open PROJ7.DOC.

Step 4: Hold down the ALT key and press the TAB key until the box shown in the middle of the screen contains the title Program Manager.

Step 5: Click the Program Manager Minimize button.

Both Word and Excel are running and the memorandum and worksheet are open. Word is the active application. Program Manager is minimized.

The next step is to tile so both Word and Excel are visible on the desktop.

TO TILE APPLICATIONS ▼

STEP 1 ▶

With Word active, click the Control-menu box.

The Control menu displays as shown in Figure 1-27.

FIGURE 1-27

STEP 2 ▶

Choose the Switch To command.

Windows displays the Task List window (Figure 1-28).

FIGURE 1-28

STEP 3 ▶

Choose the Tile button (Tile). Point to the bottom border of the Word window so the mouse pointer becomes a double-headed arrow (↕) **(Figure 1-29)**.

Windows displays two windows with Word in the left window and Excel in the right window (Figure 1-29).

FIGURE 1-29

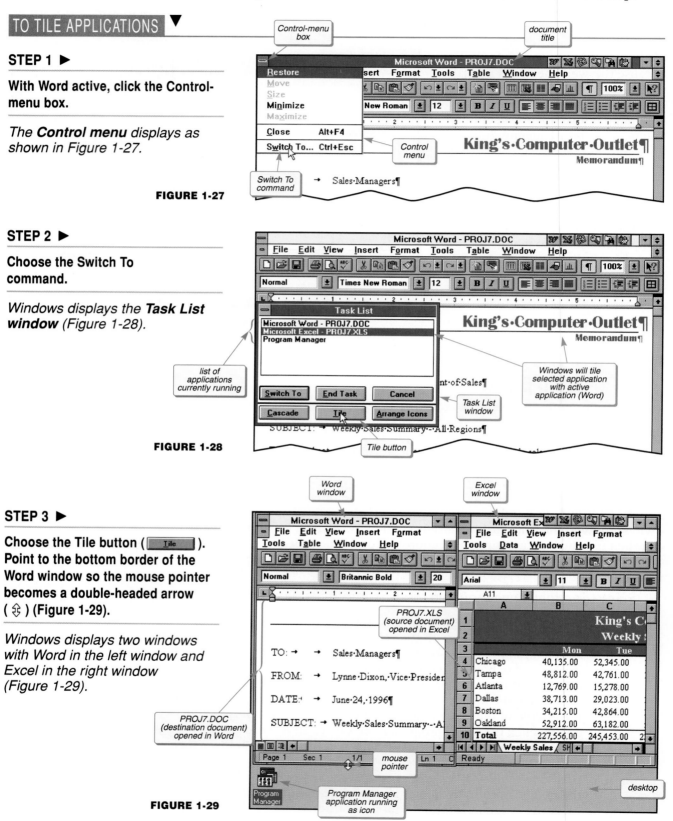

STEP 4 ▶

Drag the border to the bottom of the desktop. Do the same with the Excel window.

The Word and Excel windows display side by side as shown in Figure 1-30. Because the Excel window was the last one resized, it is the active application.

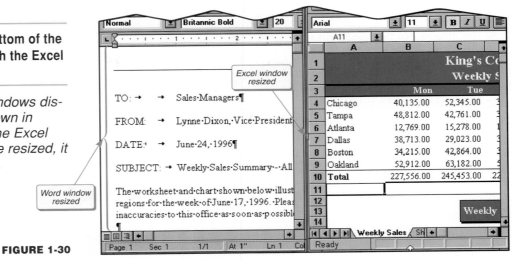

FIGURE 1-30

Besides tiling applications, you can use the Control menu (Figure 1-28) to switch to another application (similar to pressing ALT+TAB), close an application, or cascade applications. When you **cascade**, the applications windows overlap so each title bar is visible. When the applications are cascaded, you can bring any application window to the top of the desktop by clicking the application's title bar.

Using the Drag and Drop Procedure Between Tiled Applications to Copy and Embed

The following steps show how to copy and embed between the two tiled applications using the drag and drop procedure. With drag and drop, you select the worksheet range, point to the border of the range, hold down the CTRL key, drag over to the memorandum, release the left mouse button and then the CTRL key.

TO DRAG AND DROP BETWEEN TILED APPLICATIONS ▼

STEP 1 ▶

Click in the Word window and scroll down so the last paragraph mark displays. Click in the Excel window and select the range A3:G25. Point to the border of the range so the mouse pointer changes to a block arrow.

The selected range and mouse pointer display as shown in Figure 1-31.

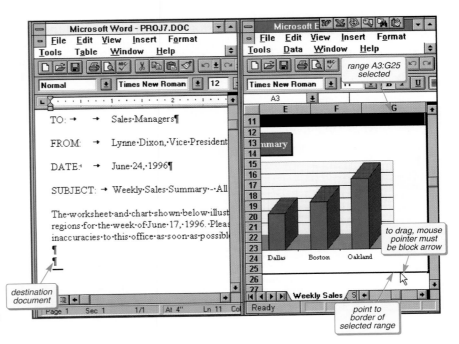

FIGURE 1-31

STEP 2 ▶

With the mouse pointer displaying as a block arrow, hold down the CTRL key so the mouse pointer changes to a block arrow with a small plus sign (↖). While holding down the CTRL key, drag the mouse to the last paragraph mark in the Word window. Release the left mouse button and then release the CTRL key.

The range A3:G25 from the worksheet is embedded into the memorandum (Figure 1-32).

FIGURE 1-32

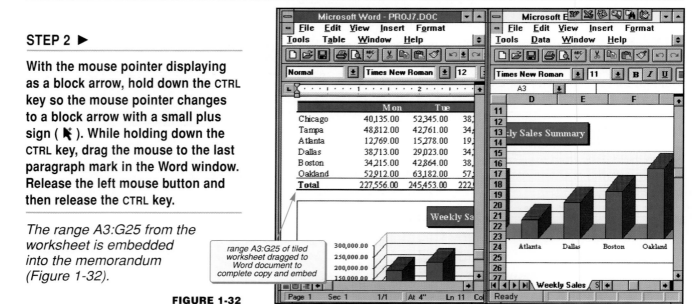

STEP 3 ▶

Click the Excel Maximize button to maximize the Excel window. Click the Microsoft Word button on the Office Manager toolbar or press ALT+TAB to activate Word. Click the Maximize button to maximize the Word window. Double-click the Control-menu box in the Word title bar to exit Word. Do not save the changes. When the Excel window displays, close Excel without saving changes to the workbook.

Consider the following important points when using the drag and drop technique between tiled applications.

1. You must select the range to copy and point to the border.
2. The mouse pointer must be a block arrow before you hold down the CTRL key.
3. You must first release the left mouse button before you release the CTRL key or Windows will move instead of copy.

▶ EMBEDDING OBJECTS USING THE OBJECT COMMAND

The prior OLE examples used the Clipboard to transfer the information between applications. An alternative method is to use the **Object command** on the Insert menu. The primary differences between using the Object command and the Clipboard are the following:

FIGURE 1-33

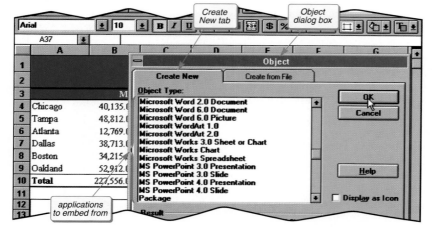

1. The Object command allows you to embed without ever leaving the destination document.
2. With the Object command, you can embed an existing file or create a new object from one of the applications on your system (Figure 1-33). You cannot, however, embed part of a document as was done when the range A3:G25 was embedded using the Paste option in the Paste Special dialog box.

In some applications, such as Word and PowerPoint, you can use the Insert Microsoft Excel worksheet button (■) on the Standard toolbar to embed an empty workbook. Once the empty workbook is embedded in the Word or PowerPoint document, you can utilize Excel's capabilities to create the workbook without ever leaving the application.

▶ PROJECT SUMMARY

This project introduced you to the three methods for copying objects between a source document and a destination document: (1) *copy and paste*; (2) *copy and embed*; and (3) *copy and link*. The *copy and paste* method is quick and easy, but limited. *The copy and embed* method makes the object part of the destination document and allows you to use the editing capabilities of the source application. The *copy and link* method establishes a link in the destination document to the object in the source document, instead of making it part of the destination document. When you edit a linked object, Windows activates the source application and opens the document that the object is part of. You learned how to copy and embed by using the drag and drop procedure between tiled applications. Finally, you learned that you can use the Object command on the Insert menu to embed objects from other applications.

▶ KEY TERMS AND INDEX

cascade *(OLE23)*
Control menu *(OLE22)*
copy and embed *(OLE3)*
copy and link *(OLE3)*
copy and paste *(OLE3)*
destination document *(OLE2)*
external links *(OLE20)*
in-place activation *(OLE12)*

internal links *(OLE20)*
link *(OLE3)*
Links command *(OLE19)*
Links dialog box *(OLE20)*
Object command *(OLE24)*
objects *(OLE2)*
OLE *(OLE3)*
Paste Link option button *(OLE16)*

Paste option button *(OLE11)*
Paste Special command *(OLE9)*
Paste Special dialog box *(OLE10)*
source application *(OLE15)*
source document *(OLE2)*
Switch To command *(OLE22)*
Task List window *(OLE22)*
tiling *(OLE21)*

QUICK REFERENCE

In Microsoft Excel, you can accomplish a task in a number of ways. The following table provides a quick reference to each task presented in this project with its available options. The commands listed in the Menu column can be executed using either the keyboard or mouse.

Task	Mouse	Menu	Keyboard Shortcuts
Copy and Embed Between Applications	Select object in source document; click Copy button; switch to destination document; from Edit menu, choose Paste Special, then select Paste option	Select object in source document; from Edit menu choose Copy; switch to destination document; from Edit menu, choose Paste Special, then select Paste option	Select object in source document; press CTRL+C; switch to destination document; from Edit menu, choose Paste Special, then select Paste option
Copy and Link Between Applications	Select object in source document; click Copy button; switch to destination document; from Edit menu, choose Paste Special, then select Paste Link option	Select object in source document; from Edit menu choose Copy; switch to destination document; from Edit menu, choose Paste Special, then select Paste Link option	Select object in source document; press CTRL+C; switch to destination document; from Edit menu, choose Paste Special, then select Paste Link option

(continued)

QUICK REFERENCE (continued)

Task	Mouse	Menu	Keyboard Shortcuts
Copy and Paste Between Applications	Select object in source document; click Copy button; switch to destination document; click Paste button	Select object in source document; from Edit menu choose Copy; switch to destination document; from Edit menu, choose Paste	Select object in source document; press CTRL+C; switch to destination document; press CTRL+V
Edit Embedded or Linked Object Without Leaving an Application	Double-click on object in Word or PowerPoint, click Excel button on Standard toolbar	From Insert menu, choose Object	
Edit Links		From Edit menu, choose Links	
Tile or Cascade	Click Control-menu box; choose Switch To		Press CTRL+ESC

S T U D E N T   A S S I G N M E N T S

STUDENT ASSIGNMENT 1
True/False

Instructions: Circle T if the statement is true or F if the statement is false.

T   F   1. An object can be an entire worksheet.

T   F   2. The source document is the one that contains the object to copy.

T   F   3. Use the Paste button on the Standard toolbar to embed an object.

T   F   4. When you copy and link, the object is saved along with the destination document.

T   F   5. OLE stands for Object Linking and Embedding.

T   F   6. When you use the copy and paste method, a range of cells is pasted into a Word document as a table.

T   F   7. When you edit an embedded object, Windows automatically updates the source document on disk.

T   F   8. Click an embedded object to edit it.

T   F   9. Use the Link command in the source document to check links.

T   F   10. Use the copy and embed method when an object is fairly stable.

T   F   11. Embed large objects, link small objects.

T   F   12. Use the copy and link method when an object is likely to change.

T   F   13. Double-click the Control-menu box of the active application to tile.

T   F   14. The copy and link method establishes a reference, or link, to the source document in the destination document.

T   F   15. Drag and drop between applications means that the object is cut from one document and pasted (embedded) into another.

T   F   16. The Undo button cannot undo a paste.

T   F   17. You can link only one document to another.

T   F   18. The Links command allows you to update a link.

T   F   19. If the Links command on the Edit menu is ghosted, then there is no link to the active document.

T   F   20. Windows cannot display two or more applications on the screen at one time.

STUDENT ASSIGNMENT 2
Multiple Choice

Instructions: Circle the correct response.

1. To exchange data with other applications so you can use the editing capabilities of the source application and save the object as part of the destination document, use the _____ method.
   a. copy and paste   b. copy and embed   c. copy and link   d. either b or c

2. To paste an object from a worksheet into a Word document as a Word table, use the _____ method.
   a. copy and paste   b. copy and embed   c. copy and link   d. either a or c

3. To paste an object so only a reference to the object is assigned to the destination document, use the _____ method.
   a. copy and paste   b. copy and embed   c. copy and link   d. none of the above

4. To paste so when you edit the object, the toolbars in the destination document change to the source application, use the _____ method.
   a. copy and paste   b. copy and embed   c. copy and link   d. undo and repeat

5. When you copy and link and the object is edited, Windows will _____.
   a. save the source document when you return to the destination document
   b. not save the source document unless you instruct it to do so
   c. save the source document when you save the destination document
   d. not save the source document even if you instruct it to do so

6. When you edit an embedded object in a destination document, Windows will _____.
   a. save the source document when you click outside the object
   b. not save the source document
   c. save the source document when you save the destination document
   d. none of the above

7. Which one of the menus on the menu bar do not refer to the embedded object when you double-click it to edit?
   a. File   b. Edit   c. Format   d. Help

8. The keyboard shortcut for displaying the Task List window is _____.
   a. CTRL+C   b. CTRL+ESC   c. CTRL+V   d. CTRL+ENTER

9. To display the Task List window, choose the Switch To command on the _____ menu.
   a. Tools   b. Edit   c. Control   d. File

10. To display applications behind one another on the desktop with the title bar of each application showing, use the _____ button in the Task List dialog box.
    a. Cascade   b. Tile   c. Switch To   d. Arrange Icons

STUDENT ASSIGNMENT 3
Understanding Button Functions

Instructions: Fill in the descriptions in the spaces provided.

1. Describe the function of the following buttons in the Task List window:

   a. Switch To (Switch To) _____

   b. End Task (End Task) _____

   c. Cancel (Cancel) _____

   d. Cascade (Cascade) _____

   e. Tile (Tile) _____

   f. Arrange Icons (Arrange Icons) _____

STUDENT ASSIGNMENT 3 (continued)

2. Describe the function of the following buttons in the Links dialog box:

a. Update Now (Update Now) _____

b. Open Source (Open Source) _____

c. Change Source (Change Source...) _____

d. Break Link (Break Link) _____

STUDENT ASSIGNMENT 4
Matching

Instructions: Match the method in column 2 with the statement in column 1.

When you want to

_____ 1. Edit the object using the source application
even when the source document is not available.

_____ 2. Include an object that is maintained separately
from the destination document.

_____ 3. Include a very large object.

_____ 4. Change a worksheet to a table in Word.

_____ 5. Include an object that changes often and
you want the latest copy in the destination
document when it is opened.

Use this method

a. copy and paste
b. copy and embed
c. copy and link

COMPUTER LABORATORY EXERCISES

COMPUTER LABORATORY EXERCISE 1
Using the Help Menu to Understand OLE, Drag and Drop, and Tiling

Part 1 Instructions: Start Excel and perform the following tasks using a computer:

1. Choose the Search for Help on command from the Help menu.
2. Type ole in the Search dialog box.
3. Use the Scroll box to find and select OLE, embedding in other applications.
4. Choose the Show Topics button.
5. With the topic Embedding a Microsoft Excel object in another application highlighted in the lower list, choose the Go To button.
6. Read the information that displays. Choose the Print button in the How To window.
7. Close the How To window.
8. Choose the Search button and scroll to OLE, linking source worksheets to dependents.
9. Select this topic and choose the Show Topics button.
10. With the topic Linking a Microsoft Excel document to a document from another application highlighted in the lower list, choose the Go To button.
11. Read the information that displays. Choose the Print button in the How To window.
12. Choose the Close button in the How To window.
13. To exit Help, double-click the Control-menu box in the Help window.

Part 2 Instructions: Start Excel and perform the following tasks using a computer:

1. Choose the Index command from the Help menu.
2. Click the O button.
3. Find Object command (Insert menu) in the list that displays and click Create from File tab.
4. Read the information that displays. Choose the Print Topic command on the File menu.
5. To exit Help, double-click the Control-menu box in the Help window.

Part 3 Instructions: Start Excel and perform the following tasks using a computer:

1. Choose the Search for Help on command on the Help menu.
2. Type `dragging, between applications` in the Search dialog box.
3. Choose the Show Topics button.
4. With Dragging data between applications highlighted in the lower box, choose the Go To button.
5. Read the information that displays. Choose the Print Topic command from the File menu.
6. Choose the Close button in the How To window.
7. Choose the Search button.
8. Type `tiling` With tiling windows, Arrange command highlighted in the upper box, choose the Show Topics button.
9. With the topic Arrange and Arrange Icons Commands (Window Menu) highlighted in the lower box, choose the Go To button.
10. Read the information that displays. Choose the Print Topic command from the File menu.
11. To exit Help, double-click the Control-menu box in the Help window.

COMPUTER LABORATORY EXERCISE 2
Object Linking and Embedding

The manager of the accounting department at the firm where you work has directed you to solve an applications problem. She would like to keep all of the branch managers up to date regarding the monthly office expenses incurred at each of the branch locations. She currently does this by using Word to generate a new memorandum each month to summarize the information she has in a worksheet in Excel. As her assistant, you have been instructed to find a way to reuse the same memorandum each month and somehow incorporate the worksheet information directly in the memorandum.

Part 1 Instructions: Start Word and open the memorandum CLE7-2.DOC from the Excel5 subdirectory on the Student Diskette that accompanies this book. Start Excel and open the worksheet CLE7-2.XLS in the Excel5 subdirectory on the Student Diskette.

Perform the tasks that follow to copy and paste the worksheet in the memorandum (Figure CLE1-2a):

1. With Excel active and the CLE7-2 workbook opened, select the range A2:E6 and click the Copy button on the Standard toolbar.
2. Switch to Word.
3. Press CTRL+END to place the insertion point at the bottom of the memorandum.
4. Click the Paste button.
5. Save the document using the filename CLE7-2A.DOC.
6. Print the document.
7. Close Word and Excel. Do not save changes to the workbook.

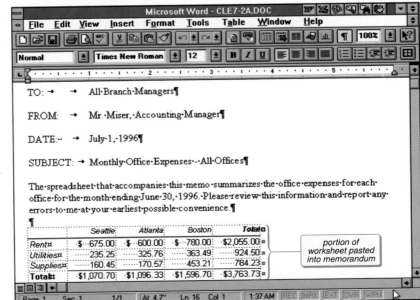

FIGURE CLE1-2a

(continued)

COMPUTER LABORATORY EXERCISE 2 (continued)

Part 2 Instructions: Start Word and open the memorandum CLE7-2.DOC from the Excel5 subdirectory on the Student Diskette. Start Excel and open the workbook CLE7-2.XLS from the Excel5 subdirectory on the Student Diskette.

Perform the tasks that follow to copy and embed the worksheet into the memorandum (Figure CLE1-2b):

1. With Excel active and the CLE7-2 workbook opened, select the range A2:F17 and click the Copy button on the Standard toolbar.
2. Switch to Word.
3. Press CTRL+END to place the insertion point at the bottom of the memorandum.
4. Choose the Paste Special command on the Edit menu and embed the object (range A2:F17 of the worksheet) on the Clipboard.
5. Save the document using the filename CLE7-2B.DOC.
6. Print the document.
7. Close Word and Excel. Do not save changes to the workbook.

Part 3 Instructions: Start Word and open the memorandum CLE7-2.DOC from the Excel5 subdirectory on the Student Diskette. Start Excel and open the worksheet CLE7-2.XLS from the Excel5 subdirectory on the Student Diskette.

Perform the tasks that follow to copy and link the worksheet (range A2:F17) to the memorandum. The memorandum should appear as shown in Figure CLE1-2b.

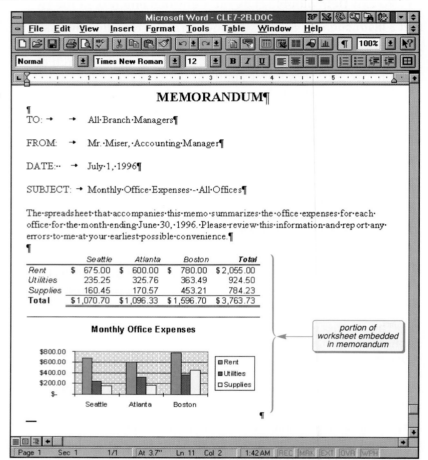

FIGURE CLE1-2b

1. With Excel active and the CLE7-2 workbook opened, select the range A2:E17 and click the Copy button on the Standard toolbar.
2. Switch to Word.
3. Press CTRL+END to place the insertion point at the bottom of the memorandum.
4. Choose the Paste Special command on the Edit menu and link the object (range A2:F17 of the worksheet) on the Clipboard to the memorandum.
5. Save the document to the Excel5 subdirectory on the Student Diskette using the filename CLE7-2C.DOC.
6. Print the document.
7. Close both Word and Excel. Do not save changes to the workbook.

COMPUTER LABORATORY EXERCISE 3
Object Linking and Embedding Clip Art

Part 1 Instructions: Start Excel and open the workbook CLE7-3.XLS from the Excel5 subdirectory on the Student Diskette. Start Word.

Perform the tasks that follow to copy and embed the clip art, shown in Figure CLE1-3a into the worksheet CLE7-3.XLS:

1. With Word active, choose the Picture command on the Insert menu and open the Windows file, blusedan.wmf (Figure CLE1-3a).
2. Select the picture in Word and click the Copy button on the Standard toolbar.
3. Switch to Excel.
4. Click a cell below the data in the worksheet.
5. Choose the Paste Special command on the Edit menu and embed the car below the data in the worksheet.
6. Select the car and resize it so it has the same width as the data in the worksheet (Figure CLE1-3b).
7. Save the workbook using the filename CLE7-3A.XLS.
8. Print the worksheet without gridlines. Click the Save button on the Standard toolbar.
9. Close Excel. Close Word. Do not save changes to the document in Word.

FIGURE CLE1-3a

FIGURE CLE1-3b

Part 2 Instructions: Start Excel and open the workbook CLE7-3.XLS from the Excel5 subdirectory on the Student Diskette. Start Word.

Perform the tasks that follow to copy and link the picture shown in Figure CLE1-3c to CLE7-3.XLS as an icon:

1. With Word active, choose the Picture command on the Insert menu and open the Windows clip art, motorcrs.wmf.
2. Select the picture and click the Copy button on the Standard toolbar.
3. Switch to Excel.
4. Click cell G1 on the worksheet.
5. Choose the Paste Special command on the Edit menu and link the flags to the worksheet as an icon. Move and resize the icon as it appears as shown in Figure CLE1-3d.
6. Select the icon and double-click to view it in Word. Switch to Excel.
7. Save the workbook using the filename CLE7-3B.XLS.
8. Print the worksheet without gridlines. Click the Save button on the Standard toolbar and close Excel.
9. Save the Word document using the filename CLE7-3B.DOC and close Word.

FIGURE CLE1-3c

FIGURE CLE1-3d

COMPUTER LABORATORY ASSIGNMENT 1
Editing a Table Pasted in a Word Document from an Excel Workbook

Purpose: To edit a table in Word that was pasted from an Excel worksheet.

Instructions: Start Word and open the document CLE7-2A.DOC. If you did not complete Part 1 of Computer Laboratory Exercise 2 on page OLE29, ask your instructor for a copy of CLE7-2A.DOC (Figure CLE1-2a on page OLE29). Add $100.00 to the rent for each city. Adjust the totals so they are correct. Save the document using the filename CLA7-1.DOC. Print the document. Close Word.

COMPUTER LABORATORY ASSIGNMENT 2
Editing a Worksheet Embedded in a Word Document

Purpose: To edit a worksheet embedded in a Word document.

Instructions: Start Word and open the document CLE7-2B.DOC. If you did not complete Part 2 of Computer Laboratory Exercise 2 on page OLE30, ask your instructor for a copy of CLE7-2B.DOC. Double-click the embedded worksheet (Figure CLE1-2b on page OLE30). Add $100.00 to the rent for each city. Save the document using the filename CLA7-2.DOC. Print the document. Close Word.

COMPUTER LABORATORY ASSIGNMENT 3
Editing a Worksheet Linked to a Word Document

Purpose: To edit a worksheet linked to a Word document.

Instructions: Start Word and open the document CLE7-2C.DOC from the Excel5 subdirectory on the Student Diskette. If you did not complete Part 3 of Computer Laboratory Exercise 2 on page OLE30, ask your instructor for a copy of CLE7-2C.DOC. Use the Links command on the Edit menu to make sure that CLE7-2.XLS is linked to CLE7-2C.DOC. Also check to be sure that CLE7-2.XLS is in the indicated directory on your Student Diskette. Double-click the linked worksheet (Figure CLE1-2b on page OLE30). Add $100.00 to the rent for each city. Save the document using the filename CLA7-3.DOC. Print the document. Close Word. Save the workbook using the filename CLA7-3.XLS. Activate Word and choose the Links command on the Edit menu. Verify that the linked workbook has changed to CLA7-3.XLS.

D A T A B A S E

USING *M*ICROSOFT *A*CCESS 2 FOR *W*INDOWS

▼

CREATING A DATABASE

You will have mastered the material in this project when you can:

▶ Describe databases and database management systems
▶ Start Access
▶ Describe the features of the Access screen
▶ Create a database
▶ Create a table
▶ Define the fields in a table
▶ Open a table
▶ Add records to an empty table
▶ Close a table

▶ Close a database
▶ Open a database
▶ Add records to a non-empty table
▶ Print the contents of a table
▶ Use a form to view data
▶ Create a graph
▶ Use Online Help
▶ Understand how to design a database to eliminate redundancy

▶ WHAT IS A DATABASE?

Creating, storing, sorting, and retrieving data are important tasks. In their personal lives, many people keep a variety of records, such as names, addresses, and phone numbers of friends and business associates, records of investments, records of expenses for tax purposes, and so on. These records must be arranged for quick access. Businesses must also be able to store and access information quickly and easily. Personnel and inventory records, payroll information, customer records, order data, and accounts receivable information are all crucial and must be readily available.

The term **database** describes a collection of data organized in a manner that allows access, retrieval, and use of that data. A **database management system**, like Access, allows you to use a computer to create a database; add, change, and delete data in the database; sort data in the database; retrieve data in the database; and create forms and reports using data in the database.

In Access, a database consists of a collection of tables. Figure 1-1 shows a sample database for an organization. It consists of two tables. The CUSTOMER table contains information about the customers of the organization. The Sales Rep (SLSREP) table contains information about the organization's sales representatives.

The rows in the tables are called records. A **record** contains information about a given person, product, or event. A row in the CUSTOMER table, for example, contains information about a specific customer.

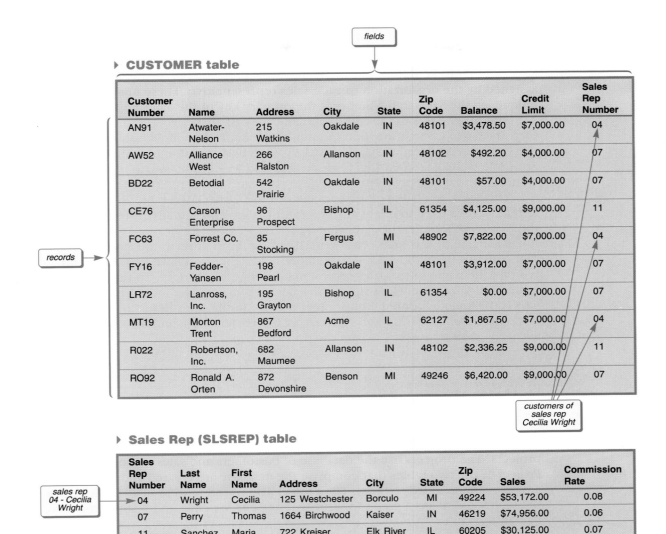

FIGURE 1-1

The columns in the tables are called fields. A **field** contains a specific piece of information within a record. In the CUSTOMER table, for example, the fourth field, City, contains the city where the customer is located.

The first field in the CUSTOMER table is the Customer Number. This is a code assigned by the organization to each customer. Like many organizations, this organization calls it a "number" even though it actually contains letters. The customer numbers have a special format. They consist of two uppercase letters, followed by a two-digit number.

These numbers are *unique*; that is, no two customers will be assigned the same number. Such a field can be used as a **unique identifier**. This simply means that a given customer number will appear in only a single record in the table. There is only one record, for example, in which the customer number is CL67. A unique identifier is also called a **primary key**. Thus, the Customer Number field is the primary key for the CUSTOMER table.

The next seven fields in the CUSTOMER table include the Name, Address, City, State, Zip Code, Balance, and Credit Limit. For example, customer AN91 is Atwater-Nelson. It is located at 215 Watkins in Oakdale, Indiana. The Zip Code is 48101. Its current balance (the amount it owes to the organization) is $3,478.50. Its credit limit (the amount its balance should not exceed) is $7,000.00.

Each customer has a single sales representative. The last field in the CUSTOMER table, Sales Rep Number, gives the number of the customer's sales representative.

The first field in the Sales Rep table, Sales Rep Number, is the number assigned by the organization to each sales representative. These numbers are unique, so the Sales Rep Number is the primary key of the Sales Rep table.

The other fields in the Sales Rep table are Last Name, First Name, Address, City, State, Zip Code, Sales, and Commission Rate. For example, sales representative 04 is Cecilia Wright. She lives at 125 Westchester in Borculo, Michigan. Her Zip Code is 49224. So far this year, she has sold $53,172.00 worth of product. Her commission rate is 8% (0.08).

The Sales Rep Number appears in both the CUSTOMER table and the Sales Rep table. It is used to relate customers and sales representatives. For example, in the CUSTOMER table, the sales representative number for customer AN91 is 04. To find the name of this sales representative, look for the row in the Sales Rep table that contains 04 in the Sales Rep Number field. Once you have found it, you will see that the name of the sales representative is Cecilia Wright. To find all the customers for whom Cecilia Wright is the sales representative, look through the CUSTOMER table for all the customers with 04 in the Sales Rep Number field. Her customers are AN91 (Atwater-Nelson), FC63 (Forrest Co.), and MT19 (Morton Trent) as shown in Figure 1-1 on the previous page.

▶ WHAT IS ACCESS?

Access is a powerful database management system (DBMS) that functions in the Windows environment and allows you to create and process data in a database. To illustrate the use of Access, this book presents a series of projects. The projects use the database of customers and sales representatives. In Project 1, the two tables that comprise the database are created and the appropriate records are added to them. The project also uses a form to display the data in the tables, as well as a graph to visually represent the data, and prints a report of data in the tables.

Database Preparation Steps

The database preparation steps give you an overview of how the database, consisting of the CUSTOMER table and the Sales Rep table shown in Figure 1-1, will be built in this project. If you are building the database in this project on a personal computer, read these thirteen steps without doing them.

1. Start Access.
2. Create the CUST database.
3. Begin the creation of the CUSTOMER table.
4. Define the fields in the CUSTOMER table.
5. Save the CUSTOMER table in the CUST database.
6. Add data records to the CUSTOMER table.
7. Print the contents of the CUSTOMER table.
8. Create and use a form to view the data in the CUSTOMER table.
9. Begin the creation of the Sales Rep table.
10. Define the fields in the Sales Rep table.
11. Save the Sales Rep table in the CUST database.
12. Add records to the Sales Rep table.
13. Create a graph that visually represents data from the Sales Rep table.

The following pages contain a detailed explanation of each of these steps.

▶ STARTING ACCESS

T o start Access, the Office Manager toolbar must display on the screen or the Microsoft Office group window must be open. Follow these steps to start Access, or ask your instructor how to start Access on your computer.

TO START ACCESS ▼

STEP 1 ▶

Place a formatted diskette in drive A.

STEP 2 ▶

If the Office Manager toolbar displays, use the mouse to point to the Microsoft Access button (🖱) (Figure 1-2). If the Office Manager toolbar does not display at the top right of your screen, then point to the Microsoft Access program-item icon (🖱) in the Microsoft Office group window.

Your Office Manager toolbar may contain more or fewer buttons than shown in Figure 1-2.

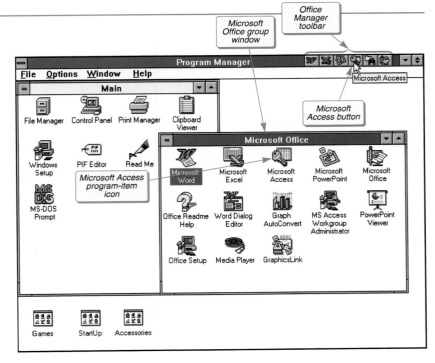

FIGURE 1-2

STEP 3 ▶

If the Office Manager toolbar displays, then with the mouse pointer pointing to the Microsoft Access button, click the left mouse button. If the Office Manager toolbar does not display at the top right of your screen, then double-click the Microsoft Access program-item icon in the Microsoft Office group window. If the Welcome to Microsoft Access 2.0 message displays, point to the Control-menu box in the MS Access Cue Cards dialog box (Figure 1-3).

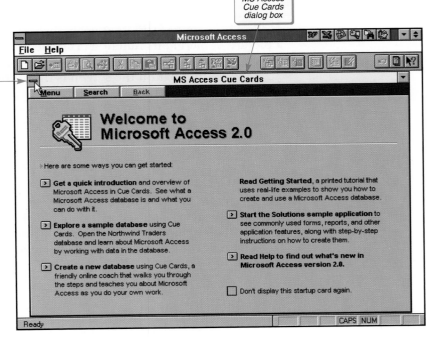

FIGURE 1-3

STEP 4 ▶

Double-click the Control-menu box to remove the message.

The Access desktop displays without the Welcome to Microsoft Access message (Figure 1-4).

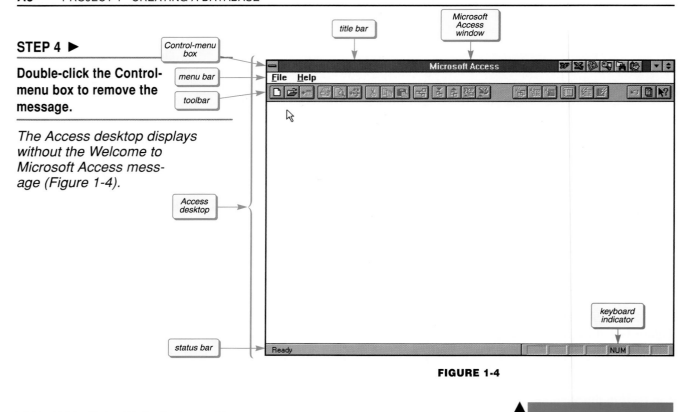

FIGURE 1-4

▶ THE DESKTOP

T he first bar on the desktop is the **title bar**. It displays the title of the product, Microsoft Access. The Control-menu box at the left end of the title bar is used to access the **Control menu**.

The second bar is the **menu bar**. It contains a list of menus. You select a menu from the menu bar using the mouse or keyboard.

The third bar is the **toolbar**. The toolbar contains buttons that allow you to perform certain tasks more quickly than using the menu bar. Each button contains a picture depicting its function. The specific buttons on the toolbar will vary, depending on the task on which you are working.

The bottom bar on the screen is the **status bar** (Figure 1-4). It contains special information appropriate for the task on which you are working. Currently, it contains the single word, Ready, which means Access is ready to accept commands.

▶ CREATING A NEW DATABASE

B efore creating the tables that comprise the database, you need to create the database itself as a file on disk. Once the database is created, all the tables, reports, and forms will automatically be placed within it.

The following steps create a new database called CUST.

TO CREATE A NEW DATABASE ▼

STEP 1 ▶

Select the File menu by pointing to the word File on the menu bar and clicking the left mouse button. Then point to the New Database command.

Access displays the File menu (Figure 1-5).

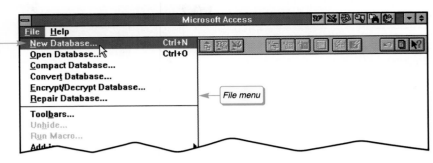

FIGURE 1-5

STEP 2 ▶

Choose the New Database command from the File menu by clicking the left mouse button.

The New Database dialog box displays (Figure 1-6).

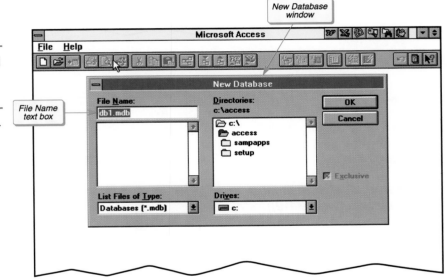

FIGURE 1-6

STEP 3 ▶

Type cust as the filename and then point to the drop-down list arrow next to the Drives list box (Figure 1-7).

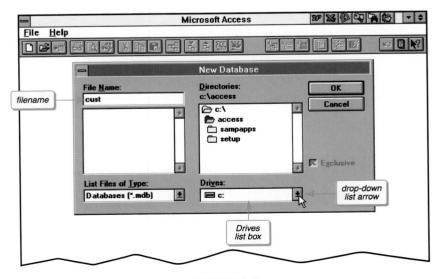

FIGURE 1-7

STEP 4 ▶

Click the drop-down list arrow and then point to a:

The list of available drives displays (Figure 1-8). Your list might be different.

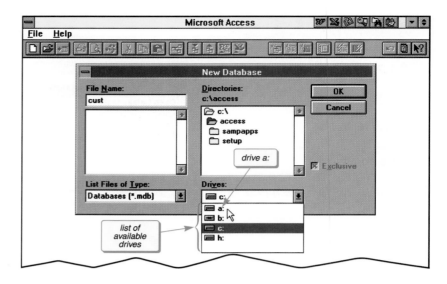

FIGURE 1-8

STEP 5 ▶

Select drive A by clicking the left mouse button and then point to the OK button (OK).

The filename is entered and the drive is selected (Figure 1-9).

STEP 6 ▶

Choose the OK button by clicking the left mouse button.

The database is created on disk. The database: CUST window displays as shown in Figure 1-11 on page A11.

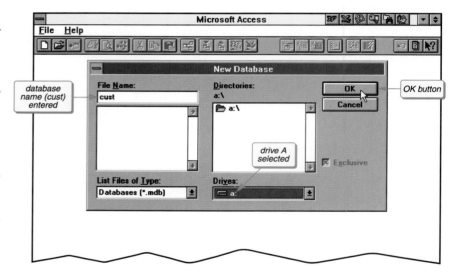

FIGURE 1-9

▶ CREATING A TABLE

An Access database consists of a collection of tables. Once you have created the database, you must create each of the tables within it. In this project, for example, you must create both the CUSTOMER and Sales Rep tables shown in Figure 1-1.

To **create a table**, you describe the **structure** of the table to Access by describing the fields within the table. For each field, you indicate the following information.

1. **Field name** — Each field in the table must have a unique name. In the CUSTOMER table (Figure 1-10 on the next page), for example, the field names are Customer Number, Name, Address, City, State, Zip Code, Balance, Credit Limit, and Sales Rep Number.
2. **Data type** — Data type indicates to Access the type of data that the field will contain. Some fields, such as Commission Rate, can contain only numbers. Others, such as Balance and Credit Limit, can contain numbers and dollar signs. Still others, such as Name and Address, can contain letters.
3. **Description** — Access allows you to enter a detailed description of the field.

You can also assign field widths to text fields (fields whose data type is "Text"). This indicates the maximum number of characters that can be stored in the field. If you do not assign a width to such a field, Access assumes the width is 50.

You must also indicate which field or fields make up the primary key; that is, the unique identifier, for the table. In the sample database, the Sales Rep Number is the primary key of the Sales Rep table and the Customer Number is the primary key of the CUSTOMER table.

To name a field, follow these rules:

1. Names can be up to 64 characters in length.
2. Names can contain letters, digits, spaces, as well as most of the punctuation symbols.
3. Names cannot contain periods (.), exclamation points (!), or square brackets ([ ]).
4. The same name cannot be used for two different fields in the same table.

Each field has a data type. This indicates the type of data that can be stored in the field. The data types you will use in this project are:

1. **Text** — The field can contain any characters.
2. **Number** — The field can contain only numbers. The numbers can be either positive or negative. Fields are assigned this type so they can be used in arithmetic operations. Fields that contain numbers but will not be used for arithmetic operations are usually assigned a data type of Text. The Sales Rep Number field, for example, is a text field because the sales representative numbers will not be involved in any arithmetic.
3. **Currency** — The field can contain only dollar amounts. The values will be displayed with dollar signs, commas, and decimal points, with two digits following the decimal point. Like numeric fields, you can use currency fields in arithmetic operations. Access automatically assigns a size to currency fields.

The field names, data types, field widths, primary key information, and descriptions for the CUSTOMER table are shown in Figure 1-10. With this information, you are ready to begin creating the table. To create the table, use the steps beginning on page A11.

▶ **Structure of CUSTOMER table**

Field Name	Data Type	Field Size	Primary Key?	Description
Customer Number	Text	4	Yes	Customer Number (Primary Key)
Name	Text	20		Customer Name
Address	Text	15		Street Address
City	Text	15		City
State	Text	2		State (two-character abbreviation)
Zip Code	Text	5		Zip Code (five-character version)
Balance	Currency			Current Balance
Credit Limit	Currency			Credit Limit
Sales Rep Number	Text	2		Number of matching Sales Representative

▶ **Data for CUSTOMER table**

Customer Number	Name	Address	City	State	Zip Code	Balance	Credit Limit	Sales Rep Number
AN91	Atwater-Nelson	215 Watkins	Oakdale	IN	48101	$3,478.50	$7,000.00	04
AW52	Alliance West	266 Ralston	Allanson	IN	48102	$492.20	$4,000.00	07
BD22	Betodial	542 Prairie	Oakdale	IN	48101	$57.00	$4,000.00	07
CE76	Carson Enterprise	96 Prospect	Bishop	IL	61354	$4,125.00	$9,000.00	11
FC63	Forrest Co.	85 Stocking	Fergus	MI	48902	$7,822.00	$7,000.00	04
FY16	Fedder-Yansen	198 Pearl	Oakdale	IN	48101	$3,912.00	$7,000.00	07
LR72	Lanross, Inc.	195 Grayton	Bishop	IL	61354	$0.00	$7,000.00	07
MT19	Morton Trent	867 Bedford	Acme	IL	62127	$1,867.50	$7,000.00	04
RO22	Robertson, Inc.	682 Maumee	Allanson	IN	48102	$2,336.25	$9,000.00	11
RO92	Ronald A. Orten	872 Devonshire	Benson	MI	49246	$6,420.00	$9,000.00	07

FIGURE 1-10

TO CREATE A TABLE ▼

STEP 1 ▶

Point to the New button (New) in the Database dialog box (Figure 1-11).

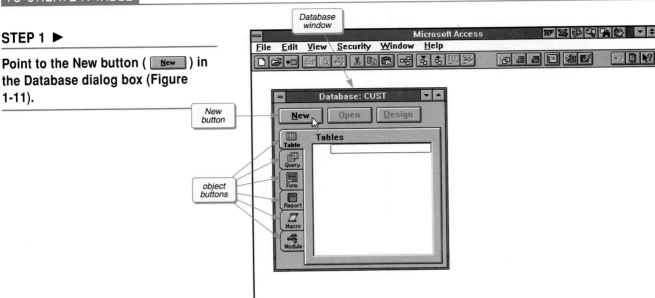

FIGURE 1-11

STEP 2 ▶

Choose the New button by clicking the left mouse button and then point to the New Table button (▣).

The New Table dialog box displays (Figure 1-12). (If you have not already determined the fields that comprise your table, you can use Table Wizards. Table Wizards guide you through the table creation by suggesting some commonly used tables and fields. If you already know the fields you need, however, Table Wizards are not particularly helpful.)

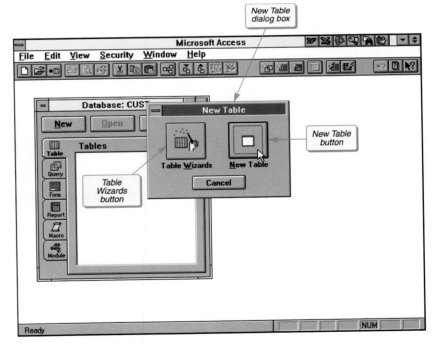

FIGURE 1-12

STEP 3 ▶

Choose the New Table button.

The Table dialog box displays (Figure 1-13). To create the table, you make entries in the Field Name, Data Type, and Description columns. You enter additional information in the Field Properties box located near the bottom of the Table dialog box. The current field indicator (▶) is currently positioned on the first field, indicating Access is ready for you to enter the name of the first field in the Field Name column.

FIGURE 1-13

The next step in creating the table is to define the fields by specifying the required details in the Table dialog box. Perform the following steps to accomplish this task.

TO DEFINE THE FIELDS IN A TABLE ▼

STEP 1 ▶

Type Customer Number **(the name of the first field) in the Field Name column and press the TAB key.**

The words Customer Number display in the Field Name column and the highlight advances to the Data Type column, indicating you can enter the data type (Figure 1-14). The word Text, one of the possible data types, currently displays. You can also use a drop-down list arrow to display a list of available data types.

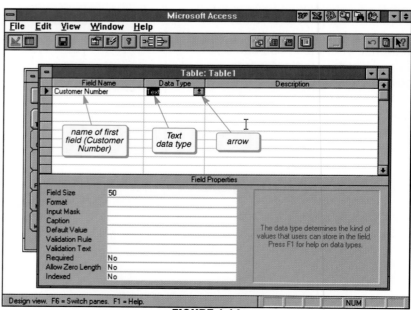

FIGURE 1-14

STEP 2 ▶

Since Text is the correct data type, press the TAB key to move the highlight to the Description column, type Customer Number (Primary Key) as the description, and then point to the Set Primary Key button ( ) on the toolbar (Figure 1-15).

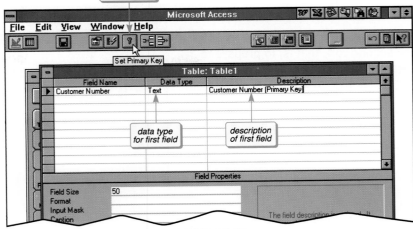

FIGURE 1-15

STEP 3 ▶

Click the Set Primary Key button to make Customer Number the primary key and then point to the Field Size text box.

Customer Number is the primary key as indicated by the key symbol that appears in front of the field (Figure 1-16). The pointer, which has changed shape to an I-beam ( ) is in the Field Size text box.

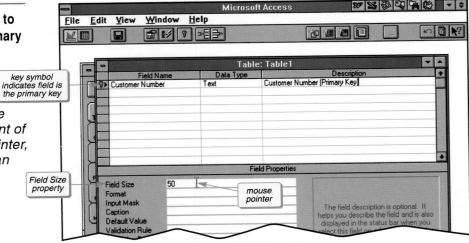

FIGURE 1-16

STEP 4 ▶

Select the Field Size text box by clicking the left mouse button. Press the BACKSPACE key twice to erase the current entry (50). Type 4 which is the size of the Customer Number field. Point to the Field Name column just below the field name Customer Number in the second row.

The Field Size is changed to 4 (Figure 1-17). The mouse pointer, an I-beam, points to the Field Name column on the second row.

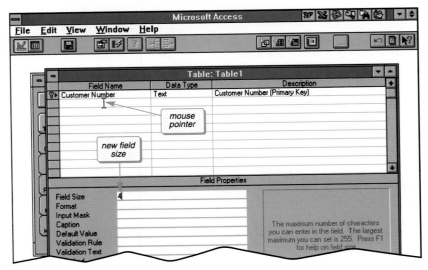

FIGURE 1-17

STEP 5 ▶

Click the left mouse button to select the second row, that is, to prepare to enter the second field.

The current field indicator moves to the second row just below the field name Customer Number (Figure 1-18).

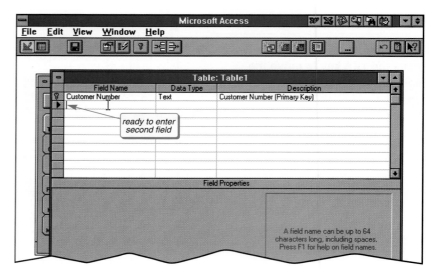

FIGURE 1-18

STEP 6 ▶

Use the techniques illustrated in Steps 1 through 5 to make the entries from the CUSTOMER table structure shown in Figure 1-10 on page A10 up through and including the name of the Balance field. You will not need to click the Set Primary Key button for any of these fields. Click the drop-down list arrow in the Data Type column and point to the Currency data type.

The additional fields are entered (Figure 1-19). A drop-down list of available data types displays in the Data Type column for the Balance field.

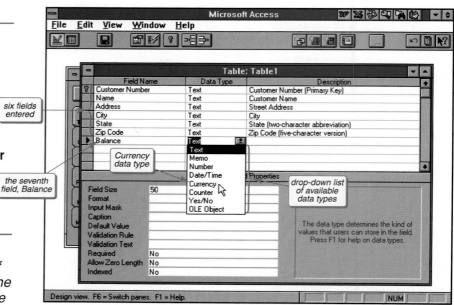

FIGURE 1-19

STEP 7 ▶

Select the Currency data type by clicking the left mouse button and then press the TAB key. Make the remaining entries from the CUSTOMER table structure shown in Figure 1-10 on page A10.

Correcting Errors in the Structure

When creating a table, check the entries carefully to ensure they are correct. If you make a mistake and discover it before you press the TAB key, you can correct the error by pressing the BACKSPACE key until the incorrect characters are removed. Then, type the correct characters. If you don't discover a mistake until later, you can correct it by pointing to the entry with the mouse, clicking the left mouse button, and typing the correct value, and then pressing the ENTER key.

If you accidentally add an extra field to the structure, select the field by pointing to the leftmost column on the row that contains the field to be deleted and then click the left mouse button. Once you have selected the field, press the DELETE key. This will remove the field from the structure.

If you forget a field, select the field that will follow the field you wish to add, select Edit, and then choose the Insert Row command. The remaining fields move down one row, making room for the missing field. Make the entries for the new field in the usual manner.

If you made the wrong field a key field, point to the Key entry for the field, click the left mouse button, and then click the Set Primary Key button.

As an alternative to these steps, you might want to start over. To do so, choose the Cancel button (Cancel) in the Create Access Table dialog box and then choose No. The original desktop displays and you can repeat the process you used earlier.

▶ SAVING A TABLE

T he CUSTOMER table structure is now complete. The final step is to save the table within the database. To do so, you must give the table a name. Table names are from one to sixty-four characters in length and can contain letters, numbers, and spaces. The two table names in this project are CUSTOMER and SLSREP.

To save the table, perform the following steps.

TO SAVE THE TABLE ▼

STEP 1 ▶

Select the File menu and point to the Save command (Figure 1-20).

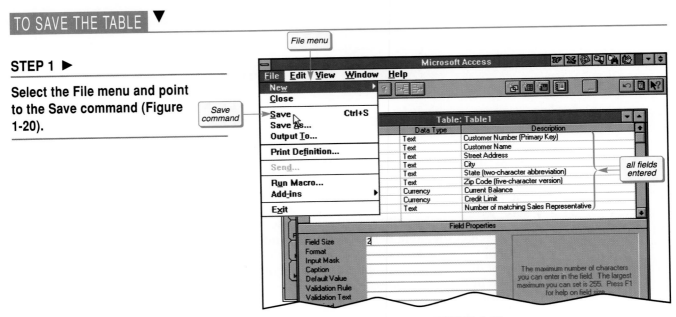

FIGURE 1-20

STEP 2 ▶

Choose the Save command by clicking the left mouse button. Type CUSTOMER (in uppercase letters) as the name of the table and point to the OK button.

The Save As dialog box displays (Figure 1-21). The name of the table is entered in the Table Name text box.

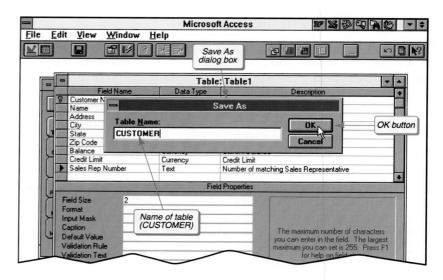

FIGURE 1-21

STEP 3 ▶

Choose the OK button. Then point to the Control-menu box (▣) in the Table: CUSTOMER window (Figure 1-22).

STEP 4 ▶

Double-click the Control-menu box to close the window.

Access closes the Table window.

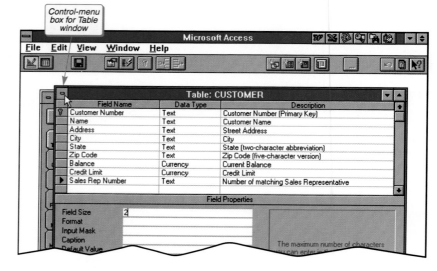

FIGURE 1-22

▶ **ADDING RECORDS TO THE CUSTOMER TABLE**

C reating a table by building the structure and saving the table is the first step in a two-step process. The second step is to add records to the table. In order to add records to a table, the table must be open. To open a table, select the table in the Database window and then choose the Open button (Open). The table displays in Datasheet view. In **Datasheet view**, the table is represented as a collection of rows and columns. It looks very much like the tables shown in Figure 1-1 on page A3.

You often add records in phases. You may, for example, not have enough time to add all the records in one session. To illustrate this process, this project begins by adding the first two records in the CUSTOMER table (Figure 1-23). The remaining records are added later.

▶ **CUSTOMER table (first 2 records)**

Customer Number	Name	Address	City	State	Zip Code	Balance	Credit Limit	Sales Rep Number
AN91	Atwater-Nelson	215 Watkins	Oakdale	IN	48101	$3,478.50	$7,000.00	04
AW52	Alliance West	266 Ralston	Allanson	IN	48102	$492.20	$4,000.00	07

FIGURE 1-23

To open the CUSTOMER table and then add records, perform the following steps.

TO ADD RECORDS TO THE CUSTOMER TABLE ▼

STEP 1 ▶

Point to the Open button in the Database window (Figure 1-24).

FIGURE 1-24

STEP 2 ▶

Choose the Open button by clicking the left mouse button and then point to the Maximize button (▲) in the Table: CUSTOMER window.

The Table: CUSTOMER window displays (Figure 1-25). The window contains the Datasheet view for the CUSTOMER table. The current record indicator is positioned on the first record. The status bar at the bottom of the window also indicates that the indicator is positioned on record 1.

FIGURE 1-25

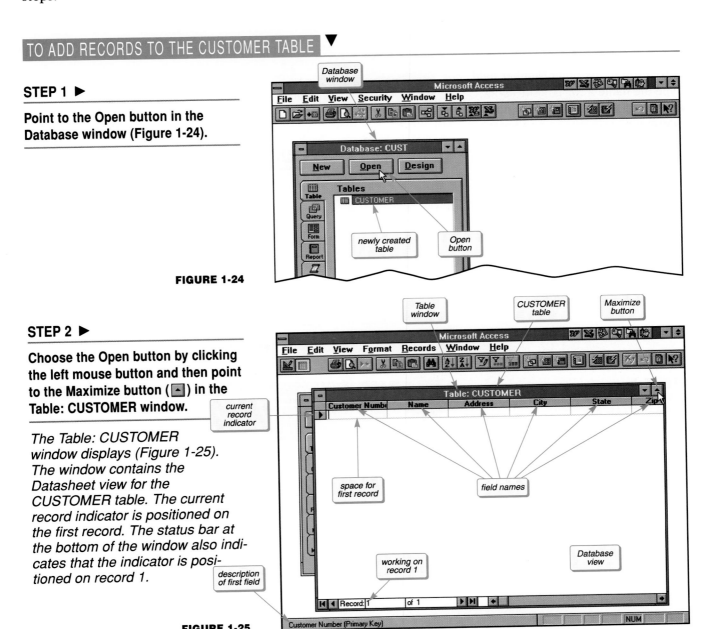

STEP 3 ▶

Click the Maximize button to maximize the window containing the table. Type AN91 which is the first customer number in Figure 1-23. Be sure you type both the A and the N in uppercase.

The customer number is entered, but the insertion point is still in the Customer Number field (Figure 1-26).

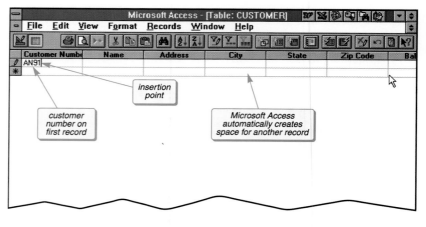

FIGURE 1-26

STEP 4 ▶

Press the TAB key to complete the entry for the Customer Number field. Type the name Atwater-Nelson and press the TAB key. Type the address 215 Watkins and press the TAB key. Type the city Oakdale and press the TAB key. Type the state IN and type the zip code, 48101

The Name, Address, City, and State fields are entered. The data for the Zip Code field displays on the screen (Figure 1-27), but the entry is not complete because you have not yet pressed the TAB key.

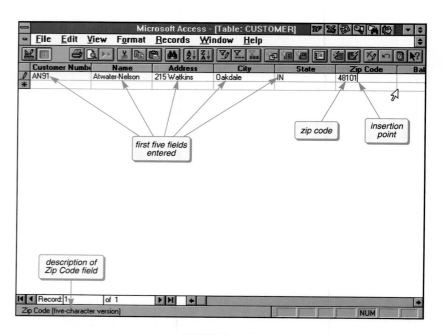

FIGURE 1-27

STEP 5 ▶

Press the TAB key.

The Zip Code is entered. The fields shift to the left so the Balance field displays on the screen, and the highlight advances to the Balance field (Figure 1-28).

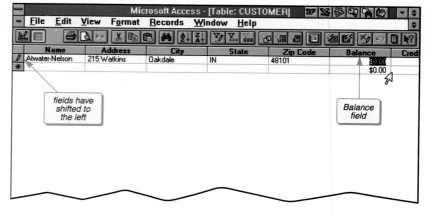

FIGURE 1-28

STEP 6 ▶

Type the balance 3478.50 and press the TAB key. Type the credit limit 7000 and press the TAB key. Type 04 (sales rep number). Be sure you type 04 rather than simply 4.

Access automatically adds dollar signs and commas to the data in the Balance and Credit Limit fields, because they are currency fields (Figure 1-29). The sales rep number has been typed, but the insertion point is still positioned on the field.

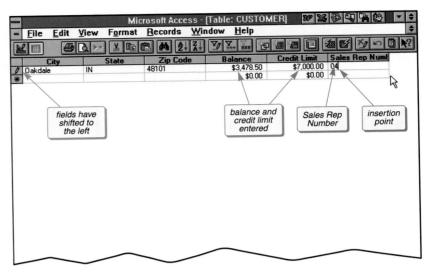

FIGURE 1-29

STEP 7 ▶

Press the TAB key.

The fields shift back to the right, the record is saved, and the insertion point moves to the customer number on the next row (Figure 1-30).

STEP 8 ▶

Use the techniques shown in Steps 2 through 7 to add the data for the second record in Figure 1-23.

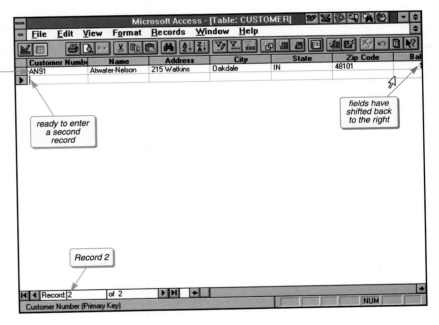

FIGURE 1-30

Closing a Table and a Database

It is a good idea to close a table as soon as you have finished working with it. It keeps the screen from getting cluttered and also prevents you from making accidental changes to the data in the table. In addition, if you will no longer work with the database, it is a good idea to close the database as well.

The process to close a table and a database is shown in the steps on the next page.

TO CLOSE A TABLE AND A DATABASE ▼

STEP 1 ▶

Point to the Control-menu box for the Table window (Figure 1-31).

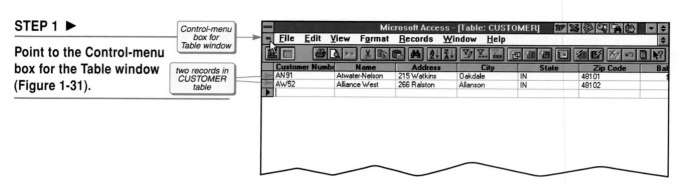

FIGURE 1-31

STEP 2 ▶

Double-click the Control-menu box to close the table and then point to the Control-menu box for the Database window (Figure 1-32).

STEP 3 ▶

Double-click the Control-menu box to close the Database window.

The Database is closed and the Database window is removed from the screen.

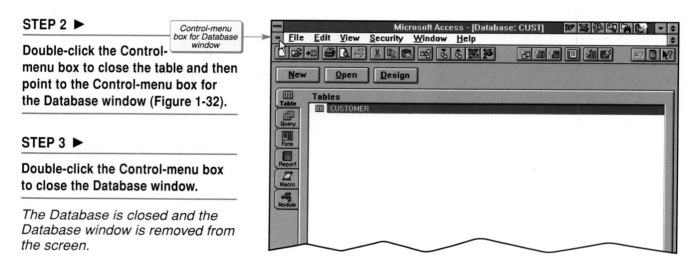

FIGURE 1-32

▶ EXITING ACCESS

T he creation of the CUSTOMER table is now complete and two records have been added to it. You could continue to add records at this time. You may not want to do this all in one session, however. If not, you can exit Access at this point. The following step exits Access.

TO EXIT ACCESS

Step 1: Double-click the Control-menu box.

Control returns to Windows Program Manager.

When you are ready to continue working, start Access using the method shown in Figure 1-2 through Figure 1-4 on pages A5 and A6. *Be sure you have inserted your diskette in drive A before you begin the process.*

▶ OPENING A DATABASE

I n order to work with any of the tables, reports, or forms in a database, the database must be open. To open a database, use the Open Database command on the File menu, as the following steps illustrate. If the database is already open, the Database window will display on the screen. In that case, the following steps are unnecessary.

TO OPEN A DATABASE ▼

STEP 1 ▶

Select the File menu and point to the Open Database command (Figure 1-33).

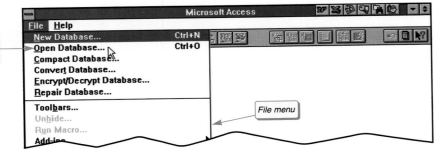

FIGURE 1-33

STEP 2 ▶

Choose the Open Database command. If the drive listed in the Drives text box is not A, change it to A by clicking the drop-down list arrow in the Drives list box and selecting A. Then point to the OK button in the Open Database dialog box.

The Open Database dialog box displays (Figure 1-34). The drive is a: and the CUST database is currently selected.

STEP 3 ▶

Choose the OK button.

The database is open and the Database window displays (Figure 1-11 on page A11).

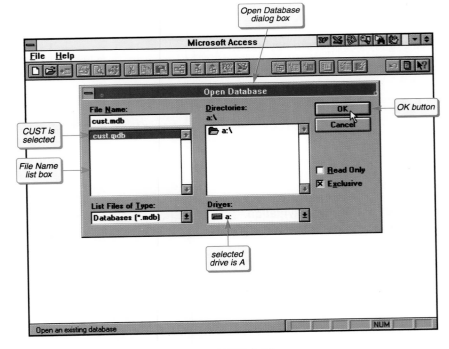

FIGURE 1-34

▶ ADDING ADDITIONAL RECORDS

Y ou can add records to a table that already contains data using a process almost identical to that used to add records to an empty table. The only difference is that you place the highlight after the last data record before you enter the additional data. To do so, use the **navigation buttons** found near the lower left-hand corner of the screen. Perform the following steps to add the remaining records to the CUSTOMER table.

TO ADD ADDITIONAL RECORDS TO A TABLE ▼

STEP 1 ▶

With the CUSTOMER table highlighted in the Database window, click the Open button.

STEP 2 ▶

When the CUSTOMER table displays, maximize the window by clicking the Maximize button.

STEP 3 ▶

Point to the Last Record navigation button (▶│) (Figure 1-35).

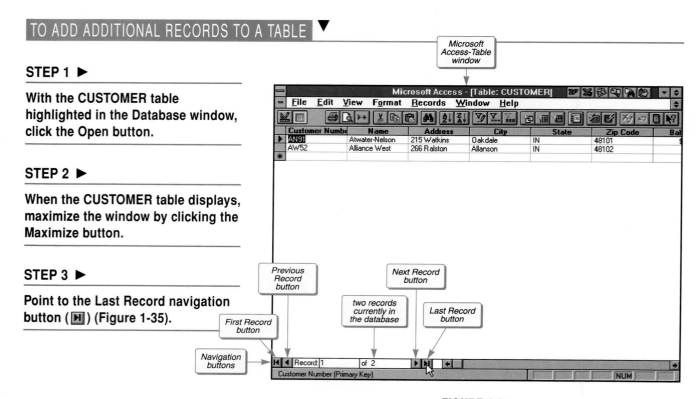

FIGURE 1-35

STEP 4 ▶

Click the Last Record navigation button and then point to the Next Record navigation button (▶).

Access positions the highlight on the last record in the table (Figure 1-36).

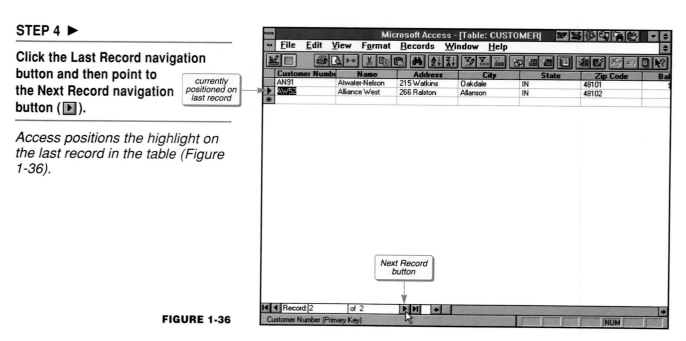

FIGURE 1-36

STEP 5 ►

Click the Next Record navigation button to move to a new record.

STEP 6 ►

Add the remaining eight records from Figure 1-37, using the same techniques you used to add the first two records.

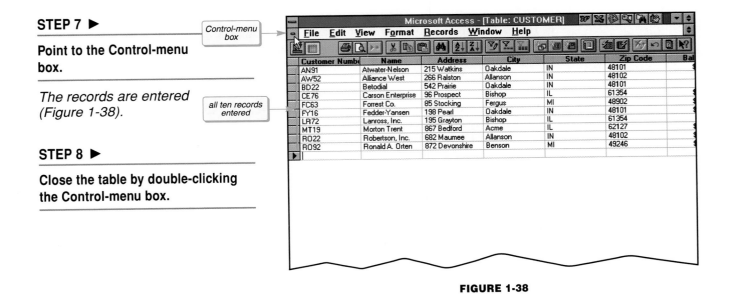

▸ **CUSTOMER table (last 8 records)**

Customer Number	Name	Address	City	State	Zip Code	Balance	Credit Limit	Sales Rep Number
BD22	Betodial	542 Prairie	Oakdale	IN	48101	$57.00	$4,000.00	07
CE76	Carson Enterprise	96 Prospect	Bishop	IL	61354	$4,125.00	$9,000.00	11
FC63	Forrest Co.	85 Stocking	Fergus	MI	48902	$7,822.00	$7,000.00	04
FY16	Fedder-Yansen	198 Pearl	Oakdale	IN	48101	$3,912.00	$7,000.00	07
LR72	Lanross, Inc.	195 Grayton	Bishop	IL	61354	$0.00	$7,000.00	07
MT19	Morton Trent	867 Bedford	Acme	IL	62127	$1,867.50	$7,000.00	04
R022	Robertson, Inc.	682 Maumee	Allanson	IN	48102	$2,336.25	$9,000.00	11
RO92	Ronald A. Orten	872 Devonshire	Benson	MI	49246	$6,420.00	$9,000.00	07

FIGURE 1-37

STEP 7 ►

Point to the Control-menu box.

The records are entered (Figure 1-38).

STEP 8 ►

Close the table by double-clicking the Control-menu box.

Control-menu box

all ten records entered

FIGURE 1-38

Access maintains the data so it is always ordered by the primary key. Because Customer Number is the primary key of the CUSTOMER table, the data in the table will automatically be arranged so the customer numbers are in alphabetical order. The data that you just entered happened to be in the correct order. If you enter a record containing a customer number that is not in alphabetical order, however, Access will automatically place it in order. You will not notice this immediately, but rather the next time you open the table.

For example, if you add a record with customer number PR29, it will appear at the end of the table. The next time you open the table, however, it will appear between the record for customer MT19 and the one for customer RO22. Records are ordered in ascending order by the primary key field.

Correcting Errors in the Data

Just as when you created the table, check the entries carefully to ensure they are correct. If you make a mistake and discover it before you press the TAB key, correct it by pressing the BACKSPACE key until the incorrect characters are removed and then typing the correct characters.

If you discover an incorrect entry later, correct the error by pointing to the entry with the mouse, clicking the left mouse button, and then making the appropriate correction. If the record you must correct is not on the screen, use the navigation buttons (Next Record, Previous Record, and so on) to move to it. If the field you want to correct is not visible on the screen, use the horizontal scroll bar along the bottom of the screen to shift all the fields until the one you want displays. Then, make the correction.

If you accidentally add an extra record, select the record by pointing to the box that immediately precedes the record and clicking the left mouse button. Then, press the DELETE key. This will remove the record from the table. If you forget a record, add it using the same procedure as for all the other records. Access will automatically place it in the correct location in the table.

Occasionally, you might attempt to add a record, but Access refuses to accept it. Instead, it gives you an error message, indicating the problem. The most likely reason for this in the CUSTOMER table is inadvertently entering a customer number that duplicates the customer number on another record.

Suppose, for example, that when you typed the fifth record (Forrest Co.), you accidentally entered the customer number for the sixth record (FY16). When you later tried to add the sixth record, Access rejected the addition, because a record with the same customer number (FY16) was already in the table. If this occurs, first check the customer numbers carefully, make any necessary corrections, and then try again to add the record.

If you cannot determine how to correct the data, you have a problem. Access will not allow you to move to any other record until you have made the correction, nor will it allow you to close the table. You are, in effect, stuck on the record. If you should ever find yourself in this situation, simply press the ESC key. This will remove the record you are trying to add from the screen. You can then move to any other record, close the table, or take any other action you desire.

▶ PREVIEWING AND PRINTING THE CONTENTS OF A TABLE

When working with a database, you will often need to obtain a printed copy of the table contents. Figure 1-39 shows a printed copy of the contents of the CUSTOMER table. Because the CUSTOMER table is substantially wider than the screen, it will also be wider than the normal printed page on Portrait orientation. **Portrait orientation** means the printout is across the width of the page. **Landscape orientation** means the printout is across the length of the page. Thus, to print the wide database table, use Landscape orientation. If you are printing the contents of a table that fits on the screen, you will not need Landscape orientation. A convenient way to change to Landscape orientation is to use Print Preview. This allows you to determine whether Landscape orientation is necessary and, if it is, to easily change the orientation to Landscape.

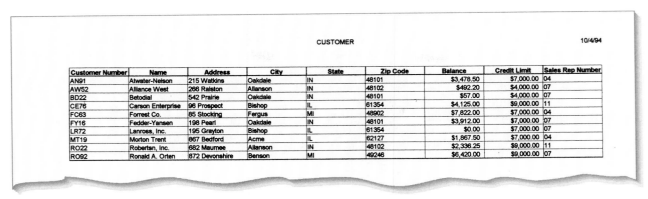

Customer Number	Name	Address	City	State	Zip Code	Balance	Credit Limit	Sales Rep Number
AN91	Atwater-Nelson	215 Watkins	Oakdale	IN	48101	$3,478.50	$7,000.00	04
AW52	Alliance West	266 Ralston	Allanson	IN	48102	$492.20	$4,000.00	07
BD22	Betodial	542 Prairie	Oakdale	IN	48101	$57.00	$4,000.00	07
CE76	Carson Enterprise	96 Prospect	Bishop	IL	61354	$4,125.00	$9,000.00	11
FC63	Forrest Co.	85 Stocking	Fergus	MI	48902	$7,822.00	$7,000.00	04
FY16	Fedder-Yansen	198 Pearl	Oakdale	IN	48101	$3,912.00	$7,000.00	07
LR72	Lanross, Inc.	195 Grayton	Bishop	IL	61354	$0.00	$7,000.00	07
MT19	Morton Trent	867 Bedford	Acme	IL	62127	$1,867.50	$7,000.00	04
RO22	Robertsn, Inc.	682 Maumee	Allanson	IN	48102	$2,336.25	$9,000.00	11
RO92	Ronald A. Orten	872 Devonshire	Benson	MI	49246	$6,420.00	$9,000.00	07

FIGURE 1-39

The following steps use Print Preview to print the CUSTOMER table.

TO PREVIEW AND PRINT THE CONTENTS OF A TABLE ▼

STEP 1 ▶

Make sure the CUSTOMER table is selected. (Because it is currently the only table in the database, it will automatically be selected, so you don't need to take any special action at this point.) Point to the Print Preview ( ) button (Figure 1-40).

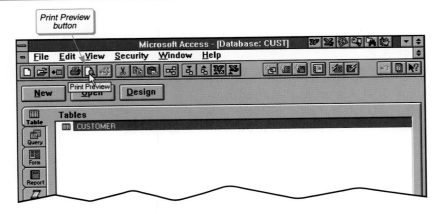

FIGURE 1-40

STEP 2 ▶

Click the Print Preview button.

The preview of the report displays (Figure 1-41). In the figure, the report displays in Portrait orientation, which will not display all fields on a page.

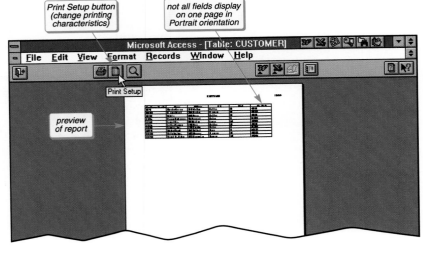

FIGURE 1-41

STEP 3 ▶

If your display is already in Landscape orientation, skip to Step 5. If it is in Portrait orientation, as in Figure 1-41 on the previous page, choose the Print Setup button (▣) by clicking the left mouse button. Point to the Landscape option button.

Access displays the Print Setup dialog box (Figure 1-42). The selected printer is the HP DeskJet 500 on LPT1:. Your printer may be different.

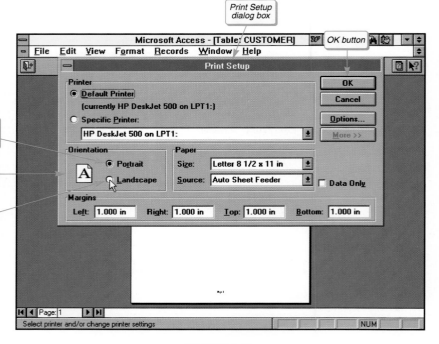

FIGURE 1-42

STEP 4 ▶

Select the Landscape option button in the Orientation area and choose the OK button in the Print Setup dialog box. Then, point to the Print button (🖨).

The orientation is changed to Landscape, as shown by the report that displays on the screen (Figure 1-43).

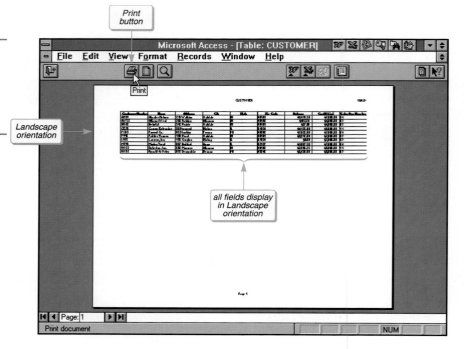

FIGURE 1-43

STEP 5 ▶

Choose the Print button by clicking the left mouse button and then point to the OK button.

The Print dialog box displays (Figure 1-44).

STEP 6 ▶

Choose the OK button in the Print dialog box.

Access displays the Printing dialog box briefly and then prints the report that was shown in Figure 1-39 on page A25.

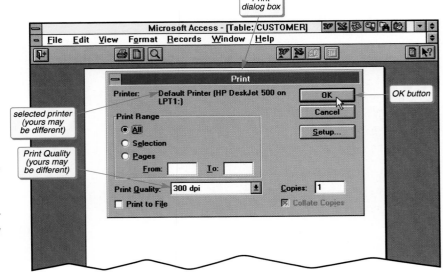

FIGURE 1-44

STEP 7 ▶

Point to the Control-menu box (Figure 1-45).

STEP 8 ▶

Double-click the Control-menu box.

Access closes the window.

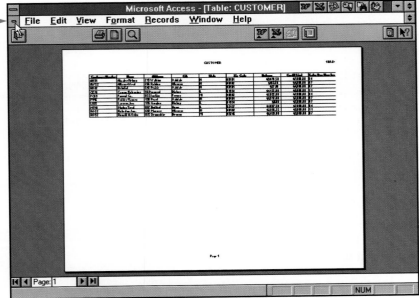

FIGURE 1-45

▶ CREATING ADDITIONAL TABLES

A database typically consists of more than one table. The sample database contains two: the CUSTOMER table and the SLSREP table. You need to repeat the process of creating a table and adding records for each table in the database. In the sample database, you need to create and add records to the SLSREP table. The structure and data for the table are given in Figure 1-46 on the next page. Perform the steps on the next page to create the table.

▸ **Structure for Sales Rep (SLSREP) table**

Field Name	Data Type	Field Size	Primary Key?	Description
Sales Rep Number	Text	2	Yes	Sales Rep Number (Primary Key)
Last Name	Text	12		Last name of sales representative
First Name	Text	8		First name of sales representative
Address	Text	15		Street address
City	Text	15		City
State	Text	2		State (two-character abbreviation)
Zip Code	Text	5		Zip Code (five-character version)
Sales	Currency			Total sales amount of sales representative
Commission Rate	Number			Commission rate

▸ **Data for Sales Rep (SLSREP) table**

Sales Rep Number	Last Name	First Name	Address	City	State	Zip Code	Sales	Commission Rate
04	Wright	Cecilia	125 Westchester	Borculo	MI	49224	$53,172.00	0.08
07	Perry	Thomas	1664 Birchwood	Kaiser	IN	46219	$74,956.00	0.06
11	Sanchez	Maria	722 Kreiser	Elk River	IL	60205	$30,125.00	0.07

FIGURE 1-46

TO CREATE THE SLSREP TABLE ▼

STEP 1 ▶

Make sure the CUST database is open. Point to the New button.

The Microsoft Access-Database: CUST window displays (Figure 1-47). If you recently maximized another window, this window will also be maximized as shown in the figure. If not, it will appear in its normal size.

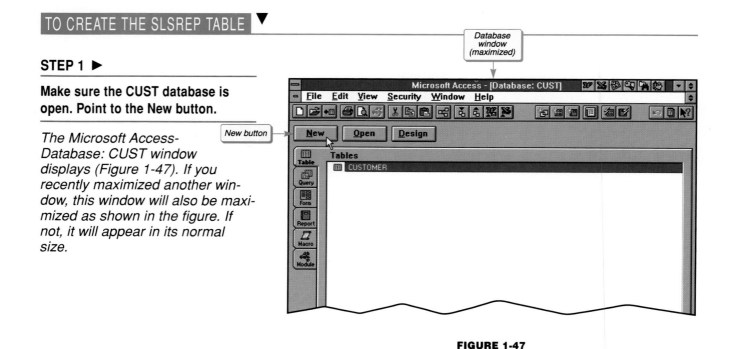

FIGURE 1-47

STEP 2 ▶

Choose the New button and then choose the New Table button. Then enter the name, data type, and description for the first field in the SLSREP table (the Sales Rep Number field). Point to the Set Primary Key button.

The entries for the first field display (Figure 1-48).

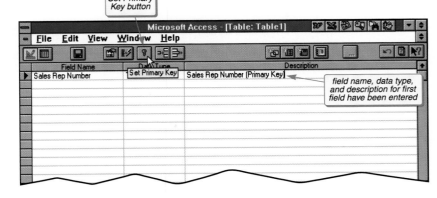

FIGURE 1-48

STEP 3 ▶

Click the Set Primary Key button to make the Sales Rep Number field the primary key and then make the remaining entries (including changing the field sizes) up through and including the name of the Commission Rate field. Click the drop-down list arrow in the Data Type column. Point to Number.

The entries display (Figure 1-49). The drop-down list of data types displays.

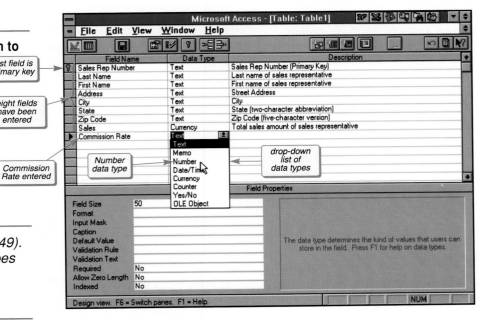

FIGURE 1-49

STEP 4 ▶

Choose the Number data type by clicking the left mouse button and then press the TAB key. Enter the description for the Commission Rate field.

STEP 5 ▶

Select the File menu, choose the Save command, type SLSREP as the name of the table, and choose the OK button. Double-click the Control-menu button to close the window.

The table is saved in the CUST database.

▶ ADDING RECORDS TO THE SLSREP TABLE

ow that you have created the SLSREP table, perform the following steps to add records to it.

TO ADD RECORDS TO THE SLSREP TABLE ▼

STEP 1 ▶

Move the highlight to the SLSREP table by pointing to the name of the table and clicking the left mouse button. Point to the Open button.

The SLSREP table is selected (Figure 1-50).

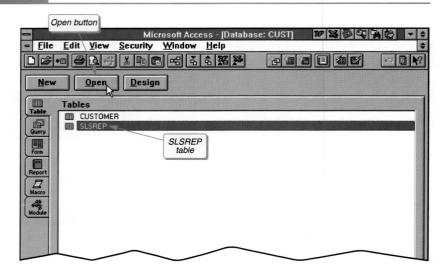

FIGURE 1-50

STEP 2 ▶

Choose the Open button and then enter the Sales Representative data from Figure 1-46 into the SLSREP table on page A28.

The datasheet displays with three records entered (Figure 1-51).

STEP 3 ▶

Close the table by double-clicking the Control-menu box.

Access closes the table and removes the datasheet from the screen.

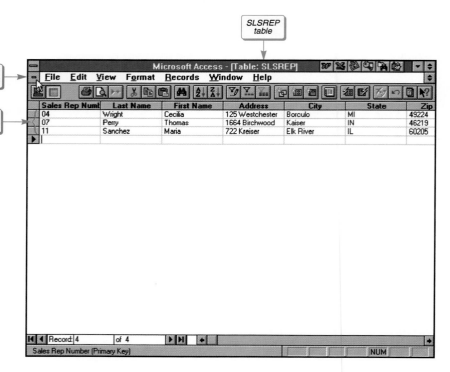

FIGURE 1-51

► USING A FORM TO VIEW DATA

I n creating tables, you have used Datasheet view, that is, the data on the screen displayed as a table. You can also use **Form view**, in which you see a **form** displaying a single record at a time.

The advantage with Datasheet view is that you can see multiple records at once. It has the disadvantage that, unless you have few fields in the table, you cannot see all the fields at the same time. With Form view, you see only a single record, but you can see all the fields in the record. The view you choose is a matter of personal preference.

The simplest way to create a form is to use the AutoForm button (🔳). To do so, first highlight the table for which the form is to be created in the Database window. Then, click the button. Perform the following steps to use the AutoForm button to create a form.

TO USE THE AUTOFORM BUTTON TO CREATE A FORM ▼

STEP 1 ►

Make sure the CUST database is open, the Database window displays, and the CUSTOMER table is highlighted. Point to the AutoForm button (Figure 1-52).

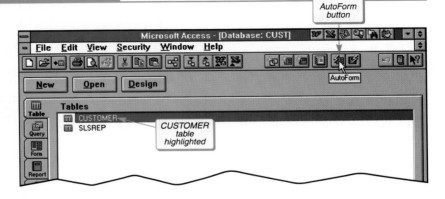

FIGURE 1-52

STEP 2 ►

Click the AutoForm button.

The form displays (Figure 1-53).

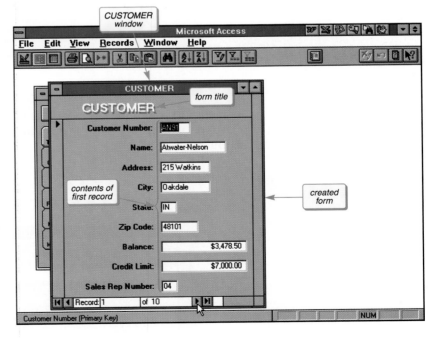

FIGURE 1-53

Using the Form

You can use Form view like you used Datasheet view. Use the navigation buttons to move between records. You can add new records or change existing ones. Press the DELETE key to delete the record displayed on the screen. In other words, you can perform database operations using either Form view or Datasheet view.

Because you can only see one record at a time in Form view, to see a different record, such as the fifth record, use the navigation buttons to move to it. To move from record to record in Form view, perform the following steps.

TO USE THE FORM

STEP 1 ▶

Point to the Next Record button (Figure 1-53).

STEP 2 ▶

Click the Next Record button four times.

The fifth record displays on the form (Figure 1-54).

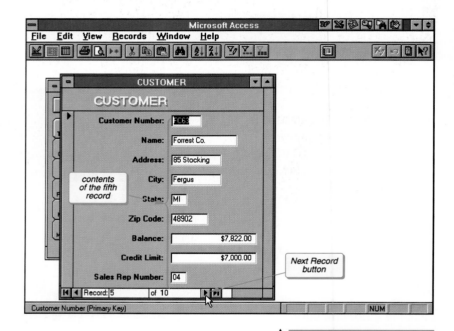

FIGURE 1-54

Closing a form is similar to closing a table. The only difference is that you will be asked if you want to save the form. The following steps close the form and save it as Customer Form.

TO CLOSE AND SAVE THE FORM

STEP 1 ▶

Point to the Control-menu box for the CUSTOMER window (Figure 1-55).

FIGURE 1-55

STEP 2 ►

Double-click the Control-menu box and then point to the Yes button (Yes).

The Microsoft Access dialog box displays, asking if you want to save the form (Figure 1-56).

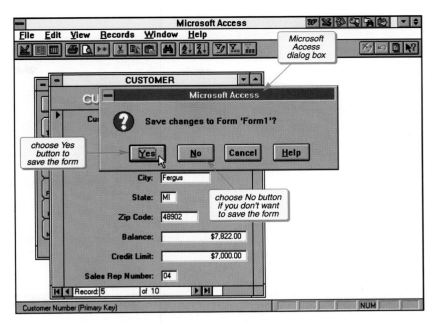

FIGURE 1-56

STEP 3 ►

Choose the Yes button, type Customer Form **as the name of the form, and point to the OK button (Figure 1-57).**

STEP 4 ►

Choose the OK button.

The form is saved as part of the database and is removed from the screen.

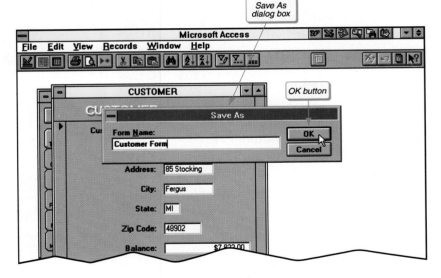

FIGURE 1-57

Using the Saved Form (Customer Form)

Once you have saved a form, you can use it at any time in the future by opening it. Opening a form is similar to opening a table. Perform the steps on the next page to open the Customer Form.

TO OPEN THE CUSTOMER FORM

STEP 1 ▶

Make sure the CUST database is open, the Database window is on the screen, and point to the Form button (▣) (Figure 1-58).

FIGURE 1-58

STEP 2 ▶

Choose the Form button.

The list of forms displays on the screen (Figure 1-59). Currently, only a single form, Customer Form, appears.

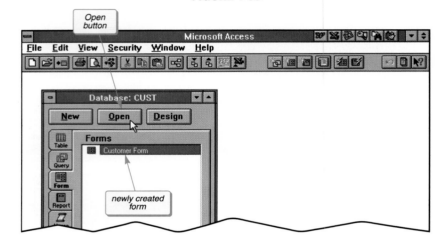

FIGURE 1-59

STEP 3 ▶

Choose the Open button.

The form displays (Figure 1-60). It can now be used in the manner described earlier.

STEP 4 ▶

Once you have finished working with the form, close it, using the steps described on page A32. You will not be asked if you want to save the form, because it has already been saved.

The form is removed from the screen and the Database window displays.

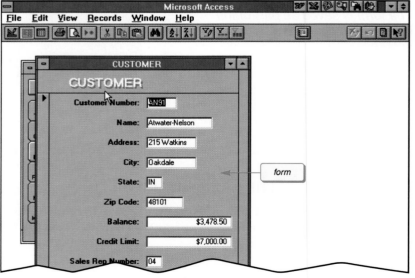

FIGURE 1-60

▶ CREATING A GRAPH

S ometimes the most effective way to present data in a database is graphically. Access contains a graphics tool that allows you to create and customize a wide variety of graphs. A **Graph Wizard** can assist in the creation of a graph.

This project creates the graph shown in Figure 1-61. It illustrates the sales figures of each of the three sales representatives. The sales representative numbers appear along the x- (horizontal) axis. The sales amounts are represented along the y- (vertical) axis. The height of each bar represents the sales amount for the corresponding sales representative.

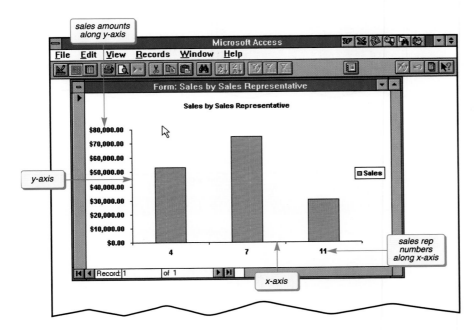

FIGURE 1-61

In creating a graph, you must select the field for the x-axis first. You can then select the field or fields for the y-axis. To create the graph shown in Figure 1-61, for example, you must select the Sales Rep Number field first and then select the Sales field. The Graph Wizard then gives you a chance to make a number of selections that affect the appearance of the final graph. In each case, the Graph Wizard makes an initial selection for you and then gives you the option of changing the selection. For the graph shown in Figure 1-61, you can simply accept the selections the Graph Wizard makes for you.

The steps on the next page illustrate the process of creating a graph.

TO CREATE A GRAPH

STEP 1 ►

Make sure the CUST database is open and the Database window is on the screen. Choose the Form button and then point to the New button (Figure 1-62).

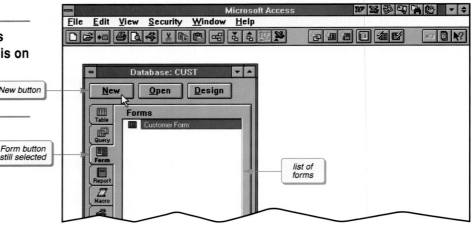

FIGURE 1-62

STEP 2 ►

Choose the New button and then click the arrow in the Select a Table/Query list box.

The list of available tables displays (Figure 1-63).

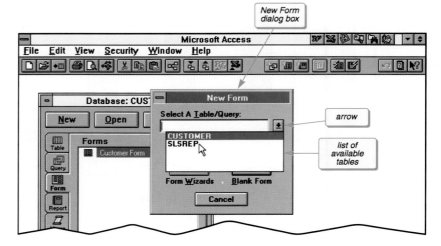

FIGURE 1-63

STEP 3 ►

Select the SLSREP table by pointing to it and clicking the left mouse button. Then, point to the FormWizards button ( ) (Figure 1-64).

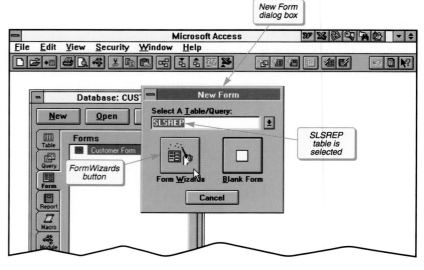

FIGURE 1-64

STEP 4 ▶

Choose the FormWizards button, select Graph, and point to the OK button.

The FormWizards dialog box displays (Figure 1-65). The Graph Wizard is selected.

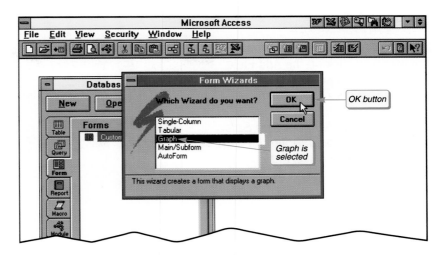

FIGURE 1-65

STEP 5 ▶

Choose the OK button and then point to the Add Field button (▣).

The Graph Wizard dialog box displays (Figure 1-66). The Sales Rep Number field is selected.

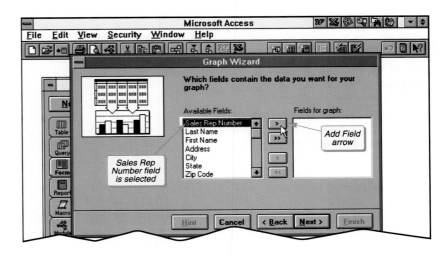

FIGURE 1-66

STEP 6 ▶

Add the Sales Rep Number as a field for the graph by clicking the Add Field button. Select the Sales field and point to the Add Field button.

Sales Rep Number is included as a field for the graph (Figure 1-67). The Sales field is selected.

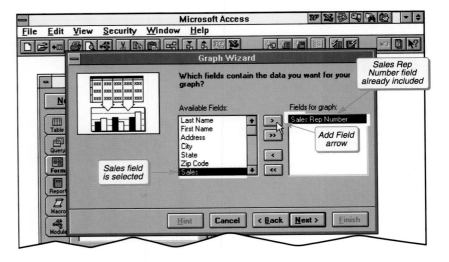

FIGURE 1-67

STEP 7 ▶

Add the Sales field to the fields for the graph by clicking the Add Field button and then point to the Next button (Next >).

The Sales Rep Number and Sales fields are both included in the list of fields for the graph (Figure 1-68).

FIGURE 1-68

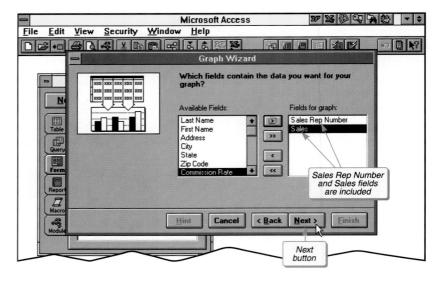

STEP 8 ▶

Choose the Next button and then point to the Next button on the following screen.

The Graph Wizard dialog box displays (Figure 1-69), requesting the method for calculating totals. The correct choice is already selected.

FIGURE 1-69

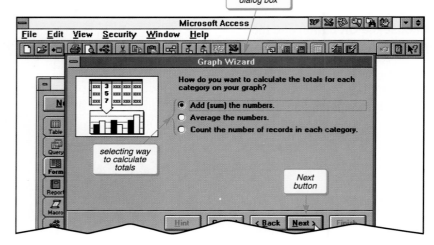

STEP 9 ▶

Choose the Next button and then point to the Next button on the following screen.

The Graph Wizard dialog box displays (Figure 1-70), requesting the type of graph. The correct type (a bar graph) is already selected.

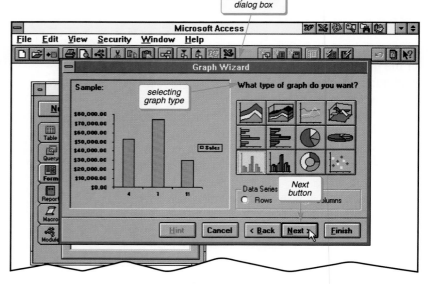

FIGURE 1-70

STEP 10 ▶

Choose the Next button and type
Sales by Sales
Representative **as the title. Point
to the Next button.**

*The Graph Wizard dialog box dis-
plays (Figure 1-71). The title has
been entered.*

FIGURE 1-71

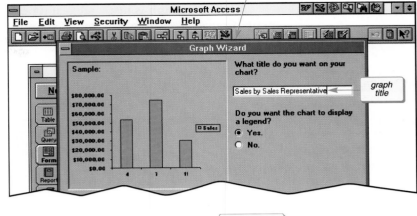

STEP 11 ▶

**Choose the Next button and then
point to the Finish button (Finish)
(Figure 1-72).**

FIGURE 1-72

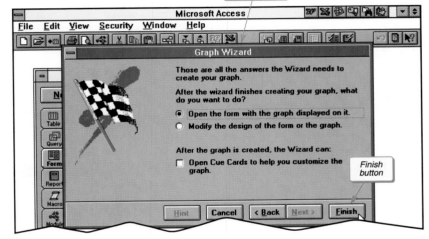

STEP 12 ▶

Choose the Finish button.

*The graph displays (Figure 1-73).
The values along the x-axis are
the sales representative numbers.
The values on the y-axis are sales
amounts. The title of the graph is
the same as the name of the table.*

FIGURE 1-73

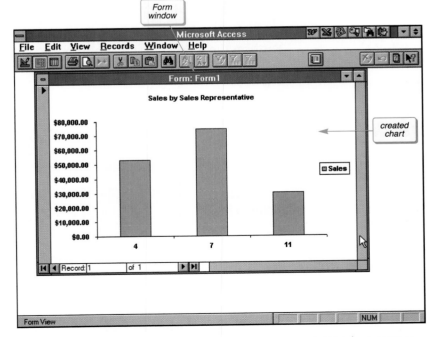

Because a graph is just a special type of form, closing and saving a form is the same process as closing and saving a graph. Perform the following steps to close and save the graph as Sales by Sales Representative.

TO CLOSE AND SAVE THE GRAPH ▼

STEP 1 ▶

Double-click the Control-menu box on the form window. Point to the Yes button.

The Microsoft Access dialog box displays, asking if you wish to save the graph (Figure 1-74).

STEP 2 ▶

Choose the Yes button. Type Sales by Sales Representative **as the name of the graph and choose the OK button.**

The graph is saved as a form in the database.

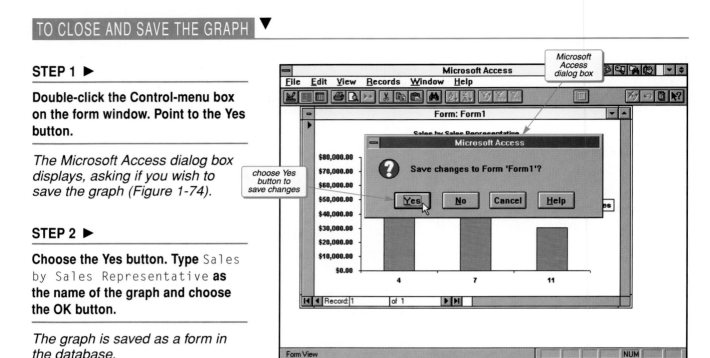

FIGURE 1-74

Printing the Saved Graph

In addition to viewing the graph on the screen, you can also print the graph. Perform the following steps to print the graph.

TO PRINT THE GRAPH ▼

STEP 1 ▶

Make sure the CUST database is open and the Database window is on the screen. Select the Sales by Sales Representative form and point to the Open button (Figure 1-75).

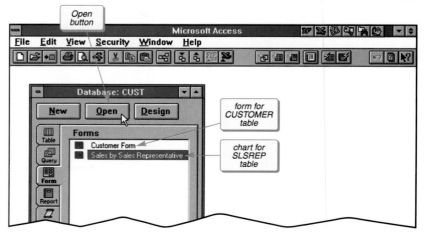

FIGURE 1-75

STEP 2 ▶

Choose the Open button. After the graph displays, point to the Print Preview button.

The File menu displays (Figure 1-76).

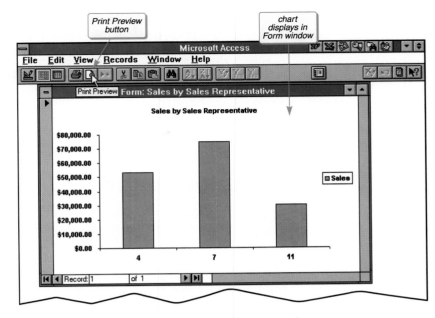

FIGURE 1-76

STEP 3 ▶

Click the Print Preview button.

A preview of the printed graph displays (Figure 1-77).

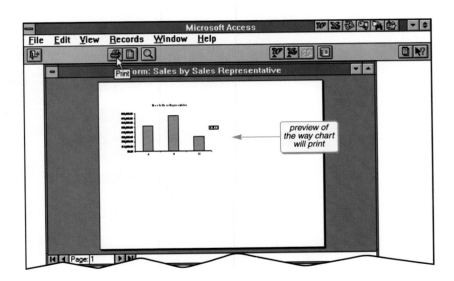

FIGURE 1-77

STEP 4 ▶

Choose the Print button.

The graph prints (Figure 1-78).

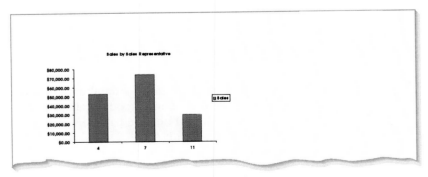

FIGURE 1-78

Closing a graph is similar to closing a form. Perform the following steps to close a graph.

TO CLOSE A GRAPH

Step 1: Double-click the Control-menu box on the Form window.

The form containing the graph is closed and removed from the screen.

▶ USING ONLINE HELP

With Access, you can obtain help at any time by using the Help menu (Figure 1-79). For most information, choose Contents, which provides a variety of ways of finding the information you need. You can also choose Search to search for a specific topic or procedure. The Cue Cards command displays a series of screens that walk you through a variety of tasks in the form of a tutorial. About Microsoft Access gives information about the version of Access and the user to whom the product is registered. Click the Help button (🔽) and then click any other button to obtain help on the other button.

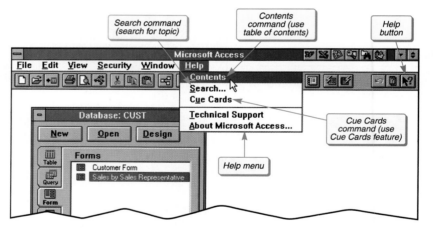

FIGURE 1-79

▶ DESIGNING A DATABASE

Database design refers to the arrangement of data into tables and fields. In the example in this project, the design is specified; but in many cases, you will have to determine the design based on what you want the system to accomplish.

With large, complex databases, the database design process can be extensive. Major sections of advanced database texts are devoted to this topic. Often, however, you should be able to design a database effectively by keeping one simple principle in mind: *Design to remove redundancy.* **Redundancy** means storing the same fact in more than one place.

▶ **CUSTOMER table**

Customer Number	Name	Address	City	St	Zip Code	Balance	Credit Limit	Sales Rep Number	Last Name	First Name	Address	City	St	Zip Code	Sales	Comm Rate
AN91	Atwater-Nelson	215 Watkins	Oakdale	IN	48101	$3,478.50	$7,000.00	04	Wright	Cecilia	125 Westchester	Borculo	MI	49224	$53,172.00	0.08
AW52	Alliance West	266 Ralston	Allanson	IN	48102	$492.20	$4,000.00	07	Perry	Thomas	1664 Birchwood	Kaiser	IN	46219	$74,956.00	0.06
BD22	Betodial	542 Prairie	Oakdale	IN	48101	$57.00	$4,000.00	07	Perry	Thomas	1664 Birchwood	Kaiser	IN	46219	$74,956.00	0.06
CE76	Carson Enterprise	96 Prospect	Bishop	IL	61354	$4,125.00	$9,000.00	11	Sanchez	Maria	722 Kreiser	Elk River	IL	60205	$30,125.50	0.07
FC63	Forrest Co.	85 Stocking	Fergus	MI	48902	$7,822.00	$7,000.00	04	Wright	Cecilia	125 Westchester	Borculo	MI	49224	$53,172.00	0.08
FY16	Fedder-Yansen	198 Pearl	Oakdale	IN	48101	$3,912.00	$7,000.00	07	Perry	Thomas	1664 Birchwood	Kaiser	IN	46219	$74,956.00	0.06
LR72	Lanross, Inc.	195 Grayton	Bishop	IL	61354	$0.00	$7,000.00	07	Perry	Thomas	1664 Birchwood	Kaiser	IN	46219	$74,956.00	0.06
MT19	Morton Trent	867 Bedford	Acme	IL	62127	$1,867.50	$7,000.00	04	Wright	Cecilia	125 Westchester	Borculo	MI	49224	$53,172.00	0.08
R022	Robertson, Inc.	682 Maumee	Allanson	IN	48102	$2,336.25	$9,000.00	11	Sanchez	Maria	722 Kreiser	Elk River	IL	60205	$30,125.50	0.07
RO92	Ronald A. Orten	872 Devonshire	Benson	MI	49246	$6,420.00	$9,000.00	07	Perry	Thomas	1664 Birchwood	Kaiser	IN	46219	$74,956.00	0.06

duplicate sales rep names

FIGURE 1-80

To illustrate, you need to maintain the following information shown in Figure 1-80. In the figure, all the data is contained in a single table. Notice that the data for a given sales representative (number, name, address, and so on) occurs on more than one record. Storing this data on multiple records is an example of redundancy, which causes several problems:

1. Redundancy wastes space on the disk. The address of sales representative 04 (Cecilia Wright), for example, should be stored only once. Storing this fact several times is wasteful.
2. Redundancy makes updating the database more difficult. If, for example, Cecilia Wright moves, her address would need to be changed in several different places.
3. A possibility of inconsistent data exists. Suppose, for example, that you change the address of Cecilia Wright on customer FC63's record to 146 Valley, but you don't change it on customer AN91's record. In both cases, the sales representative number is 04, but the addresses are different. In other words, the data is *inconsistent*.

The solution to the problem is to place the redundant data in a separate table — one in which the data will no longer be redundant. If, for example, you place the data for sales representatives in a separate table (Figure 1-81), the data for each sales rep will appear only once. Notice that you need to have the sales rep number in both tables. Without it, there would be no way to tell which sales rep was associated with which customer. All the other sales rep data, however, was removed from the CUSTOMER table and placed in the SLSREP table. This new arrangement corrects the problems:

> **Sales Rep (SLSREP) table**

Sales rep data is in separate table →

Sales Rep Number	Last Name	First Name	Address	City	State	Zip Code	Sales	Commission Rate
04	Wright	Cecilia	125 Westchester	Borculo	MI	49224	$53,172.00	0.08
07	Perry	Thomas	1664 Birchwood	Kaiser	IN	46219	$74,956.00	0.06
11	Sanchez	Maria	722 Kreiser	Elk River	IL	60205	$30,125.50	0.07

> **CUSTOMER table**

Customer Number	Name	Address	City	State	Zip Code	Balance	Credit Limit	Sales Rep Number
AN91	Atwater-Nelson	215 Watkins	Oakdale	IN	48101	$3,478.50	$7,000.00	04
AW52	Alliance West	266 Ralston	Allanson	IN	48102	$492.20	$4,000.00	07
BD22	Betodial	542 Prairie	Oakdale	IN	48101	$57.00	$4,000.00	07
CE76	Carson Enterprise	96 Prospect	Bishop	IL	61354	$4,125.00	$9,000.00	11
FC63	Forrest Co.	85 Stocking	Fergus	MI	48902	$7,822.00	$7,000.00	04
FY16	Fedder-Yansen	198 Pearl	Oakdale	IN	48101	$3,912.00	$7,000.00	07
LR72	Lanross, Inc.	195 Grayton	Bishop	IL	61354	$0.00	$7,000.00	07
MT19	Morton Trent	867 Bedford	Acme	IL	62127	$1,867.50	$7,000.00	04
R022	Robertson, Inc.	682 Maumee	Allanson	IN	48102	$2,336.25	$9,000.00	11
RO92	Ronald A. Orten	872 Devonshire	Benson	MI	49246	$6,420.00	$9,000.00	07

FIGURE 1-81

1. Because the data for each sales representative is stored only once — space is not wasted.
2. Changing the address of a sales representative is easy. You only have to change one row in the SLSREP table.
3. Because the data for a sales representative is stored only once, inconsistent data cannot occur.

Designing to omit redundancy will help you to produce good and valid database designs.

▶ PROJECT SUMMARY

Project 1 introduced you to starting Access and creating a database. You learned how to create a database, how to create the tables in a database by defining the fields within the tables, and how to add records to the tables. Once you created the tables, you learned how to print the contents of the table, as well as how to use a form to view the data in the table. Finally, you created a graph that represented the data visually.

▶ KEY TERMS AND INDEX

Q U I C K   R E F E R E N C E

In Access, you can accomplish a task in a number of different ways. The following table provides a quick reference to each task presented in this project with its available options. The commands listed in the Menu column can be executed using either the keyboard or the mouse.

Task	Mouse	Menu	Keyboard Shortcuts
Assign a Field Name			Type name, press TAB
Close a Database		From File menu, choose Close Database	
Close a Table, Form, or Graph		From Control menu, choose Close	
Create a Database		From File menu, choose New Database	
Create a Form or Graph	Click Form button in Database dialog box, click New button, click table name, click FormWizards button		
Create a Table	Click Table button in Database dialog box if not already chosen; click New button		
Delete a Field		From Edit menu, choose Delete	Press DELETE
Delete a Record		From Edit menu, choose Delete	Press DELETE
Edit Data in a Field		Type data, then press the TAB key	
Exit Access	Double-click Control-menu box on title bar	From File menu, choose Exit	Press ALT+F4
Indicate a Field Size	Click Field Size text box	From View menu, choose Table Properties	Press F6
Indicate a Field Type	Click drop-down list arrow in Data Type column, then click appropriate type		Type appropriate letter

(continued)

QUICK REFERENCE (continued)

Task	Mouse	Menu	Keyboard Shortcuts
Indicate a Key Field	Click Set Primary Key button	From Edit menu, choose Set Primary Key	
Move to the First Record	Click First Record navigation button	From Records menu, choose Go To, then choose First	
Move to the Last Record	Click Last Record navigation button	From Records menu, choose Go To, then choose Last	
Move to the Next Field	Click field; if field is not on screen, use scroll bar to make field visible, then click field		Press TAB
Move to the Next Record	Click Next Record navigation button	From Records menu, choose Go To, then choose Next	
Move to the Previous Field	Click field; if field is not on screen, use scroll bar to make field visible, then click field		Press SHIFT+TAB
Move to Previous Record	Click Previous Record navigation button	From Records menu, choose Go To, then choose Previous	
Open a Database		From File menu, choose Open Database	Use arrow keys to move highlight to name, then press ENTER
Open a Form or Graph	Click Form button in Database dialog box, click Open button, click form or graph name		Use arrow keys to move highlight to name, then press ENTER
Open a Table	Click table name, then click Open button in Database dialog box		Use arrow keys to move highlight to name, then press ENTER key
Print the Contents of a Table		From File menu, choose Print Preview	
Save a Form		From Control menu, choose Close, then choose Yes and enter name of form	
Save a Graph		From Control menu, choose Close, then choose Yes and enter name of graph	
Save a Newly Defined Table		From File menu, choose Save	
Start Access	Click Microsoft Access button on Office Manager toolbar or double-click Microsoft Access program-item icon	First select Access icon, then from File menu, choose Open	

STUDENT ASSIGNMENT 1
True/False

Instructions: Circle T if the statement is true or F if the statement is false.

T F 1. The term database describes a collection of data organized in a manner that allows access, retrieval, and use of that data.

T F 2. Table names can be from one to 64 characters in length and can include blank spaces.

T F 3. The bottom bar on an Access window is called the information bar.

T F 4. Once an Access database is created, all the tables, reports, and forms you create will automatically be placed within it.

T F 5. Field names can be no more than 64 characters in length and cannot include numeric digits.

T F 6. The only field type available for fields that must be used in arithmetic operations is Numeric.

T F 7. You can include blanks in an Access field name.

T F 8. To delete a field in a table structure, point to the leftmost column on the row that contains the field to be deleted, click the left mouse button, and press CTRL+DELETE.

T F 9. To add a field, select the field that will follow where you would like to insert the field, select Edit, and then choose the Insert Row command.

T F 10. You name a table before you define the field names, field types, and field widths.

T F 11. If you do not assign a width to a text field, Access assumes the width is 50.

T F 12. To open a database, choose the Open Database command from the File menu.

T F 13. You can use the TAB key to move to the next field in a record in Datasheet view.

T F 14. If you enter 10000 in a field that has been defined as a Currency field type, then the value will display as $10,000.00.

T F 15. Records are always ordered in the order in which they are entered.

T F 16. To delete a record from a table, point to the box that immediately precedes the record, click the left mouse button, and then press CTRL+DELETE.

T F 17. You can change records using Form view, but you can only add records using Datasheet view.

T F 18. When you create a graph, you must select the field for the x-axis first.

T F 19. The title for a graph cannot be changed and is always the same as the name of the table.

T F 20. Controlling redundancy results in an increase in consistency.

STUDENT ASSIGNMENT 2
Multiple Choice

Instructions: Circle the correct response.

1. A database is _____.
   a. the same as a file
   b. a software product
   c. a collection of data organized in a manner that allows access, retrieval, and use of that data.
   d. none of the above
2. Which of the following is not a benefit of controlling redundancy?
   a. greater consistency is maintained
   b. less space is occupied
   c. update is easier
   d. all of the above are benefits

(continued)

STUDENT ASSIGNMENT 2 (continued)

3. A field that uniquely identifies a particular record in a table is called a _____.
   a. foreign key
   b. secondary key
   c. primary key
   d. principal key
4. Access is a(n) _____.
   a. applications software package
   b. DBMS
   c. database
   d. both a and b
5. The bar on an Access Table window that gives information on the current position within a table and the number of records in a table is called the _____.
   a. title bar
   b. status bar
   c. information bar
   d. navigation bar
6. A record in Access is composed of a _____.
   a. series of databases
   b. series of files
   c. series of records
   d. series of fields
7. To create a new database, select the _____ command from the File menu.
   a. New
   b. New Database
   c. Create
   d. Create Database
8. To remove a field from a table structure, select the field and press _____.
   a. the DELETE key
   b. CTRL+D
   c. CTRL+DELETE
   d. CTRL+Y
9. To display the contents of a table on the screen before printing, use the Print Preview command from the _____ menu.
   a. Print
   b. Edit
   c. File
   d. Options
10. To close a database, select the _____ command from the File menu.
    a. Close
    b. Close Database
    c. Quit
    d. Quit Database

STUDENT ASSIGNMENT 3
Understanding Access Windows

Problem: For many of the student assignments and computer laboratory exercises in these projects, you will use the Soft database that is included in the Access2 subdirectory on the Student Diskette that accompanies this book.

The Soft database stores information about the inventory of a store that sells educational software. The Software table contains information on software that the store sells. The Vendor table contains information on the vendors who produce or market the software. The data and structure for the Software table are shown in Figure SA1-3a. The data and structure for the Vendor table are shown in Figure SA1-3b on the next page.

▶ Structure of Software Table

Field Name	Data Type	Field Size	Primary Key?	Description
Software Number	Text	4	Yes	Software Number (Primary Key)
Name	Text	15		Software Name
Category	Text	3		MTH (Mathematics); ENG (English); SCI (Science)
Quantity	Number			Number in Stock (Use Integer as the Field Size)
Price	Currency			Selling Price of Software
Vendor Code	Text	2		Software Vendor Code

▶ Data for Software Table

Software Number	Name	Category	Quantity	Price	Vendor Code
0593	Easy Calculus	MTH	8	$79.95	LS
0870	Number Crunch	MTH	5	$49.95	EI
1673	Chem Works	SCI	12	$19.95	CC
1693	Kid-Writer	ENG	22	$29.95	LS
2573	Pendulum	SCI	10	$24.95	EI
2603	Storywriter	ENG	16	$24.95	CC
3933	Math Tester	MTH	18	$39.95	AS
3963	Writing is Fun	ENG	3	$39.95	CC
4353	Rhythmetic	MTH	30	$69.95	AS
5820	Test Tube	SCI	25	$24.95	AS
5940	Science Quest	SCI	34	$89.95	EI
5950	Easy English	ENG	10	$29.95	LS

FIGURE SA1-3a

(continued)

STUDENT ASSIGNMENT 3 (continued)

▸ **Structure of Vendor table**

Field Name	Data Type	Field Size	Primary Key?	Description
Vendor Code	Text	2	Yes	Vendor Code (Primary Key)
Name	Text	20		Vendor Name
Address	Text	15		Street Address
City	Text	15		City
State	Text	2		State (two-character abbreviation)
Zip Code	Text	5		Zip Code (five-character version)
Phone Number	Text	12		Telephone Number (999-999-9999 version)

▸ **Data for Vendor table**

Vendor Code	Name	Address	City	State	Zip Code	Phone Number
AS	Academic Software	346 Adams Ave.	Philadelphia	PA	19111	215-780-3953
CC	Compuschool Co.	9661 King Pl.	Springfield	MA	01013	413-572-8292
EI	Edusoft Inc.	1625 Brook St.	Costa Mesa	CA	92688	714-336-4785
LS	Learnit Software	145 Oak Ave.	Wilmington	DE	19808	302-475-4477

FIGURE SA1-3b

Instructions:

In Figure SA1-3c, arrows point to some of the major components of the Access window. Identify the various parts of the window in the space provided and use this figure to answer the following questions.

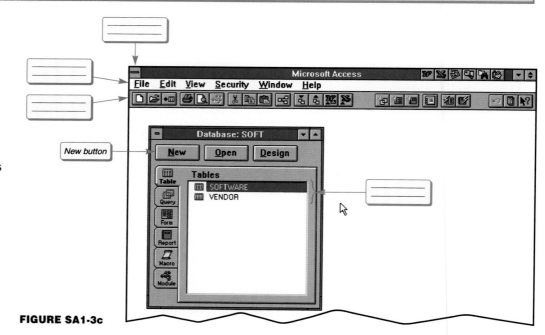

FIGURE SA1-3c

1. When would you use the New button?

_____

2. How do you close a database?

_____

STUDENT ASSIGNMENT 4
Understanding the Table Window in Design View

Instructions: Figure SA1-4 shows the Software table window in Design view. Use this figure to answer the following questions.

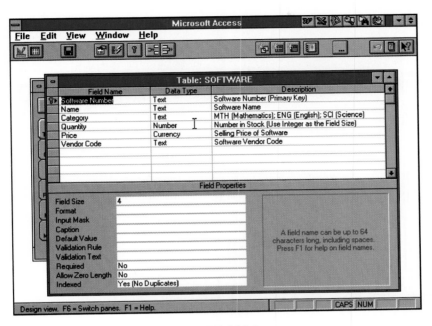

FIGURE SA1-4

1. Which fields can be used in mathematical operations?

   _____

   _____

2. What is the default field size for a field with a data type of text?

   _____

   _____

3. How do you indicate the primary key for a table?

   _____

   _____

4. Suppose you needed to insert a field for Vendor Cost immediately after the Price field. The field has a data type of currency. How would you accomplish this task?

   _____

   _____

5. Adding the Vendor Cost field was a mistake. The field needs to be deleted. How would you accomplish this task?

   _____

   _____

STUDENT ASSIGNMENT 5
Understanding a Table Window in Datasheet View

Instructions: In Figure SA1-5, arrows point to various components of the Datasheet view window. Identify the components in the space provided.

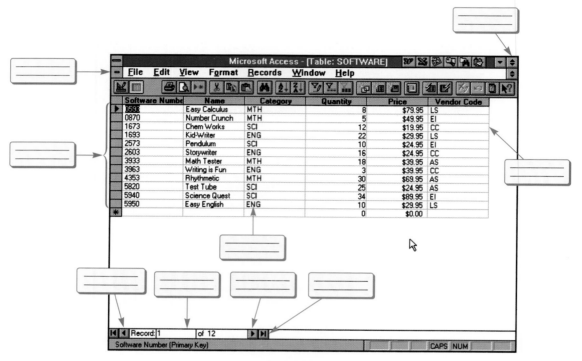

FIGURE SA1-5

STUDENT ASSIGNMENT 6
Using a Table Window in Form View

Instructions: The Form view for the first record in the Software table is shown in Figure SA1-6. Use this figure to answer the following questions.

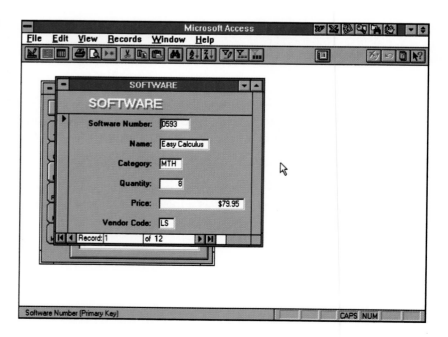

FIGURE SA1-6

1. How would you change the software name from "Easy Calculus" to "Easy Algebra"?

_____

_____

2. How would you move to the fourth record?

_____

_____

3. What would you need to enter in the Price field for the fourth record to change the Price from $29.95 to $34.00?

_____

_____

4. You have just finished changing the price for the fourth record. How would you move to the third record?

_____

_____

5. How would you add a record to the Software table?

_____

_____

C O M P U T E R   L A B O R A T O R Y   E X E R C I S E S

COMPUTER LABORATORY EXERCISE 1
Using the Help Menu

Instructions: Perform the following tasks using a computer:

1. Start Access.
2. Choose the Contents command from the Help menu.
3. Choose Search.
4. Type field properties in the Search dialog box.
5. Choose Show Topics.
6. Select the topic Setting a Field Property and then choose Go To.
7. The Help window shown in Figure CLE1-1 should display. Point to Field Size, as shown in Figure CLE1-1, and press the left mouse button.

FIGURE CLE1-1

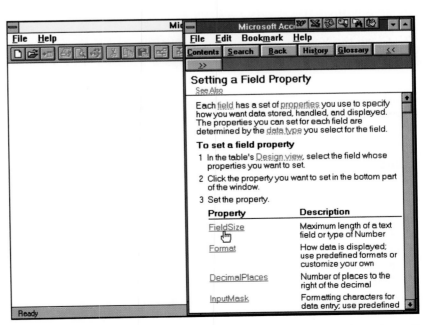

(continued)

COMPUTER LABORATORY EXERCISE 1 (continued)

8. Read the information in the Field Size Property Help window and answer the following questions.
   a. What is the maximum field size for a data type of Text?

   _____

   b. In general, why should you use the smallest possible Field Size setting?

   _____

   c. When should you use the Currency data type?

   _____

   d. When should you use the Integer data type?

   _____

9. Close the Help window.
10. Exit Access.

COMPUTER LABORATORY EXERCISE 2
Changing Data

Instructions: Start Access and open the Vendor table in the Soft database from the Access2 subdirectory on the Student Diskette that accompanies this book. Perform the following tasks:

1. Change the address for vendor code AS to `400 Gilham St.`
2. Add the following record to the Vendor table.

SC	Schoolhouse Inc.	5 Orchard Ave.	Barrington	IL	60010	708-382-4100

3. Print the Vendor table.
4. Change the address for vendor code AS back to `346 Adams Ave.` (This reverses the change you made above in task 1.)
5. Delete the extra record that you added in task 2.
6. Print the Vendor table.
7. Close the Vendor table and the Soft database.
8. Exit Access.

COMPUTER LABORATORY EXERCISE 3
Creating a Graph

Instructions: Create a graph for the Software table. Perform the following tasks:

1. Start Access.
2. Open the Soft database from the Access2 subdirectory on the Student Diskette that accompanies this book.
3. Choose the Form button and then the New button.
4. Select the Software table and choose the FormWizards button.
5. Select the Graph Wizard.
6. Select Category as the x-axis field and Quantity as the y-axis field.
7. Create the graph shown in Figure CLE1-3.

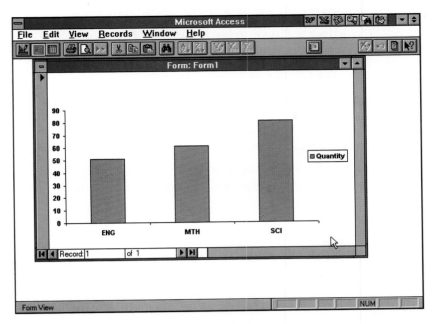

FIGURE CLE1-3

8. Print the graph.
9. Close the graph and save it as Softgraph1.
10. Close the Soft database.
11. Exit Access.

COMPUTER LABORATORY ASSIGNMENTS

Creating and Displaying a Database

Each project ends with four computer laboratory assignments. In each project, Computer Laboratory Assignment 1 involves a database of Consumer Products, Computer Laboratory Assignment 2 involves a database of Employees, Computer Laboratory Assignment 3 deals with a database containing data about Movies, and Computer Laboratory Assignment 4 deals with a database containing information about the inventory of a bookstore.

The computer laboratory assignments are cumulative. That is, the assignment for Computer Laboratory Assignment 1 in Project 2 builds on the assignment for Computer Laboratory Assignment 1 from Project 1. Thus, be sure to work through the computer laboratory assignment completely before proceeding to the next project. Otherwise, you may encounter difficulty later on.

COMPUTER LABORATORY ASSIGNMENT 1
Creating a Consumer Products Database

Purpose: To provide practice in creating and updating a database.

Problem: A wholesale distribution company needs to maintain information on the items they sell to local retail stores. The database they will use for this purpose consists of two tables. The Product table contains information on items that the distributor has in stock. The Item Class table contains information on the item class to which each product belongs. You have been assigned to create and update this database.

Instructions: The data and structure for the Product table are shown in Figure CLA1-1a. The data and structure for the Item Class table are shown in Figure CLA1-1b. You are to create both tables.

▸ **Structure of Product table**

Field Name	Data Type	Field Size	Primary Key?	Description
Product Number	Text	4	Yes	Product number (primary key)
Product Description	Text	16		Product description
Units on Hand	Number			Number of units on hand (Use Integer as the Field Size.)
Item Class Code	Text	2		Item class code
Warehouse Number	Number			Warehouse number (Use Integer as the Field Size.)
Price	Currency			Unit price

▸ **Data for Product table**

Product Number	Product Description	Units on Hand	Item Class Code	Warehouse Number	Price
AD29	Shaver	104	PC	2	59.99
AK13	Ice Cream Maker	68	HW	3	39.96
AY83	Hair Dryer	112	PC	1	16.99
BE24	Breadmaker	34	HW	3	199.96
BL07	Microwave Oven	11	AP	2	149.99
BX55	Electric Wok	95	HW	3	39.99
CA35	Refrigerator	8	AP	3	159.99
CC04	Makeup Mirror	44	PC	1	29.99
CX22	Luxury Spa	20	PC	3	109.96
CZ91	Juice Extractor	82	HW	2	49.96

FIGURE CLA1-1a

▸ **Structure of Item Class table**

Field Name	Data Type	Field Size	Primary Key?	Description
Item Class Code	Text	2	Yes	Item class code (primary key)
Item Class Description	Text	15		Item class description

▸ **Data for Item Class table**

Item Class Code	Item Class Description
AP	Appliances
HW	Housewares
PC	Personal Care

FIGURE CLA1-1b

Perform the following tasks using Access:

1. Create a new database in which to store all the files related to the products data. Call the database Items.
2. Create the Product table using the structure shown in Figure CLA1-1a. Change the Field Size for the Units On Hand and Warehouse Number fields to Integer. (Hint: Integer will store the values as whole numbers.) Use the name Product for the table.
3. Add the data shown in Figure CLA1-1a to the Product table.
4. Print the table.
5. Create the Item Class table using the field characteristics shown in Figure CLA1-1b. Use the name Class for the table.
6. Add the data shown in Figure CLA1-1b to the Class table.
7. Print the table.
8. Create and print a graph. The x-values for the graph should be item class codes and the y-values should be units on hand. Use the same graph type as that shown in Figure CLE1-3. Do not save the graph.

COMPUTER LABORATORY ASSIGNMENT 2
Creating an Employees Database

Purpose: To provide practice in creating and updating a database.

Problem: A small mail order catalog company has a database of employees. The database consists of two tables. The Employee table contains information on the employee. The Department table contains information on the department in which the employee works. You have been assigned to create and update this database.

Instructions: The data and structure for the Employee table are shown in Figure CLA1-2a on the next page. The data and structure for the Department table are shown in Figure CLA1-2b on the next page. You are to create both tables.

(continued)

COMPUTER LABORATORY ASSIGNMENT 2 (continued)

▶ **Structure of Employee table**

Field Name	Data Type	Field Size	Primary Key?	Description
Employee Number	Text	4	Yes	Employee number (primary key)
Employee Last Name	Text	12		Last name of employee
Employee First Name	Text	8		First name of employee
Department Code	Text	2		Department code
Pay Rate	Currency			Hourly pay rate

▶ **Data for Employee table**

Employee Number	Employee Last Name	Employee First Name	Department Code	Pay Rate
0011	Fitzmeyer	Luke	04	8.65
0023	McCall	Mark	04	8.10
0036	Radleman	Anne	01	9.90
0047	Pierce	Kim	02	6.30
0120	Rodgers	Andrew	03	7.75
0122	Alvarez	Maria	01	9.30
0225	Chou	Tanya	02	8.00
0226	Semple	Peter	04	6.80
0229	Lewistom	Daniel	03	9.00
0330	Garrison	Chandra	03	8.80
0337	Navarre	David	01	11.00
0441	Evanston	John	02	6.30

FIGURE CLA1-2a

▶ **Structure of Department table**

Field Name	Data Type	Field Size	Primary Key?	Description
Department Code	Text	2	Yes	Department code (primary key)
Department Name	Text	16		Name of department

▶ **Data for Department table**

Department Code	Department Name
01	Accounting
02	Customer Service
03	Purchasing
04	Shipping

FIGURE CLA1-2b

Perform the following tasks using Access:

1. Create a new database in which to store all the files related to the Employee data. Name the database Emp.
2. Create the Employee table using the structure shown in Figure CLA1-2a. Use the name Employee for the table.
3. Add the data shown in Figure CLA1-2a to the Employee table.
4. Print the table.
5. Create the Department table using the structure shown in Figure CLA1-2b. Use the name Department for the table.
6. Add the data shown in Figure CLA1-2b to the Department table.
7. Print the table.
8. Three new employees have just joined the company. Open the Employee table and add the following three employees.

Employee Number	Employee Last Name	Employee First Name	Department Code	Pay Rate
0756	Ping	Tao	03	7.10
0787	Mendes	Alberto	02	8.90
0866	Whitestone	Evelyn	03	6.90

9. Print the table.
10. Create and print a graph. The x-values for the graph should be department codes and the y-values should be pay rates. Use the same graph type as that shown in Figure CLE1-3. Do not save the graph.

COMPUTER LABORATORY ASSIGNMENT 3
Creating a Movies Database

Purpose: To provide practice in creating and updating a database.

Problem: A family has a database of video tapes they have collected. This database consists of two tables. The Movie table contains information on the movies in the collection. The Director table contains information on the individuals who directed the movie. You have been assigned to create and update this database.

Instructions: The data and structure for the Movie table are shown in Figure CLA1-3a on the next page. The data and structure for the Director table are shown in Figure CLA1-3b on the next page. You are to create both tables.

(continued)

COMPUTER LABORATORY ASSIGNMENT 3 (continued)

▶ **Structure of Movie table**

Field Name	Data Type	Field Size	Primary Key?	Description
Movie Number	Text	3	Yes	Movie number (primary key)
Movie Title	Text	21		Title of movie
Year Made	Number			Year movie was released (Use Integer as the FieldSize.)
Movie Type	Text	6		Movie category
Length	Number			Length of movie in minutes (Use Integer as the FieldSize.)
Nominations	Number			Number of award nominations (Use Integer as the FieldSize.)
Awards	Number			Number of awards (Use Integer as the FieldSize.)
Director Code	Text	2		Director code

▶ **Data for Movie table**

Movie Number	Movie Title	Year Made	Movie Type	Length	Nominations	Awards	Director Code
001	Amy Mason	1978	DRAMA	92	5	4	01
002	Breakdown	1965	SUSPEN	92	4	0	04
003	Dancing Duo	1972	COMEDY	137	3	1	04
004	The Dirty Horse	1960	WESTER	137	1	0	03
007	The Brass Ring	1949	DRAMA	82	0	0	03
008	Wild Willie	1970	WESTER	108	3	1	03
010	Murder and Mayhem	1979	COMEDY	96	3	1	01
011	Hot Potato	1964	COMEDY	120	0	0	03
012	Last Resort	1980	HORROR	95	1	0	01
013	Strange Business	1959	SUSPEN	129	6	2	03
015	House of Laughter	1969	HORROR	140	2	0	04
016	Hot Potato	1940	SUSPEN	99	0	0	02
017	My Brother Pete	1955	DRAMA	111	6	3	03
019	Caterpillars	1964	SCI FI	115	2	0	02
020	Missing Month	1941	SUSPEN	129	1	1	02

FIGURE CLA1-3a

▸ **Structure of Director table**

Field Name	Data Type	Field Size	Primary Key?	Description
Director Code	Text	2	Yes	Director code (primary key)
Director Name	Text	18		Name of director

▸ **Data for Director table**

Director Code	Director Name
01	Harhuis, Stacy
02	Greiner, Kimberly
03	Valdez, Roberto
04	Lefever, F. X.

FIGURE CLA1-3b

Perform the following tasks using Access:

1. Create a new database in which to store all the files related to the movie data. Name the database Mov.
2. Create the Movie table using the structure shown in Figure CLA1-3a. Change the Field Size for the Year Made, Length, Nominations, and Awards fields to Integer. (Hint: Integer will store the values as whole numbers.) Use the name Movie for the table.
3. Add the data shown in Figure CLA1-3a to the Movie table.
4. Print the table.
5. Create the Director table using the structure shown in Figure CLA1-3b. Use the name Director for the table.
6. Add the data shown in Figure CLA1-3b to the Director table.
7. Print the table.
8. Open the Movie table and change the title for movie number 008 to *Wild Wild Willie.*
9. The Year entry for *My Brother Pete* is incorrect. Change it to 1956.
10. Delete the record for movie number 11.
11. Print the table.
12. Create and print a graph. The x-values for the graph should be director codes and the y-values should be average movie lengths. Use the same graph type as that shown in Figure CLE1-3. (Hint: Choose Average on the Graph Wizard dialog box.) Do not save the graph.

COMPUTER LABORATORY ASSIGNMENT 4
Creating a Books Database

Purpose: To provide practice in designing, creating, and updating a database.

Problem: A small bookstore owner has a book inventory database. A report giving the data for this database is shown in Figure CLA1-4. The owner has asked you to design the database for the bookstore, that is, you must determine the tables, fields, primary keys, and field characteristics. When you have finished designing the database, you are to create the tables and then update the database.

Wednesday, January 19, 1994			BOOK				Page 1
Book Code	**Title**	**Author**	**Publisher Name**	**Publisher Code**	**Book Type**	**Price**	**Units on Hand**
0599	The Man From Now	Cara Bailey	Sampson-Irwin	SI	HOR	$5.95	1
0643	Albert's End	Cara Bailey	Sampson-Irwin	SI	HOR	$22.95	0
1129	Dark Alley	George Chan	Barnum Books	BB	MYS	$4.50	3
139X	Rain in the Morning	Robert Eton	Peabody Books	PB	FIC	$4.95	2
1778	Manspirit	Eliza Henry	Vanderveen	VN	SFI	$17.95	3
3605	City of Secrets	George Chan	Barnum Books	BB	SUS	$6.95	3
3969	A Cat for Christa	Stacy Michaels	Sandt and Shipper	SS	FIC	$4.50	1
4999	Agatha's Way	Robert Eton	Peabody Books	PB	FIC	$4.95	2
5436	The Stinkpot	Eliza Henry	Vanderveen	VN	SUS	$6.95	0
6527	Academic Murder	Elena Torres	Sampson-Irwin	SI	MYS	$21.95	4
7114	The Ragbagger	George Chan	Barnum Books	BB	MYS	$6.95	2
7802	Kites	Stacy Michaels	Sandt and Shipper	SS	FIC	$7.50	1
8160	Evil Wind	Eliza Henry	Barnum Books	BB	SUS	$5.95	2
9934	Stripes and Solids	Robert Eton	Peabody Books	PB	MYS	$9.95	3

FIGURE CLA1-4

Instructions: Create both the Book and the Publisher tables.

Perform the following tasks using Access:

1. Using the data shown in Figure CLA1-4, determine the structure for the necessary tables.
2. Create a new database in which to store the tables and other files.
3. Create the tables.
4. Determine the table names.
5. Add the data shown in Figure CLA1-4 to the tables.
6. Print the tables.
7. Create and print a graph. The x-values for the graph should be publisher codes and the y-values should be average prices. (Hint: Choose Average on the Graph Wizard dialog box.)

QUERYING A DATABASE

You will have mastered the material in this project when you can:

- State the purpose of queries
- Create a new query
- Use a query to display all records and all fields
- Run a query
- Print the answer to a query
- Close a query
- Clear a query
- Use a query to display selected fields
- Use character data in criteria in a query
- Use wildcards in criteria
- Use numeric data in criteria

- Use comparison operators
- Use compound criteria involving AND
- Use compound criteria involving OR
- Sort the answer to a query
- Join tables in a query
- Restrict the records in a join
- Use computed fields in a query
- Calculate statistics in a query
- Use grouping with statistics
- Save a query
- Use a saved query
- Graph the answer to a query

▶ WHAT ARE QUERIES?

 database management system like Access offers many useful features, among them the ability to answer questions. Figure 2-1 on the next page, for example, shows several questions:

- What is the balance of customer CE76?
- Which customers' names begin with Ro?
- Which customers are located in Oakdale?
- How much available credit do the customers currently have?
- Which customers with a $7,000 credit limit are represented by sales representative 07?

The answers to these questions, and many more, are found in the database, and Access can find the answers for you. When you pose a question to Access, or any other database management system, the question is called a query. A **query** is simply a question represented in a way that Access can understand.

Thus, to find the answer to a question, you first create a corresponding query using the techniques illustrated in this project. Once you have created the query, you instruct Access to **run the query**, that is, to perform the steps necessary to obtain the answer. When finished, Access will display the answer to your question in the format shown at the bottom of Figure 2-1.

A63

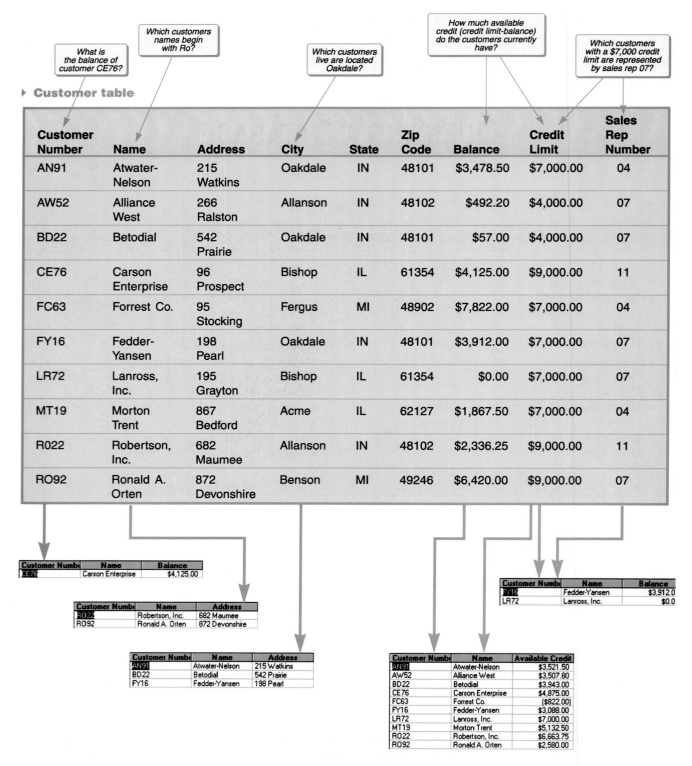

FIGURE 2-1

Starting Access and Opening the CUST Database

Before creating queries, you must first start Access. To do so, follow the same steps you used in Project 1 (see page A5). Once you have done so, you need to open the database you will use for the queries. For the queries in the text, this means you must open the CUST database (which holds the CUSTOMER and SLSREP tables you created in Project 1) by following the steps shown in Project 1 (see page A21). If you did not create the CUST database in Project 1 and intend to work through this project on a personal computer, you can open the CUST database from the subdirectory Access2 on the Student Diskette that accompanies this book.

▶ CREATING A NEW QUERY

You create a query by making entries in a special window called a **Select Query window**. Thus, once the database is open, the first step in creating a query is to create a new Select Query window. To do so, use the Query button (🔲) and then the New button in the Database window, as shown in the following steps. It is typically easier to work with the Select Query window if it is maximized. Thus, as a standard practice, maximize the Select Query window as soon as you have created it.

TO CREATE A NEW QUERY ▼

STEP 1 ▶

With the CUST database open and the Database window on the screen, point to the Query button (Figure 2-2).

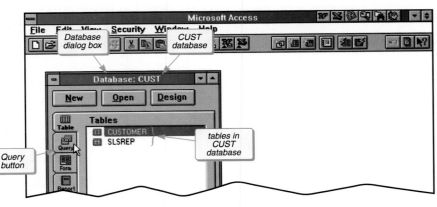

FIGURE 2-2

STEP 2 ▶

Choose the Query button.

The list of queries displays (Figure 2-3). Currently, there are none.

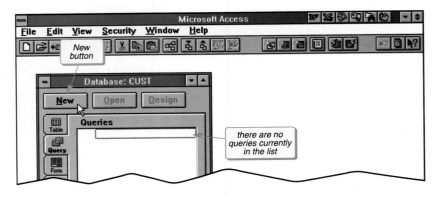

FIGURE 2-3

STEP 3 ▶

Choose the New button.

The New Query dialog box displays (Figure 2-4). For certain complex queries, Query Wizards can help you construct the query. For most queries, however, you will choose the New Query button (▣) and then construct the query yourself.

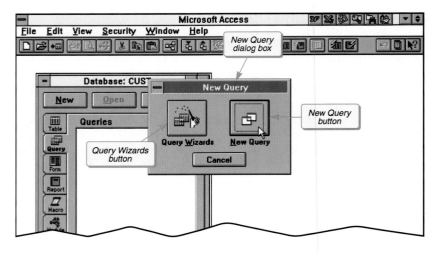

FIGURE 2-4

STEP 4 ▶

Choose the New Query button.

The Add Table dialog box displays (Figure 2-5). The list of tables in the CUST database displays in the dialog box. The CUSTOMER table is currently selected.

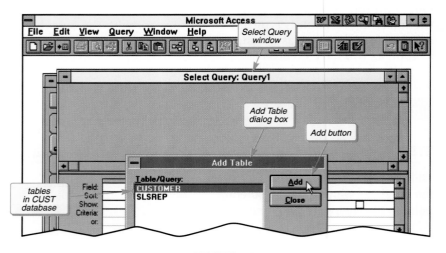

FIGURE 2-5

STEP 5 ▶

Add the CUSTOMER table to the query by choosing the Add button (Add).

A field list for the CUSTOMER table displays in the upper portion of the window (Figure 2-6).

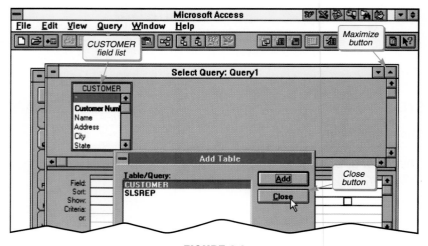

FIGURE 2-6

STEP 6 ▶

Choose the Close button (Close), maximize the Select Query window, and then point to the line that separates the upper and lower portions of the window.

*The Select Query window is maximized (Figure 2-7). The upper portion of the window contains a field list for the CUSTOMER table. The lower portion contains the **QBE grid**, the place where you specify fields to be included, sort order, and the criteria that the records you are looking for must satisfy. The name QBE comes from **query-by-example**, which is the general name for the type of approach that Microsoft Access uses for querying a database.*

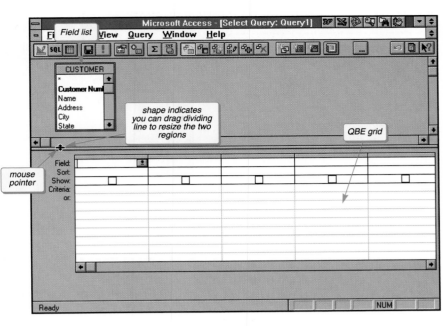

FIGURE 2-7

STEP 7 ▶

Drag the line down to the approximate position shown in Figure 2-8. Then, move the pointer to the lower edge of the field list box so that it changes shape to a heavy vertical line with two arrows (as shown in the figure).

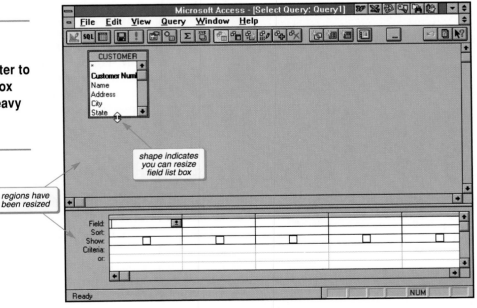

FIGURE 2-8

STEP 8 ▶

Drag the lower edge of the box down far enough so that all fields in the **CUSTOMER** table are visible.

All fields in the CUSTOMER table display (Figure 2-9).

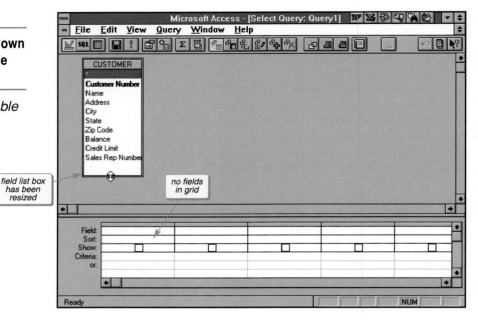

FIGURE 2-9

Once you have created a new Select Query window, you are ready to create the actual query by making entries in the QBE grid that appears in the lower portion of the window. You enter the names of the fields you want included in the **Field row** in the grid. You can also enter **criteria**, such as the fact that the customer number must be CE76, in the **Criteria row** of the grid. When you do so, only the record or records that match the criterion (Customer Number = CE76) will be included in the answer.

▶ DISPLAYING SELECTED FIELDS IN A QUERY

Only the fields that appear in the QBE grid will be included in the results of the query. Thus, to display only certain fields, place these fields in the grid and no others. If you inadvertently place the wrong field in the grid, select the Edit menu and then choose the Delete command to remove it. Alternatively, you could choose the Clear Grid command to clear the entire QBE grid and then start over.

Perform the following steps to create a query to show the customer number, name, and sales rep number for all customers by including only those fields in the QBE grid.

TO INCLUDE SELECTED FIELDS IN A QUERY ▼

STEP 1 ▶

Make sure you have maximized the
Select Query window containing a
field list for the CUSTOMER table in
the upper portion of the window and
an empty QBE grid in the lower
portion (see Figure 2-9).

STEP 2 ▶

Point to the Customer Number field
and double-click the left mouse
button to include the Customer
Number field in the query.

*The Customer Number is included
as the first field in the QBE grid
(Figure 2-10).*

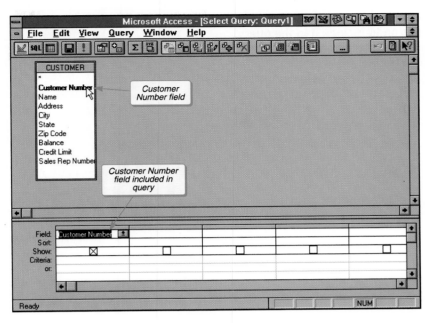

FIGURE 2-10

STEP 3 ▶

Point to the Name field and double-
click the left mouse button to
include it in the query.

*The Customer Number and
Name fields are included in
the QBE grid (Figure 2-11).*

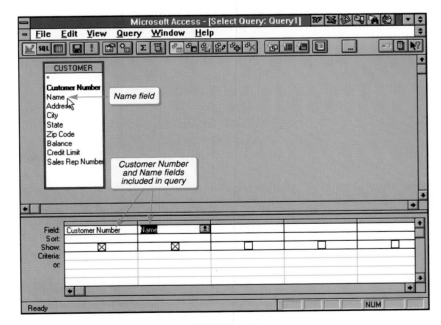

FIGURE 2-11

STEP 4 ▶

Point to the Sales Rep Number field and double-click the left mouse button to include it in the query.

The Customer Number, Name, and Sales Rep Number fields are included in the query (Figure 2-12).

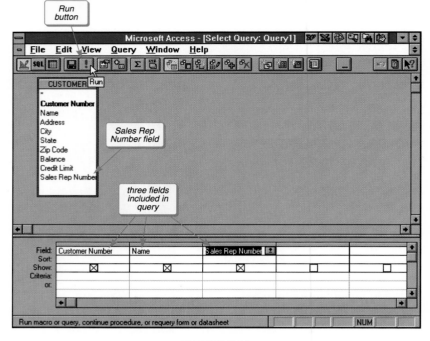

FIGURE 2-12

▶ RUNNING A QUERY

Once you have created the query, you need to run it by clicking the **Run button** (!). Access will then perform the steps necessary to obtain and display the answer. The set of records that make up the answer is called a **dynaset**, which stands for *dyna*mic *set* of records. Although it looks like a table stored on your disk, it really is not. It is constructed from data in the existing CUSTOMER table. If you were to change the data in the CUSTOMER table and then rerun this same query, the results would reflect the changes. This is the reason it is called dynamic. It changes right along with changes in the actual tables.

TO RUN A QUERY ▼

STEP 1 ▶

Click the Run button (see Figure 2-12).

The query is executed and the results display (Figure 2-13). The Run button changes to the Print Preview button. If the pointer points to the Print Preview button, the description of the button may obscure a portion of the first record.

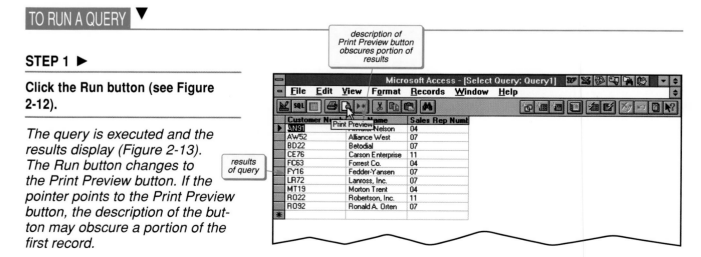

FIGURE 2-13

STEP 2 ▶

Move the mouse pointer to a position that is outside of the data and is not on the toolbar.

The data displays (Figure 2-14). No button description obscures a portion of the data. Notice that an extra blank row, marking the end of the table, displays at the end of the results. This will always be the case.

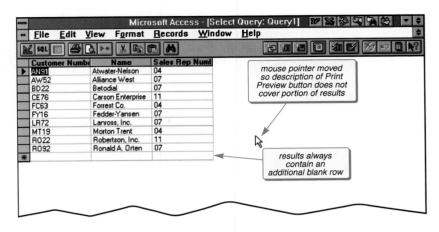

FIGURE 2-14

In all future examples, after running a query, move the mouse pointer so the description of the Print Preview button does not appear.

▶ PRINTING THE RESULTS OF A QUERY

T o print the results of a query, use the same techniques you learned in Project 1 to print the data in the table. These steps are summarized below:

TO PRINT THE RESULTS OF A QUERY ▼

STEP 1 ▶

Click the Print Preview button, as shown in Figure 2-15.

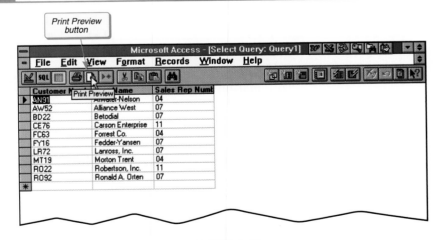

FIGURE 2-15

STEP 2 ▶

Click the Print button (Figure 2-16).

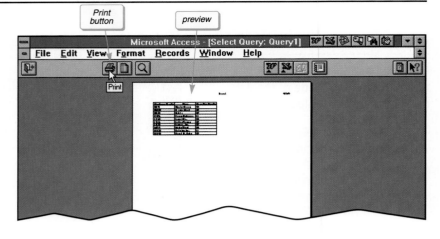

FIGURE 2-16

STEP 3 ▶

After the report prints, click the Close Window button (▣⁺) (Figure 2-17).

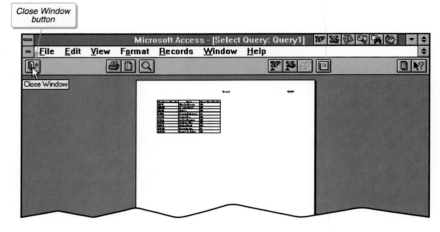

FIGURE 2-17

If the results of a query require Landscape orientation, switch to Landscape orientation before you click the Print button (as indicated in Project 1 on page A26).

▶ RETURNING TO THE SELECT QUERY WINDOW

You can examine the results of a query on your screen to see the answer to your question. You can scroll through the records, if necessary, just as you scroll through the records of any other table. You can also print a copy of the table. In any case, once you are finished working with the results, you can return to the Select Query window to ask another question. To do so, click the **Design View** button (▣) as shown in the following step.

TO RETURN TO THE SELECT QUERY WINDOW ▼

STEP 1 ▶

Click the Design View button (Figure 2-18).

The Select Query window displays once again.

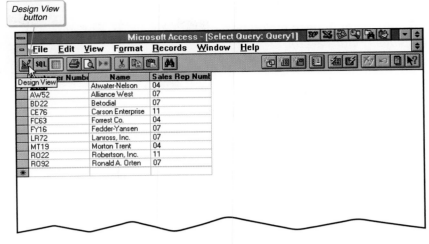

FIGURE 2-18

▶ CLOSING A QUERY

To remove the Select Query window from the desktop, close it. Access then asks if you want to save your query for future use. If you expect to need to create the same query often, save the query. For now, you will not save any queries. You will see how to save them later in the project. Perform the following steps to close a query without saving it.

TO CLOSE A QUERY ▼

STEP 1 ▶

Point to the Control-menu box for the Select Query window (Figure 2-19).

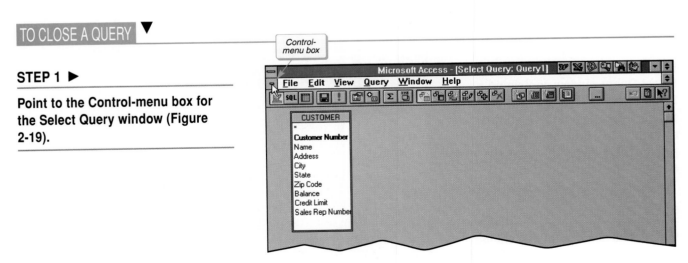

FIGURE 2-19

STEP 2 ▶

Double-click the Control-menu box.

The Microsoft Access dialog box displays (Figure 2-20).

STEP 3 ▶

Choose the No button (No) in the Microsoft Access dialog box.

The Select Query window is removed from the desktop.

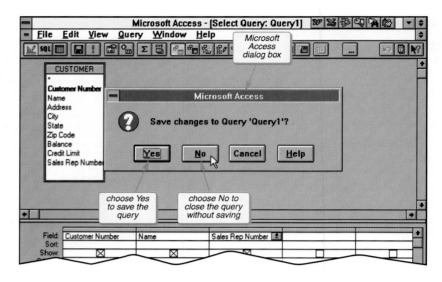

FIGURE 2-20

▶ INCLUDING ALL FIELDS IN A QUERY

I f you want to include all fields in a query, you could select each field individually. There is a simpler way, however. By selecting the asterisk (*) that appears in the field list, you are indicating that all fields are to be included. Perform the following steps to use the asterisk to include all fields.

TO INCLUDE ALL FIELDS IN A QUERY ▼

STEP 1 ▶

Be sure you have a maximized Select Query window containing a field list for the CUSTOMER table in the upper portion of the window and an empty QBE grid in the lower portion. (See Steps 1 through 8 on Pages A65 through A68.)

STEP 2 ▶

Point to the asterisk in the field list box (Figure 2-21).

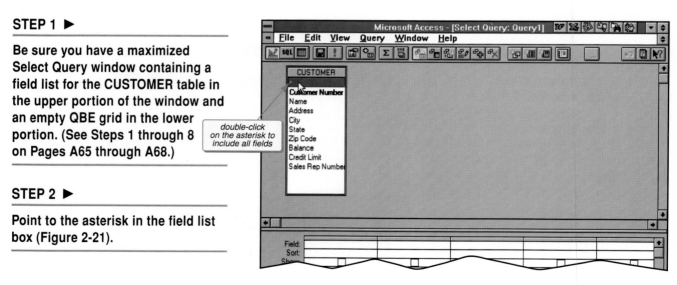

FIGURE 2-21

STEP 3 ▶

Double-click the left mouse button.

The table name, CUSTOMER, followed by an asterisk, is added to the QBE grid (Figure 2-22), indicating all fields are included.

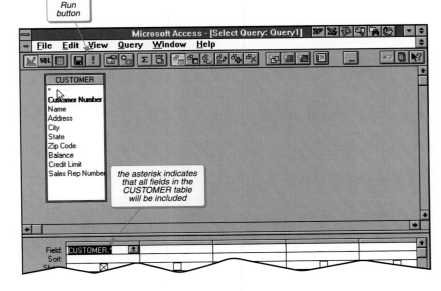

FIGURE 2-22

STEP 4 ▶

Click the Run button.

The results display and all fields in the CUSTOMER table are included (Figure 2-23).

STEP 5 ▶

Click the Design View button to return to the Select Query window.

The data sheet is replaced by the Select Query window (Figure 2-22).

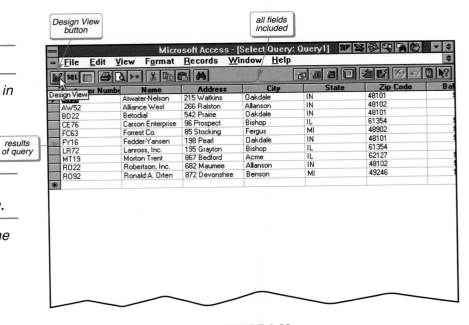

FIGURE 2-23

▶ CLEARING THE QBE GRID

I f you make mistakes as you are creating a query, you can fix them individually. Alternatively, you may simply want to clear out the entries in the QBE grid and start over. One way to clear out the entries is to close the Select Query window and then start a new query just as you did earlier. A simpler approach, however, is to choose the **Clear Grid command** from the Edit menu.

TO CLEAR A QUERY ▼

STEP 1 ▶

Click the Design View button to
return to the Select Query window,
if you have not already done so.
Select the Edit menu (Figure 2-24).

STEP 2 ▶

Choose the Clear Grid command.

*Access clears the QBE grid so
you can enter your next query.*

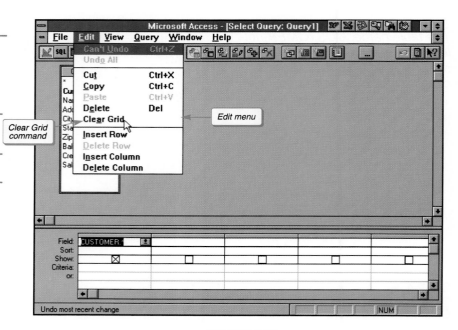

FIGURE 2-24

▶ ENTERING CRITERIA

When you use queries, you usually are looking for those records that satisfy some criterion. You might want the name of the customer whose number is CE76, for example, or the numbers, names, and addresses of those customers whose names start with Ro. To enter criteria, enter them on the **Criteria row** in the QBE grid underneath the field names to which the criteria applies. For example, to enter the fact that the customer number must be CE76, enter CE76 in the Criteria row underneath the Customer Number field. You must, of course, first add the Customer Number field to the QBE grid before you can enter the criterion.

The next examples illustrate the types of criteria that are available.

▶ USING TEXT DATA IN CRITERIA

To use text data in criteria, simply type the text in the Criteria row below the corresponding field name. Perform the following steps to query the CUSTOMER table and display the customer number, name, and balance of customer CE76.

TO USE TEXT DATA IN A CRITERIA ▼

STEP 1 ►

One-by-one, double-click the Customer Number, Name, and Balance fields to add them to the query. Then, point to the Criteria entry for the first field in the QBE grid.

The Customer Number, Name, and Balance fields are added to the QBE grid (Figure 2-25). The pointer points to the Criteria entry for the first field (Customer Number) and has changed shape to an I-beam.

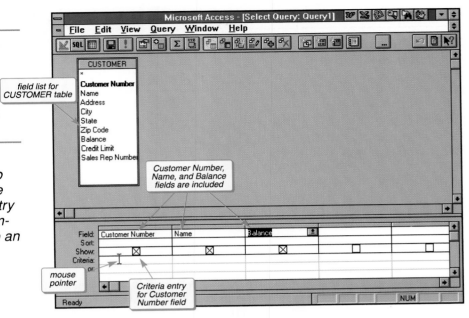

FIGURE 2-25

STEP 2 ►

Click the left mouse button and type `CE76` as the criterion for the Customer Number field.

The criterion is entered (Figure 2-26).

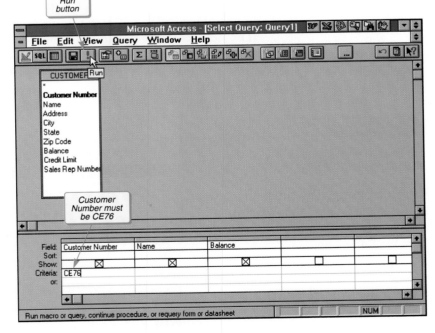

FIGURE 2-26

STEP 3 ▶

Run the query by clicking the Run button.

The results display (Figure 2-27). Only customer CE76 is included. (The extra blank row contains $0.00 in the Balance field. Unlike Text fields, which are left blank, Numeric and Currency fields in the extra row contain 0. Because Balance is a Currency field, the value displays as $0.00.)

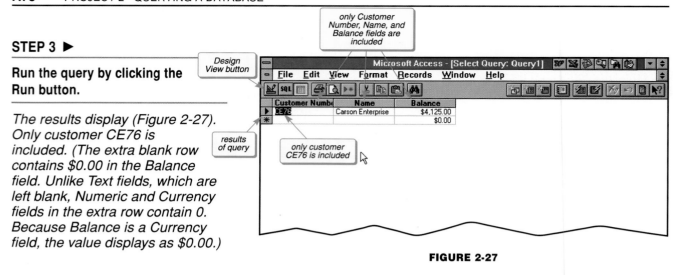

FIGURE 2-27

▶ USING WILDCARDS

Two special **wildcards** are available in Microsoft Access. Wildcards are symbols that represent any character or combination of characters.

The first of the two wildcards, the asterisk (*), represents any collection of characters. Thus Ro* represents the letters Ro, followed by any collection of characters. The other wildcard symbol is the question mark (?), which represents any individual character. Thus T?m represents the letter T, followed by any single character, followed by the letter m, such as Tim or Tom.

The next example illustrates using a wildcard to find the number, name, and address of those customers whose names begin with Ro. For this example, because you don't know how many characters will follow the Ro, the asterisk is appropriate.

TO USE A WILDCARD ▼

STEP 1 ▶

Click the Design View button to return to the Select Query window and choose the Clear Grid command from the Edit menu.

Access clears the QBE grid so you can enter your next query.

STEP 2 ▶

Include the Customer Number, Name, and Address fields in the query and then point to the Criteria entry for the second field (Figure 2-28).

FIGURE 2-28

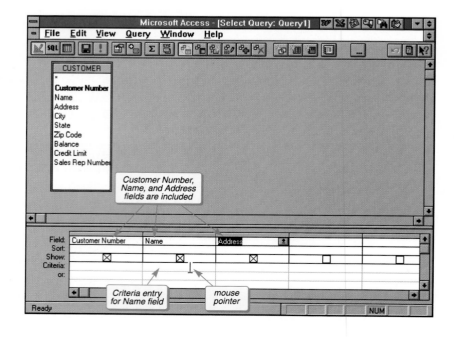

STEP 3 ▶

Click the left mouse button and type LIKE RO* **(Figure 2-29).**

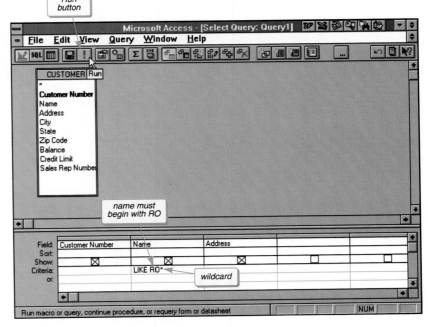

FIGURE 2-29

STEP 4 ▶

Click the Run button.

The results display (Figure 2-30). Only the customers whose names start with "Ro" are included.

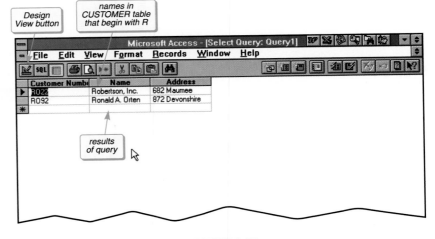

FIGURE 2-30

▶ USING CRITERIA FOR A FIELD NOT IN THE RESULT

I n some cases, you may have criteria for a particular field that should not appear in the results of the query. For example, you may wish to see the Customer Number, Name, and Address for all customers who live in Oakdale. The criteria involves the City field, which is not one of the fields to be included in the results.

In order to enter a criterion for the City field, it must be included in the QBE grid. Normally, this would also mean it would appear in the results. To prevent this from happening, remove the X from its **Show check box**, the box in the **Show row** of the grid. The steps on the next page illustrate the process by displaying the Customer Number, Name, and Address for customers living in Oakdale.

TO USE CRITERIA FOR A FIELD NOT IN THE RESULT ▼

STEP 1 ►

Click the Design View button to return to the Select Query window and choose the Clear Grid command from the Edit menu.

Access clears the QBE grid so you can enter your next query.

STEP 2 ►

Include the Customer Number, Name, Address, and City fields in the query. Enter `Oakdale` as the criterion for the City field and then point to the City field's Show check box (Figure 2-31).

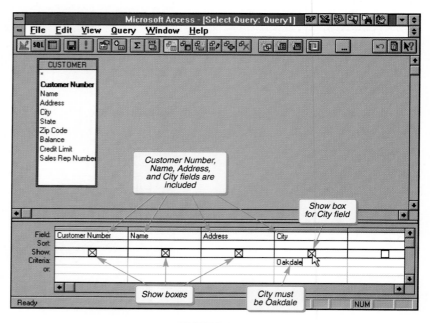

FIGURE 2-31

STEP 3 ►

Click the left mouse button to remove the X in the Show check box.

The X is removed from the Show check box for the City field (Figure 2-32), indicating it will not "show" in the result.

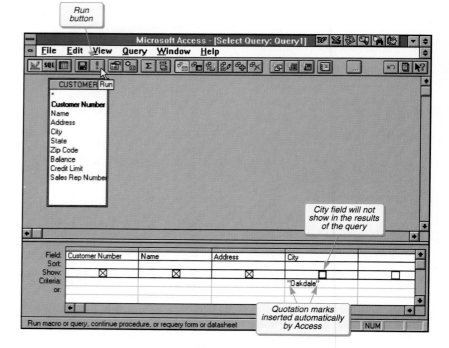

FIGURE 2-32

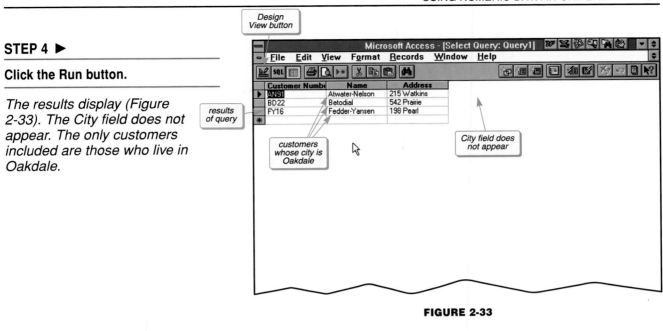

STEP 4 ▶

Click the Run button.

The results display (Figure 2-33). The City field does not appear. The only customers included are those who live in Oakdale.

FIGURE 2-33

▶ USING NUMERIC DATA IN CRITERIA

To enter a number in a criterion, type the number without any dollar signs or commas. The next example displays all customers whose credit limit is $7,000. To do so, type 7000 as a criterion for the Credit Limit field.

TO USE NUMERIC DATA IN CRITERIA ▼

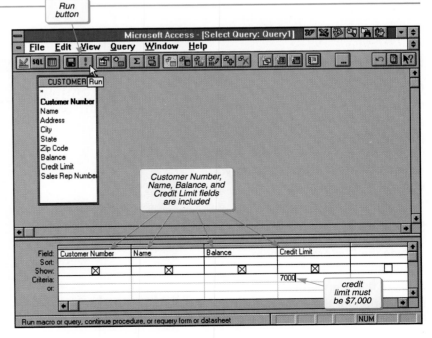

STEP 1 ▶

Click the Design View button to return to the Select Query window and choose the Clear Grid command from the Edit menu.

Access clears the QBE grid so you can enter your next query.

STEP 2 ▶

Include the Customer Number, Name, Balance, and Credit Limit fields in the query. Enter 7000 as the criterion for the Credit Limit field (Figure 2-34). Notice that there is no need to enter commas or dollar signs in the criterion.

FIGURE 2-34

STEP 3 ▶

Click the Run button.

The results display (Figure 2-35). Only those customers who have a $7,000 credit limit are included.

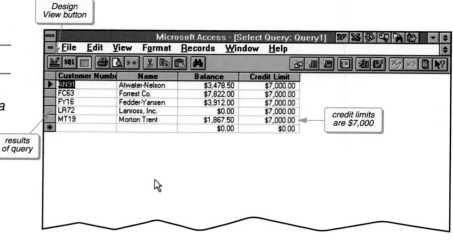

FIGURE 2-35

▶ USING COMPARISON OPERATORS

U nless you specify otherwise, Access assumes that the criteria you enter involve equality (exact matches). In the last query, for example, you were requesting those customers whose credit limit is *equal to* 7000. If you want something other than an exact match, you must enter the appropriate **comparison operator**. The choices are > (greater than), < (less than), >= (greater than or equal to), <= (less than or equal to), and NOT (not equal to).

Perform the following steps to use the > operator to find all customers whose balance is over $5,000.

TO USE A COMPARISON OPERATOR IN A CRITERION ▼

STEP 1 ▶

Click the Design View button to return to the Select Query window and choose the Clear Grid command from the Edit menu.

Access clears the QBE grid so you can enter your next query.

STEP 2 ▶

Include the Customer Number, Name, Balance, and Credit Limit fields in the query. Enter >5000 as the criterion for the Balance field (Figure 2-36).

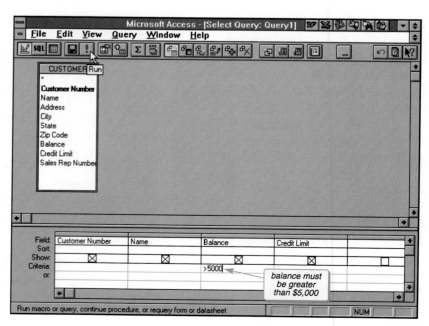

FIGURE 2-36

STEP 3 ▶

Click the Run button.

*The results display (Figure 2-37).
Only those customers who have a
balance over $5,000 are included.*

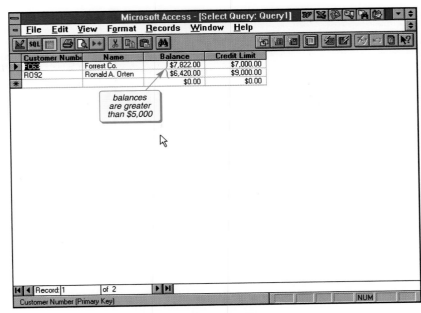

FIGURE 2-37

▶ Using Compound Criteria

O ften, you will have more than one criterion that the data for which you
are searching must satisfy. This type of criterion is called a **compound
criterion**. There are two types of compound criteria.

   In **AND criteria**, each individual criterion must be true in order for the compound criterion to be true. For example, an AND criterion would allow you to find
those customers who have a $7,000 credit limit *and* who are represented by sales
rep 07.

   OR criteria, on the other hand, are true, provided either individual criterion
is true. An OR criterion would allow you to find those customers who have a
$7,000 credit limit *or* who are represented by sales rep 07. In this case, any cus-
tomer whose credit limit is $7,000 would be included in the answer whether or
not the customer was represented by sales rep 07. Likewise, any customer represented by sales rep 07 would be included whether or not the customer had a
$7,000 credit limit.

   To combine criteria with AND, place the criteria on the same line. Perform
the steps on the next page to use an AND criterion to find those customers whose
credit limit is $7,000 and who are represented by sales rep 07.

TO USE A COMPOUND CRITERION INVOLVING "AND"

STEP 1 ▶

Click the Design View button to return to the Select Query window and choose the Clear Grid command from the Edit menu.

Access clears the QBE grid so you can enter your next query.

STEP 2 ▶

Include the Customer Number, Name, Balance, Credit Limit, and Sales Rep Number fields in the query. Then, point to the Criteria entry for the Credit Limit field (Figure 2-38).

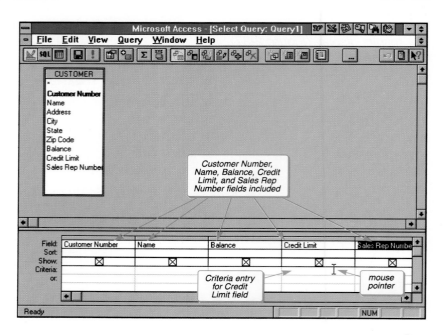

FIGURE 2-38

STEP 3 ▶

Click the left mouse button and then enter 7000 as a criterion for the Credit Limit field (Figure 2-39).

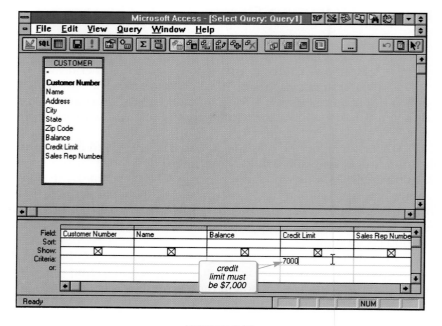

FIGURE 2-39

STEP 4 ▶

Point to the criteria entry for the Sales Rep Number field, click the left mouse button, and enter 07 **as the criterion for the Sales Rep Number field.**

The fields shift to the left (Figure 2-40). Criteria have been entered for the Credit Limit and Sales Rep Number fields.

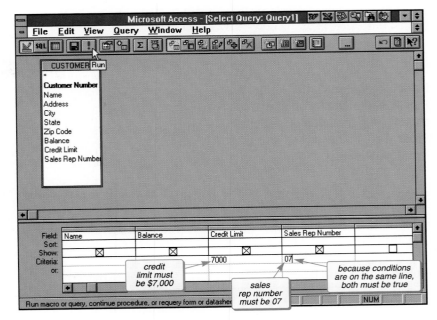

FIGURE 2-40

STEP 5 ▶

Click the Run button.

The results display (Figure 2-41). Only those customers who have a $7,000 credit limit and whose sales rep number is 07 are included.

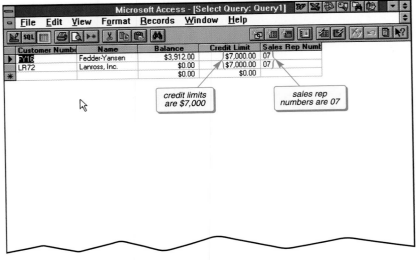

FIGURE 2-41

To combine criteria with OR, the criteria must be entered on separate lines in the Criteria portion of the grid. The steps on the next page use an OR criterion to find those customers who have a $7,000 credit limit or who are represented by sales rep 07 (or both).

TO USE A COMPOUND CRITERION INVOLVING "OR"

STEP 1 ▶

Select the Criteria entry for the Sales Rep Number field by pointing to it and clicking the left mouse button. Press the BACKSPACE key four times to delete the entry ("07").

STEP 2 ▶

Point to the second line of criteria (the line labeled "or:") for the Sales Rep Number field, click the left mouse button, and type 07.

The criteria are entered for the Credit Limit and Sales Rep Number fields on different lines (Figure 2-42).

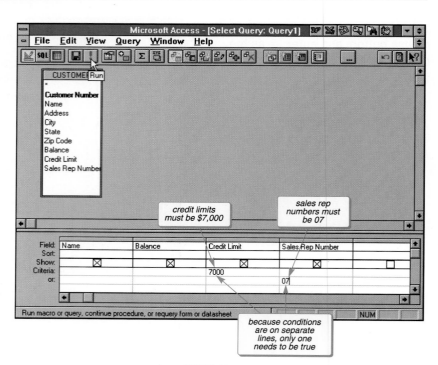

FIGURE 2-42

STEP 3 ▶

Click the Run button.

The results display (Figure 2-43). Only those customers who have a $7,000 credit limit or whose sales rep number is 07 are included.

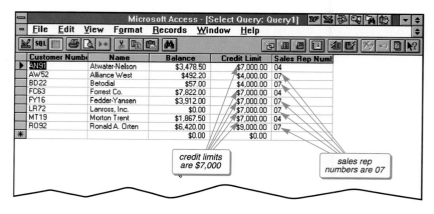

FIGURE 2-43

▶ SORTING DATA IN A QUERY

I n some queries, the order in which the records are displayed really does not matter. All you care about are the records that appear in the results. It doesn't matter which one is first or which one is last.

In other queries, however, the order can be very important. You may want to see customers' balances and may want them arranged from the highest to the lowest. Perhaps you want to see customers' addresses and want them listed by state. Further, within all the customers in a given state, you may want them to be listed by city.

To order the records in the answer to a query in a particular way, you **sort** the records. The field or fields on which the records are sorted is called the **sort key**. If you are sorting on more than one field (such as sorting by city within state), the more important field (state) is called the **major key** and the less important field (city) is called the **minor key**.

To sort in Microsoft Access, specify the sort order in the Sort line of the QBE grid underneath the field that is the sort key. If you specify more than one sort key, the sort key on the left will be the major key and the one on the right will be the minor key.

Perform the following steps to sort the data in the CUSTOMER table by state.

TO SORT DATA ▼

STEP 1 ►

Be sure you have maximized the Select Query window containing a field list for the CUSTOMER table in the upper portion of the window and an empty QBE grid in the lower portion.

STEP 2 ►

Include the State field in the QBE grid, point to the Sort entry under the State field, and click the left mouse button. Click the down arrow that appears.

The State field is included (Figure 2-44). A list of available sort orders displays.

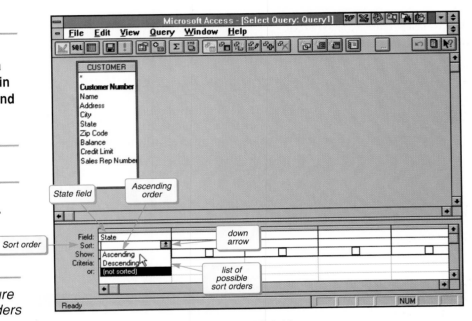

FIGURE 2-44

STEP 3 ►

Choose Ascending order by pointing to Ascending and clicking the left mouse button (Figure 2-45).

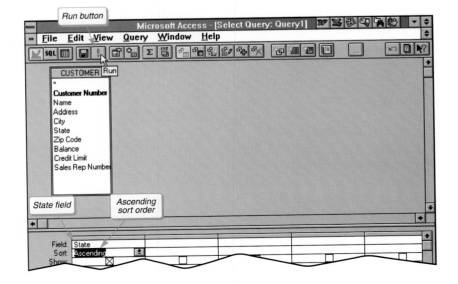

FIGURE 2-45

STEP 4 ▶

Run the query.

The results contain the state names from the CUSTOMER table (Figure 2-46). The names appear in alphabetical order. Duplicates are included.

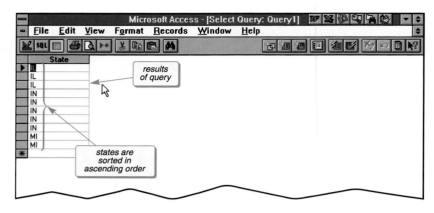

FIGURE 2-46

▶ SORTING ON MULTIPLE KEYS

T he next example lists the number, name, credit limit, and sales rep number for all customers. The data is to be sorted by sales rep number within descending credit limit. The phrase "sales rep number *within* descending credit limit" means the sales rep number is the minor key and the credit limit is the major key. It also means credit limits are to appear in descending (high-to-low) order. The following steps accomplish this by specifying the Credit Limit and Sales Rep Number fields as sort keys.

TO SORT ON MULTIPLE KEYS ▼

STEP 1 ▶

Click the Design View button to return to the Select Query window and choose the Clear Grid command from the Edit menu.

Access clears the QBE grid so you can enter your next query.

STEP 2 ▶

Include the Customer Number, Name, Credit Limit, and Sales Rep Number fields in the query. Select Descending as the sort order for the Credit Limit field and Ascending as the sort order for the Sales Rep Number field (Figure 2-47).

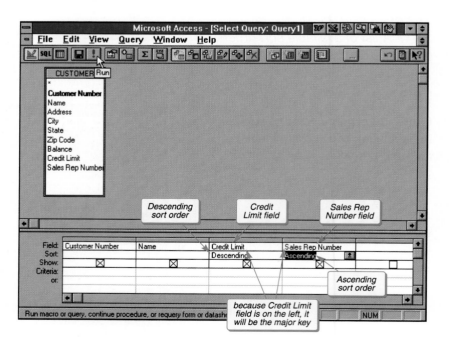

FIGURE 2-47

STEP 3 ▶

Run the query.

The results display (Figure 2-48). The customers are sorted by credit limit with the highest credit limit first. Within the collection of customers having the same credit limit, the customers are sorted by sales rep number.

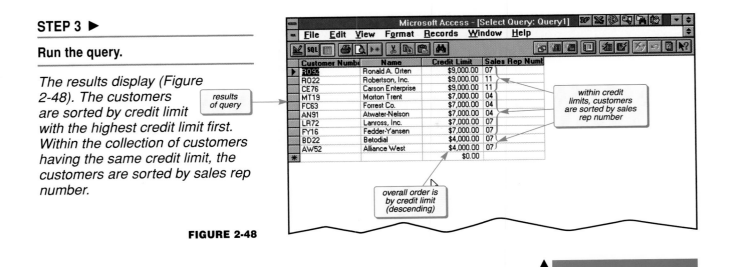

FIGURE 2-48

It is important to remember that the major key must appear to the left of the minor key in the QBE grid. If you attempted to sort the customer data by city within state, for example, but placed the City field to the left of the State field (Figure 2-49a), the City field would be considered to be the major key. This would lead to the results shown in Figure 2-49b. As you can see, the data is sorted alphabetically by city, *not by city within state*.

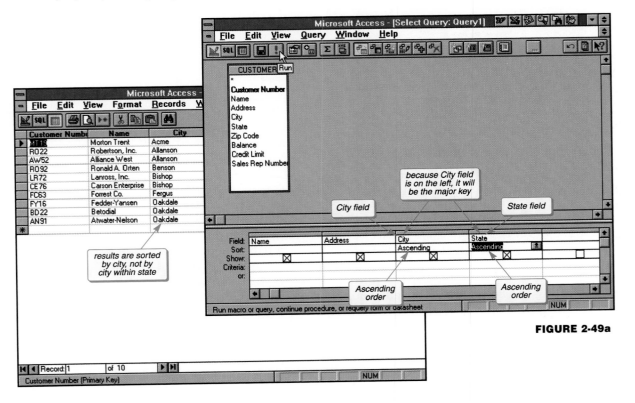

FIGURE 2-49a

FIGURE 2-49b

To sort in the correct order, add the State field to the QBE grid *before* adding the City field (Figure 2-50a). This yields the results shown in Figure 2-50b. The data is sorted by state. Within all the customers in any given state, the customers are sorted by city.

FIGURE 2-50a

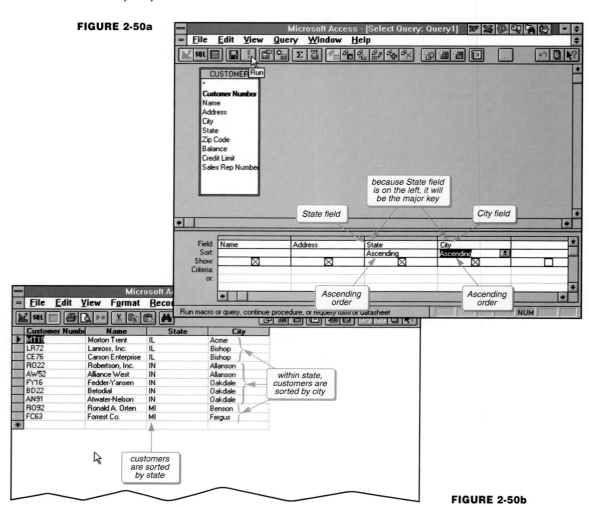

FIGURE 2-50b

▶ OMITTING DUPLICATES

As you saw earlier, when you sort data, duplicates are included. In Figure 2-46 on page A88, for example, IL appeared three times, IN appeared five times, and MI appeared twice. If you don't want duplicates included, use the Properties command and specify Yes for Unique Values only. Perform the following steps to produce a sorted list of the states in the CUSTOMER table in which each state is only listed once.

TO OMIT DUPLICATES ▼

STEP 1 ►

Click the Design View button to return to the Select Query window and choose the Clear Grid command from the Edit menu.

Access clears the QBE grid so you can enter your next query.

STEP 2 ►

Include the State field, select Ascending as the sort order, point to the second field in the QBE grid (the empty field following State), and click the left mouse button to move the insertion point. Then, select the View menu (Figure 2-51).

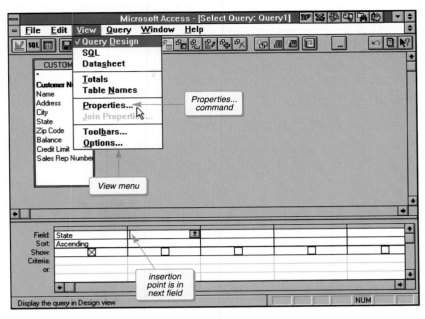

FIGURE 2-51

STEP 3 ►

Choose the Properties command.

The Query Properties dialog box displays (Figure 2-52).

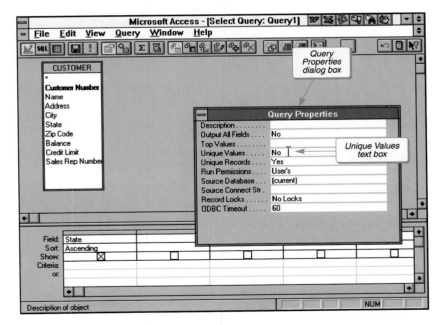

FIGURE 2-52

STEP 4 ▶

Point to the Unique Values text box, click the left mouse button, and then click the down arrow that displays to produce a list of available choices for Unique Values (Figure 2-53).

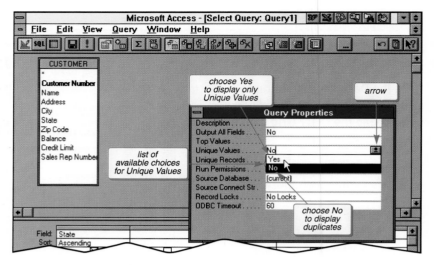

FIGURE 2-53

STEP 5 ▶

Select Yes by clicking the left mouse button and then double-click the Control-menu box for the Query Properties dialog box to close the dialog box.

STEP 6 ▶

Run the query.

The results display (Figure 2-54). The states are sorted alphabetically. Each state is included only once.

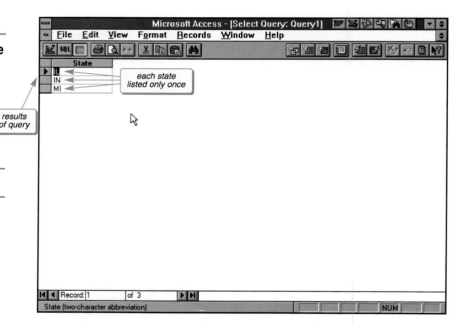

FIGURE 2-54

▶ JOINING TABLES

S uppose you want to list the number and name of each customer along with the number and name of the customer's sales rep. The customer name is in the CUSTOMER table, whereas the sales rep name is in the SLSREP table. Thus, this query cannot be satisfied using a single table. You need to **join** the tables; that is, to find records in the two tables that have identical values in matching fields (Figure 2-55). In this example, you need to find records in the CUSTOMER and the SLSREP tables that have the same value in the Sales Rep Number fields.

▸ **CUSTOMER Table**

▸ **Sales Rep (SLSREP) Table**

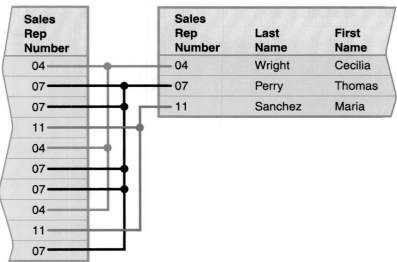

FIGURE 2-55

To join tables in Access, you must first bring field lists for both tables to the upper portion of the Select Query window. Access will draw a line between matching fields in the two tables, indicating that the tables are related. You can then select fields from either table. Access will join the tables automatically.

The first step is to add an additional table (the SLSREP table) to the query, as illustrated in the following steps.

TO JOIN TABLES ▼

STEP 1 ▶

Click the Design View button to return to the Select Query window and choose the Clear Grid command from the Edit menu.

Access clears the QBE grid so you can enter your next query.

STEP 2 ▶

Point to the Add Table button (▣) (Figure 2-56).

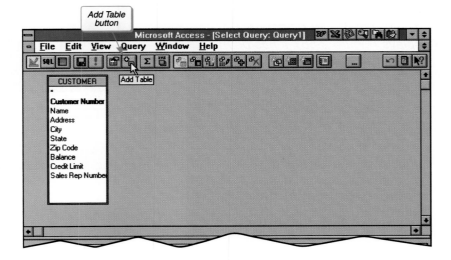

FIGURE 2-56

STEP 3 ▶

Click the Add Table button.

The Add Table dialog box displays (Figure 2-57).

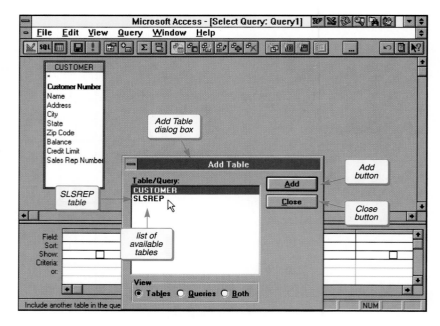

FIGURE 2-57

STEP 4 ▶

Choose the SLSREP table by pointing to it, clicking the left mouse button, and then clicking the Add button. Close the Add Table dialog box by double-clicking its Control-menu box. Expand the size of the field list so all the fields in the SLSREP table display.

A field list for the SLSREP table displays (Figure 2-58). It has been enlarged so all the SLSREP fields are visible. A line appears, joining the Sales Rep Number fields in the two field lists. This line indicates how the tables are related, that is, linked through the matching fields. If you did not name the fields the same, Access will not insert the line. You can insert it manually by pointing to one of the two matching fields and dragging the pointer to the other.

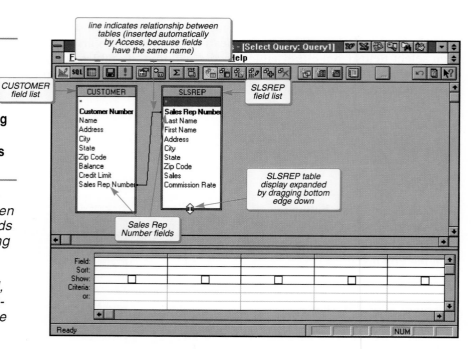

FIGURE 2-58

STEP 5 ▶

Include the Customer Number, Name, and Sales Rep Number fields from the CUSTOMER table and the Last Name and First Name fields from the SLSREP table (Figure 2-59). Notice that you don't have to choose the Sales Rep Number from both tables in order for the join to work.

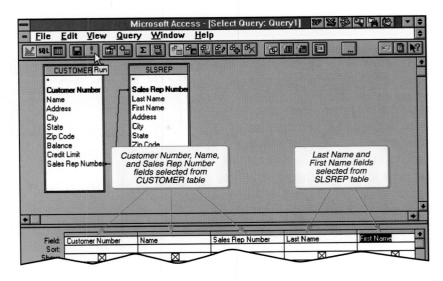

FIGURE 2-59

STEP 6 ▶

Run the query.

The results display (Figure 2-60). They contain data from the CUSTOMER table, as well as data from the SLSREP table.

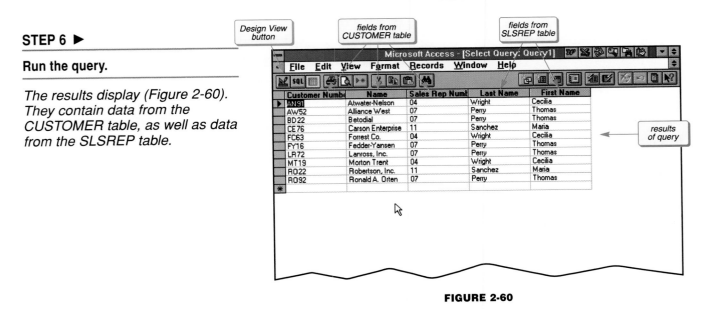

FIGURE 2-60

▶ RESTRICTING RECORDS IN A JOIN

Sometimes, you will want to join tables, but you will not want to include all possible records. In such cases, you will relate the tables and include fields just as you did before. You will also include criteria. For example, to include the same fields as in the previous query, but only those customers whose credit limit is $7,000, you will make the same entries as before and then also enter the number 7000 as a criterion for the Credit Limit field.

Perform the steps on the next page to modify the query from the previous example to restrict the records that will be included in the join.

TO RESTRICT THE RECORDS IN A JOIN ▼

STEP 1 ▶

Click the Design View button to return to the Select Query window. Add the Credit Limit field to the query and then click the right scroll arrow so it displays. Enter 7000 **as the criterion for the Credit Limit field and then click the Show check box for the Credit Limit field to remove the X.**

The Credit Limit field displays in the QBE grid (Figure 2-61). A criterion is entered for the Credit Limit field and the Show check box is blank, indicating the field will not display in the results of the query.

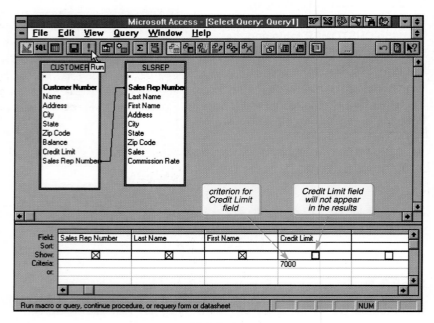

FIGURE 2-61

STEP 2 ▶

Run the query.

The results display (Figure 2-62). Only those customers with a credit limit of $7,000 appear in the result. The Credit Limit field does not display.

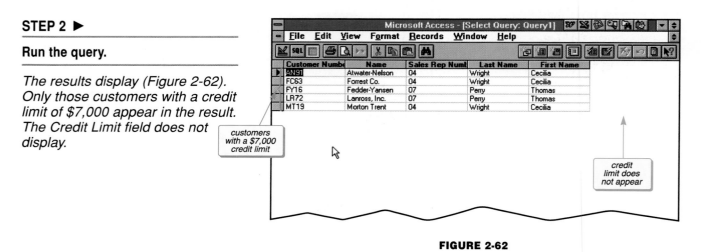

FIGURE 2-62

▶ Using Computed Fields in a Query

Suppose you want to find each customer's available credit. This poses a problem, because there is no field for available credit in the CUSTOMER table. You can compute it, however, because the available credit is equal to the credit limit minus the balance. Such a field is called a **computed field**.

To include computed fields in queries, you enter a name for the computed field, a colon, and then the expression in one of the columns in the Field row. For available credit, enter `Available Credit:[Credit Limit]-[Balance]`, for example. You can type this directly into the Field row. You will not be able to see the entire entry, however, because there is not enough room for it. A better way is to select the column in the Field row in which you wish to place the computed field and then press SHIFT+F2. A dialog box (the Zoom dialog box) will display. You can then type the expression in the Zoom dialog box.

You are not restricted to subtraction in computations. You can use addition (+), multiplication (*), or division (/). You can also include parentheses [()] in your computations to indicate which computations should be done first.

Perform the following steps to use a computed field to display the number, name, and available credit of all customers.

TO USE A COMPUTED FIELD IN A QUERY ▼

STEP 1 ▶

Be sure you have maximized the Select Query window containing a field list for the CUSTOMER table (but not the SLSREP table) in the upper portion of the window and an empty QBE grid in the lower portion. You can do this by closing the query without saving it (see page A73) and then starting over (see page A65). As an alternative, click any field in the list of fields in the SLSREP table and then choose the Remove Table command from the Query menu. This will remove the SLSREP table from the Select Query window.

STEP 2 ▶

Include the Customer Number and Name fields. Point to the Field entry in the third column in the QBE grid, click the left mouse button and, then press SHIFT+F2. Type `Available Credit:[Credit Limit]-[Balance]` in the Zoom dialog box that displays.

The Zoom dialog box displays (Figure 2-63). The expression you entered displays within the dialog box.

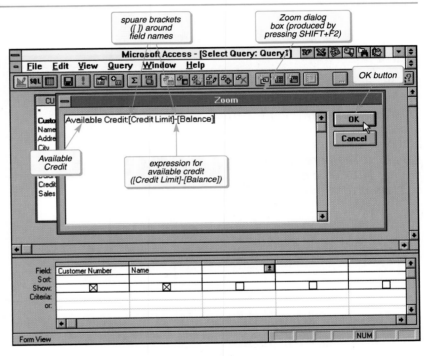

FIGURE 2-63

STEP 3 ▶

Choose the OK button.

The Zoom dialog box no longer displays (Figure 2-64). The final portion of the expression you entered displays in the third field within the QBE grid.

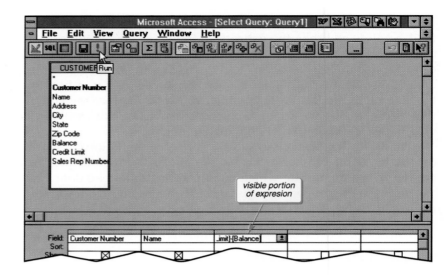

FIGURE 2-64

STEP 4 ▶

Run the query.

The results display (Figure 2-65). Microsoft Access has calculated and displayed the available credit amounts. The parentheses around $822.00 indicate it is a negative number.

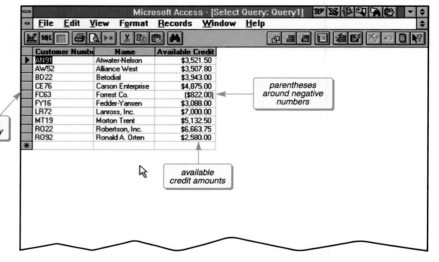

FIGURE 2-65

▶ CALCULATING STATISTICS

Microsoft Access supports the built-in functions: COUNT, SUM, AVG (average), MAX (largest value), MIN (smallest value), STDEV (standard deviation), VAR (variance), FIRST, and LAST. To use any of these in a query, you include it in the Totals row in the QBE grid. The Totals row does not routinely appear in the grid. To include it, select the View menu and then choose the Totals command.

The following example illustrates how you use these functions by calculating the average balance for all customers.

TO CALCULATE STATISTICS ▼

STEP 1 ►

Click the Design View button to return to the Select Query window and choose the Clear Grid command from the Edit menu.

Access clears the QBE grid so you can enter your next query.

STEP 2 ►

Select the View menu (Figure 2-66).

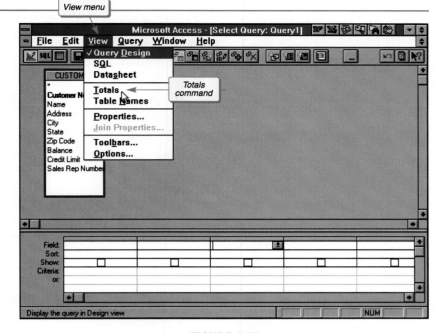

FIGURE 2-66

STEP 3 ►

Choose the Totals command and include the Balance field.

The Total row is now included in the QBE grid (Figure 2-67). The Balance field is included and the entry in the Total row is Group By. The mouse pointer, which has changed shape to an I-beam, is pointing to the Total row under the Balance field.

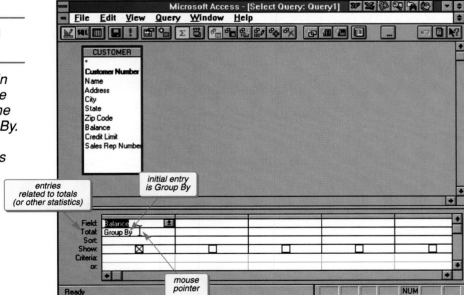

FIGURE 2-67

STEP 4 ▶

Point to the Total row under the Balance field and click the left mouse button (Figure 2-68).

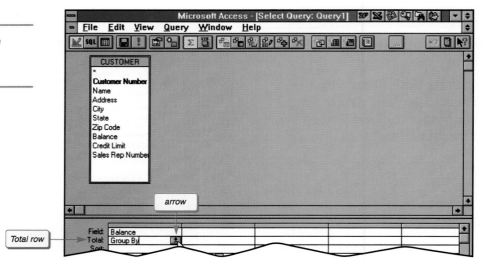

FIGURE 2-68

STEP 5 ▶

Click the down arrow that appears.

The list of available selections displays (Figure 2-69).

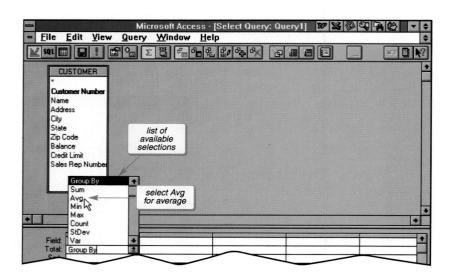

FIGURE 2-69

STEP 6 ▶

Point to Avg and click the left mouse button.

Avg is selected (Figure 2-70).

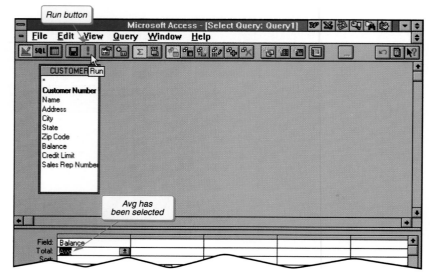

FIGURE 2-70

STEP 7 ▶

Run the query.

The result displays (Figure 2-71), showing the average balance for all customers.

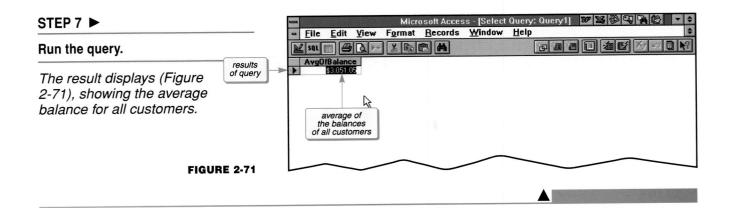

FIGURE 2-71

▶ USING CRITERIA IN CALCULATING STATISTICS

S ometimes, calculating statistics for all the records in the table is appropriate. In other cases, however, you will need to calculate the statistics for only those records that satisfy some criteria. To enter a criterion in a field, you first select Where as the entry in the Total row for the field and then enter the criterion in the Criteria row. Perform the following steps to use this technique to calculate the average balance for customers of sales rep 07.

TO USE CRITERIA IN CALCULATING STATISTICS ▼

STEP 1 ▶

Click the Design View button to return to the Select Query window and choose the Clear Grid command from the Edit menu.

Access clears the QBE grid so you can enter your next query.

STEP 2 ▶

Include totals in the query as you did in the previous example. Include the Balance field and select Avg as the calculation. Include the Sales Rep Number field in the second column on the QBE grid. Next, produce the list of available options for the Total entry just as you did when you selected Avg for the Balance field. Use the vertical scroll bar to move down through the options until the word Where displays.

The drop-down list of available selections displays (Figure 2-72).

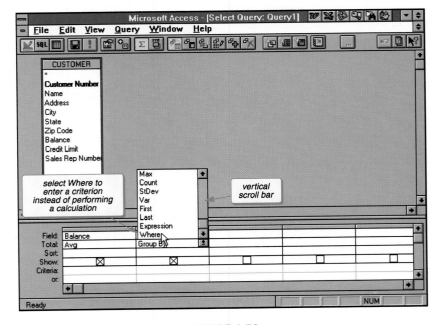

FIGURE 2-72

STEP 3 ▶

Select Where by pointing to it and clicking the left mouse button. Then, enter 07 as the criterion for the Sales Rep Number field.

Where is selected as the entry in the Total row for the Sales Rep Number field (Figure 2-73) and 07 is entered as the criterion.

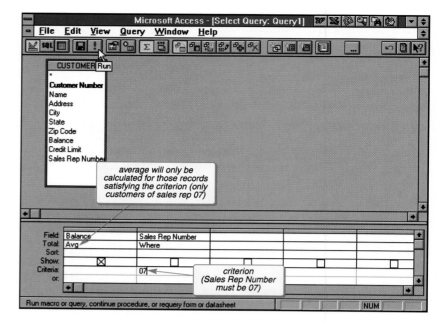

FIGURE 2-73

STEP 4 ▶

Run the query.

The result displays (Figure 2-74), giving the average balance for customers of sales rep 07.

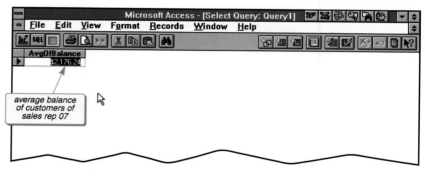

FIGURE 2-74

▶ GROUPING

A nother way statistics are often used is in combination with grouping. The statistics are then calculated for groups of records. You may, for example, need to calculate the average balance for the customers of each sales rep. You will want the average for the customers of sales rep 04, the average for customers of sales rep 07, and so on.

This type of calculation involves **grouping**, which simply means creating groups of records that share some common characteristic. In grouping by sales rep number, the customers of sales rep 04 would form one group, the customers of sales rep 07 would form a second group, and the customers of sales rep 12 would form a third group. The calculations are then made for each group. To indicate grouping in Access, select Group By as the entry in the Total row for the field to be used for grouping.

Perform the following steps to calculate the average balance for customers of each sales rep.

TO GROUP ▼

STEP 1 ▶

Click the Design View button to return to the Select Query window and choose the Clear Grid command from the Edit menu.

Access clears the QBE grid so you can enter your next query.

STEP 2 ▶

Include the Balance field and select Avg as the calculation in the first column of the QBE grid. Include the Sales Rep Number field in the second column of the QBE grid.

The Balance and Sales Rep Number fields are included (Figure 2-75). The Totals entry for the Sales Rep Number field is currently Group By, which is correct, so it doesn't need to be changed.

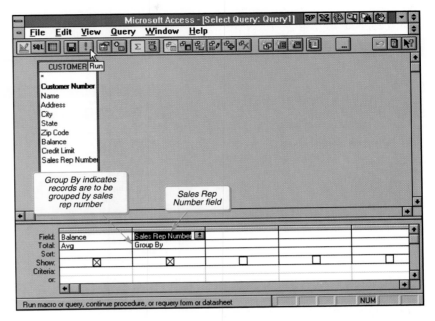

FIGURE 2-75

STEP 3 ▶

Run the query.

The results display (Figure 2-76), showing each sales rep's number along with the average balance of the customers of that sales rep.

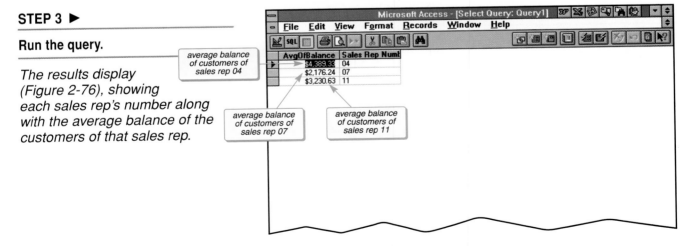

FIGURE 2-76

▶ SAVING A QUERY

In some cases, you will construct a query that you want to use again. To avoid having to repeat all your entries, save the query. To do so, close the query as before. This time, however, indicate that you want to save your work. Then assign a name to the query. The following steps illustrate the process of saving the query and calling it Average Balance by Sales Rep.

TO SAVE A QUERY ▼

STEP 1 ▶

Select the File menu.

The File menu displays (Figure 2-77).

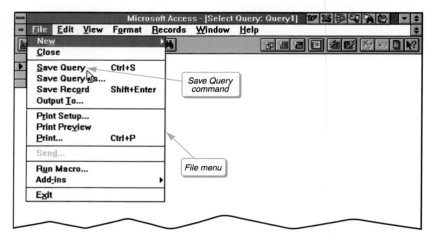

FIGURE 2-77

STEP 2 ▶

Choose the Save Query command and type Average Balance by Sales Rep

The Save As dialog box displays (Figure 2-78). The name of the query has been entered.

STEP 3 ▶

Choose the OK button.

Access saves the query as part of the CUST database.

STEP 4 ▶

Close the Select Query window by double-clicking the Control-Menu box.

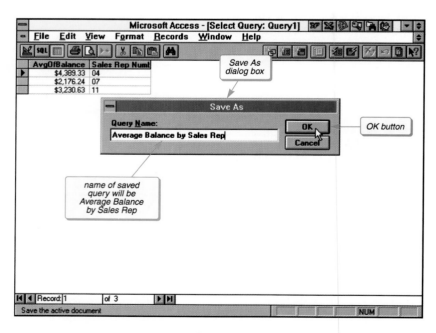

FIGURE 2-78

Once a query has been saved, you can use it at any time in the future by *opening* it and then *running* it. The query is run against the current database. Thus, if there have been changes to the data since the last time it was run, the results of the query may be different.

▶ GRAPHING THE ANSWER TO A QUERY

 graph of the results of a query can often be useful. To create a graph, use the same techniques you used in Project 1.

Sometimes, one type of graph will present the data much more clearly than another. A pie chart, for example, indicates percentages better than a bar chart. Fortunately, changing the type of graph, as well as customizing the graph in a variety of ways, is a simple process in Access. Perform the following steps to produce a pie chart that relates sales rep numbers to the average balance of customers of the sales rep.

TO GRAPH THE ANSWER TO A QUERY ▼

STEP 1 ▶

Choose the Form button and choose the New button. Click the down arrow.

The list of available tables and queries displays (Figure 2-79).

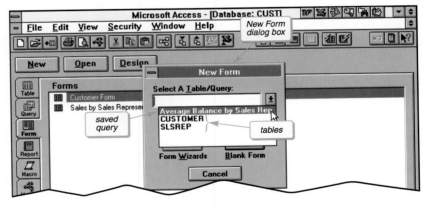

FIGURE 2-79

STEP 2 ▶

Select the Average Balance by Sales Rep query, choose the FormWizards button, select Graph, and choose the OK button. Select the Sales Rep Number field, click the Add Field button, select the AvgOfBalance field, and click the Add Field button.

The fields for the graph are selected (Figure 2-80).

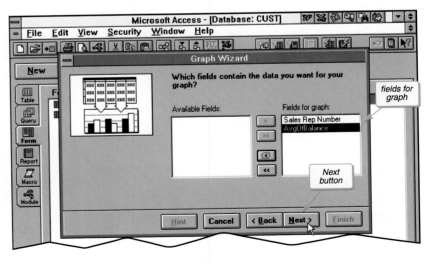

FIGURE 2-80

STEP 3 ▶

Choose the Next button and then select the pie chart as the type of chart. Then, choose the Next button.

The Graph Wizard dialog box displays (Figure 2-81). The pie chart is selected.

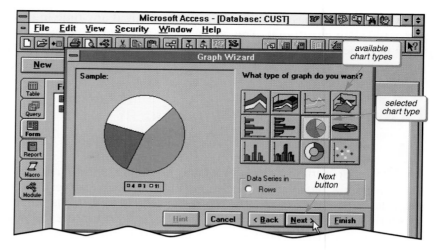

FIGURE 2-81

STEP 4 ▶

Type Average Balance by Sales Rep **as the title (Figure 2-82).**

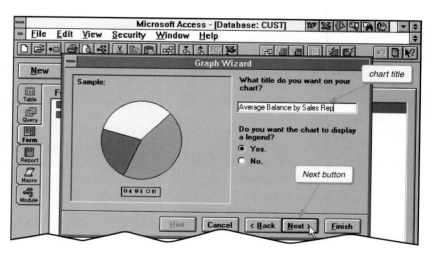

FIGURE 2-82

STEP 5 ▶

Choose the Next button and then choose the Finish button.

The graph displays (Figure 2-83).

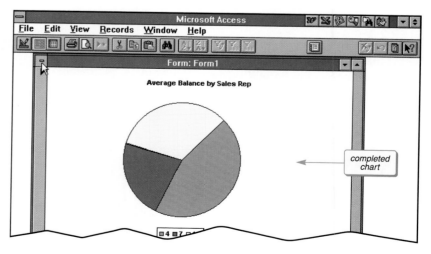

FIGURE 2-83

To remove a graph from the desktop, you need to close it. To do so, double-click its Control-menu box. You will then be asked whether or not you want to save your work.

Perform the following steps to close the graph and save it using the name Average Balance by Sales Rep (the same as the graph title).

TO CLOSE A GRAPH AND SAVE IT

STEP 1 ▶

Double-click the Form: Form1 Control-menu box and then choose the Yes button.

STEP 2 ▶

Type Average Balance by Sales Rep **as the Form Name in the Save As dialog box (Figure 2-84).**

STEP 3 ▶

Choose the OK button.

The graph is saved in the CUST database.

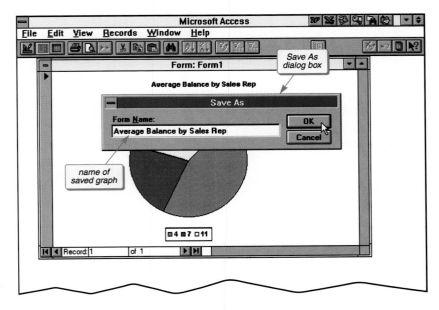

FIGURE 2-84

▶ PROJECT SUMMARY

Project 2 introduced you to querying a database using Access. You learned how to create and run queries. You learned how to use various types of criteria. You also learned how to join tables using queries. Finally, you learned how to use calculated fields and statistics, as well as how to graph the answer to a query.

▶ KEY TERMS AND INDEX

In Access, you can accomplish a task in a number of different ways. The following table provides a quick reference to each task presented in this project with its available options. The commands listed in the Menu column can be executed using either the keyboard or mouse.

Task	Mouse	Menu	Keyboard Shortcuts
Add a Table to a Query	Click Add Table button	From Query menu, choose Add Table	
Calculate Statistics	Click Totals button	From View menu, choose Totals	
Clear QBE Grid		From Edit menu, choose Clear Grid	
Close a Query		From Control menu, choose Close	
Create a Computed Field			Press SHIFT+F2, then type expression
Create a New Query	Click Query button and click New button	From File menu, choose New; choose Query	
Create an AND Criterion			Place criteria on same line in Criteria portion of QBE grid
Create an OR Criterion			Enter criteria on separate lines in Criteria portion of QBE grid
Enter a Criterion	Click criteria row for field for criterion and type criterion		Use arrow keys to move to criterion, then type criterion
Exclude Duplicates		From View menu, choose Properties; choose Yes for Unique Values only	
Graph the Answer to a Query	Click Graph button on toolbar		
Group Records in a Query		Select Group By as Totals entry for field	
Include a Field in a Query	Double-click field in field list box		
Include all Fields in a Query	Double-click asterisk in field list box		
Print the Answer to a Query	Click Print Preview button	From File menu, choose Print Preview	
Remove the Results of a Query from the Screen	Click Design View button	From View menu, choose Query Design	
Run a Query	Click Run button	From Query menu, choose Run	
Save a Query		From Control menu, choose Close	
Sort the Results of a Query	Click Sort entry under name of sort key and click drop-down list arrow		

STUDENT ASSIGNMENT 1
True/False

Instructions: Circle T if the statement is true or F if the statement is false.

T F 1. To include all the fields in a record in a query, select the asterisk (*) that appears in the field list.

T F 2. To list only certain records in a table, use a query.

T F 3. To use character data in criteria, you must enclose the text in quotation marks.

T F 4. The set of records that make up the answer to a query is called a dynaset.

T F 5. When you enter a criterion for a particular field, that field must appear in the results of the query.

T F 6. To find all customers whose balance is $100 or less, enter <=$100.00 as the criterion for the Balance field.

T F 7. To clear all the entries in a QBE grid, choose Clear Grid from the Query menu.

T F 8. When you sort a query on more than one key, the major key must appear to the left of the minor key.

T F 9. To omit duplicates from a query, choose the Query Properties command from the Query menu.

T F 10. The wildcard symbols available for use in a query are * and &.

T F 11. To create a criterion involving "Equals," you must type the equal sign (=).

T F 12. To create a compound criterion using AND, enter all criteria on the same line.

T F 13. To create a compound criterion using OR, type the word OR before the second criterion.

T F 14. To join two or more tables, use a query.

T F 15. To add an additional file to a query, choose the Add Table command from the View menu.

T F 16. To display the Totals row in the QBE grid, choose the Totals command from the Query menu.

T F 17. To use the Max function in a query, include it in the Totals row in the QBE grid.

T F 18. To calculate the total balance for customers of sales rep 04, select Sum as the entry in the Total: row for the Balance field, select Where as the entry in the Total: row for the Sales Rep Number field, and enter 04 as the criterion for the Sales Rep Number field.

T F 19. To group all records that have like values in the same field, select Group By as the entry in the Total: row of the field.

T F 20. To include computed fields in a query, enter a name for the computed field, a colon, and then the expression in one of the columns of the Criteria row.

STUDENT ASSIGNMENT 2
Multiple Choice

Instructions: Circle the correct response.

1. To list only certain records in a table use a _____.
   a. list
   b. query
   c. question
   d. answer

(continued)

STUDENT ASSIGNMENT 2 (continued)

2. To find all customers whose balance is $100 or less, enter _____ as the criterion for the Balance field.
   a. <= $100.00
   b. <=100
   c. <$100.00
   d. <100

3. To clear all the entries in a QBE grid, choose the Clear Grid command from the _____ menu.
   a. File
   b. Edit
   c. View
   d. Query

4. The wildcard symbols available for use in a query are the _____ and the _____.
   a. double period (..), asterisk (*)
   b. question mark (?), ampersand (&)
   c. double period (..), at symbol (@)
   d. question mark (?), asterisk (*)

5. Equal to (=), less than (<), and greater than (>) are examples of _____.
   a. criteria
   b. comparison operators
   c. values
   d. compound criteria

6. When two or more criteria are connected with AND or OR, the result is called a _____.
   a. compound criterion
   b. simple criterion
   c. character criterion
   d. pattern criterion

7. To add an additional file to a query, choose the _____ command from the Query menu.
   a. Add File
   b. Join Table
   c. Join File
   d. Add Table

8. Use a query to _____ tables, that is, find records in two tables that have identical values in matching fields.
   a. merge
   b. match
   c. join
   d. combine

9. Press _____ to display the Zoom dialog box and type an expression for a computed field in a query.
   a. F2
   b. SHIFT+F2
   c. ALT+F2
   d. CTRL+F2

10. To add a Totals: row to a QBE grid, choose the Totals command from the _____ menu.
    a. Query
    b. Edit
    c. View
    d. File

STUDENT ASSIGNMENT 3
Understanding the Query Design Window

Instructions: In Figure SA2-3, arrows point to the major components of the Select Query window. Identify the various parts of the Select Query window in the spaces provided. Answer the following questions about the window.

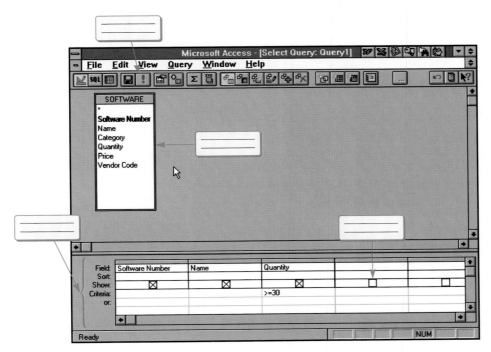

FIGURE SA2-3

1. What is the purpose of the Show: row?

2. When would you select the asterisk from the Software list?

3. What is the purpose of this query?

STUDENT ASSIGNMENT 4
Understanding Compound Criteria

Instructions: Figure SA2-4a shows a created query for the Software table using a compound criterion, and Figure SA2-4b lists the contents of the Software table. In the space below, list the answer to this query.

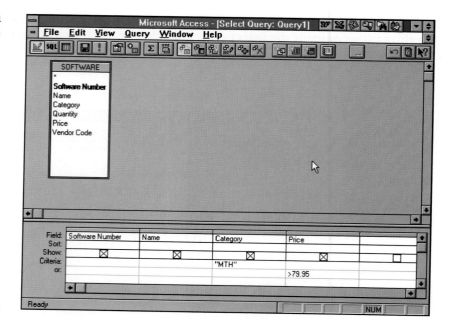

FIGURE SA2-4a

▸ **Data for Software Table**

Software Number	Name	Category	Quantity	Price	Vendor Code
0593	Easy Calculus	MTH	8	$79.95	LS
0870	Number Crunch	MTH	5	$49.95	EI
1673	Chem Works	SCI	12	$19.95	CC
1693	Kid-Writer	ENG	22	$29.95	LS
2573	Pendulum	SCI	10	$24.95	EI
2603	Storywriter	ENG	16	$24.95	CC
3933	Math Tester	MTH	18	$39.95	AS
3963	Writing is Fun	ENG	3	$39.95	CC
4353	Rhythmetic	MTH	30	$69.95	AS
5820	Test Tube	SCI	25	$24.95	AS
5940	Science Quest	SCI	34	$89.95	EI
5950	Easy English	ENG	10	$29.95	LS

FIGURE SA2-4b

STUDENT ASSIGNMENT 5
Understanding Sorting Data in a Query

Instructions: Figure SA2-5 shows a query created to sort the answer in a particular order. In the space below, list the answer to this query. Refer to Figure SA2-4b for the contents of the Software table.

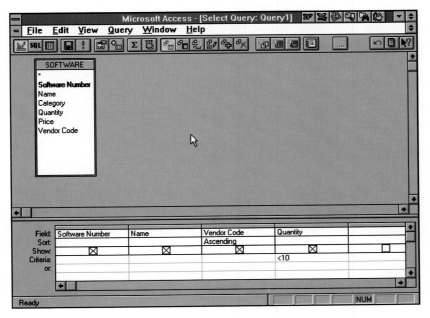

FIGURE SA2-5

STUDENT ASSIGNMENT 6
Understanding Statistics in Queries

Instructions: Figure SA2-6 shows a query created to calculate statistics. In the space below, list the answer to this query. Refer to Figure SA2-4b on page A112 for the contents of the Software table.

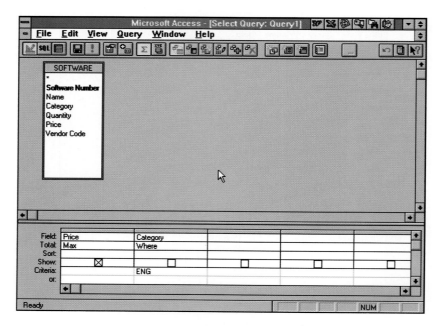

FIGURE SA2-6

COMPUTER LABORATORY EXERCISES

COMPUTER LABORATORY EXERCISE 1
Using the Help Menu

Instructions: Perform the following tasks:

1. Start Access.
2. Choose the Contents command from the Help menu.
3. Select Search.
4. Type `queries: select queries` in the Search dialog box and click the Show Topics button, as shown in Figure CLE2-1.

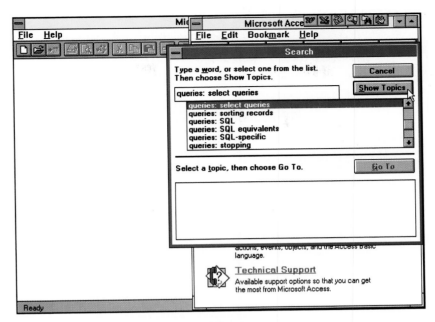

FIGURE CLE2-1

5. From the Go To list box select the phrase "Creating a Select Query" from the list.
6. Read the information and answer the following questions.
   a. In a multitable query, how can you keep track of the table with which a field is associated?

   _____

   _____

   b. What is the default query type?

   _____

   _____

   c. Do previously saved queries display in the Add Table dialog box?

   _____

   _____

7. Close the Help window.
8. Exit Access.

COMPUTER LABORATORY EXERCISE 2
Sorting and Printing a Query Answer

Instructions: Perform the following tasks:

1. Start Access.
2. Open the Soft database from the subdirectory Access2 on the Student Diskette that accompanies this book and create a new query.
3. Add the Software table to the query.
4. Include the Software Number, Name, Vendor Code, and Price fields in the QBE grid, as shown at the bottom of the screen in Figure CLE2-2 on the next page.

(continued)

COMPUTER LABORATORY EXERCISE 2 (continued)

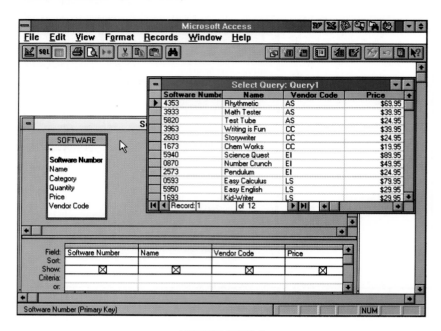

FIGURE CLE2-2

5. Sort the data by price (descending) within vendor code (ascending).
6. Run the query to generate the results shown at the top of the screen in Figure CLE2-2.
7. Print the results.
8. Close the query without saving it.
9. Exit Access.

COMPUTER LABORATORY EXERCISE 3
Performing Calculations in Queries

Instructions: Determine the on hand value of the software in the Soft database. Perform the following tasks:

1. Start Access.
2. Open the Soft database from the subdirectory Access2 on the Student Diskette that accompanies this book and create a new query for the Software table.
3. Include the Software Number, Name, Quantity and Price in the QBE grid, as shown at the bottom of the screen in Figure CLE2-3.

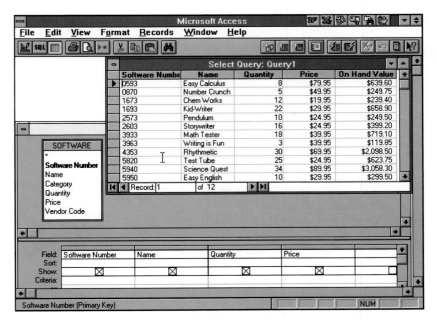

FIGURE CLE2-3

4. In the next column of the QBE grid, type `On Hand Value: [Price]*[Quantity]` in the Zoom dialog box.
5. Run the query to generate the results shown at the top of the screen in Figure CLE2-3.
6. Print the results.
7. Close the query without saving it.
8. Exit Access.

COMPUTER LABORATORY ASSIGNMENTS

COMPUTER LABORATORY ASSIGNMENT 1
Querying the Consumer Products Database

Purpose: To provide practice in creating queries and using queries.

Problem: Query the consumer products database in a variety of ways.

Instructions: Use the database created in Computer Laboratory Assignment 1 of Project 1 for this assignment. Execute each task on the computer and print the answer.

1. Open the Items database and create a new query for the Product table.
2. Display and print all the records in the table, as shown in Figure CLA2-1a on the next page.

(continued)

COMPUTER LABORATORY ASSIGNMENT 1 (continued)

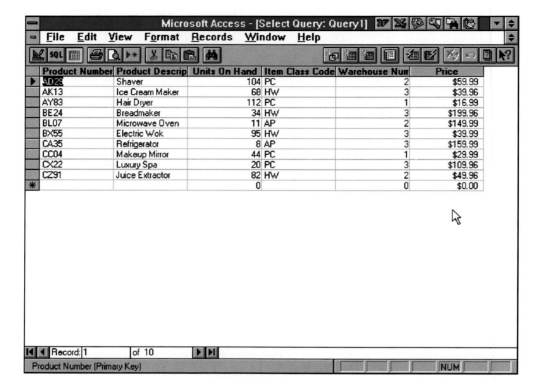

FIGURE CLA2-1a

3. Display and print the Product Number, Product Description, and Price for all records in the table.
4. Display and print the records for all products classified as Personal Care (PC).
5. Display and print the records for all products where the Product Description begins with the letter M.
6. Display and print the records for all products that have less than 20 units on hand.
7. Display and print the records for all products that have a price greater than $99.95.
8. Display and print the records for all products classified as Personal Care (PC) and that have a price greater than $39.99.
9. Display and print the records for all products classified as Housewares or that have a price less than $24.95.
10. Join the Product and Class tables. Include the Product Description, Units On Hand, Item Class Description, and Price fields in the QBE grid. Sort the records by Product Description. Display and print the results.
11. Restrict the records retrieved in task 10 above to only those products located in warehouse 3. Display and print the results.
12. Close the query without saving it and create a new query for the Product table.
13. Include the Product Number and Product Description in the QBE grid. Compute the on hand value (units on hand*price) for all records in the table. Display and print the results.
14. Display and print the average price of all products.
15. Display and print the average price for each item class.
16. Save the query you created in task 15 as Average Price by Item Class.
17. Create and print a pie chart for the Average Price by Item Class query, as shown in Figure CLA2-1b.
18. Save the graph as Average Price by Item Class, close the Items database, and exit Access.

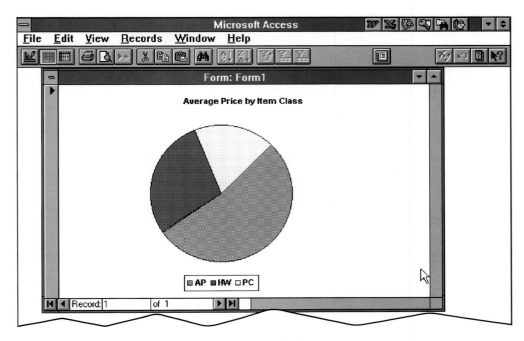

FIGURE CLA2-1b

COMPUTER LABORATORY ASSIGNMENT 2
Querying the Employee Database

Purpose: To provide practice in creating queries and using queries.

Problem: Query the employee database in a variety of ways.

Instructions: Use the database created in Computer Laboratory Assignment 2 of Project 1 for this assignment. Execute the tasks on the computer and print the answer.

1. Open the Emp database and create a new query for the Employee table.
2. Display all the records in the table and print the result, as shown in Figure CLA2-2a.

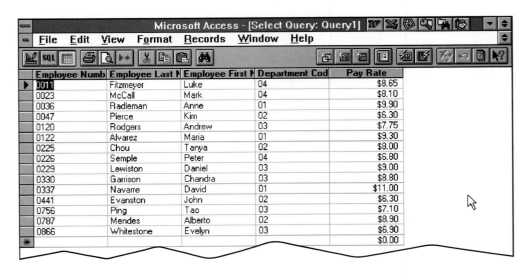

FIGURE CLA2-2a

(continued)

COMPUTER LABORATORY ASSIGNMENT 2 (continued)

3. Display and print the Employee Number, Employee Last Name, Employee First Name, and Pay Rate for all the records in the table.
4. Display and print the records for all employees who work in the department with a code 01.
5. Display and print the records for all employees whose last name starts with the letter R.
6. Display and print the records for all employees whose pay rate is less than $8.00.
7. Display and print the records for all employees who work in the department with a code 02 and who have a pay rate less than $8.00.
8. Display and print the records for all employees who work in department code 01 or whose pay rate is less than $8.00.
9. Display and print pay rates in ascending order. List each pay rate only once.
10. Join the Employee and Department tables. Display and print the Employee Number, Employee Last Name, Employee First Name, Pay Rate, and Department Name.
11. Display and print the Employee Number, Employee Last Name, Employee First Name, Department Name, and Pay Rate for all employees whose pay rate is greater than $9.00.
12. Close the query without saving it and create a new query for the Employee table.
13. Include the Employee Last Name, Employee First Name, and Pay Rate in the QBE grid. Compute the estimated weekly wage of each employee (pay rate*40). Display and print the results.
14. Display and print the highest pay rate.
15. Display and print the lowest pay rate.
16. Display and print the average pay rate for each department.
17. Save the query you created in task 16 as Average Pay Rate by Dept.
18. Create and print a pie chart for the Average Pay Rate by Dept query, as shown in Figure CLA2-2b.
19. Save the graph as Average Pay Rate by Dept, close the Emp database, and exit Access.

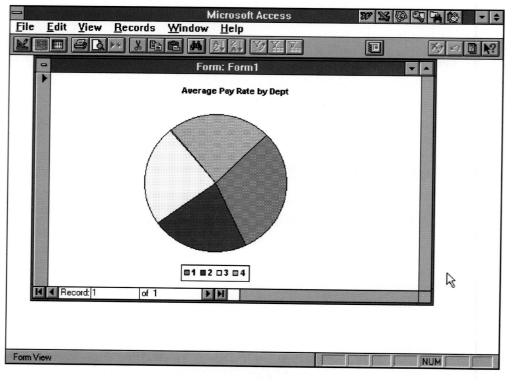

FIGURE CLA2-2b

COMPUTER LABORATORY ASSIGNMENT 3
Querying the Movie Database

Purpose: To provide practice in creating queries and using queries.

Problem: Query the movie database in a variety of ways.

Instructions: Use the database created in Computer Laboratory Assignment 3 of Project 1 for this assignment. Execute the tasks on the computer and print the answer.

1. Open the Mov database and create a new query for the Movie table.
2. Display and print all the records in the table, as shown in Figure CLA2-3a.

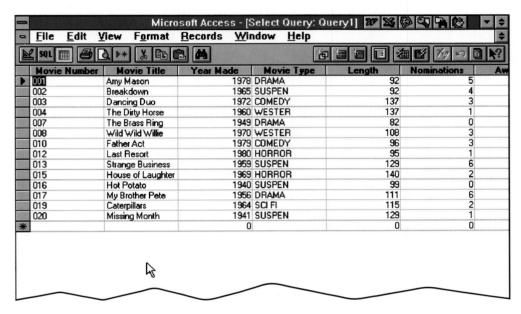

Movie Number	Movie Title	Year Made	Movie Type	Length	Nominations	Aw
001	Amy Mason	1978	DRAMA	92	5	
002	Breakdown	1965	SUSPEN	92	4	
003	Dancing Duo	1972	COMEDY	137	3	
004	The Dirty Horse	1960	WESTER	137	1	
007	The Brass Ring	1949	DRAMA	82	0	
008	Wild Wild Willie	1970	WESTER	108	3	
010	Father Act	1979	COMEDY	96	3	
012	Last Resort	1980	HORROR	95	1	
013	Strange Business	1959	SUSPEN	129	6	
015	House of Laughter	1969	HORROR	140	2	
016	Hot Potato	1940	SUSPEN	99	0	
017	My Brother Pete	1956	DRAMA	111	6	
019	Caterpillars	1964	SCI FI	115	2	
020	Missing Month	1941	SUSPEN	129	1	
		0		0	0	

FIGURE CLA2-3a

3. Display and print the Movie Title, Year Made, and Movie Type for all the records in the table.
4. Display and print the Movie Number, Movie Title, Year Made, and Director Code for all movies with a Movie Type of COMEDY.
5. Display and print all the records for movies made after 1969.
6. Display and print all the records for movies with a Movie Type of SUSPEN that have received awards.
7. Display and print all the records for movies that have a Movie Title that begins with Th.
8. Display and print all the records for movies made before 1950 or longer than 100 minutes.
9. Display and print all the records for movies that are longer than 100 minutes and that are either SUSPEN or HORROR movie types.
10. Display and print the Movie table sorted by Movie Title within director code.
11. Join the Movie and Director tables. Display and print the Movie Number, Movie Title, Movie Type, and Director Name for all records.
12. Restrict the records retrieved in task 11 above to only movies that have received award nominations. Display and print the results.
13. Display and print the Movie Title, Movie Type, Year Made, Director Name, and the difference between the number of nominations received and the number of awards received.
14. Close the query without saving it and create a new query for the Movie table.
15. Display and print the total of all movie lengths.
16. Display and print the average number of nominations for movies that have a movie type of COMEDY.

(continued)

COMPUTER LABORATORY ASSIGNMENT 3 (continued)

17. Display and print the total number of nominations by Director Code.
18. Save the query you created in task 17 as Total Nominations by Director.
19. Create and print a pie chart for the Total Nominations by Director query, as shown in Figure CLA2-3b.
20. Save the graph as Total Nominations by Director, close the Mov database, and exit Access.

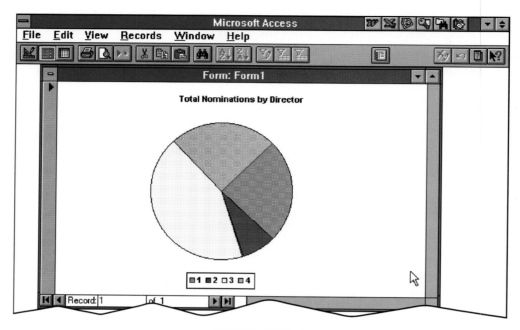

FIGURE CLA2-3b

COMPUTER LABORATORY ASSIGNMENT 4
Querying the Book Database

Purpose: To provide practice in structuring, creating, and using queries.

Problem: You are the office manager for a local bookstore. The bookstore owner is gathering some facts to assist her in making plans for the next three months. She has sent you a memo outlining the type of information she needs. You must supply her with the correct information.

Instructions: Use the database created in Computer Laboratory Assignment 4 of Project 1 for this assignment. Provide the following:

1. An inventory list sorted by author within publisher name.
2. The average price of all books and the average price for each publisher.
3. The price of the most expensive and least expensive book in the inventory.
4. A list of which books are currently not in stock.
5. A list of all books that need to be reordered. Books with less than two copies need to be reordered. For reordering purposes, she would like the Book Code, Book Title, Author, Publisher Name, and Price. The list should be in order by publisher name. She expects to ask for this list on a weekly basis.
6. The on hand value of each book.
7. A chart showing the average price for each publisher.
8. A list of each different author in the inventory.
9. A count of the number of books, grouped by book type.
10. The average price of books by book type.

▼

MAINTAINING A DATABASE

OBJECTIVES You will have mastered the material in this project when you can:

- ▶ Add records to a table
- ▶ Locate records
- ▶ Change the contents of records in a table
- ▶ Delete records from a table
- ▶ Restructure a table
- ▶ Change field characteristics
- ▶ Add a field
- ▶ Save the changes to the structure
- ▶ Update the contents of a single field
- ▶ Make the same change to all records
- ▶ Specify a required field

- ▶ Specify a range
- ▶ Specify a default value
- ▶ Specify legal values
- ▶ Specify a format
- ▶ Update a table with validation rules
- ▶ Specify referential integrity
- ▶ Delete groups of records
- ▶ Make changes to groups of records
- ▶ Create single-field and multiple-field secondary indexes
- ▶ Use a secondary index

▶ WHAT DOES MAINTAINING A DATABASE INVOLVE?

A fter creating and loading a database, you must be able to maintain it. Maintaining the database means modifying the data to keep it up-to-date, such as adding new records, changing the data for existing records, and deleting records. Updating can include mass updates or deletions, that is, to update or to delete many records at the same time.

As the needs of the organization change, you may need to **restructure** your database, that is, to change the database structure. For example, your organization may decide that customers are to be categorized by customer type, so you need to add a field for customer type to the CUSTOMER table in your database. You may also need to change the characteristics of existing fields. For example, you may find the Name field is too short to contain the name of one of your new customers, so you need to change the field's width in the CUSTOMER table structure.

To improve the efficiency of certain types of database processing, create **secondary indexes**, which are similar to indexes found in the back of books. Figure 3-1 on the next page summarizes the various types of activities involved in maintaining a database.

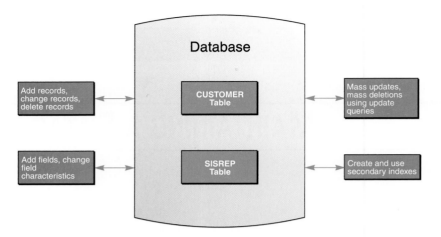

FIGURE 3-1

▶ STARTING ACCESS AND OPENING THE CUST DATABASE

Before creating queries, you must first start Access. To do so, follow the same steps you used in Project 1 (see page A5). Once you have done so, you need to open the database to be used. For this project, this means you must open the CUST database. Do so by following the steps shown in Project 1 (see page A21).

▶ ADDING, CHANGING, AND DELETING

Keeping the data in a database up-to-date requires three tasks: adding new records, changing the data in existing records, and deleting existing records.

Adding Records

In Project 1, you added records to a database using Datasheet view, that is, as you were adding records, the records were displayed on the screen in the form of a datasheet or table. When you need to add additional records, you can use the same techniques.

In Project 1, you used a form to view records. This is called **Form view**. You can also use Form view to update the data in a table. You can add new records, change existing records, or delete records. To do so, use the same techniques you used in Datasheet view. To add a record to the CUSTOMER table with a form, for example, perform the following steps. These steps use the Customer Form form you created in Project 1.

TO USE A FORM TO ADD RECORDS ▼

STEP 1 ►

With the CUST database open, point to the Form button (Figure 3-2).

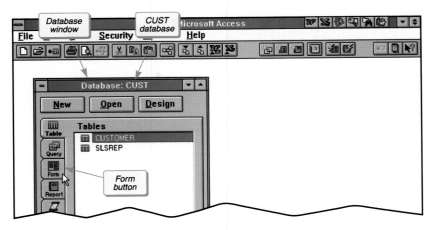

FIGURE 3-2

STEP 2 ►

Choose the Form button. Select Customer Form, and point to the Open button (Figure 3-3).

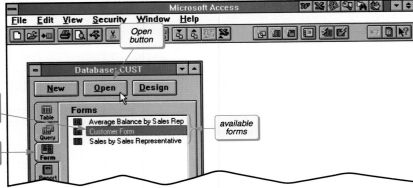

FIGURE 3-3

STEP 3 ►

Choose the Open button. Point to the Last Record button.

The screen contains a maximized version of the form for the CUSTOMER table (Figure 3-4).

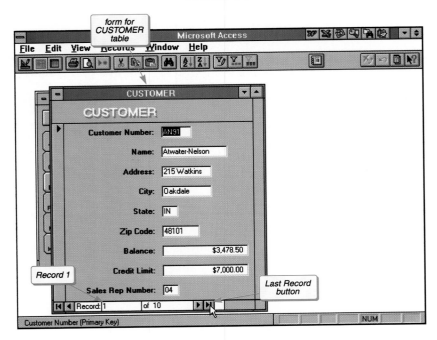

FIGURE 3-4

STEP 4 ▶

Click the Last Record button to move to the last record in the table and then point to the Next Record button.

The last record displays on the screen (Figure 3-5).

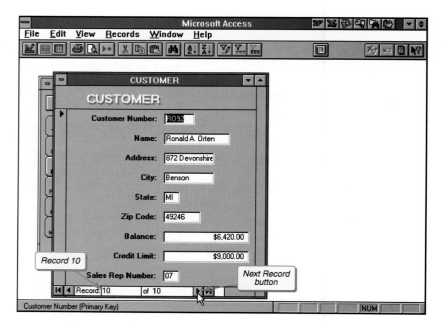

FIGURE 3-5

STEP 5 ▶

Click the Next Record button. Type the data for the new record, as shown in Figure 3-6. Press the TAB key after entering the data in each field.

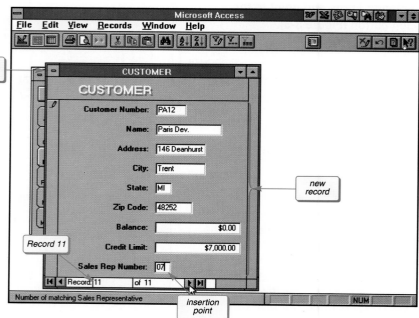

FIGURE 3-6

The record is now added to the CUSTOMER table.

Searching for a Record

In the database environment, **searching** means looking for records that satisfy some criteria. Looking for all the customers whose sales rep number is 04 is an example of searching. The queries in Project 2 were examples of searching. Access had to locate those records that satisfied the criteria.

There is also need for searching when using Form view or Datasheet view. In order to update customer FC63, for example, you first need to find the customer. In a small table, repeatedly pressing the Next Record button until customer FC63 is on the screen may not be particularly difficult. In a large table with many records, however, this would be extremely cumbersome. You need a way to be able to go directly to a record just by giving the value in some field. This is the function of the Find button ( ). Before clicking this button, move the highlight to the field for the search.

Perform the following steps first to move the highlight to the Customer Number field and then use the Find button to locate the customer whose number is FC63.

TO LOCATE RECORDS ▼

STEP 1 ▶

With the CUSTOMER table open and the form (Customer Form) for the CUSTOMER table on the screen, point to the First Record button (◄) and click it to display the first record. If the Customer Number field is not currently selected (highlighted), select it by pointing to it and clicking the left mouse button.

STEP 2 ▶

Point to the Find button (Figure 3-7).

FIGURE 3-7

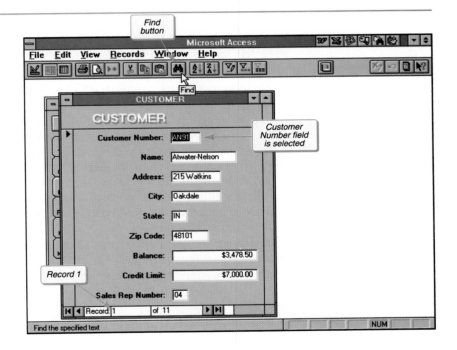

STEP 3 ▶

Click the Find button. Type FC63 and point to the Find Next button (Find Next).

The Find in field: 'Customer Number' dialog box displays (Figure 3-8). The Find What: box contains FC63.

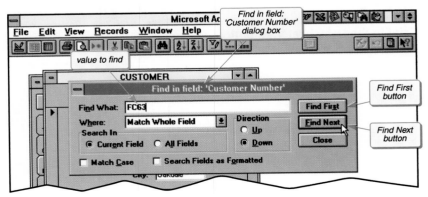

FIGURE 3-8

STEP 4 ▶

Choose the Find Next button and then choose the Close button.

Access locates the record for customer FC63 (Figure 3-9).

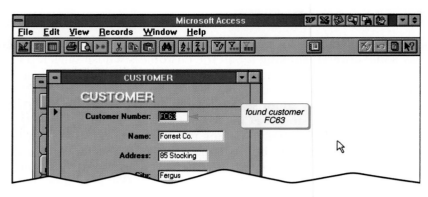

FIGURE 3-9

After locating a record that satisfies a criterion, to find the next record that satisfies the same criterion, repeat the same process. (You will not need to retype the value.)

Changing the Contents of a Record

After locating the record to be changed, move the highlight to the field to be changed by using the TAB key or by clicking the field with a mouse. Then, make the appropriate changes. (Clicking the field with a mouse automatically produces an insertion point. After pressing the TAB key, press F2 to produce an insertion point.) Normally, Access is in Insert mode, so the characters typed will be inserted at the appropriate position. To change to Overstrike mode, press the INSERT key. The letters OVR will then appear near the right-hand edge of the status bar. To return to Insert mode, press the INSERT key. In Insert mode, if the data in the field completely fills the field, no additional characters can be inserted. In this case, increase the size of the field before inserting the characters. You will see how to do this later in the project.

Perform the following steps to use Datasheet view to change the name of customer FC63 to Forrest Eccles Co. by inserting Eccles between Forrest and Co. (There is sufficient room in the field to do so.)

TO UPDATE THE CONTENTS OF A FIELD ▼

STEP 1 ▶

Point to the Datasheet View button (▦) (Figure 3-10).

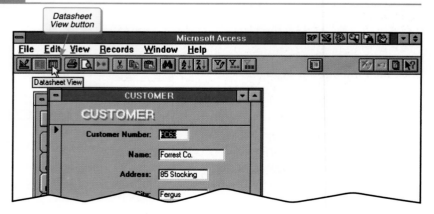

FIGURE 3-10

STEP 2 ▶

Click the Datasheet View button to move to Datasheet view and then maximize the window. Point to the position in the name field for customer FC63 for the new letters, (that is, immediately prior to the letter C of Co. (Figure 3-11). The mouse pointer appears as an I-beam.

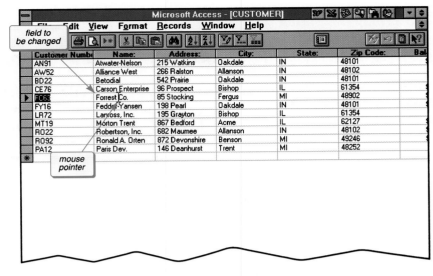

FIGURE 3-11

STEP 3 ▶

Type `Eccles` followed by a single space.

The name is now Forrest Eccles Co. (Figure 3-12).

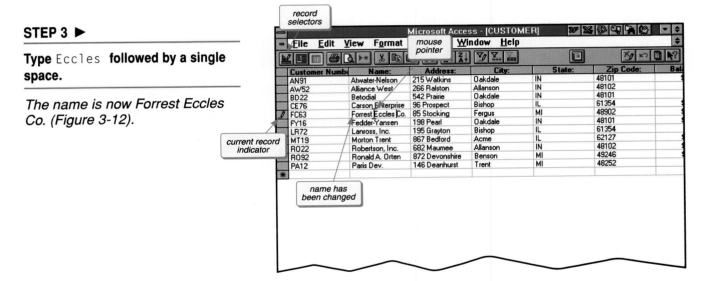

FIGURE 3-12

Deleting Records

When records are no longer needed, delete (remove) them from the table. If, for example, customer LR72 will no longer be doing business with the organization, that customer's record should be deleted. To delete a record, first locate it and then press the DELETE key. Perform the steps on the next page to delete customer LR72.

TO DELETE A RECORD ▼

STEP 1 ►

With the datasheet for the
CUSTOMER table on the
screen, point to the record
selector for the record on
which the customer number is LR72
and click the left mouse button
to select the record.

*The record is selected (Figure
3-13).*

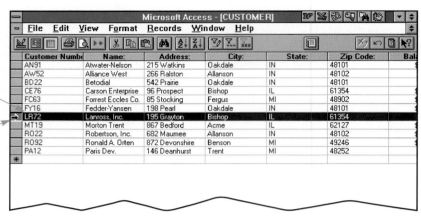

customer LR72
is selected

record
selector

FIGURE 3-13

STEP 2 ►

**Press the DELETE key to delete the
record.**

*The Microsoft Access dialog box
displays (Figure 3-14). The message indicates how many records
will be deleted.*

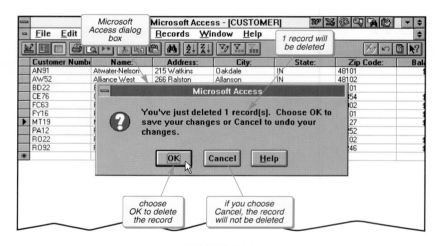

Microsoft
Access dialog
box

1 record will
be deleted

Microsoft Access

You've just deleted 1 record[s]. Choose OK to
save your changes or Cancel to undo your
changes.

OK   Cancel   Help

choose
OK to delete
the record

if you choose
Cancel, the record
will not be deleted

FIGURE 3-14

STEP 3 ►

**Choose the OK button to complete
the deletion.**

*The record is deleted
(Figure 3-15).*

record has
been deleted

STEP 4 ►

**Close the table by double-clicking
the Control-menu box.**

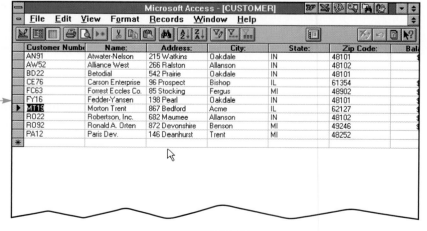

FIGURE 3-15

▶ CHANGING THE STRUCTURE

When you initially create a database, you define its **structure**; that is, you indicate the names, types, and sizes of all the fields. It would be nice if the structure you first defined would continue to be appropriate as long as you use the database. There are, however, a variety of reasons why the structure of a table might need to change. Changes in the needs of users of the database might require additional fields to be added. For example, if it is important to store the type of a customer (such as regular, discount, or special), you need to add such a field to the CUSTOMER table because it is not there already.

Characteristics of a given field might need to change. It just so happens that Carson Enterprise's name is stored incorrectly in the database. It should be Carson Lanard Enterprise. Unfortunately, there is not enough room in the Name field to hold the correct name. To accommodate this change, increase the width of the Name field.

It may turn out that a field that is currently in the table is no longer necessary. If no one ever uses a particular field, there is no point in having it in the table. Because it is occupying space and serving no useful purpose, it would be nice to remove it from the table. You will also need to delete the field from any forms, reports, or queries that include it.

To make any of these changes, choose the Design button (Design) from the database window.

Changing the Size of a Field

Perform the following steps to change the size of the Name field from 20 to 25.

TO CHANGE THE SIZE OF A FIELD ▼

STEP 1 ▶

With the Database window on the screen, the Table button (▦) selected, and the CUSTOMER table highlighted, point to the Design button (Figure 3-16).

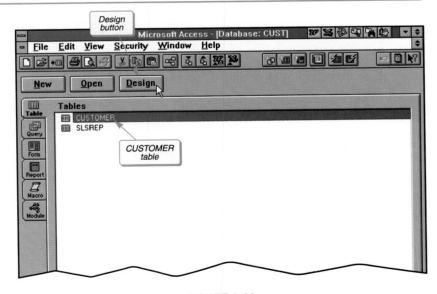

FIGURE 3-16

STEP 2 ▶

Choose the Design button, select
the Name field by clicking on its
record selector (the first column)
and then point to the Field Size
box.

*The Name field is selected (Figure
3-17). The mouse pointer, which
has changed shape to an I-beam,
points to the Field Size box.*

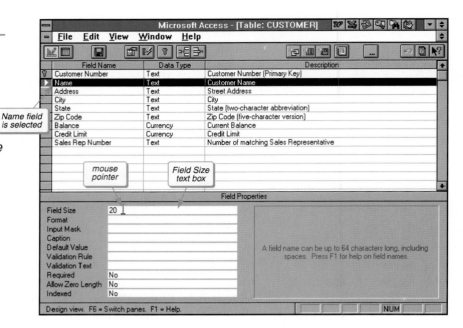

FIGURE 3-17

STEP 3 ▶

Select the entry for the size of the
Name field by clicking the left mouse
button, press the BACKSPACE key to
delete the number 0, and then
type 5 (the new size should
be 25).

*The new size displays in the
Field Size box (Figure 3-18).*

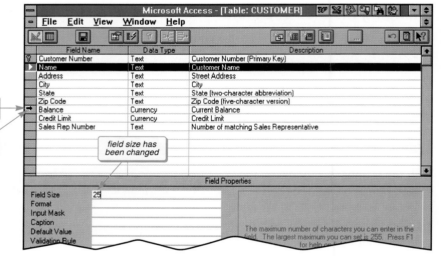

FIGURE 3-18

Adding a New Field

Perform the following steps to add a new field to a table. The field will be
called Cust Type. It will be used to indicate the type of customer. The possible
entries in this field are REG (regular customer), DSC (discount customer), and SPC
(special customer). The new field will follow the Zip Code in the list of fields, that
is, it will be the *seventh* field in the restructured table. The current seventh field
(Balance) will become the eighth field, Credit Limit will become the ninth field,
and so on.

TO ADD A FIELD TO THE CUSTOMER TABLE ▼

STEP 1 ►

Point to the record selector for the Balance field (see Figure 3-18).

STEP 2 ►

Click the left mouse button to select the Balance field and then press the INSERT key to insert a blank row.

A blank row displays in the position for the new field (Figure 3-19).

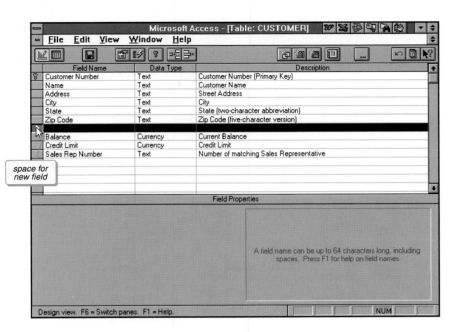

FIGURE 3-19

STEP 3 ►

Point to the Field Name column for the new field and click the left mouse button. Type Cust Type (field name) and press the TAB key. Select the Text data type by pressing the TAB key. Type Customer Type (REG, SPC, or DSC) as the description. Point to the Field Size box and click the left mouse button. Press the BACKSPACE key twice to erase the 50 and then type 3 (the size of the Cust Type field).

The entries for the new field are complete (Figure 3-20).

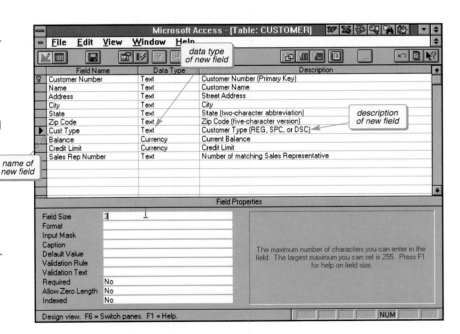

FIGURE 3-20

STEP 4 ▶

Select the File menu and point to the Save command (Figure 3-21).

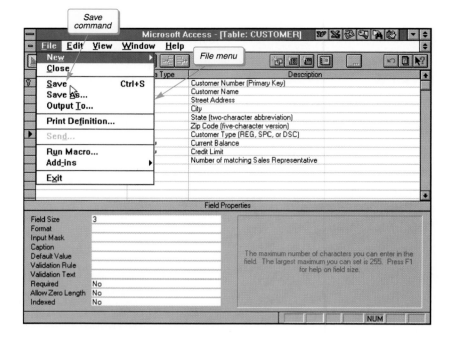

FIGURE 3-21

STEP 5 ▶

Choose the Save command and then point to the Datasheet View button (Figure 3-22).

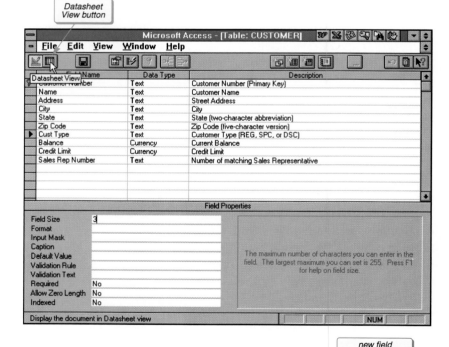

FIGURE 3-22

STEP 6 ▶

Click the Datasheet View button.

The datasheet displays (Figure 3-23). The changes to the structure have been made.

FIGURE 3-23

Updating the Restructured Database

Changes to the structure are immediately available. The customer name field is longer, although it doesn't appear that way on the screen, and the new customer number type field is included.

To make a change to a single field, such as changing the name from Carson Enterprise to Carson Lanard Enterprise, point to the field to be changed, click the left mouse button, and then type the correct value. If the record to be changed is not on the screen, use the tool bar buttons, Next Record and Previous Record, to move to it. If the field to be corrected is not visible on the screen, use the horizontal scroll bar along the bottom of the screen to shift all the fields until the correct one displays. Then, make the change.

Perform the following steps to change the name of Carson Enterprise to Carson Lanard Enterprise. These steps also increase the column width so the entire name is visible.

TO UPDATE THE CONTENTS OF A FIELD AND INCREASE THE COLUMN WIDTH ▼

STEP 1 ▶

With the CUSTOMER table open and the window containing the table maximized (Figure 3-23), point immediately in front of the letter E in Carson Enterprise. Click the left mouse button and then type `Lanard` followed by a single space.

The name is changed from Carson Enterprise to Carson Lanard Enterprise (Figure 3-24). The column is too narrow, however, for the entire name to display.

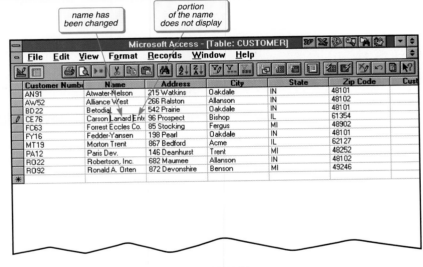

FIGURE 3-24

STEP 2 ▶

Point to the line separating the Name and Address column headings. The mouse pointer shape changes to a plus sign with two arrow heads (**+**).

The mouse pointer, which has changed shape, points to the line separating the Name and Address column headings (Figure 3-25).

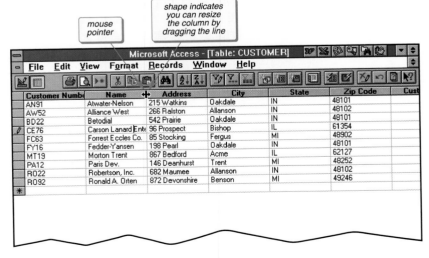

FIGURE 3-25

STEP 3 ▶

Double-click the left mouse button.

Access resizes the column to best fit the entries in it (Figure 3-26). The entire name of Carson Lanard Enterprise displays.

STEP 4 ▶

Close the table by double-clicking the Control-menu box. When asked if you wish to save the layout changes, choose the Yes button.

The name is changed and the table is closed.

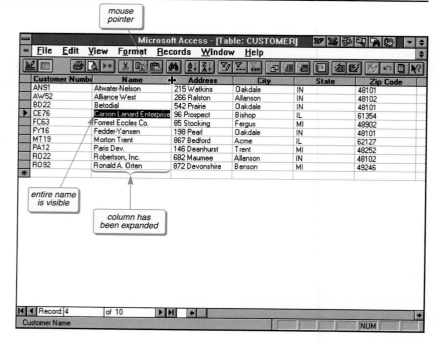

FIGURE 3-26

Updating the Contents of a New Field in a Table

The Cust Type field is blank on every record. One approach to updating the field would be to step through the entire table, changing the value on each record to what it should be. However, if most of the customers have the same type, there is a simpler approach.

Suppose, for example, that most customers are type REG (regular). You can initially set all the values to REG. The quickest and easiest way to do this is to use a special type of query called an **update query**. Later, change the type for the special and discount customers individually.

The process for creating an update query begins just like the process for creating the queries in Project 2. After selecting the table for the query, select the Update option from the Query menu. An extra row, Update To: will then appear in the QBE grid. Use this additional row to indicate the way the data will be updated.

Perform the following steps to change the value in the Cust Type field for all the records to REG.

TO MAKE THE SAME FIELD CHANGE TO ALL RECORDS IN A TABLE ▼

STEP 1 ►

Choose the Query button and then point to the New button (Figure 3-27).

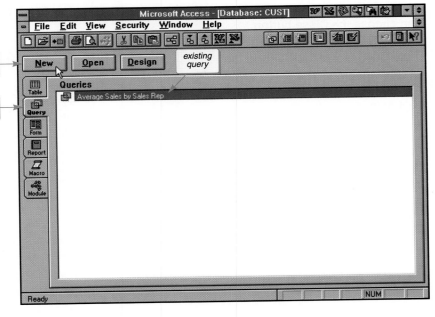

FIGURE 3-27

STEP 2 ►

Choose the New button, choose the New Query button, select the CUSTOMER table, and point to the Add button.

The Add Table dialog box displays (Figure 3-28). The CUSTOMER table is selected.

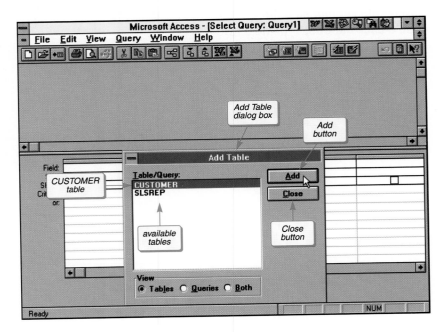

FIGURE 3-28

STEP 3 ▶

Choose the Add button to add the CUSTOMER table to the query and then choose the Close button. Adjust the size of the two portions of the Query screen, as well as the list box containing the fields in the CUSTOMER table (as in Project 2 page A67). Select the Query menu and point to the Update command.

The Microsoft Access - [Select Query: Query1] window displays (Figure 3-29). The size of the field list is adjusted so all of the fields in the CUSTOMER table display. The Query menu displays.

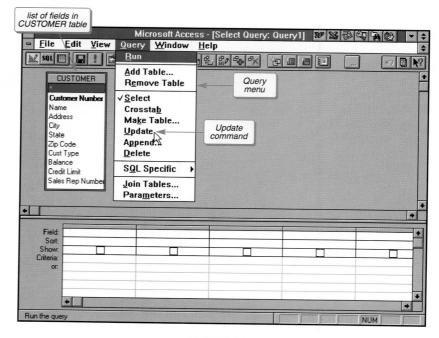

FIGURE 3-29

STEP 4 ▶

Choose the Update command by clicking the left mouse button, double-click the Cust Type field to select the field, and then point to the Update To: box in the first column of the QBE grid.

The Cust Type field is selected (Figure 3-30).

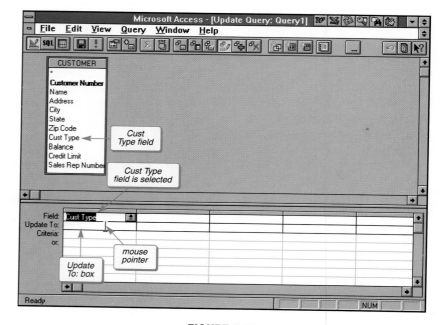

FIGURE 3-30

STEP 5 ▶

Click the left mouse button, type REG **and point to the Run button (Figure 3-31).**

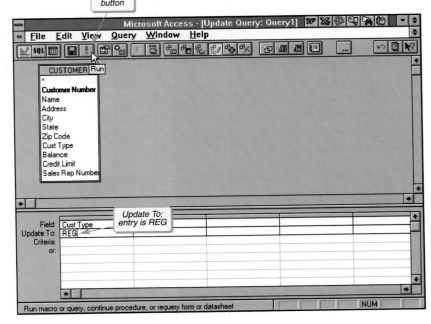

FIGURE 3-31

STEP 6 ▶

Click the Run button.

The Microsoft Access dialog box displays (Figure 3-32). The message indicates ten rows will be updated by the query.

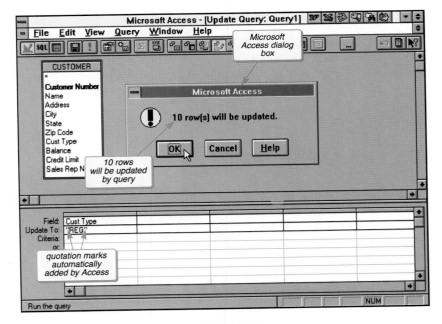

FIGURE 3-32

STEP 7 ►

Choose the OK button by clicking the left mouse button and then double-click the Control-menu box to close the query. In the Microsoft Access dialog box that displays, choose the No button (do not save the query).

STEP 8 ►

Open the CUSTOMER table. Click the right scroll arrow so the Cust Type field displays.

The CUSTOMER table that displays (Figure 3-33) shows that all entries in the Cust Type field are now REG.

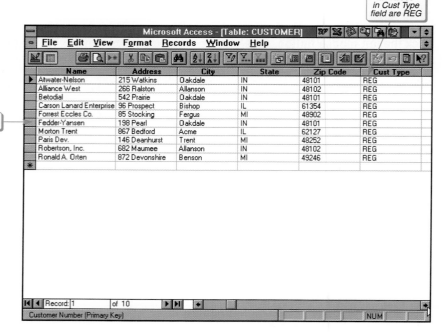

FIGURE 3-33

After changing all the customer types to REG, change the ones that should be DSC or SPC individually. Perform the following steps to change the customer types that should not be REG.

TO MAKE INDIVIDUAL CHANGES ▼

STEP 1 ►

Point immediately in front of REG in the third row and click the left mouse button. Press the DELETE key to remove REG. Type SPC and in a similar fashion, change the REG on the sixth row to DSC and the REG on the eighth row to SPC (Figure 3-34).

STEP 2 ►

Double-click the Control-menu box to close the table.

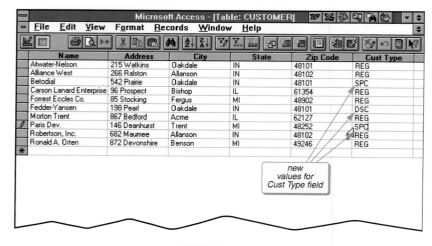

FIGURE 3-34

The Cust Type field changes are now complete.

▶ CREATING VALIDATION RULES

U p to this point in this book, you have created, loaded, queried, and updated a database. Nothing done so far, however, ensures that users only enter valid data. This section explains how to create **validation rules**, that is, rules that the data entered by a user must follow. As you will see, Access will prevent users from entering data that does not follow the rules. The steps also specify **validation text**, the message that will be displayed if a user violates the validation rule.

Validation rules can indicate a **required field**, a field in which the user must actually enter data. For example, by making the Name field a required field, a user must actually enter a name (that is, the user cannot leave it blank). Validation rules can make sure a user's entry lies within a certain **range of values**, for example, that the values in the Balance field are between 0 and 20,000. They can specify a **default value**, that is, a value that Access will display on the screen in a particular field before the user begins adding a record. To make data entry of customer numbers more convenient, you can also have lowercase letters converted automatically to uppercase. Finally, validation rules can specify a collection of legitimate entries. For example, the only legitimate entries for Customer Type are REG, SPC, and DSC.

Specifying a Required Field

Perform the following steps to specify that Name is to be a required field.

TO SPECIFY A REQUIRED FIELD ▼

STEP 1 ▶

With the Database window on the screen (Figure 3-2 on page A125) and the CUSTOMER table highlighted, choose the Design button, select the Name field, and point to the Required box.

The Design view displays (Figure 3-35). The mouse pointer (an I-beam) points to the Required box.

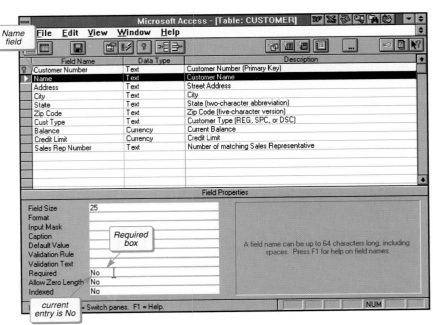

FIGURE 3-35

STEP 2 ▶

Click the left mouse button and then click the drop-down arrow that appears in the Required box. Point to Yes.

A list of available choices for the Required box displays (Figure 3-36).

STEP 3 ▶

Select Yes by clicking the left mouse button.

It is now required that the user enter data into the Name field when adding a record.

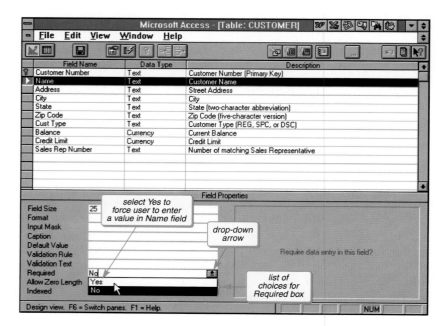

FIGURE 3-36

Specifying a Range

Perform the following steps to specify that entries in the Balance field must be between $0 and $20,000.

TO SPECIFY A RANGE ▼

STEP 1 ▶

Select the Balance field by clicking its record selector.

The Balance field is selected (Figure 3-37).

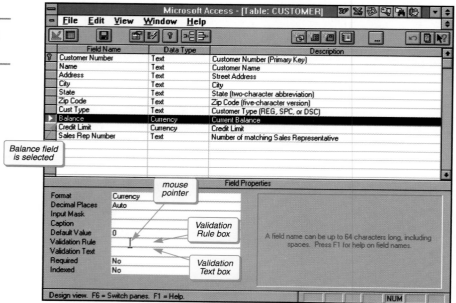

FIGURE 3-37

STEP 2 ▶

Point to the Validation Rule box and click the left mouse button to produce an insertion point in the Validation Rule box, type >=0 and <=20000 and then point to the Validation Text box (Figure 3-38).

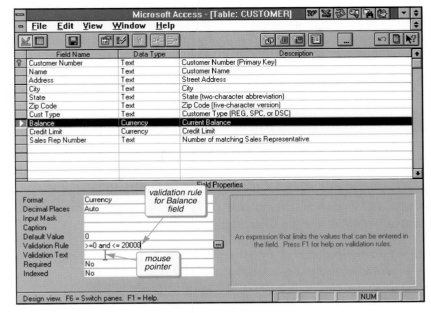

FIGURE 3-38

STEP 3 ▶

Click the left mouse button to produce an insertion point in the Validation Text box. Type the comment Balance must be between $0.00 and $20,000 You must type all the text, including the dollar signs, in the box.

The validation text is entered (Figure 3-39). Only the last portion of the wording is visible.

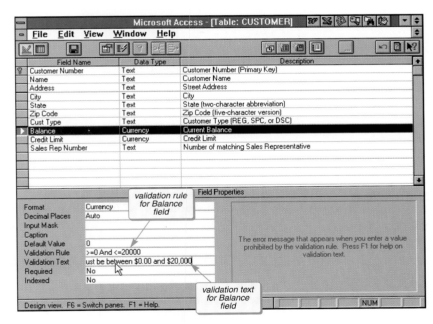

FIGURE 3-39

Users will now be prohibited from entering a balance that is either less than $0 or greater than $20,000 when they add records or change the value in the Balance field.

Specifying a Default Value

Perform the following steps to specify a default value of 7000 for the Credit Limit field. This simply means that if users do not enter a credit limit, the credit limit will be $7,000.

TO SPECIFY A DEFAULT VALUE ▼

STEP 1 ▶

Select the Credit Limit field. Point to the Default Value box, click the left mouse button, delete the 0, and type =7000

The Credit Limit field is selected. The default value is entered in the Default Value box (Figure 3-40).

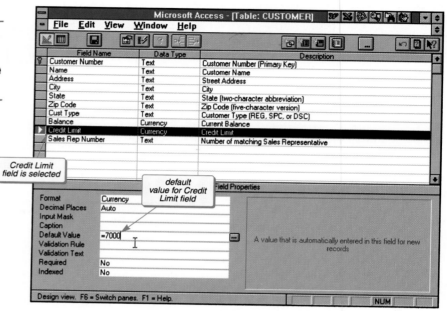

FIGURE 3-40

From this point on, if users do not make an entry in the Credit Limit field when adding records, Access will set the credit limit to $7,000.

Specifying a Collection of Legal Values

The only legal values for the Cust Type field are REG, SPC, and DSC. An appropriate validation rule for this field can make Access reject any entry other than these three possibilities. In other words, these are the only three **legal values**. Perform the following steps to specify the legal values for the Cust Type field. Unlike criteria in queries, it is essential to enclose character values, such as REG, in quotation marks.

TO SPECIFY LEGAL VALUES ▼

STEP 1 ▶

Select the Cust Type field. Point to the Validation Rule box, click the left mouse button, and type `="REG" OR ="SPC" OR ="DSC"` **Point to the Validation Text box, click the left mouse button, and type** `Cust Type must be REG, SPC, or DSC`

The Cust Type field is selected. The validation rule and validation text have been entered (Figure 3-41).

FIGURE 3-41

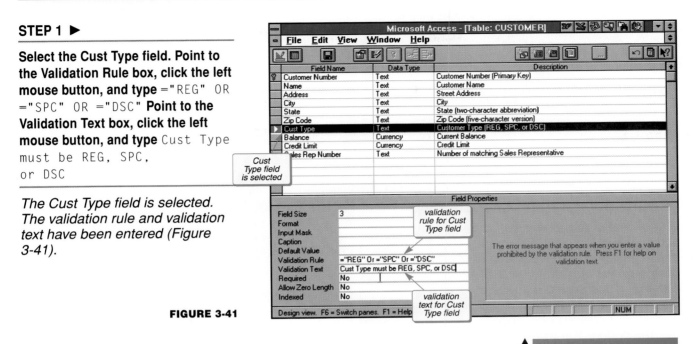

Users will now only be allowed to enter REG, SPC, or DSC in the Cust Type field when they add records or make changes to this field.

Using a Format

Perform the following steps to specify a format for the Customer Number field in the CUSTOMER table. The format symbol used in the example is >, which causes Access to automatically convert lowercase letters to uppercase. The format symbol < causes Access to automatically convert uppercase letters to lowercase.

TO SPECIFY A FORMAT ▼

STEP 1 ▶

Select the Customer Number field. Point to the Format box, click the left mouse button, and type > **(Figure 3-42).**

FIGURE 3-42

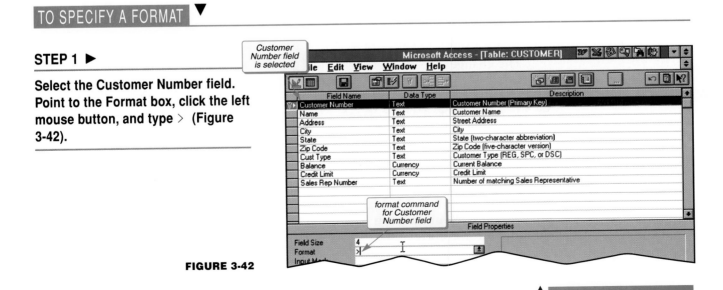

From this point on, any lowercase letters users enter in the Customer Number field when they add records or change the value in this field will automatically be converted to uppercase.

To save the validation rules, default values, and formats, perform the following steps.

TO SAVE THE VALIDATION RULES, DEFAULT VALUES, AND FORMATS ▼

STEP 1 ▶

Select the File menu and choose the Save command. Point to the No button.

The Microsoft Access dialog box displays (Figure 3-43). The message is asking if you wish to have the new rules applied to current records. If this were a database used to run a business or to solve some other critical need, choose the Yes button. You would not want to take the chance that some of the data already in the database violates the rules.

STEP 2 ▶

Because none of the rules is violated by the data in the CUSTOMER table, choose the No button by clicking the left mouse button.

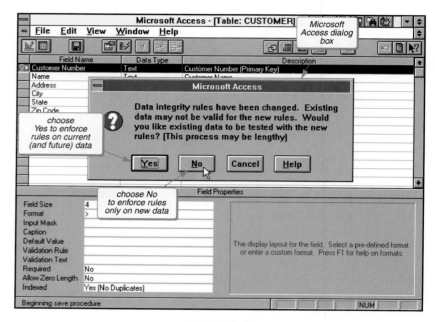

FIGURE 3-43

The changes are made.

▶ UPDATING A TABLE THAT CONTAINS VALIDATION RULES

W hen updating a table that contains validation rules, Access provides a great deal of assistance in making sure the data entered is valid. Access helps in making sure that data is formatted correctly. Access also will not accept invalid data. Entering a number that is out of the required range, for example, or entering a value that is not one of the possible choices will produce an error message in the form of a dialog box. The database will not be updated until the error is corrected.

If the customer number entered contains lowercase letters, such as ss22 (Figure 3-44), Access will automatically convert the data to SS22 (Figure 3-45).

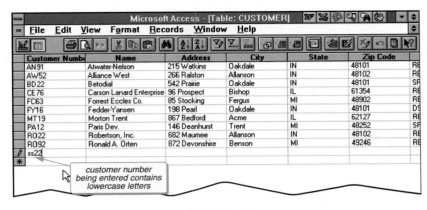

FIGURE 3-44

Access will automatically convert the data to SS22 (Figure 3-45).

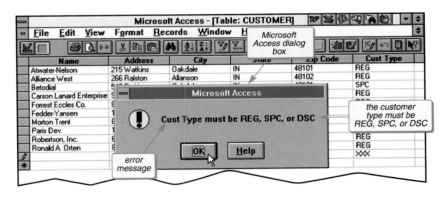

FIGURE 3-45

If the Cust Type is not valid, such as XXX, Access will display the message you specified (Figure 3-46) and will not allow the data to enter the database.

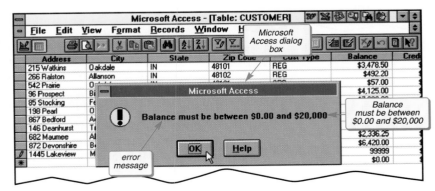

FIGURE 3-46

If the Balance is not valid, such as 99999, Access also displays the appropriate message (Figure 3-47) and refuses to accept the data.

FIGURE 3-47

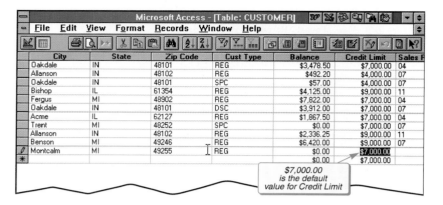

FIGURE 3-48

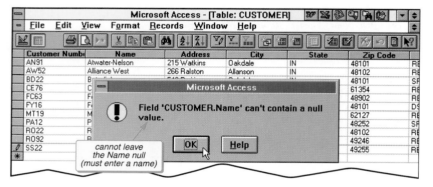

FIGURE 3-49

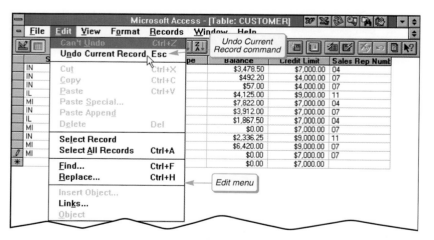

FIGURE 3-50

Instead of the Credit Limit initially appearing as $0.00, it will now appear as $7,000.00 (Figure 3-48), because 7000 is the default value for the Credit Limit field. Thus, for any customer whose credit limit is $7,000.00, there is no need to enter the value. Simply pressing the TAB key accepts the $7,000.00 that is currently displayed on the screen.

If a required field is not entered, Access indicates this fact as soon as you attempt to leave the record (Figure 3-49). This field *must* be entered before Access will move to a different record.

When a table has validation rules, it is possible to get stuck in a field. Perhaps you don't remember the validation rule you created or perhaps the one you created was incorrect. In any case, if you have entered data that violates the validation rule, you will not be able to leave the field nor can you simply close the table.

The first thing to try is to enter an acceptable entry. If this does not work, repeatedly press the BACKSPACE key to erase the contents of the field and then try to leave the field. If, for some reason, this doesn't work either, select the Undo Current Record command from the Edit menu (Figure 3-50). The record will not be added to the database; instead, it will be removed from the screen.

If you ever have to take such drastic action, you probably have a faulty validation rule. Use the techniques of the previous sections to correct the existing validation rules for the field.

▶ SPECIFYING REFERENTIAL INTEGRITY

A **foreign key** is a field in one table whose values are required to match the **primary key** of another table. For example, the sales rep number in the CUSTOMER table must match the primary key of the SLSREP table. In practice, this simply means that the sales rep number for any customer must be that of a real sales rep, that is, a sales rep currently in the SLSREP table. You should not store a customer whose sales rep number is 05, for example, if there is no sales rep 05. The property that the value in a foreign key must match to that of another table's primary key is called **referential integrity**.

In Access, to specify referential integrity, define a relationship between the tables by using the Relationships button. Access will then forbid any updates to the database that would violate the referential integrity.

The type of relationship between two tables specified by using the Relationships button is referred to as a **one-to-many relationship**. This means that one record in the first table is related to (matches) many records in the second table, but each record in the second table is related to only one record in the first. In the sample database, for example, there is a one-to-many relationship between the SLSREP table and the CUSTOMER table. One sales representative is associated with many customers, but each customer is associated with a single sales representative. In general, the table containing the foreign key will be the "many" part of the relationship.

Perform the following steps to use the Relationships button (⬚) to specify referential integrity by specifying a relationship between the SLSREP and CUSTOMER tables.

TO SPECIFY REFERENTIAL INTEGRITY ▼

STEP 1 ▶

If a datasheet is currently on the screen, double-click its Control-menu box to close it. Then, choose the Relationships button (Figure 3-51).

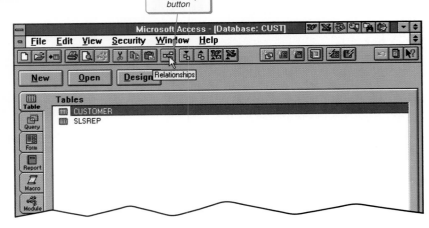

FIGURE 3-51

STEP 2 ▶

Select the SLSREP table.

The Add Table dialog box displays (Figure 3-52).

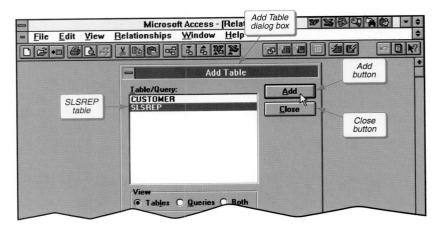

FIGURE 3-52

STEP 3 ►

Choose the Add button, select the CUSTOMER table, choose the Add button again, and then choose the Close button. Resize the Field List boxes that display so all fields are visible. Point to the Sales Rep Number field in the Field List box for the SLSREP table.

Field list boxes for the SLSREP and CUSTOMER tables display. The boxes have been resized so all fields are visible (Figure 3-53).

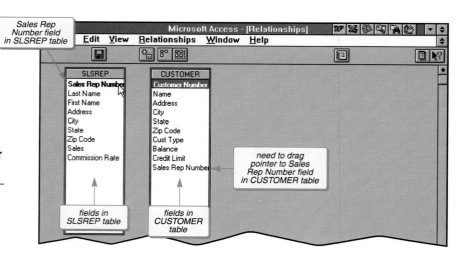

FIGURE 3-53

STEP 4 ►

Click and hold the left mouse button, drag the pointer to the Sales Rep Number field in the Field List box for the CUSTOMER table, and then release the left mouse button. Point to the Enforce Referential Integrity check box.

The Relationships dialog box displays (Figure 3-54). The correct fields (the Sales Rep Number fields) have been identified as the matching fields.

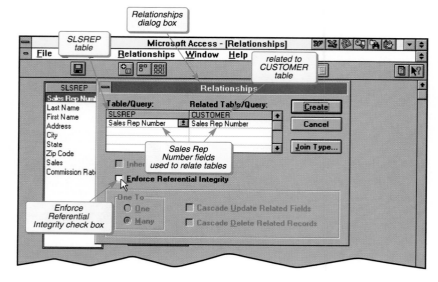

FIGURE 3-54

STEP 5 ►

Click the left mouse button to place an X in the Enforce Referential Integrity check box.

Enforce Referential Integrity is selected (Figure 3-55). This will cause Access to reject any update that would violate referential integrity.

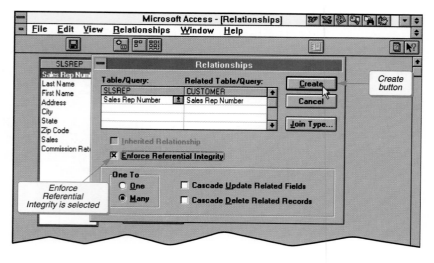

FIGURE 3-55

STEP 6 ▶

Choose the Create button
(Create).

*Access creates the relationship
and displays it visually with a line
joining the two Sales Rep Number
fields (Figure 3-56). The number 1
by the Sales Rep Number field in
the SLSREP table indicates that
the SLSREP table is the "one" part
of the relationship. The symbol at
the Customer end of the arrow
indicates that the CUSTOMER
table is the "many" part of the
relationship.*

STEP 7 ▶

Select the File menu and choose the
Save Layout command to save the
relationship.

STEP 8 ▶

Double-click the Control-menu box
to close the Microsoft Access
[Relationships] window and then
choose the Yes button.

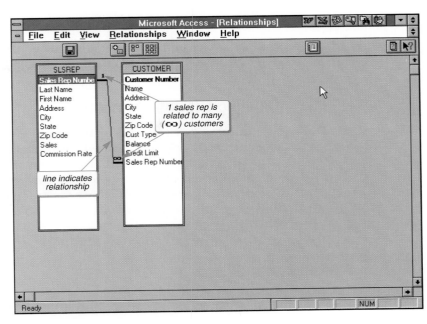

FIGURE 3-56

FIGURE 3-57

Access will now reject any
number in the Sales Rep Number
field in the CUSTOMER table that
does not match a sales rep number
in the SLSREP table. Trying to add a
customer whose sales rep number
does not match would result in the
error message shown in Figure 3-57.

Deleting a sales representative
for whom there are related customers would also cause a problem.
These customers would now have a
sales rep number that does not
match any sales representative.
Deleting Sales Rep 04 from the
SLSREP table, for example, would
cause a problem for all records in
the CUSTOMER table on which the
sales rep number is 04. To prevent
this problem, Access will forbid
such a deletion. Instead of deleting
the record, Access will display the
message shown in Figure 3-58.

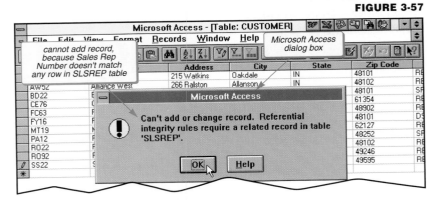

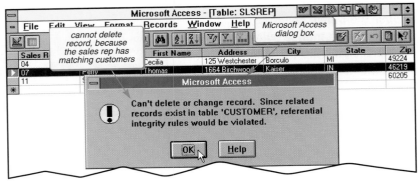

FIGURE 3-58

▶ MASS UPDATES

arlier in this project, an update query was used to change all the entries in the Cust Type column to REG. The updates can also involve criteria.

Deleting Groups of Records

In some cases, there may be several records to be deleted at a time. If, for example, territories change and customers whose zip code is 62127 are assigned to a different organization, all the customers who have this zip code should be deleted. Instead of deleting these customers individually, which would be very cumbersome, delete them in one operation by using an update query. Perform the following steps to use an update query to delete all customers whose zip code is 62127.

TO DELETE GROUPS OF RECORDS ▼

STEP 1 ▶

If there is a datasheet on the screen, close it by double-clicking its Control-menu box. Click the Query button, choose the New button, choose the New Query button, select the CUSTOMER table, choose the Add button, and then choose the Close button. Adjust the size of the two portions of the Query screen, as well as the list box containing the fields in the CUSTOMER table as in Project 2 (see page A67). Select the Query menu and point to the Delete command.

The Microsoft Access - [Select Query:Query1] window displays (Figure 3-59). All the fields in the CUSTOMER table display. The Query menu displays.

STEP 2 ▶

Choose the Delete command by clicking the left mouse button, double-click the Zip Code field to select the field, and then point to the Criteria box.

The Zip Code field displays in the Field box, indicating it is selected (Figure 3-60).

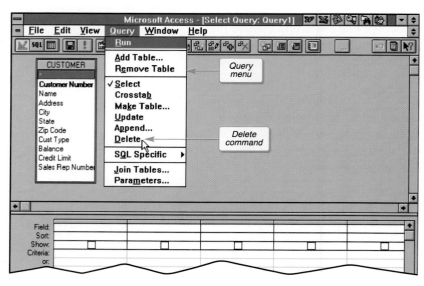

FIGURE 3-59

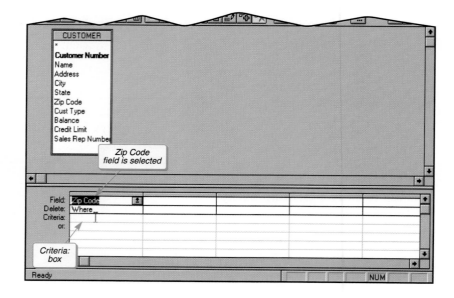

FIGURE 3-60

STEP 3 ▶

Click the left mouse button and then type 62127

The criterion is entered in the Zip Code column (Figure 3-61).

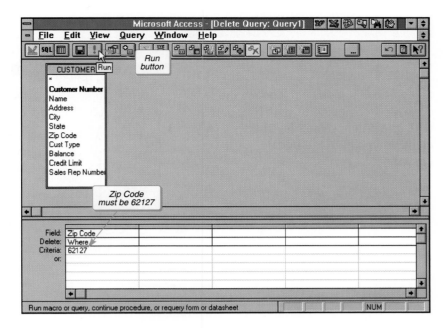

FIGURE 3-61

STEP 4 ▶

Click the Run button and then point to the OK button.

The Microsoft Access dialog box displays (Figure 3-62). The message indicates that this particular query will delete 1 row (record). Choose the NO button by double-clicking its Control-menu box.

STEP 5 ▶

Choose the OK button.

The record is deleted.

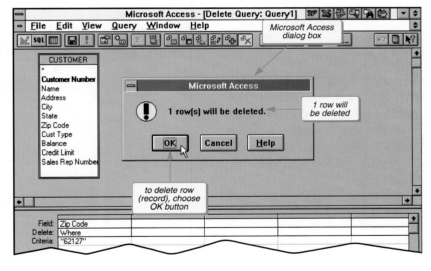

FIGURE 3-62

One customer (MT19) has been removed from the table.

Changing Groups of Records

Just as update queries can delete several records at once, they can also change several records at a time. To change the credit limit of all customers whose credit limit is currently $4,000 to $5,000 would be very cumbersome individually. Again, an update query can simplify the process. Perform the following steps to use an update query to change the credit limit of all customers whose credit limit is $4,000 to $5,000.

TO MAKE CHANGES TO GROUPS OF RECORDS ▼

STEP 1 ▶

Select the Edit menu and choose the Clear Grid command to clear the QBE grid. Then, select the Query menu and point to the Update command.

The Query menu displays (Figure 3-63).

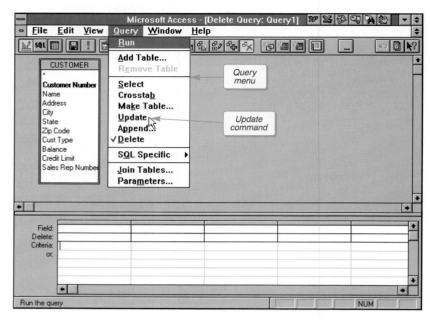

FIGURE 3-63

STEP 2 ▶

Choose the Update command by clicking the left mouse button. Next, double-click the Credit Limit field to select the field, enter 5000 as the Update To: value, and enter 4000 as the Criteria: value. Then, point to the Run button.

The Credit Limit field is selected (Figure 3-64). The value 5000 is entered in the Update To: box and the value 4000 is entered in the Criteria: box.

STEP 3 ▶

Click the Run button and then choose the OK button in the Microsoft Access dialog box.

The query executes.

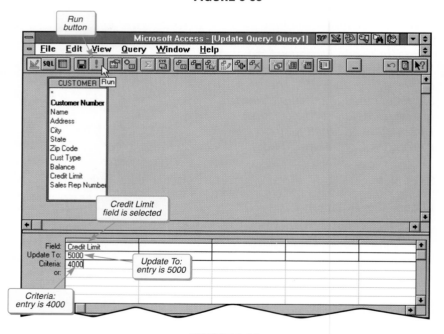

FIGURE 3-64

STEP 4 ▶

Close the query by double-clicking its Control-menu box and choose the NO button. Choose the Table button, select the CUSTOMER table, and then choose the Open button. Click the right scroll arrow three times to display the Credit Limits column.

The CUSTOMER table displays in Datasheet view (Figure 3-65). The credit limits that were $4,000 have been changed to $5,000.

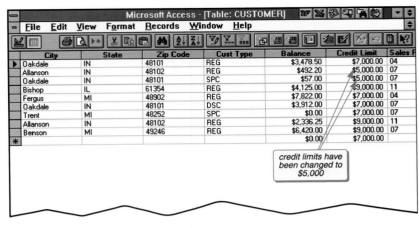

FIGURE 3-65

▶ CREATING AND USING INDEXES

Y ou are already familiar with the concept of an index. The index in the back of a book contains important words or phrases, as well as a list of pages on which the given words or phrases can be found. An index for a database table is similar. Figure 3-66, for example, shows the CUSTOMER table and an index built on customer names. In technical terms, Name is the **index key**. In this case, the items of interest are customer names instead of key words or phrases — as is the case in the back of this project (Key Terms and Index section).

▸ **INDEX ON NAME COLUMN**   ▸ **CUSTOMER Table**   **FIGURE 3-66**

Name	Record Number
Alliance West	2
Atwater-Nelson	1
Betodial	3
Carson Lanard Enterprise	4
Fedder-Yansen	6
Forrest Eccles Co.	5
Morton Trent	7
Paris Dev.	8
Robertson, Inc.	9
Ronald A. Orten	10

Record Number	Customer Number	Name	Street	City	State
1	AN31	Atwater-Nelson	215 Watkins	Oakdale	IN
2	AW52	Alliance West	266 Ralston	Allanson	IN
3	BD22	Betodial	542 Prairie	Oakdale	IN
4	CE76	Carson Lanard Enterprise	96 Prospect	Bishop	IL
5	FC63	Forrest Eccles Co.	85 Stocking	Fergus	MI
6	FY16	Fedder-Yansen	198 Pearl	Oakdale	IN
7	MT19	Morton Trent	867 Bedford	Acme	IL
8	PA12	Paris Dev.	146 Dearhurst	Trent	MI
9	RO22	Robertson, Inc	682 Maumee	Allanson	IN
10	RO92	Ronald A. Orten	872 Devonshire	Benson	MI

Each customer name occurs in the index along with the number of the record on which the customer name is located. Further, the names appear in the index in alphabetical order. To use this index to find Fedder-Yansen, for example, rapidly scan the names in the index to find Fedder-Yansen. Next, look at the corresponding record number (6) and then go immediately to record 6 in the CUSTOMER table, thus finding this customer much more rapidly than by looking through the entire CUSTOMER table one record at a time. This is the same action that Access takes when it uses an index. Thus, indexes make the process of retrieving records very fast and efficient.

There is another benefit to indexes. Indexes provide an efficient alternative to sorting. That is, if the records should appear in a certain order, it is easier to use an index instead of physically rearranging the records in the table. Physically rearranging the records in a different order, which is called sorting, can be a very time-consuming process.

To see how indexes can be used for alphabetizing records, look at the record numbers in the index (Figure 3-66 on the previous page) and suppose you used these to list all customers. That is, simply follow down the record number column, listing the corresponding customers. In this example, you would first list the customer on record 2 (Alliance West), then the customer on record 1 (Atwater-Nelson), then the customer on record 3 (Betodial), and so on. The customers would be listed alphabetically by Name without actually sorting the table.

To gain the benefits from an index, you must first create one. Access automatically creates an index on the primary key. This index is called the **primary index**. The other indexes are called secondary indexes. You must create the secondary indexes, indicating the field or fields on which the index is built.

Creating Single-Field Indexes

Perform the following steps to create two **single-field secondary indexes**. For the first one, the index key will be the Name field. For the second, the index key will be the Zip Code field. Each case needs to indicate whether to allow duplicates, that is, two records that have the same value in the index key. For example, in the secondary index for the Name field, if duplicates are not allowed, Access would not allow the addition of a customer whose name is the same as the name of a customer already in the database. In both of the indexes created in the following steps, duplicates will be allowed.

TO CREATE SINGLE-FIELD SECONDARY INDEXES ▼

STEP 1 ▶

With the CUSTOMER table open and its datasheet maximized, click the Design button. Select the Name field, point to the Indexed box, and click the left mouse button. Then, point to the drop-down arrow next to the Indexed box (Figure 3-67).

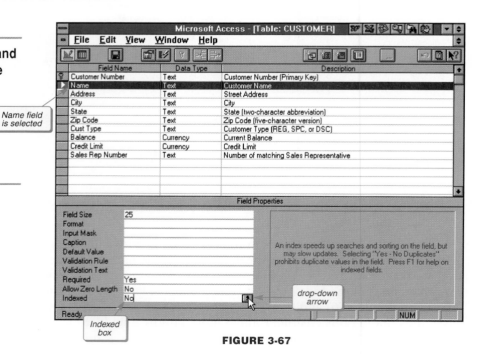

FIGURE 3-67

STEP 2 ▶

Click the drop-down arrow and point to Yes (Duplicates OK).

The Indexed list displays (Figure 3-68). The mouse pointer points to Yes (Duplicates OK).

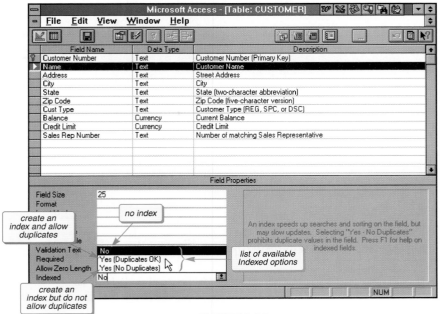

FIGURE 3-68

STEP 3 ▶

Click the left mouse button to select Yes (Duplicates OK). Select the Zip Code field, point to the Indexed box, and click the left mouse button. Click the drop-down arrow next to the Indexed box, and select Yes (Duplicates OK).

The Zip Code field is selected (Figure 3-69). The Indexed entry is Yes (Duplicates OK).

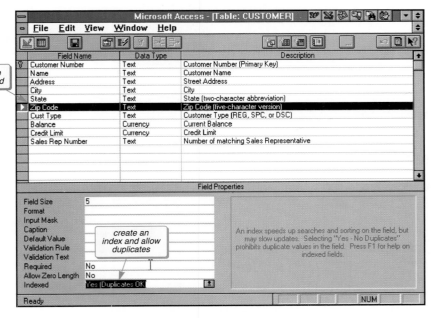

FIGURE 3-69

The indexes on the Name and Zip Code fields have now been created and are ready for use.

Creating Multiple-Field Indexes

Creating **multiple-field secondary indexes,** indexes created on more than one field, involves a different process from creating single-field secondary indexes. Select the Indexes command from the View menu and then enter the combination of fields that make up the index key. Perform the following steps to create a multiple-field secondary index with the name credbal. The key will be the combination of the Credit Limit and the Balance fields.

TO CREATE A MULTIPLE-FIELD SECONDARY INDEX ▼

STEP 1 ►

Select the View menu and point to the Indexes command (Figure 3-70).

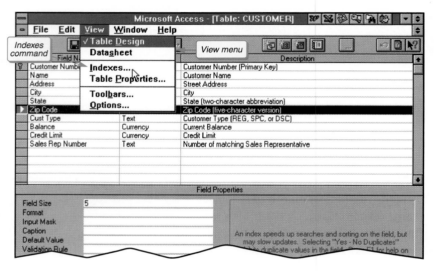

FIGURE 3-70

STEP 2 ►

Choose the Indexes command.

The Indexes: CUSTOMER dialog box displays (Figure 3-71). The index on Customer Number is the Primary index and was created automatically by Access. The indexes on Name and Zip Code are the ones just created. Use this dialog box to create additional indexes.

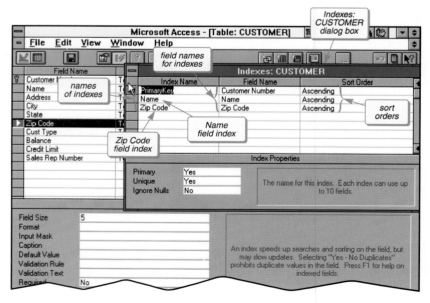

FIGURE 3-71

STEP 3 ▶

Select the Index Name entry on the row following Zip Code by pointing to it and clicking the left mouse button. Type `Credbal` as the Index name, press the TAB key, and point to the drop-down arrow.

The Index name has been entered as Credbal (Figure 3-72). An insertion point appears in the Field Name column.

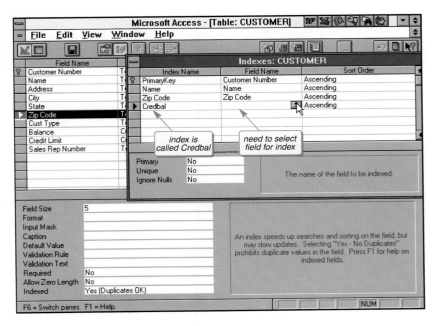

FIGURE 3-72

STEP 4 ▶

Click the left mouse button to produce a list of fields in the CUSTOMER table and point to the down scroll arrow.

A list of fields in the CUSTOMER table displays (Figure 3-73).

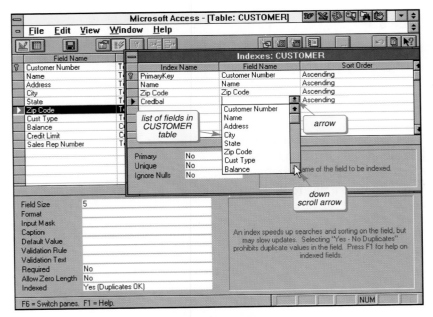

FIGURE 3-73

STEP 5 ▶

Click the down scroll arrow once to bring the Credit Limit field to the screen and then select the Credit Limit field by pointing to it and clicking the left mouse button. Press the TAB key three times to move to the Field Name entry on the following row. Select the Balance field in the same manner as the Credit Limit field. Point to the Control-menu box for the Indexes: CUSTOMER dialog box.

Credit Limit and Balance are selected as the two fields for the Credbal index (Figure 3-74). The absence of an Index name on the row containing the Balance field indicates that it is part of the previous index, Credbal.

STEP 6 ▶

Close the Indexes: CUSTOMER dialog box by double-clicking its Control-menu box.

STEP 7 ▶

Save the changes by selecting the File menu and choosing the Save command. Then, click the Datasheet View button to move to Datasheet view.

The indexes are created and the datasheet displays.

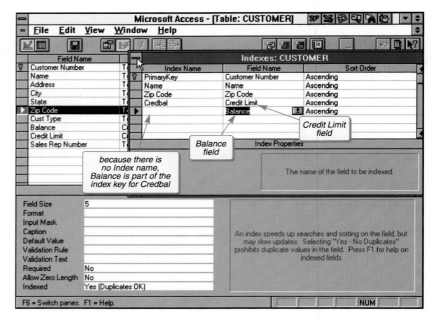

FIGURE 3-74

The indexes have now been created. Access will use them automatically, whenever possible, to improve efficiency of ordering or finding records. It will also maintain them automatically. That is, whenever the data in the CUSTOMER table is changed, Access will automatically make appropriate changes in the indexes.

Ordering Records

Recall from previous discussions that Access sequences the records by customer number whenever listing them because customer number is the primary key. To change the order in which records appear, click the Sort Ascending button (⬚) or Sort Descending button (⬚). These will reorder the records, based on the field in which the cursor is located. To sort on multiple fields, use the Edit Filter/Sort button (⬚). In sorting, Access will automatically use any appropriate secondary indexes.

Perform the following steps to order the records by customer name.

TO ORDER ROWS ON A SINGLE FIELD ▼

STEP 1 ►

Open the CUSTOMER table in Datasheet view, press the TAB key to move to the Name field, and point to the Sort Ascending button (Figure 3-75).

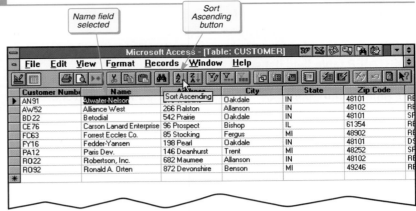

FIGURE 3-75

STEP 2 ►

Click the Sort Ascending button.

The rows are now ordered by Name (Figure 3-76).

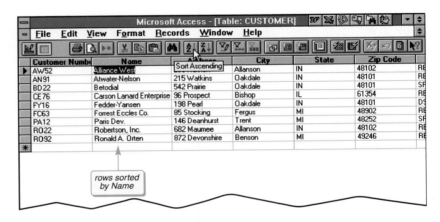

FIGURE 3-76

Perform the following steps to order records on a combination of fields.

TO ORDER ROWS ON MULTIPLE FIELDS ▼

STEP 1 ►

Point to the Edit Filter/Sort button (Figure 3-77).

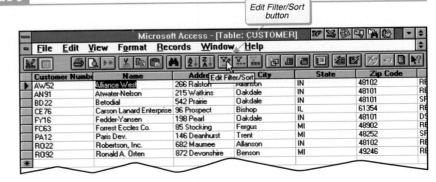

FIGURE 3-77

STEP 2 ▶

Click the Edit Filter/Sort button.
Resize the portions of the screen,
as in Project 2, and also resize the
CUSTOMER table field list so all
fields display. Select the Edit menu
and point to the Clear Grid
command.

*The Microsoft Access - [Filter:
CUSTOMERFilter1]
window displays (Figure
3-78). The Edit menu
displays.*

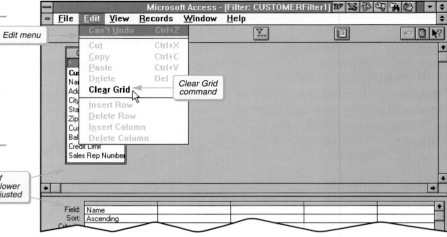

FIGURE 3-78

STEP 3 ▶

Choose the Clear Grid command.
Select the Credit Limit field by
pointing to it and double-clicking the
left mouse button. Select the Sort:
entry for the Credit Limit field and
click the drop-down arrow.

*The Credit Limit field is selected
(Figure 3-79). The list of sort
orders displays.*

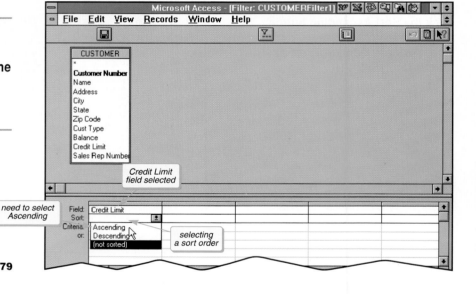

FIGURE 3-79

STEP 4 ▶

Select Ascending. Select the
Balance field by double-clicking the
left mouse button and then select
Ascending as the sort order. Point to
the Apply Filter/Sort button (▼)
(Figure 3-80).

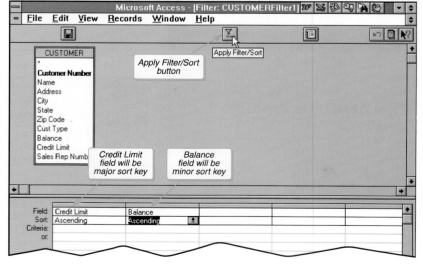

FIGURE 3-80

STEP 5 ▶

Click the Apply Filter/Sort button and then click the right scroll arrow three times so both the Balance and Credit Limit fields display.

The rows are ordered by Credit Limit. Within each group of customers having the same credit limit, the rows are ordered by Balance (Figure 3-81).

STEP 6 ▶

Close the CUSTOMER table by double-clicking its Control-menu box.

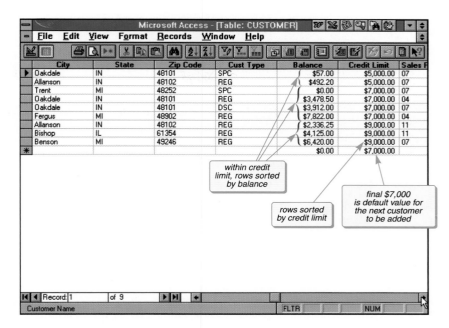

FIGURE 3-81

▶ PROJECT SUMMARY

Project 3 covered the issues involved in maintaining a database. You learned to use Form view to add records and also how to search for the next record satisfying some criteria. You learned how to change and delete records. You learned how to change the structure of a table, how to create validation rules, and how to specify referential integrity between two tables by creating relationships. You learned how to make mass changes to a table. Finally, you learned how to create and use indexes.

▶ KEY TERMS AND INDEX

default value *(A141)*
foreign key *(A148)*
Form view *(A124)*
index key *(A155)*
legal values *(A144)*
multiple-field secondary indexes
    (A158)
one-to-many relationship *(A149)*

primary index *(A156)*
primary key *(A148)*
range of values *(A141)*
referential integrity *(A149)*
required field *(A141)*
restructure *(A123)*
searching *(A127)*
secondary indexes *(A123)*

single-field secondary indexes
    (A156)
structure *(A131)*
update query *(A136)*
validation rules *(A141)*
validation text *(A141)*

In Access, you can accomplish a task in a number of different ways. The following table provides a quick reference to each task presented in this project with its available options. The commands listed in the Menu column can be executed using either the keyboard or mouse.

Task	Mouse	Menu	Keyboard Shortcuts
Add a Field		From Edit menu, choose Insert Row	Press INSERT
Add a Record	Click Last Record button, click Next Record button		
Change a Field Size	Click Field Size box		Press F6
Change a Group of Records		From Query menu, choose Update	
Create a Multiple-Field Secondary Index		From View menu, choose Indexes	
Create a Single-Field Secondary Index	Click Indexed box	From View menu, choose Indexes	Press F6, press TAB
Delete a Field		From Edit menu, choose Delete	Press DELETE
Delete a Group of Records		From Query menu, choose Delete	
Delete a Record		From Edit menu, choose Delete	Press DELETE
Escape from Editing		From Edit menu, choose Undo Current Record	Press ESC (may need to do it twice)
Increase Column Width on a Datasheet	Drag Grid Line on right edge of column		
Order Records on a Single Field	Click Sort Ascending or Sort Descending button	From Records menu, choose Quick Sort	
Order Records on Multiple Fields	Click Edit Filter/Sort button	From Records menu, choose Edit Filter/Sort	
Produce an Insertion Point in a Field	Click the field		Press F2
Restructure a Table	Click Design button	From View menu, choose Table Design	
Search for a Record	Click Find button	From Edit menu, choose Find	Press CTRL+F
Specify a Default Value	Click Default Value box		Press F6, press TAB
Specify a Format	Click Format box		Press F6, press TAB
Specify Validation Rule	Click Validation Rule box		Press F6, press TAB
Specify Validation Text	Click Validation Text box		Press F6, press TAB
Specify Relationships (Referential Integrity)	Click Relationships button	From Edit menu, choose Relationships	

STUDENT ASSIGNMENT 1
True/False

Instructions: Circle T if the statement is true or F if the statement is false.

T F 1. Access automatically sorts records by the primary index.

T F 2. Access allows secondary indexes on single fields only.

T F 3. Indexes provide an efficient alternative to sorting.

T F 4. To create an index, choose the Indexes command from the View menu on the Table Design window.

T F 5. To change the order in which records appear in a table, click the Sort Ascending or Sort Descending button.

T F 6. The quickest and easiest way to make the same change to all records is to use a query.

T F 7. To create an update query, create a New Query and choose the Update command from the Query menu.

T F 8. Only Currency and Numeric fields can be assigned default values.

T F 9. To force all letters in a field to display as uppercase, use the > symbol in the Format box.

T F 10. To sort records in a table on multiple fields, use the Edit Filter/Sort button.

T F 11. A foreign key is a field in one table whose values are required to match a primary key of another table.

T F 12. The property that the value in a foreign key must match that of another table's primary key is called entity integrity.

T F 13. To add records to a table in Form view, move to the last record in the table and click the Next Record button.

T F 14. You can add and change records using Form view, but you can only delete records using Datasheet view.

T F 15. To delete a record from a table, point to the record selector for the record, click the left mouse button, and then press DELETE.

T F 16. To search for a specific record in a table, move the highlight to the field in which you wish to search and click the Find button.

T F 17. To delete a group of records that satisfy a criteria, use a query.

T F 18. To add a field to a table structure, select the field below where you would like the new field inserted and press CTRL+N.

T F 19. To delete records that satisfy some criteria using a query, choose the Delete command from the Query menu.

T F 20. To specify referential integrity, choose Referential Integrity from the Edit menu.

STUDENT ASSIGNMENT 2
Multiple Choice

Instructions: Circle the correct response.

1. Indexes _____.
   a. provide an efficient alternative to sorting
   b. allow rapid retrieval of records
   c. allow rapid retrieval of tables
   d. both a and b

(continued)

STUDENT ASSIGNMENT 2 (continued)

2. To create a multiple-field secondary index, choose _____ from the View menu on the Table Design window.
   a. Secondary Index
   b. Define Secondary Indexes
   c. Indexes
   d. Define Indexes

3. To sort records in a table on multiple fields, use the _____ button.
   a. Sort
   b. Sort/Order
   c. Order/Range
   d. Edit Filter/Sort

4. To search for a specific record in a table, move the highlight to the field in which you wish to search and click the _____ button.
   a. Search
   b. Locate
   c. Find
   d. Locator

5. To force all letters in a field to display as uppercase, use the _____ symbol in the Format box.
   a. ?
   b. >
   c. @
   d. &

6. A _____ is a field in one table whose values are required to match a primary key of another table.
   a. secondary key
   b. auxiliary key
   c. foreign key
   d. matching key

7. The property that the value in a foreign key must match that of another table's primary key is called _____ integrity.
   a. entity
   b. referential
   c. relationship
   d. inter-relation

8. To delete records that satisfy some criteria using a query, choose the Delete command from the _____ menu.
   a. Edit
   b. Query
   c. View
   d. Select

9. To specify referential integrity, choose _____ from the Edit menu.
   a. Referential Integrity
   b. Integrity
   c. Relationships
   d. Primary Key

10. To add a field to a table structure, select the field below where you would like the new field inserted and press _____.
   a. CTRL+N
   b. CTRL+INSERT
   c. INSERT
   d. ALT+INSERT

STUDENT ASSIGNMENT 3
Understanding Form View

Instructions: Figure SA3-3 shows the first record in the Software table in Form view. Use this figure to help explain how to perform the following tasks in Form view.

1. Move from the first record to the second record.

   _____

   _____

2. Add a new record to the Software table.

   _____

   _____

3. Move to the first record in the table.

_____

_____

_____

4. Locate the record that contains the value SCI in the Category field.

_____

_____

_____

5. Locate the next record that contains the value SCI in the Category field.

_____

_____

_____

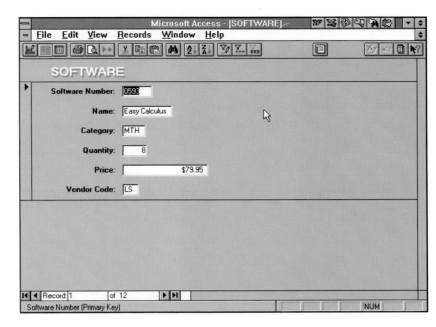

FIGURE SA3-3

STUDENT ASSIGNMENT 4
Understanding Validation Rules

Instructions: Figure SA3-4 shows the Software table in Design view. Use this figure to help explain how to create the following validation rules. For each instruction, assume that the proper field has already been selected.

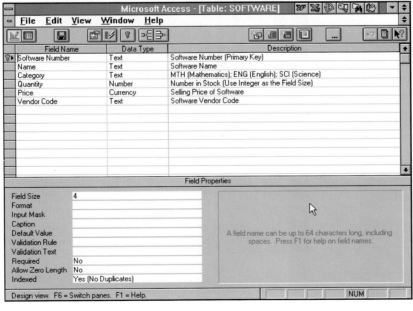

FIGURE SA3-4

(continued)

STUDENT ASSIGNMENT 4 (continued)

1. Make the Name field a required field.

   _____

   _____

2. Ensure that only MTH, ENG, or SCI are entered in the Category field.

   _____

   _____

3. Display a message to indicate the legal values for the Category field.

   _____

   _____

4. Ensure that entries in the Category field are converted to uppercase.

   _____

   _____

5. Specify that entries in the Quantity field be greater than or equal to 0 and less than or equal to 100.

   _____

   _____

STUDENT ASSIGNMENT 5
Understanding Update Queries

Instructions: Figure SA3-5 shows the Update Query window for the Software table. Use this figure to help explain how to perform the following tasks:

1. Change the price for all records from $24.95 to $26.95.

   _____

   _____

   _____

   _____

2. Change the vendor code for all records from EI to CC.

   _____

   _____

   _____

   _____

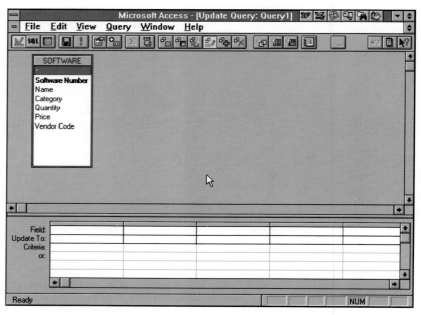

FIGURE SA3-5

3. Change the quantity to 30 for all records where the category is ENG.

_____

_____

4. Delete all records where the Category is ENG.

_____

_____

STUDENT ASSIGNMENT 6
Understanding Indexes

Instructions: Figure SA3-6 shows the Design window for the Vendor table. Use this figure to help explain how to perform the following tasks:

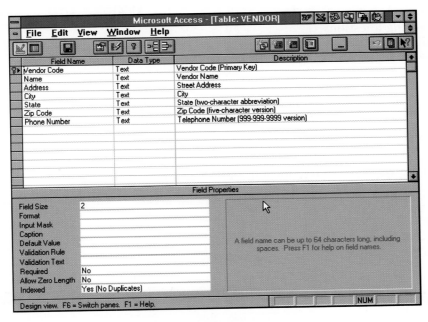

FIGURE SA3-6

1. Create an index for the Name field.

_____

_____

2. Create an index for the Zip Code field.

_____

_____

3. Create an index called statcity on the combination of the State and City fields.

_____

_____

_____

COMPUTER LABORATORY EXERCISE 1
Using the Help Menu

Instructions: Perform the following tasks:

1. Start Access.
2. Choose the Contents command from the Help menu.
3. Select Search.
4. Type `referential integrity` in the Search dialog box and select the phrase "Defining Relationships Between Tables," as shown in Figure CLE3-1.
5. Read the information and answer the following questions.
   a. How do you delete a relationship?

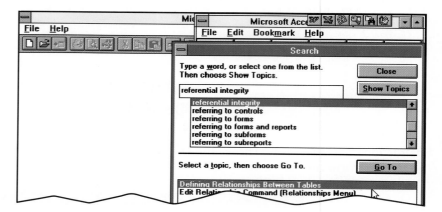

FIGURE CLE3-1

_____

b. Do the field properties for each field in the relationship have to be identical?

_____

_____

c. How do you create a second relationship between two tables?

_____

_____

6. Close the Help window.
7. Exit Access.

COMPUTER LABORATORY EXERCISE 2
Creating Validation Rules

Instructions: Perform the following tasks:

1. Start Access.
2. Open the Soft database in the subdirectory Access2 on the Student Diskette that accompanies this book and open the Software table in Design view, as shown in Figure CLE3-2.
3. Make Name a required field.

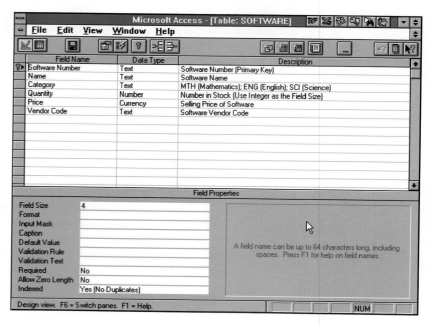

FIGURE CLE3-2

4. Ensure that all entries for the Category field are converted to uppercase.
5. Ensure that all entries for the Vendor Code field are converted to uppercase.
6. Assign a default value of 10 to the Quantity field.
7. Specify that the only legal values for the Category field are MTH, ENG, and SCI. Include a message to inform the user of these values.
8. Save the changes to the structure and open the Software table.
9. Print the table.
10. Exit Access.

COMPUTER LABORATORY EXERCISE 3
Specifying Referential Integrity

Instructions: Perform the following tasks:

1. Start Access.
2. Open the Soft database in the subdirectory Access2 on the Student Diskette that accompanies this book and choose Relationships from the Edit menu.
3. Add the Software and Vendor tables to the Relationships window, as shown in Figure CLE3-3.

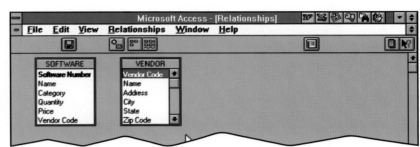

FIGURE CLE3-3

4. Resize the Field List boxes so all fields display.
5. Create a one-to-many relationship between the Vendor and Software tables.
6. Save the relationship and close the database.
7. What would now happen if you opened the Software table and added a record with a vendor code of BA?

_____

_____

8. Exit Access.

COMPUTER LABORATORY ASSIGNMENTS

COMPUTER LABORATORY ASSIGNMENT 1
Maintaining the Consumer Products Database

Purpose: To provide practice in maintaining a database.

Instructions: Use the database created in Computer Laboratory Assignment 1 of Project 1 for this assignment. Execute each task on the computer and print the results.

1. Open the Items database and open the Product table in Design view, as shown in Figure CLA3-1 on the next page.
2. Create a secondary index for the Product Description field.
3. Create a secondary index on the combination of the Item Class Code and Product Description fields. Name the index Classprod.
4. Save these changes and display the Product table in Datasheet view. _(continued)_

COMPUTER LABORATORY ASSIGNMENT 1 (continued)

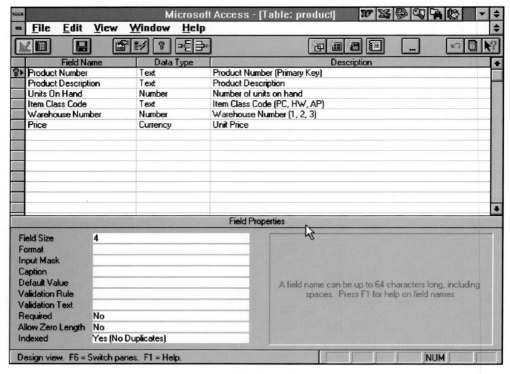

FIGURE CLA3-1

5. Order the records in the Product table by Product Description within Item Class Code.
6. Print the table.
7. Display the Design window for the Product table and change the field width of the Product Description field to 22.
8. Save the changes and display the table in Datasheet view.
9. Change the entry for Product Number CX22 from Luxury Spa to Luxury Spa & Whirlpool. If necessary, adjust the column width so the entire product description displays.
10. Print the table.
11. Create and save the following validation rules for the Product table. List the steps involved.
    a. Make Product Description a required field.

    _____

    _____

    b. Ensure that any lowercase letters entered in the Product Number will be converted to uppercase.

    _____

    _____

    c. Specify that PC, HW, and AP are the legal values for the Item Class Code field. Include validation text.

    _____

    _____

    d. Specify that warehouse numbers must be between 1 and 3.

    _____

    _____

12. Create a form for the Product table. Use the name Product Form.

13. Open the form called Product Form and add the following record to the Product table:

| CBO3 | Gas Dryer | 2 | AP | 1 | 299.99 |

14. Change to Datasheet view and print the table.
15. Create a new query for the Product table.
16. Using a query, delete all records in the Product table where the Product Description starts with the letter R. (Hint: Use a wildcard.)
17. Close the query without saving it.
18. Print the Product table.
19. Specify referential integrity between the Class table (the "one" table) and the Product table (the "many" table). List the steps involved.

_____

_____

_____

20. Close the database and Access.

COMPUTER LABORATORY ASSIGNMENT 2
Maintaining the Employee Database

Purpose: To provide practice in maintaining a database.

Instructions: Use the database created in Computer Laboratory Assignment 2 of Project 1 for this assignment. Execute each task on the computer and print the results.

1. Open the Emp database and open the Employee table in Design view, as shown in Figure CLA3-2.
2. Create a secondary index for the Employee Last Name field.

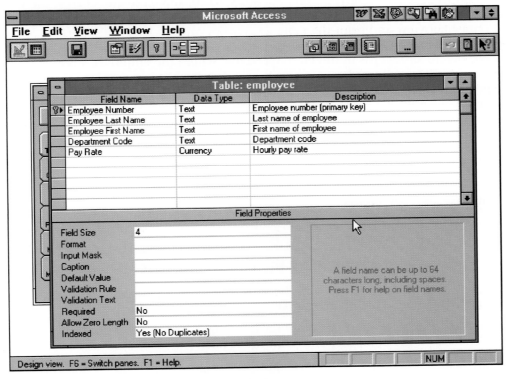

FIGURE CLA3-2   (*continued*)

COMPUTER LABORATORY ASSIGNMENT 2 (continued)

3. Create a secondary index on the combination of the Department Code and Employee Last Name fields. Name the index Deptname.
4. Create a secondary index on the combination of the Pay Rate and Employee Last Name fields. Name the index Payname.
5. Save these changes and display the Employee table in Datasheet view.
6. Order the records by Employee Last Name.
7. Print the table.
8. Order the records in the Employee table by Employee Last Name within Pay Rate.
9. Print the table.
10. Display the Design window for the Employee table and add the field Union Code to the Employee table. Define the field as Text with a width of 3. Insert the Union Code field after the Department Code field. This field will contain data on whether the employee is a union member (UNM) or non-union member (NON). Save the changes to the Employee table.
11. Create a new query for the Employee table.
12. Using this query, change all the entries in the Union Code column to UNM. This will be the status of most employees. Do not save the query.
13. Print the table.
14. Create the following validation rules for the Employee table. List the steps involved.
    a. Make Employee First Name and Employee Last Name required fields.

    _____

    b. Specify the legal values UNM and NON for the Union Code field. Include validation text.

    _____

    _____

15. Create a form for the Employee table. Use the name Employee Form.
16. Using Form view, add the following record to the Employee table.

| 0909 | Fisher | Ella | 02 | NON | 9.30 |

17. Locate the employees with Employee Numbers 0023, 0120, and 0226 and change the Union Code for each record to NON.
18. Change to Datasheet view and print the table.
19. Create a new query for the Employee table.
20. Using a query, delete all records in the Employee table where the employee's last name starts with the letter G. (Hint: Use a wildcard.)
21. Close the query without saving it.
22. Print the Employee table.
23. Specify referential integrity between the Department table (the "one" table) and the Employee table (the "many" table). List the steps involved.

    _____

    _____

24. Close the database and exit Access.

COMPUTER LABORATORY ASSIGNMENT 3
Maintaining the Movie Database

Purpose: To provide practice in maintaining a database.

Instructions: Use the database created in Computer Laboratory Assignment 3 of Project 1 for this assignment. Execute each task on the computer and print the results.

1. Open the Mov database and open the Movie table in Design view, as shown in Figure CLA3-3.

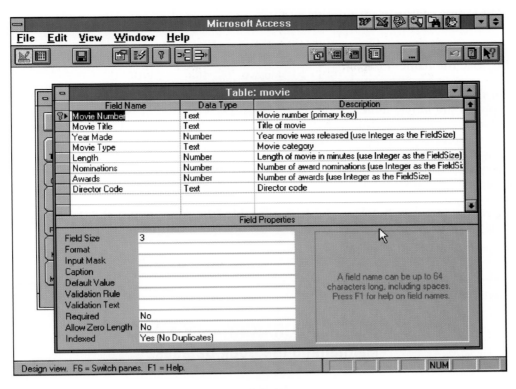

FIGURE CLA3-3

2. Create a secondary index for the Movie Title field.
3. Create a secondary index on the combination of the Movie Type and Movie Title fields. Name the index Typetitle.
4. Save these changes and display the Movie table in Datasheet view.
5. Order the records in the Movie table by Movie Title within Movie Type.
6. Print the table.
7. Display the Design window for the Movie table and change the field width of Movie Title to 25.
8. Add the field Color Type to the Movie table. Define the field as Text with a width of 5. Insert the Color Type field after the Length field. This field will contain data on whether the movie is in color (COLOR) or black and white (BW).
9. Save these changes and display the Movie table in Datasheet view.
10. Change the title for the movie Father Act to Father Act, Too.
11. Order the records by the Movie Title index.
12. Print the table.
13. Create a new query for the Movie table.
14. Using this query, change all the entries in the Color Type column to COLOR. This will be the status of most movies. Do not save the query.
15. Print the Movie table.
16. Create and save the following validation rules for the Movie table. List the steps involved.
    a. Make Movie Title a required field.

    _____

    b. Specify the legal values COLOR and BW for the Color Type field. Include validation text.

    _____

    _____

    c. Assign a default value of COLOR to the Color Type field.

    _____

(continued)

COMPUTER LABORATORY ASSIGNMENT 3 (continued)

17. Create a form for the Movie table. Use the name Move Form.

023	Mojave	1937	WESTER	97	BW	02

18. Using Form view, add the following record to the Movie table.
19. Locate the Movies with Movie Numbers 020 and 007 and change the Color Type for each record to BW.
20. Change to Datasheet view and print the table.
21. Create a new query for the Movie table.
22. Using a query, delete all records in the Movie table where the movie was made in 1940.
23. Close the query without saving it.
24. Print the Movie table.
25. Specify referential integrity between the Director table (the "one" table) and the Movie table (the "many" table). List the steps involved.

_____

26. Close the database and exit Access.

COMPUTER LABORATORY ASSIGNMENT 4
Maintaining the Book Database

Purpose: To provide practice in maintaining a database.

Problem: The bookstore owner is very pleased with the work you have done so far on the Book database. Because the business is expanding rapidly, she would like to make some changes to the database. She has sent you a list of recommended changes and has asked if you can implement them.

Instructions: Use the database created in Computer Laboratory Assignment 4 of Project 1 for this assignment. Provide printed output and/or a written explanation that confirms the changes to the database.

The following are recommended changes to the Book database:

1. The title for Book Code 7114 is actually *The Ragbagger and the Sea* not *The Ragbagger*. Change the size of the field to accommodate the correct title.
2. Customer queries can be answered more efficiently if the books can be displayed in various orders. List the books in author order. Also list the books in order by title within publisher and in order by title within book type.
3. Most books in inventory are paperback, but there are a few hardback books. Add a new field with values such as SOFT(paperback) and HARD (hardback) to indicate the cover type.
4. Currently, the only hardback books in stock are those books with a price of $17.95 or greater. Use a more efficient method than changing each record individually to make those corrections to the database.
5. Various personnel in the bookstore are updating the database. Improve the accuracy of the data entry process by adding some validation rules to the database. The following are examples.
   a. No book is priced at less than $1.99 or greater than $99.99.
   b. All Book Type and Publisher Code entries are in uppercase.
   c. The Book Title, Publisher, and Author fields are required.
   d. Publisher Code entries should match the entries in the Publisher table.
   e. SOFT and HARD are the only choices for the cover type. Most books are paperback.
   f. Any letters entered in the Book Code field are in uppercase.
6. Three copies of a new paperback book (code 6781) have just arrived that should be added to the database. However, the book publisher is not in the Publisher table. Add the book to the database. The publisher is Fraser Books (FR). The book title is *The Runaway Hero* by Megan Rustan, and it is fiction. The price is $5.95.
7. The store will no longer carry science fiction (SFI) books. Delete all science fiction books from the database.

PRESENTATION GRAPHICS

USING *M*ICROSOFT *P*OWER *P*OINT 4 FOR *W*INDOWS

BUILDING A SLIDE PRESENTATION

OBJECTIVES You will have mastered the material in this project when you can:

- Start PowerPoint
- Describe the PowerPoint window
- Use the PowerPoint Pick a Look Wizard
- Select a template
- Create a title slide
- Create a bulleted list
- Italicize text
- Change font size

- Save a presentation
- Create a new slide
- Use the PowerPoint spelling checker
- Print a transparency presentation
- Exit PowerPoint
- Open a saved presentation
- Edit a presentation
- Use PowerPoint online Help

▶ WHAT IS POWERPOINT?

PowerPoint is a complete **presentation graphics program** that allows you to produce professional-looking presentations. PowerPoint gives you the flexibility to make an informal presentation in a small conference room using overhead transparencies (Figure 1-1a), to make an electronic presentation using a projection device attached to a personal computer (Figure 1-1b), or to make a formal presentation to a large audience using 35mm slides (Figure 1-1c).

PowerPoint contains several features to assist in the creation of a presentation. The following list describes these PowerPoint features.

- *Word processing*   **Word processing** allows you to create automatic bulleted lists, combine words and images, check spelling, find and replace text, and use multiple fonts and type sizes.
- *Outlining*   **Outlining** allows you to quickly create your presentation by using an outline format. You can import outlines from Microsoft Word or other word processors.
- *Graphing*   **Graphing** allows you to create and insert charts into your presentations. Graph formats include two-dimensional (2-D) graphs: area, bar, column, combination, line, pie, xy (scatter), and three-dimensional (3-D) graphs: area, bar, column, line, and pie.

FIGURE 1-1a

FIGURE 1-1b

FIGURE 1-1c

- ▸ *Drawing* **Drawing** allows you to create diagrams using shapes, such as arcs, arrows, cubes, rectangles, stars, and triangles. Drawing also allows you to modify shapes without redrawing.
- ▸ *Clip art* **Clip art** allows you to insert artwork into your presentation without creating it yourself. There are over 1000 graphic images in the Microsoft ClipArt Gallery.
- ▸ *Presentation management* **Presentation management** allows you to control the design and arrangement of your presentation.
- ▸ *Wizards* A **wizard** is a tutorial approach to quickly and efficiently create a presentation. PowerPoint wizards make it easy to create quality presentations by prompting you for specific content and design criteria. The AutoContent Wizard asks you what are you going to talk about and what type of presentation are you going to give, such as recommending a strategy or selling a product. The Pick a Look Wizard asks you questions about the type of presentation media you are using for your presentation, such as color overheads or video screen. The Pick a Look Wizard asks you to select a format for your presentation and to select printing options. You may also select footer options, such as date, page number, and company name, or other text you might want to include on the bottom of every slide. With

either wizard, just answer the questions that display in the windows. After completing the wizard steps, your presentation is well on its way to completion.

▶ PROJECT ONE — TIPS AND TECHNIQUES FOR FINDING THE RIGHT JOB

This book presents a series of projects using PowerPoint to produce slides similar to those you would develop in an academic or business environment. Project 1 uses PowerPoint to create the overhead presentation shown in Figures 1-2a through 1-2d. The objective is to produce a presentation on Tips and Techniques for Finding the Right Job that will be presented using an overhead projector. As an introduction to PowerPoint, this project steps you through the most common type of presentation, a **bulleted list**. A bulleted list is a list of paragraphs, each preceded by a bullet. A **bullet** is a symbol (usually a heavy dot) that precedes text when the text warrants special emphasis. The first of the four slides is called the title slide (Figure 1-2a). The **title slide** introduces the presentation to the audience.

Slide Preparation Steps

The following preparation steps give you an overview of how to create the slides in Figures 1-2a, 1-2b, 1-2c, and 1-2d. If you are creating

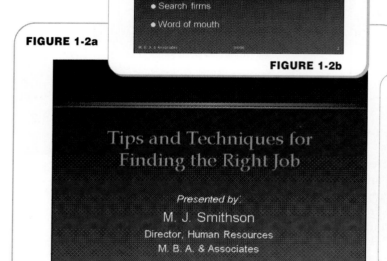

FIGURE 1-2a

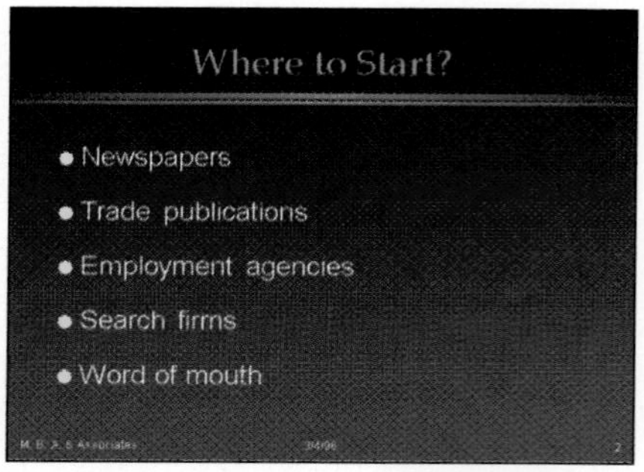

FIGURE 1-2b

FIGURE 1-2c

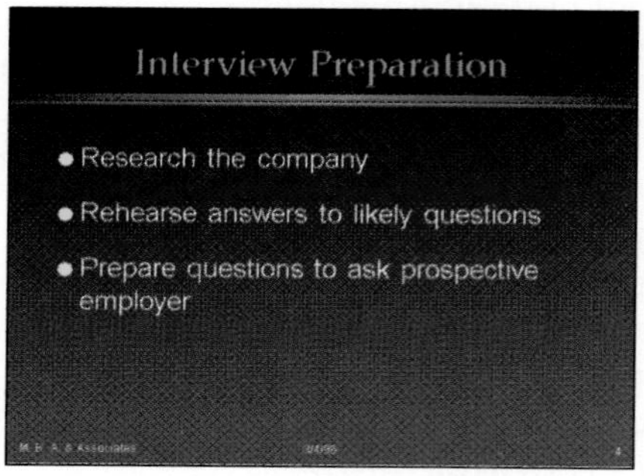

FIGURE 1-2d

these slides on a personal computer, read these steps without doing them.

1. Start PowerPoint.
2. Use Pick a Look Wizard.
3. Create a title slide.
4. Create three bulleted lists.
5. Spell check the presentation.

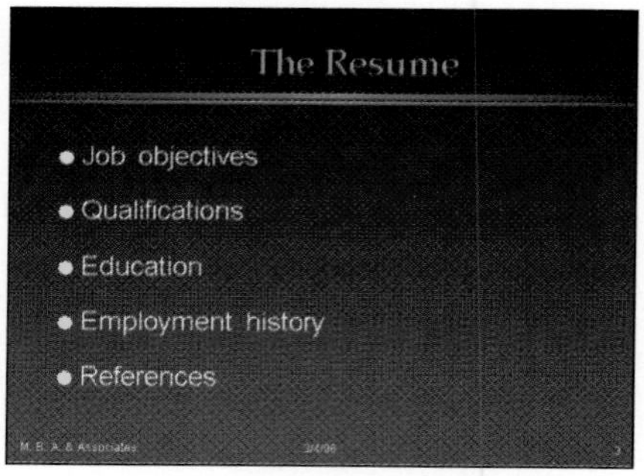

6. Save the presentation.
7. Print the presentation.
8. Exit PowerPoint.
9. Open PowerPoint.
10. View Quick Preview.
11. Make a transparency.

▶ STARTING POWERPOINT

T o start PowerPoint, the Office Manager toolbar must display on the screen or the Microsoft Office group window must be open. Follow these steps to start PowerPoint, or ask your instructor how to start PowerPoint on your computer.

TO START POWERPOINT ▼

STEP 1 ▶

If the Office Manager toolbar displays, use the mouse to point to the Microsoft PowerPoint button (🖳) (Figure 1-3). If the Office Manager toolbar does not display at the top right of your screen, then point to the Microsoft PowerPoint program-item icon (🖳) in the Microsoft Office group window.

Your Office Manager toolbar may contain more or fewer buttons than shown in Figure 1-3.

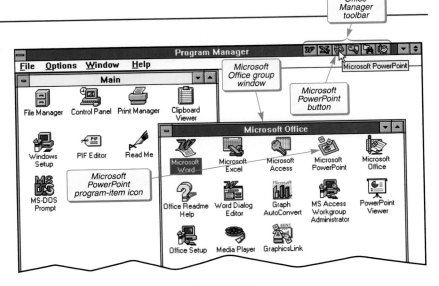

FIGURE 1-3

STEP 2 ▶

If the Office Manager toolbar displays, then with the mouse pointer pointing to the Microsoft PowerPoint button, click the left mouse button. If the Office Manager toolbar does not display at the top right of your screen, then double-click the Microsoft PowerPoint program-item icon in the Microsoft Office group window.

PowerPoint displays an empty slide and the Tip of the Day dialog box (Figure 1-4). Each time you start PowerPoint, a different tip displays.

FIGURE 1-4

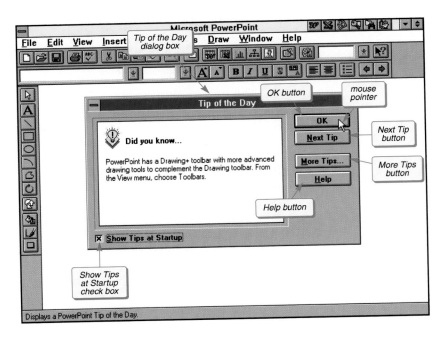

STEP 3 ▶

Choose the OK button.

The PowerPoint startup dialog box displays (Figure 1-5). The option button selected at startup depends on the option chosen the last time PowerPoint was started.

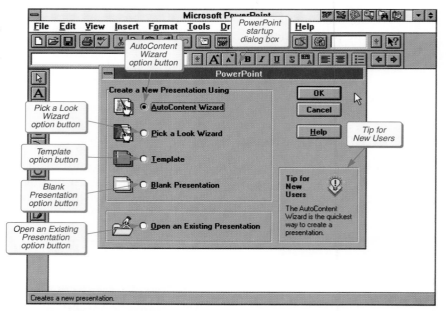

FIGURE 1-5

The Tip of the Day (Figure 1-4 on the previous page) displays each time you start PowerPoint. These tips provide helpful hints for designing and building presentations. The Next Tip button (Next Tip) in the Tip of the Day dialog box displays the next tip in the Tip of the Day library. The More Tips button (More Tips...) displays the Tip of the Day Help window where you may select the topic for which you want more information. The Help button (Help) displays the PowerPoint Help window. To discontinue the Tip of the Day dialog box at startup, click the Show Tips at Startup check box to remove the x. To reactivate the Tip of the Day at startup, choose the Tip of the Day command from the Help menu and then click the Show Tips at Startup check box to add an x.

▶ THE POWERPOINT STARTUP DIALOG BOX

Each time you start PowerPoint, the PowerPoint startup dialog box displays (Figure 1-5 above). The PowerPoint startup dialog box contains a list of option buttons. You may select only one option button from the list. The option button choices are AutoContent Wizard, Pick a Look Wizard, Template, Blank Presentation, and Open an Existing Presentation. The PowerPoint startup dialog box helps you create a new presentation or open an existing presentation.

When creating a new presentation, the AutoContent Wizard helps you decide content and order, whereas the Pick a Look Wizard helps you decide appearance and attitude. If you choose either the AutoContent Wizard or the Pick a Look Wizard option button, additional dialog boxes display. You determine the design of your slides through the selections made in these dialog boxes. The Template options allow you to choose a template. A **template** provides consistency in design and color throughout the entire presentation. The template determines the color scheme, font style and size, and layout of your presentation. The Blank Presentation option displays a blank PowerPoint slide after prompting you to choose a layout. The Open an Existing Presentation option displays the Open dialog box, where you choose the presentation you wish to open.

▶ PICK A LOOK WIZARD

T he Pick a Look Wizard presents a series of dialog boxes that prompt you for design criteria to customize the Slide Master for your presentation. The **Slide Master** is a "control" slide that holds the title and text place-holders, as well as background items that display on all your slides in the presentation. As you move from step to step in the Pick a Look Wizard, you are asked for the type of output you are using for this presentation. Your choices are black-and-white overheads, color overheads, on-screen presentation, and 35mm slides. Project 1 uses the on-screen presentation format. On-screen presentation allows you to develop your presentation in color for an on-screen slide show, yet allows you to print your presentation as either color overheads or black-and-white overheads.

In another step, you are prompted to select a template. PowerPoint designed templates specifically for the type of presentation output. The templates for on-screen presentations and 35mm slides have the most color. Color overhead templates use some color, but black-and-white overhead templates use no color. Templates may be changed at anytime during the development of your presentation. Dialog boxes display in subsequent Pick a Look Wizard steps for printing options and footer options.

By choosing option buttons and selecting check boxes, you can quickly create the look and feel of your presentation. Perform the following steps to use the Pick a Look Wizard.

TO USE THE PICK A LOOK WIZARD ▼

STEP 1 ▶

Choose the Pick a Look Wizard option button in the PowerPoint startup dialog box by pointing to it and clicking the left mouse button. Then, point to the OK button (Figure 1-6).

The black dot in the Pick a Look Wizard option button denotes it is selected. The other option buttons in the PowerPoint startup dialog box are white. You may select only one option button.

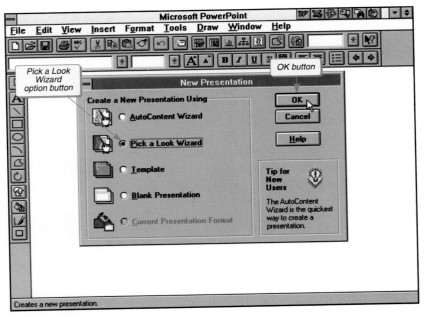

FIGURE 1-6

STEP 2 ▶

Choose the OK button. When the
Pick a Look Wizard – Step 1 of 9
dialog box displays, point to the
Next button (Next>).

*The Pick a Look Wizard – Step 1
of 9 dialog box displays (Figure
1-7).*

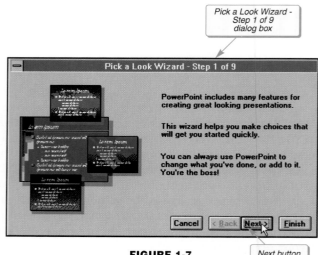

FIGURE 1-7

STEP 3 ▶

Choose the Next button. When the
Pick a Look Wizard Step 2 of 9
dialog box displays, point to the
Next button.

*The Pick a Look Wizard – Step 2
of 9 dialog box displays (Figure
1-8). The On-Screen Presentation
option button is selected.*

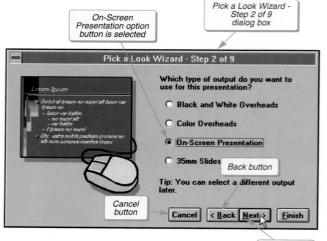

FIGURE 1-8

STEP 4 ▶

Choose the Next button.

*The Pick a Look Wizard – Step 3
of 9 dialog box displays (Figure
1-9). The Multiple Bars option button is selected. To help you select
the best template for your presentation, a preview of the Multiple
Bars template displays in the dialog box. Microsoft artists designed
the Multiple Bars template to display white text on a cyan (light
blue-green) background.*

FIGURE 1-9

STEP 5 ▶

Select the Double Lines option button by clicking the left mouse button. Then, point to the Next button.

The Double Lines option button is selected. A preview of the Double Lines template displays in the dialog box (Figure 1-10). The Double Lines template was selected because it was designed to display light colored text on a dark background. Light text on a dark background provides a stronger contrast than light text on a light background. Recall that the Multiple Bars template displayed white text on a cyan background.

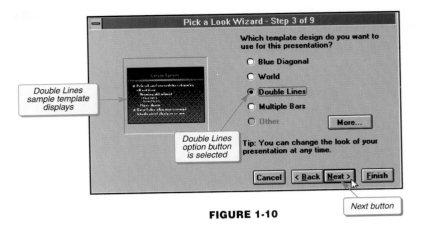

Double Lines sample template displays

Double Lines option button is selected

Next button

FIGURE 1-10

STEP 6 ▶

Choose the Next button. When the Pick a Look Wizard – Step 4 of 9 dialog box displays, point to the Speaker's Notes check box.

The Pick a Look Wizard – Step 4 of 9 dialog box displays (Figure 1-11). All four check boxes display with an x. The check boxes are used to select the different ways to print your presentation.

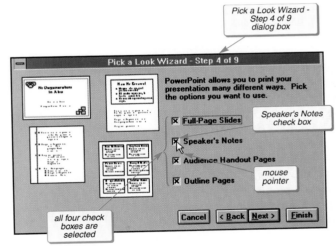

Pick a Look Wizard - Step 4 of 9 dialog box

Speaker's Notes check box

mouse pointer

all four check boxes are selected

FIGURE 1-11

STEP 7 ▶

Click the Speaker's Notes check box to remove the x.

The Speaker's Notes check box is blank, which designates you will not be prompted to add Pick a Look Wizard slide options to the speaker's notes pages (Figure 1-12).

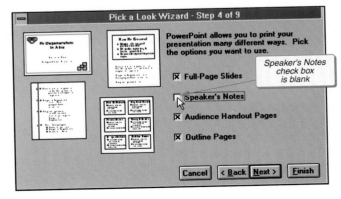

Speaker's Notes check box is blank

FIGURE 1-12

STEP 8 ►

Remove the x from the Audience Handout Pages check box and the Outline Pages check box by clicking them one at a time. Then, point to the Next button.

The Audience Handout Pages check box is blank and the Outline Pages check box is blank, which designate you won't be prompted to add Pick a Look Wizard handout options or outline options (Figure 1-13).

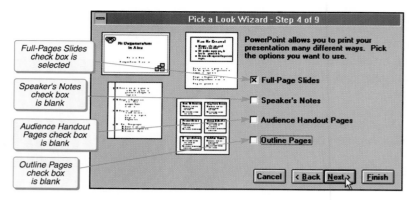

FIGURE 1-13

STEP 9 ►

Choose the Next button.

The Pick a Look Wizard – Slide Options dialog box displays (Figure 1-14). The check boxes for Name, company, or other text, Date, and Page Number are not selected. The Pick a Look Wizard – Slide Options dialog box gives you the opportunity to add text, a date, or page numbers to the footer of the Slide Master. The name used during the PowerPoint installation, M.B.A. & Associates, displays in the text box (Figure 1-14). Your screen will display the name that was used during the installation of PowerPoint on your computer. The text box is blank if PowerPoint was installed without entering a company name.

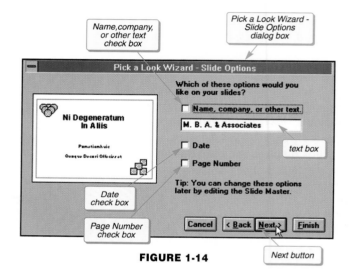

FIGURE 1-14

STEP 10 ►

Choose the Name, company, or other text check box, the Date check box, and the Page Number check box and point to the Next button.

The Name, company, or other text check box, the Date check box, and the Page Number check box each contain an x (Figure 1-15).

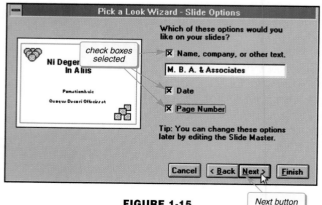

FIGURE 1-15

STEP 11 ▶

Choose the Next button. When the
Pick a Look Wizard – Step 9 of 9
dialog box displays, point to the
Finish button (Finish).

*The Pick a Look Wizard – Step 9
of 9 dialog box displays (Figure
1-16).*

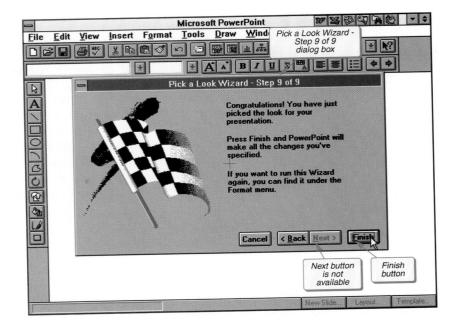

FIGURE 1-16

STEP 12 ▶

Choose the Finish button to exit
Pick a Look Wizard and go to the
first slide in your presentation.

*The first slide of the presentation
displays the Double Lines template and the slide options
selected in the Pick a Look
Wizard (Figure 1-17).*

FIGURE 1-17

Recall earlier in the Pick a Look Wizard — Slide Options dialog box you
selected options to display on every slide (Figure 1-15 on the previous page).
Because you selected options for Name, company, or other text, Date, and Page
Number, they display at the bottom of the slide.

In the Pick a Look Wizard — Step 3 of 9 dialog box (Figure 1-10 on page PP9),
you selected a template from a list of four option buttons. To see all possible templates, choose the More button (More...). Choosing the More button displays the
Presentation Template dialog box. Then, choose the desired template from the
drop-down file list in the \powerpnt\template\sldshow directory by selecting the
template of choice. When you highlight the template name by clicking it, a preview of the template displays in the lower right corner of the Presentation
Template dialog box. Once you select a template, choose the **Apply button**
(Apply) to apply it to your presentation.

▶ THE POWERPOINT WINDOW

T he basic unit of a PowerPoint presentation is a **slide**. **Objects** are the building blocks for a PowerPoint slide. A slide contains one or many objects, such as title, text, graphics, tables, charts, and drawings. In PowerPoint, you have the option of using the PowerPoint default settings or establishing your own settings. A **default setting** is a particular value for a variable that is assigned automatically by PowerPoint and that remains in effect unless canceled or overridden by the user. These settings control the placement of objects, the color scheme, the transition between slides, and other slide attributes. **Attributes** are the properties or characteristics of an object. For example, if you underline the title of the slide, the title is the object and the underline is the attribute.

PowerPoint Views

PowerPoint has five views. You may use any or all views while creating your presentation. You change views by clicking one of the view buttons found on the **View Button Bar** at the bottom of the PowerPoint screen (Figure 1-17 on the previous page). The PowerPoint window display is dependent on the view. Some views are graphical, while others are textual. The views are:

▶ **Slide view**   Slide view displays a single slide as it appears in your presentation. When creating a presentation in Slide view, you type the text and add graphic art, utilizing buttons on the toolbars.
▶ **Outline view**   Outline view displays a presentation in an outline format, showing all slide titles and text.
▶ **Slide Sorter view**   Slide Sorter view displays miniatures of the slides in your presentation. You can then copy, cut, paste, or change slide position to modify your presentation.
▶ **Notes Pages view**   Notes Pages view displays the current note page. Notes Pages view allows you to create speaker's notes to use when you give your presentation. Each notes page corresponds to a slide and includes a reduced slide image.
▶ **Slide Show view**   Slide Show view displays your slides as an electronic presentation on your computer, using the full screen.

In Project 1, you create a presentation in Slide view.

PowerPoint Window

The **PowerPoint window** in Slide view contains the title bar, the menu bar, the toolbars: Standard toolbar, Formatting toolbar, and Drawing toolbar; the status bar, the AutoLayout object area, the mouse pointer, the scroll bars, and the view buttons.

TITLE BAR   The **title bar** (Figure 1-18a) displays the name of the current PowerPoint file. Until you save your presentation, PowerPoint assigns the name Presentation.

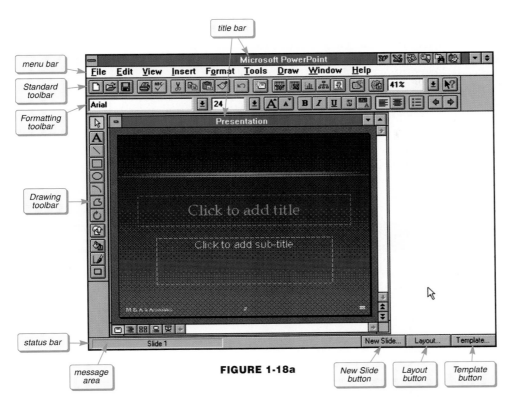

FIGURE 1-18a

MENU BAR   The **menu bar** (Figure 1-18a) displays the PowerPoint menu names. Each menu name represents a list of commands that allows you to retrieve, store, print, and change objects in your presentation. To display a menu, such as the File menu, point to the name File on the menu bar and click the left mouse button.

STATUS BAR   Located at the bottom of the PowerPoint window, the **status bar** consists of three buttons: New Slide button (New Slide...), Layout button (Layout...), and Template button (Template...), and an area to display messages (Figure 1-18a). Most of the time, the current slide number displays in the status bar. However, when you choose a command, the status bar provides a short message about that command.

NEW SLIDE BUTTON   Choosing the **New Slide button** (Figure 1-18a) inserts a new slide into a presentation after the current slide.

LAYOUT BUTTON   Choosing the **Layout button** (Figure 1-18a) displays the Slide Layout dialog box. Select a slide layout from the options in the dialog box.

TEMPLATE BUTTON   Choosing the **Template button** (Figure 1-18a) displays the Presentation Template dialog box. You may select a template anytime during the creation of your presentation.

TOOLBARS   PowerPoint **toolbars** consist of buttons that allow you to perform tasks more quickly than using the menu bar. For example, to save, you choose the Save button ( ) on the Standard toolbar. Each button face has a graphical representation that helps you remember its function. Figure 1-18b, Figure 1-18c, and Figure 1-18d on the next page illustrate the buttons on each of the three toolbars that display each time you start PowerPoint and open a presentation in Slide view. They are the Standard toolbar, the Formatting toolbar, and the Drawing toolbar. Each button will be explained in detail when it is used in the projects. PowerPoint allows you to customize all toolbars and to add toolbar buttons you use most often. Likewise, you can remove those toolbar buttons you don't use. Choose the **Customize command** in the Tools menu to alter toolbars to meet your requirements.

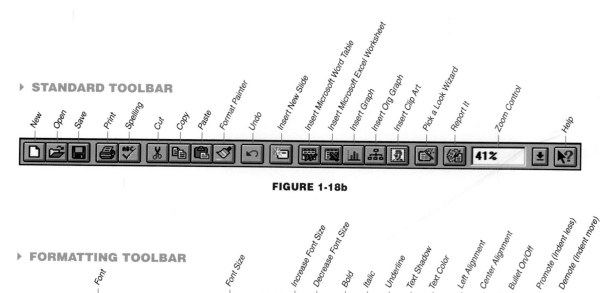

FIGURE 1-18b

FIGURE 1-18c

▶ **DRAWING TOOLBAR**

FIGURE 1-18d

STANDARD TOOLBAR   The **Standard toolbar** (Figure 1-18b) contains tools to execute the most common commands found in the menu bar, such as open, print, save, copy, cut, paste, and many more. The Standard toolbar also has a button for the **Zoom Control**. You control how large or small a document appears on the PowerPoint window with the Zoom Control.

FORMATTING TOOLBAR   The **Formatting toolbar** (Figure 1-18c) contains tools for changing text attributes. The Formatting toolbar allows you to quickly change font, font size, and alignment. It also contains tools to bold, italicize, underline, shadow, color, and bullet text. The five **attribute buttons**, Bold, Italic, Underline, Text Shadow, and Bullet, are on/off switches, or **toggles**. You choose the button once to turn the attribute on; then, you choose it again to turn the attribute off.

DRAWING TOOLBAR   The **Drawing toolbar** (Figure 1-18d) is a collection of tools for drawing lines, circles, and boxes. The Drawing toolbar also contains tools to alter the objects once you have drawn them.

SCROLL BARS   The **vertical scroll bar** (Figure 1-19), located on the right side of the PowerPoint window, allows you to move forward or backward through your presentation.

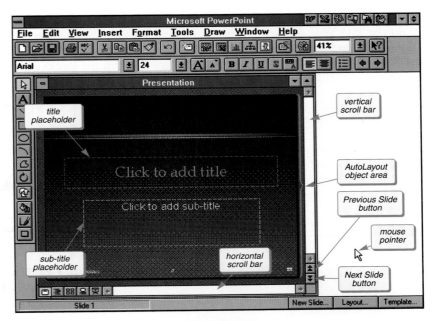

FIGURE 1-19

Choosing the **Next Slide button** ( ) (Figure 1-19), located on the vertical scroll bar, advances you to the next slide in the presentation. Clicking the **Previous Slide button** ( ) (Figure 1-19), located on the vertical scroll bar, backs you up to the slide preceding the current slide.

The **horizontal scroll bar** (Figure 1-19), located on the bottom of the PowerPoint window, allows you to display a portion of the window when you magnify the slide, such that you cannot display it in the PowerPoint window.

It should be noted that in Slide view, both the vertical and horizontal scroll bar actions are dependent upon Zoom Control. If you are in Slide view and Zoom Control is set, such that the entire slide is not visible in the Slide window, clicking the up arrow on the vertical scroll bar will display the next portion of your slide, not the previous slide. Therefore, to go to the previous slide, click the Previous Slide button. To go to the next slide, click the Next Slide button.

AUTOLAYOUT OBJECT AREA   The **AutoLayout object area** (Figure 1-19) is a collection of placeholders for title, text, clip art, graphs, or charts. These placeholders display when you create a new slide. You can change the AutoLayout anytime during the creation of your presentation by selecting the Layout button located on the status bar and then choosing another layout.

PLACEHOLDERS   Surrounded by a dotted line, **placeholders** are the empty objects on a new slide. Depending on the AutoLayout selected, placeholders display for title, text, graphs, tables, organization charts, and clip art. Once you place contents in a placeholder, the placeholder becomes an object. For example, text typed in the placeholder becomes a text object.

TITLE PLACEHOLDER   Surrounded by a dotted line, the **title placeholder** is the empty title object on a new slide (Figure 1-19). Text typed in the title placeholder becomes the title object.

SUB-TITLE PLACEHOLDER   Surrounded by a dotted line, the **sub-title placeholder** is the empty sub-title object that displays below the title placeholder on a title slide (Figure 1-19).

MOUSE POINTER The **mouse pointer** can become one of several different shapes, depending on the task you are performing in PowerPoint and the pointer's location on the screen. The different shapes will be discussed when they display in subsequent projects. The mouse pointer in Figure 1-19 on the previous page has the shape of a left-pointing block arrow ().

▶ MAXIMIZING THE POWERPOINT WINDOW

he PowerPoint window is not maximized when you start PowerPoint. Maximizing the PowerPoint window makes it easier to see the contents of the window. Perform the following steps to maximize the PowerPoint window.

TO MAXIMIZE THE POWERPOINT WINDOW ▼

STEP 1 ▶

Point to the Maximize button (▲) in the upper right corner of the PowerPoint window (Figure 1-20).

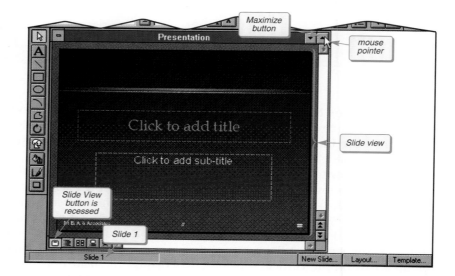

FIGURE 1-20

STEP 2 ▶

Click the left mouse button.

*The PowerPoint window fills the desktop (Figure 1-21). The **Restore button** (▲▼) replaces the Maximize button at the right side of the menu bar. Choosing the Restore button returns the PowerPoint window to its original size.*

FIGURE 1-21

▶ CREATING THE TITLE SLIDE

The purpose of the title slide is to introduce the presentation to the audience. PowerPoint assumes the first slide in a new presentation is the **title slide**. With the exception of a blank slide, PowerPoint assumes every new slide has a title. To make creating your presentation easier, any text you type after a new slide displays becomes the title object. In other words, you do not have to first select the title placeholder before typing text. The AutoLayout for the title slide has a title placeholder near the middle of the window and a sub-title placeholder directly below the title placeholder (Figure 1-21 on the previous page).

Entering the Presentation Title

The presentation title for Project 1 is Tips and Techniques for Finding the Right Job. You type the presentation title in the title placeholder on the title slide. Perform the following steps to explain how to create the title slide for Project 1.

TO ENTER THE PRESENTATION TITLE ▼

STEP 1 ▶

Type Tips and Techniques for Finding the Right Job

*Tips and Techniques for Finding the Right Job displays in the title text box (Figure 1-22). When you type the first character, a slashed outline, called the **selection box,** displays around the title placeholder. A small vertical line (|), called the **insertion point**, indicates where the next character displays. The highlighted (colored) box is the **text box,** and it indicates you are in **text mode**.*

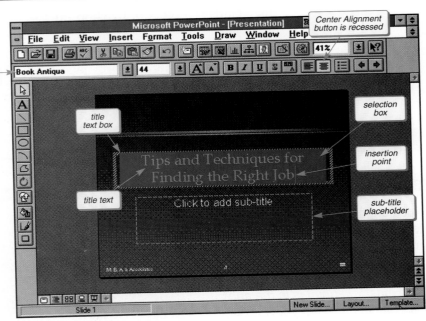

FIGURE 1-22

Notice that you do not press the ENTER key after the word Job. If you press the ENTER key after typing the title, PowerPoint creates a new paragraph. A **paragraph** is a segment of text with the same format that begins when you press the ENTER key and ends when you press the ENTER key again. Pressing the ENTER key creates a new line in a new paragraph. Therefore, do not press the ENTER key unless you want to create a two-paragraph title. Additionally, PowerPoint **line wraps** text that exceeds the width of the placeholder. Tips and Techniques for Finding the Right Job exceeds the width of the title placeholder. PowerPoint wrapped the text into two lines (Figure 1-22).

The title is centered in the window because the Double Lines template alignment attribute is centered. The Center Alignment button (▣) is recessed on the Formatting toolbar.

PRESENTATION TIP

When designing your slide title, keep in mind that uppercase letters are less distinct, making them more difficult to read than lowercase letters. For emphasis, it is acceptable to use all uppercase letters in short titles. Capitalize only the first letter in all words in long titles, except for short articles such as or, the, or an, unless the article is the first word in the title (i.e., The Road to Success).

Correcting a Mistake While Typing

If you type the wrong letter and notice the error before typing the next word, use the BACKSPACE key to erase all the characters back to and including the one that is wrong. If you mistakenly pressed the ENTER key after entering the title and the cursor is on the new line, simply press the BACKSPACE key to return the insertion point to the right of the letter b in the word Job.

You can reverse the last change made by clicking the **Undo button** (◄) on the Standard toolbar or by choosing the **Undo command** from the Edit menu.

Entering the Presentation Sub-title

The next step is to enter Presented by: M. J. Smithson, Director, Human Resources, M. B. A. & Associates into the sub-title placeholder.

TO ENTER THE PRESENTATION SUB-TITLE ▼

STEP 1 ►

Position the mouse pointer on the label, Click to add sub-title, located inside the sub-title placeholder. Then, click the left mouse button.

The insertion point is in the sub-title text box (Figure 1-23). The mouse pointer displays as an I-beam (I). The I-beam mouse pointer indicates the mouse is within a text placeholder. The selection box indicates the sub-title placeholder is selected.

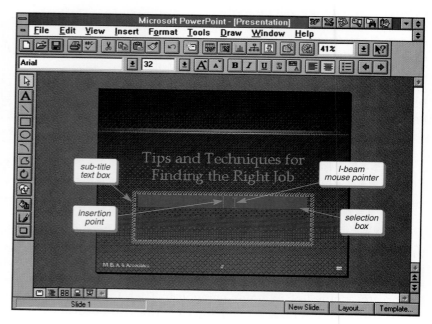

FIGURE 1-23

STEP 2 ▶

Type Presented by: **and press the** ENTER **key. Type** M. J. Smithson **and press the** ENTER **key. Type** Director, Human Resources **and press the** ENTER **key. Type** M. B. A. & Associates

The text displays in the sub-title object, as shown in Figure 1-24. The insertion point displays after the letter s in Associates.

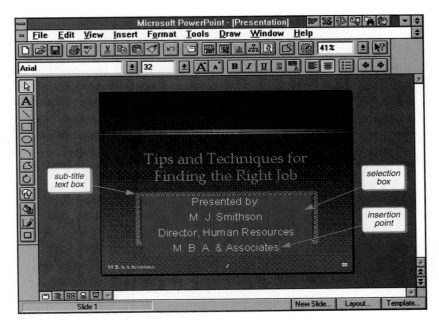

FIGURE 1-24

The previous section created a title slide using an AutoLayout for title slide. PowerPoint displayed the title slide layout because you created a new presentation. You entered text in the title placeholder without selecting the title placeholder because PowerPoint assumes every slide has a title. However, you could click the title placeholder to select it and then type your title. In general, to type text in any text placeholder, click on the text placeholder and type. You also added a sub-title that identifies the presenter. While this is not required, it is often useful information to the audience.

▶ TEXT ATTRIBUTES

This presentation is using the Double Lines template that was selected through the Pick a Look Wizard. Each template has its own text attributes. A **text attribute** is a characteristic of the text, such as font (typeface), font size, font style, or font color. You can adjust text attributes anytime before, during, or after you type the text. Recall that a template determines the color scheme, font style and size, and layout of your presentation. Most of the time, you will use that template's text attributes and color scheme. However, there are times when you want to change the way your presentation looks and still keep a particular template. PowerPoint gives you that flexibility. You can use the template you want and change the text color, the text size, the text typeface, and the text style. Table 1-1 on the next page explains the different text attributes available in PowerPoint.

▸ **TABLE 1-1**

ATTRIBUTE	DESCRIPTION
Font	Defines the appearance and shape of letters, numbers, and special characters.
Text color	Defines the color of the text. Displaying text in color requires a color monitor. Printing text in color requires a color printer or plotter.
Font size	Specifies the size of the characters on the screen. Character size is gauged by a measurement system called points. A single **point** is about 1/72 of an inch in height. Thus, a character with a point size of eighteen is about 18/72 (or 1/4) inch in height.
Text style	Defines text characteristics. Text styles include plain, italic, bold, shadowed, and underlined. Text may have one or more styles at a time.
Subscript	Defines the placement of a character in relationship to another. A subscript character displays or prints slightly below and next to another character.
Superscript	Defines the placement of a character in relationship to another. A superscript character displays or prints slightly above and immediately to one side of another character.

The next two sections explain how to change the text style and font size attributes.

▶ CHANGING THE TEXT STYLE

Text styles include plain, italic, bold, shadowed, and underlined. PowerPoint allows you to use one or more text styles in your presentation. Perform the following steps to add emphasis to the title slide by changing plain text to italic text.

TO CHANGE THE TEXT STYLE ▼

STEP 1 ▶

Point to Presented by: and triple-click the left mouse button.

The paragraph Presented by: is highlighted (Figure 1-25).

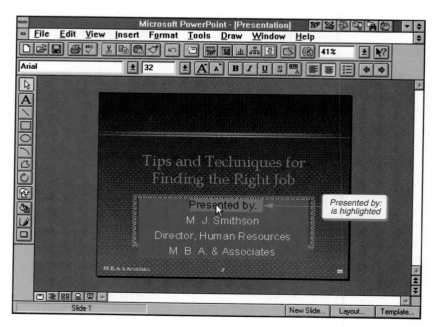

FIGURE 1-25

STEP 2 ▶

Position the mouse pointer on the Italic button (*I*) on the Formatting toolbar.

When you point to a button on a toolbar, PowerPoint displays a yellow **ToolTips** box with the corresponding name of that tool. When pointing to the Italic button, the ToolTips box displays the word Italic (Figure 1-26).

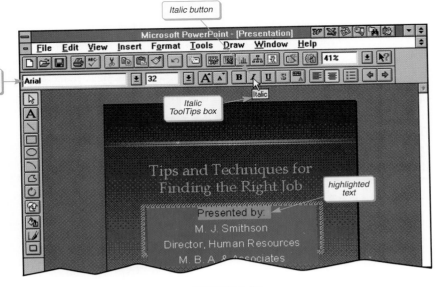

FIGURE 1-26

STEP 3 ▶

Choose the Italic button on the Formatting toolbar by clicking the left mouse button.

The text is italicized and the Italic button is recessed (Figure 1-27).

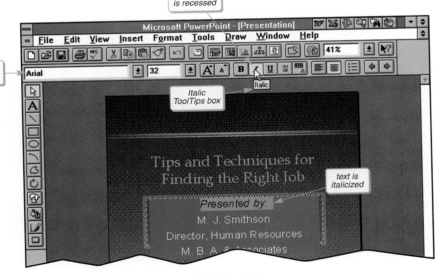

FIGURE 1-27

To remove italics from text, select the italicized text and then click the Italic button. The Italic button is recessed and the text does not have the italic text style.

▶ CHANGING THE FONT SIZE

The Double Lines template default font size is 32 points for body text and 44 points for title text. A point is 1/72 of one inch in height. Thus, a character with a point size of 44 is about 44/72, or 11/18 of one inch in height. Slide 1 requires you to decrease the font size for the following three paragraphs: (1) Presented by: (2) Director, Human Resources (3) M. B. A. & Associates. Perform the following steps on the next page to change font size.

TO CHANGE FONT SIZE ▼

STEP 1 ►

With Presented by:
highlighted, point to the
Decrease Font Size button
(▣) on the Formatting toolbar
(Figure 1-28).

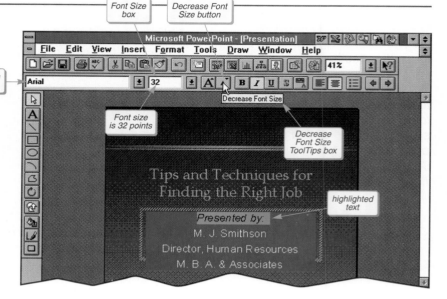

FIGURE 1-28

STEP 2 ►

Click the Decrease Font Size button
twice so 24 displays in the Font Size
box on the Formatting toolbar.

*The paragraph, Presented by:,
reduces to 24 points (Figure 1-29).
The Font Size box displays the
new font size as 24 points.*

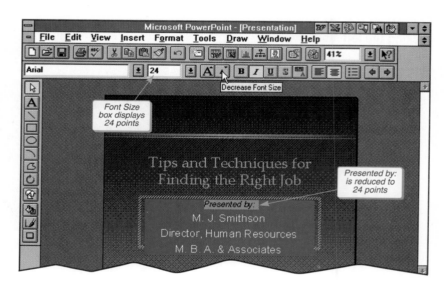

FIGURE 1-29

STEP 3 ►

Position the mouse pointer
immediately in front of the letter D in
Director.

*The mouse pointer now displays
as an I-beam because the pointer
is positioned before the letter D in
Director (Figure 1-30).*

FIGURE 1-30

STEP 4 ►

Drag the I-beam mouse pointer from the letter D in Director to the third letter s in Associates to highlight all characters in these two paragraphs (Figure 1-31).

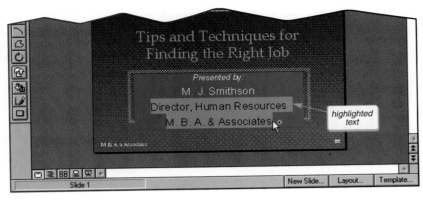

FIGURE 1-31

STEP 5 ►

Click the Decrease Font Size button twice so 24 displays in the Font Size box.

The paragraphs, Director, Human Resources and M. B. A. & Associates, reduce to 24 points. The Font Size box displays the font size as 24 points (Figure 1-32).

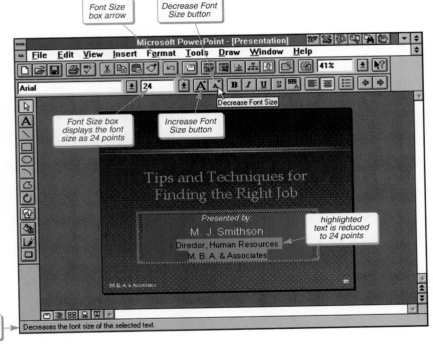

FIGURE 1-32

Instead of using the Decrease Font Size button, you can click the Font Size arrow on the Formatting toolbar to display a list of available font sizes and then click the desired point size. You may also click the Font Size box and type a font size between 1 and 999.

If you need to increase the font size, click the **Increase Font Size button** (Ａ), located next to the Decrease Font Size button on the Formatting toolbar.

PRESENTATION TIP

When designing a presentation, use the following rules as guidelines:

▶ Short lines of text are easier to read than long lines.
▶ Use bold and italic sparingly for emphasis.
▶ Use no more than two types of fonts and styles.

▶ SAVING THE PRESENTATION

While you are building your presentation, the computer stores it in main memory. It is important to save your presentation frequently because if the computer is turned off or if you lose electrical power, the presentation is lost. Another reason to save is if you run out of lab time before completing your project, you may finish the project later without having to start over. Therefore, it is mandatory to save on disk any presentation you will use later. Before you continue with Project 1, save the work completed thus far. Perform the following steps to save a presentation to drive A, using the Save button on the Standard toolbar. (It is assumed that you have a formatted disk in drive A.)

TO SAVE THE PRESENTATION ▼

STEP 1 ▶

Insert a formatted diskette in drive A and point to the Save button on the Standard toolbar (Figure 1-33).

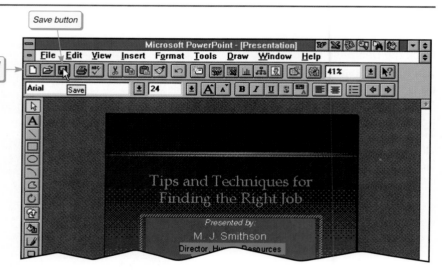

FIGURE 1-33

STEP 2 ▶

Choose the Save button.

PowerPoint displays the Save As dialog box (Figure 1-34). The default filename *.ppt displays in the File Name box. The default directory displays under Directories:. The current drive displays in the Drives box.

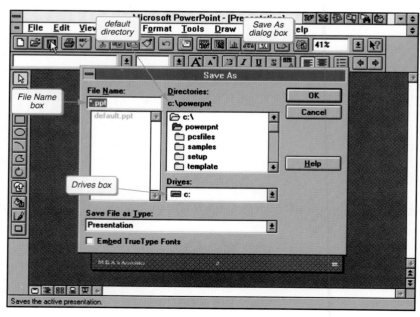

FIGURE 1-34

STEP 3 ▶

Type `proj1` in the File Name box. Do not press the ENTER key after typing the filename.

The name proj1 replaces *.ppt in the File Name box (Figure 1-35).

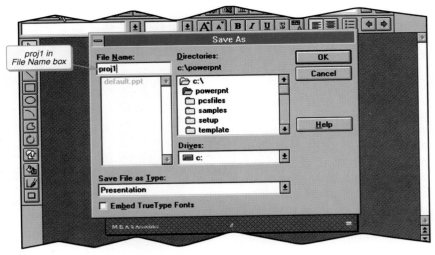

FIGURE 1-35

STEP 4 ▶

Choose the Drives box arrow and point to a:

A drop-down list of available drives displays (Figure 1-36).

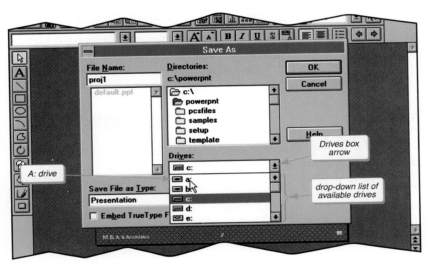

FIGURE 1-36

STEP 5 ▶

Select drive A by clicking the left mouse button.

Drive A becomes the current drive (Figure 1-37).

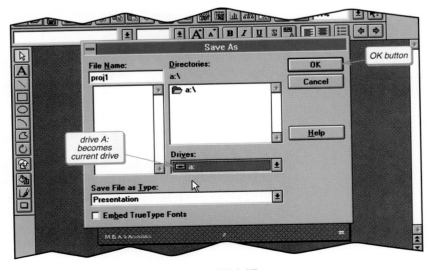

FIGURE 1-37

STEP 6 ▶

Choose the OK button in the Save As dialog box.

The Summary Info dialog box displays (Figure 1-38). The name displaying in the Author text box is the name of the person that was entered at the time PowerPoint was installed. Your screen will display a name other than M. J. Smithson. If a name was not entered during installation, the Author text box is blank. You may edit the information displayed in the Summary Info dialog box by pressing the TAB *key to advance to the next text box. Pressing the* ENTER *key when text is highlighted clears the text box. To accept the information as it displays in the Summary Info dialog box, choose the OK button.*

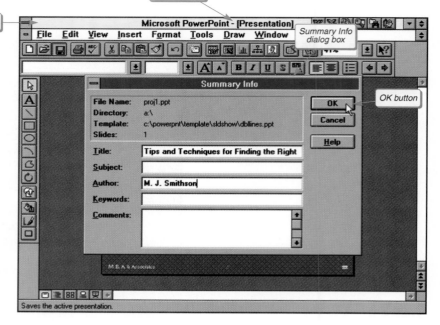

FIGURE 1-38

STEP 7 ▶

Choose the OK button in the Summary Info dialog box.

The presentation is saved to drive A under the filename PROJ1.PPT. The presentation title displays in the title bar as PROJ1.PPT (Figure 1-39).

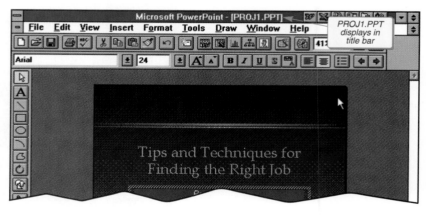

FIGURE 1-39

PowerPoint automatically appends to the filename PROJ1 the extension **.ppt**, which stands for **PowerP**oin**t**. Although the presentation PROJ1 is saved on disk, it also remains in main memory and displays on the screen.

PowerPoint filenames follow the Windows naming conventions. When saving your presentation file, use no more than eight characters, no spaces, and no reserved characters, such as a period (.), quotation mark ("), slash (/), backslash (\), brackets ([ ]), colon (:), semicolon (;), vertical bar (|), equal sign (=), or comma (,).

The Summary Info dialog box provides you with an area to store information about your presentation. Table 1-2 lists the types of information contained in the Summary Info dialog box.

▶ **TABLE 1-2**

SUMMARY INFO TYPES	CONTENTS
Title box	The presentation title.
Subject box	The presentation subject. You can state a brief description of the presentation content.
Author box	The author's name.
Keywords box	Keywords used in the presentation. Used to associate keywords with a presentation when using the **Find File command** in the File menu.
Comments box	Comments about the presentation.

It is a good practice to save periodically while you are working on a project. By doing so, you protect yourself from losing all the work you have done since the last time you saved.

▶ ADDING A NEW SLIDE

The title slide for your presentation is created. The next step is to add the first bulleted list slide in Project 1. The New Slide button adds a slide into the presentation, which is placed after the current slide. Usually when you create your presentation, you are adding slides with text, graphics, or charts. When you add a new slide, PowerPoint displays a dialog box for you to choose one of the AutoLayouts. These AutoLayouts have placeholders for various objects, such as title, text, graphics, graphs, and charts. Some placeholders provide access to other PowerPoint visuals by allowing you to double-click the placeholder. Figure 1-40 displays the twenty-one different AutoLayouts available in PowerPoint. More information about using AutoLayout placeholders to add graphics follows in subsequent projects. Perform the following steps on the next page to add a Bulleted List slide.

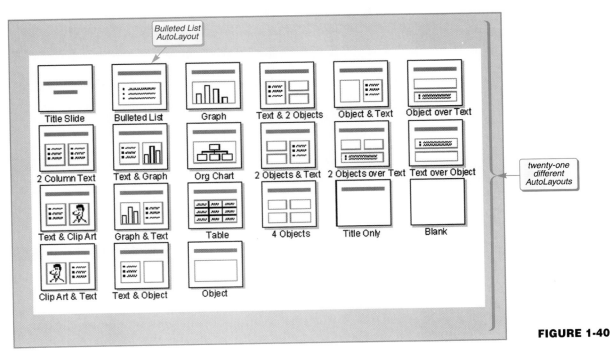

FIGURE 1-40

TO ADD A NEW SLIDE ▼

STEP 1 ►

Position the mouse pointer on the
New Slide button on the status bar
(Figure 1-41).

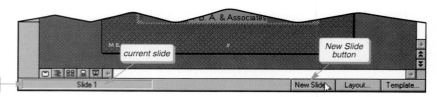

FIGURE 1-41

STEP 2 ►

Choose the New Slide button.

*The New Slide dialog box displays
(Figure 1-42). The Bulleted List
AutoLayout is selected, and the
AutoLayout title, Bulleted List, dis-
plays at the bottom right corner of
the New Slide dialog box.*

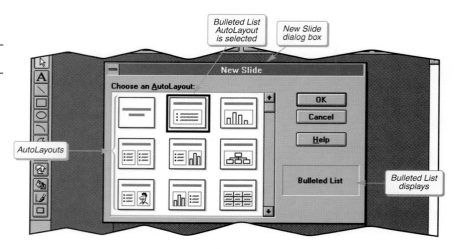

FIGURE 1-42

STEP 3 ►

**Choose the OK button in the New
Slide dialog box.**

*Slide 2 displays, keeping the
attributes of the Double Lines template (Figure 1-43).*

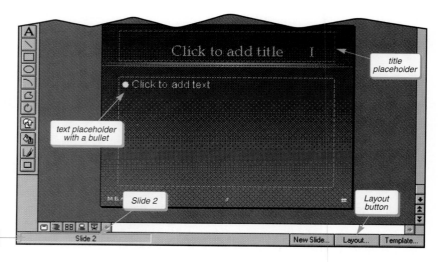

FIGURE 1-43

Because you selected the Bulleted List AutoLayout, PowerPoint displays Slide
2 with a title placeholder and a text placeholder with a bullet. You can change the
layout for a slide at any time during the creation of your presentation by clicking
the Layout button on the status bar and then selecting the AutoLayout of your
choice.

▶ CREATING THE REMAINING SLIDES IN THE PRESENTATION

 owerPoint assumes every new slide has a title. Therefore, any text you type after a new slide displays becomes the title object. The title for Slide 2 is Where to Start?. Perform the following step to enter this title.

TO TYPE THE TITLE FOR SLIDE 2 ▼

STEP 1 ▶

Type Where to Start?

The title, Where to Start?, displays in the title object (Figure 1-44).

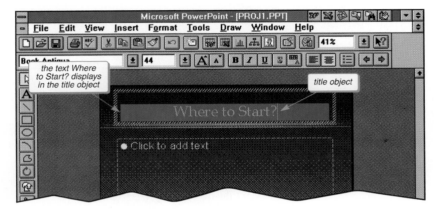

FIGURE 1-44

Selecting the Text Placeholder

Before you can type text into the text placeholder, you must first select it. Perform the following step to select the text placeholder on Slide 2.

TO SELECT THE TEXT PLACEHOLDER ▼

STEP 1 ▶

Click on the bullet paragraph, located inside the text placeholder, labeled Click to add text.

The insertion point displays immediately after the bullet on Slide 2 (Figure 1-45).

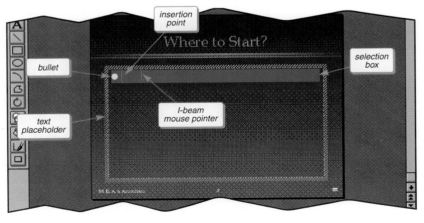

FIGURE 1-45

Typing a Bulleted List

Recall that a bulleted list is a list of paragraphs, each preceded by a bullet. Also recall that a paragraph is a segment of text ended by pressing the ENTER key. The next step is to enter the bulleted list. This bulleted list consists of the five entries shown in Figure 1-46. Perform the following steps to type a bulleted list.

TO TYPE A BULLETED LIST

Step 1: Type Newspaper and press the ENTER key.
Step 2: Type Trade publications and press the ENTER key.
Step 3: Type Employment agencies and press the ENTER key.
Step 4: Type Search firms and press the ENTER key.
Step 5: Type Word of mouth

Each time you press the ENTER key, PowerPoint places a bullet at the beginning of each new paragraph (Figure 1-46).

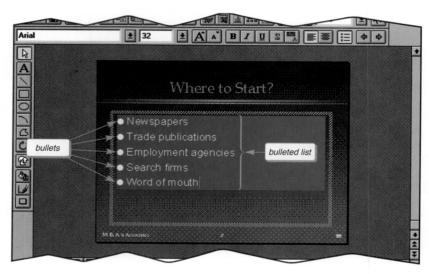

FIGURE 1-46

The ENTER key was not pressed after typing the last paragraph in Step 5. If the ENTER key is pressed, a new bullet displays after the last entry on this slide. To remove the extra bullet, press the BACKSPACE key.

TO CREATE SLIDE 3

Step 1: Add a new slide by choosing the New Slide button on the status bar.
Step 2: Select Bulleted List from the New Slide dialog box and choose the OK button.
Step 3: Type The Resume as the title for Slide 3.
Step 4: Select the text object by clicking anywhere inside the text placeholder.
Step 5: Type Job objectives and press the ENTER key.
Step 6: Type Qualifications and press the ENTER key.
Step 7: Type Education and press the ENTER key.
Step 8: Type Employment history and press the ENTER key.
Step 9: Type References

Slide 3 displays as shown in Figure 1-47.

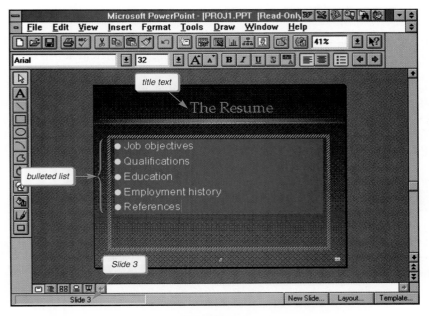

FIGURE 1-47

TO CREATE SLIDE 4

Step 1: Add a new slide by choosing the New Slide button on the status bar.

Step 2: Select Bulleted List from the New Slide dialog box and choose the OK button.

Step 3: Type `Interview Preparation` as the title for Slide 4.

Step 4: Select the text object by clicking anywhere inside the text placeholder.

Step 5: Type `Research the company` and press the ENTER key.

Step 6: Type `Rehearse answers to likely questions` and press the ENTER key.

Step 7: Type `Prepare questions to ask prospective employer`

The slide title and text object display, as shown in Figure 1-48.

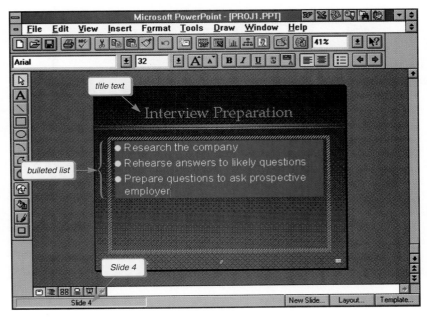

FIGURE 1-48

▶ MOVING TO ANOTHER SLIDE

When creating or editing your presentation, you will often want to display a slide other than the current one. Dragging the vertical scroll bar box up or down moves you through your presentation. The small box on the vertical scroll bar is called the **elevator** (▨) and is shown in Figure 1-49. When you drag the elevator, the **slide indicator box** (Slide 4) shows you the number of the slide you are about to display. Once you see the number of the slide you wish to display in the slide indicator box, release the left mouse button. Perform the steps below to move through your presentation using the vertical scroll bar.

TO MOVE TO ANOTHER SLIDE ▼

STEP 1 ▶

Position the mouse pointer on the elevator. Press and hold the left mouse button.

Slide 4 (Slide 4) displays in the slide indicator box (Figure 1-49).

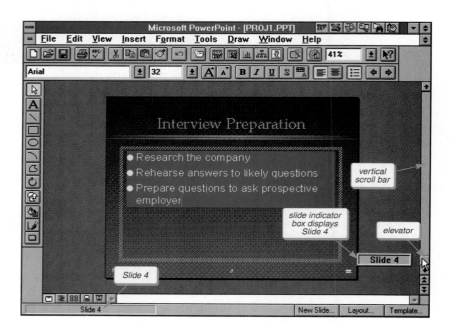

FIGURE 1-49

STEP 2 ▶

Drag the elevator up the vertical scroll bar until Slide 1 (Slide 1) displays in the slide indicator box (Figure 1-50).

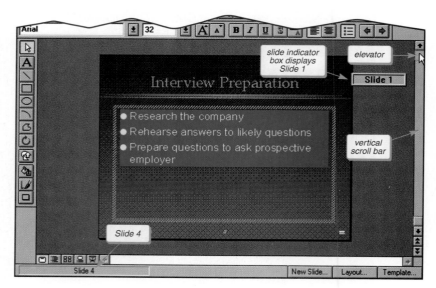

FIGURE 1-50

STEP 3 ▶

Release the left mouse button.

Slide 1 titled, Tips and Techniques for Finding the Right Job, displays in the PowerPoint window (Figure 1-51).

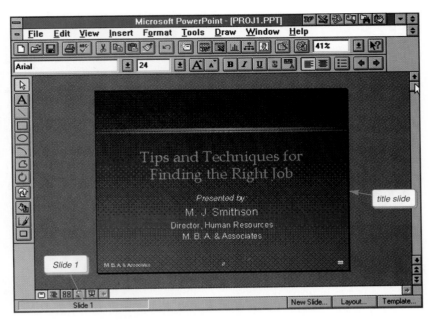

FIGURE 1-51

▶ VIEWING THE PRESENTATION USING SLIDE SHOW

The **Slide Show button** (▣), located at the bottom left of the PowerPoint window, lets you display your presentation electronically using a computer. The computer acts like a slide projector, displaying each slide on a full screen. The full screen slide hides the toolbars, menus, and other PowerPoint window elements.

TO VIEW THE TITLE SLIDE USING SLIDE SHOW ▼

STEP 1 ▶

Position the mouse pointer on the Slide Show View button, located at the bottom left of the PowerPoint window (Figure 1-52).

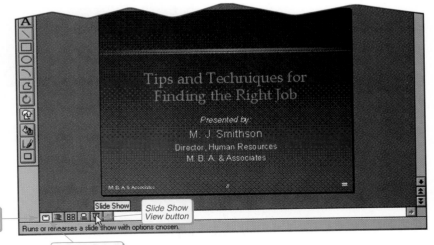

FIGURE 1-52

STEP 2 ▶

Click the left mouse button.

The title slide fills the screen (Figure 1-53). The date displaying on your screen will be different from the date displayed in Figure 1-53. The date stored as the system date displays at the bottom of the slide. The PowerPoint window is hidden.

FIGURE 1-53

STEP 3 ▶

Click the left mouse button until the last slide of the presentation, Slide 4, displays (Figure 1-54).

Each slide in your presentation displays on the screen, one slide at a time. Each time you click the left mouse button, the next slide displays.

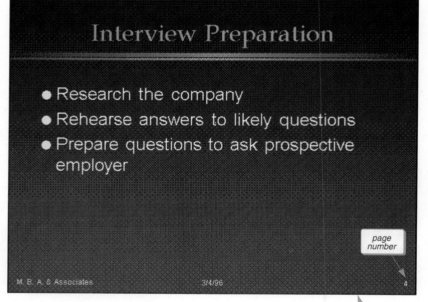

FIGURE 1-54

STEP 4 ▶

Click the left mouse button.

You have attempted to advance past the last slide in your presentation. PowerPoint exits Slide Show view after the last slide in your presentation and displays Slide 1, which was the current slide when you clicked the Slide Show View button (Figure 1-55).

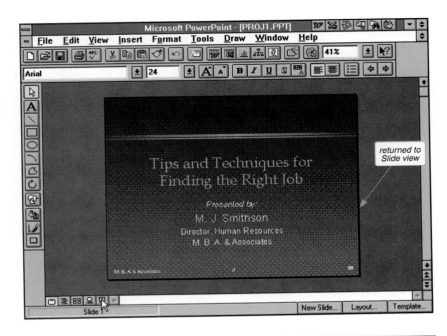

FIGURE 1-55

To use the keyboard in Slide Show view to advance through the entire presentation one slide at a time, press the PAGE DOWN key. To go back one slide at a time in Slide Show view, click the right mouse button or press the PAGE UP key. The ESC key allows you to exit from Slide Show view and return to the view you were in when you clicked the Slide Show View button.

Running slide show is an excellent way to practice a presentation prior to giving it. You can view your presentation using slide show from Slide view, Outline view, Slide Sorter view, or Notes Pages view.

▶ USING THE NEXT SLIDE BUTTON TO ADVANCE ONE SLIDE

 hen you want to advance one or two slides, it is quicker to click the Next Slide button instead of dragging the elevator on the vertical scroll bar. Perform the steps below to use the Next Slide button.

TO USE THE NEXT SLIDE BUTTON TO ADVANCE ONE SLIDE ▼

STEP 1 ▶

Position the mouse pointer on the Next Slide button (Figure 1-56).

FIGURE 1-56

STEP 2 ▶

Choose the Next Slide button.

Slide 2 displays in the PowerPoint window (Figure 1-57).

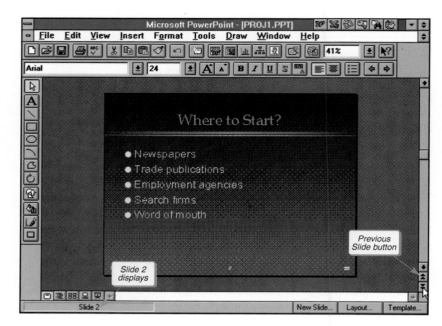

FIGURE 1-57

To return to the previous slide, choose the Previous Slide button. The Previous Slide button is located above the Next Slide button. Both the Next Slide button and the Previous Slide button advance/return the number of slides based upon the number of clicks. For example, if you double-click, you move two slides; if you triple-click, you move three slides. You may not advance beyond the last slide in your presentation or backup beyond the first slide in your presentation.

▶ CHANGING SLIDE MASTER COMPONENTS

The Slide Master contains the basic format used by all slides you create. The Slide Master has formatted placeholders for the slide title, text, and background items. These formatted placeholders are called the Master title and the Master text. The **Master title** controls the attributes and alignment of the slide title object. The **Master text** controls the main slide text attributes and alignment of the text objects.

Each template has a specially designed Slide Master. So, if you select a template but want to change a component of that template, you can override that component by changing the Slide Master. Any change to the Slide Master results in changing every slide in the presentation. For example, if you change the title text style to italic, every slide following the master changes to italicized title text.

Each view has its own master. You can access the master by pressing the SHIFT key while clicking the appropriate view button. For example, pressing the SHIFT key and clicking the Slide View button displays the Slide Master. To exit a master, click the view button to which you wish to return.

The key components most frequently changed on the Slide Master are listed in Table 1-3.

▶ **TABLE 1-3**

COMPONENT	DESCRIPTION
Font	Defines the appearance and shape of letters, numbers, and special characters.
Font size	Specifies the size of the characters on the screen. Character size is gauged by a measurement system called points. A single point is about 1/72 of an inch in height. Thus, a character with a point size of 18 is about 18/72 of an inch in height.
Text style	Text may have one or more styles at a time. Text styles include plain, italic, bold, shadowed, and underlined.
Text position	Position of text in a paragraph is left-aligned, right-aligned, centered, or justified. Justified text is proportionally spaced across the object.
Color scheme	A coordinated set of eight colors designed to complement each other. Color schemes consist of background color, line and text color, shadow color, title text color, object fill color, and three different accent colors.
Background items	Any object other than the title object or text object. Typical items include borders, graphics such as a company logo, page number, date, and time.
Page number	Inserts the special symbol used to print the slide number.
Date	Inserts the special symbol used to print the date the presentation was printed.
Time	Inserts the special symbol used to print the time the presentation was printed.

Changing Line Spacing on the Slide Master

To make the slide in the presentation easier to read, the spacing on the Slide Master is set to one line after the paragraph. When you choose the **Line Spacing command**, the Line Spacing dialog box displays. The Line Spacing dialog box allows you to adjust line spacing on the Slide Master within the paragraph, before the paragraph, and after the paragraph. Perform the following steps to change line spacing from zero lines after the paragraph to one-half of a line after the paragraph.

TO CHANGE LINE SPACING ON THE SLIDE MASTER ▼

STEP 1 ▶

Point to the Slide View button () and press and hold the SHIFT key.

When you press and hold the SHIFT key, the Slide Master ToolTips box displays Slide Master (Figure 1-58).

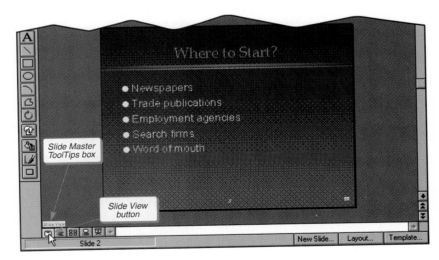

FIGURE 1-58

STEP 2 ▶

While holding down the SHIFT key, click the left mouse button, then release the SHIFT key.

The Slide Master displays (Figure 1-59).

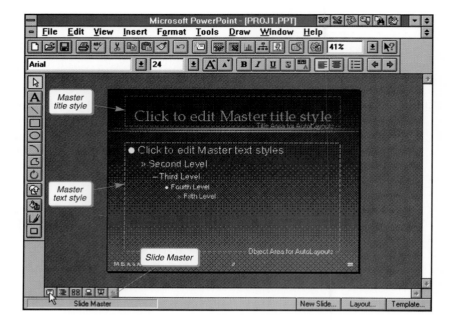

FIGURE 1-59

STEP 3 ▶

Click anywhere on the bullet paragraph, Click to edit Master text styles.

The insertion point displays at the point where you clicked (Figure 1-60). The text object area is selected.

FIGURE 1-60

STEP 4 ▶

Select the Format menu and point to the Line Spacing command (Figure 1-61).

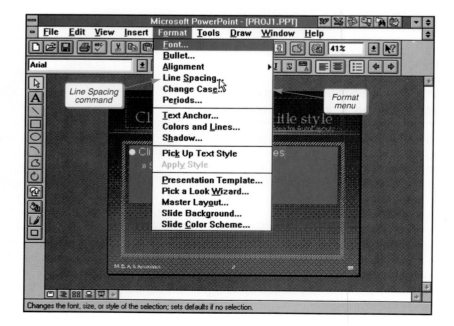

FIGURE 1-61

STEP 5 ▶

Choose the Line Spacing command from the Format menu by clicking the left mouse button.

PowerPoint displays the Line Spacing dialog box (Figure 1-62).

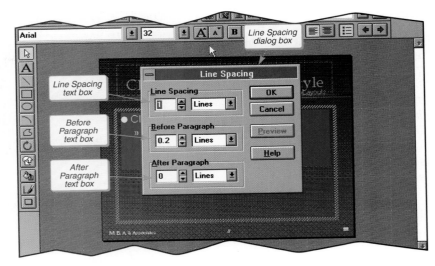

FIGURE 1-62

STEP 6 ▶

Position the mouse pointer on the up arrow next to the After Paragraph text box.

The After Paragraph text box displays the current setting, 0, for the number of lines after a paragraph (Figure 1-63).

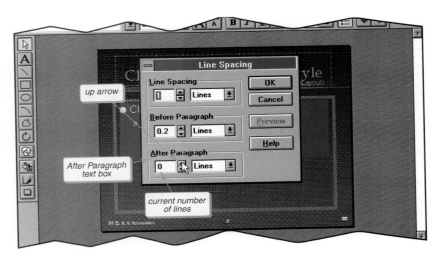

FIGURE 1-63

STEP 7 ▶

Click the up arrow next to the After Paragraph text box so 0.5 displays.

The After Paragraph text box displays 0.5 (Figure 1-64).

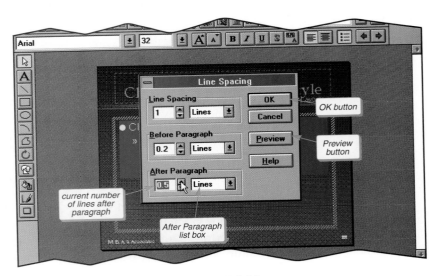

FIGURE 1-64

STEP 8 ▶

Choose the OK button in the Line Spacing dialog box.

The Slide Master text placeholder displays the new after paragraph line spacing (Figure 1-65). Depending on the video drivers installed, the spacing on your screen may appear slightly different from this figure.

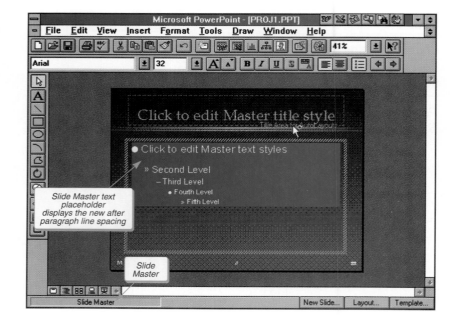

FIGURE 1-65

STEP 9 ▶

Choose the Slide View button, located at the bottom left of the PowerPoint window.

Slide 2 displays with the after paragraph line spacing set at 0.5 lines (Figure 1-66).

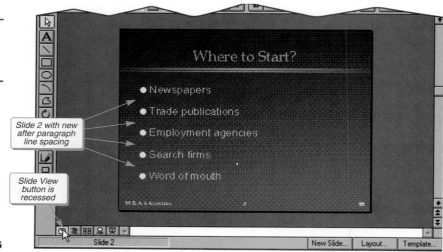

FIGURE 1-66

The after paragraph line spacing is controlled by setting the number of units after a paragraph. Units are either lines or points. Lines are the default unit. Points may be selected by clicking the arrow next to the After Paragraph line spacing drop-down list box (Figure 1-64 on page PP39). Recall from page PP20 that a single **point** is about 1/72 of an inch in height.

The placeholder at the top of the Slide Master (Figure 1-65) is for editing the Master title style. The large placeholder under the Master title placeholder is for editing the Master text styles. It is here you make changes to the various bullet levels. Changes could be made to line spacing, bullet font, text and line color, alignment, and text shadow. It is also the object area for AutoLayouts.

Sometimes, you need to change the location of text to improve the readability of a slide. Other times, you need to add blank space to a slide that appears to be cluttered or congested.

PRESENTATION TIP

Resist the temptation to regard blank space on a slide as wasted space. Blank space added for the purpose of directing the attention of the audience to specific text or graphics is called **white space**. White space is a powerful design tool. Used effectively, white space improves audience attention.

During a presentation, the audience is using several demanding, cognitive skills to interpret your information, such as:

▸ Retrieving relevant data from their long-term memory
▸ Watching the presenter for non-verbal cues (body language)
▸ Listening to and interpreting what the presenter says
▸ Comparing what is said verbally to what is said through the presenter's body language and then trying to identify any inconsistencies
▸ Formulating questions about unclear or confusing information
▸ Deciding what is important on each slide, based on the message of the text and the arrangement of the text
▸ Recognizing words and comprehending their meanings
▸ Analyzing the phrases on the slide
▸ Organizing the ideas presented in the text
▸ Incorporating the ideas with their prior knowledge and experience

▸ OVERRIDING THE SLIDE MASTER

Recall that a change to the Slide Master affects all slides in the presentation. When you changed the after paragraph line spacing in the previous section, you changed the way the sub-title displays on the title slide. In this section, you will return to the title slide and decrease the after paragraph line spacing for only the title slide. This change will override the format for the Slide Master and only change the title slide. The other slides in your presentation will retain the one line after paragraph setting, as determined in the previous section.

 **TO OVERRIDE THE SLIDE MASTER** ▼

STEP 1 ▸

Click the Previous Slide button once.

Slide 1 displays (Figure 1-67). The actual amount of space displaying on the screen depends upon the video driver. Your screen may vary from the screen in this figure.

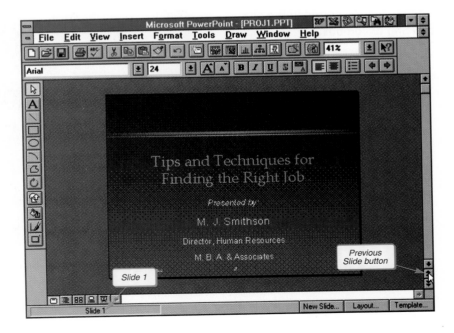

FIGURE 1-67

STEP 2 ▶

Select the sub-title text by dragging the mouse pointer from the letter P in Presented through the third letter s in Associates (Figure 1-68).

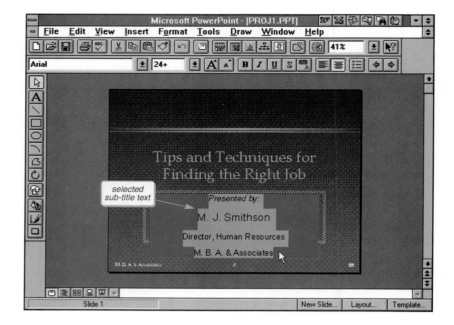

FIGURE 1-68

STEP 3 ▶

From the Format menu, choose the Line Spacing command, and click the down arrow next to the After Paragraph text box once so the After Paragraph text box displays 0 (Figure 1-69).

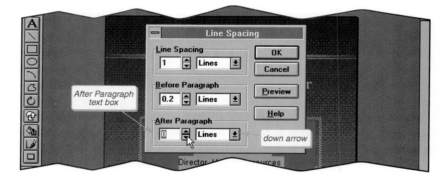

FIGURE 1-69

STEP 4 ▶

Choose the OK button in the Line Spacing dialog box.

The sub-title after paragraph line spacing returns to zero (Figure 1-70).

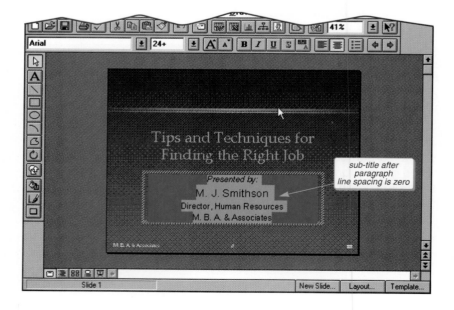

FIGURE 1-70

Changing the after paragraph line spacing to zero overrides the after paragraph line spacing format of the Slide Master. Only the title slide changed. The other three slides in your presentation still have one line after each paragraph, as formatted by the Slide Master.

▶ CHECKING SPELLING

PowerPoint checks your presentation for spelling errors using a standard dictionary contained in the Microsoft Office group. This dictionary is shared with the other Microsoft Office applications, such as Word and Excel. A **custom dictionary** is available if you want to add special words, such as proper names, cities, and acronyms. When checking a presentation for spelling errors, PowerPoint opens the standard dictionary and automatically opens the custom dictionary file, if one exists. If a word is not found in either dictionary, PowerPoint displays a dialog box. When a word appears in the dialog box, you have several options. Your options are explained in Table 1-4.

▶ **TABLE 1-4**

OPTION	DESCRIPTION
Manually correct the word	Retype the word with the proper spelling and choose Change. PowerPoint continues checking the rest of the presentation.
Ignore the misspelling	Choose Ignore when the word is spelled correctly but not found in the dictionaries. PowerPoint continues checking the rest of the presentation.
Ignore all occurrences of the misspelling	Choose Ignore All when the word is spelled correctly but not found in the dictionaries. PowerPoint continues checking the rest of the presentation.
Change to another spelling	Choose Change after selecting the proper spelling of the word from the list displayed in the Suggestions box. PowerPoint continues checking the rest of the presentation.
Change all occurrences of the misspelling to another spelling	Choose Change All after selecting the proper spelling of the word from the list displayed in the Suggestions box. PowerPoint continues checking the rest of the presentation.
Add a word to the custom dictionary	Choose Add. PowerPoint opens the custom dictionary, adds the word, and continues checking the rest of the presentation.
Suggest alternative spellings	Choose Suggest. PowerPoint lists suggested spellings. Select the correct word or type the proper spelling and then choose Change. PowerPoint continues checking the rest of the presentation.

PowerPoint begins to check spelling from the insertion point and continues to the end of the presentation. This allows you to begin the spell checking anywhere in the presentation without having to go to the first slide. Perform the following steps on the next page to use the PowerPoint spelling checker. In the following example, the name Smithson is not in the standard or custom dictionary, which causes the spelling checker to treat the name as a misspelled word. Depending on the accuracy of your typing, your presentation may have additional misspelled words.

TO CHECK THE SPELLING OF A PRESENTATION ▼

STEP 1 ►

Position the mouse pointer on the Spelling button (🔤) on the Standard toolbar (Figure 1-71).

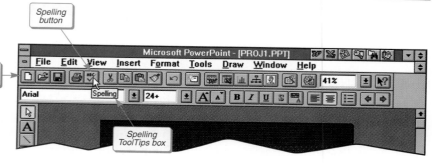

FIGURE 1-71

STEP 2 ►

Choose the Spelling button.

The Spelling dialog box displays Smithson in the Not in Dictionary box (Figure 1-72). The name Smiths displays in both the Change To box and the Suggestions box.

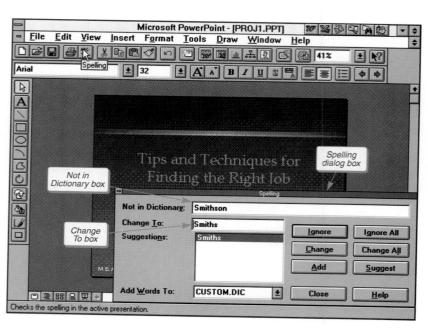

FIGURE 1-72

STEP 3 ►

Position the mouse pointer on the Ignore All button (Ignore All) in the Spelling dialog box. (Figure 1-73).

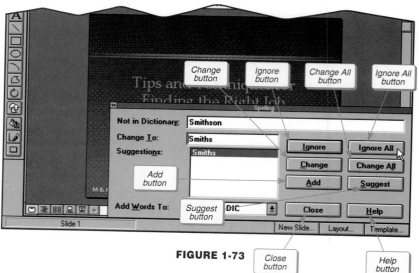

FIGURE 1-73

STEP 4 ▶

Choose the Ignore All button in the Spelling dialog box.

PowerPoint ignores all occurrences of the word Smithson and continues searching for additional misspelled words after Smithson until it returns to the slide where you began the spelling check. PowerPoint may stop on additional words depending on your typing accuracy. When PowerPoint has checked all slides for misspellings, it displays the Microsoft PowerPoint information box (Figure 1-74).

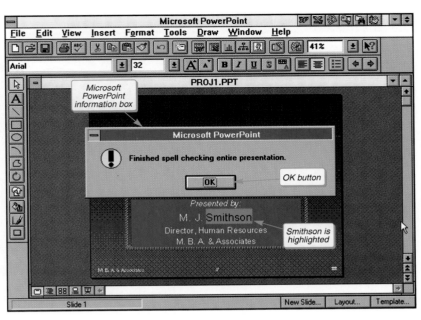

FIGURE 1-74

STEP 5

Choose the OK button in the Microsoft PowerPoint information box.

Slide 1 displays.

The PowerPoint dictionary contains commonly used English words. It does not contain proper names, abbreviations, technical terms, poetic contractions, foreign words, or antiquated terms. PowerPoint treats words not found in the dictionaries as misspellings. You may choose to ignore these misspellings or add them to the custom dictionary.

When PowerPoint encounters a word not found in either the standard dictionary or the custom dictionary, it highlights the word and places it in the Not in Dictionary box, located at the top of the Spelling dialog box. Suggestions display as long as the Always Suggest option is chosen in the Options dialog box. To display the Options dialog box, choose the **Options command** from the Tools menu.

If the spelling change suggested by the PowerPoint spelling checker is not your choice, you can select any of the words in the list of suggested words by choosing the desired word. The word you choose appears in the Change To box in the Spelling dialog box. If your choice is not in the list of suggested words, you may type your desired word directly into the Change To box. When you choose the Change button, the word in the Change To box replaces the misspelled word.

▶ VIEWING THE PRESENTATION IN SLIDE SORTER VIEW

T he presentation for Project 1 is complete. The next step is to review the presentation in Slide Sorter view. This allows you to look at several slides in one window. This is useful for proofreading your presentation. Perform the following steps on the next page to view the presentation in Slide Sorter view.

TO VIEW THE PRESENTATION IN SLIDE SORTER VIEW ▼

STEP 1 ▶

Point to the Slide Sorter View button (⊞), as shown in Figure 1-75.

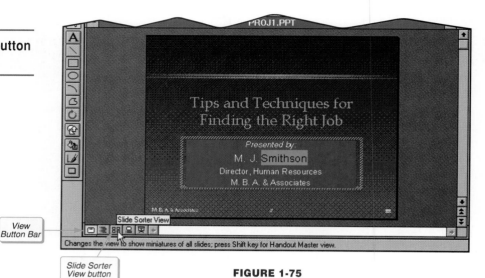

FIGURE 1-75

STEP 2 ▶

Choose the Slide Sorter View button.

All four slides in Project 1 display in Slide Sorter view (Figure 1-76). The Slide Sorter View button is recessed. The Zoom Control default setting on the Standard toolbar is 66%.

STEP 3

Choose the Slide View button at the bottom left of the PowerPoint window.

PowerPoint exits Slide Sorter view and returns to Slide view.

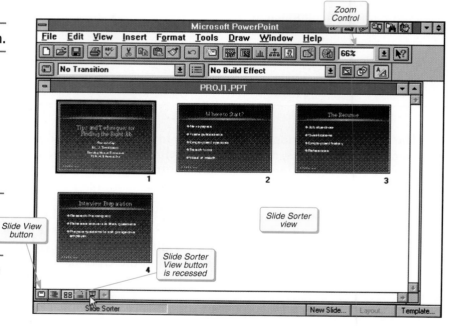

FIGURE 1-76

You can increase the size of the slide in Slide Sorter view by increasing the value in the Zoom Control box. When you increase the Zoom Control, you reduce the number of slides that display on one screen, but you increase the readability of each slide. Use the vertical scroll bar to view slides not visible in the PowerPoint window. Slide Sorter view has other features that will be introduced in later projects.

▶ SAVING AN EXISTING PRESENTATION WITH THE SAME FILENAME

S aving frequently can never be overemphasized. Prior to printing your presentation, you should save your work in the event you experience difficulties with the printer. You may occasionally encounter system problems that can only be resolved by restarting the computer. In this instance, you will need to start PowerPoint and open your presentation from the most recent copy of your presentation. As a precaution, always save your presentation before you print it. Perform the following steps to save the existing presentation.

TO SAVE AN EXISTING PRESENTATION WITH THE SAME FILENAME ▼

STEP 1 ▶

Insert your data disk into drive A. Position the mouse pointer on the Save button on the Standard toolbar (Figure 1-77).

STEP 2

Choose the Save button.

PowerPoint saves Project 1 to the disk in drive A, using the filename PROJ1.PPT as defined by the Save As dialog box earlier in this project.

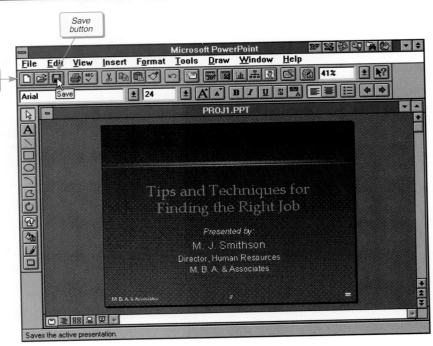

FIGURE 1-77

▶ PRINTING THE PRESENTATION

O nce you create a presentation and save it on disk, you need to print it. A printed version of the presentation is called a **hard copy**, or **printout**. The first printing of the presentation is called a **rough draft**. The rough draft allows you to proofread the presentation to check for errors and readability. After correcting errors, you will need to print the final copy of your presentation. If you made any changes to your presentation since your last save, be sure to save your presentation before you print it.

Perform the following steps on the next page to print the rough draft of the presentation.

TO PRINT THE PRESENTATION ▼

STEP 1 ►

Ready the printer according to the printer instructions. Select the File menu and point to the Print command (Figure 1-78).

FIGURE 1-78

STEP 2 ►

Choose the Print command from the File menu by clicking the left mouse button. When PowerPoint displays the Print dialog box, point to the Scale to Fit Paper check box.

PowerPoint displays the Print dialog box (Figure 1-79). The PowerPoint default settings for the Print dialog box are Print What: displays Slides; Copies: displays 1 for printing one copy of the presentation; Slide Range: the All option button is selected and the Collate Copies check box is selected.

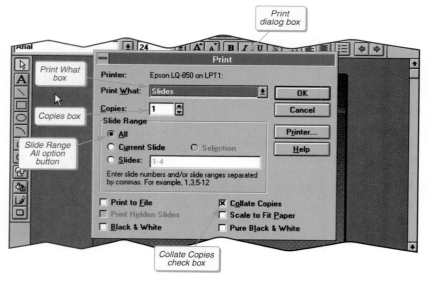

FIGURE 1-79

STEP 3 ►

Choose the Scale to Fit Paper and Pure Black & White check boxes by clicking them. Then, position the mouse pointer on the OK button.

The Scale to Fit Paper and Pure Black & White check boxes are selected (Figure 1-80). The Scale to Fit Paper option automatically resizes slides to fit the paper loaded in the printer. The Pure Black & White option turns all colors and fills to white and all text and lines to black. Pure Black & White is used for rough drafts.

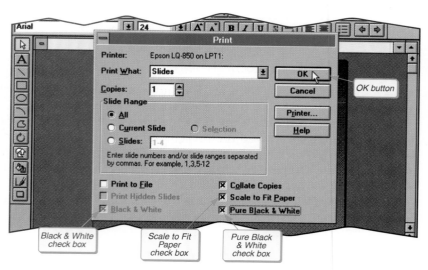

FIGURE 1-80

STEP 4 ▶

Choose the OK button.

The mouse pointer momentarily changes to an hourglass shape (⧖), and PowerPoint displays the Print Status dialog box (Figure 1-81). The presentation begins printing on the printer.

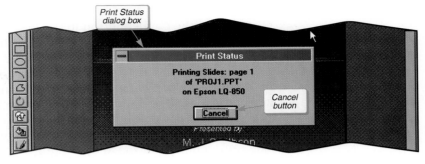

FIGURE 1-81

STEP 5 ▶

When the printer stops, retrieve the printouts of the presentation.

PROJ1 prints on four pages (Figure 1-82).

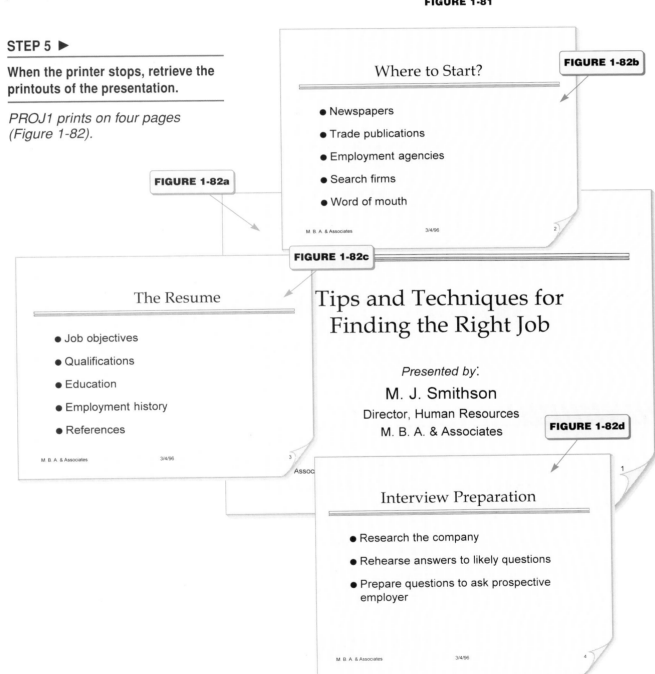

Pressing the Cancel button in the Print dialog box (Figure 1-80 on page PP48) ends the print request. Pressing the Cancel button in the Print Status dialog box (Figure 1-81 on the previous page) stops the printing process.

Selecting the Slide Range: All option button in the Print dialog box prints all the slides in the presentation (Figure 1-79 on page PP48). Selecting the Slide Range: Current Slide option button prints only the current slide. Selecting the Slide Range: Slides option button prints the range of slides you designate by entering the beginning and ending slide number in the text box. Choose the Current Slide option button or the Slides option button when you want to print a portion of your presentation.

Additionally, you may print your presentation by clicking the Print button on the Standard toolbar. PowerPoint immediately begins printing the presentation, using the settings last selected in the Print dialog box. The Print dialog box does not display. Use the Print button after selecting print options in the Print dialog box (Figure 1-80 on page PP48).

PRESENTATION TIP

One test every slide must pass is the **Floor Test**. You perform the Floor Test by placing the slide on the floor and trying to read it while you are standing. If the slide is readable, it passes the test. The slide fails the test if text is too small to read. Text too small to read during the Floor Test will be too small to read when displayed on the overhead projector. If the slide fails the Floor Test, you need to modify the slide to make text larger.

▶ EXITING POWERPOINT

The creation of the presentation is now complete. When you exit PowerPoint, PowerPoint prompts to save any changes made to the presentation since the last save, closes all PowerPoint windows, and then quits PowerPoint. Quitting PowerPoint returns control to the Program Manager. Perform the following steps to exit PowerPoint.

TO EXIT POWERPOINT ▼

STEP 1 ▶

Select the File menu and point to the Exit command (Figure 1-83).

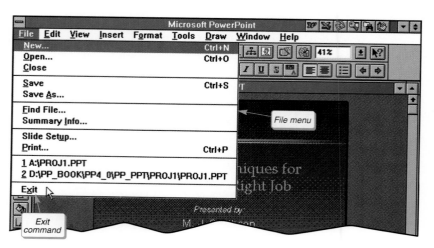

FIGURE 1-83

STEP 2 ▶

Choose the Exit command.

If you made changes to the presentation, the Microsoft PowerPoint dialog box displays, asking Save changes to "PROJ1.PPT"? (Figure 1-84). Choose the Yes button ([Yes]) to save the changes to PROJ1.PPT before exiting PowerPoint. Choose the No button ([No]) to exit PowerPoint without saving the changes to PROJ1.PPT. Choose the Cancel button ([Cancel]) to terminate the Exit command and return to the presentation. If you did not make changes to your presentation since your last save, this dialog box does not display.

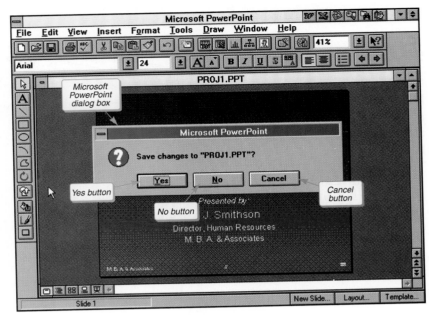

FIGURE 1-84

You can also exit PowerPoint by double-clicking the Control-menu box in the application title bar or by pressing ALT+F4.

▶ OPENING A PRESENTATION

Earlier, the presentation built in Project 1 was saved on disk using the file-name PROJ1.PPT. Once you create and save a presentation, you may have to retrieve it from disk to make changes. For example, you might want to replace the template or modify some text. After starting PowerPoint, perform the following steps to open PROJ1.PPT, using the PowerPoint dialog box.

Starting PowerPoint

Perform the following steps to start PowerPoint. Refer to Figures 1-3 through 1-5 on pages PP5 and PP6 to review these steps in detail.

TO START POWERPOINT

Step 1: Double-click the Microsoft PowerPoint program-item icon in the Micro-soft Office group window.

Step 2: Choose the OK button in the Tip of the Day dialog box.

The PowerPoint startup dialog box displays (see Figure 1-5 on page PP6).

TO OPEN A PRESENTATION ▼

STEP 1 ►

Click the Open an Existing Presentation option button, located at the bottom of the PowerPoint startup dialog box. Then, point to the OK button.

The Open an Existing Presentation option button is selected in the PowerPoint startup dialog box (Figure 1-85).

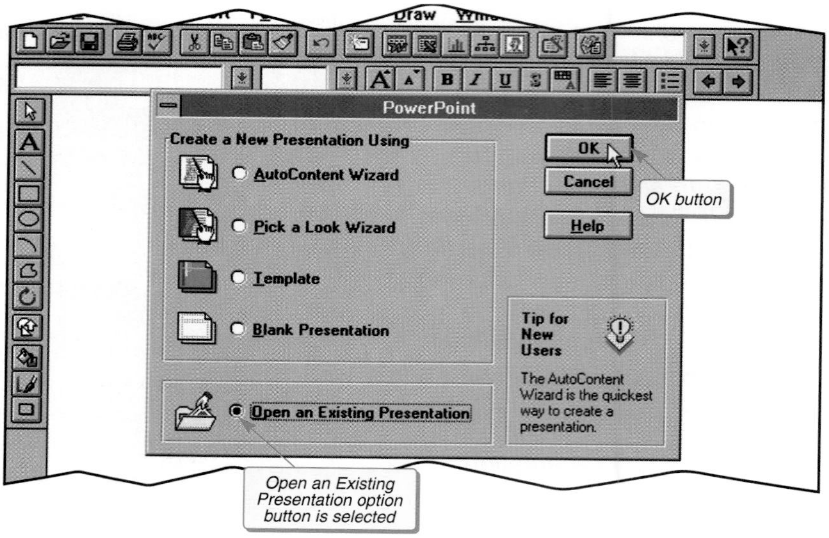

FIGURE 1-85

STEP 2 ►

Choose the OK button in the PowerPoint startup dialog box.

PowerPoint displays the Open dialog box (Figure 1-86).

FIGURE 1-86

STEP 3 ►

If drive A is not the current drive, select drive A (refer to Figures 1-36 and 1-37 on page PP25 to review this technique). Select proj1.ppt by clicking its filename in the File Name list box.

The first slide in your presentation displays in the Open dialog box (Figure 1-87).

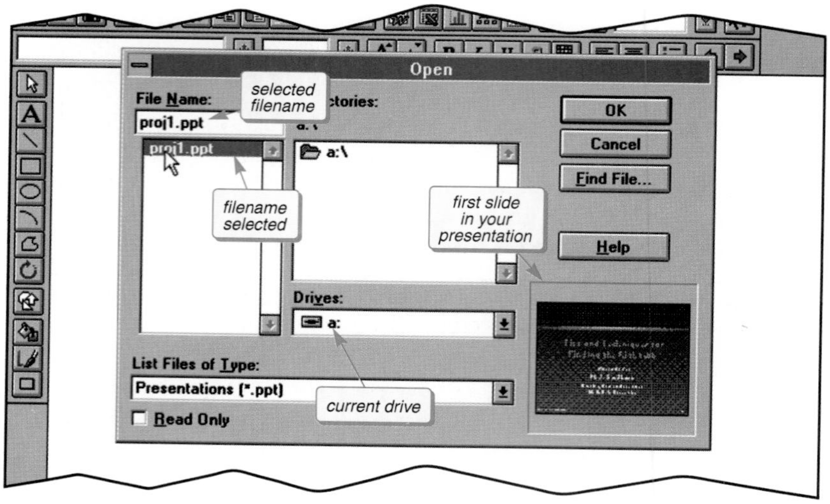

FIGURE 1-87

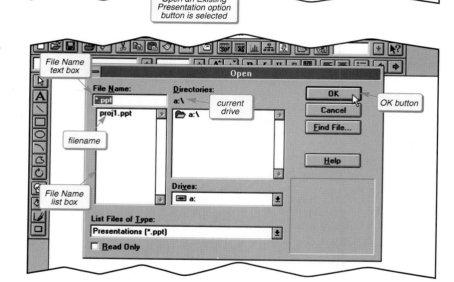

STEP 4 ▶

Choose the OK button in the Open dialog box.

PowerPoint loads the presentation with the filename PROJ1.PPT from drive A: into main memory and displays the first slide on the screen (Figure 1-88).

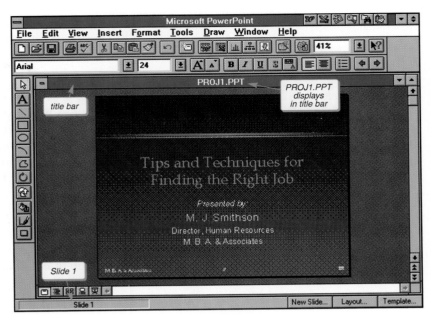

FIGURE 1-88

Project 1 is loaded into memory and Slide 1 displays on the screen. You may now correct errors or make additions to your presentation. The next section explains how to correct errors.

▶ CORRECTING ERRORS

A fter creating a presentation, you may find you must make changes. Changes may be required because a slide contains an error, because the scope of the presentation shifted, or because a slide failed the Floor Test. The next section explains the types of errors that commonly occur when creating a presentation.

Types of Corrections Made to Presentations

There are usually three types of corrections to text in a presentation: additions, deletions, or replacements.

▶ *Additions* Additions are necessary when you omit text from a slide and need to add it later. You may need to insert text in the form of a sentence, a word, or a single character. For example, you might want to add the rest of the presenter's first name on your title slide in Project 1.

▶ *Deletions* Deletions are required when text on a slide is incorrect or is no longer relevant to the presentation. For example, in Slide 4, you might want to remove the word likely from the bullet item Rehearse answers to likely questions.

▶ *Replacements* Replacements are needed when you want to revise the text in your presentation. For example, you may want to exchange one word for another. On Slide 4, you might want to substitute the words prospective employer with the word interviewer.

Editing text in PowerPoint is basically the same as editing text in a word processing package. The following steps illustrate the most common changes made to a presentation.

Inserting Text into an Existing Slide

If you forget to type a word or phrase, you can insert the text by positioning the insertion point to the right of the location where you want the text inserted. PowerPoint inserts text to the left of the insertion point. The text to the right of the insertion point moves to the right and downward to accommodate the added text. Perform the following steps to add the rest of M. J. Smithson's first name, Michael.

TO INSERT TEXT

Step 1: Position the insertion point between the letter M and the period in the second line of the sub-title text on the title slide by clicking the left mouse button.
Step 2: Type `ichael`

The title slide now shows Michael J. Smithson's first name instead of his initials. The period will be removed in the next section.

Deleting Text

There are three methods to delete text. One is to use the **BACKSPACE** key to remove text just typed. The second is to position the insertion point to the left of the text you wish to delete and then press the **DELETE** key. The third method is to drag through the text to delete and press the DELETE key. (Use the third method when deleting large sections of text.)

TO DELETE TEXT

Step 1: Position the insertion point between the letter l in Michael and the period on Slide 1.
Step 2: Press the DELETE key.

The period is deleted from Slide 1, and the text shifts to the left one space.

TO REPLACE TEXT

Step 1: Click the Next Slide button three times so Slide 4 displays.
Step 2: Drag through the words prospective employer on the last paragraph of Slide 4.
Step 3: Type `interviewer`

PowerPoint replaces the words prospective employer with the word interviewer.

▶ POWERPOINT ONLINE HELP

A t anytime while using PowerPoint, you can select the Help menu to gain access to **online Help**. The PowerPoint Help menu (Figure 1-89 below) displays several commands. Table 1-5 explains the purpose of each command.

▶ **TABLE 1-5**

COMMAND	PURPOSE
Contents command	To access the Help Contents window.
Search for Help on	To navigate around Help.
Index	To find information about PowerPoint from an alphabetical list.
Quick Preview	To watch a demonstration of PowerPoint.
Tip of the Day	To display a tip explaining an efficient way to complete a task.
Cue Cards	To display an abbreviated instruction card that stays on the screen while you work.
Technical Support	To find out what to do when you have a technical question.
About Microsoft PowerPoint	To see release information and information about how PowerPoint is using your system.

Pressing F1 displays the PowerPoint Help Contents window.

You can print the information in the Help window by choosing the **Print Topic command** from the File menu in the Help window. You close a Help window by choosing Exit from the File menu in the Help window or by double-clicking the Control-box in the title bar in the Help window.

PowerPoint's online Help has features that make it powerful and easy to use. The best way to familiarize yourself with online Help is to use it. Begin with the **How to Use Help command** in the Help menu. To get to the How to Use Help command, choose the **Contents command** from the Help menu. The PowerPoint Help menu displays. Choose the How to Use Help command from the Help menu in the PowerPoint Help dialog box. Then, choose a topic, such as Help Basics.

Viewing Quick Preview

Quick Preview is a five-minute demonstration of the features in PowerPoint. Available through the Help menu, Quick Preview gives you a quick product overview. A demonstration of the main features shows you how PowerPoint works and the types of presentations you can create.

TO VIEW QUICK PREVIEW ▼

STEP 1 ▶

Select the Help menu and point to the Quick Preview command (Figure 1-89).

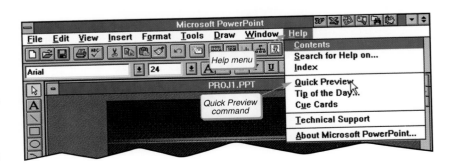

FIGURE 1-89

STEP 2 ▶

Choose the Quick Preview command.

The Quick Preview welcome window displays (Figure 1-90).

STEP 3

Choose the Click to Start (Click to Start) button.

Quick Preview begins.

FIGURE 1-90

When Quick Preview begins, four buttons display at the lower left of the Quick Preview window. Choose the Back button (< Back) to go to the previous Quick Preview window. Choose the Quit button (Quit) to exit Quick Preview. Choose the Next button to go to the subsequent Quick Preview window. Choose the Help button for information about the buttons in Quick Preview.

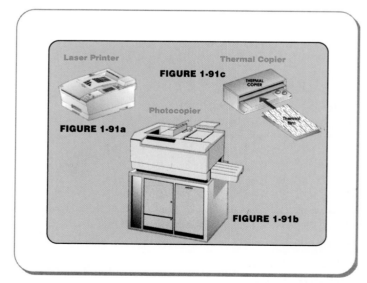

FIGURE 1-91c

FIGURE 1-91a

FIGURE 1-91b

Making a Transparency

Making a transparency is accomplished using one of several devices. One device is a printer, attached to your computer, such as an ink jet printer or a laser printer (Figure 1-91a). Transparencies produced on a printer may be black and white or color, depending on the printer. Another device is a photocopier (Figure 1-91b). A third device is a thermal copier (Figure 1-91c). A thermal copier transfers a carbonaceous substance, such as toner from a photocopier, from a paper master to an acetate film. Because each of the three devices requires a special transparency film, check the user's manual for the film requirement of your specific device.

▶ DESIGNING A PRESENTATION

hen you design a presentation, use the following preparation steps as a guide:

1. Identify the purpose of the presentation. Is this presentation selling an idea or product? Is it reporting results of a study? Is the presentation educating your audience? Whatever the purpose, your goal is to capture the attention of the audience and to explain the data or concept in a manner that is quickly and easily understood. Presentation graphics help people *see* what they *hear*. People remember:

    ▶ 10% of what they *read*
    ▶ 20% of what they *hear*
    ▶ 30% of what they *see*
    ▶ 70% of what they *see* and *hear*

2. Identify the audience. How many people will attend the presentation? Is this an informal presentation to your peers or is this a formal presentation to management or a client? The characteristics of the audience determine which presentation media to use:

    ▶ Overhead transparencies are best when you want audience interaction in a lighted room, for groups less than 40 people, or when other equipment is not available.

    ▶ An electronic presentation using a projection device attached to a personal computer is good for any size audience, depending on the projection device: up to five people when using a laptop with a 14-inch or 17-inch monitor, 25 to 50 people when using an LCD panel or projector, or up to 100 people when using a large-screen video projector. Using an electronic presentation enables you to display embedded audio and video clips into the presentation without switching to another device, such as a video cassette recorder. Use an electronic presentation when you don't have time to make slides or overheads. Be certain that you have a pre-tested system and everything works like it should.

    ▶ 35mm slides are best for a formal presentation to any size audience. 35mm slide presentations are highly recommended when audience size exceeds 50 people. 35mm slide presentations are best-suited for a non-interactive presentation because the room is dark. However, you may use 35mm slides for an interactive presentation in a semi-darkened room if you use slide colors that project in ambient light.

3. Identify the goals you expect to achieve. If you are selling a product, your presentation must focus on why this product is best for this audience. If you are reporting the results of a study, make sure you actually give the results of the study, not just the history of how you conducted the study.

4. Analyze the content. Keep to one concept per slide. Highlight the subject instead of presenting a page of text. Limit your slide to five to seven words per line and five to seven lines per slide. Don't clutter; use empty space effectively.

5. Establish a format and use it. Use one of the PowerPoint templates or create your own. Be consistent with color and text attributes. Remember to use bold and italics sparingly for emphasis and to use no more than two type fonts and styles.

Two acronyms pertain directly to presentation design:

—K.I.S. (Keep It Simple)
—C.C.C. (Clutter Creates Confusion)

▶ PROJECT SUMMARY

Project 1 introduced you to starting PowerPoint and creating a presentation. This project also illustrated how to create a bulleted list presentation. You learned about PowerPoint objects, attributes, and templates. You set the foundation of your presentation using the Pick a Look Wizard. It was here that you selected a template and information to display on every slide. Project 1 illustrated how to change the text style to italics and decrease font size on the title slide. After completing these tasks, you saved your presentation. After saving, you changed line spacing. Using the PowerPoint spelling checker, you learned how to spell check a presentation. You learned how to print a presentation, then how to exit PowerPoint, and open an existing PowerPoint presentation. You learned how to correct errors and use PowerPoint online Help. Finally, you learned preparation steps for designing a presentation.

▶ KEY TERMS AND INDEX

text box *(PP17)*
text color *(PP20)*
text mode *(PP17)*
text position *(PP37)*
text style *(PP20, PP37)*
time *(PP37)*
title bar *(PP12)*

Title box *(PP27)*
Title placeholder *(PP15)*
title slide *(PP4, PP17)*
toggles *(PP14)*
toolbars *(PP13)*
ToolTips *(PP21)*
Undo button *(PP18)*

Undo command *(PP18)*
vertical scroll bar *(PP14)*
white space *(PP41)*
wizard *(PP3)*
word processing *(PP2)*
Zoom Control *(PP46)*

Q U I C K   R E F E R E N C E

In PowerPoint, you can accomplish a task in a number of ways. The following table provides a quick reference to each task in this project with its available options. The commands listed in the Menu column can be executed using either the keyboard or mouse.

Task	Mouse	Menu	Keyboard Shortcuts
Check Spelling	Click Spelling button on Standard toolbar	From Tools menu, choose Spelling	Press F7
Context-Sensitive Help			Press F1 when dialog box displays
Decrease Font Size	Click Decrease Font Size button on Formatting toolbar	From Format menu, choose Font, then choose size	Press CTRL+SHIFT+<
Display a Presentation on a Screen	Click Slide Show button on toolbar	From File menu, choose Slide Show	
Exit PowerPoint	Double-click Control-menu box in title bar	From File menu, choose Exit	Press ALT+F4
First Slide	Drag elevator to top of vertical scroll bar		Press CTRL+PAGE UP
Help	Click Help button on Standard toolbar	Select Help menu	Press F1
Increase Font Size	Click Increase Font Size button on Formatting toolbar	From Format menu, choose Font, then choose size	Press CTRL+SHIFT+>
Italicize Text	Click Italic button on Formatting toolbar	From Text menu, choose Style, then choose Italic	Press CTRL+I
Last Slide	Drag elevator to bottom of vertical scroll bar		Press CTRL+PAGE DOWN
New Slide	Click New Slide button	From Slide menu, choose New Slide	Press CTRL+N
Next Slide	Click Next Slide button		Press PAGE DOWN
Open a Presentation	Click Open button on Standard toolbar	From File menu, choose Open	Press CTRL+O
Previous Slide	Click Previous Slide button		Press PAGE UP
Print a Presentation	Click Print button on Standard toolbar	From File menu, choose Print	Press CTRL+P
Save a Presentation	Click Save button on Standard toolbar	From File menu, choose Save	Press CTRL+S

STUDENT ASSIGNMENTS

STUDENT ASSIGNMENT 1
True/False

Instructions: Circle T if the statement is true or F if the statement is false.

T F 1. PowerPoint is a complete presentation graphics program that allows you to produce professional-looking presentations.

T F 2. The mouse pointer can become one of several different shapes, depending on the task you are performing in PowerPoint and the pointer's location on the screen.

T F 3. The basic unit of a PowerPoint presentation is the document.

T F 4. Toolbars consist of buttons that access commonly used PowerPoint tools.

T F 5. The PowerPoint file extension is PPT.

T F 6. PowerPoint allows you to create automatic bulleted lists, combine words and images, check spelling, find and replace text, and use multiple fonts and type sizes.

T F 7. Selecting Pure Black & White from the Print dialog box turns all colors and fills to black and all text and lines to white.

T F 8. The New Slide button allows you to select a template for your presentation.

T F 9. The Drawing toolbar is a collection of tools for drawing, graphing, and adding text to a slide.

T F 10. The Scale to Fit Paper option in the Print dialog box allows you to print more than one slide on one sheet of paper.

T F 11. The Print button is located on the Formatting toolbar.

T F 12. To start PowerPoint, type POWERPNT at the DOS prompt.

T F 13. When you add a slide to an open presentation, PowerPoint prompts you to choose a template.

T F 14. To view Quick Preview, choose the Quick Preview command from the View menu.

T F 15. The current slide number displays on the status bar.

T F 16. When you save a presentation, it disappears from the screen.

T F 17. When selected text has been italicized, the Italic button appears recessed.

T F 18. To save a document, click the Save button on the Formatting toolbar.

T F 19. The Pick a Look Wizard asks you questions about the type of presentation media you are using for your presentation, such as color overheads or video screen.

T F 20. PowerPoint provides five families of templates: VIDSCREN, B&WOVHD, CLROVHD, ONSCRNSL, and 35MSLIDE.

STUDENT ASSIGNMENT 2
Multiple Choice

Instructions: Circle the correct response.

1. When the mouse pointer is positioned on a menu, it has the shape of a(n) _____ .
   a. I-beam   b. hourglass   c. vertical bar   d. left-pointing block arrow

2. To save a presentation after it was saved once, use the _____ button.
   a. Save   b. Save As   c. Close   d. Exit

3. _____ displays miniature versions of a presentation.
   a. Slide view   b. Notes Pages view   c. Slide Sorter view   d. Outline view

4. Five of the major features of PowerPoint are _____ .
   a. spreadsheet, graphing, drawing, wizard, and outlining
   b. word processing, graphing, database, wizard, and outlining
   c. word processing, graphing, drawing, wizards, and outlining
   d. word processing, graphing, drawing, cut/paste, and outlining

5. To start Microsoft PowerPoint for Windows, _____ .
    a. point to the Microsoft PowerPoint program-item icon and click the left mouse button
    b. point to the Microsoft PowerPoint program-item icon and double-click the left mouse button
    c. point to File Manager and double-click the left mouse button
    d. point to the Open command on the File menu and click the left mouse button
6. Before you change the font size of a line of text, you must _____ .
    a. position the mouse pointer beside the first character in the line to be formatted
    b. highlight the first word in the line to be formatted
    c. underscore the line to be formatted
    d. highlight the line to be formatted
7. PowerPoint automatically adds the extension of _____ to a filename when you save a presentation.
    a. .DOC   b. .TXT   c. .PPT   d. .XLS
8. To erase a character to the left of the insertion point, press the _____ key.
    a. BACKSPACE   b. INSERT   c. DELETE   d. both a and c
9. When you exit PowerPoint, _____ .
    a. control is returned to Program Manager
    b. it is erased from disk
    c. it is removed from the screen
    d. both b and c
10. The template controls the placement and attributes of the _____ .
    a. body object
    b. title object
    c. title text
    d. all the above

STUDENT ASSIGNMENT 3
Understanding the PowerPoint Window

Instructions: In Figure SA1-3, arrows point to the major components of the PowerPoint window in Slide view. Identify the various parts of the window in the spaces provided.

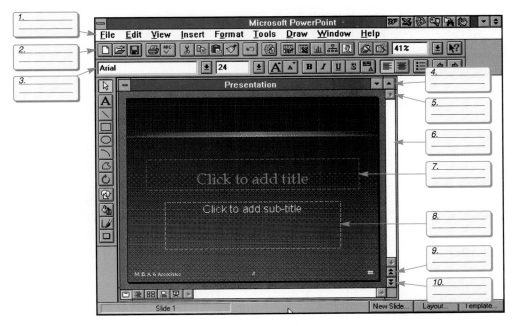

FIGURE SA1-3

STUDENT ASSIGNMENT 4
Understanding the Standard Toolbar

Instructions: In Figure SA1-4, arrows point to several buttons on the PowerPoint window. In the spaces provided, list the name and a brief explanation of each button.

Button Name	Explanation
1. _____	_____
2. _____	_____
3. _____	_____
4. _____	_____
5. _____	_____
6. _____	_____
7. _____	_____
8. _____	_____
9. _____	_____

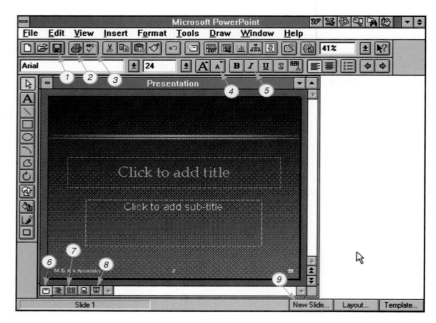

FIGURE SA1-4

STUDENT ASSIGNMENT 5
Understanding How to Change Line Spacing

Instructions: Fill in the number for each step listed below to indicate the proper sequence. These steps override the Slide Master and change the line spacing of each paragraph of the body text shown in Figure SA1-5 to 0.75 lines after each paragraph.

STEP ____: From the Format menu, choose the Line Spacing command.

STEP ____: Choose the OK button from the Line Spacing dialog box.

STEP ____: Click the down arrow next to the After Paragraph text box once so 0.75 displays.

STEP ____: Select the paragraphs to be changed by dragging the mouse pointer.

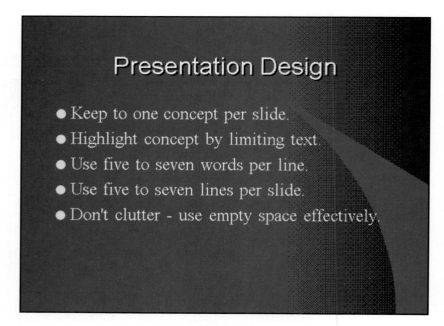

FIGURE SA1-5

STUDENT ASSIGNMENT 6
Understanding the Print Dialog Box

Instructions: Answer the following questions concerning the Print dialog box in Figure SA1-6. The numbers in the figure correspond to the numbers in the following questions.

1. What is the purpose of the Pure Black & White option?

   _____

2. What is the purpose of the Scale to Fit Paper option?

   _____

3. What is the purpose of the Slide Range All option?

   _____

4. What is the purpose of the Copies box?

   _____

5. What is the purpose of the Cancel button?

   _____

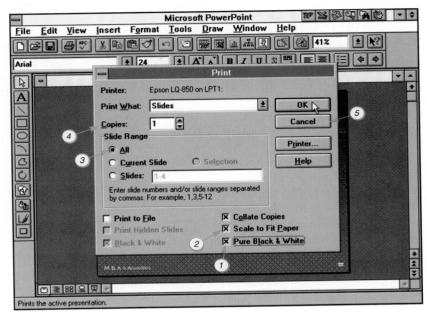

FIGURE SA1-6

COMPUTER LABORATORY EXERCISES

COMPUTER LABORATORY EXERCISE 1
Using the Quick Preview

Instructions: Perform the following tasks using a computer:

1. Start PowerPoint. From the Help menu on the menu bar, choose the Quick Preview command. Choose the Click to Start button. Read the contents of the screen. Choose the Next button. Continue until you reach the end of Quick Preview.
2. To close Quick Preview, choose the Quit button.

COMPUTER LABORATORY EXERCISE 2
Formatting a Slide

Instructions: Start PowerPoint. Open the presentation CLE1-2.PPT from the PPOINT subdirectory on the Student Diskette that accompanies this book.

(continued)

COMPUTER LABORATORY EXERCISE 2 (continued)

Perform the following tasks to change the slide so it looks like the one in Figure CLE1-2.

1. Highlight the bulleted paragraphs.
2. Select the Format menu from the menu bar and point to the Line Spacing command.
3. From the Format menu, choose the Line Spacing command by clicking the left mouse button.
4. Click the up arrow box next to the After Paragraph text box until 0.5 displays.
5. Choose the OK button from the Line Spacing dialog box.
6. Italicize the body object text.
7. Save the presentation on your data disk with the filemane CLE1-2A.
8. Print the presentation by selecting the File menu, choosing the Print button, and selecting Slides in the Print What box.
9. Choose the OK button in the Print dialog box.
10. From the File menu, choose the Exit command to exit PowerPoint.

FIGURE CLE1-2

COMPUTER LABORATORY EXERCISE 3
Spell Checking a Presentation

Instructions: Start PowerPoint. Open the presentation CLE1-3.PPT from the PPOINT subdirectory on the Student Diskette that accompanies this book. CLE1-3.PPT is shown in Figures CLE1-3a and CLE1-3b.

Perform the following tasks:

1. Choose the Spelling button from the Standard toolbar.
2. Choose the Suggest button in the Spelling dialog box to display a list of suggested spellings for the incorrect word.
3. Change the incorrect word Useer by choosing the word User from the list of suggested spellings.
4. Ignore the spelling check message regarding the acronym OLE by choosing the Ignore button.
5. Ignore PowerPoint by choosing the Ignore button.

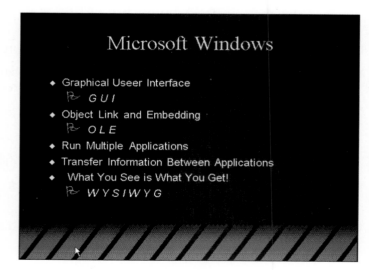

FIGURE CLE1-3a

6. Change the incorrect spacing in your presentation by positioning the insertion point between the letter r in your and the letter p in presentation and then pressing the SPACEBAR. Then, choose the Change button.
7. Save the presentation on your data disk with the filename CLE1-3A.
8. Print the slides for the corrected presentation.
9. From the File menu, choose the Exit command to exit PowerPoint.

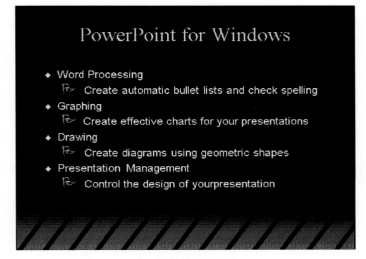

FIGURE CLE1-3b

COMPUTER LABORATORY ASSIGNMENTS

COMPUTER LABORATORY ASSIGNMENT 1
Building a Presentation Using the Pick a Look Wizard

Purpose: To become familiar with building a presentation, applying a template, printing a presentation, and saving a presentation.

Problem: You are the director of benefits for Intergalactic Pipeline. Your primary responsibility is the company insurance plan. A new health insurance plan begins the first of next month. You are presenting the 1996 health insurance coverage to the employees next week.

Instructions: Perform the following tasks:

1. Using the Pick a Look Wizard, create an On-screen presentation with the Double Lines template. Add the company name, date, and page number, as shown in Figure CLA1-1.
2. Create a title slide for Intergalactic Pipeline using your name as the presenter.
3. Add a new slide using the Bulleted List AutoLayout.
4. Type the title and body text for the slide shown in Figure CLA1-1.
5. Adjust the paragraph line spacing to 0.5 lines after each paragraph.
6. Save the presentation on your data disk with the filename CLA1-1.
7. Print the presentation slides.
8. Exit PowerPoint.

FIGURE CLA1-1

COMPUTER LABORATORY ASSIGNMENT 2
Building a Presentation Using the Pick a Look Wizard and Changing Paragraph Line Spacing

Purpose: To become familiar with building a presentation, applying a template, changing paragraph line spacing, printing a presentation, and saving a presentation.

Problem: You are the assistant manager of Maximum Savings and Loan. Your area of responsibility is the loan department. Maximum Savings and Loan is starting its annual home improvement loan campaign. You have been asked to develop a presentation on consumer credit for the home improvement loan campaign.

Instructions: Perform the following tasks:

1. Using the Pick a Look Wizard, choose the Blue Diagonal template and add company name, date, and page number, as shown in Figure CLA1-2.
2. Create a title slide using your name as the presenter.
3. Create a bulleted list for the slide shown in Figure CLA1-2.
4. Adjust the paragraph line spacing to one line after each paragraph.
5. Save the presentation on your data disk with the filename CLA1-2.
6. Print the presentation slides choosing the Print command from the File menu.
6. Exit PowerPoint.

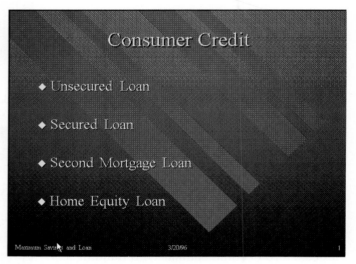

FIGURE CLA1-2

COMPUTER LABORATORY ASSIGNMENT 3
Building a Presentation Using a Template, Changing Paragraph Line Spacing, and Spell Checking

Purpose: To become familiar with designing and building a presentation, applying a template using the Pick a Look Wizard, changing paragraph line spacing, spell checking a presentation, printing a presentation, and saving a presentation.

Problem: You are the assistant director of admissions at Western State University. You have been asked by the chancellor to give a presentation on Western State University. Create a title slide and the bulleted list of the issues you plan to discuss (Figure CLA1-3). Create at least three more slides to complete the presentation. The paragraphs on the next page are excerpts from the Western State University catalog. Use the underlined passages to complete your presentation.

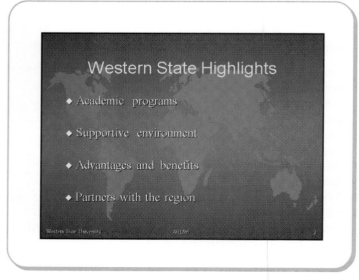

FIGURE CLA1-3

Western State University is <u>a comprehensive university dedicated to serving</u> <u>the professional, cultural, and general educational needs of the citizens of West-</u> <u>ern Arizona</u>. The university provides <u>programs that meet the professional, cul-</u> <u>tural, and general educational needs of the citizens and communities</u>. Its <u>academic programs</u> lead <u>to post baccalaureate and technical proficiency certifi-</u> <u>cates</u> and <u>associate, baccalaureate, and master's degrees</u>. Drawing upon the university's considerable computer resources, the faculty attempts to provide students with both technical skills and awareness of the social and ethical implications of new technology.

Western State University's <u>outreach activities include interactions with local</u> <u>school systems, governments, human services agencies, businesses, and indus-</u> <u>tries—interactions ranging from continuing education and special training to pro-</u> <u>fessional assistance from faculty, staff, and students</u>.

Western State University is a community committed to people as its most important resource. The institution strives to foster cultural diversity and to provide a supportive environment where students, staff, and faculty can grow and thrive, through:

- a <u>hospitable atmosphere for a student body of diverse career goals</u> <u>and ethnic backgrounds, old and young, of both sexes and all races</u>
- a <u>faculty and staff reflecting cultural diversity</u>
- <u>academic consideration of cultural differences</u>
- public programs featuring diverse speakers, performers, and programs
- <u>affirmative action hiring and student recruiting</u>
- outreach to public schools with minority students representing the broad range of citizens of the region

Western State University encourages all who are qualified or who are qualifiable to attend by:

- <u>placing a primary emphasis on educational activities</u>
- <u>offering pre-college course work</u>
- <u>offering reasonable in-state tuition rates, with state support paying</u> <u>for two-thirds of the cost of education</u>
- <u>offering financial aid</u>
- <u>providing strong student support services</u>
- scheduling classes to facilitate the teaching/learning process
- <u>offering flexible courses, scheduling, and sites</u>
- emphasizing lifelong learning

Western State University is <u>a partner with the region it serves both by help-</u> <u>ing citizens and institutions of the region and by garnering support from them to</u> <u>maintain the university's strength</u>.

Instructions: Perform the following tasks:

1. Create an On-screen presentation using the Pick a Look Wizard to add the World template. Add company name, date, and page number.
2. Create a title slide with your name as the presenter.
3. Create the bulleted list shown in Figure CLA1-3.
4. Create at least three additional slides for your presentation.
5. Adjust the after paragraph line spacing to create an appealing presentation.
6. Save the presentation on your disk with the filename CLA1-3.
7. Check the spelling of your presentation.
8. Save the presentation again.
9. Print the presentation slides.
10. Exit PowerPoint.

COMPUTER LABORATORY ASSIGNMENT 4
Designing a Slide

Purpose: To provide practice in planning, designing, and creating a presentation.

Problem: You are the director of financial aid at Western State University. You have been asked by the chancellor to give a five-slide presentation on financial aid available at Western State University. The information you will need is provided below.

To help students meet the cost of their education, Western State University provides financial assistance. The purpose of the Office of Financial Aid is to help students meet educational costs beyond those which they and their families are able to contribute.

There are three types of financial aid for college students available from federal, state, and university programs:

1. Grants or scholarships, which do not have to be repaid.
2. Loans, which must be repaid.
3. College work-study programs, where the student earns money.

To apply for financial aid, a student must:

▸ Apply for admission to Western State University as a degree-seeking student. Financial aid through the university is not available for non degree-seeking students.

▸ Apply for financial aid by submitting a Financial Aid Form (FAF) through the College Scholarship Service. This form is available through high school guidance offices and the Western State University Office of Financial Aid.

For Arizona residents only: Designate the State Student Assistance Commission of Arizona as recipient of the analysis in order to apply for the State Higher Education Award and Lilly Endowment Educational Award.

The analysis of the information provided on the form allows the university to evaluate student need for aid. If the student is eligible, the university will put together a "package" of aid to help meet the student's educational expense. Students receive an Award Notification from the Office of Financial Aid and must return the Financial Aid Acceptance Form to indicate whether they accept the types of funds awarded.

Once a student registers for classes, a bill is generated and mailed to the student. The student must then report to the Bursar's Office to have the financial aid applied to tuition and fees.

If the financial aid amount is greater than tuition and fees, the student will receive a check for the difference.

Important Dates

January 1 - March 1: File the Financial Aid Form (FAF) with the College Scholarship Service for priority consideration. Students filing after March 1 may apply only for a Pell Grant by completing the Financial Aid Form or an application for Federal Student Aid. Students filing late will be considered for campus aid as they complete their files, depending on qualifications and available funds.

June: Award Notifications will be sent out to all applicants with complete files.

Instructions: Design and create a presentation consisting of five slides. Your presentation must include a title slide with your name as the presenter. Select a template that enhances your presentation. Print the date at the bottom of each slide. Adjust after paragraph line spacing, as necessary, to make your slides appealing. Be sure to check the spelling of your presentation before printing it. Save your presentation using the filename CLA1-4. Exit PowerPoint.

▼

CREATING A PRESENTATION IN OUTLINE VIEW

OBJECTIVES You will have mastered the material in this project when you can:

▶ Create a presentation in Outline view
▶ Describe the PowerPoint window in Outline view
▶ Demote text
▶ Promote text
▶ Paste clip art into a presentation from the ClipArt Gallery

▶ Add an AutoShapes object
▶ Add text to an object
▶ Change text color
▶ Color fill an object
▶ Change slide order
▶ Print a presentation outline

▶ ## INTRODUCTION

In both the academic and business environments, you will be asked to make presentations. Most business presentations are some form of a sales presentation: selling your proposal or product to a client, convincing management to approve a new project, or persuading the board of directors to accept the fiscal budget. In all probability, sometime during your professional life, you will make a sales presentation, usually with very short notice. As an alternative to creating your presentation in Slide view, as you did in Project 1, PowerPoint provides an outlining feature to help you organize your thoughts. When the outline is complete, it becomes the foundation for your presentation.

Outlining in PowerPoint is performed in Outline view. However, unlike Slide view, where you type your text directly on the slide, Outline view allows you to type your text as if you were typing an outline on a sheet of paper. First, you would type a title for the outline, which would be the subject matter of the presentation and which would later become the title slide. Then, you would type the remainder of the outline, indenting appropriately to establish a structure or hierarchy. Once the outline is complete, you may then make your presentation more persuasive by adding graphics. This project uses outlining to create the presentation and graphics to visually support the text.

▶ PROJECT TWO — SAN BAARBO VACATIONS

Project 2 uses PowerPoint to create the four slides shown in Figures 2-1a through 2-1d. San Baarbo Vacations is a travel agency making presentations to local organizations to promote their two new vacation packages to San Juan, Puerto Rico. The purpose of the presentation is to entice members of the audience to buy one or both of the San Juan vacation packages. To persuade the audience, San Baarbo Vacations chose a template with a travel theme and included graphics to enhance the bulleted text.

Slide Preparation Steps

The following slide preparation steps summarize how to create the slides shown in Figures 2-1a through 2-1d. If you are creating these slides on a personal computer, read these steps without doing them.

1. Start the PowerPoint program.
2. Apply template travels.ppt using the Pick a Look Wizard.
3. Create the presentation in Outline view.

FIGURE 2-1b

FIGURE 2-1a

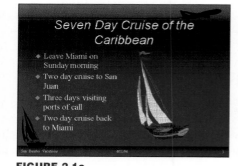

FIGURE 2-1c

FIGURE 2-1d

4. Spell check the presentation.
5. Save the presentation.
6. Change the Slide 2 slide layout to Text over Object and apply Puerto Rico clip art from the intlmaps.pcs clip art file (see Figure 2-1b).
7. Change the Slide 3 slide layout to Text and Clip Art and apply Sailboat clip art from the transprt.pcs clip art file (see Figure 2-1c).
8. Using the Seal tool on the AutoShapes toolbar, apply the seal object to Slide 4. Add yellow text to the seal object. Color fill the seal object red (see Figure 2-1d).
9. Change slide order in Outline view and in Slide Sorter view.
10. Copy and paste Slide 2 in Slide Sorter view.
11. Use the Undo button to reverse the pasting of Slide 2.

12. Save the presentation.
13. Print the presentation outline and slides.
14. Quit PowerPoint.

▶ STARTING POWERPOINT

T o start PowerPoint, the Windows Program Manager must display on the screen and the Microsoft Office group window must be open. Double-click the Microsoft PowerPoint program-item icon in the Microsoft Office group window. Then, choose the OK button in the Tip of the Day dialog box.

▶ USING ADDITIONAL FEATURES OF THE PICK A LOOK WIZARD

I n Project 1, you created a presentation by first developing the "look" of the presentation by selecting options in the Pick a Look Wizard. You selected a template and then embellished the presentation by adding the company name, the date, and the page number to the bottom of each slide. Similarly, in Project 2, you will add a template, but this time you will select the template from the template directory. Clicking the **More button** in the Pick a Look Wizard — Step 3 of 9 dialog box allows you to select a template from one of three subdirectories in the template directory. You will again add the company name, date, and a page number to the bottom of each slide. You will also add the company name, date, and a page number to each outline page. However, on the outline pages, the company name displays in the **header**, or top of the page, and the date and page number display in the **footer**, or bottom of the page.

The following steps explain how to select a template choosing the More button in the Pick a Look Wizard — Step 3 of 9 dialog box and how to add a company name, a date, and a page number to the outline pages.

Starting the Pick a Look Wizard

Recall from Project 1 that the Pick a Look Wizard is a quick way to establish the overall format of your presentation. Perform the following steps to start the Pick a Look Wizard.

TO START THE PICK A LOOK WIZARD

Step 1: Click the Pick a Look Wizard option button in the PowerPoint dialog box.

Step 2: Choose the OK button in the PowerPoint dialog box.

Step 3: Choose the Next button in the Pick a Look Wizard — Step 1 of 9 dialog box.

Step 4: Choose the Next button in the Pick a Look Wizard — Step 2 of 9 dialog box. When the Pick a Look Wizard — Step 3 of 9 dialog box displays, point to the More button.

The Pick a Look Wizard — Step 3 of 9 dialog box displays (Figure 2-2 on the next page).

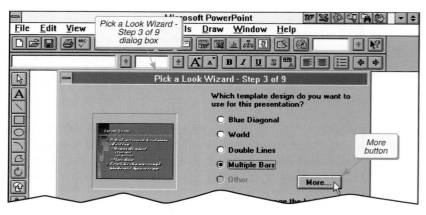

FIGURE 2-2

The next section explains how to select a template from the Presentation Template dialog box.

Selecting a Template from the Presentation Template Dialog Box

Recall from Project 1 that the Pick a Look Wizard — Step 3 of 9 dialog box displays option buttons for four templates: Blue Diagonal, World, Double Lines, and Multiple Bars. These templates are suitable for many presentations, but sometimes you want a template that adds intensity to your presentation. PowerPoint has more than 100 artist-created templates in its three template subdirectories: bwovrhd, clrovrhd, and sldshow. The bwovrhd subdirectory contains templates created for black-and-white overhead transparencies. Actually, the templates in the bwovrhd subdirectory use shades of black and gray. The clrovrhd subdirectory contains templates for color overhead transparencies. The templates designed for color overhead transparencies use shades of black and gray and include some color. The sldshow subdirectory contains templates for on-screen slide shows. The templates designed for on-screen slide shows use the most color with background color ranging from shades of gray to bright red. The best way to decide on a template is to browse through the template subdirectories until you find one that suits your presentation.

PRESENTATION TIP

The template conveys a silent message just by the use of color. Color serves many functions:

▶ Heightens the realism of the image by displaying its actual colors

▶ Points out differences and similarities

▶ Creates an emotional response

Knowing how people perceive color helps you emphasize your message. Color sets a mood for the presentation. People respond to color. The psychological basis for which some colors are "cool" (blue, green, and violet) and other colors are "hot" (red and orange) is the manner in which the human eye focuses. Warmer colors seem to reach toward the audience while cooler colors seem to pull away from the audience. The design principle to remember is light, bright colors seem to jump out from a dark background and are easiest to see. White or yellow text, used with a dark gray drop shadow, on a dark blue, green, purple, or black background is ideal.

TO SELECT A TEMPLATE FROM THE PRESENTATION TEMPLATE DIALOG BOX ▼

STEP 1 ►

Choose the More button in the Pick a Look Wizard – Step 3 of 9 dialog box. When the Presentation Template dialog box displays, point to the File Name scroll bar elevator in the File Name list box.

The Presentation Template dialog box displays (Figure 2-3). The File Name list box contains a list of templates available in the sldshow template subdirectory.

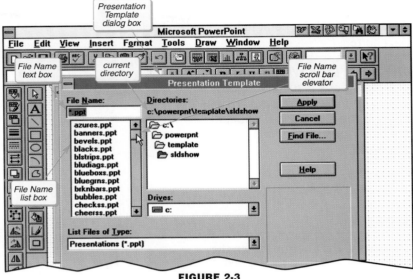

FIGURE 2-3

STEP 2 ►

Drag the File Name scroll bar elevator down to the bottom of the scroll bar. Then, point to travels.ppt in the File Name list box (Figure 2-4).

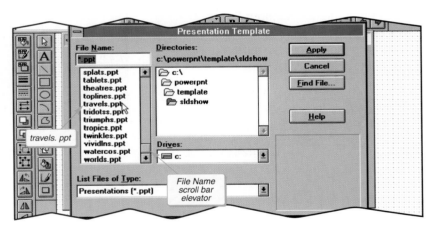

FIGURE 2-4

STEP 3 ►

Select the travels.ppt template. Then, point to the Apply button in the Presentation Template dialog box.

A preview of the travels.ppt template displays in the preview box (Figure 2-5). The filename, travels.ppt, is highlighted and displays in the File Name text box.

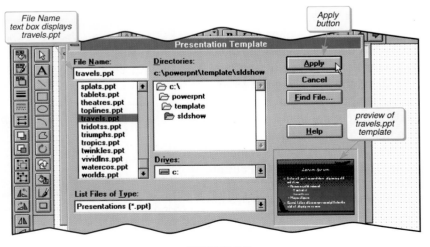

FIGURE 2-5

STEP 4 ▶

Choose the Apply button. When the Pick a Look Wizard – Step 3 of 9 dialog box displays, point to the Next button.

The Pick a Look Wizard – Step 3 of 9 dialog box displays (Figure 2-6). The travels.ppt template displays in the preview box. Notice the Other option button is selected.

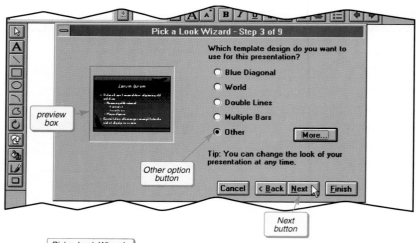

STEP 5 ▶

Choose the Next button. When the Pick a Look Wizard – Step 4 of 9 dialog box displays, remove the x in the Speaker's Notes check box and the x in the Audience Handout Pages check box by pointing to each box and clicking the left mouse button. Then, point to the Next button.

The Pick a Look Wizard – Step 4 of 9 dialog box displays (Figure 2-7). The Full-Page Slides and Outline Pages check boxes are selected.

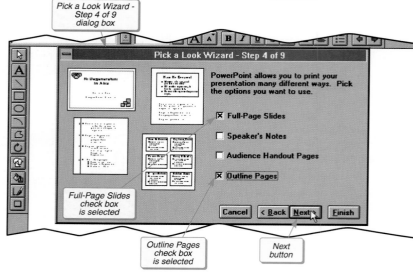

FIGURE 2-7

STEP 6 ▶

Choose the Next button. When the Pick a Look Wizard – Slide Options dialog box displays, select the check boxes for Name, company, or other text; Date; and Page Number. Drag the mouse pointer through the existing text in the Name, company, or other text box and type San Baarbo Vacations for the company name. Then, point to the Next button.

San Baarbo Vacations displays in the text box and all three check boxes are selected in the Pick a Look Wizard – Slide Options dialog box (Figure 2-8).

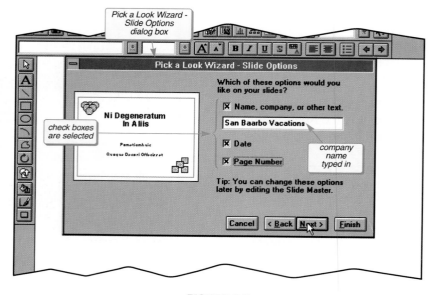

FIGURE 2-8

STEP 7 ►

Choose the Next button.

The Pick a Look Wizard – Outline Options dialog box displays (Figure 2-9). San Baarbo Vacations displays in the text box because you typed it in the Pick a Look Wizard – Slide Options dialog box. PowerPoint automatically selects the Page Number check box.

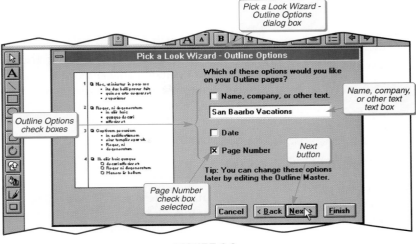

FIGURE 2-9

STEP 8 ►

Select the check box for Name, company, or other text and the check box for Date. Then, point to the Next button.

All three check boxes are selected in the Pick a Look Wizard – Outline Options dialog box (Figure 2-10).

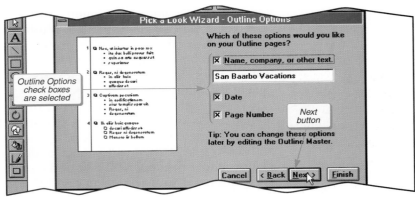

FIGURE 2-10

STEP 9 ►

Choose the Next button. When the Pick a Look Wizard – Step 9 of 9 dialog box displays, choose the Finish button.

Slide 1 displays the title slide with the travels.ppt template and the placeholders for the title and sub-title (Figure 2-11).

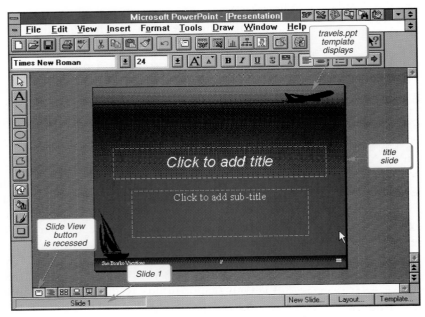

FIGURE 2-11

Maximizing the PowerPoint Window

The PowerPoint window is not always maximized when you start PowerPoint. Recall from Project 1 that maximizing the PowerPoint window makes it easier to see the contents of the window. If your window is not already maximized, click the Maximize button on the title bar. For a detailed explanation of how to maximize the PowerPoint window, see page PP16.

▶ USING OUTLINE VIEW

Outline view provides a quick and easy way to create a presentation. Outlining allows you to organize your thoughts in a structured format. An outline uses indentation to establish a hierarchy, which denotes levels of importance to the main topic. An **outline** is a summary of thoughts, presented as headings and subheadings, often used as a preliminary draft when creating a presentation. In Outline view, title text displays at the left side of the window along with a slide icon and a slide number. Indented under the title text is the body text. Graphic objects, such as pictures, graphs, or tables, do not display in Outline view. When a slide contains a graphic object, the slide icon next to the slide title displays with a small graphic on it. The slide icon is blank when a slide does not contain graphics. The attributes for text in Outline view are the same as in Slide view except for color and paragraph style.

PowerPoint limits the number of outline levels to six. PowerPoint refers to outline levels as heading levels. The outline begins with a title on **heading level one**. The title is the main topic of a slide. Text supporting the main topic begins on **heading level two** and indents under heading level one. **Heading level three** indents under heading level two and contains text to support heading level two. **Heading level four**, **heading level five**, and **heading level six** indent under heading level three, heading level four, and heading level five, respectively. Use heading levels four, five, and six as required for presentations requiring vast amounts of detail, such as scientific or engineering presentations. Business and sales presentations usually focus on summary information and use heading level one, heading level two, and heading level three.

 PRESENTATION TIP

A topic needing more than six heading levels has too much detail and may overwhelm the audience. Decompose large topics into two or more subtopics. Then, create a new slide for each group of subtopics.

The audience ultimately determines the level of detail you place on one slide. Before you create your presentation, determine who is likely to attend. Design your presentation around the amount of detail the audience wants to see. Remember, you want to keep their attention. One sure way to lose their attention is to bore them with details when a summary will suffice. Additionally, try to pace your information over several slides. The purpose of a slide is to identify ideas or concepts. This differs from a page of printed text that tells the whole story on one page. Don't expect your audience to read a slide filled with text. As the presenter, it is your responsibility to introduce the topic and then explain the details.

You may create and edit your presentation title and text in Outline view. Outline view also makes it easy to sequence slides and to relocate title and text from one slide to another.

PowerPoint can make slides from an outline created in Microsoft Word or another word processor if you save it as an RTF file or as plain text. The file extension **RTF** stands for **R**ich **T**ext **F**ormat.

TO USE OUTLINE VIEW ▼

STEP 1 ▶

Point to the Outline View button (▤) at the lower left of the PowerPoint screen (Figure 2-12).

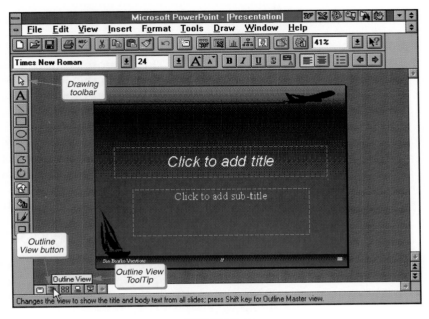

FIGURE 2-12

STEP 2 ▶

Click the Outline View button.

PowerPoint displays the Outline View window (Figure 2-13).

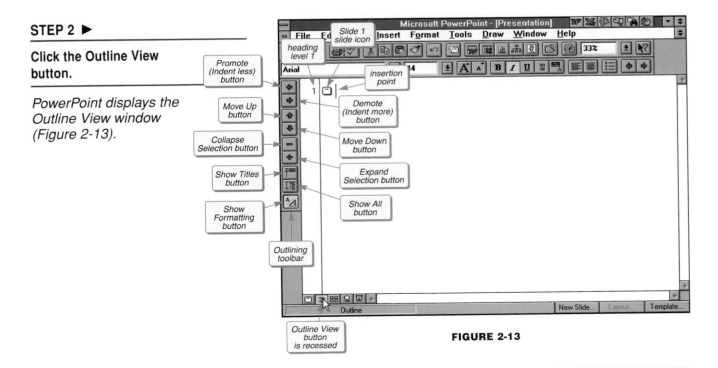

FIGURE 2-13

▶ THE POWERPOINT SCREEN IN OUTLINE VIEW

The PowerPoint screen in Outline view differs from the screen in Slide view in that the Outlining toolbar displays and the Drawing toolbar does not display. (See Figures 2-12 and 2-13 on the previous page to compare the differences.) The Outlining toolbar contains the following tools:

PROMOTE BUTTON   The **Promote (Indent less) button** (◀) moves the selected paragraph up one level in the outline hierarchy each time you click the button. Promoting a paragraph outdents or moves it to the left until you reach heading level one.

DEMOTE BUTTON   The **Demote (Indent more) button** (▶) moves the selected paragraph down one level in the outline hierarchy each time you click the button. Demoting a paragraph indents or moves it to the right. You can only demote down to the sixth heading level.

MOVE UP BUTTON   The **Move Up button** (▲) moves selected text up one paragraph at a time while maintaining its hierarchical outline level and text style. The selected text changes position with the paragraph located above it.

MOVE DOWN BUTTON   The **Move Down button** (▼) moves selected text down one paragraph at a time while maintaining its hierarchical outline level and text style. The selected text changes position with the paragraph located below it.

COLLAPSE SELECTION BUTTON   The **Collapse Selection button** (−) hides all heading levels except the slide title of the selected slide. The button is useful when you want to collapse one slide in your outline.

EXPAND SELECTION BUTTON   The **Expand Selection button** (+) displays all heading levels for the selected slide. The button is useful when you want to expand one slide in your outline.

SHOW TITLES BUTTON   The **Show Titles button** (▤) collapses all heading levels to show only the slide titles. This button is useful when you are looking at the organization of your presentation and do not care to see all the details.

SHOW ALL BUTTON   The **Show All button** (▤) expands all heading levels to display the slide title and text for all slides in the presentation.

SHOW FORMATTING BUTTON   The **Show Formatting button** (ᴬ⁄) is a toggle that displays or hides the text attributes in Outline view. This button is useful when you want to work with plain text as opposed to working with bolded, italicized, or underlined text. When printing your outline, plain text often speeds up the printing process.

▶ CREATING A PRESENTATION IN OUTLINE VIEW

In Outline view, you can view title and body text, add and delete slides, rearrange slides or slide text by dragging and dropping, promote and demote text, save the presentation, print the outline or slides, copy and paste slides or text to and from other presentations, apply a template, and import an outline.

Developing a presentation in Outline view is quick because you type the text for all slides at one time. Once you type the outline, the presentation is fundamentally complete. If you choose, you can then go to Slide view to enhance your presentation with graphics.

Creating a Title Slide in Outline View

Recall from Project 1 that the title slide introduces the presentation to the audience. Additionally, Project 2 uses the title slide to capture the attention of the audience. The travels template enhances the presentation title by displaying an airplane at the top of the slide and a sailboat at the bottom of the slide. Perform the following steps to create a title slide in Outline view.

TO CREATE A TITLE SLIDE IN OUTLINE VIEW ▼

STEP 1 ►

Type San Baarbo Vacations **and press the ENTER key.**

San Baarbo Vacations displays as the title for Slide 1 and is called heading level 1. A slide icon displays to the left of each slide title. In Outline view, the Zoom Control default setting is 33% of actual slide size. Pressing the ENTER key moves you to the next line and maintains the same heading level. Therefore, the insertion point is in position for typing the title for Slide 2 (Figure 2-14).

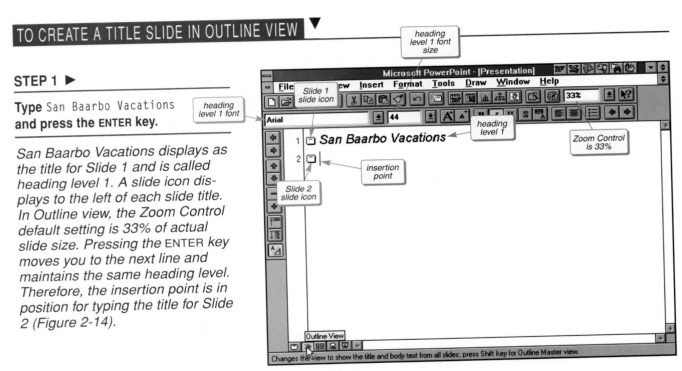

FIGURE 2-14

STEP 2 ►

Point to the Demote (Indent more) button on the Outlining toolbar (Figure 2-15).

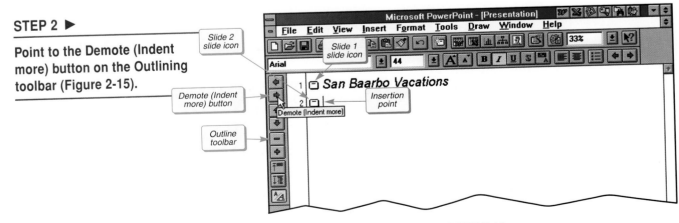

FIGURE 2-15

STEP 3 ▶

Click the Demote (Indent more) button.

The Slide 2 slide icon no longer displays (Figure 2-16). The insertion point is indented to the right and is now in position for typing the sub-title text. By default, heading level two is a sub-title on the title slide.

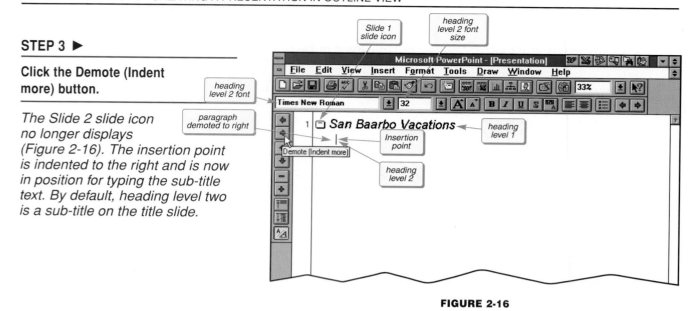

FIGURE 2-16

STEP 4 ▶

Type Presents... **and press the ENTER key. Then, type** Passport to the Caribbean

Slide 1 title text is heading level one and the sub-title text is heading level two (Figure 2-17).

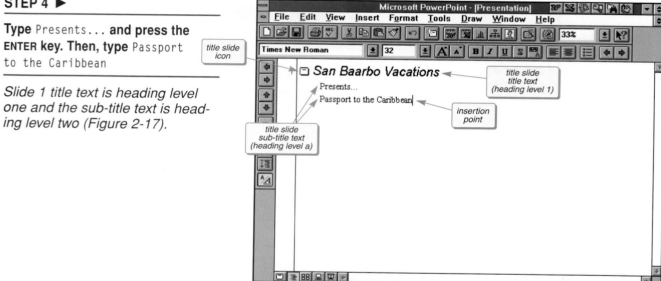

FIGURE 2-17

The title slide for Project 2 is complete. The following section explains how to add bulleted list slides in Outline view.

▶ ADDING BULLETED LIST SLIDES IN OUTLINE VIEW

R ecall that when you add a new slide, PowerPoint defaults to the Bulleted List slide layout. This is true in Outline view as well. Begin by typing your list of topics and then demoting each topic to the appropriate heading level. Each time you demote a paragraph, PowerPoint adds a bullet to the left of each heading level. Each heading level has a different bullet font.

Using Outline View to Create a Multiple Level Bulleted List Slide

Slide 2 is the first informational slide for Project 2. Slide 2 introduces the main topic: two new vacation packages offered by San Baarbo Vacations. Each vacation package displays as heading level two, and its supportive paragraph displays as heading level three. Perform the following steps to create a multiple level bulleted list slide in Outline view.

TO USE OUTLINE VIEW TO CREATE A MULTIPLE LEVEL BULLETED LIST SLIDE ▼

STEP 1 ▶

Point to the Insert New Slide button (▦) on the Standard toolbar (Figure 2-18).

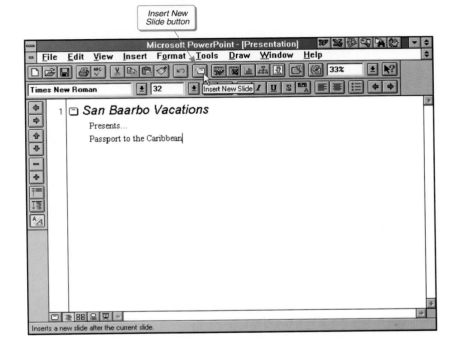

FIGURE 2-18

STEP 2 ▶

Click the Insert New Slide button.

The Slide 2 slide icon displays (Figure 2-19). The insertion point is in position to type the title for Slide 2.

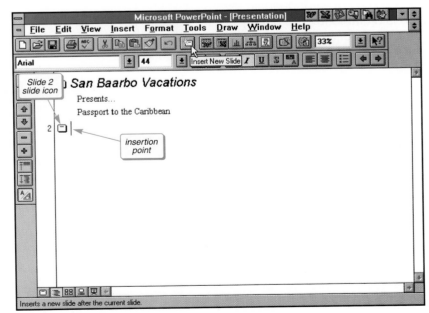

FIGURE 2-19

STEP 3 ▶

Type the title for Slide 2 San Baarbo Vacations Offers Two New Exciting Packages **and press the ENTER key. Then, click the Demote (Indent more) button on the Outlining toolbar to demote to heading level two.**

The title for Slide 2 displays and the insertion point is in position to type the first bulleted paragraph (Figure 2-20). A diamond-shaped bullet displays to the left of the insertion point.

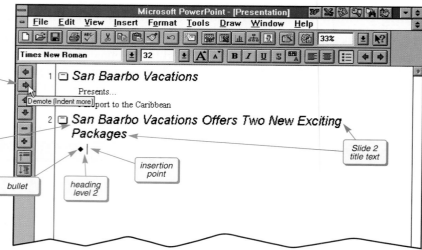

FIGURE 2-20

STEP 4 ▶

Type the first bulleted paragraph Seven day cruise of the Caribbean **and press the ENTER key. Then, click the Demote (Indent more) button on the Outlining toolbar to demote down to heading level three.**

Slide 2 displays three heading levels: the title on heading level one, the bulleted paragraph on heading level two, and the insertion point on heading level three (Figure 2-21). The bullet for heading level two is a diamond. The bullet for heading level three is a dash.

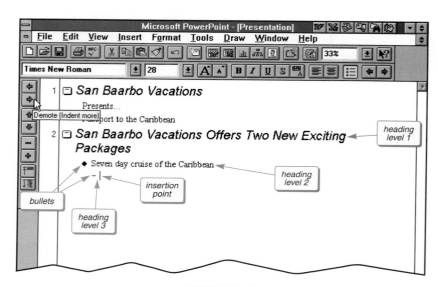

FIGURE 2-21

STEP 5 ▶

Type Seven days and six nights on the luxurious Island Queen **and press the ENTER key. Then, point to the Promote (Indent less) button on the Outlining toolbar.**

Pressing the ENTER key begins a new paragraph at the same heading level as the previous paragraph (Figure 2-22).

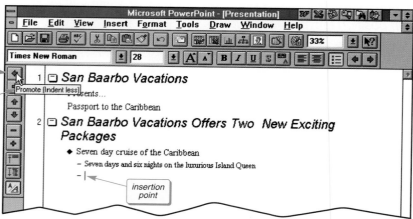

FIGURE 2-22

STEP 6 ▶

Click the Promote (Indent less) button to promote up to heading level two.

Clicking the Promote (Indent less) button moves the insertion point left and promotes the paragraph to heading level two (Figure 2-23).

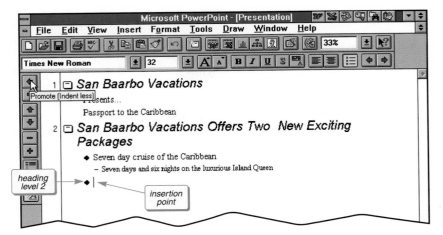

FIGURE 2-23

STEP 7 ▶

Type Special weekend flight **and press the ENTER key. Then, click the Demote (Indent more) button on the Outlining toolbar to demote down to heading level three (Figure 2-24).**

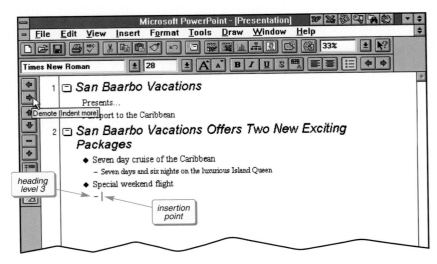

FIGURE 2-24

STEP 8 ▶

Type Three days and two nights in San Juan

Slide 2 is a multiple-level bulleted list. The title is heading level one. The major bulleted items are in heading level two. The minor bulleted items are in heading level three. The insertion point is positioned after the letter n in Juan (Figure 2-25).

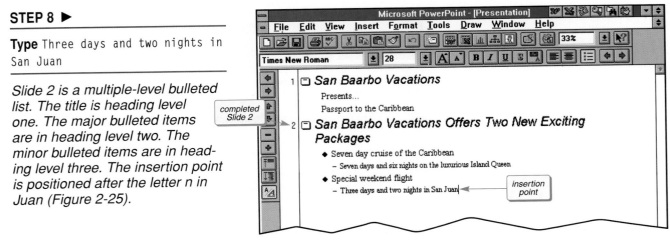

FIGURE 2-25

If your preference is to use the keyboard instead of the mouse when typing an outline, press the TAB key or the ALT+SHIFT+RIGHT ARROW keys to demote text and press the SHIFT+TAB keys or the ALT+SHIFT+LEFT ARROW keys to promote text.

When adding a new slide, click the Insert New Slide button on the Standard toolbar or the New Slide button on the status bar. If you are using the keyboard to add a new slide, press the CTRL+M keys. Still another way to add a new slide is to promote a new paragraph to heading level one. You do this by pressing the ENTER key after typing the last line of text on the current slide and then clicking the Promote (Indent less) button until the insertion point is at heading level one. A slide icon displays when you reach heading level one.

Finishing the Outline for Project 2

Now that you have the basics for creating slides in Outline view, follow the steps below to complete the outline for Project 2.

Creating the First Subordinate Slide

When developing your presentation, begin with a main topic and follow with subsequent slides to support the main topic. Placing all your information on one slide would overwhelm your audience. Therefore, decompose your presentation into several slides with three to seven bullets per slide. Perform the following steps to create the first slide that supports the main topic in Slide 2.

TO CREATE THE FIRST SUBORDINATE SLIDE

Step 1: Click the Insert New Slide button on the Standard toolbar to add a new slide.

Step 2: Type Seven Day Cruise of the Caribbean and press the ENTER key.

Step 3: Click the Demote (Indent more) button on the Outlining toolbar to demote to heading level two.

Step 4: Type Leave Miami on Sunday morning and press the ENTER key.

Step 5: Type Two day cruise to San Juan and press the ENTER key.

Step 6: Type Three days visiting ports of call and press the ENTER key.

Step 7: Type Two day cruise back to Miami

The screen displays, as shown in Figure 2-26.

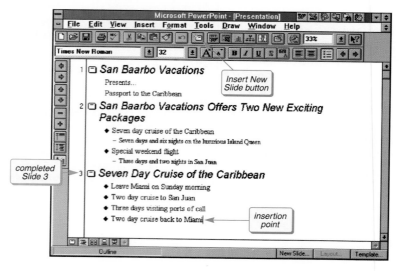

FIGURE 2-26

Creating the Second Subordinate Slide

The next step is to create the slide that supports the second bulleted item on Slide 2, Special Weekend Flight. Perform the following steps to create this subordinate slide.

TO CREATE THE SECOND SUBORDINATE SLIDE

Step 1: Click the Insert New Slide button on the Standard toolbar to add a new slide.

Step 2: Type Special Weekend Flight and press the ENTER key.

Step 3: Click the Demote (Indent more) button on the Outlining toolbar to demote to heading level two.

Step 4: Type Fly from Chicago on Friday and press the ENTER key.

Step 5: Click the Demote (Indent more) button on the Outlining toolbar to demote to heading level three.

Step 6: Type Packages from other major cities available and press the ENTER key.

Step 7: Click the Promote (Indent less) button on the Outlining toolbar to promote to heading level two.

Step 8: Type Spend two fun-filled days in San Juan and press the ENTER key.

Step 9: Click the Demote (Indent more) button on the Outlining toolbar to demote to heading level three.

Step 10: Type Sail, surf, swim, relax and press the ENTER key.

Step 11: Click the Promote (Indent less) button on the Outlining toolbar to promote to heading level two.

Step 12: Type Fly back on Sunday night

The screen displays, as shown in Figure 2-27.

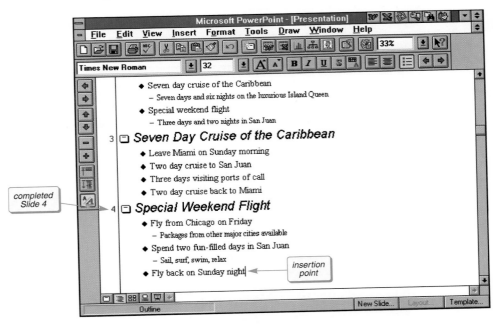

FIGURE 2-27

Saving the Presentation

Remember that it is wise to frequently save your presentation on disk. Because the outline is now complete, you should save your presentation now. For a detailed example of the steps summarized below, refer to pages PP24 through PP26 in Project 1.

TO SAVE A PRESENTATION

Step 1: Click the Save button on the Standard toolbar.
Step 2: Type proj2 in the File Name box. Do not press the ENTER key.
Step 3: Click the Drives drop-down box arrow and select the drive name a:.
Step 4: Choose the OK button from the Save As dialog box.
Step 5: Revise the information contained in the Summary Info dialog box and choose the OK button.

The presentation is saved to drive A: under the name PROJ2.PPT.

▶ CHANGING TO SLIDE VIEW

T he outline for the San Baarbo Vacation presentation is complete. Outline view displays only text for each slide. Changing to Slide view allows you to display your slides as they appear in your presentation. After creating your presentation in Outline view, use Slide view to change to a slide layout more appropriate for your presentation. For example, you might want to change to a slide layout designed for displaying text and graphics. You must be in Slide view when you add objects to a slide. Perform the following steps to switch to Slide view.

TO CHANGE TO SLIDE VIEW ▼

STEP 1 ▶

Point to the Slide 4 slide icon (▭).

The mouse pointer changes to a four-headed arrow (✛) when positioned over the slide icon in Outline view (Figure 2-28).

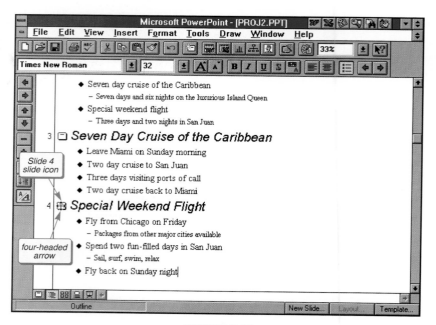

FIGURE 2-28

STEP 2 ▶

Double-click the slide icon for Slide 4.

Slide 4 displays in Slide view (Figure 2-29).

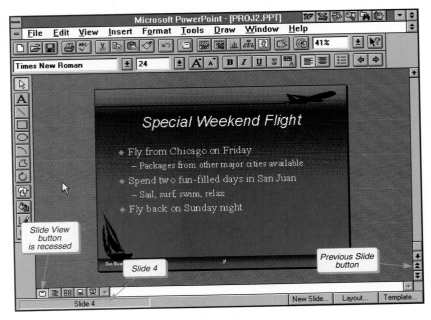

FIGURE 2-29

STEP 3 ▶

Click the Previous Slide button on the vertical scroll bar twice to display Slide 2.

Slide 2 displays in Slide view (Figure 2-30).

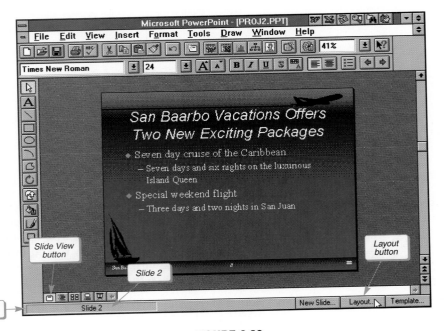

FIGURE 2-30

Recall that you could change to Slide view by clicking the Slide View button located at the lower left of the PowerPoint screen.

▶ ADDING CLIP ART TO A SLIDE

Clip art is a quick way to add professional-looking artwork to your presentation without creating the art yourself. There are over 1,000 graphic images in the PowerPoint **ClipArt Gallery**. PowerPoint combines topic-related clip art images into categories. PowerPoint stores these categories in the ClipArt Gallery. You include clip art in your presentation by selecting a clip art image from the ClipArt Gallery. Additionally, the ClipArt Gallery is shared among all Microsoft Office applications.

Table 2-1 gives you an idea of the organization of the ClipArt Gallery that accompanies PowerPoint. The table contains five of the filenames from the ClipArt Gallery and a description of the clip art contained in each file. You will be using clip art from the Transportation category and the Maps — International category. However, if PowerPoint was installed on your computer as a "typical" installation, these two categories will be missing. Contact your instructor if you are missing either clip art category when you perform the following steps. A full installation is required before all the clip art images are available for use.

▶ **TABLE 2-1**

CLIP ART CATEGORY	FILENAME	ART DESCRIPTION
Academic	ACADEMIC.PCS	46 slides, e.g., Professor, Girl Student, Boy Student.
Backgrounds	BACKGRND.PCS	58 scenic slides, e.g., Citiscape with Horizon, Mountain View, Road to Horizon.
Currency	CURRENCY.PCS	146 slides, e.g., Generic Stack of Coins, Generic Stack of Bills 1, Stack of Money.
Maps — International	INTLMAPS.PCS	180 maps, e.g., Africa, North America, Central America.
People	PEOPLE.PCS	111 artist drawings, e.g., Woman with Briefcase, Man with Briefcase, Man at Desk.
Sports & Leisure	SPORTS.PCS	41 sports symbols, e.g. Football & Goal Post, Golfer.

▶ ADDING CLIP ART OBJECTS TO YOUR PRESENTATION

The next step in creating your presentation is to add clip art to the slides. Recall that clip art is one type of object that may be added to a slide. PowerPoint makes it easy to add objects to a slide by providing several slide layouts with placeholders specifically designed for clip art and other objects (text, charts, tables, and graphs).

Changing Slide Layout

Recall from Project 1 that when you add a new slide, PowerPoint displays the AutoLayouts dialog box from which you choose one of the slide layouts. After creating a slide, you may change its layout by clicking the **Layout button** on the status bar. The Slide Layout dialog box then displays. Like the AutoLayout dialog box, the Slide Layout dialog box allows you to choose one of the twenty-one different slide layouts. As you create a presentation or as you edit an existing presentation, you may want to change the layout of a slide. With PowerPoint, you won't lose any text or graphics when you change to a new layout.

Using slide layouts eliminates the need to resize objects because PowerPoint automatically sizes the object to fit the placeholder. To keep your presentation interesting, PowerPoint includes several slide layouts to combine text with nontext objects such as clip art. The placement of the text, in relationship to the nontext object, depends on the slide layout. The nontext object placeholder may be to the right of the text, left of the text, above the text, or below the text. Additionally, some slide layouts are constructed with two nontext object placeholders. Refer to Project 1 for a list of the available slide layouts (Figure 1-40 on PP27). Perform the following steps to change the slide layout from a bulleted list to text over an object.

TO CHANGE SLIDE LAYOUT ▼

STEP 1

Point to the Layout button on the status bar (Figure 2-30 on page PP87).

STEP 2 ▶

Click the Layout button on the status bar and then point to the elevator on the Slide Layout vertical scroll bar.

The Slide Layout dialog box displays nine of the 21 available slide layouts (Figure 2-31). Bulleted List is selected because it is the current slide layout. Its name displays at the lower right of the Slide Layout dialog box.

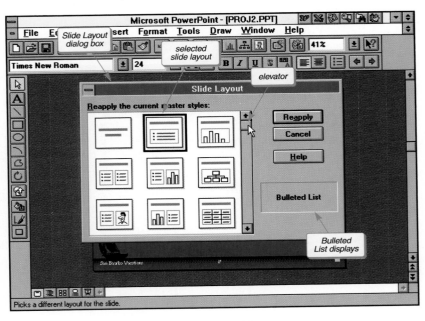

FIGURE 2-31

STEP 3 ▶

Drag the elevator to the bottom of the vertical scroll bar in the Slide Layout dialog box. Then, select the Text over Object slide layout (▦).

The Text over Object slide layout is selected (Figure 2-32). When you click a layout, its name displays in the text box at the lower right of the Slide Layout dialog box.

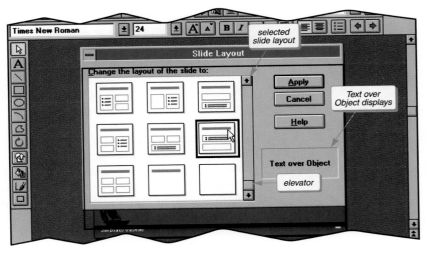

FIGURE 2-32

STEP 4 ▶

Point to the Apply button in the Slide
Layout dialog box (Figure 2-33).

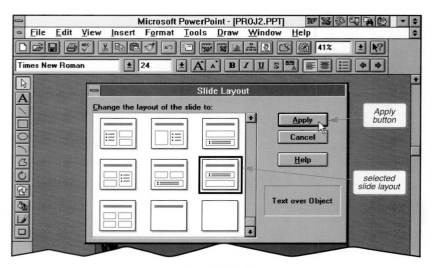

FIGURE 2-33

STEP 5 ▶

Choose the Apply button.

*Slide 2 displays with an object
placeholder at the bottom of the
slide (Figure 2-34).*

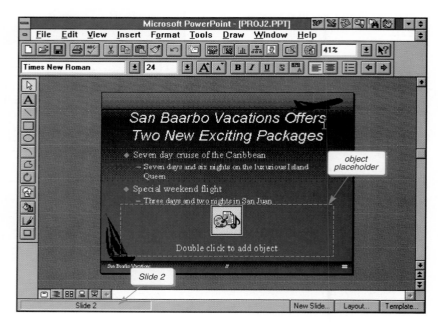

FIGURE 2-34

The object placeholder at the bottom of Slide 2 will hold a clip art image. The
next section explains how to add clip art to your presentation.

Adding Clip Art

In a presentation, clip art serves a purpose — it conveys a message. It should
not be used decoratively. Clip art should contribute to the understandability of the
slide. Before adding clip art to a presentation, ask yourself: "Does the clip art convey or support the slide topic?" If the answer is no, do not put the clip art on the
slide.

Perform the following steps to add the clip art map of Puerto Rico to Slide 2.

TO ADD CLIP ART ▼

STEP 1 ►

Point to the object placeholder at the bottom of Slide 2 (Figure 2-35).

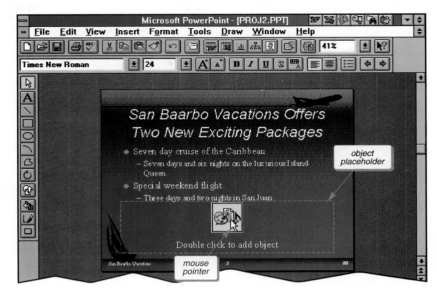

FIGURE 2-35

STEP 2 ►

Double-click the object placeholder. When the Insert Object dialog box displays, point to Microsoft ClipArt Gallery in the Object Type list box.

PowerPoint displays the Insert Object dialog box (Figure 2-36). The list of object types on your computer may look different from the one in the figure. The objects listed depend on the type of installation. If Microsoft ClipArt Gallery does not display, contact your instructor.

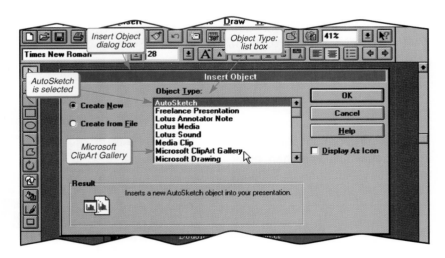

FIGURE 2-36

STEP 3 ►

Select Microsoft ClipArt Gallery. Then, point to the OK button.

Microsoft ClipArt Gallery is selected (Figure 2-37).

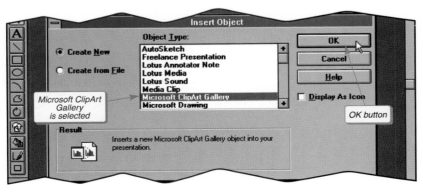

FIGURE 2-37

STEP 4 ►

Choose the OK button. When the Microsoft ClipArt Gallery – Picture in PROJ2.PPT dialog box displays, point to the elevator in the Choose a category to view below list box.

The Microsoft ClipArt Gallery – Picture in PROJ2.PPT dialog box displays with a gallery of images (Figure 2-38). The selected image is a professor in the Academic category. Your selected image may be different, depending on the clip art installed on your computer. If this is the first time clip art has been accessed after an installation, the Microsoft ClipArt Gallery dialog box displays with a message asking if you would like to add clip art from PowerPoint now? Click the Yes button. PowerPoint will then display the Microsoft ClipArt Gallery – Picture in PROJ2.PPT dialog box.

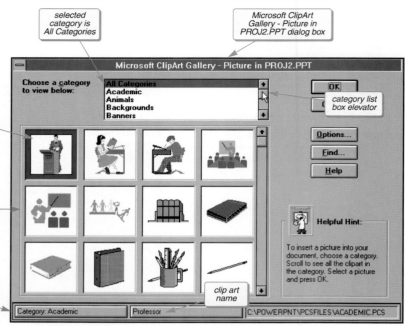

FIGURE 2-38

STEP 5 ►

Drag the elevator until Maps – International displays. Then, point to the Maps – International clip art category (Figure 2-39).

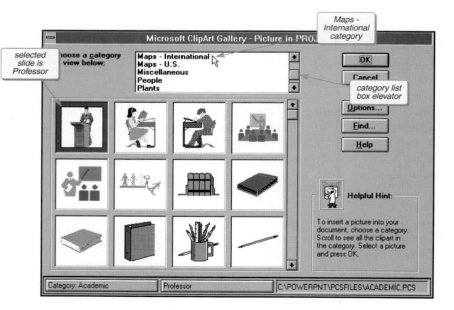

FIGURE 2-39

STEP 6 ▶

Select Maps – International and then point to the elevator in the gallery of images list box.

The selected category is Maps – International. The first image, Africa, is selected (Figure 2-40).

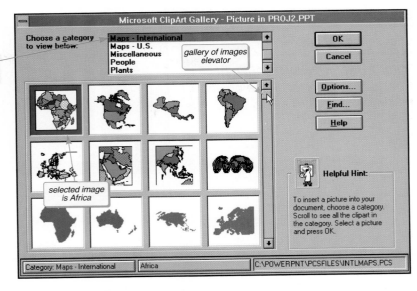

FIGURE 2-40

STEP 7 ▶

Drag the elevator down the vertical scroll bar until the map of Puerto Rico displays. Then, point to the map of Puerto Rico (Figure 2-41).

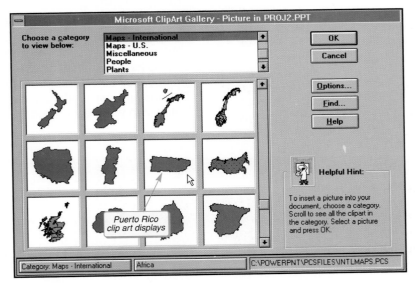

FIGURE 2-41

STEP 8 ▶

Select the map of Puerto Rico and then point to the OK button (Figure 2-42).

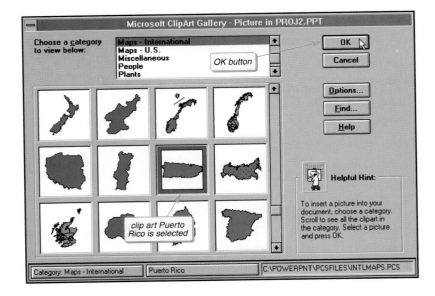

FIGURE 2-42

STEP 9 ▶

Choose the OK button.

Slide 2 displays with the map of Puerto Rico inserted in the object placeholder (Figure 2-43).

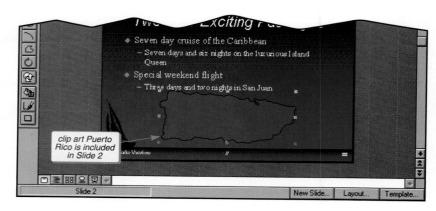

clip art Puerto Rico is included in Slide 2

FIGURE 2-43

PRESENTATION TIP

Use clip art in your presentation whenever appropriate to add power to the text. Through the use of clip art, misconceptions are reduced. If the presentation consists of words alone, the audience creates its own mental picture. The mental picture the audience creates may be different from the concept you are trying to convey. The audience will understand the concept better when clip art is included in the presentation.

▶ **TABLE 2-2**

FORMAT	FILE EXTENSION
AutoCAD Format 2-D	.dxf
AutoCAD Plot File	.adi
Compuserve GIF	.gif
Computer Graphics Metafile	.cgm
CorelDRAW!	.cdr
DrawPerfect	.wpg
Encapsulated PostScript	.eps
Hewlett-Packard Graphic Language	.hgl
Hewlett-Packard Plotter Print File	.plt
Kodak Photo CD	.pcd
Lotus 1-2-3 Graphics	.pic
Macintosh PICT	.pct
Micrografx Designer/Draw	.drw
PC Paintbrush	.pcx
Tagged Image Format	.tif
Targa	.tga
Windows Bitmaps	.dib, .bmp
Windows Device Independent Bitmap	.dib
Windows Metafile	.wmf

Besides the 1,000 graphic images in the PowerPoint ClipArt Gallery, there are additional sources for clip art, such as retailers specializing in computer software and bulletin board systems. A **bulletin board system** is a computer system that allows users to communicate with each other and share files.

Additionally, you can include pictures into your presentation. These may include scanned photographs and line art, and artwork from compact disks. To insert a picture into a presentation, the picture must be saved in a format that PowerPoint can recognize. Table 2-2 identifies the formats PowerPoint recognizes.

Changing Text Size

Recall from Project 1 that you change text size by first selecting the text and then clicking the Font Size button until the font size you want displays. Perform the following steps to change text size.

TO CHANGE TEXT SIZE

Step 1: Select Seven days and six nights on the luxurious Island Queen by triple-clicking the paragraph.

Step 2: Click the Decrease Font Size button one time.

Step 3: Select Three days and two nights in San Juan by triple-clicking the paragraph.

Step 4: Click the Decrease Font Size button one time.

The decrease in font size on Slide 2 adds white space between the text and the clip art object (Figure 2-44).

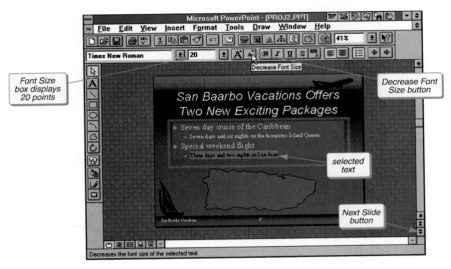

FIGURE 2-44

Changing Slide Layout for Slide 3

Recall that using a slide layout eliminates the need to resize objects because PowerPoint automatically sizes the object to fit the object placeholder. Slide 3 uses the Text & Clip Art slide layout (see Figure 2-45). Perform the following steps to change slide layout.

TO CHANGE SLIDE LAYOUT FOR SLIDE 3 ▼

STEP 1 ▶

Click the Next Slide button on the vertical scroll bar. Click the Layout button on the status bar. When the Slide Layout dialog box displays, select the Text & Clip Art slide layout (Figure 2-45).

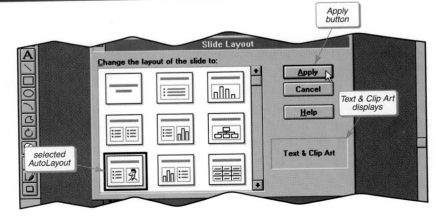

FIGURE 2-45

STEP 2 ▶

Choose the Apply button.

Slide 3 displays with a clip art placeholder at the right side of the slide (Figure 2-46).

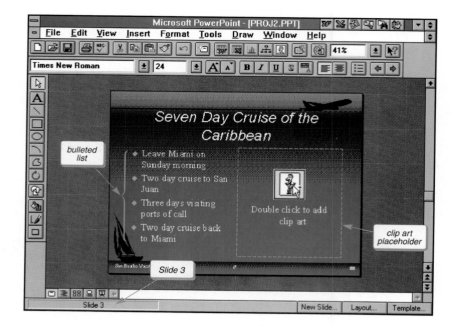

FIGURE 2-46

The next section explains how to add clip art to Slide 3.

Adding Clip Art to Slide 3

Slide 3 contains clip art of a sailboat. This clip art is called Sailboat and is located in the Transportation category. Perform the following steps to add clip art to Slide 3.

TO ADD CLIP ART TO SLIDE 3 ▼

STEP 1 ▶

Double-click the clip art placeholder at the right side of Slide 3. When the Microsoft ClipArt Gallery – Picture in PROJ2.PPT dialog box displays, drag the elevator in the Choose a category to view below list box until Transportation displays. Select the Transportation category. Drag the elevator down the vertical scroll bar in the gallery of images until the sailboat displays. Select the sailboat (Figure 2-47). Then, point to the OK button.

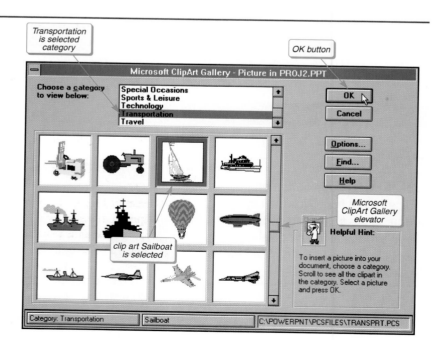

FIGURE 2-47

STEP 2 ▶

Choose the OK button.

Slide 3 displays with the sailboat inserted in the clip art placeholder (Figure 2-48).

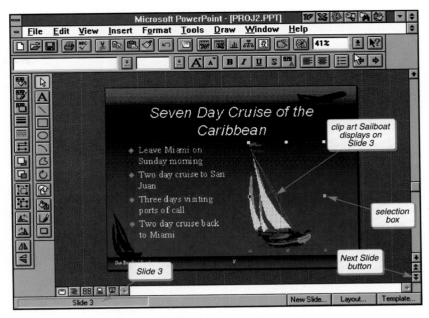

FIGURE 2-48

▶ Using the AutoShapes Toolbar

Y ou can use the PowerPoint drawing features to produce professional images and artwork for your presentation. In addition to the Drawing toolbar identified in Project 1, PowerPoint has two toolbars for adding graphics and visual support to your presentation: the AutoShapes and Drawing+ (pronounced as drawing plus) toolbars. The **AutoShapes toolbar** contains tools for drawing commonly used shapes, such as diamonds, stars, and triangles. The **Drawing+ toolbar** contains tools for modifying your graphics. For example, you could change the fill color of an object by selecting the Fill Color button (⬛) on the Drawing+ toolbar. **Fill color** is the interior color of an object.

You access the AutoShapes toolbar by clicking the AutoShapes button (⬛) on the Drawing toolbar. The AutoShapes toolbar displays twenty-four shapes. You draw a shape by clicking the button on the AutoShapes toolbar that represents the shape you wish to draw and positioning the cross-hair pointer (⬛) on the slide. Then, drag the shape until it takes on the proportions you want. Pressing and holding the SHIFT key when dragging the shape creates regular shapes. A **regular shape** is perfectly proportioned and can be inscribed within a square, such as a circle or a square. Holding the CTRL key when dragging the shape draws the shape outward from the center of the shape.

Accessing the AutoShapes Toolbar

To add a shape to your presentation, you must first access the AutoShapes toolbar. Perform the steps on the next page to access the AutoShapes toolbar.

TO ACCESS THE AUTOSHAPES TOOLBAR ▼

STEP 1 ▶

Click the Next Slide button on the vertical scroll bar and then point to the AutoShapes button on the Drawing toolbar.

Slide 4 displays (Figure 2-49).

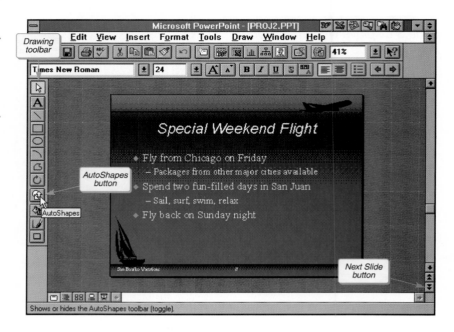

FIGURE 2-49

STEP 2 ▶

Click the AutoShapes button.

The AutoShapes toolbar displays in the PowerPoint window (Figure 2-50). The AutoShapes toolbar displays at the location it was positioned at during the last PowerPoint session.

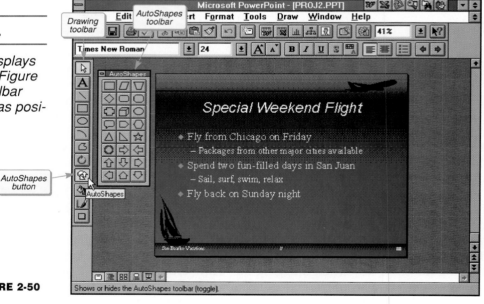

FIGURE 2-50

If the AutoShapes toolbar displays on top of your slide, you may want to move it out of your way. Move the AutoShapes toolbar by holding down the left mouse button on an open space on the toolbar (not a button) and then dragging the toolbar to another location on the PowerPoint window. When you drag the toolbar near the outer edges of the PowerPoint window, an outline of the AutoShapes toolbar displays. This outline indicates how the toolbar will display when you drop it in the new location.

Now that you have displayed the AutoShapes toolbar, you are ready to add the seal object to Slide 4. The seal object resembles a sunburst and is added to Slide 4 to persuade the audience to buy a vacation package by depicting the warm glow of the sun. Perform the following steps to add the seal object to Slide 4 using the Seal Tool button () from the AutoShapes toolbar.

TO ADD THE SEAL OBJECT TO SLIDE 4 ▼

STEP 1 ►

Click the Seal Tool on the AutoShapes toolbar (Figure 2-51).

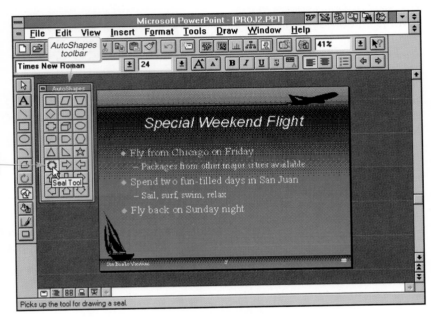

FIGURE 2-51

STEP 2 ►

Position the cross-hair pointer below the letter S in San Juan and to the right of the word relax in the paragraph Sail, surf, swim, relax (Figure 2-52).

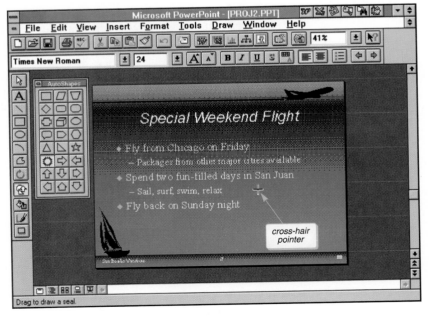

FIGURE 2-52

STEP 3 ►

Press the left mouse button and drag diagonally down and to the right until the cross-hair pointer almost touches the horizon in the travels template. Drop the seal object by releasing the left mouse button.

The seal object displays in the lower right corner of Slide 4 (Figure 2-53). When you release the left mouse button, the cross-hair pointer becomes a two-headed arrow. Eight resize handles display around the seal object. Dragging a resize handle controls the size of the shape.

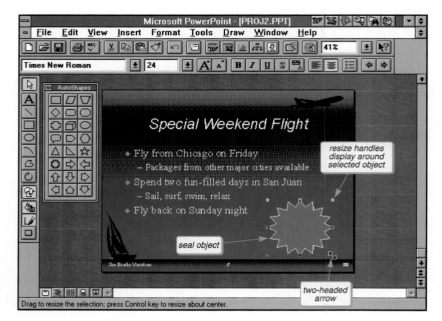

FIGURE 2-53

The two-headed pointer shows the direction in which you can resize the object. When you drag the resize handle, the two-headed arrow changes to a cross-hair pointer.

▶ ADDING TEXT TO AN OBJECT

Shapes drawn with the AutoShapes tools are objects. You can add text to any closed object drawn with the AutoShapes tools, such as rectangles, circles, and triangles. After drawing an object, just start typing. PowerPoint automatically centers your text in the object. As long as you add text immediately after drawing the object, you don't need to select it again, because it is already selected.

Adding text to an object is done for two reasons. Sometimes you add text for the purpose of labeling an object. For example, if you used PowerPoint to draw a floor plan, you could label each object simply by selecting it and typing its name. Other times, you place text inside the object to add drama to the presentation, as in Slide 4. Perform the following steps to add text to the seal object on Slide 4.

TO ADD TEXT TO AN OBJECT ▼

STEP 1

If the seal object is not selected, select it by clicking it.

STEP 2 ►

Type Fun in the Sun

The text is centered in the seal object, as shown in Figure 2-54. A selection box displays when text is typed.

FIGURE 2-54

Now that you have added text to the seal object, you will change the color of the text to yellow. The next section explains how to change text color.

► CHANGING TEXT COLOR

Using color in a presentation can have dramatic effects. Recall that people perceive colors as warm or cool. For instance, red and yellow convey a feeling of warmth, while blue and white project a feeling of coolness. Additionally, warm colors seem to reach toward the audience while cool colors seem to pull away from the audience. Changing the color of the text changes the way the audience feels about the subject matter. Because this is a sales presentation and you are trying to create an emotional response, you want the audience to crave a warm, sunny vacation. In the following steps, you will use the Text Color button (⬛) to change the color of the text within the seal object from a cool white to a warm yellow.

TO CHANGE TEXT COLOR ▼

STEP 1 ►

Select the text in the seal object by triple-clicking it or dragging the I-beam pointer through it (Figure 2-55).

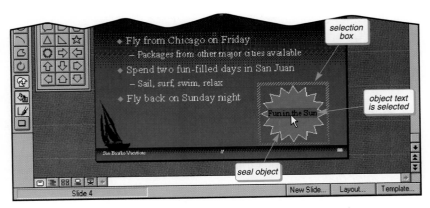

FIGURE 2-55

STEP 2 ▶

Point to the Text Color button on the Formatting toolbar (Figure 2-56).

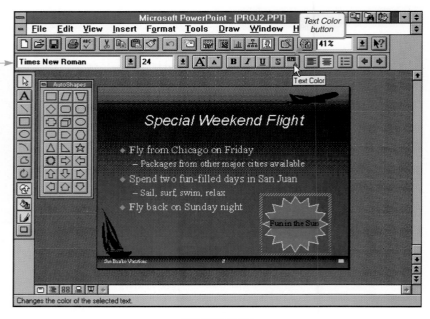

FIGURE 2-56

STEP 3 ▶

Click the Text Color button. When the Text Color drop-down list box displays, point to the Other Color command.

The Text Color drop-down list box displays (Figure 2-57). White is the current text color and is designated by the heavy black line surrounding the color sample.

FIGURE 2-57

STEP 4 ▶

Click the Other Color command. When the Other Color dialog box displays, point to the yellow color sample in the Color Palette area. Yellow is in row 1, column 5.

The Other Color dialog box displays the Color Palette (Figure 2-58). The current text color, white, displays in the preview box in the Other Color dialog box.

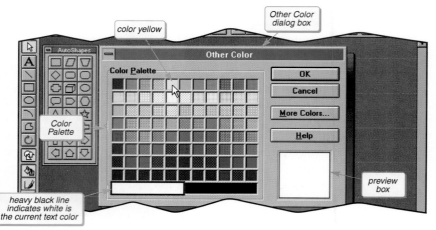

FIGURE 2-58

STEP 5 ▶

Click the yellow color sample and then point to the OK button.

The yellow color sample is selected and yellow displays in the preview box in the Other Color dialog box (Figure 2-59).

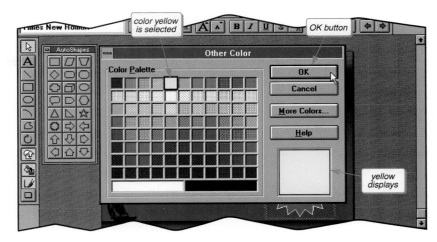

FIGURE 2-59

STEP 6 ▶

Choose the OK button.

The text in the seal object is yellow but does not display as such because the text is still highlighted (Figure 2-60).

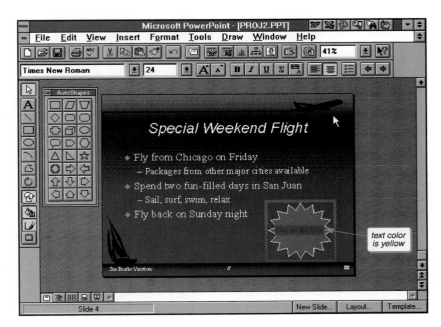

FIGURE 2-60

▶ CHANGING THE FILL COLOR OF THE SEAL OBJECT

When Slide 4 is complete, the seal object will be red. Recall from Project 1 that you want light colors on a dark background or dark colors on a light background. Because the text in the seal object is yellow, you will want to change the fill color of the seal. Additionally, you want to sell the audience a vacation to sunny San Juan. A quick way to change the fill color is to click the Fill Color button on the Drawing+ toolbar. But first, you must display the Drawing+ toolbar. The next section explains how to use the shortcut menu to display and manipulate the Drawing+ toolbar.

Shortcut Menus

In PowerPoint, the use of shortcut menus is limited. A **shortcut menu** is a menu containing frequently used PowerPoint commands. To display a toolbar shortcut menu, point to one of the toolbars and press the right mouse button. To display an editing or formatting shortcut menu, point to an object on a slide and press the right mouse button. This section discusses using the shortcut menu to work with the toolbars.

Occasionally, you may want to override a color that was determined by the default attributes of the template. You accomplish this using the Fill command. The Fill command is found on the Drawing+ toolbar as a button called Fill Color. You can quickly display the Drawing+ toolbar by using a shortcut menu. When pointing to any toolbar, press the right mouse button. The shortcut menu displays the names of the available PowerPoint toolbars. A check mark in front of the toolbar name indicates it is selected to display in the PowerPoint window. You select the toolbar by clicking on the toolbar name. The check mark displays in front of the toolbar name. You also deselect the toolbar by clicking on the toolbar name. However, when you deselect the toolbar, the check mark no longer displays in front of the name.

Two additional commands display in the shortcut menu: Toolbars and Customize. The Toolbars command displays the Toolbars dialog box, where you can select the toolbars to display on the PowerPoint window. The Customize command displays the Customize Toolbars dialog box, where you can add or delete buttons on a toolbar.

Perform the following steps to display the Drawing+ toolbar using a shortcut menu. If the Drawing+ toolbar is already displaying on your PowerPoint window (as shown in Figure 2-62), read the next two steps and proceed to the next section: Changing the Fill Color of the Seal Object.

TO DISPLAY THE DRAWING+ TOOLBAR ▼

STEP 1 ▶

Point to one of the toolbars and click the right mouse button. When the shortcut menu displays, point to Drawing+.

The shortcut menu displays (Figure 2-61). The shortcut menu displays at the location of the mouse pointer when you clicked the right mouse button. Therefore, your screen may look different from the one in Figure 2-61. A check mark displays in front of the toolbars currently selected to display on the PowerPoint window. The Drawing+ toolbar does not presently have a check mark. (If there is a check mark in front of the Drawing+ toolbar, press the ESC key to exit from the shortcut menu and proceed to Step 3.)

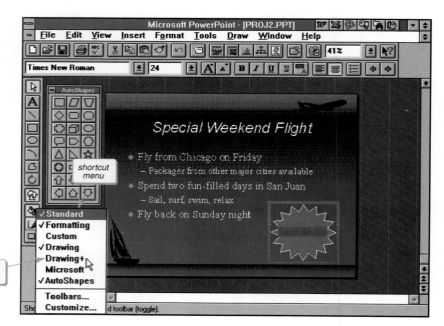

FIGURE 2-61

STEP 2 ▶

Click Drawing+ in the shortcut
menu. Then, point to the Control-
menu box on the AutoShapes
toolbar.

*The Drawing+ toolbar displays
(Figure 2-62). (You will close the
AutoShapes toolbar because it is
no longer needed for this project
and to reduce clutter on the
PowerPoint window.)*

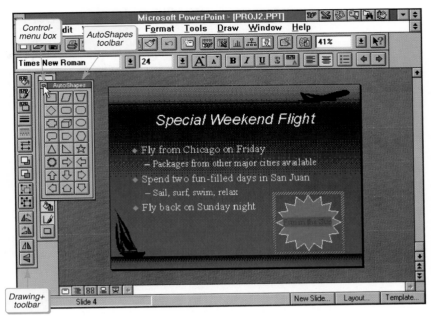

FIGURE 2-62

STEP 3 ▶

Double-click the Control-menu box
to close the AutoShapes toolbar.

*The AutoShapes toolbar no longer
displays in the PowerPoint window
(Figure 2-63). In addition to the
Standard and Formatting toolbars,
the Drawing+ and Drawing toolbars display in the PowerPoint
window. The location of your toolbars is not important because you
can drag them to a different location in the PowerPoint window.*

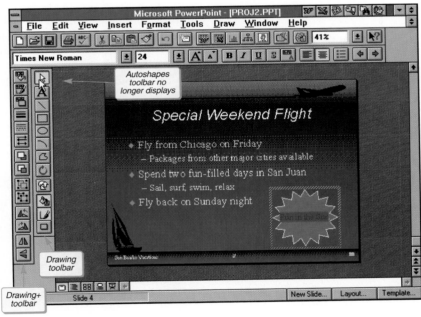

FIGURE 2-63

Instead of closing the AutoShapes toolbar, you could drag it to a new location.
If, for example, you drag it to the top of the PowerPoint window, it would display
horizontally like the Standard toolbar or the Formatting toolbar.

Changing the Fill Color of the Seal Object

Now that the Drawing+ toolbar displays in the PowerPoint window, you are ready to change the color of the seal object. You click the Fill Color button on the Drawing+ toolbar to display a drop-down box containing eight color samples and five commands. The eight color samples are the eight colors used in the color scheme for the current template. The five commands in the Fill Color drop-down box are described in Table 2-3.

▸ **TABLE 2-3**

COMMAND	DESCRIPTION
No Fill	Object is not filled, it is transparent.
Background	Fill color displays background color of the slide. Background color is determined by the template.
Shaded	Shaded creates a three-dimensional effect. There are six styles of shades: vertical, horizontal, diagonal right, diagonal left, from corner, from center.
Pattern	Displays Pattern Fill dialog box with 36 pattern styles. Two colors combine to create a pattern. Color can be assigned to the background and to the foreground of the pattern.
Other Color	Displays Color Palette of 90 color samples.

Fill color can be one solid color, two-color patterns, or shaded colors. A color-filled object is **opaque**, meaning that any objects behind the color-filled object would not display. An object with no fill is **transparent**, meaning that objects behind it would display.

Perform the following steps to change the fill color of the seal object to red.

TO CHANGE THE FILL COLOR OF THE SEAL OBJECT ▼

STEP 1 ▶

If the seal object is not selected, select it by clicking it. Then, point to the Fill Color button on the Drawing+ toolbar (Figure 2-64).

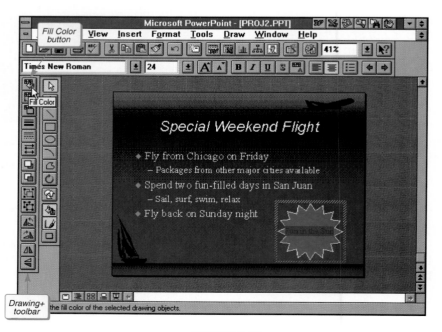

FIGURE 2-64

STEP 2 ▶

Click the Fill Color button. When the Fill Color drop-down box displays, point to the Other Color command.

The Fill Color drop-down box displays color samples and five commands (Figure 2-65). The current fill color is a two-color mix of purple and red, designated by the black border around the color sample. The color samples change each time you select a new color.

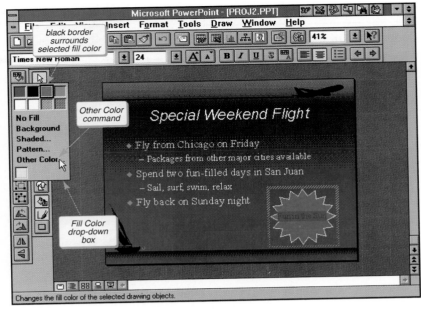

FIGURE 2-65

STEP 3 ▶

Click the Other Color command. When the Other Color dialog box displays, point to the red color sample in the Color Palette. Red is in row 1, column 2.

The Color Palette displays 90 color samples (Figure 2-66). The current fill color displays in the preview box in the Other Color dialog box.

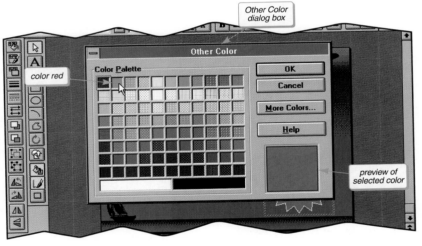

FIGURE 2-66

STEP 4 ▶

Click the red color sample and then point to the OK button.

The preview box displays the selected fill color (Figure 2-67). A black border surrounds the red color sample, which indicates it is the selected fill color.

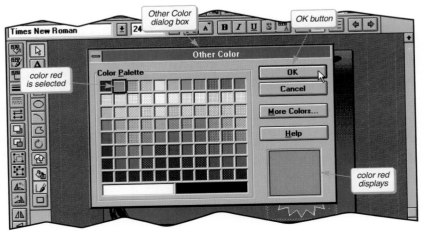

FIGURE 2-67

STEP 5 ▶

Choose the OK button. When Slide 4
displays, click outside the seal
object to deselect it.

*The seal object fill color is red and
the text is yellow (Figure 2-68).*

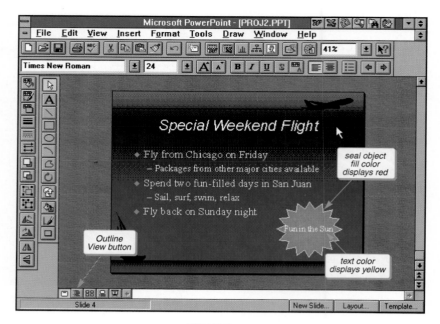

FIGURE 2-68

As an alternative to selecting a color sample and choosing the OK button,
double-click the color sample. PowerPoint returns to the slide and displays the
new fill color in the object.

Project 2 is complete and you should save the presentation again by clicking
the Save button on the Standard toolbar.

▶ EDITING THE PRESENTATION

N   ow that Project 2 is complete, you will want to review it for content and
presentation flow. If you find that your slides need to be in a different
sequence, you can easily change the slide order by dragging the slide to
its new position. You can change slide order in either Outline view or Slide Sorter
view. The next sections explain several editing features of PowerPoint. First, you
will learn how to change slide order in Outline view and then in Slide Sorter view.
You will also learn how to copy a slide and paste it into the presentation. Finally,
you will learn how to use the Undo button to reverse the last edit action.

Changing Slide Order in Outline View

In Outline view, you move the slide to its new location by dragging the slide
icon until the placement indicator displays. In Outline view, the placement indicator is a horizontal line that identifies the new position of the slide. Perform the following steps to change slide order in Outline view.

TO CHANGE SLIDE ORDER IN OUTLINE VIEW ▼

STEP 1 ▶

Click the Outline View button located at the bottom of the PowerPoint screen. When Outline view displays, position the mouse pointer over the slide icon for Slide 4.

The outline for Project 2 displays (Figure 2-69). Slide 4 is highlighted because it was the current slide in Slide view. Slides containing graphics display with graphic symbols in the slide icon. The pointer becomes a four-headed arrow when positioned over the slide icon.

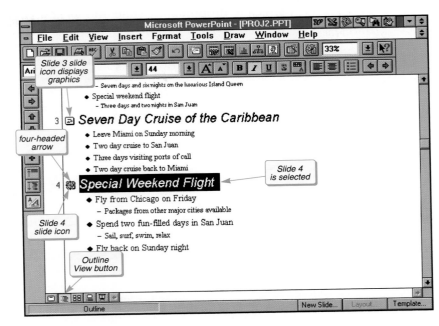

FIGURE 2-69

STEP 2 ▶

Press the left mouse button and drag the slide icon until the horizontal placement indicator displays below the paragraph, Three days and two nights in San Juan and above the paragraph Seven Day Cruise of the Caribbean. Then, drop Slide 4 above the Slide 3 slide icon by releasing the left mouse button.

Slide 4 and Slide 3 exchange positions in the presentation outline (Figure 2-70). PowerPoint automatically renumbers the slides.

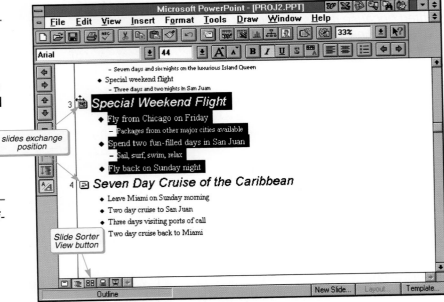

FIGURE 2-70

As you dragged the slide icon, a horizontal placement indicator displayed as soon as you moved off the slide. The placement indicator is useful for identifying the exact location to drop the slide when changing slide order in Outline view.

Changing Slide Order in Slide Sorter View

As previously stated, changing slide order in Slide Sorter view is simply dragging and dropping the slide into its new position. When you drag a slide to a new location in Slide Sorter view, the placement indicator displays to indicate where the slide will be positioned. In Slide Sorter view the **placement indicator** is a vertical dotted line with arrows at the top and bottom. The mouse pointer displays as a miniature slide icon ( ) as soon as you drag the slide. You move the slide to its new location by dragging the miniature slide icon pointer until the placement indicator displays at the location where you want to insert the slide. Because you cannot drop the slide on top of another slide in Slide Sorter view, the placement indicator appears to jump in front of a slide or after a slide as the miniature slide icon pointer moves around the window. Perform the steps below to change slide order in Slide Sorter view.

TO CHANGE SLIDE ORDER IN SLIDE SORTER VIEW ▼

STEP 1 ►

Click the Slide Sorter View button located at the bottom of the PowerPoint screen and point to Slide 3.

Project 2 displays in Slide Sorter view (Figure 2-71). Slide 3 is highlighted because it was the current slide in Outline view. PowerPoint assigns a number to each slide.

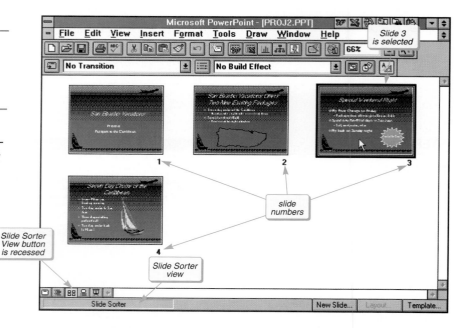

FIGURE 2-71

STEP 2 ►

Press the left mouse button and drag Slide 3 down until the placement indicator displays after Slide 4 (Figure 2-72).

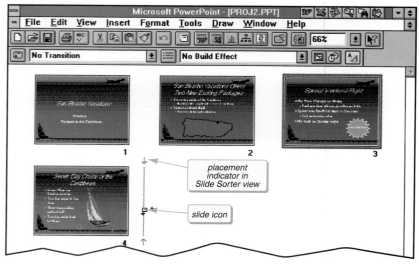

FIGURE 2-72

STEP 3 ▶

Release the left mouse button to drop Slide 3 after Slide 4.

Slide 4 and Slide 3 exchange positions (Figure 2-73). PowerPoint automatically renumbers the slides.

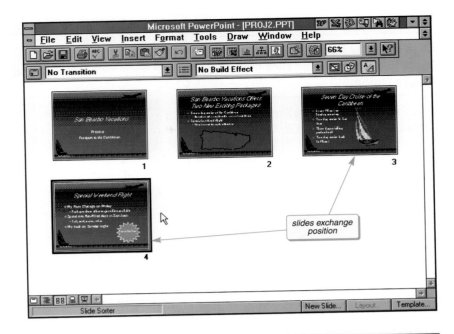

FIGURE 2-73

Copying a Slide

Occasionally you will want to copy a slide and then make changes to it. PowerPoint has a Copy command that allows you to quickly duplicate a slide or any object on a slide. After you make a copy, you will paste it someplace in your presentation. The next section explains how to copy and paste a slide in Slide Sorter view.

TO COPY AND PASTE A SLIDE IN SLIDE SORTER VIEW ▼

STEP 1 ▶

Click Slide 2 to select it and then point to the Copy button (▣) on the Standard toolbar (Figure 2-74).

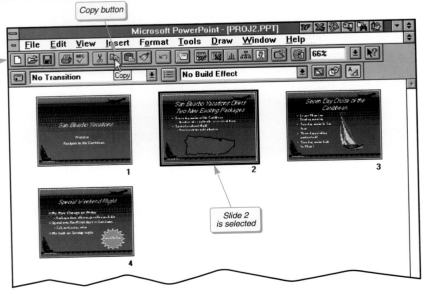

FIGURE 2-74

STEP 2 ▶

Click the Copy button and then point to the left of Slide 4 and click the left mouse button.

The insertion point displays in front of Slide 4 (Figure 2-75).

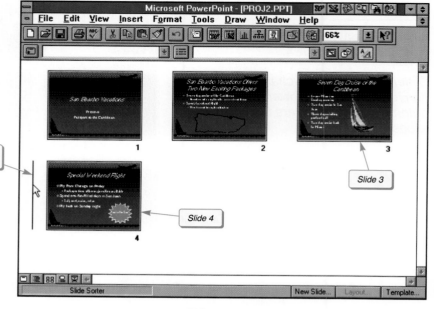

FIGURE 2-75

STEP 3 ▶

Point to the Paste button (▣) on the Standard toolbar (Figure 2-76).

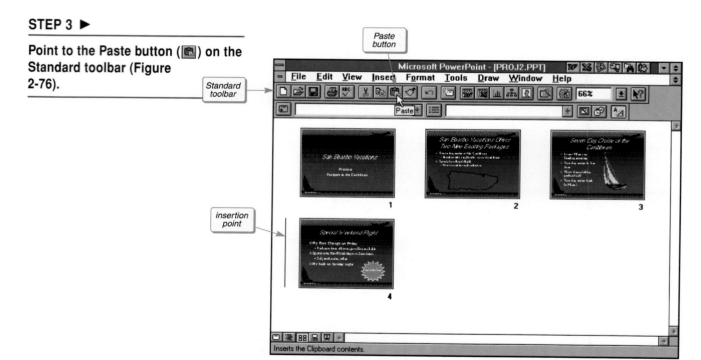

FIGURE 2-76

STEP 4 ▶

Click the Paste button.

A copy of Slide 2 displays as Slide 4 and the former Slide 4 displays as Slide 5 (Figure 2-77).

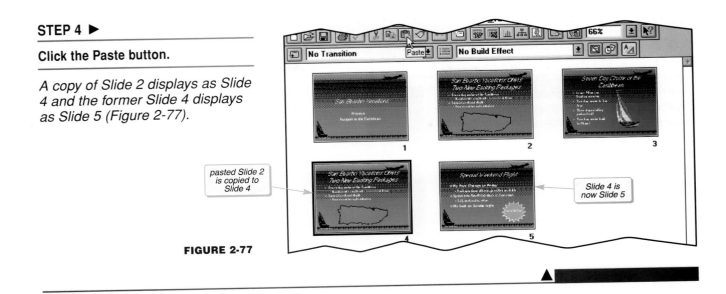

FIGURE 2-77

An alternative to clicking the Copy and Paste buttons is to use the edit shortcut menu. To access the edit shortcut menu, point to the slide you wish to copy and click the right mouse button. When the edit shortcut menu displays, choose the Copy command. To paste a slide into the presentation, point to the location at which you wish to insert. Then, click the right mouse button and choose the Paste command.

Using the Undo Button to Reverse the Last Edit

PowerPoint provides an Undo button to reverse the last edit task. For example, if you delete an object but realize you still want to display it, you could click the Undo button and the object would again display. However, PowerPoint only stores the last edit in a buffer. A **buffer** is an area used to temporarily store data. As soon as you perform another edit task, the new task replaces the previous task stored in the Undo buffer.

Peform the following steps to use the Undo button to reverse the pasting of the copy of Slide 2 performed in the previous step.

TO USE THE UNDO BUTTON TO REVERSE THE LAST EDIT ▼

STEP 1 ▶

Point to the Undo button on the Standard toolbar (Figure 2-78).

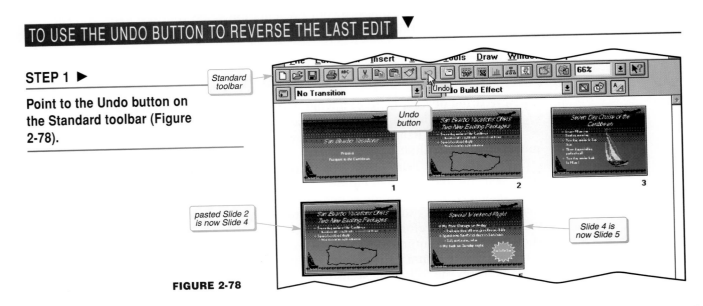

FIGURE 2-78

STEP 2 ►

Click the Undo button.

The copy of Slide 2 pasted between Slide 3 and Slide 4 is gone (Figure 2-79). The insertion point displays where the slide previously displayed. PowerPoint automatically renumbers the slides.

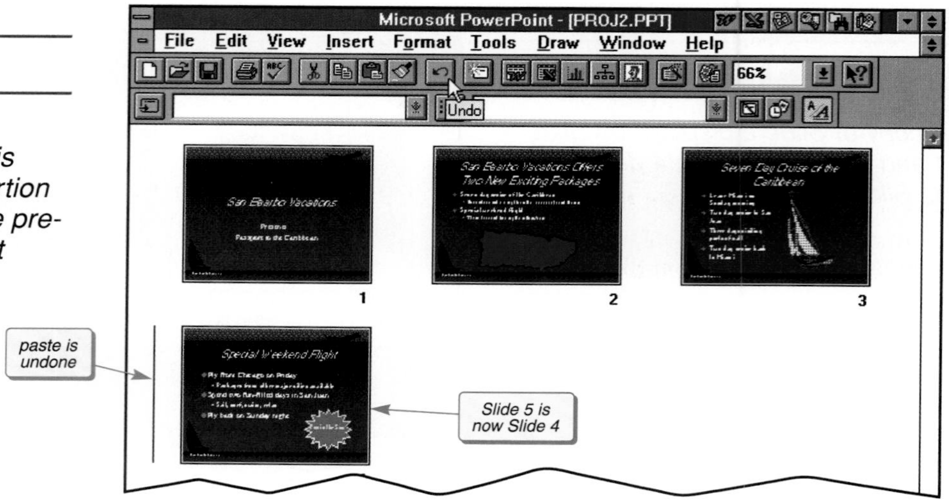

paste is undone

Slide 5 is now Slide 4

FIGURE 2-79

An added bonus to the Undo button is that because clicking the Undo button reverses or undoes your last action, you can return the presentation to the state it was in prior to clicking the Undo button the first time, by clicking the Undo button again.

The previous section on editing your presentation will save you time and effort when developing large presentations. Besides using the buttons on the toolbars, you can use a shortcut menu to cut, copy, or paste objects or slides. To use the shortcut menu, select the object or slide and then click the right mouse button. The shortcut menu displays. If you prefer to use PowerPoint menus, select the object on the slide, select the Edit menu from the menu bar, and then choose the edit command you want to use.

Checking Spelling and Saving Again

The presentation is now complete and should be checked for spelling errors. Check for spelling errors by clicking the Spelling button on the Standard toolbar.

If you made any changes to your presentation since your last save, you should save it again as PROJ2 using the Save button on the Standard toolbar.

▶ PRINTING THE PRESENTATION OUTLINE

During development of a lengthy presentation, it is often easier to review your outline in print rather than on-screen. Printing your outline is also useful for handouts or to review your subject matter prior to full development of your presentation.

Recall that the Print dialog box displays print options. When you wish to print your outline, specify Outline view in the Print What list box located in the Print dialog box. The outline prints **as last viewed** in Outline view. This means that you must select the Zoom Control to display the text the way in which you wish to print. Therefore, if you are uncertain of the Zoom Control setting, you should return to Outline view prior to printing your outline to review it. You may select the Print command from the File menu while in any view except Slide Show view. Perform the following steps to print your outline.

TO PRINT THE PRESENTATION OUTLINE ▼

STEP 1 ►

Ready the printer according to the printer instructions. Select the File menu and choose the Print command. When the Print dialog box displays, point to the arrow on the Print What drop-down list box.

PowerPoint displays the Print dialog box (Figure 2-80).

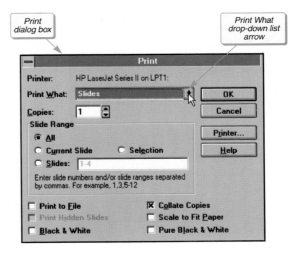

FIGURE 2-80

STEP 2 ►

Click the left mouse button and point to Outline View.

A list of print options displays (Figure 2-81).

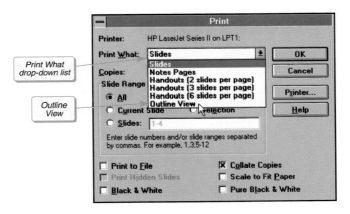

FIGURE 2-81

STEP 3 ►

Select Outline View and point to the OK button (Figure 2-82).

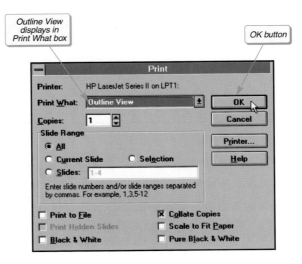

FIGURE 2-82

STEP 4 ▶

Choose the OK button.

The mouse pointer momentarily displays as an hourglass and PowerPoint displays the Print Status dialog box (Figure 2-83). The presentation outline begins printing on the printer.

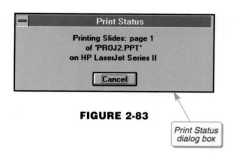

FIGURE 2-83

Print Status
dialog box

STEP 5 ▶

When the printer stops, retrieve the printout (Figure 2-84).

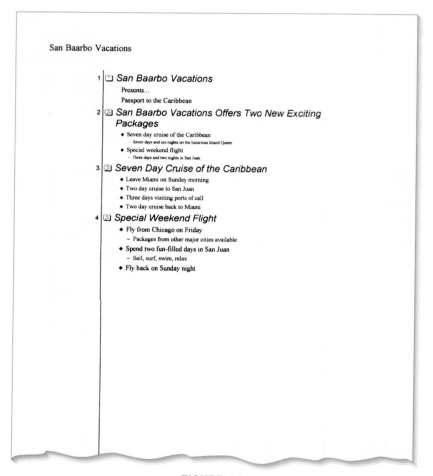

San Baarbo Vacations

1 ▢ *San Baarbo Vacations*
    Presents...
    Passport to the Caribbean

2 ▢ *San Baarbo Vacations Offers Two New Exciting Packages*
    ◆ Seven day cruise of the Caribbean
      – Seven days and six nights on the luxurious Island Queen
    ◆ Special weekend flight
      – Three days and two nights in San Juan

3 ▢ *Seven Day Cruise of the Caribbean*
    ◆ Leave Miami on Sunday morning
    ◆ Two day cruise to San Juan
    ◆ Three days visiting ports of call
    ◆ Two day cruise back to Miami

4 ▢ *Special Weekend Flight*
    ◆ Fly from Chicago on Friday
      – Packages from other major cities available
    ◆ Spend two fun-filled days in San Juan
      – Sail, surf, swim, relax
    ◆ Fly back on Sunday night

FIGURE 2-84

▶ PRINTING PRESENTATION SLIDES

Once you create a presentation, you may either print it or display it on your computer. After correcting errors, you will want to print the final copy of your presentation. If you made any changes to your presentation since your last save, be sure to save your presentation before you print.

Perform the following steps to print the presentation slides.

TO PRINT PRESENTATION SLIDES

Step 1: Ready the printer according to the printer instructions.
Step 2: From the File menu, choose the Print command.
Step 3: Click the Print What drop-down list box arrow and select Slides.
Step 4: Choose the Pure Black & White check box if printing on a noncolor printer.
Step 5: Choose the OK button in the Print dialog box.
Step 6: When the printer stops, retrieve the printout.

Your printout should look like the slides in Figures 2-85a through 2-85d.

The Print What drop-down list contains choices for printing two, three, or six slide images per page. These are labeled as Handouts [2 slides per page], Handouts [3 slides per page], and Handouts [6 slides per page]. Handouts are useful for reviewing a presentation because several slides are printed on one page. Many businesses distribute handouts before a presentation so the attendees have a hardcopy for reference.

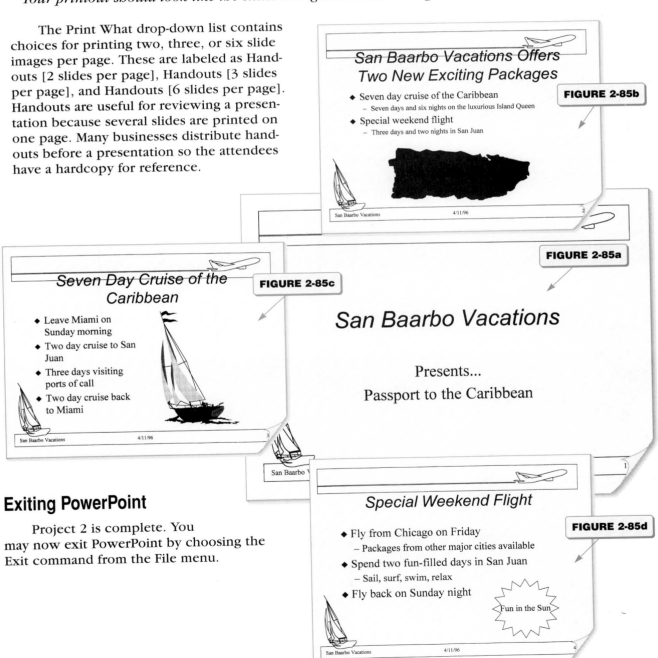

Exiting PowerPoint

Project 2 is complete. You may now exit PowerPoint by choosing the Exit command from the File menu.

▶ PROJECT SUMMARY

Project 2 introduced you to Outline view and clip art. You created a slide presentation in Outline view, where you entered all your text in the form of an outline. You arranged the text using the Promote (Indent less) and Demote (Indent more) buttons. Once your outline was complete, you changed slide layouts and added clip art. You added the seal object from the AutoShapes toolbar and then added text. You modified the text in the seal object by changing its color. You also learned how to change the fill color of an object. You edited a presentation by rearranging slide order, copying and pasting, and reversing the last edit by using the Undo button. Finally, you learned how to print your outline.

▶ KEY TERMS AND INDEX

as last viewed *(PP114)*
AutoShapes toolbar *(PP97)*
buffer *(PP113)*
bulletin board system *(PP94)*
clip art *(PP88)*
ClipArt Gallery *(PP88)*
Collapse Selection button *(PP78)*
Demote (Indent more) button *(PP78)*
Drawing+ toolbar *(PP97)*
Expand Selection button *(PP78)*
fill color *(PP97)*
footer *(PP71)*

header *(PP71)*
heading level five *(PP76)*
heading level four *(PP76)*
heading level one *(PP76)*
heading level six *(PP76)*
heading level three *(PP76)*
heading level two *(PP76)*
Layout button *(PP88)*
More button *(PP71)*
Move Down button *(PP78)*
Move Up button *(PP78)*
opaque *(PP106)*
outline *(PP76)*

Outline view *(PP76)*
placement indicator *(PP110)*
Promote (Indent less) button *(PP78)*
regular shape *(PP97)*
RTF *(PP77)*
shortcut menu *(PP104)*
Show All button *(PP78)*
Show Formatting button *(PP78)*
Show Titles button *(PP78)*
transparent *(PP106)*

QUICK REFERENCE

In PowerPoint, you can accomplish a task in a number of ways. The following table provides a quick reference to each task in this project with its available options. The commands listed in the Menu column can be executed using either the keyboard or mouse.

Task	Mouse	Menu	Keyboard Shortcuts
Change Fill Color	Click Fill Color button and click color sample	From Format menu, choose Colors and Lines, choose Fill, then choose color sample in Color drop-down list box	
Change Template	Click Template button	From Format menu, choose Presentation Template, then choose template file	
Change Layout	Click Layout button	From Format menu, choose Slide Layout, then choose a slide layout	
Change Text Color	Click Text Color button and click color sample	From Format menu, choose Font, then choose color sample in Text Color drop-down list box	

Task	Mouse	Menu	Keyboard Shortcuts
Demote a Paragraph	Click Demote (Indent more) button or select text and drag four-headed pointer right to new heading level		Press TAB or ALT+SHIFT+RIGHT ARROW
Insert a New Slide	Click Insert New Slide button on Standard toolbar or New Slide on status bar	From Insert menu, choose New Slide	Press CTRL+M
Move a Paragraph Down	Click Move Down button		Press ALT+SHIFT+DOWN ARROW
Move a Paragraph Up	Click Move Up button		Press ALT+SHIFT+UP ARROW
Promote a Paragraph	Click Promote (Indent less) button or select text and drag four-headed pointer left to new heading level		Press SHIFT+TAB or ALT+SHIFT+LEFT ARROW
Show All Text and Headings	Click Show All button		Press ALT+SHIFT+A
Show Heading Level 1	Click Show Titles button		Press ALT+SHIFT+1

S T U D E N T   A S S I G N M E N T S

STUDENT ASSIGNMENT 1
True/False

Instructions: Circle T if the statement is true or F if the statement is false.

T F 1. An outline is a summary of thoughts, presented as headings and subheadings, often used as a preliminary draft when creating a presentation.

T F 2. The Fill Color button is used to change the text color of an object.

T F 3. The placement indicator displays when you drag a slide to a new location.

T F 4. In Outline view, the subtitle on the title slide displays as heading level one.

T F 5. The Promote (Indent less) button moves the selected paragraph up one level in the outline hierarchy each time you click the button.

T F 6. Clip art is a quick way to add professional-looking artwork to your presentation without creating the art yourself.

T F 7. The insertion point displays when you drag a slide to a new location.

T F 8. Selecting a template may only be done in the Pick A Look Wizard — Step 3 of 9 dialog box.

T F 9. PowerPoint automatically sizes the object to fit the placeholder.

T F 10. Zoom Control in Outline view will affect the size of text when printing the outline.

T F 11. A bulletin board system is a computer system that allows users to communicate with each other and share files.

T F 12. Outline view provides a quick, easy way to create a presentation.

(continued)

STUDENT ASSIGNMENT 1 (continued)

T   F   13. The file extension RTF stands for Real Text Format.
T   F   14. The Slide Show button on the Standard toolbar lets you print your presentation electronically using your computer.
T   F   15. PowerPoint limits the number of outline levels to three.
T   F   16. The Color Palette displays 90 color samples.
T   F   17. To display an editing or formatting shortcut menu, point to an object on a slide and click the left mouse button.
T   F   18. A check mark in front of a toolbar name in a shortcut menu indicates it is selected to display on the PowerPoint window.
T   F   19. PowerPoint has an AutoShapes toolbar to help you add graphics and visual support to your presentation.
T   F   20. The AutoShapes toolbar contains twenty-four shapes.

STUDENT ASSIGNMENT 2
Multiple Choice

Instructions: Circle the correct response.

1. Sources of clip art include _____ .
   a. Microsoft ClipArt Gallery
   b. bulletin board systems
   c. computer software retailers
   d. all of the above
2. To display a toolbar shortcut menu, point to one of the toolbars and _____ .
   a. press the left mouse button
   b. press the F1 key
   c. press the right mouse button
   d. both a and c
3. PowerPoint has more than 100 artist-created templates in its three template subdirectories: _____ .
   a. powerpnt, template, and samples
   b. xlators, pcsifiles, and sldshow
   c. bwovrhd, clrovrhd, and sldshow
   d. none of the above
4. _____ provides a quick, easy way to create a presentation.
   a. Slide Sorter view
   b. Notes Pages view
   c. Slide Show view
   d. Outline view
5. To add a new slide to a presentation in Outline view, _____ .
   a. click the New Slide button on the status bar
   b. click the Promote (Indent less) button until the insertion point reaches heading level one
   c. press CTRL+M
   d. all of the above
6. The outline begins with a title on _____ .
   a. Outline level zero
   b. Outline level two
   c. Outline level one
   d. none of the above

7. In Outline view, move a slide by dragging the _____ to its new position.
   a. paragraph
   b. slide icon
   c. bullet
   d. none of the above
8. PowerPoint provides a(n) _____ button to reverse the last edit task.
   a. Paste   b.   Undo   c.   Edit   d.   Copy
9. The presentation outline may be printed by selecting the Print command from the File menu when in

   _____ .
   a. Notes Pages view
   b. Slide view
   c. Slide Sorter view
   d. all of the above
10. The _____ button moves selected text up one paragraph at a time while maintaining its hierarchical outline level and text style.
   a. Move Up
   b. Promote (Indent less)
   c. Move Down
   d. Demote (Indent more)

STUDENT ASSIGNMENT 3
Understanding the Outlining View Window

Instructions: Arrows in Figure SA2-3 point to the major components of a PowerPoint Outline view window. Identify the various parts of the window in the spaces provided.

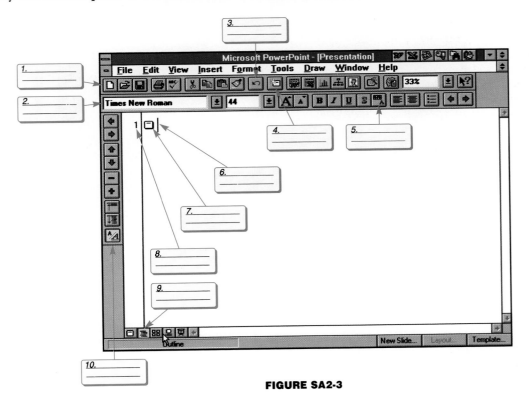

FIGURE SA2-3

ASSIGNMENT 4
Understanding the Outlining Toolbar

Instructions: In Figure SA2-4, arrows point to several of the buttons on the Outlining toolbar. In the spaces provided, briefly explain the purpose of each button.

STUDENT ASSIGNMENT 5
Understanding How to Change Slide Layout

Instructions: Assume you are in Outline view. Write numbers in front of the steps below to indicate the sequence of steps necessary to change the slide layout from Bulleted List to the slide layout shown in Figure SA2-5.

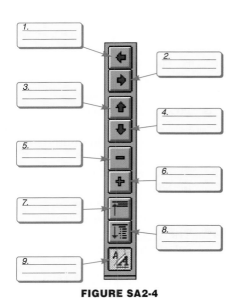

FIGURE SA2-4

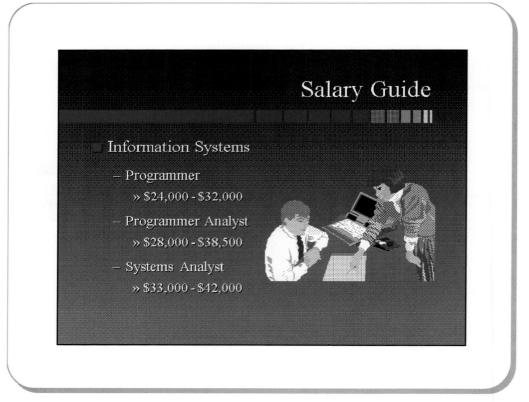

FIGURE SA2-5

STEP _____ : Click the Text & Clip Art slide layout in the Slide Layout dialog box.

STEP _____ : Click the slide icon of the slide that is changing layouts.

STEP _____ : Click the Layout button.

STEP _____ : Choose the Apply button in the Slide Layout dialog box.

STEP _____ : Click the Slide View button.

STUDENT ASSIGNMENT 6
Changing Text Color Within an Object

Instructions: Write numbers in front of the steps below to indicate the sequence of steps necessary to change the text color to black, as shown in Figure SA2-6.

FIGURE SA2-6

STEP __2__ :   Click the Text Color button on the Formatting toolbar.

STEP __1__ :   Select the text that is being changed.

STEP __4__ :   Click the black color sample in the Other Color dialog box.

STEP __5__ :   Choose the OK button in the Other Color dialog box.

STEP __3__ :   Click the Other Color command.

COMPUTER LABORATORY EXERCISE 1
Using an Outline to Create a Slide

Instructions: Start PowerPoint. Open the presentation CLE2-1.PPT from the PPOINT4 subdirectory on the Student Diskette that accompanies this book. Perform the following tasks to change the slide so it looks like the one in Figure CLE2-1.

FIGURE CLE2-1

1. Change to Slide view by clicking the Slide View button.
2. Click the Layout button and apply the Text & Clip Art slide layout.
3. Double-click on the clip art placeholder located on the slide.
4. Choose the Sports & Leisure category in the Microsoft ClipArt Gallery Picture in CLE2-1.PPT dialog box.
5. Select Football & Goal Post in the Microsoft ClipArt Gallery — Picture in CLE2-1.PPT dialog box and then choose the OK button.
6. Save the presentation on your data disk with the filename CLE2-1A using the Save As command from the File menu.
7. Print the presentation outline by selecting the File menu, choosing the Print command, selecting Outline View from the Print What drop-down list box, and then choosing the OK button in the Print dialog box.
8. Print the presentation slide by selecting the File menu, choosing the Print command, selecting Slides from the Print What drop-down list box, clicking the Pure Black & White check box, and then choosing the OK button in the Print dialog box.
9. Select the File menu and choose the Close command to close the presentation.

COMPUTER LABORATORY EXERCISE 2
Changing Slide Order

Instructions: Start PowerPoint. Open the presentation CLE2-2.PPT from the PPOINT4 subdirectory on the Student Diskette that accompanies this book.

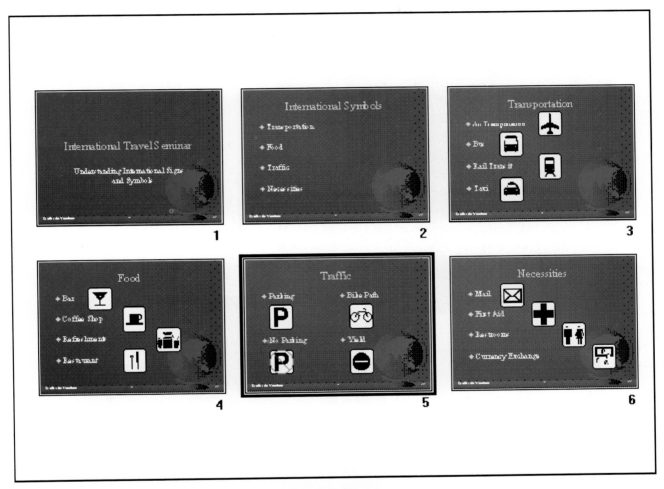

FIGURE CLE2-2

Perform the following tasks to change the slides so they look like the ones in Figure CLE2-2:

1. Change view to Slide Sorter view by clicking the Slide Sorter button.
2. Drag the title slide, Slide 5 (International Travel Seminar) and drop it in front of Slide 1 (International Symbols).
3. Drag the new Slide 5 (Food) and drop it in front of Slide 4 (Necessities).
4. Drag Slide 6 (Traffic) and drop it in front of Slide 5 (Necessities).
5. Save the presentation on your data disk with the filename CLE2-2A using the Save As command from the File Menu.
6. Print the presentation slide images by selecting the File menu, choosing the Print command, selecting Handouts (6 slides per page) from the Print What drop-down list box, clicking the Pure Black & White check box, and then choosing the OK button in the Print dialog box.
7. Choose the Close command from the File menu to close the presentation.

COMPUTER LABORATORY EXERCISE 3
Modifying a Presentation

Instructions: Start PowerPoint. Open the presentation CLE2-3.PPT from the PPOINT4 subdirectory on the Student Diskette that accompanies this book. Perform the following tasks to modify the presentation so it looks like the slides in Figure CLE2-3a and Figure CLE2-3b.

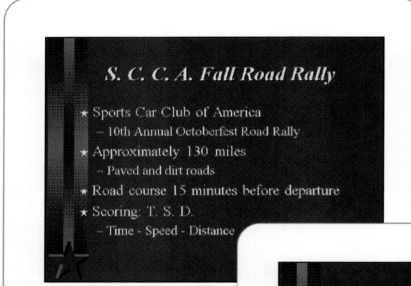

1. In Outline view, drag the mouse pointer to select Slide 2 (Sports Car Club of America) through Slide 8 (Time — Speed — Distance).
2. Click the Demote (Indent more) button one time to demote selected slides to heading level two.

FIGURE CLE2-3b

FIGURE CLE2-3a

3. Click on the paragraph, 10th Annual Octoberfest Road Rally, and click the Demote (Indent more) button one time to demote to heading level three.
4. Click on the paragraph, Paved and dirt roads, and then click the Demote (Indent more) button one time to demote to heading level three.
5. Click on the paragraph, Time — Speed — Distance, and then click the Demote (Indent more) button one time to demote to heading level three.
6. Drag the mouse pointer to select Slide 3 (Portsmith High School parking lot) through Slide 9 (Awards ceremony at end of rally) and click the Demote (Indent more) button one time to demote to heading level two.
7. Click on the paragraph, Inspections, and click the Demote (Indent more) button one time to demote to heading level three.
8. Click on the paragraph, 1 minute intervals between cars, and click the Demote (Indent more) button one time to demote to heading level three.
9. Click the Template button on the status bar.

10. Apply template dropstrs.ppt located in the c:\powerpnt\template\sldshow subdirectory.
11. Save the presentation on your data disk with the filename CLE2-3A using the Save As command from the File menu.
12. Print the presentation outline by selecting the File menu, choosing the Print command, selecting Outline View from the Print What drop-down list box, and then choosing the OK button in the Print dialog box.
13. Print the presentation slides by selecting the File menu, choosing the Print command, selecting Handouts (2 slides per page) from the Print What drop-down list box, clicking the Pure Black & White check box, and then choosing the OK button in the Print dialog box.
14. Choose the Close command from the File menu to close the presentation.

C O M P U T E R   L A B O R A T O R Y   A S S I G N M E N T S

COMPUTER LABORATORY ASSIGNMENT 1
Building a Presentation Using an Outline

Purpose: To become familiar with building a presentation using Outline view, applying a template, saving a presentation, and printing a presentation in Slide view and Outline view.

Problem: You are a marketing executive for the Fly High Golf Ball Company. Fly High is sponsoring the 1996 Midwest Open Golf Benefit. The Midwest Open Golf Benefit raises money for Dreams Come True, a foundation that grants the wishes of terminally ill children. Your responsibility is to create a presentation to promote the Midwest Open Golf Benefit.

Instructions: Perform the following tasks:

1. Start the PowerPoint program. When the New Presentation dialog box displays, click Blank Presentation and then choose the OK button.
2. When the New Slide dialog box displays, click the Bulleted List slide layout and then choose the OK button.
3. Change view to Outline view.
4. Use the outline shown in Figure CLA2-1a to create the presentation in Figure CLA2-1b, and Figure CLA2-1c on the next page.

I. Fly High Presents the 1996 Midwest Open
  A. October 12th - 15th
  B. Play the fabulous Willowdale Country Club
  C. $200,000 in prizes
  D. All proceeds donated to Dreams Come True
II. Willowdale Country Club
  A. Winner of the 1995 Pro Choice Award
  B. Designed by Amie Nicklaus
  C. Tree-lined fairways
  D. Famous 15th hole
    1. 125 yards
    2. Par 3
    3. 200 foot vertical drop
III. Prizes
  A. First place $100,000
  B. Second place $50,000
  C. Third place $25,000
  D. Fourth place $15,000
  E. Fifth place $10,000
IV. Dreams Come True
  A. Fulfills wishes of terminally ill children
  B. 5,000 wishes granted in 1995
    1. 500 trips to Disneyland
    2. 1,500 trips to Walt Disney World
    3. 3,000 Christmas in July

FIGURE CLA2-1a

(continued)

COMPUTER LABORATORY ASSIGNMENT 1 (continued)

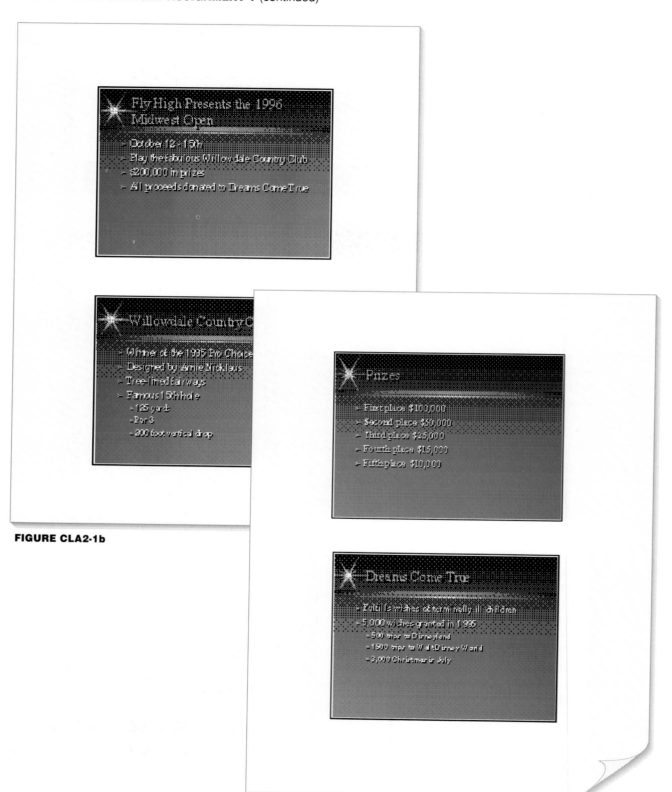

FIGURE CLA2-1b

FIGURE CLA2-1c

5. Spell check the presentation by clicking the Spelling button on the Standard toolbar.
6. Apply template sparkles.ppt located in the c:\powerpnt\template\sldshow subdirectory.
7. Save the presentation on your data disk with the filename CLA2-1 using the Save As command in the File menu.
8. Print the presentation slides by selecting the File menu, choosing the Print command, selecting Handouts (2 slides per page) from the Print What drop-down list box, clicking the Pure Black & White check box, and then choosing the OK button in the Print dialog box.
9. Print the presentation outline by selecting the File menu, choosing the Print command, selecting Outline View from the Print What drop-down list box, and then choosing the OK button in the Print dialog box.

COMPUTER LABORATORY ASSIGNMENT 2
Adding Clip Art to a Presentation

Purpose: To become familiar with adding clip art to a presentation.

Problem: As the marketing executive for Fly High Golf Ball Company, you have completed the outline for the 1996 Midwest Open Golf Benefit (Figure CLA2-1). You have decided to enhance your presentation by adding clip art. If you did not complete Computer Laboratory Assignment 1, see your instructor for a copy of presentation Figure CLA2-1.

Instructions: Perform the following tasks:

1. Open presentation CLA2-1.PPT from your data disk.
2. Click the Slide view button to display Slide 1.
3. Click the Layout button on the status bar and change the slide layout to Text & Clip Art.
4. Insert clip art, Golfer, from the Sports & Leisure category in the Microsoft ClipArt Gallery to Slide 1.
5. Increase font size of bulleted text to 32 points.

FIGURE CLA2-2a

(continued)

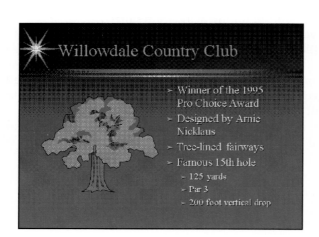

FIGURE CLA2-2b

COMPUTER LABORATORY ASSIGNMENT 3
(continued)

3. Click the Layout button on the status bar and change the slide layout to Text & Clip Art.
4. Insert clip art, Golfer, from the Sports & Leisure category in the Microsoft ClipArt Gallery to Slide 1.
5. Increase font size of bulleted text to 32 points.

FIGURE CLA2-2c

6. Click the Next Slide button to advance to Slide 2 and change the slide layout to Clip Art & Text.
7. Insert clip art, Summer Tree, from the Backgrounds category in the Microsoft ClipArt Gallery to Slide 2.
8. Click the Next Slide button to advance to Slide 3 and change the slide layout to Text & Clip Art.
9. Insert clip art, Stack of Money, from the Currency category in the Microsoft ClipArt Gallery to Slide 3.

10. Click the Next Slide button to advance to Slide 4 and change the slide layout to Text over Object.
11. Insert clip art Open Hands from the Gestures category in the Microsoft ClipArt Gallery to Slide 4.
12. Save the presentation with the filename CLA2-2 using the Save As command from the File menu.
13. Drag the elevator up the vertical scroll bar to go to Slide 1. View the presentation in Slide Show view.
14. Print the presentation by choosing Slides in the Print dialog box.

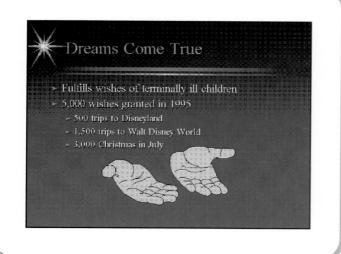

FIGURE CLA2-2d

COMPUTER LABORATORY ASSIGNMENT 3
Building a Presentation in Outline View, Selecting a Template, Demoting Paragraphs, Promoting Paragraphs, Changing Slide Order, and Adding Clip Art

Purpose: To become familiar with creating a presentation in Outline view, adding a template, adding clip art, and changing slide order.

Problem: You are a student in Management 583 — Small Business Management. You are to make an on-screen presentation on starting a home-based business. You have researched home-based businesses from information received from the U.S. Small Business Administration. You decide to enhance the presentation by adding a title slide and graphics.

Instructions: Perform the tasks on the next page:

I. Starting a home-based business

  A. Ask yourself:

    1. Why am I doing it?

    2. Can I switch between home responsibilities and business work?

    3. Do I have the discipline to maintain schedules?

    4. Can I deal with isolation?

    5. Am I a self-starter?

    6. What is my niche?

    7. Are there legal requirements?

  B. Getting Help - S.B.A.

    1. U.S. Small Business Administration

      a) Office of Business Development

    2. Offices nationwide

    3. Small Business Answer Desk

      a) 1-800-8-ASK-SBA

  C. S.B.A. Programs and Services

    1. Training programs

    2. Education programs

    3. Advisory services

    4. Publications

    5. Financial programs

    6. SBA On-line

FIGURE CLA2-3a

      a) 1-800-859-INFO

        (1) 2400 baud modem

      b) 1-800-697-INFO

        (1) 9600 baud modem

  D. Developing a Business Plan

    1. Objective and critical look at your business idea

    2. Accurate and concise description of your business

      a) What is the principal activity?

        (1) Be specific

        (2) Give product or service descriptions

      b) How will business be started?

      c) What experience do you bring to the business?

  E. Marketing

    1. Can you market your business from home?

    2. Who and what is your market?

    3. What pricing and sales terms are you planning?

    4. How will you be competitive?

(continued)

FIGURE CLA2-3b

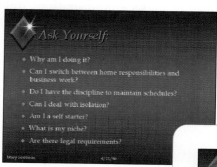

FIGURE CLA2-3c

FIGURE CLA2-3d

FIGURE CLA2-3e

FIGURE CLA2-3f

FIGURE CLA2-3g

COMPUTER LABORATORY ASSIGNMENT 3 (continued)

1. Use the Pick a Look Wizard option to apply template twinkles.ppt from the template subdirectory sldshow and include your name, the date, and page number on the slides and on the outline.

2. Create a title slide with the following information, replacing Mary Smithson with your name in the subheading.

   Starting a Home-Based Business
   Mary Smithson
   Management 583
   Small Business Management

3. Type your presentation on starting a home-based business in Outline view. The outline is shown in Figure CLA2-3a on page PP131.

4. On Slide 2, change the bulleted list font size to 24 and change the line spacing to .5 before paragraph.

5. On Slide 3, change the slide layout to Clip Art & Text and add the Two Men in Discussion clip art from the People category in the ClipArt Gallery.

6. On Slide 4, change the slide layout to Clip Art & Text and add the Sales Presentation clip art from the People category in the ClipArt Gallery. Adjust the font size so the text fits in the text placeholder.

7. On Slide 5, change the slide layout to Text & Clip Art and add the Hand Writing clip art from the Academic category. Adjust the font size so the text fits in the text placeholder.
8. On Slide 6, change the slide layout to Text over Object and add Business Meeting clip art from the People category. Adjust the font size so the text fits in the text placeholder.
9. Spell check your presentation and then save it with the filename CLA2-3 using the Save As command in the File menu.
10. Print your presentation slides and outline.

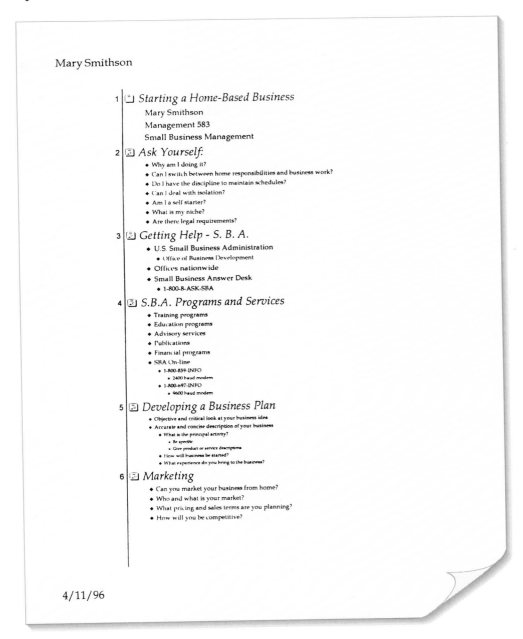

FIGURE CLA2-3h

COMPUTER LABORATORY ASSIGNMENT 4
Designing a Slide

Purpose: To provide practice in planning, designing, and creating a presentation in Outline view.

Problem: Each year, the alumni association offers a discounted travel package to its members. This year, you are the travel director for the alumni association responsible for presenting two travel packages at the alumni association's annual dinner. At the dinner, the members present will vote on the package that will be offered to all alumni association members. You are to scan through the ClipArt Gallery to select appropriate clip art. Then, research the travel packages with your local travel agency.

Instructions: Create a title slide and three informative slides in Outline view. Select an appealing template that fits the theme of your presentation. You should include appropriate clip art on each slide. Be sure to spell check your presentation. Save your presentation with the filename CLA2-4 before printing it. Print the outline with Zoom Control set at 33%. Then, print the slides.

▼

ENHANCING A PRESENTATION AND ADDING GRAPHS AND TABLES

OBJECTIVES You will have mastered the material in this project when you can:

▸ Modify an Existing Presentation
▸ Save a Presentation with a New Filename
▸ Create a graph using Microsoft Graph 5
▸ Create a table using Microsoft Word 6

▸ Add transitions to a slide show
▸ Apply build effects to a slide
▸ Set slide timing
▸ Run an automatic slide show

▸ INTRODUCTION

I n Projects 1 and 2, you learned how to create a presentation in Slide view and in Outline view. The slides within these presentations contained both text and clip art. PowerPoint has many other presentation features designed to grasp your audience's attention. For example, your slides can contain tables and graphs to pictorially represent data trends and patterns. You can also add special effects to your presentation, such as controlling the motion of one slide exiting the screen and another entering. This project incorporates these features into the slide show you began in Project 2.

▸ PROJECT THREE — SAN BAARBO VACATIONS ENHANCED

P roject 3 enhances the San Baarbo Vacation presentation created in Project 2. The original presentation promoted two vacation packages to San Juan to prospective customers. To better explain the vacation packages, the travel agency has decided to add more detail and pizzazz to the presentation. This includes a list of cabin classes, a graph of cabin fares, a list of San Juan features, and a seasonal temperature table. The travel agency is preparing for a tourism show and wants to automate the slide show to run without human intervention. Additional features are to include a visual effect to smooth the transition from one slide to the next and to build each bulleted slide line-by-line to emphasize the current bulleted paragraph.

Slide Preparation Steps

The following slide preparation steps summarize how to create the slides shown in Figures 3-1a through 3-1i. If you are creating these slides on a personal computer, read these steps without doing them.

1. Start PowerPoint.
2. Open an existing presentation and save it with a new filename.
3. Apply the template TROPICS.PPT to the presentation.
4. Change the Slide 2 slide layout to Object over Text.
5. Add a new bulleted list slide.
6. Add a new graph slide.
7. Add another bulleted list slide and save the presentation.
8. Add a table slide.
9. Add a closing slide.
10. Spell check the presentation and save it.
11. Add transition to the presentation.
12. Add build effects to the presentation and save it.
13. Automate the slide show.
14. Save the presentation and exit PowerPoint.

The following sections describe these steps in detail.

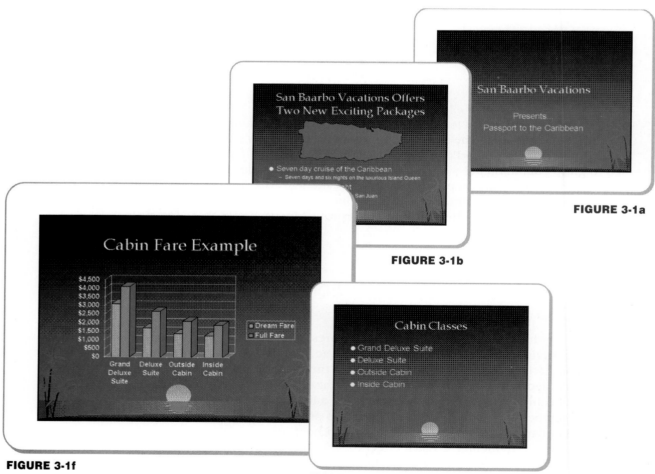

FIGURE 3-1a

FIGURE 3-1b

FIGURE 3-1f

FIGURE 3-1e

▶ MODIFYING AN EXISTING PRESENTATION

Because you are enhancing the presentation you created in Project 2, the first step in this project is to open the PROJ2.PPT file. So that the original Project 2 presentation remains intact, you will save the PROJ2.PPT file with a new filename: PROJ3.PPT. You will then make modifications to the new file's existing slides and add four new slides. The steps on the following pages illustrate these procedures.

Starting PowerPoint

To start PowerPoint, the Windows Program Manager must display on the screen and the Microsoft Office group window must be open. Double-click the Microsoft PowerPoint program-item icon in the Microsoft Office group window. Then, choose the OK button in the Tip of the Day dialog box.

Opening a Presentation

The San Baarbo Vacations presentation was saved in Project 2 using the file-name PROJ2.PPT. Therefore, the first step is to open PROJ2.PPT, as shown below.

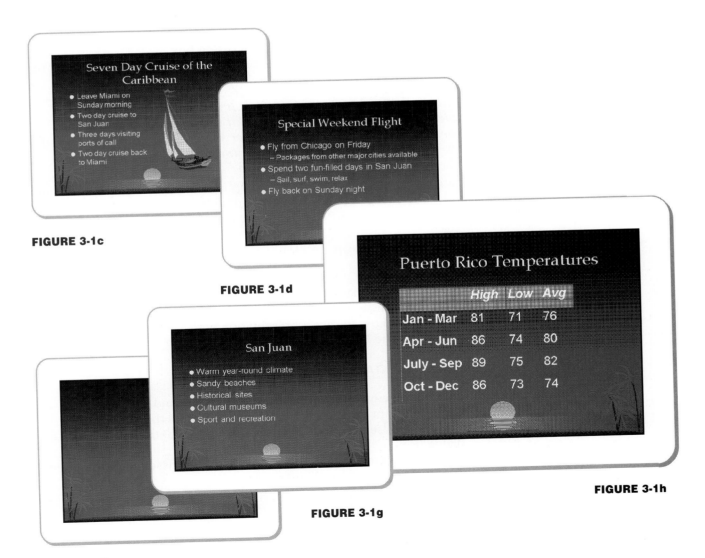

FIGURE 3-1c

FIGURE 3-1d

FIGURE 3-1g

FIGURE 3-1h

FIGURE 3-1i

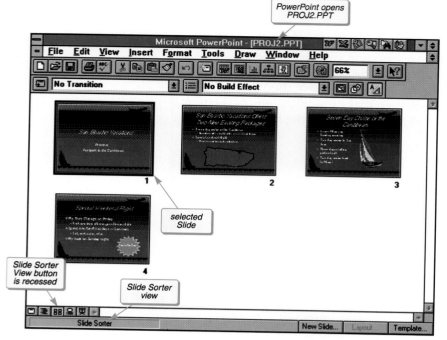

FIGURE 3-2

TO OPEN AN EXISTING PRESENTATION

Step 1: Insert the diskette containing the file PROJ2.PPT into drive A.

Step 2: Select the Open an Existing Presentation option in the PowerPoint startup dialog box.

Step 3: Choose the OK button in the PowerPoint startup dialog box.

Step 4: If necessary, click the Drives box arrow and select drive A in the Open dialog box.

Step 5: Select proj2.ppt by clicking its filename in the File Name list box.

Step 6: Choose the OK button in the Open dialog box.

Step 7: If necessary, click the Maximize button on the PROJ2.PPT title bar to maximize the PowerPoint window.

PowerPoint opens PROJ2.PPT and displays it in Slide Sorter view, which was the view it was in last time you saved it (Figure 3-2). If your screen differs from Figure 3-2, click the Slide Sorter View button at the bottom of the screen. The PowerPoint window is maximzed.

An alternative to using the OK button in Step 6 is to double-click the filename PROJ2.PPT in the File Name list box. When you double-click a filename, the Open dialog box disappears and PowerPoint opens the presentation.

Saving the Presentation with a New Filename

Because you want the PROJ2.PPT presentation to remain unchanged, you should save it with a new filename, such as PROJ3.PPT. Then, make any necessary revisions to the new file. Essentially, you are making a duplicate copy of a file. The following steps illustrate how to save a presentation with a new filename using the Save As command from the File menu.

TO SAVE THE PRESENTATION WITH A NEW FILENAME

Step 1: From the File menu, choose the Save As command.

Step 2: Type `proj3` in the File Name box. Do not press the ENTER key.

Step 3: With drive A set as the default, choose the OK button in the Save As dialog box.

Step 4: When the Summary Info dialog box displays, revise the information and then choose the OK button.

The presentation is saved to drive A with the filename PROJ3.PPT (Figure 3-3).

Changing Templates

Because San Baarbo Vacations is modifying the contents of this presentation, the travel agency will also give it a new look by changing the template. Recall from Project 1 that a template may be changed at any time during the development of the presentation. Perform the steps below to change the template from TRAVELS.PPT to TROPICS.PPT.

TO CHANGE TEMPLATES

Step 1: Click the Template button on the status bar.

Step 2: Drag the File Name scroll bar elevator to the bottom of the scroll bar. Then, select the tropics.ppt template in the File Name list box.

Step 3: Choose the Apply button in the Presentation Template dialog box.

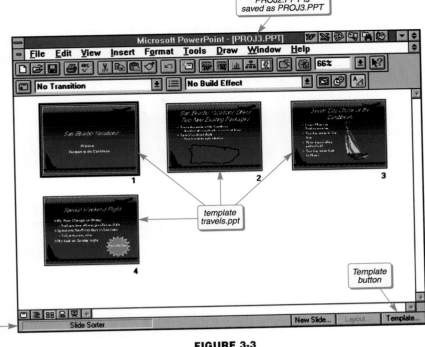

FIGURE 3-3

The slides display with the new template: tropics.ppt (Figure 3-4).

The TROPICS.PPT template places palm trees at the bottom of the slide with the sun rising over the ocean. Changing the template is a quick and easy way to change the focus of a presentation, depending on your target audience.

Changing Slide Layout

Slide 2 in the presentation currently has the Text over Object slide layout; that is, the bulleted list displays above the graphic of Puerto Rico. However, you would prefer that the graphic display above the text. Thus, perform the following steps to change the slide layout to Object over Text. For a detailed explanation of this procedure, refer to pages PP89 and PP90 in Project 2.

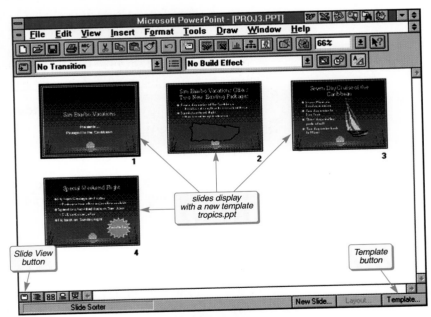

FIGURE 3-4

TO CHANGE SLIDE LAYOUT

Step 1: Click the Slide View button at the bottom of the screen to change views.

Step 2: Click the Next Slide button on the vertical scroll bar one time to display Slide 2.

Step 3: Click the Layout button on the status bar.

Step 4: Select the Object over Text slide layout (▥) by clicking it.

Step 5: Choose the Apply button in the Slide Layout dialog box.

Slide 2 changes to the Object over Text slide layout (Figure 3-5). The clip art map of Puerto Rico displays above the bulleted paragraphs.

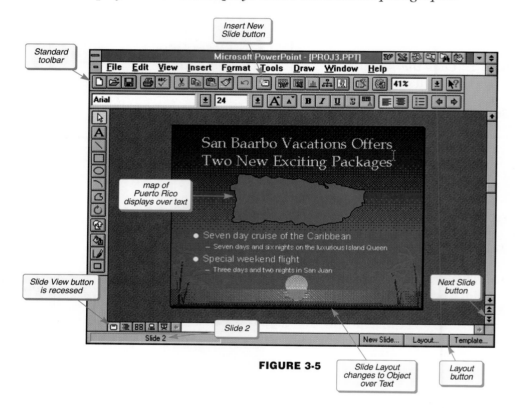

FIGURE 3-5

An alternative to choosing the Apply button in Step 5 is to double-click the slide layout in the Slide Layout dialog box. When you double-click a slide layout, the Slide Layout dialog box disappears, and PowerPoint displays the slide with the new layout.

Deleting an Object

Slide 4 currently has a seal object in its lower right corner. To alter the look of your presentation, you decide to remove this object, as shown in the steps below.

TO DELETE AN OBJECT

Step 1: Click the Next Slide button twice to display Slide 4.

Step 2: Select the seal object by clicking it. Be sure to select the whole object and not just the text within the object.

Step 3: Press the DELETE key.

The seal object is deleted from Slide 4 (Figure 3-6).

If you accidentally delete text instead of the entire object, click the Undo button on the Standard toolbar. Then, repeat Steps 2 and 3.

Adding a New Slide to the Presentation

The next step is to add a fifth slide to the presentation that outlines the four major types of cabin classes. Recall that you add a new slide by clicking the Insert New Slide button on the Standard toolbar. Perform the following steps to add a bulleted list slide to the presentation.

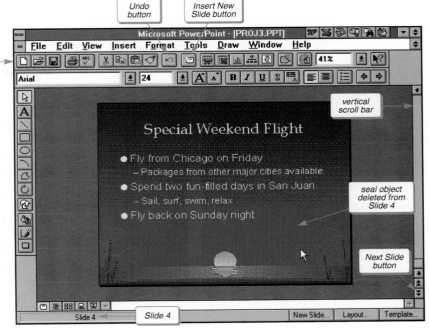

FIGURE 3-6

TO ADD A NEW SLIDE TO THE PRESENTATION

Step 1: Click the Insert New Slide button on the Standard toolbar.
Step 2: Select Bulleted List from the New Slide dialog box by double-clicking it.
Step 3: Type Cabin Classes as the title for Slide 5.
Step 4: Select the text object by clicking anywhere inside the text placeholder.
Step 5: Type Grand Deluxe Suite and press the ENTER key.
Step 6: Type Deluxe Suite and press the ENTER key.
Step 7: Type Outside Cabin and press the ENTER key.
Step 8: Type Inside Cabin

Slide 5 is complete (Figure 3-7).

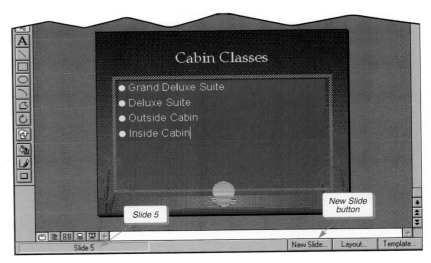

FIGURE 3-7

From the previous steps, you can see that you can add a new slide to the end of a presentation by simply clicking the Insert New Slide button.

▶ USING MICROSOFT GRAPH TO CREATE A COLUMN GRAPH

G raphs are used to display trends and magnitudes to your audience. The next slide in this presentation contains a column graph that compares costs between cabin class fares (Figure 3-8). In the column graph for this project, each column represents the cost of a cabin. Full fares are the usual and customary costs for a room; dream fares are promotional rates, usually lower in cost than the full fare. Full fare columns are a different color from dream fare columns; the respective colors of these two fares are indicated in the **legend** on the graph. A legend is an explanatory table or list of symbols appearing on a graph. By scanning the graph, you can easily see that the highest cabin fare is in the Grand Deluxe Suite.

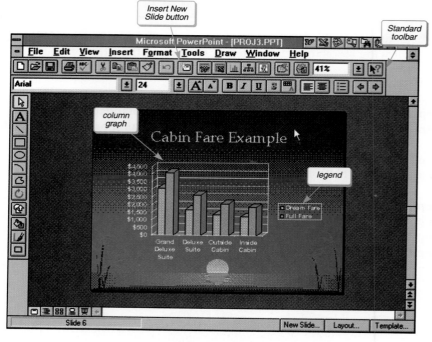

FIGURE 3-8

PowerPoint comes with a **supplementary application** called **Microsoft Graph 5**, which allows you to create graphs within PowerPoint. When you open a supplementary application, its menus, buttons, tools, etc., are available to you directly on the PowerPoint screen. This concept of bringing the application to you is called **OLE**, or **Object Linking and Embedding**. The graph you create is actually an **embedded object** because it is created in another application, Microsoft Graph, and inserted into your presentation.

Creating a graph requires several steps. First, you add a new slide with the graph layout. Next, you open the Graph application into the PowerPoint screen. Then, you decide on the graph type. For example, you can display the data using a bar graph, a column graph, a pie graph, or one of the other fourteen graph types. Table 3-1 summarizes the most often used graph types. Finally, you enter and format the data for the graph.

▸ **TABLE 3-1**

GRAPH ICON	GRAPH TYPE	DESCRIPTION
▤	Bar Graph	Shows individual figures at a specific time or illustrates comparisons. The categories on a bar graph are organized vertically, and the values are organized horizontally, placing more emphasis on comparisons and less emphasis on time. Also available in 3-D (three-dimensional).
▥	Column Graph	Shows variation over a period of time or illustrates comparisons between items. Although similar to a bar graph, a column graph's categories are organized horizontally, and its values are organized vertically. Also available in 3-D.
▨	Line Graph	Shows trends or changes in data over a period of time at even intervals. A line graph emphasizes time flow and rate of change, instead of the amount of change.
◑	Pie Graph	Shows the proportion of parts to a whole. This graph type is useful for emphasizing a significant element. A pie graph always contains one data series. If you select more than one data series, only one will display in your graph. Also available in 3-D.

The steps on the following pages explain in detail how to create the column graph for this project.

Adding a New Slide with the Graph AutoLayout

Because you want the column graph on a new slide, you will select the Graph AutoLayout as shown in these steps.

TO ADD A NEW SLIDE WITH THE GRAPH AUTOLAYOUT

Step 1: Click the Insert New Slide button on the Standard toolbar.
Step 2: Double-click the Graph AutoLayout (▥) in the New Slide dialog box.

Slide 6 displays the graph placeholder (Figure 3-9).

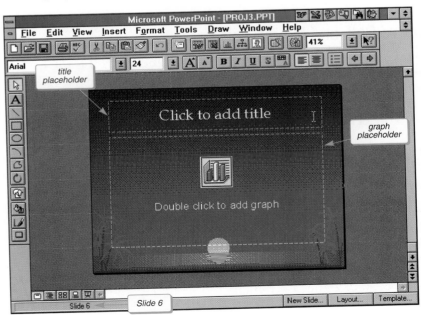

FIGURE 3-9

The Datasheet

The **datasheet** (Figure 3-10), a Microsoft Graph window, is a rectangular grid containing columns (vertical) and rows (horizontal). A column letter above the grid, called the **column heading**, identifies each column. A row number on the left side of the grid, called the **row heading**, identifies each row.

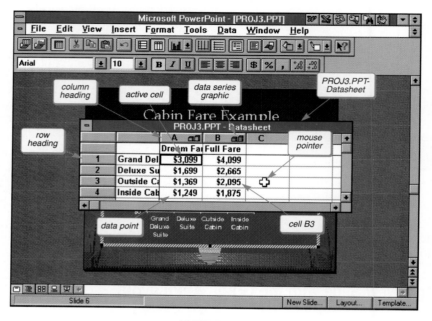

FIGURE 3-10

The datasheet contains numbers, called **data points**, in the rows and columns. Microsoft Graph (referred to as Graph) uses the data points to create the graph that displays in the presentation. Notice in Figure 3-10 that behind the Datasheet window is the column graph that represents the data points in the datasheet. The datasheet can contain a maximum of 4,000 rows and 4,000 columns.

Cell, Active Cell, and Mouse Pointer

The intersection of each column and row is a cell. A **cell** is the basic unit of the datasheet into which you enter data. A cell is identified by its **cell reference**, which is the coordinates of the intersection of a column and a row. To identify a cell, specify the column letter first, followed by the row number. For example, cell B3 refers to the cell located at the intersection of column B and row 3 (Figure 3-10).

One cell on the datasheet, designated the **active cell**, is the one in which you can enter data points. The active cell is identified by a heavy black border surrounding the cell. For example, the active cell in Figure 3-10 is cell A1.

The mouse pointer in Graph becomes one of several shapes, depending on the task you are performing and the pointer's location on the screen. The mouse pointer in Figure 3-10 has the shape of a block plus sign (⊕), which indicates it is positioned on a cell in the datasheet.

Opening the Graph Application into the PowerPoint Window

In order to create the column graph in Slide 6, you must first open the Graph application. Recall that OLE brings this supplementary application to the PowerPoint window and makes the menus, buttons, tools, etc., in the Graph application available on the PowerPoint screen. Once open, Graph displays a Datasheet window in a work area in the middle of the PowerPoint screen, as shown in the steps below.

TO OPEN THE GRAPH APPLICATION INTO THE POWERPOINT WINDOW ▼

STEP 1

Type Cabin Fare Example

PowerPoint displays the title of Slide 6 in the title placeholder.

STEP 2 ▶

Double-click the graph placeholder (see Figure 3-9) in the middle of Slide 6.

Graph displays the PROJ3.PPT — Datasheet window in a work area on the PowerPoint screen (Figure 3-11). Notice that sample data displays in the datasheet in the Datasheet window. The data points in the sample datasheet are plotted in a graph on Slide 6, which is positioned behind the Datasheet window. You can change the data points in the sample datasheet.

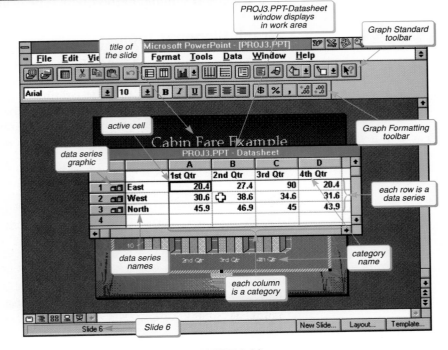

FIGURE 3-11

Graph displays default data in the sample datasheet to help you create your graph. A **data series** is a single row or a single column of data points on the datasheet. Each data series displays as a set of **data markers** on the graph, such as bars, lines, or pie slices.

In Figure 3-11, notice that the default data series is a single row; that is, each row in the datasheet is represented by a cluster of columns in the graph. The **data series names** display in the column to the left of the data points in the datasheet and in a legend in the graph. In the sample datasheet, East, West, and North are the data series names. Because the rows in this datasheet are the data series, each column in the datasheet is called a **category**. In this case, **category names** display in the column above the data points in the datasheet and below the columns in the graph. In the sample datasheet, 1st Qtr, 2nd Qtr, 3rd Qtr, and 4th Qtr are the category names.

Graph plots the data based on the data points you enter and the **orientation** you choose. The default orientation is data series in rows; that is, rows in the datasheet are plotted as columns in the graph. Later in this project, you will change the orientation to data series in columns.

A data series graphic displays to the right of the data series name in the datasheet to indicate the current graph type and the color of the data series. For example, in Figure 3-11 the data series graphic ( ) for East indicates the current graph type is a column graph, and the East data series is colored orange in the graph.

The default graph type is a 3-D column graph. If your graph type differs from the one in Figure 3-11, choose the Chart Type command from the Format menu and select 3-D Column in the Chart Type dialog box.

Graph Standard Toolbar

Notice in Figure 3-11 that the Standard toolbar buttons have changed. This is because you are no longer working in PowerPoint; instead, you are working in Graph. Later, when you exit the Graph application, the PowerPoint Standard toolbar will reappear. The Graph Standard toolbar contains buttons to help you complete the most frequently used actions in Graph. Table 3-2 illustrates the Graph Standard toolbar's buttons and their functions.

▸ **TABLE 3-2**

ICON	NAME	FUNCTION
	Import Data Button	Imports data from another application. The data you import is inserted into the datasheet and displayed graphically in the graph window.
	Import Chart Button	Imports an existing graph from Microsoft Excel.
	View Datasheet Button	Displays the datasheet window, allowing you to edit or format the data.
	Cut Button	Removes the selection and places it on the Clipboard.
	Copy Button	Copies the selection and places it on the Clipboard.
	Paste Button	Pastes the contents of the Clipboard into the selection.
	Undo Button	Reverses the last command you chose, if possible, or deletes the last entry you typed.
	By Row Button	Associates graph data series with rows on the datasheet.
	By Column Button	Associates graph data series with columns on the datasheet.
	Chart Type Button	Displays a palette of fourteen graph types. Clicking any one applies that graph type to active graph.
	Vertical Gridlines Button	Controls whether major vertical gridlines, indicating large groupings of values or categories, are visible on the graph.

ICON	NAME	FUNCTION
	Horizontal Gridlines Button	Controls whether major horizontal gridlines, indicating large groupings of values, are visible on the graph.
	Legend Button	Adds a legend to the right of the plot area and resizes the plot area to accommodate the legend. If the graph already has a legend, clicking the Legend button removes it.
	Text Box Button	Draws a text box in which you can type text on a worksheet; lets you add unattached, or "floating", text to a graph.
	Drawing Button	Displays the Drawing toolbar.
	Color Button	Changes the foreground color of a selected object.
	Pattern Button	Changes the pattern and pattern color of a selected object.
	Help Button	Adds a question mark (?) to the mouse pointer so you can get information about commands or screen elements.

Graph Formatting Toolbar

Like the Standard toolbar, the Formatting toolbar in Graph is different from the Formatting toolbar in PowerPoint. The Formatting toolbar displays directly below the Standard toolbar. If your screen does not display a Formatting toolbar, choose the Toolbars command from the View menu; then, select the Formatting check box in the Toolbars dialog box and choose the OK button. Table 3-3 explains the function of the buttons and boxes on the Graph Formatting toolbar.

▸ TABLE 3-3

ICON	NAME	FUNCTION
Arial	Font Box	Lists the available fonts.
10	Font Size Box	Lists the available sizes for the font selected in the Font Box.
B	Bold Button	Applies bold formatting to characters in cells, text boxes, or graph text.
I	Italic Button	Applies italic formatting to characters in cells, text boxes, or graph text.
U	Underline Button	Applies a single underline to characters in cells, text boxes, or graph text.
	Align Left Button	Aligns the contents of text boxes or graph text to the left.
	Center Button	Centers the contents of text boxes or graph text.

(continued)

ICON	NAME	FUNCTION
〓	Align Right Button	Aligns the contents of text boxes or graph text to the right.
$	Currency Style Button	Applies the currently defined Currency style to selected cells.
%	Percent Style Button	Applies the curently defined Percent style to selected cells.
,	Comma Style Button	Applies the currently defined Comma style to selected cells.
←.0 .00	Increase Decimal Button	Adds one decimal place to the number format each time you click the button.
.00 →.0	Decrease Decimal Button	Removes one decimal place from the number format each time you click the button.

Deleting Data from Columns in the Datasheet

The sample datasheet is a four-column datasheet containing columns A, B, C, and D (see Figure 3-11 on page PP145). San Baarbo Vacations is creating a two-column graph to compare the Dream Fare and the Full Fare (see Figure 3-8 on page PP142). Thus, the next step is to delete the data from columns C and D in the sample datasheet, as shown in the following steps.

TO DELETE DATA FROM COLUMNS IN THE DATASHEET ▼

STEP 1 ▶

Point to the column C heading (Figure 3-12a).

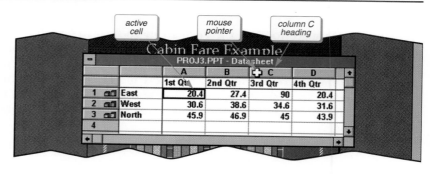

FIGURE 3-12a

STEP 2 ▶

Select columns C and D by dragging the mouse pointer through the column C and D headings.

Columns C and D are selected (Figure 3-12b). Selected columns are highlighted.

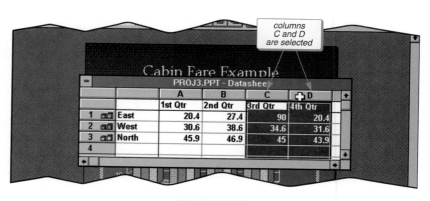

FIGURE 3-12b

STEP 3 ►

Press the DELETE **key.**

The data in columns C and D is deleted (Figure 3-13). Notice that the graph behind the Datasheet window changes to reflect the deleted columns; that is, the 3rd Qtr and 4th Qtr columns have been removed from the graph.

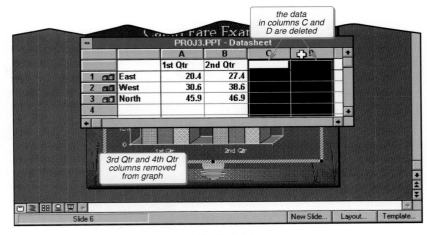

FIGURE 3-13

Selecting a Cell in a Datasheet

In order to enter data into a cell, you must first select it. One way to **select a cell** (make it active) is to use the mouse to move the mouse pointer (the block plus sign) to the active cell and click the left mouse button.

Another method to select a cell is to use the arrow keys that are located to the right of the type-writer area on the keyboard. An **arrow key** selects the cell adjacent to the active cell in the direction of the arrow on the key. The ENTER key selects the cell immediately below the active cell. Table 3-4 summarizes the keys you press to move to various locations in the datasheet.

▸ **TABLE 3-4**

TO MOVE	PRESS
One cell	One of the arrow keys
Down one cell (immediately below an active cell)	ENTER
To beginning of a row	HOME
To first data cell (cell A1)	CTRL+HOME
To end of row (last occupied column)	END
To lower right cell containing data	CTRL+END
Down one window	PAGE DOWN
Up one window	PAGE UP
Right one window	ALT+PAGE DOWN
Left one window	ALT+PAGE UP
Up or down to the edge of the current data region	CTRL+DOWN ARROW or CTRL+UP ARROW
Left or right to the edge of the current data region	CTRL+LEFT ARROW or CTRL+RIGHT ARROW

Pressing the END key moves the insertion point to column D at the end of the current row. This is because you deleted the data in columns C and D, and Graph still recognizes column D as the last occupied column. Until you close the presentation, the graph and corresponding datasheet are not reset. Therefore, if you open the presentation, return to the datasheet, and then press the END key, the insertion point would then move to column B of the current row.

Entering Category Names

Recall that the category names in the sample datasheet display above the data points and below the columns in the graph. The current category names are 1st Qtr and 2nd Qtr. You can change these default category names. To do this, you select the appropriate cell and then enter the text, as described in the steps on the next page.

TO ENTER THE CATEGORY NAMES ▼

STEP 1 ▶

Select the first cell under the column A heading, containing 1st Qtr as the category name, by pointing to the cell and clicking the left mouse button.

The cell becomes the active cell as designated by the heavy border around it (Figure 3-14). The mouse pointer is also in the cell.

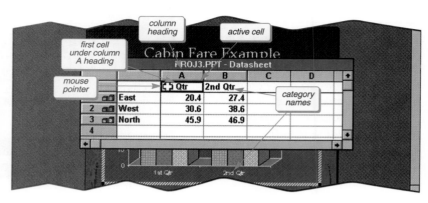

FIGURE 3-14

STEP 2 ▶

Type Dream Fare

When you type the first character, the heavy border disappears and an insertion point displays in the cell. Dream Fare displays left-aligned in the first cell under the column A heading (Figure 3-15). When you enter text into a datasheet cell, Graph automatically left-aligns it within the cell. Notice that the category name, Dream Fare, is too large for the cell and spills into the cell to its immediate right.

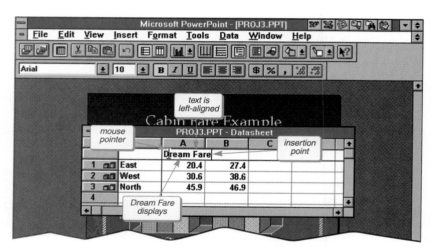

FIGURE 3-15

STEP 3 ▶

Press the RIGHT ARROW key.

*Graph enters the category name, Dream Fare, beneath the column A heading, and the first cell under the column B heading, containing the category name 2nd Qtr, becomes the active cell (Figure 3-16). Because a category name is in the cell to the right of Dream Fare, Graph **truncates**, or chops off, the right-most characters of the category name in the datasheet. The graph, however, displays the category name in its entirety. Notice that the graph changes to reflect the new category name; that is, Dream Fare replaces 1st Qtr.*

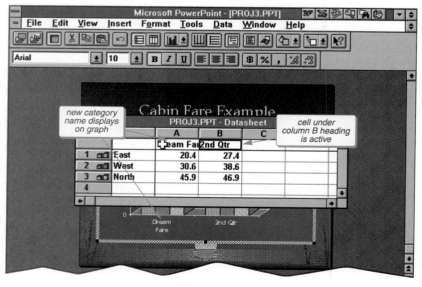

FIGURE 3-16

STEP 4 ▶

Type Full Fare

The category names are now complete (Figure 3-17).

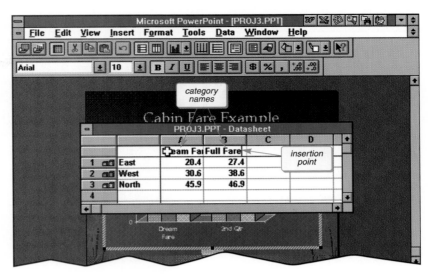

FIGURE 3-17

Although the category names display in the cell as you type them, they are not actually *entered* into the cell until you press an arrow key or the ENTER key, or until you click another cell. (This explains why the category name Full Fare does not yet display on the graph.)

Entering the Data Series Names

The next step in developing the datasheet, and its associated graph, in Project 3 is to enter the data series names in the column to the right of the row headings. Recall that the data series names display to the left of the data points in the datasheet and in the legend on the graph. The default data series names are East, West, and North. The process of changing these default data series names is similar to changing the category names and is described below.

TO ENTER THE DATA SERIES NAMES ▼

STEP 1 ▶

Select the first cell to the right of the row 1 heading, containing East as the data series name.

The cell immediately to the right of the row 1 heading becomes the active cell (Figure 3-18).

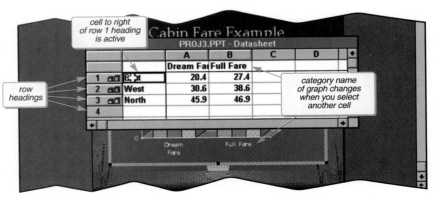

FIGURE 3-18

STEP 2 ▶

Type Grand Deluxe Suite **and press the DOWN ARROW key.**

Graph enters the data series name, Grand Deluxe Suite, in the first cell to the right of the row 1 heading. The first cell to the right of the row 2 heading becomes the active cell (Figure 3-19). Because there is a data point to the right of Grand Deluxe Suite, this data series name is truncated in the cell. The legend, which is hidden behind the Datasheet window, displays the data series in its entirety.

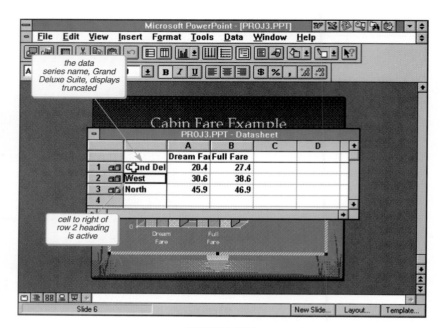

FIGURE 3-19

STEP 3 ▶

Type Deluxe Suite **in the first cell to the right of the row 2 heading and press the DOWN ARROW key. Type** Outside Cabin **in the first cell to the right of the row 3 heading and press the DOWN ARROW key. Type** Inside Cabin **in the first cell to the right of the row 4 heading.**

The data series names are complete (Figure 3-20). Notice that the Inside Cabin data series name displays in its entirety because you did not press an arrow key or the ENTER key after typing it.

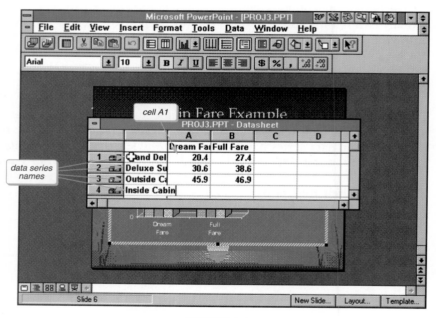

FIGURE 3-20

Entering the Data Points

In Graph, you can enter data points into cells to represent amounts. Recall that a cell containing a data point is referenced by its column and row coordinates. For example, the first cell containing a data point in Figure 3-20 is cell A1. Again, Graph displays default data points in these cells. Perform the following steps to change the default data points in the datasheet.

TO ENTER THE DATA POINTS ▼

STEP 1 ▶

Select cell A1, which contains the default data point 20.4.

Cell A1 becomes the active cell (Figure 3-21).

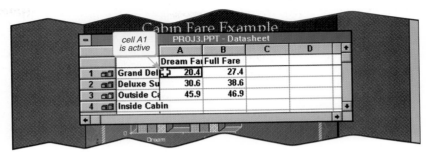

FIGURE 3-21

STEP 2 ▶

Type 3099

The data point 3099 displays in the active cell, which is cell A1 (Figure 3-22). (Data points are entered without using a dollar sign. The data points on the datasheet are formatted with a dollar sign later in this project.)

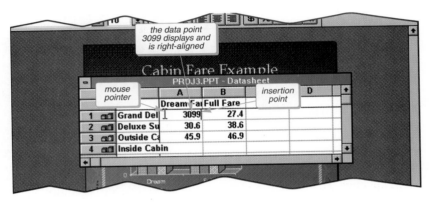

FIGURE 3-22

STEP 3 ▶

Press the RIGHT ARROW key.

Graph enters the data point 3099 in cell A1, and cell B1 becomes the active cell (Figure 3-23). Notice that data points are right-aligned in a cell.

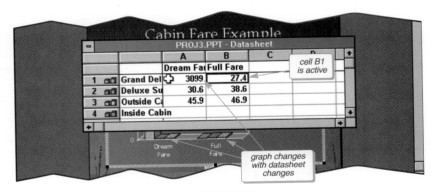

FIGURE 3-23

STEP 4 ▶

Type 4099

The data point 4099 displays in the active cell B1 (Figure 3-24).

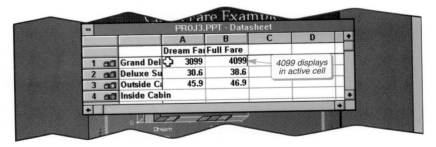

FIGURE 3-24

STEP 5 ▶

Select cell A2 by clicking it.

Cell A2 becomes the active cell (Figure 3-25).

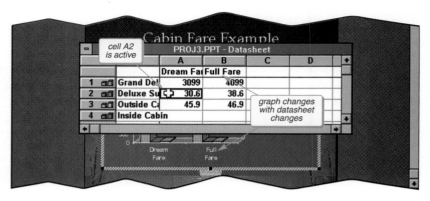

FIGURE 3-25

STEP 6 ▶

Enter 1699 **in cell A2,** 2665 **in cell B2,** 1369 **in cell A3,** 2095 **in cell B3,** 1249 **in cell A4, and** 1875 **in cell B4. Do not press an arrow key or the ENTER key after typing cell B4's entry.**

The datasheet entries are complete (Figure 3-26).

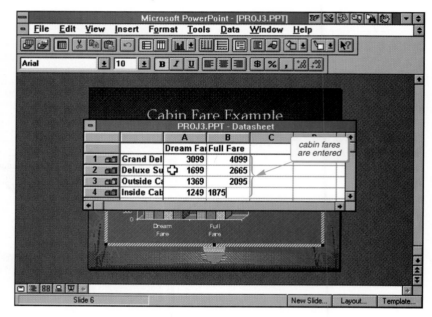

FIGURE 3-26

If your screen scrolls up at the end of Step 6, click the up arrow on the Datasheet window vertical scroll bar to bring the entire datasheet back into view.

If you need to modify the contents of a cell, click the cell and type the correct name or data point.

The next section explains how to format the datasheet using the Graph Formatting toolbar. For a detailed explanation of the Graph Formatting toolbar, see Table 3-3 on page PP147.

Formatting Data Points on the Datasheet

Changing the format of the data points on the datasheet allows you to represent currency and percentages, insert commas, and increase or decrease the number of positions after the decimal point. Perform the following steps to format the data points on the datasheet to represent dollar amounts.

TO FORMAT DATA POINTS ON THE DATASHEET ▼

STEP 1 ▶

Select columns A and B by dragging the mouse pointer through the column A and B headings.

Columns A and B are selected (Figure 3-27).

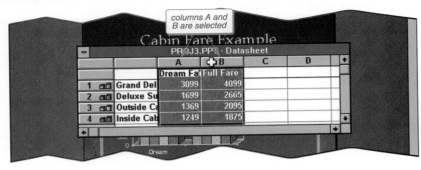

FIGURE 3-27

STEP 2 ▶

Point to the Currency Style button (💲) on the Formatting toolbar (Figure 3-28).

Recall that the PowerPoint window is displaying the Graph Formatting toolbar, not the PowerPoint Formatting toolbar.

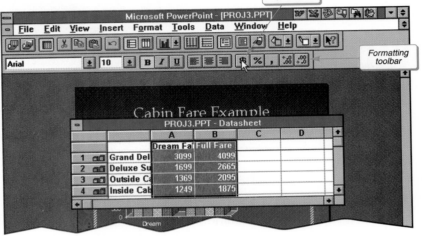

FIGURE 3-28

STEP 3 ▶

Click the Currency Style button.

The currency style is applied to the data points in the selected cells (Figure 3-29). That is, the data points display with dollar signs, commas, and two decimal positions.

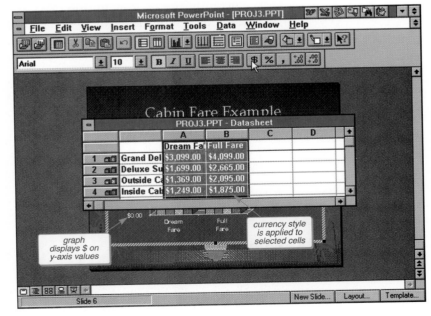

FIGURE 3-29

STEP 4 ▶

Click the Decrease Decimal button ( ) on the Formatting toolbar two times.

The decimal points are removed from the data points in the selected cells (Figure 3-30). Thus, the data points display as whole numbers. Each time you click the Decrease Decimal button, one decimal position is removed from the data points in the selected cells.

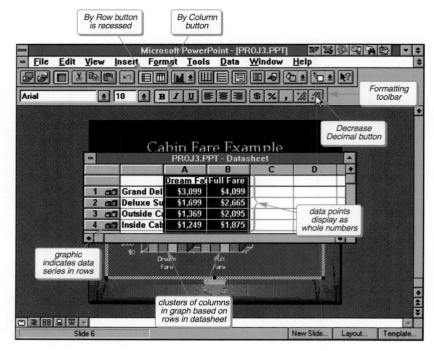

FIGURE 3-30

Changing Graph's Orientation

Recall that Graph plots the data based on the data points you enter and the orientation you choose. Recall also that the default orientation is data series in rows; that is, rows in the datasheet are plotted as clusters of columns in the graph. However, you want the data series in columns. That is, columns in the datasheet should be plotted as columns in the graph.

Currently, the By Row button ( ) on the Standard toolbar is recessed, indicating the data series is in rows. The By Column button ( ) on the Standard toolbar associates the data series plotted on the graph with columns on the datasheet. Perform the following steps to change the graph's orientation from data series in rows to data series in columns.

TO CHANGE A GRAPH'S ORIENTATION ▼

STEP 1 ►

Click the By Column button on the Standard toolbar.

The data series are now based on the columns in the datasheet (Figure 3-31).

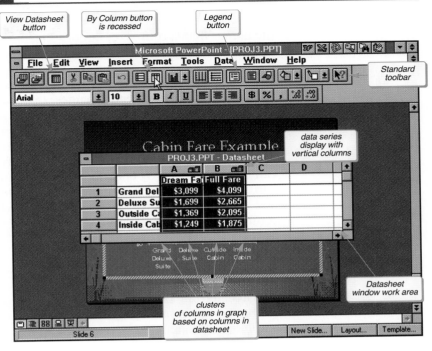

FIGURE 3-31

STEP 2 ►

Click outside the Datasheet window work area.

The Graph application closes and the PowerPoint application reappears. The Cabin Fare Example graph displays in the PowerPoint window (Figure 3-32). A legend displays to the right of the graph to identify the different data series displayed.

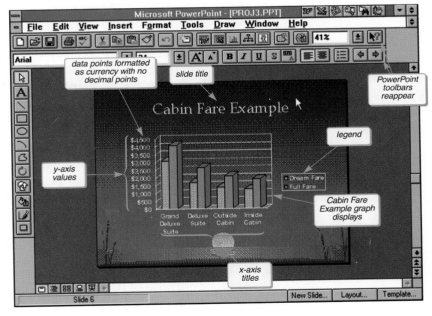

FIGURE 3-32

Several major changes occur on the datasheet when you click the By Column button in Figure 3-31 on the previous page. First, the By Column button is recessed. Second, the data series names and category names are swapped; that is, the names beneath the column headings become the data series names, and the names to the right of the row headings become the category names. Third, because the data series and category names have switched, the words beneath the columns in the graph change to the new data series names, and the legend changes to the new category names. Instead of two data series names, the graph has four data series names. Finally, the data series graphic displays in the column header above the data series, instead of the row heading to left of the data series.

If, for some reason, you want to edit the graph, simply double-click it to open the Graph application. If you need to modify the contents of the datasheet, you can display it again by clicking the View Datasheet button (▥) on the Graph Standard toolbar. If you accidentally delete the legend from an existing graph, you can add it again by clicking the Legend button on the Graph Standard toolbar. Then, to return to PowerPoint, simply click anywhere outside the Datasheet window work area.

Changing Graph Types

Recall from Table 3-1 on page PP143 that the four most common graph types are bar graph, column graph, line graph, and pie graph. Project 3 uses the column graph to compare costs between cabin class fares.

If, for some reason, you wanted to change the graph type, you would click the Chart Type button on the Graph Standard toolbar. When the Chart Type drop-down list displays, select one of the graph types. To help you determine what the graph will look like, the Chart Type drop-down list displays a graphic of each of the fourteen graph types.

When you select a new graph type, several changes occur. First, the graph displays as the new graph type. Second, depending on the graph type selected, names beneath the column and row headings may switch position with each other. Finally, the data series graphic in the datasheet displays reflecting the new graph type.

Adding Data Labels

Data labels add detail to the graph by placing a label on the graph for a data series, an individual data point, or for all the data points in the graph. Data for the data label comes directly from the datasheet. Thus, if a data point value changes, so does the data label.

It is sometimes useful to add the actual number value of the data point onto the chart. For example, in a column graph with wide value ranges between data points, placing the actual value next to the column eliminates the guessing of the data point. This is because the data point value would display on the graph.

Another purpose of data labels is to show percentages. For example, in a pie graph you are illustrating one data series as the whole pie. Each pie wedge represents one data point in the datasheet. Therefore, displaying data labels as a percentage on the pie graph shows the exact contribution of the data point to the data series. This is often useful when making budget presentations.

To add data labels to a graph, you must be in Microsoft Graph 5 and the menu bar must display. From the Insert menu, choose the Data Labels command. When the Data Labels dialog box displays, select the option button for the type of data label you wish to display. Then, choose the OK button.

Adding Another Slide to the Presentation

You want to add another slide to your presentation that describes the climate and attractions at San Juan, as shown in these steps.

**TO ADD ANOTHER SLIDE
TO THE PRESENTATION**

Step 1: Click the Insert New Slide button on the Standard toolbar.

Step 2: Double-click the Bulleted List AutoLayout in the New Slide dialog box.

Step 3: Type San Juan as the title for Slide 7.

Step 4: Select the text object by clicking anywhere inside the text placeholder.

Step 5: Type Warm year-round climate and press the ENTER key.

Step 6: Type Sandy beaches and press the ENTER key.

Step 7: Type Historical sites and press the ENTER key.

Step 8: Type Cultural museums and press the ENTER key.

Step 9: Type Sport and recreation

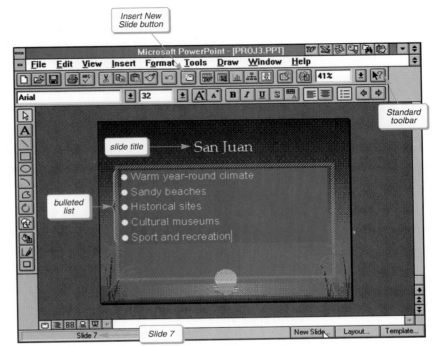

FIGURE 3-33

Slide 7 displays as shown in Figure 3-33.

Saving the Presentation

Because several changes have been made since your last save, you should save the presentation again with the same filename by clicking the Save button on the Standard toolbar.

▶ ADDING A TABLE

The next slide in this presentation contains a table that shows the temperatures for Puerto Rico (Figure 3-34). The rows in the table display each quarter in a year, and the columns display high, low, and average temperatures. Including the headings, the table contains four columns and five rows.

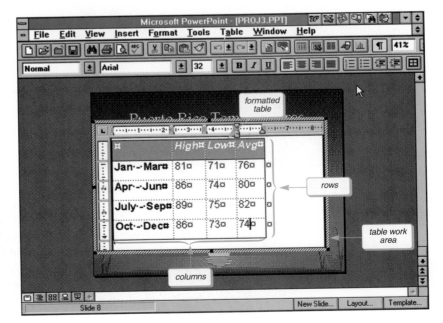

FIGURE 3-34

A **table** is a collection of columns and rows. Similar to a datasheet, the intersection of a column and a row on a table is called a cell. Cells are filled with data. The major difference between a table and a datasheet is that a graph is generated from data points on a datasheet; that is, the datasheet does not display on the slide, whereas, the data in a table displays on the slide in its column-row format. Another difference between a table and a datasheet is that the data you enter within a cell of a table wordwraps just as the text does between the margins of a document, instead of being truncated as in a cell in a datasheet.

Like the graph, a table is actually an embedded object because it is created in Microsoft Word 6. When you instruct PowerPoint to insert a table on a slide, Word opens and its menus, buttons, tools, etc., are available to you directly on the PowerPoint screen.

Creating a table requires several steps. First, you add a new slide with the table layout. Next, you open the Word application into the PowerPoint screen. Then, you enter headings and data into the table. Finally, you format the table so it looks more professional. The following pages contain a detailed outline of these steps.

Adding a Slide with the Table AutoLayout

Because you want the table on a separate slide, you add a new slide with the Table AutoLayout, as shown in these steps.

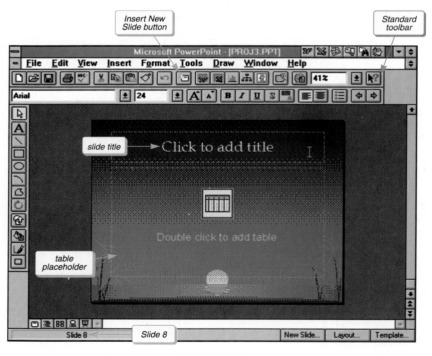

FIGURE 3-35

TO ADD A NEW SLIDE WITH THE TABLE AUTOLAYOUT

Step 1: Click the Insert New Slide button on the Standard toolbar.

Step 2: Double-click the Table AutoLayout (▦) in the New Slide dialog box.

Slide 8 displays the table placeholder (Figure 3-35).

Opening the Word Application and Inserting a Table

In order to create the table in Slide 8, you must first open the Word application. Recall that OLE brings this supplementary application to the PowerPoint window and makes the menus, buttons, tools, etc., from the Word application available on the PowerPoint screen. Once open, Word displays an Insert Word Table dialog box in a work area in the middle of the PowerPoint screen. You establish the number of columns and rows in the dialog box to insert a table, as shown in the steps below.

TO OPEN THE WORD APPLICATION AND INSERT A TABLE ▼

STEP 1

Type Puerto Rico Temperatures

PowerPoint displays the title of Slide 8 in the title placeholder.

STEP 2 ►

Double-click the table placeholder in the Table AutoLayout.

Word displays the Insert Word Table dialog box on the PowerPoint screen (Figure 3-36). The table is currently set to display two columns and two rows. Your table should have four columns and five rows.

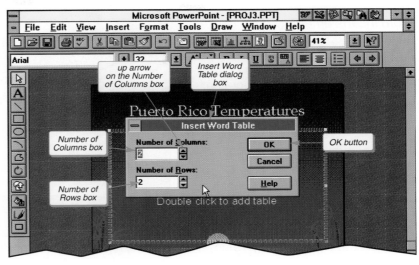

FIGURE 3-36

STEP 3 ►

Click the up arrow next to the Number of Columns box two times.

The number 4 displays in the Number of Columns box, which indicates four columns are in this table (Figure 3-37).

FIGURE 3-37

STEP 4 ►

Click the up arrow next to the Number of Rows box three times.

The number 5 displays in the Number of Rows box, which indicates are five rows are in this table (Figure 3-38).

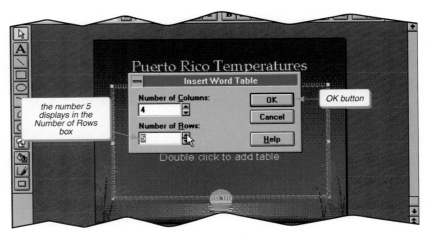

FIGURE 3-38

STEP 5 ▶

Choose the OK button.

Word inserts an empty table containing four columns of equal width and five rows of equal height (Figure 3-39). The insertion point is in the first cell (column 1, row 1) of the table.

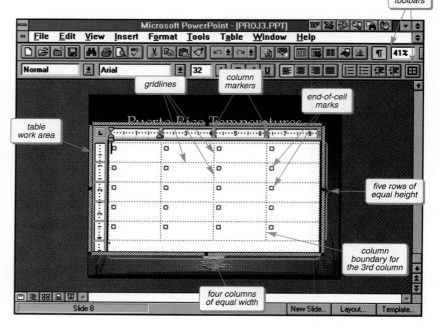

FIGURE 3-39

Notice in Figure 3-39 that the PowerPoint toolbars and menus have been replaced with the Word toolbars and menus.

The table displays on the screen with dotted **gridlines**. If your table does not have gridlines, choose the Gridlines command from the Table menu. Word does not print the table with gridlines; instead, the gridlines display to help you identify in which row and column you are working.

The vertical gridline immediately to the right of a column is called the **column boundary**. You decrease the width of a column by dragging the column boundary to the left. You increase the width of the column by dragging the column boundary to the right. You can also change column widths by dragging the **column markers** on the horizontal ruler.

Each cell has an **end-of-cell mark**, which is used to select a cell; that is, you point to the end-of-cell mark and click it to select a cell. The end-of-cell marks are currently left-aligned within each cell, indicating the data will be left-aligned. The alignment buttons on the Formatting toolbar change the alignment of a cell's contents.

To advance from one cell to the next, press the TAB key. To advance from one row to the next, also press the TAB key or click in the cell; do not press the ENTER key. The ENTER key is used to begin new paragraphs within a cell.

Adding Column Headings

Each column containing data should be identified with a heading. Perform the following steps to add column headings to the table.

STEP 1 ►

Click the cell located in column 2, row 1. Type High

The word High displays left-aligned in the cell (Figure 3-40). Recall that the alignment of cell data is controlled by the alignment of the end-of-cell marks.

FIGURE 3-40

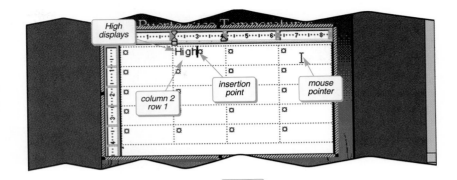

STEP 2 ►

Press the TAB key. Type Low **and press the TAB key. Type** Avg

The table displays three column headings (Figure 3-41).

FIGURE 3-41

The column headings are complete. The next step is to fill in the rows of the table.

Filling in the Rows

As you fill in each row of the table, you should first label the row with a row heading. Then, complete the row with the data in the appropriate column. Perform the following steps to fill in the rows for the Puerto Rico Temperature table.

STEP 1 ►

Click the cell in column 1, row 2. Type Jan - Mar **(Be sure to press the SPACEBAR before and after the hyphen.)**

The row heading is left-aligned in the cell (Figure 3-42).

FIGURE 3-42

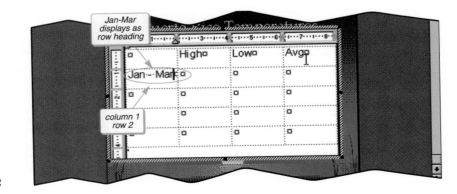

STEP 2 ▶

Press the TAB key and type 81

The high temperature for January through March displays left-aligned in the cell (Figure 3-43).

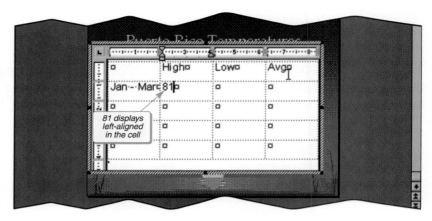

FIGURE 3-43

STEP 3 ▶

Press the TAB key. Type 71 **and press the TAB key. Type** 76

The high, low, and average temperatures for the months of January through March are entered (Figure 3-44).

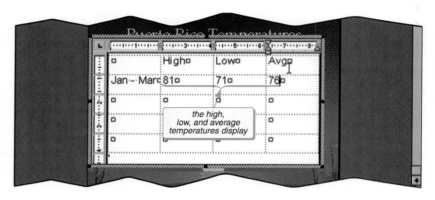

FIGURE 3-44

STEP 4 ▶

Press the TAB key. Type Apr - Jun **and press the TAB key. Type** 86 **and press the TAB key. Type** 74 **and press the TAB key. Type** 80 **and press the TAB key. Type** July - Sep **and press the TAB key. Type** 89 **and press the TAB key. Type** 75 **and press the TAB key. Type** 82 **and press the TAB key. Type** Oct - Dec **and press the TAB key. Type** 86 **and press the TAB key. Type** 73 **and press the TAB key. Type** 74

The table is complete (Figure 3-45).

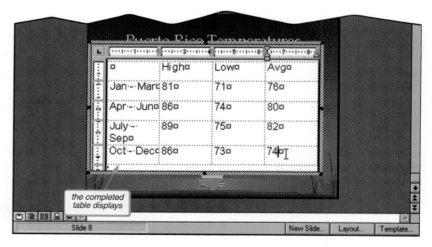

FIGURE 3-45

Notice that the cell containing the row heading July – Sep wrapped in the cell because the heading is too long to fit on one line in the cell. When you format the table in the next section, the contents of this cell will no longer wordwrap.

Formatting the Table

Because PowerPoint creates tables using Microsoft Word, the table may be automatically formatted using Word's Table AutoFormat command, which provides thirty-four predefined formats for tables. These predefined formats vary the borders, shading, colors, and fonts for the cells within a table. Perform the following steps to format the table with the Table AutoFormat command.

TO FORMAT THE TABLE ▼

STEP 1 ►

With the insertion point and mouse pointer somewhere in the table, click the right mouse button to display a shortcut menu. Point to the Table AutoFormat command in the shortcut menu.

Word displays a shortcut menu for tables (Figure 3-46).

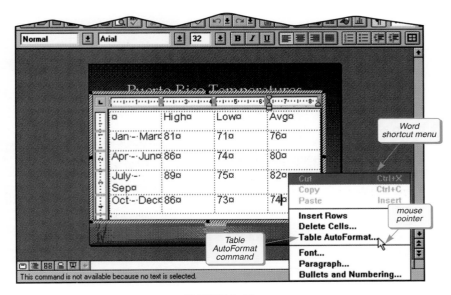

FIGURE 3-46

STEP 2 ►

Choose the Table AutoFormat command.

The Table AutoFormat dialog box displays (Figure 3-47). The first predefined table format, Simple 1, is selected in the Formats list, and a preview of the selected format displays in the Preview area.

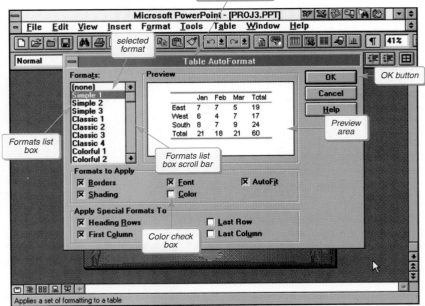

FIGURE 3-47

STEP 3 ▶

Select Classic 4 in the Formats list box by clicking it.

Word displays a preview of the Classic 4 format (Figure 3-48).

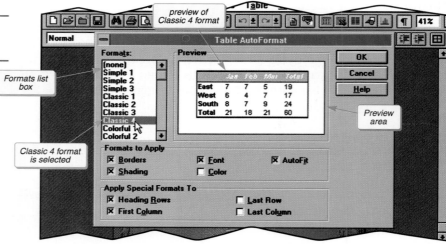

FIGURE 3-48

STEP 4 ▶

If it is not already selected, click the Color check box in the Formats to Apply area.

The table displays in color because the Color check box is selected (Figure 3-49).

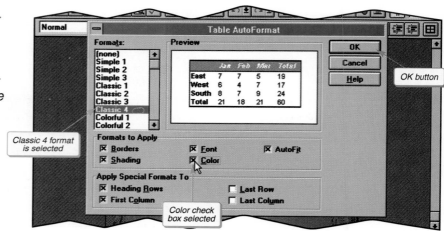

FIGURE 3-49

STEP 5 ▶

Choose the OK button.

The Table AutoFormat dialog box closes and the table displays with the Classic 4 format (Figure 3-50). Notice that the cell containing the July - Sep heading no longer word-wraps. Because the AutoFit check box was selected in the Table Auto-Format dialog box, Word redefines the column width based on the cell containing the longest data item.

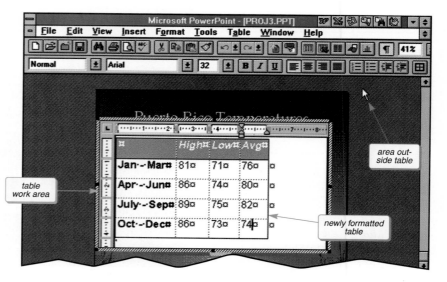

FIGURE 3-50

STEP 6 ▶

Click outside the table work area.

The Word application closes and the PowerPoint application reappears. The table displays on Slide 8 in the PowerPoint window (Figure 3-51). Because the table does not fill the table placeholder, it appears to be left-aligned on the slide.

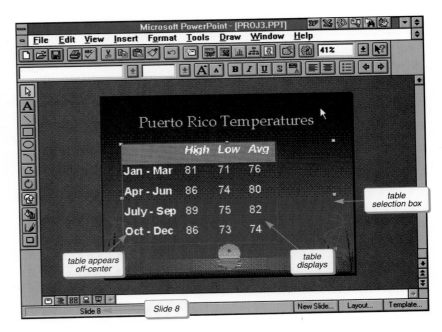

FIGURE 3-51

If, at a later time, you want to edit the table, simply double-click it to open the Word application. When your revisions are complete, click outside the table work area to return to PowerPoint.

Moving the Table Object

You want the table to begin directly beneath the letter P in the Puerto Rico Temperatures title object. Thus, you want to move the table. Because the table is an object, you can drag it just like you do any other object, as shown in these steps.

TO MOVE THE TABLE OBJECT ▼

STEP 1 ▶

Point to the center of the table. Then, press and hold the left mouse button.

When you press and hold the left mouse button, a dotted box outlines the table object (Figure 3-52). As you move, the outline box follows your pointer to show you where the table will be placed when you release the mouse button.

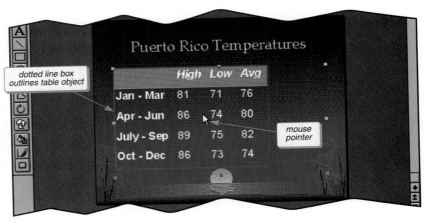

FIGURE 3-52

STEP 2 ▶

Drag the table to the right until the left edge of the outline box aligns with the letter P in Puerto Rico (Figure 3-53).

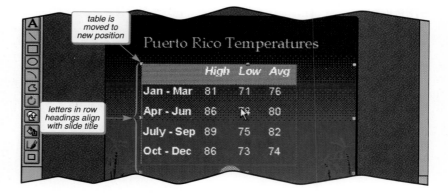

FIGURE 3-53

STEP 3 ▶

Release the left mouse button.

Word drops the table into place on Slide 8 (Figure 3-54). Recall that the procedure of moving an object with the mouse is called dragging and dropping.

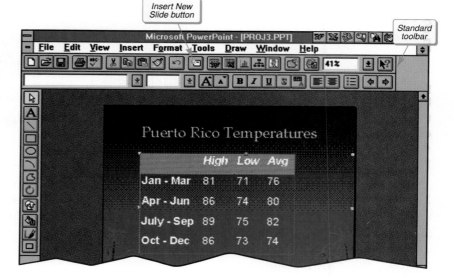

FIGURE 3-54

The revisions to the San Baarbo Vacations presentation are complete. However, the travel agency has decided to end the presentation with a blank slide, instead of returning to the PowerPoint screen. Thus, the next section adds a blank slide to the end of the presentation.

Adding a Blank Slide to End the Presentation

Recall that when you advance past the last slide in Slide Show view, PowerPoint returns to the PowerPoint screen. To prevent the audience from seeing the PowerPoint screen, it is a good practice to end your presentation with a **closing slide**.

PRESENTATION TIP
The last slide of your presentation should be a closing slide, which may be a summary, a closing thought, or simply a blank slide. Using a blank slide to end an on-screen presentation gives the presentation a clean ending.

Perform the following steps to add a blank slide to the end of the presentation.

TO ADD A BLANK SLIDE

Step 1: Click the Insert New
Slide button on the
Standard toolbar.
Step 2: Double-click the Blank
AutoLayout (☐) in
the New Slide dialog
box.

*Slide 9 displays only the trop-
ics template (Figure 3-55).*

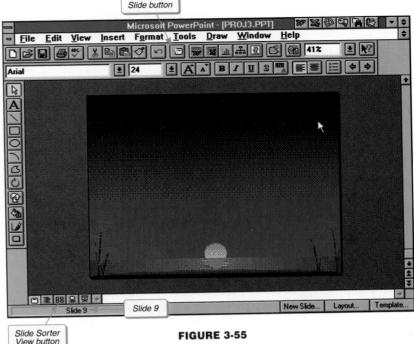

FIGURE 3-55

Spell Checking a Presentation

You should spell check your
presentation before saving it again
by clicking the Spelling but-ton on
the Standard toolbar. For a detailed
explanation of spell checking a presentation, refer to pages PP44 and
PP45 in Project 1.

Saving the Presentation

Because several changes have been made since your last save, you should save
the presentation again with the same filename by clicking the Save button on the
Standard toolbar.

▶ ADDING SPECIAL EFFECTS

P owerPoint provides many special effects to make your slide show presentation look professional. Two of these special effects are called transition
and build. With these special effects, you control how slides enter and
exit the screen and how the contents of a bulleted slide display. The following
pages discuss each of the special effects in detail.

Adding Transitions to a Slide Show

PowerPoint allows you to control the way you advance from one slide to the
next by adding transitions to an on-screen slide show. **Transitions** are special
visual effects that display when you move one slide off the screen and bring on the
next one. PowerPoint has over forty different transitions. The transition name char-
acterizes the visual effect that displays.

You set slide transitions through the Transition Effects box or the Transition
button on the Slide Sorter toolbar, which displays when you are in Slide Sorter
view.

Slide Sorter Toolbar

In Slide Sorter view, the Slide Sorter toolbar displays beneath the Standard
toolbar — in place of the Formatting toolbar. The Slide Sorter toolbar contains

tools to help you quickly add special effects to your slide show. Table 3-5 explains the function of the buttons and boxes on the Slide Sorter toolbar.

▶ **TABLE 3-5**

ICON	NAME	FUNCTION
⊡	Transition Button	Displays the Transition dialog box, which lists special effects used for slide changes during a slide show.
No Transition ⬇	Transition Effects Box	Displays a list of transition effects. Selecting a transition effect from the list applies it to the selected slide(s) and demonstrates it in the preview box.
▤	Build Button	Displays the Build dialog box which contains special effects to apply to a slide series. For example, building a slide on the screen, one bulleted paragraph at a time.
No Build Effect ⬇	Build Effects Box	Displays a list of build effects.
▨	Hide Slide Button	Excludes a slide from the presentation without deleting it.
⏲	Rehearse Timings Button	Records the amount of time spent on each slide during a presentation rehearsal.
ᴬ⁄ᴀ	Show Formatting Button	Displays or hides character formatting attributes.

Adding Transitions to a Slide Show

In the San Baarbo Vacations presentation, you want the Strips Right-Down transition between slides; that is, all slides begin stacked on top of one another, like a deck of cards. As you click the mouse to view the next screen, the current slide exits the screen by shrinking down toward the bottom right corner of the screen until it is gone. Perform the following steps to add the Strips Right-Down transition to the San Baarbo Vacations presentation.

TO ADD TRANSITIONS TO A SLIDE SHOW ▼

STEP 1 ▶

Click the Slide Sorter View button at the bottom of the PowerPoint screen. Select Slide 9 by clicking it.

PowerPoint displays the presentation in Slide Sorter view (Figure 3-56). Depending on the last slide you viewed, your screen may display differently. Slide 9 is selected. Slide 9 currently does not have a transition effect, as noted in the Transition Effects box on the Slide Sorter toolbar.

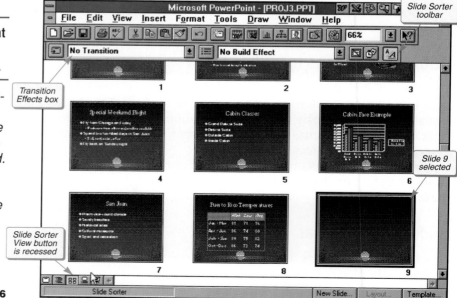

FIGURE 3-56

STEP 2 ▶

Select the Edit menu and point to the Select All command (Figure 3-57).

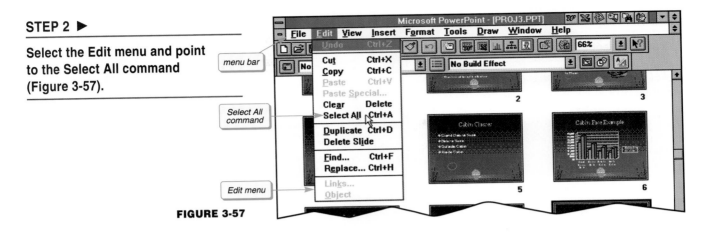

FIGURE 3-57

STEP 3 ▶

Choose the Select All command.

All of the slides in the presentation are selected, as indicated by the heavy border around each slide (Figure 3-58).

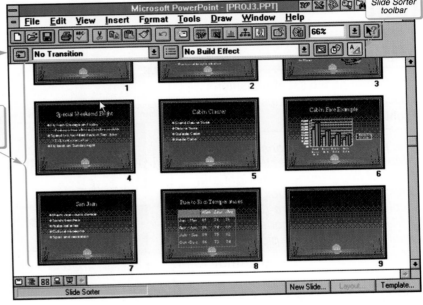

FIGURE 3-58

STEP 4 ▶

Click the Transition button on the Slide Sorter toolbar.

The Transition dialog box displays (Figure 3-59). Currently, this presentation does not have a transition effect. The preview box displays a sample picture, a dog in this case. Each time you select an effect, it is demonstrated on the sample picture in the preview box.

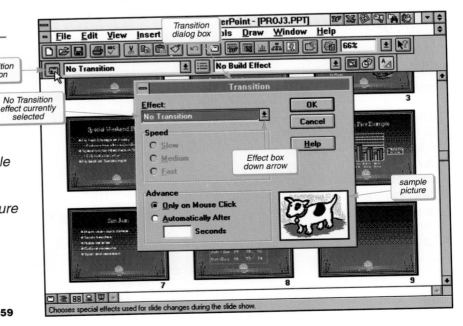

FIGURE 3-59

STEP 5 ▶

Click the Effect box arrow.

A list of transition effects displays (Figure 3-60).

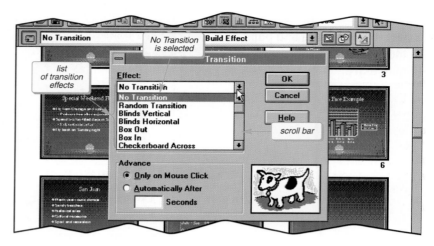

FIGURE 3-60

STEP 6 ▶

Scroll through the list of transition effects and click the Strips Right-Down effect.

The preview box demonstrates the Strips Right-Down effect by stripping the dog picture to the right and down off the preview box and then displaying a key picture (Figure 3-61). To see the demonstration again, simply click the picture in the preview box.

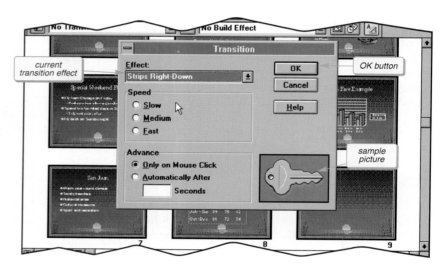

FIGURE 3-61

STEP 7 ▶

Click the Slow option button in the Speed box.

When you click the Slow option button, the preview box demonstrates the effect and speed of the transition (Figure 3-62). The key picture slowly moves down and to the right of the preview box as the dog picture displays.

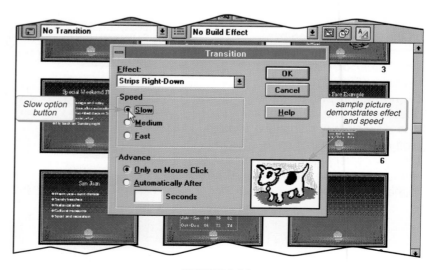

FIGURE 3-62

STEP 8 ▶

Choose the OK button.

PowerPoint displays the presentation in Slide Sorter view (Figure 3-63). A transition icon (▢) displays under each slide, which indicates that transition effects have been added to the slides. The transition effect currently applied to the selected slide(s) displays in the Transition Effects box.

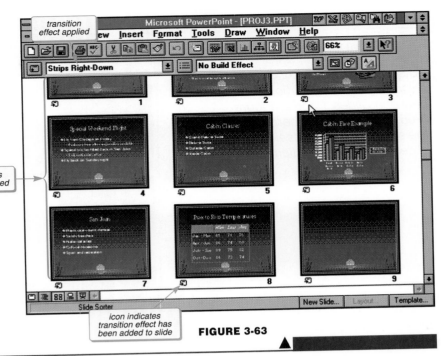

FIGURE 3-63

Transition has been applied to the entire presentation. When you have finalized your presentation, you should select the Fast option button in the Transition dialog box because you do not want to emphasize the transition. The next step in creating this slide show is to add special effects to individual slides.

Applying Build Effects

Build effects are applied to bulleted slides. This special effect instructs PowerPoint to progressively disclose each bulleted paragraph, one at a time, during the running of a slide show. PowerPoint has thirty build effects and the capability to dim the other bulleted paragraphs already on the slide when a new paragraph is displayed.

On Slide 1, you want to apply the Fly From Left effect. When you display a slide with this effect, bulleted paragraph *flies* in from the left edge of the screen to its proper location on the slide each time you click the mouse. Perform the following steps to apply build effects to an existing bulleted slide.

TO APPLY BUILD EFFECTS ▼

STEP 1 ▶

If Slide 1 does not currently display, drag the elevator to the top of the vertical scroll bar to display it.

This presentation currently does not have any build effects, as designated in the Build Effects box (Figure 3-64). All slides in the presentation are currently selected. You need to deselect the slides before you select Slide 2.

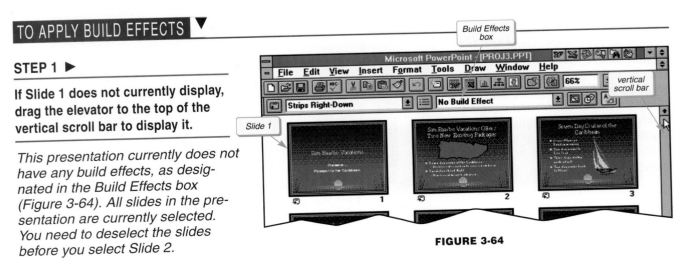

FIGURE 3-64

STEP 2 ▶

Click between Slide 1 and Slide 2.

No slides in the presentation are selected and the insertion point is between Slides 1 and 2 (Figure 3-65). (Clicking anywhere outside the selected slides deselects the slides in the presentation.)

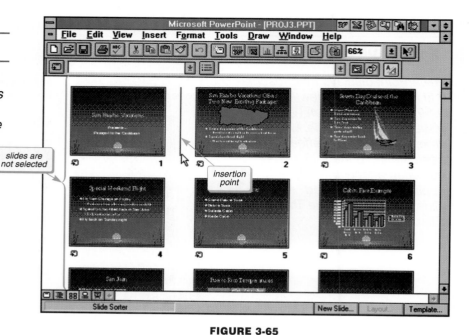

FIGURE 3-65

STEP 3 ▶

Select Slide 2 by clicking it.

Slide 2 is the only selected slide in the presentation (Figure 3-66). Slide 2 currently does not have any build effects.

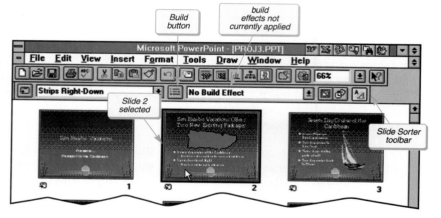

FIGURE 3-66

STEP 4

Click the Build button on the Slide Sorter toolbar.

The Build dialog box displays (Figure 3-67). PowerPoint displays the defaults for the Dim Previous Points and Effect boxes. The default color is controlled by the color scheme of the template. The defaults are not used in the slide until their check boxes are selected.

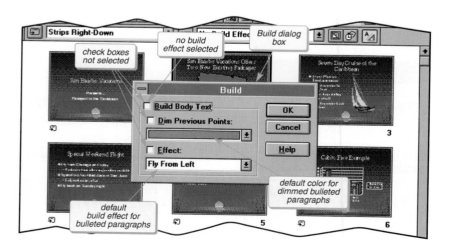

FIGURE 3-67

STEP 5 ▶

Click the Effect check box.

The Effect check box is selected (Figure 3-68) The Build Body Text check box is automatically selected when either the Dim Previous Points or Effect check box is selected. Fly From Left, the default effect, displays in the Effect box.

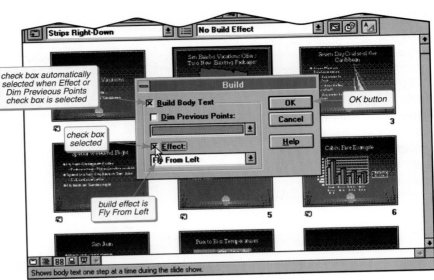

FIGURE 3-68

STEP 6 ▶

Choose the OK button in the Build dialog box.

A build icon (::::) displays under Slide 2 and to the right of the transition icon, which indicates that build effects have been applied to the slide (Figure 3-69).

STEP 7

Click between Slide 1 and Slide 2.

No slides in the presentation are selected and the insertion point is between Slides 1 and 2 (Figure 3-65 above).

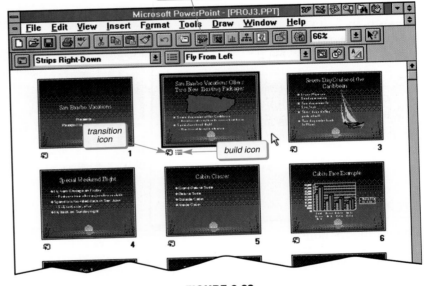

FIGURE 3-69

The Fly From Left build effect has been applied to Slide 2. The next section applies this same build effect to the remaining bulleted slides in the presentation.

Applying a Build Effect to the Remaining Bulleted Slides

The next step is to apply the Fly From Left build effect to Slides 3, 4, 5, and 7 in the San Baarbo Vacations presentation. These slides are **noncontiguous**; that is, not consecutive. To select noncontiguous slides, you press and hold the SHIFT key while clicking each slide, then release the SHIFT key called (**SHIFT+click**). Use the SHIFT+click technique to apply the build effect to the remaining bulleted slides in the presentation as shown in these steps.

TO APPLY A BUILD EFFECT TO THE REMAINING BULLETED SLIDES ▼

STEP 1 ►

Press and hold the SHIFT key and click Slide 3, Slide 4, and Slide 5. Release the SHIFT key. Drag the vertical scroll bar elevator until Slide 7 displays. Then, press and hold the SHIFT key and click Slide 7. Release the SHIFT key.

Slides 3, 4, 5, and 7 are selected (Figure 3-70).

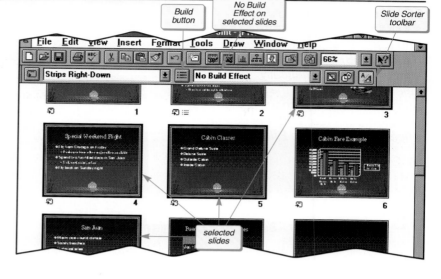

FIGURE 3-70

STEP 2 ►

Click the Build button on the Slide Sorter toolbar. When the Build dialog box displays, click the Effect check box.

PowerPoint automatically selects the Build Body Text check box when the Effect check box is selected (Figure 3-71). Fly From Left displays in the Effect box.

FIGURE 3-71

STEP 3 ►

Choose the OK button.

The Fly From Left build effect is applied to the selected slides (Figure 3-72).

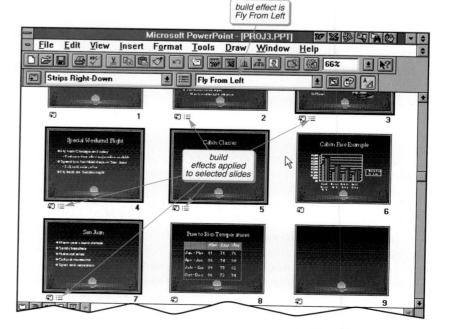

FIGURE 3-72

The revisions to the San Baarbo Vacations presentation are complete.

Dim Previous Points

When you added the Fly From Left build effect, you selected the Effect check box in the Build dialog box. You could have also selected the Dim Previous Points check box, which tells PowerPoint to change the color of the previous bulleted paragraph as a new one displays on the screen. You can accept the default dim color displayed in the Dim Previous Points color box, or you can click the box arrow and select a different dim color. Because of the many color choices, you should experiment with your presentation to decide the color best suited for your presentation. Many times, you will decide not to select the Dim Previous Points check box because you could not find a dim color to enhance your presentation, as is the case in the San Baarbo Vacation presentation.

Saving the Presentation Again

Because several changes have been made since your last save, you should save the presentation again with the same filename by clicking the Save button on the Standard toolbar.

▶ RUNNING AN AUTOMATIC SLIDE SHOW

In Project 1, you were introduced to using Slide Show view to look at your presentation one slide at a time. You will now use Slide Show view to run an **automatic slide show**. The automatic slide show will display each slide for a period of time. The time is set using the **Rehearse Timings button**. The Rehearse Timings button, found on the Slide Sorter toolbar, allows you to run a slide show and rehearse your presentation. While you are running the slide show, PowerPoint keeps track of the length of time each slide is displayed and then sets the timing accordingly. Once timings are set, you must tell PowerPoint to use these times to run the automatic slide show.

PRESENTATION TIP
Allow an average of two minutes for each slide in your presentation. Some slides will take longer to explain, while others will take less. Rehearsing your presentation will help you determine the proper amount of time for each slide. Allow at least two to three minutes for the closing slide to wrap up your presentation.

TO SET SLIDE TIMINGS ▼

STEP 1 ▶

Point to the Rehearse Timings button on the Slide Sorter toolbar (Figure 3-73).

FIGURE 3-73

STEP 2 ▶

Click the Rehearse Timings button on the Slide Sorter toolbar.

PowerPoint begins the slide show and displays Slide 1 (Figure 3-74). A timer box displays at the lower left of the slide. The timer accumulates until you click the left mouse button.

Slide 1

Timer box displays number of seconds slide is on screen

FIGURE 3-74

STEP 3 ▶

Click the left mouse button when you finish rehearsing Slide 1.

PowerPoint displays the title and clip art for Slide 2 (Figure 3-75). The timer resets to zero each time a new slide displays and then begins accumulating seconds until the next slide displays.

Slide 2 title

Slide 2

timer resets to zero each time a new slide displays

FIGURE 3-75

STEP 4 ▶

Click the left mouse button when you are ready to display the first bulleted paragraph.

PowerPoint displays the first bulleted paragraph and any demoted paragraphs (Figure 3-76). The timer displays the total elapsed time since Slide 2 first displayed on the screen.

first bulleted paragraph and any demoted paragraphs display

timer displays elapsed time since slide first displayed on screen

FIGURE 3-76

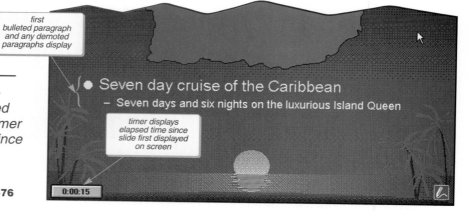

STEP 5 ▶

Click the left mouse button to display each of the remaining bulleted paragraphs on Slide 2. When you finish rehearsing Slide 2, click the left mouse button to rehearse Slide 3. Continue rehearsing your presentation until you reach Slide 9, the slide that displays only the tropics template. When Slide 9 displays, allow the timer to accumulate for two to three minutes. Click the left mouse button.

PowerPoint returns to Slide Sorter view and displays the Microsoft PowerPoint information box (Figure 3-77). The information box displays a message identifying the total time for the slide show and a question asking to record the slide timings in Slide Sorter view. In this figure, the total time used during the presentation rehearsal was 9 minutes and 10 seconds. Depending on your rehearsal, your time will differ.

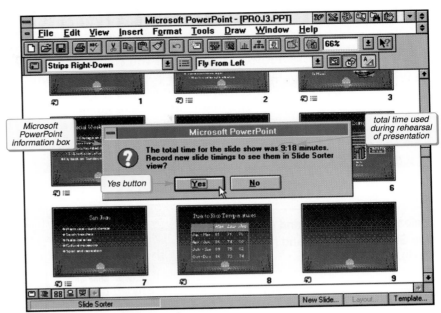

FIGURE 3-77

STEP 6 ▶

Choose the Yes button.

PowerPoint displays the amount of time each slide displays before the next slide replaces it (Figure 3-78). The time is listed as minutes and seconds. If you wanted to run the rehearsal again before setting the timings, you would choose the No button from Figure 3-77 in Step 5 above.

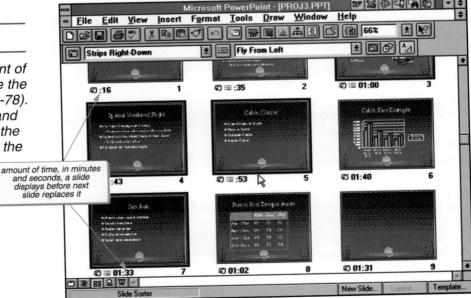

FIGURE 3-78

The timings for each slide have been established during the rehearsal. The next step is to activate the automatic slide show.

Using Slide Timings for Automatic Slide Show

By default, PowerPoint manually advances slides in a slide show. Recall in Projects 1 and 2 that you clicked the mouse pointer to move through your presentation. In order for PowerPoint to automatically run your presentation based on your rehearsal timings, you need to change the option to advance the slides. Perform the following steps to change the advance option.

TO CHANGE THE ADVANCE OPTION FROM MANUAL TO SLIDE TIMINGS ▼

STEP 1 ▶

Select the View menu and point to the Slide Show command (Figure 3-79).

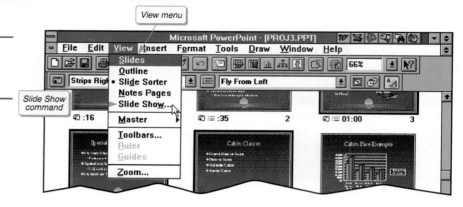

FIGURE 3-79

STEP 2 ▶

Choose the Slide Show command. When the Slide Show dialog box displays, select the Use Slide Timings option button. Then, point to the Show button (Show).

The Slide Show dialog box contains options for which slides to include in the slide show and options for how to advance the slides in the slide show (Figure 3-80). The default settings are for all slides and manual advance. You are using the slide timings to advance your presentation so you have selected the Use Slide Timings option. The Show button will activate the automatic slide show so you can test your timings.

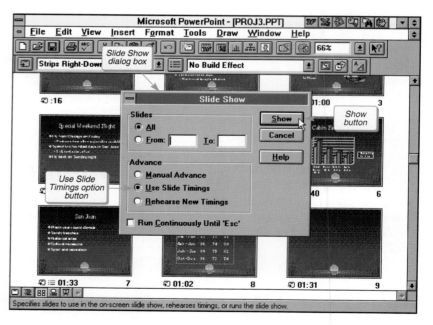

FIGURE 3-80

STEP 3

Choose the Show button.

PowerPoint begins the automatic slide show with the timings you used in your rehearsal.

PowerPoint moves through the slide show. To interrupt or exit the slide show, press the ESC key. Table 3-6 contains slide show shortcuts.

PRESENTATION TIP
Practice running your automatic slide show several times before presenting it to an audience.

Saving the Presentation and Exiting PowerPoint

The presentation is complete. Because several changes have been made since your last save, you should save the presentation again with the same filename by clicking the Save button on the Standard toolbar.

You may now exit PowerPoint by choosing the Exit command from the File menu.

▶ PROJECT SUMMARY

Project 3 enhanced the San Baarbo Vacations presentation started in Project 2. The first step was to save the presentation with a new name so as to preserve the original Project 2 presentation. You then changed templates to give the presentation a new look. Next, you deleted the seal object on Slide 4 because it was no longer applicable to the presentation. You then added a new bulleted list to explain available cabin classes. Next, you added a graph to illustrate the differences in cabin fares. To create the graph, you used Microsoft Graph 5 and completed a datasheet. Next, you added a bulleted list to explain the many features of San Juan. To further support the presentation, you added a temperature table using Microsoft Word 6.

Once the presentation was complete, you added special effects to the slide show. First, you added a transition effect to strip the current slide off the screen down and to the right. Then, you created build effects to display each bulleted paragraph independently of the others. At the end of the project, you rehearsed your presentation to establish timings to run an automatic slide show. Finally, you changed the PowerPoint advance option to allow PowerPoint to run your slide show automatically.

▶ **TABLE 3-6**

TASK	SHORTCUT
Go to slide <number>	<Number>+ENTER
Black/unblack screen	B, . (period)
White/unwhite screen	W, , (comma)
Show/hide pointer	A, = (equal)
Stop/restart automatic show	S, + (plus)
End show	ESC, CTRL+Break, - (hyphen)
Erase screen annotations	E
Use new time	T
Use original time	O
Advance on mouse click	M
Advance to hidden slide	H
Go to Slide 1	Press and hold both mouse buttons for two seconds
Advance to next slide	Click mouse button, SPACEBAR, N, RIGHT ARROW, DOWN ARROW, PAGE DOWN
Return to previous slide	Click right mouse button, BACKSPACE, P, LEFT ARROW, UP ARROW PAGE UP

▶ KEY TERMS AND INDEX

active cell *(PP144)*
arrow key *(PP149)*
automatic slide show *(PP177)*
build effects *(PP175)*
category *(PP145)*
category names *(PP145)*
cell *(PP144)*
cell reference *(PP144)*
closing slide *(PP168)*
column boundary *(PP162)*
column heading *(PP144)*
column markers *(PP162)*
data labels *(PP158)*

data markers *(PP145)*
data points *(PP144)*
data series *(PP145)*
data series names *(PP145)*
datasheet *(PP144)*
embedded object *(PP142)*
end-of-cell mark *(PP162)*
gridlines *(PP162)*
legend *(PP142)*
Microsoft Graph 5 *(PP142)*
noncontiguous *(PP175)*
Object Linking and Embedding
   (OLE) *(PP142)*

OLE *(PP142)*
orientation *(PP146)*
Rehearse Timings button
   (PP177)
row heading *(PP144)*
select a cell *(PP149)*
SHIFT+click *(PP175)*
supplementary application
   (PP142)
table *(PP160)*
transitions *(PP169)*
truncates *(PP150)*

Q U I C K   R E F E R E N C E

In PowerPoint, you can accomplish a task in a number of ways. The following table provides a quick reference to each task in this project with its available options. The commands listed in the Menu column can be executed using either the keyboard or mouse.

Task	Mouse	Menu	Keyboard Shortcuts
Add a Legend	Click Legend button on Graph Standard toolbar	From Graph Data menu, choose Legend	
Add a Transition	Click Transition button on Slide Sorter toolbar	From Tools menu, choose Transition	
Change the Graph Orientation	Click By Row or click By Column button on Graph Standard toolbar	From Graph Data menu, choose Series in Rows or choose Series in Columns	
Clear Cell(s)		From Edit menu, choose Clear	Press DELETE
Create a Build Slide	Click Build button on Slide Sorter toolbar	From Tools menu, choose Build	
Delete a Datasheet Cell		From Graph Edit menu, choose Delete	
Delete a Database Column			Press CTRL+HYPHEN
Delete a Database Row			Press CTRL+HYPHEN
Delete a Table Column		From Word Table menu, choose Delete Cells	
Delete a Table Row		From Word Table menu, choose Delete Cells	

Task	Mouse	Menu	Keyboard Shortcuts
Insert a Graph	Double-click in graph placeholder or click Insert Graph button or double-click in empty object placeholder	From Insert menu, choose Microsoft Graph	
Insert a Table	Double-click in table placeholder or click Insert Table button or double-click in empty object placeholder	From Insert menu, choose Microsoft Word Table	
Save a Presentation with a Different Filename		From File menu, choose Save As	Press F12
Select All Cells in Tables		From Word menu, choose Select All	Press CTRL+A
Select All Slides (Slide Sorter		From Edit menu, choose Select All	Press CTRL+A
Select a Cell	Click in cell		
Select a Database Column	Click in column heading		
Select a Database Row	Click in row heading		
Select a Graph Type	Click Chart Type button on Graph Standard toolbar	From Format menu, choose Chart Type	
Select Noncontiguous Slides	SHIFT+click slide		
Choose Slide Sorter view	Click Slide Sorter View button	From View menu, choose Slide Sorter	Press CTRL+ALT+P
Start Slide Show	Click Slide Show View button	From View menu, choose Slide Show	
View a Datasheet	Click View Datasheet button on Graph Standard toolbar	From View menu or Graph menu, choose Datasheet	

S T U D E N T   A S S I G N M E N T S

STUDENT ASSIGNMENT 1
True/False

Instructions: Circle T if the statement is true or F if the statement is false.

T F   1. Double-clicking the graph placeholder closes PowerPoint and opens Microsoft Graph.

T F   2. In a datasheet, pressing the ENTER key selects the cell adjacent to the active cell.

T F   3. A legend is an explanatory table or list of symbols appearing on a graph.

T F 4. Clicking the Currency button on the Graph Formatting toolbar inserts dollar signs and two decimal positions to the selected data points.

T F 5. A cell is the basic unit of the datasheet.

T F 6. A data series is a single row or a single column of data points on the table.

T F 7. A column heading is a letter identifying a column in a table.

T F 8. Microsoft Word truncates category names to fit in the datasheet cell.

T F 9. In a datasheet, a row number on the left side of the grid is called the row heading.

T F 10. Clicking the By Row button on the Graph Formatting toolbar changes the orientation to associate the chart data series with horizontal rows on the datasheet.

T F 11. When you open a supplementary application, such as Microsoft Graph, its menus, buttons, and tools are available to you directly on the PowerPoint screen.

T F 12. You change the width of a table column by dragging the column boundary or by dragging a column marker on the horizontal ruler.

T F 13. In a table, each cell has an end-of-cell mark, which is used to select a cell.

T F 14. Transitions are special visual effects that emphasize the current bulleted paragraph by building a slide one bulleted paragraph at a time.

T F 15. A cell is identified by its cell reference, which is the coordinates of the intersection of a column and a row.

T F 16. Once applied, build effects instruct PowerPoint to progressively disclose each bulleted paragraph, one at a time, during the running of a slide show.

T F 17. The datasheet is a rectangular grid containing horizontal columns and vertical rows.

T F 18. A table is actually an embedded object because it is created in Microsoft Word 6.

T F 19. The numbers representing data in a datasheet are called data points.

T F 20. Microsoft Word wordwraps text entries to fit into a cell.

STUDENT ASSIGNMENT 2
Multiple Choice

Instructions: Circle the correct response.

1. Microsoft Graph uses the data points to create the _____ that displays in the presentation.
   a. graph   b. datasheet   c. table   d. all of the above

2. To identify a cell, specify the _____ first, followed by the _____ .
   a. row letter, column number   c. column number, row letter
   b. column letter, row number   d. row number, column letter

3. To select noncontiguous slides, hold down the _____ key while clicking each slide.
   a. SHIFT   b. ALT   c. TAB   d. CTRL

4. The datasheet uses the _____ toolbars.
   a. PowerPoint   b. Word 6   c. Graph 5   d. Office

5. A cell is _____ .
   a. a basic unit of a datasheet   c. the intersection of each column and row
   b. identified by its cell reference   d. all of the above

6. When entering data into a table, press the _____ key to advance to the next cell.
   a. SHIFT   b. ENTER   c. TAB   d. both b and c

7. The _____ toolbar displays buttons for adding transition and build effects to slides in a slide show.
   a. Special Effects   b. Formatting   c. Standard   d. Slide Sorter

8. Click the _____ button to create a slide that progressively discloses each bulleted paragraph.
   a. Transition   b. Build   c. Rehearse Timings   d. both a and b

9. To add a new slide, click the _____ .
   a. Insert New Slide button on the Standard toolbar
   b. AutoLayout button on the status bar
   c. New Slide button on the Formatting toolbar
   d. both a and c

STUDENT ASSIGNMENT 3
Understanding the Datasheet Window

Instructions: Arrows in Figure SA3-3 point to the major components of a Graph Datasheet window. Identify the various parts of the window in the spaces provided.

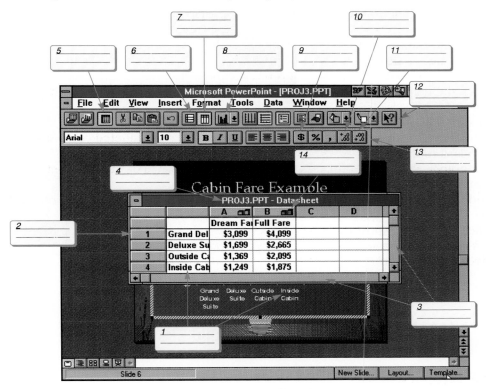

FIGURE SA3-3

STUDENT ASSIGNMENT 4
Understanding the Slide Sorter Toolbar

Instructions: Arrows in Figure SA3-4 point to buttons on the Slide Sorter toolbar. In the spaces provided, identify and briefly explain the purpose of each button and box.

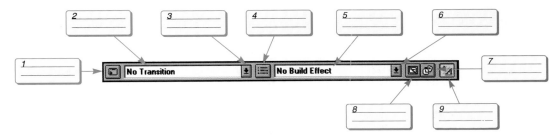

FIGURE SA3-4

STUDENT ASSIGNMENT 5
Understanding How to Add a Graph

Instructions: Assume you are in Slide view and are adding a graph to the end of a presentation. Fill in the step numbers below to indicate the sequence necessary to add the graph shown in Figure SA3-5.

Step ____: Click Decrease Decimal button.
Step ____: Type the slide title.
Step ____: Click outside the Datasheet window work area to display graph in slide.
Step ____: Double-click the graph placeholder.
Step ____: Delete data in columns C and D.
Step ____: Click the Insert New Slide button on the Standard toolbar.
Step ____: Select data points.
Step ____: Type column headings, data series names, and data points into datasheet.
Step ____: Double-click the Graph AutoLayout in the New Slide dialog box.
Step ____: Click Currency Style button.

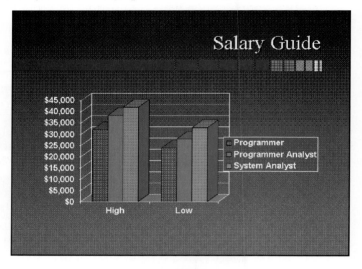

FIGURE SA3-5

STUDENT ASSIGNMENT 6
Understanding How to Add Build Effects

Instructions: Assume you are in Slide view and are adding build effects to all bulleted list slides in your presentation. Fill in the step numbers below to indicate the sequence necessary to add build effects.

Step ____: Click between any two slides to deselect the bulleted list slides.
Step ____: Click the Effect check box.
Step ____: Click the Slide Sorter View button.
Step ____: Choose the OK button in the Build dialog box.
Step ____: Select all bulleted list slides in the presentation.
Step ____: Click the Build button on the Slide Sorter toolbar.

COMPUTER LABORATORY EXERCISES

COMPUTER LABORATORY EXERCISE 1
Using PowerPoint Help

Instructions: Start PowerPoint. Open a blank presentation and choose the Title Slide AutoLayout. Perform the following tasks:

1. From the Help menu, choose the Search for Help on command. Type slide show when the Search dialog box displays. Choose the Show Topics button. If it is not already selected, select About Creating and Running Slide Shows. Choose the Go To button. Read the information. From the File menu, choose the Print Topic command.

2. Scroll down the screen until the See also section displays. Jump to Running a slide show by clicking it. Read and print the information on running a slide show. Click the Tip button (**Tip**) at the top of the screen. Read the tip. Click the Back button (**Back**) to return to About Creating and Running Slide Shows.
3. Jump to Setting slide timings by clicking it. Read and print the information on setting slide timings.
4. Scroll until the See also section displays. Jump to Hints for creating and running slide shows. Read and print the information on hints for creating and running slide shows. Click the Back button.
5. Exit Help by choosing the Exit command from the File menu.

COMPUTER LABORATORY EXERCISE 2
Adding a Table to a Presentation

Instructions: Start PowerPoint. Open the presentation CLE3-2.PPT from the PPOINT4 subdirectory on the Student Diskette that accompanies this book. Perform the following tasks to add a table so the presentation looks like the one in Figures CLE3-2a through CLE3-2c.

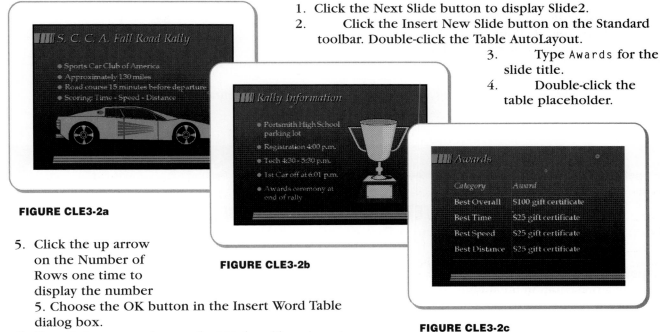

1. Click the Next Slide button to display Slide2.
2.   Click the Insert New Slide button on the Standard toolbar. Double-click the Table AutoLayout.
3.   Type Awards for the slide title.
4.   Double-click the table placeholder.

FIGURE CLE3-2a

FIGURE CLE3-2b

FIGURE CLE3-2c

5. Click the up arrow on the Number of Rows one time to display the number 5. Choose the OK button in the Insert Word Table dialog box.
6. Type Category and press the TAB key. Type Award and press the TAB key. Type Best Overall and press the TAB key. Type $100 gift certificate and press the TAB key. Type Best Time and press the TAB key. Type $25 gift certificate and press the TAB key. Type Best Speed and press the TAB key. Type $25 gift certificate
7. With the insertion point and mouse pointer somewhere in the table, click the right mouse button to display a shortcut menu. Point to the Table AutoFormat command.
8. Select Classic 1 in the Formats list box. Choose the OK.
9. Click outside the table window work area to close Word and to display the table in Slide 3.
10. Save the presentation with the filename CLE3-2 on your data disk.
11. Print the presentation by selecting Slides in the Print What box and by selecting the Pure Black & White check box.
12. From the File menu, choose the Close command to close the presentation.

COMPUTER LABORATORY EXERCISE 3
Converting a Presentation into an Automatic Slide Show

Instructions: Start PowerPoint. Open the presentation CLA2-2.PPT from your data disk. If you did not complete Computer Laboratory Assignment 2 in Project 2, see your instructor for a copy. Perform the following tasks to change the presentation to an automatic slide show.

1. If the presentation is not in Slide Sorter view, click the Slide Sorter View button.
2. SHIFT+click all slides in the presentation.
3. Click the Transition button on the Slide Sorter toolbar.
4. Click the down arrow on the Effect box. Select Checkerboard Across from the Effect drop-down list box. Select the Automatically After option button. Type 20 in the Automatically After text box. Choose the OK button.
5. Click the Build button on the Slide Sorter toolbar.
6. Select the Dim Previous Points check box. Select Cyan (light blue-green), which is located in column 2 row 2 in the Dim Previous Points color drop-down list box.
7. Select the Effect check box. Click the arrow on the Effect box. Scroll down and select Wipe Right from the Effect drop-down list box. Choose the OK button.
8. From the View menu, choose the Slide Show command. Select the Use Slide Timings option button in the Slide Show dialog box. Choose the Show button.
9. Watch the presentation.
10. Save the presentation with the filename CLE3-3.
11. Print the presentation by selecting Slides (with Builds) in the Print What box and by selecting the Pure Black & White check box.
12. From the File menu, choose the Close command to close the presentation.

·COMPUTER LABORATORY ASSIGNMENTS

COMPUTER LABORATORY ASSIGNMENT 1
Building a Presentation with a Graph

Purpose: To become familiar with creating a presentation in Outline view, adding clip art, and inserting a graph.

Problem: You are the Director of Safety for Intergalactic Pipeline. You are to present the annual safety review to all department managers tomorrow afternoon. You have established your agenda. After reviewing the accident statistics, you decide a graph would best represent the five-year accident history. You decide to emphasize the company's safety goal and objectives. You also decide on a plan of action to meet the company's goal.

I.   Annual Safety Review
    A.   T. P. Hamilton
    B.   Director of Safety
    C.   Intergalactic Pipeline
II.   Agenda
    A.   Accident history
    B.   Safety goal & objectives
    C.   Plan of action
III. Accident History
IV.   Safety Goal & Objectives
    A.   Goal
       1.   Accident-free work place
    B.   Objectives
       1.   Reduce accidents by 20% per year
       2.   Eliminate preventable accidents
V.   Plan of Action
    A.   Pre-plan every job
       1.   Job safety analysis sheet
       2.   Material safety data sheet
    B.   Train employees
       1.   Proper use of tools and equipment
    C.   Inspect equipment
       1.   Repair or replace damaged equipment

FIGURE CLA3-1a

Instructions: Perform the following tasks:

Year	Total Accidents	Chargeable	Non-Chargeable	Preventable
1991	399	187	214	67
1992	357	148	209	52
1993	323	153	170	65
1994	306	106	200	68
1995	300	89	211	77

1. Create the presentation in Figures CLA3-1b through CLA3-1e using the outline in Figure CLA3-1a. Substitute your name for T. P. Hamilton on the title slide.

2. Click the Template button on the status bar. Double-click the BLUEBOXS.PPT template.

3. Select Slide 2 by clicking it. Click the Slide View button to switch to Slide view. Double-click the Object over Text slide layout. From the Microsoft ClipArt Gallery, choose the People category, and insert the Group Meeting clip art.

4. Click the Next Slide button to display Slide 3. Click the Layout button on the status bar. Double-click the Graph slide layout.

5. Open Graph by double-clicking the graph placeholder. Complete the datasheet using the data in the table below.

6. Click outside the Datasheet window work area to close Graph and to display Slide 3.

7. Click the Next Slide button to display Slide 4. Double-click the Text and Clip Art slide layout. Double-click the clip art placeholder. From the Microsoft ClipArt Gallery, choose the People category, and insert Construction Worker clip art.

8. Save the presentation on your data disk with the filename CLA3-1.

9. Print the presentation using the Pure Black & White option in the Print dialog box.

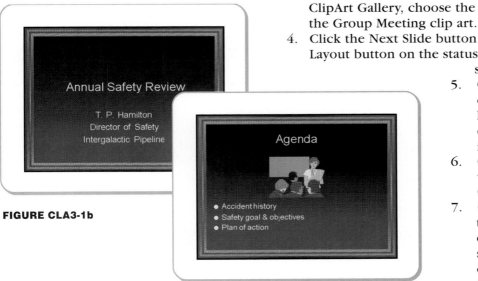

FIGURE CLA3-1b

FIGURE CLA3-1c

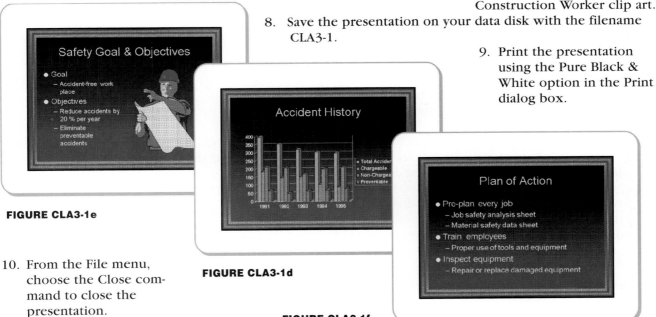

FIGURE CLA3-1e

FIGURE CLA3-1d

FIGURE CLA3-1f

10. From the File menu, choose the Close command to close the presentation.

COMPUTER LABORATORY ASSIGNMENT 2
Building a Presentation with a Table

Purpose: To become familiar with adding a table into a presentation.

Problem: You are the public relations officer for Metropolitan Transportation. Recently, your company re-evaluated all of its service areas. In order to improve community relations, you are speaking at a town hall meeting to announce the increases in service.

Instructions: Perform the following tasks:

1. Create the presentation in Figures CLA3-2b through CLA3-2e using the outline in Figure CLA3-2a.

2. Click the Template button on the status bar. Double-click the TOPLINES.PPT template.

3. Click the Slide View button and display Slide 1. Substitute your name for Linda Johnson on the title slide. Reduce the font size of Presented by to 24 points.

4. Click the Next Slide button to display Slide 2. Click the Layout button on the status bar. Double-click the Text & Clip Art slide layout.

5. Double-click the clip art placeholder. From the Microsoft ClipArt Gallery, choose the Transportation category, and insert the Bus clip art.

6. Click the Next Slide button to display Slide 3. Click the Layout button on the status bar. Double-click the Table slide layout.

7. Open the table work area by double-clicking the table placeholder. Create a table that has five columns and seven rows. Complete the table using the data below.

8. Spell check the contents of the table by clicking the Spelling button on the Word Standard toolbar.

I. Metropolitan Transportation
   A. Presented by:
   B. Linda Johnson
   C. Public Relations Officer
II. Improved Services
   A. Revised bus schedule
      1. Increased routes
      2. More bus stops
   B. Clean buses
   C. Friendly drivers
   D. No rate increase
III. Bus Schedule
IV. Community Programs
   A. Senior citizen discount - 5%
   B. Children under 12 ride free with paid adult
   C. Discounted weekend fares
   D. Discounted commuter fares

FIGURE CLA3-2a

Bus Number	502	504	506	509
1st & Maple	6:40	7:40	8:40	9:40
1st & Elm	6:50	7:50	8:50	9:50
2nd & Oak	7:00	8:00	9:00	10:00
2nd & Pine	7:15	8:15	9:15	10:15
3rd & Water	7:30	8:30	9:30	10:30
4th & College	7:45	8:45	9:45	10:45

9. Point to the center of the table and click the right mouse button to display a shortcut menu. Choose the Table AutoFormat command. Select the Classic 1 format. Choose the OK button.

10. Click outside the table to close Word and display the table in Slide 3.

11. Spell check the presentation in PowerPoint by clicking the Spelling button on the Standard toolbar.

12. Save the presentation on your data disk with the filename CLA3-2.

13. Print the presentation.

14. From the File menu, choose the Close command to close the presentation.

FIGURE CLA3-2b

FIGURE CLA3-2c

FIGURE CLA3-2d

FIGURE CLA3-2e

COMPUTER LABORATORY ASSIGNMENT 3
Adding Special Effects into a Presentation and Running a Slide Show

Purpose: To become familiar with adding transition effects, build effects, and running an automatic slide show.

Problem: Your instructor was so impressed with your presentation on starting a home-based business, he invited you to present it again at the Management Department's annual recognition dinner. You want to improve the presentation by adding slide transitions and build effects. You also decide to make the presentation an automatic slide show.

Instructions: Open CLA2-3 from your data disk. If you did not complete Computer Laboratory Assignment 3 in Project 2, see your instructor for a copy.

Instructions: Perform the following tasks:

1. Save the presentation with the filename CLA3-3 on your data disk.
2. If not already in Slide Sorter view, click the Slide Sorter View button.
3. From the Edit menu, choose the Select All command.
4. Click the Transition button. Select Random Transition from the Effect drop-down list. Choose the OK button.
5. Click the Build button. Select the Dim Previous Points check box. Select fuchsia from the Dim Previous Points color drop-down list. Fuchsia is the color sample in column 3, row 1. Select the Effect check box. Select Random Effects from the Effect drop-down list. Choose the OK button.
6. Click the Rehearse Timings button. When the title slide displays, click the left mouse button to display the rest of the slide. Rehearse the entire presentation to set slide timings. When the Microsoft PowerPoint information box displays, click the Yes button.
7. From the View menu, choose the Slide Show command. Select the Use Slide Timings option. Choose the Show button in the Slide Show dialog box.
8. Print the presentation by selecting Slides (with Builds) in the Print What box and by selecting the Pure Black & White check box.
9. From the File menu, choose the Close command to close the presentation.

COMPUTER LABORATORY ASSIGNMENT 4
Designing, Creating, and Running a Slide Show

Purpose: To become familiar with designing, creating, and running an automatic slide show.

Problem: You have been invited to speak to students enrolled in a personal finance course at the local community college. You are presenting information about the different types of mortgage loans and the costs associated with owning a home. Design and create an automatic slide show. Select an appropriate template. The presentation should consist of at least six slides, of which four should include a title slide, a table, a graph, and a closing slide. Use clip art where appropriate. Obtain the following information about mortgage loans from at least four lending institutions: institution name, loan type (fixed or variable), term (length of loan in years), interest rate, and points. Create a table to organize the mortgage loan information. Obtain a list of average home costs for the current year and previous four years. Create a bar graph illustrating the annual fluctuation in the average cost of a home. Add transition and build effects to the slide show. Set timings and run the automatic slide show. Be sure to spell check the presentation before saving it with the filename CLA3-4 on your data disk. Submit a copy of the automatic slide show on disk saved as CLA3-4 along with printouts of the slides using Slides (with Build) in pure black and white. From the File menu, choose the Close command to close the presentation.

INDEX